READINGS IN

WESTERN CIVILIZATION

VOLUME ONE—SPRING

SECOND EDITION

PROVIDENCE COLLEGE

Development of Western Civilization Program

Tapestry Press, Ltd.
Acton, MA 01720

Printed in the United States of America.

ISBN 1-56888-612-8

Front Cover: "School of Athens" (Vatican, Stanza della Segnatura [fres.], 1508–12) by Raphael. All rights reserved.

All possible effort has been made to locate the copyright owner or holder of the copyrighted material included in this book. If any rights have been inadvertently infringed upon, the publisher asks to be excused and agrees to make corrections to any subsequent editions or reprintings.

Acknowledgments:

Pp. 22-92: Selections from *The Song of Roland*, translated by Dorothy L. Sayers. Copyright © 1971 by Penguin Classics. All rights reserved.

Pp. 107–113: From *The Art of Courtly Love* by Andreas Capellanus, translated by J. J. Parry, 1941. Copyright renewed 1960; Columbia University Press 1990 reprint of 1941. All rights reserved.

Pp. 128-275: *Inferno* and *Purgatorio* by Dante Alighieri, translated by Tony Esolen. Reprinted by permission of Tony Esolen. All rights reserved.

Pp. 421–426: "Sonnets" by Francis Petrarch from *Petrarch: Selected Poems* by Anthony Mortimer, University of Alabama Press, 1977. Reprinted by permission of Anthony Mortimer. All rights reserved.

Pp. 427–449: "The Book of the Courtier" from *The Courtier* by Baldasar Castiglione, translated by Charles Singleton. Copyright © 1959 by Anchor Books/Doubleday. All rights reserved.

Pp. 692–744: "Essays" by Michel de Montaigne from *Essays* by Michel de Montaigne, translated by Donald M. Frame. Copyright © 1958, 1986 by Stanford University Press. All rights reserved.

CONTENTS

PROLOGUE

Readings in Western Civilization are three custom anthologies designed for the Providence College Western Civilization Program. The selected primary works represent an attempt to include the most obvious works and ideas which have shaped our western cultural identities.

As cultural studies in colleges and universities have expanded to be global, so too the commercial anthologies that service such courses have grown to include selections from world literatures, with the increased breadth accompanied by increased heft and cost. The western focus which these custom volumes contain, partial as it is, reflects a conscious effort to provide depth and focus on the western heritages by which we, in the west (regardless of race, ethnicity, or place of origin), have been historically shaped—at least up until the nineteenth century. The Providence College Western Civilization Program, and these volumes, trace that cultural bias, expanding the inclusions to the global as the past moves to the present and cultural influences are no longer contained by geography.

The idea of creating custom anthologies means that the selections can be altered and supplemented as needs, interests, and themes suggest. These volumes are not collections of perfect texts perfectly edited. Many translations are arguably the best to be had; many translations and texts are from public domain sources, and in these cases the editors tried not to sacrifice quality to cost. In this they may not have always succeeded. The volumes therefore constitute an open invitation to students and instructors to read carefully, question thoughtfully, and make suggestions for ongoing improvement of the present work.

Brian Barbour
Terrie Curran

1. THE LIFE OF CHARLEMAGNE
(c. 830)

Einhard

(trans. by Samuel Epes Turner)

Einhard (c. 775–840) was educated in the Frankish monastery of Fulda and joined Charlemagne's palace school in 792 under the leadership of the British scholar, Alcuin. After Charlemagne's death in 814, he became secretary to Charlemagne's son, Louis the Pious, and drew upon the royal archives, as well as personal knowledge for biographical material of Charlemagne. He looked to the Roman historian, Suetonius, whose Life of Augustus *served as his chief model for organization. Like Suetonius, Einhard relies minimally on chronology, allocating major attention to the achievements of his subject. He is extremely diplomatic concerning personal matters such as Charlemagne's concubines, focusing more on Charlemagne's public life as military leader, administrator, and especially his promotion of learning, of the Church, and of building projects. This first medieval biography of a layperson was very popular through the Middle Ages and provides a valuable historical perspective on the era, the subject, and the biographer.*

EINHARD'S PREFACE

Since I have taken upon myself to narrate the public and private life, and no small part of the deeds, of my lord and foster-father, the most excellent and most justly renowned King Charles, I have condensed the matter into as brief a form as possible. I have been careful not to omit any facts that could come to my
5   knowledge, but at the same time not to offend by a prolix style those minds that despise everything modern, if one can possibly avoid offending by a new work men who seem to despise also the masterpieces of antiquity, the works of most learned and luminous writers. Very many of them, l have no doubt, are men devoted to a life of literary leisure, who feel that the affairs of the present
10   generation ought not to be passed by, and who do not consider everything done today as unworthy of mention and deserving to be given over to silence and oblivion, but are nevertheless seduced by lust of immortality to celebrate the glorious deeds of other times by some sort of composition rather than to deprive posterity of the mention of their own names by not writing at all.

15   Be this as it may, I see no reason why I should refrain from entering upon a task of this kind, since no man can write with more accuracy than I of events that took place about me, and of facts concerning which I had personal knowledge, ocular demonstration as the saying goes, and I have no means of ascertaining whether or not any one else has the subject in hand.

20   In any event, I would rather commit my story to writing, and hand it down to posterity in partnership with others, so to speak, than to suffer the most glorious life of this most excellent king, the greatest of all the princes of his day, and his illustrious deeds, hard for men of later times to imitate, to be wrapped in the darkness of oblivion.

25   But there are still other reasons, neither unwarrantable nor insufficient, in my opinion, that urge me to write on this subject, namely, the care that King Charles bestowed upon me in my childhood, and my constant friendship with himself and his children after I took up my abode at court. In this way he strongly endeared me to himself, and made me greatly his debtor as well in death as in life,

30   so that were I unmindful of the benefits conferred upon me, to keep silence concerning the most glorious and illustrious deeds of a man who claims so much at my hands, and suffer his life to lack due eulogy and written memorial, as if he had never lived, I should deservedly appear ungrateful, and be so considered, albeit my powers are feeble, scanty, next to nothing indeed, and not at all adapted to write

35   and set forth a life that would tax the eloquence of a Cicero.

        I submit the book. It contains the history of a very great and distinguished man; but there is nothing in it to wonder at besides his deeds, except the fact that I, who am a barbarian, and very little versed in the Roman language, seem to suppose myself capable of writing gracefully and respectably in Latin, and to

40   carry my presumption so far as to disdain the sentiment that Cicero is said in the first book of the Tusculan Disputations to have expressed when speaking of the Latin authors. His words are: "It is an outrageous abuse both of time and literature for a man to commit his thoughts to writing without having the ability either to arrange them or elucidate them, or attract readers by some charm of

45   style." This dictum of the famous orator might have deterred me from writing if I had not made up my mind that it was better to risk the opinions of the world, and put my little talents for composition to the test, than to slight the memory of so great a man for the sake of sparing myself.

THE LIFE OF THE EMPEROR CHARLES

1. The Merovingian Family

        The Merovingian family, from which the Franks used to choose their kings, is

50   commonly said to have lasted until the time of Childeric [III, 743-752] who was deposed, shaved, and thrust into the cloister by command of the Roman Pontiff Stephen [II (or III) 752-757]. But although, to all outward appearance, it ended with him, it had long since been devoid of vital strength, and conspicuous only

from bearing the empty epithet Royal; the real power and authority in the kingdom
55   lay in the hands of the chief officer of the court, the so-called Mayor of the Palace,
and he was at the head of affairs. There was nothing left for the King to do but to
be content with his name of King, his flowing hair, and long beard, to sit on his
throne and play the ruler, to give ear to the ambassadors that came from all
quarters, and to dismiss them, as if on his own responsibility, in words that were,
60   in fact, suggested to him, or even imposed upon him. He had nothing that he could
call his own beyond this vain title of King and the precarious support allowed by
the Mayor of the Palace in his discretion, except a single country seat, that
brought him but a very small income. There was a dwelling house upon this, and a
small number of servants attached to it, sufficient to perform the necessary offices.
65   When he had to go abroad, he used to ride in a cart, drawn by a yoke of oxen
driven, peasant-fashion, by a Ploughman; he rode in this way to the palace and to
the general assembly of the people, that met once a year for the welfare of the
kingdom, and he returned him in like manner. The Mayor of the Palace took charge
of the government and of everything that had to be planned or executed at home or
70   abroad.

2. Charlemagne's Ancestors

At the time of Childeric's deposition, Pepin, the father of King Charles, held
this office of Mayor of the Palace, one might almost say, by hereditary right; for
Pepin's father, Charles [Martel 715-41], had received it at the hands of his father,
Pepin, and filled it with distinction. It was this Charles that crushed the tyrants
75   who claimed to rule the whole Frank land as their own, and that utterly routed
the Saracens, when they attempted the conquest of Gaul, in—two great battles—
one in Aquitania, near the town of Poitiers, and the other on the River Berre, near
Narbonne—and compelled them to return to Spain. This honor was usually
conferred by the people only upon men eminent from their illustrious birth and
80   ample wealth. For some years, ostensibly under King Childeric, Pepin, the father of
King Charles, shared the duties inherited from his father and grandfather most
amicably with his brother, Carloman. The latter, then, for reasons unknown,
renounced the heavy cares of an earthly crown and retired to Rome [747]. Here he
exchanged his worldly garb for a cowl, and built a monastery on Mt. Oreste, near
85   the Church of St. Sylvester, where he enjoyed for several years the seclusion that
he desired, in company with certain others who had the same object in view. But
so many distinguished Franks made the pilgrimage to Rome to fulfill their vows,
and insisted upon paying their respects to him, as their former lord, on the way,
that the repose which he so much loved was broken by these frequent visits, and
90   he was driven to change his abode. Accordingly when he found that his plans
were frustrated by his many visitors, he abandoned the mountain, and withdrew
to the Monastery of St. Benedict, on Monte Cassino, in the province of Samnium
[754], and passed the rest there in the exercise of religion.

3. Charlemagne's Accession

Pepin, however, was raised by decree of the Roman pontiff, from the rank of
Mayor of the Palace to that of King, and ruled alone over the Franks for fifteen
years or more [752-768]. He died of dropsy [Sept. 24, 768] in Paris at the close of
the Aquitanian War, which he had waged with William, Duke of Aquitania, for
nine successive years, and left his two sons, Charles and Carloman, upon whom,
by the grace of God, the succession devolved. The Franks, in a general assembly of
the people, made them both kings [Oct. 9, 786] on condition that they should divide
the whole kingdom equally between them, Charles to take and rule the part that
had to belonged to their father, Pepin, and Carloman the part which their uncle,
Carloman had governed. The conditions were accepted, and each entered into the
possession of the share of the kingdom that fell to him by this arrangement; but
peace was only maintained between them with the greatest difficulty, because
many of Carloman's party kept trying to disturb their good understanding, and
there were some even who plotted to involve them in a war with each other. The
event, however, which showed the danger to have been rather imaginary than
real, for at Carloman's death his widow fled to Italy with her sons and her
principal adherents, and without reason, despite her husband's brother, put
herself and her children under the protection of Desiderius, King of the Lombards.
Carloman had succumbed to disease after ruling two years in common with his
brother, and at his death Charles was unanimously elected King of the Franks.

4. Plan of This Work

It would be folly, I think, to write a word concerning Charles' birth and
infancy, or even his boyhood, for nothing has ever been written on the subject, and
there is no one alive now who can give information on it. Accordingly, I
determined to pass that by as unknown, and to proceed at once to treat of his
character, his deeds, and such other facts of his life as are worth telling and
setting forth, and shall first give an account of his deed at home and abroad, then
of his character and pursuits, and lastly of his administration and death, omitting
nothing worth knowing or necessary to know.

5. Aquitanian War

His first undertaking in a military way was the Aquitanian War, begun by
his father but not brought to a close; and because he thought that it could be
readily carried through, he took it up while his brother was yet alive, calling
upon him to render aid. The campaign once opened, he conducted it with the
greatest vigor, notwithstanding his brother withheld the assistance that he had
promised, and did not desist or shrink from his self-imposed task until, by his
patience and firmness, he had completely gained his ends. He compelled Hunold,
who had attempted to seize Aquitania after Waifar's death, and renew the war

130 then almost concluded, to abandon Aquitania and flee to Gascony. Even here he
gave him no rest, but crossed the River Garonne, built the castle of Fronsac, and
sent ambassadors to Lupus, Duke of Gascony, to demand the surrender of the
fugitive, threatening to take him by force unless he were promptly given up to him.
Thereupon Lupus chose the wiser course, and not only gave Hunold up, but
135 submitted himself, with the province which he ruled, to the King.

6. Lombard War

After bringing this war to an end and settling matters in Aquitania (his
associate in authority had meantime departed this life), he was induced [in 773],
by the prayers and entreaties of Hadrian [I, 772-795], Bishop of the city of Rome,
to wage war on the Lombards. His father before him had undertaken this task at
140 the request of Pope Stephen [II or III, 752-757], but under great difficulties, for
certain leading Franks, of whom he usually took counsel, had so vehemently
opposed his design as to declare openly that they would leave the King and go
home. Nevertheless, the war against the Lombard King Astolf had been taken up
and very quickly concluded [754]. Now, although Charles seems to have had
145 similar, or rather just the same grounds for declaring war that his father had, the
war itself differed from the preceding one alike in its difficulties and its issue.
Pepin, to be sure, after besieging King Astolf a few days in Pavia, had compelled
him to give hostages, to restore to the Romans the cities and castles that he had
taken, and to make oath that he would not attempt to seize them again; but Charles
150 did not cease, after declaring war, until he had exhausted King Desiderius by a
long siege [773], and forced him to surrender at discretion; driven his son Adalgis,
the last hope of the Lombards, not only from his kingdom, but from all Italy [774];
restored to the Romans all that they had lost; subdued Hruodgaus, Duke of Friuli
[776], who was plotting revolution; reduced all Italy to his power, and set his son
155 Pepin as king over it. [781] At this point I should describe Charles' difficult
passage over the Alps into Italy, and the hardships that the Franks endured in
climbing the trackless mountain ridges, the heaven-aspiring cliffs and ragged
peaks, if it were not my purpose in this work to record the manner of his life
rather than the incidents of the wars that he waged. Suffice it to say that this war
160 ended with the subjection of Italy, the banishment of King Desiderius for life, the
expulsion of his son Adalgis from Italy, and the restoration of the conquests of the
Lombard kings to Hadrian, the head of the Roman Church.

7. Saxon War

At the conclusion of this struggle, the Saxon war, that seems to have been only
laid aside for the time, was taken up again. No war ever undertaken by the Frank
165 nation was carried on with such persistence and bitterness, or cost so much labor,
because the Saxons, like almost all the tribes of Germany, were a fierce people,
given to the worship of devils, and hostile to our religion, and did not consider it

dishonorable to transgress and violate all law, human and divine. Then there
were peculiar circumstances that tended to cause a breach of peace every day.
170   Except in a few places, where large forests or mountain ridges intervened and
made the bounds certain, the line between ourselves and the Saxons passed almost
in its whole extent through an open country, so that there was no end to the
murders, thefts and arsons on both sides. In this way the Franks became so
embittered that they at last resolved to make reprisals no longer, but to come to
175   open war with the Saxons [772]. Accordingly war was begun against them, and
was waged for thirty-three successive years with great fury; more, however, to the
disadvantage of the Saxons than of the Franks. It could doubtless have been
brought to an end sooner, had it not been for the faithlessness of the Saxons. It is
hard to say how often they were conquered, and, humbly submitting to the King,
180   promised to do what was enjoined upon them, without hesitation the required
hostages, gave and received the officers sent them from the King. They were
sometimes so much weakened and reduced that they promised to renounce the
worship of devils, and to adopt Christianity, but they were no less ready to
violate these terms than prompt to accept them, so that it is impossible to tell which
185   came easier to them to do; scarcely a year passed from the beginning of the war
without such changes on their part. But the King did not suffer his high purpose
and steadfastness—firm alike in good and evil fortune—to be wearied by any
fickleness on their part, or to be turned from the task that he had undertaken, on
the contrary, he never allowed their faithless behavior to go unpunished, but
190   either took the field against them in person, or sent his counts with an army to
wreak vengeance and exact righteous satisfaction. At last, after conquering and
subduing all who had offered resistance, he took ten thousand of those that lived
on the banks of the Elbe, and settled them, with their wives and children, in many
different bodies here and there in Gaul and Germany [804]. The war that had
195   lasted so many years was at length ended by their acceding to the terms offered by
the King; which were renunciation of their national religious customs and the
worship of devils, acceptance of the sacraments of the Christian faith and religion,
and union with the Franks to form one people.

Charles himself fought but two pitched battles in this war, although it was a
200   long protracted one on Mount Osning [783], at the place called Detmold, and again
on the bank of the river Hase, both in the space of little more than a month. The
enemy were so routed and overthrown in these two battles that they never
afterwards ventured to take the offensive or to resist the attacks of the King,
unless they were protected by a strong position. A great many of the Frank as well
205   as of the Saxon nobility, men occupying the highest posts of honor, perished in this
war, which only came to an end after the lapse of thirty-two years [804]. So many
and grievous were the wars that were declared against the Franks in the
meantime, and skillfully conducted by the King, that one may reasonably question
whether his fortitude or his good fortune is to be more admired. The Saxon war
210   began two years [772] before the Italian war [773]; but although it went on
without interruption, business elsewhere was not neglected, nor was there any

shrinking from other equally arduous contests. The King, who excelled all the princes of his time in wisdom and greatness of soul, did not suffer difficulty to deter him or danger to daunt him from anything that had to be taken up or carried
215 through, for he had trained himself to bear and endure whatever came, without yielding in adversity, or trusting to the deceitful favors of fortune in prosperity.

8. Spanish Expedition

In the midst of this vigorous and almost uninterrupted struggle with the Saxons, he covered the frontier by garrisons at the proper points, and marched over the Pyrenees into Spain at the head of all the forces that he could muster. All
220 the towns and castles that he attacked surrendered, and up to the time of his homeward march he sustained no loss whatever; but on his return through the Pyrenees he had cause to rue the treachery of the Gascons. That region is well adapted for ambuscades by reason of the thick forests that cover it; and as the army was advancing in the long line of march necessitated by the narrowness of
225 the road, the Gascons, who lay in ambush [778] on the top of a very high mountain, attacked the rear of the baggage train and the rear guard in charge of it, and hurled them down to the very bottom of the valley.[1] In the struggle that ensued they cut them off to a man; they then plundered the baggage, and dispersed with all speed in every direction under cover of approaching night. The lightness of their
230 armor and the nature of the battle ground stood the Gascons in good stead on this occasion, whereas the Franks fought at a disadvantage in every respect, because of the weight of their armor and the unevenness of the ground. Eggihard, the King's steward; Anselm, Count Palatine; and Roland, Governor of the March of Brittany, with very many others, fell in this engagement. This ill turn could not be avenged
235 for the nonce, because the enemy scattered so widely after carrying out their plan that not the least clue could be had as to their whereabouts.

9. Submission of the Bretons and Beneventans

Charles also subdued the Bretons [786], who lived on the sea coast, in the extreme western part of Gaul. When they refused to obey him, he sent an army against them, and compelled them to give hostages, and to promise to do his
240 bidding. He afterwards entered Italy in person with his army [787], and passed through Rome to Capua, a city in Campania, where he pitched his camp and threatened the Beneventans with hostilities unless they should submit themselves to him. Their duke, Aragis, escaped the danger by sending his two sons, Rumold and Grimold, with a great sum of money to meet the King, begging him to accept
245 them as hostages, and promising for himself and his people compliance with all the King's commands, on the single condition that his personal attendance should not be required. The King took the welfare of the people into account rather than the

---

[1]This is the total historical basis for the *Song of Roland* (c. 1100).

250

stubborn disposition of the Duke, accepted the proffered hostages, and released him from the obligation to appear before him in consideration of his handsome gift. He retained the younger son only as hostage, and sent the elder back to his father, and returned to Rome, leaving commissioners with Aragis to exact the oath of allegiance, and administer it to the Beneventans. He stayed in Rome several days in order to pay his devotions at the holy places, and then came back to Gaul [787].

10. Tassilo and the Bavarian Campaign

255

260

265

270

At this time, on a sudden, the Bavarian war broke out, but came to a speedy end. It was due to the arrogance and folly of Duke Tassilo. His wife, a daughter of King Desiderius, was desirous of avenging her father's banishment through the agency of her husband, and accordingly induced him to make a treaty with the Huns, the neighbors of the Bavarians on the east, and not only to leave the King's commands unfulfilled, but to challenge him to war. Charles' high spirit could not brook Tassilo's insubordination, for it seemed to him to pass all bounds; accordingly he straightway summoned his troops from all sides for a campaign against Bavaria and appeared in person with a great army on the river Lech, which forms the boundary between the Bavarians and the Alemanni. After pitching his camp upon its banks, he determined to put the Duke's disposition to the test by an embassy before entering the province. Tassilo did not think that it was for his own or his people's good to persist, so he surrendered himself to the King, gave the hostages demanded, among them his own son Theodo, and promised by oath not to give ear to any one who should attempt to turn him from his allegiance; so this war, which bade fair to be very grievous, came very quickly to an end. Tassilo, however, was afterward summoned to the King's presence [788], and not suffered to depart, and the government of the province that he had had in charge was no longer entrusted to a duke, but to counts.

11. Slavic War

275

280

After these uprisings had been thus quelled, war was declared against the Slavs who are commonly known among us as Wilzi, but properly, that is to say in their own tongue, are called Welatabians. The Saxons served in this campaign as auxiliaries among the tribes that followed the King's standard at his summons, but their obedience lacked sincerity and devotion. War was declared because the Slavs kept harassing the Abodriti, old allies of the Franks, by continual raids, in spite of all commands to the contrary. A gulf of unknown length, but nowhere more than a hundred miles wide, and in many parts narrower, stretches off towards the east from the Western Ocean.[2] Many tribes have settlements on its shores; the Danes and Swedes, whom we call Northmen, on the northern shore and all the adjacent islands; but the southern shore is inhabited by the Slava and the Aôsti;

---

[2]The Baltic Sea

285 and various other tribes. The Welatabians, against whom the King now made war, were the chief of these; but in a single campaign [789], which he conducted in person, he so crushed and subdued them that they did not think it advisable thereafter to refuse obedience to his commands.

12. War with the Huns

290 The war against the Avars, or Huns, followed [791], and, except the Saxon war, was the greatest that he waged; he took it up with more spirit than any of his other wars, and made far greater preparations for it. He conducted one campaign in person in Pannonia, of which the Huns then had possession. He entrusted all subsequent operations to his son, Pepin, and the governors of the provinces, to counts even, and lieutenants. Although they most vigorously prosecuted the war, it only came to a conclusion after a seven years' struggle. The utter depopulation of
295 Pannonia, and the site of the Khan's palace, now a desert, where not a trace of human habitation is visible bear witness to how many battles were fought in those years, and how much blood was shed. The entire body of the Hun nobility perished in this contest, and all its glory with it. All the money and treasure that had been years amassing was seized, and no war in which the Franks have ever
300 engaged within the memory of man brought them such riches and such booty. Up to that time the Huns had passed for a poor people, but so much gold and silver was found in the Khan's palace, and so much valuable spoil taken in battle, that one may well think that the Franks took justly from the Huns what the Huns had formerly taken unjustly from other nations. Only two of the chief men of the
305 Franks fell in this war—Eric, Duke of Friuli, who was killed in Tarsatch [799], a town on the coast of Liburnia by the treachery of the inhabitants; and Gerold, Governor of Bavaria, who met his death in Pannonia, slain [799], with two men that were accompanying him, by an unknown hand while he was marshaling his forces for battle against the Huns, and riding up and down the line encouraging
310 his men. This war was otherwise almost a bloodless one so far as the Franks were concerned, and ended most satisfactorily, although by reason of its magnitude it was long protracted.

13. Danish War

The Saxon war next came to an end as successful as the struggle had been long. The Bohemian [805-806] and Linonian [808] wars that next broke out could
315 not last long; both were quickly carried through under the leadership of the younger Charles. The last of these wars was the one declared against the Northmen called Danes. They began their career as pirates, but afterward took to laying waste the coasts of Gaul and Germany with their large fleet. Their King Godfred was so puffed with vain aspirations that he counted on gaining empire
320 over all Germany, and looked upon Saxony and Frisia as his provinces. He had already subdued his neighbors the Abodriti, and made them tributary, and boasted

that he would shortly appear with a great army before Aix-la-Chapelle,[3] where
the King held his court. Some faith was put in his words, empty as they sound, and
it is supposed that he would have attempted something of the sort if he had not
325 been prevented by a premature death. He was murdered [810] by one of his own
bodyguard, and so ended at once his life and the war that he had begun.

14. Extent of Charlemagne's Conquests

Such are the wars, most skillfully planned and successfully fought, which this
most powerful king waged during the forty-seven years of his reign. He so largely
increased the Frank kingdom, which was already great and strong when he
330 received it at his father's hands, that more than double its former territory was
added to it. The authority of the Franks was formerly confined to that part of
Gaul included between the Rhine and the Loire, the Ocean and the Balearic Sea; to
that part of Germany which is inhabited by the so-called Eastern Franks, and is
bounded by Saxony and the Danube, the Rhine and the Saale—this stream
335 separates the Thuringians from the Sorabians; and to the country of the Alemanni
and Bavarians. By the wars above mentioned he first made tributary Aquitania,
Gascony, and the whole of the region of the Pyrenees as far as the River Ebro,
which rises in the land of the Navarrese, flows through the most fertile districts of
Spain, and empties into the Balearic Sea, beneath the walls of the city of Tortosa.
340 He next reduced and made tributary all Italy from Aosta to Lower Calabria,
where the boundary line runs between the Beneventans and the Greeks, a
territory more than a thousand miles long; then Saxony, which constitutes no
small part of Germany, and is reckoned to be twice as wide as the country
inhabited by the Franks, while about equal to it in length; in addition, both
345 Pannonias, Dacia beyond the Danube, and Istria, Liburnia, and Dalmatia, except
the cities on the coast, which he left to the Greek Emperor for friendship's sake,
and because of the treaty that he had made with him. In time, he vanquished and
made tributary all the wild and barbarous tribes dwelling in Germany between
the Rhine and the Vistula, the Ocean and the Danube, all of which speak very
350 much the same language, but differ widely from one another in customs and dress.
The chief among them are the Welatabians, the Sorabians, the Abodriti, and the
Bohemians, and he had to make war upon these; but the rest, by far the larger
number, submitted to him of their own accord.

15. Foreign Relations

He added to the glory of his reign by gaining the good will of several kings
355 and nations; so close, indeed, was the alliance that he contracted with Alfonso [II
791-842] King of Galicia and Asturias, that the latter, when sending letters or
ambassadors to Charles, invariably styled himself his man. His munificence won

---

[3]Charlemagne's court, also called Aachen.

the kings of the Scots also to pay such deference to his wishes that they never gave
him any other title than lord or themselves than subjects and slaves; there are
360   letters from them extant in which these feelings in his regard are expressed. His
relations with Aaron, King of the Persians, who ruled over almost the whole of
the East, India excepted, were so friendly that this prince preferred his favor to
that of all the kings and potentates of the earth, and considered that to him alone
marks of honor and munificence were due. Accordingly, when the ambassadors
365   sent by Charles to visit the most holy sepulcher and place of resurrection of our
Lord and Savior presented themselves before him with gifts, and made known
their master's wishes, he not only granted what was asked, but gave possession of
that holy and blessed spot. When they returned, he dispatched his ambassadors
with them, and sent magnificent gifts, besides stuffs, perfumes, and other rich
370   products of the Eastern lands. A few years before this, Charles had asked him for
an elephant, and he sent the only one that he had. The Emperors of Constantinople,
Nicephorus [I 802-811], Michael [I, 811-813], and Leo [V, 813-820], made
advances to Charles, and sought friendship and alliance with him by several
embassies; and even when the Greeks suspected him of designing to wrest the
375   empire from them, because of his assumption of the title Emperor, they made a close
alliance with him, that he might have no cause of offense. In fact, the power of the
Franks was always viewed by the Greeks and Romans with a jealous eye, whence
the Greek proverb "Have the Frank for your friend, but not for your neighbor."

16. Public Works

This King, who showed himself so great in extending his empire and subduing
380   foreign nations, and was constantly occupied with plans to that end, undertook
also very many works calculated to adorn and benefit his kingdom, and brought
several of them to completion. Among these, the most deserving of mention are the
basilica of the Holy Mother of God at Aix-la-Chapelle, built in the most admirable
manner, and a bridge over the Rhine at Mayence, half a mile long, the breadth of
385   the river at this point. This bridge was destroyed by fire [May, 813] the year
before Charles died, but, owing to his death so soon after, could not be repaired,
although he had intended to rebuild it in stone. He began two palaces of beautiful
workmanship; one near his manor called Ingelheim, not far from Mayence; the
other at Nimeguen, on the Waal, the stream that washes the south side of the island
390   of the Batavians. But, above all, sacred edifices were the object of his care
throughout his whole kingdom; and whenever he found them falling to ruin from
age, he commanded the priests and fathers who had charge of them to repair them,
and made sure by commissioners that his instructions were obeyed. He also fitted
out a fleet for the war with the Northmen; the vessels required for this purpose
395   were built on the rivers that flow from Gaul and Germany into the Northern
Ocean. Moreover, since the Northmen continually overran and laid waste the
Gallic and German coasts, he caused watch and ward to be kept in all the
harbors, and at the mouths of rivers large enough to admit the entrance of vessels,

400 to prevent the enemy from disembarking; and in the South, in Narbonensis and Septimania, and along the whole coast of Italy as far as Rome, he took the same precautions against the Moors, who had recently begun their piratical practices. Hence, Italy suffered no great harm in his time at the hands of the Moors, nor Gaul and Germany from the Northmen, save that the Moors got possession of the Etruscan town of Civita Vecchia by treachery, and sacked it, and the Northmen

405 harried some of the islands in Frisia off the German coast.

17. Private Life

Thus did Charles defend and increase as well as beautify his kingdom, as is well known; and here let me express my admiration of his great qualities and his extraordinary constancy alike in good and evil fortune. I will now forthwith proceed to give the details of his private and family life. After his father's death,

410 while sharing the kingdom with his brother, he bore his unfriendliness and jealousy most patiently, and, to the wonder of all, could not be provoked to be angry with him. Later he married a daughter of Desiderius, King of the Lombards, at the insistence of his mother; but he repudiated her at the end of a year for some reason unknown, and married Hildegard, a woman of high birth, of Suabian

415 origin. He had three sons by her—Charles, Pepin and Louis—and as many daughters - Hruodrud, Bertha, and Gisela. He had three other daughters besides these—Theoderada, Hiltrud, and Ruodhaid—two by his third wife, Fastrada, a woman of East Frankish (that is to say, of German) origin, and the third by a concubine, whose name for the moment escapes me. At the death of Fastrada [794],

420 he married Liutgard, an Alemannic woman, who bore him no children. After her death [June 4, 800] he had three concubines—Gersuinda, a Saxon by whom he had Adaltrud; Regina, who was the mother of Drogo and Hugh; and Ethelind, by whom he had Theodoric. Charles' mother, Berthrada, passed her old age with him in great honor; he entertained the greatest veneration for her; and there was never

425 any disagreement between them except when he divorced the daughter of King Desiderius, whom he had married to please her. She died soon after Hildegard, after living to three grandsons and as many granddaughters in her son's house, and he buried her with great pomp in the Basilica of St. Denis, where his father lay. He had an only sister, Gisela, who had consecrated herself to a religious life

430 from girlhood, and he cherished as much affection for her as for his mother. She also died a few years before him in the nunnery where she passed her life.

The plan that he adopted for his children's education was, first of all, to have both boys and girls instructed in the liberal arts, to which he also turned his own attention. As soon as their years admitted, in accordance with the custom of the

435 Franks, the boys had to learn horsemanship, and to practise war and the chase, and the girls to familiarize themselves with cloth-making, and to handle distaff and spindle, that they might not grow indolent through idleness, and he fostered in them every virtuous sentiment. He only lost three of all his children before his death, two sons and one daughter, Charles, who was the eldest, Pepin, whom he

440   had made King of Italy, and Hruodrud, his oldest daughter. whom he had
betrothed to Constantine [VI, 780-802], Emperor of the Greeks. Pepin left one son,
named Bernard, and five daughters, Adelaide, Atula, Guntrada, Berthaid and
Theoderada. The King gave a striking proof of his fatherly affection at the time of
Pepin's death [810]: he appointed the grandson to succeed Pepin, and had the

445   granddaughters brought up with his own daughters. When his sons and his
daughter died, he was not so calm as might have been expected from his
remarkably strong mind, for his affections were no less strong, and moved him to
tears. Again, when he was told of the death of Hadrian [796], the Roman Pontiff,
whom he had loved most of all his friends, he wept as much as if he had lost a

450   brother, or a very dear son. He was by nature most ready to contract friendships,
and not only made friends easily, but clung to them persistently, and cherished
most fondly those with whom he had formed such ties. He was so careful of the
training of his sons and daughters that he never took his meals without them when
he was at home, and never made a journey without them; his sons would ride at his

455   side, and his daughters follow him, while a number of his body-guard, detailed for
their protection, brought up the rear. Strange to say, although they were very
handsome women, and he loved them very dearly, he was never willing to marry
any of them to a man of their own nation or to a foreigner, but kept them all at
home until his death, saying that he could not dispense with their society. Hence,

460   though otherwise happy, he experienced the malignity of fortune as far as they
were concerned; yet he concealed his knowledge of the rumors current in regard to
them, and of the suspicions entertained of their honor.

18. Conspiracies Against Charlemagne

By one of his concubines he had a son, handsome in face, but hunchbacked,
named Pepin, whom I omitted to mention in the list of his children. When Charles

465   was at war with the Huns, and was wintering in Bavaria [792], this Pepin
shammed sickness, and plotted against his father in company with some of the
leading Franks, who seduced him with vain promises of the royal authority. When
his deceit was discovered, and the conspirators were punished, his head was
shaved, and he was suffered, in accordance with his wishes, to devote himself to a

470   religious life in the monastery of Prüm. A formidable conspiracy against Charles
had previously been set on foot in Germany, but all the traitors were banished,
some of them without mutilation, others after their eyes had been put out. Three of
them only lost their lives; they drew their swords and resisted arrest, and, after
killing several men, were cut down, because they could not be otherwise

475   overpowered. It is supposed that the cruelty of Queen Fastrada was the primary
cause of these plots, and they were both due to Charles' apparent acquiescence in
his wife's cruel conduct, and deviation from the usual kindness and gentleness of
his disposition. All the rest of his life he was regarded by everyone with the
utmost love and affection, so much so that not the least accusation of unjust rigor

480   was ever made against him.

19. Charlemagne's Treatment of Foreigners

He liked foreigners, and was at great pains to take them under his protection.
There were often so many of them, both in the palace and the kingdom, that they
might reasonably have been considered a nuisance; but he, with his broad
humanity, was very little disturbed by such annoyances, because he felt himself
485 compensated for these great inconveniences by the praises of his generosity and
the reward of high renown.

20. Personal Appearance

Charles was large and strong, and of lofty stature, though not
disproportionately tall (his height is well known to have been seven times the
length of his foot); the upper part of his head was round, his eyes very large and
490 animated, nose a little long, hair fair, and face laughing and merry. Thus his
appearance was always stately and dignified, whether he was standing or sitting;
although his neck was thick and somewhat short, and his belly rather prominent;
but the symmetry of the rest of his body concealed these defects. His gait was firm,
his whole carriage manly, and his voice clear, but not so strong as his size led one
495 to expect. His health was excellent, except during the four years preceding his
death, when he was subject to frequent fevers; at the last he even limped a little
with one foot. Even in those years he consulted rather his own inclinations than
the advice of physicians, who were almost hateful to him, because they wanted
him to give up roasts, to which he was accustomed, and to eat boiled meat instead.
500 In accordance with the national custom, he took frequent exercise on horseback
and in the chase, accomplishments in which scarcely any people in the world can
equal the Franks. He enjoyed the exhalations from natural warm springs, and
often practiced swimming, in which he was such an adept that none could surpass
him; and hence it was that he built his palace at Aix-la-Chapelle, and lived there
505 constantly during his latter years until his death. He used not only to invite his
sons to his bath, but his nobles and friends, and now and then a troop of his
retinue or body guard, so that a hundred or more persons sometimes bathed with
him.

21. Dress

He used to wear the national, that is to say, the Frank, dress—next to his skin
510 a linen shirt and linen breeches, and above these a tunic fringed with silk; while
hose fastened by bands covered his lower limbs, and shoes his feet, and he
protected his shoulders and chest in winter by a close-fitting coat of otter or
marten skins. Over all he flung a blue cloak, and he always had a sword girt
about him, usually one with a gold or silver hilt and belt; he sometimes carried a
515 jewelled sword, but only on great feast-days or at the reception of ambassadors
from foreign nations. He despised foreign costumes, however handsome, and never

allowed himself to be robed in them, except twice in Rome, when he donned the Roman tunic, chlamys, and shoes; the first time at the request of Pope Hadrian, the second to gratify Leo, Hadrian's successor. On great feast-days he made use of
520 embroidered clothes, and shoes bedecked with precious stones; his cloak was fastened by a golden buckle, and he appeared crowned with a diadem of gold and gems; but on other days his dress varied little from the common dress of the people.

22. Habits

Charles was temperate in eating, and particularly so in drinking, for he abominated drunkenness in anybody, much more in himself and those of his
525 household; but he could not easily abstain from food, and often complained that fasts injured his health. He very rarely gave entertainments, only on great feast-days, and then to large numbers of people. His meals ordinarily consisted of four courses, not counting the roast, which his huntsmen used to bring in on the spit; he was more fond of this than of any other dish. While at table, he listened to reading
530 or music. The subjects of the readings were the stories and deeds of olden time; he was fond, too, of St. Augustine's books, and especially of the one entitled "The City of God." He was so moderate in the use of wine and all sorts of drink that he rarely allowed himself more than three cups in the course of a meal. In summer after the midday meal, he would eat some fruit, drain a single cup, put off his
535 clothes and shoes, just as he did for the night, and rest for two or three hours. He was in the habit of awaking and rising from bed four or five times during the night. While he was dressing and putting on his shoes, he not only gave audience to his friends, but if the Count of the Palace told him of any suit in which his judgment was necessary, he had the parties brought before him forthwith, took cognizance
540 of the case, and gave his decision, just as if he were sitting on the Judgment-seat. This was not the only business that he transacted at this time, but he performed any duty of the day whatever, whether he had to attend to the matter himself, or to give commands concerning it to his officers.

23. Studies

Charles had the gift of ready and fluent speech, and could express whatever he had to say with the utmost clearness. He was not satisfied with command of his
545 native language merely, but gave attention to the study of foreign ones, and in particular was such a master of Latin that he could speak it as well as his native tongue; but he could understand Greek better than he could speak it. He was so eloquent, indeed, that he might have passed for a teacher of eloquence. He most
550 zealously cultivated the liberal arts, held those who taught them in great esteem, and conferred great honors upon them. He took lessons in grammar from the deacon Peter of Pisa, at that time an aged man. Another deacon, Albin of Britain, surnamed Alcuin, a man of Saxon extraction, who was the greatest scholar of the day, was his teacher in other branches of learning. The King spent much time and

555   labor with him studying rhetoric, dialectics, and especially astronomy; he learned
to reckon, and used to investigate the motions of the heavenly bodies most
curiously, with an intelligent scrutiny. He also tried to write, and used to keep
tablets and blanks in bed under his pillow, that at leisure hours he might accustom
his hand to form the letters; however, as he did not begin his efforts in due season,
560   but late in life, they met with ill success.

24. Piety

He cherished with the greatest fervor and devotion the principles of the
Christian religion, which had been instilled into him from infancy. Hence it was
that he built the beautiful basilica at Aix-la-Chapelle, which he adorned with
gold and silver and lamps, and with rails and doors of solid brass. He had the
565   columns and marbles for this structure brought from Rome and Ravenna,[4] for he
could not find such as were suitable elsewhere. He was a constant worshipper at
this church as long as his health permitted, going morning and evening, even after
nightfall, besides attending mass; and he took care that all the services there
conducted should be administered with the utmost possible propriety, very often
570   warning the sextons not to let any improper or unclean thing be brought into the
building or remain in it. He provided it with a great number of sacred vessels of
gold and silver and with such a quantity of clerical robes that not even the
doorkeepers who fill the humblest office in the church were obliged to wear their
everyday clothes when in the exercise of their duties. He was at great pains to
575   improve the church reading and psalmody, for he was well skilled in both
although he neither read in public nor sang, except in a low tone and with others.

25. Generosity

He was very forward in succoring the poor, and in that gratuitous generosity
which the Greeks call alms, so much so that he not only made a point of giving in
his own country and his own kingdom, but when he discovered that there were
580   Christians living in poverty in Syria, Egypt, and Africa, at Jerusalem, Alexandria,
and Carthage, he had compassion on their wants, and used to send money over the
seas to them. The reason that he zealously strove to make friends with the kings
beyond seas was that he might get help and relief to the Christians living under
their rule.
585   He cherished the Church of St. Peter the Apostle at Rome above all other holy
and sacred places, and heaped its treasury with a vast wealth of gold, silver, and
precious stones. He sent great and countless gifts to the popes; and throughout his
whole reign the wish that he had nearest at heart was to re-establish the ancient
authority of the city of Rome under his care and by his influence, and to defend

---

[4]His architect, Odo of Metz, borrowed heavily from Justinian's sixth century church at
Ravenna, St.Vitale.

590 and protect the Church of St. Peter, and to beautify and enrich it out of his own store above all other churches. Although he held it in such veneration, he only repaired to Rome to pay his vows and make his supplications four times during the whole forty-seven years that he reigned.

27. Charlemagne Crowned Emperor

When he made his last journey thither, he also had other ends in view. The
595 Romans had inflicted many injuries upon the Pontiff Leo, tearing out his eyes and cutting out his tongue, so that he had been compelled to call upon the King for help [Nov 24, 800]. Charles accordingly went to Rome, to set in order the affairs of the Church, which were in great confusion, and passed the whole winter there. It was then that he received the titles of Emperor and Augustus [Dec 25, 800], to which he
600 at first had such an aversion that he declared that he would not have set foot in the Church the day that they were conferred, although it was a great feast-day, if he could have foreseen the design of the Pope. He bore very patiently with the jealousy which the Roman emperors showed upon his assuming these titles, for they took this step very ill; and by dint of frequent embassies and letters, in which
605 he addressed them as brothers, he made their haughtiness yield to his magnanimity, a quality in which he was unquestionably much their superior.

28. Reforms

It was after he had received the imperial name that, finding the laws of his people very defective (the Franks have two sets of laws, very different in many particulars), he determined to add what was wanting, to reconcile the
610 discrepancies, and to correct what was vicious and wrongly cited in them. However, he went no further in this matter than to supplement the laws by a few capitularies, and those imperfect ones; but he caused the unwritten laws of all the tribes that came under his rule to be compiled and reduced to writing . He also had the old rude songs that celebrate the deeds and wars of the ancient kings written
615 out for transmission to posterity. He began a grammar of his native language. He gave the months names in his own tongue, in place of the Latin and barbarous names by which they were formerly known among the Franks. He likewise designated the winds by twelve appropriate names; there were hardly more than four distinctive ones in use before. He called January, Wintarmanoth; February,
620 Hornung; March, Lentzinmanoth; April, Ostarmanoth; May, Winnemanoth; June, Brachmanoth; July, Heuvimanoth; August, Aranmanoth; September, Witumanoth; October, Windumemanoth; November, Herbistmanoth; December, Heilagmanoth. He styled the winds as follows; Subsolanus, Ostroniwint; Eurus, Ostsundroni; Euroauster, Sundostroni; Auster, Sundroni; Austro-Africus, Sundwestroni;
625 Africus, Westsundroni; Zephyrus, Westroni; Caurus, Westnordroni; Circius, Nordwestroni; Septentrio, Nordroni; Aquilo, Nordostroni; Vulturnus, Ostnordroni.

28. Coronation of Louis—Charlemagne's Death

630

635

640

645

Toward the close of his life [813], when he was broken by ill-health and old age, he summoned Louis, King of Aquitania, his only surviving son by Hildegard, and gathered together all the chief men of the whole kingdom of the Franks in a solemn assembly. He appointed Louis, with their unanimous consent, to rule with himself over the whole kingdom and constituted him heir to the imperial name; then, placing the diadem upon his son's head, he bade him be proclaimed Emperor and his step was hailed by all present favor, for it really seemed as if God had prompted him to it for the kingdom's good; it increased the King's dignity, and struck no little terror into foreign nations. After sending his son back to Aquitania, although weak from age he set out to hunt, as usual, near his palace at Aix-la-Chapelle, and passed the rest of the autumn in the chase, returning thither about the first of November [813]. While wintering there, he was seized, in the month of January, with a high fever [Jan 22, 814], and took to his bed. As soon as he was taken sick, he prescribed for himself abstinence from food, as he always used to do in case of fever, thinking that the disease could be driven off, or at least mitigated, by fasting. Besides the fever, he suffered from a pain in the side, which the Greeks call pleurisy; but he still persisted in fasting, and in keeping up his strength only by draughts taken at very long intervals. He died January twenty-eighth, the seventh day from the time that he took to his bed, at nine o'clock in the morning, after partaking of the holy communion, in the seventy-second year of his age and the forty-seventh of his reign.

29. Burial

650

655

660

His body was washed and cared for in the usual manner, and was then carried to the church, and interred amid the greatest lamentations of all the people. There was some question at first where to lay him, because in his lifetime he had given no directions as to his burial; but at length all agreed that he could nowhere be more honorably entombed than in the very basilica that he had built in the town at his own expense, for love of God and our Lord Jesus Christ, and in honor of the Holy and Eternal Virgin, His Mother. He was buried there the same day that he died, and a gilded arch was erected above his tomb with his image and an inscription. The words of the inscription were as follows: "In this tomb lies the body of Charles, the Great and Orthodox Emperor, who gloriously extended the kingdom of the Franks, and reigned prosperously for forty-seven years. He died at the age of seventy,[5] in the year of our Lord 814, the 7th Indiction, on the 28th day of January."

---

[5]Einhard gives two different ages for Charles at his death: above (line 647) at 72, and here at 70; as Charles was born in April 742, he was 70 years and 10 months old at his death.

30. Omens of Death

Very many omens had portended his approaching end, a fact that he had recognized as well as others. Eclipses both of the sun and moon were very frequent during the last three years of his life, and a black spot was visible on the sun for the space of seven days. The gallery between the basilica and the palace, which he had built at great pains and labor, fell in sudden ruin to the ground on the day of the Ascension of our Lord. The wooden bridge over the Rhine at Mayence, which he had caused to be constructed with admirable skill, at the cost of ten years' hard work, so that it seemed as if it might last forever, was so completely consumed in three hours by an accidental fire that not a single splinter of it was left, except what was under water. Moreover, one day in his last campaign into Saxony against Godfred, King of the Danes, Charles himself saw a ball of fire fall suddenly from the heavens with a great light, just as he was leaving camp before sunrise to set out on the march. It rushed across the clear sky from right to left, and everybody was wondering what was the meaning of the sign, when the horse which he was riding gave a sudden plunge, head foremost, and fell, and threw him to the ground so heavily that his cloak buckle was broken and his sword belt shattered; and after his servants had hastened to him and relieved him of his arms, he could not rise without their assistance. He happened to have a javelin in his hand when he was thrown, and this was struck from his grasp with such force that it was found lying at a distance of twenty feet or more from the spot. Again, the palace at Aix-la-Chapelle frequently trembled, the roofs of whatever buildings he tarried in kept up a continual crackling noise, the basilica in which he was afterwards buried was struck by lightning, and the gilded ball that adorned the pinnacle of the roof was shattered by the thunderbolt and hurled upon the bishop's house adjoining. In this same basilica, on the margin of the cornice that ran around the interior, between the upper and lower tiers of arches, a legend was inscribed in red letters, stating who was the builder of the temple, the last words of which were Karolus Princeps. The year that he died it was remarked by some, a few months before his decease, that the letters of the word Princeps were so effaced as to be no longer decipherable. But Charles despised, or affected to despise, all these omens, as having no reference whatever to him.

31. Will

It had been his intention to make a will, that he might give some share in the inheritance to his daughters and the children of his concubines; but it was begun too late and could not be finished. Three years before his death, however, he made a division of his treasures, money, clothes, and other movable goods in the presence of his friends and servants, and called them to witness it, that their voices might insure the ratification of the disposition thus made. He had a summary drawn up of his wishes regarding this distribution of his property, the terms and text of which are as follows:

"In the name of the Lord God, the Almighty Father, Son, and Holy Ghost. This is the inventory and division dictated by the most glorious and most pious Lord Charles, Emperor Augustus, in the 811th year of the Incarnation of our Lord Jesus Christ, in the 43d year of his reign in France and 37th in Italy, the 11th of his
705   empire, and the 4th Indiction, which considerations of piety and prudence have determined him, and the favor of God enabled him, to make of his treasures and money ascertained this day to be in his treasure chamber. In this division he is especially desirous to provide not only that the largess of alms which Christians usually make of their possessions shall be made for himself in due course and
710   order out of his wealth, but also that his heirs shall be free from all doubt, and know clearly what belongs to them, and be able to share their property by suitable partition without litigation or strife. With this intention and to this end he has first divided all his substance and movable goods ascertained to be in his treasure chamber on the day aforesaid in gold, silver, precious stones, and royal
715   ornaments into three lots and has subdivided and set off two of the said lots into twenty-one parts, keeping the third entire. The first two lots have been thus subdivided into twenty one parts because there are in his kingdom twenty-one recognized metropolitan cities, and in order that each archbishopric may receive by way of alms, at the hands of his heirs and friends, one of the said parts, and
720   that the archbishop who shall then administer its affairs shall take the part given to it, and share the same with his suffragans in such manner that one third shall go to the Church, and the remaining two thirds be divided among the suffragans. The twenty-one parts into which the first two lots are to be distributed, according to the number of recognized metropolitan cities, have been set apart one from
725   another, and each has been put aside by itself in a box labeled with the name of the city for which it is destined. The names of the cities to which this alms or largess is to be sent are as follows: Rome, Ravenna, Milan, Friuli, Grado, Cologne, Mayence, Salzburg, Treves, Sens, Besanáon, Lyons, Rouen, Rheims, Arles, Vienne, Moutiers-en-Tarantaise, Embrun, Bordeaux, Tours, and Bourges. The third lot, which he
730   wishes to be kept entire, is to be bestowed as follows: While the first two lots are to be divided into the parts aforesaid, and set aside under seal, the third lot shall be employed for the owner's daily needs, as property which he shall be under no obligation to part with in order to the fulfillment of any vow, and this as long as he shall be in the flesh, or consider it necessary for his use. But upon his death, or
735   voluntary renunciation of the affairs of this world, this said lot shall be divided into four parts, and one thereof shall be added to the aforesaid twenty-one parts; the second shall be assigned to his sons and daughters, and to the sons and daughters of his sons, to be distributed among them in just and equal partition; the third, in accordance with the custom common among Christians, shall be devoted
740   to the poor, and the fourth shall go to the support of the men servants and maid servants on duty in the palace. It is his wish that to this said third lot of the whole amount, which consists, as well as the rest, of gold and silver shall be added all the vessels and utensils of brass iron and other metals together with the arms, clothing, and other movable goods, costly and cheap, adapted to diverse uses, as

745   hangings, coverlets, carpets, woolen stuffs, leathern articles, pack-saddles, and whatsoever shall be found in his treasure chamber and wardrobe at that time, in order that thus the parts of the said lot may be augmented, and the alms distributed reach more persons. He ordains that his chapel—that is to say, its church property, as well that which he has provided and collected as that which came to

750   him by inheritance from his father shall remain entire, and not be disseyered by any partition whatever. If, however, any vessels, books or other articles be found therein which are certainly known not to have been given by him to the said chapel, whoever wants them shall have them on paying their value at a fair estimation. He likewise commands that the books which he has collected in his

755   library in great numbers shall be sold for fair prices to such as want them, and the money received therefrom given to the poor. It is well known that among his other property and treasures are three silver tables, and one very large and massive golden one. He directs and commands that the square silver table, upon which there is a representation of the city of Constantinople, shall be sent to the Basilica

760   of St. Peter the Apostle at Rome, with the other gifts destined therefore; that the round one, adorned with a delineation of the city of Rome, shall be given to the Episcopal Church at Ravenna; that the third, which far surpasses the other two in weight and in beauty of workmanship, and is made in three circles, showing the plan of the whole universe, drawn with skill and delicacy, shall go, together with

765   the golden table, fourthly above mentioned, to increase that lot which is to be devoted to his heirs and to alms.

    This deed, and the dispositions thereof, he has made and appointed in the presence of the bishops, abbots, and counts able to be present, whose names are hereto subscribed: Bishops—Hildebald, Ricolf, Arno, Wolfar, Bernoin, Laidrad,

770   John, Theodulf, Jesse, Heito, Waltgaud. Abbots—Fredugis, Adalung, Angilbert, Irmino. Counts—Walacho, Meginher, Otulf, Stephen, Unruoch, Burchard, Meginhard, Hatto, Rihwin, Edo, Ercangar, Gerold, Bero, Hildiger, Rocculf.
    Charles' son Louis who by the grace of God succeeded him, after examining this summary, took pains to fulfill all its conditions most religiously as soon as

775   possible after his father's death.

2. THE SONG OF ROLAND (SELECTIONS)
(c. 1100)

(trans. by Dorothy L. Sayers)

The Song of Roland *was composed as a rally song for the Crusades (see Pope Urban II's Call for the first Crusade, 1095). The anonymous poet bases the story on a slim historical event mentioned in Einhard's* Life of Charlemagne: *in 778 Charlemagne's rear guard was ambushed in the Pyrenees by Basque marauders and Roland was slain. This "chanson de geste" (song of great deeds) updates the event into being a clash between Christians and Saracens (Spanish Muslims), which becomes universalized into a battle between good and evil, loyalty and betrayal. The conflicts occur on the obvious political level and on more subtle moral levels: what loyalty entails—to God, to one's lord, to relatives and friends, and to oneself. The poem not only serves to remind the Christian Crusaders of the villainy of the enemy but, as important, it provides a reshaping of classical heroic values into Christian heroic values.*

1

Carlon the King, our Emperor Charlemayn,
Full seven years long has been abroad in Spain,
He's won the highlands as far as to the main;
No castle more can stand before his face,
5   City nor wall is left for him to break,
Save Saragossa in its high mountain place;
Marsilion holds it, the king who hates God's name,
Mahound he serves, and to Apollyon[1] prays:
He'll not escape the ruin that awaits.

                                AOI[2]

2

10   Marsilion sat in Saragossa town,
He sought an orchard where shade was to be found,

---

[1]*Apollyon* (Apollo)—an ignorant attribution; the Christian author knows little of the tenets or diety of the Muslim faith.

[2]*AOI*—A cry or cheer that acts as a refrain.

2. The Song of Roland (Selections)

On a bright dais of marble he lies down;
By twenty thousand his vassals stand around.
He calls before him all his dukes and his counts:
15   "Listen, my lords, what affliction is ours!
The Emperor Charles that wears fair France's crown
Invades our country our fortunes to confound.
I have no host but before him gives ground,
I find no force his forces for to flout;
20   Wise men of wit, give counsel to me now,
Save me from death and loss of my renown."
There's ne'er a paynim utters a single sound,
Till Blancandrin, Valfonda's lord, speaks out.

3

Blancandrin's wise amid the paynim horde;
25   He was for valour a mighty knight withal,
And fit of wit for to counsel his lord.
He tells the king; "Be you afeared for naught,
But send to Charles in his pride and his wrath
Your faithful service and your friendship henceforth.
30   Promise him lions and bears and hounds galore,
Sev'n hundred camels and a thousand mewed hawks,[3]
Four hundred pack-mules with gold and silver store,
And fifty wagons, a wagon-train to form,
Whence he may give his soldiers[4] rich rewards.
35   Say, in this land he has made enough war;
To Aix[5] in France let him go home once more;
At Michaelmas you'll follow to his court,
There you'll submit unto the Christian law,
And be his man by faith and fealty sworn.
40   Hostages too, if for sureties he call,
You'll let him have, ten maybe or a score;
'Twere good we send the sons our wives have borne:
I'll send mine own, though he should die therefor.
Better by far the heads of them should fall

---

[3]*mewed hawks*—hawks which have got over their moult, and are consequently in good
condition.

[4]*soldiers*—these are the mercenaries, who received their pay (*solde*) directly from the King
in cash, as distinct from the feudal vassalage, who were maintained by their respective
lords. Many of them were knights-errant, without territorial attachment, who wandered
about offering their services to whoever would employ them.

[5]*Aix*—Aachen was the imperial city of Charlemagne, who rebuilt its palace and chapel
and granted it many special privileges. He was reputed to have been born there and
certainly died and was buried there in 814.

45   Than we should lose honour, estate and all.
      And be reduced to beggary and scorn."

                                                        AOI
                              4

      Quoth Blancandrin: "I swear by my right hand
      And beard that flutters about my girdle-span,
      Straightway you'll see the Frenchman's host disband:
50   They'll hurry home to France, their native land,
      When each within his favourite haunt is back,
      Charles in his chapel at Aix will take his stand,
      And there he'll hold high feast at Michaelmas.
      The time will pass, the trysted hour elapse:
55   No news of us, no message will he have.
      Fierce is the king, a cruel-hearted man;
      Our sureties' heads he'll smite off with the axe.
      Better their heads should fall into their laps
      Than that fair Spain should fall from out our hands,
60   And we should suffer grave losses and mishap."
      The Paynims say: "There is some truth in that."

                              5

      The King Marsile had ended the debate;
      He calls before him Clarin of Balagate,
      Estramarin, and Eudropin his mate;
65   And Garlon Longbeard and Priamon he names,
      And Machiner and his uncle Matthay,
      Johun of Outremer, and Malabayn,
      And Blancandrin; these ten make up the tale,
      Ten matchless villains, to whom he's said his say:
70   "Barons, my lords, get you to Charlemayn,
      Who sits at siege, Cordova town to take.
      Bear each in hand an olive-branch displayed;
      Peace and submission are signified that way.
      If you contrive this treaty to arrange,
75   Of gold and silver I'll give you goodly weight,
      And lands and fiefs as much as heart can crave."
      The Paynims answer: "That will be ample pay."

                                                        AOI

2. The Song of Roland (Selections)

6

Marsile the king his conference had ceased.
He tells his men: "My barons, go with speed;
80   Bear in your hands boughs of the olive tree.
On my behalf King Charlemayn beseech,
For his God's sake to show me clemency.
Say, this month's end in truth he shall not see
Ere I shall seek him with thousand vassals leal.
85   The law of Christ I'll then and there receive,
In faith and love I will his liegeman be.
I'll send him sureties if thus he shall decree."
Quoth Blancandrin: "Be sure he'll grant your plea."

                                            AOI

7

Marsilion sent for ten mules white as snow,
90   (A gift that erst Suatilia's king bestowed),
Their saddles silver, their bridles all of gold.
Now are they mounted, the men who are to go;
All in their hands the olive-branches hold.
They came to Carlon that hath France in control;
95   They'll trap him somehow, for it is fated so.

                                            AOI

8

The Emperor Charles is glad and full of cheer.
Cordova's taken, the outer walls are pierced,
His catapults have cast the towers down sheer;
Rich booty's gone to all his chevaliers,
100   Silver and gold and goodly battle-gear.
In all the city no paynim now appears
Who is not slain or turned to Christian fear.
The Emperor sits in a great orchard near,
Having about him Roland and Olivere,
105   Samson the duke, and Anseis the fierce,
Geoffrey d'Anjou the King's gonfalonier,
And Gerin too, and with him too Gerier;
And where these were was many another fere[6]—
Full fifteen thousand of France the fair and dear.

---

[6]*fere*—companion.

110 Upon white carpets they sit, those noble peers,
   For draughts and chess the chequer-boards are reared;
   To entertain the elder lords revered;
   Young bachelors disport with sword and spear.
   Beneath a pine beside an eglantier[7]
115 A faldstool stands all of the red gold clear;
   Of fairest France there sits the king austere.
   White are his locks, and silver is his beard,
   His body noble, his countenance severe:
   If any seek him, no need to say, "Lo, here!"
120 From off their steeds lit down the messengers,
   Well did they greet him with shows of love sincere.

9

   Before them all Blancandrin forward stood;
   And hailed the King: "God give His grace to you,
   The glorious God to whom worship is due.
125 Thus speaks the king, Marsilion, great in rule:
   Much hath he studied the saving faith and true.
   Now of his wealth he would send you in sooth
   Lions and bears, leashed greyhounds not a few,
   Sev'n hundred camels, a thousand falcons mewed,
130 And gold and silver borne on four hundred mules;
   A wagon-train of fifty carts to boot,
   And store enough of golden bezants good
   Wherewith to pay your soldiers as you should.
   Too long you've stayed in this land to our rue:
135 To Aix in France return you at our suit.
   Thither my liege will surely follow you,
   [And will become your man in faith and truth,
   And at your hand hold all his realm in feu!"]
   With lifted hands to God the Emperor sues;
140 Then bows his head and so begins to brood.
AOI

10

   The Emperor bode long time with downcast eyes;
   He was a man not hasty in reply,
   But wont to speak only when well advised.
   When he looked up, his glance was stem and high.

---

[7]*eglantier*—wild-rose bush.

145   He told the envoys: "Fair is your speech and fine;
         Yet King Marsile is foe to me and mine.
         In all these words and offers you recite
         I find no warrant wherein I may confide."
         "Sureties for this", the Saracen replies,
150   "Ten or fifteen or twenty we'll provide.
         One of my sons I'll send, on pain to die;
         Others, yet nobler, you'll have, as I divine.
         When in your palace high feast you solemnize
         To great St Michael of Peril-by-the-Tide,[8]
155   He'll follow you, on that you may rely,
         And in those baths[9] God made you by His might
         He would turn Christian and there would be baptized."
         Quoth Charles: "He yet may save his soul alive."

                                                    AOI

11

         Fair was the ev'ning and clearly the sun shone;
160   The ten white mules Charles sends to stall anon;
         In the great orchard he bids men spread aloft
         For the ten envoys a tent where they may lodge,
         With sergeants[10] twelve to wait on all their wants.
         They pass the night there till the bright day draws on.
165   Early from bed the Emperor now is got;
         At mass and matins he makes his orison.
         Beneath a pine straightway the King is gone,
         And calls his barons to council thereupon;
         By French advice whate'er he does is done.

                                                    AOI

12

170   The Emperor goes beneath a tall pine-tree,
         And to his council he calls his barony:

---

[8]*St Michael of Peril-by-the-Tide*—("St M. in periculo maris"). The name was originally given to the monastery built on the great island rock called Mont St Michel, off the coast of Normandy. Later it came to be applied to the Archangel himself, "*St Michel del Peril*".

[9]*baths*—the curative mineral springs for which Aix is still celebrated, and which were held to be of miraculous origin.

[10]*sergeants*—the word "sergeant", meaning primarily "servant", was applied generally to almost any man, under the rank of knight, who exercised any kind of office in a lord's household or on his estate. In military use, it denoted a tenant doing military service, especially one who was in attendance on a knight in the field. The "sergeant" marched and fought on horseback, but was more lightly armed than the "chevalier".

There Duke Ogier,[11] Archbishop Turpin meet,
Richard the Old[12] and his nephew Henri,
Count Acelin the brave of Gascony,
175   Miles, and his cousin the Lord Tibbald of Rheims,
Gerin likewise and Gerier are convened;
And County Roland, there with the rest came he,
And Oliver, noble and good at need;
All French of France, thousand and more, maybe;
180   And Ganelon that wrought the treachery.
So starts that council which came to such sore grief.

AOI

13

"Barons, my lords", began the Emperor Carlon,
"From King Marsile come envoys, seeking parley.
He makes me offers of treasure overpassing:
185   Of lions and bears and hounds to the leash mastered,
Sev'n hundred camels, and falcons mewed and hearty,
Four hundred mules with Arab gold all charged,
And fifty wagons well-laden in a cart-train.
But now to France he urges my departure,
190   And to my palace at Aix he'll follow after,
There change his faith for one of more advantage,
Become a Christian and of me hold his marches.
But his true purpose—for that I cannot answer."
The French all say: "We'd best be very guarded."

AOI

14

195   The Emperor Charles had finished all his speech.
The County Roland, who fiercely disagrees,
Swift to oppose springs up upon his feet:
He tells the King: "Nevermore trust Marsile!
Seven years long in land of Spain we've been.
200   I won for you both Noples and Commibles,
I took Valterna, the land of Pine I seized,
And Balagate, and Seville and Tudele.

---

[11]*Ogier the Dane*—this semi-historical hero boasts a *Chanson de Geste* devoted to his exploits, and figures in many others.
[12]*Richard the Old*—his historical prototype is Richard I of Normandy, who lived (943–996) later than Charlemagne's time, but has been attracted into the Carolingian cycle by the natural tendency of epic to accumulate famous names regardless of chronology.

Then wrought Marsile a very treacherous deed:
He sent his Paynims by number of fifteen,
205   All of them bearing boughs of the olive tree,
And with like words he sued to you for peace.
Then did you ask the French lords for their rede;[13]
Foolish advice they gave to you indeed.
You sent the Paynim two counts of your meinie:
210   Basan was one, the other was Basile.
He smote their heads off in hills beneath Haltile.
This war you've started wage on, and make no cease;
To Saragossa lead your host in the field,
Spend all your life, if need be, in the siege,
215   Revenge the men this villain made to bleed!"

                                                 AOI

15

The Emperor Charles sat still with his head bended;
He stroked his beard and his moustaches gently;
Nor good nor ill he answers to his nephew.
The French are silent, Guènes[14] alone excepted;
220   But he leaps up, strides into Carlon's presence,
And full of pride begins thus to address him.
He tells the King: "Trust not a brawling fellow,
Me nor another; seek only your own welfare.
If King Marsile informs you by this message
225   He'll set his hands in yours, and fealty pledge you,
And hold all Spain from you, at your good pleasure,
And to that faith we follow give acceptance,
The man who tells you this plea should be rejected
Cares nothing, Sire, to what death he condemns us.
230   Counsel of pride must not grow swollen-headed;
Let's hear wise men, turn deaf ears to the reckless."

                                                 AOI

16

Naimon at this stood forth before them all:
No better vassal was ever seen in hall.
He tells the King: "Well have you heard, my lord,
235   The arguments Count Ganelon sets forth.

---

[13]*rede*—counsel.
[14]*Guènes*—the alternate name for Ganelon.

There's weight in them, and you should give them thought.
The King Marsile is vanquished in the war,
You've taken from him his castles and his forts,
With catapults you've broken down his walls,
240   You've burned his cities and his armies outfought.
Now that he comes on your mercy to call
Foul sin it were to vex him any more.
Since he'll find sureties his good faith to support,
We should make haste to cut this great war short."
245   The French all say: "The Duke speaks as he ought."

                                      AOI

17

"Barons, my lords, whom shall we send anon
To Saragossa, to King Marsilion?"
"I, by your leave," saith Naimon, "will begone,
Therefore on me bestow the glove and wand."
250   "You are my wisest", the King makes answer prompt:
"Now by the beard my cheek and chin upon,
You shall not go so far this twelvemonth long.
Hence! sit you down, for we summon you not!"

18

"Barons, my lords, whom shall we send of you
255   To Saragossa, the Sarsen[15] king unto?"
"Myself", quoth Roland, "may well this errand do."
"That shall you not", Count Oliver let loose;
"You're high of heart and stubborn of your mood,
You'd land yourself, I warrant, in some feud.
260   By the King's leave this errand I will do."
The King replies: "Be silent there, you two!
Nor you nor he shall on that road set foot.
By this my beard that's silver to the view,
He that names any of the Twelve Peers shall rue!"
265   The French say nothing: they stand abashed and mute.

19

Then from their ranks arose Turpin of Rheims;
He tells the King: "Leave your French lords at ease;

---

[15]*Sarsen*—Saracen.

Full sev'n long years in this land have you been,
Much have they suffered of perils and fatigue;
270   Pray you then, Sire, give wand and glove to me;
The Saracen of Spain I'll seek and see,
And in his looks his purpose will I read."
The Emperor answers with anger in his mien:
"On that white carpet sit down and hold your peace;
275   Be still, I say, until I bid you speak."

                                            AOI

20

The Emperor said: "My free and knightly band,
Come choose me out some baron of my land
To bring my message to King Marsilion's hand."
Quoth Roland: "Guènes my step-sire is the man."
280   The French all say: "Indeed, he is most apt;
If he's passed over you will not find his match."
Count Ganelon is furious out of hand;
His great furred gown of marten he flings back
And stands before them in his silk bliaut clad.
285   Bright are his eyes, haughty his countenance,
Handsome his body, and broad his bosom's span;
The peers all gaze, his bearing is so grand.
He says to Roland: "Fool! what has made thee mad?
I am thy step-sire, and all these know I am,
290   And me thou namest to seek Marsilion's camp!
If God but grant I ever thence come back
I'll wreak on thee such ruin and such wrack
That thy life long my vengeance shall not slack."
Roland replies: "This is all boast and brag!
295   Threats cannot fright me, and all the world knows that
To bear this message we must have a good man;
I'll take your place if the King says I can."

                                            AOI

21

Quoth Ganelon: "My place thou shalt not take;
Thou'rt not my vassal, nor I thy suzerain.
300   Charles for his service commands me to obey.
I'll seek Marsile in Saragossa's gates;
But rather there some deadly trick I'll play

Than not find vent for my unbounded rage."
When Roland heard him, then he laughed in his face.

AOI

22

305 When Ganelon sees Roland laugh outright
He's fit to burst for anger and despite,
And very nearly goes clean out of his mind.
He tells the Count: "I love you not, not I;
You've picked on me unfairly, out of spite.
310 Just Emperor, here I stand before your eyes,
Ready to do whatever you think right.

23

To Saragossa I see that I must shift me;
There's no return for him that journeys thither.
Bethink you well that my wife is your sister,
315 A son she bare me, fairest of goodly children,
Baldwin," (quoth he) "and a champion he will be.
To him I leave all my lands and my living;
No more I'll see him; take care, Sir, of your kinsman."
Quoth Charles: "Your heart is too tender within you;
320 Go now you must, for even so I bid you."

AOI

24

Then said the King: "Stand forward, Ganelon,
Here at my hand receive the glove and wand;
You've heard the French—you are the man they want."
"Messire," said Guènes, "Roland hath done this wrong!
325 I'll never love him the whole of my life long,
Nor Oliver his friend and fellow fond,
Nor the Twelve Peers by whom he's doted on;
Sire, in your presence I defy the whole lot."
Then said the King: "Your passion is too hot;
330 I bid you go and so you must begone."
"Well may I go, but safeguard have I not,
Basile had none, nor Basan none, God wot."

AOI

2. The Song of Roland (Selections)

25

The King holds out to him his right-hand glove;
Fain would Count Guènes be an hundred miles off!
335   When he would take it, it fell into the dust.
"God! what is this?" cry all the French at once;
"For sure this message will bring us great ill-luck."
"My lords," quoth Guènes, "you'll know it soon enough."

26

"Sire, give me leave" quoth Guènes, "hence to hie;
340   Since go I must, it boots not to abide."
"Go", said the King, "by Jesu's leave and mine."
With his right hand he's absolved him and signed,[16]
And to his care letter and wand consigned.

27

Guènes the Count to his lodging makes speed,
345   Of his array he setteth him to seek
The best he has to serve him for this need.
His golden spurs he buckles on his heels,
Girds to his side Murgleys his brand of steel,
And mounts him up on Tachëbrun his steed;
350   His stirrup's held by Guinëmer his eme.[17]
Then might you see full many a brave knight weep,
Saying to him: "Woe worth your valour's meed!
In the King's court these many years you've been,
A noble vassal by all were you esteemed.
355   He that named you for this gear by his rede
Charlemayn's self shall not save him nor shield:
No right had Roland to have contrived this scheme;
For you're a man sprung of a noble breed."
Then they said, "Sir, take us with you, we plead."
360   Guènes replied: "God forbid it should be!
Best die alone nor slay good knights with me.
Sirs, you'll return to fair France presently:
On my behalf my wife I bid you greet,
And Pinabel that is my friend and peer.
365   Baldwin my son, whom you know well, I ween,

---

[16]*absolved him and signed*—i.e. pronounced the absolution over him, making the sign of the cross.
[17]*eme*—uncle.

Him shall you help and accept for your liege."
Then he sets forth and on his way goes he.

AOI

28

Under tall olives the County Guènes rides;
The Paynim envoys he's caught up in good time,
370 And Blancandrin drops back with him behind.
Now each to other begins to speak with guile.
Blancandrin says: "Charles is a wondrous wight!
Pulia he's ta'en, Calabria likewise,
And unto England passed over the salt tide
375 To win St Peter the tribute of the isle.[18]
What seeks he here, warring in our confines?"
"Such is his pleasure", Count Ganelon replies;
"In all the world you will not find his like."

AOI

29

Quoth Blancandrin: "The French are men of worth,
380 Yet to their lord they do a scurvy turn,
These dukes and counts, when they counsel such work;
Both him and others they harry to their hurt."
"There's none," quoth Guènes, "who merits such ill words,
Save only Roland, for whom 'twill be the worse.
385 But now, the Emperor in the cool shade conversed;
Up came his nephew all in his byrny girt,
Fresh with his booty from Carcassone returned.
Roland in hand a golden apple nursed
And showed his uncle, saying, 'Take it, fair sir;
390 The crowns I give you of all the kings on earth.'
One day his pride will undo him for sure,
Danger of death day by day he incurs.
If one should slay him some peace might be preserved."

AOI

30

Quoth Blancandrin: "Roland's a villain fell,
395 Presuming thus all folk on earth to quell,

---

[18]*the tribute of the isle*—The annual tribute known as "Peter's Pence", paid by England to the See of Rome, was of Anglo-Saxon origin, and instituted in the eighth or ninth century, though not in consequence of political or military pressure by Charlemagne.

2. The Song of Roland (Selections)

And every land under his yoke compel!
Whom does he count on to lend his arms such strength?"
Ganelon answers: "He counts upon the French;
They'll never fail him, they love him far too well.
400　　Silver and gold he gives them for largesse,
Horses and mules, silks and accoutrements.
And everything the Emperor wants, he gets—
He'll win for him all lands 'twixt east and west."

AOI

31

So long rides Guènes with Blancandrin that day
405　　Till each to each has pledged his truth and faith
They will seek means Count Roland for to slay.
So long they ride, they come by road and way
To Saragossa, and by a yew draw rein.
A faldstool[19] stood beneath a pine-tree's shade,
410　　With silken cloth of Alexandria draped;
There sat the King that bore the rule in Spain.
Full twenty thousand Saracens stood arrayed.
Not one of them has any word to say,
So eagerly upon the news they wait.
415　　And here come Guènes and Blancandrin apace!

32

Blancandrin came before Marsilion,
And by the hand held County Ganelon;
Saith to the King: "Save you, sir, by Mahond,
And by Apollyon, whose blest faith we extol!
420　　To Charles we gave your message every jot;
Both of his hands he lifted up aloft
And praised his God; further, he answered not.
One of his nobles, you see, he's sent along—
A lord of France, of most illustrious stock;
425　　From him you'll hear if peace is won or lost."
"We'll hear him," quoth Marsile; "let him say on."

AOI

---

[19]*faldstool*—a folding stool or chair.

33

Now Ganelon had giv'n this matter thought,
And with great cunning he now begins to talk,
Even as a man that's to the manner born.
430 He tells the King: "God have you in His ward,
The glorious God whom we ought to adore!
King Charlemayn, the Great, thus sends you word:
You must receive the faith of Christ Our Lord,
And as your fief half Spain he will award.
435 If you refuse to accept this accord,
You shall be taken and fettered by main force,
And haled away to Aix, into his court,
There to be doomed and done with once for all;
There shall you die in shamefulness and scorn."
440 On hearing this Marsile was quite distraught;
He held a dart with golden feathers wrought,
And would have struck him, but he was overborne.

AOI

34

The King Marsile has all his colour changed.
Grasping the shaft, his javelin he shakes.
445 When Guènes sees it he sets hand to his blade,
Two fingers' breadth forth of the scabbard hales,
And says to it: "Full bright you are and brave!
In the King's court I've borne you many a day!
Ne'er shall the Emperor of France have cause to say
450 I died alone in strange lands far away;
Before their bravest the price of you have paid!"
The Paynims cry: "We must prevent this fray."

35

The wiser Paynims remonstrate with him so
That King Marsile has sunk back on this throne.
455 Quoth the Caliph: "You put us to reproach,
Thinking to threaten this Frenchman with a blow!
It is your business to listen and take note."
Saith Ganelon: "All this, sir, must I thole.[20]
For all the gold God made, I'll not forgo,

---

[20]*thole*—endure.

460 No, not for all the wealth your land can boast,
  To speak the message—so I'm but given scope—
  Which Charles the King, that mighty man of mould,
  Has sent by me to this his mortal foe."
  He had on him a sable-fur-lined cloak
465 Covered with silk which Alexandria wove;
  He flings it down for Blancandrin to hold,
  But of his sword he nowise will let go;
  In his right hand he grasps the hilts of gold,
  The Paynims say: "Lo there a baron bold!"
               AOI

36

470 Guènes approached the King and thus addressed him:
  He saith to him: "You do vainly to vex you.
  Carlon thus bids you, that hath France in possession:
  The Christian faith must of you be accepted,
  And one half Spain he will give you in tenure;
475 The other half is for Roland his nephew;
  A right proud partner you'll have there for co-tenant!
  If these conditions should by you be rejected,
  In Saragossa he'll besiege and invest you,
  And by main force you shall be seized and fettered.
480 Thence to his city of Aix you'll go directly.
  You shall not ride on palfrey nor on destrier,
  Nor for the road shall you have mule nor jennet;
  On some poor screw of a pack-ass he'll set you;
  And you will lose your head there by his sentence.
485 See now, the Emperor has written you this letter."
  To the right hand of the Moor he presents it.

37

  The King Marsile for very rage went white;
  He breaks the seal and flings the wax aside,
  Looks at the letter and reads what is inside.
490 "These words to me Carlon the French King writes:
  I'm to remember his grief and his despite
  For those two brothers, Basan and Basil hight,
  Whom I beheaded in Haltoye-on-the-Height;
  And if I value the purchase of my life,
495 Must send my uncle the Caliph as his prize;
  Else nevermore will he be friend of mine."

Marsilion's son at this broke in and cried:
"Ganelon's words are madness out of mind!
This is too much—he shall not rest alive;
500   Give him to me and justice he shall find!"
When Guènes heard, he shook his blade on high,
And set his back to the trunk of the pine.

38

Unto the orchard the King Marsile repairs;
Of his best men he takes with him a share,
505   And thither came Blancandrin white of hair,
And Jurfaret, who is his son and heir,
And the Caliph, his eme and officer.
Quoth Blancandrin: "Call in that Frenchman there:
He'll serve our ends, to this I've heard him swear."
510   "Fetch him yourself, 'twere best", the King declares.
In his right hand Count Ganelon he bare
Into the orchard where king and council were.
So they begin to plot the treacherous snare.

                             AOI

39

"Guènes, fair sir," said Marsile, "I allow,
515   Something too lightly I treated you just now
When in my fury I would have struck you down;
But by these pelts of sable fur I vow,
Which of good gold are worth five hundred pounds,
Richly I'll quite you ere the next day be out."
520   "This I refuse not", said Ganelon the Count;
"God, if He please, shall balance the account."

                             AOI

40

"Truly, Count Guènes," then said the King Marsile.
"I have in mind your right good friend to be.
Of Charlemayn fain would I hear you speak.
525   He's very old, a hard life his has been;
Two hundred years and more I know he's seen;
In lands so many his body he's fatigued,
Hard strokes so many he's taken on his shield,
Rich kings so many he's brought to beggary—

530 When will he weary of fighting in the field?"
 "That's not his way", said Guènes, "in the least.
 None knows the Emperor, or looks upon his mien,
 But says of him: 'A right great man is he.'
 Howe'er I sounded his praise and his esteem,
535 His worth and honour would still outrun my theme.
 His mighty valour who could proclaim in speech?
 God kindled in him a courage so supreme,
 He'd rather die than fail his knights at need."

AOI

41

 The Paynim said: "I marvel in my thought,
540 At Charlemayn, that is so old and hoar!
 I know he's lived two hundred years and more.
 In lands so many his body he's forworn,
 Sharp strokes so many of lance and spear has borne,
 Rich kings so many beggared and brought to naught—
545 When will he weary of going to the wars?"
 "Never", said Guènes, "while Roland still bears sword;
 There's none so valiant beneath the heavens broad,
 Oliver too, his friend, is a brave lord;
 And the Twelve Peers whom Charles so much adores
550 Protect the vanward with knights a thousand score;
 Charles is secure, he fears no man at all."

AOI

42

 The Paynim said: "I marvel in my mind
 At Charlemayn whose head is old and white.
 Two hundred years, I know, have passed him by.
555 In lands so many he's conquered far and wide,
 Lance-thrusts so many he's taken in the strife,
 Rich kings so many brought to a beggar's plight—
 When will he weary of going forth to fight?"
 "Never", said Guènes, "while Roland sees the light;
560 'Twixt east and west his valour has no like,
 Oliver too, his friend, is a brave knight;
 And the twelve Peers, in whom the King delights,
 With twenty thousand Frenchmen to vanward ride:
 Charles is secure, he fears no man alive."

AOI

43

565   "Guènes, fair sir," then said the King directly,
       "I have an army, you will not find a better,
       Four hundred thousand good knights as I may reckon:
       Can I give battle to Carlon and his Frenchmen?"
       Guènes replies: "Not you, and so I tell you,
570   For of your Paynims the losses would be deadly.
       Leave all this folly, come to your sober senses.
       Send to the Emperor so huge a heap of treasure
       That all the French will marvel at its splendour.
       For twenty sureties, that you will likewise send him,
575   Back to fair France Charles will return contented,
       Leaving behind a rear-guard to protect him.
       With them, I warrant, will be Roland his nephew,
       Oliver too, the valorous and gentle.
       Dead are these Counts, if you will give me credit.
580   Carlon will see his great pride fall'n and ended;
       He'll have no heart to fight with you from henceforth."
                                                         AOI

44

       "Guènes, fair sir," [the King Marsilion cries,]
       "What must I do to bring Roland to die?"
       "I'll tell you that", Count Ganelon replies.
585   "At Sizer Gate[21] the King will have arrived,
       Leaving a rear-guard to keep the pass behind.
       There'll be his nephew Count Roland, the great knight,
       Oliver too, on whom he most relies,
       With twenty thousand good Frenchmen at their side.
590   An hundred thousand send of your Paynim kind,
       And these shall first engage the French in fight.
       Of the French force the loss will not be light—
       Yours will be slaughtered, and that I'll not disguise!
       The like assault you'll launch a second time,
595   And, first or last, Roland will not get by.
       You will have done a deed of arms full fine;
       You'll ne'er again see war in all your life.
                                                         AOI

---

[21]*Sizer Gate: Port de Sizer*, or *Sizer* (the spelling varies)—this is the pass now called the Col de Cize, which cuts through the Pyrenees on the road running from St-Jean-Pied-de-Port by way of Roncevaux to Pampeluna, and forms the "Gate of Spain".

2. The Song of Roland (Selections)

45

Whoso should smite the County Roland dead,
From Carlon's body then were the right hand reft;
600   The wondrous armies would dwindle off and melt,
Nor could Charles gather so great a host afresh;
Our fathers' land[22] would thus find peace and rest."
When he heard this Marsile fell on his neck,
And straightway bad them unlock his treasure-chests.

                                         AOI

46

605   Then said Marsile: "One thing alone remains:
There's no good bond where there is no good faith;
Give me your oath Count Roland to betray."
Guènes replies: "It shall be as you say."
Upon the relics of his good sword Murgleys
610   He sware the treason and sware his faith away.

                                         AOI

47

There was a faldstool of ivory all wrought;
Marsile commands a volume[23] to be brought
Of Termagant's and of Mahomet's law;
The Saracen of Spain thereon has sworn
615   That in the rear-guard Count Roland shall be sought;
If there he find him, he'll fight with his whole force,
And do his best to slay him once for all.
Guènes replies: "And may it so befall!"

                                         AOI

48

Lo, now! there comes a Paynim, Valdebron;
620   He stands before the King Marsilion,
And gaily laughing he says to Ganelon:
"Here, take my sword, a better blade is none.

---

[22] *Our fathers' land*—Tere Majur (*terram majorum*): the land of one's ancestors, the Fatherland—i.e. France. The phrase is often put into the mouths even of Saracen speakers, as though it were a proper name. (Some editors translate it simply "the Great Land", *terram majorem*.)
[23] *a volume*—the Koran?

A thousand mangons[24] are in the hilt thereof;
'Tis yours, fair sir, for pure affection,
625   For help against Roland the champion,
If in the rear-guard we find him as we want."
Quoth Ganelon to him: "It shall be done."
They kiss each other the cheek and chin upon.

49

Thereafter comes a Paynim, Climborin,
630   And laughing gaily to Ganelon begins:
"Come, take my helm, I ne'er saw none so rich:
[Above the nasal a carbuncle there is.
out of pure friendship I offer you this gift]
If against Roland you'll aid us by your wit
635   That we may bring a shameful death on him."
"It shall be done", quoth Ganelon to this;
They kissed each other upon the mouth and chin.

                                      AOI

50

Then to the Count Queen Bramimonda spoke:
"Dearly, fair sir, I love you, by my troth,
640   My king so lauds you, and his vassals also.
This pair of owches[25] on your wife I bestow,
Heavy with jacinth and amethyst and gold;
More worth are they than all the wealth of Rome,
The like of them your Emperor never owned."
645   He takes the jewels and thrusts them in his poke.[26]

                                        AOI

51

The King calls Malduit, the keeper of his treasure:
"King Carlon's gifts, have you yet got them ready?"
And he replies, "Yea, sire, in ample measure:
Sev'n hundred camels laden with precious metal,
650   And twenty sureties, the noblest under heaven."

                                        AOI

---

[24] *mangons*—the mangon is a Saracen gold coin.
[25] *owches*—brooches?.
[26] *poke*—pouch.

2. The Song of Roland (Selections)

52

Marsilion's hand on Guènes' shoulder lies;
He says to him: "You are both bold and wise.
Now by that faith which seems good in your eyes
Let not your heart turn back from our design.
655 Treasure I'll give you, a great and goodly pile,
Ten mule-loads gold, digged from Arabian mines;
No year shall pass but you shall have the like.
Take now the keys of this great burg of mine,
Offer King Charles all its riches outright.
660 Make sure that Roland but in the rear-guard rides,
And if in pass or passage I him find
I'll give him battle right bitter to abide."
"I think", said Guènes, "that I am wasting time."
He mounts his horse and on his journey hies.

AOI

53

665 The Emperor now returns upon his way
And has arrived before the town of Gayne
(Count Roland took it and all its wall down-razed,
An hundred years thereafter it lay waste;)
And there the King for news of Guènes waits,
670 And for the tribute of the great land of Spain.
In the white dawn, at breaking of the day,
Into the camp the County Guènes came.

AOI

54

Early that day the Emperor leaves his bed.
Matins and mass the King has now heard said;
675 On the green grass he stood before his tent.
Roland was with him, brave Oliver as well,
Naimon the Duke and many another yet.
Then perjured Guènes the traitor comes to them
And starts to speak with cunning false pretence.
680 He tells the King: "To you (whom God defend!)
Of Saragossa the keys I here present.
I bring you also wealth to your heart's content,

And twenty sureties: [27]see they be closely kept.
The valiant king, Marsile, this message sends:
685   The Caliph's absence he prays you'll not resent.
Mine own eyes saw four hundred thousand men
In hauberk armed, some having laced their helms,
And girt with swords whose hilts were richly gemmed,
Attend him forth; to the sea-shore they went.
690   The faith of Christ they'd keep not, nor accept,
And for this cause they from Marsilion fled.
But ere they'd sailed four leagues, maybe, or less,
Black wind and storm and tempest on them fell;
They were all drowned; they'll ne'er be seen again.
695   Had he been living I would have had him fetched.
Now, as regards the Paynim King himself.
Believe me, sire, before a month is sped
He'll follow you to France, to your own realm.
There he'll receive the faith that you profess,
700   There with joined hands to you his fealty pledge,
And hold from you in fief the Spanish realm."
Then said the King: "The name of God be blest!
Well have you done: I shall reward you well."
Throughout the host a thousand trumpets swell,
705   The French strike camp, their goods on sumpters set;
Home to fair France behold them all addressed.

AOI

55

King Charlemayn has spoiled the Spanish borders,
He's taken castles, put cities to the slaughter;
Now the King says he has ended his warfare.
710   Home to fair France the Emperor turns his horses.

* * * * *28

Pennon to lancehead Count Roland now has corded;
High on a hillock he displays it abroad there.
In fields all round the French set up their quarters.
Through the wide valleys the Paynim hosts go forward,

---

[27] *twenty sureties*—this is the last we hear of the hostages, whose ultimate fate is not mentioned.
[28] The scribe has perhaps omitted a line or two here, mentioning where Charlemagne and his army have got to. We learn from laisse 58 that they have reached the entrance to the pass, at the foot of the Pyrenees.

715   [All fully armed,] accoutred in their corslets,
Their helms laced on, and their swords in the sword-belt,
Shields on their necks, and their lances well ordered.
High on the mountains in a thicket they've halted:
Four hundred thousand they wait there for the morning;
720   God! it is grievous that the French have no warning!

                                              AOI

56

The day goes down, dark follows on the day.
The Emperor sleeps, the mighty Charlemayn.
He dreamed he stood in Sizer's lofty gate,
Holding in hand his ashen lance full great.
725   Count Ganelon takes hold of it, and shakes,
And with such fury he wrenches it and breaks
That high as heaven the flinders fly away.
Carlon sleeps on, he sleeps and does not wake.

57

After this dream he had another dream:
730   That in his chapel at Aix in France was he;
In his right arm a fierce bear[29] set its teeth.
Forth from Ardennes he saw a leopard speed,
That with rash rage his very body seized.
Then from the hall ran in a greyhound fleet,
735   And came to Carlon by gallops and by leaps.
From the first brute it bit the right ear clean,
And to the leopard gives battle with great heat.
The French all say the fight is good to see,
But none can guess which shall the victor be.
740   Carlon sleeps on; he wakes not from his sleep.

                                              AOI

58

The night is past and the clear dawn is showing.
[A thousand trumpets] are sounded for the hosting.
The Emperor rides full lordly in his going.
"Barons, my lords," quoth Charlemayn, "behold now
745   These lofty passes, these narrows winding closely—

---

[29]*a fierce bear*, etc.: the bear is presumably Ganelon, as in laisse 186; the leopard, Marsilion; the greyhound, Roland.

Say, who shall have the rearguard now to hold them?"
Quoth Ganelon: "I name my nephew Roland;
You have no baron who can beat him for boldness."
When the King heard, a stern semblance he showed him:
750   "A fiend incarnate you are indeed", he told him;
"Malice hath ta'en possession of you wholly!
Who then should keep the vanguard[30] of my progress?"
Quoth Ganelon: "Ogier the Dane I vote for;
You have no baron can do it with more prowess."

AOI

59

755   When Roland hears what he's appointed to,
He makes reply as knighthood bids him do:
"My noble stepsire, I owe you gratitude
That I'm assigned the rearguard at your suit.
Charles, King of France, the loss shall never rue
760   Of steed or palfrey thereby, I warrant you,
No saddle-beast, nor hinny neither mule,
Pack-horse nor sumpter thereby he shall not lose,
Save first the sword have paid the reckoning due."
Quoth Ganelon: "I know it; you speak truth."

AOI

60

765   When Roland hears that to the rearward guard
His stepsire names him, he speaks in wrath of heart:
"Ah! coward wretch, foul felon, baseborn carle,
Didst think the glove would fall from out my grasp
As did the wand[31] from thine, before King Charles?"

AOI

61

770   "Just Emperor," then besought Count Roland bold,
"From your right hand deliver me your bow;[32]

---

[30]*who then should keep the vanguard?*—i.e. in Roland's place, since he usually takes command there with the other peers.

[31]*the wand*—the mention of the wand, here and in L. 774, seems to be a lapse of memory on the poet's part. Actually (LL. 333–335) it was the glove that Ganelon let fall.

[32]*your bow*—the use of a bow as the token of an appointment does not seem to be very usual, nor is it clear why Charlemagne should have one in his hand, since the bow was not

No man, I swear, shall utter the reproach
That I allowed it to slip from out my hold
As did the wand that Ganelon let go."
775   The Emperor sits with his head bended low,
On cheek and chin be plucks his beard for woe,
He cannot help but let the tears o'erflow.

62

Straightway thereon comes Naimon to the King—
No better vassal in court did ever sit.
780   He says to him: "You've listened to all this;
The County Roland is angered to the quick;
The rear-guard now has been adjudged to him
And you've no baron can ever make him quit.
Give him the bow now bended in your grip,
785   And find good men to aid him in this shift."
So the King gives it, and Roland seizes it.

63

To Roland then the King his uncle said:
"Nephew, fair sir, hear now and heed me well:
Half of my army I'll leave you for this stead;
790   Keep them with you and you'll be safe with them."
The Count said: "No; I never will consent;
May God confound me if I shame my descent!
A thousand score I'll keep of valiant French.
Safe through the passes go you with confidence;
795   Never fear man so long as I draw breath."
                                     AOI

64

Roland the Count mounts on his destrier.
Comes then to him his comrade Oliver,
And Gerin comes and brave Count Gerier,
And Othon comes and so does Berenger,
800   Old Anseis, and Astor, great of worth,
And Gerard[33] too, Roussillon's haughty earl;

---

reckoned as a "noble" weapon, except for use in hunting. Later MSS substitute, or add, the more customary glove or standard.

[33]*Gerard of Roussillon*—not Roussillon in the Pyrenees, but a hill in Burgundy (now Mont Lassois), near the Abbey of Pothières, which was founded, together with the Abbey of

And with them comes the rich Duke Gaïfer.
Quoth the Archbishop: "By Heav'n, I'm with you, sirs!"
"And so am I," Walter the Count affirms,
805　"I'm Roland's man,[34] him am I bound to serve!"
Knights twenty thousand they choose for followers.

AOI

65

To Walter Hum Count Roland gives command:
"A thousand French take, of our own French land,
And hold the gorges and heights on either hand;
810　Nor let the Emperor lose from his side one man."
Quoth Walter: "Mine to do as you demand."
With thousand French of France their own dear land
On gorge and hill Count Walter holds the flanks;
Come what come may he'll never quit his stand
815　Till from the sheath have flashed sev'n hundred brands.
King Almeric,[35] lord of Balferna's strand,
That day shall give hard battle to their band.

66

High are the hills, the valleys dark and deep,
Grisly the rocks, and wondrous grim the steeps.
820　The French pass through that day with pain and grief,
The bruit of them was heard full fifteen leagues.
But when at length their fathers' land they see,
Their own lord's land, the land of Gascony,
Then they remember their honours and their fiefs,
825　Sweethearts and wives whom they are fain to greet,
Not one there is for pity doth not weep.
Charles most of all a boding sorrow feels,
His nephew's left the Spanish gates to keep;
For very ruth he cannot choose but weep.

AOI

Vézelay by the historical Gerard. His exploits are celebrated in the *Chanson de Geste* which bears his name.
[34]*man*—i.e. vassal.
[35]The engagement between Almeric and Walter Hum is not described in the poem; its results are mentioned in laisse 152.

2. The Song of Roland (Selections)

67

830   All the twelve peers in Spain are left behind,
Full twenty thousand stout Frenchmen at their side;
Valiant they are, and have no fear to die.
To land of France the Emperor homeward hies.
And still his face beneath his cloak he hides.
835   Close at his rein the good Duke Naimon rides;
He asks the King: "What troubles thus your mind?"
"This is ill done", quoth Charles, "to ask me why!
So much I grieve I cannot choose but sigh.
Through Ganelon fair France is ruined quite.
840   An angel showed me a vision in the night,
How in my hand he broke my lance outright,
He that my nephew to the rear-guard assigned.
In foreign marches[36] abandoned, Roland bides—
God! if I lose him I shall not find his like."

                                            AOI

68

845   King Charlemayn from tears cannot refrain;
Full hundred thousand, the French grieve for his sake,
And for Count Roland are wondrously afraid.
Him has the false lord Ganelon betrayed;
Vast the reward the paynim king has paid:
850   Silver and gold, and cloth of silk and saye,[37]
Horses and mules, camels and beasts of prey.
Marsile has called the barony of Spain;
His viscounts, counts, almanzors stand arrayed,
Dukes and emirs, and youths of high estate;
855   Four hundred thousand he's summoned in three days.
In Saragossa he bids his tabors play;
Mahound their idol high on the tower they raise,
And every Paynim adores and gives it praise.
Then by forced marches their army hastes away,
860   Through Terracerta[38] they ride by hill and dale.
Now have they seen French gonfalons displayed.
The twelve companions who in the rear-guard wait
Mean to give battle, and none shall say them nay.

---

[36]*marches*—the frontier region of a province; the province itself.
[37]*saye*—a fine cloth of silk and wool.
[38]*Terracerta*—Tere Certaine—possibly Cerdagne, the region about Catalonia.

69

865

Marsilion's nephew[39] trips out before the throng,
Riding a mule which he whips with a wand;
He tells his uncle with laughter on his tongue:
"Fair sir and king, I've served you well and long;
Much have I suffered, much labour undergone,
Many fields fought, and many battles won!

870

First blow at Roland[40] is the reward I want;
With my sharp sword I'll split him through the sconce!
Yea, if I find good favour with Mahond,
I'll set Spain free, unloosing of her bonds
From Gate of Spain to Durstant and beyond.

875

Charles will lose heart, the French will yield anon,
You shall be quit of wars your whole life long."
He gets the glove from King Marsilion.

AOI

70

Marsilion's nephew holds the glove in his fist:
Unto his uncle thus proudly he begins:

880

"Fair sire and king, you've made me a great gift.
Find me twelve lords, the best that you can pick.
'Gainst the twelve peers our valour for to pit."
The first that answers is Falsaron to wit,
He was own brother unto Marsile the king:

885

"You and I, nephew, will gladly go to it.
In very deed this battle will we give
To Carlon's rearward that guards his host for him:
The thing is done! by us they'll all be killed."

AOI

71

King Corsablis now springs from out the host,

890

Barbarian born, the magic art he knows.
Like a brave man thus valiantly he spoke:
"No coward I, no, not for all God's gold!"

---

[39] *Marsilion's nephew*—his name, as we learn in L. 1195, is Adelroth.

[40] *first blow at Roland (le colp de Roland)*—the privilege of striking the first blow in the battle was much sought after. Much later, we find Malpramis, the son of the Emir Baligant, similarly demanding of his father the honour (*le colp*) in the battle with Charlemagne. The commander-in-chief bestows the honour by handing over his glove in token (L. 878).

2. The Song of Roland (Selections)

* * * * *41

Malprimis of Brigale comes spurring bold,
He'll run afoot swifter than steed can go;
895 With a loud voice before Marsile he boasts:
"I'll bear my body with you to Roncevaux:
if I find Roland I'll fight till he's laid low."

72

From Balaguet there cometh an Emir;
His form is noble his eyes are bold and clear,
900 When on his horse he's mounted in career
He bears him bravely armed in his battle-gear
And for his courage he's famous far and near;
Were he but Christian, right knightly he'd appear.
Before Marsile he cries for all to hear:
905 "To Roncevaux", saith he, "my course I'll steer;
If I find Roland, then death shall be his weird,42
And Oliver's, and all of the Twelve Peers!
The French shall die the death in shame and tears.
King Charlemayn, the dotard old and blear,
910 Will soon be sick of waging warfare here!
Spain shall be ours in peace this many a year!"
The King Marsile pours thanks into his ears.

AOI

73

Comes an Almanzor, a lord of Moriane,
There's no worse villain in all the land of Spain,
915 Before Marsilion his bragging boast he makes:
"To Roncevaux I'll lead my people straight,
Full twenty thousand with spear and lance arrayed.
If I meet Roland I'll kill him, by my faith!
No day shall dawn but Carlon shall bewail."

AOI

41A few lines seem to have been omitted here, completing Corsablis' speech of defiance.
42*weird*—doom.

74

920   And next there comes Turgis of Tortelosa;
        A count he is, and the whole city owneth;
        A right ill will to Christian men he showeth.
        Before Marsile with the rest he enrols him.
        He tells the King: "Fear not for any foeman!
925   Mahound's worth more than St Peter the Roman;
        Serve him; the field is ours and ours the trophy!
        To Roncevaux I go to meet with Roland;
        There shall he die; he shall have help of no man.
        See here my sword, how long it is and noble;
930   'Gainst Durendal I'll measure it right boldly;
        Which shall prevail you'll not be long in knowing.
        The French shall die if they dare to oppose us;
        Carlon the old shall be grieving and groaning;
        Crown nevermore shall he wear from that moment."

75

935   And Escremiz of Valterne is the next;
        He owns that fief, and he's a Saracen;
        Before Marsile he shouts amid the press:
        "To Ronceval I go to stoop their crests.
        If I find Roland, there shall he lose his head,
940   And Oliver, who's captain of the rest;
        The whole Twelve Peers are all marked out for death.
        The French shall die and France shall be bereft.
        Few men of worth to Carlon shall be left."

                                                    AOI

76

        Next comes a Paynim, called Estorgan by name,
945   Estramarin his comrade with him came;
        Foul felons both and knavish traitors they.
        Then said Marsile: "My lords, draw near, I pray;
        Through Roncevaux you mean to force your way,
        And lead my troops, and lend us your best aid."
950   And they reply: "Command, and we obey.
        Both Oliver and Roland we'll assail,
        Of the Twelve Peers none shall survive the fray.
        Sharp are our swords and goodly are the blades,
        All in hot blood we'll dye them red this day;

955 The French shall die, and Carlon shall bewail.
A gift we'll make you of the home of their race;
Come with us, King, and see how goes the game,
And as a gift we'll give you Charlemayn."

77

Then comes at speed Margaris of Seville,
960 Who holds his land as far as Cazmarin.
Ladies all love him, so beautiful he is,
She that beholds him has a smile on her lips,
Will she or nill she, she laughs for very bliss,
And there's no Paynim his match for chivalry.
965 He joins the throng and cries unto the King
Loudest of all: "Never you fear a whit!
In Roncevaux this Roland I'll go kill,
Nor Oliver shall any longer live;
All the Twelve Peers we'll cut in little bits.
970 Lo! here my sword with golden pummel gilt!
Th' Emir of Primes gave it me for a gift,
I swear I'll dye it vermilion to the hilt.
The French shall die and France in shame shall sit.
Old greybeard Charles shall never live, I think,
975 One day but what he'll rage and weep for this.
France can be ours in a year if we will;
In Saint-Denis[43] we'll eat and sleep our fill."
The Paynim. King makes deep salaam to him.
                                                        AOI

78

980 And last there comes Chernubles of Munigre;
His unshorn hair hangs trailing to his feet.
He for his sport can shoulder if he please
More weight than four stout sumpter-mules can heave.
He dwells in regions wherein, so 'tis believed,
985 Sun never shines nor springs one blade of wheat,
No rain can fall, no dew is ever seen,
There, every stone is black as black can be,
And some folk say it's the abode of fiends.
Chernubles saith: "My sword's girt in the sheath;
990 In Roncevaux red blood shall dye it deep.

---

[43]*Saint-Denis*—a town near Paris with a famous abbey, founded by Dagobert in 626, the burial-place of the Kings of France.

Should Roland cross my path, that doughty chief,
And I not smite him, never put faith in me!
To this my blade his Durendal shall yield,
The French shall die, and France be left bereaved."
995   This said, the whole Twelve Champions are convened;
One hundred thousand stout Saracens they lead.
Each one afire with zeal to do great deeds.
Beneath a pine-grove they arm them for the field.

79

    Now are the Paynims in Sarsen hauberks dight
1000   Whereof the most with triple mail are lined;
Good Saragossa helms they lace on tight,
Swords of Viana steel gird on their thighs;
Spears of Valence they have, and shields full fine,
Their gonfalons are scarlet, blue, and white.
1005   They leave their mules, their palfreys leave behind,
And mount their steeds; in serried ranks they ride.
Fair was the day, the sun shone clear and bright,
No piece of harness but glittered in the light.
A thousand trumpets ring out for more delight.
1010   Great is the noise; it reaches the French lines.
Quoth Oliver: "I think, companion mine,
We'll need this day with Saracens to fight."
Roland replies: "I hope to God you're right!
Here must we stand to serve on the King's side.
1015   Men for their lords great hardship must abide,
Fierce heat and cold endure in every clime,
Lose for his sake, if need be, skin and hide.
Look to it now! Let each man stoutly smite!
No shameful songs be sung for our despite!
1020   Paynims are wrong, Christians are in the right!
Ill tales of me shall no man tell, say I!"

                                            AOI

80

    Oliver's climbed upon a hilly crest,
Looks to his right along a grassy cleft,
And sees the Paynims and how they ride addressed.
1025   To his companion Roland he calls and says:
"I see from Spain a tumult and a press—
Many bright hauberks, and many a shining helm!

A day of wrath, they'll make it for our French.
Ganelon knew it, false heart and traitor fell;
1030   When to the Emperor he named us for this stead!"
Quoth Roland: "Silence, Count Oliver, my friend!
He is my stepsire, I will have no word said."

81

Oliver's climbed a hill above the plain,
Whence he can look on all the land of Spain,
1035   And see how vast the Saracen array;
All those bright helms with gold and jewels gay,
And all those shields, those coats of burnished mail,
And all those lances from which the pennons wave;
Even their squadrons defy all estimate,
1040   He cannot count them, their numbers are so great;
Stout as he is, he's mightily dismayed.
He hastens down as swiftly as he may,
Comes to the French and tells them all his tale.

82

Quoth Oliver: "The Paynim strength I've seen;
1045   Never on earth has such a hosting been:
A hundred thousand in van ride under shield
Their helmets laced, their hauberks all agleam
Their spears upright, with heads of shining steel.
You'll have such battle as ne'er was fought on field.
1050   My lords of France, God give you strength at need!
Save you stand fast, this field we cannot keep."
The French all say: "Foul shame it were to flee!
We're yours till death; no man of us will yield."

                                      AOI

83

Quoth Oliver: "Huge are the Paynim hordes,
1055   And of our French the numbers seem but small,
Companion Roland, I pray you sound your horn,
That Charles may hear and fetch back all his force."
Roland replies: "Madman were I and more,
And in fair France my fame would suffer scorn.
1060   I'll smite great strokes with Durendal my sword,
I'll dye it red high as the hilt with gore.

This pass the Paynims reached on a luckless morn;
I swear to you death is their doom therefor."

AOI

84

"Companion Roland, your Olifant[44] now sound!
1065   King Charles will hear and turn his armies round;
He'll succour us with all his kingly power."
Roland replies: "May never God allow
That I should cast dishonour on my house
Or on fair France bring any ill renown!
1070   Rather will I with Durendal strike out,
With this good sword, here on my baldrick bound;
From point to hilt you'll see the blood run down.
Woe worth the Paynims that e'er they made this rout!
I pledge my faith, we'll smite them dead on ground."

AOI

85

1075   "Companion Roland, your Olifant now blow;
Charles in the passes will hear it as he goes,
Trust me, the French will all return right so."
"Now God forbid", Roland makes answer wroth,
"That living man should say he saw me go
1080   Blowing of horns for any Paynim foe!
Ne'er shall my kindred be put to such reproach.
When I shall stand in this great clash of hosts
I'll strike a thousand and then sev'n hundred strokes,
Blood-red the steel of Durendal shall flow.
1085   Stout are the French, they will do battle bold,
These men of Spain shall die and have no hope."

86

Quoth Oliver: "Herein I see no blame:
I have beheld the Saracens of Spain;
They cover all the mountains and the vales,
1090   They spread across the hillsides and the plains;
Great is the might these foreigners display,

---

[44]*Olifant*—the word (which is a form of "elephant") means (a) ivory, (b) a horn made of ivory, and is used specifically, almost as a proper name, to denote Roland's horn, made of an elephant's tusk, and adorned with gold and jewels about the rim.

And ours appears a very small array."
"I thirst the more", quoth Roland, "for the fray.
God and His angels forbid it now, I pray,
1095   That e'er by me fair France should be disfamed!
I'd rather die than thus be put to shame;
If the King loves us it's for our valour's sake."

87

Roland is fierce and Oliver is wise
And both for valour may bear away the prize.
1100   Once horsed and armed the quarrel to decide,
For dread of death the field they'll never fly.
The counts are brave, their words are stern and high.
Now the false Paynims with wondrous fury ride.
Quoth Oliver: "Look, Roland, they're in sight.
1105   Charles is far off, and these are very nigh;
You would not sound your Olifant for pride;
Had we the Emperor we should have been all right.
To Gate of Spain turn now and lift your eyes,
See for yourself the rear-guard's woeful plight.
1110   Who fights this day will never more see fight."
Roland replies: "Speak no such foul despite!
Curst be the breast whose heart knows cowardise!
Here in our place we'll stand and here abide:
Buffets and blows be ours to take and strike!"

                                                  AOI

88

1115   When Roland sees that battle there must be
Leopard nor lion ne'er grew so fierce as he.
He calls the French, bids Oliver give heed:
"Sir friend and comrade, such words you shall not speak!
When the King gave us the French to serve this need
1120   These twenty thousand he chose to do the deed;
And well he knew not one would flinch or flee.
Men must endure much hardship for their liege,
And bear for him great cold and burning heat,
Suffer sharp wounds and let their bodies bleed.
1125   Smite with your lance and I with my good steel,
My Durendal the Emperor gave to me:
And if I die, who gets it may agree
That he who bore it, a right good knight was he."

89

	Then to their side comes the Archbishop Turpin,
1130	Riding his horse and up the hillside spurring.
	He calls the French and preaches them a sermon:
	"Barons, my lords, Charles picked us for this purpose;
	We must be ready to die in our King's service.
	Christendom needs you, so help us to preserve it.
1135	Battle you'll have, of that you may be certain,
	Here come the Paynims—your own eyes have observed them.
	Now beat your breasts and ask God for His mercy:
	I will absolve you and set your souls in surety.
	If you should die, blest martyrdom's your guerdon;
1140	You'll sit on high in Paradise eternal."
	The French alight and all kneel down in worship;
	God's shrift and blessing the Archbishop conferreth,
	And for their penance he bids them all strike firmly.

90

	The French rise up and on their feet stand close;
1145	All of their sins are shriven and made whole,
	And the Archbishop God's blessing has bestowed.
	Then on swift steeds they leap to saddlebow.
	Armed with the arms prescribed by knightly code;
	All are now ready into the field to go.
1150	Count Roland said to Oliver right so:
	"Sir my companion, too true the word you spoke,
	That all of us by Ganelon were sold.
	He's ta'en his wage of wealth and goods and gold.
	The Emperor's vengeance I think will not be slow!
1155	Marsile the King has bargained for our bones:
	He'll need the sword to fetch his purchase home."

AOI

91

	Through Gate of Spain Roland goes riding past
	On Veillantif, his swiftly-running barb;
	Well it becomes him to go equipped in arms,
1160	Bravely he goes, and tosses up his lance,
	High in the sky he lifts the lancehead far,
	A milk-white pennon is fixed above the shaft
	Whose falling fringes whip his hands on the haft.

2. The Song of Roland (Selections)

Nobly he bears him, with open face he laughs;
1165 And his companion behind him follows hard;
The Frenchmen all acclaim him their strong guard.
On Saracens he throws a haughty glance
But meek and mild looks on the men of France,
To whom he speaks out of a courteous heart:
1170 "Now, my lord barons, at walking pace—advance!
Looking for trouble these Paynims ride at large—
A fine rich booty we'll have ere this day's past;
Never French king beheld the like by half."
E'en as he speaks, their battles join and charge.

AOI

92

1175 Quoth Oliver: "I have no more to say:
To sound your horn for help you would not deign,
So here you are, you've not got Charlemayn;
Little he knows, brave heart! he's not to blame.
Nor those with him, nowise in fault are they.
1180 Ride forward then and do the best you may!
Barons my lords, hold firm amid the fray!
Now for God's sake be resolute, I pray,
To strike hard blows, to give them and to take.
King Carlon's war-cry forget not to proclaim!"
1185 A mighty shout the Frenchmen give straightway;
Whoso had heard the cry "Mountjoy"[45] they raise
He would remember its valiance all his days.
They charge—Lord God, was ever sight so brave?
They spur their steeds to make the greater haste,
1190 They fall afighting—there is no other way—
The Saracens join battle undismayed;
Paynims and Franks are fighting face to face.

93

Now Adelroth, (he was King Marsile's nephew),
Before the host comes first of all his fellows;
1195 With evil words the French he thus addresses:

---

[45]*Mountjoy*—a mountjoy (montjoie) was a mound or cairn of stones set up to mark the site of a victory. The old French war-cry, "Montjoie St-Denis!" or, briefly, "Montjoie!" derived from the cairn set up at Saint-Denis on the site of the saint's martyrdom (his spiritual victory). Others derive "Montjoie" from the Hill of Rama, called "Mons Gaudii," from which pilgrims obtained their first view of Jerusalem.

"Villainous Franks, with us you have to reckon!
You've been betrayed by him that should protect you,
Your king lacked wit who in the passes left you.
Fair France will lose her honour in this venture;
1200   From Carlon's body the right arm will be severed."
When Roland hears him, God! but his rage is reckless!
He spurs his horse, gives full rein to his mettle,
His blow he launches with all his mightiest effort;
The shield he shatters, and the hauberk he rendeth,
1205   He splits the breast and batters in the breast-bone,
Through the man's back drives out the backbone bended,
And soul and all forth on the spear-point fetches;
Clean through he thrusts him, forth of the saddle wrenching,
And flings him dead a lance-length from his destrier;
1210   Into two pieces he has broken his neckbone.
No less for that he speaks to him and tells him:
"Out on thee, churl! no lack-wit is the Emperor,
He is none such, nor loved he treason ever;
Right well he did who in the passes left us,
1215   Neither shall France lose honour by this venture.
First blood to us! Go to it, gallant Frenchmen!
Right's on our side, and wrong is with these wretches!"
AOI

* * * * *

104

Great is the battle and crowded the mellay,
Nor does Count Roland stint of his strokes this day;
1220   While the shaft holds he wields his spear amain—
Fifteen great blows ere it splinters and breaks.
Then his bare brand, his Durendal, he takes;
Against Chernubles he spurs his steed in haste,
Splits through the helm with carbuncles ablaze,
1225   Through the steel coif, and through scalp and through brain
'Twixt the two eyes he cleaves him through the face;
Through the bright byrny close-set with rings of mail,
Right through the body, through the fork and the reins,
Down through the saddle with its beaten gold plates,
1230   Through to the horse he drives the cleaving blade,
Seeking no joint through the chine carves his way,
Flings horse and man dead on the grassy plain.
"Foul befal, felon, that e'er you sought this fray!

Mahound", quoth he, "shall never bring you aid.
1235   Villains like you seek victory in vain."

105

The County Roland throughout the field goes riding;
With Durendal, good sword, he stabs and slices,
The toll he takes of Saracens is frightful.
Would you had seen him, dead man on dead man piling,
1240   Seen the bright blood about his pathway lying!
Bloody his hauberk and both his arms with fighting,
His good horse bloody from crest to withers likewise;
Oliver too doth never cease from striking,
And the Twelve Peers are not a whit behindhand,
1245   And all the French are hammering and smiting;
The Paynims fall, some dead and others dying.
Quoth the Archbishop: "Right blessèd be our knighthood";
He shouts "Mountjoy!" war-cry of Charles the mighty.

                                      AOI

106

And Oliver goes riding through the press;
1250   His spear is broken, only the shaft is left.
Against a Paynim, Malun, he rides addrest,
Smashes the shield with flowers and gold bedecked,
Both of his eyes he smites out of his head,
So that his brains around his feet are spread,
1255   And flings the corpse amid sev'n hundred dead.
Turgis he's slain, and slain Esturgot next,
Till to the grips the spear-shaft splits in shreds.
Roland cries out: "What are you doing, friend?
I'd give no groat for sticks in such a stead!
1260   Here iron avails, and steel and nothing else.
Where is your sword that Hauteclaire is y-clept,[46]
With its gold hilts and pummel crystal-gemmed?"
"I've had no time to draw," Oliver said,
"I've been so busy with striking right and left."

                                      AOI

---

[46]*y-clept*—named.

107

1265	Dan[47] Oliver has drawn his goodly brand,
	As his friend Roland so urgently demands;
	Now will he prove him a stout knight of his hands!
	He smites a Paynim, Justin of Val Ferrat;
	Clean through the middle the skull of him he cracks,
1270	The saffron[48] byrny splits, and his breast and back,
	And saddle, brave with gems and golden bands,
	And through the spine the horse in sunder hacks,
	And dead on field flings all before him flat.
	"I'll call you brother," quoth Roland," after that!
1275	'Tis for such strokes our Emperor loves a man."
	The shout "Mountjoy!" goes up on every hand.

AOI

108

	Gerin the Count bestrides his steed Sorel,
	Gerier his comrade on Passëcerf is set;
	Eagerly both loose rein and spur ahead
1280	And go to strike a Paynim, Timozel,
	One on the shield, the other on the chest.
	Both spears at once are broken in his breast,
	Flat in the fallow straightway they fling him dead—
	I do not know, I never have heard tell,
1285	Which of the two was the more swift and snell.[49]
	[And Engelier, Knight of Bordeaux, he next
	Slew Esprevere, that son was to Burel.][50]
	Archbishop Turpin has o'erthrown Siglorel,
	The sorcerer, who'd once been down to Hell,
1290	With Jupiter[51] for guide, by magic spells.
	Quoth Turpin then: "Ear-marked was he for death!"
	Roland replies: "The churl has made an end.
	Oliver, brother, such strokes delight me well!"

---

[47] *Dan* (Dominus)—lord.

[48] *saffron*—burnished with a yellow varnish made from bismuth oxide.

[49] *snell*—speedy.

[50] These two lines have been telescoped in the text, and are thus emended by most editors.

[51] *Jupiter*—like Apollo, the classical Jove has been demoted to the status of demon.

2. The Song of Roland (Selections)

109

1295

Fiercer and still more fierce the battle grows;
Both French and Paynims deal wondrous heavy strokes,
Some in attacking, and some in parrying blows.
How many spears are bloodied there and broke!

1300

What gonfalons, what banners rent and strown!
How many French in flower of youth laid low,
Whom wives and mothers shall never more behold,
Nor those of France who wait them on the road!
King Charlemayn must weep and wail for woe;

1305

What help in that? he cannot save his folk.
Ill did Count Guènes serve Carlon, when he rode
To Saragossa and all his people sold;
Thereby he lost life and limbs of his own
When at Aix after they judged him to the rope,[52]

1310

And of his kin thirty were hanged also,
Who ne'er had thought such death should be their dole.

AOI

110

Fierce is the battle and wondrous grim the fight.
Both Oliver and Roland boldly smite,
Thousands of strokes the stout Archbishop strikes,

1315

The whole Twelve Peers are not a whit behind,
And the French ranks lay on with all their might.
Heaped by the hundred thousands of Paynims lie,
None can escape unless he turns and flies,
Will he or nill he, there must he leave his life.

1320

There France must lose the noblest of her knights,
They'll see no more their kindred and their sires,
Nor Charles, who scans the pass with anxious eyes.
Throughout all France terrific tempests rise,
Thunder is heard, the stormy winds blow high,

1325

Unmeasured rain and hail fall from the sky,
While thick and fast flashes the levin bright,
And true it is the earth quakes far and wide.
Far as from Saintes to Michael-of-the-Tide,
From Besançon to Wissant Port, you'd find

1330

There's not a house but the walls crack and rive.
Right at high noon a darkness falls like night,

---

[52]*to the rope*—but in any event, a much more horrible death is meted out to Ganelon much later.

Save for the lightning there's not a gleam of light;
None that beholds it but is dismayed for fright,
And many say: "This is the latter time,
1335   The world is ending, and the Great Doom is nigh."
They speak not true, they cannot read the signs:
'Tis Roland's death calls forth this mighty cry.

111

The French have fought with valour and success;
By scores and thousands lie Paynim corpses spread,
1340   Of hundred thousand scarce two will fight again.
Quoth the Archbishop: "Right valiant are our men,
The like of these hath no lord under heav'n.
Thus it is written in the Gestes of the French:[53]
Our Emperor's power was never rivalled yet."
1345   They search the field for their maimed and their dead,
With grief and sorrow the eyes of them are wet,
With love and pity for their kindred and friends.
Now falls upon them Marsile with all his strength.

                                                    AOI

112

The King Marsile comes riding up a gorge
1350   With all his army about him in great force;
He has assembled twenty huge battle-hordes.
Such flash of helms with gems and gold adorned!
Such shields, such byrnies with burnished saffron wrought!
Sev'n hundred trumpets are sounding the assault;
1355   Through all the country the noise of them goes forth.
"Brother," quoth Roland, "friend Oliver, sweet lord,
It is our death false Ganelon has sworn;
The treason's plain, it can be hid no more;
A right great vengeance the Emperor will let fall.
1360   But we must bide a fearful pass of war.
No man has ever beheld the like before.
I shall lay on with Durendal my sword,
You, comrade, wield that great Hauteclaire of yours.
In lands how many have we those weapons borne!

---

[53]*The Gestes of the French*—the chronicle, to which the poet from time to time refers, and from which he claims to derive his information.

2. The Song of Roland (Selections)

1365   Battles how many victoriously fought!
     Ne'er shall base ballad be sung of them in hall!"

AOI

113

     Marsile beholds his slaughtered chivalry.
     He bids his trumpets and horns sound instantly
     And then sets forward with his great company.
1370   Then first rides out a Saracen, Abisme,
     In all that host was none more vile than he,
     With evil vice and crimes he's dyed full deep,
     In Mary's Child, God's Son, he's no belief,
     And black he is as melted pitch to see.
1375   Better he loves murder and treachery
     Than all the gold that is in Galicie
     None ever saw him in mirth or jollity;
     But bold he is and rash to a degree,
     And for that reason he's loved by King Marsile.
1380   He bears a dragon to rally his meinie.[54]
     The good Archbishop observes him, much displeased,
     He'd like to hit him on sight, that's how he feels,
     And to himself he says quite quietly:
     "This Sarsen looks right heretic to me.
1385   'Twere best by far to go and kill the beast;
     I never loved cowards nor coward deeds."

AOI

114

     Th' Archbishop opens the battle up anew;
     He rides a charger that from Grossayle he took
     (That was a king in Denmark, whom he slew).
1390   A steed he is swiftly-running and smooth,
     Flat in the knee and hollow in the hoof,
     Short in the thigh and ample in the croup,
     Long in the flank and the back well set up,
     White of his tail and yellow of his Plume,
1395   Small of his ears and his head tawny-hued;[55]
     Here is a horse no courser could outdo.

---

[54]*meinie*—household.

[55]With this classic enumeration of the good points of a horse compare Shakespeare, *Venus and Adonis* 295–298. The two descriptions have much in common, except that the mediaeval writer attaches much more importance to colour.

Him the Archbishop, of his valour right good,
Spurs on Abisme, and none shall stay his mood.
He rides to strike him on his target of proof
1400   Wondrous with topaz and amethyst to boot,
With carbuncle ablaze, and beryl blue
(Emir Galafe gave it him for a boon
Whom in Val Metas a devil gave it to.)
Turpin lays on, nor spares; I tell you true,
1405   After he hit it it was not worth a sou!
From flank to flank he splits his body through,
And flings him dead wherever he finds room.
The French all cry: "A valiant blow and shrewd!
Right strong to save is our Archbishop's crook!"

115

1410   Now can the French count up the Paynim might
They see it filling the plains from side to side.
They urge on Roland and Oliver likewise
And the Twelve Peers to flee for all their lives;
To whom straightway the Prelate speaks his mind:
1415   "Barons, my lords, these shameful thoughts put by;
By God I charge you, hold fast and do not fly,
Lest brave men sing ill songs in your despite.
Better it were to perish in the fight.
Soon, very soon we all are marked to die,
1420   None of us here will see to-morrow's light;
One thing there is I promise you outright:
To you stand open the gates of Paradise,
There with the holy sweet Innocents to bide."
His words so fill them with courage and delight
1425   There's none among them but shouts "Mountjoy" on high.
AOI

116

A Saracen, of Saragossa Town
Was there, the lord of half that city round—
Climborin namely, that traitor false and foul
Which took the oath of Ganelon the Count
1430   And then for friendship kissed him upon the mouth
And with his helm and carbuncle endowed;
Our Fatherland he swore he'd disrenown,
And from the Emperor would snatch away the crown.

2. The Song of Roland (Selections)

Now he comes riding on Barbëmouche his mount—
1435   Fleeter was never swallow nor falcon found—
Slacks rein, spurs hard its mettle to arouse,
On Engelier the Gascon forward bounds.
Buckler nor byrny avails against him now,
Into the midriff lance-point and pennon plough,
1440   From breast to back the shaft runs through and out,
A whole spear's length he hurls him dead on ground.
"Fit for destruction is all this gear!" he shouts;
"Paynims, strike hard! carve your way through the rout!"
"God!" say the French, "one of our best is down!"
                                          AOI

117

1445   Count Roland calls to Oliver his friend:
"Fair sir, companion, see, Engelier is dead;
No better man had we for knightliness."
The Count replies: "God give me fair revenge!"
In his steed's flanks the golden spurs he sets,
1450   He grasps Hauteclaire, whose steel is all dyed red,
He deals the Paynim a mighty stroke and dread,
Twists out the blade, down falls the Saracen;
The Adversary[56] bears off his soul to Hell.
Then he goes on, slays Duke Alfayen next,
1455   From Escababa he hews away the head,
And seven Arabs unhorses then pell-mell:
That lot at least will never fight again.
"My friend is angry", the County Roland said:
"Fighter for fighter he matches me right well;
1460   'Tis for such strokes King Carlon loves us best!"
Aloud he cries: "Strike on, my valiant men!"
                                          AOI

118

Elsewhere, behold a Paynim, Valdabron,
Was godfather to King Marsilion;
He owns a navy four hundred dromonds[57] strong,
1465   And to his service no seaman but is bond.
He captured Salem by fraud in times bygone,

---

[56] *the Adversary*—i.e. Satan.
[57] *dromond(s)*—a large and very swift mediaeval sailing-ship, used both for war and commerce.

And sacked the Temple of good King Solomon,
Murdering there the Patriarch by the font.
He took the oath of County Ganelon,
1470 And sword and mangons gave him as pledge thereon.
He rides a horse that he calls Gramimond,
Never of speed was peregrine more prompt.
With the sharp spur he urges it headlong;
The great Duke Samson straightway he falls upon.
1475 He splits the shield, he bursts the habergeon,
Drives through his body spear-head and gonfalon,
Flings him from saddle a full spear's length along:
"Paynims!" he cries, "we'll beat them yet! Lay on!"
"God!" say the French, "there's a brave baron gone!"

                                                  AOI

119

1480 When the Count Roland sees Samson thus laid low
Well may you guess how he is grieved of soul.
He spurs his horse and speeds to smite the foe
With Durendal, more worth than finest gold.
By might and main the Baron deals the stroke
1485 Full on the helm that is all gemmed with gold;
The skull he splits, byrny and breast are broke,
Cloven the saddle, that is all gemmed with gold;
Through the beast's back deep down the weapon goes;
Like it or leave it, he has destroyed them both.
1490 The Paynims say: "This is a bitter blow!"
"I love you not," quoth Roland, "by my troth;
Yours is the outrage, yours is the lying boast!"

                                                  AOI

120

An African there was of Afric, too,
Was called Malquiant, the son of King Malcude;
1495 Harnessed he is in gold from head to foot,
None in the sun so glitters to the view,
He rides a horse that he calls Saut-Perdu;
No steed could rival the swiftness of its hoofs.
He strikes Anseïs in mid-shield square and true,
1500 He shears away the scarlet and the blue,
Rips the mailed skirt of the hauberk of proof,
Into the body drives the steel and the wood.

2. The Song of Roland (Selections)

The Count falls dead, his days have met their doom.
The French all say: "Brave lord, alack for you!"

121

1505   Archbishop Turpin goes riding through the field;
Ne'er was mass sung by any tonsured priest
That of his body could do such valiant deeds!
He hails the Paynim: "God send the worst to thee!
Thou hast slain one for whom my whole heart grieves."
1510   Into a gallop he urges his good steed,
He strikes him hard on his Toledo shield,
And lays him dead upon the grassy green.

122

There was a Paynim, and Grandoyne was he called,
King Capuel's son, from Cappadocia's shores,
1515   Mounted on Marmor, for so he names his horse,
Swifter of speed than any bird that soars.
He slacks the rein and he goes spurring forth,
And runs to strike Gerin with all his force.
From off his neck he splits the red shield shorn,
1520   From off his body he rips the byrny torn,
Into his heart the pennon blue he's borne,
And down he flings him dead on a rocky tor.
Gerin his comrade he smites down afterward,
Berenger next, Guy of St Antoine fall;
1525   And then he strikes the mighty duke Astorge,
(Envers-on-Rhône and Valence called him lord),
And lays him dead; for joy the Paynims roar;
The French all say: "What loss we have to mourn!"
                                             AOI

123

The County Roland grips fast his blood-red blade;
1530   Well has he heard how the French are dismayed;
His heart grieves so, 'tis like to split in twain.
In hails the Paynim: "God send thee all His plagues!
Thou hast slain one for whom I'll make thee pay!"
He spurs his horse that gladly runs apace;
1535   Let win who may, they're at it, face to face.
                                             AOI

124

The Prince Grandoyne was a good knight and gallant,
Strong of his hands and valorous in battle;
Athwart him now comes Roland the great captain;
He'd never met him, but he knew him instanter.
1540   By his proud aspect, and by his noble stature,
His haughty looks, and his bearing and manner.
He cannot help it, a mortal fear unmans him;
Fain would he fly, but what's the good? he cannot.
The Count assails him with such ferocious valour
1545   That to the nasal the whole helmet is shattered,
Cloven the nose and the teeth and the palate,
The jaz'rain[58] hauberk and the breastbone and backbone,
Both silver bows from off the golden saddle;
Horseman and horse clean asunder he slashes,
1550   Lifeless he leaves them and the pieces past patching.
The men of Spain fall a-wailing for sadness:
The French all cry: "What strokes! and what a champion!"

125

Fierce is the battle and marvellous and great.
The Frenchmen ply their burnished spears amain.
1555   There had you seen how many men in pain,
How many wounded and bleeding there and slain!
Heaped up pell-mell they lie, on back or face.
The Saracens cannot endure the strain;
Will they or nill they they flee across the plain,
1560   And the French forces with all their might give chase.

                         AOI

126

Wondrous the battle, and it grows faster yet;
The French fight on with rage and fury fell,
They lop off wrists, hew ribs and spines to shreds,
They cleave the harness through to the living flesh;
1565   On the green ground the blood runs clear and red.
[The Paynims say: "We cannot stand the stress,]
French Fatherland, be curst of Mahomet!
Your sons are bravest of all the sons of men."

---

58 *jazerain*—a kind of chain-mail made in Algiers (Al-Djezair).

2. The Song of Roland (Selections)

1570 There's none of them but cries: "Marsile to help!
Ride, ride, O King, for we are hard bested."

127

Roland the Count calls out to Olivere:
"Fair sir, companion, confess that for this gear
Our lord Archbishop quits him like any peer;
Earth cannot match him beneath the heavens' sphere,
1575 Well does he know to handle lance and spear."
The Count replies: "Let's aid him now and here!"
At this the French lay on the lustier,
Hard are their strokes, the fight is very fierce,
And for the Christians the losses are severe.
1580 Who then had seen Roland and Olivere
Smite with their swords and through all the press pierce!
And the Archbishop goes thrusting with his spear.
Of those they slew the numbers are writ clear
In many charters and tales of chroniclers:
1585 More than four thousand as in the Geste appears.
Four great assaults they've borne with right good cheer;
Then comes a fifth, doleful and dread and drear.
All the French knighthood has fallen in career;
Sixty alone by God's grace persevere;
1590 These ere they die will sell their bodies dear.
AOI

128

When County Roland sees all his brave men down,
To Oliver his friend he cries aloud:
"For God's sake, comrade, fair sir, what think you now?
See what good knights lie here upon the ground!
1595 Well may we pity this fair sweet France of ours,
Thus left so barren of all her knighthood's flower.
Why aren't you here, O friend and Emperour?
Oliver, brother, what way is to be found?
How send him news of what is come about?"
1600 Oliver said: "And how should I know how?
I'd rather die than we should lose renown."
AOI

129

	"I'll sound", quoth Roland, "my Olifant straightway;
	When Carlon hears, passing through Gate of Spain,
	I pledge my word, the French will turn again."
1605	Quoth Oliver: "It would be foul disdain,
	And to your kindred the reproach would be great:
	All their lives long they'd not live down the shame.
	When I desired you, why then you said me nay;
	If now you do it, of me you'll get no praise.
1610	Blow if you will—such conduct is not brave.
	Nay, but how deep in blood your arms are bathed!"
	The Count replies: "I've struck good blows this day."

AOI

130

	Said Roland then: "Full grievous is this fight.
	I'll sound my horn, and Charles will hear the cry."
1615	Quoth Oliver: " 'Twould ill beseem a knight.
	I asked you, comrade, and you refused, for pride.
	Had Charles been here, then all would have gone right;
	He's not to blame, nor the men at his side.
	Now by my beard (quoth he) if e'er mine eyes
1620	Again behold my sister Aude the bright,
	Between her arms never you think to lie."

AOI

131

	Quoth Roland: "Why so angry with me, friend?"
	And he: "Companion, you got us in this mess.
	There is wise valour, and there is recklessness:
1625	Prudence is worth more than foolhardiness.
	Through your o'erweening you have destroyed the French;
	Ne'er shall we do service to Charles again.
	Had you but given some heed to what I said,
	My lord had come, the battle had gone well,
1630	And King Marsile had been captured or dead.
	Your prowess, Roland, is a curse on our heads.
	No more from us will Charlemayn have help,
	Whose like till Doomsday shall not be seen of men.

Now you will die, and fair France will be shent;[59]
1635 Our loyal friendship is here brought to an end;
A bitter parting we'll have ere this sun set."

AOI

132

When the Archbishop thus hears them in dispute,
With his gold spurs he pricks his steed anew,
Draws near to them and utters this rebuke:
1640 "Lord Oliver, and you, Lord Roland, too,
Let's have no quarrel, o'God's name, 'twixt you two.
It will not save us to sound the horn, that's true;
Nevertheless, 'twere better so to do.
Let the King come; his vengeance will be rude;
1645 None shall to Spain ride home with merry news.
After, our French will light them down on foot,
Seek out our bodies and limbs in sunder hewn,
Lay us on biers borne upon sumpter-mules,
And weep for us with grief right pitiful;
1650 In the church-close we shall have burial due,
And not be food for dogs and swine and wolves."
Quoth Roland, "Sir, your words are right and good."

AOI

133

Roland has set Olifant to his lips,
Firmly he holds it and blows it with a will.
1655 High are the mountains, the blast is long and shrill,
Thirty great leagues the sound went echoing.
King Carlon heard it and all who rode with him.
"Lo, now, our men are fighting", quoth the King.
Guènes retorts: "If any man said this
1660 Except yourself, it were a lie, methinks."

AOI

134

The County Roland with pain and anguish winds
His Olifant, and blows with all his might.
Blood from his mouth comes spurting scarlet-bright

---

[59]*shent*—put to shame.

He's burst the veins of his temples outright.
1665   From hand and horn the call goes shrilling high:
King Carlon hears it who through the passes rides,
Duke Naimon hears, and all the French beside.
Quoth Charles: "I hear the horn of Roland cry!
He'd never sound it but in the thick of fight."
1670   "There is no battle", Count Ganelon replies;
"You're growing old, your hair is sere and white,
When you speak thus, you're talking like a child.
Full well you know Roland's o'erweening pride;
'Tis strange that God endures him so long time!
1675   Took he not Noples against your orders quite?
The Paynims made a sally from inside,
And there gave battle to Roland the great knight;
So he swilled down the field—a brave device
To keep the bloodstains from coming to your eyes!
1680   For one small hare he'll blow from morn till night;
Now to the Peers he's showing-off in style.
Who dare attack him ! No man beneath the sky!
Ride on, ride on! Why loiter here the while?
Our Fathers' land lies distant many a mile."

                                                    AOI

135

1685   Count Roland's mouth with running blood is red;
He's burst asunder the temples of his head;
He sounds his horn in anguish and distress.
King Carlon hears, and so do all the French.
Then said the King: "This horn is long of breath."
1690   "'Tis blown", quoth Naimon, "with all a brave man's strength;
Battle there is, and that I know full well.
He that would stay you is but a traitor fell.
To arms! let sound your battle-cry to heav'n!
Make haste to bring your gallant household help!
1695   You hear how Roland makes desperate lament!"

136

The Emperor Charles lets sound his horns aloft.
The French light down and arm themselves anon
With helm and hauberk and gilded swords girt on;
Goodly their shields, their lances stiff and strong,
1700   Scarlet and white and blue the gonfalons.

2. The Song of Roland (Selections)

Straightway to horse the warrior lords have got;
Swift through the passes they spur and never stop.
Each unto other they speak and make response:
"Might we reach Roland ere he were dead and gone,
1705   We'ld strike good strokes beside him in the throng."
What use is that? They have delayed too long.

137

Vespers draws on and shining is the day;
Against the sun glitters their armed array,
Hauberk and helm flash back a mighty blaze,
1710   So many shields their painted flowers display,
Such store of spears with gilded pennons gay!
The Emperor rides right wrathful on his way.
And all the French in anger and dismay;
There is not one but weeps for very rage;
1715   For Roland's sake they're grievously afraid.
The King arrests Count Ganelon straightway;
He's turned him over to the cooks in his train;
The master-cook he calls, Besgun by name:
"Guard me him well, as fits a man so base,
1720   For all my house this villain has betrayed!"
Besgun takes charge, with five-score kitchen knaves,
The best and worst that serve in that estate.
They pluck the beard from off his chin and face,
With four sound thumps each gives him a good baste,
1725   With sticks and faggots they pound him and they paste,
And round his neck they fasten a strong chain,
Right well they chain him like a bear in a cage;
Now on a pack-horse they've hoisted him in shame;
Till Carlon want him 'tis they will keep him safe.
                                                    AOI

138

1730   Huge are the hills and shadowy and high,
Deep in the vales the living streams run by.
The trumpets sound before them and behind,
All with one voice to Olifant reply.
In wrath of heart the Emperor Carlon rides,
1735   And all the French in sorrow and in ire;
There's none but grieves and weeps from out his eyes;
They all pray God to safeguard Roland's life

Till they may come to battle by his side;
Once they are with him they'll make it a great fight.
1740   What use is that? their prayers are empty quite,
Too long they've lingered, they cannot come in time.

                                                              AOI

139

King Charlemayn rides on in anger grim,
Over his byrny flows the white beard of him;
All the French barons beside him spur full swift;
1745   There's none of them but is with fury filled
Not to be aiding Roland the Paladin
Now that he's fighting the Spanish Sarrasins.
He's hurt so sore, I fear he cannot live.
God! and what men, those sixty with him still!
1750   Better had never nor captain nor yet king.

                                                              AOI

140

Roland surveys the mountains and the fells;
How many French he sees there lying dead!
Like a good knight he makes them this lament:
"Barons, my lords, may God of His largesse
1755   Bring all your souls to Paradise the blest,
Amid bright flowers to make their hallowed beds!
I never saw braver or truer men.
So long you served me unceasingly and well,
So many lands conquered for Carlon's realm!
1760   The Emperor bred you alas! to what sad end!
O dearest land, fair nursery of the French,
By what hard hap art thou this day bereft!
Barons of France, for me you go to death,
Nought can I give you of safeguard or defence;
1765   Now aid you God, who ne'er failed any yet!
Oliver, brother, you shall not lack my help.
Though none should slay me I'll die of grief no less;
Sweet sir, companion, let's go and fight afresh!"

2. The Song of Roland (Selections)

141

	The County Roland returns into the field
1770	And like a warrior his Durendal he wields;
	Faldron de Puy through the midriff he cleaves
	With four-and-twenty besides, of great esteem.
	Never on vengeance was any man so keen.
	E'en as the deer before the deerhound flees
1775	So before Roland the Paynims show their heels.
	Quoth the Archbishop: "Well done, well done indeed!
	Valour like this becomes a knight of breed
	That bears his arms and sits a goodly steed;
	Forward and fierce in battle should he be,
1780	Else he's not worth a single penny-piece,
	Best he turn monk in monastery meek
	And for our sins pray daily on his knees-"
	Quoth Roland: "Strike, spare none of them," saith he.
	At this the French renew the fight with speed;
1785	Therein the Christians endure great loss and grief.

142

	When it is known no prisoners will be made
	Men fight back fiercely, and stubborn is the fray;
	Therefore the French grow very lions for rage.
	Here comes Marsile, e'en as a baron brave,
1790	Riding a horse, and Gaignun is its name.
	Full upon Bevon he rides and spurs amain,
	That held all Beaune and Dijon for domain.
	The shield he shatters, and the hauberk he breaks,
	And lays him dead, he need not strike again.
1795	And Ivon next and Ivor too, his mate,
	And Gerard too of Roussillon he slays.
	Roland the Count, who is not far away,
	Cries to the Paynim: "God damn your soul, I say!
	These my companions by treason you have slain!
1800	Ere we go hence a bitter price you'll pay,
	And you shall learn the name of my good blade!"
	He rides to strike him, e'en as a baron brave;
	From his sword-arm he shears the hand away.
	And Jurfaret the Fair he next waylays,
1805	Marsilion's son, and slices off his pate.
	The Paynims cry: "Mahound! Mahound to aid!
	Venge us on Carlon, all you gods of our faith!

Into our land he's sent this evil race!
Come life come death they'll never quit the place."
1810   Then one to other cries: "Fly then! fly in haste!"
An hundred thousand have fled the field straightway;
They'll not return, call after them who may.

AOI

143

What help is that? Marsile has taken flight,
Yet there remains his uncle Marganice,
1815   That governs Carthage, Alfrere and Garamile,
And Ethiope, a land accursed and vile.
In his command are all the Negro tribes;
Thick are their noses, their ears are very wide;
Full fifty thousand are gathered in their fines,
1820   Boldly and fast and furiously they ride,
Yelling aloud the Paynim battle-cry.
Then Roland said: "Here are we doomed to die;
Full well I know we cannot long survive.
Fail not, for shame, right dear to sell your lives.
1825   Lift up, my lords, your burnished blades and fight!
Come life, come death, the foe shall pay the price,
Lest we should bring fair France into despite!
When on this field Carlon my lord sets eyes
He'll see what toll we've taken of their might:
1830   Fifteen dead Paynims for each of us he'll find;
Nor fail to bless us for this our great emprise."[60]

AOI

144

When Roland looks on these accursed tribesmen—
As black as ink from head to foot their hides are,
With nothing white about them but their grinders—
1835   Then said the Count: "'Tis true beyond denial,
Right well I know it, this day shall death betide us.
I'll to the throng; Frenchmen, fight on beside me!"
Quoth Oliver: "The devil take the hindmost!"
The French hear this and once more fall a-fighting.

AOI

---

[60]*emprise*—enterprise, feat of arms.

2. The Song of Roland (Selections)

145

1840   When Paynims see how few the French are grown
They plume themselves, puffed up with pride and hope:
"Now to the Emperor," they say, "his crimes come home!"
Marganice comes, riding a sorrel colt;
He spurs him hard with rowels all of gold,
1845   And from behind deals Oliver a blow;
Deep in his back the burnished mail is broke,
That the spear's point stands forth at his breast-bone.
He saith to him: "You've suffered a sore stroke;
Charlemayn sent you to the pass for your woe.
1850   Foul wrong he did us, 'tis good he lose his boast:
I've well requited our loss on you alone."

                                           AOI

146

Oliver feels that he is hurt to death;
He grasps his sword Hauteclaire the keen of edge,
Smites Marganice on his high golden helm,
1855   Shearing away the flowers and crystal gems,
Down to the teeth clean splits him through the head,
Shakes loose the blade and flings him down and dead;
Then saith: "Foul fall you, accursèd Paynim wretch!
Charles has had losses, so much I will confess:
1860   But ne'er shall you, back to the land you left,
To dame or damsel return to boast yourself
That e'er you spoiled me to the tune of two pence,
Or made your profit of me or other men."
This done, to Roland he cries aloud for help.

                                           AOI

147

1865   Oliver feels he's wounded mortally;
His thirst for vengeance can never glutted be.
Amid the press he strikes right valiantly;
He breaks asunder the spear-shaft and the shield,
Splits chines and saddles and lops off hands and feet.
1870   Whoso had seen him hew Paynims piece from piece,
Throw one on other their bodies down in heaps,
Might well remember that flower of knightly deeds!
And Carlon's war-cry he fails not to repeat,

But still "Mountjoy!" goes shouting loud and clear.
1875   He calls to Roland his comrade and his peer:
"Sir, my companion, draw nigh and stand with me;
We must this day be parted to our grief "

                                             AOI

148

Oliver's face, when Roland on him looks,
Is grey and ghastly, discoloured, wan with wounds,
1880   His bright blood sprays his body head to foot;
Down to the ground it runs from him in pools.
"God!" says the Count, "I know not what to do!
Fair sir, companion, woe worth your mighty mood!—
Ne'er shall be seen a man to equal you.
1885   Alas, fair France! what valiant men and true
Must thou bewail this day, cast down and doomed!
Bitter the loss the Emperor has to rue!"
So much he says, and in the saddle swoons.

                                             AOI

149

See Roland now swooning in saddle laid,
1890   And Oliver that unto death is maimed;
He's bled so much that his eyes are all glazed,
Or far or near he can see nothing straight,
Nor recognise a single living shape;
So when he comes to where his comrade waits,
1895   On the gold helm be smites at him amain,
Down to the nasal he splits the jewelled Plates,
Only his head is not touched by the blade.
Then Roland, stricken, lifts his eyes to his face,
Asking him low and mildly as he may:
1900   "Sir, my companion, did you mean it that way?
Look, I am Roland, that loved you all my days;
You never sent me challenge or battle-gage."[61]
Quoth Oliver: "I cannot see you plain;
I know your voice; may God see you and save.
1905   And I have struck you; pardon it me, I pray."
Roland replies: "I have taken no scathe;

---

[61]*challenge or battle-gage*—Roland wonders whether Oliver is still angry with him, but cannot believe that he would bear arms against him without having sent him a formal challenge, accompanied by the usual token of defiance.

2. The Song of Roland (Selections)

I pardon you, myself and in God's name."
Then each to other bows courteous in his place.
With such great love thus is their parting made.

150

1910   Oliver feels the coming pangs of death;
Both of his eyes are turning in his head,
Now he is blind wholly, and wholly deaf.
He lights from horse and to his knees he gets
And makes confession aloud, and beats his breast,
1915   Then clasps his hands and lifts them up to Heav'n;
In Paradise he prays God give him rest,
And France the Fair and Carlon prays Him bless,
And his companion Roland above all men.
His heart-strings crack, he stoops his knightly helm,
1920   And sinks to earth, and lies there all his length.
Dead is the Count, his days have reached their end.
The valiant Roland weeps for him and laments,
No man on earth felt ever such distress.

151

When Roland sees his friend and comrade die,
1925   And on the ground face down beholds him lie,
With tender words he bids him thus goodbye:
"Sir, my companion, woe worth your valiant might!
Long years and days have we lived side by side,
Ne'er didst thou wrong me nor suffer wrong of mine.
1930   Now thou art dead I grieve to be alive."
Having thus said, the Marquis[62] swoons outright
On his steed's back, that Veillantif is hight;
He's kept from falling by the gold stirrups bright;
Go as he may, they hold him still upright.

152

1935   Or ever Roland comes to himself again
And has recovered and rallied from his faint,
Fearful disaster his fortunes have sustained;
All of the French are lost to him and slain;
Sole, the Archbishop and Walter Hum remain.
1940   Walter has come down from the heights again;

---

[62]*marquis*—the title means "lord of the marches" (see note on L. 844). Roland was Lord of the Marches of Brittany.

Well has he striven against the men of Spain,
His men are dead, mown down by Paynim blades;
Will he or nill he, he flees towards the vale,
And upon Roland he cries aloud for aid:
1945 "Where art thou, where, great county, warrior brave?
While thou wast there I never was dismayed.
Walter am I, who Maëlgut o'ercame,
Nephew am I to Droön white with age;
Thou for my valour wast wont to love me aye!
1950 My lance is shattered, my shield is split in twain,
Battered and broken is my hauberk of mail,
A spear has pierced me [through the midst of my reins;]
Death is upon me, yet dear I made them pay."
Lo! at that word Roland hears him and wakes;
1955 He spurs his horse and comes to him in haste.

AOI

153

Roland is filled with grief and anger sore;
In the thick press he now renews his war.
Of those of Spain he's overthrown a score,
And Walter six, the Archbishop five more.
1960 The Paynims say: "These men are worst of all!
Let none escape alive; look to it, lords!
Who fears the onset, let shame be his reward!
Who lets these go, may he be put to scorn!"
Then once again the hue and cry breaks forth;
1965 From every side pour in the Paynim hordes.

AOI

154

The County Roland is mighty of his mood,
Walter de Hum well-famed for knightlihood,
And the Archbishop a warrior tried and proved;
Betwixt their valours there's not a pin to choose.
1970 In the thick press they smite the Moorish crew.
A thousand Paynims dismount to fight on foot,
And forty thousand horsemen they have, to boot,
Yet 'gainst these three, my troth! they fear to move.
They hurl against them their lances from aloof,
1975 Javelins, jereeds, darts, shafts and spears they loose.
in the first shock brave Walter meets his doom.
Turpin of Rheims has his shield split in two,

His helm is broken, his head has ta'en a wound,
His hauberk's pierced, the mail-rings burst and strewn,
1980   By four sharp spears his breast is stricken through,
Killed under him his horse rolls neck and croup;
Th' Archbishop's down, woe worth the bitter dule.[63]

AOI

155

Turpin of Rheims, finding himself o'erset,
With four sharp lance-heads stuck fast within his breast.
1985   Quickly leaps up, brave lord, and stands erect.
He looks on Roland and runs to him and says
Only one word: "I am not beaten yet!
True man failed never while life in him was left."
He draws Almace, his steel-bright brand keen-edged;
1990   A thousand strokes he strikes amid the press.
Soon Charles shall see he spared no foe he met,
For all about him he'll find four hundred men,
Some wounded, some clean through the body cleft,
And some of them made shorter by the head.
1995   So tells the Geste; so he that fought there tells:
The worthy Giles,[64] whom God with marvels blessed,
In Laön minster thus-wise the charter penned;
Who knows not this knows nought of what befel.

156

The County Roland fights bravely as he may,
2000   But his whole body in heat and sweat is bathed,
And all his head is racked with grievous pain
From that great blast which brake his temples' veins.
Fain would he know if Charles is bringing aid;
His Olifant he grasps, and blows full faint.
2005   The Emperor halts, hearing the feeble strain:
"My lords," quoth he, "this tells a woeful tale;
Roland my nephew is lost to us this day,
That call proclaims his breath is nigh to fail.
Whoso would reach him must ride with desperate haste
2010   Sound through the host! bid every trumpet play!"
Full sixty thousand so loud their clarions bray

---

[63]*dule*—grief.
[64]*the worthy Giles*—St Giles, who had a hermitage in Provence, and became the hero of many legends.

The hills resound, the valleys ring again.
The Paynims hear, no lust to laugh have they:
"We'll soon have Charles to reckon with," they say.

AOI

157

2015   The Paynims say: "The Emperor's turned about;
Of those of France hark how the trumpets sound!
If Carlon comes, we shall have rack and rout,
If Roland lives, once more he'll war us down,
We shall not keep one foot of Spanish ground."
2020   Straightway four hundred helmed warriors rally round,
The finest fighters that in the field are found;
A fearful onslaught they'll make upon the Count;
Truly Lord Roland has got his work cut out.

158

Whenas Count Roland sees their assault begin,
2025   Right fierce he makes him, and strong and menacing;
While life is in him he'll never quail or quit.
He sits his horse that is named Veillantif,
Into his flanks the golden spurs he pricks
And sets upon them where most the press is thick.
2030   The Lord Archbishop, brave Turpin, rides with him.
Paynim to paynim cries: "Comrade, go to it!
Have we not heard the Frankish trumpets ring?
Charles is returning, the great, the mighty king!"

159

The County Roland ne'er loved a recreant,
2035   Nor a false heart, nor yet a braggart jack,
Nor knight that was not a good man of his hands.
He cried to Turpin, the Churchman militant,
"Sir, you're on foot, I'm on my horse's back;
For love of you here will I make my stand,
2040   And side by side we'll take both good and bad.
I'll not desert you for any mortal man.
Go we together these Paynims to attack;
The mightiest blows are those of Durendal."
Quoth the Archbishop: "'Twere shame our strokes to slack;
2045   Carlon is coming, our vengeance shall not lack."

2. The Song of Roland (Selections)

160

2050

2055

2060

The Paynims say: "Why were we ever born?
Woe worth the while! our day of doom has dawned.
Now have we lost our peerage and our lords,
The mighty Carlon comes on with all his force,
Of those of France we hear the shrilling horns,
The cry 'Mountjoy!' sounds fearfully abroad.
So grim of mood is Roland in his wrath
No man alive can put him to the sword.
Let fly at him, and then give up the war."
So they let fly; spears, lances they outpour,
Darts and jereeds and feathered shafts galore.
The shield of Roland is pierced and split and scored,
The mail-rings riven, and all his hauberk torn,
Yet in his body he is not touched at all,
Though under him, with thirty wounds and more,
His Veillantif is stricken dead and falls.
The Paynims flee, abandoning the war;
Count Roland's left amid the field, unhorsed.

AOI

161

2065

2070

2075

2080

In wrath and grief away the Paynims fly;
Backward to Spain with headlong haste they hie.
The County Roland cannot pursue their flight,
Veillantif's lost, he has no steed to ride;
Will he or nill he, he must on foot abide,
He's turned to aid Archbishop Turpin's plight,
And from his head the gilded helm untied,
Stripped off the hauberk of subtle rings and bright,
And all to pieces has cut the bliaut fine
Wherewith to bandage his wounds that gape so wide.
Then to his breast he clasps and lifts him light
And gently lays him upon the green hill-side,
With fair soft speech entreating on this wise:
"Ah, noble sir, pray give me leave awhile;
These friends of ours, we loved so well in life,
We must not leave them thus lying where they died.
I will go seek them, find, and identify,
And lay them here together in your sight."
"Go and return," the Bishop makes reply;
"Thanks be to God, this field is yours and mine."

162

2085

Roland departs and through the field is gone;
Alone he searches the valleys and high rocks.
[And there he finds Ivor, and there Ivon],
Gerier and Gerin, the good companions,

2090

[And Engelier whom Gascony begot];
And he has found Berenger and Oton,
And after finds Anseïs and Samson,
And finds Gerard the Old, of Roussillon.
He lifts them up, brave baron, one by one,

2095

To the Archbishop he carries them anon,
And by his knees ranges them all along.
The Bishop weeps, he cannot stint thereof;
He lifts his hand and gives them benison,
And after saith: "Alack, brave champions!

2100

May your souls rest with the all-glorious God
In Paradise, amid the rose-blossoms.
I too am dying and sorrow for my lot,
Who the great Emperor no more may look upon."

163

Roland once more unto the field repairs,

2105

And has sought out his comrade Oliver.
Close to his breast he lifts him, and with care
As best he may to the Archbishop bears
And on his shield lays with the others there;
The Bishop signs and shrives them all with prayer.

2110

With tears renewed their sorrow is declared,
And Roland saith: "Fair fellow Oliver,
You were own son unto Duke Renier
That held the marches of the Vale of Runers.
To shatter shield or break lance anywhere,

2115

And from their seat proud men to overbear,
And cheer the brave with words of counsel fair,
And bring the cruel to ruin and despair,
No knight on earth was valiant as you were."

164

The County Roland, seeing his peers lie dead,

2120

And Oliver, who was his dearest friend,
Begins to weep for ruth and tenderness;

Out of his cheeks the colour all has fled,
He cannot stand, he is so deep distressed,
He swoons to earth, he cannot help himself
2125   "Alas, for pity, sweet lord!" the Bishop saith.

165

When the Archbishop saw Roland faint and fallen,
So sad was he, he never had been more so;
He reaches out; he's taken Roland's horn up.
In Ronceval there runs a stream of water;
2130   Fain would he go there and fetch a little for him.
With feeble steps he turns him thither, falt'ring;
He is so weak, that he cannot go forward,
For loss of blood he has no strength to call on.
Ere one might cover but a rood's length in walking
2135   His heart has failed him, he has fallen face-foremost;
The pangs of death have seized him with great torment.

166

The County Roland has rallied from his faint,
Gets to his feet, though he's in grievous pain,
And looks about him over hill, over vale.
2140   Beyond his comrades, upon the grass-green plain,
There he beholds the noble baron laid,
The great Archbishop, vice-gerent of God's name.
He beats his breast with eyes devoutly raised,
With folded hands lifted to Heaven he prays
2145   That God will give him in Paradise a place.
Turpin is dead that fought for Charlemayn;
In mighty battles, and in preaching right brave,
Still against Paynims a champion of the Faith;
Blest mote he be, the Lord God give him grace!

                                AOI

167

2150   The County Roland sees the Archbishop lie;
He sees his bowels gush forth out of his side
And on his brow the brain laid bare to sight.
Midst of his breast where the key-bones divide,
Crosswise he lays his comely hands and white,
2155   And thus laments him as native use requires:

"Ah, debonair, thou good and noble knight!
Now I commend thee to the great Lord of might,
Servant more willing than thee He shall not find.
Since the Apostles no prophet was thy like,
2160   For to maintain the Faith, and win mankind.
May thy soul meet no hindrance in her flight!
May Heaven's gate to her stand open wide!"

168

Now Roland feels that he is at death's door;
Out of his ears the brain is running forth.
2165   Now for his peers he prays God call them all,
And for himself St Gabriel's aid implores;
Then in each hand he takes, lest shame befal,
His Olifant and Durendal his sword.
Far as a quarrel flies from a cross-bow drawn,
2170   Toward land of Spain he goes, to a wide lawn,
And climbs a mound where grows a fair tree tall,
And marble stones[65] beneath it stand by four.
Face downward there on the green grass he falls,
And swoons away, for he is at death's door.

169

2175   High are the hills and very high the trees are;
Four stones there are set there, of marble gleaming.
The County Roland lies senseless on the greensward.
A Saracen is there, watching him keenly;
He has feigned death, and lies among his people,
2180   And has smeared blood upon his breast and features.
Now he gets up and runs towards him fleetly;
Strong was he, comely and of valour exceeding.
Now in his rage and in his overweening
He falls on Roland, his arms and body seizing;
2185   He saith one word: "Now Carlon's nephew's beaten.
I'll take his sword, to Araby I'll reive[66] it."
But as he draws it Roland comes to, and feels him.

---

[65] *marble stones*—probably posts such as were used to mark a frontier.
[66]*reive*—steal away.

2. The Song of Roland (Selections)

170

	Roland has felt his good sword being stol'n;
	Opens his eyes and speaks this word alone:
2190	"Thou'rt none of ours, in so far as I know."
	He takes his horn, of which he kept fast hold,
	And smites the helm, which was all gemmed with gold;
	He breaks the steel and the scalp and the bone,
	And from his head batters his eyes out both,
2195	And dead on ground he lays the villain low;
	Then saith: "False Paynim, and how wast thou so bold,
	Foully or fairly, to seize upon me so?
	A fool he'll think thee who hears this story told.
	Lo, now! the mouth of my Olifant's broke;
2200	Fallen is all the crystal and the gold."

171

	Now Roland feels his sight grow dim and weak;
	With his last strength he struggles to his feet;
	All the red blood has faded from his cheeks.
	A grey stone stands before him at his knee:
2205	Ten strokes thereon he strikes, with rage and grief;
	It grides, but yet nor breaks nor chips the steel.
	"Ah! " cries the Count, "St Mary succour me!
	Alack the day, Durendal, good and keen!
	Now I am dying, I cannot fend for thee.
2210	How many battles I've won with you in field!
	With you I've conquered so many goodly fiefs
	That Carlon holds, the lord with the white beard!
	Let none e'er wield you that from the foe would flee—
	You that were wielded so long by a good liege!
2215	The like of you blest France shall never see."

172

	Count Roland smites the sardin stone amain.
	The steel grides loud, but neither breaks nor bates.
	Now when he sees that it will nowise break
	Thus to himself he maketh his complaint:
2220	"Ah, Durendal! so bright, so brave, so gay!
	How dost thou glitter and shine in the sun's rays!
	When Charles was keeping the vales of Moriane,
	God by an angel sent to him and ordained

	He should bestow thee on some count-capitayne.
2225	On me he girt thee, the noble Charlemayn.
	With this I won him Anjou and all Bretayn,
	With this I won him Poitou, and conquered Maine;
	With this I won him Normandy's fair terrain,
	And with it won Provence and Acquitaine,
2230	And Lombardy and all the land Romayne,
	Bavaria too, and the whole Flemish state,
	And Burgundy and all Apulia gained;
	Constantinople in the King's hand I laid;
	In Saxony he speaks and is obeyed;
2235	With this I won Scotland, [Ireland and Wales,][67]
	And England, where he set up his domain;
	What lands and countries I've conquered by its aid,
	For Charles to keep whose beard is white as may!
	Now am I grieved and troubled for my blade;
2240	Should Paynims get it, 'twere worse than all death's pains.
	Dear God forbid it should put France to shame!"

173

	Count Roland smites upon the marble stone;
	I cannot tell you how he hewed it and smote;
	Yet the blade breaks not nor splinters, though it groans;
2245	Upward to heaven it rebounds from the blow.
	When the Count sees it never will be broke,
	Then to himself right softly he makes moan:
	"Ah, Durendal, fair, hallowed, and devote,
	What store of relics lie in thy hilt of gold!
2250	St Peter's tooth, St Basil's blood, it holds,
	Hair of my lord St Denis, there enclosed,
	Likewise a piece of Blessed Mary's robe;
	To Paynim hands 'twere sin to let you go;
	You should be served by Christian men alone,
2255	Ne'er may you fall to any coward soul!
	Many wide lands I conquered by your strokes
	For Charles to keep whose beard is white as snow,
	Whereby right rich and mighty is his throne."

---

[67]The text is corrupt; but either Ireland or Wales is certainly intended, and possibly both.

2. The Song of Roland (Selections)

174

2260
Now Roland feels death press upon him hard;
It's creeping down from his head to his heart.
Under a pine-tree he hastens him apart,
There stretches him face down on the green grass,
And lays beneath him his sword and Olifant.
He's turned his head to where the Paynims are,
2265
And this he doth for the French and for Charles,
Since fain is he that they should say, brave heart,
That he has died a conquerer at the last.
He beats his breast full many a time and fast,
Gives, with his glove, his sins into God's charge.
2270
                                                                    AOI

175

Now Roland feels his time is at an end;
On the steep hill-side, toward Spain he's turned his head,
And with one hand he beats upon his breast;
Saith: "Mea culpa; Thy mercy, Lord, I beg
2275
For all the sins, both the great and the less,
That e'er I did since first I drew my breath
Unto this day when I'm struck down by death."
His right-hand glove he unto God extends;
Angels from Heaven now to his side descend.
                                                                    AOI

176

2280
The County Roland lay down beneath a pine;
To land of Spain he's turned him as he lies,
And many things begins to call to mind:
All the broad lands he conquered in his time,
And fairest France, and the men of his line,
2285
And Charles his lord, who bred him from a child;
He cannot help but weep for them and sigh.
Yet of himself he is mindful betimes;
He beats his breast and on God's mercy cries:
"Father most true, in whom there is no lie,
2290
Who didst from death St Lazarus make to rise,
And bring out Daniel safe from the lions' might,
Save Thou my soul from danger and despite
Of all the sins I did in all my life."

His right-hand glove he's tendered unto Christ,
2295   And from his hand Gabriel accepts the sign.
Straightway his head upon his arm declines;
With folded hands he makes an end and dies.
God sent to him His Angel Cherubine,
And great St Michael of Peril-by-the-Tide;
2300   St Gabriel too was with them at his side;
The County's soul they bear to Paradise.

[*The poem continues with the return of Charlemagne and his forces who bury their dead comrades; upon returning to Aix, Charlemagne has Ganelon put on trial and subsequently executed.*]

3. POPE URBAN II:
CALL FOR THE CRUSADES
CLERMONT, FRANCE 1095
(c. 1120)

Robert the Monk

(trans. by Dana C. Munro)

Robert's is one of several accounts by persons present at Urban's speech delivered at the Council of Clermont in 1095. However, apart from the major thrust of calling Christian Europe to unite in the name of Christ against Muslim oppression in Jerusalem and the East, the accounts differ in length and rhetorical style. Robert's version is most impressive for its rhetorical exhortation by description of the horrors perpetrated, by recollection of past great Christian heroes such as Charlemagne, and by the strength of conviction that God is on their side ("It is the will of God!").

[For other versions of the speech, see http://www.fordham.edu/halsall/source/urban2-5vers.html]

Oh, race of Franks, race from across the mountains, race chosen and beloved by God as shines forth in very many of your works set apart from all nations by the situation of your country, as well as by your Catholic faith and the honor of the Holy Church! To you our discourse is addressed and for you our exhortation

5 is intended. We wish you to know what a grievous cause has led us to your country, what peril threatening you and all the faithful has brought us.

From the confines of Jerusalem and the city of Constantinople a horrible tale has gone forth and very frequently has been brought to our ears, namely, that a race from the kingdom of the Persians, an accursed race, a race utterly alienated

10 from God, a generation forsooth which has not directed its heart and has not entrusted its spirit to God, has invaded the lands of those Christians and has depopulated them by the sword, pillage and fire; it has led away a part of the captives into its own country, and a part it has destroyed by cruel tortures; it has either entirely destroyed the churches of God or appropriated them for the rites of

15 its own religion. They destroy the altars, after having defiled them with their uncleanness. They circumcise the Christians, and the blood of the circumcision they either spread upon the altars or pour into the vases of the baptismal font.

When they wish to torture people by a base death, they perforate their navels, and dragging forth the extremity of the intestines, bind it to a stake; then with flogging they lead the victim around until the viscera having gushed forth the victim falls prostrate upon the ground. Others they bind to a post and pierce with arrows. Others they compel to extend their necks and then, attacking them with naked swords, attempt to cut through the neck with a single blow. What shall I say of the abominable rape of the women? To speak of it is worse than to be silent. The kingdom of the Greeks is now dismembered by them and deprived of territory so vast in extent that it cannot be traversed in a march of two months. On whom therefore is the labor of avenging these wrongs and of recovering this territory incumbent, if not upon you? You, upon whom above other nations God has conferred remarkable glory in arms, great courage, bodily activity, and strength to humble the hairy scalp of those who resist you.

Let the deeds of your ancestors move you and incite your minds to manly achievements; the glory and greatness of king Charles the Great, and of his son Louis, and of your other kings, who have destroyed the kingdoms of the pagans, and have extended in these lands the territory of the holy church. Let the holy sepulchre of the Lord our Saviour, which is possessed by unclean nations, especially incite you, and the holy places which are now treated with ignominy and irreverently polluted with their filthiness. Oh, most valiant soldiers and descendants of invincible ancestors, be not degenerate, but recall the valor of your progenitors.

But if you are hindered by love of children, parents and wives, remember what the Lord says in the Gospel, "He that loveth father or mother more than me, is not worthy of me." "Every one that hath forsaken houses, or brethren, or sisters, or father, or mother, or wife, or children, or lands for my name's sake shall receive an hundredfold and shall inherit everlasting life." Let none of your possessions detain you, no solicitude for your family affairs, since this land which you inhabit, shut in on all sides by the seas and surrounded by the mountain peaks, is too narrow for your large population; nor does it abound in wealth; and it furnishes scarcely food enough for its cultivators. Hence it is that you murder one another, that you wage war, and that frequently you perish by mutual wounds. Let therefore hatred depart from among you, let your quarrels end, let wars cease, and let all dissensions and controversies slumber. Enter upon the road to the Holy Sepulchre; wrest that land from the wicked race, and subject it to yourselves. That land which as the Scripture says "floweth with milk and honey," was given by God into the possession of the children of Israel. Jerusalem is the navel of the world; the land is fruitful above others, like another paradise of delights. This the Redeemer of the human race has made illustrious by His advent, has beautified by residence, has consecrated by suffering, has redeemed by death, has glorified by burial. This royal city, therefore, situated at the centre of the world, is now held captive by His enemies, and is in subjection to those who do not know God, to the worship of the heathens. She seeks therefore and desires to be liberated, and does not cease to implore you to come to her aid. From you especially she asks succor, because, as we have already said, God has conferred upon you above all nations great glory in arms. Accordingly undertake this journey for the remission of your sins, with the assurance of the imperishable glory of the kingdom of heaven.

65

When Pope Urban had said these and very many similar things in his urbane discourse, he so influenced to one purpose the desires of all who were present, that they cried out, "It is the will of God! It is the will of God!" When the venerable Roman pontiff heard that, with eyes uplifted to heaven he gave thanks

70 to God and, with his hand commanding silence, said:

Most beloved brethren, today is manifest in you what the Lord says in the Gospel, "Where two or three are gathered together in my name there am I in the midst of them." Unless the Lord God had been present in your spirits, all of you would not have uttered the same cry. For, although the cry issued from numerous

75 mouths, yet the origin of the cry was one. Therefore I say to you that God, who implanted this in your breasts, has drawn it forth from you. Let this then be your war-cry in combats, because this word is given to you by God. When an armed attack is made upon the enemy, let this one cry be raised by all the soldiers of God: It is the will of God! It is the will of God!

80 And we do not command or advise that the old or feeble, or those unfit for bearing arms, undertake this journey; nor ought women to set out at all, without their husbands or brothers or legal guardians. For such are more of a hindrance than aid, more of a burden than advantage. Let the rich aid the needy; and according to their wealth, let them take with them experienced soldiers. The

85 priests and clerks of any order are not to go without the consent of their bishop; for this journey would profit them nothing if they went without permission of these. Also, it is not fitting that laymen should enter upon the pilgrimage without the blessing of their priests.

Whoever, therefore, shall determine upon this holy pilgrimage and shall make

90 his vow to God to that effect and shall offer himself to Him as a living sacrifice, holy, acceptable unto God, shall wear the sign of the cross of the Lord on his forehead or on his breast. When truly having fulfilled his vow he wishes to return, let him place the cross on his back between his shoulders. Such, indeed, by the twofold action will fulfill the precept of the Lord, as He commands in the

95 Gospel, "He that taketh not his cross and followeth after me, is not worthy of me."

4. TRAVELS IN WEST AFRICA (SELECTIONS)

Ibn Battúta
(1304–1368)

Ibn Battúta (1304-1368) was born in Tangier, North Africa where he studied Islamic law. He was one of the most traveled men of his time or any time. In his lifetime, he journeyed over 73,000 miles—the equivalent of three times around the circumference of the globe. In 1325 (the year after Marco Polo died), Ibn Battúta set out on his first journey—a traditional Islamic pilgrimage or hajj *to Mecca. Instead of returning home, however, he traveled to Iraq and Persia, back to Mecca, then to the coastal cities of East Africa, back to Mecca a third time, off to Constantinople, then to India for eight years where he worked as a* quadi *(Islamic legal scholar or judge). He was then sent on a diplomatic mission to China, a few years later returned to Mecca for the fourth time, and then finally home to Tangier. The following year he traveled to Islamic Spain, and shortly after took a final journey by camel caravan across the Sahara Desert to the African kingdom of Malli. In all his travels he almost never stepped outside the world of Islam, since there were Islamic communities all over the world, including Constantinople, India, China and Africa. The following excerpt is from his* Rihla *or travel account. It is the final chapter in which he narrates his journey to the Islamic kingdom of Malli in West Africa.*

CHAPTER XIV

From Marrákush I travelled with the suite of our master [the Sultan] to Fez, where I took leave of our master and set out for the Negrolands. I reached the town of Sijilmása, a very fine town, with quantities of excellent dates. The city of Basra rivals it in abundance of dates, but the Sijilmása dates are better, and the kind called *Írár* has no equal in the world. I stayed there with the learned Abú
5 Muhammad al-Bushrí, the man whose brother I met in the city of Qanjanfú in China. How strangely separated they are! He showed me the utmost honour.

At Sijilmása I bought camels and a four months' supply of forage for them. Thereupon I set out on the 1st Muharram of the year [seven hundred and] fifty-
10 three [18th February 1352] with a caravan including, amongst others, a number of the merchants of Sijilmása. After twenty-five days we reached Tagházá, an unattractive village, with the curious feature that its houses and mosques are built of blocks of salt, roofed with camel skins. There are no trees there, nothing but

sand. In the sand is a salt mine; they dig for the salt, and find it in thick slabs, lying
15 one on top of the other, as though they had been tool-squared and laid under the
surface of the earth. A camel will carry two of these slabs. No one lives at
Tagházá except the slaves of the Massúfa tribe, who dig for the salt; they subsist
on dates imported from Dar'a and Sijilmása, camels' flesh, and millet imported
from the Negrolands. The negroes come up from their country and take away the
20 salt from there. At Íwálátan a load of salt brings eight to ten *mithqáls*; in the town
of Mállí it sells for twenty to thirty, and sometimes as much as forty. The negroes
use salt as a medium of exchange, just as gold and silver is used [elsewhere]; they
cut it up into pieces and buy and sell with it. The business done at Tagházá, for all
its meanness, amounts to an enormous figure in terms of hundredweights of gold-
25 dust.

We passed ten days of discomfort there, because the water is brackish and the
place is plagued with flies. Water supplies are laid in at Tagházá for the crossing
of the desert which lies beyond it, which is a ten-nights' journey with no water on
the way except on rare occasions. We indeed had the good fortune to find water in
30 plenty, in pools left by the rain. One day we found a pool of sweet water between
two rocky prominences. We quenched our thirst at it and then washed our clothes.
Truffles are plentiful in this desert and it swarms with lice, so that people wear
string necklaces containing mercury, which kills them. At that time we used to go
ahead of the caravan, and when we found a place suitable for pasturage we
35 would graze our beasts. We went on doing this until one of our party was lost in
the desert; after that I neither went ahead nor lagged behind. We passed a caravan
on the way and they told us that some of their party had become separated from
them. We found one of them dead under a shrub, of the sort that grows in the sand,
with his clothes on and a whip in his hand. The water was only about a mile
40 away from him.

We came next to Tásarahlá, a place of subterranean water-beds, where the
caravans halt. They stay there three days to rest, mend their waterskins, fill them
with water, and sew on them covers of sackcloth as a precaution against the
wind. From this point the *takshíf* is despatched. The *takshíf* is a name given to any
45 man of the Massúfa tribe who is hired by the persons in the caravan to go ahead
to Íwálátan, carrying letters from them to their friends there, so that they may take
lodgings for them. These persons then come out a distance of four nights' journey to
meet the caravan, and bring water with them. Anyone who has no friend in
Íwálátan writes to some merchant well known for his worthy character, who
50 then undertakes the same services for him. It often happens that the *takshíf* perishes
in this desert, with the result that the people of Íwálátan know nothing about the
caravan, and all or most of those who are with it perish. That desert is haunted by
demons; if the *takshíf* be alone, they make sport of him and disorder his mind, so
that he loses his way and perishes. For there is no visible road or track in these
55 parts—nothing but sand blown hither and thither by the wind. You see hills of
sand in one place, and afterwards you will see them moved to quite another place.
The guide there is one who has made the journey frequently in both directions, and

60 who is gifted with a quick intelligence. I remarked, as a strange thing, that the
guide whom we had was blind in one eye, and diseased in the other, yet he had the
best knowledge of the road of any man. We hired the *takshif* on this journey for a
hundred gold *mithqáls;* he was a man of the Massúfa. On the night of the seventh
day [from Tásarahlá] we saw with joy the fires of the party who had come out to
meet us.

65 Thus we reached the town of Íwálátan [Walata] after a journey from
Sijilmása of two months to a day. Íwálátan is the northernmost province of the
negroes, and the sultan's representative there was one Farbá Husayn, *farbá*
meaning deputy [in their language]. When we arrived there, the merchants
deposited their goods in an open square, where the blacks undertook to guard
70 them, and went to the *farbá*. He was sitting on a carpet under an archway, with his
guards before him carrying lances and bows in their hands, and the headmen of the
Massúfa behind him. The merchants remained standing in front of him while he
spoke to them through an interpreter, although they were close to him, to show his
contempt for them. It was then that I repented of having come to their country,
because of their lack of manners and their contempt for the whites.

75 I went to visit Ibn Baddá, a worthy man of Salá [Sallee, Rabát], to whom I
had written requesting him to hire a house for me, and who had done so. Later on
the *mushríf* [inspector] of Íwálátan, whose name was Manshá Jú, invited all those
who had come with the caravan to partake of his hospitality. At first I refused to
attend, but my companions urged me very strongly, so I went with the rest. The
80 repast was served—some pounded millet mixed with a little honey and milk, put in
a half calabash shaped like a large bowl. The guests drank and retired. I said to
them "Was it for this that the black invited us?" They answered "Yes; and it is in
their opinion the highest form of hospitality." This convinced me that there was no
good to be hoped for from these people, and I made up my mind to travel [back to
85 Morocco at once] with the pilgrim caravan from Íwálátan. Afterwards, however,
I thought it best to go to see the capital of their king [at Mállí].

My stay at Íwálátan lasted about fifty days; and I was shown honour and
entertained by its inhabitants. It is an excessively hot place, and boasts a few
small date-palms, in the shade of which they sow watermelons. Its water comes
90 from underground waterbeds at that point, and there is plenty of mutton to be had.
The garments of its inhabitants, most of whom belong to the Massúfa tribe, are of
fine Egyptian fabrics. Their women are of surpassing beauty, and are shown more
respect than the men. The state of affairs amongst these people is indeed
extraordinary. Their men show no signs of jealousy whatever; no one claims
95 descent from his father, but on the contrary from his mother's brother. A person's
heirs are his sister's sons, not his own sons. This is a thing which I have seen
nowhere in the world except among the Indians of Malabar. But those are
heathens; *these* people are Muslims, punctilious in observing the hours of prayer,
studying books of law, and memorizing the Koran. Yet their women show no
100 bashfulness before men and do not veil themselves, though they are assiduous in
attending the prayers. Any man who wishes to marry one of them may do so, but

they do not travel with their husbands, and even if one desired to do so her family would not allow her to go.

105　The women there have "friends" and "companions" amongst the men outside their own families, and the men in the same way have "companions" amongst the women of other families. A man may go into his house and find his wife entertaining her "companion" but he takes no objection to it. One day at Íwálátan I went into the qádí's house, after asking his permission to enter, and found with him a young woman of remarkable beauty. When I saw her I was shocked and 110　turned to go out, but she laughed at me, instead of being overcome by shame, and the qádí said to me "Why are you going out? She is my companion." I was amazed at their conduct, for he was a theologian and a pilgrim to boot. I was told that he had asked the sultan's permission to make the pilgrimage that year with his "companion" (whether this one or not I cannot say) but the sultan would not 115　grant it.

When I decided to make the journey to Málí, which is reached in twenty-four days from Íwálátan if the traveller pushes on rapidly, I hired a guide from the Massúfa (for there is no necessity to travel in a company on account of the safety of that road), and set out with three of my companions. On the way there are many 120　trees, and these trees are of great age and girth; a whole caravan may shelter in the shade of one of them. There are trees which have neither branches nor leaves, yet the shade cast by their trunks is sufficient to shelter a man. Some of these trees are rotted in the interior and the rain-water collects in them, so that they serve as wells and the people drink of the water inside them. In others there are bees and 125　honey, which is collected by the people. I was surprised to find inside one tree, by which I passed, a man, a weaver, who had set up his loom in it and was actually weaving.

A traveller in this country carries no provisions, whether plain food or seasonings, and neither gold nor silver. He takes nothing but pieces of salt and 130　glass ornaments, which the people call beads, and some aromatic goods. When he comes to a village the womenfolk of the blacks bring out millet, milk, chickens, pulped lotus fruit, rice, *fúní* (a grain resembling mustard seed, from which *kuskusú* and gruel are made), and pounded haricot beans. The traveller buys what of these he wants, but their rice causes sickness to whites when it is eaten, and the *fúní* is 135　preferable to it.

Ten days after leaving Íwálátan we came to the village of Zágharí, a large village, inhabited by negro traders called *wanjaráta*, along with whom live a community of whites of the 'Ibádite sect. It is from this village that millet is carried to Íwálátan. After leaving Zágharí we came to the great river, that is the Nile, on 140　which stands the town of Kársakhú. The Nile flows from there down to Kábara, and thence to Zágha.[1] In both Kábara and Zágha there are sultans who owe allegiance to the king of Málí. The inhabitants of Zágha are of old standing in Islam; they show great devotion and zeal for study. Thence the Nile descends to

---

[1]The river he refers to is actually the Niger River.

145 Tumbuktú and Gawgaw [Gogo], both of which will be described later; then to the town of Múlí in the land of the Límís, which is the frontier province of [the kingdom of] Mállí; thence to Yúfí, one of the largest towns of the negroes, whose ruler is one of the most considerable of the negro rulers. It cannot be visited by any white man because they would kill him before he got there.[2] From Yúfí the Nile

150 descends to the land of the Núba [Nubians], who profess the Christian faith, and thence to Dunqula [Dongola], which is their chief town. The sultan of Dunqula is called Ibn Kanz ad-Dín; he was converted to Islám in the days of [Sultan] al-Malik an-Násir [of Egypt]. Thence it descends to Janádil [the Cataracts], which is the end of the negro territories and the beginning of the province of Uswán [Aswan] in Upper Egypt.

155 I saw a crocodile in this part of the Nile, close to the bank; it looked just like a small boat. One day I went down to the river to satisfy a need, and lo, one of the blacks came and stood between me and the river. I was amazed at such lack of manners and decency on his part, and spoke of it to someone or other. He answered " His purpose in doing that was solely to protect you from the

160 crocodile, by placing himself between you and it."

We set out thereafter from Karsakhú and came to the river of Sansara, which is about ten miles from Mállí. It is their custom that no persons except those who have obtained permission are allowed to enter the city. I had already written to the white community [there] requesting them to hire a house for me, so when I

165 arrived at this river, I crossed by the ferry without interference. Thus I reached the city of Mállí, the capital of the king of the blacks. I stopped at the cemetery and went to the quarter occupied by the whites, where I asked for Muhammad ibn al-Faqíh. I found that he had hired a house for me and went there. His son-in-law brought me candles and food, and next day Ibn al-Faqíh himself came to visit me,

170 with other prominent residents. I met the qádí of Mállí, 'Abd ar-Rahmán, who came to see me; he is a negro, a pilgrim, and a man of fine character. I met also the interpreter Dúghá, who is one of the principal men among the blacks. All these persons sent me hospitality-gifts of food and treated me with the utmost generosity—may God reward them for their kindnesses! Ten days after our

175 arrival we ate a gruel made of a root resembling colocasia, which is preferred by them to all other dishes. We all fell ill—there were six of us—and one of our number died. I for my part went to the morning prayer and fainted there. I asked a certain Egyptian for a loosening remedy and he gave me a thing called *baydar*, made of vegetable roots, which he mixed with aniseed and sugar, and stirred in water. I

180 drank it off and vomited what I had eaten, together with a large quantity of bile. God preserved me from death but I was ill for two months.

The sultan of Mállí is Mansá Sulaymán, *mansá* meaning [in Mande] sultan, and Sulaymán being his proper name.[3] He is a miserly king, not a man from whom

---

[2]By "white man," Ibn Battúta means any Muslim from North Africa.

[3]The following is a brief account of the early negro empires.

The earliest Sudanic empire was that of Ghána (which was really the title of its later Soninke rulers). This empire was founded about the fourth century, apparently by some

one might hope for a rich present. It happened that I spent these two months
185   without seeing him, on account of my illness. Later on he held a banquet in
commemoration of our master [the late sultan of Morocco] Abu'l-Hasan, to which
the commanders, doctors, qádí and preacher were invited, and I went along with
them. Reading-desks were brought in, and the Koran was read through, then they
prayed for our master Abu'l-Hasan and also for Mansá Sulaymán. When the
190   ceremony was over I went forward and saluted Mansá Sulaymán. The qádí, the
preacher, and Ibn al-Faqíh told him who I was, and he answered them in their
tongue. They said to me "The sultan says to you 'Give thanks to God,'" so I said
"Praise be to God and thanks under all circumstances."

When I withdrew the [sultan's] hospitality gift was sent to me. It was taken
195   first to the qádí's house, and the qádí sent it on with his men to Ibn al-Faqíh's
house. Ibn al-Faqíh came hurrying out of his house bare-footed, and entered my
room saying "Stand up; here comes the sultan's stuff and gift to you. So I stood up
thinking [since he had called it "stuff"] that it consisted of robes of honour and
money, and lo! it was three cakes of bread, and a piece of beef fried in native oil,
200   and a calabash of sour curds. When I saw this I burst out laughing, and thought it
a most amazing thing that they could be so foolish and make so much of such a
paltry matter.

For two months after this hospitality gift was sent to me I received nothing
further from the sultan, and then followed the month of Ramadán. Meanwhile I
205   used to go frequently to the palace where I would salute him and sit alongside the
qádí and the preacher. I had a conversation with Dúghá the interpreter, and he
said "Speak in his presence, and I shall express on your behalf what is
necessary." When the sultan held an audience early in Ramadán, I rose and stood
before him and said to him: "I have travelled through the countries of the world
210   and have met their kings. Here have I been four months in your country, yet you
have neither shown me hospitality, nor given me anything. What am I to say of you
before [other] rulers?" The sultan replied "I have not seen you, and have not been

white immigrants. The site of its capital seems to have changed more than once. From the
ninth to the eleventh century the Soninke of Kumbi were masters of the Ghána empire,
until its destruction by the Almoravids of Morocco in 1076. A number of small states were
constituted on its ruins, and one of these, the Soninke dynasty of the Kannte, whose
capital was at Sosso (to the weft of Sansanding), recaptured Ghána in 1203 and restored
the Soninke empire. To this was due also the foundation of Waláta, as the Muslim
inhabitants of Ghána, refusing to live under infidel rule, established themselves at the
water-point of Waláta or Bírú (see note 6). The conqueror, Sumanguru, was killed in battle
in 1235 with the Malinke, whose king Sunjáta or Mári Játa annexed the Soninke empire,
was converted to Islam (see p. 329), and established the new capital at Málli. He captured
and destroyed Ghána in 1240, and died in 1255. After a succession of rulers, the next
emperor of importance was Músá (Ibn Battúta's Mansá Musá), in whose reign (1307-32)
the Málli empire reached its widest dimensions. Músá was the grandson of a sister of
Sunjáta. The reign of his son and successor Mansá Maghán (1332-6) marks a brief
retrogression, but under Músá's brother Sulaymán (1336-59), the Málli regained much of
their power and prestige. With his death there set in a sharp decline, accentuated by civil
wars. The Málli kingdom, however, still remained the most powerful of the Niger states
until the rise of the Songhay kingdom (see note 32), and did not finally disappear until
1670.

told about you." The qádí and Ibn al-Faqíh rose and replied to him, saying "He has already saluted you, and you have sent him food." Thereupon he gave orders
215 to set apart a house for my lodging and to pay me a daily sum for my expenses. Later on, on the night of the 27th Ramadán, he distributed a sum of money which they call the *Zakáh* [alms] between the qádí, the preachers, and the doctors. He gave me a portion along with them of thirty- three and a third *mithqáls*, and on my departure from Má“lí he bestowed on me a gift of a hundred gold *mithqáls*.

220 On certain days the sultan holds audiences in the palace yard, where there is a platform under a tree, with three steps; this they call the *pempi*. It is carpeted with silk and has cushions placed on it. [Over it] is raised the umbrella, which is a sort of pavilion made of silk, surmounted by a bird in gold, about the size of a falcon. The sultan comes out of a door in a corner of the palace, carrying a bow in
225 his hand and a quiver on his back. On his head he has a golden skull-cap, bound with a gold band which has narrow ends shaped like knives, more than a span in length. His usual dress is a velvety red tunic, made of the European fabrics called *mutanfas*. The sultan is preceded by his musicians, who carry gold and silver guimbris [two-stringed guitars], and behind him come three hundred armed slaves.
230 He walks in a leisurely fashion, affecting a very slow movement, and even stops from time to time. On reaching the *pempi* he stops and looks round the assembly, then ascends it in the sedate manner of a preacher ascending a mosque-pulpit. As he takes his seat the drums, trumpets, and bugles are sounded. Three slaves go out at a run to summon the sovereign's deputy and the military commanders, who enter
235 and sit down. Two saddled and bridled horses are brought, along with two goats, which they hold to serve as a protection against the evil eye. Dúghá stands at the gate and the rest of the people remain in the street, under the trees.

The negroes are of all people the most submissive to their king and the most abject in their behaviour before him. They swear by his name, saying *Mansá*
240 *Sulaymán ki.*[4] If he summons any of them while he is holding an audience in his pavilion, the person summoned takes off his clothes and puts on worn garments, removes his turban and dons a dirty skullcap, and enters with his garments and trousers raised knee-high. He goes forward in an attitude of humility and dejection, and knocks the ground hard with his elbows, then stands with bowed
245 head and bent back listening to what he says. If anyone addresses the king and receives a reply from him, he uncovers his back and throws dust over his head and back, for all the world like a bather splashing himself with water. I used to wonder how it was they did not blind themselves. If the sultan delivers any remarks during his audience, those present take off their turbans and put them
250 down, and listen in silence to what he says. Sometimes one of them stands up before him and recalls his deeds in the sultan's service, saying "I did so-and-so on such a day" or "I killed so-and-so on such a day." Those who have knowledge of this confirm his words, which they do by plucking the cord of the bow and releasing it [with a twang], just as an archer does when shooting an arrow. If the

---

[4]*I.e.* "The Emperor Sulayman has commanded," in Mandingo.

255   sultan says "Truly spoken" or thanks him, he removes his clothes and "dusts."
       That is their idea of good manners.

                                    * * * * *

       I was at Máilí during the two festivals of the sacrifice and the fast-breaking.
       On these days the sultan takes his seat on the *pempi* after the midafternoon prayer.
260   The armour-bearers bring in magnificent arms—quivers of gold and silver, swords
       ornamented with gold and with golden scabbards, gold and silver lances, and
       crystal maces. At his head stand four amírs driving off the flies, having in their
       hands silver ornaments resembling saddle-stirrups. The commanders, qádí, and
       preacher sit in their usual places. The interpreter Dúghá comes with his four
265   wives and his slave-girls, who are about a hundred in number. They are wearing
       beautiful robes, and on their heads they have gold and silver fillets, with gold and
       silver balls attached. A chair is placed for Dúghá to sit on. He plays on an
       instrument made of reeds, with some small calabashes at its lower end, and chants
       a poem in praise of the sultan, recalling his battles and deeds of valour. The
270   women and girls sing along with him and play with bows. Accompanying them are
       about thirty youths, wearing red woollen tunics and white skull-caps; each of
       them has his drum slung from his shoulder and beats it. Afterwards come his boy
       pupils who play and turn wheels in the air, like the natives of Sind. They show a
       marvellous nimbleness and agility in these exercises and play most cleverly with
275   swords. Dúghá also makes a fine play with the sword. Thereupon the sultan
       orders a gift to be presented to Dúghá and he is given a purse containing two
       hundred *mithqáls* of gold dust, and is informed of the contents of the purse before
       all the people. The commanders rise and twang their bows in thanks to the sultan.
       The next day each one of them gives Dúghá a gift, every man according to his rank.
280   Every Friday after the *'asr* prayer, Dúghá carries out a similar ceremony to this
       that we have described.

       On feast-days, after Dúghá has finished his display, the poets come in. Each of
       them is inside a figure resembling a thrush, made of feathers, and provided with a
       wooden head with a red beak, to look like a thrush's head. They stand in front of
285   the sultan in this ridiculous make-up and recite their poems. I was told that their
       poetry is a kind of sermonizing in which they say to the sultan: "This *pempi*
       which you occupy was that whereon sat this king and that king, and such and
       such were this one's noble actions and such and such the other's. So do you too do
       good deeds whose memory will outlive you." After that, the chief of the poets
290   mounts the steps of the *pempi* and lays his head on the sultan's lap, then climbs to
       the top of the *pempi* and lays his head first on the sultan's right shoulder and then
       on his left, speaking all the while in their tongue, and finally he comes down again.
       I was told that this practice is a very old custom amongst them, prior to the
       introduction of Islám, and that they have kept it up.

295   The negroes disliked Mansá Sulaymán because of his avarice. His
       predecessor was Mansá Maghá, and before him reigned Mansá Músá, a generous
       and virtuous prince, who loved the whites and made gifts to them. It was he who
       gave Abú Isháq as-Sáhilí four thousand *mithqáls* in the course of a single day. I

300   heard from a trustworthy source that he gave three thousand *mithqáls* on one day to Mudrik ibn Faqqús, by whose grandfather his own grandfather, Sáraq Játa, had been converted to Islám.

       The negroes possess some admirable qualities. They are seldom unjust, and have a greater abhorrence of injustice than any other people. Their sultan shows no mercy to anyone who is guilty of the least act of it. There is complete security in
305   their country. Neither traveller nor inhabitant in it has anything to fear from robbers or men of violence. They do not confiscate the property of any white man who dies in their country, even if it be uncounted wealth. On the contrary, they give it into the charge of some trustworthy person among the whites, until the rightful heir takes possession of it. They are careful to observe the hours of
310   prayer, and assiduous in attending them in congregations, and in bringing up their children to them. On Fridays, if a man does not go early to the mosque, he cannot find a corner to pray in, on account of the crowd. It is a custom of theirs to send each man his boy [to the mosque] with his prayer-mat; the boy spreads it out for his master in a place befitting him [and remains on it] until he comes to the mosque.
315   Their prayer-mats are made of the leaves of a tree resembling a date-palm, but without fruit.

       Another of their good qualities is their habit of wearing clean white garments on Fridays. Even if a man has nothing but an old worn shirt, he washes it and cleans it, and wears it to the Friday service. Yet another is their zeal for learning
320   the Koran by heart. They put their children in chains if they show any backwardness in memorizing it, and they are not set free until they have it by heart. I visited the qádí in his house on the day of the festival. His children were chained up, so I said to him "Will you not let them loose?" He replied "I shall not do so until they learn the Koran by heart." Among their bad qualities are the
325   following. The women servants, slave-girls, and young girls go about in front of everyone naked, without a stitch of clothing on them. Women go into the sultan's presence naked and without coverings, and his daughters also go about naked. Then there is their custom of putting dust and ashes on their heads, as a mark of respect, and the grotesque ceremonies we have described when the poets recite
330   their verses. Another reprehensible practice among many of them is the eating of carrion, dogs, and asses.

       The date of my arrival at Mállí was 14th Jumáda I., [seven hundred and] fifty-three [28th June 1352] and of my departure from it 22nd Muharram of the year fifty-four [27th February 1353]. I was accompanied by a merchant called Abú
335   Bakr ibn Ya'qúb. We took the Míma road. I had a camel which I was riding, because horses are expensive, and cost a hundred *mithqáls* each. We came to a wide channel which flows out of the Nile and can only be crossed in boats. The place is infected with mosquitoes, and no one can pass that way except by night. We reached the channel three or four hours after nightfall on a moonlit night. On
340   reaching it I saw sixteen beasts with enormous bodies, and marvelled at them, taking them to be elephants, of which there are many in that country. Afterwards I saw that they had gone into the river, so I said to Abú Bakr "What kind of

animals are these?" He replied "They are hippopotami which have come out to
pasture ashore." They are bulkier than horses, have manes and tails, and their
345   heads are like horses' heads, but their feet like elephants' feet. I saw these
hippopotami again when we sailed down the Nile from Tumbuktú to Gawgaw.
They were swimming in the water, and lifting their heads and blowing. The men in
the boat were afraid of them and kept close to the bank in case the hippopotami
should sink them.

350   They have a cunning method of catching these hippopotami. They use spears
with a hole bored in them, through which strong cords are passed. The spear is
thrown at one of the animals, and if it strikes its leg or neck it goes right through it.
Then they pull on the rope until the beast is brought to the bank, kill it and eat its
flesh. Along the bank there are quantities of hippopotamus bones.

355   We halted near this channel at a large village, which had as governor a negro,
a pilgrim, and man of fine character, named Farbá Maghá. He was one of the
negroes who made the pilgrimage in the company of Sultan Mansá Músá. Farbá
Maghá told me that when Mansá Músá came to this channel, he had with him a
qádí, a white man. This qádí attempted to make away with four thousand *mithqáls*
360   and the sultan, on learning of it, was enraged at him and exiled him to the country
of the heathen cannibals. He lived among them for four years, at the end of which
the sultan sent him back to his own country. The reason why the heathens did not
eat him was that he was white, for they say that the white is indigestible because
he is not "ripe," whereas the black man is "ripe" in their opinion.

365   Sultan Mansá Sulaymán was visited by a party of these negro cannibals,
including one of their amírs. They have a custom of wearing in their ears large
pendants, each pendant having an opening of half a span. They wrap themselves in
silk mantles, and in their country there is a gold mine. The sultan received them
with honour, and gave them as his hospitality-gift a servant, a negress. They killed
370   and ate her, and having smeared their faces and hands with her blood came to the
sultan to thank him. I was informed that this is their regular custom whenever they
visit his court. Someone told me about them that they say that the choicest parts of
women's flesh are the palm of the hand and the breast.

    We continued our journey from this village which is by the channel, and came
375   to the town of Qurí Mansá. At this point the camel which I was riding died. Its
keeper informed me of its death, but when I went out to see it, I found that the
blacks had already eaten it, according to their usual custom of eating carrion. I
sent two lads whom I had hired for my service to buy me a camel at Zághari, and
waited at Qurí Mansá for six days till they returned with it.

380   I travelled next to the town of Míma and halted by some wells in its outskirts.
Thence we went on to Tumbuktú, which stands four miles from the river. Most of
its inhabitants are of the Massúfa tribe, wearers of the face-veil. Its governor is
called Farbá Músá. I was present with him one day when he had just appointed
one of the Massúfa to be amir of a section. He assigned to him a robe, a turban, and
385   trousers, all of them of dyed cloth, and bade him sit upon a shield, and the chiefs of
his tribe raised him on their heads. In this town is the grave of the meritorious poet

Abú Isháq as-Sáhilí, of Gharnáta [Granada], who is known in his own land as at-Tuwayjin ["Little Saucepan"].

390 From Tumbuktú I sailed down the Nile on a small boat, hollowed out of a single piece of wood. We used to go ashore every night at the villages and buy whatever we needed in the way of meat and butter in exchange for salt, spices, and glass beads. I then came to a place the name of which I have forgotten, where there was an excellent governor, a pilgrim, called Farbá Sulaymán. He is famous for his courage and strength, and none ventures to pluck his bow. I have not seen anyone

395 among the blacks taller or bulkier than him. At this town I was in need of some millet, so I visited him (it was on the Prophet's birthday) and saluted him. He took me by the hand, and led me into his audience hall. We were served with a drink of theirs called *daqnú*, which is water containing some pounded millet mixed with a little honey or milk. They drink this in place of water, because if they drink plain

400 water it upsets them. If they have no millet they mix the water with honey or milk. Afterwards a green melon was brought in and we ate some of it.

A young boy, not yet full-grown, came in, and Farbá Sulaymán, calling him, said to me "Here is your hospitality-gift; keep an eye on him in case he escapes." So I took the boy and prepared to withdraw, but he said " Wait till the food

405 comes." A slave-girl of his joined us; she was an Arab girl, of Damascus, and she spoke to me in Arabic. While this was going on we heard cries in his house, so he sent the girl to find out what had happened. She returned to him and told him that a daughter of his had just died. He said " I do not like crying, come, we shall walk to the river," meaning the Nile, on which he has some houses. A horse was

410 brought, and he told me to ride, but I said "I shall not ride if you are walking," so we walked together. We came to his houses by the Nile, where food was served, and after we had eaten I took leave of him and withdrew. I met no one among the blacks more generous or upright than him. The boy whom he gave me is still with me.

* * * * *

5. THE ART OF COURTLY LOVE (SELECTIONS)
(c. 1185)

Andreas Capellanus

(trans. by J. J. Parry)

Andreas Capellanus was chaplain at the court of Marie of Champagne who supposedly commissioned him to compose the work as a code for lovers. It is a puzzling work for several reasons: the first two books are in the cynical vein of Ovid (from whom they draw much) and thus immoral from medieval Christian perspective; the third book (rarely read!) is a retraction, claiming the previous material to be a joke and reasserting Christian teachings on proper relationships. The influence of the first two books was wide in romance literature and engenders debate as to the extent courtly love behavioral prescripts (and romance literature) reflect actual life or were useful as a form of "escapism" in literature.

AUTHOR'S PREFACE

I am greatly impelled by the continual urging of my love for you, my revered friend Walter, to make known by word or mouth and to teach you by my writings the way in which a state of love between two lovers may be kept unharmed and likewise how those who do not love may get rid of the darts of Venus that are
5   fixed in their hearts. You tell me that you are a new recruit of Love, and, having recently been wounded by an arrow of his, you do not know how to manage your horse's reins properly and you cannot find any cure for yourself. How serious this is and how it troubles my soul no words of mine can make clear to you. For I know, having learned from experience, that it does not do the man who owes
10 obedience to Venus's services any good to give careful thought to anything except how he may always be doing something that will entangle him more firmly in his chains; he thinks he has nothing good except what may wholly please his love. Therefore, although it does not seem expedient to devote oneself to things of this kind or fitting for any prudent man to engage in this kind of hunting, nevertheless,
15 because of the affection I have for you, I can by no means refuse your request; because I know clearer than day that after you have learned the art of love your

-107-

progress in it will be more cautious, in so far as I can I shall comply with your desire.

BOOK ONE: INTRODUCTION TO THE TREATISE ON LOVE

20 We must first consider what love is, whence it gets its name, what the effect of love is between what persons love may exist, how it may be acquired, retained, increased, decreased, and ended, what are the signs that one's love is returned, and what one of the lovers ought to do if the other is unfaithful.

CHAPTER I. WHAT LOVE IS

Love is a certain inborn suffering derived from the sight of and excessive meditation upon the beauty of the opposite sex, which causes each one to wish
25 above all things the embraces of the other and by common desire to carry out all of love's precepts in the other's embrace.

That love is suffering is easy to see, for before the love becomes equally balanced on both sides there is no torment greater, since the lover is always in fear that his love may not gain its desire and that he is wasting his efforts. He
30 fears, too, that rumors of it may get abroad, and he fears everything that might harm it in any way, for before things are perfected a slight disturbance often spoils them. If he is a poor man, he also fears that the woman may scorn his poverty; if he is ugly, he fears that she may despise his lack of beauty or may give her love to a more handsome man; if he is rich, he fears that his parsimony in the
35 past may stand in his way. To tell the truth, no one can number the fears of one single lover. This kind of love, then, is a suffering, which is felt by only one of the persons and may be called "single love." But even after both are in love the fears that arise are just as great, for each of the lovers fears that what he has acquired with so much effort may be lost through the effort of someone else, which is
40 certainly much worse for a man than if, having no hope, he sees that his efforts are accomplishing nothing, for it is worse to lose the things you are seeking than to be deprived of a gain you merely hope for. The lover fears, too, that he may offend his loved one in some way; indeed he fears so many things that it would be difficult to tell them.
45 That this suffering is inborn I shall show you clearly, because if you will look at the truth and distinguish carefully you will see that it does not arise out of any action, only from the reflection of the mind upon what it sees does this suffering come. For when a man sees some woman fit for love and shaped according to his taste, he begins at once to lust after her in his heart; then the more
50 he thinks about her the more he burns with love, until he comes to a fuller meditation. Presently he begins to think about the fashioning of the woman and to differentiate her limbs, to think about what she does, and to pry into the secrets of her body, and he desires to put each part of it to the fullest use. Then after he has come to this complete meditation, love cannot hold the reins, but he proceeds at

55 once to action; straightway he strives to get a helper and to find an intermediary. He begins to plan how he may find favor with her, and he begins to seek a place and a time opportune for talking; he looks upon a brief hour as a very long year, because he cannot do anything fast enough to suit his eager mind. It is well known that many things happen to him in this manner. This inborn suffering comes,
60 therefore, from seeing and meditating. Not every kind of meditation can be the cause love, an excessive one is required; for a restrained thought does not, as a rule, return to the mind, and so love cannot arise from it.

CHAPTER IV: WHAT THE EFFECTS OF LOVE IS

Now it is the effect of love that a true lover cannot be degraded with any avarice. Love causes a rough and uncouth man to be distinguished for his
65 handsomeness; it can endow a man even of the humblest birth with nobility of character; it blesses the proud with humility; and the man in love becomes accustomed to performing many services gracefully for everyone. O what a wonderful thing is love, which makes a man shine with so many virtues and teaches everyone, no matter who he is, so many good traits of character! There is
70 another thing about love that we should not praise in few words: it adorns a man, so to speak, with the virtue of chastity, because he who shines with the light of one love can hardly think of embracing another woman, even a beautiful one. For when he thinks deeply of his beloved the sight of any other woman seems to his mind rough and rude.

CHAPTER V: WHAT PERSONS ARE FIT FOR LOVE

75 We must now see what persons are fit to bear the arms of love. You should know that everyone of sound mind who is capable of doing the work of Venus may be wounded by one of Love's arrows unless prevented by age, or blindness, or excess of passion. Age is a bar, because after the sixtieth year in a man and the fiftieth in a woman, although one may have intercourse his passion cannot
80 develop into love; because at that age the natural heat begins to lose its force, and the natural moisture is greatly increased, which leads a man into various difficulties and troubles him with various ailments, and there are no consolations in the world for him except food and drink. Similarly, a girl under the age of twelve and a boy before the fourteenth year do not serve in love's army.
85 However, I say and insist that before his eighteenth year a man cannot be a true lover, because up to that age he is overcome with embarrassment over any little thing, which not only interferes with the perfecting of love, but even destroys it if it is well perfected. But we find another even more powerful reason, which is that before this age a man has no constancy, but is changeable in every way, for such a
90 tender age cannot think about the mysteries of love's realm. Why love should kindle in a woman at an earlier age than in a man I shall perhaps show you elsewhere.

95　　Blindness is a bar to love, because a blind man cannot see anything upon which his mind can reflect immoderately, and so love cannot arise in him, as I have already fully shown. But I admit that this is true only of the acquiring of love, for I do not deny that a love which a man acquires before his blindness may last after he becomes blind.

100　　An excess of passion is a bar to love, because are men who are slaves to such passionate desire that they cannot be held in the bonds of love; men who, after they have thought long about some woman or even enjoyed her, when they see another woman straightway desire her embraces, and they forget about the services they have received from their first love and they feel no gratitude for them. Men of this kind lust after every woman they see; their love is like that of a shameless dog. They should rather, I believe, be compared to asses, for they are

105　　moved only by that low nature which shows that men are on the level of the other animals rather than by that true nature which sets us apart from all the other animals by the difference of reason. Of such lovers I shall speak elsewhere.

* * *

　　To my request [for a list of rules of love], he answered, You have been permitted to see our mightily works that through you our glory may be revealed to

110　　those who know it not, and that this sight which you now see may be a means of salvation for many ladies. We therefore command and firmly enjoin upon you that wherever you find a lady of any worth departing from our pathway by refusing to submit herself to love's engagements, you shall take care to relate to her what you have seen here and shall cause her to leave her erroneous ideas so that she may

115　　escape such very heavy torments and find a place here in glory. Know, then, that the chief rules in love are these twelve that follow.

　　　　Thou shalt avoid avarice like the deadly pestilence and shalt embrace its opposite.

　　　　Thou shalt keep thyself chaste for the sake of her whom thou lovest.

120　　　　Thou shalt not knowingly strive to break up a correct love affair that someone else is engaged in.

　　　　Thou shalt not choose for they love anyone whom a natural sense of shame forbids thee to marry.

　　　　Be mindful completely to avoid falsehood.

125　　　　Thou shalt not have many who know of thy love affair.

　　　　Being obedient in all things to the commands of ladies, thou shalt ever strive to ally thyself to the service of Love.

　　　　In giving and receiving love's solaces let modesty be ever present.

　　　　Thou shalt speak no evil.

130　　　　Thou shalt not be a revealer of love affairs.

　　　　Thou shalt be in all things polite and courteous.

　　　　In practicing the solaces of love thou shalt not exceed the desires of thy lover.

[Some of the other, more controversial "rules" Andreas Capellanus includes in other sections are:

135   Marriage should not be a deterrent to love.
         Love cannot exist in the individual who cannot be jealous.
         A double love cannot obligate an individual.
         Love constantly waxes and wanes.
         Love is reinforced by jealousy.
140   Suspicion of the beloved generates jealousy and therefore intensifies love.
         Eating and sleeping diminish greatly when one is aggravated by love.
         The lover's every deed is performed with the thought of his beloved in mind.]

BOOK TWO, CHAPTER III

         It also decreases love if one discovers any infamy in the lover or hears of any
         avarice, bad character, or any kind of unworthiness; so it does for him to have an
145   affair with another woman, even if he is not in love with her. Love decreases, too,
         if the woman finds that her lover is foolish and indiscreet, or if he seems to go
         beyond reasonable bounds in his demands for love, or if she sees that he has no
         regard for her modesty and will not forgive her bashfulness. For a faithful lover
         ought to prefer love's greatest pains to making demands which deprive his beloved
150   of her modesty or taking pleasure in making fun of her blushes; he is not called a
         lover, but a betrayer, who would consider only his own passions and who would
         be unmindful of the good of his beloved. Love decreases, too, if the woman
         considers that her lover is cowardly in battle, or sees that he is unrestrained in
         his speech or spoiled by the vice or arrogance. For nothing appears more seemly in
155   the character of any lover at all than that he should be clad in the garment of
         humility and wholly lack the nakedness of pride. The utterance of silly and
         foolish words frequently decreases love. Many men, when with a woman, think
         that they will please her if they utter the first silly words that come into their
         heads, which is really a great mistake. The man who thinks he can please a wise
160   woman by doing something foolish shows a great lack of sense.
         Other things which weaken love are blasphemy against God or His saints,
         mockery of the ceremonies of the Church, and a deliberate withholding of charity
         from the poor. We find that love decreases very sharply if one is unfaithful to his
         friend, or if he brazenly says one thing while he deceitfully conceals a different
165   idea in his heart. Love decreases, too, if the lover piles up more wealth than is
         proper, or if he is too ready to go to law over trifles. We could tell you many more
         things about the weakening of love, but we leave you to find these out for yourself,
         for we see that you are so devoted to the practice of love as to neglect all other
         business and so determined to love that nothing in the art of love can escape you,
170   since there is not a thing in it that you leave undiscussed. But we do not want you
         to overlook the fact that when love has definitely begun to decline, it quickly
         comes to an end unless something comes to save it.

CHAPTER IV: HOW LOVE MAY COME TO AN END

Now having treated briefly of the lessening of love we shall try next to add
for you an explanation of how it may come to an end. First of all we see that love
175   comes to an end if one of the lovers breaks faith or tries to break faith with the
other, or if he is found to go astray from the Catholic religion. It comes to an end
also after it has been openly revealed and made known to men. So, too if one of the
lovers has plenty of money and does not come to the aid of the other who is in
great need and lacks a great many things, then love usually becomes very cheap
180   and comes to an ignominious end. An old love also ends when a new one begins,
because no one can love two people at the same time.

CHAPTER VII: VARIOUS DECISIONS IN LOVE CASES[1]

Now then, let us come to various decisions in cases of love:
I. A man who was greatly enamoured of a certain woman devoted his whole
heart to the love of her. But when she saw that he was in love with her, she
185   absolutely forbade him to love. When she discovered that he was just as much in
love with her as ever, she said to him one day, I know it is true that you have
striven a very long time for love, but you can never get it unless you are willing to
make me a firm promise that you will always obey all my commands and that if
you oppose them in any way you will be willing to lose my love completely. The
190   man answered her, My lady, God forbid that I should ever be so much in error as
to oppose your commands in anything; so, since what you ask is very pleasing, I
gladly assent to it. After he had promised this she immediately ordered him to make
no more effort to gain her love and not to dare to speak a good word of her to
others. This was a heavy blow to the lover, yet he bore it patiently. But one day
195   when this lover and some other knights were with some ladies he heard his
companions speaking very shamefully about his lady and saying things about her
reputation that were neither right nor proper. He endured it for a while with an
ill grace, but when he saw that they kept on disparaging the lady he burst out
violently against them and began to accuse them of slander and to defend his
200   lady's reputation. When all this came to her ears she said that he ought to lose her
love completely because by praising her he had violated her commands.
This point the Countess of Champagne explained as follows in her decision.
She said that the lady was too severe in her command, because she was not
ashamed to silence him by an unfair sentence after he had wholly submitted
205   himself to her will and after she had given him the hope of her love by binding him
to her with a promise which no honourable woman can break without a reason.
Nor did the aforesaid lover sin at all when he tried to deliver a well-deserved
rebuke to those who were slandering his lady. For although he did make such a

---

[1]These (and other) cases were brought before Marie of Champagne's "Court of Love" for
judgement, the outcome of which formed the basis for the "Rules of Love."

210 promise in order the more easily to obtain her love, it seems unfair of the woman to lay upon him the command that he should trouble himself no more with love for her.

IV. Another question like this came up: two men who were in all things absolutely equal began to pay court at the same time and in the same manner and demanded urgently that they be loved. Therefore it was asked which man's love

215 could be chosen in such a case. We are taught by the admonition of the same countess that in such a case the man who asks first should be given the preference; but if their proposals seem to be simultaneous, it is not unfair to leave it to the woman to choose the one of the two toward whom she finds her heart inclining.

IX. A certain man asked the same lady to make clear where there was the

220 greater affection between lovers or between married people. The lady gave him a logical answer. She said: We consider that marital affection and the true love of lovers are wholly different and arise from entirely different sources, and so the ambiguous nature of the word prevents the comparison of the things and we have to place them in different classes. Comparisons of more or less are not valid when

225 things are grouped together under an ambiguous heading and the comparison is made in regard to that ambiguous term. It is no true comparison to say that a name is simpler than a body or that the outline of a speech is better arranged than the delivery.

XIV. A certain lady, while her lover was on an expedition overseas and she

230 had no hope of his early return and nearly everybody had given up all hope that he would ever come, sought for herself another lover. But a confidant of the first lover, who was very much grieved by the lady's change of faith, forbade her this new love. The woman did not accept his advice and defended herself by saying, If a woman who is left a widow by the death of her lover may seek a new love after

235 two years have elapsed, this should be much more permissible for a woman who is left a widow while her lover is still alive and who for this length of time hasn't had the satisfaction of any messenger or letter from him, especially when there has been no lack of messengers. After the question had been disputed pro and con for a long time it was refereed to the Countess of Champagne, who settled it with this

240 decision. It is not right for the lady to give up her love because her lover has been away for a long time (unless she knows that he was the first to fail in his love or that he has clearly been unfaithful) in cases in which it is obvious that his absence is due to necessity or to some especially praiseworthy cause. Nothing should bring more joy to the soul of a woman who is in love than to hear from distant

245 regions the praise of her lover or to know that he is respected by honourable assemblages of great men. That he is said to have refrained from communicating with her by letters or messengers may be considered great prudence on his part, since he my not reveal this secret to any third party.

6. EXCERPTS FROM LANCELOT, OR THE KNIGHT OF THE CART
(c. 1170)

Chretien de Troyes

(trans. by W. W. Comfort)

Chretien tells us in his preface that he was commissioned by Marie of Champagne to compose a story incorporating the precepts of courtly love which she had had Andreas Capellanus compile and describe in his Art of Courtly Love. *The result was this tale of the love of Lancelot and Gwenyvere, a romance significant for depicting the psychology of love as the hero experiences psychomachia, or battles within his psyche (i.e., between Love and Reason). Chretien may have had some difficulty with the assignment since he never finished the tale (it was completed by another poet); he composed many other chivalric tales of proper love and tales of spiritual quests for the holy grail. Yet his tale of illicit love and daring chivalric adventures came to represent the epitome of 'romance' and subsequent authors (notably Malory) revised and popularized the Arthurian material that Chretien shaped.*

[For the complete tale Chretien composed, see http://sunsite.berkeley.edu/ OMACL/Lancelot/]

PREFACE

Since my lady of Champagne wishes me to undertake to write a romance, I shall very gladly do so, being so devoted to her service as to do anything in the world for her, without any intention of flattery. But if one were to introduce any flattery upon such an occasion, he might say, and I would subscribe to it, that this

5 lady surpasses all others who are alive, just as the south wind which blows in May or April is more lovely than any other wind. But upon my word, I am not one to wish to flatter my lady. I will simply say: "The Countess is worth as many queens as a gem is worth of pearls and sards." Nay I shall make no comparison, and yet it is true in spite of me; I will say, however, that her command has more to

10 do with this work than any thought or pains that I may expend upon it. Here Chretien begins his book about the Knight of the Cart. The material and the

treatment of it are given and furnished to him by the Countess, and he is simply trying to carry out her concern and intention. Here he begins the story.

[*Queen Quinevere has been abducted by Meleagant, and two Knights of the Round Table, Lancelot and Gawain, set out to rescue her.*]

LANCELOT MOUNTS THE CART

He had overtaken a cart. In those days such a cart served the same purpose as
15　does a pillory now; and in each good town where there are more than three thousand such carts nowadays, in those times there was only one, and this, like our pillories, had to do service for all those who commit murder or treason, and those who are guilty of any delinquency, and for thieves who have stolen others' property or have forcibly seized it on the roads. Whoever was convicted of any
20　crime was placed upon a cart and dragged through all the streets, and he lost henceforth all his legal rights, and was never afterward heard, honored, or welcomed in any court. The carts were so dreadful in those days that the saying was then first used: "When thou dost see and meet a cart, cross thyself and call upon God, that no evil may befall thee." The knight on foot, and without a lance,
25　walked behind the cart, and saw a dwarf sitting on the shafts, who held, as a driver does, a long goad in his hand. Then he cries out: "Dwarf, for God's sake, tell me now if thou has seen my lady, the Queen, pass by here." The miserable, low-born dwarf would not give him any news of her, but replied: "If thou wilt get up into the cart I am driving thou shalt hear tomorrow what has happened to the
30　Queen." Then he kept on his way without giving further heed. The knight hesitated only for a couple of steps before getting in. Yet, it was unlucky for him that he shrank from the disgrace, and did not jump in at once; for he will later rue his delay. But common sense, which is inconsistent with love's dictates, bids him refrain from getting in, warning him and counseling him to do and undertake
35　nothing for which he may reap shame and disgrace. Reason, which dares thus speak to him, reaches only his lips, but not his heart; but love is enclosed within his heart, bidding him and urging him to mount at once upon the cart. So he jumps in, since love will have it so, feeling no concern about the shame, since he is prompted by love's commands. And my lord Gawain presses on in haste after the
40　cart, and when he finds the knight sitting in it, his surprise is great. "Tell me," he shouted to the dwarf, "if thou knowest anything of the Queen?" And he replied: "If thou art so much thy own enemy as is this knight who is sitting here, get in with him, if it be thy pleasure, and I will drive thee along with him." When my lord Gawain heard that, he considered it great foolishness, and said that he would not
45　get in, for it would be dishonorable to exchange a horse for a cart. "Go on, and wherever thy journey lies, I will follow after thee."

APPROACHES TO BADEMAGUS KINGDOM: WATER-BRIDGE AND SWORD-BRIDGE

They advanced through the woods until it might be six o'clock, and then at a crossroads they met a damsel, whom they both saluted, each asking and requesting her to tell them, if she knows, whither the Queen has been taken. Replying
50 intelligently, she said to them: "If you would pledge me your word, I could set you on the right road and path, and I would tell you the name of the country and of the knight who is conducting her; but whoever would essay to enter that country must endure sore trials, for before he could reach there he must suffer much." Then my lord Gawain replies: "Damsel, so help me God I promise to place all my strength at
55 your disposal and service, whenever you please, if you will tell me now the truth." And he who had been on the cart did not say that he would pledge her all his strength; but he proclaims, like one whom love makes rich, powerful and bold for any enterprise, that at once and without hesitation he will promise her anything she desires, and he puts himself altogether at her disposal. "Then I will
60 tell you the truth," says she. Then the damsel relates to them the following story: "In truth, my lords, Meleagant, a tall and powerful knight, son of the King of Gorre, has taken her off into the kingdom whence no foreigner returns, but where he must perforce remain in servitude and banishment." Then they ask her: "Damsel, where is this country? Where can we find the way thither?" She replies:
65 "That you shall quickly learn; but you may be sure that you will meet with many obstacles and difficult passages, for it is not easy to enter there except with the permission of the king, whose name is Bademagu; however, it is possible to enter by two very perilous paths and by two very difficult passage-ways. One is called the water-bridge, because the bridge is under water and there is the same amount
70 of water beneath it as above it, so that the bridge is exactly in the middle; and it is only a foot and a half in width and in thickness. This choice is certainly to be avoided, and yet it is the less dangerous of the two. In addition there are a number of other obstacles of which I will say nothing. The other bridge is still more impracticable and much more perilous, never having been crossed by man. It is just
75 like a sharp sword, and therefore all the people call it the sword-bridge. Now I have told you all the truth I know." But they ask of her once again: "Damsel, deign to show us the two passages." To which the damsel makes reply: "This road here is the most direct to the water-bridge, and that one yonder leads straight to the sword-bridge." Then the knight, who had been on the cart, says: "Sire, I am ready
80 to share with you without prejudice; take one of these two routes, and leave the other one to me; take whichever you prefer." In truth, my lord Gawain replies, "Both of them are hard and dangerous: I am not skilled in making such a choice, and hardly know which of them to take; but it is not right for me to hesitate when you have left the choice to me; I will choose the water-bridge." The other answers:
85 "Then I must go uncomplainingly to the sword-bridge, which I agree to do." Thereupon they all three part, each one commending the others very courteously to God. And when she sees them departing, she says: "Each one of you owes me a

90

favor of my choosing, whenever I may choose to ask it. Take care not to forget that." "We shall surely not forget it, sweet friend," both the knights call out. Then each one goes his own way, and he of the cart is occupied with deep reflections, like one who has no strength or defense against love which holds him in its sway. His thoughts are such that he totally forgets himself and he knows not whether he is alive or dead, forgetting even his own name, not knowing whether he is armed or not, or whither he is going or whence he came. Only one creature he has in mind,

95

and for her his thought is so occupied that he neither sees nor hears naught else. And his horse bears him along rapidly, following no crooked road, but the best and the most direct; and thus proceeding unguided, he brings him into an open plain.

LANCELOT KEEPS HIS PROMISE TO THE DAMSEL, BUT, OUT OF LOVE FOR GUINEVERE, REFRAINS FROM LOVE-MAKING

In the midst of the hall a bed had been set up, the sheets of which were by no

100

means soiled, but were white and wide and well spread out. The bed was not of shredded straw or of coarse spreads. But a covering of two silk cloths had been laid upon the couch. The damsel lay down first, but without removing her chemise. He had great trouble in removing his hose and in untying the knots. He sweated with the trouble of it all; yet, in the midst of all the trouble, his promise impels and

105

drives him on. Is this then an actual force? Yes, virtually so; for he feels that he is duty bound to take his place by the damsel's side. It is his promise that urges him and dictates his act. So he lies down at once, but like her, he does not remove his shirt. He takes good care not to touch her; and when he is in bed, he turns away from her as far as possible, and speaks not a word to her, like a monk to whom

110

speech is forbidden. Not once does he look at her, nor show her any courtesy. Why not? Because his heart does not go out to her. She was certainly very fair and winsome, but not everyone is pleased and touched by what is fair and winsome. The knight has only one heart, and this one is really no longer his, but has been entrusted to someone else, so that he cannot bestow it elsewhere. Love, which

115

holds all hearts beneath its sway, requires it to be lodged in a single place. All hearts? No, only those which it esteems. And he whom love deigns to control ought to prize himself the more. Love prized his heart so highly that it constrained it in a special manner, and made him so proud of his distinction that I am not inclined to find fault with him, if he lets alone what love forbids, and remains fixed where it

120

desires. The maiden clearly sees and knows that he dislikes her company and would gladly dispense with it, and that, having no desire to win her love, he would not attempt to woo her. So she said: "My lord, if you will not feel hurt, I will leave and return to bed in my own room, and you will be more comfortable. I do not believe that you are pleased with my company and society. Do not esteem

125

me less if I tell you what I think. Now take your rest all night, for you have so well kept your promise and I have no right to make further request of you. So I commend you to God, and shall go away." Thereupon she arises; the knight does not object,

but rather gladly lets her go, like one who is the devoted lover of some one else; the damsel clearly perceived this, and went to her room, where she undressed
130 completely and retired, saying to herself: "Of all the knights I have ever known, I never knew a single knight whom I would value the third part of an angevin in comparison with this one. As I understand the case, he has on hand a more perilous and grave affair than any ever undertakes by a knight; and may God grant that he succeed in it." Then she fell asleep, and remained in bed until the next
135 day's dawn appeared.

LANCELOT CROSSES THE SWORD-BRIDGE—PAINFULLY

At the end of this very difficult bridge they dismount from their steeds and gaze at the wicked looking stream, which is as swift and raging; as black and turgid, as fierce and terrible as if it were the devil's stream; and it is so dangerous and bottomless that anything falling into it would be as completely lost as if it fell
140 into the salt sea. And the bridge, which spans it, is as different from any other bridge; for there never was such a one as this. If anyone asks of me the truth, there never was such a bridge, nor one whose flooring was bad. The bridge across the cold stream consisted of a polished, gleaming sword; but the sword was stout and stiff, and was as long as two lances. At each end there was a tree-trunk in which
145 the sword was firmly fixed. No one need fear to fall because of its breaking or bending, for its excellence was such that it could support a great weight. But the two knights who were with the third were much discouraged; for they surmised that two lions or two leopards would be found tied to a great rock at the other end of the bridge. The water and the bridge and the lions combine so to terrify them
150 that they both tremble with fear, and say: "Fair sire, consider well what confronts you; for it is necessary and needful to do so. This bridge is badly made and built, and the construction of it is bad. If you do not change your mind in time, it will be too late to repent. You must consider which of several alternatives you will choose. Suppose that than one could hold in the winds and forbid them to blow, or
155 keep the birds from singing, or re-enter one's mother's womb and be born again— all of which is as impossible as to empty the sea of its water; but even supposing that you got across, can you think and suppose that those two fierce lions that are chained on the other side will not kill you, and suck the blood from your veins, and eat your flesh and then gnaw your bones? For my part, I am bold enough,
160 when I even dare to look and gaze at them. If you do not care, they will certainly devour you. Your body will soon be torn and rent apart, for they will show you no mercy. So take pity on us now, and stay here in our company. It would be wrong for you to expose yourself intentionally to such mortal peril." And he, laughing, replies to them: "Gentlemen, receive my thanks and gratitude for the
165 concern you feel for me; it comes from your love and kind hearts. I know full well that you would not like to see any mishap come to me; but I have faith and confidence in God, that He will protect me to the end. I fear the bridge and stream no more than I fear this dry land; so I intend to prepare and make the dangerous

170 attempt to cross. I would rather die than turn back now." The others have nothing more to say; but each weeps with pity and heaves a sigh. Meanwhile he prepares, as best he may, to cross the stream, and he does a very marvelous thing in removing the armor from his feet and hands. He will be in a sorry state when he reaches the other side. He is going to support himself with his bare hands and feet upon the sword, which was sharper than a scythe, for he had not kept on his feet either sole

175 or upper or hose. But he felt no fear of wounds upon his hands or feet; he preferred to maim himself rather than to fall from the bridge and be plunged in the water from which he could never escape. In accordance with this determination, he passes over with great pain and agony, being wounded in the hands, knees, and feet. But even this suffering assuages and relieves the pain. Creeping on his hands,

180 feet, and knees, he proceeds until he reaches the other side. Then he recalls and recollects the two lions which he thought he had seen from the other side; but, on looking about, he does not see so much as a lizard or anything else to do him harm. He raises his hand before his face and looks at his ring, and by this test he proves that neither of the lions is there which he thought he had seen, and that he had

185 been enchanted and deceived; for there was not a living creature there. When those who had remained behind upon the bank saw that he had safely crossed, their joy was natural; but they do not know of his injuries. He, however, considers himself fortunate not to have suffered anything worse. The blood from his wounds drips on his shirt on all sides.

LANCELOT FINALLY ENCOUNTERS GUINEVERE, BUT SHE REJECTS HIM

190 When the Queen saw the king holding Lancelot by the hand, she rose before the king [Bagdemagu], but she looked displeased with clouded brow, and she spoke not a word. "Lady, here is Lancelot come to see you," says the king; "you ought to be pleased and satisfied." "I, sire? He cannot please me. I care nothing about seeing him." "Come now, lady," says the king who was very frank and

195 courteous, "what induces you to act like this? You are too scornful toward a man who has served you so faithfully that he has repeatedly exposed his life to mortal danger on this journey for your sake, and who has defended and rescued you from my son Meleagant who has deeply wronged you." "Sire, truly he has made poor use of his time. I shall never deny that I feel no gratitude toward him." Now

200 Lancelot is dumbfounded; but he replies very humbly like a polished lover: "Lady, certainly I am grieved at this, but I dare not ask your reason." The Queen listened as Lancelot voiced his disappointment, but in order to grieve and confound him, she would not answer a single word, but returned to her room, and Lancelot followed her with his eyes and heart until she reached the door; but she was not

205 long in sight, for the room was close by. His eyes would gladly have followed her, had that been possible; but the heart, which is more lordly and masterful in its strength, went through the door after her, while the eyes remained behind weeping with the body. And the king said privately to him: "Lancelot, I am amazed at what

210 this means, and how it comes about that the Queen cannot endure the sight of you, and that she is so unwilling to speak with you. If she is ever accustomed to speak with you, she ought not to be niggardly now or avoid conversation with you, after what you have done for her. Now tell me, if you know, why and for what misdeed she has shown you such a countenance." "Sire, I did not notice that just now; but she will not look at me or hear my words, and that distresses and grieves me

215 much." "Surely," says the king, "she is in the wrong, for you have risked your life for her."

AT THEIR NEXT MEETING, GUINEVERE REVEALS LANCELOT'S "CRIME"

This time the Queen did not lower her eyes to the ground, but she went to meet him cheerfully, honoring him all she could, and making him sit down by her side. Then they talked together at length of all that was upon their hearts, and love

220 furnished them with so much to say that topics did not lack. And when Lancelot sees how well he stands, and that all he says finds favor with the Queen, he says to her in confidence: "Lady, I marvel greatly why you received me with such a countenance when you saw me the day before yesterday, and why you would not speak a word to me; I almost died of the blow you gave me, and I had not the

225 courage to dare to question you about it, as I now venture to do. I am ready now, Lady, to make amends, when you have told me what has been the crime which has caused me such distress." Then the Queen replies: "What? Did you not hesitate for shame to mount the cart? You showed you were loath to get in, when you hesitated for two whole steps. That is the reason why I would neither address nor look at

230 you." "May God save me from such a crime again," Lancelot replies, "and may God show me no mercy, if you were not quite right! For God's sake, lady, receive my amends at once." The Queen replies; "I pardon you willingly." "Thank you for that lady," he then says; "but I cannot tell you here all that I should like to say; I should like to talk with you more at leisure, if possible." Then the Queen indicates

235 a window by her glance rather than with her finger, and says: "Come through the garden to-night and speak with me at yonder window, when every one inside has gone to sleep. You will not be able to get in; I shall be able to touch you only with my lips or hand, but, if you please, I will stay there until morning for love of you. Our bodies cannot be joined, for close beside me in my room lies Kay the seneschal,

240 who is still suffering from his wounds. And the door is not open, but is tightly closed and guarded well. When you come, take care to let no spy catch sight of you." "Lady," says he, "if I can help it, no spy shall see me who might think or speak evil of us." Then, having agreed upon this plan, they separate very joyfully.

LANCELOT, IGNORING HIS WOUNDS, CONSUMMATES HIS LOVE FOR GUINEVERE

245

250

255

260

265

270

275

280

Then the Queen retires, and he prepares to loosen the window. Seizing the bars, he pulls and wrenches them until he makes them bend and drags them from their places. But the iron was so sharp that the end of his little finger was cut to the nerve, and the first joint of the next finger was torn; but he who is intent upon something else paid no heed to any of his wounds or to the blood trickling down. Though the window is not low, Lancelot gets through it quickly and easily. First he finds Kay asleep in his bed, then he comes to the bed of the Queen, whom he adores and before whom he kneels, holding her more dear than the relic of any saint. And the Queen extends her arms to him, and embracing him, presses him tightly against her bosom, drawing him into the bed beside her and showing him every possible satisfaction; her love and her heart go out to him. It is love that prompts her to treat him so; and if she feels great love for him, he feels a hundred thousand times as much for her. For there is no love at all in other hearts compared with what there is in his; in his heart love was so completely embodied that it was niggardly toward all other hearts. Now Lancelot possesses all he wants when the Queen voluntarily seeks his company and love, and when he holds her in his arms, and she holds him in hers. Their sport is so agreeable and sweet, as they kiss and fondle each other, that in truth such a marvelous joy comes over them as was never heard or known. But their joy will not be revealed by me, for in a story it has no place. Yet, the most choice and delightful satisfaction was precisely that of which our story must not speak. That night Lancelot's joy and pleasure were very great. But, to his sorrow, day comes and he must leave his mistress' side. It cost him such pain to leave her that he suffered a real martyr's agony. His heart now stays where the Queen remains; he has not the power to lead it away, for it finds such pleasure in the Queen that it has no desire to leave her; so his body goes, and his heart remains. But enough of his body stays behind to spot and stain the sheets with the blood which has fallen from his fingers. Full of sighs and tears, Lancelot leaves in great distress. He grieves that no time is fixed for another meeting, but it cannot be. Regretfully he leaves by the window through which he has entered so happily. He was so badly wounded in the fingers that they were in a sorry state; yet he straightened the bars and set them in their place again, so that from neither side, either before or behind, was it evident that anyone had drawn out or bent any of the bars. When he leaves the room, he bows and acts precisely as if he were before a shrine; then he goes with a heavy heart, and reaches his lodging without being recognized by anyone. He throws himself naked upon his bed without awakening anyone, and then for the first time he is surprised to notice the cuts in his fingers; but he is not at all concerned, for he is very sure that the wound was caused by dragging the window bars from the wall. Therefore he was not at all worried, for he would rather have had both arms dragged from his body than not enter through the window. But he would have been very angry and distressed, if he had thus injured and wounded himself under any other circumstances.

7. LETTER FROM HELOISE TO ABELARD
(c. 1125)

(trans. by C. K. Scott Moncrieff)

The love affair between the scholar and theologican Abelard and his seventeen-year-old pupil Heloise is one of the most famous real medieval romances. When Heloise became pregnant, she argued that marriage would curtail Abelard's career, but they were nonetheless secretly wed. Heloise's uncle, the canon Fulbert, angered at what he saw as a betrayal of trust, had Abelard castrated. Intellectually as well, Abelard faced enemies: his radical philosophical views earned him condemnation and he was forced to retreat to the monastery at Cluny, while Heloise became a nun. Their letters are enmeshed in controversy over authenticity, but their powerful love is amply referenced in many contemporary works.

To her master, nay father, to her husband, nay brother; his handmaid, nay daughter, his spouse, nay sister: to ABELARD, Heloise.

Your letter written to a friend for his comfort, beloved, was lately brought to me by chance. Seeing at once from the title that it was yours, I began the more
5   ardently to read it in that the writer was so dear to me, that I might at least be refreshed by his words as by a picture of him whose presence I have lost. Almost every line of that letter, I remember, was filled with gall and wormwood, to wit those that related the miserable story of our conversion, and thy unceasing crosses, my all.
10   Thou did indeed fulfil in that letter what at the beginning of it thou had promised thy friend, namely that in comparison with thy troubles he should deem his own to be nothing or but a small matter. After setting forth thy former persecution by thy masters, then the outrage of supreme treachery upon thy body, thou has turned thy pen to the execrable jealousy and inordinate assaults of thy
15   fellow-pupils also, namely Alberic of Rheims and Lotulph the Lombard; and what by their instigation was done to that famous work of thy theology, and what to thyself, as it were condemned to prison, thou hast not omitted.

From these thou come to the machinations of thine Abbot and false brethren, and the grave detraction of thee by those two pseudo-apostles, stirred up against
20   thee by the aforesaid rivals, and to the scandal raised by many of the name of Paraclete given to the oratory in departure from custom: and then, coming to those intolerable and still continuing persecutions of thy life, thou hast carried to the end the miserable story of that cruellest of extortioners and those wickedest of

25   monks, whom thou call thy sons. Which things I deem that no one can read or hear with dry eyes, for they renewed in fuller measure my griefs, so diligently did they express each several part, and increased them the more, in that thou related that thy perils are still growing, so that we are all alike driven to despair of thy life, and every day our trembling hearts and throbbing bosoms await the latest rumor of thy death.

30   And so in His Name Who still protects thee in a certain measure for Himself, in the Name of Christ, as His handmaids and thine, we beseech thee to deign to inform us by frequent letters of those shipwrecks in which thou still art tossed, that thou may have us at least, who alone have remained to thee, as partners in thy grief or joy. For they are wont to bring some comfort to a grieving man who grieve

35   with him, and any burden that is laid on several is borne more easily, or transferred. And if this tempest should have been stilled for a space, then all the more hasten thou to write, the more pleasant thy letter will be. But whatsoever it be of which thou may write to us, thou wilt confer no small remedy on us; if only in this that thou wilt show thyself to be keeping us in mind.

40   For how pleasant are the letters of absent friends Seneca himself by own example teaches us, writing thus in a certain passage to his friend Lucilius: "Because thou write me often, I thank thee. For in the one way possible thou show thyself to me. Never do I receive a letter from thee, but immediately we are together." If the portraits of our absent friends are pleasant to us, which renew

45   our memory of them and relieve our regret for their absence by a false and empty consolation, how much more pleasant are letters which bring us the written characters of the absent friend. But thanks be to God, that in this way at least no jealousy prevents thee from restoring to us thy presence, no difficulty impedes thee, no neglect (I beseech thee) need delay thee.

50   Thou has written to thy friend the comfort of a long letter, considering his difficulties, no doubt, but treating of thine own. Which diligently recording, whereas thou did intend them for his comfort, thou hast added greatly to our desolation, and while thou wert anxious to heal his wounds has inflicted fresh wounds of grief on us and made our former wounds to ache again. Heal, I beseech

55   thee, the wounds that thou thyself hast given, who art so busily engaged in healing the wounds given by others. Thou has indeed humored thy friend and comrade, and paid the debt as well of friendship as of comradeship; but by a greater debt thou hast bound thyself to us, whom it behooves thee to call not friends but dearest friends, not comrades but daughters, or by a sweeter and a holier name, if

60   any can be conceived.

As to the greatness of the debt which binds thee to us neither argument nor evidence is lacking, that any doubt be removed; and if all men be silent the fact itself cries aloud. For of this place thou, after God, art the sole founder, the sole architect of this oratory, the sole builder of this congregation. Nothing did thou

65   build here on the foundations of others. All that is here is thy creation. This wilderness, ranged only by wild beasts or by robbers, had known no habitation of men, had contained no dwelling. In the very lairs of the beasts, in the very

lurking places of the robbers, where the name of God is not heard, thou did erect a divine tabernacle, and did dedicate the Holy Ghost's own temple. Nothing did thou borrow from the wealth of kings or princes, when thou could have obtained so much and from so many, that whatsoever was wrought here might be ascribed to thee alone. Clerks or scholars flocking in haste to thy teaching ministered to thee all things needful, and they who lived upon ecclesiastical benefices, who knew not how to make but only how to receive oblations, and had hands for receiving, not for giving, became lavish and importunate here in the offering of oblations.

Thine, therefore, truly thine is this new plantation in the divine plan, for the plants of which, still most tender, frequent irrigation is necessary that they may grow. Frail enough, from the weakness of the feminine nature, is this plantation; it is infirm, even were it not new. Wherefore it demands more diligent cultivation and more frequent, after the words of the Apostle: "I have planted, Apollos watched; but God gave the increase." The Apostle had planted, by the doctrines of his preaching, and had established in the Faith the Corinthians, to whom he wrote. Thereafter Apollos, the Apostle's own disciple, had watered them with sacred exhortations, and so by divine grace the increment of virtues was bestowed on them. Thou are tending the vineyard of another's vine which thou did not plant, which is turned to thine own bitterness, with admonitions often wasted and holy sermons preached in vain. Think of what thou owe to thine own, who thus spend thy care on another's. Thou teach and reprove rebels, nor gain than aught. In vain before the swine dost thou scatter the pearls of divine eloquence. Who gives so much thought to the obstinate, consider what thou owe to the obedient. Who bestows so much on thine enemies, meditate what thou owe to thy daughters.[1] And to say nothing of the rest, think by what a debt thou are bound to me, that what thou owe to the community of devoted women thou may pay more devotedly to her who is thine alone.

How many grave treatises in the teaching, or in the exhortation, or for the comfort of holy women the holy Fathers composed, and with what diligence they composed them, thine excellence knows better than our humility. Wherefore to no little amazement thine oblivion moves the tender beginnings of our conversion, that neither by reverence for God, nor by love of us, nor by the examples of the holy Fathers hast thou been admonished to attempt to comfort me, as I waver and am already crushed by prolonged grief, either by speech in thy presence or by a letter in thine absence. And yet thou know thyself to be bound to me by a debt so much greater in that thou are tied to me more closely by the pact of the nuptial sacrament; and that thou art the more beholden to me in that I ever, as is known to all, embraced thee with an unbounded love. Thou know, dearest, all men know what I have lost in thee, and in how wretched a case that supreme and notorious betrayal took me myself also from me with thee, and that my grief is immeasurably greater from the manner in which I lost thee than from the loss of thee.

---

[1] She means the convent nuns, not biological daughters.

7. Letter from Heloise to Abelard

110 And the greater the cause of grief, the greater the remedies of comfort to be applied. Not, however, by another, but by thee thyself, that thou who art alone in the cause of my grief may be alone in the grace of my comfort. For it is thou alone that can make me sad, can make me joyful or can comfort me. And it is thou alone that owes me this great debt, and for this reason above all that I have at once
115 performed all things that you did order, till that when I could not offend thee in anything I had the strength to lose myself at thy behest. And what is more, and strange it is to relate, to such madness did my love turn that what alone it sought it cast from itself without hope of recovery when, straightway obeying thy command, I changed both my habit and my heart, that I might show thee to be the
120 one possessor both of my body and of my mind. Nothing have I ever (God knows) required of thee save myself, desiring thee purely, not what was thine. Not for the pledge of matrimony, nor for any dowry did I look, not my own passions or wishes but thine (as thou thyself know) was I zealous to gratify.

And if the name of wife appears more sacred and more valid, sweeter to me is
125 ever the word friend, or, if thou be not ashamed, concubine or whore. To wit that the more I humbled myself before thee the fuller grace I might obtain from thee, and so also damage less the fame of thine excellence. And thou thyself wert not wholly unmindful of that kindness in the letter of which I have spoken, written to thy friend for his comfort. Wherein thou hast not disdained to set forth sundry
130 reasons by which I tried to dissuade thee from our marriage, from an ill-starred bed; but were silent as to many, in which I preferred love to wedlock, freedom to a bond. I call God to witness, if Augustus, ruling over the whole world, were to deem me worthy of the honor of marriage, and to confirm the whole world to me, to be ruled by me forever, dearer to me and of greater dignity would it seem to be
135 called thy strumpet than his empress.

For it is not by being richer or more powerful that a man becomes better; one is a matter of fortune, the other of virtue. Nor should she deem herself other than venal who weds a rich man rather than a poor, and desires more things in her husband than himself. Assuredly, whomsoever this concupiscence leads into
140 marriage deserves payment rather than affection; for it is evident that she goes after his wealth and not the man, and is willing to prostitute herself, if she can, to a richer. As the argument advanced (in Aeschines) by the wise Aspasia to Xenophon and his wife plainly convinces us. When the wise woman aforesaid had propounded this argument for their reconciliation, she concluded as follows: "For
145 when ye have understood this, that there is not a better man nor a happier woman on the face of the earth; then ye will ever and above all things seek that which ye think the best; thou to be a husband of so excellent a wife, and she to be married to so excellent a husband." A blessed sentiment, assuredly, and more than philosophic, expressing wisdom itself rather than philosophy. A holy error and a
150 blessed fallacy among the married, that a perfect love should preserve their bond of matrimony unbroken, not so much by the continence of their bodies as by the purity of their hearts. But what error shows to the rest of women the truth has made manifest to me. Since what they thought of their husbands, that I, that the

155 entire world not so much believed as knew of thee. So that the more genuine my
love was for thee, the further it was removed from error.

For who among kings or philosophers could equal thee in fame? What
kingdom or city or village did not burn to see thee? Who I ask, did not hasten to
gaze upon thee when thou appeared in public, nor on thy departure with straining
160 neck and fixed eye follow thee? What wife, what maiden did not yearn for thee in
thine absence, nor burn in thy presence? What queen or powerful lady did not
envy me my joys and my bed? There were two things, I confess, in thee especially,
wherewith thou could at once captivate the heart of any woman; namely the arts
of making songs and of singing them. Which we know that other philosophers
165 have seldom followed. Wherewith as with a game, refreshing the labor of
philosophic exercise, thou has left many songs composed in amatory measure or
rhythm, which for the suavity both of words and of tune being oft repeated, have
kept thy name without ceasing on the lips of all; since even illiterates the
sweetness of thy melodies did not allow to forget thee. It was on this account
chiefly that women sighed for love of thee. And as the greater part of thy songs
170 descanted of our love, they spread my fame in a short time through many lands, and
inflamed the jealousy of many against me. For what excellence of mind or body did
not adorn thy youth? What woman who envied me then does not my calamity now
compel to pity one deprived of such delights? What man or woman, albeit an
enemy at first, is not now softened by the compassion due to me?

175 And, though exceedingly guilty, I am, as thou know, exceedingly innocent. For
it is not the deed but the intention that makes the crime.[2] It is not what is done but
the spirit in which it is done that equity considers. And in what state of mind I
have ever been towards thee, only thou, who hast knowledge of it, can judge. To
thy consideration I commit all, I yield in all things to thy testimony. Tell me one
180 thing only, if thou can, why, after our conversion, which thou alone did decree, I
am fallen into such neglect and oblivion with thee that I am neither refreshed by
thy speech and presence nor comforted by a letter in thine absence. Tell me, one
thing only, if thou can, or let me tell thee what I feel, nay what all suspect.
Concupiscence joined thee to me rather than affection, the ardor of desire rather
185 than love. When therefore what thou desired ceased, all that thou had exhibited at
the same time failed. This, most beloved, is not mine only but the conjecture of all,
not peculiar but common, not private but public. Would that it seemed thus to me
only, and thy love found others to excuse it, by whom my grief might be a little
quieted. Would that I could invent reasons by which in excusing thee I might cover
190 in some measure my own vileness.

Give thy attention, I beseech thee, to what I demand; and thou wilt see this to
be a small matter and most easy for thee. While I am cheated of thy presence, at
least by written words, whereof thou hast an abundance, present to me the
sweetness of thine image. In vain may I expect thee to be liberal in things if I must
195 endure thee niggardly in words. Until now I believed that I deserved more from

---

[2]This was one of Abelard's controversial ideas.

thee when I had done all things for thee, persevering still in obedience to thee. Who indeed as a girl was allured to the asperity of monastic conversation not by religious devotion but by thy command alone. Wherein if I deserve nought from thee, thou may judge my labor to have been vain. No reward for this may I expect
200   from God, for the love of Whom it is well known that I did not anything. When thou hastened to God, I followed thee in the habit, nay preceded thee. For as though mindful of the wife of Lot, who looked back from behind him, thou delivered me first to the sacred garments and monastic profession before thou gave thyself to God. And for that in this one thing thou should have had little trust in
205   me, I vehemently grieved and was ashamed. For I (God knows) would without hesitation precede or follow thee to the Vulcanian fires according to thy word. For not with me was my heart, but with thee. But now, more than ever, if it be not with thee, it is nowhere. For without thee it cannot anywhere exist. But so act that it may be well with thee, I beseech thee. And well with thee will it be if it find thee
210   propitious, if thou give love for love, little for much, words for deeds. Would that thy love, beloved, had less trust in me, that it might be more anxious! But the more confident I have made thee in the past, the more neglectful now I find thee. Remember, I beseech thee, what I have done, and pay heed to what thou owe me. While with thee I enjoyed carnal pleasures, many were uncertain whether I did so
215   from love or from desire. But now the end shows in what spirit I began. I have forbidden myself all pleasures that I might obey thy will. I have reserved nothing for myself, save this, to be now entirely thine. Consider therefore how great is thine injustice, if to me who deserve more thou pay less, nay nothing at all, especially when it is a small thing that is demanded of thee, and right easy for thee
220   to perform.

     And so in His Name to whom thou has offered thyself, before God I beseech thee that in whatsoever way thou can restore to me thy presence, to wit by writing me some word of comfort. To this end alone that, thus refreshed, I may give myself with more alacrity to the service of God. When in time past thou sought me out for
225   temporal pleasures, thou visited me with endless letters, and by frequent songs did set thy Heloise on the lips of all men. With me every public place, each house resounded. How more rightly should thou excite me now towards God, whom thou excited then to desire. Consider, I beseech thee, what thou owe me, pay heed to what I demand; and my long letter with a brief ending I conclude. Farewell, my all.

8. INFERNO AND PURGATORIO

Dante Alighieri
(1265–1321)

(trans. by Tony Esolen)

Dante Alighieri (1265–1321) gives us in literature what the architects of the Gothic cathedrals give us in stone: a sweeping but unified treatment of all that is, in Heaven, on earth, and under the earth. His Divine Comedy *takes the reader on a pilgrimage into the deepest reaches of Hell, then up the mountain of Purgatory, and finally to the starry realms of Heaven, where even theological language must give way to mystical vision. It is, perhaps, the greatest poem ever written; it certainly is the most comprehensive.*

The selection below forms the first part of Dante's poem, the Inferno. *Even though sin involves inherent disorder in the human soul, the structure of Hell, like the structure of a medieval* summa, *is rational and orderly. The pilgrim Dante, who has lost his way in the tangles of the world, is led by the ancient Roman poet Virgil (usually taken to be a personification of Reason) down each of ten concentric rings, with the sins growing progressively more wicked as one descends. At the bottom of Hell, locked in ice, is Lucifer, the epitome of pride, to punish whose rebellion Hell was first created. Sin, and not merely the punishment for sin, entails a loss of liberty. In Dante's Christian Aristotelianism, man and angel are both made by God to be free and to enjoy the vision of God eternally. That is our* telos, *the perfection of our nature. It beckons us, and we are to respond in love. The* Inferno *shows the futility, the hopelessness, and the unreason of choosing something or someone else as the final object of our desire.*

INFERNO

CANTO ONE

*Lost in a **dark wood** and threatened by **three beasts**, Dante is rescued by **Virgil**, who proposes a journey to the other world.*

In the middle of the journey of our life
  I found myself in a dark wilderness,
    for I had wandered from the straight and true.

How hard a thing it is to tell about,
5   that wilderness so savage, dense, and harsh,
    it brings back all my fear in the mere thought!
It was so bitter, death is hardly more—
    but to reveal the good that came to me,
    I shall relate the other things I saw.
10 How I had entered, I can't bring to mind,
    I was so full of sleep just at that point
    when I first left the way of truth behind.
But when I reached the foot of a high hill,
    right where the valley opened to its end—
15   the valley that had pierced my heart with fear—
I raised my eyes and saw its shoulders robed
    with the rays of that wandering light of Heaven[1]
    that leads all men aright on every road.
That quieted a bit the dread that stirred
20   trembling within the waters of my heart
    all through that night of misery I endured.
And as a man with labored breathing drags
    his legs out of the water and, ashore,
    fixes his eyes upon the dangerous sea,
25 So too my mind, while still a fugitive,
    turned back to gaze again upon that pass
    which never let a man escape alive.
When I had given my weary body rest,
    I struck again over the desert slope,
30   ever the firmer foot the one below,
And look! just where the steeper rise began,
    a leopard light afoot and quick to lunge,
    all covered in a pelt of flecks and spots,
Who stood before my face and would not leave,
35   but did so check me in the path I trod,
    I often turned to go the way I came.
The hour was morning at the break of dawn;
    the sun was mounting higher with those stars[2]
    that shone beside him when the Love Divine
40 In the beginning made their beauty move;
    and so they were a cause of hope for me
    to get free of that beast of flashy hide—
The waking hour and that sweet time of year;
    but hope was not so strong that I could stand

---

[1]*that . . . Heaven:* the sun
[2]*those stars:* the constellation Aries; it is springtime

45   bold when a lion stepped before my eyes!
      This one seemed to be coming straight for me,
        his head held high, his hunger hot with wrath—
        seemed to strike tremors in the very air!
      Then a she-wolf, whose scrawniness seemed stuffed

50   with all men's cravings, sluggish with desires,
        who had made many live in wretchedness—
      So heavily she weighed my spirit down,
        pressing me by the terror of her glance,
        I lost all hope to gain the mountaintop.

55   And as a gambler, winning with a will,
        happening on the time when he must lose,
        turns all his thoughts to weeping, and despair,
      So I by that relentless beast; who came
        against me, step by step, and drove me back

60   to where the sun is silent evermore.
      Now while I stumbled to the deepest wood
        before my eyes appeared the form of one
        who seemed hoarse, having held his words so long.
      And when I saw him in that endless waste,

65   "Mercy upon me, mercy!" I cried out,
        "Whatever you are, a shade, or man in truth!"
      He answered me: "No man; I was a man,
        and both my parents came from Lombardy,
        and Mantua they called their native land.

70   In the last days of Julius I was born,
        and lived in Rome under the good Augustus
        in the time of the false and cheating gods.
      I was a poet, and I sang of how
        that just son of Anchises[3] came from Troy

75   when her proud towers and walls were burnt to dust.
      But you, why do you turn back to such pain?
        Why don't you climb that hill that brings delight,
        the origin and cause of every joy?"
      "Then are you—are you Virgil? And that spring

80   swelling into so rich a stream of verse?"
      I answered him, my forehead full of shame.
      "Honor and light of every poet, may
        my long study avail me, and the love
        that made me search the volume of your work.

85   You are my Teacher, my authority;

---

[3]*son of Anchises:* Aeneas, legendary founder of Rome; celebrated by Virgil in his epic, the *Aeneid*

you alone are the one from whom I took
 the style whose loveliness has honored me.
See there the beast that makes me turn aside.
 Save me from her, O man renowned and wise!
90 She sets the pulses trembling in my veins!"
"It is another journey you must take,"
 replied the poet when he saw me weep,
 "if you wish to escape this savage place,
Because this beast that makes you cry for help
95 never lets any pass along her way,
 but checks his path until she takes his life.
So vicious is her nature, so ill-bent,
 she never stuffs her ravenous will enough,
 but after feeding hungers all the more.
100 Many a living soul takes her to wife
 and many shall, until the Greyhound comes,
 he who will make her die in misery.
Not land, not lucre will he feed upon,
 but wisdom, love, and strength shall be his meat,
105 and by the cloth of felt he will be born.
He will bring health to humbled Italy,
 the land for which the maid Camilla died,
 and Nisus, Turnus, and Euryalus.
Through every village he will hunt her down
110 until at last he drives her back to Hell,
 whence envy set her loose upon the world.
And so I judge it would be best for you
 to follow me, and I will be your guide,
 leading you out through an eternal place,
115 Where you will hear the groans of hopeless men,[4]
 will look upon the sorrowing souls of old,
 crying in torment for the second death;
Then you will look upon those souls content
 to wait in fire,[5] because they hope someday
120 to come among the nation of the blessed.
If you then wish to rise and go to them,
 another soul[6] will come, worthier than I—
 with her I'll leave you when I go my way.
For that great Emperor who reigns above,
125 because I was a rebel to His law,

---

[4]*hopeless men:* the souls in Hell, longing for a "second death" which will not come
[5]*content to wait in fire:* the souls in Purgatory, who will all be saved
[6]*another soul:* Beatrice

           will not allow me entry to his realm.
           Everywhere He commands, from there He rules,
               there stand His city and His lofty throne.
               Happy the man He chooses for His house!"
130   "Poet," I said to him, "I beg of you,
               by that same God you never knew, that I
               may flee this evil and the worse to come,
           Lead me now to the place you tell me of,
               so I may see Saint Peter's gate,[7] and those
135   you say are dwelling in such misery."
           He set on, and I held my pace behind.

---

[7] *Saint Peter's gate:* the gates of Purgatory

CANTO TWO

To settle Dante's doubts about his worthiness to take the journey, Virgil tells of how **Beatrice** *came down from Heaven to beg his help.*

So the day wore away, and the dark air
  released the living souls that dwell on earth
  from all their labors. I alone remained,
Girding myself to bear and battle through
5   the journey, and the pity of my heart—
  which memory never straying shall recount.
O Muses, O high genius, help me now!
  O memory that engraved the things I saw,
  here shall your worth be manifest to all.
10 "Poet," I started, "you who guide my steps,
  see to my strength, make sure it will suffice,
  before you trust me to so hard a road.
You tell of Silvius' father[8] who went down
  to the immortal world still in the flesh—
15   and with his flesh's senses all aware.
Yet if the Adversary of all evil[9]
  showed him this grace, it does not seem unfit
  to intellects that see the great result,
Both who and what was meant to spring from him;
20   for he was chosen in the Heaven of heavens
  father of sacred Rome and her command,
And these, if we would speak the truth, were set
  firmly in place to be the holy throne
  where the successor to great Peter[10] sits.
25 Upon this journey which you celebrate
  he learned of things which were the cause of both
  his triumph, and the mantle of the Pope.
Later, the Chosen Vessel[11] also went
  to bring back comfort, strengthening the faith
30   which is the first step on salvation's way.
But I? Who grants my coming? And for what?
  I'm not Aeneas, I'm not Saint Paul! No one—
  not I myself—could think me worthy—so
If I should enter on this quest, I fear

---

[8]*Silvius' father:* In book six of the *Aeneid,* Aeneas goes to the underworld to learn of his own destiny and that of the Rome which he is to found.
[9]*Adversary . . . evil:* God
[10]*successor . . . Peter:* the Pope
[11]*Chosen Vessel:* St. Paul had a vision of Paradise; cf. 2 Cor. 12:1–5

35   it would be mad and foolish. But you're wise,
      you understand me better than my words."
    And as a man who unwills what he wills,
      changing his plan for every little thought,
      till he withdraws from any kind of start,
40   So did I turn my mind on that dark verge,
      for thinking ate away the enterprise
      so prompt in the beginning to set forth.
    "If I have understood your words aright,"
      replied the shade of that greathearted man,
45   "your spirit has been bruised by cowardice,
    Which many a time so weighs a man's heart down
      it turns him from a glorious enterprise—
      as shadows fool the horse that shies away.
    That you may slip this worry and go free,
50   I'll tell you why I came and what I heard
      when first I pitied you your misery.
    I was among the souls in Limbo[12] when
      so lovely and blest a Lady[13] called to me
      I asked her for the grace of a command.
55   Her eyes were flashing brighter than the stars,
      and she addressed me with an angel's voice,
      sweetly and softly, in such words as these:
    'O kind and gracious soul of Mantua,
      whom the world still renowns and ever shall,
60   whose fame will last as long as earth endures,
    The friend I love—and not a fortune-friend—
      has been so checked along his journey up
      the desert slope, he has turned back for dread,
    And from what I have heard of him in Heaven
65   I fear he may have wandered so far wrong,
      my rising for his help may come too late.
    Go then, and with the beauty of your words,
      and any skill you have to set him free,
      help him, that I may be consoled. I am
70   The blessed Beatrice who bid you go;
      love makes me speak, and bade me hasten from
      the place that stirs my longing to return.
    When I shall stand before my Lord, I vow
      often to speak to him in praise of you.'

---

[12]*Limbo:* literally, the Edge: a state suspended between salvation and damnation. See Canto Four below.
[13]*Lady:* Beatrice

75   Then she fell silent, and I thus began:
          "O Lady of that power whereby alone
            the human race transcends all mortal things
            dwelling below the circle of the moon,
         What you command is such a grace indeed,
80   it would be late, had I obeyed already!
          Show me your will, for that is all you need.
         But tell me why it does not worry you
            to descend to this center of the world
            from that vast realm you burn to see again."
85   "Because you wish to know things to the core,"
          replied the Lady, "I will tell in brief
          why I am not afraid to enter here.
         The only things that justly cause us fear
          are those that have the power to do us harm;
90   the others, not at all. By the free gift
         Of God I have been fashioned in such form,
          no misery you feel can touch me now,
          no flame of these hell-fires can harrow me.
         A gentle Lady in Heaven[14] was so moved
95   with pity for that soul whose way is barred,
          she broke the unbending sentence from above.
         She called to Lucy,[15] making this request:
          'Your faithful follower now has need of you;
          I give him over to your loving care.'
100   Lucy, the foe of every cruelty,
          arose and hastened to the place where I
          sat beside Rachel of the ancient days.
         'Beatrice, true praise of God, why do you not
          come to the aid of him who loved you so
105   that for your sake he left the common crowd?
         Do you not hear him weeping piteously?
          Do you not see the death he wrestles with
          upon the flood-tide violent as the sea?'
         No man was ever quicker in the world
110   to seize his profit or to flee his harm
          than I was, when I heard the words she spoke,
         Leaving my blessed seat to come down here
          to rest my trust upon your noble speech,
          which honors you and those who heed it well."

---

[14]*Lady in Heaven:* Mary

[15]*Lucy:* Saint Lucia, for whom Dante may have had a special devotion; she assists him also in Purgatory, cf. *Pg.* ix.52–63.

115 When she had finished speaking to me so,
    she turned her glistening eyes all bright with tears—
    which made me all the readier to go,
And so I came to you as she desired,
    raising you from the beast that faced you down
120   and stole from you the short way up the hill.
What is it, then? Why stand here, why delay?
    Why let such cowardice come take your heart?
    Why are you not afire and bold and free,
Seeing that three such ladies blessed in Heaven
125   care for your healing from their court above,
    and what I tell you holds forth so much good?"
As little flowers shut small and bowed beneath
    the frost of night, when the sun brightens them,
    rise open-petaled on their stems upright,
130 So did my weary courage surge again,
    and such sweet boldness rushed into my heart
    I cried out as a man at last set free,
"O Lady of compassion and my help!
    And you most gracious who obeyed her wish
135   soon as you heard the truth she spoke to you!
Your words have put my heart in order now,
    kindling so great a longing to set on
    you've turned me to our first intention—go!
Go, for we two now share one will alone:
140   you are my guide, my teacher, and my lord."
    So did I say to him. Then we set forth,
Taking the deep and savage-wooded path.

CANTO THREE

*Virgil and Dante enter the **gates of Hell**. There they meet the **small-souled**, those unnamed spirits whose cowardice relegates them to the mere vestibule of the lower world. Passing onward, they come to the **River Acheron**, whose ferryman, **Charon**, ushers the gathered souls to their eternal misery.*

I AM THE WAY INTO THE CITY OF WOE,
I AM THE WAY INTO ETERNAL PAIN,
I AM THE WAY TO GO AMONG THE LOST.

JUSTICE CAUSED MY HIGH ARCHITECT TO MOVE:
5   DIVINE OMNIPOTENCE CREATED ME,
THE HIGHEST WISDOM, AND THE PRIMAL LOVE.

8. *Dante*/Inferno III

BEFORE ME THERE WERE NO CREATED THINGS
BUT THOSE THAT LAST FOREVER—AS DO I.
ABANDON ALL HOPE YOU WHO ENTER HERE.

10 I saw these words of dark and harsh intent
    engraved upon the archway of a gate.
    "Teacher," I said, "their sense is hard for me."
  And he to me, as one who read my thoughts:
    "Here you must leave distrust and doubt behind,
15   here you must put all cowardice to death.
  We have come to the place I spoke about,
    where you would see the souls who dwell in pain,
    for they have lost the good of intellect."
  And after he had laid his hand on mine
20   with cheerful countenance, strengthening my resolve,
    he led me to the secret things below.
  There sighs and moans and utter wailing swept
    resounding through the dark and starless air;
    I heard them for the first time, and I wept.
25 Shuddering din of strange and various tongues,
    sorrowful words and accents pitched with rage,
    shrill and harsh voices, blows of hands with these
  Raised up a tumult ever swirling round
    in that dark air untinted by a dawn,
30   as sand-grains whipping when the whirlwind blows.
  Said I—a blind of horror held my brain—
    "My Teacher, what are all these cries I hear?
    Who are these people conquered by their pain?"
  And he to me: "This state of misery
35   is clutched by those sad souls whose works in life
    merited neither praise nor infamy.
  Here they're thrown in among that petty choir
    of angels who were for themselves alone,
    not rebels, and not faithful to the Lord.
40 Heaven drives them out—its beauty would be marred;
    nor will the deep abyss receive their souls,
    lest they bring glory to the wicked there."
  And I: "Teacher, what weighs upon their hearts?
    What grief is it that makes them wail so loud?"
45   And he responded, "A few words will do.
  These souls, immortal, have no hope for death,
    and their blind lives crept grovelling so low
    they leer with envy at every other lot.
  The world allows no rumor of them now;

50 mercy and justice hold them in contempt.
    Let's say no more about them. Look, and pass."
   And I, beholding, saw a banner fly,
    whirling about and racing with such speed
    it seemed that it would scorn to stand, or pause;
55 And all behind that flag in a long file
    so numerous a host of people ran,
    I had not thought death had unmade so many.
   When I had recognized a few of these,
    I saw and knew at once the shade of him,
60 the craven one,[16] who made the great denial.
   Immediately I understood the truth:
    this was the low sect of those paltry souls
    hateful to God and to his enemies.
   These worthless wretches who had never lived
65 were pricked to motion now perpetually
    by flies and wasps that stung their naked limbs
   And ran the blood in furrows down their faces,
    which, mixed with tears, collected at their feet
    where loathsome maggots gorged and multiplied.
70 When I had turned my gaze ahead, I saw
    a band of people gathered at the banks
    of a broad river. "Teacher, if I may,
   Let me know of those people, and what law
    makes them appear so eager to cross over,
75 from what I make out through the feeble light."
   And he responded, "These things will be made
    plain to you when we fix our steps upon
    the melancholy shores of Acheron."
   Then with eyes fallen low and full of shame,
80 fearing that I had burdened him with talk,
    I held my words until we reached the stream.
   And look here—coming at us in a boat,
    an old man, hair and lank skin blanched with age,
    hollering, "Woe to you, O crooked souls!
85 Hope never more to look upon the sky!
    I come to lead you to the other shore,
    into eternal darkness—fire and ice!
   And as for you there, you the living soul,
    get away from these others who are dead."
90 But when he saw that I would not depart

---

[16]*the craven one:* probably Pope Celestine V, who abdicated the papacy in 1294, giving way
to Dante's nemesis, Boniface VIII

He said, "Another way, another port
  will bring your passage to the shore—not here.
  A lighter boat must carry you across."
  "Quit grumbling, Charon," said my guide. "Be still!
95   No questions—only know that this is willed
  where power is power to do whatever it will."
Then at once slumped to rest the goatish jowls
  of the punt-man of that liver-colored swamp,
  whose furious eyes yet flashed with wheels of fire.
100   But when they heard the old man's cruel words
  those naked and exhausted souls turned white,
  gnashing their teeth with fury for their fate—
Hurled blasphemy at God and at their parents,
  at the whole human race, the place, the time,
105   and the seed of their begetting and their birth.
Then all these people, wailing bitterly,
  gathered upon the cursed riverbank
  that waits each man who does not fear the Lord.
Charon the demon, eyes of fiery coal,
110   signals them all to get into the boat—
  smacks with his oar the soul that lags behind.
As in the fall when leaves are lifted off,
  one drops—another—till the naked branch
  sees all its garment lying on the earth,
115   So the bad seed of Adam one by one
  toss themselves from the shore at Charon's sign,
  as hawks returning to the master's call.
They cross the murky waters, and before
  they disembark upon the farther side,
120   another throng has gathered at the shore.
My gracious Teacher spoke to me: "My son,
  all souls that die beneath the wrath of God
  from every nation here collect in one,
And they are prompt to cross the river, for
125   Justice Divine so goads and spurs them on,
  that what they fear turns into their desire.
No good soul ever passes by these ways,
  and so, if Charon rails about you, well—
  you know how to interpret what he says."
130   He finished; and the gloomy plains of Hell
  shook with such might that though the terror's past
  it bathes me in a sweat to think of it.
That tear-drenched land heaved forth a sudden blast,
  flashing a lightning bolt as red as fire

135   that vanquished all my senses, and I fell
          As a man falls whom sleep has overcome.

CANTO FOUR

Dante and Virgil now descend into the abyss. They enter the first of the concentric rings of Hell, that of **Limbo,** *the Rim, where dwell, neither in joy nor in suffering, all unbaptized infants and those men and women who lived virtuously but who lacked the true faith. There they meet* **Homer** *and the great poets of old, and* **Aristotle** *and the great philosophers.*

       Thunder! the great boom broke so hard upon
          the deep sleep in my head, I shook myself—
          starting as one awakened by main force—
       Then I stood up and turned my rested eyes
5   about me, peering steadily, to see
          what kind of place it was where I awoke.
       In truth, I found myself upon the brink
          of the valley of the sorrowful abyss
          thundering with the roar of endless woe.
10   So dark it was and deep and bleared with mist,
          that though I fixed my gaze upon the bottom
          I still could not discern a single thing.
       "Into the blind world let us now descend,"
          began the poet, his face as pale as death,
15   "I will go first, and you will follow me."
       And I—for I had seen his color turn—
          replied, "How should I go, when you fear too,
          you who have been my courage when I doubt?"
       "The anguish of the souls who dwell down here,"
20   he answered me, "has painted in my face
          the pity you have taken to be fear.
       We must be moving on. The road is long."
          So he set forth, and so he made me enter
          into the first belt circling the abyss.
25   As far as I could tell from listening, here
          there were no wails, but only sighs, that made
          a trembling in the everlasting air.
       They rose from sorrow, without punishment,
          of the vast throngs of people sighing there,
30   of men and women and of infants too.
       "You don't ask," my good Teacher said to me,
          "who are these souls you look upon? Before
          you go on in your journey, you must know

They did not sin. If they had merits, these
35   were not enough—baptism they did not have,
          the one gate to the faith which you believe.
       And if they lived before the Christian faith,
          they did not give God homage as they ought;
          and of these people I myself am one.
40   For such a falling-short, and for no crime,
          we all are lost, and suffer only this:
          hopeless, we live forever in desire."
       When I heard this, great sorrow seized my heart,
          for I saw men of great distinction there
45   hovering in Limbo at the edge of Hell.
       "Tell me, my Teacher, tell me, my good lord,"
          I started—for I wanted to confirm
          the faith that conquers every path that strays,
       "Has anyone ever left here by his own
50   or by another's merits, to be blessed?"
       He heard the meaning mantled by my words
       And said, "I had just entered in this state
          when I saw coming One[17] of power and might,
          crowned with the glorious sign of victory.
55   From us he took the shade of our first father,[18]
          the shades of his son Abel and of Noah,
          of Moses who, obedient, gave the Law,
       Of patriarch Abraham, David the king,
          of Israel with his father and his sons
60   and Rachel, whom so long he labored for,[19]
       And many others, and he made them blessed.
          And you should also know that, before these,
          salvation came for not one human soul."
       We did not leave off walking while he spoke
65   but went on through the forest all the way—
          I mean the forest thicketed with souls.
       We hadn't ventured far from where I'd slept
          when there before us blazed a ring of light
          quelling the darkness that surrounded it.
70   We were still quite a little length away
          but close enough for me to see in part
          that people to be honored held that place.
       "O you who honor knowledge and all art,

---

[17]*One:* Christ, in the Harrowing of Hell between his death and resurrection
[18]*first father:* Adam
[19]*Rachel . . . for:* Jacob (Israel) worked for his father-in-law Laban for fourteen years to win Rachel's hand in marriage; cf. Gen. 29:15–30

who are these here so favored that they dwell
75   distinguished from the manner of the rest?"
And he: "The honored name, which still resounds
        their glory in your life above, has won
        such grace from Heaven, that it exalts them here."
And suddenly I heard a voice call out:
80   "Honor the highest prince of poetry!
        His shade which had departed has returned."
And when the voice had ceased, and all was still,
        I saw four mighty shades approaching us,
        with neither joy nor sadness in their eyes.
85 "Behold that shade whose right hand wields the sword,"
        my worthy Teacher thus began to say,
        "who comes before the others as their lord.
Homer the sovereign poet is that soul;
        Horace the satirist comes after him,
90   Ovid comes third, and Lucan is the last.
Because we come together in that name
        of 'poet' which the one soul spoke alone,
        they do me honor—and in this do well."
So did I see united that sweet school
95   of the lord of the most exalted song
        that like an eagle soars above the rest.
When they had talked together for a while
        they turned to me, and beckoned me to come,
        bringing unto my Teacher's lips a smile,
100   And greeted me, and honored me so well
        that they included me among their band,
        and made me sixth in that academy.
So we proceeded till we reached the light,
        speaking of things best kept in silence here,
105   as in that place to speak of them was right.
Before a noble castle then we came,
        by lofty walls encircled seven times,
        roundabout guarded by a lovely stream.
Over this stream we passed as on dry land;
110   then with those sages through the seven gates
        I entered, and we reached a fresh green field,
Where I saw souls whose eyes were grave and slow,
        whose looks were marked with great authority.
        Seldom they spoke, and held their voices low.
115   We drew away to one side of the plain
        to a place high and free and filled with light,
        that we might see them all. And there before me

On meadows bright as fine-enamelled green,
   the spirits of the great were shown to me—
120   glory it is, to see what I have seen!
I saw Electra with a numerous train—
   among them I knew Hector and Aeneas,
   and full-armed Caesar with his falcon eye.
I saw Penthesilea and Camilla
125   there on the other side, and King Latinus
   who sat beside his child Lavinia.
I saw that Brutus who drove Tarquin out,
   Lucretia, Julia, Martia, and Cornelia;
   and, sitting by himself, the Saladin.
130 And when I raised the lashes of my eye
   I saw the Master of all those who know[20]
   among his wisdom-seeking family.
All look upon him there, all honor him;
   I saw the souls of Socrates and Plato
135   where they stood nearer to him than the rest;
Democritus, who posits that the world
   is ruled by chance; Thales, Empedocles,
   Zeno, Diogenes, and Heraclitus,
And Anaxagoras, and the good collector
140   of herbals Dioscorides, and Orpheus,
   Cicero, Livy, moral Seneca,
Geometrician Euclid, Ptolemy,
   Hippocrates and Galen, Avicenna,
   and the great Commenter, Averroes.
145 I give no reckoning of them all—the length
   of what I have to do so drives me on,
   often my words fall short of the event.
The company of six is cut by two,
   and my wise guide leads me another way,
150   out of the quiet, into the trembling air—
Into a place where nothing ever shines.

---

[20]*the Master . . . know:* Aristotle

CANTO FIVE

Now the poets descend into the realm of the damned. After they meet and defy **Minos,** *the monstrous judge over all of the entering souls, they enter the second circle, that of the* **Lustful.** *Here they listen to the tale of* **Paolo and Francesca,** *noble young people murdered in the act of adulterous love.*

So I descended from the outer ring
    down to the next, which belts less space about
    but far more pain, for souls to wail its sting.
Horrible Minos grunts there like a bull,
5   weighs all the sins and sends the wicked down
    according to how far he winds his tail.
I mean that when one born in evil hour
    appears before him, he confesses all,
    and then judge Minos, the sin-connoisseur,
10   Discerns what place in Hell is fit for him:
    belts himself with his tail as many times
    as there are grades the sinner must descend.
Before him ever stand a crowd of souls:
    they step up one by one to testify,
15   they speak and hear and then are flung below.
"You who come to this sanctuary of pain,"
    said Minos when he saw me, leaving off
    the duties of so great a role, "Beware!
Watch how you enter and in whom you trust!
20   Don't be fooled by the broad and easy gate."
    My guide to him: "Enough! Why must you shout?
You shall not bar him, for he comes by fate.
    No questions—only know that this is willed
    where power is power to do whatever it will."
25   I now begin to hear arising wails
    of sorrow; I have come where the great cries
    batter me like a wave pounding the shore.
It is a place where all light is struck dumb,
    moaning as when high winds from east and west
30   wrestle upon the sea in a fierce storm.
That hellish cyclone that can never rest
    snatches the spirits up in its driving whirl,
    whisks them about and beats and buffets them,
And when they fall before the ruined slope,
35   ah then the shrieking, the laments, the cries!
    then they hurl curses at the power of God.
I learned that such a torment was designed

for the damned who were wicked in the flesh,
who made their reason subject to desire.
40 And as a flock of starlings winter-beaten
founder upon their wings in widening turns,
so did that whirlwind whip those evil souls,
Flinging them here and there and up and down;
nor were they ever comforted by hope—
45 no hope for rest, or even lesser pain.
And as the cranes go cawing out their songs,
forming a long streak in the air, I saw
approaching us and trailing cries of woe
Shades blown our way by the great battling winds,
50 so I said, "Teacher, tell me, who are those
spirits so lashed and scourged in the black air?"
"The first among those souls whose history
you wish to hear," he then responded, "was
empress of men of many languages.
55 She had so rotted with the lecher's vice
she altered 'lust' to 'just' by her decree,
to bleach the scandal that she brought herself.
Semiramis is she, of whom we read
that she was Ninus' heir, his whorish wife;
60 she held the land where now the Sultan rules.
Next is that amorous soul[21] who slew herself
and to Sychaeus' ashes broke her vow;
then Cleopatra, steeped in lechery.
Helen of Troy then see, for whom ten years
65 of ill revolved; and see the great Achilles,
who fell in his last combat, against Love.
See Paris, Tristan . . ." And he pointed out
innumerable shades and named them all,
whom Love had severed from our life on earth.
70 When I had heard my learned Teacher name
the courtly ladies and the knights of old,
a whelm of pity left me at a loss,
And "Poet," I began, "I greatly long
to speak to those two shades who fly as one
75 and seem so lightly carried on the wind."
And he responded: "You shall see them when
they sail nearer to us; then beg them by
the love that drives them on, and they will come."

---

[21]*amorous soul:* Dido, Queen of Carthage, who fell in love with Aeneas and committed suicide when, at the command of the gods, he left her to journey to Italy. Her story is told by Virgil in the *Aeneid,* books 1–4.

Soon as the wind had swerved their flight our way,
80   I cried, "O weary spirits, if Another[22]
         does not forbid it, come and speak with us!"
As turtledoves who heed the loving call—
         with firm and lifted wings they shear the air
         and fly to the sweet dove-cote, swift of will—
85   So did they veer away from Dido's flock
         and come to us through that malignant air,
         such force had the affection of my cry.
"O living spirit, courteous and good,
         traveling the black night to visit us
90   who left the world dyed purple with our blood,
Were He who rules the universe our friend,
         we would entreat him, praying for your peace,
         for you have pitied our ill-twisted fate.
All that you please to hear and speak about
95   we two will hear and speak with you, as long
         as the wind falls in silence. Where the Po
Rushes with all its tributaries down
         to its sea-harbor, that it may have peace,
         is situated the town where I was born.
100   Love that flames soonest in the gentle heart
         seized him for that sweet body which was snatched
         from me—and how it happened hurts me still.
Love, which allows no loved one not to love,
         seized me with such a strong delight in him
105   that, as you see, it will not leave me yet.
Love led us to one death. The realm of Cain[23]
         waits for the man who quenched us of our lives."
         Such were the words they offered. And I bowed
My head to hear the story of those souls
110   and what they suffered; bowed so low, at last
         the poet said, "What are you thinking of?"
When I could speak I thus began, "Alas,
         what great desire, what sweet and tender thoughts
         have led these lovers to this woeful pass!"
115   Turning to them once more I spoke again.
         "Francesca," I began, "your torments move
         my heart to weep in pity for your pain.
But tell me: in the season of sweet sighs,

---

[22]*Another:* i.e., God

[23]*Cain:* Cain, who slew his brother Abel (Gen. 4), lends his name to a region near the bottom of Dante's Hell where those who betrayed their own kinsmen are punished. See below, canto xxxii.

how did it happen, what made Love give way
120   that you should know the truth of those desires?"
And she to me: "There is no greater grief
      than to recall a time of happiness
      while plunged in misery—as your Teacher knows.
But if so great a longing urges you
125   to know about the first root of our love,
      then I will tell you, speaking through my tears.
One day we two were reading for delight
      about how love had mastered Lancelot;
      we were alone and innocent and felt
130 No cause to fear. And as we read, at times
      we went pale, as we caught each other's glance,
      but we were conquered by one point alone.
For when we read that the much-longed-for smile[24]
      accepted such a gentle lover's kiss,
135   this man, whom nothing will divide from me,
Trembled to place his lips upon my mouth.
      A pander was that author, and his book!
      That day we did not read another page."
And the while one spirit told their tale,
140   the other wept so sadly that I fell
      swooning for pity, faint and cold as death,
And like a corpse I dropped, insensible.

---

[24]*smile:* that of Guinevere, wife of King Arthur

CANTO SIX

After eluding **Cerberus,** *the triple-headed beast of Hell, the poets enter the second ring, where the* **Gluttonous** *are punished in a storm of cold rain. There Dante speaks with* **Ciacco,** *a fellow Florentine who foretells strife for a city divided by injustice and greed.*

In coming to—my mind had shut its door,
   pitying those two kinsmen and their tale,
   confounding me and covering me with sadness—
I see new forms of torment all about
5   and new tormented souls, wherever I move,
   wherever I turn, wherever I set my gaze.
At the third ring am I, where the rain falls
   eternally, accursed, ponderous, cold—
   changeless in rhythm, changeless in quality.
10   Thick knobs of hail, snow, water foul as ink
   pour down forever through the gloomy air
   and soak into the ground to make it stink.
Cerberus the bizarre and cruel beast
   with his three gullets barks like a great dog
15   over the spirits drowning in that paste.
His eyes are bloody, his scruff is slick and black,
   his paunch is huge, his paw-hands clawed like hooks
   to snatch and skin and shred the souls to bits.
The downpour makes the spirits yowl like dogs;
20   they roll upon one side to shield the other—
   those desecrating wretches turn and turn!
When Cerberus the great worm discovered us
   he bared his fangs and opened his maws wide,
   his muscles taut and not one holding still.
25   My guide spread out his palms and shoveled up
   two big fistfuls of mud and chucked them down
   the monster's ravenous funnels. As a dog
Yammering in an agony of greed,
   straining to eat and nothing else, shuts up
30   soon as he sinks his fangs into his feed,
So did those greasy mugs of Cerberus
   the demon, who so thunders at the souls
   they wish they could go deaf. We took our way,
Passing above the shadows in the press
35   of that thick rain; and fixed our soles upon
   what seemed their persons, but was emptiness.
Each one of them, flat on the earth, lay prone,

until one jerked himself up to a sit
as soon as he perceived us passing by.
40 "O you, led through this low world," said the shade,
"regard me well! You may know who I am—
for you were made before I was unmade."
And I: "Perhaps the anguish you endure
has cast you from my memory, for it seems
45 I've never looked upon your face before.
But tell me who you are, sent to a place
so painful, and with such a punishment—
though some are harsher, none is more unpleasant."
And he to me: "Your city,[25] so stuffed full
50 with envy that the sack's mouth spews it up,
once held me in the calm and sunlit life.
You fellow citizens called me Ciacco—'Hog.'
For that sin of the throat that damns the soul,
as you can see, I'm flattened by the rain.
55 And I am not the only sad soul here,
for all these others suffer the same pain
for the same fault." And he spoke nothing more.
And I responded: "Ciacco, your distress
weighs on my heart and summons me to tears.
60 But tell me, if you know, to what will come
The citizens of our party-sundered town:
are there just men among us? And tell why
we are assailed by such disharmony."
And he: "After a struggle long and tense
65 they'll come to bloodshed, and the backwoods side
will chase the other out with great offense.
Then by his force[26] who waits his chance to strike,
that party will collapse within three years
and then the other climbs to power again,
70 Long holding high their foreheads in their pride,
and despite all the cries and accusations,
heaping great burdens on the other side.
Two men are just, but no one heeds their words.
Avarice, pride, and envy are the three
75 principal flames that kindle in their hearts."
He put an end here to his grievous speech.
And I to him: "I wish to learn yet—please,
do me the favor, speak a little more.

---

[25]*your city*: Florence
[26]*his force*: that of Pope Boniface VIII, interfering in Florentine politics

Those worthy men Tegghiaio, Farinata,
80 Jacopo Rusticucci, Arrigo, Mosca,
  the rest who set their minds to merit well,
Say where they are and let me know their state,
  for a great longing presses me to know
  if Heaven sweetens or Hell poisons them."
85 "They dwell among the blackest souls below,"
  said he, "weighed to the pit by different faults.
  Go far enough and you will find them all.
But when you have returned to the sweet world,
  I beg, remember me to someone there;
90 I say no more, and no more will respond."
His eyes that held me rolled a-squint—he stared
  at me a moment, hung his head, and fell
  flat with the other sinners, blind as they.
And my guide said to me: "He wakes no more
95 till roused by the angelic trump of doom
  when he will go to face the hostile Power.[27]
Each man shall see again his woeful tomb,
  shall reassume his flesh and form, and hear
  his sentence thundering through eternity."
100 So we passed on through that polluted mix
  of soul and slush, with slow and thoughtful steps,
  touching awhile upon the life to come,
And I said, "Teacher, for these torments here—
  after the final Sentence will they grow,
105 or ease a bit, or stew as sharp as now?"
He: "Turn to your philosophy again,
  which shows that when a thing at last is whole
  it feels more pleasure—so it feels more pain.
For all that these accursed folk cannot
110 come to their true perfection and man's end,
  they look to be more 'perfect' then than now."
Down that wide-bending road we took our way,
  saying a great deal more than I repeat,
  until we reached the edge of the descent.
115 There we found Plutus,[28] the great enemy.

---

[27]*hostile Power*: God, as judge
[28]*Plutus*: classical god of wealth

8. *Dante*/Inferno VII

CANTO SEVEN

Passing by, in contempt, the jabbering **Plutus,** *guardian of the fourth circle, Dante and Virgil see where the unnamed* **Avaricious,** *in teams of misers and squanderers, roll enormous boulders at each other while jeering about each other's vices. Virgil explains to Dante the role of* **Fortune** *in the governance of the world. Continuing, they come upon the fifth circle, which is the* **River Styx,** *where the* **Wrathful** *and the* **Sullen** *are punished.*

"Pape Satan, pape Satan aleppe!"
    so Plutus chopped out with his clucking voice,
    and that most gracious sage, aware of all,
Strengthened my heart: "Though he has power enough,
5   let your fears never hurt you. He will not
    steal from us our descending down this bluff."
Then he turned back to face those blood-puffed lips
    and said, "Shut up, you cursed wolf of Hell!
    Swallow your rage and let it gnaw your guts!
10   His passage to the hollows has its cause.
    It is willed from on high, whence Michael brought
    vengeance against the arrogant revolt."[29]
As in a fresh breeze when a ship's mast snaps,
    the sails once puffed and stretched fall in a heap;
15   so did that cruel beast drop to the earth.
So we descended into the fourth purse,
    taking more of that sad embankment which
    bags all the evil of the universe.
Justice of God! Who else but you crams in
20   all of the strange new toils and pains I saw?
    And why are we so laid to waste in sin?
As at Charybdis[30] when two sea-waves wheel
    head-on and smash over the whirlpool—so
    the people in this ring must dance their reel.
25   I saw far more than I had elsewhere seen,
    howling on one side, howling on the other,
    popping their chests with force to roll huge weights.
They bashed those stones together front to front,
    then straight off each side turned about and yelled,
30   "Why do you fritter?" "Why the fists so tight?"
So in the dismal circle they went round

---

[29]*Michael . . . revolt:* the archangel Michael, punishing the revolt led by Satan. See Rev. 12:7–12

[30]*Charybdis:* in Greco-Roman mythology, the name for a dangerous whirlpool in the straits between Italy and Sicily

on either hand to the point opposite,
hollering out their poetry of shame,
And when they'd gotten halfway round the ring,
35   they turned around to have another joust.
And I said, for my heart was nearly pierced,
"My Teacher, show me who these people are,
and let me know if they were all ordained,
those on our left with hair clipped like a clerk's."
40   And he to me: "In the first life, each soul
you see here was so cross-eyed in his mind,
he held no measure when he saved or spent.
Their voices yap that judgment loud enough
when they come to the two points of the ring,
45   where their opposing vices split them off.
Those whose heads have no cap of hair to crop
were all clerks, even popes and cardinals,
whom avarice browbeats, bullying to the top."
"Teacher," said I, "among this mob of such,
50   I'll wager I can recognize a few
who got their fingers dirty in this sin!"
And he: "Forget it, it's an empty thought.
The nothing-knowing life that made them foul
dims them beyond all recognition now.
55   They will butt head to head forevermore.
From the tomb these will rise with their fists shut,
and these with half the hair ripped from their scalps.
Ill-giving and ill-keeping snatched from them
the lovely world, and set them in this brawl.
60   I will not prettify it by my words.
Now you can see, my son, how short a jest
are the good things assigned to Fortune's care—
for which the human race squabble and squall,
For all the gold that lies beneath the moon
65   and all that has, could never give a moment
of rest to one of these exhausted souls."
"My Teacher," I said then, "tell me this too.
What is that Fortune you have touched upon,
that holds the world's goods in so fierce a clutch?"
70   And he: "Oh, you are simpletons indeed!
How deep the ignorance that injures you!
I'll give you the bare truth, that you may feed.
He whose transcendent wisdom passes all

fashioned the heavens and gave each sphere a guide[31]
75   that every part might shine to every part,
    Distributing the splendor equally.
     Similarly for things that shine on earth
     He chose a general minister and guide
    To scramble now and then the empty goods
80   from race to race, from one blood to another,
     past all defense man's shrewdness might devise,
    And so this nation rises to command
     and that one droops, just as her judgments please—
     as hidden as a serpent in the grass.
85   Your wisdom cannot duel hers: she sees
     ahead, she judges, and she follows through
     in her realm as the other heavenly powers
    In theirs. Her many changes know no truce;
     she must go swiftly, by necessity—
90   so many men step up to take their turn!
    She is the one so cursed and crucified
     by the same people who should give her praise,
     slanderously accusing her of wrong,
    But she is blessed, and she does not hear.
95   With all the other creatures fashioned first[32]
     she dwells in gladness and she turns her sphere.
    Let us descend to greater misery now,
     for every star is sinking which had climbed
     when I set out. We must not stay too long."
100   We cut the circle to the other bank,
     passing a spring that boiled and bubbled over
     into a trench that led the stream away.
    Dark was that water, of a purplish black,
     and we companions of its murky waves
105   walked down below along its cursed track.
    It flows into a swamp whose name is Styx,
     this gloomy little brook, descending to
     the bottom of the gray, malignant slope.
    And I, who gazed intently as I stood,
110   saw people in that slough all slimed with mud,
     stripped naked, and their faces torn with rage.
    They thumped each other not with hands alone
     but with the head, the chest, the feet, the teeth!—
     snapping to rip each other limb from limb.

---

[31]*guide:* an angel, called an Intelligence, to govern each of the planetary spheres
[32]*creatures . . . first:* the angels

115 "Son," my good Teacher said, "now you may see
  the souls of those whom wrath has overcome;
  and you should take it for a certainty
That underwater here are souls who sigh
  and make the river bubble to the top,
120 as you may see wherever you turn your eye.
Stuck in the mire they say: 'Sullen we were
  up in the sweet air gladdened by the sun,
  bearing the smoke of sluggishness in our hearts.
Now we are sullen here in this black bog.'
125 Such is the hymn they gargle in the throat.
  They cannot get the words out whole and clear."
So in a wide arc we walked round that pond
  between the dry slope and the rotten squelch,
  eyes turned upon the souls who gulped down mud.
130 To the foot of a tower at last we came.

CANTO EIGHT

The poets are ferried over the **Styx** *by the angry boatman* **Phlegyas**. *On their way, they encounter the wrathful* **Filippo Argenti**, *drive him off when he tries to harass them, and watch in pleasure as the others rip him to pieces. Finally they land at the shores of inner Hell, outside the walls of the city of* **Dis**, *where they are refused entry by the fallen angels.*

Continuing, I say that long before
  we'd arrived at the foot of the high tower,
  we raised our eyes up to the top—for there
Were placed two little lights, and in reply
5 another signal flickered far away,
  so far, the eye could hardly make it out.
To the sea of all wisdom then I turned:
  "What does this signal mean? That other fire,
  what does it answer? And who's sending them?"
10 "Over the nasty water you can find
  already what we're waiting for," said he,
  "if the bog's fumes don't hide it from your sight."
No arrow shot a-whistling from the cord
  could ever fly so swiftly through the air
15 as in that instant a small boat I saw
Coming in our direction on the water,
  one oarsman only at her helm, who cried,
  "Traitor! I've got you now, you wicked soul!"
"Phlegyas, Phlegyas, holler all you want!"

20 my lord replied. "This time it's all in vain.
  You'll have us only while we cross the slough."
 As when a man who hears of a big fraud
  pulled off on him, resents it, seethes with grief—
  so Phlegyas chafed, his anger shut inside.
25 After my guide went down into the boat
  he bade me enter too, and only then
  did the craft seem to carry any weight.
 Soon as my guide and I were in the skiff
  that ancient prow went cutting through more water
30 than when it ferried other souls across.
 While we were racing over the dead pond,
  before me rose a spirit full of slime—
  "And who are you, who come before your hour?"
 And I to him: "I've come, but not to stay.
35 But who are you, made ugly by such filth?"
  And he: "You see that I am one who weeps."
 And I to him: "Well, then, accursed spirit,
  keep to your weeping and your misery!
  I know you, fouled and mucked though you may be."
40 Then he flung out both hands to grab the skiff—
  at that my wary Teacher shoved him off,
  "Get out of here! Run with the other dogs!"
 Then round my neck he clasped me in his arms
  and kissed my face and said, "Indignant soul!
45 Blessed be she whose womb bore fruit in you!
 That one on earth was full of arrogance.
  No good or gracious deed adorns his name—
  and so his shade is full of fury here.
 Up there how many think themselves great kings
50 who will be stuck like swine here in this sty,
  leaving a name to spit on in contempt."
 "Teacher," I said, "I've got a hankering
  to see them dunk that spirit in this swill
  before we leave the lake and disembark."
55 And he replied, "You will enjoy your fill
  before the farther beach comes into sight.
  Such a desire is good to satisfy."
 Soon after that I saw the mud-melee
  rake him apart just as I could have wished—
60 for which I praise and thank God to this day.
 "Get Filippo Argenti!" they all yelled,
  and that short-tempered shade from Florence turned
  gnashing his teeth against his peevish self.

We left him there—of him I tell no more,
65   but such a cry of grief pounded my ears
       I fixed my gaze wide-eyed to see the shore.
The good Teacher advised me, "Now, my son,
       we draw near to the city they call Dis,
       with its great hosts, with its grave citizens."
70   "Teacher," said I, "already I discern
       the turrets of its mosques behind the moat.
       Like iron from the forge they glow and burn."
And he replied, "The everlasting flames
       its heart ignites make it as red as fire,
75   flaring within these nether depths of Hell."
We sped along into the deep-trenched moats
       that fortify that never-solaced land;
       the city seemed to loom with iron walls.
Not without taking first a long turn round
80   we came to where the boatman hollered, "Out!
       This is the entrance—here's where you get off!"
More than a thousand of those angels rained
       from Heaven I saw upon the garrison,
       jeering, "Who's this who has no death to show
85   But travels through the kingdom of the dead?"
       And my wise Teacher made a sign to say
       that he desired to speak with them aside.
Then they played a bit closer their great scorn
       and said, "You come alone, and let him go
90   who was so hot to come into this reign.
Let him go back alone on his mad way!
       Let him try, if he can. For you who've led
       him down so dark a country—here you'll stay."
Consider, Reader, whether I was not
95   distressed on hearing those accursed words!
       For I believed I never would return.
"Beloved guide, in every trial yet
       you who have been my best assurance, most
       faithful to keep me safe from any threat,"
100   Said I, "don't leave me so undone and lost!
       If we are not permitted to go on,
       let's trace our footsteps back again at once!"
And that lord who had guided me so far
       said, "Have no fear. No one can take from us
105   our passage on—granted by One so great.
Wait for me here, and feed upon good hope
       to fortify your soul in its fatigue.

I will not leave you in the lower world."
So saying, the sweet father goes his way,
110   leaves me behind, while I remain in doubt,
   with yes and no at combat in my head.
I couldn't hear the words he put to them,
   but not long would they stand with him in place
   when back inside the gates they scrambled, where
115 Our adversaries slammed them in the face
   of my good master, who remained outside,
   and turned to me, with slow and measured steps.
His eyes were bowed to earth, his brow was shorn
   of all his boldness, as he sighed and said,
120   "Who are these here to block my going down
To the houses of pain? But you"—to me—
   "ignore my anger. No dismay. They'll bustle
   to fight it, but I'll have the victory.
This insolence of theirs is nothing new.
125   They showed it once at a less secret gate,[33]
   whose locks and bars stand broken even now.
On it are etched those words of death you saw.
   Already someone's[34] coming down the slope,
   passing through all the rings without a guide—
130 One who will breach these city gates for us."

---

[33]*gate:* the gates of Hell
[34]*someone:* the angel of the next canto

CANTO NINE

*While waiting for the **angel from Heaven**, the poets see the **Furies** upon the ramparts, and hear them call for the Gorgon, **Medusa,** the sight of whom would turn a man to stone. Virgil shields Dante from looking at her. At last the angel arrives and opens the gates. Dante and Virgil now enter the sixth circle, where the **Heretics** are confined to tombs of fire.*

That color cowardice had bleached upon
 my countenance, when I saw my leader turn,
 all the more swiftly checked it in his own.
He held himself as one who listens hard,
5 for the eye could not travel very far
 through that black air and through those briars of fog.
"Yet it must be . . . we have to win this fight.
 If not—but such a person offered it!
 How long it seems before our helper comes!"
10 I saw well how he covered up his speech,
 veiling his start with what came afterwards,
 whose words were very different from the first,
Yet what he said dismayed me even so,
 because I drew out of his cut-off word
15 a meaning worse, perhaps, than he intended.
"Down to the bottom of this dismal shell
 has anyone descended from the rim,
 whose severed hope is his sole pain in Hell?"
I asked this question. "Rarely," he replied,
20 it comes about that one of us will make
 the journey here along the path I take.
It's true that I've come down here once before,
 conjured to by the cruel witch Erichtho
 who summoned souls to animate the corpse.
25 My flesh had not been stripped of me for long
 when I was forced to come inside these walls
 to drag a spirit back from Judas' ring.
That is the lowest and the blackest place,
 the farthest from the Heaven that turns all things.
30 I know the journey well, so rest assured.
This quagmire which exhales so great a stink
 runs like a belt around the city of woe,
 which we can't enter without anger now."
He said more, which my mind cannot recall,
35 because my eyes were wholly focused on
 the lofty tower up to the searing top,

Where in a moment there had risen erect
    three hellish Furies stained and dyed in blood,
    members and gestures of the female sex,
40 Gartered with greenest hydras round their waists;
    adders and small horned vipers formed their hair,
    twisting about the temples of those beasts.
And he, who knew those shabby handmaids of
    Hecate, queen of everlasting woe,
45   said to me, "See the fierce Erinyes there!
Megara is the Fury on the left;
    she is Alecto wailing on the right;
    Tisiphone in the center." That was all.
And each one clawed her nails to cleave her chest,
50   beat her breasts with her palms and shrieked so loud
    I flinched, and to the poet's side I pressed.
"Medusa, come! Let's turn this one to stone!"
    they cried together, staring down at us.
    "We blundered, letting Theseus get away."
55 "Quick, turn your back and cover up your face,
    for should you see the Gorgon if she shows,
    there would be no returning up above!"
So did my Teacher say, and he himself
    turned me around, and since he did not trust
60   my own, he shut my eyes with his hands too.
O you whose intellects see clear and whole,
    gaze on the doctrine that is hidden here
    beneath the unfamiliar verses' veil.
And now above the water churned with scum
65   broke such a fearful crash it sent the shakes
    through either shore—the roarings such as come
Whenever a headstrong gale is raised by war
    of heat and cold massed in the atmosphere:
    it batters the woods with nothing to hold it back,
70 Slashes and beats limbs down and sweeps them off,
    drives onward in its arrogance of dust,
    and sets the shepherds and the beasts to flee.
He freed my eyes and said, "Now strain the nerve
    of your sight there above the ancient sludge
75   where the smoke is the bitterest." As frogs
Are quick to vanish in the water when
    they see their enemy the serpent come,
    and squat and crouch all quiet at the bottom,
I saw more than a thousand souls destroyed
80   scurry away before the steps of one

who passed the waters of the Styx, dry-shod.
    He swept his left arm out in front of him,
        clearing the gross air from before his face—
        and that alone for him seemed wearisome.
85 I saw he was a herald sent from Heaven,
        turned to my Teacher, but he made a sign
        that I should hold my peace, and bow to him.
    O how he seemed to me so full of scorn!
        Came to the gate, and with a little wand
90   opened it; there was nothing to resist.
    "O you despicable race cast out from Heaven,"
        upon the horrible threshold he began,
        "where do you fetch this pride that feeds on you!
    Why do you kick your heels against the will
95   of Him whose ends can never be cut short,
        who many a time has made your torments grow?
    What good is it to butt your heads at fate?
        Your Cerberus did so, if you may recall,
        and he still wears his chin and jowls skinned bald."
100 Then he turned back along the filthy road
        without a word to us, as if he were
        someone with other business on his mind
    Than what may press and sting the man before him;
        and so we made our way into that city—
105   his holy words had made us confident.
    Without a battle then we went inside,
        and I, who had a wish to scout the site
        and the condition of the spirits barred
    Inside that stronghold, see a stretching plain
110   wherever I turn my gaze, on every side,
        full of the cruellest punishments and pain.
    As at Arles, near the mud-flats of the Rhone,
        or as at Pola, near Quarnero Bay
        which bathes and shuts the bounds of Italy,
115 The crammed-in tombs make all the ground uneven,
        so did the tombs in this place, everywhere,
        except the manner made it harsher still,
    For flames were sown among those open graves
        and fired them to so great a temperature
120   that iron forged red-hot requires no more.
    All of their slabs hung open, and there came
        out of their mouths such bitter lamentation—
        well, they that made it seemed in misery!
    "Teacher," I said, "who are those people there

125   entombed within the arks, who can be heard
         by the great sighs of sorrow from inside?"
       "These are the patriarchs of heresy,"
         he said, "with all their followers, every sect.
         More than you'd think lie packed into these tombs.
130   Heretics here are buried like with like,
         and hot and less hot are their monuments."
         And after he turned right, we took our path
       Between the tortures and the battlements.

CANTO TEN

*In the sixth circle, Dante speaks to the Epicurean heretic **Farinata,** valorous leader of one of the Florentine factions and an important figure in the city's civil war. While they are speaking, they are interrupted by **Cavalcante de' Cavalcanti,** the father of Dante's friend and fellow poet Guido Cavalcanti; he is dismayed to hear, as he thinks, that Guido is dead. Dante resumes speaking with Farinata, who prophesies **Dante's exile from Florence,** and explains to Dante the limits of **the knowledge of the damned.***

       Now he proceeded down a secret track
         between the torments and the city wall,
         my Teacher, with me close behind his back.
       "O highest peak of virtue," I began,
5   "who lead me at your pleasure round these rings,
         speak to me, let my wish be satisfied.
       The people who are lying in these graves,
         can they be seen? The lids have all been raised
         and no one seems on guard." And he to me:
10   "These will be bolted on the day of doom
         when from the Valley of Jehosophat
         the souls bring back their bodies to the tomb.
       On this side, in his cemetery, lies
         that Epicurus with his followers who
15   put it that spirit dies when body dies.
       Now as for your request, soon it will be
         fulfilled for you in here—that, and another
         desire you silently withhold from me."
       "Good leader, if I hide my heart from you,"
20   said I, "I do it only to speak less—
         that's what you've often said that I should do."
       "O Tuscan, you who speak with modest grace,
         alive and traveling through the city of fire,
         may it please you to pause here in this place.

25   Your speech and accent make it clear to me
          you were born in the noble fatherland[35]
          I may have punished once too bitterly."
      This sound suddenly burst forth from inside
          one of the arks of stone, and in some fear
30   I drew a little closer to my guide.
      "What are you doing? Turn around!" said he.
          "Look upon Farinata risen there!
          His full height from the waist up you will see."
      I had already fixed my eyes on his;
35   who raised himself with great chest and great brow,
          surging as if he held all Hell in scorn.
      And with his prompt and spirited hand my guide
          pushed me towards him among the sepulchers,
          saying, "Make sure each word you utter counts."
40   At the foot of his tomb I stood, and he
          looked at me for a little, till he asked,
          with some disdain, "Who were your family?"
      I who was eager to obey him did
          not hide the matter, but revealed it all,
45   at which he raised his eyebrow just a bit
      And said, "They were bold enemies of mine,
          fierce to my party and my ancestors,
          for which twice over I sent them scattering."
      "If they were twice cast out, they twice returned,"
50   I thus responded, "and from every side,
          an art which yours, it seems, have not well learned."
      Then next to him out of the lidless tomb
          arose a shadow visible to the chin;
          I think he must have risen to his knees.
55   He looked around me, searched, as if he longed
          to see if someone else was there with me,
          and when his little hope was quenched, he wept
      And said, "If through this dungeon of the blind
          you go by means of genius at its height,
60   where is my son?[36] Why is he not with you?"
      And I: "I haven't come here on my own.
          He who stands waiting leads me through this place
          for one[37] your Guido, maybe, held in scorn."
      I'd read his name already by his words

---

[35]*fatherland:* Tuscany; specifically, Florence
[36]*my son:* the poet Guido Cavalcanti
[37]*one:* Beatrice

65   and by the manner of his punishment,
          so I replied in full. But suddenly
      He drew upright and cried, "What do you mean?
          You said 'he held'—isn't he still alive?
          Has the sweet sunlight ceased to strike his eyes?"
70   And when he noticed I was hesitant
          and didn't answer him immediately,
          he fell back, and did not come out again.
      But he at whose request I'd stopped to speak,
          that man of great soul, never turned his neck,
75   or bent his trunk, or changed his countenance,
      But went on speaking as he had at first.
          "If they," said he, "have badly learned that art,
          that tortures me more than this bed of fire.
      Yet fifty times the moon will not re-burn—
80   that face of Hecate, the queen of Hell—
          before you find how hard that is to learn.
      As you hope to go back to the sweet world,
          tell me, why are those people pitiless
          against my side in every law they pass?"
85   Said I, "The great rout and the massacre
          that blushed the river Arbia red with blood,
          are why our temple sounds with such a prayer."
      He shook his head a little, with a sigh.
          "There I was not alone—nor would have moved
90   with all the others, had there been no cause.
      "But when each man agreed to wipe away
          Florence from off the earth, I was alone,
          her sole defender in the sight of all."
      "Ah, as your seed may ever hope for peace,"
95   I begged him, "please, untie this knot for me
          which twists my judgment all in tangles here.
      If I've heard right, it seems that you can see
          what time will bring before it comes to pass—
          not so, for things that happen currently."
100   "As a man with bad vision," he replied,
          "we dimly see things far away. So much
          splendor the sovereign Lord still shines on us.
      When things draw near, or happen, emptiness
          is all we see. If no one brings us news,
105   we can know nothing of your human state.
      Now you can understand that evermore
          dead will be all our knowledge from the time
          the future ends, and Judgment shuts the door."

Then I said—for I felt remorse's sting—
110   "Will you now tell that soul who fell away,
    his son is still on earth among the living?
If at first I was silent in reply,
    let him know I was caught in that mistake,
    dwelling upon the doubt you've solved for me."
115 And now my Teacher called me to return,
    so I besought the soul to hurry on
    and tell me who stood with him in that tomb.
"More," he said, "than a thousand lie with me;
    "Frederick the Second and the Cardinal.
120   About the rest I have no more to say."
At that he hid his form within. So towards
    the ancient poet I turned my steps, and mulled
    the spirit's speech to me, his hostile words.
And as we walked in silence, by and by
125   the poet said, "Why are you lost in thought?"
    And so I satisfied him in reply.
"Save in your memory everything you've heard
    against you," that wise man commanded me,
    "and now listen to this," he said and pointed.
130   "When you shall come before the radiance
    of that sweet soul[38] whose lovely eye sees all,
    from her you'll learn the journey of your life."
Then straight to the left hand he took his way;
    we left the walls and towards the center walked
135   along a path that struck into a pit
Whose loathsome stench rose to the very top.

---

[38]*that sweet soul:* i.e., Beatrice

CANTO ELEVEN

At the inner rim of the sixth circle, the poets find the tombstone of **Pope Anastasius.**
Before they descend further, Virgil explains to Dante **the structure of lower Hell.**
The final three rings punish sins of **violence, fraud,** *and* **treachery,** *with the ring of
violence subdivided according to the one violated: one's neighbor, oneself, or God—
either in God's own person, or in His handmaid, Nature.*

At the edge of a ring of broken stones
   heaped in a tumble down to the steep pit,
   we came upon a crueller pack of woe,
Where for the overwhelming stink that breathed
5   horribly from the depths of the abyss,
   we drew away a bit, and made our screen
The great slab of a tomb, on which I read
   these words engraved: "I guard Pope Anastasius.
   Photinus drew him from the straight and true."
10   "We should take our descent a little slow,
   letting our sense grow used to the foul air
   a little—then we will not mind it so."
So said the Teacher. "Let's not lose the time,"
   said I to him, "but find some recompense."
15   "That's just what I've been thinking of," said he.
 "My son, down in the pit below these rocks,"
   he began, "there are three rings, small and smaller
   as you go down, like those you've left above.
They are all filled with spirits of the damned.
20   So that the sight of them will be enough,
   hear how and why Hell stows them where they're crammed.
All malice meriting the hate of God
   has for its end injustice. All such ends
   afflict the sufferer by force, or fraud.
25   Since fraud's an evil owned by man alone,
   God hates it more; and so the fraudulent
   sink further down, assailed by greater pain.
The violent fill the first ring, but because
   there are three persons force is used against,
30   the ring is delved with three rounds, each distinct.
Against one's neighbor or oneself or God
   one can use force—against their persons or
   their property, as I shall now explain.
Violent death and vicious wounds are sins
35   against one's neighbor; and his property
   may suffer arson, ruin, and forced loss,

So homicides and all who strike for hate,
   spoilers and beasts of prey, are tortured there
   in the first round, in all their separate packs.
40   Men can raise violent hands against themselves
   and their own goods; so in the second round
   it's fit that they repent—to no avail—
Who robbed themselves of life on earth above,
   gambled their substance, melted all their wealth,
45   or wept for things that should have brought them joy.
One can use force against the Deity,
   cursing it, or denying it in one's heart,
   or scorning Nature and her generous goods;
And so the narrowest round seals with its mark
50   Sodomites,[39] and the usurers of Cahors,[40]
   and those who utter scorn of God at heart.
Now fraud—which bites at every conscience—can
   be used on one who puts his faith in you
   or one who pockets no such confidence.
55   This latter type of fraud appears to cut
   only that bond of love which Nature makes;
   thus to the second circle for their nest
Go flatterers, swindling sorcerers, hypocrites,
   impostors, pickers of purses, simonists,
60   panders and greasy palms and all such filth.
The other fraud forgets two bonds of love,
   one made by Nature, and one added on,
   from which a special faith to keep is born;
So at the bottom of the universe
65   where Satan sits, in the lowest ring of all,
   traitors are laid to waste eternally."
"Teacher, your explanation is quite clear,"
   said I, "and you have pieced out very well
   this chasm and all the people it confines.
70   But tell me, those up there in the swamp's slime,
   those windswept spirits, those the rain beats down,
   those tongues that jeer when they collide each time,
Why aren't they also in this city of rust
   to suffer, if God holds them in His wrath?
75   If He does not, how is their suffering just?"
And he to me: "How is it that your mind
   goes madly wandering so far from itself?

---

[39] *Sodomites:* homosexuals
[40] *Cahors:* French town, proverbial in the Middle Ages for being a nest of usurers

In what direction have you turned its gaze?
Don't you remember the Philosopher[41]—
80   his Ethics, where he treats at length the three
      propensities which Heaven does not will,
Incontinence and malice and deranged
      bestiality? And how incontinence
      offends God less, is taxed with lesser blame?
85   So if you study his conclusion well,
      and bring back to your mind who those souls are
      who bear their penalties in upper Hell,
You will perceive why they are sundered from
      these villains here, and why less angrily
90   Heaven's vengeance brings on them its hammering blows."
"O sun that clears and cures all troubled sight,
      you please me so much when you solve these things—
      no less than knowledge, doubt is a delight!
Could you go back a little, though," said I,
95   "when you said usury's an offense against
      God's bounty? There's a riddle to untie."
"Whoever understands Philosophy
      and heeds it, notes, not in one place alone,
      how Nature takes her course," he said to me,
100   "From Intellect divine and from its art,
      and in your Physics, if you gloss it well,
      you'll find, not many pages from the start,
That your art strives to follow, as it may,
      Nature—you are the pupil, she the teacher.
105   So we might say that human industry
Is the grandchild of God. From these two things—
      remember the first part of Genesis—
      man must derive his life and his advance,
And since the usurer takes a different path,
110   setting his hope in something else, he sins,
      despising Nature and her follower.
But now I'd like to move, so follow me,
      for the Fish flash their tails on the horizon,
      the Bear[42] is full northwest, and still ahead
115   There lies our way to venture down the slope."

---

[41]*the Philosopher:* Aristotle
[42]*the Fish . . . the Bear:* Pisces and Ursa Major. It is almost dawn of the next day.

CANTO TWELVE

*The poets descend into the seventh circle, guarded by the beast of violence, **the** Minotaur**. At the base of the embankment they meet **the Centaurs**, led by **Chiron**, who shoot arrows at murderers who must stand in the **River Phlegethon**, a boiling stream as red as blood. The centaur **Nessus** identifies the sinners for them and carries Dante across the ford.*

This descent was a jagged-bouldered one,
    and, for the loathsome thing before the bank,
    a place which any eye would gladly shun.
As at the Slips of Mark that struck the flank
5   of the River Adige this side of Trent,
    because of earthquake or support too weak,
To the plain from the very mountaintop
    the rock-face is so smashed-in and destroyed
    it makes a path for someone up above;
10   Such was the way to go down this gorge here,
    and at the ruptured margin of the ditch
    there lay outstretched the Infamy of Crete[43]
Conceived within the counterfeited cow;
    and when he saw us two, he champed himself,
15   crumpled in wrath and eaten up inside.
Turning to him, my wise one cried, "Perhaps
    you think you've got the Duke of Athens[44] here,
    the one who slew you in the world above?
Clear away, beast! For this man has not come
20   taught by your clever sister and her clue,
    but goes about to view your punishments."
And as a bull who's snapped his harness-ropes
    when the death-blow's already set him reeling—
    he cannot charge, but leaps this way and that;
25   So did I see the furious Minotaur.
    "Run to the gap," the wary poet cried,
    "better go down while he is blind with rage!"
We picked our way then down that garbage-dump
    of fallen rocks, which slid and shifted as
30   I trod on them with unaccustomed weight.
He noticed I was thinking as I walked.
    "This ruin guarded by the bestial wrath
    I doused just now—perhaps you're wondering

---

[43] *Infamy of Crete:* the Minotaur
[44] *Duke of Athens:* Theseus

How it collapsed. Know then, that other time
35   when I descended to the deepest Hell,
     the cliff had not yet crumbled. But not long,
As far as I can judge, before He[45] came
     who made the glorious raid on Lucifer
     and raised up spirits from the highest ring,
40   Every side of this deep and stinking hole
     shivered as if the universe felt love—
     which some believe has often turned the world
Back to the chaos of its origin;
     and at that instant this old cliffside, here
45   and elsewhere, shook and toppled. But look down,
Fix your eyes on the valley, for we draw
     near to the river of blood which seethes all men
     who injured others by their violence."
O foolish wrath and blind cupidity,
50   that dig their spurs in us through our short lives,
     then cruelly drench us for eternity!
I saw a deep moat bent into an arc
     so that its arms encircled the whole plain,
     as my escort had said. Between this moat
55   And the foot of the cliff, hot on the trace
     ran centaurs, armed with arrows for their bows,
     as in the world they galloped at the chase.
When they saw us come down, they stopped at once
     and three of their platoon approached us with
60   bows slung, and arrows picked to fly. And one
Cried from afar, "You who descend the banks,
     which of the tortures have you come for? Tell
     from where you stand—if not, I draw my bow."
"We will make our response," my Teacher said,
65   "to Chiron, when we reach him. As for you,
     your will was always hot—to your own harm."
He nudged me, saying, "That one's Nessus, who
     died for his theft of lovely Deianira,
     and made himself a vengeance for himself.
70   He in the middle, gazing at his chest,
     is great Chiron, who nursed and raised Achilles;
     the other, Pholus, ever filled with wrath.
They go by thousands round about the moat,
     arrowing souls who try to pluck themselves
75   out of the blood more than their faults allot."

---

[45]*He:* Christ

So we approached those quick and sleek-limbed beasts;
    Chiron took out a dart, and with the nock
    smoothed back the beard from both sides of his jaws.
When he had thus uncovered his large mouth
80   he said to his companions, "Have you marked
    how things move at the touch of him in back?
The feet of dead men are not known for that."
    And my good guide, beside his chest by now
    where the two natures meld in company,
85   Replied, "He is alive indeed, and I
    must show him the dark valley all alone;
    not for delight, but by necessity.
One left her song of alleluia to
    give me this strange commission I fulfill;
90   he is no thief, nor I a thieving soul.
But by that power through which I move my steps
    along so wild a trail of savagery,
    give us one of your troop to keep beside us,
To show us where to wade across the stream,
95   and carry this one here upon his croup—
    he is no spirit walking through the air."
Chiron then turned aside by his right breast
    and said to Nessus, "Go back, be their guide.
    If troops get in your way, make them clear out."
100   Along the bubbling of the blood-red stream
    now with the trusty escort we moved on,
    where all the boiling spirits shriek and scream.
I saw some people plunged up to the brow,
    and, "These are tyrants," the huge centaur said,
105   "who thrust their hands for plunder and for blood.
Here they wail for their ruthlessness in crime;
    here's Alexander and fierce Dionysus
    who grieved his Sicily so long a time.
That forehead there whose fur is so jet-black
110   is Azzolino, and the blond one there,
    Obizzo of the Estes. For a fact,
He was snuffed by his bastard son above."
    At that I turned to the poet, but he said,
    "Let him speak to you first now. I will follow."
115   A little further on the centaur stopped
    beside a band who stuck out to the throat
    above that seething river. To one side,
He pointed out a solitary shade.

"That spirit[46] sabered, in the lap of God,
120   the heart which still drips blood beside the Thames."
Then I saw people lifting from the brew
   the head and all the trunk besides; of these
   I recognized the forms of quite a few.
At every step the blood subsided so,
125   until it cooked only the spirit's feet;
   that was our crossing for the realms below.
"Just as you see the bubbling river here
   grow shallower as we go," the centaur said,
   "you should know too that farther down the moat
130 The riverbed sinks lower, step by step,
   until you reach the deeper holes again
   where it is fitting that the tyrants groan.
The divine justice skewers on that side
   Attila the Hun, who was a scourge on earth,
135   Pyrrhus and Sextus, and perpetually
Squeezes the tears these boiling waves unbar
   from Rinier Pazzo and Rinier Corneto,
   who on the highways waged their thieving war."
We reached the banks; he turned and crossed the ford.

---

[46]*that spirit:* Henry de Montfort, who slew Henry, brother of the English king Edward I

CANTO THIRTEEN

*Dante and Virgil now find themselves in a dark, thorny forest. It is the second round of the seventh circle, that of the **Suicides** and the **Spoilers** of their own substance, who committed violence against themselves. Here the Suicides are imprisoned in thorn-trees, and the Spoilers are hunted through the forest by snapping dogs. Dante speaks to **Pier della Vigne**, a poet and courtier who slew himself rather than endure slander. Then they encounter the Spoilers **Lano da Siena** and **Jacopo da Sant'Andrea**—the latter bringing harm to the tree of an **unnamed Florentine**.*

    Nessus had not arrived at the far shore
      when we had made our way into a wood,
      a place unmarked by any kind of path.
    Its leaves not green, but dingy and dull black;
5   no slender limbs, but hunched with knots and gnarls;
      no hanging fruit, but sticks and poisonous thorns.
    Not those fierce beasts that hate the harrowed farms
      between Corneto and Cecina find
      such tangled boles and thickets harsh with brush.
10   Here the disgusting Harpies[47] build their nests
      who chased the Trojans from the Strophades
      with sad announcement of the harm to come.
    They have broad wings, a human face and neck,
      claws on the foot and feathers on the paunch.
15   They cry their wailing from those alien trees.
    "Before you enter further, you should know
      that you are now within the second round,"
      said my good Teacher, "and you shall be so
    Until you reach the horrifying sand.
20   Keep your eyes open, then, and you'll see things
      which if I told you of, you'd not believe."
    I heard from all sides heaving cries of woe
      but saw no one to make them anywhere,
      so I stood lost, bewildered. I believe
25   That he believed that I believed they came,
      so many voices, from behind those trunks,
      from people hiding on account of us.
    And so the Teacher said, "If you snap clean
      some little twig from off one of these plants,
30   the thoughts you're thinking will be left like stumps."
    At that I reached my hand out gingerly

---

[47]*Harpies:* in classical mythology, ministers of divine vengeance, part woman, part vulture. For their chasing the Trojans, see the *Aeneid* 3.210–35.

and from a thorn-tree plucked a little branch
and its trunk cried, "Why do you hack at me?"
When it had darkened with its dripping blood
35   it cried anew, "Why do you mangle me?
Isn't there any pity in your soul?
Once we were men, now we are stubs and stakes.
Your hand might well have felt more sympathy
even if we had been the souls of snakes."
40   As when you light one end of a green log,
the air inside that forces its way out
will squeak and sputter at the other end,
So from the splintered limb came forth at once
both blood and speech; at which I let it drop,
45   and stood there like a man in fear. "If he
Could have believed at first, O injured soul,"
my guide so wise responded, "what
he's only read about within my rhyme,
Never would he have stretched his hand against you.
50   But since the thing was unbelievable,
I made him do what I myself regret.
But tell him who you were: to mend the deed
maybe he'll make your memory green again
back in the world above, when he returns."
55   "You speak so sweetly, I must take the bait,"
the trunk replied. "May it not weigh you down
if I should lime myself and speak a bit.
I was the guardian of Frederick's[48] heart,
the Emperor's trusted man who held the keys,
60   locking, unlocking with so soft an art
I stole most of the other courtiers from
his secrets. In that glorious duty I
kept faith so well, I lost my sleep, and wore
My pulse away. But she who never turns
65   her eyes from Caesar's house—the harlot Envy,
vice of the court and death for all mankind,
Inflamed against me every other soul,
and the inflamed inflamed Augustus[49] so,
that my glad honors turned to mournful gloom.
70   My spirit, relishing the taste of scorn,
thinking that I could flee their scorn in death,
made me against myself, though just, unjust.

---

[48]*Frederick:* Holy Roman Emperor, Frederick II
[49]*Augustus:* i.e., Frederick⁴

By the bizarre roots of this tree I swear
    I never broke the faith I owed my lord,
75   so worthy to be honored by all men.
If either of you goes back to the world,
    prop up my reputation, which still lies
    beneath the blow that Envy dealt it then."
The poet paused a while, then turned to me.
80   "Since he is silent now, don't lose the time,
    but speak, if you would like to ask him more."
But I replied, "Whatever you believe
    will satisfy me, ask it—I cannot,
    such is the pity pressing on my heart."
85 So he began, "O soul locked in this cell—
    so let him freely do you the good turn
    you have requested—may it please you, tell
How the soul's grafted here inside these knobs,
    and, if you can, if ever anyone
90   can shuck such knotted members and go free."
Then the trunk gusted out a sigh of grief,
    turning the breath into a voice, and spoke,
    "The answer to your question will be brief.
When the ferocious soul that plucks itself
95   from its own body leaves it and departs,
    judge Minos sends it to this seventh shelf.
Into the woods it falls, no chosen place.
    Wherever Fortune's crossbow slings it, there
    it puts its roots down like the rankest weed.
100 It shoots into a sapling, a wild plant.
    The Harpies chew its foliage for their feed,
    cause pain, and for that pain create a vent.
We too will come to take our sloughed-off skins,
    but none of us will put them on again:
105   it is not just to have what one has stripped.
Here we will drag our bodies through the dust,
    and on this sad wood's branches they will hang,
    each by the thorns of its assaulting soul."
We were still waiting for the broken branch,
110   believing that he wanted to say more,
    when we were startled by a sudden noise,
As when a hunter posting in the woods
    senses at once the wild boar and the chase
    come near—he hears the beast, the trampled brush—
115 So look there now, two spirits at our left,
    naked and clawed to ribbons, hard in flight,

smashing through all the thickets in the woods.
The one in front: "Run quickly, quickly, death!"
  The other one, who seemed to lag too far,
120   hollered, "Lano, your legs were not so deft
In the tilt at the Toppo riverbank!"[50]
  Then—failing in his breath perhaps—he made
  himself a tangled hideout with a bush.
Behind, were all the forest could contain
125   of black bitches running in ravenous greed,
  as fast as greyhounds that have slipped the chain.
Into the squatting soul they sunk their teeth
  and tore apart his muscles into shreds;
  then carried off those members ripped in pain.
130 And then my escort took me by the hand
  and led me to the little shrub that wept
  for all its bloody branches, torn in vain.
"O Jacopo," said he, "of Sant'Andrea!
  How did it help to make a screen of me?
135   Is it my fault you led a wicked life?"
My Teacher then approached the soul, and said,
  "Who were you, who through all your broken sticks
  puff out your sorrowing speech with drops of blood?"
And he to us: "O souls who have arrived
140   to witness the dishonor done to me,
  the slaughter that has torn my leaves away,
Gather them at the foot of this sad bush.
  My city[51] changed its patron from the god
  of war to John the Baptist, on its coins—
145 For which his art will ever make her grieve.
  And if there were no fragments of Mars left
  in stone upon the bridge over the Arno,
Those citizens who built her base anew
  upon the ashes left by the great Hun[52]
150   would find that all their labor was in vain.
I made myself a gallows of my house."

---

[50]*tilt . . . riverbank:* A battle in 1288, in which Lano sought his own death because he had squandered all his means
[51]*My city:* Florence, whose gold coins were stamped with the image of John the Baptist; Dante decries the loss of courtly valor and the emergence of a society based on greed
[52]*the great Hun:* Attila is meant, though it was the Goth Totila who actually besieged Florence in the 5th century.

CANTO FOURTEEN

*Taking leave of the Florentine, Dante and Virgil move on to the third round of the seventh circle, that of the **Violent against God.** These are punished in a **rain of fire** which kindles the desert sands beneath them. They are also divided into three groups, the first of which, the **Blasphemers,** must lie flat on the burning sands. After Virgil rebukes the blasphemer **Capaneus,** he identifies the five rivers of the other world, and describes how the four that flow in Hell spring from the tears of the **Old Man of Crete.***

> The love I cherished for my native land
>   so wrung my heart, I gathered the strewn fronds
>   and gave them back to him, whose voice had grown
> Already faint. Then to the edge we came,
> 5   passing the second to the third round, where
>   a fearful work of justice can be seen.
> To show most clearly these unheard-of things,
>   I say we had arrived at a flat moor
>   whose bed was bare, refusing every plant.
> 10 The woeful forest garlands it about,
>   as it was circled by the dismal moat.
>   We halted in our steps right at the rim.
> Its floor was all one packed and parched expanse
>   of sand—of fashion like the Libyan plains
> 15 pressed by the feet of Cato long ago.
> Vengeance of God! How much should you be feared
>   by everyone who reads my tale and learns
>   of what was made so clear before my eyes!
> For there I saw great flocks of naked souls
> 20 mightily weeping in their misery,
>   subject, apparently, to different rules:
> Some lay flat on their backs upon the ground;
>   and some were sitting huddled at the knees;
>   and others roved about continually.
> 25 The greatest number were of those who ran;
>   the least, who took their tortures lying down—
>   but their tongues were the freest in their cries.
> Over the desert, in a gentle fall,
>   there rained broad flakes of fire, as in the Alps
> 30 the snow comes falling on a windless day.
> As in those torrid parts of India
>   over his army Alexander saw
>   flames fall from Heaven and strike the earth still strong,
> For which, looking ahead, he had his troops

35   trample them out before they fed each other—
    easier to extinguish one by one—
   So the eternal fire descended here,
    sparking the sand like fuel beneath the flint,
    doubling the sorrows of the damned. Without
40   A moment's pause their miserable hands
    jittered their polka here there everywhere
    brushing the burns of fresh flakes from their skin.
   "Teacher," I started, "you who overcome
    all things, except the stubborn demons who
45   came out against us at their kingdom's gate,
   Who's that huge one who doesn't seem to mind
    the fire, but lies and twists his face for spite,
    so that the rains don't seem to ripen him?"
   And he himself, who picked up what I said,
50   hearing me ask my guide about him, cried,
    "What I was living, so am I still, dead!
   Jove can go break his blacksmith's[53] back with work
    from whom in wrath he took the thunderbolt
    that ran me through on my last day on earth—
55   Or wear the others out in endless shifts
    under Mount Aetna at the pitch-black forge
    hollering, 'Vulcan, help, I need your help!',
   As he did on the Phlegran battlefield,
    hurling his lance through me with all his force—
60   he'd get from me no joy in his revenge."
   At that my guide spoke out so loud and strong,
    I had not heard him speak so loud before:
    "Your pride has not cooled off, O Capaneus,
   And in that you are punished all the more!
65   No other torture than your own mad rage
    would bring your fury its most fitting pain."
   He turned to me then, with his lips composed,
    and said, "One of the seven kings was he
    who besieged Thebes. The man held God in scorn,
70   Still thinks Him worthless, as his words attest—
    but, as I told him, his despisings are
    the fittest decoration for his chest.
   Now follow me, and watch that you don't set
    your feet upon the scorching sand, but keep
75   a straight path at the margin of the wood."

---

[53]*blacksmith:* Vulcan, the crippled blacksmith of the Greco-Roman gods, whose forge was said to be inside the volcanic Mount Aetna

We walked in silence, till we came upon
    a narrow river gushing from the forest.
    It makes me shiver yet, so red it was!
As hot springs bubble up at Bulicame,
80   where whores divert the brook to separate baths,
    so did that stream cut through the desert sand.
Both its embankments and its bed were stone,
    as were the channel's margins on each side,
    so I surmised we'd cross the desert here.
85   "Of all the things I've shown you up to now,
    from when we entered through the gate of Hell,
    crossing whose threshold no one is refused,
Nothing you've seen is as remarkable
    as is this river here before your eyes,
90   which cools and quenches all the flames above it."
This from my guide; at which I begged him to
    let me partake more largely of that food
    for which he had aroused the appetite.
"Far in the sea a country lies in waste,"
95   the poet then began, "whose name is Crete.
    Under its ancient king[54] the world was chaste.
There stood a mountain lush with leaf and spring,
    Mount Ida, as they called it in those days;
    now it is barren, like an aged thing.
100   The goddess Rhea chose it for a crib
    to trust her son[55] to, and, to hide him better,
    her followers made a racket when he wailed.
Deep in that hill a huge old man stands tall;
    his back turned to the delta of the Nile,
105   he stares at Rome, as at his looking-glass.
His head is fashioned all of finest gold;
    his arms and chest are silver unalloyed;
    then he is bronze down to the torso's fork,
Below which all is iron, choice and pure,
110   except his right foot, which is mere baked clay.
    He leans more weight on that, than on the other.
Each part, except the gold, is rotted through
    by a long fissure made by trickling tears,
    which form a stream, and tunnel through that cave.
115   They fall into this valley, rock to rock;
    make Acheron, and Styx, and Phlegethon,

---

[54]*ancient king:* Saturn, in the so-called Golden Age
[55]*her son:* Jupiter

then they go lower by this narrow duct
Till there are no more mountains to descend,
    where they make Cocytus. What that dead pool is,
120   you will soon see. Here let the matter end."
And I to him: "Then if this present stream
    comes guttering down from our world up above,
    why do we see it only at this hem?"
And he to me: "You know this place is round,
125   and even though you've traveled a long way
    and tended to the left while going down,
You have not yet gone all around the ring.
    So let it not bring wonder to your face
    should there appear before us some new thing."
130 "Teacher, where can you find the Phlegethon
    and Lethe? Those tears form the first, you say,
    and you are silent on the other one."
"All of your questions bring delight to me,
    but the boiling red stream," he said, "should solve
135   your first one with no trouble. You shall see
The River Lethe, but not in this gulch—
    you'll see it where the spirits go to bathe
    when their repented sins are wiped away.
But now it's time for us to leave these woods.
140   Follow behind me on the walk of stone;
    there is no burning sand upon the rim,
And the flames are extinguished overhead."

CANTO FIFTEEN

*Still in the third round of the seventh circle, walking along the channel's wall, Dante
and Virgil meet the second group of the **Violent against God: the Sodomites**, who
must run continually through the hailing fire. One of their group, a Florentine
politician and poet named **Brunetto Latini**, recognizes his protégé Dante and
discusses with him Dante's own future and that of Florence. After naming some of
the others who shared his sin, Brunetto must hurry away.*

Along one of the rims of stone we came,
    where the mist of the river makes a shade,
    shielding the water and the banks from flame.
As do the Dutch who fear the hurling tide
5   smashing the coast between Bruges and Wissant—
    they build a dike to shunt the sea aside;
And as the Paduans along the Brent
    defend their towns and villages before

the mountains of Carinthia feel the heat,
10   In such a fashion were these bulwarks made,
     although their master-builder made them not
     so thick or tall—whoever he might be.
We had already left the woods behind
     so far, that even had I turned to look,
15   I never could have made out where it was,
When following the dike we met a band
     of spirits coming towards us, and each one
     stared at us hard as one is wont to stare
At someone in the dark of the new moon,
20   knitting their brows to keep us keen in sight
     as an old tailor threads the needle's eye.
And while this family was watching us
     one of them knew me and he seized me by
     my tunic's hem and cried, "What wonder's this!"
25   And I, when he'd stretched out his arm to me,
     so fixed my eyes upon his crusted looks
     that even the charred features could not keep
My intellect from recognizing them,
     and lowering my hand towards his face
30   I answered, "Ser Brunetto, are *you* here?"
Said he, "May it not trouble you, my son,
     if Brunetto Latino turns a while
     to walk with you, and lets the file go on."
And I: "I beg you, please, with all my heart!
35   And if you wish me to sit down with you,
     if he with whom I go is pleased, I shall."
"My son," said he, "whoever of this flock
     stops for an instant, lies a hundred years
     and cannot fan away the flames that strike.
40   So let's go on; I'll follow at your feet,
     then will I join my company again,
     who go and mourn their everlasting loss."
I did not dare to come down from that road
     to walk beside him, but I bowed my head
45   as one who, walking, shows his reverence.
And he began, "What chance or destiny
     has brought you here before your final day?
     And who is he who leads your pilgrimage?"
"Up there in life beneath the quiet stars
50   I lost my way," I answered, "in a valley,
     before I reached the fullness of my age.
I turned my shoulders on it yesterday:

this soul appeared as I was falling back,
 and by the road through Hell he leads me home."
55 "Follow your star and you will never fail
 to find your glorious port," he said to me,
 "if in that lovely life I judged you well.
And if I hadn't died when you were young,
 seeing the heavens smile on you so kindly,
60 I would have given you strength to do your work.
But those ungrateful people of ill-will
 who in old days came down from Fiesole[56]
 and smack still of the granite and the hill,
Will grow to hate you for your doing good—
65 justly so, for among the bitter sorbs
 the sweet fig should not bloom. About their brood,
The world has long reported them as blind—
 a people greedy, envious, and proud.
 Clean yourself of the customs of their kind!
70 Such honor will your fortune hold for you
 that both sides will be hungry for your life,
 but let the grass be far from the goat's tooth.
Let the beasts of Fiesole provender
 upon themselves, and never touch the plant,
75 if any can still sprout in their manure,
Wherein there lives again the holy seed
 of those old Romans who remained behind
 when men had built that nest of vice and greed."[57]
"If I could have my wishes heard in full,"
80 I answered him, "you would not even now
 be banished from our life. It moves my heart,
But in my mind your image is set firm,
 how like a father, gentle and beloved,
 you taught me in the world from time to time
85 How man achieves an everlasting name;
 and in my words as long as I shall live
 I shall declare my gratitude to you.
I'll write down what you tell of my life's course
 and save it, with the other prophecies,
90 to be glossed by a Lady[58] who will know—
If I arrive to see her. Let this much

---

[56]*Fiesole:* mountain-town above Florence; Dante is suggesting that the true founders of Florence were not the noble Romans who dwelt there first, but the uncouth Fiesolans who came later
[57]*nest . . . greed:* i.e., Florence
[58]*Lady:* Beatrice

be clear to you: unless my conscience scolds me,
    I'm ready for whatever Fortune wills.
My ears have heard such pledges made before.
95   Let Fortune turn her wheel which way she likes
    for all that—and the farmer turn his hoe!"
And then my Teacher turned his cheek to me,
    catching my glance behind him on the right.
    "One who takes note has listened well," said he.
100   Continuing with Ser Brunetto, I
    walk on and ask him of the worthiest
    and the most famous of his company.
And he to me: "To know of some, is well;
    it merits praise to pass the rest in silence;
105   the time's too short for such a tale to tell.
Know, in a word, that they were scholars all,
    great men of letters, clerks of wide renown,
    made filthy in the world by the same fall.
Pedagogue Priscian's with that wretched mob,
110   Francis d'Accorso with him; and note there,
    in case you hanker after such a scab,
Him whom the Servant of all Servants[59] switched
    from Arno's see to Bacchiglione's, where
    he left his sinews stretched in wickedness.
115   I'd tell of more, but can't go further on
    talking and walking with you, for I see
    fresh smoke arising from the sands ahead.
People approach with whom I must not be.
    In one thing I still live: I ask no more,
120   but trust my *Treasure* to your memory."
Then he turned round, and seemed like those who strip
    to race for the green banner through the fields
    about Verona; and of those he seemed
The one who wins, and not the one who loses.

---

[59] *Servant of all Servants:* the Pope; here, Boniface VIII, who moved the sodomite bishop Andrea da Mozzi from Florence to Vicenza, on the River Bacchiglione

CANTO SIXTEEN

*Continuing in the third round of the seventh ring, that of the **Violent against God**,
the poets encounter **three noble Florentines,** who discuss with Dante the corruption
of their native city. Moving on towards the precipice that forms the edge of this ring,
Virgil asks Dante for his belt and casts it into the chasm below, summoning up the
monster **Geryon,** symbol of **Fraud.***

We had now come where one can hear the tumble
   of rushing waters into the next ring,
   as bees about the beehive hum and rumble;
When three shades hastening all together went
5   off from a squad of spirits passing by
   under the rain of bitter punishment.
They came toward us and cried out this demand:
   "Stop, you who in your habit seem to be
   another citizen of our crooked land!"
10 Alas, what scars I saw on every member,
   old and fresh wounds, carved into them by fire!
   It gives me sadness even to remember.
My learned master waited on their cries;
   turning his eyes to me, "Hold on," he said.
15   "One should be courteous to men like these.
And if this place's nature sent no flame
   arrowing down, I'd say it was less fit
   that they should run to you, than you to them."
They recommenced their ancient litany
20 while we were waiting; when they reached our side
   a wheel they fashioned of themselves all three.
As naked champions, muscles slicked with oil,
   warily searching where and when to seize
   their chance before the jabs and punches fly—
25 So these wheeled in a ring; each turned his eye
   in my direction, cocked his neck to go
   opposite to his feet, continually.
And, "If the miseries of this shifting sand
   cause you to hold our prayers and us in scorn,"
30 began one, "and our features scorched and skinned,
Still, let our reputations bend your soul
   to tell us who you are, with living feet
   scraping securely through the pit of Hell.
The man whose tracks you see me trample on,
35 though he goes naked, scalded of his hair,
   was of a higher rank than you believe:

The grandson of the womanly Gualdrada,
    Guido Guerra his name; and in his life
    he achieved much by judgment, and the sword.
40   He who comes after me to thresh the sand
    was Tegghiaio Aldobrandi, whose advice
    should have been welcomed in the world above.
I who am crucified with them, in life
    was Jacopo Rusticucci. Far the worst
45   was the harm done me by my shrewish wife."
Had I a covering from the rain of fire
    I'd have leapt off and cast myself among them,
    and think my Teacher would have suffered it—
But since I'd have been burnt and baked, my fear
50   overpowered the good will that made me crave
    to clasp within my arms the three down there.
"Sorrow, not loathing," I began to say,
    "had fixed itself so deep within my heart
    it will be long before it's stripped away,
55   And did so just as soon as he, my lord,
    uttered the words that made me think that men
    of honor, such as you, were coming near.
I am your countryman, and ever have
    heard tell of your good works and honored names—
60   heard, and recounted them with reverent love.
I leave the chaff and go for the sweet fruit
    promised me by my guide, whose word is true:
    but I must fall to Hell's dead center first."
"May your limbs long enjoy your soul as guide,"
65   the spirit then responded, "and your fame
    shine forth its light long after you have died,
Tell us if courtesy and valor dwell
    within our city as they used to do,
    or if they have departed from them all.
70   Borsiere, who came to suffer here with us
    not long since, and who goes there with his troop,
    troubles us deeply with the bitter news."
"Outsiders and their sudden wash of wealth
    beget in you such arrogance and excess,
75   Florence, you feel already your ill-health."
So I cried out, with proud and lifted head.
    As men change glances when they meet the truth,
    so did those three, on hearing what I said.
"If you shall ever pay so slight a fee
80   to satisfy a question," all replied,

"happy are you whose speech is bold and free!
Yet if you do escape this murky lair
   and turn to see the lovely stars again,
   when you'll rejoice in saying, 'I was there,'
85 Please, speak about us to the living." Then
   they broke their wheel and fled on feet as swift
   as slender wings. One could not say "amen"
As quickly as the three had disappeared,
   so to my Teacher also it seemed time
90   for us to take our leave. I followed him,
And not long had we ventured, when so near
   was the roar of the water's cataract,
   words were almost impossible to hear.
As that stream[60] in the western Appennines,
95   first among those that from Mount Viso fall
   in the direction of the rising sun,
Called "Quietwater" in the hills above
   before it tumbles down the valleys to
   its bed at Forli, where that name is gone,
100 Thunders at Saint Benedict of the Alps
   because it plummets at a single leap
   where it should brim over a thousand steps—
So too down from a shattered side of cliff
   echoed the crash of that polluted brook.
105   Much longer, and it would have drummed us deaf.
About my waist I wore a rope for belt
   and once or twice considered using it
   to snare the leopard with the gaudy pelt.
But when I'd loosened it and slipped it off,
110   as my guide had commanded me to do,
   I gave it to him, knotted and wound up.
At that he swung about on his right side
   and flung it far away over the edge
   of the deep chasm before us. To myself
115 I said, "Some strange new thing must correspond
   to the strange gesture my good Teacher makes
   and seconds with his gaze." Ah, men, beware!
How watchful you must be when you are near
   one who not only sees the action, but
120   can peer beneath and read your thoughts themselves!
He said to me: "You will soon see arise
   what I await, and what you only dream.

---

[60]*that stream*: the Montone, called the Acquacheta ("Quietwater") near its source

Soon it will be unveiled before your eyes."
Knowing a truth whose face appears a lie,
125   a man should always keep his lips shut tight
long as he can, lest he be tagged with shame
Though he has told the truth: but I cannot
keep silent here; and, Reader, by the notes
of this my Comedy, I swear—and may
130   They keep in favor long—through that thick air
I saw a figure swimming in the night,
such as would stun the surest heart with wonder,
Just as a diver surfacing, who goes
below to pry an anchor loose from rocks
135   or something hidden in the sea, extends
His arms and tucks his legs to thrust again.

CANTO SEVENTEEN

The monster of Fraud, **Geryon,** *lands on the brink. Virgil instructs Dante to walk further along the stone dike, to witness the last group of the* **Violent against God:** *the nameless* **Usurers,** *who take the rain of fire sitting down, and who can only be identified by the insignia of the purses hung round their necks. When Dante returns, the poets descend into the circle of the* **Fraudulent,** *flying on the back of Geryon.*

"Behold the beast with the barbed tail, who flies
past mountains, scattering armies, smashing walls!
Behold the beast whose stench sickens the world!"
So did my guide begin, speaking to me
5   and signaling the beast to come to land
at the end of the stone walk on the dike.
And that disgusting likeness of deceit
arrived, and lugged his head and chest ashore,
but did not draw his tail onto the beach.
10   He had the features of an honest man,
so kindly was his countenance at the skin,
but the trunk down below was serpentine;
His paws were furry to the shoulder-tops,
and his back and his breast and both his sides
15   were parti-colored all in whorls and knots.
Not Turks nor Tartars weaving carpets weave
more colors for their groundwork or their fringe;
Arachne never set them on her loom.
As barges sometimes mooring at the shore
20   stand part within the water, part on land,
and as among those Germans swilling beer

The beaver dips his tail into the brook
to seize his prey, this worst of beasts stood here
on the stone rim, the cut-off of the sand.
25 Out into empty space it flicked its tail,
coiling the venomous fork to keep it high
which armed its bone-point like a scorpion's flail.
"Now we must veer a little," said my guide,
"and take our way down to that vicious beast
30 who waits there, crouching." So to the right side
We turned, descending down the bank of stone,
and took nine or ten steps upon its verge
to keep clear of the sand and hailing flame.
And when we had come up to it, I saw
35 souls sitting a bit further up the dunes
near the edge of the chasm. My teacher then:
"In order that you may bring back with you
the full experience of this round," he said,
"go and observe the habits of that crew.
40 But clip your conversation, keep it short.
While you are gone I'll haggle with this beast
that he may yield the use of his strong back."
And so along the seventh circle's cape
I went on, all alone, until I came
45 to where the mournful people sat in pain.
Sorrowing streams broke from their eyes, and here
and there with restless hands they tried to get
relief from fire-flakes or the scalding ground,
Not unlike dogs who in the sweltering days
50 snap with the snout or scratch with flurrying paw
when they are bit by fleas or gnats or flies.
When I had turned my eyes to stare at some
upon whose faces fell the dolorous fire,
not one could I make out; yet I observed
55 That round the neck of each one hung a pouch
of its own color and insignia.
Each seemed to gorge his eyes upon that feast.
And as I walked beside them, noting well,
I saw in azure on a purse of gold
60 a face and rampant figure of a lion.
The chariot of my vision rolling on,
I saw another purse as red as blood
showing a goose whiter than butter. One
Who bore a fat and farrowing sow of blue
65 for the insignia of his silver sack,

said, "What are you doing in this gutter, you?
Get lost. And just because you're still alive,
   know that Vitaliano from my town
will someday sit in Hell at my left side.
70   I am a Paduan with these Florentines.
   They thunder and they thunder in my ears,
   'Salute the coming of the sovereign knight
Who brings the bag with the three goats!'" He made
   a face then, screwing up his mouth and sticking
75   his tongue out, like an ox that licks its nose.
Fearing that if I stayed much longer there
   I'd irk the man who warned me to be quick,
   I turned my back on those defeated souls.
I found my leader had already climbed
80   upon the hunch of that fierce animal,
   and said to me, "Be fearless now and strong.
Now we go down the pit by stairs like these.
   Climb on in front— I want to stay between
   to guard you from the venom of its tail."
85   As one who shudders with the four-day chills
   of quartan fever, nails already blue,
   shivers all over at the sight of shade,
So did I shudder at his words, but shame
   rose up against me with its threats which make
90   a servant brave before his valiant lord.
I took my seat upon its cursed back,
   trying, trying to say, but my voice couldn't
   come as I thought, "Please, hold on to me tight."
But he who came so often to my aid
95   in times of doubt and peril, when I mounted,
   secured me with his arms and bore me up
And called out, "You can go now, Geryon.
   Be slow on the descent, keep the turns wide.
   Remember the new weight you carry down."
100   And as a little boat from off the quay
   slips steadily backwards, so he shoved away,
   and when he felt himself entirely free
He swung his tail around to meet his chest,
   swerved and stretched out and darted like an eel,
105   sweeping the air behind him with his paws.
I don't think Phaethon felt greater fright
   when he let drop his chariot's reins, and seared
   that streak into the sky, which we still see,
Nor when poor Icarus felt the melting wax

110   unfeathering himself about the loins,
           his father crying, "You're going the wrong way!",
       Than was the fear I felt when I saw air
           on every side of me, and every sight
           extinguished but the savage serpent there.
115   Slowly, slowly it swam and took its course
           wheeling, descending; as I could not tell
           but for the breeze below, and on my cheek.
       Now on the right hand I could hear the gorge
           thunder beneath us with a horrible crash,
120   and so I leaned and stared into the gulf.
       Then I was more afraid of falling off
           for I saw flames below and heard the wails,
           trembled, and huddled tighter with my thighs.
       Now I saw what could not be seen before,
125   marking our turning and our plummeting
           by the great evils nearing on all sides.
       As the trained falcon long upon the wing
           causes the falconer to cry, "You fall!"
           when without catching sight of call or prey
130   It droops down in a hundred languid turns
           where it had taken off with speed, and perches
           far from its master, peevish and dismayed,
       So by the very foot of the sheer rock
           Geryon landed at the bottom and—
135   free of the burden of our persons—shot
       Vanishing like an arrow from the string.

CANTO EIGHTEEN

*Dante and Virgil enter the **eighth circle,** that of the **Fraudulent.** Called **Malebolge,**
this circle is itself divided into ten pockets or ditches, each punishing a different
sort of fraud. In the **first ditch,** Dante sees **Seducers** and **Panderers** whipped by
demons; there he meets **Venedico Caccianemico,** and Virgil directs his attention to
Jason, the Argonaut. Crossing to the **second ditch** by means of a rock-formation that
runs like a bridge from end to end of Malebolge, they see the **Flatterers,** plunged in
excrement, among whom they identify **Alessio Interminei** and the whore **Thais.***

       There is a place in Hell called Malebolge,
           "Pouches of Evil," all of iron-gray stone,
           just like the ring that circles it above.
       Right in the center of this wicked plain
5   a broad and plummeting basin drops from sight—
           its structure I will speak of, in its place.

This strip of Hell that thus remains goes round
   between the hole and the hard precipice;
   into ten separate pockets it is split.
10 As where defenders of a city's walls
   dig trench on trench about the fortresses,
   the rings of ditches form a pattern there
Similar to the pattern made by these;
   and as from sill to the next stronghold's sill
15   small bridges lead the way to the last edge,
So from the cliff's base rock-ribs cut their way
   across the gutters here and up their banks,
   converging at the hole that chops them short.
Here, shaken from the monster Geryon's back,
20   we found ourselves; the poet then set out
   to the left, and I followed in his track.
On our right hand we saw new misery,
   new torments, and new handlers of the lash,
   and this first pocket was stuffed full with them.
25 The sinners at the bottom were all nude:
   those near approached us while the far ones went
   in our direction, but with greater strides.
As Romans in the year of jubilee,
   for the great hosts of pilgrims on the bridge,
30   found a way to move traffic steadily,
For on one side the travelers have to face
   Castle Sant'Angelo, going towards Saint Peter's,
   while those upon the other face the hill.
Over the blackish stone and everywhere
35   I saw horned devils ply their thick-boled whips,
   thirsty for blood, lashing the sinners' backs.
Ah, how the first strokes made them lift their heels!
   Yes, no one stood and waited for another
   or yet a third! And as I walked along,
40 My glance happened to light on one of them
   and I broke out directly, "For a fact,
   I haven't fasted from the sight of him."
To get a better view I set my feet,
   and my guide, sweet and courteous, halted too,
45   permitting me to walk a short way back.
And that scourged spirit thought to hide himself,
   lowering his brow. It did him little good!
   "O you who cast your eyes upon the earth,
If your face and its features aren't false,
50   are Venedico Caccianemico.

But what has dipped you in so sharp a sauce?"
And he to me: "Against my will I'll tell,
    for your clear speech recalls that world of old
    and has a power upon me to compel.
55 I was the man who pushed Ghisolabella
    my sister to the bed of the Marchese,
    no matter how they tell the dirty tale.
I'm not the only Bolognese who weeps
    here in this ditch—the place is full of us!
60   More than the tongues that say not 'si' but 'sipa'
Between the rivers Savena and Reno.
    Want witness for it, something you can trust?
    Only recall the avarice of our hearts."
So he spoke, but a demon slashed at him
65   with his rough horsewhip, crying, "Off with you,
    Pimp! We're no whores for you to swindle here!"
Then I rejoined my leader and my guide,
    and soon we came upon a place where juts
    a stone reef from the chasm's rocky side.
70 We scrambled up this bridge quite easily,
    and turning right upon its jagged back
    we left those endless circlings all behind.
When we were at the summit of its arch
    where it gapes underneath and gives the flogged
75   a passage through, my guide said, "Stop and let
Sight of these others born in evil hour
    strike you. You haven't seen their faces yet,
    for they were walking the same way we walked."
So from that ancient bridge we watched the track
80   of sinners from the other band; here too
    the lash made sure their paces were not slack.
And my good Teacher, though I did not ask,
    said, "Look at that great figure coming there,
    who does not seem to shed a tear for pain.
85 What kingliness his image still retains!
    Jason—who with his brave heart and his wits
    deprived the Colchians of the golden fleece.
He came ashore upon the isle of Lemnos
    after the ruthless women boldly put
90   their fathers, sons, and brothers all to death.
With acts of love and words of sweetest skill
    he fooled the pretty girl Hypsiphile,
    who'd fooled the rest in leading them to kill.
He left her great with child and all alone;

95   such fault condemns him to such punishment.
       What he did to Medea also earns
Its vengeance here. Seducers go with him,
       all liars. That's enough for you to know
       of this first ditch and those clamped in its fangs."
100   Our narrow path over the bridge now met
       the second bank, and where they crossed they made
       a buttress for another arch beyond.
Here in the second pouch we came upon
       people who whimpered, sniveling, runny-nosed,
105   who slapped and smacked themselves with open palms.
The walls were fungus-crusted, thick with mold
       which rose in vapors from below and clung,
       making a nauseous brawl with eyes and nose.
So hollow was the bottom of this pouch
110   we had no vantage point to see a soul
       until we climbed the summit of the arch.
So there we climbed, and in the trench I saw
       people plunged deep in just the sort of dung
       you dump from human privies and latrines.
115   And while I searched the bottom with my eyes
       I saw a man, his head so shit-besmeared
       you couldn't tell if he were lay or priest,
Who yelled: "Why does your hunger make you choke
       to stare at me and not the other filth?"
120   And I: "Because, if I remember well,
I saw you when you wore your haircut dry,
       Alessio Interminei, from Lucca!
       That's why I gaze upon you more than all."
Then he, smacking his pumpkin-pate for spite,
125   "They've sunk me down here, all my flatteries,
       with which my mouth was never plastered tight."
And after that my guide, "Pray, stretch your gaze,"
       he said to me, "a little further on,
       until your eye can reach the filthy face
130   Of that hair-rumpled and disgusting wench
       who claws herself with shit beneath her nails,
       now standing up, now squatting on her haunch.
Thais she is, the whore whose lover asked,
       "Do I have lots of what it takes to please you?"
135   and she replied, "Oh yes, you're marvelous!"
I think our sights have had their fill of this."

CANTO NINETEEN

*Dante and Virgil pass to the **third ditch of Malebolge,** where the **Simonists**—those who use church offices for profiteering—are plunged headfirst in font-like holes in the stone, with the soles of their feet anointed and set afire. Here Dante meets the soul of **Pope Nicholas III,** who at first mistakes him for **Boniface VIII,** then prophesies Boniface's damnation and that of a succeeding pope, **Clement V.** Dante replies with a vigorous attack against the corruption of the papacy.*

O Simon Magus,[61] O you wretched crew
 of his disciples! The things of God should be
 espoused to righteousness and love, and you
Rapacious wolves, you pander them for gold,
5 foul them for silver! Sound the trumpet now
 for you—for this third pocket is your place.
We had already reached the following tomb,
 climbing the ledge until the spot we reached
 hung plumb above the middle of the moat.
10 O highest Wisdom, how much art you show
 in Heaven, on earth, and in the evil world!
 How justly does your power apportion all!
I saw that on both walls and on the ground
 the livid iron stone was full of holes,
15 all of a size, and every one was round.
No bigger, and no narrower they appeared
 than the holes in my lovely baptistery
 of San Giovanni, made for holy fonts,
One of which, and not many years ago,
20 I had to break to save a boy from drowning—
 and let men take that for the stamp of truth.
Out of the mouth of every hole there stuck
 a sinner's feet and legs up to the fat
 above the knee; the rest remained inside.
25 And everywhere the soles were set afire,
 making them kick and wrench their joints so hard
 they'd have snapped twisted ropes or cords in two.
As flame upon a thing anointed goes
 darting and dancing on the peel, so here
30 flames flickered from their heels up to the toes.
"Who's that one, Teacher, in his painful wrath,

---

[61]*Simon Magus:* Simon was a magician who wished to purchase from the apostles the gift of the Holy Spirit (Acts 8:9–24); he gives his name to the sin of turning church offices to profit.

kicking more than the others of his lot,"
said I, "whose soles are licked by redder flame?"
"Come with me, if you like," he said, "along
35   that farther bank, which slopes more easily.
You'll learn of him and of his twisted wrong."
"As a thing pleases you, it pleases me.
    You are my lord, you know I never part
from what you will, and know my silent thoughts."
40 And so we crossed to the fourth bank, and turned,
    descending by the weaker hand until
we reached the narrow-walked and riddled base.
My gentle Teacher kept me by his hip
    till we came to the rotten hole of him
45   who mourned his evil living with his shanks.
"Whoever you may be whose up is down,
    O wretched spirit planted like a stake,"
said I, "give us a few words, if you can."
There I stood like the friar who hears the sins
50   of a faithless assassin, head in grave,
who calls him back to hold death off awhile,
And he cried, "Are you standing there already,
    you standing there already, Boniface?[62]
The future's book deceived me by some years!
55 So quickly glutted, are you, with the wealth
    for which you didn't fear to wed by guile
the lovely Bride,[63] then rend and sell her flesh?"
I was as one who takes for mockery
    someone's response he does not understand,
60   and cannot fathom how he should reply.
Then Virgil said, "Say this to him at once:
    'I am not he, I am not he you think.'"
As he instructed, so was my response.
At that the spirit writhed and wrenched his feet
65   and, sighing, with a voice of grief and tears,
replied, "Well then what do you want from me?
If you're so interested in who I was
    that you've come down the embankment just for that,
know that I wore the mantle of the Pope;
70 and was Orsini, "the bear's son," indeed,
    so eager to advance my cubs, on earth
I stashed great wealth and here I stash myself.

---

[62]*Boniface:* Pope Boniface VIII
[63]*the lovely Bride:* the Church

Under my head the others all are crammed—
   my predecessor popes in simony,
75   squashed flat into the fissure of the stone.
I in my turn will tumble lower when
   he comes, the one whom I mistook you for
   when I asked what I asked so suddenly.
But longer is the time that I'll have spent
80   with my feet cooked and body upside-down
   than he'll be planted with his feet on fire,
For after him will come a filthier work[64]
   out of the west, a shepherd without laws,
   such as must top both him and me together.
85   A modern Jason, he, from Maccabees:
   and as the first one's king was pliable,
   so he who governs France will bend for him."
I may have been too bold, I just don't know,
   or mad, when in this measure I replied:
90   "Oh, tell me, how much treasure did He want
Out of Saint Peter, did Our Lord, before
   he placed the keys in his authority?
   Surely he asked no more than 'Follow me.'
And neither Peter nor the others squeezed
95   cash from Matthias when he drew the lot
   to take the place the wicked Judas lost.
Then stay right where you are, you're punished well!
   Make sure you guard those evil-gotten coins
   that made you bold to battle with Anjou![65]
100 And were it not that even here in Hell
   I'm ruled by reverence for those Highest Keys
   you once held in the happy life above,
I would use words still heavier than these—
   for the world is made dismal by your greed,
105   raising the crooked, trampling down the good.
About you shepherds was the prophecy
   of the Evangelist,[66] when he saw her
   who sits upon the seas, whoring with kings;
The woman who was born with seven heads,
110 who from ten horns, the Ten Commandments, took
   her strength, so long as virtue pleased her spouse.[67]

---

[64]*a filthier work:* Pope Clement V, whom Dante accuses of collusion with the king of France, Philip IV, the Fair

[65]*Anjou:* Charles of Anjou

[66]*the Evangelist:* St. John; cf. Rev. 17, the description of the Whore of Babylon

[67]*her spouse:* the Pope, here seen as wedded to the Church

Silver and gold you've made into your god!
   How can we tell you from the idolater?
   He prays to one god—to a hundred, you.
115   Constantine, to what evil it gave birth,
   not your conversion, no, but your Donation[68]
   taken up the first rich Pope on earth!"
And while I sang the notes of such a song,
   anger or conscience bit him to the quick
120   and made him kick his soles with violence.
But those words pleased my guide, I well believe,
   for all the while he listened to the sound
   of spoken truth, his lips were calm and glad.
Taking me in his arms, he helped me up,
125   and, holding me against his breast, he climbed
   back up the bank the same way we went down.
It did not weary him to clutch me tight,
   bearing me to the summit of the arch,
   the ferry from the fourth to the fifth rim.
130   Here he set down his burden, tenderly,
   for here the rock was battered in and steep,
   a strenuous crossing for a mountain goat.
From there another valley came in sight.

---

[68]*Donation:* the so-called Donation of Constantine, whereby the emperor ceded temporal authority in Italy to the Pope

8. *Dante/Inferno XX*

CANTO TWENTY

*In the **fourth ditch of Malebolge**, the poets see the **Diviners,** who weep from heads wrenched backwards on their shoulders. After pointing out some of the notable soothsayers of ancient myth, Virgil tells the story of the **witch Manto,** who gave her name to his native city, Mantua. Finally, he shows Dante the fraudulent magicians of the present age.*

Now of new punishment my verse must tell,
    lending the matter for the twentieth canto
    of my first song, of spirits drowned in Hell.
I was disposed already to look down
5   upon the bottom of the pouch in sight,
    bathed as it was in anguish and laments,
And I saw people in that rounding vale
    walking, silently weeping, slow and solemn,
    as men on earth proceed in litanies.
10   And when my eyes observed them further down,
    they seemed miraculously screwed-about
    between the chin and where the torso starts,
For backwards to the kidneys turned the face,
    and backwards always did they have to go,
15   for they had lost the sight of things ahead.
Maybe in wrenchings of paralysis
    a man may be so wholly twisted round;
    I've never seen it, and I have my doubts.
Reader, so may God let you gather fruit
20   from this your reading, place yourself with me
    and think how I could keep my own face dry
When I looked on our human image there
    so gone awry and twisted, that the eyes
    shed tears that trickled down the buttocks' crack.
25   I leaned upon an outcrop of the bridge
    and surely wept; I wept so, that my guide
    said, "Even now, with all the other fools!
Here pity lives the best when it is dead.
    Who is more wicked than the man who longs
30   to make God's judgment yield to human force?
Lift up your head, lift it up, look at him
    for whom the Thebans saw the earth yawn open,
    at which they cried, 'Where are you tumbling to,
'Amphiaraus? Leaving the war so soon?'
35   And tumbled to the pit until he came
    to Minos, he who snatches everyone.

See how he's made a breast out of his back;
    because he wished to see too far ahead,
    now he looks back and walks a backward path.

40 See there Tiresias, he whose figure changed
    when he became a female from a male,
    converting every member, every limb,

Who had to beat apart, first, with a stick,
    two serpents twined about in intercourse,

45   before he gained his manly plumes again.

Aruns is he, his back to the Greek's[69] belly,
    who in the hills of Luni, harrowed by
    the Carrarese who live down in the valley,

Dwelt in a cave among those marble cliffs,

50   and spent his nights watching the sea and stars,
    with not a thing to cut his vision short.

The woman there who covers up her breasts—
    her back's to you—with tresses loosed and wild,
    and on that side wears all her hairy parts,

55 Was Manto, who went searching many lands
    till settling in the place where I was born.
    Please, hear me on this topic for a bit.

After Tiresias her father died,
    and Bacchus' city, Thebes, became a slave,

60   this woman roved a long time through the world.

Above in lovely Italy lies a lake
    at the foot of the Alps that cut the Tyrol
    from German lands: its name is Benaco.

All of the hills from Garda to Pennino

65   to Val Camonica are watered by
    the thousand springs that flow into that lake.

There in the middle is a spot the bishops
    from Brescia and from Trent and from Verona
    could bless as theirs, if they should go that way.

70 Peschiera, strong and handsome front for war
    against the Brescians and the Bergamasks,
    lies to the south, on the more level shore.

Here all the water which cannot be held
    within the lap of Benaco must fall,

75   making a river flowing through green fields.

From the point where that stream begins to flow,
    they call it Mincio, and not Benaco,
    all the way to Governolo and the Po.

---

[69]*the Greek:* Tiresias; Aruns is following him

Not far on in its course it finds the flats
80   and spreads itself and turns into a marsh;
        and sometimes in the summer it grows rank.
      Passing by here the brutish virgin saw
        an island in the middle of the swamp,
        untilled, and naked of inhabitants.
85   And there, to flee all human intercourse,
        she settled with her slaves to ply her arts,
        and lived, and left her empty corpse behind.
      The men who then were scattered roundabout
        gathered upon that island, rendered strong
90   by the marsh circling round it like a moat.
      They built a city over those dead bones,
        and, from her name who first picked out the place,
        drawing no lots, they called it 'Mantua.'
      The folk inside were once more numerous,
95   before the mad and stupid Casalodi
        let Pinamonte play him for a fool.
      And so I warn you, if you ever hear
        of any other founding of my town,
        let no deception cheat you of the truth."
100   "Teacher," I said, "for me your arguments
        possess such certainty and seize my trust,
        that all the others are extinguished coals.
      But tell me of these people in procession:
        do you see any soul worthy of note?
105   My mind keeps coming back to that alone."
      And so he said, "That one who from his cheek
        spreads his beard down upon his swarthy back
        was a diviner, when the men of Greece
      Waged war,[70] with hardly a boy left in the crib—
110   and scanned the heavens with Calchas for that point
        to cut the ropes in Aulis and set sail.
      Eurypylus his name, as I have sung
        in my high tragedy, in a certain place;
        you know it well, who know the whole of it.
115   That other who's so skinny in the flanks
        was Michael Scot, and he without a doubt
        knew how to play the tricks of sorcery.
      Bonatti, there; and see Asdente, a cobbler
        who now would like to have attended more
120   to string and leather; his regrets come late.

---

[70]*war:* the Trojan War

See the sad women there who left the loom,
   the thread and spindle, to be fortune-tellers,
   casting their spells with herbs and waxen dolls.
But come now, for the figure in the moon—
125   Cain and his bush of thorns—is in the west,
   setting into the sea south of Seville,
And last night it was round and at the full.
   You should recall it, for from time to time
   it did not hurt you in those endless woods."
130   So we continued walking as he spoke.

CANTO TWENTY-ONE

*Here at the **sixth ditch of Malebolge**, where the **Grafters** are punished, Dante catches sight of a great **lake of boiling tar**, when suddenly an **unnamed Demon** shouts to his fellows, the **Evilclaws**, and pitches the **Alderman of Lucca** into the lake. Virgil instructs Dante to hide for a few moments while he speaks to **Eviltail**, the leader of the platoon of Evilclaws. Finally, Eviltail assigns a troop of ten demons, led by **Curlybeard**, to escort Dante and Virgil to the next bridge, which, as we will learn, does not exist.*

And so from one bridge to the next we came,
   talking of things I do not care to sing
   within my Comedy, and reached the top,
And rested there to see the other crack
5   of Evil Pouches, and their useless cries;
   and what we looked upon was wondrous black.
As sailors in the Arsenal of Venice
   boil the whole winter long the tight-grip tar
   to caulk the loosened planks of hulls and keels,
10   For there's no sailing then—so this one builds
   himself a brand new boat, that one stops up
   the ribs of his that's made a lot of trips;
They hammer at the prow or at the poop,
   and some carve oars and some twist cords for rope,
15   some stitch the jib or patch the mainsail up—
So boiled below us a thick pot of pitch,
   never by fire but by the art of God,
   leaving the banks all sticky in this ditch.
I saw the tar, but in it I could see
20   nothing but bubbles that the boiling raised,
   puffing and swelling big until they popped.
While down below attentively I gazed,
   my guide hollered to me, "Look out, look out!"

and grabbed me from the spot where I was standing.
25 I turned as one who can't just wait to see
      (although his valor fails for sudden fear)
      whatever thing it is that he must flee,
Who looks but takes no time in getting out—
      and there behind us, scrambling up the ridge,
30   I saw a devil coming, black as Hell.
Ah, how his face was fiercer than a beast's!
      How cruel his behavior seemed to me,
      his wings spread open and his feet that flew!
Over his shoulder, spiked and hunched for pride,
35   he slung a sinner by the ankles both
      and snagged him by the sinews of his feet.
He shouted from our bridge, "Hey, Evilclaws!
      One of the aldermen of Santa Zita![71]
      Stick this one under while I go for more,
40 For that's a town that's got 'em stocked in force.
      Everyone takes a bribe except Bonturo!
      A 'no,' for money, turns into 'of course.'"
He flung him down, and over the rough ridge
      he sped—no mastiff ever ran so fast,
45   snapping his chain to catch the fleeing thief.
That soul plunged in, and bobbed up with his rear.
      Sneaking behind the bridge the demons cried,
      "The Holy Face[72] has got no business here!
The Serchio[73] is no swimming-hole like this!
50   Unless you want to taste our hooks, make sure
      no part of you sticks up out of the pitch."
When they'd harpooned him with a hundred prongs
      they jeered, "You do your jigs here under cover,
      so grab the cash in hiding, if you can!"
55 Just so, the cooks will make their scullery-boys
      stick forks into a pot of stew to keep
      the hunks of meat from bobbing to the top.
Said my good Teacher then: "So that they don't
      know that you're here, go squat behind some rock
60   and get yourself a hideout, and remember,
No matter what offense they do to me,
      don't be afraid—I've got things reckoned up,
      for I've been through this wrangling place before."

---

[71]*One . . . Santa Zita:* one of the magistrates of Lucca
[72] *Holy Face:* black-faced icon of Christ, in the church of Santa Zita, in Lucca
[73]*Serchio:* river flowing through Lucca

Then he passed over from the bridge's head,
65   and as he reached the bank of the sixth ditch
      he had to show some boldness in his brow.
With just such storm and such a frenzied rage
      dogs race out in the track of the poor soul
      who stands stock-still and begs from where he is,
70   As rushed the demons from beneath the pier
      and turned their grappling-hooks against his face,
      but he cried, "Better make no mischief here!
Before you snag me on your hooks, you'd best
      get one of you to come and hear me out,
75   and then decide to stick the fork in me."
And they all hollered, "Eviltail should go!"
      One of them stepped up—all the rest stood pat—
      saying, "What good does he think this will do?"
"Eviltail, do you really think you see
80   me coming here," my Teacher said, "secure
      from every obstacle you've put before me,
Without the favor and the will of God?
      So let me go, since it is willed in Heaven
      that I should show someone this savage road."
85   At that, so disappointed was his pride
      he let the hook fall clanking to his feet
      and said, "There won't be any stabbing now."
And then my guide to me: "O you who sit
      among the rocks all crouched and huddled up,
90   you can come back to me now, safe and sound."
So I came out and hurried up to him,
      and all the devils made as if to lunge,
      so that I feared they wouldn't keep the deal;
As once I saw foot-soldiers grow afraid
95   when they marched with safe-conduct from Caprona,
      surrounded by so many enemies.
I pressed myself close to my leader's side
      from head to toe, and never let my eyes
      turn from their faces, for they were not kind.
100   They cocked their hooks and said, one to the next,
      "Want I should touch him on the rump a bit?"
      And they replied, "Go on and give it to him!"
The demon who was speaking to my guide
      heard it and wheeled around immediately
105   and said, "At ease, at ease there, Crumplehead!"
Then said to us: "There's no way down this ridge.
      The arch is smashed and toppled to the ground

that used to serve the sixth ditch for a bridge.
But if you do still want to go on down,
110　come along by this bank. It's not too far
　　before you'll find another ridge to cross.
As of five hours from now, by yesterday
　　one thousand and two hundred sixty-six
　　years will be finished since the road collapsed.
115　I'm sending some of these my boys down there
　　to check if someone's airing himself out.
　　Go on with them. They won't do any harm.
March forward, Tramplefrost and Hellerkin!"
　　so he began to them, "and Larddog, you,
120　and Curlybeard, you lead the troop of ten.
And Stormbreath, go along, and Dragonsnout,
　　with Dogscratcher and tusky Swinetooth too,
　　and Gobgoblin and Redfroth howling mad.
Go all around to search the boiling glue,
125　keep these men safe until that other ridge,
　　the one that crosses all the dens intact."
"Oh no, Teacher!" said I. "What's this I see?
　　Let's go alone, if you can find the way,
　　without an escort—I don't want one, me!
130　If you're as wary as you've ever been,
　　don't you see how they grin and grit their teeth
　　and arch their brows to threaten us with pain?"
And he to me: "You mustn't be afraid.
　　Let them go grit their teeth if they think best.
135　They do it for the boiled meat in the pitch."
Then the platoon turned sharp left on the bank,
　　but first they'd stuck their tongues between their teeth
　　and blown it at their sergeant for a sign,
And he had made a bugle of his arse.

CANTO TWENTY-TWO

*Still in the **sixth ditch of Malebolge**, the demons led by Curlybeard harpoon a
Navarrese bribe-taker, who names others in the lake, and escapes from the
Evilclaws by pretending to trick some of his comrades into coming out. Enraged, the
demon Hellerkin flies after him to no avail, and becomes entangled in a scuffle with
his fellow Demon, Tramplefrost. They both fall into the boiling pitch.*

I've seen, in my day, cavalry break camp,
　　storm to attack, and muster for parade,
　　and sometimes beat retreat to save their lives;

I have seen scouts ride horseback through your lands,
5   O Aretines, and raiding-parties rush,
     and clashing tournaments and galloping jousts;
Sometimes with trumpet-blasts, sometimes with bells,
     with drums, with signals from the battlements,
     with native gear and that of other lands;
10   But never a mounted knight or squad afoot
     or boat that waits the lantern or the stars
     have I seen move for so bizarre a flute.
With the ten demons then we took our way.
     What savage company! But as they say,
15   'In church with saints, and in the stews with swine.'
For all that, I attended to the tar,
     to witness each particular of this pouch
     and of the people it must stew and char.
As do the dolphins when they make a sign
20   to sailors by the arching of their backs
     that they should save their ship before it storms,
So, sometimes, to alleviate the pain,
     one of the sinners showed his backside up
     then hid it like a lightning-flash again.
25   As at the water's edge beside a ditch
     the bullfrogs perch with muzzles sticking out,
     and hide the legs and all the bulging paunch,
So stood these sinners everywhere you'd scout,
     but soon as they saw Curlybeard draw near,
30   so too they dunked beneath the bubbling pitch.
I saw—it makes my heart shake to this day—
     one wait too long, as it can happen that
     this frog stays out while that one darts away,
And Dogscratcher, right there in front of him,
35   hooked him and dragged him by the tar-clogged locks,
     and pulled him like an otter from a pond.
(I knew the names of every devil there,
     for I had noted them when they were picked,
     and later heard what they would call themselves.)
40   "Hey, Redfroth, set your nails in this one here!
     Claw him and strip the leather from his back!"
     the cursed demons hollered all together.
"My Teacher, please," I asked him, "if you can,
     discover who he is whose wretched luck
45   has put him in his adversaries' hands."
My guide then walked up to the man in tar
     and asked him where he came from, and he answered,

"I was born in the kingdom of Navarre.
My mother made me servant to a lord;
50   she'd gotten pregnant by a worthless rogue,
one who destroyed himself and all his wealth.
Then I was a valet for the good king
Thibault, and there I started to take bribes,
and in this heat I pay the reckoning."
55   And Swinetooth, from whose mouth on each side stuck
a tusk like a wild boar's, gave him to feel
how one of them could rip his stitches out.
The rat had fallen in with wicked cats!
Curlybeard fenced him with his arms stretched wide—
60   "Keep clear, you! This one's getting skewered by me."
And to my Teacher then he turned his face:
"Ask him what else you'd like to know of him,
before somebody else rips him apart."
So then the guide: "Now tell us, if you know
65   if there are any souls from Italy
under the tar?" And that one said, "Just now
I left a spirit from a land nearby.
I wish I were still covered up with him,
I wouldn't have to fear the hook or claw!"
70   Said Stormbreath: "We've put up with this too long!"
and with his grappler snagged him by the arm,
yanked it and tore away a muscle whole.
Dragonsnout also wanted to join in
and give it to him in the legs—but their
75   sergeant wheeled round and round with angry eye.
When they had held their peace a little while,
my leader did not pause, but asked the sinner,
who was still gazing on his open wound,
"Who was that man you say you left behind
80   unluckily, to come upon the shore?"
"That was Friar Gomita," he replied,
"he of Sardinia, vessel of all fraud,
who had his master's enemies in hand
and treated them to earn the praise of all.
85   For he took bribes and let them off scot-free—
those are his words. In other duties too
no small-time, but the king of grafters, he.
And Michel Zanche, lord of Logodoro,
hangs with him, and their tongues are never tired
90   of talking of their damned Sardinia.
Oh no, that other demon bares his fangs!

I'd tell you a lot more, but I'm afraid
he's setting up to scratch me on the mange!"
The big commander turned to the Gobgoblin,
95   who rolled his crazy eyes before he struck,
and said, "Get over there, you filthy crow!"
"If you would like to see or hear some more,"
the spirit, terrified, resumed at once,
"Tuscans, Lombards, I'll make 'em all come out,
100   But have the Evilclaws step back a bit
so they won't be afraid of their revenge,
and I, while standing in this very spot,
Though I'm just one, I'll see that seven appear!
I'll whistle, which is what we always do
105   whenever we perceive the coast is clear."
The Larddog raised his muzzle at those words
and shook his head and said, "It's all a trick,
a nasty trick so he can jump back in!"
And he—who had a wealth of snares in him—
110   replied, "I'm quite a trickster, if I can
wheedle worse sorrow for my mates below."
Hellerkin couldn't hold back, so he said,
contrary to the others, "If you dive,
I won't come at your traces at a gallop,
115   But I'll be batting wings above the pitch!
Let's leave the edge and hide behind the slope
and see if you can beat us by yourself."
O Reader, hear this new sport! Each one turned
his eyes an instant at the opposite shore—
120   Larddog the first, who had resisted most.
He chose his moment well, that Navarrese:
planted his heels and at a single leap
slipped from the plotting of his enemies.
Each of the devils was stung with shame for that,
125   he most of all who brought on the mistake,
so he set off and cried, "I've got you now!"
But to no good: his wings could never fly
as fast as fear. So that one went below
and this one flapped his wings to pull up short,
130   Just as a duck who sees the hawk swoop down
aiming for her—she dives at once, and he
has to come back above, ruffled and vexed.
Tramplefrost took the joke in rage, and flew
right after Hellerkin, eager to see
135   that soul escape so he could start a brawl;

And when the barterer had disappeared
  he turned his talons to his fellow demon
  and clutched him in a hold above the trench.
The other was a full-grown falcon too
140   if it should come to talons, and they both
  fell in the middle of the boiling pool.
The heat did its dis-grappling pretty quick,
  but for all that there was no getting up
  with wings so limed and clotted in the tar.
145 Curlybeard, groaning with the rest of them,
  commanded four to fly to the far side,
  harpoons and all; and with the greatest speed
The demons flew to man the posts assigned,
  and stuck their hooks into their glued-up fellows
150 who were already cooked beneath the crust.
And so we left them in that tangled mess.

CANTO TWENTY-THREE

*Virgil and Dante **escape from the Evilclaws** by sliding down the steep bank into the **seventh ditch of Malebolge**. Here, walking with leaden cloaks painted with gold, go the **Hypocrites**. Dante speaks to two friars, **Catalano and Loderingo,** whose hypocrisy set the stage for civil bloodshed in his native Florence. While speaking to them, he observes the high priest **Caiaphas,** crucified to the floor of Hell. From Catalano, Virgil finally learns of the treachery of the Eviltails in the ditch above.*

Silent, alone, no escort at our side,
  we set out, one before and one behind,
  as Friars Minor[74] walk in single file.
The skirmish we'd just seen reminded me
5   of one of Aesop's fables, where he tells
  about the frog and mouse who crossed the stream,
For "presently" and "soon" are not so close
  as those are, if you fix your mind on them
  and pair them from beginning to the end.
10 And as one thought will jump into the next,
  so from this thought another one was born,
  which made me twice as frightened as before.
"These demons took a hurt on our account
  and were well-mocked," so I thought to myself,
15   "and you can trust it rankles a good deal.
If you wind wrath around the spool with hate,

---

[74]*Friars Minor:* Franciscans, the "little friars"

they should be coming back thirstier for blood
than the dog who snaps a rabbit in his teeth."
Then I could feel the hair curl on my flesh,
20   and, standing back a bit, intent with fear,
I said, "Please, Teacher, if you don't move fast
And hide yourself and me, I'm fearful of
the Evilclaws—they're gaining on us now!
What I imagine, I can almost feel!"
25   And he: "Were I a pane of leaded glass[75]
your outer form would not reflect as soon
as I receive the image of your thoughts.
Now above all they walk along with mine;
their gestures and expressions are the same.
30   So I've devised a single plan from both.
If the slope at the right bank will allow,
we can descend into the other ditch
and flee the hunting you imagine now."
He'd hardly got two words out for his plan
35   when I caught sight of them not far away,
their wings spread wide to overtake and snatch.
All of a sudden my guide seized me—as
a mother who is wakened by a noise
and sees the leaping flames beside her bed,
40   Seizes her child and flees and does not stop,
having more care for him than for herself,
with no more than a smock to hide her shame—
And from the neck of the rough slope of rock
he took flat on his back the tumbled scarp
45   that plugs the near side of the ditch beyond.
Water that gushes down the sluice to turn
the wheel of a great grindstone at a mill,
not even at the paddles falls so fast
As fell my master down that bordering stone,
50   bearing me on his chest as he slid down—
not as his fellow or friend, but as his son.
And hardly had his feet touched at the base
when they had reached the summit over us;
but now we need have no more doubts of them.
55   For though high Providence has willed that they
be ministers of pain in the fifth ditch,
all power to leave that ditch, it takes away.
Down there we found a painted populace

---

[75]*pane . . . glass:* a mirror

who walked about with slow, slow steps, and wept;
60   exhaustion and defeat dwelt in each face.
They all wore hooded capes with cowls that hung
over their eyes, cut in the ample style
they like to use at Cluny for the monks.
The outsides all were gilt in blinding gold;
65   inside, all lead; so heavy, the lead cloaks
Frederick made felons wear were light as straw.
O weary mantle for eternity!
Still we turned to the left and walked with them,
and listened to their moans attentively.
70   But for that heavy burden the tired crew
went slow, so slow, that when we moved the hip
the company we walked beside was new.
"Please, find someone," I therefore asked my guide,
"whom we might recognize by deed or name.
75   We can walk still, and look from side to side."
And one who heard the Tuscan in my speech
cried from behind us, "Hold your feet a bit,
you who go racing through the troubled air.
It may be I can give you what you need."
80   At that, my guide turned round to me to say,
"Wait, and then at the sinner's pace proceed."
So there I stood, and saw two spirits show
great haste to reach me—haste of will, seen in
their faces; for their burdens made them slow
85   As did the crowded way. They came; they looked
sidelong at me, and did not say a word.
Turned to each other then, and commented:
"This one's alive, it seems. His throat, it moves.
And if they *are* dead, by what privilege
90   can they go on without the stole of lead?"
To me: "O Tuscan, who have come unto
the brotherhood of long-faced hypocrites,
do not think ill to tell us who you are."
And I to them: "In the great town that stands
95   on the sweet Arno I was born, and bred;
this is the body I have always had.
But who are you, distilled in drops of woe,
so many, that run coursing down the cheek?
What is your punishment that glitters so?"
100   And one replied to me: "Our yellow capes
are made of lead so heavy, that the weight
causes the scales, as you have heard, to creak.

We two were Jolly Friars, Bolognese:
    I Catalano, Loderingo he.
105   Your city called us in to keep the peace.
They took us both together for a place
    a single man would hold, and what we were,
    the ruins on the Gardingo leave a trace."
"O friars," I began, "your evil deeds—"
110   but said no more, for suddenly I caught
    sight of one crucified upon the ground,
nailed with three stakes. He saw me—and he wrenched
    and writhed, and puffed his sobs into his beard,
    and brother Catalan, who noticed, said,
115   "That soul[76] you wonder at, who lies transfixed,
    advised the Pharisees that it was fit
    to martyr one man[77] for the people's sake.
Naked he lies, spread-eagled in the road,
    as you may see, and by necessity
120   he feels the weight of all the passing souls.
His father-in-law[78] is racked in this same ditch
    along with all the other councilors
    who sowed the seeds of evil for the Jews."
Then I saw Virgil in astonishment
125   stare at the spirit stretched out in a cross,
    humiliated in the banishment
That never ends. And to the friar he turned,
    saying, "Let it not displease you, if you may,
    but tell if there's a passage on the right
130   Over which we can both get out of here,
    so that we needn't call on the black angels[79]
    and make them come to take us from this hole."
And he responded: "Nearer than you hope
    there is a ridge that starts at Dis's wall
135   and arches over all the savage pits
But one, because it's broken at this point
    and can't be crossed. You can climb up the ruins
    on that side there, heaped over the next ditch."
My guide stood still a moment, his head bowed,
140   then said, "He gave a bad account of things,
    that one who hooks the sinners." And the friar:

---

[76]*that soul:* Caiaphas the High Priest
[77]*one man:* Jesus; see John 11:50
[78]*father-in-law:* Annas
[79]*the black angels:* the Evilclaws

"When I was at Bologna[80] I heard tell
  of all the devil's vices, and I heard
  he was a liar and the father of lies."
145 At that my guide set out with greater strides,
    some anger darkening in his countenance,
    and I too left the heavy-laden souls
And followed after his beloved feet.

---

[80]*Bologna:* the University of Bologna

CANTO TWENTY-FOUR

*The poets climb over to the **seventh ditch of Malebolge**, where they see the **Thieves**, harried and transmuted by serpents. Dante recognizes a church-robber, **Vanni Fucci**, who for sheer spite prophesies hardship for Dante and his party in Florence.*

When the year's young in season, and the spray
   washes the sunbeams in Aquarius,
   and the nights dwindle south towards half a day,
When the frost paints a copy on the ground
5   of her white sister's snowy image, but
   her feather's sharpness doesn't last for long;
The peasant lad who finds his fodder's low
   gets up and takes a look, and smacks his thigh,
   thinking the countryside's all white with snow,
10   Goes inside grumbling, fretting up and down,
   like a poor wretch who can't tell what to do,
   comes back out, and puts new hope in his pack,
Seeing the world has changed its face so soon,
   and takes his staff and drives his little flock
15   to forage in the fields. So too with me:
My Teacher made me downcast for a while
   when I perceived the trouble in his brow;
   but then he laid the plaster on the sore,
For when we reached the ruined bridge, my guide
20   turned to me with that sweet and gracious look
   which I'd first seen below the mountainside.
He looked upon the ruins quietly,
   considering in himself which way to go,
   then spread his arms, and took me by the hand.
25   And like a man who judges while he works
   and therefore always seems to see ahead,
   so, as he helped me to the summit of
A jutting rock, he saw another crag
   and said, "Cling tight to that one and climb up,
30   but test it first to see if it will hold."
That was no way for those with cowls of lead,
   for we—he lightly, I with struggle—could
   hardly mount up the ridge from jag to jag.
And if it weren't that the belt that rings
35   this ditch was shorter than the one before,
   I cannot speak for him, but I'd have been
Defeated. But since Evil Pouches tilt
   down towards the lowest sink in the abyss,

the lie of every valley makes it so
40 That one side rises higher than the next;
    and so at last we reached where the last stone
    had tumbled from the shattered bridge. My breath
Had been milked dry out of the lungs, so hard
    that when I scrambled up, I could do nothing
45 but sit at the first level place. "You must
Shake off your sluggishness," the Teacher said,
    "for no one comes to fame who sits in soft
    pillows of down, or lies at ease in bed,
And when his life is wasted utterly
50 he leaves such traces of himself behind
    as smoke in air or foam upon the sea.
Get up, then! Conquer your distress, with that
    brave soul that wins through every fight, unless
    it should turn weak beneath the flesh's weight.
55 It won't suffice for you, to leave the damned.
    For you shall have to climb a longer stair:
    Turn that to profit, if you understand."
At that I rose, and made myself appear
    furnished with better breathing than I felt,
60 and said, "Let's go, for I am bold and strong."
Over the arching reef we took our way,
    rocky and narrow and difficult it was,
    and pitched more steeply than the last. And as
We walked I spoke a bit, not to seem faint,
65 when came a voice out of the seventh ditch,
    ill-suited to form words. But what it said
I do not know, though I was on the hump
    of the stone arch that makes the crossing there.
    Whoever it was seemed quick to get away.
70 I leaned to look below, but living eyes
    could not pierce to the bottom through the dark,
    so I said, "Teacher, please, let's go across
To the next belt and then climb down the wall.
    I hear from here but I can't understand—
75 look down, but can't make out a thing at all."
"No other answer will I give," said he,
    "than to comply. An honorable request
    ought to be met with action, silently."
Then we descended from the bridge's head
80 where it adjoins the slope of the eighth pit,
    and then the pouch was manifest to me,
For there I saw a terrifying mass

of serpents, of such different shapes and sorts,
   the thought still wastes the color in my face.
85   Let Libya with its deserts boast no more!
    If it breeds Spearers, Slitherers, hot Chelydri,
    Cencri erect and twin-head Amphisboenes,
   Never so many nor so venomous pests
    has it and all of Ethiopia shown,
90   and all the land that looms on the Red Sea.
   Through this most wretched and malignant throng
    . ran people, naked, frightened, without hope
    to find a hiding-hole or antidote.
   Their wrists were strapped behind their backs by snakes
95   which round the kidneys squeezed the head and tail
    and formed a bulging knot above the groin.
   And look—right at a sinner near our ledge
    there flashed a snake who fixed him with its fangs
    just where the neck is knotted to the back.
100   A man can't scrawl an I or O as fast
    as he ignited and went up in flames
    and disappeared in a collapse of ash;
   And after he lay strewn and thus destroyed,
    his body's dust collected on its own
105   and suddenly returned to what it was.
   So the great wise men of the ancient days
    held that the Phoenix died and was reborn
    at the approach of the five-hundredth year;
   Who in her life feeds not on herb or grain,
110   but balsamum and tears of frankincense,
    and myrrh and spikenard make her funeral bed.
   And as a man who falls[81] and can't say how—
    by demon's force that yanks him to the earth,
    or other blockage binding a man's powers—
115   When he comes to, he gazes round, all lost,
    bewildered by the suffocating fit
    he has endured, and as he looks, breathes deep:
   Such was the sinner when he stood once more.
    O power of God, how stern your rigor is,
120   which deals such blows and lets the vengeance pour!
   My guide then asked the spirit who he was,
    and he replied, "I rained from Tuscany
    not long ago, into this savage throat.
   I loved the life of beasts and not of men,

---

[81]*a man who falls:* a man afflicted with the "falling disease," epilepsy

125   bastard mule that I was. I'm Vanni Fucci,
      Beast, and Pistoia was my worthy den."
I to my guide: "Tell him not to sneak off,
      and ask of him what fault shoved him down here.
      I knew him as a man of wrath and blood."[82]

130   The sinner heard, and did not stall for time,
      but turned the focus of his sight to me,
      and his face reddened with a sullen shame.
Said he: "It pains me that you've caught me here
      plunged in the misery where you see me now,

135   more than it pained me to be snatched from life.
I can't refuse to answer what you ask.
      I'm put down here because I was a thief,
      filched the fair Vestments from the Sacristy—
The blame was wrongly laid on someone else.

140   But if you get outside this dungeon's night,
      so that this sight of me won't bring you pleasure,
Open your ears and hear what I foretell.
      Pistoia first will slim itself of Blacks;[83]
      Florence renews her people and her ways,

145   Then will the war-god draw his thunderbolt
      from Val di Magra, wrapped in darkening clouds,
      and with a headlong and tempestuous surge
Battle it on the Plains of Piceno,
      where he will split the clouds with sudden fire

150   and strike down every White upon the field.
I've told you this for spite, to bring you grief."

---

[82]*a man of wrath and blood:* Dante is wondering why this spirit is here and not with the centaurs

[83]*Blacks:* The Blacks and Whites are parties in the continuing strife besetting Florence. Fucci foretells what will result in the exile of Dante (a member of the White Party).

CANTO TWENTY-FIVE

Vanni Fucci is led away in punishment by serpents. The poets continue among the **Thieves,** *in the* **seventh ditch of Malebolge.** *There they see the thieving centaur* **Cacus,** *and witness the strange* **metamorphoses** *of three of the thieves.*

At the end of his prophecy the thief
    raised both his hands with the two figs[84] pricked out—
    "Take that, O God—I fling them in your face!"
From that point on the snakes were friends to me,
5   for one enwound itself around his neck
    as if it said, "I want you to shut up,"
And then a second slithered through his arms
    and noosed them with so tight a knot in front
    he couldn't give those arms a jerk or jolt.
10   Pistoia, Pistoia! Why should you not decide
    once and for all to burn yourself to ash—
    since you surpass your seed in wickedness!
In all the circles of the darkest Hell
    I'd seen no soul so haughty against God—
15   not he who tumbled from the walls of Thebes.[85]
He fled—he could not speak another word;
    and then there came a centaur mad with rage,
    hollering, "Where's that rebel, where's he gone!"
I don't believe the marsh-flats of Maremma
20   bring forth as many vipers as his hunch
    had crawling up to where our mouth begins.
Upon his shoulders, right behind the neck,
    there perched a dragon with his wings spread wide,
    scorching whatever soul he hit upon.
25   My Teacher said, "This one is Cacus, who
    dwelt in the cave beneath the Aventine[86]
    and there left many a pool of human blood.
He does not share his brother centaurs' walk,
    on account of the sneaking theft he made
30   of the great herd of cattle near his rock;
But all his shifty deeds came to an end
    under the club of Hercules, who gave him
    a hundred blows. He didn't feel the tenth."
While he spoke and the Centaur galloped by,

---

[84]*figs:* an obscene gesture, made by sticking the thumb between the index and middle
fingers
[85]*he who tumbled . . . Thebes:* Capaneus; see above, canto xiv.
[86]*Aventine:* the Roman hill where Cacus dwelt. The tale is told in the *Aeneid,* 8.190–267.

35   three spirits suddenly appeared below.
      My guide was not aware of them, nor I,
  Until they shouted at us, "Who are you!"
    at which we broke our conversation off,
    and our attention turned to them alone.
40   I didn't recognize them, but it happened,
    as it does sometimes follow by mere chance,
    one of them had to name another one
  And said, "Where is that Cianfa lurking now?"
    Whereupon, that my guide would stand and watch,
45   I laid my finger to my lips. O Reader,
  It's no great cause for wonder if you're slow
    to trust what I'm about to tell you now,
    for I, who saw it, hardly can believe.
  I held my eyebrows raised to look their way,
50   and there! a snake with six feet flings itself
    and clings to one of them with all his length.
  It strapped the belly with its middle feet
    and clutched the arms by the anterior,
    then sunk its fangs to bite through either cheek;
55   It stretched its hind feet straight along the thighs
    and flipped its tail between them and on up
    the sinner's loins to clamp behind his back.
  No ivy ever gripped its barbs about
    a tree so tightly as that horrible beast
60   twisted the other's members with its own.
  They glued and fused together, as if formed
    out of hot wax, and saw their colors melt
    so neither one seemed what it was before,
  As when a flame is set below a scrap
65   of parchment, and a brownish hue appears,
    which, while the white is dying, is not black.
  The other two cried out as they looked on:
    "Alas, Agnel, how you have changed yourself!
    Already, see, you're neither two nor one!"
70   Already indeed their two heads had formed one,
    and there appeared two figures mingled in
    one face, where the two faces had been lost.
  Out of four bands of flesh they formed two arms;
    the thighs and calves, the belly and the chest
75   made members that no man has ever seen.
  Each former countenance was cancelled out;
    the image in perversion seemed both two
    and nothing—and as such it slunk away.

As the green lizard under the sharp lash
80   of the dog days, darting from hedge to hedge,
crosses the road quick as a lightning-flash,
So came a little serpent lit with wrath
after the bellies of the other two,
as black and livid as a peppercorn.
85   In that part where the foetus takes its food
it fixed itself on one of them, and bit:
then fell stretched out before him on the ground.
The bitten man then stared, but did not speak:
rather, with feet set firm, he yawned, as if
90   assailed by fever or by drowsiness.
The man glared at the snake, the snake at him.
This through the wound and that one through its mouth
sent violent clouds of smoke that rose and merged.
Be silent, Lucan, where you touch upon
95   wretched Sabellus and Nasidius,
and listen to the arrow I shoot now.
Be silent, Ovid, with your Arethusa
and Cadmus, where your poem turns
this to a serpent, that one to a spring;
100   I hold no grudge, for never front to front
did you transmute two natures so their forms
were ready to change matter with each other.
They corresponded in the following way,
for the snake split his tail into a fork
105   while the man pressed his feet together tight.
The legs all the way up the thigh began
to cling together, so that soon no trace
appeared of any juncture. The forked tail
Assumed in turn the figure that was lost
110   by the man there; his scaly hide grew soft
as flesh, while the man's hardened. Then I saw
His arms recede into the shoulder-pits
while the two short feet of the serpent stretched
and grew as long as the man's limbs had shrunk.
115   Then its hind feet, twisted and wound in one,
became the member which a man must hide,
while the wretch saw two paws grow from his own.
As the smoke veiled the one soul and the other
with a new color, and on this side made
120   the hair sprout up and stripped the hair from that,
The one got up, the other fell to earth,
but never turned their evil flashing eyes

beneath whose gaze they interchanged their snouts:
He who was standing drew his face-flesh in
125 towards the temples, and with the extra matter
  the ears protruded from his hollow cheeks,
And what did not run backwards to the ears
  composed a nose out of the excess flesh
  and swelled the lips as fat as lips must swell.
130 He who lay on the ground lengthened his snout
  and drew the two ears back into his head,
  just as a snail retracts its horns inside,
And the tongue, which was single and well-made
  for speech, now cleaves in two, while the tongue's fork
135 closes within the other, and the smoke
Subsides. The soul who had become a beast
  slithered across the valley with a hiss
  and he behind the serpent spoke and spat.
He turned his brand new shoulders on the snake
140 and to the third one said: "Let Buoso go
  creeping on all fours down the road, like me!"
So did I see the seventh ballast change
  and change again; and if my pen has left
  matters a little tangled, let the strange
145 Nature of it excuse me. And though my eye
  was slightly dazed and my mind somewhat faint,
  they could not sneak away so secretly
That I could overlook Puccio Sciancato,
  the only soul that did not suffer change
150 out of the three companions. And the third
Was he, Gaville, on whose account you mourn.

CANTO TWENTY-SIX

After an invective against the corruption of Florence, Dante resumes his account. The poets proceed to the **eighth ditch of Malebolge,** *where the* **Evil Counselors** *are wholly swathed in flames, and speak through the tongue of fire at the top. Dante asks Virgil to call upon a certain twin-tongued flame, where dwell the souls of* **Ulysses and Diomedes.** *Ulysses recounts how he and his men died on their voyage into the southern hemisphere, far beyond the Pillars of Hercules.*

Florence, rejoice! Your fame's so great to tell,
  you beat your wings over the land and seas
  and spread your name throughout the deeps of Hell!
Among the thieves I found five citizens,
5 five of your finest, and that brings me shame,

nor do you climb in greater reverence.
But if our dreams before the dawn come true,
    shortly you'll feel what Prato (not to mention
    the other towns) longs to have fall on you.
10   It would be fine had it already come.
    Then let it, since it must! The more I age,
    the more your punishment will sadden me.
We took our leave up the projecting rocks
    that left us pale as ivory, going down;
15   my guide climbed up, and pulled me after him,
And following the solitary way
    among the shards and boulders of the ridge,
    the foot could not move on without the hand.
Then did I grieve, and now I grieve again,
20   when I direct my mind to what I saw,
    and put my genius under tighter rein
Lest without virtue's guidance it run loose:
    that if my stars, or grace, has given me good,
    I won't begrudge myself in its abuse.
25   But as a peasant resting on a hill
    in that warm time of year when he who sheds
    light on the world hides less than usual,
When the mosquito follows on the fly,
    sees crowds of fireflies in the twilight dell
30   down by the vineyard or the fields he's tilled;
With just so many flickering fire-lights shone
    the eighth pouch, as I noticed just as soon
    as I could see the bottom of the pit.
And as that prophet[87] who avenged himself
35   with murderous bears, looked on the chariot of
    Elijah,[88] horses galloping steep to heaven:
He could not follow its parting with his eyes
    but saw no more than one bright burst of fire
    like a small cloud, ascending higher and higher—
40   So every flame moves through this trench's throat
    and not one flickering light reveals the theft,
    for each one stows away a sinner's soul.
I stood erect upon the bridge to look,
    and would have fallen headlong with no push
45   had I not kept a handhold on the rock.

---

[87] *that prophet:* Elisha, taunted by boys, cursed them; they were immediately slain by bears from the woods. See 2 Kings 2:23–24.
[88] *Elijah:* Elisha's teacher, who was taken up into Heaven by a chariot of fire; see 2 Kings 2:9–12

Seeing me so intent to learn, my guide
    explained, "In every flame there dwells a soul.
    The fires that light them swaddle them inside."
"My Teacher," I responded, "what you say
50   makes me more certain; but I'd thought already
    that it was so, and wished to ask you this:
What spirit dwells within that double fire
    divided at the top as if it rose
    from Polynices' and his brother's[89] pyre?"
55   And he replied: "That flame tortures Ulysses
    and Diomedes, and as two they meet
    God's vengeance, as they sinned and met His wrath.
For they bemoan their ambush in that flame,
    their wooden horse in Troy, which was the gate
60   through which the noble seed of Rome first came;
There they weep for the artful trick which brought
    sorrow to Deidamia[90] even in death,
    and bear the punishment for Pallas' shrine."[91]
"If they can speak from there inside those flares,"
65   said I, "Teacher, I pray with all my heart,
    and pray again up to a thousand prayers,
That you will not decline to let me stay
    until the twin-horned fire comes near—you see
    what great desire has made me bend their way!"
70   And he to me: "Your prayer is worthy of
    the highest praise, and therefore I agree:
    but you must hold your own tongue in restraint.
I understand your wish, so let me speak,
    for they might take your language in disdain
75   and shy away from us, since they were Greek."
And when the flame at last had come our way
    and it seemed to my guide the time and place,
    in such a form as this I heard him say,
"O you who are two souls within one fire,
80   if ever I earned your favor while I lived,
    if ever I earned your favor, great or small,
When in the world I wrote my lofty verse,

---

[89]*Polynices' . . . brother's:* Dante is referring to the twin sons of Oedipus, Polynices and Eteocles, who fought for control of Thebes after the death of their father, and who slew each other in battle.

[90]*Deidamia:* the girl who loved Achilles; Ulysses and Diomedes engineered a trick to jilt her on the isle of Scyros and join them in the Trojan War

[91]*Pallas' shrine:* the Palladium, tutelary image of the goddess Pallas Athena; stolen from Troy by Ulysses and Diomedes

    do not depart, but tell us, one of you,
      where you were lost, and where you went to die."
85   The greater horn upon the ancient flame
      began to quiver into murmuring,
      just like a torch-light wearied by the wind,
    And then, leading the flame-tip here and there,
      as if that were the very tongue that spoke,
90   it flung a voice without, and said, "When I
    Left Circe, who had lured away from me
      more than a year on her isle near Gaeta,
      before Aeneas gave that cape its name,
    Neither the sweet affection for my son,
95   nor piety due my father, nor the love
      I owed Penelope to bring her joy,
    Could rout from me the burning to go forth
      to gain experience of the world, and learn
      of every human vice, and human worth.
100 I sent myself on the deep open sea
      with only a boat and that small troop of men,
      my friends, who never had abandoned me.
    I saw the shores of either continent
      up to Spain and Morocco, saw Sardinia,
105   and all the other isles that ocean bathes.
    I and my comrades were stiff-limbed and old
      when we arrived within the narrow mouth[92]
      where Hercules once set his warning signs
    Lest man should dare to venture past the mark:
110   on the right hand I left Seville behind,
      and on the left, Ceuta. Then I spoke:
    "O brothers, who have borne innumerable
      dangers to reach the setting of the sun,
      from these few hours remaining to our watch,
115   From time so short in which to live and feel,
      do not refuse experience of the lands
      beyond the sun, the world where no one dwells.
    Think well upon your nation and your seed!
      For you were never made to live like brutes,
120   but to pursue the good in mind and deed."
    I made my comrades' appetites so keen
      to take the journey, by this little speech,
      I hardly could have held them after that.
    Turning our aft-side to the morning sun

---

[92]*narrow mouth:* the Straits of Gibraltar

125   we made wings of our oars for the mad flight,
      gradually gaining to the left, so far
That nightfall now revealed the southern pole
      and all its stars, while ours were sunk so low
      they never rose above the ocean's rim.
130   Five times the light of the moon's underside
      was kindled for the earth, and five times quenched,
      since we'd set out upon the arduous pass,
When far off there appeared a mountain-shore,
      hazy and dark, which seemed to loom so high,
135   no man had seen so high a peak before.
We cheered, but soon that cheering turned to woe,
      for then a whirlwind born from the strange land
      battered our little vessel on the prow.
Three times the boat and all the sea were whirled,
140   and at the fourth, to please Another's[93] will,
      the aft tipped in the air, the prow went down,
Until the ocean closed above our bones."

---

[93]*Another's:* i.e., God

CANTO TWENTY-SEVEN

*Still in the **eighth ditch of Malebolge**, Dante encounters another of the **Evil Counselors**, Guido da Montefeltro, who tells of his corruption by **Pope Boniface VIII**, and of his death and damnation.*

The flame had risen upright and was still,
   for it would speak no more, and went its way,
   as the sweet poet gave it leave to go,
Whereon another soul who came behind
5   turned our eyes to the summit of his flame
   by the strange garbled noise it spluttered out.
As the Sicilian bull that bellowed first
   with its inventor's[94] cries—and justly so—
   who'd smoothed its brazen contours with his file,
10   Would bellow with the tortured wretch's voice
   so loudly that, though it was made of bronze,
   the instrument itself seemed pierced in pain;
So here, finding at first the flame entire
   and every passage shut, the wretched words
15   converted to the language of the fire.
But when the voice had traveled all the way
   to the flame's tip, it quivered with that motion
   the tongue imparted, and we heard it say:
"O you to whom I now direct my voice,
20   who spoke in Lombard when you said just now,
   'Go, then, I won't provoke you any more,'
Though I've come somewhat late to take my turn,
   let it not vex you to remain and talk.
   You see it does not vex me—and I burn!
25   If into this blind dungeon you've been spilt
   recently from my lovely Italy,
   that sweet land and the scene of all my guilt,
Tell if Romagna is at peace or war:
   for I came from the hills between Urbino
30   and the peak that sets free the Tiber's flow."
I was still leaning out and looking down
   intently, when the poet touched my side.
   "Your turn to talk," he said. "Italian, he."
And I—who had determined what to say,

---

[94]*inventor:* the Athenian Perillus constructed a brazen bull for Phalaris, tyrant of Agrigentum in Sicily. The bull was hollow, allowing victims to be shut inside, while a fire was lit from below; the mouth was so formed as to turn the cries into bellowing. Fittingly, Perillus himself was the first victim.

35 began to speak. "O spirit down below
    hidden in flame," I said without delay,
  "Romagna is not and has never been
    free of the war within her tyrants' hearts;
    but I left none in open tyranny.
40 Ravenna stands as it has stood for years:
    the eagle of Polenta's brooding there
    and shadows Cervia with its spreading wings.
  Forli, that passed the trial of long siege
    and heaped the slaughtered Frenchmen in the field,
45 finds herself once more under the Green Paws.
  The mastiff and his puppy from Verrucchio,
    who had Montagna slain by treachery,
    suck the blood of their enemies—nothing new.
  The Lion Cub in the White Lair controls
50 the towns on the Lamone and the Santerno,
    who changes parties when the seasons change.
  And Cesena, washed by the Savio,
    just as it lies between the plains and hills,
    lives neither free nor under tyranny.
55 And now I ask you, tell me who you are,
    do not begrudge me more than I have you—
    so may the world long see your name endure."
  After the fire had made its hollow roar,
    such as it does, the keen point of the flame
60 danced here and there, and breathed out this reply,
  "If I believed that my response was heard
    by anyone returning to the world,
    this flame would stand and never stir again,
  But since no man has ever come alive
65 out of this gulf of Hell, if I hear true,
    I'll answer, with no fear of infamy.
  I was a man of arms, then wore the cord
    of a lay friar, thinking to make amends,
    and doubtless my belief would have come true
70 Had the Great Priest[95]—may he be dragged to Hell!—
    not pitched me back into my former faults.
    Listen to how and why, for I shall tell.
  While I yet wore the form of bones and flesh
    my mother gave me, all my actions were
75 not those that mark the lion, but the fox.
  Clever expedients and covered ways—

---

[95]*Great Priest:* Pope Boniface VIII

I worked them all so artfully, my fame
resounded at the limits of the earth.
Yet when I saw that I had reached the age
80   at which a man should reel the hawsers in
and let his sails come down, the deeds which once
I took delight in, now I wearied of,
confessed, repented, gave my freedom over.
Wretch that I am, it would have done me good!
85   But the prince of the modern Pharisees—
engaged in battle near the Lateran
and never against Saracens or Jews,
For all his enemies were Christian men,
and none turned traitor at the siege of Acre,
90   or plied his business in the Sultan's lands—
Cared neither for his papal dignity,
his holy orders, nor my friar's cord
which used to make men leaner in the waist.
As Constantine once summoned Pope Sylvester
95   to cure his leprosy on Mount Soracte,
so this one in the fever of his pride
Called me as his physician for the cure
and asked me for a plan, and I was silent,
because his words seemed drunken. But he pressed,
100   'Let your heart not be troubled. In advance
I will absolve you. Show me what to do
to batter Palestrina to the ground.
I hold the power to bar and unbar Heaven,
you know; for there are two of them, those keys
105   my predecessor[96] did not hold so dear.'
His ponderous words kept pushing me until
silence seemed the more perilous course. Said I,
'Father, because you cleanse me of that sin
Into which I am falling—well, be long
110   on promises and short on keeping them.
This gains the triumph for your lofty throne.'
The day I died, Saint Francis came for me,
but one of the black angels said to him,
'Don't cheat me now! Don't carry him away!
115   This one belongs with all my slaves down there,
because he gave his counsel to defraud.
Since then I've itched to snatch him by the hair!

---

[96]*my predecessor*: Pope Celestine V, who, under pressure from Boniface, abdicated the papacy

One who does not repent can't be absolved,
    nor can a man repent and will at once:
120   the law of contradiction rules it out.'
Ah, sorrow! When I woke to my position
    and heard him say as he grabbed hold, 'Perhaps
    you hadn't thought that I was a logician.'
He bore me off to Minos, and that judge
125   twisted his tail eight times round his rough back,
    and biting it in a mad burst of rage
He bellowed, 'To the thieving fire with this,'
    so where you see me I am lost forever,
    and, garbed in fire, I go in bitterness."
130   When he had finished what he had to say,
    the sorrowing flame departed from us, twisting
    and buffeting the arrow of the fire.
But we continued on, my guide and I,
    over the rock-ridge up the arch beyond
135   which spans the trench in which they pay the fee
Who heap up woe by severing what was joined.

CANTO TWENTY-EIGHT

*The poets now move on to the **ninth ditch of Malebolge**, where devils with swords slash open the **Schismatics**—sowers of discord on earth. They meet **Mohammed**; the Tuscan leaders **Pier da Medicina** and **Mosca dei Lamberti**; the instigator of Julius Caesar, **Curio**; and the Provencal poet and warrior, **Betrand de Born**.*

Who could ever—even with words set loose in prose—
    tell in full—though he told it many times—
    of all the blood and wounds I witnessed now?
Certainly every tongue would fall too short
5   on account of our language and our minds
    which lack the bosom to contain so much.
If you assembled all who ever fell
    in the fortune-battered fields of Puglia
    and found the sorrow of bloodshed at the hands
10   Of Trojans or of Hannibal, who piled
    a giant heap of rings from dead men's fingers
    in the long Punic War, as Livy writes,
Who does not stray—and added all who felt
    the grievous blows of Robert Guiscard's march,
15   with all the men whose bones lie heaped up still
At Ceperan, where every Pugliese chief
    turned traitor—and the bones near Tagliacozzo,

where old Alardo triumphed weaponless,
And had one show his limbs lopped off, and one
20   his members gored, it would be nothing to
the fashion of the filth in the ninth ditch.
A barrel with the mid-stave split apart
    is not—as I saw one there—so burst wide,
    from the chin severed down to where we fart.
25   His bowels and guts dangled between the legs;
    the organs showed, and that repugnant bag
    that turns whatever we gobble into shit.
While my mind clung entirely to this sight,
    he looked at me and with his two hands tore
30   his chest apart: "See how I split the haunch!
Look at Mohammed and his mangled trunk!
    Before me in his weeping goes Ali,
    slashed down the face from cowlick to the chin.
And all the other souls you witness here
35   sowed scandal, discord, schism when alive,
    and therefore they are cloven as you see.
Behind us is a devil who sets us right,
    for to the cruel slicing of his sword
    he subjects every spirit in the file
40   When we've gone once around the painful road,
    and every wound we suffer closes up
    before we come to face the steel again.
But who are you there gazing from the ridge,
    maybe to dawdle going to the pains
45   they've judged to fit the crimes that *you've* confessed?"
"Death has not caught him yet," my Teacher said,
    "nor is he led to torments here by sin,
    but to give him complete experience
I who am dead must lead him into Hell,
50   down the abyss from one round to the next.
    This is as true as that I speak to you."
When they heard what he said, more than a hundred
    stood stock-still in the trench to stare at me,
    forgetting all their tortures as they wondered.
55   "Well then, tell Fra Dolcin to arm himself—
    you who, perhaps, will see the sunlight soon,
    if he'd like not to follow me to Hell
Immediately—with lots of food supplies,
    lest snow bring victory to the Novarese
60   which wouldn't have come easy otherwise."
Raising one foot suspended in the air,

Mohammed spoke these words to me, then stretched
   toe to the ground to walk and leave us there.
   Another, with a hole bored through his throat
65   and his nose severed clear up to the eyes,
   and only one ear left, stood in the moat
With all the rest to gape at me in wonder,
   but he was first to open up his pipe,
   all red with blood and visible outside,
70 And said, "O you whom sin does not condemn,
   and whom I saw above in Italy,
   unless too close a likeness has deceived me—
Remember me, Pier da Medicina,
   if ever you return to the sweet plains
75   that from Vercelli slope to Marcabo.
And let the two princes of Fano know,
   tell milord Guido and tell Angiolello,
   unless the prophecies of Hell are vain,
They will be pitched out of their boat at sea,
80   stones hung about their necks near La Cattolica
   by a fierce tyrant[97] in his treachery.
From Cyprus west all the way to Majolica[98]
   Neptune has never seen so great a crime,
   neither by pirates, nor by men of Greece.
85 That treacherous prince who squints out of one eye,
   who holds the land whereof one here with me
   would just as soon have fasted from the sight,
Will have them come to parley, then arrange
   that they should have no need of prayer or vow
90   to get them past Focara's windy cape."
And I to him: "Then please, make clear to me,
   if you would have me tell of you above,
   who's he, who hates the sight of Rimini?"
At that he put his hand upon the jaw
95   of a companion, prying the mouth open,
   hollering, "This one here, who doesn't talk.
Driven from Rome, this spirit drowned the doubts
   in Caesar, by affirming that a man
   who is prepared delays to his own loss."
100 Oh, how he seemed to me downcast and cold,
   with his tongue sliced in half down to the gullet,
   this Curio, whose speech was once so bold!

---

[97]*tyrant:* the one-eyed Malatestino Malatesta, prince of Rimini
[98]*Majolica:* Majorca

And one whose hands both left and right were lopped,
   raising his dripping stumps in the dark air
105   so that the blood that fell befouled his face,
Cried out, "Remember Mosca too, who said,
   alas, 'A thing that's done with has an end,'
   which sowed the seeds of ill for Tuscany."
I added: "And brought death to your whole line,"
110   at which, accumulating woe on woe,
   he went away as one beset with gloom
And madness. I remained to view the band,
   and saw a thing I'd be afraid to tell
   alone, without more proof to back my word,
115   But my good conscience makes me feel secure,
   that trusty friend that frees a man beneath
   the armor of his knowing he is pure.
Clearly I saw, and the sight still comes back,
   a trunk without a head come walking on
120   just like the others of that sullen pack,
That held the chopped-off head by the long hanks,
   a-hanging like a lantern from his hand,
   and the head gaped at us and said, "Ah, me!"
He made himself a lamp unto himself,
125   and they were two in one and one in two.
   How that can be, He knows Who steers the helm.
When he arrived just at the bridge's foot
   he lifted the arm high with the whole head,
   to bring these words the closer to our sides:
130   "Now look upon the grievous punishment,
   you who yet breathe and go to view the dead—
   see whether any is as great as mine!
That you may bring back news about me, know
   I am Bertran de Born, the one who roused
135   the English prince against his sire and king.[99]
I set the father and the son at war;
   the wicked goadings of Achitophel
   for Absalom and David did no more.
Because I sundered two such persons joined,
140   sundered I carry now my brains, alas,
   from their stem in this trunk. Thus you may see
The rule of retribution work in me."

---

[99]*English prince . . . king:* Prince Henry and Henry II of England, his father

CANTO TWENTY-NINE

*Before they leave the ditch of the Schismatics, Dante notices the mutilated shade of a kinsman, **Geri del Bello**, threatening him. When the poets come to the **tenth ditch of Malebolge**, where the **Falsifiers** are punished by nauseating and detestable diseases, they meet two **Alchemists, Graffolino and Capocchio**. The canto ends with an invective against **the stupidity of the Sienese.***

The mob of souls and all their various wounds
   had made my lights so full and drunk with tears,
   I longed to stay a little while and weep.
But Virgil: "What are you still gazing at?
5   Why does your sight still prop itself down there
   among the dismal amputated shades?
You did not do so at the other moats.
   Think, if you're going to number all the spirits,
   twenty-two miles the valley turns about.
10 The moon's already set beneath our feet;
   the time conceded us is short enough.
   There's more to see which you have not yet seen."
"If you had paid attention to the cause,"
   straightaway I responded, "why I gazed,
15 you might have granted me a longer pause."
Meanwhile he set out, and I followed him,
   my guide, as I was making my reply
   and adding to it, "In that cavity
Where I was keeping at my post to look,
20   I think a spirit of my own blood mourns
   the wickedness that down there costs so much."
"There is no need," my Teacher said to me,
   "to break your thoughts upon him anymore.
   Attend to something else, and let him stay
25 Where he must stay. I saw him near the bridge
   pointing you out and hurling threats at you,
   and heard them call his name: Geri del Bello.
Your mind was then so seized by him who once
   was lord of Hautefort,[100] you didn't look
30   in his direction until he had gone."
"My Guide, the violent death he had to die
   which hasn't been avenged by anyone
   who should be party to his shame," said I,
"makes him indignant, as I guess, and so

---

[100]*lord of Hautefort:* Bertrand de Born

35   he takes his leave and does not speak to me.
        That made me feel more pity for his fate."
      So we conversed as we went walking, right
        to where the ridge would first reveal the pit
        down to the bottom, if there were more light.
40   When we arrived at the last cloister of
        Pouches of Evil, and our eyes could see
        the lay-brothers it housed, I was so stung
      With arrows of unusual laments,
        they seemed to steel the tips in sympathy—
45   and so I blocked my ears up with both hands.
      If you threw all the sick in the sick-houses
        of Val di Chiana in malaria season,
        and the diseases of Maremma's flats
      And of Sardinia, into the same ditch—
50   such pain was here, and it made just such stink
        as comes from members dying of the rot.
      Over the final slope of the long ridge
        we two descended, turning still to left,
        and then my power of sight came more alive
55   Down towards the bottom, where the minister
        of God on high, Justice infallible,
        punishes counterfeits whose sins on earth
      It enters in its book. No greater gloom
        did all the sick of Aegina behold,
60   when the air was so full of pestilence
      That every living thing down to the worm
        dropped dead, all of them, and the ancient folk,
        as the old poets hold for certain truth,
      Restored their progeny from the seed of ants,
65   than was the gloom in that dark valley, seeing
        the spirits languish in their separate sheaves.
      Some on another's stomach or his back
        lay sprawled, while others dragged their shifting forms
        on all fours down the melancholy track.
70   Step by slow step we took our silent way,
        listening to and watching the diseased,
        who could not raise their persons from the ground.
      I saw two sitting propped, as one fry-pan
        leans on another fry-pan in the oven,
75   spotted from head to foot with scabby crusts,
      And I've not seen a currycomb so fast
        scrubbed by the stable-boy whose master's coming,
        or by one waked against his will to hurry,

As did each soul rake himself with the bite
80   of fingernails in the great maddening itch,
        itch that will never find relief or rest,
And scraped the nails down the long stretch of scab
        like a knife slicing scales from off a pike
        or other fish whose scales are bigger yet.
85   "O you whose fingers strip your sheet-mail off,"
        my guide began to speak to one of them,
        "and sometimes dig the nail to tug and pinch,
Tell us if an Italian in this ditch
        is to be found—so may your nail suffice
90   to do this labor for eternity."
"We whom you see so laid to waste, we two
        are both Italian," said the one, in tears,
        "but you who ask this of us, who are you?"
And my guide said, "I am one who descends
95   with this man yet alive from ledge to ledge,
        for I intend to show him all of Hell."
Then they broke off their mutual prop and stay
        and each one, trembling, turned to look at me,
        with all who heard it on the ricochet.
100   Towards my side then the good Teacher drew
        and said, "Say anything you want to them,"
        and I began thus, as he wished me to:
"So may your name not steal itself away
        from human memory in the former world,
105   but live through many turnings of the sun,
Tell me then who you are, and from what city;
        let not your tedious and repulsive pains
        make you ashamed to show yourselves to me."
"Arezzo was my city," one replied.
110   "Albert of Siena burnt me at the stake,
        but why I'm damned here is not why I died.
It's true I said to him, speaking in jest,
        'I can rise up into the air and fly!',
        and he, a fickle sort with not much brains,
115   Wanted to learn the art. For this alone—
        I did not make him Daedalus![101]—he had
        me burned by him who held him as his son.
But Minos who can never be deceived
        condemned me to this last pouch of the ten,

---

[101]*Daedalus:* the mythical Greek inventor who devised waxen wings with which to escape from the island of Crete

120   for alchemy I practiced in the world."
        I to the poet: "Now was there ever a folk
          as vain and stupid as the Sienese?
          Surely not even Frenchmen, not by far!"
        The other leprous spirit overheard

125   and answered me: "And that's not counting Stricca
          who had the knack to keep his spending down,
        And Niccolo who was the first above
          to sow into that garden lush with weeds
          the luxury of seasoning with the clove,

130   Nor does it count the Squanderers' Brigade
          among whom Caccia chucked his lands and vines
          and the Bedazzled showed what sense he made.
        But if you'd like to know who backs your cry
          against the Sienese, sharpen your sight

135   until my features give you the reply,
        And you will see that I'm Capocchio's shade,
          who made false metals by my alchemy,
          and, if my eyes see true, you should recall
        How fine an ape of Nature's works I was."

CANTO THIRTY

*Still in the **tenth ditch of Malebolge**, Dante sees two frenzied spirits running like dogs and tearing into the other sufferers; they are the shades of the **Impostors, Gianni Schicchi and Myrrha**. Then the poets meet the swollen hydroptic, **Master Adam**, a **Counterfeiter**, who finds himself in a scuffle with **Sinon**, the **Liar** who played the Trojans false in the affair of the Horse. After Virgil rebukes Dante for evidently enjoying the brawl, the poets leave.*

        Back in the days when Juno's wrath was fired
          against the Theban blood by Semele,
          and she avenged herself against them twice,
        She made King Athamas grow so insane

5   that when he saw his wife with either arm
          carrying the burden of his two young sons,
         He cried, "Let's lay the nets so I can catch
          the lioness and the lion-cubs at the pass!"
        And then he thrust his ruthless clutches forth

10   And snatched the one, Learchus—whirled him round
          and brained him on a stone; then with the other
          the mother leapt into the sea and drowned.
        And when the wheel of fortune turned about
          to bring Troy down for all its daring pride,

15   and king and kingdom were at once wiped out,
     Pathetic Hecuba,[102] in captive gloom,
       seeing the strangling of Polyxena
       her daughter, and the sad discovered doom
     Of murdered Polydorus on the shore,
20   frenzied and mad, went howling like a dog,
       so badly had her grief twisted her mind.
     But none so fury-ridden in Thebes or Troy
       had ever lunged with such ferocity
       to bite at beasts or even rip men's limbs,
25   As I saw two souls, naked, pale as death,
       tearing away and snapping as they ran,
       like the tusked swine who's set loose from the sty.
     One of them got Capocchio, sunk his tusk
       into the neck, and as he dragged him off,
30   he made him rake his gut on the hard ground.
     The Aretine remaining, all atremble,
       said to me, "That mad demon's Gianni Schicchi,
       who in his frenzy mangles us like that."
     Said I, "Oh, let that other swine not stick
35   its tusks into your back, but tell us, please,
       who it may be, before it dashes off."
     "That is the ancient soul of wicked Myrrha
       who strayed beyond the bounds of lawful love,"
       said he, "when she became her father's lover.
40   This girl went to her father's bed to sin,
       falsified in another woman's form;
       that other counterfeiter dared to fake
     Buoso Donati at the point of death
       so he could win the princess of the stables,
45   entering his last will and testament."
     When the two shades whom I'd been watching passed
       in their furious rage, I turned to look
       upon the others born in evil hour.
     I saw one sinner shaped like a fat lute,
50   or would be, if you chopped off at the groin
       the legs which make a man into a fork.
     The heavy dropsy that distorts the limbs
       with ill-drained humors, bloating up the paunch
       so big with fluid that it dwarfs the face,
55   Puffed up his mouth, as a consumptive man
       driven by thirst curls back his upper lip

---

[102]*Hecuba:* Queen of Troy

and draws the lower one down to touch the chin.
"O you who are without a punishment—
and I don't know why—in this wretched world,"

60   said he to us, "behold, and listen to
The miserable state of Master Adam.
   Alive, I had all I could want, and now,
   alas, I long for one small water drop.
The little rushing brooks that splash their way

65   down the green hills of Casentino to
the Arno, with their stream-beds cold and moist,
Are ever before me, and it's not in vain,
   for their sweet image dries me out far worse
than this which wastes the flesh within my face.

70   The rigid justice sifting me like wheat
   has drawn a cause from where my sins took place
to set my thirsty sighs to faster flight.
There stands Romena castle, where I coined
   counterfeit money with the Baptist's stamp,

75   for which I left my body burnt above.
But if I could see here the mournful souls
   of Guido, Alexander, or their brother—
for Branda's fountain I'd not trade that sight!
And if those raving shades that run around

80   this dungeon tell the truth, one's here already—
what good is that to me? My limbs are bound!
Yet if I were still barely light enough
   to go but one inch in a hundred years,
   I'd have set out upon the path by now,

85   Culling him out from all this loathsome dross,
   though it's eleven miles around the ditch
   and not less than a half a mile across.
On their account I'm in this household here:
   they led me on to stamp the florins with

90   the three carats of trash instead of gold."
And I to him: "Who are those wretched things,
   the two who steam like sweaty hands in winter,
   lying tight on your border at the right?"
"I found them here—they haven't turned once since,

95   when I rained down into this garbage-pot,
   nor do I think they'll ever turn again.
This one's the lying woman[103] who accused

---

[103]*lying woman:* Potiphar's wife, who falsely charged the Hebrew Joseph with rape; see Gen. 39

Joseph; that's the Greek liar, Sinon of Troy:
    sharp fever burns their grease and makes that stench."
100   And one of them, who took it as a spite
    perhaps, that he was given so black a name,
    banged with his fist that swollen bag of guts.
It boomed as if it were a kettledrum,
    and Master Adam gave him no less back
105   but smacked him in the face with a free arm,
And said to him, "Although the heaviness
    so weighs my members down that I can't move,
    I have one arm that still can do the job."
And he replied, "Those arms were not so free
110   when you were strapped and burning at the stake,
    but when you coined, you moved them readily!"
And the hydroptic, "There you do tell truth,
    but you were not so true a witness when
    Priam the Trojan asked you for the truth."
115   "I told a lie, and you lied with your coins,"
    said Sinon. "I'm here for a single sin,
    but you, for more than any other fiend!"
"Recall, you perjurer, the Trojan horse,"
    responded he who had the bloated paunch,
120   "and let it pain you that the whole world knows."
"And let the thirst that cracks your tongue pain you,"
    said the Greek, "and that watery rot which makes
    a hedge out of your guts to block your eyes!"
The money-maker then: "So let your mouth
125   be gashed to shreds by your disease, as always,
    for if I thirst and fluid stuffs my bag,
You have the burning migraine in the skull,
    and you'd need few words to invite you to
    take one lick of Narcissus' glassy pool."
130   I was entirely fixed upon those two
    when said my Teacher, "You keep looking there
    and in a while *I'll* pick a fight with *you*."
And when I heard the anger in his voice
    I turned with such embarrassment and shame
135   it haunts my memory still. But as a man
Who dreams disaster or a grievous loss,
    dreaming, he longs for it to be a dream,
    yearning for what's the case, as if it weren't,
So was I then, when I could not reply,
140   wanting to make apology, and I
    apologized indeed—unwittingly.

"Less shame would wash away a greater fault,"
   my Teacher said, "than yours has been, and so
   unburden all the sadness from your mind.
145 Be sure that I am ever at your side,
   if fortune ever welcomes you again
   where people brawl like that and do not tire.
To want to hear it, is a base desire."

CANTO THIRTY-ONE

*The poets now descend to the **tenth and final circle** of Hell, that of the **Traitors**. They are conveyed to the bottom of that sink by **Antaeus**, one of **the Giants**, along with **Nimrod** and **Ephialtes**, punished in chains here for their presumption.*

The very tongue that stung me with rebuke
   so that I flushed with shame in either cheek,
   then brought the medicine to soothe the shame;
As I have heard the lance of Peleus
5   and of his son Achilles used to give
   wounds with the first touch, healing with the next.
We turned our back upon the wretched pit,
   with no more conversation as we crossed
   upon the inner ridge that circles it.
10 Here it was less than night and less than day,
   and I could hardly see in front of me,
   but heard instead the deep blast of a horn
Loud enough to make roaring thunder faint,
   and as it took its course it turned my eyes
15   to focus on the place from which it came.
After the bloody rout, when the great Charles[104]
   had lost his army and the holy war,
   never so terribly in Roncesvalles
Did Roland blow his horn. And when I turned
20   I soon caught sight, or so it seemed, of towers,
   many and tall. "Teacher, what land is this?"
I asked, and he replied, "Because you race
   ahead too great a distance through the darkness,
   imagination tangles you in knots.
25 You'll see it well, when you've arrived, how much
   your senses have deceived you from afar;
   so spur yourself a bit and hurry on."
He took me by the hand affectionately.

---

[104]*Charles:* Charlemagne

"Before we go much farther, you should know,
30   lest it should strike you as a shock," said he,
"That those things aren't towers, but giants, sunk
    into the basin there behind its banks,
    and each one visible from the navel up."
As when a fog begins to float away,
35   little by little, sight re-figures things
    which had lain hidden in the thickened air,
So in that dark dense vapor, piercing through
    as I came near and nearer to the brink,
    my errors fled from me, and my fear grew,
40   For, as upon the circling ramparts of
    Montereggion there stands a crown of towers,
    so here with half their persons high above
The limits of the inner sink of Hell
    tower the horrible giants, whom Jupiter
45   still menaces with thundering in the skies.
Then I discerned the face of one indeed,
    shoulders and chest and great part of the trunk,
    and both arms hanging at his flanks. No doubt
Nature did very well, when she left off
50   the art of making living things like those,
    depriving Mars of such executors.
And if she still, without regret, creates
    the whale and elephant, consider well
    and you will find her wiser and more just,
55   For where you join to evil will and might
    the instrument of reason in the mind,
    no shelter for mankind can ever stand.
I thought his face had the same length and bulk
    as the bronze pine-cone hanging at Saint Peter's,
60   with a like measure for his other bones;
So the banks of the basin, like a loin-cloth
    from the waist down, still showed enough of him
    above, that if they tried to grab his hair
Three lanky Frisians would have failed their boast,
65   for I could count thirty great spans of him
    down from the place a man will clasp his cloak.
"*Raphel ma-i amecche zabi almi,*"
    the savage mouth began to shout at us;
    no sweeter psalm was fit for such as he.
70   And my guide turned against him: "Stupid soul!
    Grab your horn tight and vent yourself with it
    when wrath or any passion seizes you!

Feel round your neck and there you'll find the strap
   that keeps it tied, O spirit of confusion—
75   and see it make the stripe across your chest."
To me then, "He incriminates himself.
   He's Nimrod;[105] owing to his evil plan
   there's no one language used in all the world.
Let's leave him and not toss our words away,
80   for no one's ever heard the tongue he speaks,
   and every tongue is gibberish to him."
So we walked further onward, to the left,
   and at the distance of a crossbow-shot
   we found another giant, fiercer far
85   And mightier in bulk. I cannot say
   what sort of craftsman bound him, but a chain
   ran like a belt five times around his body
From the neck to the waist, and strapped his arms,
   the left pinned tight against his chest, the right
90   behind his back. "This piece of arrogance,"
My guide explained, "wanted to try his power
   against the power of the highest Jove,
   and this is what he merits for his pains.
Ephialtes—who fought in the great test
95   when warring giants put the gods to fear.
   The arms he raised, he'll never move again."
And I to him: "If it can be arranged,
   I'd like my eyes to have experience
   of Briareus, the immeasurable."
100   And he responded, "You will see Antaeus
   nearby, for he can speak and is unchained.
   He'll set us at the bottom of all crime.
The one you'd like to see is far off there,
   and is in chains, just like this giant here,
105   except he's more ferocious in his looks."
No earthquake ever shook so strong a tower
   with violence to match Ephialtes
   who on a sudden shook. Then more than ever
I was afraid that I might die—the dread
110   would have sufficed alone to bring it on,
   had I not seen the bonds that held him bound.
So we proceeded further, and we came
   to where Antaeus rose a good seven yards,

---

[105]*Nimrod:* according to tradition, the builder of the Tower of Babel; see Gen. 10:8–12, 11:1–9

besides his head, out of the rock-rimmed gulf.

115 "O you who in that valley[106] touched by fate—
where Scipio was made the heir of glory
when Hannibal turned tail with all his troops—
Once slew a thousand lions for your prey,
and who, if you had fought in the great war

120 beside your brother Titans, some do think
The Sons of Earth would have enjoyed the day,
do not take it in scorn to set us down
where the cold locks the Cocytus in ice.
Don't make us seek Tityus or Typhoeus:

125 this man can give you what you long for here,
so bend and do not turn your face askew,
For in the world he can still bring you fame.
He lives, and looks to live for many years,
unless grace calls him home before his time."

130 So said the Teacher; and the giant in haste
reached down those hands which once made Hercules
feel their hard grip, and took hold of my guide,
And Virgil, when he felt it, said to me,
"Come over here, let me hold on to you,"

135 and made one bundle of himself and me.
As it appears to one who stands beneath
the Garisenda tower that leans, when clouds
pass by to make the sight impending—so
Antaeus seemed to me who stood intent

140 to watch him lean; and there were moments when
I wished we had another road to go.
But softly at the bottom which devours
Judas and Lucifer, he set us down,
nor did he linger after he had bent

145 But straightened like a mast upon a ship.

---

[106]*that valley:* at Zama, near present-day Tunis, in north Africa; there the Roman general
Scipio defeated the great Carthaginian, Hannibal, to end the Second Punic War

CANTO THIRTY-TWO

*The poets now walk over the frozen **River Cocytus**. They are in the **tenth circle**, among the **Traitors**. Here in the region called **Caina**, frozen in the ice, with their heads bowed, are the **Betrayers of Kindred**. Dante meets **Camiscion de' Pazzi**, who identifies for him the **Brothers of Mangona**, who slew each other. Proceeding to a second zone, **Antenora**, Dante encounters the **Betrayers of Nation or Party**, among whom is the Florentine traitor **Bocca degli Abati**, who betrays for Dante the identities of others there with him.*

Had I the bitter and crack-throated rhymes
    fit for the miserable hole towards which
    all of the other beetling ridges thrust,
I would squeeze out the juice of my invention
5   more fully, but because I have no such,
    not without fear I bring myself to speak:
It is no jesting enterprise to tell—
    not for the tongue that calls "mama" and "dada"—
    about the universal sink of Hell.
10   But let those Ladies[107] now assist my verse
    who helped Amphion raise the walls of Thebes;
    so may my words not differ from the fact.
You rabble, worst of ill-created things,
    who stand fixed in a place which speech abhors—
15   better had you been born as sheep or goats!
When we arrived down in that gloomy well
    far lower than the giants' feet above,
    and I was gazing still at the high wall,
I heard a voice cry out, "Watch where you step!
20   Go on, but do not tread upon the heads
    of the exhausted brothers, spirits damned."
At that I turned, and saw before my feet
    a lake of ice, which in the terrible cold
    looked not like frozen water, but like glass.
25   So thick an ice-veil never blocks the course
    of the Danube in wintry Austria,
    nor of the Don under the frigid sky,
As was this ice; and if Mount Tambernic
    had fallen on it, or Mount Pietrapan,
30   even its edge would not have made a creak.
As the frog in the summer sits to croak,
    his mug above the pond, while hazy dreams

---

[107] *those Ladies:* the Muses

of gleaning come upon the peasant girl,
So were the grieving spirits, livid gray,
35   fixed in the ice up to where shame appears,
      chattering their teeth like storks that snap their bills.
Each held his face down low, while every mouth
      gave evidence of the cold, and every eye
      testified to the sorrow in the heart.
40   When I had looked about awhile, I glanced
      down at my feet; and saw two spirits so
      tight-pressed, their heads of hair had grown ensnarled.
"O you who hold your chests in such a clench,"
      said I, "who are you?" And they wried their necks,
45   and when they'd raised their faces straight towards me
Their eyes, which had been moist already, spilled
      tears through the eyelids, which the ice froze shut
      back in the sockets with its locking grip.
Never a clamp clamped plank to plank so hard,
50   for which they were so overcome with wrath
      they butted head to head like two he-goats.
And one whose ears the frost had bitten off
      said to us, ever keeping his head low,
      "What mirror are you staring at in us?
55   If you would like to know who these two are,
      the vale of the Bisenzo was the home
      both for their father Albert and for them.
From the same womb they came. And you could search
      all of Caina, and you'd never find
60   souls fitter to be fixed in aspic here,
Not him whose chest and shadow were gored through
      by one blow from the hand of Arthur,[108] not
      Foccaccia, not this one who burdens me
With his head in my way to block my sight,
65   whose name above was Sassol Mascheroni.
      You'll know of him if you're from Tuscany.
So you won't weary me with talk, I was
      Camiscion de' Pazzi, and await
      Carlino, who will make my crime seem less."
70   After, I saw a thousand faces, turned
      wolfish for cold, at which I shuddered then
      and shall whenever I see a frozen bog.
And while we went down to the central hole

---

[108] *not him . . . Arthur:* Mordred, bastard son and betrayer of King Arthur, slain by him in Arthur's final battle

where sinks the whole world's heaviness, and I
75   was trembling in the everlasting chill,
If it was fortune, destiny, or will,
        who knows, but as I walked among the heads
        I stubbed my foot hard on one spirit's face.
He wailed and yelled, "Why do you trample me?
80   Unless you come to add to the revenge
        for Montaperti,[109] why this injury?"
And I: "My Teacher, wait for me a bit.
        I want to clear a doubt I have of him;
        then make me hurry on as you see fit."
85   So my guide paused, and I replied to him
        who kept on spitting out his blasphemies,
        "Who are you, slinging such rebuke at others?"
"And who are you who go through Antenora
        kicking," he answered, "others' cheeks so hard,
90   if I were living, it would be too rough!"
"*But I'm alive*, and can be good to you,"
        was my response, "if you should look for fame:
        I'll make a note of you with all the rest."
And he to me: "I crave the opposite.
95   Get lost, then! Don't torment me any more.
        You don't know how to flatter for this pit."
I caught him by the dog-hair on his nape
        and said, "I think you'd better tell your name,
        or I won't leave a hair left in your scalp!"
100   And he: "Rip out my locks then, strip me bald!
        I still won't tell or show you who I am,
        not if you pounced on me a thousand times!"
I'd wound his hanks already in my hand
        and yanked them out in bunches as he yowled
105   and huddled his eyes low, when someone yelled,
"Hey, Bocca, what the hell's the fuss? It's not
        enough to play the snare-drum with your jaws,
        you've got to bark too? What's got into you?"
"Now," said I, "speak no more, it's fine with me,
110   vile traitor that you are, for I'll bring back
        the truth about you, to your infamy."
"Go away," he replied. "Tell what you like!
        But don't keep mum if you get out of here
        about that soul whose tongue was quick to speak.
115   He weeps for the *argent* he took from France.

---

[109]*Montaperti:* battle in 1260, at which Bocca betrayed Dante's party

'I saw,' you can go say, 'the one from Duera
   down where the sinners are kept fresh in ice.'
And if they ask of you, 'Who else was there?',
   here at your side's that son of Beccheria
120   whose gullet Florence sliced the axe-head through,
And I do think Soldanier's farther on
   with Ganelon and Tebaldello, who
   opened Faenza's gates when the town slept."
We had already left him, when I saw
125   two frozen in one hole in such a way
   that one man's head was as the other's hood,
And as a hunk of bread is chewed in hunger,
   so did the top soul tear his teeth into
   the other, where the neck adjoins the brain,
130   Not otherwise than as Tydeus gnawed
   Melanippus' temples in his hate-filled rage;
   so did he gnaw the brains, the flesh, the skull.
"O you who show by such a beast-like sign
   your hatred of the one you feed upon,
135   tell me the reason, and I'll set this deal,"
Said I, "that if your hate has a just cause,
   knowing his crime and who you are, I will
   make you a good trade in the world above,
Unless my tongue should wither to the root."

CANTO THIRTY-THREE

Still in **Antenora** *among the* **Betrayers of Nation or Party,** *Dante hears the tale of* **Count Ugolino,** *who now takes his revenge by gnawing upon the brains of* **Archbishop Ruggieri,** *the man who treacherously imprisoned Ugolino and his four sons in a tower and let them starve. The poets continue to the third zone,* **Ptolomea,** *where souls go, even before the death of their bodies, when they become* **Betrayers of Guests.** *Here he finds* **Brother Alberigo** *and* **Ser Branca D'Oria.**

He raised his mouth up from that savage feed,
   the sinner did, and wiped it on the hair
   of the head he was spoiling from behind.
Then he began: "You want me to recount
5   all the despair and pain that break my heart
   even in thought, before I tell my tale.
But if my words must be the seed to sprout
   infamy for this traitor whom I gnaw,
   you'll see me weeping, speaking through my tears.
10   I don't know who you are or by what way

you've come down here, but from the speech I hear
you seem no doubt to be a Florentine.
Then you should know I was Count Ugolino,
and this here is Ruggieri, the Archbishop.
15 I'll tell you now why I'm so close to him.
That on account of his malicious plots,
trusting myself to him, I was first seized
then put to death, there is no need to say,
Yet what you can't have heard a thing about,
20 the cruelty of the death I suffered, now
you'll hear, and know if he has done me wrong!
A little window in the Eagle Cage,
now called the Tower of Hunger after me,
a tower which shall be barred for others yet,
25 Had shown me through its hole the passing moon
several times over, when a nightmare came
and tore in two the veil of things to come.
This one appeared to me as lord and master,
chasing the wolf and wolf-pups to the hills
30 obstructing Lucca from the Pisan's sight.
Leading his famished bitches in the hunt,
the Gualandi, Sismondi, and Lanfranchi[110]
took their positions and assumed the front.
A short run—then the father and his sons
35 appeared exhausted, and I dreamed I saw
the fangs of hounds ripping their sides apart.
When I awoke before the break of dawn
I heard my small sons sobbing in their dreams,
for they were with me, and they asked for bread.
40 You must be cruel if you don't grieve now
thinking of what my heart foretold—and if
now you don't weep, when do you weep at all?
Then they awakened, and the hour drew near
when food was always brought us, but we grew
45 afraid, as each of us recalled his dreams;
And I could hear them nailing up the door
of the horrible tower; and gazed upon
the faces of my sons, and spoke no more.
I did not weep, I had so turned to stone;
50 *they* wept. And my little Anselm said,
'Father, why do you stare like that? What's wrong?'
Therefore I did not weep or make reply

---

[110]*Gualandi . . . Lanfranchi:* families in Ruggieri's employ

all that long day and all the night to follow,
until the next sun came into the world.

55 When a weak glint of daylight made its way
into our prison of sorrow, and I saw
my own face in the four that looked at me,
I bit both hands for grief; and they, who thought
that I was longing for some food to eat,
60 suddenly rose and came to me and said,
'Father, for us it would be much less pain
if you ate us instead! You clothed us with
this wretched flesh, now strip it off again.'
I calmed myself lest they grow sadder still;
65 that day and all the next we did not speak.
Why did you not then open, O hard earth!
And when we had arrived at the fourth day,
my Gaddo fell outstretched before my feet,
saying, 'Papa, why don't you help me?' There
70 He died. As clearly as you see me here
I watched the other three drop, one by one,
the fifth and sixth days. Then I flung myself,
Already blind, groping upon each one—
two days I called their names, when they were dead.
75 Then hunger did what sorrow could not do."
Having said that, he turned his eyes askance
and took the wretched skull between his teeth,
tough as a dog's that gnaws down to the bone.
Ah, Pisa, vile disgrace of all the folk
80 in the sweet land where 'si' is uttered! Since
your neighbor towns are slow to punish you,
May the isles of Capraia and Gorgona
uproot themselves to plug the Arno's mouth,
that everyone who dwells in you may drown!
85 For if Count Ugolino suffered blame,
having betrayed you of your fortresses,
you for your part should not have nailed his sons
To such a cross! O Thebes renewed and young,
their tender ages made them innocent—
90 Brigata, Hugh, and the other two my song
Remembers here. We passed on, where the ice
swaddles another clan in its coarse wrap—
their heads not bowed, but all turned up and back.
Weeping itself forbids the souls to weep,
95 and pain which finds a barrier in their eyes
turns back within to make the agony grow;

For the first teardrops form an icy knot,
   and as a helmet-vizor of hard glass
   they fill the sockets full beneath the brow.
100 And even though, as in a callus, all
   sensation ceased to linger in my face
   because of the great cold, I felt a trace
Of a breeze striking me, and so I said,
   "Teacher, what makes this motion of the air?
105 I thought that every wind was spent down here."
And he to me: "You will come soon enough
   where your own eyes will give you the reply,
   seeing what makes this blast of wind come down."
One of the wretches in the frosty crust
110 cried to us then, "O cruel souls, so wicked
   that you are given the lowest place of all,
Lift the hard veils from off my face, that I
   may vent the grief my heart has soaked me with,
   one moment, till the tears freeze up again."
115 So I to him: "You'd like my help, then tell
   your name. If I don't clear your eyes, may I
   go to the bottom of this icy Hell!"
So he replied, "I'm Brother Alberigo,
   the man who served the fruit in the bad garden.
120 Here I'm paid back with interest, date for fig."
"Oh," said I, "are you dead already then?"
   And he responded, "How my body stands
   up in the world above, I do not know.
Such privilege has this realm of Ptolomea,
125 that oftentimes the soul drops down to Hell
   before the Fates have cut the thread of life.
And that you may, with greater will, shave off
   the tears hardened to glass upon my face,
   know that as soon as any soul betrays
130 As I betrayed, his body's snatched away
   and taken by a demon, who controls it
   until the time arrives for it to die.
The soul then falls headlong into this tank.
   Perhaps his body still appears above,
135 the shade who chirps his winter song behind me;
You may well know, for you have just come down.
   He is Ser Branca D'Oria; many years
   have passed since he was thus encased in ice."
Said I, "I think you play me for a fool!
140 For Branca D'Oria never died, but eats

and drinks and sleeps and puts his trousers on."
"Up in the trench," said he, "of Evilclaws,
   the pocket with the sticky bubbling pitch,
   judge Michel Zanche hadn't yet arrived
145 Before Ser Branca left his body for
   a devil—and a kinsman did the same,
   one who assisted in the treachery.
But now reach out your hand, open my eyes."
   And so I did not open them: to be
150   villainous to him was a courtesy.
Ah, Genoese, you aliens to all
   morality and full of every taint,
   why have you not been scattered from the world?
For with the wickedest soul Romagna bore
155   I found such one of yours who for his works
   already bathes his soul in Cocytus,
Whose body up above still seems alive.

CANTO THIRTY-FOUR

*The poets now arrive at the lowest sinkhole of Hell, **Judecca,** where the **Betrayers of Benefactors** are punished, most of them completely encased in ice. Here Dante beholds **Satan** himself, chewing, in his three mouths, **Judas Iscariot, Brutus,** and **Cassius.** With Dante on his back, Virgil climbs down the matted hide of Satan, reaches **the center of the earth,** and wheels about. The poets are now on the far side of the center, towards the southern hemisphere. They exit through a cavern and look upon the stars again.*

"The standards of the King of Hell advance
   towards us, and therefore look ahead and see,"
   my Teacher said, "if you can make him out."
A turning windmill far off would appear,
5   when a thick fog begins to lift away
   or night descends upon our hemisphere,
Like the strange edifice I then descried;
   but as there was no shelter from the wind
   so cold, I huddled back behind my guide.
10 With fear I set these words in verse! It was
   where the shades are all covered up in ice,
   and clearly seen, like wisps of straw in glass.
Some souls lie prone and some stand straight; of those
   some have their heads up, others have their soles,
15   and some bend over, face to feet, like bows.
When we'd walked far enough to reach the place

where my instructor thought it well to show me
   the creature who once had the lovely face,
He stopped me, stepped away from where I stood,
20   saying, "Behold there, Dis![111] Behold the place
   where you must arm yourself with fortitude."
How faint I then became, how turned to ice,
   Reader, ask not, I will not write it down,
   for any words I used would not suffice.
25   I did not die, did not remain alive.
   Think for yourself, if wisdom buds in you,
   what I became, deprived of life and death.
The emperor of the reign of misery
   from his chest up emerges from the ice;
30   closer the measure of a giant and me
Than of a giant and his arms alone;
   and if one limb is so enormous, you
   can see how vast the rest must be. If once
He was as fair as he is ugly now,
35   and raised his brow against his Maker still,
   he well is made the source of every woe.
But when I saw three faces in his head,
   how great a marvel it appeared to me!
   One face in front, and it was ruddy red;
40   The other two were joined to it upon
   the middle of the shoulder on each side,
   and joined above, where the cock sports his crown;
And the right was a kind of yellowish white,
   and where the Nile comes rolling to the plains,
45   the faces are the color on the left.
Beneath each face extended two huge wings,
   large enough to suffice for such a bird;
   I never saw a sail at sea so broad.
They had no feathers, but were black and scaled
50   like a bat's wings, and those he flapped, and flapped,
   and from his flapping raised three gales that swept
Cocytus, and reduced it all to ice.
   With his six eyes he wept, and down three chins
   dribbled his tears and slaver slick with blood.
55   In every mouth he gnashed his teeth to grind
   a sinner, as a thresher crushes flax,
   so there were three he put to such great pain.
For him in front the bites were nothing to

---

[111]*Dis:* Satan

60   the scraping claws that peeled away his back
   and often left it nude of any skin.
  "The soul up there whose punishment is worst,"
   the Teacher said, "is Judas Iscariot,
   whose feet stick out and who is chewed headfirst.
  Of the two others with their heads hung down,
65   the one who hangs from the black snout is Brutus:
   see how he writhes, and does not speak a word!
  Cassius the last, who looks so squarely built.
   But night is rising, and it's time to leave,
   for Hell has nothing more for us to see."
70   Just as he wished, I clasped him round the neck,
   and then he chose the moment and the place,
   just when the wings were open far enough,
  To grapple to the devil's matted side,
   clambering down from clump to clump between
75   the fur in tangles and the frozen crust.
  When we had reached the joint that turns the thigh,
   just at the thickening of the hip, my guide,
   with struggle, with his breath in agony,
  Reversed his head to face the devil's shanks,
80   and he clutched at the fur like one who climbs.
   I thought that we were turning back to Hell.
  "Hold on tight now, for by such stairs as these,"
   my Teacher panted, like a weary man,
   "one must depart from so much wickedness."
85   He came out through a fissure in a rock
   and set me down upon a ledge to sit,
   then joined me with a quick and careful step.
  I raised my eyes and thought that I would see
   Lucifer as I'd left him, but I saw
90   his legs held straight up in the air before me,
  And if I was bewildered then, let those
   thick-headed people judge who do not see
   what was that point[112] which I had passed beyond.
  "Come on," my Teacher said. "Up on your feet.
95   The way is long, the road is difficult,
   the sun already shines in the third hour."
  That was no palace hall or entryway
   we took then, but a cavern nature carved,
   where the footing was bad and the light dim.
100   "Before I pull my roots out of the pit,

---

[112]*that point:* the center of the earth

Teacher," I said when I could stand upright,
   "to clear an error speak with me a bit:
Where is the ice? The Devil, why is he
   fixed upside-down? How has the sun so soon
105   gone all the way to morning?" "You believe
You're on the far side of the center still,
   there where I grabbed the hide of the evil worm,"[113]
   said he, "who gnaws a hole into the world.
And so you were, as long as I climbed down,
110   but when I turned, you passed beyond the point
   towards which all weight from every side is drawn.
You're underneath the hemisphere which lies
   opposite that which spans the earth's dry land,[114]
   under whose zenith He was put to death,
115   He who was born and who lived without sin.[115]
   You have your feet upon a little sphere
   which constitues Judecca's other side.
Whenever it's morning here, it's evening there,
   and he who made a ladder with his hide
120   is there still fixed just as he was before.
He fell from Heaven on this side of the earth,
   and all the land that once was here took flight
   in fear of him, shrouded him in the sea,
And went north to our hemisphere, and maybe
125   the land we're walking on fled from him too,
   leaving the hole below us when it rose."
As far as you can go from Beelzebub[116]
   inside the cavern-tomb, there is a place
   where not by sight, but by its sound one finds
130   A little rushing stream that courses down
   a hollow it has eaten in a rock,
   taking a winding way, with easy slope.
Upon this hidden path my guide and I
   entered, to go back to the world of light,
135   and without any care to rest at ease,
He first and I behind, we climbed so high
   that through a small round opening I saw
   some of the turning beauties of the sky.
And we came out to see, once more, the stars.

---

[113]*evil worm:* Satan

[114]*that . . . land:* the northern hemisphere, which covers Europe and most of Asia and Africa

[115]*He . . . sin:* Christ

[116]*Beelzebub:* "Lord of the Flies," i.e., Satan

PURGATORIO

CANTO ONE

Dante and Virgil find themselves at the base of the **Mountain of Purgatory,** *just before the dawn. There they meet* **Cato of Utica,** *the reverend old man who serves as the guardian of the mountain. Following Cato's instructions, Virgil washes Dante's face and girds him with a humble reed.*

My little ship of ingenuity
   now hoists her sails to speed through better waters,
   leaving behind so harsh and cruel a sea,
For I will sing about that second reign
5   where human spirits purge their sins and grow
   worthy to climb at last to Paradise.
But here let the dead poetry arise,
   O holy Muses, for I am your own,
   and here, Calliope, strike a higher key
10   Accompanying my song with that sweet air
   which made the miserable Magpies[1] feel
   a blow that turned all pardon to despair.
Sweet sapphire of the morning in the east,
   gathering in the starlit atmosphere
15   pure from the zenith to the nearest ring,
Brought back the joy of looking on the skies
   as soon as I had come from the dead air
   which had oppressed with grief my heart and eyes.
That radiant star[2] that sheds its love like rain
20   made all the orient heavens smile with light,
   veiling the Fishes in her lovely train.
I turned to the right hand, and set my mind
   to scan the southern pole, and saw four stars[3]
   no man has seen since they who bore mankind
25   Saw them in Eden. What joy shone in their flame!
   O widowed region of the northern stars,
   you who have been deprived the sight of them!
When of that vision I had taken leave
   and turned a little towards the other pole,

---

[1]*Magpies:* The Pierides, sisters who, in Greek mythology, challenged the Muses to a contest in singing poetry. They lost. For their presumption, they were turned into chattering magpies.

[2]*star:* Venus, in the constellation Pisces

[3]*four stars:* Probably not the Southern Cross; rather, four stars representing the four cardinal virtues: Prudence, Temperance, Fortitude, and Justice.

30   where the Great Bear had disappeared below,
     I saw beside me an old man, alone,
       so reverend in his bearing and his look,
       no father claims more honor from his son.
     Long was his beard, a sable streaked with gray,
35   similar to the color of his hair:
       upon his breast in double bands it lay.
     The rays of the four holy stars on high
       adorned his face with such a brilliant light,
       it seemed the sun shone full upon his eye.
40   "Who are you who against the hidden stream
       have fled the prison of eternity?"
       said he, moving his venerable beard.
     "Who was your guide? What lamp has led your feet,
       issuing from the sea of that deep night
45   that ever darkens the infernal pit?
     Are the abyss's laws so broken? Or
       have all the heavens altered in their plan,
       to let the damned come to my rocky shore?"
     A gentle nudge I felt from my guide's hand,
50   and by his words and signs and touch he made
       my brow incline in reverence, my knees bend.
     "I come not on my own," responded he.
       "A Lady came from Heaven, and by her prayers
       I went to help him with my company.
55   But since it is your will that we should more
       fully reveal the truth about our state,
       my will cannot refuse. This man has not
     Yet seen the final setting of his sun,
       but by his folly it had drawn so near,
60   it left him very little time to turn.
     As I have said, to him then was I sent
       to rescue him, to free his soul: there was
       no other way but that by which I went.
     I've shown him all the people steeped in crime;
65   now I intend to show those souls that purge
       their sins under your custody. The time
     Would grow too long to tell our pilgrimage;
       from on high comes the power that is my help,
       leading him here to look on you at last
70   And hear your words. Favor his coming, then!
       He seeks his freedom—and how dear that is,
       he who refused his life for it knows well.
     You know it—for you did not find it bitter

to die for liberty in Utica,[4]
75   where you sloughed off the garment that will shine
So bright on the Great Day. We have not broken
    the eternal laws: for he still lives, and I,
    whom Minos does not bind, come from the ring
Where the chaste eyes of Martia still beseech you,
80   O holy breast, to hold her as your own.
    For her love then incline to grant our prayer.
Your seven realms above, let us go through:
    I will bring back to her our thankfulness,
    if to be named below can honor you."
85 "In life my Martia did so please my eyes,"
    said he, "that any favor she desired
    I granted to her. But now that she lies
Dwelling in death beyond the evil river,
    by that law set when first I left that world,
90   she can no longer move me, now nor ever.
But if a heavenly Lady guides your way
    and moves your steps, you have no need to flatter.
    Beg in her name: there is no more to say.
Go, therefore, and be sure you gird his waist
95   with a smooth, simple reed, and wash his face
    of all the grime of Hell, and all the dust.
No cloud should take his vision by surprise
    who steps before this mount's first minister—
    for he is one who comes from Paradise.
100 Lower and lower down about this isle,
    where the waves pound against the mountain's shore,
    reeds grow in the soft mud. No other plant
That breaks out into leaf, or stands upright
    with stiffened trunk, can long survive the place,
105   but yield at last to all the battering waves.
Do not return this way as you go up.
    The sun arising now will show you where
    to climb the mountain at its gentlest slope."
At that he vanished, and without a word
110   I raised myself and pressed close to my guide,
    casting my eyes upon him. He began:
"My son, follow my footsteps as we turn
    to go back down the plain, which slopes from here
    unto the lowest limit of the isle."

---

[4]*die for liberty:* Cato committed suicide rather than live under the reign of Julius Caesar, whom he failed to defeat in battle. For Dante, Cato's action was not one of disdain for life, but a sacrifice for liberty.

115 The dawn had driven the last twilight hour
       in flight before it, so that far away
       I saw the ocean trembling at the shore.
     We walked along that solitary plain
       as one who turns to find the road he's lost
120   and, till he finds it, seems to walk in vain.
     When we had come where dew is slow to fade,
       lying where it resists the warming sun,
       gathering in the hidden cool and shade,
     My master gently ran his open hands
125   over the little tufts of grass, and I,
       who understood the reason for his art,
     Presented him my cheeks, still stained and teared.
       He wiped them, and at last discovered all
       the color that the smoke of Hell had bleared.
130 At that we came to the deserted strand
       upon whose waters no man ever sailed
       who lived to tell it in his native land.
     He girt me there, as was Another's will.
       O wonder to behold! For when he chose
135   and plucked the lowly reed, in sudden grace
     Another was reborn to take its place.

CANTO TWO

Still at the base of the mountain, the poets see a boat approaching from the sea. It is guided by an angel, and is filled with spirits, in a state of grace, arriving at the mountain to purge their sins. Here Dante meets **Casella,** *an old friend who used to set Dante's poems to music. While Dante and the rest are listening to Casella sing, Cato interrupts the festivities.*

     To that horizon[5] had the sun now come,
       the arc that circles both the hemispheres,
       whose zenith stands above Jerusalem,
     And opposite Night, traversing the same way,
5   rose from the Ganges with those Scales he drops
       when length of darkness conquers length of day,
     So that the white and rosy cheeks of dawn,
       the lovely heavens, where I was standing, turned
       yellowish-orange in the aging sun.

---

[5]*that horizon:* The mountain of Purgatory occupies the point on the "horizon," or great circle round the earth, directly opposite Jerusalem. This particular circle is the ecliptic, the apparent path of the sun around the earth, and indeed its "zenith" or highest point lies above Jerusalem, on the Tropic of Cancer.

10 We were still walking by the sea, as those
       who dwell upon the journey they will make—
       the body lingers, while the spirit goes—
    When look! just as, surprised by morning haze,
       through the dense veils of mist to westward, Mars
15   sets in the sea with all his blushing rays,
    Such a light now appeared—ah may I see
       that light once more!—surpassing any flight,
       so swiftly did it move across the sea.
    And in the moment when I turned my sight
20   to ask my guide about it, glancing back
       I saw it had grown greater and more bright,
    And then from either side I saw a glow
       of something seeming-white, and gradually
       another gleam emerging from below.
25 My Teacher all the while spoke not a word
       as the two gleams at last appeared as wings,
       but when he recognized the helmsman, cried,
    "Now fold your hands in prayer! Fall to your knees!
       Behold, it is the herald of the Lord!
30   Now you will see such ministers as these.
    See how he holds all human means in scorn:
       he wants no oar between the shores so far
       nor other sail, but spreads his wings alone.
    See how he lifts his pennons to the sky,
35   sweeping the air with his eternal feathers,
       changeless—unlike the flesh of those who die."
    And as that Bird of Heaven drew more near,
       my eyes could not endure the glorious sight,
       so bright and dazzling did he now appear,
40 And down I cast them; and he came ashore
       upon a skiff so swift and sleek and light
       it swallowed up no water as it sped.
    The heavenly Pilot stood upon the bow,
       his beauty blessing even those who read.
45   More than a hundred souls sat toward the prow:
    "When from the land of Egypt Israel came,"
       they sang together in a single voice
       with all the verses written in that psalm.
    He gave the signal of the holy Cross
50   at which they cast themselves upon the beach;
       then turned and left as swiftly as he'd come.
    The crowd remaining stood like forest-folk
       in a strange place, looking about themselves

as one who tests and touches something new.
55 From every side the arrows of the sun
    shot daylight, as the keenness of his rays
    had from the noonday hunted Capricorn,
When the new people raised their eyes to us
    and asked, "Please, if you know it, show the way
60 we can climb up the mountain." "You perhaps
Believe that we've got some experience of
    this place," responded Virgil, "but we two
    are pilgrims like yourselves. A little while
Ahead of you we came by another way—
65 a road which was so harsh and difficult,
    climbing the mountain now will seem like play."
The spirits, who had marked the way I moved
    in breathing, saw that I was still alive
    and they turned pale with wonder. As the crowds
70 Will jostle in a rush, and no man's shy,
    when comes the messenger with olive-branch
    to bring the tidings to the town—so they,
Those spirits blessed by fate, those happy souls,
    fixed their gaze on my face, as if forgetting
75 that they must go to beautify themselves.
And one of them in pressing forward came
    to take me in his arms with such warm love
    he moved me in return to do the same.
Oh empty shadows, solid though you seem!
80 Three times behind his back I clasped my hands,
    returning empty to my breast each time.
Wonder, I think, was blushing in my face,
    at which the shade stepped backwards with a smile,
    and I, in following, made to try again,
85 When he most sweetly said that I should cease.
    And then at last I knew him, and I begged him
    to speak with me a little, at his ease.
"As in my mortal body," he replied,
    "I loved you then, so now I love you, free—
90 But you, why do you travel on this side?"
"Casella, friend, the journey I am on,
    I go that I may take it once again;
    but why were you deprived of so much time?"
And he to me: "No one has done me wrong,
95 if he who at his pleasure bids us climb
    into his ship, denied my crossing here
    Till now. From a just will he fashions his,

and in truth these three months he's taken up
each soul who wished to enter, all in peace,
100 And I, who then had turned beside the sea
just where the Tiber's water meets the salt,
was received by the angel, graciously.
To that mouth now he turns his wing, for on
the Tiber's shore is gathered every soul
105 who does not fall to face the Acheron."
"If no new law has claimed your memory
or seized your practice of those songs of love
with which you used to calm the grief in me,"
said I, "oh let it please you now awhile
110 to soothe my soul, which has, in coming here,
walked with my body many a weary mile."
"The love that speaks its reasons in my mind,"
so sweetly did he then begin to sing,
I can still hear the sweetness of his sound.
115 And so my Teacher and that throng of souls
and I stood listening so contentedly
it seemed our minds were touched by nothing else
But the notes of his song; we all held still,
when look! the honorable old man cried,
120 "What's this, you sluggish souls! Get to the hill!
What lingering, what carelessness down here!
Hurry to scrape away the scales which keep
the Lord from being manifest in you!"
As when a flock of pigeons in a field,
125 quietly pecking for the tasty seeds,
their heads not cocked to show their usual pride,
If something should appear which scares 'em, they
all of a sudden leave their feed behind,
for they're assailed by more important care—
130 So did I see that newly-gathered flock
scatter as men who go they don't know where,
leaving the song and fleeing to the rock—
Nor with less haste did we depart from there.

FROM CANTO FIVE

*Below the realm where purgation actually begins, Dante speaks to several souls who repented at the brink of violent death; among them, **Bonconte da Montefeltro** and **La Pia**. These souls, like all late repenters, dwell in Ante-Purgatory, where they must wait a certain time before they are allowed to ascend the mountain.*

. . . Another then: "Ah may that longing be
    fulfilled which pulls you up the lofty mountain,
    assist *my* longing by your piety!
I was from Montefeltro, I'm Bonconte!
5   My kin and widow take no care for me,
    that's why I walk so humbly in this file."
And I: "What force or falling-out of war
    led you so far afield from Campaldino
    that no one saw your body anymore?"
10 "Oh," he replied, "by Casentino's hills
    rushes a stream they call the Archiano,
    born in the Apennines above the Hermitage.
Just where it empties and its name turns vain
    I arrived with an arrow in the throat
15   fleeing afoot and spattering the plain.
And there at once my sight and speech were gone;
    I ended with 'Maria' on my lips
    and fell, and left my flesh to lie alone
It's truth I tell—tell it to all alive!
20   God's angel took me, and the one from hell
    hollered, 'Hey you from Heaven, why deprive
Me of his soul? He sheds one little tear
    and you bear his immortal part away!
    I'll have a different rule for this part here.'
25 You know well how the watery mists arise
    and gather in the cooling atmosphere
    till condensation makes it rain again?
That evil will that ever seeks the wrong
    now joined with intellect and stirred the smoke
30   and wind, by natural powers that make him strong,
And all the valley from the Giant Yoke
    to Pratomagno, when the day was quenched,
    he cloaked in fog, and made the skies so thick
That back to water turned the full-soaked air
35   and the rain battered down in trench and ditch,
    filling them fuller than the earth could bear,

And when it reached the rapids of the hills
    it crashed in ruin to the royal stream,
    rushing so fast that nothing could restrain it.
40   There at its mouth my body stiff and cold
    it found and swept into the Arno and
    loosened the cross I made upon my chest,
Folding my arms when I was overcome;
    then swirled me past the banks into the deep
45   till the flood's pillage pinned and buried me."
"Oh when you have returned into the world
    and rested from the long and weary way,"
    after the second soul another called,
"Please then remember me; I am La Pia.
50   Siena made me, and the dark Maremma
    unmade me. How it happened he well knows
who jewelled my hand when I became his spouse."

FROM CANTO TEN

Dante has reached the first of the seven rings around the mountain of Purgatory, where **pride,** *the most serious of the Seven Deadly Sins, is purged away. Before he meets the souls, he sees, in living sculptures, examples of the virtue that destroys pride:* **humility.**

We hadn't moved our steps upon the ring
    when I observed that as the cliff-wall turned
    rising at less than perpendicular,
It was all gleaming marble and adorned
5   with figures so well-carved that not alone
    would the great Polycletus[6] there be scorned
But Nature too. The angel who came down
    with the decree that brought to earth the peace
    for which men wept so many years, which freed
10   The gates of Heaven forbidden, now to us
    appeared so true and real, engraven there
    in sweet and courteous pose, he did not seem
A silent form. You'd swear you heard him say
    "Hail!"—for the one who opened Heaven's high love
15   was there in image, she who turned the key,
And in her pose was stamped the spoken word,
    exactly as a seal in molten wax:
    "Behold, I am the handmaid of the Lord."

---

[6]*Polycletus:* famous Greek sculptor

Said the sweet Teacher, at whose side I stood
20   nearest the heart, "You should not keep your mind
    upon the same place always." So I moved
In eye and glance, and then I saw, behind
    Mary, in that direction where my guide
    was standing when he moved me to attend,
25   Another story sculpted in the rock.
    I leapt past Virgil and I drew up near
    the better to behold it. Cut into
That marble were the oxen made to bear
    the wagon and the holy Ark,[7] whose fall
30   should make men not assigned a duty fear
To take it up. In front came people, all
    parted in seven bands, who made one sense
    of mine say "no," the other, "yes, they sing,"
And so too with the smoke of frankincense—
35   the image set at strife the eyes and nose
    with yes and no. Before the holy vessel,
Leading the way in dance and reveling,
    his skirts tucked high, the humble psalmist came,
    at once appearing more and less than king.
40   Figured forth at a window opposite
    in a great palace, Michal stared in gloom,
    the woman who despised him in her heart.
From where I stood I walked a little way
    to view from right up front another story
45   graven behind Michal and gleaming white:
For there was told in sculpture the high glory
    of all the Roman principate, whose worth
    moved Gregory to his greatest victory,
I speak of Trajan, Emperor of Rome;
50   and an old widow at his horse's rein
    stood as one shedding tears and stooped in sorrow.
Crowded about him pressed the cavalry,
    and high above them stirring in the breeze
    appeared the Eagles in the field of gold.
55   The poor old woman among all of these
    seemed to say, "Justice, Lord! Avenge my son!
    He's murdered, and the sorrow breaks my heart,"
And he responded, "Wait till I return,"
    and she, as one whom grief compels to haste,

---

[7] *Ark:* The Ark of the Covenant. David recaptured it from the Philistines and brought it back into Jerusalem, singing and dancing before it. His wife, Michal, scorned him for it, and the Lord punished her with sterility; cf. 2 Sam. 6.

60   "What if you never do return, my Lord?"
     "The man who takes my place, he'll see it done."
       And she: "What will his good deed do for you?
       He performs his, and you forget your own,"
     Whence his reply, "Take comfort, then. To do
65   my duty now before I move, is right.
       Justice demands it, pity holds me here."
     No new or strange thing ever strikes the sight
       of Him who made this speech that can be seen,
       new to us, for on earth it is not so.
70   And while I gazed on them with great delight—
       the images of such humility,
       the dearer for the hand that fashioned them—
     "Look over there," the poet whispered to me,
       "people are coming, but their steps are slow.
75   They'll send us to the levels higher up."
     My eyes, which were content in gazing so,
       eager as ever to behold new things,
       were not slow now to turn and look his way.
     Reader, I want you not to lose the power
80   of your good resolution and intent,
       hearing how God demands we pay the debt:
     Don't dwell upon the form of punishment
       but on what follows; think that at the worst
       it cannot last beyond the day of Doom.
85   "Teacher," said I, "the things I see approaching,
       they don't seem to be people . . . Who knows what?
       I don't know, with the raving of my eyes!"
     "Their heavy torment makes them crouch and squat
       down to the earth so low, these eyes of mine,"
90   said he, "first had to tussle with my thought.
     But fix your gaze and let your sight untwine
       what comes our way beneath those stones, and soon
       you will discover how they're pummeled here."
     Weary, pathetic Christians in your pride,
95   your vision toddles in the intellect
       while in your backward paces you confide,
     Do you not see that we are only worms
       born to form the angelic butterfly
       which flits to justice free of its cocoon?
100   About what do your spirits crow so high,
       defective insects all of you—like grubs
       falling short of their form's maturity?
     Sometimes to prop a roof or ceiling up

you'll see the corbel sculpted like a man
105   bearing the weight, knees crushed against his chest,
Begetting agony in those who see—
    what's not true makes you feel truly oppressed—
    so I saw them, when I looked carefully.
According to the heaviness in fact
110   they were hunched more or less by what they bore,
    and those who showed most patience in the act
Seemed to say through their tears, "I can no more."

FROM CANTO ELEVEN

*Dante meets the soul of the once-proud **Oderisi da Gubbio,** a famed illuminator of manuscripts. Oderisi inveighs against the foolish pride of man, then points out the soul of the Sienese warlord **Provenzan Salvani,** rewarded for an act of remarkable humility.*

In hearing him I held my countenance low
    and one of them, not the one speaking, wrenched
    his form under the load that stuck him fast,
Saw me and recognized me and called out,
5   struggling to keep his eyes fixed upon me
    who, bowed and huddled, walked with them about.
"Say!" I began, "aren't you Oderisi,
    glory of Gubbio and glory of that art
    they call *'illumination' a Paris?"*
10 "Brother, there shines more laughter in the leaves
    touched by the pen of Franco Bolognese:
    now all the glory is his, and mine in part.
Never would I have been so courteous
    while I was living, for my heart would heed
15   only my great desire for excellence.
Here for such pride we pay the penalty,
    nor would I be here now, if in an hour
    I still could sin, I had not turned to God.
O empty glorying in human power!
20   How short a day the branch remains in leaf—
    if it's not overcome by duller times!
In painting it was Cimabue's belief
    he held the field; now Giotto's got the cry
    and Cimabue's fame is dim. So too
25 The glory of Italian poetry,
    one Guido seized it from the other, and
    he may be born who'll chase the two of them

Out of the nest. The rumor of the world
    is but a breath, a breeze blown here and there
30   which changes name because it changes place.
After a thousand years what greater fame
    will be yours if you shed your flesh when old
    than if you died before you left off babbling
'Baba' and 'Dada'?—and to eternity
35   those years are shorter than a twitching brow
    to the long turning of the slowest sphere.
All Tuscany once held him in acclaim
    who takes so little of the path ahead;
    and now Siena hardly peeps his name,
40   Although he was the lord there when the mad
    fury of Florence was destroyed, for Florence
    was just as proud then as she's now a whore.
Your name is like the color of the grass,
    it comes and goes, and it turns brown and dry
45   in the same sun that made its seedlings green."
"Your truthful words instill humility
    into my heart, and plane my swelling pride.
    But him, the last you spoke of—who is he?"
"He's Provenzan Salvani," he replied,
50   "here for his being so presumptuous
    as to rake all Siena to his hands.
From the day of his death without repose—
    such is the coin by which the over-daring
    must pay the debt—he's gone as now he goes."
55   And I: "If any spirit who delays
    his penitence until the brink of life
    must wait down there and cannot climb up here
Until the time of all his days has passed,
    unless he is assisted by good prayer,
60   why was *his* coming yielded clear and free?"
"At the time when he lived in fullest pride,
    in the Field of Siena deliberately
    he set himself and put his shame aside,
And there, to free his friend from all the pains
65   he suffered in the prison of Anjou,
    he did what made him shudder in his veins.[8]
No more—I know my words seem dark to you,
    but before long your fellow Florentines

---

[8]*he did . . . veins:* He begged for alms in the public square of Siena.

will work so as to help *you* gloss them too.
70   His action freed him from those bonds below."

FROM CANTO TWENTY-ONE

*Dante and Virgil have just left the ring of the **avaricious**, when they feel the earth tremble and hear shouts of glory to God. Suddenly a third soul appears, walking with them. He turns out to be the spirit of **Statius**, a Roman poet of the first century.*

"... Now I perceive the net that binds your feet,"
     said my wise leader, "how you rip the snare,
     why the earth quakes, and why the crowds rejoice.
Then be so kind, please, tell me who you were:
5   and in your words give me to understand
     why all those centuries have found you here."
"In the days when the high King[9] helped the good
     Emperor Titus to avenge the holes
     through which the blood sold by Iscariot flowed,"
10   Said he, "I lived there with a poet's name,
     the name most honorable, and long-enduring.
     As yet I had no faith, for all my fame.
The spirit of my melody was so sweet
     Rome called me from Toulouse to decorate
15   my temples with the poet's myrtle crown.
Statius the people call me to this day:
     I sang of Thebes, and of the great Achilles,
     but with the second burden fell mid-way.
The brilliant seeds which set my love afire
20   flashed from the divine flame which kindled me
     and lit the lamps of many a thousand more,
Of the *Aeneid* I mean: for all I am
     of poet, it was my mamma, and my nurse.
     Without it, all my work weighs not a dram.
25   And I'd consent to spend an extra year—
     could I have lived on earth when Virgil lived—
     suffering for my sins in exile here!"
And Virgil seemed to ask me, "Please, be still,"
     turning a silent glance my way—but man
30   cannot do everything by power of will,
For smiles and tears follow so swiftly from
     the fountain of their passion, they will least

---

[9]*King:* God, avenging the death of Jesus by allowing the Romans to destroy Jerusalem in 70 A.D.

obey the will in those whose hearts are true.
I flashed the faintest glimmer of a smile,
35   at which the shade fell silent, and beheld
my eyes, the truest imprint of the soul,
And said, "Now be so good to tell me why—
may all your labor come to a good end—
you showed that little twinkle in the eye?"
40   Between this side and that one I was penned:
for the one poet urged me on to speak,
the other wished my silence. When I sighed
My Teacher heard and yielded. "Have no fear.
Speak to him, tell him what he wants to know,
45   what he has shown such interest to hear."
"You may be wondering, soul of ancient days,"
said I, "about the smile upon my lips.
But now be seized with wonder, be amazed,
For he who guides my eyes to look on high
50   is that same Virgil from whose lofty verse
you took the strength to sing of men and gods.
All other reasons, set aside as false,
if you were guessing why I smiled. Believe
the words you spoke about him were the cause."
55   Already he had fallen to the knee
to clasp my Teacher's feet, who said, "No, brother;
you are a shade, and it's a shade you see."
Rising, he said, "Now you can tell the great
measure of love for you which burns in me,
60   when I forget our emptiness, and treat
Shadows as if they had solidity."

FROM CANTO TWENTY-TWO

Statius explains to Virgil why he needed to spend time in the ring of avarice, and how he became a Christian.

"... But tell me, and forgive me as a friend,
if I'm too bold and let the reins slip free,
and talk with me as friends will talk together,
How could greed find a harbor in your heart
5   amidst all of the wisdom you possessed
in the study and practice of your art?"
Statius was moved to smile at this request,
then answered, "All you say is dear to me,
all is a sign of love. To speak the truth,

10   Often a false suspicion's given by
      externals, the appearance of a thing
      whose actual explanation may yet lie
    Hidden beneath. You found me in that ring,
      and so your question leads me to suppose
15   you believe I was avaricious in
    That other life. But that was far from me;
      know, my immoderate spending has required
      thousands of months to pay the penalty.
    Had I not turned my reasoning the right way,
20   pondering your verse that seems to shout in anger
      against the nature of humanity,
    'Why do you, holy hunger[10] after gold,
      not guide the appetites of mortal men,'
      I'd be a jouster where the rocks are rolled.
25   Then I perceived that you can stretch your wings
      too wide in spending, and repented it,
      as I repented all my other sins.
    How many men will rise with scalps bald-cropped
      by ignorance, which steals your chance to turn
30   in life, and when your breath has nearly stopped!
    And know that any fault that butts its horn
      against the horn of an opposing sin,
      withers its green in the same ring with it,
    So if I happened to be settled in
35   one place with those who weep for avarice,
      it was to purge away the opposite."
    "Now when you sang the bloody war in Thebes,
      the swords that brought Jocasta double grief,"
      said the singer of the shepherds,[11] "by the strings
40   Touched by the fingers of the Muse for you,
      the faith seems not to have made you faithful yet,
      and without faith, all that a man may do
    Will not suffice. What candle, then, what sun
      scattered the darkness that you might turn sail,
45   following the Fisherman?" "You were the one,"
    Said he, "who first invited me to drink
      of the springs in the grottoes on Parnassus;
      and then you lit for me the way to God.
    You did as one upon the road at night

---

[10]*holy hunger:* Dante interprets Virgil as saying that there is a correct and temperate appetite for the good things of the world.
[11]*singer ... shepherds:* Virgil, who also wrote pastoral poetry

50   who holds a torch that those behind may see,
         though he himself's unaided by the light,
      Saying, 'From Heaven descends a newborn son;
         the morning of humanity returns,
         and a new age of justice has begun.'[12]
55   A poet you made me, and a Christian too . . ."

---

[12]Statius is quoting Virgil's Fourth Eclogue, traditionally interpreted in the Middle Ages as an unwitting prophecy of the birth of Christ.

FROM CANTO TWENTY-SEVEN

*The poets must pass through a **barrier of fire** separating the seventh ring of Purgatory, where **lust** is punished, from the top of the mountain and Earthly Paradise. When Dante reaches the top, he hears Virgil declare him free.*

> . . . I joined my hands and stretched them to the flames,
>   gazing, seeing too sharply in my mind
>   bodies I'd seen die burning at the stake.
> My worthy guides then turned around to me
> 5   and Virgil said, "My son, there may indeed
>   be torment here, but death can never be!
> Remember, just remember! When we soared
>   on Geryon's back I led you safely down—
>   what will I do now that you're near the Lord?
> 10   Stand in this fire's belly a thousand years—
>   you must believe it for a certainty—
>   you would not lose one hair upon your head.
> If you think what I tell you is a lie,
>   come closer, test it for yourself, come here,
> 15   put your hands to your tunic's hem, and try!
> Now set aside, set aside all your fear—
>   turn round this way—be confident, come in."
>   Yet I stood firm, against my conscience. When
> He saw me stiffened and immovable,
> 20   he said, a little troubled, "Son, look now—
>   what's keeping you from Beatrice is this wall."
> As Pyramus upon the verge of death,
>   hearing the name of Thisbe, raised his brow
>   to look upon her, though his crimson blood
> 25   Had stained the mulberry; so to my wise guide
>   I turned, my stiffness softened, at the name
>   which ever rises fresh within my mind.
> At that he shook his head at me and smiled—
>   "Now really, do we want to stay back there?"
> 30   as when a promised fruit persuades a child.
> Into the flames he walked ahead of me,
>   asking Statius to come in back of us,
>   who'd walked between us all along the way.
> The blazes there inside did so surpass
> 35   all measure, that to feel the cool again
>   I would have thrown myself in boiling glass.
> But my sweet father spoke of Beatrice
>   with every step he took, to comfort me:

"I think I can already see her eyes."
40   And we were guided by a singing voice
         from past the flames, and, turning toward the sound,
         we came out where you climb to reach the peak.
      "O all ye blessed of my Father, come,"
         resounded from within a dazzling gleam
45   too mighty for my eyes to look upon.
      "The evening falls, the sun goes down to rest.
         Do not pause, but determine to press on
         before the heavens darken in the west."
      . . .

      In the first shimmerings of the break of day—
50   which cheer the pilgrims as they see them rise,
         when they've stopped for the night not far away
      From the home they draw near—from all the skies
         the darkness fled, and with it fled my sleep.
         Seeing my teachers risen, I arose.
55   "That sweet fruit searched for in so many trees
         by mortal men in all their restless care,
         today will set your hungry heart at ease."
      In such words then did Virgil speak to me:
         never did New Year's auguries proclaim
60   such welcome tidings of felicity.
      Will above will now surged in such delight
         to climb the top, that with each step I took
         I felt my feathers growing for the flight.
      And when we'd left that stairway all behind,
65   racing to reach the highest step of all,
         upon me Virgil fixed his eyes, and said,
      "The temporal and eternal fires, my son,
         you now have witnessed, and have reached the part
         where I discern no further on my own.
70   I've led you here by strength of mind, and art;
         take your own pleasure for your leader now.
         You've left the steep and narrow ways behind.
      Behold the sun which shines in front of you;
         behold the grass, the flowers, the little trees,
75   which, of its own, this earth brings forth to grow.
      While we await the glad and lovely eyes
         whose tears first made me come to you, you may
         sit here or walk among them, as you please.
      No longer wait for what I do or say.
80   Your judgment now is free and whole and true;

to fail to follow its will would be to stray.
Lord of yourself I crown and mitre you."[13]

---

[13]*Lord . . . you:* Virgil's last words in the *Divine Comedy.* Dante is now free of the taint of sin, and thus needs neither Church nor State for a guide.

CANTO THIRTY

*Walking through Earthly Paradise, Dante sees a long procession of elders, symbolic of the Word of God, led by a Griffon—a beast which is half lion, half bird—symbolic of Christ. The Griffon draws a chariot, in which **Beatrice** appears. Dante turns to Virgil to describe his reawakened love, but Virgil is gone. Beatrice proceeds to remind Dante of his sinfulness, which she presents as his infidelity to her.*

When the First Heaven's wain of seven lights—
   which never knew a rising or a fall,
   nor ever a cloud to veil them from men's sights
But sin; which points our duty to us all,
5   just as the lower seven for sailors do,
   that he who turns the helm may come to port—
Had stopped in place, the people who speak true,
   those first between the candles and the Griffon,
   turned to the chariot as to their peace,
10   And one, like to a herald sent from Heaven,
   cried out three times, the rest all following,
   singing, *"Come out of Lebanon, my bride."*
As the blest at the latest summoning
   will each one rise up ready from the grave,
15   their new-robed voices alleluiaing,
From the divine car a hundred cries
   were raised *to answer one so venerable;*
   heralds and ministers of eternal life.
"Blessed are you who come," they said, and all
20   above and round with flowers they strewed the way,
   saying, *"O give the lilies, with full hands!"*
I have seen, at the dawning of the day,
   a flush of rose across the eastern sky,
   and all the west adorned with lovely calm,
25   When the face of the newborn sun is so
   veiled by the tempering mists that shade the air,
   for a long time the eye sustains the sight;
So too now from within a mist of flowers
   that leapt like spray from the angelic hands
30   and fell within the chariot and without,
In a white veil girded with olive bands
   a Lady appeared to me—her mantle, green,
   above her vestments red as living flame.
My spirit, which had passed so long a time
35   since it had felt the crushing glory of
   her presence, now a-tremble, mute with awe,

Knowing more than my eyes had knowledge of,
    by means of hidden power that moved from her,
    felt the great might of all its ancient love.
40   And when that lofty virtue struck my sight,
    which long ago had pierced my heart with wonder,
    before I'd passed the seasons of a boy,
At once I turned left with the anxious look
    of a child running for his mama when
45   he's scared of something, or he's hurt himself,
To say to Virgil, "Not one drop of blood
    runs in my veins that isn't trembling now!
    I know the traces of the ancient flame—"
But Virgil had deprived us of himself,
50   Virgil the sweetest father, Virgil, he
    in whom I trusted that I might be healed,
Nor all the world our mother Eve once lost
    could keep my cheeks from growing moist with dew,
    and my eyes darkened, weeping bitterly.
55   "Dante, because Virgil has gone away,
    do not weep now, now's not the time to weep;
    another sword must make you cry today."
Astern or at the bow an admiral
    will stand and watch the sailors tend the beams,
60   heartening them to do their duties well;
So on the chariot's left side did I see
    (when I turned at the uttering of my name,
    recorded here out of necessity)
The Lady who was veiled when first she came
65   beneath the flowers of the angelic feast,
    turning her gaze to me across the stream.
Although the veil descending from her head,
    wreathed with the fronds that grace Minerva's tree,
    did not allow her to be clearly seen,
70   Regally in the scornful look she cast
    did she continue, as an orator
    reserves his hottest speeches for the last:
"Look well—I'm Beatrice, I am in truth!
    How did you deign to come upon the hill?
75   Do you not know that man is happy here?"
With fallen eyes I looked below into
    the clear spring, but when I beheld myself
    I turned them to the grass, the shame was so
Heavy upon my forehead. She seemed to me
80   like a severe mother speaking to her child,

who tastes the tang of her harsh piety.
She said no more; and all the angels sang
    at once, *"O Lord, I placed my hope in you,"*
    but past the words *"my feet"* they did not go.

85   As snow among the living beams of trees
      upon the mountain-spine of Italy,
      blown upon by the Slavic winds, will freeze;
Then turns to liquid, layer upon layer,
    from the breath of the land that knows no shade,
90   and looks like candles dripping in the flame,
So was I too at first, no sighs, no tears,
    until the singing of the choir whose notes
    follow the notes of the eternal spheres.
But when, in sweet and tempered melody,
95   I heard them take my part, as if they said,
    "Lady, why do you take his strength away?"
That ice which gripped me hard about the heart
    became water and breath, and with great stress
    came out through the mouth's sobs and through the eyes.
100   She who was standing ever motionless
    upon the chariot's left, then turned her words
    to speak unto the pious substances:
"You keep your watch in the eternal day,
    so neither dreams nor darkness robs your view
105   of one step of the centuries on their way,
So my reply is more for him than you—
    the one who weeps upon the farther shore,
    to make his sorrow measured to his sin."

In the rest of the Purgatorio, Dante weeps for his errors and is forgiven by Beatrice, who allows him the grace to look upon her face, unveiled. Dante is then immersed in the waters of the two paradisal rivers, Lethe (in which one forgets the guilt of one's sins) and Eunoe (which restores to us the memory of our good deeds). Thus prepared and purified, he stands with Beatrice on the mountaintop, ready to ascend to the stars.

9. THE CANTERBURY TALES (SELECTIONS)

Geoffrey Chaucer
(1340?–1400)

Chaucer's lifetime witnessed the major turbulent events of the late Middle Ages: the Hundred Years War, Black Death, Avignon Papacy, Western Schism, and Peasant's Revolt—and though he makes only oblique reference to them, the societal effects of these upheavals is subtly woven into the fabric of The Canterbury Tales. *He is the first English poet to draw upon his contemporary world, providing individualized portraits of figures from all walks of medieval life. The pilgrimage they undertake to Canterbury Cathedral is recorded by Geffrey, the persona ("mask") for the author, whose own character colors all that he sees and hears. The multiple perspectives we get on each pilgrim—from Geffrey's descriptions, to their own actions, reactions, tales, and motivations—create the first "rounded" characters in English literature; their psychological realism has been appreciated and variously interpreted in every subsequent age.*

CHAUCER'S MIDDLE ENGLISH: THE FIRST EIGHTEEN LINES OF THE GENERAL PROLOGUE TO *THE CANTERBURY TALES:*

Whan that Aprill with his shoures soote
The droghte of March hath perced to the roote,
And bathed every veyne in swich licour
Of which vertu engendred is the flour;
5   Whan Zephirus eek with his sweete breeth
Inspired hath in every holt and heeth
The tendre croppes, and the yonge sonne
Hath in the Ram his halve cours yronne,
And smale foweles maken melodye,
10   That slepen al the nyght with open ye—
So priketh hem nature in hir corages—
Thanne longen folk to goon on pilgrimages,
And palmeres for to seken straunge strondes,
To ferne halwes, kowthe in sondry londes;
15   And specially from every shires ende
Of Engelond to Caunterbury they wende,

The hooly blisful martir for to seeke,
That hem hath holpen whan that they were seke.

GENERAL PROLOGUE TO
THE CANTERBURY TALES

When April with his showers sweet with fruit
The drought of March has pierced unto the root
And bathed each vein with liquor that has power
To generate therein and sire the flower;
5   When Zephyr[1] also has, with his sweet breath,
Quickened again, in every holt and heath,
The tender shoots and buds, and the young sun
Into the Ram[2] one half his course has run,
And many little birds make melody
10   That sleep through all the night with open eye
(So Nature pricks them on to ramp and rage)—
Then do folk long to go on pilgrimage,
And palmers to go seeking out strange strands,[3]
To distant shrines well known in sundry lands
15   And specially from every shire's end
Of England they to Canterbury wend,
The holy blessed martyr[4] there to seek
Who helped them when they lay so ill and weak.
Befell that, in that season, on a day
20   In Southwark,[5] at the Tabard, as I lay
Ready to start upon my pilgrimage
To Canterbury, full of devout homage,
There came at nightfall to that hostelry
Some nine and twenty in a company
25   Of sundry persons who had chanced to fall
In fellowship, and pilgrims were they all
That toward Canterbury town would ride.
The rooms and stables spacious were and wide,
And well we there were eased, and of the best.
30   And briefly, when the sun had gone to rest,
So had I spoken with them, every one,
That I was of their fellowship anon,

---

[1]the West wind, usually signaling spring.
[2]the zodiac sign of Aries, March 12 to April 11.
[3]pilgrims traveling to foreign shores.
[4]St. Thomas à Becket, martyred in 1170 in Canterbury Cathedral; his blood was said to heal the sick.
[5]Then on the south shore of the Thames river, a suburb of London.

And made agreement that we'd early rise
To take the road, as you I will apprise.
35   But none the less, whilst I have time and space,
Before yet farther in this tale I pace,
It seems to me accordant with reason
To inform you of the state of every one
Of all of these, as it appeared to me,
40   And who they were, and what was their degree,
And even how arrayed there at the inn;
And with a knight thus will I first begin.

A **KNIGHT** there was, and he a worthy man,
Who, from the moment that he first began
45   To ride about the world, loved chivalry,
Truth, honour, freedom and all courtesy.
Full worthy was he in his liege-lord's war,
And therein had he ridden (none more far)
As well in Christendom as heathenesse,
50   And honoured everywhere for worthiness.
At Alexandria,[6] he, when it was won;
Full oft the table's roster he'd begun
Above all nations' knights in Prussia.
In Latvia raided he, and Russia,
55   No christened man so oft of his degree.
In far Granada at the siege was he
Of Algeciras, and in Belmarie.
At Ayas was he and at Satalye
When they were won; and on the Middle Sea
60   At many a noble meeting chanced to be.
Of mortal battles he had fought fifteen,
And he'd fought for our faith at Tramissene
Three times in lists, and each time slain his foe.
This self-same worthy knight had been also
65   At one time with the lord of Palatye
Against another heathen in Turkey:
And always won he sovereign fame for prize.
Though so illustrious, he was very wise
And bore himself as meekly as a maid.
70   He never yet had any vileness said,
In all his life, to whatsoever wight.[7]

---

[6]The Knight has had a long and distinguished career fighting for Christian Europe against Muslims, barbarians, and Moors.
[7]creature, person.

He was a truly perfect, gentle knight.
But now, to tell you all of his array,
His steeds were good, but yet he was not gay.
75   Of simple fustian wore he a jupon
Sadly discoloured by his habergeon;[8]
For he had lately come from his voyage
And now was going on this pilgrimage.

With him there was his son, a youthful **SQUIRE,**
80   A lover and a lusty bachelor,
With locks well curled, as if they'd laid in press.
Some twenty years of age he was, I guess.
In stature he was of an average length,
Wondrously active, aye, and great of strength.
85   He'd ridden sometime with the cavalry
In Flanders, in Artois, and Picardy,
And borne him well within that little space
In hope to win thereby his lady's grace.
Prinked out he was, as if he were a mead,
90   All full of fresh-cut flowers white and red.
Singing he was, or fluting, all the day;
He was as fresh as is the month of May.
Short was his gown, with sleeves both long and wide.
Well could be sit on horse, and fairly ride.
95   He could make songs and words thereto indite,
Joust, and dance too, as well as sketch and write.
So hot he loved that, while night told her tale,
He slept no more than does a nightingale.
Courteous he, and humble, willing and able,
100   And carved before his father at the table.[9]

A **YEOMAN**[10] had he, nor more servants, no,
At that time, for he chose to travel so;
And he was clad in coat and hood of green.
A sheaf of peacock arrows bright and keen
105   Under his belt he bore right carefully
(Well could he keep his tackle yeomanly:
His arrows had no draggled feathers low),
And in his hand he bore a mighty bow.
A cropped head had he and a sun-browned face.

---

[8]His simple attire—coarse cloth, rusty coat-of-mail—indicates his priorities.
[9]Carving was a duty and an art.
[10]A Yeoman served his lord in military service and/or on the manor in peacetime.

110	Of woodcraft knew he all the useful ways.
	Upon his arm he bore a bracer gay,
	And at one side a sword and buckler, yea,
	And at the other side a dagger bright,
	Well sheathed and sharp as spear point in the light;
115	On breast a Christopher of silver sheen.[11]
	He bore a horn in baldric all of green;
	A forester he truly was, I guess.
	There was also a nun, a **PRIORESS,**
	Who, in her smiling, modest was and coy;
120	Her greatest oath was but "By Saint Eloy!"
	And she was known as Madam Eglantine.
	Full well she sang the services divine,
	Intoning through her nose, becomingly;
	And fair she spoke her French, and fluently,
125	After the school of Stratford-at-the-Bow,[12]
	For French of Paris was not hers to know.
	At table she had been well taught withal,
	And never from her lips let morsels fall,
	Nor dipped her fingers deep in sauce, but ate
130	With so much care the food upon her plate
	That never driblet fell upon her breast.
	In courtesy she had delight and zest.
	Her upper lip was always wiped so clean
	That in her cup was no iota seen
135	Of grease, when she had drunk her draught of wine.
	Becomingly she reached for meat to dine.
	And certainly delighting in good sport,
	She was right pleasant, amiable—in short.
	She was at pains to counterfeit the look
140	Of courtliness, and stately manners took,
	And would be held worthy of reverence.
	But, to say something of her moral sense,
	She was so charitable and piteous
	That she would weep if she but saw a mouse
145	Caught in a trap, though it were dead or bled.
	She had some little dogs, too, that she fed
	On roasted flesh, or milk and fine white bread.
	But sore she'd weep if one of them were dead,

---

[11]St. Christopher medal, once the patron saint of travelers.

[12]A suburb of London at which there was a convent school evidently teaching French, but not up to the Parisian standard.

Or if men smote it with a rod to smart:
150 For pity ruled her, and her tender heart.
Right decorous her pleated wimple was;
Her nose was fine; her eyes were blue as glass;
Her mouth was small and therewith soft and red;
But certainly she had a fair forehead;
155 It was almost a full span broad, I own,
For, truth to tell, she was not undergrown.
Neat was her cloak, as I was well aware.
Of coral small about her arm she'd bear
A string of beads and gauded all with green;
160 And therefrom hung a brooch of golden sheen
Whereon there was first written a crowned "A,"
And under, *Amor vincit omnia.*[13]

Another little **NUN** with her had she,
Who was her chaplain; and of **PRIESTS** she'd **THREE**.

165 A **MONK** there was, one made for mastery,
An outrider,[14] who loved his venery;[15]
A manly man, to be an abbot able.
Full many a blooded horse had he in stable:
And when he rode men might his bridle hear
170 A-jingling in the whistling wind as clear,
Aye, and as loud as does the chapel bell
Where this brave monk was of the cell.
The rule of Maurus or Saint Benedict,[16]
By reason it was old and somewhat strict,
175 This said monk let such old things slowly pace
And followed new-world manners in their place.
He cared not for that text a clean-plucked hen
Which holds that hunters are not holy men;
Nor that a monk, when he is cloisterless,
180 Is like unto a fish that's waterless;
That is to say, a monk out of his cloister.
But this same text he held not worth an oyster;
And I said his opinion was right good.
What? Should he study as a madman would
185 Upon a book in cloister cell? Or yet

---

[13]"Love conquers all."
[14]One charged with supervising the outlying properties.
[15]hunting, but also with a pun on Venus, goddess of love.
[16]Authors of rules regulating all aspects of monastic living based on vows of poverty, chastity, obedience, and stability.

Go labour with his hands and swink and sweat,[17]
As Austin bids? How shall the world be served?
Let Austin have his toil to him reserved.[18]
Therefore he was a rider day and night;

190 Greyhounds he had, as swift as bird in flight.
Since riding and the hunting of the hare
Were all his love, for no cost would he spare.
I saw his sleeves were purfled[19] at the hand
With fur of grey, the finest in the land;

195 Also, to fasten hood beneath his chin,
He had of good wrought gold a curious pin:
A love-knot in the larger end there was.
His head was bald and shone like any glass,
And smooth as one anointed was his face.

200 Fat was this lord, he stood in goodly case.
His bulging eyes he rolled about, and hot
They gleamed and red, like fire beneath a pot;
His boots were soft; his horse of great estate.
Now certainly he was a fine prelate:

205 He was not pale as some poor wasted ghost.
A fat swan loved he best of any roast.
His palfrey was as brown as is a berry.

A **FRIAR** there was, a wanton and a merry,
A limiter,[20] a very festive man.

210 In all the Orders Four[21] is none that can
Equal his gossip and his fair language.
He had arranged full many a marriage
Of women young, and this at his own cost.
Unto his order he was a noble post.

215 Well liked by all and intimate was he
With franklins[22] everywhere in his country,
And with the worthy women of the town:
For at confessing he'd more power in gown
(As he himself said) than it good curate,

220 For of his order he was licentiate.
He heard confession gently, it was said,
Gently absolved too, leaving naught of dread.

---

[17]work; a monk's life was to be one of work, study, and prayer.
[18]St. Augustine had mandated manual labor for monks.
[19]trimmed with fur.
[20] assigned to beg (mendicant) and preach in a designed district.
[21]The four orders of Friars are Dominicans, Franciscans, Carmelites, and Augustinians.
[22]gentleman farmers.

He was an easy man to give penance
When knowing he should gain a good pittance;
225   For to a begging friar, money given
Is sign that any man has been well shriven.
For if one gave (he dared to boast of this),
He took the man's repentance not amiss.
For many a man there is so hard of heart
230   He cannot weep however pains may smart.
Therefore, instead of weeping and of prayer,
Men should give silver to poor friars all bare.
His tippet was stuck always full of knives
And pins, to give to young and pleasing wives.
235   And certainly he kept a merry note:
Well could he sing and play upon the rote.
At balladry he bore the prize away.
His throat was white as lily of the May;
Yet strong he was as ever champion.
240   In towns he knew the taverns, every one,
And every good host and each barmaid too—
Better than begging lepers, these he knew.
For unto no such solid man as he
Accorded it, as far as he could see,
245   To have sick lepers for acquaintances.
There is no honest advantageousness
In dealing with such poverty-stricken curs;
It's with the rich and with big victuallers.
And so, wherever profit might arise,
250   Courteous he was and humble in men's eyes.
There was no other man so virtuous.
He was the finest beggar of his house;
A certain district being farmed to him,
None of his brethren dared approach its rim;
255   For though a widow had no shoes to show,
So pleasant was his *In principio*,[23]
He always got a farthing ere he went.
He lived by pickings, it is evident.
And he could romp as well as any whelp.
260   On love days could he be of mickle help.
For there he was not like a cloisterer,
With threadbare cope as is the poor scholar,
But he was like a lord or like a pope.
Of double worsted was his semi-cope,

---

[23]Latin, "in the beginning," the opening words of the gospel of John.

265   That rounded like a bell, as you may guess.
        He lisped a little, out of wantonness,
        To make his English soft upon his tongue;
        And in his harping, after he had sung,
        His two eyes twinkled in his head as bright
270   As do the stars within the frosty night.
        This worthy limiter was named Hubert.

        There was a **MERCHANT** with forked beard, and girt
        In motley gown, and high on horse he sat,
        Upon his head a Flemish beaver hat;
275   His boots were fastened rather elegantly.
        He spoke his notions out right pompously,
        Stressing the times when he had won, not lost.
        He would the sea were held at any cost
        Across from Middleburgh to Orwell town.
280   At money-changing he could make a crown.
        This worthy man kept all his wits well set;
        There was no one could say he was in debt,
        So well he governed all his trade affairs
        With bargains and with borrowings and with shares.
285   Indeed, he was a worthy man withal,
        But, sooth to say, his name I can't recall.

        A **CLERK**[24] from Oxford was with us also,
        Who'd turned to getting knowledge, long ago.
        As meagre was his horse as is a rake,
290   Nor he himself too fat, I'll undertake,
        But he looked hollow and went soberly.
        Right threadbare was his overcoat; for he
        Had got him yet no churchly benefice,
        Nor was so worldly as to gain office.
295   For he would rather have at his bed's head
        Some twenty books, all bound in black and red,
        Of Aristotle and his philosophy
        Than rich robes, fiddle, or gay psaltery.
        Yet, and for all he was philosopher,
300   He had but little gold within his coffer;
        But all that he might borrow from a friend
        On books and learning he would swiftly spend,
        And then he'd pray right busily for the souls
        Of those who gave him wherewithal for schools.

---

[24] A clerk was a university student studying for a church position.

305   Of study took he utmost care and heed.
Not one word spoke he more than was his need;
And that was said in fullest reverence
And short and quick and full of high good sense.
Pregnant of moral virtue was his speech;
310   And gladly would he learn and gladly teach.

A **SERGEANT OF THE LAW,** wary and wise,
Who'd often gone to Paul's walk[25] to advise,
There was also compact of excellence.
Discreet he was, and of great reverence;
315   At least he seemed so, his words were so wise.
Often he sat as justice in assize,
By patent or commission from the crown;
Because of learning and his high renown,
He took large fees and many robes could own.
320   So great a purchaser was never known.
All was fee simple[26] to him, in effect,
Wherefore his claims could never be suspect.
Nowhere a man so busy of his class,
And yet he seemed much busier than he was.
325   All cases and all judgments could he cite
That from King William's time[27] were apposite.
And he could draw a contract so explicit
Not any man could fault therefrom elicit;
And every statute he'd verbatim quote.
330   He rode but badly in a medley coat,
Belted in a silken sash, with little bars,
But of his dress no more particulars.

There was a **FRANKLIN** in his company;
White was his beard as is the white daisy.
335   Of sanguine temperament by every sign,
He loved right well his morning sop in wine.
Delightful living was the goal he'd won,
For he was Epicurus'[28] very son,
That held opinion that a full delight
340   Was true felicity, perfect and right.
A householder, and that a great, was he;

---

[25]The porch of St. Paul's Cathedral was a popular meeting point.
[26]owned outright.
[27]William the Conqueror (1066–1087).
[28]Greek philosopher whose teachings on minimizing pain came to be seen as making pleasure the chief goal of life.

Saint Julian[29] he was in his own country.
His bread and ale were always right well done;
A man with better cellars there was none.
345 Baked meat was never wanting in his house,
Of fish and flesh, and that so plenteous
It seemed to snow therein both food and drink
Of every dainty that a man could think.
According to the season of the year
350 He changed his diet and his means of cheer.
Full many a fattened partridge did he mew,
And many a bream and pike in fish-pond too.
Woe to his cook, except the sauces were
Poignant and sharp, and ready all his gear.
355 His table, waiting in his hall alway,[30]
Stood ready covered through the livelong day.
At county sessions was he lord and sire,
And often acted as a knight of shire.
A dagger and a trinket-bag of silk
360 Hung from his girdle, white as morning milk.
He had been sheriff and been auditor;
And nowhere was a worthier vavasor.[31]

A **HABERDASHER** and a **CARPENTER**,

An **ARRAS-MAKER, DYER,** and **WEAVER**

365 Were with us, clothed in similar livery,
All of one sober, great fraternity.
Their gear was new and well adorned it was;
Their weapons were not cheaply trimmed with brass,
But all with silver; chastely made and well
370 Their girdles and their pouches too, I tell.
Each man of them appeared a proper burges[32]
To sit in guildhall on a high dais.
And each of them, for wisdom he could span,
Was fitted to have been an alderman;
375 For chattels they'd enough, and, too, of rent;
To which their goodwives gave a free assent,
Or else for certain they had been to blame.
It's good to hear "Madam" before one's name,

---

[29] patron saint of hospitality.

[30] In the medieval world, the table in the great hall would normally be dismantled and hung up when not in use.

[31] feudal landholder; country gentleman.

[32] burgher, city merchant, or businessman.

And go to church when all the world may see,
380   Having one's mantle borne right royally.

A **COOK** they had with them, just for the nonce,
To boil the chickens with the marrow-bones,
And flavour tartly and with galingale.
Well could he tell a draught of London ale.
385   And he could roast and seethe and broil and fry,
And make a good thick soup, and bake a pie.
But very ill it was, it seemed to me,
That on his shin a deadly sore had he;
For sweet blanc-mange,[33] he made it with the best.

390   There was a **SAILOR,** living far out west;
For aught I know, he was of Dartmouth town.
He sadly rode a hackney, in a gown,
Of thick rough cloth falling to the knee.
A dagger hanging on a cord had he
395   About his neck, and under arm, and down.
The summer's heat had burned his visage brown;
And certainly he was a good fellow.
Full many a draught of wine he'd drawn, I trow,
Of Bordeaux vintage, while the trader slept.
400   Nice conscience was a thing he never kept.
If that he fought and got the upper hand,
By water he sent them home to every land.
But as for craft, to reckon well his tides,
His currents and the dangerous watersides,
405   His harbours, and his moon, his pilotage,
There was none such from Hull to far Carthage.
Hardy and wise in all things undertaken,
By many a tempest had his beard been shaken.
He knew well all the havens, as they were,
410   From Gottland to the Cape of Finisterre,
And every creek in Brittany and Spain;
His vessel had been christened Madeleine.

With us there was a **DOCTOR OF PHYSIC;**
In all this world was none like him to pick
415   For talk of medicine and surgery;

---

[33]a stew with a white sauce.

For he was grounded in astronomy.[34]
He often kept a patient from the pall
By horoscopes and magic natural.
Well could he tell the fortune ascendent
420 Within the houses for his sick patient.
He knew the cause of every malady,
Were it of hot or cold, of moist or dry,
And where engendered, and of what humour;[35]
He was a very good practitioner.
425 The cause being known, down to the deepest root,
Anon he gave to the sick man his boot.
Ready he was, with his apothecaries,
To send him drugs and all electuaries;[36]
By mutual aid much gold they'd always won—
430 Their friendship was a thing not new begun.
Well read was he in Esculapius,[37]
And Deiscorides, and in Rufus,
Hippocrates, and Hali, and Galen,
Serapion, Rhazes, and Avicen,
435 Averrhoes, Gilbert, and Constantine,
Bernard and Gatisden, and John Damascene.
In diet he was measured as could be,
Including naught of superfluity,
But nourishing and easy. It's no libel
440 To say he read but little in the Bible.
In blue and scarlet he went clad, withal,
Lined with a taffeta and with sendal;[38]
And yet he was right chary of expense;
He kept the gold he gained from pestilence.
445 For gold in physic is a fine cordial,
And therefore loved he gold exceeding all.

There was a house**WIFE COME FROM BATH,** or near,
Who—sad to say—was deaf in either ear.
At making cloth she had so great a bent
450 She bettered those of Ypres and even of Ghent.[39]

---

[34]A common practice for physicians was to chart the propitious moments for cures according to the position of the stars and one's birth sign.

[35]Diseases were thought to be caused by an imbalance of the four bodily humours which corresponded to the four elements (air, earth, fire, water).

[36]medicines.

[37]The following are authors of ancient and medieval treatises on medicine.

[38]silk.

[39]Flemish cloth-making centers.

In all the parish there was no goodwife
Should offering make before her, on my life;
And if one did, indeed, so wroth was she
It put her out of all her charity.
455 Her kerchiefs were of finest weave and ground;
I dare swear that they weighed a full ten pound
Which, of a Sunday, she wore on her head.
Her hose were of the choicest scarlet red,
Close gartered, and her shoes were soft and new.
460 Bold was her face, and fair, and red of hue.
She'd been respectable throughout her life,
With five churched husbands bringing joy and strife,
Not counting other company in youth;
But thereof there's no need to speak, in truth.
465 Three times she'd journeyed to Jerusalem;[40]
And many a foreign stream she'd had to stem;
At Rome she'd been, and she'd been in Boulogne,
In Spain at Santiago, and at Cologne.
She could tell much of wandering by the way:
470 Gap-toothed[41] was she, it is no lie to say.
Upon an ambler easily she sat,
Well wimpled, aye, and over all a hat
As broad as is a buckler or a targe;
A rug was tucked around her buttocks large,
475 And on her feet a pair of sharpened spurs.
In company well could she laugh her slurs.
The remedies of love she knew, perchance,
For of that art she'd learned the old, old dance.

There was a good man of religion, too,
480 A country **PARSON,** poor, I warrant you;
But rich he was in holy thought and work.
He was a learned man also, a clerk,
Who Christ's own gospel truly sought to preach;
Devoutly his parishioners would he teach.
485 Benign he was and wondrous diligent,
Patient in adverse times and well content,
As he was ofttimes proven; always blithe,
He was right loath to curse to get a tithe,
But rather would he give, in case of doubt,

---

[40]She is an experienced pilgrim and has been to the most-famous shrines.
[41]derived from "goat-toothed," the goat being a symbol of Dionysius, the god of fertility;
hence, being "gap-toothed" was suggestive of being very sexual.

490   Unto those poor parishioners about,
        Part of his income, even of his goods.
        Enough with little, coloured all his moods.
        Wide was his parish, houses far asunder,
        But never did he fail, for rain or thunder,
495   In sickness, or in sin, or any state,
        To visit to the farthest, small and great,
        Going afoot, and in his hand, a stave.
        This fine example to his flock he gave,
        That first he wrought and afterwards he taught;
500   Out of the gospel then that text he caught,
        And this figure he added thereunto—
        That, if gold rust, what shall poor iron do?
        For if the priest be foul, in whom we trust,
        What wonder if a layman yield to lust?
505   And shame it is, if priest take thought for keep,
        A shitty shepherd, shepherding clean sheep.
        Well ought a priest example good to give,
        By his own cleanness, how his flock should live.
        He never let his benefice for hire,
510   Leaving his flock to flounder in the mire,
        And ran to London, up to old Saint Paul's
        To get himself a chantry there for souls,
        Nor in some brotherhood did he withhold;
        But dwelt at home and kept so well the fold
515   That never wolf could make his plans miscarry;
        He was a shepherd and not mercenary.
        And holy though he was, and virtuous,
        To sinners he was not impiteous,
        Nor haughty in his speech, nor too divine,
520   But in all teaching prudent and benign.
        To lead folk into Heaven but by stress
        Of good example was his busyness.
        But if some sinful one proved obstinate,
        Be who it might, of high or low estate,
525   Him he reproved, and sharply, as I know.
        There is nowhere a better priest, I trow.
        He had no thirst for pomp or reverence,
        Nor made himself a special, spiced conscience,
        But Christ's own lore, and His apostles' twelve
530   He taught, but first he followed it himselve.

        With him there was a **PLOWMAN,** was his brother,
        That many a load of dung, and many another

        Had scattered, for a good true toiler, he,
        Living in peace and perfect charity.
535   He loved God most, and that with his whole heart
        At all times, though he played or plied his art,
        And next, his neighbour, even as himself.
        He'd thresh and dig, with never thought of pelf,[42]
        For Christ's own sake, for every poor wight,
540   All without pay, if it lay in his might.
        He paid his taxes, fully, fairly, well,
        Both by his own toil and by stuff he'd sell.
        In a tabard[43] he rode upon a mare.
        There were also a reeve and miller there;
545   A summoner, manciple and pardoner,
        And these, beside myself, made all there were.

        The **MILLER** was a stout churl, be it known,
        Hardy and big of brawn and big of bone;
        Which was well proved, for when he went on lam
550   At wrestling, never failed he of the ram.
        He was a chunky fellow, broad of build;
        He'd heave a door from hinges if he willed,
        Or break it through, by running, with his head.
        His beard, as any sow or fox, was red,
555   And broad it was as if it were a spade.
        Upon the coping of his nose he had
        A wart, and thereon stood a tuft of hairs,
        Red as the bristles in an old sow's ears;
        His nostrils they were black and very wide.
560   A sword and buckler bore he by his side.
        His mouth was like a furnace door for size.
        He was a jester and could poetize,
        But mostly all of sin and ribaldries.
        He could steal corn and full thrice charge his fees;
565   And yet he had a thumb of gold, begad.
        A white coat and blue hood he wore, this lad.
        A bagpipe he could blow well, be it known,
        And with that same he brought us out of town.

        There was a **MANCIPLE**[44] from an inn of court,
570   To whom all buyers might quite well resort

---

[42]money.
[43]work smock.
[44]a steward for a college of lawyers ("inn of court").

To learn the art of buying food and drink;
For whether he paid cash or not, I think
That he so knew the markets, when to buy,
He never found himself left high and dry.
575   Now is it not of God a full fair grace
That such a vulgar man has wit to pace
The wisdom of a crowd of learned men?
Of masters had he more than three times ten,
Who were in law expert and curious;
580   Whereof there were a dozen in that house
Fit to be stewards of both rent and land
Of any lord in England who would stand
Upon his own and live in manner good,
In honour, debtless (save his head were wood),
585   Or live as frugally as he might desire;
These men were able to have helped a shire
In any case that ever might befall;
And yet this manciple outguessed them all.

The **REEVE**[45] he was a slender, choleric man
590   Who shaved his beard as close as razor can.
His hair was cut round even with his ears;
His top was tonsured like a pulpiteer's.[46]
Long were his legs, and they were very lean,
And like a staff, with no calf to be seen.
595   Well could he manage granary and bin;
No auditor could ever on him win.
He could foretell, by drought and by the rain,
The yielding of his seed and of his grain.
His lord's sheep and his oxen and his dairy,
600   His swine and horses, all his stores, his poultry,
Were wholly in this steward's managing;
And, by agreement, he'd made reckoning
Since his young lord of age was twenty years;
Yet no man ever found him in arrears.
605   There was no agent, hind, or herd who'd cheat
But he knew well his cunning and deceit;
They were afraid of him as of the death.
His cottage was a good one, on a heath;
By green trees shaded with this dwelling-place.
610   Much better than his lord could he purchase.

---

[45] A reeve oversees the supplies on a manor estate.
[46] Clergy shaved their heads, leaving only a thin ring of short hair (tonsure).

Right rich he was in his own private right,
Seeing he'd pleased his lord, by day or night,
By giving him, or lending, of his goods,
And so got thanked—but yet got coats and hoods.
615   In youth he'd learned a good trade, and had been
A carpenter, as fine as could be seen.
This steward sat a horse that well could trot,
And was all dapple-grey, and was named Scot.
A long surcoat of blue did he parade,
620   And at his side he bore a rusty blade.
Of Norfolk was this reeve of whom I tell,
From near a town that men call Badeswell.
Bundled he was like friar from chin to croup,
And ever he rode hindmost of our troop.

625   A **SUMMONER**[47] was with us in that place,
Who had a fiery-red, cherubic face,
For eczema he had; his eyes were narrow
As hot he was, and lecherous, as a sparrow;
With black and scabby brows and scanty beard;
630   He had a face that little children feared.
There was no mercury,[48] sulphur, or litharge,
No borax, ceruse, tartar, could discharge,
Nor ointment that could cleanse enough, or bite,
To free him of his boils and pimples white,
635   Nor of the bosses resting on his cheeks.
Well loved he garlic, onions, aye and leeks,
And drinking of strong wine as red as blood.
Then would he talk and shout as madman would.
And when a deal of wine he'd poured within,
640   Then would he utter no word save Latin.
Some phrases had he learned, say two or three,
Which he had garnered out of some decree;
No wonder, for he'd heard it all the day;
And all you know right well that even a jay
645   Can call out "Wat" as well as can the pope.
But when, for aught else, into him you'd grope,
'Twas found he'd spent his whole philosophy;
Just "*Questio quid juris*"[49] would he cry.
He was a noble rascal, and a kind;

---

[47]a lesser churchman who summoned accused persons to ecclesiastical court.
[48]various sorts of ointments for curing skin diseases.
[49]"What is the point of law on the question?"

650   A better comrade 'twould be hard to find.
        Why, he would suffer, for a quart of wine,
        Some good fellow to have his concubine
        A twelve-month, and excuse him to the full
        (Between ourselves, though, he could pluck a gull).
655   And if he chanced upon a good fellow,
        He would instruct him never to have awe,
        In such a case, of the archdeacon's curse,
        Except a man's soul lie within his purse;
        For in his purse the man should punished be.
660   "The purse is the archdeacon's Hell," said he.
        But well I know he lied in what he said;
        A curse ought every guilty man to dread
        (For curse can kill, as absolution save),
        And 'ware *significavit*[50] to the grave.
665   In his own power had he, and at ease,
        The boys and girls of all the diocese,
        And knew their secrets, and by counsel led.
        A garland had he set upon his head,
        Large as a tavern's wine-bush on a stake;
670   A buckler had he made of bread they bake.

        With him there rode a gentle **PARDONER**[51]
        Of Rouncival, his friend and his compeer;
        Straight from the court of Rome had journeyed he.
        Loudly he sang "Come hither, love, to me,"
675   The summoner joining with a burden round;
        Was never horn of half so great a sound.
        This pardoner had hair as yellow as wax,
        But lank it hung as does a strike of flax;
        In wisps hung down such locks as he'd on head,
680   And with them he his shoulders overspread;
        But thin they dropped, and stringy, one by one.
        But as to hood, for sport of it, he'd none,
        Though it was packed in wallet all the while.
        It seemed to him he went in latest style,
685   Dishevelled, save for cap, his head all bare.
        As shiny eyes he had as has a hare.
        He had a fine veronica[52] sewed to cap.

---

[50]a writ transferring a guilty party from jurisdiction under the ecclesiastical court to the civil court.
[51]a lesser churchman whose function was to distribute pardons from the pope to lessen time for oneself or another in purgatory.
[52]Veronica's veil, which was said to have the imprint of Christ's face on it.

His wallet lay before him in his lap,
Stuffed full of pardons brought from Rome all hot.

690 A voice he had that bleated like a goat.
No beard had he, nor ever should he have,
For smooth his face as he'd just had a shave;
I think he was a gelding or a mare.
But in his craft, from Berwick unto Ware,

695 Was no such pardoner in any place.
For in his bag he had a pillowcase
The which, he said, was Our True Lady's veil:
He said he had a piece of the very sail
That good Saint Peter had, what time he went

700 Upon the sea, till Jesus changed his bent.
He had a latten cross set full of stones,
And in a bottle had he some pig's bones.
But with these relics, when he came upon
Some simple parson, then this paragon

705 In that one day more money stood to gain
Than the poor dupe in two months could attain.
And thus, with flattery and suchlike japes,
He made the parson and the rest his apes.
But yet, to tell the whole truth at the last,

710 He was, in church, a fine ecclesiast.
Well could he read a lesson or a story,
But best of all he sang an offertory;
For well he knew that when that song was sung,
Then might he preach, and all with polished tongue.

715 To win some silver, as he right well could;
Therefore he sang so merrily and so loud.

Now have I told you briefly, in a clause,
The state, the array, the number, and the cause
Of the assembling of this company

720 In Southwark, at this noble hostelry
Known as the Tabard Inn, hard by the Bell.
But now the time is come wherein to tell
How all we bore ourselves that very night
When at the hostelry we did alight.

725 And afterward the story I engage
To tell you of our common pilgrimage.
But first, I pray you, of your courtesy,
You'll not ascribe it to vulgarity
Though I speak plainly of this matter here,

730 Retailing you their words and means of cheer;

Nor though I use their very terms, nor lie.
For this thing do you know as well as I:
When one repeats a tale told by a man,
He must report, as nearly as he can,
735 Every least word, if he remember it,
However rude it be, or how unfit;
Or else he may be telling what's untrue,
Embellishing and fictionizing too.
He may not spare, although it were his brother;
740 He must as well say one word as another.
Christ spoke right broadly out, in holy writ,
And, you know well, there's nothing low in it.
And Plato says, to those able to read:
"The word should be the cousin to the deed."
745 Also, I pray that you'll forgive it me
If I have not set folk, in their degree
Here in this tale, by rank as they should stand.
My wits are not the best, you'll understand.
Great cheer our **HOST** gave to us, every one,
750 And to the supper set us all anon;
And served us then with victuals of the best.
Strong was the wine and pleasant to each guest.
A seemly man our good host was, withal,
Fit to have been a marshal in some hall;
755 He was a large man, with protruding eyes,
As fine a burgher as in Cheapside lies;
Bold in his speech, and wise, and right well taught,
And as to manhood, lacking there in naught.
Also, he was a very merry man,
760 And after meat, at playing he began,
Speaking of mirth among some other things,
When all of us had paid our reckonings;
And saying thus: "Now masters, verily
You are all welcome here, and heartily:
765 For by my truth, and telling you no lie,
I have not seen, this year, a company
Here in this inn, fitter for sport than now.
Fain would I make you happy, knew I how.
And of a game have I this moment thought
770 To give you joy, and it shall cost you naught.
"You go to Canterbury; may God speed
And the blest martyr soon requite your meed.
And well I know, as you go on your way,
You'll tell good tales and shape yourselves to play;

775 For truly there's no mirth nor comfort, none,
    Riding the roads as dumb as is a stone;
    And therefore will I furnish you a sport,
    As I just said, to give you some comfort.
    And if you like it, all, by one assent,
780 And will be ruled by me, of my judgment,
    And will so do as I'll proceed to say,
    Tomorrow, when you ride upon your way,
    Then, by my father's spirit, who is dead,
    If you're not gay, I'll give you up my head.
785 Hold up your hands, nor more about it speak."
    Our full assenting was not far to seek;
    We thought there was no reason to think twice,
    And granted him his way without advice,
    And bade him tell his verdict just and wise,
790 "Masters," quoth he, "here now is my advice;
    But take it not, I pray you, in disdain;
    This is the point, to put it short and plain,
    That each of you, beguiling the long day,
    Shall tell two stories as you wend your way
795 To Canterbury town; and each of you
    On coming home, shall tell another two,
    All of adventures he has known befall.
    And he who plays his part the best of all,
    That is to say, who tells upon the road
800 Tales of best sense, in most amusing mode,
    Shall have a supper at the others' cost
    Here in this room and sitting by this post,
    When we come back again from Canterbury.
    And now, the more to warrant you'll be merry,
805 I will myself, and gladly, with you ride
    At my own cost, and I will be your guide.
    But whosoever shall my rule gainsay
    Shall pay for all that's bought along the way.
    And if you are agreed that it be so,
810 Tell me at once, or if not, tell me no,
    And I will act accordingly. No more."
    This thing was granted, and our oaths we swore,
    With right glad hearts, and prayed of him, also,
    That he would take the office, nor forgo
815 The place of governor of all of us,
    Judging our tales; and by his wisdom thus
    Arrange that supper at a certain price,
    We to be ruled, each one, by his advice

820

In things both great and small; by one assent,
We stood committed to his government.
And thereupon, the wine was fetched anon;
We drank, and then to rest went every one,
And that without a longer tarrying.
Next morning, when the day began to spring,

825

Up rose our host, and acting as our cock,
He gathered us together in a flock,
And forth we rode, a jog-trot being the pace,
Until we reached Saint Thomas' watering-place.
And there our host pulled horse up to a walk,

830

And said: "Now, masters, listen while I talk.
You know what you agreed at set of sun.
If even-song and morning-song are one,
Let's here decide who first shall tell a tale.
And as I hope to drink more wine and ale,

835

Whoso proves rebel to my government
Shall pay for all that by the way is spent.
Come now, draw cuts, before we farther win,
And he that draws the shortest shall begin.
Sir knight," said he, "my master and my lord,

840

You shall draw first as you have pledged your word.
Come near," quoth he, "my lady prioress:
And you, sir clerk, put by your bashfulness,
Nor ponder more; out hands, flow, every man!"
At once to draw a cut each one began,

845

And, to make short the matter, as it was,
Whether by chance or whatsoever cause,
The truth is, that the cut fell to the knight,
At which right happy then was every wight.
Thus that his story first of all he'd tell,

850

According to the compact, it befell,
As you have heard. Why argue to and fro?
And when this good man saw that it was so,
Being a wise man and obedient
To plighted word, given by free assent,

855

He slid: "Since I must then begin the game,
Why, welcome be the cut, and in God's name!
Now let us ride, and hearken what I say."
And at that word we rode forth on our way;
And he began to speak, with right good cheer,

860

His tale anon, as it is written here.

9. *Chaucer*/The Canterbury Tales (General Prologue)

[*The Knight tells a charming romance, wherein fairness in a love triangle wins out through chivalry and noble behavior; the Miller, animated by jealousy arising from his very different background, thinks he will best the Knight with a like story.*]

THE MILLER'S PROLOGUE

The Words Between the Host
and the Miller

Now when the knight had thus his story told,
In all the rout there was nor young nor old
But said it was a noble story, well
Worthy to be kept in mind to tell;
5   And specially the gentle folk, each one.
Our host, he laughed and swore, "So may I run,
But this goes well; unbuckled is the mail;
Let's see now who can tell another tale:
For certainly the game is well begun.
10   Now shall you tell, sir monk, if't can be done,
Something with which to pay for the knight's tale."
The miller, who with drinking was all pale,
So that unsteadily on his horse he sat,
He would not take off either hood or hat,
15   Nor wait for any man, in courtesy,
But all in Pilate's voice[53] began to cry,
And by the Arms and Blood and Bones he swore,
"I have a noble story in my store,
With which I will requite the good knight's tale."
20   Our host saw, then, that he was drunk with ale,
And said to him: "Wait, Robin, my dear brother,
Some better man shall tell us first another:
Submit and let us work on profitably."
"Now by God's soul," cried he, "that will not I!
25   For I will speak, or else I'll go my way."
Our host replied: "Tell on, then, till doomsday!
You are a fool, your wit is overcome."
"Now hear me," said the miller, "all and some!
But first I make a protestation round
30   That I'm quite drunk, I know it by my sound:
And therefore, if I slander or mis-say,
Blame it on ale of Southwark, so I pray;
For I will tell a legend and a life
Both of a carpenter and of his wife,

---

[53]Pontius Pilate was characterized in medieval plays by having a loud, hoarse voice.

35	And how a scholar set the good wright's cap."[54]
	The reeve replied and said: "Oh, shut your trap,
	Let be your ignorant drunken ribaldry!
	It is a sin, and further, great folly
	To asperse any man, or him defame,
40	And, too, to bring upon a man's wife shame.
	There are enough of other things to say."
	This drunken miller spoke on in his way,
	And said: "Oh, but my dear brother Oswald,
	The man who has no wife is no cuckold.
45	But I say not, thereby, that you are one:
	Many good wives there are, as women run,
	And ever a thousand good to one that's bad,
	As well you know yourself, unless you're mad.
	Why are you angry with my story's cue?
50	I have a wife, begad, as well as you,
	Yet I'd not, for the oxen of my plow,
	Take on my shoulders more than is enow,
	By judging of myself that I am one;
	I will believe full well that I am none.
55	A husband must not be inquisitive
	Of God, nor of his wife, while she's alive.
	So long as he may find God's plenty there,
	For all the rest he need not greatly care."
	What should I say, except this miller rare
60	He would forgo his talk for no man there,
	But told his churlish tale in his own way:
	I think I'll here re-tell it, if I may.
	And therefore, every gentle soul, I pray
	That for God's love you'll hold not what I say
65	Evilly meant, but that I must rehearse,
	All of their tales, the better and the worse,
	Or else prove false to some of my design.
	Therefore, who likes not this, let him, in fine,
	Turn over page and choose another tale:
70	For he shall find enough, both great and small,
	Of stories touching on gentility,
	And holiness, and on morality;
	And blame not me if you do choose amiss.
	The miller was a churl, you well know this;
75	So was the reeve, and many another more,
	And ribaldry they told from plenteous store.

---

[54]i.e., "reset the carpenter's cap," or, gave him horns, made him a cuckold.

Be then advised, and hold me free from blame;
Men should not be too serious at a game.

THE MILLER'S TALE

Once on a time was dwelling in Oxford
80 A wealthy lout who took in guests to board,
And of his craft he was a carpenter.
A poor scholar was lodging with him there,
Who'd learned the arts, but all his phantasy
Was turned to study of astrology;
85 And knew a certain set of theorems
And could find out by various stratagems,
If men but asked of him in certain hours
When they should have a drought or else have showers,
Or if men asked of him what should befall
90 To anything—I cannot reckon them all.
This clerk was called the clever Nicholas;
Of secret loves he knew and their solace;
And he kept counsel, too, for he was sly
And meek as any maiden passing by.
95 He had a chamber in that hostelry,
And lived alone there, without company,
All garnished with sweet herbs of good repute;
And he himself sweet-smelling as the root
Of licorice, valerian, or setwall.[55]
100 His Almagest,[56] and books both great and small,
His astrolabe,[57] belonging to his art,
His algorism stones—all laid apart
On shelves that ranged beside his lone bed's head;
His press was covered with a cloth of red.
105 And over all there lay a psaltery
Whereon he made an evening's melody,
Playing so sweetly that the chamber rang;
And *Angelus ad virginem*[58] he sang;
And after that he warbled the King's Note:
110 Often in good voice was his merry throat.
And thus this gentle clerk his leisure spends
Supported by some income and his friends.

---

[55]herbs and spices of strong aroma.
[56]an astronomical treatise by Ptolemy (2nd c.).
[57]an instrument to calculate the position of the stars.
[58]a hymn of the Annunciation, "The Angel Addresses the Virgin."

This carpenter had lately wed a wife
Whom he loved better than he loved his life;
115   And she was come to eighteen years of age.
Jealous he was and held her close in cage.
For she was wild and young, and he was old,
And deemed himself as like to be cuckold.
He knew not Cato,[59] for his lore was rude:
120   That vulgar man should wed similitude.
A man should wed according to estate,
For youth and age are often in debate.
But now, since he had fallen in the snare,
He must endure, like other folk, his care.
125   Fair was this youthful wife, and therewithal
As weasel's was her body slim and small.
A girdle wore she, barred and striped, of silk.
An apron, too, as white as morning milk
About her loins, and full of many a gore;
130   White was her smock, embroidered all before
And even behind, her collar round about,
Of coal-black silk, on both sides, in and out;
The strings of the white cap upon her head
Were, like her collar, black silk worked with thread,
135   Her fillet was of wide silk worn full high:
And certainly she had a lickerish[60] eye.
She'd thinned out carefully her eyebrows two,
And they were arched and black as any sloe.
She was a far more pleasant thing to see
140   Than is the newly budded young pear-tree;
And softer than the wool is on a wether.
Down from her girdle hung a purse of leather,
Tasselled with silk, with latten[61] beading sown.
In all this world, searching it up and down,
145   So gay a little doll, I well believe,
Or such a wench, there's no man can conceive.
Far brighter was the brilliance of her hue
Than in the Tower the gold coins minted new.
And songs came shrilling from her pretty head
150   As from a swallow's sitting on a shed.
Therewith she'd dance too, and could play and sham
Like any kid or calf about its dam.

---

[59]Dionysius Cato supposedly wrote a book of maxims widely used in grammar schools.
[60]lecherous.
[61]brass spangles.

Her mouth was sweet as bragget or as mead[62]
Or hoard of apples laid in hay or weed.
155 Skittish she was as is a pretty colt,
Tall as a staff and straight as cross-bow bolt.
A brooch she wore upon her collar low,
As broad as boss of buckler did it show;
Her shoes laced up to where a girl's legs thicken.
160 She was a primrose, and a tender chicken
For any lord to lay upon his bed,
Or yet for any good yeoman to wed.
Now, sir, and then, sir, go befell the case,
That on a day this clever Nicholas
165 Fell in with this young wife to toy and play,
The while her husband was down Osney way,
Clerks being as crafty as the best of us;
And unperceived he caught her by the puss,
Saying: "Indeed, unless I have my will,
170 For secret love of you, sweetheart, I'll spill."
And held her hard about the hips, and how!
And said: "O darling, love me, love me now,
Or I shall die, and pray you God may save!"
And she leaped as a colt does in the trave,
175 And with her head she twisted fast away,
And said: "I will not kiss you, by my fay!
Why, let go," cried she, "let go, Nicholas!
Or I will call for help and cry 'alas!'
Do take your hands away, for courtesy!"
180 This Nicholas for mercy then did cry,
And spoke so well, importuned her so fast
That she her love did grant him at the last,
And swore her oath, by Saint Thomas of Kent,
That she would be at his command, content,
185 As soon as opportunity she could spy.
"My husband is so full of jealousy,
Unless you will await me secretly,
I know I'm just as good as dead," said she.
"You must keep all quite hidden in this case."
190 "Nay, thereof worry not," said Nicholas,
"A clerk has lazily employed his while
If he cannot a carpenter beguile."
And thus they were agreed, and then they swore
To wait a while, as I have said before.

---

[62]drinks made from fermented honey.

195	When Nicholas had done thus every whit
	And patted her about the loins a bit,
	He kissed her sweetly, took his psaltery,
	And played it fast and made a melody.
	Then fell it thus, that to the parish kirk,
200	The Lord Christ Jesus' own works for to work,
	This goodwife went, upon a holy day;
	Her forehead shone as bright as does the May,
	So well she'd washed it when she left off work.
	Now there was of that church a parish clerk
205	Whose name was (as folk called him) Absalom.
	Curled was his hair, shining like gold, and from
	His head spread fanwise in a thick bright mop;
	'Twas parted straight and even on the top;
	His cheek was red, his eyes grey as a goose;
210	With Saint Paul's windows cut upon his shoes,
	He stood in red hose fitting famously.
	And he was clothed full well and properly
	All in a coat of blue, in which were let
	Holes for the lacings, which were fairly set.
215	And over all he wore a fine surplice
	As white as ever hawthorn spray, and nice.
	A merry lad he was, so God me save,
	And well could he let blood, cut hair, and shave,
	And draw a deed or quitclaim, as might chance.
220	In twenty manners could he trip and dance,
	After the school that reigned in Oxford, though,
	And with his two legs swinging to and fro;
	And he could play upon a violin;
	Thereto he sang in treble voice and thin;
225	And as well could he play on his guitar.
	In all the town no inn was, and no bar,
	That he'd not visited to make good cheer,
	Especially were lively barmaids there.
	But, truth to tell, he was a bit squeamish
230	Of farting and of language haughtyish.
	This Absalom, who was so light and gay,
	Went with a censer on the holy day,
	Censing the wives like an enthusiast;
	And on them many a loving look he cast,
235	Especially on this carpenter's goodwife.
	To look at her he thought a merry life,
	She was so pretty, sweet, and lickerous.
	I dare well say, if she had been a mouse

And he a cat, he would have mauled her some.
240 This parish clerk, this lively Absalom
Had in his heart, now, such a love-longing
That from no wife took he an offering;
For courtesy, he said, he would take none.
The moon, when it was night, full brightly shone,
245 And his guitar did Absalom then take,
For in love-watching he'd intent to wake.
And forth he went, jolly and amorous,
Until he came unto the carpenter's house
A little after cocks began to crow;
250 And took his stand beneath a shot-window
That was let into the good wood-wright's[63] wall.
He sang then, in his pleasant voice and small,
"Oh now, dear lady, if your will it be,
I pray that you will have some ruth on me,"
255 The words in harmony with his string-plucking.
This carpenter awoke and heard him sing,
And called unto his wife and said, in sum:
"What, Alison! Do you hear Absalom,
Who plays and sings beneath our bedroom wall?"
260 And she said to her husband, therewithal:
"Yes, God knows, John, I bear it, truth to tell."
So this went on; what is there better than well?
From day to day this pretty Absalom
So wooed her he was woebegone therefrom.
265 He lay awake all night and all the day;
He combed his spreading hair and dressed him gay;
By go-betweens and agents, too, wooed he,
And swore her loyal page he'd ever be.
He sang as tremulously as nightingale;
270 He sent her sweetened wine and well-spiced ale
And waffles piping hot out of the fire,
And, she being town-bred, mead for her desire.
For some are won by means of money spent,
And some by tricks, and some by long descent.
275 Once, to display his versatility,
He acted Herod on a scaffold high.
But what availed it him in any case?
She was enamoured so of Nicholas
That Absalom might go and blow his horn;
280 He got naught for his labour but her scorn.

---

[63]carpenter's.

And thus she made of Absalom her ape,
And all his earnestness she made a jape.
For truth is in this proverb, and no lie,
Men say well thus: It's always he that's nigh
285   That makes the absent lover seem a sloth.
For now, though Absalom be wildly wroth,
Because he is so far out of her sight,
This handy Nicholas stands in his light.
Now bear you well, you clever Nicholas!
290   For Absalom may wail and sing "Alas!"
And so it chanced that on a Saturday
This carpenter departed to Osney;
And clever Nicholas and Alison
Were well agreed to this effect: anon
295   This Nicholas should put in play a wile
The simple, jealous husband to beguile;
And if it chanced the game should go a-right,
She was to sleep within his arms all night,
For this was his desire, and hers also.
300   Presently then, and without more ado,
This Nicholas, no longer did he tarry,
But softly to his chamber did he carry
Both food and drink to last at least a day,
Saying that to her husband she should say—
305   If he should come to ask for Nicholas—
Why, she should say she knew not where he was,
For all day she'd not seen him, far or nigh;
She thought he must have got some malady,
Because in vain her maid would knock and call;
310   He'd answer not, whatever might befall.
And so it was that all that Saturday
This Nicholas quietly in chamber lay,
And ate and slept, or did what pleased him best,
Till Sunday when the sun had gone to rest.
315   This simple man with wonder heard the tale,
And marvelled what their Nicholas might ail,
And said: "I am afraid, by Saint Thomas,
That everything's not well with Nicholas.
God send he be not dead so suddenly!
320   This world is most unstable, certainly;
I saw, today, the corpse being borne to kirk
Of one who, but last Monday, was at work.
Go up," said he unto his boy anon,
"Call at his door, or knock there with a stone,

325   Learn how it is and boldly come tell me."
            The servant went up, then, right sturdily,
            And at the chamber door, the while he stood,
            He cried and knocked as any madman would—
            "What! How! What do you, Master Nicholay?
330   How can you sleep through all the livelong day?"
            But all for naught, he never heard a word;
            A hole he found, low down upon a board,
            Through which the house cat had been wont to creep;
            And to that hole he stooped, and through did peep,
335   And finally he ranged him in his sight.
            This Nicholas sat gaping there, upright,
            As if he'd looked too long at the new moon.
            Downstairs he went and told his master soon
            In what array he'd found this self-same man.
340   This carpenter to cross himself began,
            And said: "Now help us, holy Frideswide!
            Little a man can know what shall betide.
            This man is fallen, with his astromy,
             Into some madness or some agony;
345   I always feared that somehow this would be!
            Men should not meddle in God's privity.
            Aye, blessed always be the ignorant man,
            Whose creed is, all he ever has to scan!
            So fared another clerk with astromy;
350   He walked into the meadows for to pry
            Into the stars, to learn what should befall,
            Until into a clay-pit he did fall;
            He saw not that. But yet, by Saint Thomas,
            I'm sorry for this clever Nicholas.
355   He shall be scolded for his studying,
            If not too late, by Jesus, Heaven's King!
            "Get me a staff, that I may pry before,
            The while you, Robin, heave against the door.
            We'll take him from this studying, I guess."
360   And on the chamber door, then, he did press.
            His servant was a stout lad, if a dunce,
            And by the hasp he heaved it up at once;
            Upon the floor that portal fell anon.
            This Nicholas sat there as still as stone,
365   Gazing, with gaping mouth, straight up in air.
            This carpenter thought he was in despair,
            And took him by the shoulders, mightily,
            And shook him hard, and cried out, vehemently:

"What! Nicholay! Why how now! Come, look down!
370 Awake, and think on Jesus' death and crown!
I cross you from all elves and magic wights!"
And then the night-spell said he out, by rights,
At the four corners of the house about,
And at the threshold of the door, without:—
375 "O Jesus Christ and good Saint Benedict,
Protect this house from all that may afflict,
For the night hag the white Paternoster!—
Where hast thou gone, Saint Peter's sister?"
And at the last this clever Nicholas
380 Began to sigh full sore, and said: "Alas!
Shall all the world be lost so soon again?"
This carpenter replied: "What say you, then?
What! Think on God, as we do, men that swink."[64]
This Nicholas replied: "Go fetch me drink;
385 And afterward I'll tell you privately
A certain thing concerning you and me;
I'll tell it to no other man or men."
This carpenter went down and came again,
And brought of potent ale a brimming quart;
390 And when each one of them had drunk his part,
Nicholas shut the door fast, and with that
He drew a seat and near the carpenter sat.
He said: "Now, John, my good host, lief and dear,
You must upon your true faith swear, right here,
395 That to no man will you this word betray;
For it is Christ's own word that I will say,
And if you tell a man, you're ruined quite;
This punishment shall come to you, of right,
That if you're traitor you'll go mad—and should!"
400 "Nay, Christ forbid it, for His holy blood!"
Said then this simple man: "I am no blab,
Nor, though I say it, am I fond of gab.
Say what you will, I never will it tell
To child or wife, by Him that harried Hell!"
405 "Now, John," said Nicholas, "I will not lie;
But I've found out, from my astrology,
As I have looked upon the moon so bright,
That now, come Monday next, at nine of night,
Shall fall a rain so wildly mad as would
410 Have been, by half, greater than Noah's flood.

---

[64]work.

This world," he said, "in less time than an hour,
Shall all be drowned, so terrible is this shower;
Thus shall all mankind drown and lose all life."
This carpenter replied: "Alas, my wife!
415   And shall she drown? Alas, my Alison!"
For grief of this he almost fell. Anon
He said: "Is there no remedy in this case?"
"Why yes, good luck," said clever Nicholas,
"If you will work by counsel of the wise;
420   You must not act on what your wits advise.
For so says Solomon, and it's all true,
'Work by advice and thou shalt never rue.'
And if you'll act as counseled and not fail,
I undertake, without a mast or sail,
425   To save us all, aye you and her and me.
Haven't you heard of Noah, how saved was he,
Because Our Lord had warned him how to keep
Out of the flood that covered earth so deep?"
"Yes," said this carpenter, "long years ago."
430   "Have you not heard," asked Nicholas, "also
The sorrows of Noah and his fellowship
In getting his wife to go aboard the ship?
He would have rather, I dare undertake,
At that time, and for all the weather black,
435   That she had one ship for herself alone.
Therefore, do you know what would best be done?
This thing needs haste, and of a hasty thing
Men must not preach nor do long tarrying.
"Presently go, and fetch here to this inn
440   A kneading-tub, or brewing vat, and win
One each for us, but see that they are large,
Wherein we may swim out as in a barge,
And have therein sufficient food and drink
For one day only; that's enough, I think.
445   The water will dry up and flow away
About the prime of the succeeding day.
But Robin must not know of this, your knave,
And even Jill, your maid, I may not save;
Ask me not why, for though you do ask me,
450   I will not tell you of God's privity.
Suffice you, then, unless your wits are mad,
To have as great a grace as Noah had.
Your wife I shall not lose, there is no doubt,
Go, now, your way, and speedily about,

455 But when you have, for you and her and me,
Procured these kneading-tubs, or beer-vats, three,
Then you shall hang them near the roof-tree high,
That no man our purveyance may espy.
And when you thus have done, as I have said,
460 And have put in our drink and meat and bread,
Also an axe to cut the ropes in two
When the flood comes, that we may float and go,
And cut a hole, high up, upon the gable,
Upon the garden side, over the stable,
465 That we may freely pass forth on our way
When the great rain and flood are gone that day—
Then shall you float as merrily, I'll stake,
As does the white duck after the white drake.
Then I will call, 'Ho, Alison! Ho, John!
470 Be cheery, for the flood will pass anon.'
And you will say, 'Hail. Master Nicholay!
Good morrow, I see you well, for it is day!'
And then shall we be barons all our life
Of all the world, like Noah and his wife.
475 But of one thing I warn you now, outright.
Be well advised, that on that very night
When we have reached our ships and got aboard,
Not one of us must speak or whisper word,
Nor call, nor cry, but sit in silent prayer;
480 For this is God's own bidding, hence—don't dare!
Your wife and you must hang apart, that in
The night shall come no chance for you to sin
Either in looking or in carnal deed.
These orders I have told you, go, God speed!
485 Tomorrow night, when all men are asleep,
Into our kneading-tubs will we three creep
And sit there, still, awaiting God's high grace.
Go, now, your way, I have no longer space
Of time to make a longer sermoning.
490 Men say thus: 'Send the wise and say no thing.'
You are so wise it needs not that I teach;
Go, save our lives, and that I do beseech."
This silly carpenter went on his way.
Often he cried "Alas!" and "Welaway!"
495 And to his wife he told all, privately;
But she was better taught thereof than he
How all this rigmarole was to apply.
Nevertheless she acted as she'd die,

And said: "Alas! Go on your way anon,
500   Help us escape, or we are lost, each one;
I am your true and lawfully wedded wife;
Go, my dear spouse, and help to save our life."
Lo, what a great thing is affection found!
Men die of imagination, I'll be bound,
505   So deep an imprint may the spirit take.
This hapless carpenter began to quake;
He thought now, verily, that he could see
Old Noah's flood come wallowing like the sea
To drown his Alison, his honey dear.
510   He wept, he wailed, he made but sorry cheer,
He sighed and made full many a sob and sough.[65]
He went and got himself a kneading-trough
And, after that, two tubs he somewhere found
And to his dwelling privately sent round,
515   And hung them near the roof, all secretly.
With his own hand, then, made he ladders three,
To climb up by the rungs thereof, it seems,
And reach the tubs left hanging to the beams;
And those he victualled, tubs and kneading-trough,
520   With bread and cheese and good jugged ale, enough
To satisfy the needs of one full day.
But ere he'd put all this in such array,
He sent his servants, boy and maid, right down
Upon some errand into London town.
525   And on the Monday, when it came on night,
He shut his door, without a candle-light,
And ordered everything as it should be.
And shortly after up they climbed, all three;
They sat while one might plow a furlong-way.
530   "Now, by Our Father, hush!" said Nicholay,
And "Hush!" said John, and "Hush!" said Alison.
This carpenter, his loud devotions done,
Sat silent, saying mentally a prayer,
And waiting for the rain, to hear it there.
535   The deathlike sleep of utter weariness
Fell on this wood-wright even (as I guess)
About the curfew time, or little more;
For travail of his spirit he groaned sore,
And soon he snored, for badly his head lay.
540   Down by the ladder crept this Nicholay,

---

[65]groan.

And Alison, right softly down she sped.
Without more words they went and got in bed
Even where the carpenter was wont to lie.
There was the revel and the melody!
545 And thus lie Alison and Nicholas,
In joy that goes by many an alias,
Until the bells for lauds began to ring
And friars to the chancel went to sing.
This parish clerk, this amorous Absalom,
550 Whom love has made so woebegone and dumb,
Upon the Monday was down Osney way,
With company, to find some sport and play;
And there he chanced to ask a cloisterer,
Privately, after John the carpenter.
555 This monk drew him apart, out of the kirk,[66]
And said: "I have not seen him here at work.
Since Saturday; I think well that he went
For timber, that the abbot has him sent;
For he is wont for timber thus to go,
560 Remaining at the grange a day or so;
Or else he's surely at his house today;
But which it is I cannot truly say."
This Absalom right happy was and light,
And thought: "Now is the time to wake all night;
565 For certainly I saw him not stirring
About his door since day began to spring.
So may I thrive, as I shall, at cock's crow,
Knock cautiously upon that window low
Which is so placed upon his bedroom wall.
570 To Alison then will I tell of all
My love-longing, and thus I shall not miss
That at the least I'll have her lips to kiss.
Some sort of comfort shall I have, I say,
My mouth's been itching all this livelong day;
575 That is a sign of kissing at the least.
All night I dreamed, too, I was at a feast.
Therefore I'll go and sleep two hours away
And all this night then will I wake and play."
And so when time of first cock-crow was come,
580 Up rose this merry lover, Absalom,
And dressed him gay and all at point-device,
But first he chewed some licorice and spice

---

[66]church (still used in Scots' English).

So he'd smell sweet, ere he had combed his hair.
Under his tongue some bits of true-love rare,
585   For thereby thought he to be more gracious.
He went, then, to the carpenter's dark house.
And silent stood beneath the shot-window;
Unto his breast it reached, it was so low;
And he coughed softly, in a low half tone:
590   "What do you, honeycomb, sweet Alison?
My cinnamon, my fair bird, my sweetie,
Awake, O darling mine, and speak to me!
It's little thought you give me and my woe,
Who for your love do sweat where'er I go.
595   Yet it's no wonder that I faint and sweat;
I long as does the lamb for mother's teat.
Truly, sweetheart, I have such love-longing
That like a turtle-dove's my true yearning;
And I can eat no more than can a maid."
600   "Go from the window, Jack-a-napes," she said,
"For, s'help me God, it is not 'come kiss me.'
I love another, or to blame I'd be,
Better than you, by Jesus, Absalom!
Go on your way, or I'll stone you therefrom,
605   And let me sleep, the fiends take you away!"
"Alas," quoth Absalom, "and welaway!
That true love ever was so ill beset!
But kiss me, since you'll do no more, my pet,
For Jesus' love and for the love of me."
610   "And will you go, then, on your way?" asked she.
"Yes truly, darling," said this Absalom.
"Then make you ready," said she, "and I'll come!"
And unto Nicholas said she, low and still:
"Be silent now, and you shall laugh your fill."
615   This Absalom plumped down upon his knees,
And said: "I am a lord in all degrees;
For after this there may be better still
Darling, my sweetest bird, I wait your will."
The window she unbarred, and that in haste.
620   "Have done," said she, "come on, and do it fast,
Before we're seen by any neighbour's eye."
This Absalom did wipe his mouth all dry;
Dark was the night as pitch, aye dark as coal,
And through the window she put out her hole.
625   And Absalom no better felt nor worse,
But with his mouth he kissed her naked arse

Right greedily, before he knew of this.
Aback he leapt—it seemed somehow amiss,
For well he knew a woman has no beard;
630   He'd felt a thing all rough and longish haired,
And said, "Oh fie, alas! What did I do?"
"Teehee!" she laughed, and clapped the window to;
And Absalom went forth a sorry pace.
"A beard! A beard!" cried clever Nicholas,
635   "Now by God's corpus, this goes fair and well!"
This hapless Absalom, he heard that yell,
And on his lip, for anger, he did bite;
And to himself he said, "I will requite!"
Who vigorously rubbed and scrubbed his lips
640   With dust, with sand, with straw, with cloth, with chips,
But Absalom, and often cried "Alas!
My soul I give now unto Sathanas,
For rather far than own this town," said he,
"For this despite, it's well revenged I'd be.
645   Alas," said he, "from her I never blenched!"
His hot love was grown cold, aye and all quenched;
For, from the moment that he'd kissed her arse,
For paramours he didn't care a curse,
For he was healed of all his malady;
650   Indeed all paramours he did defy,
And wept as does a child that has been beat.
With silent step he went across the street
Unto a smith whom men called Dan Jarvis,
Who in his smithy forged plow parts, that is
655   He sharpened shares and coulters busily.
This Absalom he knocked all easily,
And said: "Unbar here, Jarvis, for I come."
"What! Who are you?"
"It's I, it's Absalom."
660   "What! Absalom! For Jesus Christ's sweet tree,
Why are you up so early? *Ben'cite!*[67]
What ails you now, man? Some gay girl, God knows,
Has brought you on the jump to my bellows;
By Saint Neot, you know well what I mean."
665   This Absalom cared not a single bean
For all this play, nor one word back he gave;
He'd more tow on his distaff, had this knave,
Than Jarvis knew, and said he: "Friend so dear,

---

[67]"Bless me."

This red-hot coulter in the fireplace here,
670 Lend it to me, I have a need for it,
And I'll return it after just a bit."
Jarvis replied: "Certainly, were it gold
Or a purse filled with yellow coins untold,
Yet should you have it, as I am true smith;
675 But eh, Christ's foe! What will you do therewith?"
"Let that," said Absalom, "be as it may;
I'll tell you all tomorrow, when it's day"—
And caught the coulter then by the cold steel
And softly from the smithy door did steal
680 And went again up to the wood-wright's wall.
He coughed at first, and then he knocked withal
Upon the window, as before, with care.
This Alison replied: "Now who is there?
And who knocks so? I'll warrant it's a thief."
685 "Why no," quoth he, "God knows, my sweet roseleaf,
I am your Absalom, my own darling!
Of gold," quoth he, "I have brought you a ring;
My mother gave it me, as I'll be saved;
Fine gold it is, and it is well engraved;
690 This will I give you for another kiss."
This Nicholas had risen for a piss,
And thought that it would carry on the jape
To have his arse kissed by this jack-a-nape.
And so he opened window hastily,
695 And put his arse out thereat, quietly,
Over the buttocks, showing the whole bum;
And thereto said this clerk, this Absalom,
"O speak, sweet bird, I know not where thou art."
This Nicholas just then let fly a fart
700 As loud as it had been a thunder-clap,
And well-nigh blinded Absalom, poor chap;
But he was ready with his iron hot
And Nicholas right in the arse he got.
Off went the skin a hand's-breadth broad, about,
705 The coulter burned his bottom so, throughout,
That for the pain he thought that he should die.
And like one mad he started in to cry,
"Help! Water! Water! For God's dear heart!"
This carpenter out of his sleep did start,
710 Hearing that "Water!" cried as madman would,

And thought, "Alas, now comes down Noel's flood!"[68]
He struggled up without another word
And with his axe he cut in two the cord,
And down went all; he did not stop to trade
715   In bread or ale till he'd the journey made,
And there upon the floor he swooning lay.
Up started Alison and Nicholay
And shouted "Help!" and "Hello!" down the street.
The neighbours, great and small, with hastening feet
720   Swarmed in the house to stare upon this man,
Who lay yet swooning, and all pale and wan;
For in the falling he had smashed his arm.
He had to suffer, too, another harm,
For when he spoke he was at once borne down
725   By clever Nicholas and Alison.
For they told everyone that he was odd;
He was so much afraid of "Noel's" flood,
Through fantasy, that out of vanity
He'd gone and bought these kneading-tubs, all three,
730   And that he'd hung them near the roof above;
And that he had prayed them, for God's dear love,
To sit with him and bear him company.
The people laughed at all this fantasy;
Up to the roof they looked, and there did gape,
735   And so turned all his injury to a jape.
For when this carpenter got in a word,
'Twas all in vain, no man his reasons heard;
With oaths impressive was so sworn down,
That he was held for mad by all the town;
740   For every clerk did side with every other.
They said: "The man is crazy, my dear brother."
And everyone did laugh at all this strife.
Thus futtered was the carpenter's goodwife,
For all his watching and his jealousy;
745   And Absalom has kissed her nether eye;
And Nicholas is branded on the butt.
This tale is done, and God save all the rout!

[*The Monk has just been telling a series of dreadful "tragedies" when he is interrupted by the Knight who courteously wishes to spare the group more misery.*]

---

[68]John is confusing Noah and Noel (French for "Christmas").

THE PROLOGUE TO THE NUN'S PRIEST'S TALE

"Hold!" cried the knight. "Good sir, no more of this,
What you have said is right enough, and is
Very much more; a little heaviness
Is plenty for the most of us, I guess.
5   For me, I say it's saddening, if you please,
As to men who've enjoyed great wealth and ease,
To hear about their sudden fall, alas!
But the contrary's joy and great solace,
As when a man has been in poor estate
10   And he climbs up and waxes fortunate,
And there abides in all prosperity.
Such things are gladsome, as it seems to me,
And of such things it would be good to tell."
"Yea," quoth our host, "and by Saint Paul's great bell,
15   You say the truth; this monk, his clapper's loud.
He spoke how 'Fortune covered with a cloud'
I know not what, and of a 'tragedy,'
As now you heard, and gad! no remedy
It is to wail and wonder and complain
20   That certain things have happened, and it's pain.
As you have said, to hear of wretchedness.
Sir monk, no more of this, so God you bless!
Your tale annoys the entire company;
Such talking is not worth a butterfly;
25   For in it is no sport nor any game.
Wherefore, sir monk, Don Peter by your name,
I pray you heartily tell us something else,
For truly, but for clinking of the bells
That from your bridle hang on either side,
30   By Heaven's king, Who for us all has died,
I should, ere this, have fallen down for sleep,
Although the mud had never been so deep;
Then had your story all been told in vain.
For certainly, as all these clerks complain,
35   'Whenas a man has none for audience,
It's little help to speak his evidence.'
And well I know the substance is in me
To judge of things that well reported be.
Sir, tell a tale of hunting now, I pray."
40   "Nay," said this monk, "I have no wish to play;
Now let another tell, as I have told."
Then spoke our host out, in rude speech and bold,

And said he unto the nun's priest anon:
"Come near, you priest, come hither, you Sir John,
45 Tell us a thing to make our hearts all glad;
Be blithe, although you ride upon a jade.
What though your horse may be both foul and lean?
If he but serves you, why, don't care a bean;
Just see your heart is always merry. So."
50 "Yes, sir," said he, "yes, host, so may I go,
For, save I'm merry, I know I'll be blamed."
And right away his story has he framed,
And thus he said unto us, every one,
This dainty priest, this goodly man, Sir John.

THE NUN'S PRIEST'S TALE

55 A widow poor, somewhat advanced in age,
Lived, on a time, within a small cottage
Beside a grove and standing down a dale.
This widow, now, of whom I tell my tale,
Since that same day when she'd been last a wife
60 Had led, with patience, her strait simple life,
For she'd small goods and little income-rent;
By husbanding of such as God had sent
She kept herself and her young daughters twain.
Three large sows had she, and no more, 'tis plain,
65 Three cows and a lone sheep that she called Moll.
Right sooty was her bedroom and her hall,
Wherein she'd eaten many a slender meal.
Of sharp sauce, why she needed no great deal,
For dainty morsel never passed her throat;
70 Her diet well accorded with her coat.
Repletion never made this woman sick;
A temperate diet was her whole physic,
And exercise, and her heart's sustenance.
The gout, it hindered her nowise to dance,
75 Nor apoplexy spun within her head;
And no wine drank she, either white or red;
Her board was mostly garnished, white and black,
With milk and brown bread, whereof she'd no lack,
Broiled bacon and sometimes an egg or two,
80 For a small dairy business did she do.
A yard she had, enclosed all roundabout
With pales, and there was a dry ditch without,
And in the yard a cock called Chanticleer.

In all the land, for crowing, he'd no peer.
85 His voice was merrier than the organ gay
On Mass days, which in church begins to play;
More regular was his crowing in his lodge
Than is a clock or abbey horologe.
By instinct he'd marked each ascension down
90 Of equinoctial value in that town;
For when fifteen degrees had been ascended,
Then crew he so it might not be amended.
His comb was redder than a fine coral,
And battlemented like a castle wall.
95 His bill was black and just like jet it shone;
Like azure were his legs and toes, each one;
His spurs were whiter than the lily flower;
And plumage of the burnished gold his dower.
This noble cock had in his governance
100 Seven hens to give him pride and all pleasance,
Which were his sisters and his paramours
And wondrously like him as to colours,
Whereof the fairest hued upon her throat
Was called the winsome Mistress Pertelote.
105 Courteous she was, discreet and debonnaire,
Companionable, and she had been so fair
Since that same day when she was seven nights old,
That truly she had taken the heart to hold
Of Chanticleer, locked in her every limb;
110 He loved her so that all was well with him.
But such a joy it was to hear them sing,
Whenever the bright sun began to spring,
In sweet accord, "My love walks through the land."
For at that time, and as I understand,
115 The beasts and all the birds could speak and sing.
So it befell that, in a bright dawning,
As Chanticleer 'midst wives and sisters all
Sat on his perch, the which was in the hall,
And next him sat the winsome Pertelote,
120 This Chanticleer he groaned within his throat
Like man that in his dreams is troubled sore.
And when fair Pertelote thus heard him roar,
She was aghast and said: "O sweetheart dear,
What ails you that you groan so? Do you hear?
125 You are a sleepy herald. Fie, for shame!"
And he replied to her thus: "Ah, madame,
I pray you that you take it not in grief:

By God, I dreamed I'd come to such mischief,
Just now, my heart yet jumps with sore affright.
130   Now God," cried he, "my vision read aright
And keep my body out of foul prison!
I dreamed, that while I wandered up and down
Within our yard, I saw there a strange beast
Was like a dog, and he'd have made a feast
135   Upon my body, and have had me dead.
His colour yellow was and somewhat red;
And tipped his tail was, as were both his ears,
With black, unlike the rest, as it appears;
His snout was small and gleaming was each eye.
140   Remembering how he looked, almost I die;
And all this caused my groaning, I confess."
"Aha," said she, "fie on you, spiritless!
Alas!" cried she, "for by that God above,
Now have you lost my heart and all my love;
145   I cannot love a coward, by my faith.
For truly, whatsoever woman saith,
We all desire, if only it may be,
To have a husband hardy, wise, and free,
And trustworthy, no niggard, and no fool,
150   Nor one that is afraid of every tool,
Nor yet a braggart, by that God above!
How dare you say, for shame, unto your love
That there is anything that you have feared?
Have you not man's heart, and yet have a beard?
155   Alas! And are you frightened by a vision?
Dreams are, God knows, a matter for derision.
Visions are generated by repletions
And vapours and the body's bad secretions
Of humours overabundant in a wight.
160   Surely this dream, which you have had tonight,
Comes only of the superfluity
Of your bilious irascibility,
Which causes folk to shiver in their dreams
For arrows and for flames with long red gleams,
165   For great beasts in the fear that they will bite,
For quarrels and for wolf whelps great and slight;
Just as the humour of melancholy
Causes full many a man, in sleep, to cry,
For fear of black bears or of bulls all black,
170   Or lest black devils put them in a sack.
Of other humours could I tell also,

That bring, to many a sleeping man, great woe;
But I'll pass on as lightly as I can.
"Lo, Cato, and he was a full wise man,
175   Said he not, we should trouble not for dreams?
Now, sir," said she, "when we fly from the beams,
For God's love go and take some laxative;
On peril of my soul, and as I live,
I counsel you the best, I will not lie,
180   That both for choler and for melancholy
You purge yourself; and since you shouldn't tarry,
And on this farm there's no apothecary,
I will myself go find some herbs for you
That will be good for health and pecker too;
185   And in our own yard all these herbs I'll find,
The which have properties of proper kind
To purge you underneath and up above.
Forget this not, now, for God's very love!
You are so very choleric of complexion.
190   Beware the mounting sun and all dejection,
Nor get yourself with sudden humours hot;
For if you do, I dare well lay a groat
That you shall have the tertian fever's pain,
Or some ague that may well be your bane.
195   A day or two you shall have digestives
Of worms before you take your laxatives
Of laurel, centuary, and fumitory,
Or else of hellebore purificatory,
Or caper spurge, or else of dogwood berry,
200   Or herb ivy, all in our yard so merry;
Peck them just as they grow and gulp them in.
Be merry, husband, for your father's kin!
Dread no more dreams. And I can say no more."
"Madam," said he, "gramercy for your lore.
205   Nevertheless, not running Cato down,
Who had for wisdom such a high renown,
And though he says to hold no dreams in dread,
By God, men have, in many old books, read
Of many a man more an authority
210   That ever Cato was, pray pardon me,
Who say just the reverse of his sentence,
And have found out by long experience
That dreams, indeed, are good significations,
As much of joys as of all tribulations
215   That folk endure here in this life present.

There is no need to make an argument;
The very proof of this is shown indeed.
"One of the greatest authors that men read
Says thus: That on a time two comrades went

220 On pilgrimage, and all in good intent;
And it so chanced they came into a town
Where there was such a crowding, up and down,
Of people, and so little harbourage,[69]
That they found not so much as one cottage

225 Wherein the two of them might sheltered be.
Wherefore they must, as of necessity,
For that one night at least, part company;
And each went to a different hostelry
And took such lodgment as to him did fall.

230 Now one of them was lodged within a stall,
Far in a yard, with oxen of the plow;
That other man found shelter fair enow,
As was his luck, or was his good fortune,
Whatever 'tis that governs us, each one.

235 "So it befell that, long ere it was day,
This last man dreamed in bed, as there he lay,
That his poor fellow did unto him call,
Saying: 'Alas! For in an ox's stall
This night shall I be murdered where I lie.

240 Now help me, brother dear, before I die.
Come in all haste to me.' 'Twas thus he said.
This man woke out of sleep, then, all afraid;
But when he'd wakened fully from his sleep,
He turned upon his pillow, yawning deep,

245 Thinking his dream was but a fantasy.
And then again, while sleeping, thus dreamed he.
And then a third time came a voice that said
(Or so he thought): 'Now, comrade, I am dead;
Behold my bloody wounds, so wide and deep!

250 Early arise tomorrow from your sleep,
And at the west gate of the town,' said he,
'A wagon full of dung there shall you see,
Wherein is hid my body craftily;
Do you arrest this wagon right boldly.

255 They killed me for what money they could gain.'
And told in every point how he'd been slain,
With a most pitiful face and pale of hue.

---

[69]lodging space.

And trust me well, this dream did all come true;
For on the morrow, soon as it was day,
260   Unto his comrade's inn he took the way;
And when he'd come into that ox's stall,
Upon his fellow he began to call.
"The keeper of the place replied anon,
And said he: 'Sir, your friend is up and gone;
265   As soon as day broke he went out of town.'
This man, then, felt suspicion in him grown,
Remembering the dream that he had had,
And forth he went, no longer tarrying, sad,
Unto the west gate of the town, and found
270   A dung-cart on its way to dumping-ground,
And it was just the same in every wise
As you have heard the dead man advertise;
And with a hardy heart he then did cry
Vengeance and justice on this felony:
275   'My comrade has been murdered in the night,
And in this very cart lies, face upright.
I cry to all the officers,' said he,
'That ought to keep the peace in this city.
Alas, alas, here lies my comrade slain!'
280   "Why should I longer with this tale detain?
The people rose and turned the cart to ground,
And in the center of the dung they found
The dead man, lately murdered in his sleep.
"O Blessed God, Who art so true and deep!
285   Lo, how Thou dost turn murder out alway!
Murder will out, we see it every day.
Murder's so hateful and abominable
To God, Who is so just and reasonable,
That He'll not suffer that it hidden be;
290   Though it may skulk a year, or two, or three,
Murder will out, and I conclude thereon.
Immediately the rulers of that town,
They took the carter and so sore they racked
Him and the host, until their bones were cracked,
295   That they confessed their wickedness anon,
And hanged they both were by the neck, and soon.
"Here may men see that dreams are things to dread.
And certainly, in that same book I read,
Right in the very chapter after this
300   (I spoof not, as I may have joy and bliss),
Of two men who would voyage oversea,

For some cause, and unto a far country,
If but the winds had not been all contrary,
Causing them both within a town to tarry,
305   Which town was builded near the haven-side.
But then, one day, along toward eventide,
The wind did change and blow as suited best.
Jolly and glad they went unto their rest.
And were prepared right early for to sail;
310   But unto one was told a marvelous tale.
For one of them, a-sleeping as he lay,
Did dream a wondrous dream ere it was day.
He thought a strange man stood by his bedside
And did command him, he should there abide,
315   And said to him: 'If you tomorrow wend,
You shall be drowned; my tale is at an end.'
He woke and told his fellow what he'd met
And prayed him quit the voyage and forget;
For just one day he prayed him there to bide.
320   His comrade, who was lying there beside,
Began to laugh and scorned him long and fast.
'No dream,' said he, 'may make my heart aghast,
So that I'll quit my business for such things.
I do not care a straw for your dreamings,
325   For visions are but fantasies and japes.
Men dream, why, every day, of owls and apes,
And many a wild phantasm therewithal;
Men dream of what has never been, nor shall.
But since I see that you will here abide,
330   And thus forgo this fair wind and this tide,
God knows I'm sorry; nevertheless, good day!'
"And thus he took his leave and went his way.
But long before the half his course he'd sailed,
I know not why, nor what it was that failed,
335   But casually the vessel's bottom rent,
And ship and men under the water went,
In sight of other ships were there beside,
The which had sailed with that same wind and tide.
"And therefore, pretty Pertelote, my dear,
340   By such old-time examples may you hear
And learn that no man should be too reckless
Of dreams, for I can tell you, fair mistress,
That many a dream is something well to dread.
"Why, in the 'Life' of Saint Kenelm I read
345   (Who was Kenelphus' son, the noble king

Of Mercia), how Kenelm dreamed a thing;
A while ere he was murdered, so they say,
His own death in a vision saw, one day.
His nurse interpreted, as records tell,
350   That vision, bidding him to guard him well
From treason; but he was but seven years old,
And therefore 'twas but little he'd been told
Of any dream, so holy was his heart.
By God! I'd rather than retain my shirt
355   That you had read this legend, as have I.
Dame Pertelote, I tell you verily,
Macrobius, who wrote of Scipio
The African[70] a vision long ago,
He holds by dreams, saying that they have been
360   Warnings of things that men have later seen.
"And furthermore, I pray you to look well
In the Old Testament at Daniel,
Whether he held dreams for mere vanity.
Read, too, of Joseph, and you there shall see
365   Where dreams have sometimes been (I say not all)
Warnings of things that after did befall.
Consider Egypt's king, Dan Pharaoh,
His baker and his butler, these also,
Whether they knew of no effect from dreams.
370   Whoso will read of sundry realms the themes
May learn of dreams full many a wondrous thing.
Lo, Croesus, who was once of Lydia king,
Dreamed he not that he sat upon a tree,
Which signified that hanged high he should be?
375   Lo, how Andromache, great Hector's wife,
On that same day when Hector lost his life,
She dreamed upon the very night before
That Hector's life should be lost evermore,
If on that day he battled, without fail.
380   She warned him, but no warning could avail;
He went to fight, despite all auspices,
And so was shortly slain by Achilles.
But that same tale is all too long to tell,
And, too, it's nearly day, I must not dwell
385   Upon this; I but say, concluding here,
That from this vision I have cause to fear
Adversity; and I say, furthermore,

---

[70]Macrobius (5th c.) wrote a commentary on Cicero's "Dream of Scipio [Africanus]."

	That I do set by laxatives no store,
	For they are poisonous, I know it well.
390	Them I defy and love not, truth to tell.
	"But let us speak of mirth and stop all this;
	My lady Pertelote, on hope of bliss,
	In one respect God's given me much grace;
	For when I see the beauty of your face,
395	You are so rosy-red beneath each eye,
	It makes my dreadful terror wholly die.
	For there is truth in *In principio*
	Mulier est hominis confusio[71]
	(Madam, the meaning of this Latin is,
400	Woman is man's delight and all his bliss).
	For when I feel at night your tender side,
	Although I cannot then upon you ride,
	Because our perch so narrow is, alas!
	I am so full of joy and all solace
405	That I defy, then, vision, aye and dream."
	And with that word he flew down from the beam,
	For it was day, and down went his hens all;
	And with a cluck he them began to call,
	For he had found some corn within the yard.
410	Regal he was, and fears he did discard.
	He feathered Pertelote full many a time
	And twenty times he trod her ere 'twas prime.
	He looked as if he were a grim lion
	As on his toes he strutted up and down;
415	He deigned not set his foot upon the ground.
	He clucked when any grain of corn he found,
	And all his wives came running at his call.
	Thus regal, as a prince is in his hall,
	I'll now leave busy Chanticleer to feed,
420	And with events that followed I'll proceed.
	When that same month wherein the world began,
	Which is called March, wherein God first made man,
	Was ended, and were passed of days also,
	Since March began, full thirty days and two,
425	It fell that Chanticleer, in all his pride,
	His seven wives a-walking by his side,
	Cast up his two eyes toward the great bright sun
	(Which through the sign of Taurus now had run
	Twenty degrees and one, and somewhat more),

[71]"In the beginning, woman is man's ruin."

430   And knew by instinct and no other lore
      That it was prime, and joyfully he crew,
      "The sun, my love," he said, "has climbed anew
      Forty degrees and one, and somewhat more.
      My lady Pertelote, whom I adore,
435   Mark now these happy birds, hear how they sing,
      And see all these fresh flowers, how they spring;
      Full is my heart of revelry and grace."
      But suddenly he fell in grievous case;
      For ever the latter end of joy is woe.
440   God knows that worldly joys do swiftly go;
      And if a rhetorician could but write,
      He in some chronicle might well indite
      And mark it down as sovereign in degree.
      Now every wise man, let him hark to me:
445   This tale is just as true, I undertake,
      As is the book of Launcelot of the Lake,
      Which women always hold in such esteem.
      But now I must take up my proper theme.
      A brant-fox, full of sly iniquity,
450   That in the grove had lived two years, or three,
      Now by a fine premeditated plot
      That same night, breaking through the hedge, had got
      Into the yard where Chanticleer the fair
      Was wont, and all his wives too, to repair;
455   And in a bed of greenery still he lay
      Till it was past the quarter of the day,
      Waiting his chance on Chanticleer to fall,
      As gladly do these killers one and all
      Who lie in ambush for to murder men.
460   O murderer false, there lurking in your den!
      O new Iscariot, O new Ganelon!
      O false dissimulator, Greek Sinon[72]
      That brought down Troy all utterly to sorrow!
      O Chanticleer, accursed be that morrow
465   When you into that yard flew from the beams!
      You were well warned, and fully, by your dreams
      That this day should hold peril damnably.
      But that which God foreknows, it needs must be,
      So says the best opinion of the clerks.
470   Witness some cleric perfect for his works,

---

[72]Judas Iscariot betrayed Christ; Ganelon was the traitor to Roland; Sinon betrayed the Trojans by urging acceptance of the Trojan Horse (which was filled with Greek warriors). These three traitors are the ones Dante has Satan gnaw in his three mouths.

That in the schools there's a great altercation
In this regard, and much high disputation
That has involved a hundred thousand men.
But I can't sift it to the bran with pen,
475   As can the holy Doctor Augustine,
Or Boethius, or Bishop Bradwardine,[73]
Whether the fact of God's great foreknowing
Makes it right needful that I do a thing
(By needful, I mean, of necessity);
480   Or else, if a free choice he granted me,
To do that same thing, or to do it not,
Though God foreknew before the thing was wrought;
Or if His knowing constrains never at all,
Save by necessity conditional.
485   I have no part in matters so austere;
My tale is of a cock, as you shall hear,
That took the counsel of his wife, with sorrow,
To walk within the yard upon that morrow
After he'd had the dream whereof I told.
490   Now women's counsels oft are ill to hold;
A woman's counsel brought us first to woe,
And Adam caused from Paradise to go,
Wherein he was right merry and at ease.
But since I know not whom it may displease
495   If woman's counsel I hold up to blame,
Pass over, I but said it in my game.
Read authors where such matters do appear,
And what they say of women, you may hear.
These are the cock's words, they are none of mine;
500   No harm in women can I e'er divine.
All in the sand, a-bathing merrily,
Lay Pertelote, with all her sisters by,
There in the sun; and Chanticleer so free
Sang merrier than a mermaid in the sea
505   (For Physiologus[74] says certainly
That they do sing, both well and merrily).
And so befell that, as he cast his eye
Among the herbs and on a butterfly,
He saw this fox that lay there, crouching low.
510   Nothing of urge was in him, then, to crow;

---

[73]Three medieval theologians who grappled with the problem of God's omniscience and man's free will.
[74]a collection of lore on real and fantastic animals.

But he cried "Cock-cock-cock" and did so start
As man who has a sudden fear at heart.
For naturally a beast desires to flee
From any enemy that he may see,
515 Though never yet he's clapped on such his eye.
When Chanticleer the fox did then espy,
He would have fled but that the fox anon
Said: "Gentle sir, alas! Why be thus gone?
Are you afraid of me, who am your friend?
520 Now, surely, I were worse than any fiend
If I should do you harm or villainy.
I came not here upon your deeds to spy;
But, certainly, the cause of my coming
Was only just to listen to you sing.
525 For truly, you have quite as fine a voice
As angels have that Heaven's choirs rejoice;
Boethius to music could not bring
Such feeling, nor do others who can sing.
My lord your father (God his soul pray bless!)
530 And too your mother, of her gentleness,
Have been in my abode, to my great ease;
And truly, sir, right fain am I to please.
But since men speak of singing, I will say
(As I still have my eyesight day by day),
535 Save you, I never heard a man so sing
As did your father in the grey dawning;
Truly 'twas from the heart, his every song.
And that his voice might ever be more strong,
He took such pains that, with his either eye,
540 He had to blink, so loudly would he cry,
A-standing on his tiptoes therewithal,
Stretching his neck till it grew long and small.
And such discretion, too, by him was shown,
There was no man in any region known
545 That him in song or wisdom could surpass.
I have well read, in Dan Burnell the Ass,[75]
Among his verses, how there was a cock,
Because a priest's son gave to him a knock
Upon the leg, while young and not yet wise,
550 He caused the boy to lose his benefice.
But, truly, there is no comparison

---

[75]a 12th c. work by Nigel Wireker in which a cock gains revenge by crowing late on the day
of ordination for the priest.

With the great wisdom and the discretion
Your father had, or with his subtlety.
Now sing, dear sir, for holy charity,
555   See if you can your father counterfeit."
This Chanticleer his wings began to beat,
As one that could no treason there espy,
So was he ravished by this flattery.
Alas, you lords! Full many a flatterer
560   Is in your courts, and many a cozener,
That please your honours much more, by my fay,
Than he that truth and justice dares to say.
Go read the Ecclesiast[76] on flattery;
Beware, my lords, of all their treachery!
565   This Chanticleer stood high upon his toes,
Stretching his neck, and both his eyes did close,
And so did crow right loudly, for the nonce;
And Russel Fox, he started up at once,
And by the gorget grabbed our Chanticleer,
570   Flung him on back, and toward the wood did steer,
For there was no man who as yet pursued.
O destiny, you cannot be eschewed!
Alas, that Chanticleer flew from the beams!
Alas, his wife recked nothing of his dreams!
575   And on a Friday fell all this mischance.
O Venus, who art goddess of pleasance,
Since he did serve thee well, this Chanticleer,
And to the utmost of his power here,
More for delight than cocks to multiply,
580   Why would'st thou suffer him that day to die?
O Gaufred,[77] my dear master sovereign,
Who, when King Richard Lionheart was slain
By arrow, sang his death with sorrow sore,
Why have I not your faculty and lore
585   To chide Friday,[78] as you did worthily?
(For truly, on a Friday slain was he.)
Then would I prove how well I could complain
For Chanticleer's great fear and all his pain.
Certainly no such cry and lamentation
590   Were made by ladies at Troy's debolation,
When Pyrrhus with his terrible bared sword

---

[76]Ecclesiasticus, a book of the Roman Bible.

[77]Geoffrey de Vinsauf, a 12th c. poetic manual, one example being an elaborate account of the death of Richard I (Lionheart).

[78]Friday (*vendredi* in French) is Venus' day, when erratic things supposedly happen.

Had taken old King Priam by the beard
And slain him (as the Aeneid tells to us),
As made then all those hens in one chorus
595   When they had caught a sight of Chanticleer.
But fair Dame Pertelote assailed the ear
Far louder than did Hasdrubal's good wife
When that her husband bold had lost his life,
And Roman legionaries burned Carthage;
600   For she so full of torment was, and rage,
She voluntarily to the fire did start
And burned herself there with a steadfast heart.
And you, O woeful hens, just so you cried
As when base Nero burned the city wide
605   Of Rome, and wept the senators' stern wives
Because their husbands all had lost their lives,
For though not guilty, Nero had them slain.
Now will I turn back to my tale again.
This simple widow and her daughters two
610   Heard these hens cry and make so great ado,
And out of doors they started on the run
And saw the fox into the grove just gone,
Bearing upon his back the cock away.
And then they cried, "Alas, and weladay!
615   Oh, oh, the fox!" and after him they ran,
And after them, with staves, went many a man;
Ran Coll, our dog, ran Talbot and Garland,
And Malkin with a distaff in her hand;
Ran cow and calf and even the very hogs,
620   So were they scared by barking of the dogs
And shouting men and women all did make,
They all ran so they thought their hearts would break.
They yelled as very fiends do down in Hell;
The ducks they cried as at the butcher fell;
625   The frightened geese flew up above the trees;
Out of the hive there came the swarm of bees;
So terrible was the noise, ah ben'cite!
Certainly old Jack Straw and his army
Never raised shouting half so loud and shrill
630   When they were chasing Flemings for to kill,
As on that day was raised upon the fox.
They brought forth trumpets made of brass, of box,
Of horn, of bone, wherein they blew and pooped,
And therewithal they screamed and shrieked and whooped;
635   It seemed as if the heaven itself should fall!

And now, good men, I pray you hearken all.
Behold how Fortune turns all suddenly
The hope and pride of even her enemy!
This cock, which lay across the fox's back,
640   In all his fear unto the fox did clack
And say: "Sir, were I you, as I should be,
Then would I say (as God may now help me!),
'Turn back again, presumptuous peasants all!
A very pestilence upon you fall!
645   Now that I've gained here to this dark wood's side,
In spite of you this cock shall here abide.
I'll eat him, by my faith, and that anon!'"
The fox replied: "In faith, it shall be done!"
And as he spoke that word, all suddenly
650   This cock broke from his mouth, full cleverly,
And high upon a tree he flew anon.
And when the fox saw well that he was gone,
"Alas," quoth he, "O Chanticleer, alas!
I have against you done a base trespass
655   In that I frightened you, my dear old pard,
When you I seized and brought from out that yard;
But, sir, I did it with no foul intent;
Come down, and I will tell you what I meant.
I'll tell the truth to you, God help me so!"
660   "Nay then," said he, "beshrew us both, you know,
But first, beshrew myself, both blood and bones,
If you beguile me, having done so once,
You shall no more, with any flattery,
Cause me to sing and close up either eye.
665   For he who shuts his eyes when he should see,
And wilfully, God let him ne'er be free!"
"Nay," said the fox, "but, God give him mischance
Who is so indiscreet in governance
He chatters when he ought to hold his peace."
670   Lo, such it is when watch and ward do cease,
And one grows negligent with flattery.
But you that hold this tale a foolery,
As but about a fox, a cock, a hen,
Yet do not miss the moral, my good men.
675   For Saint Paul says that all that's written well
Is written down some useful truth to tell.
Then take the wheat and let the chaff lie still.
And now, good God, and if it be Thy will,

680 As says Lord Christ, so make us all good men
And bring us into His high bliss. Amen.

THE HOST'S INVITATION TO THE PARDONER

"You, bon ami, you pardoner," he said,
"Tell us some pleasant tale or jest, anon."
"It shall be done," said he, "by Saint Ronan!
But first," he said, "just here, at this ale-stake,
5 I will both drink and eat a bite of cake."
But then these gentle folk began to cry:
"Nay, let him tell us naught of ribaldry;
Tell us some moral thing, that we may hear
Wisdom, and then we gladly will give ear."
10 "I grant it, aye," said he, "but I must think
Upon some seemly tale the while I drink."

THE PROLOGUE TO THE PARDONER'S TALE

Radix malorum est Cupiditas:[79] *Ad Thimotheum, sexto.*

"Masters," quoth he, "in churches, when I preach,
I am at pains that all shall hear my speech,
15 And ring it out as roundly as a bell,
For I know all by heart the thing I tell.
My theme is always one, and ever was:
'Radix malorum est cupiditas.'
First I announce the place whence I have come,
20 And then I show my pardons, all and some.
Our liege-lord's seal on my patent perfect,
I show that first, my safety to protect,
And then no man's so bold, no priest nor clerk,
As to disturb me in Christ's holy work;
25 And after that my tales I marshal all.
Indulgences of pope and cardinal,
Of patriarch and bishop, these I do
Show, and in Latin speak some words, a few,
To spice therewith a bit my sermoning
30 And stir men to devotion, marvelling.
Then show I forth my hollow crystal-stones,
Which are crammed full of rags, aye, and of bones;
Relics are these, as they think, every one.

---

[79]"Love of money is the root of evil."

Then I've in latten[80] box a shoulder bone
35   Which came out of a holy Hebrew's sheep.
'Good men,' say I, 'my words in memory keep;
If this bone shall be washed in any well,
Then if a cow, calf, sheep, or ox should swell
That's eaten snake, or been by serpent stung,
40   Take water of that well and wash its tongue,
And 'twill be well anon; and furthermore,
Of pox and scab and every other sore
Shall every sheep be healed that of this well
Drinks but one draught; take heed of what I tell.
45   And if the man that owns the beasts, I trow,
Shall every week, and that before cock-crow,
And before breakfast, drink thereof a draught,
As that Jew taught of yore in his priestcraft,
His beasts and all his store shall multiply.
50   And, good sirs, it's a cure for jealousy;
For though a man be fallen in jealous rage,
Let one make of this water his pottage
And nevermore shall he his wife mistrust,
Though he may know the truth of all her lust,
55   Even though she'd taken two priests, aye, or three.
'Here is a mitten, too, that you may see.
Who puts his hand therein,' I say again,
'He shall have increased harvest of his grain,
After he's sown, be it of wheat or oats,'
60   Just so he offers pence or offers groats.
Good men and women, one thing I warn you.
If any man be here in church right now
That's done a sin so horrible that he
Dare not, for shame, of that sin shriven be,
65   Or any woman, be she young or old,
That's made her husband into a cuckold,[81]
Such folk shall have no power and no grace
To offer to my relics in this place.
But whoso finds himself without such blame,
70   He will come up and offer, in God's name,
And I'll absolve him by authority
That has, by bull, been granted unto me.'
By this fraud have I won me, year by year,
A hundred marks, since I've been pardoner.

---

[80]brass.
[81]a fool on account of his wife's having sex with another man.

75   I stand up like a scholar in pulpit,
    And when the ignorant people all do sit,
    I preach, as you have heard me say before,
    And tell a hundred false japes, less or more.
    I am at pains, then, to stretch forth my neck,
80   And east and west upon the folk I beck,
    As does a dove that's sitting on a barn.
    With hands and swift tongue, then, do I so yarn
    That it's a joy to see my busyness.
    Of avarice and of all such wickedness
85   Is all my preaching, thus to make them free
    With offered pence, the which pence come to me.
    For my intent is only pence to win,
    And not at all for punishment of sin.
    When they are dead, for all I think thereon
90   Their souls may well black-berrying have gone!
    For, certainly, there's many a sermon grows
    Ofttimes from evil purpose, as one knows;
    Some for folks' pleasure and for flattery,
    To be advanced by all hypocrisy,
95   And some for vainglory, and some for hate.
    For, when I dare not otherwise debate,
    Then do I sharpen well my tongue and sting
    The man in sermons, and upon him fling
    My lying defamations, if but he
100 Has wronged my brethren or—much worse—wronged me.
    For though I mention not his proper name,
    Men know whom I refer to, all the same,
    By signs I make and other circumstances.
    Thus I pay those who do us displeasances.
105 Thus spit I out my venom under hue
    Of holiness, to seem both good and true.
    But briefly my intention I'll express;
    I preach no sermon, save for covetousness.
    For at my theme is yet, and ever was,
110 'Radix malorum est cupiditas.'
    Thus can I preach against that self-same vice
    Which I indulge, and that is avarice.
    But though myself be guilty of that sin,
    Yet can I cause these other folk to win
115 From avarice and really to repent.
    But that is not my principal intent.
    I preach no sermon, save for covetousness;
    This should suffice of that, though, as I guess.

	Then do I cite examples, many a one,
120	Out of old stories and of time long gone,
	For vulgar people all love stories old;
	Such things they can re-tell well and can hold.
	What? Think you that because I'm good at preaching
	And win me gold and silver by my teaching
125	I'll live of my free will in poverty?
	No, no, that's never been my policy!
	For I will preach and beg in sundry lands;
	I will not work and labour with my hands,
	Nor baskets weave and try to live thereby,
130	Because I will not beg in vain, say I.
	I will none of the apostles counterfeit;
	I will have money, wool, and cheese, and wheat,
	Though it be given by the poorest page,
	Or by the poorest widow in village,
135	And though her children perish of famine.
	Nay! I will drink good liquor of the vine
	And have a pretty wench in every town.
	But hearken, masters, to conclusion shown:
	Your wish is that I tell you all a tale.
140	Now that I've drunk a draught of musty ale,
	By God, I hope that I can tell something
	That shall, in reason, be to your liking.
	For though I am myself a vicious man,
	Yet I would tell a moral tale, and can,
145	The which I'm wont to preach more gold to win.
	Now hold your peace! My tale I will begin."

THE PARDONER'S TALE

	In Flanders, once, there was a company
	Of young companions given to folly,
	Riot and gambling, brothels and taverns;
150	And, to the music of harps, lutes, gitterns,
	They danced and played at dice both day and night.
	And ate also and drank beyond their might,
	Whereby they made the devil's sacrifice
	Within that devil's temple, wicked wise,
155	By superfluity both vile and vain.
	So damnable their oaths and so profane
	That it was terrible to hear them swear;

Our Blessed Saviour's Body did they tear;[82]
They thought the Jews had rent Him not enough;
160 And each of them at others' sins would laugh.
Then entered dancing-girls of ill repute,
Graceful and slim, and girls who peddled fruit,
Harpers and bawds and women selling cake,
Who do their office for the Devil's sake,
165 To kindle and blow the fire of lechery,
Which is so closely joined with gluttony;
I call on holy writ, now, to witness
That lust is in all wine and drunkenness.
Lo, how the drunken Lot unnaturally
170 Lay with his daughters two, unwittingly;
So drunk he was he knew not what he wrought.
Herod, as in his story's clearly taught,
When full of wine and merry at a feast,
Sitting at table idly gave behest
175 To slay John Baptist, who was all guiltless.
Seneca says a good word too, doubtless;
He says there is no difference he can find
Between a man that's quite out of his mind
And one that's drunken, save perhaps in this
180 That when a wretch in madness fallen is,
The state lasts longer than does drunkenness.
O gluttony; full of all wickedness,
O first cause of confusion to us all,
Beginning of damnation and our fall,
185 Till Christ redeemed us with His blood again!
Behold how dearly, to be brief and plain,
Was purchased this accursed villainy;
Corrupt was all this world with gluttony!
Adam our father, and his wife also,
190 From Paradise to labour and to woe
Were driven for that vice, no doubt; indeed
The while that Adam fasted, as I read,
He was in Paradise; but then when he
Ate of the fruit forbidden of the tree,
195 Anon he was cast out to woe and pain.[83]
O gluttony, of you we may complain!
Oh, knew a man how many maladies
Follow on excess and on gluttonies,

---

[82]by swearing by parts of Christ's body.
[83]Adam's sin of eating the apple was frequently interpreted as the sin of gluttony.

	Surely he would be then more moderate
200	In diet, and at table more sedate.
	Alas! The throat so short, the tender mouth,
	Causing that east and west and north and south,
	In earth, in air, in water men shall swink[84]
	To get a glutton dainty meat and drink!
205	Of this same matter Paul does wisely treat:
	"Meat for the belly and belly for the meat:
	And both shall God destroy," as Paul does say.
	Alas! A foul thing is it, by my fay,
	To speak this word, and fouler is the deed,
210	When man so guzzles of the white and red
	That of his own throat makes he his privy,
	Because of this cursed superfluity.
	The apostle, weeping, says most piteously:
	"For many walk, of whom I've told you, aye,
215	Weeping I tell you once again they're dross,
	For they are foes of Christ and of the Cross,
	Whose end is death, whose belly is their god."
	O gut! O belly! O you stinking cod,
	Filled full of dung, with all corruption found!
220	At either end of you foul is the sound.
	With how great cost and labour do they find
	Your food! These cooks, they pound and strain and grind;
	Substance to accident they turn with fire,
	All to fulfill your gluttonous desire!
225	Out of the hard and riven bones knock they
	The marrow, for they throw nothing away
	That may go through the gullet soft and sweet;
	With spicery, with leaf, bark, root, replete
	Shall be the sauces made for your delight,
230	To furnish you a sharper appetite.
	But truly, he that such delights entice
	Is dead while yet he wallows in this vice.
	A lecherous thing is wine, and drunkenness
	Is full of striving and of wretchedness.
235	O drunken man, disfigured is your face,
	Sour is your breath, foul are you to embrace,
	And through your drunken nose there comes a sound
	As if you snored out "Samson, Samson" round;
	And yet God knows that Samson drank no wine.
240	You fall down just as if you were stuck swine;

---

[84]work.

Your tongue is loose, your honest care obscure;
For drunkenness is very sepulture
Of any mind a man may chance to own.
In whom strong drink has domination shown
245   He can no counsel keep for any dread.
Now keep you from the white and from the red,
And specially from the white wine grown at Lepe
That is for sale in Fish Street or in Cheap.
This wine of Spain, it mixes craftily
250   With other wines that chance to be near by,
From which there rise such fumes, as well may be,
That when a man has drunk two draughts, or three,
And thinks himself to be at home in Cheap,
He finds that he's in Spain, and right at Lepe,—
255   Not at Rochelle nor yet at Bordeaux town,
And then will he snore out "Samson, Samson."
But hearken, masters, one word more I pray:
The greatest deeds of all, I'm bold to say,
Of victories in the Old Testament,
260   Through the True God, Who is omnipotent,
Were gained by abstinence and after prayer:
Look in the Bible, you may learn this there.
Lo, Attila, the mighty conqueror,
Died in his sleep, in shame and dishonour,
265   And bleeding at the nose for drunkenness;
A great captain should live in soberness.
Above all this, advise yourself right well
What was commanded unto Lemuel—
Not Samuel, but Lemuel, say I—[85]
270   The Bible's words you cannot well deny:
Drinking by magistrates is called a vice.
No more of this, for it may well suffice.
And now that I have told of gluttony,
I'll take up gambling, showing you thereby
275   The curse of chance, and all its evils treat;
From it proceeds false swearing and deceit,
Blaspheming, murder, and—what's more—the waste
Of time and money; add to which, debased
And shamed and lost to honour quite is he,
280   Who once a common gambler's known to be.
And ever the higher one is of estate,

---

[85]Chaucer is indicating to his scribe not to be overzealous "correcting" the spelling of the less familiar name of Lemuel.

The more he's held disgraced and desolate.
And if a prince plays similar hazardry[86]
In all his government and policy,
285   He loses in the estimate of men
His good repute, and finds it not again.
Chilon, who was a wise ambassador,
Was sent to Corinth, all in great honour,
From Lacedaemon, to make alliance.
290   And when he came, he noticed there, by chance,
All of the greatest people of the land
Playing at hazard there on every hand.
Wherefore, and all as soon as it might be,
He stole off home again to his country,
295   And said: "I will not thus debase my name;
Nor will I take upon me so great shame
You to ally with common hazarders.
Send, if you will, other ambassadors;
For, my truth, I say I'd rather die
300   Than you with gamblers like to them ally.
For you that are so glorious in honours
Shall never ally yourselves with hazarders
By my consent, or treaty I have made."
This wise philosopher, 'twas thus he said.
305   Let us look, then, at King Demetrius.
The king of Parthia, as the book tells us,
Sent him a pair of golden dice, in scorn,
Because the name of gambler he had borne;
Wherefore he marked his reputation down
310   As valueless despite his wide renown.
Great lords may find sufficient other play
Seemly enough to while the time away.
Now will I speak of oaths both false and great,
A word or two, whereof the old books treat.
315   Great swearing is a thing abominable,
And vain oaths yet more reprehensible.
The High God did forbid swearing at all,
As witness Matthew; but in especial
Of swearing says the holy Jeremiah,
320   "Thou shalt not swear in vain, to be a liar,
But swear in judgment and in righteousness";
But idle swearing is a wickedness.
Behold, in the first table of the Law,

---

[86]gambling.

That should be honoured as High God's, sans flaw,
325 This second one of His commandments plain:
"Thou shalt not take the Lord God's name in vain."
Nay, sooner He forbids us such swearing
Than homicide or many a wicked thing;
I say that, as to order, thus it stands;
330 'Tis known by him who His will understands
That the great second law of God is that.
Moreover, I will tell you full and flat,
That retribution will not quit his house
Who in his swearing is too outrageous.
335 "By God's own precious heart, and by His nails,
And by the blood of Christ that's now at Hales,
Seven is my chance, and yours is five and trey!"
"By God's good arms, if you do falsely play,
This dagger through your heart I'll stick for you!"
340 Such is the whelping of the bitched bones two:
Perjury, anger, cheating, homicide.
Now for the love of Christ, Who for us died,
Forgo this swearing oaths, both great and small;
But, sirs, now will I tell to you my tale.
345 Now these three roisterers, whereof I tell,
Long before prime was rung by any bell,
Were sitting in a tavern for to drink;
And as they sat they heard a small bell clink
Before a corpse being carried to his grave;
350 Whereat one of them called unto his knave:
"Go run," said he, "and ask them civilly
What corpse it is that's just now passing by,
And see that you report the man's name well."
"Sir," said the boy, "it needs not that they tell.
355 I learned it, ere you came here, full two hours;
He was, by gad, an old comrade of yours;
And he was slain, all suddenly, last night,
When drunk, as he sat on his bench upright;
An unseen thief, called Death, came stalking by,
360 Who hereabouts makes all the people die,
And with his spear he clove his heart in two
And went his way and made no more ado.
He's slain a thousand with this pestilence;
And, master, ere you come in his presence,
365 It seems to me to be right necessary
To be forewarned of such an adversary:
Be ready to meet him for evermore.

My mother taught me this, I say no more."
"By holy Mary," said the innkeeper,
370   "The boy speaks truth, for Death has slain, this year,
A mile or more hence, in a large village,
Both man and woman, child and hind and page.
I think his habitation must be there;
To be advised of him great wisdom 'twere,
375   Before he did a man some dishonour."
"Yea, by God's arms!" exclaimed this roisterer,
"Is it such peril, then, this Death to meet?
I'll seek him in the road and in the street,
As I now vow to God's own noble bones!
380   Hear, comrades, we're of one mind, as each owns;
Let each of us hold up his hand to other
And each of us become the other's brother,
And we three will go slay this traitor Death;
He shall be slain who's stopped so many a breath,
385   By God's great dignity, ere it be night."
Together did these three their pledges plight
To live and die, each of them for the other,
As if he were his very own blood brother.
And up they started, drunken, in this rage,
390   And forth they went, and towards that village
Whereof the innkeeper had told before.
And so, with many a grisly oath, they swore
And Jesus' blessed body once more rent—
"Death shall be dead if we find where he went."
395   When they had gone not fully half a mile,
Just as they would have trodden over a stile,
An old man, and a poor, with them did meet.
This ancient man full meekly them did greet,
And said thus: "Now, lords, God keep you and see!"
400   The one that was most insolent of these three
Replied to him: "What? Churl of evil grace,
Why are you all wrapped up, except your face?
Why do you live so long in so great age?"
This ancient man looked upon his visage
405   And thus replied: "Because I cannot find
A man, nay, though I walked from here to Ind,
Either in town or country who'll engage
To give his youth in barter for my age;
And therefore must I keep my old age still,
410   As long a time as it shall be God's will.
Not even Death, alas! my life will take;

Thus restless I my wretched way must make,
And on the ground, which is my mother's gate,
I knock with my staff early, aye, and late,
415 And cry: 'O my dear mother, let me in!
Lo, how I'm wasted, flesh and blood and skin!
Alas! When shall my bones come to their rest?
Mother, with you fain would I change my chest,
That in my chamber so long time has been,
420 Aye! For a haircloth rag to wrap me in!'
But yet to me she will not show that grace,
And thus all pale and withered is my face.
"But, sirs, in you it is no courtesy
To speak to an old man despitefully,
425 Unless in word he trespass or in deed.
In holy writ you may, yourselves, well read
'Before an old man, hoar upon the head,
You should arise.' Which I advise you read,
Nor to an old man any injury do
430 More than you would that men should do to you
In age, if you so long time shall abide;
And God be with you, whether you walk or ride.
I must pass on now where I have to go."
"Nay, ancient churl, by God it sha'n't be so,"
435 Cried out this other hazarder, anon;
"You sha'n't depart so easily, by Saint John!
You spoke just now of that same traitor Death,
Who in this country stops our good friends' breath.
Hear my true word, since you are his own spy,
440 Tell where he is or you shall rue it, aye,
By God and by the holy Sacrament!
Indeed you must be, with this Death, intent
To slay all us young people, you false thief."
"Now, sirs," said he, "if you're so keen, in brief,
445 To find out Death, turn up this crooked way,
For in that grove I left him, by my fay,
Under a tree, and there he will abide;
Nor for your boasts will he a moment hide.
See you that oak? Right there you shall him find.
450 God save you, Who redeemed all humankind,
And mend your ways!"—thus said this ancient man.
And every one of these three roisterers ran
Till he came to that tree; and there they found,
Of florins of fine gold, new-minted, round,
455 Well-nigh eight bushels full, or so they thought.

No longer, then, after this Death they sought,
But each of them so glad was of that sight,
Because the florins were so fair and bright,
That down they all sat by this precious hoard.
460   The worst of them was first to speak a word.
"Brothers," said he, "take heed to what I say;
My wits are keen, although I mock and play.
This treasure here Fortune to us has given
That mirth and jollity our lives may liven,
465   And easily as it's come, so will we spend.
Eh! By God's precious dignity! Who'd pretend,
Today, that we should have so fair a grace?
But might this gold be carried from this place
Home to my house, or if you will, to yours—
470   For well we know that all this gold is ours—
Then were we all in high felicity.
But certainly by day this may not be;
For men would say that we were robbers strong,
And we'd, for our own treasure, hang ere long.
475   This treasure must be carried home by night
All prudently and slyly, out of sight.
So I propose that cuts among us all
Be drawn, and let's see where the cut will fall;
And he that gets the short cut, blithe of heart
480   Shall run to town at once, and to the mart,
And fetch us bread and wine here, privately.
And two of us shall guard, right cunningly,
This treasure well; and if he does not tarry,
When it is night we'll all the treasure carry
485   Where, by agreement, we may think it best."
That one of them the cuts brought in his fist
And bade them draw to see where it might fall;
And it fell on the youngest of them all;
And so, forth toward the town he went anon.
490   And just as soon as he had turned and gone,
That one of them spoke thus unto the other:
"You know well that you are my own sworn brother,
So to your profit I will speak anon.
You know well how our comrade is just gone;
495   And here is gold, and that in great plenty,
That's to be parted here among us three.
Nevertheless, if I can shape it so
That it be parted only by us two,
Shall I not do a turn that is friendly?"

500 The other said: "Well, now, how can that be?
He knows well that the gold is with us two.
What shall we say to him? What shall we do?"
"Shall it be secret?" asked the first rogue, then,
"And I will tell you in eight words, or ten,
505 What we must do, and how bring it about."
"Agreed," replied the other, "Never doubt,
That, on my word, I nothing will betray."
"Now," said the first, "we're two, and I dare say
The two of us are stronger than is one.
510 Watch when he sits, and soon as that is done
Arise and make as if with him to play;
And I will thrust him through the two sides, yea,
The while you romp with him as in a game,
And with your dagger see you do the same;
515 And then shall all this gold divided be,
My right dear friend, just between you and me;
Then may we both our every wish fulfill
And play at dice all at our own sweet will."
And thus agreed were these two rogues, that day,
520 To slay the third, as you have heard me say.
This youngest rogue who'd gone into the town,
Often in fancy rolled he up and down
The beauty of those florins new and bright.
"O Lord," thought he, "if so be that I might
525 Have all this treasure to myself alone,
There is no man who lives beneath the throne
Of God that should be then so merry as I."
And at the last the Fiend, our enemy,
Put in his thought that he should poison buy
530 With which he might kill both his fellows; aye,
The Devil found him in such wicked state,
He had full leave his grief to consummate;
For it was utterly the man's intent
To kill them both and never to repent.
535 And on he strode, no longer would he tarry,
Into the town, to an apothecary,
And prayed of him that he'd prepare and sell
Some poison for his rats, and some as well
For a polecat that in his yard had lain,
540 The which, he said, his capons there had slain,
And fain he was to rid him, if he might,
Of vermin that thus damaged him by night.
The apothecary said: "And you shall have

A thing of which, so God my spirit save,
545 In all this world there is no live creature
     That's eaten or has drunk of this mixture
     As much as equals but a grain of wheat,
     That shall not sudden death thereafter meet;
     Yea, die he shall, and in a shorter while
550 Than you require to walk but one short mile;
     This poison is so violent and strong."
     This wicked man the poison took along
     With him boxed up, and then he straightway ran
     Into the street adjoining, to a man,
555 And of him borrowed generous bottles three;
     And into two his poison then poured he;
     The third one he kept clean for his own drink.
     For all that night he was resolved to swink
     In carrying the florins from that place.
560 And when this roisterer, with evil grace,
     Had filled with wine his mighty bottles three,
     Then to his comrades forth again went he.
     What is the need to tell about it more?
     For just as they had planned his death before,
565 Just so they murdered him, and that anon.
     And when the thing was done, then spoke the one:
     "Now let us sit and drink and so be merry,
     And afterward we will his body bury."
     And as he spoke, one bottle of the three
570 He took wherein the poison chanced to be
     And drank and gave his comrade drink also,
     For which, and that anon, lay dead these two.
     I feel quite sure that Doctor Avicena[87]
     Within the sections of his Canon never
575 Set down more certain signs of poisoning
     Than showed these wretches two at their ending.
     Thus ended these two homicides in woe;
     Died thus the treacherous poisoner also.
     O cursed sin, full of abominableness!
580 O treacherous homicide! O wickedness!
     O gluttony, lechery, and hazardry!
     O blasphemer of Christ with villainy,
     And with great oaths, habitual for pride!
     Alas! Mankind, how may this thing betide
585 That to thy dear Creator, Who thee wrought,

---

[87]Avicenna, an 11th c. Arabic philosopher, composed a Canon of Medicine.

And with His precious blood salvation bought,
Thou art so false and so unkind, alas!
Now, good men, God forgive you each trespass,
And keep you from the sin of avarice.
590 My holy pardon cures and will suffice,
So that it brings me gold, or silver brings,
Or else, I care not—brooches, spoons or rings.
Bow down your heads before this holy bull!
Come up, you wives, and offer of your wool!
595 Your names I'll enter on my roll, anon,
And into Heaven's bliss you'll go, each one.
For I'll absolve you, by my special power,
You that make offering, as clean this hour
As you were born.
600 And lo, sirs, thus I preach.
And Jesus Christ, who is our souls' great leech,
So grant you each his pardon to receive;
For that is best; I will not you deceive.
But, sirs, one word forgot I in my tale;
605 I've relics in my pouch that cannot fail,
As good as England ever saw, I hope,
The which I got by kindness of the pope.
If gifts your change of heart and mind reveal,
You'll get my absolution while you kneel.
610 Come forth, and kneel down here before, anon,
And humbly you'll receive my full pardon;
Or else receive a pardon as you wend,
All new and fresh as every mile shall end,
So that you offer me each time, anew,
615 More gold and silver, all good coins and true.
It is an honour to each one that's here
That you may have a competent pardoner
To give you absolution as you ride,
For all adventures that may still betide.
620 Perchance from horse may fall down one or two,
Breaking his neck, and it might well be you.
See what insurance, then, it is for all
That I within your fellowship did fall,
Who may absolve you, both the great and less,
625 When soul from body passes, as I guess.
I think our host might just as well begin,
For he is most-enveloped in all sin.
Come forth, sir host, and offer first anon,
And you shall kiss the relics, every one,

630 Aye, for a groat! Unbuckle now your purse."
"Nay, nay," said he, "then may I have Christ's curse!
It sha'n't be," said he, "as I've hope for riches,
Why, you would have me kissing your old breeches,
And swear they were the relics of a saint,
635 Though with your excrement 'twere dabbed like paint.
By the cross Saint Helen found in Holy Land,
I would I had your ballocks in my hand
Instead of relics in a reliquary;
Let's cut them off, and them I'll help you carry;
640 They shall be shrined within a hog's fat turd."
This pardoner, he answered not a word;
So wrathy was he no word would he say.
"Now," said our host, "I will no longer play
With you, nor any other angry man."
645 But at this point the worthy knight began,
When that he saw how all the folk did laugh:
"No more of this, for it's gone far enough;
Sir pardoner, be glad and merry here;
And you, sir host, who are to me so dear,
650 I pray you that you kiss the pardoner.
And, pardoner, I pray you to draw near,
And as we did before, let's laugh and play."
And then they kissed and rode forth on their way.

THE CLERK'S PROLOGUE

"Sir clerk of Oxford," our good host then said,
"You ride as quiet and still as is a maid
But newly wedded, sitting at the board;
This day I've heard not from your tongue a word.
5 Perhaps you mull a sophism that's prime,
But Solomon says, each thing to its own time.
"For God's sake, smile and be of better cheer,
It is no time to think and study here.
Tell us some merry story, if you may;
10 For whatsoever man will join in play,
He needs must to the play give his consent.
But do not preach, as friars do in Lent,
To make us, for our old sins, wail and weep,
And see your tale shall put us not to sleep.
15 "Tell us some merry thing of adventures.

Your terms, your colours, and your speech-figures,[88]
Keep them in store till so be you indite
High style, as when men unto kings do write.
Speak you so plainly, for this time, I pray,
20   That we can understand what things you say."
This worthy clerk, benignly he answered.
"Good host," said he, "I am under your yard;
You have of us, for now, the governance,
And therefore do I make you obeisance
25   As far as reason asks it, readily.
I will relate to you a tale that
Learned once, at Padua, of a worthy clerk,
As he proved by his words and by his work.
He's dead, now, and nailed down—within his chest,
30   And I pray God to give his soul good rest!
"Francis Petrarch, the laureate poet,
Was this clerk's name, whose rhetoric so sweet
Illumed all Italy with poetry,
As did Lignano with philosophy,
35   Or law, or other art particular;
But Death, that suffers us not very far,
Nor more, as 'twere, than twinkling of an eye,
Has slain them both, as all of us shall die.
"But forth, to tell you of this worthy man,
40   Who taught this tale to me, as I began,
I say that first, with high style he indites,
Before the body of his tale he writes,
A proem to describe those lands renowned,
Saluzzo, Piedmont, and the region round,
45   And speaks of Apennines, those hills so high
That form the boundary of West Lombardy,
And of Mount Viso, specially, the tall,
Whereat the Po, out of a fountain small,
Takes its first springing and its tiny source
50   That eastward ever increases in its course
Toward Emilia, Ferrara, and Venice;
The which is a long story to devise.
And truly, in my judgment reluctant
It is a thing not wholly relevant,
55   Save that he introduces thus his gear:
But this is his tale, which you now may hear.

---

[88]rhetorical devices; the Host is afraid the Clerk will be too learned in his tale.

THE CLERK'S TALE

There is, in the west side of Italy,
Down at the foot of Mount Viso the cold,
A pleasant plain that yields abundantly,

60   Where many a tower and town one may behold,
That were there founded in the times of old.
With many another fair delightful sight;
Saluzzo is this noble region bright.
A marquis once was lord of all that land,

65   As were his noble ancestors before;
Obedient and ready to his hand
Were all his lieges, both the less and more.
Thus in delight he lived, and had of yore,
Beloved and feared, through favour of Fortune,

70   Both by his lords and by the common run.
Therewith he was, to speak of lineage,
Born of the noblest blood of Lombardy,
With person fair, and strong, and young of age,
And full of honour and of courtesy;

75   Discreet enough to lead his nation, he;
Save in some things wherein he was to blame,
And Walter was this young lord's Christian name.
I blame him thus, that he considered naught
Of what in coming time might him betide,

80   But on his present wish was all his thought,
As, he would hunt and hawk on every side;
Well-nigh all other cares would he let slide,
And would not, and this was the worst of all,
Marry a wife, for aught that might befall.

85   That point alone his people felt so sore
That in a flock one day to him they went,
And one of them, the wisest in all lore,
Or else because the lord would best consent
That he should tell him what the people meant,

90   Or else that he could make the matter clear,
He to the marquis spoke as you shall hear.
"O noble marquis, your humanity
Assures us, aye, and gives us hardiness
As often as there is necessity

95   That we to you may tell our heaviness.
Accept, lord, now of your great nobleness
That we with sincere hearts may here complain,
Nor let your ears my humble voice disdain.

"Though I have naught to do in this matter
100 More than another man has in this place,
Yet for as much as you, most honoured sir,
Have always showed me favour and much grace,
I dare the more to ask of you a space
Of audience, to set forth our request,
105 And you, my lord, will do as you like best.
"For truly, lord, so well do we like you
And all your works (and ever have), that we—
We could not, of ourselves, think what to do
To make us live in more felicity,
110 Save one thing, lord, and if your will it be,
That to be wedded man you hold it best,
Then were your people's hearts at utter rest.
"But bow your neck beneath that blessed yoke
Of sovereignty and not of hard service,
115 The which men call espousal or wedlock;
And pray think, lord, among your thoughts so wise,
How our days pass and each in different guise;
For though we sleep or wake or roam or ride,
Time flies, and for no man will it abide.
120 "And though your time of green youth flower as yet,
Age creeps in always, silent as a stone;
Death threatens every age, nor will forget
For any state, and there escapes him none:
And just as surely as we know, each one,
125 That we shall die, uncertain are we all
What day it is when death shall on us fall.
"Accept then of us, lord, the true intent,
That never yet refused you your behest,
And we will, lord, if you will give consent,
130 Choose you a wife without delay, at least,
Born of the noblest blood and the greatest
Of all this land, so that it ought to seem
Honour to God and you, as we shall deem.
"Deliver us from all our constant dread
135 And take yourself a wife, for High God's sake;
For if it so befell, which God forbid,
That by your death your noble line should break
And that a strange successor should come take
Your heritage, woe that we were alive!
140 Wherefore we pray you speedily to wive."
Their humble prayer and their so earnest cheer
Roused in the marquis' heart great sympathy.

"You'd have me," he replied, "my people dear,
Do what I've never yet thought necessary.
145   I have rejoiced in my fond liberty,
That men so seldom find in their marriage;
Where I was free, I must be in bondage.
"Nevertheless, I see your true intent,
And know there's always sense in what you say;
150   Wherefore of my free will, will I consent
To wed a wife, as soon as ever I may.
But whereas you have offered here today
To choose a wife for me, I you release
From that, and pray that you thereof will cease.
155   "For God knows well that children oft retain
Naught of their worthy elders gone before;
Goodness comes all from God, not of the strain
Whereof they were engendered; furthermore
I trust in God's great goodness, and therefore
160   My marriage and my state and all my ease
I leave to Him to do with as He please.
"Let me alone in choosing of my wife,
That burden on my own back I'll endure;
But I pray you, and charge you on your life,
165   That what wife I may take, me you'll assure
You'll honour her life's tenure,
In word and deed, both here and everywhere,
As if she were an emperor's daughter fair.
"And furthermore, this shall you swear, that you
170   Against my choice shall neither grouse nor strive;
Since I'm forgoing liberty, and woo
At your request, so may I ever thrive
As, where my heart is set, there will I wive;
And save you give consent in such manner,
175   I pray you speak no more of this matter."
With hearty will they swore and gave assent
To all this, and no one of them said nay;
Praying him, of his grace, before they went,
That he would set for them a certain day
180   For his espousal, soon as might be; yea,
For still the people had a little dread
Lest that the marquis would no woman wed.
He granted them the day that pleased him best
Whereon he would be married, certainly,
185   And said he did all this at their request;
And they with humble hearts, obediently,

Kneeling upon their knees full reverently,
All thanked him there, and thus they made an end
Of their design and homeward did they wend.
190   And thereupon he to his officers
Ordered that for the fete they should provide,
And to his household gentlemen and squires,
Such charges gave as pleased him to decide;
And all obeyed him: let him praise or chide,
195   And each of them did all his diligence
To show unto the fete his reverence.
Explicit prima pars.

Incipit secunda pars.
Not far from that same honoured palace where
200   This marquis planned his marriage, at this tide,
There stood a hamlet, on a site most fair,
Wherein the poor folk of the countryside
Stabled their cattle and did all abide,
And where their labour gave them sustenance
205   After the earth had yielded abundance.
Amongst these humble folk there dwelt a man
Who was considered poorest of them all;
But the High God of Heaven sometimes can
Send His grace to a little ox's stall;
210   Janicula men did this poor man call.
A daughter had he, fair enough to sight;
Griselda was this young maid's name, the bright.
If one should speak of virtuous beauty,
Then was she of the fairest under sun;
215   Since fostered in dire poverty was she,
No lust luxurious in her heart had run;
More often from the well than from the tun
She drank, and since she would chaste virtue please,
She knew work well, but knew not idle ease.
220   But though this maiden tender was of age,
Yet in the breast of her virginity
There was enclosed a ripe and grave courage;
And in great reverence and charity
Her poor old father fed and fostered she;
225   A few sheep grazing in a field she kept,
For she would not be idle till she slept.
And when she homeward came, why she would bring
Roots and green herbs, full many times and oft,
The which she'd shred and boil for her living,

230 And made her bed a hard one and not soft;
     Her father kept she in their humble croft
     With what obedience and diligence
     A child may do for father's reverence.
     Upon Griselda, humble daughter pure,
235 The marquis oft had looked in passing by,
     As he a-hunting rode at adventure;
     And when it chanced that her he did espy,
     Not with the glances of a wanton eye
     He gazed at her, but all in sober guise,
240 And pondered on her deeply in this wise:
     Commending to his heart her womanhood,
     And virtue passing that of any wight,
     Of so young age in face and habitude.
     For though the people have no deep insight
245 In virtue, he considered all aright
     Her goodness, and decided that he would
     Wed only her, if ever wed he should.
     The day of wedding came, but no one can
     Tell who the woman is that bride shall be;
250 At which strange thing they wondered, many a man,
     And they said, marvelling, in privacy:
     "Will not our lord yet leave his vanity?
     Will he not wed? Alas, alas, the while!
     Why will he thus himself and us beguile?"
255 Nevertheless, this marquis has bade make,
     Of jewels set in gold and in rich azure,
     Brooches and rings, all for Griselda's sake,
     And for her garments took he then the measure
     By a young maiden of her form and stature,
260 And found all other ornaments as well
     That for such wedding would be meet to tell.
     The time of mid-morn of that very day
     Approached when this lord's marriage was to be;
     And all the palace was bedecked and gay,
265 Both hall and chambers, each in its degree;
     With kitchens stuffed with food in great plenty,
     There might one see the last and least dainty
     That could be found in all of Italy.
     This regal marquis, splendidly arrayed,
270 With lords and ladies in his company
     (Who to attend the feasting had been prayed)
     And of his retinue the bachelory,
     With many a sound of sundry melody,

Unto the village whereof I have told,
275 In this array the nearest way did hold.
Griselda who, God knows, was innocent
That for her sake was all this fine array,
To fetch some water, to a fountain went,
Yet she returned soon, did this lovely may,
280 For she had heard it said that on this day
The marquis was to wed, and if she might,
She was full fain to see the glorious sight.
She thought: "With other maidens I will stand
(Who are my friends) within our door, and see
285 The marchioness, and therefore I'll turn hand
To do at home, as soon as it may be,
The household work that's waiting there for me;
And then I'll be at leisure to behold
Her, if they this way to the castle hold."
290 And as across her threshold she'd have gone,
The marquis came, and for her did he call;
And she set down her water jar anon
Beside the threshold, in an ox's stall,
And down upon her two knees did she fall
295 And, kneeling, with grave countenance, was still
Till she had heard what was his lordship's will.
This thoughtful marquis spoke unto this maid
Full soberly, and said in this manner:
"Griselda, where's your father?" so he said.
300 And she, with reverence and with humble cheer,
Answered: "My lord, he is but inside here."
And in she went without more tarrying
And to the marquis did her father bring.
He by the hand then took this ancient man
305 And said, when he had led him well aside:
"Janicula, I neither will nor can
Conceal my love, nor my heart's longing hide.
If you but acquiesce, whate'er betide,
Your daughter will I take, before I wend,
310 To be my wife until her life's dear end.
"You love me, and I know it well today,
And are my faithful liege, and were of yore;
And all that pleases me, I dare well say,
Pleases you too; especially therefore
315 Assure me on the point I made before—
Can we together in this compact draw,
And will you take me as your son-in-law?"

This sudden word the man astonished so
That red he grew, abashed, and all quaking
320   He stood; nor could he answer further, no,
Than but to say: "O Lord, I am willing
To do your will; but against your liking
I'll do no thing; you are my lord so dear
That what you wish governs this matter here."
325   "Then I will," said this marquis, quietly,
"That in your chamber you and I and she
Have consultation, and do you know why?
Because I'd ask her if her will it be
To be my wife and so be ruled by me;
330   And all this shall be done in your presence,
I will not speak without your audience."
And while in chamber they three were about
Their business, whereof you'll hereafter hear,
The people crowded through the house without
335   And wondered by what honest method there
So carefully she'd kept her father dear.
But more Griselda wondered, as she might,
For never before that saw she such a sight.
No wonder, though, astonishment she felt
340   At seeing so great a guest within that place;
With people of his sort she'd never dealt,
Wherefore she looked on with a pallid face.
But briefly through the matter now to race,
These are the very words the marquis said
345   To this most modest, truly constant maid.
"Griselda," said he, "You shall understand
It's pleasing to your father and to me
That I wed you, and even it may stand,
As I suppose, that you would have it be.
350   But these demands must I first make," said he,
"And since it shall be done in hasty wise,
Will you consent, or will you more advise?
"I say this: Are you ready with good heart
To grant my wish, and that I freely may,
355   As I shall think best, make you laugh or smart,
And you to grumble never, night or day?
And too, when I say 'yea' you say not 'nay'
By word or frown to what I have designed.
Swear this, and here I will our contract bind."
360   Wondering upon this word, quaking for fear,
She said: "My lord, unsuited, unworthy

Am I to take the honour you give me here;
But what you'd have, that very thing would I.
And here I swear that never willingly,
365 In deed or thought, will I you disobey,
To save my life, and I love life, I say."
"This is enough, Griselda mine," cried he.
And forth he went then with full sober cheer
Out at the door, and after him came she,
370 And to the people who were waiting near,
"This is my wife," he said, "who's standing here.
Honour her, all, and love her, all, I pray,
Who love me; and there is no more to say."
And so that nothing of her former gear
375 She should take with her to his house, he bade
That women strip her naked then and there;
Whereat these ladies were not over-glad
To handle clothes wherein she had been clad.
Nevertheless, this maiden bright of hue
380 From head to foot they clothed her all anew.
Her hair they combed and brushed, which fell untressed
All artlessly, and placed a coronal
With their small fingers on her head, and dressed
Her robes with many jewels great and small;
385 Of her array how shall I tell withal?
Scarcely the people knew her for fairness,
So transformed was she in her splendid dress.
This marquis her has married with a ring
Brought for the purpose there; and then has set
390 Upon a horse, snow-white and well ambling,
And to his palace, without longer let,
With happy following folk and more they met,
Convoyed her home, and thus the day they spent
In revelry until the sun's descent.
395 And briefly forth throughout this tale to chase,
I say that unto this new marchioness
God has such favour sent her, of His grace,
It seemed in no way true, by likeliness,
That she was born and bred in humbleness,
400 As in a hovel or an ox's stall,
But rather nurtured in an emperor's hall.
To everyone she soon became so dear
And worshipful, that folk where she had dwelt
And from her birth had known her, year by year,
405 Although they could have sworn it, scarcely felt

That to Janicula, with whom I've dealt,
She really was a daughter, for she seemed
Another creature now, or so they deemed.
For though she ever had been virtuous,
410   She was augmented by such excellence
Of manners based on noble goodness thus,
And so discreet and wise of eloquence,
So gentle and so worthy reverence,
And she could so the people's hearts embrace,
415   That each her loved that looked upon her face.
Not only in Saluzzo, in the town,
Was published wide the goodness of her name,
But throughout many a land where she'd renown
If one said well, another said the same;
420   So widespread of her goodness was the fame
That men and women came; the young and old
Went to Saluzzo, her but to behold.
Thus Walter lowly, nay, but royally,
Wedded, by Fortune's grace, right honourably,
425   In the good peace of God lived easily
At home, and outward grace enough had he;
And since he saw that under low degree
Is virtue often hid, the people fairly
Held him a prudent man, and that's done rarely.
430   Not only this Griselda through her wit
Knew how with wifely arts her home to bless,
But also, when there was a need for it,
The people's wrongs she knew how to redress.
There was no discord, rancour, heaviness
435   In all that land that she could not appease,
And wisely bring them all to rest and ease.
Although her husband from the court were gone,
If gentlemen, or less, of her country
Were angered, she would bring them all at one;
440   So wise and so mature of speech was she,
And judgments gave of so great equity,
Men felt that God from Heaven her did send
People to save and every wrong to amend.
Not long Griselda had, it seems, been wed
445   Before a daughter to her lord she bore,
Though of a son she'd rather have gone to bed.
Glad were the marquis and the folk therefor;
For though a girl-child came thus all before,
She might well to a boy-child yet attain,

450   Since barren she was not, it now was plain.
       Explicit secunda pars.

       Incipit tercia pars.
       It happened, as it has sometimes before,
       That when this child had sucked a month or so,
455   This marquis in his heart such longing bore
       To test his wife, her patience thus to know,
       He could not in his heart the chance forgo
       This marvelous desire his wife to try;
       'Twas needless, God knows, thus to peek and pry,
460   He had sufficiently tried her before
       And found her ever good; what needed it
       That he should test her ever more and more?
       Though some men praise it for a subtle wit,
       Yet I say that to him 'twas no credit
465   To try his wife when there was never need,
       Putting her heart to anguish and to dread.
       In doing which the marquis took this turn:
       He came alone by night to where she lay
       And with a troubled look and features stern
470   He said to her: "Griselda mine, that day
       When I removed you from your poor array
       And placed you in a state of nobleness—
       You have not all forgotten that, I guess.
       "I say, Griselda, this your dignity
475   Wherein I have so placed you, as I trow,
       Has not made you forgetful now to be
       That I raised you from poor estate and low
       For any good you might then have or know.
       Take heed of every word that now I say,
480   There's no one else shall hear it, by my fay.
       "You know and well enough how you came here
       Into this house, it is not long ago,
       And though to me you are both lief and dear,
       Unto my nobles you are not; and so
485   They say that unto them 'tis shame and woe
       To be your subjects and compelled to serve
       You who are village-born and naught deserve.
       "And specially, since that girl-child you bore,
       These things they've said—of this there is no doubt;
490   But I desire, as I have done before,
       To live at peace with all the folk about;
       I cannot in this matter leave them out.

I must do with your daughter what is best,
Not as I would, but under men's behest.
495 "And yet, God knows, the act is hard for me;
And only with your knowledge would I bring
The deed to pass, but this I would," said he,
"That you assent with me to this one thing.
Show now that patience in your life's dealing
500 You told me of and swore to in your village
The day that marked the making of our marriage."
When she had heard all this, this she received
With never a word or change of countenance;
For, as it seemed, she was in no way grieved.
505 She said: "Lord, all lies at your own pleasance;
My child and I, with hearty obeisance,
Are all yours, and you may save us or kill
That which is yours; do you what thing you will.
"There is no thing, and so God my soul save,
510 That you may like displeasing unto me;
I do not wish a single thing to have,
Nor dread a thing to lose, save only ye;
This will is in my heart and aye shall be,
Nor length of time nor death may this deface,
515 Nor turn my passion to another place."
Glad was this marquis of her answering,
And yet he feigned as if he were not so;
All dreary were his face and his bearing
When it came time from chamber he should go.
520 Soon after this, a quarter-hour or so,
He privily told all of his intent
Unto a man, whom to his wife he sent.
A kind of sergeant was this serving man,
Who had proved often faithful, as he'd found,
525 In matters great, and such men often can
Do evil faithfully, as can a hound.
The lord knew this man loved him and was bound;
And when this sergeant learned his lordship's will
He stalked into the chamber, grim and still.
530 "Madam," said he, "you must forgive it me,
Though I do that to which I am constrained;
You are so wise you know well, it may be,
That a lord's orders may not well be feigned;
They may be much lamented or complained,
535 But men must needs their every wish obey,
And thus will I; there is no more to say.

This child I am commanded now to take"—
And spoke no more, but seized that innocent
Pitilessly, and did a gesture make
540   As if he would have slain it ere he went,
Griselda, she must suffer and consent;
And so, meek as a lamb, she sat there, still,
And let this cruel sergeant do his will.
Suspicious of repute was this same man,
545   Suspect his face, suspect his word also,
Suspect the time when this thing he began,
Alas! Her daughter that she had loved so,
She thought he'd slay it right there, whether or no.
Nevertheless, she neither wept nor sighed,
550   Doing the marquis' liking though she died.
At last she found her voice and thus began,
And meekly to the sergeant then she prayed
That, as he was a worthy, gentle man,
She might kiss her child once before his blade;
555   And on her breast this little child she laid,
With sad face, and so kissed it and did press
And lulled it and at last began to bless.
And thus she said in her benignant voice:
"Farewell, my child that I no more shall see;
560   But now I've crossed you thus, I will rejoice
That of the Father blessed may you be,
Who died for us upon the bitter tree.
Your soul, my little child, to Him I give;
This night you die for my sake—though I live."
565   I think that to a nurse in such a case
It had been hard this pitiful thing to see;
Well might a mother then have cried "Alas!"
But so steadfastly serious was she
That she endured all her adversity,
570   And to the sergeant she but meekly said:
"I give you now again your little maid.
Go now," said she, "and do my lord's behest,
But one thing will I pray you, of your grace,
That, save my lord forbade you, at the least
575   Bury this little body in some place
Where beasts nor birds will tear its limbs and face."
But no word to that purpose would he say,
But took the child and went upon his way.
This sergeant went unto his lord again
580   And of Griselda's words and of her cheer

He told him point by point, all short and plain,
And so presented him his daughter dear.
A little pity felt the marquis here;
Nevertheless, he held his purpose still,
585 As great lords do when they will have their will;
And bade the sergeant that he privily
Should softly swaddle the young child and wrap
With all the necessaries, tenderly,
And in a coffer or some garment lap;
590 But upon pain his head should meet mishap
No man should know the least of his intent,
Nor whence he came, nor whither that he went;
But to Bologna, to his sister dear
Who then was of Panago the countess,
595 He should take it, and tell of matters here,
Asking of her she do her busyness
This child to foster in all nobleness;
And whose the child was, that he bade her hide
From everyone, for aught that might betide.
600 The sergeant goes and has fulfilled this thing;
But to this marquis now return must we;
For soon he went to see her, wondering
If by his wife's demeanour he might see,
Or by her conversation learn that she
605 Were changed in aught; but her he could not find
Other than ever serious and kind.
As glad, as humble, as busy in service,
And even in love, as she was wont to be,
Was she to him at all times in each wise;
610 And of her daughter not a word spoke she.
No strange nor odd look of adversity
Was seen in her, and her dear daughter's name
She never named in earnest nor in game.
Explicit tercia pars.

615 *Sequitur pars quarta.*
In this way over them there passed four years
Ere she with child was; but as High God would,
A boy-child then she bore, as it appears,
By Walter, fair and pleasing to behold.
620 And when folk this word to the father told,
Not only he but all the people raised
Their joyous hymns to God and His grace praised.
When he was two years old and from the breast

Weaned by his nurse, it chanced upon a day
625 This marquis had another wish to test
And try his wife yet further, so they say.
Oh, needless her temptation in this way!
But wedded men no measure can observe
When they've a wife who's patient and will serve.
630 "Wife," said this marquis, "you have heard before,
My people bear our marriage with ill will;
Particularly since my son you bore
Now it is worse than ever, all this ill.
Their murmurs all my heart and courage kill,
635 For to my ears come words so aimed to smart
That they have well-nigh broken all my heart.
"Now they say this: 'When Walter's dead and gone,
Then shall Janicula's base blood succeed
And be our lord, for other have we none!'
640 Such words my people say, 'tis true, indeed!
Well ought I of such murmurs to take heed;
For truly do I fear the populace,
Though they say nothing plainly to my face.
"I would exist in peace, if that I might;
645 Wherefore I am determined utterly
That as his sister served I, and by night,
Just so will I serve him full secretly;
And thus I warn you, that not suddenly
Out of yourself for woe you start or stray;
650 Be patient in this sorrow, so I pray."
"I have," said she, "I said thus, and ever shall:
I'll have no thing, or not have, that's certain,
Save as you wish; nothing grieves me at all,
Even though my daughter and my son are slain
655 At your command, and that, I think, is plain.
I have had no part in my children twain
But sickness first, and after, woe and pain.
"You are our master; do with your own thing
Just as you like; no counsel ask of me.
660 For, as I left at home all my clothing
When first I came to you, just so," said she,
"Left will and all my liberty,
And took your clothing; wherefore do I pray
You'll do your pleasure, I'll your wish obey.
665 "For certainly, if I had prescience
Your will to know ere you your wish had told,
I would perform it without negligence;

But now I know the wish that you unfold,
To do your pleasure firmly will I hold;
670　For knew I that my death would give you ease,
Right gladly would I die, lord, you to please.
"For death can offer no loss that is known
Compared to your love's loss." And when, I say,
He saw his wife's great constancy, then down
675　He cast his eyes, and wondered at the way
She would in patience all his will obey;
And forth he went with dreary countenance,
But in his heart he knew a great pleasance.
This ugly sergeant in the very wise
680　That he her daughter took away, so he
(Or worse, if worse than this men could devise)
Has taken her son, the child of such beauty.
And always yet so all-patient was she
That she no sign gave forth of heaviness,
685　But kissed her son and so began to bless;
Save this: She prayed him that, and if he might,
Her son he'd bury in an earthen grave,
His tender limbs, so delicate to sight,
From ravenous birds and from all beasts to save.
690　But she no answer out of him could have.
He went his way as if he cared nor thought,
But to Bologna tenderly 'twas brought.
This marquis wondered ever more and more
Upon her patience; and indeed if he
695　Had not known truly in her years before
That she had loved her children perfectly,
He would have thought that out of subtlety
And malice, or from some urge more savage
She suffered this with calm face and courage.
700　But well he knew that, next himself, 'twas plain
She loved her children best in every wise.
But now to ask of women I am fain,
Whether these trials should not the man suffice?
What could an obdurate husband more devise
705　To prove her wifehood and her faithfulness,
And he continuing in his stubbornness?
But there are folk to such condition grown
That, when they do a certain purpose take,
They cannot quit the intent they thus own,
710　But just as they were bound unto a stake
They will not from that first hard purpose shake.

Just so this marquis fully was purposed
To test his wife, as he was first disposed.
He watched her, if by word or countenance
715 She show a change toward him, or in courage;
But never could he find a variance.
She was aye one in heart and in visage;
And aye the farther that she went in age,
The more true, if such thing were possible,
720 She was in love, and painstaking, as well.
From which it seemed that, as between those two,
There was but one will, for, to Walter's quest,
The same thing was her sole desire also,
And—God be thanked!—all fell out for the best.
725 She showed well that, in all this world's unrest,
A wife, of her volition, nothing should
Will to be done, save as her husband would.
The scandal of this Walter widely spread,
That, of his cruel heart, he'd wickedly
730 (Because a humble woman he had wed)
Murdered his two young children secretly.
Such murmurs went among them commonly.
No wonder, either, for to people's ear
There came no word but they'd been murdered there.
735 For which, whereas the people theretofore
Had loved him, now the scandal of such shame
Caused them to hate where they had loved before;
To be a murderer brings a hateful name.
Nevertheless, in earnest nor in game
740 Would he from this his cruel plan be bent;
To test his wife was all his fixed intent.
Now when his daughter was twelve years of age,
He to the court of Rome (in subtle wise
Informed of his design) sent his message,
745 Commanding them such bulls they should devise
As for his cruel purpose would suffice,
How that the pope, for Walter's people's rest,
Bade him to wed another, and the best.
I say, he ordered they should counterfeit
750 A papal bull and set it forth therein
That he had leave his first wife now to quit,
By papal dispensation, with no sin,
To stop all such dissension as did win
Between his folk and him; thus said the bull,
755 The which thing they did publish to the full.

The ignorant people, as no wonder is,
Supposed of course that things were even so;
But when Griselda's ears caught word of this,
I judge that then her heart was filled with woe.
760 But she, for ever steadfast, still did show
Herself disposed, this humble meek creature,
The adversity of Fortune to endure.
Abiding ever his wish and pleasure still,
To whom she had been given, heart and all;
765 He was her worldly hope, for good or ill;
But to tell all this briefly, if I shall,
This marquis wrote, in letter personal,
The devious working of his whole intent
And secretly 'twas to Bologna sent.
770 Unto Panago's count, who had, we know,
Wedded his sister, prayed he specially
To bring him home again his children two,
In honourable estate, all openly.
But one more thing he prayed him, utterly,
775 That he to no one, whoso should inquire,
Would tell who was their mother or their sire,
But say: The maiden married was to be
Unto Saluzzo's marquis, and anon.
And as this count was asked, so then did he;
780 For on day set he on his way was gone
Toward Saluzzo, with lords many a one,
In rich array, this maiden there to guide,
With her young brother riding at her side.
So toward her marriage went this fresh young maid
785 Clad richly and bedecked with jewels clear;
Her brother with her, boyishly arrayed,
And all anew, was now in his eighth year.
And thus in great pomp and with merry cheer
Toward Saluzzo went they on their way,
790 And rode along together day by day.
Explicit quarta pars.

Sequitur pars quinta.
Meanwhile, according to his wicked way,
This marquis, still to test his wife once more,
795 Even to the final proof of her, I say,
Fully to have experience to the core
If she were yet as steadfast as before,
He on a day in open audience

Loudly said unto her this rude sentence:
800 "Truly, Griselda, I'd much joy, perchance,
When you I took for wife, for your goodness
And for your truth and your obedience,
Not for your lineage nor your wealth, I guess;
But now I know, in utter certainness,
805 That in great lordship, if I well advise,
There is great servitude in sundry wise.
"I may not act as every plowman may;
My people have constrained me that I take
Another wife, and this they ask each day;
810 And now the pope, hot rancour thus to slake,
Consents, I dare the thing to undertake;
And truly now this much to you I'll say,
My new wife journeys hither on her way.
"Be strong of heart and leave at once her place,
815 And that same dower that you brought to me,
Take it again, I grant it of my grace;
Return you to your father's house," said he;
"No man may always have prosperity;
With a calm heart I urge you to endure
820 The stroke of Fortune or of adventure."
And she replied again, of her patience:
"My lord," said she, "I know, and knew alway,
How that between your own magnificence
And my poor state, no person can or may
825 Make a comparison in an equal way.
I never held me worthy or of grade
To be your wife, no, nor your chambermaid.
"And in this house, where lady you made me
(The High God do I take now to witness,
830 And as He truly may my soul's joy be),
I never held me lady nor mistress,
But only servant to your worthiness;
And ever shall, while my life may endure,
Beyond all worldly beings, that is sure.
835 "That you so long, of your benignity,
Have held me here in honour in this way,
Where I was never worthy, once, to be,
For that, thank God and you—to God I pray
He will reward you. There's no more to say.
840 Unto my father gladly will I wend
And dwell with him until my life shall end.
"Where I was fostered when an infant small,

There will I lead my life till I be dead,
A widow, clean in body, heart, and all.
845   For, since I gave to you my maidenhead,
And am your true and lawful wife, wedded,
May God forbid such a lord's wife to take
Another man for husband or love's sake.
"And of your new wife, may God of His grace
850   Grant you but joy and all prosperity:
For I will gladly yield to her my place,
Wherein so happy I was wont to be,
For since it pleases you, my lord," said she,
"Who have been all my heart's ease and its rest,
855   That I shall go, I'll go when you request.
But whereas now you proffer me such dower
As first I brought to you, it's in my mind
That 'twas my wretched clothes and nothing fair.
The which to me were hard now for to find.
860   O my good God! How noble and how kind
You seemed then, in your speech and in your face.
The day we married in that humble place.
"But truth is said—at least I find it true
For actually its proof is seen in me-
865   Old love is not the same as when it's new.
But truly, lord, for no adversity,
Though I should die of all this, shall it be
That ever in word or deed I shall repent
That I gave you my heart in whole intent.
870   "My lord, you know that, in my father's place,
You stripped from me my poor and humble weed
And clothed me richly, of your noble grace.
I brought you nothing else at all indeed,
Than faith and nakedness and maidenhead.
875   And here again my clothing I restore,
And, too, my wedding-ring, for evermore.
"The rest of all your jewels, they will be
Within your chamber, as I dare maintain;
Naked out of my father's house," said she,
880   "I came, and naked I return again.
To follow aye your pleasure I am fain,
But yet I hope it is not your intent
That smockless from your palace I be sent.
"You could not do so base and shameful thing
885   That the same womb in which your children lay
Should, before all the folk, in my walking,

Be seen all bare; and therefore do I pray
Let me not like a worm go on my way.
Remember that, my own lord, always dear,
890 I was your wife, though I unworthy were.
"Wherefore, as guerdon for my maidenhead,
The which I brought, but shall not with me bear,
Let them but give me, for my only meed,
Such a poor smock as I was wont to wear,
895 That I therewith may hide the womb of her
Who was your wife; and here I take my leave
Of you, my own dear lord, lest you should grieve."
"The smock," said he, "that you have on your back,
Let it stay there and wear it forth," said he.
900 But firmness in so saying the man did lack;
But went his way for ruth and for pity.
Before the folk her body then stripped she,
And in her smock, with head and feet all bare,
Toward her father's hovel did she fare.
905 The folk they followed, weeping and with cries,
And Fortune did they curse as they passed on;
But she with weeping did not wet her eyes,
And all this while of words she said not one.
Her father, who had heard this news anon,
910 Cursed then the day and hour when from the earth,
A living creature, nature gave him birth.
For, beyond any doubt, this poor old man
Had always feared the marquis soon would tire,
And doubted since the marriage first began,
915 If when the lord had satisfied desire,
He would not think a wife of station higher,
For one of his degree, had been more right,
And send her thence as soon as ever he might.
To meet his daughter hastily went he,
920 For he, by noise of folk, knew her coming;
And with her old coat, such as it might be,
He covered her, full sorrowfully weeping;
But the coat over her he could not bring,
For poor the cloth, and many days had passed
925 Since on her marriage day she wore it last.
Thus with her father, for a certain space,
Did dwell this flower of wifely meek patience,
Who neither by her words nor in her face,
Before the people nor in their absence,
930 Showed that she thought to her was done offense;

Nor of her high estate a remembrance
Had she, to judge by her calm countenance.
No wonder, though, for while in high estate,
Her soul kept ever full humility;
935   No mouth complaining, no heart delicate,
No pomp, no look of haughty royalty,
But full of patience and benignity,
Discreet and prideless, always honourable,
And to her husband meek and firm as well.
940   Men speak of Job and of his humbleness,
As clerks, when they so please, right well can write
Concerning men, but truth is, nevertheless,
Though clerks' praise of all women is but slight,
No man acquits himself in meekness quite
945   As women can, nor can be half so true
As women are, save this be something new.
Explicit quinta pars.

Sequitur pars sexta.
Now from Bologna is Panago come,
950   Whereof the word spread unto great and less,
And in the ears of people, all and some,
It was told, too, that a new marchioness
Came with him, in such pomp and such richness
That never had been seen with human eye
955   So noble array in all West Lombardy.
The marquis, who had planned and knew all this,
Before this count was come, a message sent
To poor Griselda, who had lost her bliss;
With humble heart and features glad she went
960   And on her knees before her lord she bent.
No pride of thought did her devotion dim;
She wisely and with reverence greeted him.
He said, "Griselda, hear what I shall say:
This maiden, who'll be wedded unto me,
965   Shall be received with splendour of array
As royally as in my house may be,
And, too, that everyone in his degree
Have his due rank in seating and service,
And high pleasance, as I can best devise.
970   "I have not serving women adequate
To set the rooms in order as I would.
And so I wish you here to regulate
All matters of the sort as mistress should.

You know of old the ways I think are good,
975 And though you're clothed in such a slattern's way,
Go do at least your duty as you may."
"Not only am I glad, my lord," said she,
"To do your wish, but I desire also
To serve you and to please in my degree;
980 This without wearying I'll always do.
And ever, lord, in happiness or woe,
The soul within my heart shall not forgo
To love you best with true intent, I know."
Then she began to put the house aright,
985 To set the tables and the beds to make;
And was at pains to do all that she might,
Praying the chambermaids, for good God's sake,
To make all haste and sweep hard and to shake;
And she, who was most serviceable of all,
990 Did every room array, and his wide hall.
About mid-morning did this count alight,
Who brought with him these noble children twain,
Whereat the people ran to see the sight
Of their array, so rich was all the train;
995 And for the first time did they not complain,
But said that Walter was no fool, at least,
To change his wife, for it was for the best.
For she was fairer far, so thought they all,
Than was Griselda, and of younger age,
1000 And fairer fruit betwixt the two should fall,
And pleasing more, for her high lineage;
Her brother, too, so fair was of visage,
That, seeing them, the people all were glad,
Commending now the sense the marquis had.
1005 "O storm-torn people! Unstable and untrue!
Aye indiscreet, and changing as a vane,
Delighting ever in rumour that is new,
For like the moon aye do you wax and wane;
Full of all chatter, dear at even a jane;
1010 Your judgment's false, your constancy deceives,
A full great fool is he that you believes!"
Thus said the sober folk of that city,
Seeing the people staring up and down,
For they were glad, just for the novelty,
1015 To have a young new lady of their town.
No more of this I'll mention or make known;
But to Griselda I'll myself address

To tell her constancy and busyness.
Full busy Griselda was in everything
1020 That to the marquis' feast was pertinent;
Nothing was she confused by her clothing,
Though rude it was and somewhat badly rent.
But with a glad face to the gate she went,
With other folk, to greet the marchioness,
1025 And afterward she did her busyness.
With so glad face his guests she did receive,
And with such tact, each one in his degree,
That no fault in it could a man perceive;
But all they wondered much who she might be
1030 That in so poor array, as they could see,
Yet knew so much of rank and reverence;
And worthily they praised her high prudence.
In all this while she never once did cease
The maiden and her brother to commend
1035 With kindness of a heart that was at peace,
So well that no man could her praise amend.
But at the last, when all these lords did wend
To seat themselves to dine, then did he call
Griselda, who was busy in his hall.
1040 "Griselda," said he, as it were in play,
"How like you my new wife and her beauty?"
"Right well," said she, "my lord, for by my fay
A fairer saw I never than is she.
I pray that God give her prosperity;
1045 And so I hope that to you both He'll send
Great happiness until your lives shall end.
"One thing I beg, my lord, and warn also,
That you prick not, with any tormenting,
This tender maid, as you've hurt others so;
1050 For she's been nurtured in her up-bringing
More tenderly, and, to my own thinking,
She could not such adversity endure
As could one reared in circumstances poor."
And when this Walter thought of her patience,
1055 Her glad face, with no malice there at all,
And how so oft he'd done to her offence,
And she aye firm and constant as a wall,
Remaining ever blameless through it all,
This cruel marquis did his heart address
1060 To pity for her wifely steadfastness.
"This is enough, Griselda mine!" cried he,

"Be now no more ill pleased nor more afraid;
I have your faith and your benignity,
As straitly as ever woman's was, assayed
1065   In high place and in poverty arrayed.
Now know I well, dear wife, your steadfastness."
And he began to kiss her and to press.
And she, for wonder, took of this no keep;
She heard not what the thing was he had cried;
1070   She fared as if she'd started out of sleep,
Till from bewilderment she roused her pride.
"Griselda," said he, "by our God Who died,
You are my wife, no other one I have,
Nor ever had, as God my soul may save!

1075   "This is your daughter, whom you have supposed
Should be my wife; the other child truly
Shall be my heir, as I have aye purposed;
You bore him in your body faithfully.
I've kept them at Bologna secretly;
1080   Take them again, for now you cannot say
That you have lost your children twain for aye.
"And folk that otherwise have said of me,
I warn them well that I have done this deed
Neither for malice nor for cruelty,
1085   But to make trial in you of virtue hid,
And not to slay my children, God forbid!
But just to keep them privily and still
Till I your purpose knew and all your will."
When she heard this, she swooned and down did fall
1090   For pitiful joy, and after her swooning
Both her young children to her did she call,
And in her arms, full piteously weeping,
Embraced them, and ail tenderly kissing,
As any mother would, with many a tear
1095   She bathed their faces and their sunny hair.
Oh, what a pitiful thing it was to see
Her swooning, and her humble voice to hear!
"Thanks, lord, that I may thank you now," said she,
"That you have saved to me my children dear!
1100   Now I am ready for death right here;
Since I stand in your love and in your grace,
Death matters not, nor what my soul may face!
"O young, O dear, O tender children mine,
Your woeful mother thought for long, truly,
1105   That cruel hounds, or birds, or foul vermin

Had eaten you; but God, of His mercy,
And your good father, all so tenderly,
Have kept you safely." And in swoon profound
Suddenly there she fell upon the ground.
1110   And in her swoon so forcefully held she
Her children two, whom she'd had in embrace,
That it was hard from her to set them free,
Her arms about them gently to unlace.
Oh, many a tear on many a pitying face
1115   Ran down, of those were standing there beside;
Scarcely, for sympathy, could they abide.
But Walter cheered her till her sorrow fled;
And she rose up, abashed, out of her trance;
All praised her now, and joyous words they said,
1120   Till she regained her wonted countenance.
Walter so honoured her by word and glance
That it was pleasing to observe the cheer
Between them, now again together here.
These ladies, when they found a tactful way,
1125   Withdrew her and to her own room were gone,
And stripped her out of her so rude array,
And in a cloth of gold that brightly shone,
Crowned with a crown of many a precious stone
Upon her head, once more to hall they brought
1130   Her, where they honoured her as all they ought.
Thus had this heavy day a happy end,
For everyone did everything he might
The day in mirth and revelry to spend
Till in the heavens shone the stars' fair light.
1135   For far more grand in every person's sight
This feast was, and of greater cost, 'twas said,
Than were the revels when they two were wed.
Full many a year in high prosperity
They lived, these two, in harmony and rest,
1140   And splendidly his daughter married he
Unto a lord, one of the worthiest
In Italy; and then in peace, as best
His wife's old father at his court he kept
Until the soul out of his body crept.
1145   His son succeeded to his heritage
In rest and peace, after the marquis' day,
And wedded happily at proper age,
Albeit he tried his wife not, so they say.
This world is not so harsh, deny who may,

1150 As in old times that now are long since gone,
And hearken what this author says thereon.
This story's told here, not that all wives should
Follow Griselda in humility,
For this would be unbearable, though they would,
1155 But just that everyone, in his degree,
Should be as constant in adversity
As was Griselda; for that Petrarch wrote
This tale, and in a high style, as you'll note.
For since a woman once was so patient
1160 Before a mortal man, well more we ought
Receive in good part that which God has sent;
For cause he has to prove what He has wrought.
But He tempts no man that His blood has bought,
As James says, if you his epistle read;
1165 Yet does He prove folk at all times, indeed,
And suffers us, for our good exercise,
With the sharp scourges of adversity
To be well beaten oft, in sundry wise;
Not just to learn our will; for truly He,
1170 Ere we were born, did all our frailty see;
But for our good is all that He doth give.
So then in virtuous patience let us live.
But one word, masters, hearken ere I go:
One hardly can discover nowadays,
1175 In all a town, Griseldas three or two;
For, if they should be put to such assays,
Their gold's so badly alloyed, in such ways,
With brass, that though the coin delight the eye,
'Twill rather break in two than bend, say I.
1180 But now, for love of the good wife of Bath,
Whose life and all whose sex may God maintain
In mastery high, or else it were but scathe,
I will with joyous spirit fresh and green
Sing you a song to gladden you, I ween;
1185 From all such serious matters let's be gone;
Hearken my song, which runs in this way on:
Griselda's dead, and dead is her patience,
In Italy both lie buried, says the tale;
For which I cry in open audience,
1190 That no man be so hardy as to assail
His own wife's patience, in a hope to find
Griselda, for 'tis certain he shall fail!
O noble wives, full of a high prudence,

Let not humility your free tongue nail,
1195   Nor let some clerk have cause for diligence
To write of you, so marvelous detail
As of Griselda, patient and so kind;
Lest Chichevache swallow you in her entrail!
Nay, follow Echo, that holds no silence,
1200   But answers always like a countervail;
Be not befooled, for all your innocence,
But take the upper hand and you'll prevail.
And well impress this lesson on your mind,
For common profit, since it may avail.
1205   Strong-minded women, stand at your defence,
Since you are strong as camel and don't ail,
Suffer no man to do to you offence;
And slender women in a contest frail,
Be savage as a tiger there in Ind;
1210   Clatter like mill, say I, to beat the male.
Nay, fear them not, nor do them reverence;
For though your husband be all armed in mail,
The arrows of your shrewish eloquence
Shall pierce his breast and pierce his aventail.
1215   In jealousy I counsel that you bind,
And you shall make him cower as does a quail.
If you are fair to see, in folks' presence,
Show them your face and with your clothes regale;
If you are foul, be lavish of expense,
1220   To gain friends never cease to do travail;
Be lightsome as a linden leaf in wind,
And let him worry, weep and wring and wail!

[*As the pilgrims near Canterbury Cathedral, the Parson takes his turn to tell a tale, which is a long and appropriate sermon to set an appropriate mood; his prologue suggests Chaucer may have envisioned this tale to be the ending of the journey.*]

THE PARSON'S PROLOGUE

What time the manciple his tale had ended,
The sun down from the south line had descended
So low that he was not, unto my sight,
Degrees full nine and twenty yet in height.
5   Four of the clock it was then, as I guess:
Four feet eleven, little more or less,
My shadow was extended then and there,
A length as if the shadow parted were

In six-foot equal parts, as I have shown.

10 Therewith the moon's high exaltation known,
I mean the sign of Libra,[89] did ascend
As we were entering a village-end;
Whereat our host, since wont to guide was he,
As in this case, our jolly company,

15 Said in this wise: "Now, masters, every one,
We lack no tales except a single one.
My judgment is fulfilled and my decree,
I think that we have heard from each degree.
Almost fulfilled is all my ordinance;

20 I pray to God to give him right good chance
Who tells to us this story pleasantly.
Sir priest," he asked, "can you a vicar be?
Are you a parson? Tell truth, by your fay!
Be what you will, break not our jolly play;

25 For every man, save you, has told his tale,
Unbuckle, show us what is in your mail;
For truly, I think, judging by your cheer,
You should knit up a mighty matter here.
Tell us a fable now, by Cock's dear bones!"

30 This parson then replied to him at once:
"You'll get no foolish fable told by me;
For Paul, when writing unto Timothy,
Reproves all those that veer from truthfulness
And tell false fables and such wretchedness.

35 Why should I sow chaff out of my own fist
When I may sow good wheat, if I but list?
But if, I say, you something wish to hear
In which the moral virtues will appear,
And if you now will give me audience,

40 I will right gladly, in Christ's reverence,
Give you such lawful pleasure as I can.
But trust me, since I am a Southern man,
I can't romance with 'rum, ram, ruff', by letter,[90]
And, God knows, rhyme I hold but little better;

45 But if you wish the truth made plain and straight,
A pleasant tale in prose I will relate
To weave our feast together at the end.
May Jesus, of His grace, the wit me send
To show you, as we journey this last stage,

---

[89]sign of the scales, judgment.
[90]The Parson is referring to alliterative poetry.

50   The way of that most perfect pilgrimage
         To heavenly Jerusalem on high.
         And if you will vouchsafe, anon shall I
         Begin my tale, concerning which, I pray,
         Choose what you will, I can no better say.
55   Yet this my meditation is, I own,
         Perhaps not free from errors to be shown
         By clerks, since I am not a learned man;
         I do but grasp the meaning as I can.
         Therefore, I do protest, I shall prepare
60   To take what comes, and all correction bear."
         When he had spoken thus, we all agreed,
         For, as it seemed to us, 'twas right indeed
         To end with something virtuous in its sense,
         And so to give him time and audience.
65   We bade our host that he to him convey
         The wish of all that he begin straightway.
         Our host, he had the very words for all.
         "Sir priest," said he, "may good to you befall!
         Say what you wish, and we will gladly hear."
70   And after that he added, for his ear:
         "Tell us," he said, "your meditation grown,
         But pray make haste, the sun will soon be down;
         Be fruitful, tell us in a little space,
         And to do well God send to you His grace!"
75   *Explicit prohemium.*

[*Chaucer never finished* The Canterbury Tales, *but before he died, he reviewed his entire literary production with some pleasure and with some misgivings here in what is traditionally called his Retraction.*]

Now do I pray all those who hear this little treatise, or read it, that, if there be within it anything that pleases them, they thank Our Lord Jesus Christ, from Whom proceeds all understanding and all goodness. And if there be anything that displeases them, I pray them, also, that they impute it to the fault of my ignorance and not to my intention, which would fain have better said if I had had knowledge. For our Book[91] says, "All that is written is written for our instruction"; and that was my intention. Wherefore I meekly beseech you that, for the sake of God's mercy, you pray for me that Christ have mercy upon me and forgive me my trespasses and especially for my translations and the writing of worldly vanities, the which I withdraw in my retractions: as, *The Book of Troilus;* also *The Book of Fame; The Book of the Nineteen Ladies; The Book of the Duchess;*

---

[91]Paul's Letter to the Romans 15:4.

The Book of Saint Valentine's Day, Of the Parliament of Birds; The Tales of Canterbury, those that tend toward sin; *The Book of the Lion;*[92] and many another book, were they in my remembrance; and many a song and many a lecherous lay,—as to which may Christ, of His great mercy, forgive me the sin. But for the translation of Boethius's *de Consolatione,* and other books of legends of saints, and homilies, and of morality and devotion—for those I thank Our Lord Jesus Christ and His Blessed Mother and all the saints of Heaven; beseeching them that they, henceforth unto my life's end, send me grace whereof to bewail my sins, and to study for the salvation of my soul:—and grant me the grace of true penitence, confession, and expiation in this present life; through the benign grace of Him Who is King of kings and Priest over all priests, Who redeemed us with the precious blood of His heart; so that I may be one of those, at the day of doom, that shall be saved: *Qui cum patre et Spiritu Sanctuo vivis et regnas Deus per onmia saecula.*[93] Amen.

---

[92]This is the only work Chaucer mentions that is not extant.
[93]"Who with the Father and Holy Spirit lives and reigns God for all time."

10. THE DECAMERON (SELECTIONS)
(1348-1353)

Giovanni Boccaccio
(1313-1375)

Boccaccio is one of the three great medieval Italian poets, along with Dante and Petrarch, whose works forecast the dawning of the Renaissance. Like his friend Petrarch, Boccaccio pioneered the revival of classical learning and appreciation of its secular values. His Decameron, a collection of a hundred tales (ten told each day for ten days), is occasioned by the Black Death which encourages a group of seven women and three gentlemen friends to flee Florence for the clean air of the countryside where the plan is to ride out the worst of the disaster and make the most of their time by enjoying good food, company, and story telling. The Preface provides a valuable contemporary description of the plague's physical, psychological, and sociological effects, as well as introducing the circumstances for the story telling. The stories themselves are a mix of humor, satire, and some light instruction; they share an earthly perspective focusing on human (sexual) relationships and the human comedy.

THE INDUCTION OF THE AUTHOR TO THE FOLLOWING DISCOURSES

Gracious Ladies, so often as I consider with my self and observe respectively, how naturally you are inclined to compassion; as many times do I acknowledge, that this present work of mine, will (in your judgement) appear to have but a harsh and offensive beginning, in regard of the mournful remembrance it bears at the very
5   entrance of the last Pestilential mortality, universally hurtful to all that beheld it, or otherwise came to knowledge of it. But for all that, I desire it may not be so dreadful to you, to hinder your further proceeding in reading, as if none were to look thereon, but with sighs and tears. For, I could rather wish, that so fearful a beginning, should seem but as an high and steep hill appears to them, that attempt
10   to travel far on foot and ascending the same with some difficulty, come afterward to walk upon a goodly even plain, which causes the more contentment in them, because the attaining thereto was hard and painful. For even as pleasures are cut off by grief and anguish; so sorrows cease by joys most sweet and happy arriving.
The year of our blessed Savior's incarnation, 1348, that memorable mortality
15   happened in the excellent City, far beyond all the rest in Italy; which plague, by

operation of the superior bodies, or rather for our enormous iniquities, by the just anger of God was sent upon us mortals. Some few years before, it took beginning in the eastern parts, sweeping thence an innumerable quantity of living souls: extending it self afterward from place to place westward, until it seized on the said City. Where neither humane skill or providence could use any prevention, notwithstanding it was cleansed of many annoyances, by diligent officers thereto deputed: besides prohibition of all sickly persons' entrance, and all possible provision daily used for conservation of such as were in health, with incessant prayers and supplications of devout people, for the assuaging of so dangerous a sickness.

About the beginning of the year, it also began in very strange manner, as appeared by diverse admirable effects; yet not as it had done in the east countries, where Lord or Lady being touched therewith, manifest signs of inevitable death followed thereon, by bleeding at the nose. But here it began with young children, male and female, either under the armpits, or in the groin by certain swellings, in some to the bigness of an apple, in others like an egg, and so in diverse greater or lesser, which (in their vulgar language) they termed to be a botch or boil. In very short time after, those two infected parts were grown mortiferous [i.e. deadly], and would disperse abroad indifferently to all parts of the body; whereupon, such was the quality of the disease, to show itself by black or blue spots, which would appear on the arms of many; others on their thighs, and every part else of the body: in some great and few, in others small and thick.

Now, as the boil (at the beginning) was an assured sign of near approaching death, so proved the spots likewise to such as had them: for the curing of which sickness it seemed, that the physician's counsel, the virtue of medicines, or any application else, could not yield any remedy, but rather it plainly appeared, that either the nature of the disease would not endure it, or ignorance in the physicians could not comprehend from whence the cause proceeded, and so by consequent, no resolution was to be determined. Moreover, beside the number of such as were skillful in art, many more both women and men, without ever having any knowledge in physic, became physicians: so that not only few were healed, but (well near) all died within three days after the said signs were seen; some sooner, and others later, commonly without either fever, or any other accident.

And this pestilence was yet of far greater power or violence; for, not only healthful persons speaking to the sick, coming to see them, or airing clothes in kindness to comfort them, was an occasion of ensuing death: but touching their garments, or any food whereon the sick person fed, or anything else used in his service, seemed to transfer the disease from the sick to the sound, in very rare and miraculous manner. Among which matter of marvel, let me tell you one thing, which if the eyes of many (as well as mine own) had not seen, hardly could I be persuaded to write it, much less to believe it, albeit a man of good credit should report it. I say, that the quality of this contagious pestilence was not only of such efficacy, in taking and catching it one from another, either men or women: but it extended further, even in the apparent view of many, that the clothes, or anything

60   else, wherein one died of that disease, being touched, or lain on by any beast, far
from the kind or quality of man, they did not only contaminate and infect the said
beast, were it dog, cat, or any other; but also it died very soon after.

Mine own eyes (as formerly I have said) among diverse others, one day had
evident experience hereof: for some poor ragged clothes of linen and wool, torn
65   from a wretched body dead of that disease, and hurled in the open street; two
swine going by, and (according to their natural inclination) seeking for food on
every dunghill, tossed and tumbled the cloths with their snouts, rubbing their
heads likewise upon them; and immediately, each turning twice or thrice about,
they both fell down dead on the said clothes, as being fully infected with the
70   contagion of them; which accident, and other the like, if not far greater, begat
diverse fears and imaginations in them that beheld them, all tending to a most
inhumane and uncharitable end; namely, to fly thence from the sick, and touching
anything of theirs, by which means they thought their health should be safely
warranted.

75   Some there were, who considered with themselves, that living soberly, with
abstinence from all superfluity; it would be a sufficient resistance against all
hurtful accidents. So combining themselves in a sociable manner, they lived as
separatists from all other company, being shut up in such houses, where no sick
body should be near them. And there, for their more security, they used delicate
80   viands and excellent wines, avoiding luxury, and refusing speech to one another,
not looking forth at the windows, to hear no cries of dying people, or see any
corpses carried to burial; but having musical instruments, lived there in all
possible pleasure. Others, were of a contrary opinion, who vowed that there was
no other remedy more certain, for a disease so desperate, than to drink hard, be
85   merry among themselves, singing continually, walking everywhere, and satisfying
their appetites with whatsoever they desired, laughing, and mocking at every
mournful accident, and so they vowed to spend day and night: for now they would
go to one tavern, then to another, living without any rule or measure; which they
might very easily do, because every one of them, (as if he were to live no longer in
90   this world) had even forsaken all things that he had. By means whereof, the most
part of the houses were become common, and all strangers might do the like (if they
pleased to adventure it) even as boldly as the lord or owner, without any let
[hindrance] or contradiction.

Yet in all this their beastly behavior, they were wise enough to shun (so much
95   as they might) the weak and sickly. In misery and affliction of our City, the
venerable authority of the laws, as well divine as humane, was even destroyed, as
it were, through want of the lawful ministers of them. For they being all dead, or
lying sick with the rest, or else lived so solitary, in such great want of servants
and attendants, as they could not execute any office, whereby it was lawful for
100   every one to do as he pleased.

Between these two aforementioned extremities of life, there were others of a
more moderate temper, not being so daintily dieted as the first, nor drinking so
dissolutely as the second; but used all things sufficient for their appetites, and

without shutting up themselves, walked abroad, some carrying sweet nosegays of
105 flowers in their hands, others odoriferous herbs, and others diverse kinds of
spiceries [herbs and spices], holding them to their noses, and thinking them most
comfortable for the brain, because the air seemed to be much infected by the
noisome smell of dead carcasses, and other hurtful odors. Some others there were
also of more inhumane mind (albeit perhaps it might be the surest) saying, that
110 there was no better remedy against the pestilence, nor yet so good, as to fly away
from it, which argument mainly moving them, and caring for nobody but
themselves, very many, both men and women, forsook the City, their own houses,
their parents, kindred, friends, and goods, flying to other men's dwellings
elsewhere. As if the wrath of God, in punishing the sins of men with this plague,
115 would fall heavily upon none but such as were enclosed within the City walls; or
else persuading themselves that not any should there be left alive, but that the final
ending of all things was come.

Now albeit these persons in their diversity of opinions died not all, so
undoubtedly they did not all escape; but many among them becoming sick, and
120 making a general example of their flight and folly, among them that could not stir
out of their beds, they languished more perplexedly than the other did. Let us omit,
that one Citizen fled after another, and one neighbour had not any care of another,
Parents nor kindred never visiting them, but utterly they were forsaken on all
sides: this tribulation pierced into the hearts of men, and with such a dreadful
125 terror, that one Brother forsook another, the Uncle the Nephew, the Sister the
Brother, and the Wife her Husband: nay, a matter much greater, and almost
incredible; Fathers and Mothers fled away from their own Children, even as if
they had no way appertained to them. In regard whereof, it could be no otherwise,
but that a countless multitude of men and women fell sick; finding no charity
130 among their friends, except a very few, and subject to the avarice of servants, who
attended them constrainedly (for great and unreasonable wages), yet few of those
attendants to be found anywhere too. And they were men or women but of base
condition, as also of grosser understanding, who never before had served in any
such necessities, nor indeed were any way else to be employed; but to give the sick
135 person such things as he called for, or to await the hour of his death; in the
performance of which service, oftentimes for gain, they lost their own lives.

In this extreme calamity, the sick being thus forsaken of neighbors, kindred,
and friends, standing also in such need of servants; a custom came up among them,
never heard of before, that there was not any woman, how noble, young, or fair
140 soever she was, but falling sick, she must of necessity have a man to attend her,
were he young or otherwise, respect of shame or modesty no way prevailing, but
all parts of her body must be discovered to him, which (in the like urgency) was
not to be seen by any but women: whereon ensued afterward, that upon the parties
healing and recovery, it was the occasion of further dishonesty, which many being
145 more modestly curious of, refused such disgraceful attending, choosing rather to
die, than by such help to be healed. In regard whereof, as well through the want of
convenient remedies, (which the sick by no means could attain unto) as also the

violence of the contagion, the multitude of them that died night and day, was so
great, that it was a dreadful sight to behold, and as much to hear spoken of. So that
150   mere necessity (among them that remained living) begat new behaviours, quite
contrary to all which had been in former times, and frequently used among the City
Inhabitants.

The custom of precedent days (as now again it is) was, that women, kindred,
neighbours, and friends, would meet together at the deceased party's house, and
155   there, with them that were of nearest alliance, express their hearts' sorrow for
their friend's loss. If not thus, they would assemble before the door, with many of
the best Citizens and kindred, and (according to the quality of the deceased) the
Clergy met there likewise, and the dead body was carried (in comely manner) on
men's shoulders, with funeral pomp of Torch light, and singing, to the Church
160   appointed by the deceased. But these seemly orders, after the fury of the pestilence
began to increase, they in like manner altogether ceased, and other new customs
came in their place; because not only people died, without having any women
about them, but infinites [i.e., many] also past out of this life, not having any
witness, how, when, or in what manner they departed. So that few or none there
165   were, to deliver outward show of sorrow and grieving: but instead thereof,
diverse declared idle joy and rejoicing, a use soon learned of immodest women,
having put off all feminine compassion, yea, or regard of their own welfare.

Very few also would accompany the body to the grave, and they not any of
the Neighbours, although it had been an honourable Citizen, but only the meanest
170   kind of people, such as were grave-makers, coffin-bearers, or the like, that did
these services only for money, and the Bier being mounted on their shoulders, in all
hast they would run away with it, not perhaps to the Church appointed by the
dead, but to the nearest at hand, having some four or six poor Priests following,
with lights or no lights, and those of the silliest; short service being said at the
175   burial, and the body irreverently thrown into the first open grave they found.
Such was the pitiful misery of poor people, and diverse, who were of better
condition, as it was most lamentable to behold; because the greater number of them,
under hope of healing, or compelled by poverty, kept still within their house weak
and faint, thousands falling sick daily, and having no help, or being succoured any
180   way with food or remedy, all of them died, few or none escaping.

Great store there were, that died in the streets by day or night, and many more
beside, although they died in their houses; yet first they made it known to their
neighbours, that their lives perished, rather by the noisome smell of dead and
putrified bodies, than by any violence of the disease in themselves. So that of these
185   and the rest, dying in this manner every where, the neighbours observed one
course of behaviour, (moved thereto no less by fear, that the smell and corruption
of dead bodies should harm them, than charitable respect of the dead) that
themselves when they could, or being assisted by some bearers of corpses, when
they were able to procure them, would haul the bodies (already dead) out of their
190   houses, laying them before their doors, where such as passed by, especially in the
mornings, might see them lying in no mean numbers. Afterward, Biers were brought

thither, and such as might not have the help of Biers, were glad to lay them on tables; and Biers have been observed, not only to be charged with two or three dead bodies at once, but many times it was seen also, that the wife with the husband, two or three Brethren together; yea, the Father and the Mother, have thus been carried along to the grave upon one Bier.

Moreover, oftentimes it has been seen, that when two Priests went with one Cross to fetch the body; there would follow (behind) three or four bearers with their Biers, and when the Priests intended the burial but of one body, six or eight more have made up the advantage, and yet none of them being attended by any seemly company, lights, tears, or the very least decency, but it plainly appeared, that the very like account was then made of Men or Women, as if they had been Dogs or Swine. Wherein might manifestly be noted, that that which the natural course of things could not show to the wise, with rare and little loss, to wit, the patient support of miseries and misfortunes, even in their greatest height: not only the wise might now learn, but also the very simplest people; and in such sort, that they should always be prepared against all infelicities whatsoever.

Hallowed ground could not now suffice, for the great multitude of dead bodies, which were daily brought to every Church in the City, and every hour in the day; neither could the bodies have proper place of burial, according to our ancient custom: wherefore, after that the Churches and Church-yards were filled, they were constrained to make use of great deep ditches, wherein they were buried by hundreds at once, ranking dead bodies along in graves, as Merchandises are laid along in ships, covering each after other with a small quantity of earth, and so they filled at last up the whole ditch to the brim.

Now, because I would wander no further in every particularity concerning the miseries happening in our City, I tell you that extremities running on in such manner as you have heard, little less spare was made in the Villages round about; wherein (setting aside enclosed Castles which were now filled like to small Cities) poor Labourers and Husbandmen, with their whole Families, died most miserably in outhouses, yea, and in the open fields also; without any assistance of remedy, or help of servants; and likewise in the highways, or their ploughed lands by day or night indifferently, yet not as men, but like brute beasts.

By means whereof, they became lazy and slothful in their daily endeavours, even like to our Citizens; not minding or meddling with their wonted affairs: but, as a waiting for death every hour, employed all their pains, not in caring any way for themselves, their cattle, or gathering the fruits of the earth, or any of their accustomed labours; but rather wasted and consumed, even such as were for their instant sustenance. Whereupon, it fell so out, that their Oxen, Asses, Sheep, and Goats, their Swine, Pullen [chickens], yea their very Dogs, the truest and faithfulest servants to men, being beaten and banished from their houses, went wildly wandering abroad in the fields, where the Corn grew still on the ground without gathering, or being so much as reaped or cut. Many of the aforesaid beasts (as endowed with reason) after they had pastured themselves in the day time,

235   would return full fed at night home to their houses, without any government of Herdsmen, or any other.

    How many fair Palaces! How many goodly Houses! How many noble habitations, filled before with families of Lords and Ladies, were then to be seen empty, without any one there dwelling, except some silly servant? How many
240   Kindreds, worthy of memory! How many great inheritances! And what plenty of riches were left without any true successors? How many good men! How many worthy Women! How many valiant and comely young men, whom none but Galen, Hippocrates, and Aesculapius (if they were living) could have been reputed any way unhealthful; were seen to dine at morning with their Parents, Friends, and
245   familiar confederates, and went to sup in another world with their Predecessors?

    It is no mean breach to my brain, to make repetition of so many miseries; wherefore, being willing to part with them as easily as I may: I say that our City being in this case, void of inhabitants, it came to pass (as afterward I understood by some of good credit) that in the venerable Church of S. Marie la Neuve, on a
250   Tuesday morning, there being then no other person, after the hearing of divine Service, in mourning habits (as the season required) returned thence seven discrete young Gentlewomen, all allied together either by friendship, neighborhood, or parentage. She among them that was most entered into years, exceeded not eight and twenty; and the youngest was no less then eighteen; being of Noble descent,
255   fair form, adorned with exquisite behaviour, and gracious modesty.

    Their names I could report, if just occasion did not forbid it, in regard of the occasions following by them related, and because times hereafter shall not tax them with reproof; the laws of pleasure being more straited nowadays (for the matters before revealed) then at that time they were, not only to their years but to
260   many much riper. Neither will I likewise minister matter to rash heads (over-ready in censuring commendable life) any way to impair the honesty of Ladies, by their idle detracting speeches. And therefore, to the end that what each of them saith may be comprehended without confusion, I purpose to style them by names, wholly agreeing, or (in part) conformable to their qualities. The first and most aged, we
265   will name Pampinea; the second Fiametta; the third Philamena; the fourth Emilia; the fifth Lauretta; the sixth Neiphila; and the last we term (not without occasion) Elissa, or Eliza. All of them being assembled at a corner of the Church, not by any deliberation formerly appointed, but merely by accident, and sitting, as it were in a round ring: after diverse sighs severely delivered, they conferred on sundry
270   matters answerable to the sad quality of the time, and within a while after, Madam Pampinea began in this manner:

    "Fair Ladies, you may (no doubt as well as I) have often heard, that no injury is offered to any one, by such as make use but of their own right. It is a thing natural for every one which is born in this World, to aid, conserve, and defend her
275   life so long as she can; and this right has been so powerfully permitted, that although it has sometimes happened, that (to defend themselves) men have been slain without any offence: yet Laws have allowed it to be so, in whose solicitude lies the best living of all mortals. How much more honest and just is it then for us,

and for every other well-disposed person, to seek for (without wronging any) and
to practise all remedies that we can, for the conservation of our lives? When I
well consider what we have here done this morning, and many other already past
(remembering withal what likewise is proper and convenient for us), I conceive
(as all you may do the like) that every one of us has due respect of herself, and then
I marvel not, but rather am much amazed (knowing none of us to be deprived of a
Woman's best judgement) that we seek not after some remedies for ourselves,
against that which every one among us ought (in reason) to fear.

"Here we meet and remain (as it seems to me) in no other manner than as if we
would or should be witnesses to all the dead bodies at rest in their grave; or else
to listen, when the religious Sisters here dwelling (whose number now are well-
near come to be none at all) sing Service at such hours as they ought to do; or else
to acquaint all comers hither (by our mourning habits) with the quality and
quantity of our heart's miseries. And when we part hence, we meet with none but
dead bodies; or sick persons transported from one place to another; or else we see
running through the City (in most offensive fury) such as (by authority of public
Laws) were banished hence, only for their bad and brutish behaviour in contempt
of those Laws, because now they know that the executors of them are dead and
sick. And if not these, more lamentable spectacles present themselves to us, by the
base rascality of the City; who being fatted with our blood, term themselves
Grave-makers, and in mere contemptible mockeries of us, are mounted on
horseback, galloping everywhere, reproaching us with our losses and misfortunes,
with lewd and dishonest songs: so that we can hear nothing else but such and such
are dead, and such and such lie dying: here hands wringing, and everywhere most
pitiful complaining.

"If we return home to our houses (I know not whether your case be
answerable to mine) when I can find none of all my Family, but only my poor
waiting Chambermaid; so great are my fears, that the very hair on my head
declares my amazement, and wheresoever I go or sit down, methinks I see the
ghosts and shadows of deceased friends, not with such lovely looks as I was wont
to behold them, but with most horrid and dreadful regards, newly stolen upon
them I know not how. In these respects, both here, elsewhere, and at home in my
house, methinks I am always ill, and much more (in mine own opinion) than any
other body, not having means or place of retirement, as all we have, and none to
remain here but only we.

"Moreover, I have often heard it said, that in tarrying or departing, no
distinction is made in things honest or dishonest; only appetite will be served; and
be they alone or in company, by day or night, they do whatsoever their appetite
desires: not secular persons only, but such as are recluses, and shut up within
Monasteries, breaking the Laws of obedience, and being addicted to pleasures of
the flesh, are become lascivious and dissolute, making the world believe, that
whatsoever is convenient for other women, is no way unbecoming for them, as
thinking in that manner to escape.

"If it be so, as manifestly it makes show of itself, What do we here? What stay
we for? And whereon do we dream? Why are we more careless of our health than
all the rest of the Citizens? Repute we ourselves less precious than all the other?
325   Or do we believe that life is linked to our bodies with stronger chains, than to
others, and that therefore we should not fear anything that has power to offend
us? We err therein, and are deceived. What brutishness were it in us, if we should
urge any such belief? So often as we call to mind, what and how many gallant
young men and women, have been devoured by this cruel pestilence; we may
330   evidently observe a contrary argument.

"Wherefore, to the end, that by being over-scrupulous and careless, we fall
not into such danger, whence when we would—perhaps cannot—recover our
selves by any means: I think it mete (if your judgement therein shall jump with mine)
that all of us as we are (at least, if we will do as diverse before us have done, and
335   yet daily endeavour to do) shunning death by the honest example of other, make
our retreat to our Country houses, wherewith all of us are sufficiently furnished,
and there to delight ourselves as best we may, yet without transgressing (in any
act) the limits of reason. There shall we hear the pretty birds sweetly singing, see
the hills and plains verdantly flowering; the Corn waving in the field like the
340   billows of the Sea, infinite store of goodly trees, and the Heavens more fairly open
to us, then here we can behold them. And although they [the Heavens] are justly
displeased, yet will they not there deny us better beauties to gaze on, than the
walls in our City (emptied of Inhabitants) can afford us.

"Moreover, the Air is much fresh and clear, and generally, there is far greater
345   abundance of all things whatsoever, needful at this time for preservation of our
health, and less offence or molestation than we find here.

"And although Country people die, as well as here our Citizens do, the grief
notwithstanding is so much the less, as the houses and dwellers there are rare, in
comparison to them in our City. And beside, if we well observe it, here we forsake
350   no particular person, but rather we may term ourselves forsaken; in regard that
our Husbands, Kindred, and Friends, either dying, or flying from the dead, have
left us alone in this great affliction, even as if we were no way belonging unto
them. And therefore, by following this counsel, we cannot fall into any
reprehension; whereas if we neglect and refuse it, danger, distress , and death
355   (perhaps) may ensue thereon.

"Wherefore, if you think good, I would allow it for well done, to take our
waiting women, with all such things as are needful for us, and (as this day) betake
ourselves to one place, tomorrow to another, taking there such pleasure and
recreation, as so sweet a season liberally bestows on us. In which manner we may
360   remain, till we see (if death otherwise prevent us not) what end the gracious
Heavens have reserved for us. I would have you also to consider, that it is no less
seemly for us to part hence honestly, than a great number of other Women to
remain here immodestly."

The other Ladies and Gentlewomen, having heard Madam Pampinea, not only
365   commended her counsel, but desiring also to put it in execution, had already

particularly consulted with themselves by what means they might instantly depart from thence. Nevertheless, Madam Philomena, who was very wise, spake thus:

"Albeit fair Ladies, the case propounded by Madam Pampinea has been very well delivered; yet (for all that) it is against reason for us to rush on, as we are over ready to do. Remember that we are all women, and no one among us is so childish but may consider, that when we shall be so assembled together, without providence or conduct of some man, we can hardly govern ourselves. We are frail, offensive, suspicious, weak spirited, and fearful: in regard of which imperfections, I greatly doubt (if we have no better direction than our own) this society will sooner dissolve itself, and (perchance) with less honour to us, than if we never had begun it. And therefore it shall be expedient for us to provide before we proceed any further." Madam Eliza hereon thus replied:

"Most true it is, that men are the chief or head of women, and without their order, seldom times do any matters of ours sort to recommendable end. But what means shall we make for men? We all know well enough, that the most part of our friends are dead, and such as are living, some be dispersed here, others there, into diverse places and companies, where we have no knowledge of their being; and to accept of strangers, would seem very inconvenient; wherefore as we have such care of our health, so should we be as respective withal, in ordering our intention, that wheresoever we aim at our pleasure and contentment, reproof and scandal may by no means pursue us."

While this discourse thus held among the Ladies, three young Gentlemen came forth of the Church (yet not so young, but the youngest had attained to five and twenty years) in whom neither malice of the time, loss of friends or kindred, nor any fearful conceit [idea] in themselves, had the power to quench affection, but (perhaps) might a little cool it, in regard of the queazy season. One of them called himself Pamphilus, the second Philostratus, and the last Dioneus. Each of them was very affable and well conditioned, and walked abroad (for their greater comfort in such a time of tribulation) to try if they could meet with their fair friends, who (happily) might all three be among these seven, and the rest kin unto them in one degree or other. No sooner were these Ladies espied by them, but they met with them also in the same advantage; whereupon Madam Pampinea (amiably smiling) said:

"See how graciously Fortune is favourable to our beginning, by presenting our eyes with three so wise and worthy young Gentlemen, who will gladly be our guides and servants, if we do not disdain them the office." Madam Neiphila began immediately to blush, because one of them had a Love in the company, and said; "Good Madam Pampinea take heed what you say, because (of mine own knowledge) nothing can be spoken but good of them all; and I think them all to be absolutely sufficient for a far greater employment than is here intended, as being well worthy to keep company not only with us, but them of more fair and precious esteem than we are. But because it appears plainly enough, that they bear affection to some here among us, I fear, if we should make the motion, that some dishonor or reproof may ensue thereby, and yet without blame either in us or them."

410   "That is nothing at all," answered Madam Philomena, "let me live honestly, and my Conscience not check me with any crime; speak then who can to the contrary, God and truth shall enter arms for me. I wish that they were as willing to come, as all we are to bid them welcome: for truly (as Madam Pampinea said) we may very well hope, that Fortune will further us to our purposed journey."

415   The other Ladies hearing them speak in such manner, not only were silent to themselves, but all with one accord and consent said that it were well done to call them, and to acquaint them with their intention, entreating their company in so pleasant a voyage. Whereupon, without any more words, Madam Pampinea mounting on her feet (because one of the three was her Kinsman) went towards

420   them, as they stood respectively observing them; and (with a pleasing countenance) giving them a gracious salutation, declared to them their deliberation, desiring (on behalf of all the rest) that with a brotherly and modest mind, they would vouchsafe to bear them company.

     The Gentlemen imagined at the first apprehension that this was spoken in

425   mockage of them; but when they better perceived that her words tended to solemn earnest, they made answer, That they were all heartily ready to do them any service. And without any further delaying, before they departed thence, took order for their aptest furnishing with all convenient necessaries, and sent word to the place of their first appointment. On the morrow, being Wednesday, about break of

430   day, the Ladies, with certain of their attending Gentlewomen, and the three Gentlemen having three servants to wait on them, left the City to begin their journey; and having travelled about a league's distance, arrived at the place of their first purpose of stay, which was seated on a little hill, distant (on all sides) from any high way, plentifully stored with fair spreading Trees, affording no

435   mean delight to the eye. On the top of all, stood a stately Palace, having a large and spacious Court in the midst round girded with Galleries, Halls, and Chambers, every one separate alone by themselves, and beautified with Pictures of admirable cunning. Nor was there any want of Gardens, Meadows, and other most pleasant Walks, with Wells and Springs of fair running waters, all encompassed with

440   branching Vines, fitter for curious and quaffing bibbers, than women sober, and singularly modest.

     This Palace the company found fully fitted and prepared, the beds in the Chambers made and daintily ordered, thickly strewed with variety of flowers, which could not but give them the greater contentment. Dioneus, who (above the

445   other) was a pleasant young gallant, and full of infinite witty conceits, said:

     "Your wit (fair Ladies) has better guided us hither, than our providence: I know not how you have determined to dispose of your cares; as for mine own, I left them at the City gate when I came thence with you; and therefore let your resolution be to spend the time here in smiles and singing, (I mean, as may fittest

450   agree with your dignity) or else give me leave to go seek my sorrows again, and so to remain discontented in our desolate City." Madam Pampinea having in like manner shaken off her sorrows, delivering a modest and bashful smile, replied in this manner:

"Dioneus, well have you spoken; it is fit to live merrily, and no other occasion made us forsake the sick and sad City. But, because such things as are without mean or measure are subject to no long continuance, I, who began the motion, whereby this society is thus assembled, and aim at the long lasting thereof, do hold it very convenient, that we should all agree to have one chief Commander among us, in whom the care and providence should consist for direction of our merriment, performing honour and obedience to the party, as to our Patron and sole Governour. And because every one may feel the burden of solicitude, as also the pleasure of commanding, and consequently have a sensible taste of both, whereby no envy may arise on any side, I could wish that each one of us (for a day only) should feel both the burden and honour, and the person so to be advanced, shall receive it from the election of us all. As for such as are to succeed, after him or her that has had the day's dominion, the party thought fit for succession must be named so soon as night approaches. And being in this eminence (according as he or she shall please), he may order and dispose how long the time of his rule shall last, as also of the place and manner, where best we may continue our delight."

These words were highly pleasing to them all, and by general voice, Madame Pampinea was chosen Queen for the first day. Whereupon, Madame Philomena ran presently to a Bay-tree, because she had often heard what honour belonged to those branches, and how worthy of honour they were, that rightfully were crowned with them, plucking off diverse branches, she made of them an apparent and honourable Chaplet, placing it (by general consent) upon her head; and this so long as their company continued, manifested to all the rest, the signal of Dominion and Royal greatness.

After that Madame Pampinea was thus made Queen, she commanded public silence, and causing the Gentlemen's three servants and the waiting women also (being four in number) to be brought before her, thus she began:

"Because I am to give the first example to you all, whereby proceeding on from good to better, our company may live in order and pleasure, acceptable to all, and without shame to any; I create Parmeno (servant to Dioneus) Master of the Household, he taking the care and charge of all our Train, and for whatsoever pertains to our Hall service. I appoint also, that Silisco, servant to Pamphilus, shall be our Dispenser and Treasurer, performing that which Parmeno shall command him. Likewise that Tindaro serve as Groom of the Chamber, to Philostratus his Master, and the other two, when his fellows impeached by their offices, cannot be present. Misia my Chambermaid, and Licisca, belonging to Philomena, shall serve continually in the Kitchen, and diligently make ready such Viands [meats, i.e. food] as shall be delivered them by Parmeno. Chimera, waiting woman to Lauretta, and Stratilia, pertaining to Fiametta, shall have the charge and government of the Ladies' Chambers, and preparing all places where we shall be present. Moreover, we will and command every one of them (as they desire to deserve our grace) that wheresoever they go or come, or whatsoever they hear or see, they bring us tidings of them."

After she had summarily delivered them these orders, very much commended of every one, she arose fairly, saying: "Here we have Gardens, Orchards, Meadows, and other places of sufficient pleasure, where everyone may sport and recreate
500   themselves: but so soon as the ninth hour strikes, then all to meet here again, to dine in the cool shade."

This jocund company having received licence from their Queen to disport themselves, the Gentlemen walked with the Ladies into a goodly Garden, making Chaplets and Nosegayes of diverse flowers, and singing silently to themselves.
505   When they had spent the time limited by the Queen, they returned into the house, where they found that Parmeno had effectually executed his office. For, when they entered into the hall, they saw the Tables covered with delicate white Napery, and the glasses looking like silver, they were so transparently clear, all the room beside strewed with Flowers of Juniper. When the Queen and all the rest had
510   washed, according as Parmeno gave order, so every one was seated at the Table: the Viands (delicately dressed) were served in, and excellent wines plentifully delivered, none attending but the three servants, and little or no loud Table-talk passing among them.

Dinner being ended, and the Tables withdrawn (all the Ladies, and the
515   Gentlemen likewise, being skilful both in singing and dancing, and playing on instruments artificially [artfully]) the Queen commanded, that diverse Instruments should be brought, and (as she gave charge) Dioneus took a Lute, and Fiametta a Viola de gamba, and began to play an excellent dance. Whereupon, the Queen with the rest of the Ladies, and the other two young Gentlemen (having sent their
520   attending servants to dinner) paced forth a dance very majestically. And when the dance was ended, they sung sundry excellent Canzonets, outwearing so the time, until the Queen commanded them all to rest, because the hour did necessarily require it. The Gentlemen having their Chambers far severed from the Ladies, curiously strewed with flowers, and their beds adorned in exquisite manner, as
525   those of the Ladies, were not a jot inferior to them; the silence of the night bestowed sweet rest on them all. In the morning, the Queen and all the rest being risen, accounting over much sleep to be very hurtful, they walked abroad into a goodly Meadow, where the grass grew verdantly, and the beams of the Sun heated not over-violently, because the shades of fair spreading Trees, gave a temperate
530   calmness, cool and gentle winds fanning their sweet breath pleasingly among them. All of them being there set down in a round ring, and the Queen in the midst, as being the appointed place of eminence, she spake:

"You see (fair company) that the Sun is highly mounted, the heat (elsewhere) too extreme for us, and therefore here is our fittest refuge, the air being so cool,
535   delicate, and acceptable, and our folly well worthy of reprehension if we should walk further and speed worse. Here are Tables, Cards, and Chess, as your dispositions may be addicted. But if mine advice might pass for current, I would admit none of those exercises, because they are too troublesome both to them that play, and such as look on. I could rather wish, that some quaint discourse might
540   pass among us, a tale or fable related by someone, to urge the attention of all the

rest. And so wearing out the warmth of the day, one pretty Novel [tale] will draw on another, until the Sun be lower declined, and the heat's extremity more diminished, to solace ourselves in some other place, as to our minds shall seem convenient. If therefore what I have said be acceptable to you (I purposing to follow in the same course of pleasure), let it appear by your immediate answer; for, till the Evening, I think we can devise no exercise more commodious for us."

* * * * *

SEVENTH DAY, NINTH TALE (Translated by John Payne, 1909)

Lydia and Pyrrhus (Told by Pamfilus)

[*Lydia, wife of Nicostratus, loves Pyrrhus, who to assure himself thereof, asks three things of her, all of which she does, and therewithal enjoys him in presence of Nicostratus, and makes Nicostratus believe that what he saw was not real.*]

"Methinks, worshipful ladies, there is no venture, though fraught with gravest peril, that whoso loves ardently will not make: of which truth, exemplified though it has been in stories not a few, I purpose to afford you yet more signal proof in one which I shall tell you; wherein you will hear of a lady who in her enterprises owed far more to the favour of Fortune than to the guidance of reason: wherefore I should not advise any of you rashly to follow in her footsteps, seeing that Fortune is not always in a kindly mood, nor are the eyes of all men equally holden.

In Argos, that most ancient city of Achaia, the fame of whose kings of old time is out of all proportion to its size, there dwelt of yore Nicostratus, a nobleman, to whom, when he was already verging on old age, Fortune gave to wife a great lady, Lydia by name, whose courage matched her charms. Nicostratus, as suited with his rank and wealth, kept not a few retainers and hounds and hawks, and was mightily addicted to the chase.

Among his dependents was a young man named Pyrrhus, a gallant of no mean accomplishment, and goodly of person and beloved and trusted by Nicostratus above all other. Of whom Lydia grew mighty enamoured, insomuch that neither by day nor by night might her thoughts stray from him: but, whether it was that Pyrrhus wist [knew] not her love, or would have none of it, he gave no sign of recognition; whereby the lady's suffering waxing more than she could bear, she made up her mind to declare her love to him; and having a chambermaid, Lusca by name, in whom she placed great trust, she called her, and said:

"Lusca, tokens thou have had from me of my regard that should ensure thy obedience and loyalty; wherefore have a care that what I shall now tell thee reach the ears of none but him to whom I shall bid thee impart it.

"Thou see, Lusca, that I am in the prime of my youth and lustihead [sensuality], and have neither lack nor stint of all such things as folk desire, save

575 only, to be brief, that I have one cause to repine, to wit, that my husband's years so far outnumber my own. Wherefore with that wherein young ladies take most pleasure I am but ill provided, and, as my desire is no less than theirs, 'tis now some while since I determined that, if Fortune has shown herself so little friendly to me by giving me a husband so advanced in years, at least I will not be mine own enemy by sparing to devise the means whereby my happiness and health may be

580 assured; and that herein, as in all other matters, my joy may be complete, I have chosen, thereto to minister by his embraces, our Pyrrhus, deeming him more worthy than any other man, and have so set my heart upon him that I am ever ill at ease save when he is present either to my sight or to my mind, insomuch that, unless I forgather with him without delay, I doubt not that 'twill be the death of me.

585 "And so, if thou hold my life dear, thou will show him my love on such wise as thou may deem best, and make my suit to him that he be pleased to come to me, when thou shall go to fetch him."

"That gladly will I," replied the chambermaid; and as soon as she found convenient time and place, she drew Pyrrhus apart, and, as best she knew how,

590 conveyed her lady's message to him. Which Pyrrhus found passing strange to hear, for 'twas in truth a complete surprise to him, and he doubted the lady did but mean to try [test] him.

Wherefore he presently, and with some asperity, answered thus:—"Lusca, believe I cannot that this message comes from my lady: have a care, therefore, what

595 thou say, and if, perchance, it does come from her, I doubt she does not mean it; and if, perchance, she does mean it, why, then I am honoured by my lord above what I deserve, and I would not for my life do him such a wrong: so have a care never to speak of such matters to me again."

Lusca, nowise disconcerted by his uncompliant tone, rejoined:—"I shall

600 speak to thee, Pyrrhus, of these and all other matters, wherewith I may be commissioned by my lady, as often as she shall bid me, whether it pleases or irks thee; but thou art a blockhead."

So, somewhat chafed, Lusca bore Pyrrhus' answer back to her lady, who would fain [nearly] have died, when she heard it, and some days afterwards

605 resumed the topic, saying:—"Thou know, Lusca, that 'tis not the first stroke that fells the oak; wherefore, methinks, thou wert best go back to this strange man, who is minded to evince his loyalty at my expense, and choosing a convenient time, declare to him all my passion, and do thy best endeavour that the affair be carried through; for if it should thus lapse, 'twould be the death of me; besides which, he

610 would think we had but trifled with him, and, whereas 'tis his love we would have, we should earn his hatred."

So, after comforting the lady, the maid hied [hastened] her in quest of Pyrrhus, whom she found in a gladsome and propitious mood, and thus addressed:—"'Tis not many days, Pyrrhus, since I declared to thee how ardent is the flame with

615 which thy lady and mine is consumed for love of thee, and now again I do thee to wit [know] thereof, and that, if thou shalt not relent of the harshness that thou did manifest the other day, thou may rest assured that her life will be short: wherefore

I pray thee to be pleased to give her solace of her desire, and should thou persist in thy obduracy, I, that gave thee credit for not a little sense, shall deem thee a great
620   fool. How flattered thou should be to know thyself beloved above all else by a lady so beauteous and high-born! And how indebted should thou feel thyself to Fortune, seeing that she has in store for thee a boon so great and so suited to the cravings of thy youth, ay, and so like to be of service to thee upon occasion of need! Bethink thee, if there be any of thine equals whose life is ordered more
625   agreeably than thine will be if thou but be wise. Which of them will thou find so well furnished with arms and horses, clothes and money as thou shall be, if thou but give my lady thy love? Receive, then, my words with open mind; be thyself again; bethink thee that 'tis Fortune's way to confront a man but once with smiling mien [face, demeanor] and open lap, and, if he then accept not her bounty, he has
630   but himself to blame, if afterward he find himself in want, in beggary.

      "Besides which, no such loyalty is demanded between servants and their masters as between friends and kinsfolk; rather 'tis for servants, so far as they may, to behave towards their masters as their masters behave towards them. Think that, if thou had a fair wife or mother or daughter or sister that found
635   favour in Nicostratus' eyes, he would be so scrupulous on the point of loyalty as thou art disposed to be in regard of this lad? Thou art a fool if so thou do believe. Hold it for certain, that, if blandishments and supplications did not suffice, he would, whatever thou might think of it, have recourse to force. Observe we, then, towards them and theirs the same rule which they observe towards us and ours.
640   Take the boon that Fortune offers thee; repulse her not; rather go thou to meet her, and hail her advance; for be sure that, if thou do not so, to say nought of thy lady's death, which will certainly ensue, thou thyself will repent thee thereof so often that thou will be fain of death."

      Since he had last seen Lusca, Pyrrhus had repeatedly pondered what she had
645   said to him, and had made his mind up that, should she come again, he would answer her in another sort, and comply in all respects with the lady's desires, provided he might be assured that she was not merely putting him to the proof; wherefore he now made answer:—

      "Lo, now, Lusca, I acknowledge the truth of all that thou says but, on the
650   other hand, I know that my lord is not a little wise and wary, and, as he has committed all his affairs to my charge, I sorely misdoubt me that 'tis with his approbation, and by his advice, and but [only] to prove [test] me, that Lydia does this: wherefore let her do three things which I shall demand of her for my assurance, and then there is nought that she shall crave of me, but I will certainly
655   render her prompt obedience. Which three things are these:—first, let her in Nicostratus' presence kill his fine sparrow-hawk, then she must send me a lock of Nicostratus' beard, and lastly one of his best teeth."

      Hard seemed these terms to Lusca, and hard beyond measure to the lady, but Love, that great factor of enterprise, and master of stratagem, gave her resolution
660   to address herself to their performance: wherefore through the chambermaid she sent him word that what he required of her she would do, and that without either

reservation or delay; and therewithal she told him, that, as he deemed Nicostratus so wise, she would contrive that they should enjoy one another in Nicostratus' presence, and that Nicostratus should believe that 'twas a mere show. Pyrrhus, therefore, anxiously expected [awaited] what the lady would do.

665

Some days thus passed, and then Nicostratus gave a great breakfast, as was his frequent wont, to certain gentlemen, and when the tables were removed, the lady, robed in green samite, and richly adorned, came forth of her chamber into the hall wherein they sat, and before the eyes of Pyrrhus and all the rest of the company hied [hastened] her to the perch on which stood the sparrow-hawk that Nicostratus so much prized, and loosed him, and, as if she were minded to carry him on her hand, took him by the jesses [leg strap] and dashed him against the wall so that he died.

670

Whereupon:—"Alas! my lady, what hast thou done?" exclaimed Nicostratus: but she vouchsafed no answer, save that, turning to the gentlemen that had sat at meat with him, she said:—"My lords, ill fitted were I to take vengeance on a king that had done me despite, if I lacked the courage to be avenged on a sparrow-hawk. You are to know that by this bird I have long been cheated of all the time that ought to be devoted by gentlemen to pleasuring their ladies; for with the first streaks of dawn Nicostratus has been up and got him to horse, and hawk on hand hied [hastened] him to the champaign [field] to see him fly, leaving me, such as you see me, alone and ill content abed. For which cause I have oftentimes been minded to do that which I have now done, and have only refrained therefrom, that, biding my time, I might do it in the presence of men that should judge my cause justly, as I trust you will do."

675

680

685

Which hearing, the gentlemen, who deemed her affections no less fixed on Nicostratus than her words imported, broke with one accord into a laugh, and turning to Nicostratus, who was sore displeased, fell a saying:—"Now well done of the lady to avenge her wrongs by the death of the sparrow-hawk!" and so, the lady being withdrawn to her chamber, they passed the affair off with diverse pleasantries, turning the wrath of Nicostratus to laughter.

690

Pyrrhus, who had witnessed what had passed, said to himself: Nobly indeed has my lady begun, and on such wise [way] as promises well for the felicity of my love. God grant that she so continue

695

And even so Lydia did: for not many days after she had killed the sparrow-hawk, she, being with Nicostratus in her chamber, from caressing passed to toying and trifling with him and he, sportively pulling her by the hair, gave her occasion to fulfil the second of Pyrrhus' demands; which she did by nimbly laying hold of one of the lesser tufts of his beard, and, laughing the while, plucking it so hard that she tore it out of his chin. Which Nicostratus somewhat resenting:—"Now what cause hast thou," quoth she, "to make such a wry face? 'Tis but that I have plucked some half-dozen hairs from thy beard. Thou did not feel it as much as did I but now thy tugging of my hair."

700

And so they continued jesting and sporting with one another, the lady jealously guarding the tuft that she had torn from the beard, which the very same

705

day she sent to her cherished lover. The third demand caused the lady more thought; but, being amply endowed with wit, and powerfully seconded by Love, she failed not to hit upon an apt expedient.

710 Nicostratus had in his service two lads, who, being of gentle birth, had been placed with him by their kinsfolk, that they might learn manners, one of whom, when Nicostratus sat at meat, carved before him, while the other gave him to drink. Both lads Lydia called to her, and gave them to understand that their breath smelt, and admonished them that, when they waited on Nicostratus, they should hold their heads as far back as possible, saying never a word of the matter to any.

715 The lads believing her, did as she bade them.

Whereupon she took occasion to say to Nicostratus: "Hast thou marked what these lads do when they wait upon thee?"

"Troth, that have I," replied Nicostratus; "indeed I have often had it in mind to ask them why they do so."

720 "Nay," rejoined the lady, "spare thyself the pains; for I can tell thee the reason, which I have for some time kept close, lest it should vex thee; but as I now see that others begin to be aware of it, it need no longer be withheld from thee. 'Tis for that thy breath stinks shrewdly [perceptibly] that they thus avert their heads from thee: 'twas not wont to be so, nor know I why it should be so; and 'tis

725 most offensive when thou art in converse with gentlemen; and therefore 'twould be well to find some way of curing it."

"I wonder what it could be," returned Nicostratus; "is it perchance that I have a decayed tooth in my jaw?"

"That may well be," quoth Lydia: and taking him to a window, she caused

730 him open his mouth, and after regarding it on this side and that:—"Oh! Nicostratus," quoth she, "how could thou have endured it so long? Thou hast a tooth here, which, by what I see, is not only decayed, but actually rotten throughout; and beyond all manner of doubt, if thou let it remain long in thy head, 'twill infect its neighbours; so 'tis my advice that thou out with it before the matter

735 grows worse."

"My judgment jumps with thine," quoth Nicostratus; "wherefore send without delay for a surgeon [i.e. barber] to draw it."

"God forbid," returned the lady, "that surgeon come hither for such a purpose; methinks, the case is such that I can very well dispense with him, and

740 draw the tooth myself. Besides which, these surgeons do these things in such a cruel way, that I could never endure to see thee or know thee under the hands of any of them: wherefore my mind is quite made up to do it myself, that, at least, if thou shalt suffer too much, I may give it over at once, as a surgeon would not do."

And so she caused the instruments that are used on such occasions to be

745 brought her, and having dismissed all other attendants save Lusca from the chamber, and locked the door, made Nicostratus lie down on a table, set the pincers in his mouth, and clapped them on one of his teeth, which, while Lusca held him, so that, albeit he roared for pain, he might not move, she wrenched by main force from his jaw, and keeping it close, took from Lusca's hand another and

750   horribly decayed tooth, which she showed him, suffering and half dead as he was, saying:—"See what thou had in thy jaw; mark how far gone it is."

   Believing what she said, and deeming that, now the tooth was out, his breath would no more be offensive, and being somewhat eased of the pain, which had been extreme, and still remained, so that he murmured not little, by diverse
755   comforting applications, he quitted the chamber: whereupon the lady forthwith sent the tooth to her lover, who, having now full assurance of her love, placed himself entirely at her service.

   But the lady being minded to make his assurance yet more sure, and deeming each hour a thousand till she might be with him, now saw fit, for the more ready
760   performance of the promise she had given him, to feign sickness; and Nicostratus, coming to see her one day after breakfast, attended only by Pyrrhus, she besought him for her better solacement, to help her down to the garden. Wherefore Nicostratus on one side, and Pyrrhus on the other, took her and bore her down to the garden, and set her on a lawn at the foot of a beautiful pear-tree: and after they
765   had sat there a while, the lady, who had already given Pyrrhus to understand what he must do, said to him:—"Pyrrhus, I should greatly like to have some of those pears; get thee up the tree, and shake some of them down."

   Pyrrhus climbed the tree in a trice, and began to shake down the pears, and while he did so:—"Fie! Sir," quoth he, "what is this you do? And you, Madam,
770   have you no shame, that you suffer him to do so in my presence? Think you that I am blind? 'Twas but now that you were gravely indisposed. Your cure has been speedy indeed to permit of your so behaving: and as for such a purpose you have so many goodly chambers, why betake you not yourselves to one of them, if you must needs so disport yourselves? 'Twould be much more decent than to do so in
775   my presence."

   Whereupon the lady, turning to her husband:—"Now what can Pyrrhus mean?" said she. "Is he mad ? "

   "Nay, Madam," quoth Pyrrhus; "mad am not I. Think you I see you not?"

   Whereat Nicostratus marvelled not a little; and:—"Pyrrhus," quoth he, "I
780   verily believe thou dream."'

   "Nay, my lord," replied Pyrrhus, "not a whit do I dream; neither do you; rather you wag it with such vigour, that, if this pear-tree did the like, there would be never a pear left on it."

   Then the lady:—"What can this mean?" quoth she: "can it be that it really
785   seems to him to be as he says? Upon my hope of salvation, were I but in my former health, I would get me up there to judge for myself what these wonders are which he professes to see."

   Whereupon, as Pyrrhus in the pear-tree continued talking in the same strange strain:—"Come down," quoth Nicostratus; and when he was down:—"Now
790   what," said Nicostratus, "is it thou say thou see up there?"

   "I suppose," replied Pyrrhus, "that you take me to be deluded or dreaming: but as I must needs tell you the truth, I saw you lying upon your wife, and then, when I came down, I saw you get up and sit you down here where you now are."

795 "Therein," said Nicostratus, "thou were certainly deluded, for, since thou climbed the pear-tree, we have not budged a jot, save as thou see." Then said Pyrrhus:—"Why make more words about the matter? See you I certainly did; and, seeing you, I saw you lying upon your own."

Nicostratus' wonder now waxed momently [increased moment by moment], insomuch that he said:—"I am minded to see if this pear-tree be enchanted, so that
800 whoso is in it sees marvels;" and so he got him[self] up into it. Whereupon the lady and Pyrrhus fell to disporting them[selves], and Nicostratus, seeing what they were about, exclaimed:—"Ah lewd woman, what is this thou do? And thou, Pyrrhus, in whom I so much trusted!" And so saying, he began to climb down.

Meanwhile the lady and Pyrrhus had made answer:—"We are sitting here:"
805 and seeing him descending, they placed themselves as they had been when he had left them, whom Nicostratus, being come down, no sooner saw, than he fell a rating them.

Then quoth Pyrrhus:—"Verily, Nicostratus, I now acknowledge, that, as you said a while ago, what I saw when I was in the pear-tree was but a false show,
810 albeit I had never understood that so it was but that I now see and know that thou have also seen a false show. And that I speak truth, you may sufficiently assure yourself, if you but reflect whether 'tis likely that your wife, who for virtue and discretion has not her peer among women, would, if she were minded so to dishonour you, see fit to do so before your very eyes. Of myself I say nought albeit
815 I had liefer [rather] be hewn in pieces than that I should so much as think of such a thing, much less do it in your presence. Wherefore 'tis evident that 'tis some illusion of sight that is propagated from the pear-tree; for nought in the world would have made me believe that I saw not you lying there in carnal intercourse with your wife, had I not heard you say that you saw me doing that which most
820 assuredly, so far from doing, I never so much as thought of."

The lady then started up with a most resentful mien [demeanor], and burst out with:—"Foul fall thee, if thou know so little of me as to suppose that, if I were minded to do thee such foul dishonour as thou say thou did see me do, I would come hither to do it before thine eyes! Rest assured that for such a purpose, were it
825 ever mine, I should deem one of our chambers more meet, and it should go hard but I would so order the matter that thou should never know of it."

Nicostratus, having heard both, and deeming that what they both averred must be true, to wit, that they would never have ventured upon such an act in his presence, passed from chiding to talk of the singularity of the thing, and how
830 marvellous it was that the vision should reshape itself for everyone that climbed the tree.

The lady, however, made a show of being distressed that Nicostratus should so have thought of her, and:—"Verily," said she, "no woman, either I nor another, shall again suffer loss of honour by this pear-tree: run, Pyrrhus, and bring hither
835 an axe, and at one and the same time vindicate thy honour and mine by felling it, albeit 'twere better far Nicostratus' skull should feel the weight of the axe, seeing that in utter heedlessness he so readily suffered the eyes of his mind to be blinded;

for, albeit this vision was seen by the bodily eye, yet ought the understanding by no means to have entertained and affirmed it as real."

840   So Pyrrhus presently hied [hastened] to fetch the axe, and returning therewith felled the pear; whereupon the lady, turning towards Nicostratus:—"Now that this foe of my honour is fallen," said she, "my wrath is gone from me."

Nicostratus then craving her pardon, she graciously granted it him, bidding him never again to suffer himself to be betrayed into thinking such a thing of her,

845   who loved him more dearly than herself. So the poor duped husband went back with her and her lover to the palace, where not seldom in time to come Pyrrhus and Lydia took their pastime together more at ease. God grant us the like.

TENTH DAY, FIFTH TALE (Translated by John Payne, 1909)

A Garden in January (Told by Emilia)

[*Madonna Dianora craves of Messer Ansaldo a garden that shall be as fair in January as in May. Messer Ansaldo binds himself to a necromancer, and thereby gives her the garden. Her husband gives her leave to do Messer Ansaldo's pleasure: he, being apprised of her husband's liberality, releases her from her promise; and the necromancer releases Messer Ansaldo from his bond, and will take nought of his.*]

Each of the gay company had with superlative commendation extolled [the previous speaker] Messer Gentile to the skies, when the king bade Emilia follow

850   suit; and with a good courage, as burning to speak, thus Emilia began:—"Delicate my ladies, none can justly say that 'twas not magnificently done of Messer Gentile; but if it be alleged that 'twas the last degree of magnificence, 'twill perchance not be difficult to show that more was possible, as is my purpose in the little story that I shall tell you."

855   In Friuli, a country which, though its air is shrewd [piercing], is pleasantly diversified by fine mountains and not a few rivers and clear fountains, is a city called Udine, where dwelt of yore a fair and noble lady, Madonna Dianora by name, wife of a wealthy grandee named Giliberto, a very pleasant gentleman, and debonair. Now this lady, for her high qualities, was in the last degree beloved by

860   a great and noble baron, Messer Ansaldo Grandense by name, a man of no little consequence, and whose fame for feats of arms and courtesy was spread far and wide. But, though with all a lover's ardor he left nought undone that he might do to win her love, and to that end frequently plied her with his ambassages [i.e., requests], 'twas all in vain. And the lady being distressed by his importunity, and

865   that, refuse as she might all that he asked of her, he nonetheless continued to love her and press his suit upon her, bethought her how she might rid herself of him by requiring of him an extraordinary and, as she deemed, impossible feat.

So one day, a woman that came oftentimes from him to her being with her:— "Good woman," said she, "thou have many a time affirmed that Messer Ansaldo

870   loves me above all else; and thou have made proffer to me on his part of wondrous

rich gifts which I am minded he keep to himself, for that I could never bring myself to love him or pleasure him for their sake; but, if I might be certified that he loves me as much as thou say, then without a doubt I should not fail to love him, and do his pleasure; wherefore, so he give me the assurance that I shall require, I shall be
875   at his command."

"What is it, Madam," returned the good woman, "that you would have him do?"

"This," replied the lady, "I would have this next ensuing January, hard by this city, a garden full of green grass and flowers and flowering trees, just as if it
880   were May; and if he cannot provide me with this garden, bid him never again send either thee or any other to me, for that, should he harass me any further, I shall no longer keep silence, as I have hitherto done, but shall make my complaint to my husband and all my kinsmen, and it shall go hard but I will be quit of him."

The gentleman being apprised of his lady's stipulation and promise,
885   notwithstanding that he deemed it no easy matter, nay, a thing almost impossible, to satisfy her, and knew besides that 'twas but to deprive him of all hope that she made the demand, did nevertheless resolve to do his endeavour to comply with it, and causing search to be made in diverse parts of the world, if any he might find to afford him counsel or aid, he lit upon one, who for a substantial reward offered
890   to do the thing by necromancy [magic].

So Messer Ansaldo, having struck the bargain with him for an exceeding great sum or money, gleefully expected [awaited] the appointed time. Which being come with extreme cold, insomuch that there was nought but snow and ice, the adept [magician] on the night before the calends of January wrought with his
895   spells to such purpose that on the morrow, as was averred by eye-witnesses, there appeared in a meadow hard by the city one of the most beautiful gardens that was ever seen, with no lack of grass and trees and fruits of all sorts. At sight whereof Messer Ansalsdo was overjoyed and caused some of the finest fruits and flowers it contained to be gathered, and privily presented to his lady, whom overjoyed, he
900   bade come and see the garden that she had craved, that thereby she might have assurance of his love, and mind her of the promise that she had given him and confirmed with an oath, and, as a loyal lady, take thought for its performance.

When she saw the flowers and fruits, the lady, who had already heard not a few folk speak of the wondrous garden, began to repent her of her promise. But for
905   all that, being fond of strange sights, she hied [hastened] her[self] with many other ladies of the city to see the garden, and having gazed on it with wonderment, and commended it not a little, she went home the saddest woman alive, bethinking her to what it bound her: and so great was her distress that she might not well conceal it; but, being written on her face, 'twas marked by her husband, who was minded
910   by all means to know the cause thereof.

The lady long time kept silence: but at last she yielded to his urgency, and discovered to him the whole matter from first to last. Whereat Giliberto was at first very wroth [angry]; but on second thoughts, considering the purity of the lady's purpose, he was better advised, and dismissing his anger:—"Dianora,"

915   quoth he, "'tis not the act of a discreet or virtuous lady to give ear to messages of such a sort, nor to enter into any compact touching her chastity with any man on any terms. Words that the ears convey to the heart have a potency greater than is commonly supposed, and there is scarce aught that lovers will not find possible. 'Twas then ill done of thee in the first instance to hearken, as afterwards to make

920   the compact; but, for that I know the purity of thy soul, that thou may be quit of thy promise, I will grant thee that which, perchance, no other man would grant, being also swayed thereto by fear of the necromancer [magician], whom Messer Ansaldo, should thou play him false, might peradventure, cause to do us a mischief. I am minded, then, that thou go to him, and contrive, if on any wise thou can, to get

925   thee quit of this promise without loss of virtue; but if otherwise it may not be, then for the nonce [one time] thou may yield him thy body, but not thy soul."

     Whereat the lady, weeping, would none of such a favour at her husband's hands. But Giliberto, for all the lady's protestations, was minded that so it should be.

930   Accordingly, on the morrow about dawn, apparelled none too ornately, preceded by two servants and followed by a chambermaid, the lady hied [hastened] her[self] to Messer Ansaldo's house. Apprised that his lady was come to see him, Messer Ansaldo, marvelling not a little, rose, and having called the necromancer [magician]:—"I am minded," said he, "that thou see what goodly gain

935   I have gotten by thine art."

     And the twain having met, the lad Ansaldo gave way to no unruly appetite, but received her with a seemly obeisance [respect]; and then the three repaired to a goodly chamber, where there was a great fire, and having caused the lady to be seated, thus spoke Ansaldo:—"Madam, if the love that I have so long borne you

940   merit any guerdon [reward], I pray you that it be not grievous to you to discover to me the true occasion of your coming to me at this hour, and thus accompanied."

     Shamefast, and the tears all but standing in her eyes, the lady made answer:— "Sir, 'tis neither love that I bear you, nor faith that I pledged you, that brings me hither, but the command of my husband, who, regarding rather the pains you have

945   had of your unbridled passion than his own or my honour, has sent me hither; and for that he commands it, I, for the nonce [moment], am entirely at your pleasure."

     If Messer Ansaldo had marvelled to hear of the lady's coming, he now marvelled much more, and touched by Giliberto's liberality, and passing from passion to compassion:—"Now, God forbid, Madam," said he, "that, it being as

950   you say, I should wound the honour of him that has compassion on my love; wherefore, no otherwise than as if you were my sister shall you abide here, while you are so minded, and be free to depart at your pleasure; nor crave I aught of you but that you shall convey from me to your husband such thanks as you shall deem meet for courtesy such as his has been, and entreat me ever henceforth as your

955   brother and servant."

     Whereat overjoyed in the last degree:—"Nought," said the lady, "by what I noted of your behaviour, could ever have caused me to anticipate other sequel of my coming hither than this which I see is your will and for which I shall ever be your debtor."

960   She then took her leave, and, attended by a guard of honour, returned to Giliberto, and told him what had passed; between whom and Messer Ansaldo there was thenceforth a most close and loyal friendship.

     Now the liberality shown by Giliberto towards Messer Ansaldo, and by Messer Ansaldo towards the lady, having been marked by the necromancer 965 [magician] , when Messer Ansaldo made ready to give him the promised reward:— "Now God forbid," said he, "that, as I have seen Giliberto liberal [generous] in regard of his honour, and you liberal in regard of your love, I be not in like manner liberal in regard of my reward, which accordingly, witting [knowing] that 'tis in good hands, I am minded that you keep."

970   The knight was abashed [embarrassed], and strove hard to induce him to take, if not the whole, at least a part of the money; but finding that his labour was in vain, and that the necromancer, having caused his garden to vanish after the third day, was minded to depart, he bade him adieu. And the carnal love he had for the lady being spent, he burned for her thereafter with a flame of honourable 975 affection.

     Now what shall be our verdict in this case, lovesome ladies? A lady, as it were dead, and a love grown lukewarm for utter hopelessness! Shall we set a liberality shown in such a case above this liberality of Messer Ansaldo, loving yet as ardently, and hoping, perchance, yet more ardently than ever, and holding 980 in his hands the prize that he had so long pursued? Folly indeed should I deem it to compare that liberality with this.

* * * * *

TENX DAY, TENTH TALE (Translated by John Payne, 1909)

The Story of Patient Griselda (Told by Dioneus)

[*The Marquis of Saluzzo, overborne by the entreaties of his vassals, consents to take a wife, but, being minded to please himself in the choice of her, takes a husbandman's daughter. He has two children by her, both of whom, he causes her to believe, he has put to death. Afterwards, feigning to be tired of her and to have taken another wife, he turns her out of doors in her shift and brings his daughter into the house in guise of his bride; but, finding her patient under it all, he brings her home again, and shows her their children, now grown up, and honours her, and causes her to be honoured, as Marchioness.*]

     Ended the king's long story, with which all seemed to be very well pleased, said Dioneo with a laugh:—"The good man that looked that night to cause the bogey's tail to droop, would scarce have contributed two pennyworth of all the

985 praise you bestow on Messer Torello:" then, witting [knowing] that it now only remained for him to tell, thus he began:—

Gentle my ladies, this day, it seems, is dedicated to Kings and folk of the like quality [the story theme of the day]; wherefore, that I stray not too far from you, I am minded to tell you somewhat of a Marquis. a piece of mad folly, albeit there

990 came good thereof to him in the end. The which I counsel none to copy, for that great pity 'twas that it turned out well with him.

There was in olden days a certain Marquis of Saluzzo, Gualtieri by name, a young man, but head of the house, who, having neither wife nor child, passed his time in nought else but in hawking and hunting, and of taking a wife and begetting

995 children had no thought; wherein he should have been accounted very wise: but his vassals, brooking it ill, did oftentimes entreat him to take a wife, that he might not die without an heir, and they be left without a lord; offering to find him one of such a pattern, and of such parentage, that he might marry with good hope, and be well content with the sequel.

1000 To whom:—"My friends," replied Gualtieri, "you enforce me to that which I had resolved never to do, seeing how hard it is to find a wife whose ways accord well with one's own, and how plentiful is the supply of such as run counter thereto, and how grievous a life he leads who chances upon a lady that matches ill with him. And to say that you think to know the daughters by the qualities of their

1005 fathers and mothers, and thereby you would argue to provide me with a wife to my liking, is but folly; for I know not how you may penetrate the secrets of their mothers so as to know their fathers; and granted that you do know them, daughters oftentimes resemble neither of their parents.

"However, as you are minded to rivet these fetters upon me, I am content that

1010 so it be; and that I may have no cause to reproach any but myself, should it turn out ill, I am resolved that my wife shall be of my own choosing; but of this rest assured, that, no matter whom I choose, if she receive not from you the honour due to a lady, you shall prove to your great cost, how sorely I resent being thus constrained by your importunity to take a wife against my will."

1015 The worthy men replied that they were well content, so only he would marry without more ado. And Gualtieri, who had long noted with approval the mien [demeanor] of a poor girl that dwelt on a farm hard by his house, and found her fair enough, deemed that with her he might pass a tolerably happy life. Wherefore he sought no further, but forthwith resolved to marry her; and having sent for her

1020 father, who was a very poor man, he contracted with him to take her to wife.

Which done, Gualtieri assembled all the friends he had in those parts, and:— "My friends," said he, "you were and are minded that I should take a wife, and rather to comply with your wishes, than for any desire that I had to marry, I have made up my mind to do so. You remember the promise you gave me, to wit, that,

1025 whomsoever I should take, you would pay her the honour due to a lady. Which promise I now require you to keep, the time being come when I am to keep mine. I have found hard by here a maiden after mine own heart, whom I purpose to take to wife, and to bring hither to my house in the course of a few days. Wherefore

1030 bethink you, how you may make the nuptial feast splendid, and welcome her with all honour; that I may confess myself satisfied with your observance of your promise, as you will be with my observance of mine."

The worthy men, one and all, answered with alacrity that they were well content, and that, whoever she might be, they would entreat her as a lady, and pay her all due honour as such. After which, they all addressed them to make goodly

1035 and grand and gladsome celebration of the event, as did also Gualtieri. He arranged for a wedding most stately and fair, and bade thereto a goodly number of his friends and kinsfolk, and great gentlemen and others of the neighbourhood, and therewithal he caused many a fine and costly robe to be cut and fashioned to the figure of a girl who seemed to him of the like proportions as the girl that he

1040 purposed to wed; and laid in store, besides, of girdles and rings, with a costly and beautiful crown, and all the other paraphernalia of a bride.

The day that he had appointed for the wedding being come, about half tierce [c. 9.30 am] he got him to horse with as many as had come to do him honour, and having made all needful dispositions:—"Gentlemen," quoth he, "'tis time to go

1045 bring home the bride."

And so away he rode with his company to the village; where, being come to the house of the girl's father, they found her returning from the spring with a bucket of water, making all the haste she could, that she might afterwards go with the other women to see Gualtieri's bride come by. Whom Gualtieri no sooner saw,

1050 than he called her by her name, to wit, Griselda, and asked her where her father was.

To whom she modestly made answer:—"My lord, he is in the house."

Whereupon Gualtieri dismounted, and having bidden the rest await him without, entered the cottage alone; and meeting her father, whose name was

1055 Giannucolo:—"I am come," said he, "to wed Griselda, but first of all there are some matters I would learn from her own lips in thy presence."

He then asked her, whether, if he took her to wife, she would study to comply with his wishes, and be not wroth [angry], no matter what he might say or do, and be obedient, with not a few other questions of a like sort to all which she

1060 answered, ay.

Whereupon Gualtieri took her by the hand, led her forth, and before the eyes of all his company, and as many other folk as were there, caused her to strip naked, and let bring the garments that he had had fashioned for her, and had her forthwith arrayed therein—and upon her unkempt head let set a crown; and then,

1065 while all wondered:—"Gentlemen," quoth he, "this is she whom I purpose to make my wife, so she be minded to have me for husband."

Then, she standing abashed and astonished, he turned to her, saying:—"Griselda, wilt thou have me for thy husband?"

To whom:—"Ay, my lord," answered she.

1070 "And I will have thee to wife," said he, and married her before them all. And having set her upon a palfrey, he brought her home with pomp.

The wedding was fair and stately, and had he married a daughter of the King of France, the feast could not have been more splendid. It seemed as if, with the change of her garb, the bride had acquired a new dignity of mind and mien [demeanor]. She was, as we have said, fair of form and feature; and therewithal she was now grown so engaging and gracious and debonair, that she showed no longer as the shepherdess, and the daughter of Giannucolo, but as the daughter of some noble lord, insomuch that she caused as many as had known her before to marvel. Moreover, she was so obedient and devoted to her husband, that he deemed himself the happiest and luckiest man in the world.

And likewise so gracious and kindly was she to her husband's vassals, that there was none of them but loved her more dearly than himself, and was zealous to do her honour, and prayed for her welfare and prosperity and aggrandisement, and instead of, as erstwhile, saying that Gualtieri had done foolishly to take her to wife, now averred that he had not his like in the world for wisdom and discernment, for that, save to him, her noble qualities would ever have remained hidden under her sorry apparel and the garb of the peasant girl. And in short she so comported herself as in no long time to bring it to pass that, not only in the marquisate, but far and wide besides, her virtues and her admirable conversation were matter of common talk, and, if aught had been said to the disadvantage of her husband, when he married her, the judgment was now altogether to the contrary effect.

She had not been long with Gualtieri before she conceived and in due time she was delivered of a girl; whereat Gualtieri made great cheer. But, soon after, a strange humour took possession of him, to wit, to put her patience to the proof by prolonged and intolerable hard usage; wherefore he began by afflicting her with his gibes, putting on a vexed air, and telling her that his vassals were most sorely dissatisfied with her by reason of her base condition [lowly birth], and all the more so since they saw that she was a mother, and that they did nought but most ruefully murmur at the birth of a daughter.

Whereto Griselda, without the least change of countenance or sign of discomposure, made answer:—"My lord, do with me as thou may deem best for thine own honour and comfort, for well I know that I am of less account than they, and unworthy of this honourable estate to which of thy courtesy thou hast advanced me." By which answer Gualtieri was well pleased, witting that she was in no degree puffed up with pride by his, or any other's, honourable entreatment of her.

A while afterwards, having in general terms given his wife to understand that the vassals could not endure her daughter, he sent her a message by a servant. So the servant came, and:—"Madam," quoth he with a most dolorous mien [demeanor], "so I value my life, I must needs do my lord's bidding. He has bidden me take your daughter," and he said no more, but the lady by what she heard, and read in his face, and remembered of her husband's words, understood that he was bidden to put the child to death.

1115   Whereupon she presently took the child from the cradle, and having kissed and blessed her, albeit she was very sore at heart, she changed not countenance, but placed it in the servant's arms, saying:—"See that thou leave nought undone that my lord and thine has charged thee to do, but leave her not so that the beasts and the birds devour her, unless he have so bidden thee."

1120   So the servant took the child, and told Gualtieri what the lady had said; and Gualtieri, marvelling at her constancy, sent him with the child to Bologna, to one of his kinswomen, whom he besought to rear and educate the child with all care, but never to let it be known whose child she was.

     Soon after it befell that the lady again conceived, and in due time was
1125 delivered of a son, whereat Gualtieri was overjoyed. But, not content with what he had done, he now even more poignantly afflicted the lady; and one day with a ruffled mien [annoyed aspect]:—"Wife," said he, "since thou gave birth to this boy, I may on no way live in peace with my vassals, so bitterly do they reproach me that a grandson of Giannucolo is to succeed me as their lord; and therefore I
1130 fear that, so I be not minded to be sent a-packing hence, I must even do herein as I did before, and in the end put thee away, and take another wife."

     The lady heard him patiently, and answered only: "My lord, study how thou may content thee and best please thyself, and waste no thought upon me, for there is nought I desire save in so far as I know that 'tis thy pleasure."

1135   Not many days after, Gualtieri, in like manner as he had sent for the daughter, sent for the son, and having made a show of putting him to death, provided for his, as for the girl's, nurture at Bologna. Whereat the lady showed no more discomposure of countenance or speech than at the loss of her daughter: which Gualtieri found passing strange, and inwardly affirmed that there was never
1140 another woman in the world that would have so done. And but that he had marked that she was most tenderly affectionate towards her children, while 'twas well pleasing to him, he had supposed that she was tired of them, whereas he knew that 'twas of her discretion that she so did.

     His vassals, who believed that he had put the children to death, held him
1145 mightily to blame for his cruelty, and felt the utmost compassion for the lady. She, however, said never aught to the ladies that condoled with her on the death of her children, but that the pleasure of him that had begotten them was her pleasure likewise.

     Years not a few had passed since the girl's birth, when Gualtieri at length
1150 deemed the time come to put his wife's patience to the final proof. Accordingly, in the presence of a great company of his vassals he declared that in no way might he longer brook to have Griselda to wife, that he confessed that in taking her he had done a sorry thing and the act of a stripling, and that he therefore meant to do what he could to procure the Pope's dispensation to put Griselda away, and take
1155 another wife: for which cause being much upbraided by many worthy men, he made no other answer but only that needs must it so be.

     Whereof the lady being apprised, and now deeming that she must look to go back to her father's house, and perchance tend the sheep, as she had aforetime, and

1160   see him, to whom she was utterly devoted, engrossed by another woman, did inwardly bewail herself sorely but still with the same composed mien with which she had borne Fortune's former buffets, she set herself to endure this last outrage.

Nor was it long before Gualtieri by counterfeit letters, which he caused to be sent to him from Rome, made his vassals believe that the Pope had thereby given him a dispensation to put Griselda away, and take another wife. Wherefore,
1165   having caused her to be brought before him, he said to her in the presence of not a few:—"Wife, by license granted me by the Pope, I am now free to put thee away, and take another wife; and, for that my forbears have always been great gentlemen and lords of these parts, whereas thine have ever been husbandman, I purpose that thou go back to Giannucolo's house with the dowry that thou brought me;
1170   whereupon I shall bring home a lady that I have found, and who is meet to be my wife."

'Twas not without travail most grievous that the lady, as she heard this announcement, got the better of her woman's nature, and suppressing her tears, made answer:—"My lord, I ever knew that my low degree was in no way
1175   congruous with your nobility, and acknowledged that the rank I had with you was of your and God's bestowal, nor did I ever make as if it were mine by gift, or so esteem it, but still accounted it as a loan. 'Tis your pleasure to recall it, and therefore it should be, and is, my pleasure to render it up to you. So, here is your ring, with which you espoused me; take it back. You bid me take with me the
1180   dowry that I brought you; which to do will require neither paymaster on your part nor purse nor packhorse on mine; for I am not unmindful that naked was I when you first had me. And if you deem it seemly that that body in which I have borne children, by you begotten, be beheld of all, naked will I depart; but yet, I pray you, be pleased, in guerdon [payment] for the virginity that I brought you and
1185   take not away, to suffer me to bear hence upon my back a single shift—I crave no more—besides my dowry."

There was nought of which Gualtieri was so fain as to weep; but yet, setting his face as a flint, he made answer:—"I allow thee a shift to thy back; so get thee hence." All that stood by besought him to give her a robe, that she, who had been
1190   his wife for thirteen years and more, might not be seen to quit his house in so sorry and shameful a plight, having nought on her but a shift. But their entreaties went for nothing: the lady in her shift, and barefoot and bareheaded, having bade them adieu, departed the house, and went back to her father amid the tears and lamentations of all that saw her.

1195   Giannucolo, who had ever deemed it a thing incredible that Gualtieri should keep his daughter to wife, and had looked for this to happen every day, and had kept the clothes that she had put off on the morning that Gualtieri had wedded her, now brought them to her; and she, having resumed them, applied herself to the petty drudgery of her father's house, as she had been wont, enduring with fortitude this
1200   cruel visitation of adverse Fortune.

Now no sooner had Gualtieri dismissed Griselda, then he gave his vassals to understand that he had taken to wife a daughter of one of the Counts of Panago.

He accordingly made great preparations as for the nuptials, during which he sent
for Griselda. To whom, being come, quoth he:—"I am bringing hither my new bride,
and in this her first home-coming I purpose to show her honour; and thou know
that women I have none in the house that know how to set chambers in due order,
or attend to the many other matters that so joyful an event requires; wherefore do
thou, that understand these things better than another, see to all that needs be
done, and bid hither such ladies as thou may see fit, and receive them, as if thou
wert the lady of the house, and then, when the nuptials are ended, thou may go
back to thy cottage."

Albeit each of these words pierced Griselda's heart like a knife, for that, in
resigning her good fortune, she had not been able to renounce the love she bore
Gualtieri, nevertheless:—"My lord," she made answer, "I am ready and prompt to
do your pleasure."

And so, clad in her sorry garments of coarse cloth, she entered the house,
which, but a little before, she had quitted in her shift, and addressed her to sweep
the chambers, and arrange arras and cushions in the hall and make ready the
kitchen, and set her hand to everything, as if she had been a paltry serving-wench:
nor did she rest until she had brought all into such meet and seemly trim as the
occasion demanded. This done, she invited in Gualtieri's name all the ladies of
those parts to be present at his nuptials, and awaited the event.

The day being come, still wearing her sorry weeds, but in heart and soul and
mien [comportment] the lady, she received the ladies as they came, and gave each a
gladsome greeting.

Now Gualtieri, as we said, had caused his children to be carefully nurtured
and brought up by a kinswoman of his at Bologna, which kinswoman was
married into the family of the Counts of Panago and, the girl being now twelve
years old, and the loveliest creature that ever was seen, and the boy being about
six years old, he had sent word to his kinswoman's husband at Bologna, praying
him to be pleased to come with this girl and boy of his to Saluzzo, and to see that
he brought a goodly and honourable company with him, and to give all to
understand that he brought the girl to him to wife, and on no wise to disclose to
any, who she really was.

The gentleman did as the Marquis bade him, and within a few days of his
setting forth arrived at Saluzzo about breakfast-time with the girl and her
brother, and a noble company, and found all the folk of those parts, and much
people besides, gathered there in expectation of Gualtieri's new bride. Who, being
received by the ladies, was no sooner come into the hall, where the tables were set,
than Griselda advanced to meet her, saying with hearty cheer:—"Welcome, my
lady."

So the ladies, who had with much instance, but in vain, besought Gualtieri,
either to let Griselda keep in another room, or at any rate to furnish her with one
of the robes that had been hers, that she might not present herself in such a sorry
guise before the strangers, sat down to table; and the service being begun, the eyes
of all were set on the girl, and every one said that Gualtieri had made a good

exchange, and Griselda joined with the rest in greatly commending her, and also her little brother.

1250 And now Gualtieri, sated at last with all that he had seen of his wife's patience, marking that this new and strange turn made not the least alteration in her demeanor, and being well assured that 'twas not due to apathy, for he knew her to be of excellent understanding, deemed it time to relieve her of the suffering which he judged her to dissemble under a resolute front; and so, having called her to him in presence of them all he said with a smile:—"And what think thou of our

1255 bride? "

"My lord," replied Griselda, "I think mighty well of her; and if she be but as discreet as she is fair—and so I deem her—I make no doubt but you may reckon to lead with her a life of incomparable felicity; but with all earnestness I entreat you, that you spare her those tribulations which you did once inflict upon another that

1260 was yours, for I scarce think she would be able to bear them, as well because she is younger, as for that she has been delicately nurtured, whereas that other had known no respite of hardship since she was but a little child."

Marking that she made no doubt but that the girl was to be his wife, and yet spoke never a whit the less sweetly, Gualtieri caused her to sit down beside him,

1265 and:—"Griselda," said he, "'Tis now time that thou see the reward of thy long patience, and that those who have deemed me cruel and unjust and insensitive, should know that what I did was done of purpose aforethought, for that I was minded to give both thee and them a lesson, that thou might learn to be a wife, and they in like manner might learn how to take and keep a wife, and that I might beget

1270 me perpetual peace with thee for the rest of my life; whereof being in great fear, when I came to take a wife, lest I should be disappointed, I therefore, to put the matter to the proof, did, and how sorely thou know, harass and afflict thee. And since I never knew thee either by deed or by word to deviate from my will, I now, deeming myself to have of thee that assurance of happiness which I desired, am

1275 minded to restore to thee at once all that, step by step, I took from thee, and by extremity of joy to compensate the tribulations that I inflicted on thee.

"Receive, then, this girl whom thou suppose to be my bride, and her brother, with glad heart, as thy children and mine. These are they, whom by thee and many another it has long been supposed that I did ruthlessly to death, and I am thy

1280 husband, that loves thee more dearly than aught else, deeming that other there is none that has the like good cause to be well content with his wife."

Which said, he embraced and kissed her; and then, while she wept for joy, they rose and hied [hastened] them there where sat the daughter, all astonished to hear the news, whom, as also her brother, they tenderly embraced, and explained

1285 to them, and many others that stood by, the whole mystery. Whereat the ladies, transported with delight, rose from table and betook them with Griselda to a chamber, and, with better omen, divested her of her sorry garb, and arrayed her in one of her own robes of state; and so, in guise of a lady (howbeit in her rags she had showed as no less) they led her back into the hall.

1290   Wondrous was the cheer which there they made with the children; and, all overjoyed at the event, they revelled and made merry, and prolonged the festivities for several days; and very discreet they pronounced Gualtieri, albeit they censured as intolerably harsh the probation to which he had subjected Griselda, and most discreet beyond all compare they accounted Griselda.

1295   Some days after, the Count of Panago returned to Bologna, and Gualtieri took Giannucolo from his husbandry, and established him in honour as his father-in-law, wherein to his great solace he lived for the rest of his days. Gualtieri himself, having mated his daughter with a husband of high degree, lived long and happily thereafter with Griselda, to whom he ever paid all honour.

1300   Now what shall we say in this case but that even into the cots of the poor the heavens let fall at times spirits divine, as into the palaces of kings souls that are fitter to tend hogs than to exercise lordship over men? Who but Griselda had been able, with a countenance not only tearless, but cheerful, to endure the hard and unheard-of trials to which Gualtieri subjected her? Who perhaps might have

1305   deemed himself to have made no bad investment, had he chanced upon one, who, having been turned out of his house in her shift, had found means so to dust the pelisse [cloak] of another as to get herself thereby a fine robe.

* * * * *

CONCLUSION OF THE AUTHOR (Translated by Richard Aldington, 1930)

Most noble ladies, for whose delight I have given myself over to this long task, I believe that with the aid of divine grace it is more through your pious

1310   prayers than any merit of mine that I have carried out what I promised to do at the beginning of this work. So now, after giving thanks, first to God and then to you, I shall rest my pen and weary hand. I know that these tales can expect no more immunity than any others, as I think I showed in the beginning of the Fourth Day; and so before I rest, I mean to reply to certain objections which might be made by

1315   you or others.

Some of you may say that in writing these tales I have taken too much license, by making ladies sometimes say and often listen to matters which are not proper to be said or heard by virtuous ladies. This I deny, for there is nothing so unchaste but may be said chastely if modest words are used; and this I think I have done.

1320   But suppose it to be true—and I shall not strive with you, for you are certain to win—I reply that I have many arguments ready. First, if there is any license in some of them, the nature of the stories demanded it; and if any understanding person looks at them with a reasonable eye he will see that they could not be related otherwise, unless I had altered them entirely. And if there are a few words

1325   rather freer than suits the prudes, who weigh words more than deeds and take more pains to appear than to be good, I say that I should no more be reproved for having written them than other men and women are reproved for daily saying

-411-

"hole," "peg," "mortar," "pestle," "sausage," "Bologna sausage," and the like things. My pen should be allowed no less power than is permitted the painter's brush; the painters are not censured for allowing Saint Michele to slay the serpent with a sword or lance and Saint Giorgio to kill the dragon as he pleases. They make Christ male and Eve female, and they fasten sometimes with one nail, sometimes with two, the feet of Him who died for the human race on the Cross.

In addition, anyone can see that these things were not told in church, where everything should be treated with reverent words and minds (although you will find plenty of license in the stories of the church); nor were they told in a school of philosophers, where virtue is as much required as anywhere else; nor among churchmen or other philosophers in any place; but they were told in gardens, in pleasure places, by young people who were old enough not to be led astray by stories, and at a time when everyone threw his cap over the mill and the most virtuous were not reproved for it.

But, such as they are, they may be amusing or harmful, like everything else, according to the persons who listen to them. Who does not know that wine is a most excellent thing, if we may believe Cinciglione and Scolaio, while it is harmful to a man with a fever? Are we to say wine is wicked because it is bad for those who are feverish? Who does not know that fire is most useful and even necessary to mankind? And because it sometimes destroys houses, villages and towns, shall we say it is bad? Weapons defend the safety of those who wish to live in peace, but they also kill men, not through any wrong in them but through the wickedness of those who use them ill.

No corrupt mind ever understands words healthily. And just as such people do not enjoy virtuous words, so the well-disposed cannot be harmed by words which are somewhat less than virtuous, any more than mud can sully sunlight or earthy filth the beauty of the skies.

What books, what words, what letters are more holy, more worthy, more to be revered than those of the divine Scripture? Yet many people by perversely interpreting them have sent themselves and others to perdition. Everything in itself is good for something, and if wrongly used may be harmful in many ways; and I say the same of my tales.

Whoever wants to turn them to bad counsel or bad ends will not be forbidden by the tales themselves, if by any chance they contain such things and are twisted and turned to produce them. Those who want utility and good fruits from them, will not find them denied nor will the tales ever be thought anything but useful and virtuous if they are read at the times and to the persons for which they are intended.

Those who have to say paternosters and play the hypocrite to their confessor can leave them alone; my tales will run after nobody asking to be read. And yet bigots say and even do such little trifles from time to time!

There will also be people to say that if some of the tales here were absent it would be all the better. Granted. But I could only write down the tales which were related; if they had told better ones, I should have written them down better.

But suppose that I was both the inventor and the scribe (which I was not), I say
that I am not ashamed that they are not all good, because there is no one save God
alone, who can do everything well and perfectly. Charlemagne, who first devised
the Paladins, could not make enough of them to form an army. In a multitude of
things we must be prepared to find diverse qualities. No field was ever so well
cultivated that it contained no nettles, briars and thorns mingled with better
plants.

Moreover since I was speaking to simple young women such as most of you
are, it would have been folly for me to go seeking and striving to find such
exquisite things and to take pains to speak with great measure. However, those
who read these tales can leave those they dislike and read those they like. I do not
want to deceive anybody, and so all these tales bear written at the head a tide
explaining what they contain.

I suppose some people will say that some of the tales are too long. I reply that
for those who have something else to do it is folly to read the tales, even when they
are short. A long time has passed between the day when I began to write and now
when I have come to the end of my labours; but I have not forgotten that I said my
work is offered to those ladies who are unoccupied, and not to others. To those
who read for pastime, no tale can be too long if it succeeds in its object. Brevity
befits students, who labour to spend time usefully, not to make it pass; but not you,
ladies, who have unoccupied all that time you do not spend in love pleasures.
None of you has studied at Athens, Bologna or Paris; and so one must chatter a
little more volubly for you than for those who have sharpened their wits by study.

I have no doubt that others will say that the things related are too full of jests
and jokes, and that it ill befits a grave and weighty man to write such things. To
them I must offer thanks and do thank them that they are so zealously tender of my
good fame. But I shall reply to their objection. I confess I am weighty, and have
often weighed myself.

But, speaking to those who have not weighed me, I must observe that I am not
grave but so light that I float in water. Considering that the friars' sermons, which
are made to censure men's sins, are full of jokes and jests and railleries, I think
that such things do not go ill in my tales, which are written to drive away ladies'
melancholy.

However, if the tales make them laugh too much, they can easily cure that by
reading the lamentations of Jeremiah, the passion of the Saviour and the penitence
of Mary Magdalene. Who can doubt that there will be others who will say that I
have a wicked poisonous tongue, because in some places I have written the truth
about the friars? I mean to pardon those who say that, because it cannot be
believed but that they are moved except by just cause, since the friars are good men
who avoid poverty for the love of God, and do good service to the ladies and say
nothing about it. And if they did not all smell a little of the goat, their company
would be most pleasant.

Yet I confess that there is no stability in the things of this world and that
everything changes. So may it have chanced with my tongue. I do not trust my own

judgment, which I always avoid in matters concerning myself, but one of my women neighbours the other day told me I have the best and sweetest tongue in the world. But, to speak the truth, when that happened there were not many of my tales left to finish. And so let what I have said suffice, as a reply to those who make these objections.

1420

I leave it to every lady to say and think what she pleases; for me it is time to end my words, giving thanks humbly to Him who by His aid and after so much labour has brought me to the desired end.

And you, fair ladies, rest in peace in His grace; and if in reading any of these tales you find any pleasure, remember me.

1425

11. *Letter to Dionisio and Sonnets (Selections)*

Francis Petrarch
(1302-1374)

(trans. by James Harvey Robinson and Henry W. Rolfe)

Petrarch is a transition figure between the Middle Ages and the Renaissance not only by virtue of his dates, but for his work as a scholar and Italian vernacular poet. He was rooted in the transcendental values of the medieval world—and lived much of his life in Avignon (then seat of the Papacy) and Rome. He was also drawn to the humanism of the classical world and encouraged the study of Greek and Latin. The two pulls on his being—the heavenly and the earthly—are evident in his 'Letter to Dioniso' in which he recognizes both comfort from Christian values, and curiosity for this world characteristic of humanism. As a scholar, he sought out, restored, and translated classical texts, hoping to foster a new Golden Age in Christian Europe; as a poet, he was an innovator in content and form (especially the sonnet which he invented). His three hundred sixty six 'rimes', inspired by his passion for Laura (an enigmatic figure), record the course of their affair, and explore in detail the conflicting passions of love: the nuances of pleasure and pain, sensuality and guilt, the claims of the flesh and of the spirit. Though he helped foster the rebirth of classical learning and a new direction for Europe, his fame rests with his 'rimes', which, in their elegance and technical perfection, launched a new direction for lyric poetry.

LETTER TO DIONISIO DA BORGO SAN SEPOLCRO

Today I made the ascent of the highest mountain in the region, which is not improperly called Ventosum. My only motive was the wish to see what so great an elevation had to offer. I have had the expedition in mind for many years; for as you know, I have lived in this region from infancy, having been cast here by that fate which determines the affairs of men. Consequently the mountain, which is visible from a great distance, was ever before my eyes, and I conceived the plan of some time doing what I have at last accomplished today. The idea took hold upon me with especial force when, in re-reading Livy's History of Rome, yesterday, I happened upon the place where Philip of Macedon, the same who waged war

10   against the Romans, ascended Mount Haemus in Thessaly, from whose summit he
     was able, it is said, to see two seas, the Adriatic and the Euxine. Whether this be
     true or false, I have not been able to determine, for the mountain is too far away,
     and writers disagree. Pomponius Mela, the cosmographer—not to mention others
     who have spoken of this occurrence—admits its truth without hesitation; Titus

15   Livius, on the other hand, considers it false. I, assuredly, should not have left the
     question long in doubt, had that mountain been as easy to explore as this one. Let
     us leave this matter to one side, however, and return to my mountain here,—it
     seems to me that a young man in private life may well be excused for attempting
     what an aged king could undertake without arousing criticism.

20   When I came to look about for a companion I found, strangely enough, that
     hardly one among my friends seemed suitable, so rarely do we meet with just the
     right combination of personal tastes and characteristics, even among those who
     are dearest to us. This one was too apathetic, that one over-anxious; this one too
     slow, that one too hasty; one was too sad, another over-cheerful; one more simple,

25   another more sagacious, than I desired. I feared this one's taciturnity and that
     one's loquacity. The heavy deliberation of some repelled me as much as the lean
     incapacity of others. I rejected those who were likely to irritate me by a cold want
     of interest, as well as those who might weary me by their excessive enthusiasm.
     Such defects, however grave, could be borne with at home, for charity suffereth all

30   things, and friendship accepts any burden; but it is quite otherwise on a journey,
     where every weakness becomes much more serious. So, as I was bent upon
     pleasure and anxious that my enjoyment should be unalloyed, I looked about me
     with unusual care, balanced against one another the various characteristics of my
     friends, and without committing any breach of friendship I silently condemned

35   every trait which might prove disagreeable on the way. And—would you believe
     it?—I finally turned homeward for aid, and proposed the ascent to my only
     brother, who is younger than I, and with whom you are well acquainted. He was
     delighted and gratified beyond measure by the thought of holding the place of a
     friend as well as a brother.

40   At the time fixed we left the house, and by evening reached Malaucene, which
     lies at the foot of the mountain, to the north. Having rested there a day, we finally
     made the ascent this morning, with no companions except two servants; and a most
     difficult task it was. The mountain is a very steep and almost inaccessible mass of
     stony soil. But, as the poet[1] has well said, "Remorseless toil conquers all." It was

45   a long day, the air fine. We enjoyed the advantages of vigour of mind and strength
     and agility of body, and everything else essential to those engaged in such an
     undertaking, and so had no other difficulties to face than those of the region itself.
     We found an old shepherd in one of the mountain dales, who tried, at great length,
     to dissuade us from the ascent, saying that some fifty years before he had, in the

50   same ardour of youth, reached the summit, but had gotten for his pains nothing
     except fatigue and regret, and clothes and body torn by the rocks and briars. No

---

[1]Virgil, *Georgics* I, 145–46.

one, so far as he or his companions knew, had ever tried the ascent before or after
him. But his counsels increased rather than diminished our desire to proceed,
since youth is suspicious of warnings. So the old man, finding that his efforts were
55   in vain, went a little way with us, and pointed out a rough path among the rocks,
uttering many admonitions, which he continued to send after us even after we had
left him behind. Surrendering to him all such garments or other possessions as
might prove burdensome to us, we made ready for the ascent, and started off at a
good pace. But, as usually happens, fatigue quickly followed upon our excessive
60   exertion, and we soon came to a halt at the top of a certain cliff. Upon starting on
again we went more slowly, and I especially advanced along the rocky way with
a more deliberate step. While my brother chose a direct path straight upon the
ridge, I weakly took an easier one which really descended. When I was called
back, and the right road was shown me, I replied that I hoped to find a better way
65   round on the other side, and that I did not mind going farther if the path were only
less steep. This was just an excuse for my laziness; and when the others had
already reached a considerable height I was still wandering in the valleys. I had
failed to find an easier path, and had only increased the distance and difficulty of
the ascent. At last I became disgusted with the intricate way I had chosen, and
70   resolved to ascend without much ado. When I reached my brother, who, while
waiting for me, had ample opportunity for rest, I was tired and irritated. We
walked along together for a time, but hardly had we passed the first spur when I
forgot about the circuitous route which I had just tried, and took a lower one
again. Once more I followed an easy, roundabout path through winding valleys,
75   only to find myself soon in my old difficulty. I was simply trying to avoid the
exertion of the ascent; but no human ingenuity can alter the nature of things, or
cause anything to reach a height by going down. Suffice it to say that, much to my
vexation and my brother's amusement, I made this same mistake three times or more
during a few hours.
80   After being frequently misled in this way, I finally sat down in a valley and
transferred my winged thoughts from things corporeal to the immaterial,
addressing myself as follows:—"What thou hast repeatedly experienced today in
the ascent of this mountain, happens to thee, as to many, in the journey toward the
blessed life. But this is not so readily perceived by men, since the motions of the
85   body are obvious and external while those of the soul are invisible and hidden.
Yes, the life which we call blessed is to be sought for on a high eminence, and strait
is the way that leads to it. Many, also, are the hills that lie between, and we must
ascend, by a glorious stairway, from strength to strength. At the top is at once the
end of our struggles and the goal for which we are bound. All wish to reach this
90   goal, but, as Ovid says, "To wish is little; we must long with the utmost eagerness
to gain our end." Thou certainly dost ardently desire, as well as simply wish,
unless thou deceivest thyself in this matter, as in so many others. What, then, doth
hold thee back? Nothing, assuredly, except that thou wouldst take a path which
seems at first thought, more easy, leading through low and worldly pleasures. But
95   nevertheless in the end, after long wanderings, thou must perforce either climb the

steeper path, under the burden of tasks foolishly deferred, to its blessed culmination, or lie down in the valley of thy sins, and (I shudder to think of it!), if the shadow of death overtake thee, spend an eternal night amid constant torments." These thoughts stimulated both body and mind in a wonderful degree
100 for facing the difficulties which yet remained. Oh, that I might traverse in spirit that other road for which I long day and night, even as today I overcome material obstacles by my bodily exertions! And I know not why it should not be far easier, since the swift immortal soul can reach its goal in the twinkling of an eye, without passing through space, while my progress today was necessarily slow, dependent
105 as I was upon a failing body weighed down by heavy members.

One peak of the mountain, the highest of all, the country people call "Sonny," why, I do not know, unless by antiphrasis, as I have sometimes suspected in other instances; for the peak in question would seem to be the father of all surrounding ones. On its top is a little level place, and here we could at least rest our tired
110 bodies.

Now, my father, since you have followed the thoughts that spurred me on in my ascent, listen to the rest of the story, and devote one hour I pray you, to reviewing the experiences of my entire day. At first, owing to the unaccustomed quality of the air and the effect of the great sweep of view spread out before me, I
115 stood like one dazed. I beheld the clouds under our feet, and what I had read of Athos and Olympus seemed less incredible as I myself witnessed the same things form a mountain of less fame. I turned my eyes toward Italy, wither my heart most inclined. The Alps, rugged and snow-capped, seemed to rise close by, although they were really at a great distance; the very same Alps through which that fierce
120 enemy of the Roman name once made his way, bursting the rocks, if we may believe the report, by the application of vinegar. I sighed, I must confess, for the skies of Italy, which I beheld rather with my mind than with my eyes. An inexpressible longing came over me to see once more my friend and my country. At the same time I reproached myself for this double weakness, springing, as it did, from a soul not
125 yet steeled to manly resistance. And yet there were excuses for both of these cravings, and a number of distinguished writers might be summoned to support me.

Then a new idea took possession of me, and I shifted my thoughts to a consideration of time rather than place. "Today it is ten years since, having completed thy youthful studies, thou didst leave Bologna. Eternal God! In the name
130 of immutable wisdom, think what alterations in thy character this intervening period has beheld! I can calmly recall past storms. The time may come when I can review in due order all the experiences of the past, saying with St. Augustine, 'I desire to recall my foul actions and the carnal corruption of my soul, not because I love them, but that I may the more love thee, O my God.' Much that is doubtful and
135 evil still clings to me, but what I once loved, that I love no longer. And yet what am I saying? I still love it, but with shame, but with heaviness of heart. Now, at last, I have confessed the truth. So it is, I love, but love what I would not love, what I would that I might hate. Though loath to do so, though constrained, though sad and sorrowing, still I do love, and I feel in my miserable self the truth of the

140 well known words, 'I will hate if I can; if not, I will love against my will.' Three
years have not yet passed since that perverse and wicked passion which had a
firm grasp upon me and held undisputed sway in my heart began to discover a
rebellious opponent, who was unwilling longer to yield obedience. These two
adversaries have joined in close combat for the supremacy, and for a long time
145 now a harassing and doubtful war has been waged in the field of my thoughts."

Thus I turned over the ten years in my mind, and then, fixing my anxious gaze
on the future, I asked myself, "If, perchance, thou shouldst prolong this uncertain
life of thine for yet two lustres, and shouldst make an advance toward virtue
proportionate to the distance to which thou hast departed from thine original
150 infatuation during the past two years, since the new longing first encountered the
old, couldst thou, on reaching thy fortieth year, face death, if not with complete
assurance, at least with hopefulness, calmly dismissing from thy thoughts the
residuum of life as it faded into old age?"

These and similar reflections occurred to me, my father. I rejoiced in my
155 progress, mourned my weaknesses, and commiserated the universal instability of
human conduct. I had well-nigh forgotten where I was and our object in coming;
but at last I dismissed my anxieties, which were better suited to other
surroundings, and resolved to look about me and see what we had come to see. The
sinking sun and the lengthening shadows of the mountains were already warning
160 us that the time was near at hand when we must go. As if suddenly wakened from
sleep, I turned about and gazed toward the west. I was unable to discern the
summits of the Pyrenees, which form the barrier between France and Spain; not
because of any intervening obstacle that I know of but owing simply to the
insufficiency of our mortal vision. But I could see with utmost clearness, off to the
165 right, the mountains of the region about Lyons, and to the left the bay of
Marseilles and the waters that lash the shores of Aigues Mortes, altho' all these
places were so distant that it would require a journey of several days to reach
them. Under our very eyes flowed the Rhone.

While I was thus dividing my thoughts, now turning my attention to some
170 terrestrial object that lay before me, now raising my soul, as I had done my body,
to higher planes, it occurred to me to look into my copy of St. Augustine's
Confessions, a gift that I owe to your love and that I always have about me, in
memory of both the author and the giver. I opened the compact little volume, small
indeed in size, but of infinite charm, with the intention of reading whatever came
175 to hand, for I could happen upon nothing that would be otherwise than edifying
and devout. Now it chanced that the tenth book presented itself. My brother,
waiting to hear something of St. Augustine's from my lips, stood attentively by. I
call him, and God too, to witness that where I first fixed my eyes it was written:
"And men go about to wonder at the heights of the mountains, and the mightily
180 waves of the sea, and the wide sweep of rivers, and the circuit of the ocean, and
the revolution to the stars, but themselves they consider not." I was abashed, and
asking my brother (who was anxious to hear more), not to annoy me I closed the
book, angry with myself that I should still be admiring earthly things who might

185 long ago have learned from even the pagan philosophers that nothing is wonderful but the soul, which, when great itself, finds nothing great outside itself. Then, in truth, I was satisfied that I had seen enough of the mountain; I turned my inward eye upon myself, and from that time not a syllable fell from my lips until we had reached the bottom again. Those words had given me occupation enough, for I could not believe that it was by a mere accident that I happened upon them. What I

190 had there read I believed to be addressed to me and to no other, remembering that St. Augustine had once suspected the same thing in his own case, when, on opening the book of the Apostle,[2] as he himself tells us, the first words that he saw there were, "Not in rioting and drunkenness, not in chambering and wantonness, not in strife and envying. But put ye on the Lord Jesus Christ, and make not provision

195 for the flesh, to fulfil the lusts thereof."

The same thing happened earlier to St. Anthony, when he was listening to the Gospel[3] where it is written, "If thou wilt be perfect, go and sell that thou hast, and give to the poor, and thou shalt have treasure in heaven: and come and follow me." Believing this scripture to have been read for his especial benefit, as his

200 biographer Athanasius says, he guided himself by its aid to the Kingdom of Heaven. And as Anthony on hearing these words waited for nothing more, and as Augustine upon reading the Apostle's admonition sought no farther, so I concluded my reading in the few words which I have given. I thought in silence of the lack of good counsel in us mortals, who neglect what is noblest in ourselves,

205 scatter our energies in all directions, and waste ourselves in a vain show, because we look about us for what is to be found only within. I wondered at the natural nobility of our soul, save when it debases itself of its own free will, and deserts its original estate, turning what God has given it for its honour into dishonour. How many times, think you, did I turn back that day, to glance at the summit of the

210 mountain, which seemed scarcely a cubit high compared with the range of human contemplation,—when it is not immersed in the foul mire of earth? with every downward step I asked myself this: If we are ready to endure a little nearer heaven, how can a soul struggling toward God, up to the steeps of human pride and human destiny, fear any cross or prison or sting of fortune? How few, I

215 thought, but are diverted from their path by the fear of difficulties or the love of ease! How happy the lot of those few, if any such ere be! It is to them, assuredly, that the poet[4] was thinking, when he wrote:

Happy the man who is skilled to understand
Nature's hid causes; who beneath his feet
220 All terrors casts, and death's relentless doom,
And the loud roar of greedy Acheron.

---

[2]Paul, in his Letter to the Romans 13.13–14.
[3]Matthew 19:21.
[4]Virgil, *Georgics* II, 490–92.

How earnestly should we strive, not to stand on mountain-tops but to trample beneath us those appetites which spring from earthly impulses.

225 With no consciousness of the difficulties of the way, amidst these preoccupations which I have so frankly revealed, we came, long after dark, but with the full moon lending us its friendly light, to the little inn which we had left that morning before dawn. The time during which the servants have been occupied in preparing our supper, I have spent in a secluded part of the house, hurriedly jotting down these experiences on the spur of the moment, lest, in case my task were

230 postponed, my mood should change on leaving the place, and so my interest in writing flag.

You will see, my dearest father, that I wish nothing to be concealed from you, for I am careful to describe to you not only life in general but even my individual reflections. And I beseech you, in turn, to pray that these vague and wandering

235 thoughts of mine may some time become firmly fixed, and, after having been vainly tossed about from one interest to another, may direct themselves at last toward the single, true, certain, and everlasting good.

SONNETS (SELECTIONS)

(trans. by Anthony Mortimer)

I

All you that hear in scattered rhymes the sound
of sighs on which I used to feed my heart
in my first youthful error when, in part,
I was another man, now left behind;

5 for the vain hopes, vain sorrows of my mind,
the tears and discourse of my varied art,
in any who have played a lover's part
pardon and pity too I hope to find.

But now I see too well how I became
10 a tale for common gossip everywhere,
so that I grow ashamed of what I am;

and of my raving still the fruit is shame
and penitence, and last the knowledge clear
that all the world loves is a passing dream.

III

It was that very day on which the sun
in awe of his creator dimmed the ray,
when I was captured, with my guard astray,
for your fine eyes, my lady, bound me then.

5   It hardly seemed the time for me to plan
defence against Love's stroke; I went my way
secure, unwary; so upon that day
of general sorrow all my pains began.

Love found me with no armour for the fight,
10   my eyes an open highway to the heart,
eyes that are now a vent for tears to flow.

And yet he played no honourable part,
wounding me with his shaft in such a state;
he saw you armed and dared not lift the bow.

XIII

When sometimes Love is borne in her sweet face
and comes among the other ladies there,
as each one suddenly seems much less fair,
by so much does my will to love increase.

5   I bless the time, the very hour, the place,
that raised my eyes up to a height so rare,
and say: my soul, your thankfulness declare
that you were rendered worthy of such grace.

From her there comes to you the thought of love
10   which, if you follow, leads to highest good,
careless of all that other men regard;

from her there comes the blithe and graceful mood
that shows the fittest path to heaven above:
and thus my hope already seems to thrive.

XLIX

Though from all lies I have preserved your fame,
giving you all the honour that I may,

ungrateful tongue, you do not yet repay
my faith with honour, but with wrath and shame;

5   for when I need you most to help my aim
in pleading for compassion, then you stay
more cold than ever, and what words you say
have the imperfect utterance of a dream.

And you, my sorrowing tears, each night you go
10   along with me when I would be alone,
and when my peace is near, then you depart;

and you, so prompt to give me grief and pain,
sighs, then you come so brokenly and slow:
my looks alone fail not to speak the heart.

CXXXII

And if this be not love, what is it then?
but if it is love, God, what can love be?
if good, why mortal bitterness to me?
if ill, why is it sweetness that torments?

5   If willingly I burn, why these laments?
if not my will, what use can weeping be?
O living death, delightful agony,
how can you do so much where none consents?

And if I do consent, wrongly I grieve.
10   By such cross winds my fragile bark is blown
I drift unsteered upon the open seas:

in wisdom light, with error so weighed down
that I myself know not the thing I crave,
and burn in winter, and in summer freeze.

CXXXIV

I find no peace, and have no arms for war,
and fear and hope, and burn and yet I freeze,
and fly to heaven, lying on earth's floor,
and nothing hold, and all the world I seize.

5 My jailer opens not, nor locks the door,
 nor binds me to her, nor will loose my ties;
 Love kills me not, nor breaks the chains I wear,
 nor wants me living, nor will grant me ease.

 I have no tongue, and shout; eyeless, I see;
10 I long to perish, and I beg for aid;
 I love another, and myself I hate.

 Weeping I laugh, I feed on misery,
 by death and life so equally dismayed:
 for you, my lady, am I in this state.

CXCIX

 You lovely hand that grip my heart so tight,
 my life enclosing in a little space,
 a hand in which both heaven and nature place
 all study, every art, to show their might;

5 and those five pearls of orient colour bright,
 that only in my wounds leave such sharp trace,
 sweet slender fingers, now Love has the grace
 to bare you for a while to my delight.

 Spotless and delicate and dearest glove,
10 fresh roses and pure ivory encasing,
 when had the world such gentle spoils to show?

 If I could thus the lovely veil remove!
 But O the transience of human things:
 even this is theft, and I must let it go.

CCLXVII

 Alas the lovely face, the sweet regard,
 alas the graceful bearing, proud and kind!
 Alas the speech by which the rebel mind
 was humbled and the coward given heart!

5 And O alas the smile that sent the dart
 which now makes death the only hope I find!
 Most royal soul, worthy to rule mankind
 if you had not descended here so late!

Still must I breathe in you, still burn again,
10   since I was yours; and, robbed of you, the less
can any other sorrow grieve the mind.

With hope you filled me and desire
when I parted from the highest living bliss:
but all your words were taken by the wind.

CCXCII

The eyes I spoke of once in words that burn,
the arms and hands and feet and lovely face
that took me from myself for such a space
of time and marked me out from other men;

5   the waving hair of unmixed gold that shone,
the smile that flashed with the angelic rays
that used to make this earth a paradise,
are now a little dust, all feeling gone;

and yet I live, grief and disdain to me,
10   left where the light I cherished never shows,
in fragile bark on the tempestuous sea.

Here let my loving song come to a close,
the vein of my accustomed art is dry,
and this, my lyre, turned at last to tears.

CCCII

My thoughts had lifted me to where she stood
whom I still seek and find on earth no more;
among the souls that the third circle bore,
she came with greater beauty and less pride.

5   She took my hand and said: "If hope can guide,
you will again be with me in this sphere:
for I am she who gave you so much war
and closed my day before the eventide.

No human mind can understand my bliss:
10   you I await and what you loved so much,
the veil I left below where now it lies."

Why did she loose my hand? why did she cease?
for at that holy and unsullied speech
I almost could have stayed in Paradise.

CCCLXIV

For twenty-one long years Love made me burn,
glad in the fire, hopeful in my pain;
my lady took my heart to heaven's domain,
and still he gave me ten more years to mourn;

5   now I am weary, and my life I spurn
for so much error that has almost slain
the seed of virtue, and what years remain,
high God, to you devoutly I return,

contrite and sad for every misspent year,
10   for time I should have put to better use
in seeking peace and shunning passions here.

Lord, having pent me in this prison close,
from everlasting torment draw me clear;
I know my fault and offer no excuse.

12. THE BOOK OF THE COURTIER (SELECTIONS)
(1528)

Baldasar Castiglione

(trans. by Charles Singleton)

The Renaissance revival of classical values, explosion in learning, increase in wealth and social mobility, made 'how to' manuals popular among the literate population of Europe. As Machiavelli composed his controversial manual for Princes, so Castiglione provides his readers with an idealized antidote to the Prince's relativist morality. Influenced by Plato's Symposium *and* Republic, The Courtier *is both a demonstration and a discourse on the art of becoming an accomplished aristocratic gentleman, a 'Renaissance Man.' The discussions over four evenings at the palace of the Duke of Urbino examine the physical, mental, and spiritual education necessary for a courtier and cover a wide range of topics of concern to the Renaissance humanists. The courtier is especially selected as exemplar, for in his capacity as advisor to kings and princes, he must not only be accomplished in dress, manners, martial and cultured arts, but be politically astute and know how to discern seeming from actual, the false from the true. The humanist education prescribed in* The Courtier *constitutes the philosophic rationale for a liberal arts education.*

BOOK I

To Messer Alfonso Ariosto

[1] I have long wondered, dearest messer Alfonso, which of two things was the more difficult for me: to deny you what you have repeatedly and so insistently asked of me, or to do it. For, on the one hand, it seemed very hard for me to deny a thing—especially when it was something praiseworthy—to one whom I love most
5   dearly and by whom I feel I am most dearly loved; yet, on the other hand, to undertake a thing which I was not sure I could finish seemed unbecoming to one who esteems just censure as much as it ought to be esteemed. Finally, after much thought, I have resolved that I would try in this to see how much aid to diligence might be had from affection and the intense desire that I have to please, which, in
10   things generally, is so wont to increase men's industry.

Now, you have asked me to write my opinion as to what form of Courtiership most befits a gentleman living at the courts of princes, by which he can have both the knowledge and the ability to serve them in every reasonable thing, thereby winning favor from them and praise from others: in short, what manner of man he must be who deserves the name of Perfect Courtier, without defect of any kind. Wherefore, considering this request, I say that, had it not seemed to me more blameworthy to be judged by you to be wanting in love than by others to be wanting in prudence, I should have eschewed this labor, out of fear of being thought rash by all who know what a difficult thing it is to choose, from among so great a variety of customs as are followed at the courts of Christendom, the most perfect form and, as it were, the flower of Courtiership. For custom often makes the same things pleasing and displeasing to us; whence it come about sometimes that the customs, dress, ceremonies, and fashions that were once prized become despised; and, contrariwise, the despised become prized. Hence, it is clearly seen that usage is more powerful than reason in introducing new things among us and in blotting out old things; and anyone who tries to judge of perfection in such matters is often deceived. For which reason, since I am well aware of this and of many another difficulty in the matter whereof it is proposed that I should write, I am forced to excuse myself somewhat and to submit evidence that this is an error (if indeed it can be called error) which I share with you, so that, if I am to be blamed for it, that blame will be shared by you, because your having put upon me a burden beyond my powers must not be deemed a lesser fault than my own acceptance of it.

So let us now make a beginning of our subject, and, if that be possible, let form such a Courtier that any prince worthy of being served by him, even though he have but small dominion, may still be called a very great lord.

In these books we shall not follow any set order or rule of distinct precepts, as is most often the custom in teaching anything whatever, but, following the manner of many ancient writers, and to revive a pleasant memory, we shall rehearse some discussions which took place among men singularly qualified in such matters. And even though I was not present and did not take part in them, being in England at the time when they occurred, I learned of them shortly thereafter from a person who gave me a faithful report of them; and I shall attempt to recall them accurately, in so far as my memory permits, so that you may know what was judged and thought in this matter by men worthy of the highest praise, and in whose judgment on all things one may have unquestioned faith. Nor will it be beside the purpose to give some account of the occasion of the discussions that took place, so that in due order we may come to the end at which our discourse aims.

[2] On the slopes of the Apennines toward the Adriatic, at almost the center of Italy, is situated, as everyone knows, the little city of Urbino. And although it sits among hills that are perhaps not as pleasant as those we see in many other places, still it has been blessed by Heaven with a most fertile and bountiful countryside, so that, besides the wholesomeness of the air, it abounds in all the

55   necessities of life. But among the greater blessings that can be claimed for it, this I
      believe to be the chief, that for a long time now it has been ruled by excellent lords
      (even though, in the universal calamity of the wars of Italy, it was deprived of
      them for a time). But, to look no further, we can cite good proof thereof in the
      glorious memory of Duke Federico, who in his day was the light of Italy. Nor are
60   there wanting many true witnesses still living who can testify to his prudence,
      humanity, justice, generosity, undaunted spirit, to his military prowess, signally
      attested by his many victories, the capture of impregnable places, the sudden
      readiness of his expeditions, the many times when with but small forces he routed
      large and very powerful armies, and the fact that he never lost a single battle; so
65   that not without reason may we compare him to many famous men among the
      ancients.

          Among his other laudable deeds, he built on the rugged site of Urbino a palace
      thought by many the most beautiful to be found anywhere in all Italy and he
      furnished it so well with every suitable thing that it seemed not a palace but a city
70   in the form of a palace; and furnished it not only with what is customary, such as
      silver vases, wall hangings of the richest cloth of gold, silk, and other like things,
      but for ornament he added countless ancient statues of marble and bronze, rare
      paintings, and musical instruments of every sort; nor did he wish to have anything
      there that was not most rare and excellent. Then, at great expense, he collected
75   many very excellent and rare books in Greek, Latin, and Hebrew, all of which he
      adorned with gold and silver, deeming these to be the supreme excellence of his
      great palace.

          [3] Following then the course of nature and being already sixty-five years
      old, he died as gloriously as he had lived, leaving as his successor his only son, a
80   child ten years of age and motherless, named Guidobaldo. This boy, even as he
      was heir to the state, seemed to be heir to all his father's virtues as well, and in his
      remarkable nature began at once to promise more than it seemed right to expect of a
      mortal; so that men judged none of the notable deeds of Duke Federico to be greater
      than his begetting such a son. But Fortune, envious of so great a worth, set herself
85   against his glorious beginning with all her might, so that, before Duke Guido had
      reached the age of twenty, he fell sick of the gout, which grew upon him with
      grievous pain, and in a short time so crippled all his members that he could not
      stand upon his feet or move. Thus, one of the fairest and ablest persons in the
      world was deformed and marred at a tender age.

90   And not even content with this, Fortune opposed him so in his every
      undertaking that he rarely brought to a successful issue anything he tried to do;
      and, although he was very wise in counsel and undaunted in spirit, it seemed that
      whatever he undertook always succeeded ill with him whether in arms or
      anything, great or small; all of which is attested by his many and diverse
95   calamities, which he always bore with such strength of spirit that his virtue was
      never overcome by Fortune; nay, despising her storms with stanch heart, he lived
      in sickness as if in health, and in adversity as if most fortunate, with the greatest
      dignity and esteemed by all. So that, although he was infirm of body in this way,

100 he campaigned with a most honorable rank in the service of their Serene Highnesses Kings Alfonso and Ferdinand the Younger of Naples; and later with Pope Alexander VI, as well as the signories of Venice and Florence.

Then when Julius II became Pope, the Duke was made Captain of the Church; during which time, and following his usual style, he saw to it that his household was filled with very noble and worthy gentlemen, with whom he lived on the most
105 familiar terms, delighting in their company; in which the pleasure he gave others was not less than that which he had from them, being well versed in both Latin and Greek and combining affability and wit with the knowledge of an infinitude of things. Besides this, so much did the greatness of his spirit spur him on that, even though he could not engage personally in chivalric activities as he had once
110 done, he still took the greatest pleasure in seeing others so engaged; and by his words, now criticizing and now praising each man according to his desserts, he showed clearly how much judgment he had in such matters. Wherefore, in jousts and tournaments, in riding, in the handling of every sort of weapon, as well as in revelries, in games, in musical performances, in short, in all exercises befitting
115 noble cavaliers, everyone strove to show himself such as to deserve to be thought worthy of his noble company.

[4] Thus, all the hours of the day were given over to honorable and pleasant exercises both of the body and of the mind; but because, owing to his infirmity, the Duke always retired to sleep very early after supper, everyone usually repaired
120 to the rooms of the Duchess . . . [where] gentle discussion and innocent pleasantries were heard. . . . [Messer Federico proposes the following game:]

[12] "I would have our game this evening be this, that one of this company be chosen and given the task of forming in words a perfect Courtier, setting forth all the conditions and particular qualities that are required of anyone who deserves
125 this name; and that everyone be allowed to speak out against those things which seem not right, as in the schools of the philosophers it is permitted to offer objections to anyone maintaining a thesis.

Messer Federico was going on his discourse when signora Emilia interrupted him, saying: "This, should it please the Duchess, shall be our game for the present."
130 "It does please me," the Duchess replied.

Whereupon nearly all of those present began to say, both to the Duchess and among themselves, that this was the finest game that could possibly be played. And no one waited for the other's answer, but all urged signora Emilia to decide who should begin. And she, turning to the Duchess, said: "Madam, will you
135 command him who it most pleases you have this task, for I do not wish, in choosing one rather than another, to appear to decide which I judge to be more capable than the others in this matter, and so offend anyone."

The Duchess replied: "Nay, make the choice yourself, and take care lest you set others an example of not obeying, prompting them to refuse obedience in their
140 turn."

[14] "Thus, I would have our Courtier born of a noble and genteel family; because it is far less becoming for one of low birth to fail to do virtuous things

than for one of noble birth, who, should he stray from the path of his forebears, stains the family name, and not only fails to achieve anything but loses what has been achieved already. For noble birth is like a bright lamp that makes manifest and visible deeds both good and bad, kindling and spurring on to virtue as much for fear of dishonor as for hope of praise. And since this luster of nobility does not shine forth in the deeds of the lowly born, they lack that spur, as well as that fear of dishonor, nor do they think themselves obliged to go beyond what was done by their forebears; whereas to the wellborn it seems a reproach not to attain at least to the mark set them by their ancestors. Hence, it almost always happens that, in the profession of arms as well as in other worthy pursuits, those who are most distinguished are men of noble birth, because nature has implanted in everything that hidden seed which gives a certain force and quality of its own essence to all that springs from it, making it like itself: as we can see not only in breeds of horses and other animals, but in trees as well, the shoots of which nearly always resemble the trunk; and if they sometimes degenerate, the fault lies with the husbandman. And so it happens with men, who, if they are tended in the right way, are almost always like those from whom they spring, and often are better; but if they lack someone to tend them properly, they grow wild and never attain their full growth.

"It is true that, whether favored by the stars or by nature, some men are born endowed with such graces that they seem not to have been born, but to have been fashioned by the hands of some god, and adorned with every excellence of mind and body; even as there are many others so inept and uncouth that we cannot but think that nature brought them into the world out of spite and mockery. And just as the latter, for the most part, yield little fruit even with constant diligence and good care, so the former with little labor attain to the summit of the highest excellence. And take, as an example, Don Ippolito d'Este, Cardinal of Ferrara, who enjoyed such a happy birth that his person, his appearance, his words, and all his actions are so imbued and ruled by this grace that, although he is young, he evinces among the most aged prelates so grave an authority that he seems more fit to teach than to be taught. Similarly, in conversing with men and women of every station, in play, in laughter, in jest, he shows a special sweetness and such gracious manners that no one who speaks with him or even sees him can do otherwise than feel an enduring affection for him.

"But, to return to our subject, I say that there is a mean to be found between such supreme grace on the one hand and such stupid ineptitude on the other, and . . . those who are not so perfectly endowed by nature can, with care and effort, polish and in great part correct their natural defects. Therefore, besides his noble birth, I would wish the Courtier favored in this other respect, and endowed by nature not only with talent and with beauty of countenance and person, but with that certain grace which we call an 'air', which shall make him at first sight pleasing and lovable to all who see him; and let this be an adornment informing and attending all his actions, giving the promise outwardly that such a one is worthy of the company and the favor of every great lord. . . .

[17] "But to come to some particulars: I hold that the principal and true profession of the Courtier must be that of arms; which I wish him to exercise with vigor; and let him be known among the others as bold, energetic, and faithful to

190 whomever he serves. And the repute of these good qualities will be earned by exercising them in every time and place, inasmuch as one may not ever fail therein without great blame. And, just as among women the name of purity, once stained, is never restored, so the reputation of a gentleman whose profession is arms, if ever in the least way he sullies himself through cowardice or other disgrace,

195 always remains defiled before the world and covered with ignominy. Therefore, the more our Courtier excels in this art, the more will he merit praise . . . let the man we are seeking be exceedingly fierce, harsh and always among the first, wherever the enemy is; and in every other place, humane, modest, reserved, avoiding ostentation above all things as well as that impudent praise of himself by which a

200 man always arouses hatred and disgust in all who hear him. . . .

[22] "There are also other exercises which, although not immediately dependent upon arms, still have much in common therewith and demand much manly vigor; and chief among these is the hunt, it seems to me, because it has a certain resemblance to war. It is a true pastime for great lords, it befits a Courtier,

205 and one understands why it was so much practiced among the ancients. He should also know how to swim , jump, run, throw stones; for, besides their usefulness in war, it is frequently necessary to show one's prowess in such things, whereby a good name is to be won, especially with the crowd (with whom one must reckon after all). Another noble exercise and most suitable for a man at court is the game

210 of tennis which shows off the disposition of body, the quickness and litheness of every member, and all the qualities that are brought out by almost every other exercise. Nor do I deem vaulting on horseback to be less worthy, which, though it is tiring and difficult, serves more than anything else to make a man agile and dextrous; and besides its usefulness, if such agility is accompanied by grace, in my

215 opinion it makes a finer show than any other.

"If, then, our courtier is more than fairly expert in such exercises, I think he ought to put aside all others, such as vaulting on the ground, rope-walking, and the like, which smack of the juggler's trade and little befit a gentleman.

"But since one cannot always engage in such strenuous activities (moreover,

220 persistence causes satiety, and drives away the admiration we have for rare things), we must always give variety to our lives by changing our activities. Hence, I would have our Courtier descend sometimes to quieter and more peaceful exercises. And, in order to escape envy and to enter agreeably into the company of others, let him do all that others do, yet never depart from comely conduct, but

225 behave himself with that good judgment which will not allow him to engage in any folly; let him laugh, jest, banter, frolic, and dance, yet in such a manner as to show always that he is genial and discreet; and let him be full of grace in all that he does or says."

[24] "As I will remember, Count, it seems to me you have repeated several

230 times this evening that the Courtier must accompany his actions, his gestures, his

habits, in short, his every movement, with grace. And it strikes me that you require this in everything as that seasoning without which all the other properties and good qualities would be of little worth. And truly I believe that everyone would easily let himself be persuaded of this, because, by the very meaning of the word, it

235 can be said that he who has grace finds grace. But since you have said that this is often a gift of nature and the heavens, and that, even if it is not quite perfect, it can be much increased by care and industry, those men who are born as fortunate and as rich in such treasure as some we know have little need, it seems to me, of any teacher in this, because such benign favor from heaven lifts them, almost in spite of

240 themselves, higher than they themselves had desired, and makes them not only pleasing but admirable to everyone. Therefore I do not discuss this, it not being in our power to acquire it of ourselves. But as for those who are less endowed by nature and are capable of acquiring grace only if they put forth labor, industry, and care, I would wish to know by what art, by what discipline, by what method,

245 they can gain this grace, both in bodily exercises, in which you deem it to be so necessary, and in every other thing they do or say. Therefore, since by praising this quality so highly you have, as I believe, aroused in all of us an ardent desire, according to the task given you by signora Emilia, you are still bound to satisfy it."

* * * *

250 [26] "But, having thought many times already about how this grace is acquired (leaving aside those who have it from the stars), I have found quite a universal rule which in this matter seems to me valid above all others, and in all human affairs whether in word or deed: and that is to avoid affectation in every way possible as though it were some very rough and dangerous reef; and (to

255 pronounce a new word perhaps) to practice in all things a certain *sprezzatura* [nonchalance], so as to conceal all art and make whatever is done or said appear to be without effort and almost without any thought about it. And I believe much grace comes of this: because everyone knows the difficulty of things that are rare and well done; wherefore facility in such things causes the greatest wonder;

260 whereas, on the other hand, to labor and, as we say, drag forth by the hair of the head, shows an extreme want of grace, and causes everything, no matter how great it may be, to be held in little account.

"Therefore we may call that art true art which does not seem to be art; nor must one be more careful of anything than of concealing it, because if it is

265 discovered, this robs a man of all credit and causes him to be held in slight esteem. And I remember having read of certain most excellent orators in ancient times who, among the other things they did, tried to make everyone believe that they had no knowledge whatever of letters; and, dissembling their knowledge, they made their orations appear to be composed in the simplest manner and according to the

270 dictates of nature and truth rather than of effort and art; which fact, had it been

known, would have inspired in the minds of the people the fear that they could be duped by it.

"So you see how art, or any intent effort, if it is disclosed, deprives everything of grace. Who among you fails to laugh when our messer Pierpaolo
275 dances after his own fashion, with those capers of his, his legs stiff on tiptoe, never moving his head, as if he were a stick of wood, and all this so studied that he really seems to be counting his steps? What eye is so blind as not to see in this the ungainliness of affectation; and not to see the grace of that cool *disinvoltura* [ease] (for when it is a matter of bodily movements many call it that) in many of the men
280 and women here present, who seem in words, in laughter, in posture not to care; or seem to be thinking more of everything than of that, so as to cause all who are watching them to believe that they are almost incapable of making a mistake?"

* * * *

[34] Then signor Morello said: "If this Courtier of ours speaks with so much elegance and gravity, I fear there may be those among us who will not understand
285 him."

"Nay," replied the Count, "all will understand him, because words that are easy to understand can still be elegant. Nor would I have him always speak of grave matters, but of amusing things, of games, jests, and jokes, according to the occasion; but sensibly in everything, with readiness and a lucid fullness; nor must
290 he show vanity or a childish folly in any way. Then, whenever he speaks of anything that is obscure or difficult, I would have him explain his meaning down to a fine point, with precision in both words and thoughts, making every ambiguity clear and plain in a manner that is careful but not tiresome. Likewise, when occasion demands, let him know how to speak with dignity and force, and
295 how to stir up those sentiments which are latent within us, kindling and moving them as the need may be; and speak at other times with such simple candor as to make it seem that nature herself is speaking, to soften such sentiments and inebriate them with sweetness, and all this with such ease as to cause the one who listens to believe that with little effort he too could attain to such excellence—but
300 who, when he tries, discovers that he is very far from it.

* * * *

[44] "I would have him more than passably learned in letters, at least in those studies which we call the humanities. Let him be conversant not only with the Latin language, but with Greek as well, because of the abundance and variety of things that are so divinely written therein. Let him be versed in the poets, as
305 well as in the orators and historians, and let him be practiced also in writing verse and prose, especially in our own vernacular; for, besides the personal satisfaction he will take in this, in this way he will never want for pleasant entertainment with the ladies, who are usually fond of such things. And if, because

of other occupations or lack of study, he does not attain to such a perfection that
310   his writings should merit great praise, let him take care to keep them under cover
so that others will not laugh at him, and let him show them only to a friend who
can be trusted; because at least they will be of profit to him in that, through such
exercise, he will be capable of judging the writing of others. For it very rarely
happens that a man who is unpracticed in writing, however learned he may be,
315   can ever wholly understand the toils and industry of writers, or taste the
sweetness and excellence of styles, and those intrinsic niceties that are often found
in the ancients.

BOOK III

[4]   Then the Magnifico, turning to the Duchess, said: "Since it is your
pleasure, Madam, I will say what I have to say, but with great fear that I shall
give no satisfaction. Certainly, it would cause me far less toil to imagine a lady
worthy of being the queen of the world than to imagine a perfect Court Lady,
5   because I do not know where to find any model for the latter; whereas, for the
Queen, I should not need to go very far, since it would be enough for me to set forth
the divine accomplishments of a lady whom I know and, in contemplating those
accomplishments, set all my thoughts to expressing clearly in words what many
see with their eyes; and if I could do no more, I should have performed my task by
10   merely uttering her name."
Then said the Duchess: "Do not exceed bounds, signor Magnifico, but hold to
the order given, and describe the Court Lady so that such a noble lady may have
someone capable of serving her worthily."
The Magnifico continued: "Then, Madam, in order to show that your
15   commands can induce me to attempt what I do not even know how to do, I will
speak of this excellent Lady as I would wish her to be; and when I have fashioned
her to my taste, and since then I may not have another, like Pygmalion I will take
her for my own. And, though signor Gasparo has said that the same rules which
serve for the Courtier serve also for the Lady, I am of a different opinion; for
20   although some qualities are common to both and are as necessary for a man as for
a woman, there are yet others that befit a woman more than a man, and others that
befit a man and to which a woman ought to be a complete stranger. I say this of
bodily exercises; but above all I think that in her ways, manners, words, gestures,
and bearing, a woman ought to be very unlike a man; for just as he must show a
25   certain solid and sturdy manliness, so it is seemly for a woman to have a soft and
delicate tenderness, with an air of womanly sweetness in her every movement,
which, in her going and staying, and in whatever she says, shall always make her
appear the woman without any resemblance to a man.
"Now, if this precept be added to the rules which these gentlemen have taught
30   the Courtier, then I think she ought to be able to follow many such and adorn
herself with the best accomplishments, as signor Gasparo says. For I hold that
many virtues of the mind are as necessary to a woman as to a man; also, gentle

birth; to avoid affectation, to be naturally graceful in all her actions, to be mannerly, clever, prudent, not arrogant, not envious, not slanderous, not vain, not
35   contentious, not inept, to know how to gain and hold the favor of her mistress and of all others, to perform well and gracefully the exercises that are suitable for women. And I do think that beauty is more necessary to her than to the Courtier, for truly that woman lacks much who lacks beauty. Also she must be more circumspect, and more careful not to give occasion for evil being said of her, and
40   conduct herself so that she may not only escape being sullied by guilt but even by the suspicion of it, for a woman has not so many ways of defending herself against false calumnies as a man has. But since Count Ludovico has set forth in great detail the chief profession of the Courtier, and has insisted that this be arms, I think it is also fitting to state what I judge that of the Court Lady to be, and when I
45   have done this I shall think to have discharged the greater part of my assignment.

    [5] "Leaving aside, then, those virtues of the mind which she is to have in common with the Courtier (such as prudence, magnanimity, continence, and many others), as well as those qualities that befit all (such as kindness, discretion, ability to manage her husband's property and house and children, if she is
50   married, and all qualities that are requisite in a good mother), I say that, in my opinion, in a Lady who lives at court a certain pleasing affability is becoming above all else, whereby she will be able to entertain graciously every kind of man with agreeable and comely conversation suited to the time and place and to the station of the person with whom she speaks, joining to serene and modest manners,
55   and to that comeliness that ought to inform all her actions, a quick vivacity of spirit whereby she will show herself a stranger to all boorishness; but with such a kind manner as to cause her to be thought no less chaste, prudent, and gentle than she is agreeable, witty, and discreet: thus, she must observe a certain mean (difficult to achieve and, as it were, composed of contraries) and must strictly
60   observe certain limit and not exceed them.

    "Now, in her wish to be thought good and pure, this Lady must not be so coy, or appear so to abhor gay company or any talk that is a little loose, as to withdraw as soon as she finds herself involved, for it might easily be thought that she was pretending to be so austere in order to hide something about herself which
65   she feared others might discover; for manners so unbending are always odious. Yet, on the other hand, for the sake of appearing free and amiable she must not utter unseemly words or enter into any immodest and unbridled familiarity or into ways such as might cause others to believe about her what is perhaps not true; but when she finds herself present at such talk, she ought to listen with a light blush of
70   shame.

    "Likewise, she must avoid an error into which I have seen many women fall, which is to gossip and eagerly listen to evil spoken of other women. For those who when they hear of the unchaste ways of other women, bristle and pretend that the thing is incredible and that a woman so immodest is a monster, in making
75   so much of the fault give cause to think that they might be guilty of it themselves. And those others who continually go about prying into other women's love

affairs, relating them in such detail and with such glee, appear envious and desirous that everyone should know of this case in order that the same thing may not through error be imputed to them; and thus they emit certain laughs and assume
80 certain attitudes, making it evident that they relish it all. And the result of this is that men, although they appear to listen to them willingly, usually conceive a bad opinion of such women and have little respect for them, and take these ways of theirs to be an invitation to go further; and they often do go so far with them that it quite justly brings shame upon them, and in the end they esteem them so little as to
85 care nothing for their company, and even come to despise them. On the other hand, there is no man so profligate and so forward as not to have reverence for those women who are esteemed to be good and virtuous, because a certain gravity, tempered with wisdom and goodness, is like a shield against the insolence and brutishness of presumptuous men; wherefore we see that a word, a laugh, or an act
90 of kindness, however small, coming from a virtuous woman is more esteemed by everyone than all the blandishments and caresses of those who so openly show their want of shame—and if they are not unchaste, by their wanton laughter, loquacity, insolence, and scurrilous behavior of this sort, they appear to be so.

[6] "And since words that have no subject matter of importance are vain and
95 puerile, the Court Lady must have not only the good judgment to recognize the kind of person with whom she is speaking, but must have knowledge of many things, in order to entertain that person graciously; and let her know how in her talk to choose those things that are suited to the kind of person with whom she is speaking, and be careful lest, unintentionally, she might sometimes utter words
100 that could offend him. Let her take care not to disgust him by indiscreet praise of herself or by being too prolix. Let her not proceed to mingle serious matters with playful or humorous discourse, or mix jests and jokes with serious talk. Let her not show ineptitude in pretending to know what she does not know, but let her seek modestly to do herself credit in what she does know—in all things avoiding
105 affectation, as has been said. In this way she will be adorned with good manners; she will perform with surpassing grace the bodily exercises that are proper to women; her discourse will be fluent and most prudent, virtuous, and pleasant; thus, she will be not only loved but revered by everyone, and perhaps worthy of being considered the equal of this great Courtier, both in qualities of mind and
110 body."

[11] Then signor Gasparo said: "... it should have been enough for you to make this Court Lady beautiful, discreet, chaste, affable, and able to entertain (without getting a bad name) in dancing music, games, laughter, witticisms, and the other things that we see going on at court every day; but wish to give her
115 knowledge of everything in the world, and allow her those virtues that have so rarely been seen in men during the past centuries, is something one cannot endure or listen to at all.

"Now, that women are perfect creatures, and consequently have less dignity than men, and that they are not capable of the virtues that men are capable of, is
120 something I am not disposed to maintain, because the worthiness of the ladies here

present would be enough to prove me wrong: but I do say that very learned men have written that, since nature always intends and plans to make things most perfect, she would constantly bring forth men if she could; and that when a woman is born, it is a defect or mistake of nature, and contrary to what she would wish to
125   do: as is seen too in the case of one who is born blind, or lame, or with some other defect; and, in trees, the many fruits that never ripen. Thus, a woman can be said to be a creature produced by chance and accident. That such is the case, consider a man's actions and a woman's, and conclude from these regarding the perfection of the one and the other. Nevertheless, since these defects in women are the fault of
130   nature that made them so, we ought not on that account to despise them, or fail to show them the respect which is their due. But to esteem them to be more than what they are seems a manifest error to me."

BOOK IV

[5] [Signor Ottaviano is speaking:] "Therefore, I think that the aim of the perfect Courtier, which we have not spoken of up to now, is so to win for himself, by means of the accomplishments ascribed to him by these gentlemen, the favor and mind of the prince whom he serves that he may be able to tell him, and always will
5   tell him, the truth about everything he needs to know, without fear or risk of displeasing him; and that when he sees the mind of his prince inclined to a wrong action, he may dare to oppose him and in a gentle manner avail himself of the favor acquired by his good accomplishments, so as to dissuade him of every evil intent and bring him to the path of virtue. And thus, having in himself the goodness which
10   these gentlemen attributed to him, together with readiness of wit, charm, prudence, knowledge of letters and of many other things—the Courtier will in every instance be able adroitly to show the prince how much honor and profit will come to him and to his realm from justice, liberality, magnanimity, gentleness, and the other virtues that befit a good prince; and, on the other hand, how much infamy and
15   harm result from the vices opposed to these virtues. . . .
[13] "Therefore, as in the arts, so likewise in virtue it is necessary to have a master who, by his teaching and good reminders, shall stir and awaken in us those moral virtues of which we have the seed enclosed and planted in our souls; and, like a good husbandman, cultivate them and open the way for them by removing
20   from about us the thorns and tares of our appetites which often so over-shadow and choke our minds as not to let them flower or produce those fair fruits which alone we should desire to see born in the human heart.
"In this way, then, justice and shame, which you say Jove sent upon earth to all men, are natural in each one of us. But even as a body without eyes, however
25   robust it may be, often goes astray in moving toward some object, so the root of these virtues which are potentially innate in our minds, often comes to nothing if it is not helped by cultivation. For if it is to pass to action and to a perfect operation, nature alone does not suffice, as has been said, but the practice of art and reason is required to purify and clear the soul by lifting from it the dark veil of ignorance,

30   from which almost all the errors of men proceed—because if good and evil were
      well recognized and understood, no one would fail to prefer good and eschew
      evil. Hence, virtue can almost be called a kind of prudence and a knowledge of
      how to choose the good, and vice a kind of imprudence and ignorance that brings
      us to judge falsely; for men never choose evil, thinking it to be evil, but are deceived
35   by a certain semblance of the good."

      [14] Then signor Gasparo replied: "There are, however, many who know
      well that they are doing evil and yet do it; and this because they put the present
      pleasure which they feel before the punishment which they fear will befall them:
      like thieves, murderers, and other such men."

40   Signor Ottaviano said: "True pleasure is always good and true suffering
      always evil; therefore these men deceive themselves in taking false pleasure for
      true, and true suffering for false; wherefore through false pleasures they often
      incur true sufferings. Therefore the art that teaches how to distinguish the true
      from the false can indeed be learned; and the virtue by which we choose what is
45   truly good and not what falsely appears so can be called true knowledge, more
      profitable to human life than any other, because it removes ignorance, from which,
      as I have said, all evils spring."

                                    * * * *

      [32] [Signor Ottaviano continues:] "Next, I should show him that, of the
      duties that fall to the prince, the most important is justice; for the maintenance
50   whereof wise and proved men ought to be appointed to office, whose prudence
      should be true prudence joined to goodness—otherwise it is not prudence but
      cunning; and when this goodness is wanting, the skill and subtlety of prosecutors
      lead only to the ruin and destruction of law and justice, and, for all that the errors
      are theirs, the blame must fall on him who put them in office.

55   "I should tell how from justice springs that piety toward God which all men
      must have, and especially princes, who ought to love Him above all else, and direct
      all their actions to Him as to the true end; and, as Xenophon said, honor and love
      Him always, but much more when they enjoy prosperity, so that afterward they
      may with more reason feel confident in asking His mercy when they experience
60   some adversity. For it is not possible to govern rightly either one's self or others
      without God's help, Who sometimes to the good sends good fortune as His minister
      to save them from grievous perils; and sometimes adverse fortune to prevent their
      being so lulled by prosperity as to forget Him or human prudence, which often
      remedies ill fortune, as a good player remedies bad throws of the dice by placing
65   his board well. Nor would I neglect to urge the prince to be truly religious—not
      superstitious or given to the folly of incantations and soothsaying; for should he
      join divine piety and true religion to human prudence, he will have good fortune
      on his side and a protecting God ever to increase his prosperity in peace and
      war. . . ."

70   [49] Then signor Gasparo said: "I remember that last evening, in discussing the accomplishments of the Courtier, these gentlemen wished him to be in love; and since, in summarizing what has been said so far, we might conclude that a Courtier who has to lead his prince to virtue by his worth and authority will almost have to be old (because knowledge very rarely comes before a certain age, and

75   especially knowledge in those things that are learned through experience)—I do not know how it can be fitting for him, if he is advanced in age, to be in love. For, as has been said this evening, love is not a good thing in old men, and those things which in young men are the delights, courtesies, and elegances so pleasing to women, in old men amount to madness and ridiculous ineptitude, and whoever

80   indulges in them will cause some women to despise him and others to deride him. So if this Aristotle of yours, as an old Courtier, were in love and did the things that young lovers do (like some whom we have seen in our time), I fear he would forget to instruct his prince, and children would perhaps mock him behind his back, and women would scarcely have any pleasure from him except to poke fun at

85   him."

Then signor Ottaviano said: "As all the other accomplishments assigned to the Courtier suit him, even though he be old, I do not think that we ought at all to deprive him of this happiness of loving."

"Nay," said signor Gasparo, "to deprive him of love is to give him a further

90   perfection and to make him live happily, free of misery and calamity."

[51] Whereupon messer Pietro, having first remained silent for a while, made ready as if to speak of something important, then said: "Gentlemen, in order to show that old men can love not only without blame but sometimes more happily than young men, I am obliged to enter upon a little discourse to explain what love

95   is, and wherein lies the happiness that lovers can have. So I beg you to follow me attentively, for I hope to bring you to see that there is no man here to whom it is unbecoming to be in love, even though he were fifteen or twenty years older than signor Morello."

Then after there was some laughter among the company, messer Pietro

100   continued: "I say, then, that, according to the definition of ancient sages, love is nothing but a certain desire to enjoy beauty; and, as our desire is only for things that are known, knowledge must always precede desire, which by its nature turns to the good but in itself is blind and does not know the good. Therefore nature has ordained that to every cognitive power there shall be joined an appetitive power;

105   and as in our soul there are three modes of cognition, namely, by sense, by reason, and by intellect: so, from sense comes appetite, which we have in common with animals; from reason comes choice, which is proper to man; from intellect, whereby man can communicate with the angels, comes will. Thus, even as sense knows only those things which the senses perceive, appetite desires these and no other; and

110   even as intellect is turned solely to the contemplation of intelligible things, the will feeds only upon spiritual good. Being by nature rational and placed as in the middle between these two extremes, man can choose (by descending to sense or rising to intellect) to turn his desires now in one direction and now in the other.

In these two ways, therefore, men can desire beauty, which name is universally
115   applied to all things, whether natural or artificial, that are made in the good
proportion and due measure that befit their nature.

[52] "But to speak of the beauty we have in mind, namely, that only which is
seen in the human person and especially in the face, and which prompts the ardent
desire we call love, we will say that it is an effluence of the divine goodness,
120   which (although it is shed, like the sun's light, upon all created things), when it
finds a face well proportioned and composed of a certain radiant harmony of
various colors set off by light and shadow and by measured distance and limited
outline, infuses itself therein and shines forth most beautifully and adorns and
illumines with grace and a wondrous splendor the object wherein it shines, like a
125   sunbeam striking upon a beautiful vase of polished gold set with precious gems.
Thus, it agreeably attracts the eyes of men to itself, and, entering through them,
impresses itself upon the soul, and moves and delights it throughout with a new
sweetness; and, by kindling it, inspires it with a desire of itself.

"Then, seized with a desire to enjoy this beauty as something good, if the soul
130   allows itself to be guided by the judgment of sense, it falls into very grave errors,
and judges that the body in which this beauty is seen is the chief cause thereof; and
hence, in order to enjoy that beauty, it deems it necessary to join itself as closely to
that body as it can, which is mistaken; hence, whoever thinks to enjoy that beauty
by possessing the body deceives himself, and is moved, not by true knowledge
135   through rational choice, but by false opinion through sensual appetite: wherefore
the pleasure that is consequent upon this is necessarily false and mistaken.

"Hence, all those lovers who satisfy their unchaste desires with the women
they love meet with one of two evils: for as soon as they have what they desired,
either they feel satiety and tedium or conceive a hatred for the beloved object, as if
140   appetite repented of its error and recognized the deceit practiced upon it by the
false judgment of sense, through which it judged what is bad to be good; or else
they remain in the same desire and yearning, like those who have not actually
attained the end they were seeking. And although, because of the blind opinion
with which they are inebriated, they seem to feel pleasure at the moment, as sick
145   men sometimes dream of a draught from some clear spring, still they are not
satisfied or quieted. And since quiet and satisfaction always follow upon the
possession of the desired good, if that were the true and good end of their desire,
they would remain quiet and satisfied upon possessing it; but they do not. Nay,
deceived by that resemblance, they soon return to their unbridled desire, and in the
150   same turmoil they felt before, once more they experience that furious and burning
thirst for what in vain they hope to possess perfectly. Such lovers therefore love
most unhappily: for either they never attain their desires, which is great
unhappiness, or if they do attain them, they find that they have attained their woe,
and their miseries become even greater miseries; because, both in the beginning and
155   in the midst of this love of theirs, they never feel anything save anguish, torments,
sorrows, sufferings, toils: so that to be pale, dejected, to be in continual tears and

sighs, to be always silent or lamenting, to long for death, in short, to be most unhappy, such are the conditions that are said to befit lovers.

[53] "The cause, then, of this ruin in the minds of men is chiefly sense, which

160   is very potent in youth, because the vigor of flesh and blood in that time of life gives it as much strength as it takes away from reason, and thus easily induces the soul to follow appetite. For, finding itself deep in an earthly prison, and deprived of spiritual contemplation in exercising its office of governing the body, the soul of itself cannot clearly perceive the truth; wherefore, in order to have knowledge, it

165   is obliged to turn to the senses as to its source of knowledge; and so it believes them and bows before them and lets itself be guided by them, especially when they have so much vigor that they almost force it; and being fallacious, they fill it with errors and false opinions.

"Thus, it nearly always happens that young men are wrapped up in this love

170   which is sensual and is an outright rebel to reason; and so they make themselves unworthy of enjoying the graces and benefits which love bestows upon its true subject; nor do they feel any pleasures in love save those which unreasoning animals feel, whereas their distress is far more grievous.

"Therefore on this premise (which is most valid) I affirm that the contrary

175   happens to those who are of a maturer age. For if the latter (when the soul is already less oppressed by the weight of the body, and when the natural heat begins to diminish) are smitten by beauty and direct their desire thereto, guided by rational choice, they are not duped then, but come into perfect possession of beauty. And thus good always comes to them from that possession; because beauty

180   is good; hence, it follows the true love of beauty is most good and holy, always working a good effect in the minds of those who check the perversity of sense with the bridle of reason; which the old can do far more easily than the young. . . ."

[55] Then Count Ludovico said: "Do you think, signor Morello, that beauty is always as good as messer Pietro Bembo says?"

185   "Certainly I do not," replied signor Morello. "Nay, I remember having seen many beautiful women who were very bad, cruel, and spiteful, and this seems to be almost always the case, for beauty makes them proud, and pride makes them cruel."

Count Ludovico said, laughing: "Perhaps they seem cruel to you because they

190   do not grant you what you want; but be instructed by messer Pietro Bembo as to how old men ought to desire beauty, and what they ought to seek in women, and with what they ought to be satisfied; and if you do not go beyond those limits, you shall see that they will be neither proud nor cruel, and will grant you what you wish."

195   Then signor Morello seemed a little annoyed, and said: "I have no wish to know what does not concern me; but be instructed yourself as to how this beauty ought to be desired by young men who are less vigorous and sturdy than their elders."

[56] Here messer Federico, in order to calm signor Morello and to change the

200   subject, did not let Count Ludovico reply, but interrupted him and said: "Perhaps

signor Morello is not entirely wrong in saying that beauty is not always good; for women's beauty is often the cause of countless evils, hatreds, wars, deaths, and destructions in the world; to which the fall of Troy bears sure witness. And, for the most part, beautiful women are either proud or cruel, or brazen (as has been said); but this last signor Morello would not consider to be a fault. There are also many wicked men who are graced with fair looks, and it seems that nature made them so to the end that they might be better able to deceive, and that this fair appearance is like the bait on the hook."

Then messer Pietro Bembo said: "You must not believe that beauty is not always good."

Here Count Ludovico, in order to return to the original subject, interrupted and said: "Since signor Morello is not concerned to know that which so deeply touches him, teach it to me and show me how old men acquire this happiness of love, for it will not trouble me if I am thought old, provided only that I profit by it."

[57] Messer Pietro laughed and said: "I wish first to drive error from the minds of these gentlemen, then I will satisfy you too." And so, beginning again, he said: "Gentlemen, I would not have any of us, like profane and sacrilegious men, incur the wrath of God in speaking ill of beauty, which is a sacred thing. Therefore, in order that signor Morello and messer Federico may be warned and not lose their sight like Stesichorus (which is a most fitting punishment for anyone who despises beauty), I say that beauty springs from God and is like a circle, the center of which is goodness. And hence, as there can be no circle without a center, there can be no beauty without goodness. Thus, a wicked soul rarely inhabits a beautiful body, and for that reason outward beauty is a true sign of inner goodness. And this grace is impressed upon the body in varying degree as an index of the soul, by which it is outwardly known, as with trees in which the beauty of the blossoms is a token of the excellence of the fruit. The same is true of the human body, as we see from the physiognomists, who often discover in the face the character and sometimes the thoughts of men; and what is more, in animals too we discern by the outward aspect the inner qualities which impress themselves upon the body in the degree that is possible. Think how clearly we read anger, ferocity, and pride in the face of the lion, the horse, and the eagle; and a pure and simple innocence in lambs and doves; a cunning guile in foxes and wolves, and so with nearly all other animals.

[58] "Hence the ugly are also wicked, for the most part, and the beautiful are good: and we may say that beauty is the pleasant, cheerful, charming, and desirable face of the good, and that ugliness is the dark, disagreeable, unpleasant, and sorry face of evil. And if you will consider all things, you will find that those which are good and useful always have the grace of beauty in them as well. Behold the constitution of this great fabric of the world, which was made by God for the health and conservation of every created thing, the round heaven, adorned with so many divine lamps, and the earth in the center, surrounded by the elements and sustained by its own weight; the sun, which in its revolving illumines the

245 whole, and in winter approaches the lowest sign, then by degrees climbs in the other direction; and the moon, which derives her light from it, according as it approaches her or draws away from her; and the five other stars which separately travel the same course. These things have an influence upon one another through the coherence of an order so precisely constituted that, if they

250 were in the least changed, they could not exist together, and the world would fall into ruin; and they also have such beauty and grace that the mind of man cannot imagine anything more beautiful.

"Think now how man is constituted, who may be called a little world: in whom we see every part of his body precisely framed, necessarily by skill, and not

255 by chance; and then the form taken as a whole is so beautiful that it would be difficult to decide whether it is utility or grace that is given more to human features and the rest of the body by all the parts, such as the eyes, nose, mouth, ears, arms, breast, and the other members. The same can be said of all the animals: look at the feathers of birds, the leaves and branches of trees, which nature gives

260 them to preserve their being, yet they also have the greatest loveliness.

"Leave nature, and come to art: what is so necessary in ships as the prow, the sides, the yards, the mast, the sails, the helm, the oars, the anchors, and the rigging? Yet all these things are so comely that to one who looks upon them they appear to be devised as much to please as to be useful. Columns and architraves support

265 lofty galleries and palaces, yet they are not therefore less pleasing to the eyes of one who looks upon them than they are useful to the buildings. When men first began to build, they put that middle ridge in their temples and houses, not in order that the buildings might have more grace, but in order that the water might flow off nicely on either side; yet comeliness was soon added to usefulness, so that if a

270 temple were built under a sky where no hail or rain ever fell, it would not seem to have any dignity or beauty if it did not have the ridge of a roof.

[59] "Thus, to call them beautiful is to bestow much praise, not only on things but on the world itself. We are praising when we say beautiful sky, beautiful earth, beautiful sea, beautiful rivers, beautiful lands, beautiful woods, trees,

275 gardens; beautiful cities, beautiful churches, houses, armies. In fine, this gracious and sacred beauty is the supreme adornment of all things; and we may say that the good and the beautiful are somehow one and the same thing is immediately caused by the beauty of the soul, which (as partaker of true divine beauty) graces and beautifies whatever it touches, and especially if the body which it inhabits is not

280 of such base material that the soul cannot impress its character thereon. Therefore beauty is the true trophy of the soul's victory, when with divine power she holds sway over material nature, and by her light conquers the darkness of the body. Hence, we should not say that beauty makes women proud or cruel, even though it may seen so to signor Morello; nor should we impute to beautiful women those

285 enmities, deaths, and destructions of which the unbridled appetites of men are the cause. I will not deny, of course, that it is possible to find beautiful women in the world who are also immodest, but this is not at all because their beauty inclines them to immodesty; nay, it turns them from it and leads them to the path of virtuous

conduct, through the tie that beauty has with goodness. But sometimes a bad
upbringing, the continual urgings of their lovers, gifts, poverty, hope, deceits, fear,
and a thousand other causes can overcome even the steadfastness of beautiful and
good women; and by way of these or similar causes beautiful men can also become
wicked. . . .

[62] [Pietro Bembo continues:] "Therefore when the fair aspect of some
beautiful woman meets his eye, joined to such comely behavior and gentle manners
that he (as one well versed in love) feels that his spirit accords with hers; and as
soon as he notices that his eyes seize upon her image and carry it to his heart; and
when his soul begins to take pleasure in contemplating her and to feel an influence
within that stirs and warms it little by little; and when those lively spirits which
shine forth from her eyes continue to add fresh fuel to the fire—then, at the start,
he ought to administer a quick remedy and arouse his reason, and therewith arm
the fortress of his heart, and so shut out sense and appetite that they cannot enter
there by force or deception. Thus, if the flame is extinguished, the danger is also
extinguished; but if it continues to live and grow, then the Courtier, feeling himself
caught, must firmly resolve to avoid all ugliness of vulgar love, and must enter into
the divine path of love, with reason as his guide. And first he must consider that
the body wherein this beauty shines is not the source from which it springs, but,
rather, that beauty (being an incorporeal thing and, as we have said, a heavenly
ray) loses much of its dignity when it chances to be conjoined with base and
corruptible matter; for the more perfect it is, the less it partakes of matter, and is
most perfect when entirely separated therefrom. And he must consider that, just as
one cannot hear with his palate or smell with his ears, so also beauty can in no
way be enjoyed, nor can the desire it excites in our minds be satisfied through the
sense of touch, but only by way of that sense whereof this beauty is the true object,
namely, the faculty of sight.

"Therefore let him keep aloof from the blind judgment of sense, and with his
eyes enjoy the radiance of his Lady, her grace, her amorous sparkle, the smiles, the
manners and all the other pleasant ornaments of her beauty. Likewise with his
hearing let him enjoy the sweetness of her voice, the modulation of her words, the
harmony of her music (if his lady love be a musician). Thus, he will feed his soul
on the sweetest food by means of these two senses—which partake little of the
corporeal, and are reason's ministers—without passing to any unchaste appetite
through desire for the body.

"Then let him obey, please, and honor his Lady with all reverence, and hold
her dearer than himself, and put her convenience and pleasure before his own, and
love in her the beauty of her mind no less than that of her body. Let him take care
therefore not to allow her to fall into any error, but through admonishment and
good precepts let him always seek to lead her to modesty, temperance, and true
chastity, and see to it that no thoughts arise in her except those that are pure and
free of all blemish of vice; and thus, by sowing virtue in the garden of her fair
mind, he will gather fruits of the most beautiful behavior, and will taste them with

wondrous delight. And this will be the true engendering and expression of beauty in beauty, which some say is the end of Love.

335   "In such a way our Courtier will be most acceptable to his Lady, and she will always show herself obedient, sweet, and affable to him, and as desirous of pleasing him as of being loved by him; and the wishes of both will be most virtuous and harmonious, and so they will both be very happy."

    [65] All were most attentive to Bembo's discourse; and he, pausing a moment, and seeing that no one else spoke, said: "Since you have had me begin to teach 340 happy love to our Courtier who is not young, I wish to lead him even a little further; for it is very dangerous to stop at this point, seeing that the soul is most inclined in the direction of the senses, as we have said several times; and, although reason may choose wisely in its operation and be aware that beauty does not originate in the body, and although it may put a bridle upon unseemly desires, still 345 the continual contemplation of beauty in the body often perverts sound judgment. And even if no other evil resulted therefrom, absence from the beloved brings much suffering with it, because the influence of that beauty gives the lover a wondrous delight when it is present and, by warming his heart, arouses and melts certain dormant and congealed powers in his soul, which, being nourished by the warmth 350 of love, well up around his heart, and send forth through the eyes the spirits that are most subtle vapors made of the purest and brightest part of the blood, that receive the image of her beauty and shape it with a thousand various ornaments. Hence, the soul delights and, as in a stupor, feels, together with the pleasure, the fear and reverence that we are wont to have for sacred things, and judges that it 355 has found its paradise.

    [66] "Therefore the lover who considers beauty only in the body loses this good and this happiness as soon as his beloved lady, by her absence, leaves his eyes deprived of their splendor, and consequently leaves his soul widowed of its good. For when her beauty is thus far away, that amorous influence does not 360 warm his heart as when she was present; wherefore his pores become dry, yet the memory of her beauty still stirs those powers of his soul a little, so that they seek to scatter the spirits abroad; and these, finding the ways shut, have no exit, and yet seek to go forth; and shut in thus, they prick the soul with these goads and cause it to suffer painfully, as children do when the teeth begin to come through the 365 tender gums. And from this come the tears, the sighs, the anguish, and the torments of lovers, because the soul is always in travail and affliction, and wellnigh enters into a furor until such time as the cherished beauty appears to it again; and then suddenly it is quieted and breathes easily, and, being wholly intent upon that beauty, it feeds on sweetest food, nor would it ever depart from so delightful a 370 spectacle.

    "Hence, to escape the torment of this absence and to enjoy beauty without suffering, the Courtier, aided by reason, must turn his desire entirely away from the body and to beauty alone, contemplate it in its simple and pure self, in so far as he is able, and in his imagination give it a shape distinct from all matter; and thus 375 make it loving and dear to his soul, and there enjoy it; and let him keep it with him day and night, in every time and place, without fear of ever losing it, remembering always that the body is something very different from beauty, and not only does not increase beauty but lessens its perfection.

380 "In this way our Courtier who is no longer young will be spared the bitterness and calamities that the young almost always experience: such as jealousies, suspicions, disdain, anger, despairs, and certain wrathful furors by which they are often led so into error that some of them not only beat the women whom they love, but take their own lives. He will do no injury to the husband, father, brothers, or kinsfolk of his beloved Lady; he will in no way defame her; he

385 will never be forced to do the hard thing of curbing his eyes and tongue in order not to disclose his desires to others, or to endure suffering at partings or during absences; for he will always carry his precious treasure with him, shut up in his heart, and will also, by the force of his own imagination, make her beauty much more beautiful than in reality it is.

390 [67] "But among such blessings the lover will find another much greater still, if he will make use of this love as a step by which to mount to a love far more sublime; which he will succeed in doing if he continually considers within himself how narrow a bond it is to be limited always to contemplating the beauty of one body only; and therefore, in order to go beyond such a close limit, he will bring

395 into his thought so many adornments that, by putting together all beauties, he will form a universal concept and will reduce the multitude of these to the unity of that single beauty which sheds itself on human nature generally. And thus he will no longer contemplate the particular beauty of one woman, but that universal beauty which adorns all bodies; and so, dazzled by this greater light, he will not concern

400 himself with the lesser, and, burning with a better flame, he will feel little esteem for what at first he so greatly prized.

"This degree of love, although it is very noble and such that few attain thereto, can still not be called perfect; for, since the imagination is a corporeal faculty, and has no knowledge if not through those principles that are furnished it

405 by the sense, it is not wholly purged of material darkness; and hence, although it may consider this universal beauty in the abstract and in itself alone, yet it does not discern that beauty clearly or without a certain ambiguity, because of the likeness which the shapes in the fantasy have to the body. Wherefore, those who attain this love are like little birds beginning to put on feathers, that although

410 with their weak wings they can lift themselves a little in flight, yet dare not go far from their nest or trust themselves to the winds and open sky.

[68] "Therefore, when our Courtier shall have reached this goal, although he may be called a very happy lover by comparison with those who are submerged in the misery of sensual love, still I would not have him be satisfied, but rather go

415 forward boldly along the lofty path, following the guide that leads him to the goal of true happiness. And thus, instead of going outside himself in thought (as all must who choose to contemplate bodily beauty alone), let him turn within himself, in order to contemplate that beauty which is seen by the eyes of the mind, which begin to be sharp and clear-sighted when those of the body lose the flower of their

420　delight. Then the soul, which has departed from vice and is purged by the study of true philosophy and is given to a spiritual life and is practiced in the things of the intellect, facing toward the contemplation of its own substance, as if wakened from deepest sleep, opens those eyes which all have and few use, and sees in itself a ray of that light which is the true image of the angelic beauty communicated to it,

425　and of which it then communicates a faint image to the body. Thus, when it has grown blind to earthly things, the soul acquires a very keen perception of heavenly things; and sometimes when the native forces of the body are rendered inoperative by assiduous contemplation, or are bound by sleep, then, being no longer fettered by them, the soul senses a certain hidden savor of true angelic

430　beauty, and, ravished by the splendor of that light, begins to kindle and to pursue it so eagerly that it is almost drunk and beside itself in its desire to unite itself to that beauty, thinking to have found the footprint of God, in the contemplation of which it seeks—to rest in its blessed end. And thus, burning with this most happy flame, it rises to its noblest part, which is the intellect; and there, no longer

435　darkened by the obscure night of earthly things, it beholds divine beauty; but still it does not yet quite enjoy that beauty perfectly, because it contemplates it in its own particular intellect merely, which is unable to comprehend vast universal beauty. Wherefore, not content with bestowing this blessing, love gives the soul a greater happiness; for, just as from the particular beauty of one body it guides the

440　soul to the universal beauty of all bodies, so in the highest stage of perfection beauty guides it from the particular intellect to the universal intellect. Hence, the soul, aflame with the most holy fire of true divine love, flies to unite itself with the angelic nature; and not only completely abandons the senses, but has no longer any need of reason's discourse; for, transformed into an angel, it understands all

445　things intelligible, and without any veil or cloud views the wide sea of pure divine beauty, and receives it into itself, enjoying that supreme happiness of which the senses are incapable.

　　　[69] "If, then, the beauties which every day with these clouded eyes of ours we see in corruptible bodies (but which are nothing but dreams and the thinnest

450　shadows of beauty) seem to us so fair and full of grace that they kindle in us a most ardent fire and one of such delight that we judge no felicity able to equal what we sometimes feel when a single glance from a woman's beloved eyes reach us—what happy marvel, what blessed awe, must we think is that which fills the souls that attain to the vision of divine beauty! What sweet flame, what delightful

455　burning, must we think that to be which springs from the fountain of supreme and true beauty-which is the source of every other beauty, which never increases or diminishes: always beautiful, and in itself most simple and equal in every part; like only to itself, and partaking of none other; but so beautiful that all other beautiful things are beautiful because they participate in its beauty.

460　"This is that beauty which is indistinguishable from the highest good, which by its light calls and draws all things unto itself, and not only gives intellect to intellectual things, reason to rational things, sense and desire to sensual things, but to plants also and to stones it communicates motion and the natural instinct

proper to them, as an imprint of itself. Therefore this love is as much greater and
465 happier than the others as the cause that moves it is more excellent; and hence, just
as material fire refines gold, so this most sacred fire in our souls destroys and
consumes what is mortal therein, and quickens and beautifies that celestial part
which, in the senses, was at first dead and buried. This is the Pyre whereon the
poets record that Hercules was burned atop Mount Oeta, and by such burning
470 became divine and immortal after death. This the Burning Bush of Moses, the
Cloven Tongues of Fire, the Fiery Chariot of Elias, which doubles grace and
happiness in the souls of those who are worthy to behold it, when they leave this
earthly baseness and fly toward heaven.

"Therefore let us direct all the thoughts and powers of our souls to this most
475 holy light, that shows us the path leading to heaven; and, following after it and
divesting ourselves of those passions wherewith we were clothed when we fell,
by the ladder that bears the image of sensual beauty at its lowest rung, let us
ascend to the lofty mansion where heavenly, lovely, and true beauty dwells,
which lies hidden in the inmost secret recesses of God, so that profane eyes cannot
480 behold it. Here we shall find a most happy end to our desires, true rest from our
labors, the sure remedy for our miseries, most wholesome medicine for our
illnesses, safest refuge from the dark storms of this life's tempestuous sea."

13. *UTOPIA*
(1515–1516)

Thomas More

(trans. by Henry Morley)

Thomas More, both Sir and Saint, was "a man for all seasons" and supreme exemplar of integrity in the Renaissance. He was a scholar, rose to be chancellor under Henry VIII, and for his refusal to acknowledge Henry as the head of the Church in England (after Henry's divorce from Catherine of Aragon), More was beheaded. His scholarly curiosity, creative imagination, and reliance on rationality are evident in his Utopia. *In the vein of Plato's* Republic, *More composed the work to stimulate discussion about the nature and purpose of the commonweal by offering a fictional account ("utopia" means "nowhere") of a far-off island. That he composed it in Latin (and never published it in England) with a fictional narrator, Raphael Hythloday ("speaker of nonsense"), to report about the Utopian rational society, indicates More's need to veil implicit criticism of contemporary conditions in England.*

BOOK I.

Henry the Eighth, the unconquered King of England, a prince adorned with all the virtues that become a great monarch, having some differences of no small consequence with Charles the most serene prince of Castile, sent me into Flanders, as his ambassador, for treating and composing matters between them. I was
5 colleague and companion to that incomparable man Cuthbert Tonstal, whom the king with such universal applause lately made Master of the Rolls; but of whom I will say nothing; not because I fear that the testimony of a friend will be suspected, but rather because his learning and virtues are too great for me to do them justice, and so well known, that they need not my commendations unless I
10 would, according to the proverb, "Show the sun with a lanthorn." Those that were appointed by the prince to treat with us met us at Bruges, according to agreement; they were all worthy men. The Margrave of Bruges was their head, and the chief man among them; but he that was esteemed the wisest, and that spoke for the rest, was George Temse, the Provost of Casselsee; both art and nature had
15 concurred to make him eloquent: he was very learned in the law; and as he had a great capacity, so by a long practice in affairs he was very dextrous at

unravelling them. After we had several times met without coming to an agreement, they went to Brussels for some days to know the prince's pleasure. And since our business would admit it, I went to Antwerp. While I was there, among many that
20 visited me, there was one that was more acceptable to me than any other, Peter Giles, born at Antwerp, who is a man of great honour, and of a good rank in his town, though less than he deserves; for I do not know if there be anywhere to be found a more learned and a better bred young man: for as he is both a very worthy and a very knowing person, so he is so civil to all men, so particularly kind to his
25 friends, and so full of candour and affection, that there is not perhaps above one or two anywhere to be found that is in all respects so perfect a friend. He is extraordinarily modest, there is no artifice in him; and yet no man has more of a prudent simplicity: his conversation was so pleasant and so innocently cheerful, that his company in a great measure lessened any longings to go back to my
30 country, and to my wife and children, which an absence of four months had quickened very much. One day as I was returning home from Mass at St. Mary's, which is the chief church, and the most frequented of any in Antwerp, I saw him by accident talking with a stranger, who seemed past the flower of his age; his face was tanned, he had a long beard, and his cloak was hanging carelessly about him,
35 so that by his looks and habit I concluded he was a seaman. As soon as Peter saw me, he came and saluted me; and as I was returning his civility, he took me aside, and pointing to him with whom he had been discoursing, he said, "Do you see that man? I was just thinking to bring him to you." I answered, "He should have been very welcome on your account." "And on his own too," replied he, "if you knew
40 the man, for there is none alive that can give so copious an account of unknown nations and countries as he can do; which I know you very much desire." Then said I, "I did not guess amiss, for at first sight I took him for a seaman." "But you are much mistaken," said he, "for he has not sailed as a seaman, but as a traveller, or rather a philosopher. This Raphael, who from his family carries the name of
45 Hythloday, is not ignorant of the Latin tongue, but is eminently learned in the Greek, having applied himself more particularly to that than to the former, because he had given himself much to philosophy, in which he knew that the Romans have left us nothing that is valuable, except what is to be found in Seneca and Cicero. He is a Portuguese by birth, and was so desirous of seeing the world, that he
50 divided his estate among his brothers, run the same hazard as Americus Vesputius, and bore a share in three of his four voyages, that are now published; only he did not return with him in his last, but obtained leave of him almost by force, that he might be one of those twenty-four who were left at the farthest place at which they touched, in their last voyage to New Castile. The leaving him thus did not a little
55 gratify one that was more fond of travelling than of returning home, to be buried in his own country; for he used often to say, that the way to heaven was the same from all places; and he that had no grave, had the heaven still over him. Yet this disposition of mind had cost him dear, if God had not been very gracious to him; for after he, with five Castilians, had travelled over many countries, at last, by
60 strange good fortune, he got to Ceylon, and from thence to Calicut where he very

happily found some Portuguese ships; and, beyond all men's expectations, returned to his native country." When Peter had said this to me, I thanked him for his kindness, in intending to give me the acquaintance of a man whose conversation he knew would be so acceptable; and upon that Raphael and I embraced each other.

65 After those civilities were past which are usual with strangers upon their first meeting, we all went to my house, and entering into the garden, sat down on a green bank, and entertained one another in discourse. He told us, that when Vesputius had sailed away, he and his companions that stayed behind in New Castile, by degrees insinuated themselves into the affections of the people of the

70 country, meeting often with them, and treating them gently: and at last they not only lived among them without danger, but conversed familiarly with them; and got so far into the heart of a prince, whose name and country I have forgot, that he both furnished them plentifully with all things necessary, and also with the conveniences of travelling; both boats when they went by water, and waggons

75 when they travelled over land: he sent with them a very faithful guide, who was to introduce and recommend them to such other princes as they had a mind to see: and after many days' journey, they came to towns, and cities, and to commonwealths, that were both happily governed and well peopled. Under the equator, and as far on both sides of it as the sun moves, there lay vast deserts that were parched with

80 the perpetual heat of the sun; the soil was withered, all things looked dismally, and all places were either quite uninhabited, or abounded with wild beasts and serpents, and some few men, that were neither less wild nor less cruel than the beasts themselves. But as they went farther, a new scene opened, all things grew milder, the air less burning, the soil more verdant, and even the beasts were less

85 wild: and at last there were nations, towns, and cities, that had not only mutual commerce among themselves, and with their neighbours, but traded both by sea and land, to very remote countries. There they found the conveniences of seeing many countries on all hands, for no ship went any voyage into which he and his companions were not very welcome. The first vessels that they saw were flat-

90 bottomed, their sails were made of reeds and wicker woven close together, only some were of leather; but afterwards they found ships made with round keels, and canvas sails, and in all respects like our ships; and the seamen understood both astronomy and navigation. He got wonderfully into their favour, by showing them the use of the needle, of which till then they were utterly ignorant. They sailed

95 before with great caution, and only in summertime, but now they count all seasons alike, trusting wholly to the loadstone, in which they are perhaps more secure than safe; so that there is reason to fear that this discovery, which was thought would prove so much to their advantage, may by their imprudence become an occasion of much mischief to them. But it were too long to dwell on all that he told

100 us he had observed in every place; it would be too great a digression from our present purpose: whatever is necessary to be told, concerning those wise and prudent institutions which he observed among civilized nations, may perhaps be related by us on a more proper occasion. We asked him many questions concerning all these things, to which he answered very willingly; only we made no inquiries

105   after monsters, than which nothing is more common; for everywhere one may hear of ravenous dogs and wolves, and cruel men-eaters; but it is not so easy to find states that are well and wisely governed.

    As he told us of many things that were amiss in those new-discovered countries, so he reckoned up not a few things from which patterns might be taken
110   for correcting the errors of these nations among whom we live; of which an account may be given, as I have already promised, at some other time; for at present I intend only to relate those particulars that he told us of the manners and laws of the Utopians: but I will begin with the occasion that led us to speak of that commonwealth. After Raphael had discoursed with great judgment on the many
115   errors that were both among us and these nations; had treated of the wise institutions both here and there, and had spoken as distinctly of the customs and government of every nation through which he had passed, as if he had spent his whole life in it; Peter being struck with admiration, said, "I wonder, Raphael, how it comes that you enter into no king's service, for I am sure there are none to whom
120   you would not be very acceptable: for your learning and knowledge, both of men and things, is such, that you would not only entertain them very pleasantly, but be of great use to them, by the examples you could set before them, and the advices you could give them; and by this means you would both serve your own interest, and be of great use to all your friends."—"As for my friends," answered he, "I need
125   not be much concerned, having already done for them all that was incumbent on me; for when I was not only in good health, but fresh and young, I distributed that among my kindred and friends which other people do not part with till they are old and sick; when they then unwillingly give that which they can enjoy no longer themselves. I think my friends ought to rest contented with this, and not to expect
130   that for their sakes I should enslave myself to any king whatsoever."—"Soft and fair," said Peter, "I do not mean that you should be a slave to any king, but only that you should assist them, and be useful to them."—"The change of the word," said he, "does not alter the matter."—"But term it as you will," replied Peter, "I do not see any other way in which you can be so useful, both in private to your
135   friends, and to the public, and by which you can make your own condition happier."—"Happier!" answered Raphael, "is that to be compassed in a way so abhorrent to my genius? Now I live as I will, to which I believe few courtiers can pretend. And there are so many that court the favour of great men, that there will be no great loss if they are not troubled either with me or with others of my
140   temper." Upon this, said I, "I perceive, Raphael, that you neither desire wealth nor greatness; and indeed I value and admire such a man much more than I do any of the great men in the world. Yet I think you would do what would well become so generous and philosophical a soul as yours is, if you would apply your time and thoughts to public affairs, even though you may happen to find it a little uneasy to
145   yourself: and this you can never do with so much advantage, as by being taken into the counsel of some great prince, and putting him on noble and worthy actions, which I know you would do if you were in such a post; for the springs both of good and evil flow from the prince, over a whole nation, as from a lasting

150 fountain. So much learning as you have, even without practice in affairs, or so great a practice as you have had, without any other learning, would render you a very fit counsellor to any king whatsoever."—"You are doubly mistaken," said he, "Mr. More, both in your opinion of me, and in the judgment you make of things: for as I have not that capacity that you fancy I have; so, if I had it, the public would not be one jot the better, when I had sacrificed my quiet to it. For most

155 princes apply themselves more to affairs of war than to the useful arts of peace; and in these I neither have any knowledge, nor do I much desire it: they are generally more set on acquiring new kingdoms, right or wrong, than on governing well those they possess. And among the ministers of princes, there are none that are not so wise as to need no assistance, or at least that do not think themselves so

160 wise, that they imagine they need none; and if they court any, it is only those for whom the prince has much personal favour, whom by their fawnings and flatteries they endeavour to fix to their own interests: and indeed Nature has so made us, that we all love to be flattered, and to please ourselves with our own notions. The old crow loves his young, and the ape her cubs. Now if in such a Court, made up of

165 persons who envy all others, and only admire themselves, a person should but propose anything that he had either read in history, or observed in his travels, the rest would think that the reputation of their wisdom would sink, and that their interest would be much depressed, if they could not run it down: and if all other things failed, then they would fly to this, that such or such things pleased our

170 ancestors, and it were well for us if we could but match them. They would set up their rest on such an answer, as a sufficient confutation of all that could be said; as if it were a great misfortune, that any should be found wiser than his ancestors; but though they willingly let go all the good things that were among those of former ages, yet if better things are proposed they cover themselves obstinately

175 with this excuse of reverence to past times. I have met with these proud, morose, and absurd judgments of things in many places, particularly once in England."— "Was you ever there?" said I.—"Yes, I was," answered he, "and stayed some months there, not long after the rebellion in the west was suppressed with a great slaughter of the poor people that were engaged in it.

180 "I was then much obliged to that reverend prelate, John Morton, Archbishop of Canterbury, Cardinal, and Chancellor of England: a man," said he, "Peter (for Mr. More knows well what he was), that was not less venerable for his wisdom and virtues, than for the high character he bore. He was of a middle stature, not broken with age; his looks begot reverence rather than fear; his conversation was

185 easy, but serious and grave; he sometimes took pleasure to try the force of those that came as suitors to him upon business, by speaking sharply, though decently to them, and by that he discovered their spirit and presence of mind, with which he was much delighted, when it did not grow up to impudence, as bearing a great resemblance to his own temper; and he looked on such persons as the fittest men

190 for affairs. He spoke both gracefully and weightily; he was eminently skilled in the law, had a vast understanding, and a prodigious memory; and those excellent talents with which Nature had furnished him, were improved by study and

experience. When I was in England the king depended much on his counsels, and the government seemed to be chiefly supported by him; for from his youth he had been all along practised in affairs; and having passed through many traverses of fortune, he had with great cost acquired a vast stock of wisdom, which is not soon lost when it is purchased so dear. One day when I was dining with him there happened to be at table one of the English lawyers, who took occasion to run out in a high commendation of the severe execution of justice upon thieves, who, as he said, were then hanged so fast, that there were sometimes twenty on one gibbet; and upon that he said he could not wonder enough how it came to pass, that since so few escaped, there were yet so many thieves left who were still robbing in all places. Upon this, I who took the boldness to speak freely before the Cardinal, said, there was no reason to wonder at the matter, since this way of punishing thieves was neither just in itself nor good for the public; for as the severity was too great, so the remedy was not effectual; simple theft not being so great a crime that it ought to cost a man his life, no punishment how severe soever being able to restrain those from robbing who can find out no other way of livelihood. 'In this,' said I, 'not only you in England, but a great part of the world imitate some ill masters that are readier to chastise their scholars than to teach them. There are dreadful punishments enacted against thieves, but it were much better to make such good provisions by which every man might be put in a method how to live, and so be preserved from the fatal necessity of stealing and of dying for it.'—'There has been care enough taken for that,' said he, 'there are many handicrafts, and there is husbandry, by which they may make a shift to live unless they have a greater mind to follow ill courses.'—'That will not serve your turn,' said I, 'for many lose their limbs in civil or foreign wars, as lately in the Cornish rebellion, and some time ago in your wars with France, who being thus mutilated in the service of their king and country, can no more follow their old trades, and are too old to learn new ones: but since wars are only accidental things, and have intervals, let us consider those things that fall out every day. There is a great number of noblemen among you, that are themselves as idle as drones, that subsist on other men's labour, on the labour of their tenants, whom, to raise their revenues, they pare to the quick. This indeed is the only instance of their frugality, for in all other things they are prodigal, even to the beggaring of themselves: but besides this, they carry about with them a great number of idle fellows, who never learned any art by which they may gain their living; and these, as soon as either their lord dies, or they themselves fall sick, are turned out of doors; for your lords are readier to feed idle people, than to take care of the sick; and often the heir is not able to keep together so great a family as his predecessor did. Now when the stomachs of those that are thus turned out of doors, grow keen, they rob no less keenly; and what else can they do? for when, by wandering about, they have worn out both their health and their clothes, and are tattered, and look ghastly, men of quality will not entertain them, and poor men dare not do it; knowing that one who has been bred up in idleness and pleasure, and who was used to walk about with his sword and buckler, despising all the neighbourhood with an insolent scorn, as far below him, is not fit for the spade and mattock: nor will he serve a poor man for so small a hire, and in so low a diet as he can afford to give him.' To this he answered, 'This sort of men ought to be particularly cherished, for in them consists the force of the

240   armies for which we have occasion; since their birth inspires them with a nobler sense of honour, than is to be found among tradesmen or ploughmen.'—'You may as well say,' replied I, 'that you must cherish thieves on the account of wars, for you will never want the one, as long as you have the other; and as robbers prove sometimes gallant soldiers, so soldiers often prove brave robbers; so near an

245   alliance there is between those two sorts of life. But this bad custom, so common among you, of keeping many servants, is not peculiar to this nation. In France there is yet a more pestiferous sort of people, for the whole country is full of soldiers, still kept up in time of peace; if such a state of a nation can be called a peace: and these are kept in pay upon the same account that you plead for those idle retainers

250   about noblemen; this being a maxim of those pretended statesmen that it is necessary for the public safety, to have a good body of veteran soldiers ever in readiness. They think raw men are not to be depended on, and they sometimes seek occasions for making war, that they may train up their soldiers in the art of cutting throats; or as Sallust observed, for keeping their hands in use, that they

255   may not grow dull by too long an intermission. But France has learned to its cost, how dangerous it is to feed such beasts. The fate of the Romans, Carthaginians, and Syrians, and many other nations and cities, which were both overturned and quite ruined by those standing armies, should make others wiser: and the folly of this maxim of the French, appears plainly even from this, that their trained

260   soldiers often find your raw men prove too hard for them; of which I will not say much, lest you may think I flatter the English. Every day's experience shows, that the mechanics in the towns, or the clowns in the country, are not afraid of fighting with those idle gentlemen, if they are not disabled by some misfortune in their body, or dispirited by extreme want, so that you need not fear that those well-

265   shaped and strong men (for it is only such that noblemen love to keep about them, till they spoil them) who now grow feeble with ease, and are softened with their effeminate manner of life, would be less fit for action if they were well bred and well employed. And it seems very unreasonable, that for the prospect of a war, which you need never have but when you please, you should maintain so many

270   idle men, as will always disturb you in time of peace, which is ever to be more considered than war. But I do not think that this necessity of stealing arises only from hence; there is another cause of it more peculiar to England.'—'What is that?' said the Cardinal.—'The increase of pasture,' said I, 'by which your sheep, which are naturally mild, and easily kept in order, may be said now to devour

275   men, and unpeople, not only villages, but towns; for wherever it is found that the sheep of any soil yield a softer and richer wool than ordinary, there the nobility and gentry, and even those holy men the abbots, not contented with the old rents which their farms yielded, nor thinking it enough that they, living at their ease, do no good to the public, resolve to do it hurt instead of good. They stop the course of

280   agriculture, destroying houses and towns, reserving only the churches, and

enclose grounds that they may lodge their sheep in them. As if forests and parks had swallowed up too little of the land, those worthy countrymen turn the best inhabited places in solitudes; for when an insatiable wretch, who is a plague to his country, resolves to inclose many thousand acres of ground, the owners, as

285   well as tenants, are turned out of their possessions, by tricks, or by main force, or being wearied out with ill usage, they are forced to sell them. By which means those miserable people, both men and women, married and unmarried, old and young, with their poor but numerous families (since country business requires many hands), are all forced to change their seats, not knowing whither to go; and

290   they must sell almost for nothing their household stuff, which could not bring them much money, even though they might stay for a buyer. When that little money is at an end, for it will be soon spent; what is left for them to do, but either to steal and so to be hanged (God knows how justly), or to go about and beg? And if they do this, they are put in prison as idle vagabonds; while they would willingly work,

295   but can find none that will hire them; for there is no more occasion for country labour, to which they have been bred, when there is no arable ground left. One shepherd can look after a flock, which will stock an extent of ground that would require many hands, if it were to be ploughed and reaped. This likewise in many places raises the price of corn. The price of wool is also so risen, that the poor

300   people who were wont to make cloth are no more able to buy it; and this likewise makes many of them idle. For since the increase of pasture, God has punished the avarice of the owners, by a rot among the sheep, which has destroyed vast numbers of them; to us it might have seemed more just had it fell on the owners themselves. But suppose the sheep should increase ever so much, their price is not

305   like to fall; since though they cannot be called a monopoly, because they are not engrossed by one person, yet they are in so few hands, and these are so rich, that as they are not pressed to sell them sooner than they have a mind to it, so they never do it till they have raised the price as high as possible. And on the same account it is, that the other kinds of cattle are so dear, because many villages being

310   pulled down, and all country labour being much neglected, there are none who make it their business to breed them. The rich do not breed cattle as they do sheep, but buy them lean, and at low prices; and after they have fattened them on their grounds, sell them again at high rates. And I do not think that all the inconveniences this will produce are yet observed; for as they sell the cattle dear,

315   so if they are consumed faster than the breeding countries from which they are brought can afford them, then the stock must decrease, and this must needs end in great scarcity; and by these means this your island, which seemed as to this particular the happiest in the world, will suffer much by the cursed avarice of a few persons; besides this, the rising of corn makes all people lessen their families

320   as much as they can; and what can those who are dismissed by them do, but either beg or rob? And to this last, a man of a great mind is much sooner drawn than to the former. Luxury likewise breaks in apace upon you, to set forward your poverty and misery; there is an excessive vanity in apparel, and great cost in diet; and that not only in noblemen's families, but even among tradesmen, among the

325   farmers themselves, and among all ranks of persons. You have also many infamous houses, and besides those that are known, the taverns and alehouses are no better; add to these, dice, cards, tables, football, tennis, and quoits, in which money runs fast away; and those that are initiated into them, must in the conclusion betake themselves to robbing for a supply. Banish these plagues, and give orders that

330   those who have dispeopled so much soil, may either rebuild the villages they have pulled down, or let out their grounds to such as will do it: restrain those engrossings of the rich, that are as bad almost as monopolies; leave fewer occasions to idleness; let agriculture be set up again, and the manufacture of the wool be regulated, that so there may be work found for those companies of idle

335   people whom want forces to be thieves, or who now being idle vagabonds, or useless servants, will certainly grow thieves at last. If you do not find a remedy to these evils, it is a vain thing to boast of your severity in punishing theft, which though it may have the appearance of justice, yet in itself is neither just nor convenient. For if you suffer your people to be ill educated, and their manners to

340   be corrupted from their infancy, and then punish them for those crimes to which their first education disposed them, what else is to be concluded from this, but that you first make thieves and then punish them?'

       "While I was talking thus, the counsellor who was present had prepared an answer, and had resolved to resume all I had said, according to the formality of a

345   debate, in which things are generally repeated more faithfully than they are answered; as if the chief trial to be made were of men's memories. 'You have talked prettily for a stranger,' said he, 'having heard of many things among us which you have not been able to consider well; but I will make the whole matter plain to you, and will first repeat in order all that you have said, then I will show how much

350   your ignorance of our affairs has misled you, and will in the last place answer all your arguments. And that I may begin where I promised, there were four things—' 'Hold your peace,' said the Cardinal, 'this will take up too much time; therefore we will at present ease you of the trouble of answering, and reserve it to our next meeting, which shall be to-morrow, if Raphael's affairs and yours can admit of it.

355   But, Raphael,' said he to me, 'I would gladly know upon what reason it is that you think theft ought not to be punished by death? Would you give way to it? Or do you propose any other punishment that will be more useful to the public? For since death does not restrain theft, if men thought their lives would be safe, what fear or force could restrain ill men? On the contrary, they would look on the

360   mitigation of the punishment as an invitation to commit more crimes.' I answered, 'It seems to me a very unjust thing to take away a man's life for a little money; for nothing in the world can be of equal value with a man's life: and if it is said, that it is not for the money that one suffers, but for his breaking the law, I must say, extreme justice is an extreme injury; for we ought not to approve of these terrible

365   laws that make the smallest offences capital, nor of that opinion of the Stoics, that makes all crimes equal, as if there were no difference to be made between the killing a man and the taking his purse, between which, if we examine things impartially, there is no likeness nor proportion. God has commanded us not to kill,

370 and shall we kill so easily for a little money? But if one shall say, that by that law we are only forbid to kill any, except when the laws of the land allow of it; upon the same grounds, laws may be made in some cases to allow of adultery and perjury: for God, having taken from us the right of disposing, either of our own or of other people's lives, if it is pretended that the mutual consent of man in making laws can authorize manslaughter in cases in which God has given us no example,

375 that it frees people from the obligation of the divine law, and so makes murder a lawful action; what is this, but to give a preference to human laws before the divine? And if this is once admitted, by the same rule men may in all other things put what restrictions they please upon the laws of God. If by the Mosaical law, though it was rough and severe, as being a yoke laid on an obstinate and servile

380 nation, men were only fined, and not put to death for theft, we cannot imagine that in this new law of mercy, in which God treats us with the tenderness of a father, He has given us a greater license to cruelty than He did to the Jews. Upon these reasons it is, that I think putting thieves to death is not lawful; and it is plain and obvious that it is absurd, and of ill consequence to the commonwealth, that a thief

385 and a murderer should be equally punished; for if a robber sees that his danger is the same, if he is convicted of theft as if he were guilty of murder, this will naturally incite him to kill the person whom otherwise he would only have robbed, since if the punishment is the same, there is more security, and less danger of discovery, when he that can best make it is put out of the way; so that terrifying

390 thieves too much, provokes them to cruelty.

"'But as to the question, what more convenient way of punishment can be found? I think it is much more easier to find out that, than to invent anything that is worse; why should we doubt but the way that was so long in use among the old Romans, who understood so well the arts of government, was very proper for

395 their punishment? They condemned such as they found guilty of great crimes, to work their whole lives in quarries, or to dig in mines with chains about them. But the method that I liked best, was that which I observed in my travels in Persia, among the Polylerits, who are a considerable and well-governed people. They play a yearly tribute to the King of Persia; but in all other respects they are a free

400 nation, and governed by their own laws. They lie far from the sea, and are environed with hills; and being contented with the productions of their own country, which is very fruitful, they have little commerce with any other nation; and as they, according to the genius of their country, have no inclination to enlarge their borders; so their mountains, and the pension they pay to the Persian,

405 secure them from all invasions. Thus they have no wars among them; they live rather conveniently than with splendour, and may be rather called a happy nation, than either eminent or famous; for I do not think that they are known so much as by name to any but their next neighbours. Those that are found guilty of theft among them, are bound to make restitution to the owner, and not as it is in

410 other places, to the prince, for they reckon that the prince has no more right to the stolen goods than the thief; but if that which was stolen is no more in being, then the goods of the thieves are estimated, and restitution being made out of them, the

415 remainder is given to their wives and children: and they themselves are condemned to serve in the public works, but are neither imprisoned, nor chained, unless there happened to be some extraordinary circumstances in their crimes. They go about loose and free, working for the public. If they are idle or backward to work, they are whipped; but if they work hard, they are well used and treated without any mark of reproach, only the lists of them are called always at night, and then they are shut up. They suffer no other uneasiness, but this of constant labour; for as

420 they work for the public, so they are well entertained out of the public stock, which is done differently in different places. In some places, whatever is bestowed on them, is raised by a charitable contribution; and though this way may seem uncertain, yet so merciful are the inclinations of that people, that they are plentifully supplied by it; but in other places, public revenues are set aside for

425 them; or there is a constant tax of a poll-money raised for their maintenance. In some places they are set to no public work, but every private man that has occasion to hire workmen, goes to the market-places and hires them of the public, a little lower than he would do a freeman: if they go lazily about their task, he may quicken them with the whip. By this means there is always some piece of work or

430 other to be done by them; and beside their livelihood, they earn somewhat still to the public. They all wear a peculiar habit, of one certain colour, and their hair is cropped a little above their ears, and a piece of one of their ears is cut off. Their friends are allowed to give them either meat, drink, or clothes, so they are of their proper colour; but it is death, both to the giver and taker, if they give them money;

435 nor is it less penal for any freeman to take money from them, upon any account whatsoever: and it is also death for any of these slaves (so they are called) to handle arms. Those of every division of the country are distinguished by a peculiar mark; which it is capital for them to lay aside, to go out of their bounds, or to talk with a slave of another jurisdiction; and the very attempt of an escape is

440 no less penal than an escape itself; it is death for any other slave to be accessory to it; and if a freeman engages in it he is condemned to slavery. Those that discover it are rewarded; if freemen, in money; and if slaves, with liberty, together with a pardon for being accessory to it; that so they might find their account, rather in repenting of their engaging in such a design, than in persisting in it.

445 "These are their laws and rules in relation to robbery; and it is obvious that they are as advantageous as they are mild and gentle; since vice is not only destroyed, and men preserved, but they treated in such a manner as to make them see the necessity of being honest, and of employing the rest of their lives in repairing the injuries they have formerly done to society. Nor is there any hazard

450 of their falling back to their old customs: and so little do travellers apprehend mischief from them, that they generally make use of them for guides, from one jurisdiction to another; for there is nothing left them by which they can rob, or be the better for it, since as they are disarmed, so the very having of money is a sufficient conviction: and as they are certainly punished if discovered, so they

455 cannot hope to escape; for their habit being in all the parts of it different from what is commonly worn, they cannot fly away, unless they would go naked, and

even then their cropped ear would betray them. The only danger to be feared from them, is their conspiring against the government: but those of one division and neighbourhood can do nothing to any purpose, unless a general conspiracy were laid amongst all the slaves of the several jurisdictions, which cannot be done, since they cannot meet or talk together; nor will any venture on a design where the concealment would be so dangerous, and the discovery so profitable. None are quite hopeless of recovering their freedom, since by their obedience and patience, and by giving good grounds to believe that they will change their manner of life for the future, they may expect at last to obtain their liberty: and some are every year restored to it, upon the good character that is given of them.—When I had related all this, I added, that I did not see why such a method might not be followed with more advantage, than could ever be expected from that severe justice which the counsellor magnified so much. To this he answered, that it could never take place in England, without endangering the whole nation. As he said this, he shook his head, made some grimaces, and held his peace, while all the company seemed of his opinion, except the Cardinal, who said that it was not easy to form a judgment of its success, since it was a method that never yet had been tried. 'But if,' said he, 'when the sentence of death was passed upon a thief, the prince would reprieve him for a while, and make the experiment upon him, denying him the privilege of a sanctuary; and then if it had a good effect upon him, it might take place; and if it did not succeed, the worst would be, to execute the sentence on the condemned persons at last. And I do not see,' added he, 'why it would be either unjust, inconvenient, or at all dangerous, to admit of such a delay: in my opinion, the vagabonds ought to be treated in the same manner; against whom, though we have made many laws, yet we have not been able to gain our end.' When the Cardinal had done, they all commended the motion, though they had despised it when it came from me; but more particularly commended what related to the vagabonds, because it was his own observation.

"I do not know whether it be worth while to tell what followed, for it was very ridiculous; but I shall venture at it, for as it is not foreign to this matter, so some good use may be made of it. There was a jester standing by, that counterfeited the fool so naturally, that he seemed to be really one. The jests which he offered were so cold and dull, that we laughed more at him than at them; yet sometimes he said, as it were by chance, things that were not unpleasant; so as to justify the old proverb, 'That he who throws the dice often, will sometimes have a lucky hit.' When one of the company had said, that I had taken care of the thieves, and the Cardinal had taken care of the vagabonds, so that there remained nothing but that some public provision might be made for the poor, whom sickness or old age had disabled from labour. 'Leave that to me,' said the fool, 'and I shall take care of them; for there is no sort of people whose sight I abhor more, having been so often vexed with them, and with their sad complaints; but as dolefully soever as they have told their tale, they could never prevail so far as to draw one penny from me: for either I had no mind to give them anything, or when I had a mind to do it, I had nothing to give them: and they now know me so well, that they will not lose their labour, but let me pass without giving me any trouble, because they hope for nothing, no more in faith than if I were a priest: but I would have a law made, for sending all these beggars to monasteries, the men to the Benedictines to be made lay-brothers, and the women to be nuns.' The Cardinal smiled, and approved of it

505 in jest; but the rest liked it in earnest. There was a divine present, who though he was a grave morose man, yet he was so pleased with this reflection that was made on the priests and the monks, that he began to play with the fool, and said to him, 'This will not deliver you from all beggars, except you take care of us friars.'— 'That is done already,' answered the fool, 'for the Cardinal has provided for you,

510 by what he proposed for restraining vagabonds, and setting them to work, for I know no vagabonds like you.' This was well entertained by the whole company, who looking at the Cardinal, perceived that he was not ill pleased at it; only the friar himself was vexed, as may be easily imagined, and fell into such a passion, that he could not forbear railing at the fool, and calling him knave, slanderer,

515 backbiter, and son of perdition, and then cited some dreadful threatenings out of the Scriptures against him. Now the jester thought he was in his element, and laid about him freely. 'Good friar,' said he, 'be not angry, for it is written, "In patience possess your soul."'—The friar answered (for I shall give you his own words), 'I am not angry, you hangman; at least I do not sin in it, for the Psalmist says, "Be ye

520 angry, and sin not."'—Upon this the Cardinal admonished him gently, and wished him to govern his passions. 'No, my lord,' said he, 'I speak not but from a good zeal, which I ought to have; for holy men have had a good zeal, as it is said, "The zeal of thy house hath eaten me up;" and we sing in our church, that those who mocked Elisha as he went up to the house of God, felt the effects of his zeal; which

525 that mocker, that rogue, that scoundrel, will perhaps feel.'—'You do this perhaps with a good intention,' said the Cardinal; 'but in my opinion, it were wiser in you, and perhaps better for you, not to engage in so ridiculous a contest with a fool.'— 'No, my lord,' answered he, 'that were not wisely done; for Solomon, the wisest of men, said, "Answer a fool according to his folly"; which I now do, and show him

530 the ditch into which he will fall, if he is not aware of it; for if the many mockers of Elisha, who was but one bald man, felt the effect of his zeal, what will become of one mocker of so many friars, among whom there are so many bald men? We have likewise a Bull, by which all that jeer us are excommunicated.'—When the Cardinal saw that there was no end of this matter, he made a sign to the fool to

535 withdraw, turned the discourse another way; and soon after rose from the table, and dismissing us, went to hear causes.

"Thus, Mr. More, I have run out into a tedious story, of the length of which I had been ashamed, if, as you earnestly begged it of me, I had not observed you to hearken to it, as if you had no mind to lose any part of it. I might have contracted

540 it, but I resolved to give it you at large, that you might observe how those that despised what I had proposed, no sooner perceived that the Cardinal did not dislike it, but presently approved of it, fawned so on him, and flattered him to such a degree, that they in good earnest applauded those things that he only liked in jest.

545 And from hence you may gather , how little courtiers would value either me or my counsels."

To this I answered, "You have done me a great kindness in this relation; for as everything has been related by you, both wisely and pleasantly, so you have made me imagine that I was in my own country, and grown young again, by recalling that good Cardinal to my thoughts, in whose family I was bred from my
550 childhood: and though you are upon other accounts very dear to me, yet you are the dearer, because you honour his memory so much; but after all this I cannot change my opinion; for I still think that if you could overcome that aversion which you have to the Courts of Princes, you might, by the advice which it is in your power to give, do a great deal of good to mankind; and this is the chief design that
555 every good man ought to propose to himself in living: for your friend Plato thinks that nations will be happy, when either philosophers become kings, or kings become philosophers; it is no wonder if we are so far from that happiness, while philosophers will not think it their duty to assist kings with their councils."—
"They are not so base-minded," said he, "but that they would willingly do it;
560 many of them have already done it by their books, if those that are in power would but hearken to their good advice. But Plato judged right, that except kings themselves became philosophers, they who from their childhood are corrupted with false notions, would never fall in entirely with the councils of philosophers, and this he himself found to be true in the person of Dionysius.

565 "Do not you think, that if I were about any king, proposing good laws to him, and endeavouring to root out all the cursed seeds of evil that I found in him, I should either be turned out of his Court, or at least be laughed at for my pains? For instance, what could it signify if I were about the King of France, and were called into his cabinet-council, where several wise men, in his hearing, were
570 proposing many expedients: as by what arts and practices Milan may be kept; and Naples, that had so oft slipped out of their hands, recovered; how the Venetians, and after them the rest of Italy, may be subdued; and then how Flanders, Brabant, and all Burgundy, and some other kingdoms which he has swallowed already in his designs, may be added to his empire. One proposes a league with the Venetians,
575 to be kept as long as he finds his account in it, and that he ought to communicate councils with them, and give them some share of the spoil, till his success makes him need or fear them less, and then it will be easily taken out of their hands. Another proposes the hiring the Germans, and the securing the Switzers by pensions. Another proposes the gaining the Emperor by money, which is
580 omnipotent with him. Another proposes a peace with the King of Arragon, and in order to cement it, the yielding up the King of Navarre's pretensions. Another thinks the Prince of Castile is to be wrought on, by the hope of an alliance; and that some of his courtiers are to be gained to the French faction by pensions. The hardest point of all is what to do with England: a treaty of peace is to be set on
585 foot, and if their alliance is not to be depended on, yet it is to be made as firm as possible; and they are to be called friends, but suspected as enemies: therefore the Scots are to be kept in readiness, to be let loose upon England on every occasion:

590 and some banished nobleman is to be supported underhand (for by the league it
cannot be done avowedly) who has a pretension to the crown, by which means
that suspected prince may be kept in awe. Now when things are in so great a
fermentation, and so many gallant men are joining councils, how to carry on the
war, if so mean a man as I should stand up, and wish them to change all their
councils, to let Italy alone and stay at home, since the kingdom of France was
indeed greater than could be well governed by one man; that therefore he ought not
595 to think of adding others to it: and if after this, I should propose to them the
resolutions of the Achorians, a people that lie on the south-east of Utopia, who
long ago engaged in war, in order to add to the dominions of their prince another
kingdom, to which he had some pretensions by an ancient alliance. This they
conquered, but found that the trouble of keeping it was equal to that by which it
600 was gained; that the conquered people were always either in rebellion or exposed
to foreign invasions, while they were obliged to be incessantly at war, either for
or against them, and consequently could never disband their army; that in the
meantime they were oppressed with taxes, their money went out of the kingdom,
their blood was spilt for the glory of their king, without procuring the least
605 advantage to the people, who received not the smallest benefit from it even in time
of peace; and that their manners being corrupted by a long war, robbery and
murders everywhere abounded, and their laws fell into contempt; while their king,
distracted with the care of two kingdoms, was the less able to apply his mind to
the interests of either. When they saw this, and that there would be no end to these
610 evils, they by joint councils made an humble address to their king, desiring him to
choose which of the two kingdoms he had the greatest mind to keep, since he could
not hold both; for they were too great a people to be governed by a divided king,
since no man would willingly have a groom that should be in common between him
and another. Upon which the good prince was forced to quit his new kingdom to
615 one of his friends (who was not long after dethroned), and to be contented with
his old one. To this I would add, that after all those warlike attempts, the vast
confusions, and the consumption both of treasure and of people that must follow
them; perhaps upon some misfortune, they might be forced to throw up all at last;
therefore it seemed much more eligible that the king should improve his ancient
620 kingdom all he could, and make it flourish as much as possible; that he should love
his people, and be beloved of them; that he should live among them, govern them
gently, and let other kingdoms alone, since that which had fallen to his share was
big enough, if not too big for him. Pray how do you think would such a speech as
this be heard?"—"I confess," said I, "I think not very well."
625 "But what," said he, "if I should sort with another kind of ministers, whose
chief contrivances and consultations were, by what art the prince's treasures
might be increased. Where one proposes raising the value of specie when the king's
debts are large, and lowering it when his revenues were to come in, that so he
might both pay much with a little, and in a little receive a great deal: another
630 proposes a pretence of a war, that money might be raised in order to carry it on,
and that a peace be concluded as soon as that was done; and this with such

appearances of religion as might work on the people, and make them impute it to the piety of their prince, and to his tenderness for the lives of his subjects. A third offers some old musty laws, that have been antiquated by a long disuse; and

635 which, as they had been forgotten by all the subjects, so they had been also broken by them; and proposes the levying the penalties of these laws, that as it would bring in a vast treasure, so there might be a very good pretence for it, since it would look like the executing a law, and the doing of justice. A fourth proposes the prohibiting of many things under severe penalties, especially such as were

640 against the interest of the people, and then the dispensing with these prohibitions upon great compositions, to those who might find their advantage in breaking them. This would serve two ends, both of them acceptable to many; for as those whose avarice led them to transgress would be severely fined, so the selling licenses dear would look as if a prince were tender of his people, and would not

645 easily, or at low rates, dispense with anything that might be against the public good. Another proposes that the judges must be made sure, that they may declare always in favour of the prerogative, that they must be often sent for to Court, that the king may hear them argue those points in which he is concerned; since how unjust soever any of his pretensions may be, yet still some one or other of them,

650 either out of contradiction to others, or the pride of singularity, or to make their court, would find out some pretence or other to give the king a fair colour to carry the point: for if the judges but differ in opinion, the clearest thing in the world is made by that means disputable, and truth being once brought in question, the king may then take advantage to expound the law for his own profit; while the judges

655 that stand out will be brought over, either out of fear or modesty; and they being thus gained, all of them may be sent to the bench to give sentence boldly, as the king would have it: for fair pretences will never be wanting when sentence is to be given in the prince's favour. It will either be said that equity lies of his side, or some words in the law will be found sounding that way, or some forced sense will

660 be put on them; and when all other things fail, the king's undoubted prerogative will be pretended, as that which is above all law; and to which a religious judge ought to have a special regard. Thus all consent to that maxim of Crassus, that a prince cannot have treasure enough, since he must maintain his armies out of it: that a king, even though he would, can do nothing unjustly; that all property is in

665 him, not excepting the very persons of his subjects: and that no man has any other property, but that which the king out of his goodness thinks fit to leave him. And they think it is the prince's interest, that there be as little of this left as may be, as if it were his advantage that his people should have neither riches nor liberty; since these things make them less easy and less willing to submit to a cruel and

670 unjust government; whereas necessity and poverty blunts them, makes them patient, beats them down, and breaks that height of spirit, that might otherwise dispose them to rebel. Now what if after all these propositions were made, I should rise up and assert, that such councils were both unbecoming a king, and mischievous to him: and that not only his honour but his safety consisted more in his people's

675 wealth, than in his own; if I should show that they choose a king for their own

sake, and not for his; that by his care and endeavours they may be both easy and safe; and that therefore a prince ought to take more care of his people's happiness than of his own, as a shepherd is to take more care of his flock than of himself. It is also certain, that they are much mistaken that think the poverty of a nation is a

680 means of the public safety. Who quarrel more than beggars? Who does more earnestly long for a change, than he that is uneasy in his present circumstances? And who run to create confusions with so desperate a boldness, as those who have nothing to lose, hope to gain by them? If a king should fall under such contempt or envy, that he could not keep his subjects in their duty, but by

685 oppression and ill usage, and by rendering them poor and miserable, it were certainly better for him to quit his kingdom, than to retain it by such methods, as makes him while he keeps the name of authority, lose the majesty due to it. Nor is it so becoming the dignity of a king to reign over beggars, as over rich and happy subjects. And therefore Fabricius, a man of a noble and exalted temper, said, he

690 would rather govern rich men, than be rich himself; since for one man to abound in wealth and pleasure, when all about him are mourning and groaning, is to be a gaoler and not a king. He is an unskilful physician, that cannot cure one disease without casting his patient into another: so he that can find no other way for correcting the errors of his people, but by taking from them the conveniences of life,

695 shows that he knows not what it is to govern a free nation. He himself ought rather to shake off his sloth, or to lay down his pride; for the contempt or hatred that his people have for him, takes its rise from the vices in himself. Let him live upon what belongs to him, without wronging others, and accommodate his expense to his revenue. Let him punish crimes, and by his wise conduct let him endeavour

700 to prevent them, rather than be severe when he has suffered them to be too common: let him not rashly revive laws that are abrogated by disuse, especially if they have been long forgotten, and never wanted; and let him never take any penalty for the breach of them, to which a judge would not give way in a private man, but would look on him as a crafty and unjust person for pretending to it. To these things I

705 would add, that law among the Macarians, a people that lie not far from Utopia, by which their king, on the day on which he begins to reign, is tied by an oath confirmed by solemn sacrifices, never to have at once above a thousand pounds of gold in his treasures, or so much silver as is equal to that in value. This law, they tell us, was made by an excellent king, who had more regard to the riches of his

710 country than to his own wealth; and therefore provided against the heaping up of so much treasure, as might impoverish the people. He thought that moderate sum might be sufficient for any accident; if either the king had occasion for it against rebels, or the kingdom against the invasion of an enemy; but that it was not enough to encourage a prince to invade other men's rights, a circumstance that was the

715 chief cause of his making that law. He also thought that it was a good provision for that free circulation of money, so necessary for the course of commerce and exchange: and when a king must distribute all those extraordinary accessions that increase treasure beyond the due pitch, it makes him less disposed to oppress his

subjects. Such a king as this will be the terror of ill men, and will be beloved by all
720 the good.

"If, I say, I should talk of these or such like things, to men that had taken their
bias another way, how deaf would they be to all I could say?"—"No doubt, very
deaf," answered I; "and no wonder, for one is never to offer at propositions or
advice that we are certain will not be entertained. Discourses so much out of the
725 road could not avail anything, nor have any effect on men whose minds were
prepossessed with different sentiments. This philosophical way of speculation is
not unpleasant among friends in a free conversation, but there is no room for it in
the Courts of Princes where great affairs are carried on by authority."—"That is
what I was saying," replied he, "that there is no room for philosophy in the
730 Courts of Princes."—"Yes, there is," said I, "but not for this speculative
philosophy that makes everything to be alike fitting at all times: but there is
another philosophy that is more pliable, that knows its proper scene,
accommodates itself to it, and teaches a man with propriety and decency to act that
part which has fallen to his share. If when one of Plautus's comedies is upon the
735 stage and a company of servants are acting their parts, you should come out in the
garb of a philosopher, and repeat out of 'Octavia' a discourse of Seneca's to Nero,
would it not be better for you to say nothing than by mixing things of such
different natures to make an impertinent tragi-comedy? For you spoil and corrupt
the play that is in hand when you mix with it things of an opposite nature, even
740 though they are much better. Therefore go through with the play that is acting the
best you can, and do not confound it because another that is pleasanter comes into
your thoughts. It is even so in a commonwealth, and in the councils of princes; if ill
opinions cannot be quite rooted out, and you cannot cure some received vice
according to your wishes, you must not therefore abandon the commonwealth, for
745 the same reasons you should not forsake the ship in a storm because you cannot
command the winds. You are not obliged to assault people with discourses that
are out of their road, when you see that their received notions must prevent your
making an impression upon them. You ought rather to cast about and to manage
things with all the dexterity in your power, so that if you are not able to make
750 them go well they may be as little ill as possible; for except all men were good
everything cannot be right, and that is a blessing that I do not at present hope to
see."—"According to your arguments," answered he, "all that I could be able to
do would be to preserve myself from being mad while I endeavoured to cure the
madness of others; for if I speak truth, I must repeat what I have said to you; and
755 as for lying, whether a philosopher can do it or not, I cannot tell, I am sure I
cannot do it. But though these discourses may be uneasy and ungrateful to them, I
do not see why they should seem foolish or extravagant: indeed if I should either
propose such things as Plato has contrived in his commonwealth, or as the
Utopians practise in theirs, though they might seem better, as certainly they are,
760 yet they are so different from our establishment, which is founded on property,
there being no such thing among them, that I could not expect that it would have
any effect on them; but such discourses as mine, which only call past evils to mind

and give warning of what may follow, have nothing in them that is so absurd that they may not be used at any time, for they can only be unpleasant to those who are

765 resolved to run headlong the contrary way; and if we must let alone everything as absurd or extravagant which by reason of the wicked lives of many may seem uncouth, we must, even among Christians, give over pressing the greatest part of those things that Christ hath taught us, though He has commanded us not to conceal them, but to proclaim on the house-tops that which He taught in secret. The

770 greatest parts of His precepts are more opposite to the lives of the men of this age than any part of my discourse has been; but the preachers seemed to have learned that craft to which you advise me, for they observing that the world would not willingly suit their lives to the rules that Christ has given, have fitted His doctrine as if it had been a leaden rule, to their lives, that so some way or other they might

775 agree with one another. But I see no other effect of this compliance except it be that men become more secure in their wickedness by it. And this is all the success that I can have in a Court, for I must always differ from the rest, and then I shall signify nothing; or if I agree with them, I shall then only help forward their madness. I do not comprehend what you mean by your casting about, or by the bending and

780 handling things so dexterously, that if they go not well they may go as little ill as may be; for in Courts they will not bear with a man's holding his peace or conniving at what others do. A man must barefacedly approve of the worst counsels, and consent to the blackest designs: so that he would pass for a spy, or possibly for a traitor, that did but coldly approve of such wicked practices: and

785 therefore when a man is engaged in such a society, he will be so far from being able to mend matters by his casting about, as you call it, that he will find no occasions of doing any good: the ill company will sooner corrupt him, than be the better for him: or if notwithstanding all their ill company, he still remains steady and innocent, yet their follies and knavery will be imputed to him; and by mixing

790 counsels with them, he must bear his share of all the blame that belongs wholly to others.

"It was no ill simile by which Plato set forth the unreasonableness of a philosopher's meddling with government. If a man, says he, was to see a great company run out every day into the rain, and take delight in being wet; if he knew

795 that it would be to no purpose for him to go and persuade them to return to their houses, in order to avoid the storm, and that all that could be expected by his going to speak to them would be that he himself should be as wet as they, it would be best for him to keep within doors; and since he had not influence enough to correct other people's folly, to take care to preserve himself.

800 "Though to speak plainly my real sentiments, I must freely own, that as long as there is any property, and while money is the standard of all other things, I cannot think that a nation can be governed either justly or happily; not justly, because the best things will fall to the share of the worst men; nor happily, because all things will be divided among a few (and even these are not in all

805 respects happy), the rest being left to be absolutely miserable. Therefore when I reflect on the wise and good constitution of the Utopians, among whom all things

are so well governed, and with so few laws; where virtue hath its due reward, and yet there is such an equality, that every man lives in plenty; when I compare with them so many other nations that are still making new laws, and yet can never

810 bring their constitution to a right regulation, where notwithstanding every one has his property; yet all the laws that they can invent have not the power either to obtain or preserve it, or even to enable men certainly to distinguish what is their own from what is another's; of which the many lawsuits that every day break out, and are eternally depending, give too plain a demonstration; when, I say, I balance

815 all these things in my thoughts, I grow more favourable to Plato, and do not wonder that he resolved not to make any laws for such as would not submit to a community of all things: for so wise a man could not but foresee that the setting all upon a level was the only way to make a nation happy, which cannot be obtained so long as there is property: for when every man draws to himself all that he can

820 compass, by one title or another, it must needs follow, that how plentiful soever a nation may be, yet a few dividing the wealth of it among themselves, the rest must fall into indigence. So that there will be two sorts of people among them, who deserve that their fortunes should be interchanged; the former useless, but wicked and ravenous; and the latter, who by their constant industry serve the public more

825 than themselves, sincere and modest men. From whence I am persuaded, that till property is taken away there can be no equitable or just distribution of things, nor can the world be happily governed: for as long as that is maintained, the greatest and the far best part of mankind will be still oppressed with a load of cares and anxieties. I confess without taking it quite away, those pressures that lie on a

830 great part of mankind may be made lighter; but they can never be quite removed. For if laws were made to determine at how great an extent in soil, and at how much money every man must stop, to limit the prince that he might not grow too great, and to restrain the people that they might not become too insolent, and that none might factiously aspire to public employments; which ought neither to be

835 sold, nor made burthensome by a great expense; since otherwise those that serve in them would be tempted to reimburse themselves by cheats and violence, and it would become necessary to find out rich men for undergoing those employments which ought rather to be trusted to the wise. These laws, I say, might have such effects, as good diet and care might have on a sick man, whose recovery is

840 desperate: they might allay and mitigate the disease, but it could never be quite healed, nor the body politic be brought again to a good habit, as long as property remains; and it will fall out as in a complication of diseases, that by applying a remedy to one sore, you will provoke another; and that which removes the one ill symptom produces others, while the strengthening one part of the body weakens

845 the rest."—"On the contrary," answered I, "it seems to me that men cannot live conveniently, where, all things are common: how can there be any plenty, where every man will excuse himself from labour? For as the hope of gain doth not excite him, so the confidence that he has in other men's industry may make him slothful: if people come to be pinched with want, and yet cannot dispose of anything as their

850 own; what can follow upon this but perpetual sedition and bloodshed, especially

when the reverence and authority due to magistrates falls to the ground? For I cannot imagine how that can be kept up among those that are in all things equal to one another."—"I do not wonder," said he, "that it appears so to you, since you have no notion, or at least no right one, of such a constitution: but if you had been

855 in Utopia with me, and had seen their laws and rules, as I did, for the space of five years, in which I lived among them; and during which time I was so delighted with them, that indeed I should never have left them, if it had not been to make the discovery of that new world to the Europeans; you would then confess that you had never seen a people so well constituted as they."—"You will not easily

860 persuade me," said Peter, "that any nation in that new world is better governed than those among us. For as our understandings are not worse than theirs, so our government, if I mistake not, being more ancient, a long practice has helped us to find out many conveniences of life: and some happy chances have discovered other things to us, which no man's understanding could ever have invented."—"As for

865 the antiquity, either of their government, or of ours," said he, "you cannot pass a true judgment of it, unless you had read their histories; for if they are to be believed, they had towns among them before these parts were so much as inhabited. And as for those discoveries, that have been either hit on by chance, or made by ingenious men, these might have happened there as well as here. I do not

870 deny but we are more ingenious than they are, but they exceed us much in industry and application. They knew little concerning us before our arrival among them; they call us all by a general name of the nations that lie beyond the Equinoctial Line; for their Chronicle mentions a shipwreck that was made on their coast 1,200 years ago; and that some Romans and Egyptians that were in the ship, getting safe

875 ashore, spent the rest of their days amongst them; and such was their ingenuity, that from this single opportunity they drew the advantage of learning from those unlooked-for guests, and acquired all the useful arts that were then among the Romans, and which were known to these shipwrecked men: and by the hints that they gave them, they themselves found out even some of those arts which they could

880 not fully explain; so happily did they improve that accident, of having some of our people cast upon their shore. But if such an accident has at any time brought any from thence into Europe, we have been so far from improving it, that we do not so much as remember it; as in after-times perhaps it will be forgot by our people that I was ever there. For though they from one such accident made themselves masters of

885 all the good inventions that were among us; yet I believe it would be long before we should learn or put in practice any of the good institutions that are among them. And this is the true cause of their being better governed, and living happier than we, though we come not short of them in point of understanding or outward advantages."—Upon this I said to him, "I earnestly beg you would describe that

890 island very particularly to us. Be not too short, but set out in order all things relating to their soil, their rivers, their towns, their people, their manners, constitution, laws, and, in a word, all that you imagine we desire to know. And you may well imagine that we desire to know everything concerning them, of which we are hitherto ignorant."—"I will do it very willingly," said he, "for I

895   have digested the whole matter carefully; but it will take up some time."—"Let us go then," said I, "first and dine, and then we shall have leisure enough."

He consented. We went in and dined, and after dinner came back, and sat down in the same place. I ordered my servants to take care that none might come and interrupt us. And both Peter and I desired Raphael to be as good as his word.

900   When he saw that we were very intent upon it, he paused a little to recollect himself, and began in this manner.

BOOK II.

The island of Utopia is in the middle two hundred miles broad, and holds almost at the same breadth over a great part of it; but it grows narrower towards both ends. Its figure is not unlike a crescent: between its horns, the sea comes in

905   eleven miles broad, and spreads itself into a great bay, which is environed with land to the compass of about five hundred miles, and is well secured from winds. In this bay there is no great current, the whole coast is, as it were, one continued harbour, which gives all that live in the island great convenience for mutual commerce; but the entry into the bay, occasioned by rocks on the one hand, and

910   shallows on the other, is very dangerous. In the middle of it there is one single rock which appears above water, and may therefore be easily avoided, and on the top of it there is a tower in which a garrison is kept, the other rocks lie under water, and are very dangerous. The channel is known only to the natives, so that if any stranger should enter into the bay, without one of their pilots, he would run great

915   danger of shipwreck; for even they themselves could not pass it safe, if some marks that are on the coast did not direct their way; and if these should be but a little shifted, any fleet that might come against them, how great soever it were, would be certainly lost. On the other side of the island there are likewise many harbours; and the coast is so fortified, both by nature and art, that a small number of men can

920   hinder the descent of a great army. But they report (and there remains good marks of it to make it credible) that this was no island at first, but a part of the continent. Utopus that conquered it (whose name it still carries, for Abraxa was its first name) brought the rude and uncivilized inhabitants into such a good government, and to that measure of politeness, that they now far excel all the rest of mankind;

925   having soon subdued them, he designed to separate them from the continent, and to bring the sea quite round them. To accomplish this, he ordered a deep channel to be dug fifteen miles long; and that the natives might not think he treated them like slaves, he not only forced the inhabitants, but also his own soldiers, to labour in carrying it on. As he set a vast number of men to work, he beyond all men's

930   expectations brought it to a speedy conclusion. And his neighbours who at first laughed at the folly of the undertaking, no sooner saw it brought to perfection, than they were struck with admiration and terror.

There are fifty-four cities in the island, all large and well built: the manners, customs, and laws of which are the same, and they are all contrived as near in the

935   same manner as the ground on which they stand will allow. The nearest lie at

least twenty-four miles distance from one another, and the most remote are not so far distant, but that a man can go on foot in one day front it, to that which lies next it. Every city sends three of their wisest senators once a year to Amaurot, to consult about their common concerns; for that is chief town of the island, being situated near the centre of it, so that it is the most convenient place for their assemblies. The jurisdiction of every city extends at least twenty miles: and where the towns lie wider, they have much more ground: no town desires to enlarge its bounds, for the people consider themselves rather as tenants than landlords. They have built over all the country, farmhouses for husbandmen, which are well contrived, and are furnished with all things necessary for country labour. Inhabitants are sent by turns from the cities to dwell in them; no country family has fewer than forty men and women in it, besides two slaves. There is a master and a mistress set over every family; and over thirty families there is a magistrate. Every year twenty of this family come back to the town, after they have stayed two years in the country; and in their room there are other twenty sent from the town, that they may learn country work from those that have been already one year in the country as they must teach those that come to them the next from the town. By this means such as dwell in those country farms are never ignorant of agriculture, and so commit no errors, which might otherwise be fatal, and bring them under a scarcity of corn. But though there is every year such a shifting of the husbandmen, to prevent any man being forced against his will to follow that hard course of life too long; yet many among them take such pleasure in it, that they desire leave to continue in it many years. These husbandmen till the ground, breed cattle, hew wood, and convey it to the towns, either by land or water, as is most convenient. They breed an infinite multitude of chickens in a very curious manner; for the hens do not sit and hatch them, but vast number of eggs are laid in a gentle and equal heat, in order to be hatched, and they are no sooner out of the shell, and able to stir about, but they seem to consider those that feed them as their mothers, and follow them as other chickens do the hen that hatched them. They breed very few horses, but those they have are full of mettle, and are kept only for exercising their youth in the art of sitting and riding them; for they do not put them to any work, either of ploughing or carriage, in which they employ oxen; for though their horses are stronger, yet they find oxen can hold out longer; and as they are not subject to so many diseases, so they are kept upon a less charge, and with less trouble; and even when they are so worn out, that they are no more fit for labour, they are good meat at last. They sow no corn, but that which is to be their bread; for they drink either wine, cyder, or perry, and often water, sometimes boiled with honey or liquorice, with which they abound; and though they know exactly how much corn will serve every town, and all that tract of country which belongs to it, yet they sow much more, and breed more cattle than are necessary for their consumption; and they give that overplus of which they make no use to their neighbours. When they want anything in the country which it does not produce, they fetch that from the town, without carrying anything in exchange for it. And the magistrates of the town take care to see it given them; for they meet generally in

980 the town once a month upon a festival day. When the time of harvest comes, the magistrates the country send to those in the towns, and let them know how many hands they will need for reaping the harvest; and the number they call for being sent to them, they commonly despatch it all in one day.

OF THEIR TOWNS, PARTICULARLY OF AMAUROT.

He that knows one of their towns, knows them all, they are so like one
985 another, except where the situation makes some difference. I shall therefore describe one of them; and none is so proper as Amaurot; for as none is more eminent, all the rest yielding in precedence to this, because it is the seat of their supreme council; so there was none of them better known to me, I having lived five years altogether in it.
990 It lies upon the side of a hill, or rather a rising ground: its figure is almost square, for from the one side of it, which shoots up almost to the top of the hill, it runs down in a descent for two miles to the river Anider; but it is a little broader the other way that runs along by the bank of that river. The Anider rises about eighty miles above Amaurot in a small spring at first; but other brooks falling into
995 it, of which two are more considerable than the rest. As it runs by Amaurot, it is grown half a mile broad; but it still grows larger and larger, till after sixty miles course below it, it is lost in the ocean, between the town and the sea, and for some miles above the town, it ebbs and flows every six hours, with a strong current. The tide comes up for about thirty miles so full, that there is nothing but salt water
1000 in the river, the fresh water being driven back with its force; and above that, for some miles, the water is brackish; but a little higher, as it runs by the town, it is quite fresh; and when the tide ebbs, it continues fresh all along to the sea. There is a bridge cast over the river, not of timber, but of fair stone, consisting of many stately arches; it lies at that part of the town which is farthest from the sea, so that
1005 ships without any hindrance lie all along the side of the town. There is likewise another river that runs by it, which though it is not great, yet it runs pleasantly, for it rises out of the same hill on which the town stands, and so runs down through it, and falls into the Anider. The inhabitants have fortified the fountain-head of this river, which springs a little without the towns; that so if they should
1010 happen to be besieged, the enemy might not be able to stop or divert the course of the water, nor poison it; from thence it is carried in earthen pipes to the lower streets; and for those places of the town to which the water of that small river cannot be conveyed, they have great cisterns for receiving the rain-water, which supplies the want of the other. The town is compassed with a high and thick wall,
1015 in which there are many towers and forts; there is also a broad and deep dry ditch, set thick with thorns, cast round three sides of the town, and the river is instead of a ditch on the fourth side. The streets are very convenient for all carriage, and are well sheltered from the winds. Their buildings are good, and are so uniform, that a whole side of a street looks like one house. The streets are
1020 twenty feet broad; there lie gardens behind all their houses; these are large but

enclosed with buildings, that on all hands face the streets; so that every house has
both a door to the street, and a back door to the garden. Their doors have all two
leaves, which, as they are easily opened, so they shut of their own accord; and
there being no property among them, every man may freely enter into any house
1025 whatsoever. At every ten years end they shift their houses by lots. They cultivate
their gardens with great care, so that they have both vines, fruits, herbs, and
flowers in them; and all is so well ordered, and so finely kept, that I never saw
gardens anywhere that were both so fruitful and so beautiful as theirs. And this
humour of ordering their gardens so well, is not only kept up by the pleasure they
1030 find in it, but also by an emulation between the inhabitants of the several streets,
who vie with each other; and there is indeed nothing belonging to the whole town
that is both more useful and more pleasant. So that he who founded the town,
seems to have taken care of nothing more than of their gardens; for they say, the
whole scheme of the town was designed at first by Utopus, but he left all that
1035 belonged to the ornament and improvement of it, to be added by those that should
come after him, that being too much for one man to bring to perfection. Their
records, that contain the history of their town and state, are preserved with an
exact care, and run backwards 1,760 years. From these it appears that their
houses were at first low and mean, like cottages, made of any sort of timber, and
1040 were built with mud walls and thatched with straw. But now their houses are
three stories high: the fronts of them are faced either with stone, plastering, or
brick; and between the facings of their walls they throw in their rubbish. Their
roofs are flat, and on them they lay a sort of plaster, which costs very little, and
yet is so tempered that it is not apt to take fire, and yet resists the weather more
1045 than lead. They have great quantities of glass among them, with which they glaze
their windows. They use also in their windows a thin linen cloth, that is so oiled
or gummed that it both keeps out the wind and gives free admission to the light.

OF THEIR MAGISTRATES.

Thirty families choose every year a magistrate, who was anciently called the
Syphogrant, but is now called the Philarch; and over every ten Syphogrants, with
1050 the families subject to them, there is another magistrate, who was anciently called
the Tranibor, but of late the Archphilarch. All the Syphogrants, who are in
number 200, choose the Prince out of a list of four, who are named by the people of
the four divisions of the city; but they take an oath before they proceed to an
election, that they will choose him whom they think most fit for the office. They
1055 give their voices secretly, so that it is not known for whom every one gives his
suffrage. The Prince is for life, unless he is removed upon suspicion of some design
to enslave the people. The Tranibors are new chosen every year, but yet they are
for the most part continued. All their other magistrates are only annual. The
Tranibors meet every third day, and oftener if necessary, and consult with the
1060 Prince, either concerning the affairs of the state in general, or such private
differences as may arise sometimes among the people; though that falls out but

seldom. There are always two Syphogrants called into the council-chamber, and these are changed every day. It is a fundamental rule of their government, that no conclusion can be made in anything that relates to the public, till it has been first debated three several days in their council. It is death for any to meet and consult concerning the state, unless it be either in their ordinary council, or in the assembly of the whole body of the people.

These things have been so provided among them, that the Prince and the Tranibors may not conspire together to change the government, and enslave the people; and therefore when anything of great importance is set on foot, it is sent to the Syphogrants; who after they have communicated it to the families that belong to their divisions, and have considered it among themselves, make report to the senate; and upon great occasions, the matter is referred to the council of the whole island. One rule observed in their council, is, never to debate a thing on the same day in which it is first proposed; for that is always referred to the next meeting, that so men may not rashly, and in the heat of discourse, engage themselves too soon, which might bias them so much, that instead of consulting the good of the public, they might rather study to support their first opinions, and by a perverse and preposterous sort of shame, hazard their country rather than endanger their own reputation, or venture the being suspected to have wanted foresight in the expedients that they at first proposed. And therefore to prevent this, they take care that they may rather be deliberate than sudden in their motions.

OF THEIR TRADES, AND MANNER OF LIFE.

Agriculture is that which is so universally understood among them, that no person, either man or woman, is ignorant of it; they are instructed in it from their childhood, partly by what they learn at school, and partly by practice; they being led out often into the fields, about the town, where they not only see others at work, but are likewise exercised in it themselves. Besides agriculture, which is so common to them all, every man has some peculiar trade to which he applies himself, such as the manufacture of wool, or flax, masonry, smith's work, or carpenter's work; for there is no sort of trade that is in great esteem among them. Throughout the island they wear the same sort of clothes without any other distinction, except what is necessary to distinguish the two sexes, and the married and unmarried. The fashion never alters; and as neither disagreeable nor uneasy, so it is suited to the climate, and calculated both for their summers and winters. Every family makes their own clothes; but all among them, women as well men, learn one or other of the trades formerly mentioned. Women, for the most part, deal in wool and flax, which suit best with their weakness, leaving the ruder trades to the men. The same trade generally passes down from father to son, inclinations often following descent; but if any man's genius lies another way, he is by adoption translated into a family that deals in the trade to which he is inclined: and when that is to be done, care is taken not only by his father, but by the magistrate, that he may be put to a discreet and good man. And if after a person has learned one trade, he desires to acquire another, that is also allowed, and is managed in the same manner as the former. When he has learned both, he follows that which he likes best, unless the public has more occasion for the other.

1105

The chief, and almost the only business of the Syphogrants, is to take care that no man may live idle, but that every one may follow his trade diligently: yet they do not wear themselves out with perpetual toil, from morning to night, as if they were beasts of burden, which as it is indeed a heavy slavery, so it is everywhere the common course of life amongst all mechanics except the Utopians; but they dividing the day and night into twenty-four hours, appoint six of these for work; three of which are before dinner; and three after. They then sup, and at eight o'clock, counting from noon, go to bed and sleep eight hours. The rest of their time besides that taken up in work, eating and sleeping, is left to every man's discretion; yet they are not to abuse that interval to luxury and idleness, but must employ it in some proper exercise according to their various inclinations, which is for the most part reading. It is ordinary to have public lectures every morning before daybreak; at which none are obliged to appear but those who are marked out for literature; yet a great many, both men and women of all ranks, go to hear lectures of one sort or other, according to their inclinations. But if others, that are not made for contemplation, choose rather to employ themselves at that time in their trades, as many of them do, they are not hindered, but are rather commended, as men that take care to serve their country. After supper, they spend an hour in some diversion, in summer in their gardens, and in winter in the halls where they eat; where they entertain each other, either with music or discourse. They do not so much as know dice, or any such foolish and mischievous games: they have, however, two sorts of games not unlike our chess; the one is between several numbers, in which one number, as it were, consumes another: the other resembles a battle between the virtues and the vices, in which the enmity in the vices among themselves, and their agreement against virtue, is not unpleasantly represented; together with the special oppositions between the particular virtues and vices; as also the methods by which vice either openly assaults or secretly undermines virtue; and virtue on the other hand resists it. But the time appointed for labour is to be narrowly examined, otherwise you may imagine, that since there are only six hours appointed for work, they may fall under a scarcity of necessary provisions. But it is so far from being true, that this time is not sufficient for supplying them with plenty of all things, either necessary or convenient; that it is rather too much; and this you will easily apprehend, if you consider how great a part of all other nations is quite idle. First, women generally do little, who are the half of mankind; and if some few women are diligent, their husbands are idle: then consider the great company of idle priests, and of those that are called religious men; add to these all rich men, chiefly those that have estates in land, who are called noblemen and gentlemen, together with their families, made up of idle persons, that are kept more for show than use; add to these, all those strong and lusty beggars, that go about pretending some disease, in excuse for their begging; and upon the whole account you will find that the number of those by whose labours mankind is

1110

1115

1120

1125

1130

1135

1140

1145

supplied, is much less than you perhaps imagined. Then consider how few of those that work are employed in labours that are of real service; for we who measure all things by money, give rise to many trades that are both vain and superfluous, and serve only to support riot and luxury. For if those who work were employed only in such things as the conveniences of life require, there would be such an abundance of them, that the prices of them would so sink, that tradesmen could not be maintained by their gains; if all those who labour about useless things, were set to more profitable employments, and if all they that languish out their lives in sloth and idleness, every one of whom consumes as much as any two of the men that are at work, were forced to labour, you may easily imagine that a small proportion of time would serve for doing all that is either necessary, profitable, or pleasant to mankind, especially while pleasure is kept within its due bounds. This appears very plainly in Utopia, for there, in a great city, and in all the territory that lies round it, you can scarce find five hundred, either men or women, by their age and strength, are capable of labour, that are not engaged in it; even the Syphogrants, though excused by the law, yet do not excuse themselves, but work, that by their examples they may excite the industry of the rest of the people. The like exemption is allowed to those, who being recommended to the people by the priests, are by the secret suffrages of the Syphogrants privileged from labour, that they may apply themselves wholly to study; and if any of these fall short of those hopes that they seemed at first to give, they are obliged to return to work. And sometimes a mechanic, that so employs his leisure hours, as to make a considerable advancement in learning, is eased from being a tradesman, and ranked among their learned men. Out of these they choose their ambassadors, their priests, their Tranibors, and the Prince himself, anciently called their Barzenes, but is called of late their Ademus.

And thus from the great numbers among them that are neither suffered to be idle, nor to be employed in any fruitless labour, you may easily make the estimate how much may be done in those few hours in which they are obliged to labour. But besides all that has been already said, it is to be considered that the needful arts among them are managed with less labour than anywhere else. The building or the repairing of houses among us employ many hands, because often a thriftless heir suffers a house that his father built to fall into decay, so that his successor must, at a great cost, repair that which he might have kept up with a small charge: it frequently happens, that the same house which one person built at a vast expense, is neglected by another, who thinks he has a more delicate sense of the beauties of architecture; and he suffering it to fall to ruin, builds another at no less charge. But among the Utopians, all things are so regulated that men very seldom build upon a new piece of ground; and are not only very quick in repairing their houses, but show their foresight in preventing their decay: so that their buildings are preserved very long, with but little labour; and thus the builders to whom that care belongs are often without employment, except the hewing of timber, and the squaring of stones, that the materials may be in readiness for raising a building very suddenly, when there is any occasion for it. As to their clothes, observe how

little work is spent in them: while they are at labour, they are clothed with leather and skins, cast carelessly about them, which will last seven years; and when they appear in public they put on an upper garment, which hides the other; and these are all of one colour, and that is the natural colour of the wool. As they need less
1195   woollen cloth than is used anywhere else, so that which they make use of is much less costly. They use linen cloth more; but that is prepared with less labour, and they value cloth only by the whiteness of the linen, or the cleanness of the wool, without much regard to the fineness of the thread: while in other places, four or five upper garments of woollen cloth, of different colours, and as many vests of
1200   silk, will scarce serve one man; and while those that are nicer think ten too few, every man there is content with one, which very often serves him two years. Nor is there anything that can tempt a man to desire more; for if he had them, he would neither be the warmer, nor would he make one jot the better appearance for it. And thus, since they are all employed in some useful labour, and since they content
1205   themselves with fewer things, it falls out that there is a great abundance of all things among them: so that it frequently happens, that for want of other work, vast numbers are sent out to mend the highways. But when no public undertaking is to be performed, the hours of working are lessened. The magistrates never engage the people in unnecessary labour, since the chief end of the constitution is to regulate
1210   labour by the necessities of the public, and to allow all the people as much time as is necessary for the improvement of their minds, in which they think the happiness of life consists.

OF THEIR TRAFFIC.

But it is now time to explain to you the mutual intercourse of this people, their commerce, and the rules by which all things are distributed among them.
1215   As their cities are composed of families, so their families are made up of those that are nearly related to one another. Their women, when they grow up, are married out; but all the males, both children and grandchildren, live still in the same house, in great obedience to their common parent, unless age has weakened his understanding; and in that case, he that is next to him in age comes in his room.
1220   But lest any city should become either too great, or by any accident be dispeopled, provision is made that none of their cities may contain above six thousand families, besides those of the country round it. No family may have less than ten, and more than sixteen persons in it; but there can be no determined number for the children under age. This rule is easily observed, by removing some of the children
1225   of a more fruitful couple to any other family that does not abound so much in them. By the same rule, they supply cities that do not increase so fast, from others that breed faster; and if there is any increase over the whole island, then they draw out a number of their citizens out of the several towns, and send them over to the neighbouring continent; where, if they find that the inhabitants have more soil
1230   than they can well cultivate, they fix a colony, taking the inhabitants into their society, if they are willing to live with them; and where they do that of their own

accord, they quickly enter into their method of life, and conform to their rules, and this proves a happiness to both nations: for according to their constitution, such care is taken of the soil, that it becomes fruitful enough for both, though it might be otherwise too narrow and barren for any one of them. But if the natives refuse to conform themselves to their laws, they drive them out of those bounds which they mark out for themselves, and use force if they resist. For they account it a very just cause of war, for a nation to hinder others from possessing a part of that soil, of which they make no use, but which is suffered to lie idle and uncultivated; since every man has by the law of Nature a right to such a waste portion of the earth as is necessary for his subsistence. If an accident has so lessened the number of the inhabitants of any of their towns, that it cannot be made up from the other towns of the island, without diminishing them too much, which is said to have fallen out but twice since they were first a people, when great numbers were carried off by the plague; the loss is then supplied by recalling as many as are wanted from their colonies; for they will abandon these, rather than suffer the towns in the island to sink too low.

But to return to their manner of living in society, the oldest man of every family, as has been already said, is its governor. Wives serve their husbands, and children their parents, and always the younger serves the elder. Every city is divided into four equal parts, and in the middle of each there is a market-place: what is brought thither, and manufactured by the several families, is carried from thence to houses appointed for that purpose, in which all things of a sort are laid by themselves; and thither every father goes and takes whatsoever he or his family stand in need of, without either paying for it, or leaving anything in exchange. There is no reason for giving a denial to any person, since there is such plenty of everything among them; and there is no danger of a man's asking for more than he needs; they have no inducements to do this, since they are sure that they shall always be supplied. It is the fear of want that makes any of the whole race of animals either greedy or ravenous; but besides fear, there is in man a pride that makes him fancy it a particular glory to excel others in pomp and excess. But by the laws of the Utopians, there is no room for this. Near these markets there are others for all sorts of provisions, where there are not only herbs, fruits, and bread, but also fish, fowl, and cattle. There are also, without their towns, places appointed near some running water, for killing their beasts, and for washing away their filth; which is done by their slaves: for they suffer none of their citizens to kill their cattle, because they think that pity and good-nature, which are among the best of those affections that are born with us, are much impaired by the butchering of animals: nor do they suffer anything that is foul or unclean to be brought within their towns, lest the air should be infected by ill smells which might prejudice their health. In every street there are great halls that lie at an equal distance from each other, distinguished by particular names. The Syphogrants dwell in those that are set over thirty families, fifteen lying on one side of it, and as many on the other. In these halls they all meet and have their repasts. The stewards of every one of them come to the market-place at an appointed hour; and

1280

according to the number of those that belong to the hall, they carry home provisions. But they take more care of their sick than of any others: these are lodged and provided for in public hospitals: they have belonging to every town four hospitals, that are built without their walls, and are so large that they may pass for little towns: by this means, if they had ever such a number of sick persons, they could lodge them conveniently, and at such a distance, that such of them as are sick of infectious diseases may be kept so far from the rest that there can be no danger of contagion. The hospitals are furnished and stored with all things that are convenient for the ease and recovery of the sick; and those that are put in them are looked after with such tender and watchful care, and are so constantly attended by their skilful physicians, that as none is sent to them against their will, so there is scarce one in a whole town that, if he should fall ill, would not choose rather to go thither than lie sick at home.

1285

After the steward of the hospitals has taken for the sick whatsoever the physician prescribes, then the best things that are left in the market are distributed equally among the halls, in proportion to their numbers, only, in the first place, they serve the Prince, the chief priest, the Tranibors, the ambassadors, and strangers, if there are any, which indeed falls out but seldom, and for whom there are houses well furnished, particularly appointed for their reception when they come among them. At the hours of dinner and supper, the whole Syphogranty being called together by sound of trumpet, they meet and eat together, except only such as are in the hospitals, or lie sick at home. Yet after the halls are served, no man is hindered to carry provisions home from the market-place; for they know that none does that but for some good reason; for though any that will may eat at home, yet none does it willingly, since it is both ridiculous and foolish for any to give themselves the trouble to make ready an ill dinner at home, when there is a much more plentiful one made ready for him so near hand.

1290

1295

1300

All the uneasy and sordid services about these halls are performed by their slaves; but the dressing and cooking their meat, and the ordering their tables, belong only to the women, all those of every family taking it by turns. They sit at three or more tables, according to their number; the men sit towards the wall, and the women sit on the other side, that if any of them should be taken suddenly ill, which is no uncommon case amongst women with child, she may, without disturbing the rest, rise and go to the nurse's room, who are there with the suckling children; where there is always clean water at hand, and cradles in which they may lay the young children, if there is occasion for it, and a fire that they may shift and dress them before it. Every child is nursed by its own mother, if death or sickness does not intervene; and in that case the Syphogrants' wives find out a nurse quickly, which is no hard matter; for any one that can do it, offers herself cheerfully; for as they are much inclined to that piece of mercy, so the child whom they nurse considers the nurse as its mother. All the children under five years old sit among the nurses, the rest of the younger sort of both sexes, till they are fit for marriage, either serve those that sit at table; or if they are not strong enough for that, stand by them in great silence, and eat what is given them; nor

1305

1310

1315

1320   have they any other formality of dining. In the middle of the first table, which stands across the upper end of the hall, sit the Syphogrant and his wife; for that is the chief and most conspicuous place; next to him sit two of the most ancient, for there go always four to a mess. If there is a temple within that Syphogranty, the priest and his wife sit with the Syphogrant above all the rest: next them there is a

1325   mixture of old and young, who are so placed, that as the young are set near others, so they are mixed with the more ancient; which they say was appointed on this account, that the gravity of the old people, and the reverence that is due to them, might restrain the younger from all indecent words and gestures. Dishes are not served up to the whole table at first, but the best are first set before the old, whose

1330   seats are distinguished from the young, and after them all the rest are served alike. The old men distribute to the younger any curious meats that happen to be set before them, if there is not such an abundance of them that the whole company may be served alike.

        Thus old men are honoured with a particular respect; yet all the rest fare as

1335   well as they. Both dinner and supper are begun with some lecture of morality that is read to them; but it is so short, that it is not tedious nor uneasy to them to hear it: from hence the old men take occasion to entertain those about them, with some useful and pleasant enlargements; but they do not engross the whole discourse so to themselves, during their meals, that the younger may not put in for a share: on

1340   the contrary, they engage them to talk, that so they may in that free way of conversation find out the force of every one's spirit, and observe his temper. They despatch their dinners quickly, but sit long at supper; because they go to work after the one, and are to sleep after the other, during which they think the stomach carries on the concoction more vigorously. They never sup without music; and

1345   there is always fruit served up after meat; while they are at table, some burn perfumes, and sprinkle about fragrant ointments and sweet waters: in short, they want nothing that may cheer up their spirits: they give themselves a large allowance that way, and indulge themselves in all such pleasures as are attended with no inconvenience. Thus do those that are in the towns live together; but in the

1350   country, where they live at great distance, every one eats at home, and no family wants any necessary sort of provision, for it is from them that provisions are sent unto those that live in the towns.

OF THE TRAVELLING OF THE UTOPIANS.

        If any man has a mind to visit his friends that live in some other town, or desires to travel and see the rest of the country, he obtains leave very easily from

1355   the Syphogrant and Tranibors, when there is no particular occasion for him at home: such as travel, carry with them a passport from the Prince, which both certifies the license that is granted for travelling, and limits the time of their return. They are furnished with a waggon and a slave, who drives the oxen, and looks after them: but unless there are women in the company, the waggon is sent back at

1360   the end of the journey as a needless encumbrance: while they are on the road, they carry no provisions with them; yet they want nothing, but are everywhere treated as if they were at home. If they stay in any place longer than a night, every one follows his proper occupation, and is very well used by those of his own trade: but if any man goes out of the city to which he belongs, without leave, and is found

1365 rambling without a passport, he is severely treated, he is punished as a fugitive, and sent home disgracefully; and if he falls again into the like fault, is condemned to slavery. If any man has a mind to travel only over the precinct of his own city, he may freely do it, with his father's permission and his wife's consent; but when he comes into any of the country houses, if he expects to be entertained by them, he

1370 must labour with them and conform to their rules: and if he does this, he may freely go over the whole precinct; being thus as useful to the city to which he belongs, as if he were still within it. Thus you see that there are no idle persons among them, nor pretences of excusing any from labour. There are no taverns, no alehouses nor stews among them; nor any other occasions of corrupting each other, of getting into

1375 corners, or forming themselves into parties: all men live in full view, so that all are obliged, both to perform their ordinary task, and to employ themselves well in their spare hours. And it is certain that a people thus ordered must live in great abundance of all things; and these being equally distributed among them, no man can want, or be obliged to beg.

1380 In their great council at Amaurot, to which there are three sent from every town once a year, they examine what towns abound in provisions, and what are under any scarcity, that so the one may be furnished from the other; and this is done freely, without any sort of exchange; for according to their plenty or scarcity, they supply, or are supplied from one another; so that indeed the whole

1385 island is, as it were, one family. When they have thus taken care of their whole country, and laid up stores for two years, which they do to prevent the ill consequences of an unfavourable season, they order an exportation of the overplus, both of corn, honey, wool, flax, wood, wax, tallow, leather, and cattle; which they send out commonly in great quantities to other nations. They order a

1390 seventh part of all these goods to be freely given to the poor of the countries to which they send them, and sell the rest at moderate rates. And by this exchange, they not only bring back those few things that they need at home (for indeed they scarce need anything but iron), but likewise a great deal of gold and silver; and by their driving this trade so long, it is not to be imagined how vast a treasure they

1395 have got among them: so that now they do not much care whether they sell off their merchandise for money in hand, or upon trust. A great part of their treasure is now in bonds; but in all their contracts no private man stands bound, but the writing runs in the name of the town; and the towns that owe them money, raise it from those private hands that owe it to them, lay it up in their public chamber, or

1400 enjoy the profit of it till the Utopians call for it; and they choose rather to let the greatest part of it lie in their hands who make advantage by it, than to call for it themselves: but if they see that any of their other neighbours stand more in need of it, then they call it in and lend it to them: whenever they are engaged in war, which is the only occasion in which their treasure can be usefully employed, they make

1405   use of it themselves. In great extremities or sudden accidents they employ it in hiring foreign troops, whom they more willingly expose to danger than their own people: they give them great pay, knowing well that this will work even on their enemies, that it will engage them either to betray their own side, or at least to desert it, and that it is the best means of raising mutual jealousies among them: for

1410   this end they have an incredible treasure; but they do not keep it as a treasure, but in such a manner as I am almost afraid to tell, lest you think it so extravagant, as to be hardly credible. This I have the more reason to apprehend, because if I had not seen it myself, I could not have been easily persuaded to have believed it upon any man's report.

1415   It is certain that all things appear incredible to us, in proportion as they differ from [our] own customs. But one who can judge aright, will not wonder to find, that since their constitution differs so much from ours, their value of gold and silver should be measured by a very different standard; for since they have no use for money among themselves, but keep it as a provision against events which

1420   seldom happen, and between which there are generally long intervening intervals; they value it no farther than it deserves, that is, in proportion to its use. So that it is plain, they must prefer iron either to gold or silver: for men can no more live without iron, than without fire or water; but Nature has marked out no use for the other metals, so essential as not easily to be dispensed with. The folly of men has

1425   enhanced the value of gold and silver, because of their scarcity. Whereas, on the contrary, it is their opinion that Nature, as an indulgent parent, has freely given us all the best things in great abundance, such as water and earth, but has laid up and hid from us the things that are vain and useless.

    If these metals were laid up in any tower in the kingdom, it would raise a

1430   jealousy of the Prince and Senate, and give birth to that foolish mistrust into which the people are apt to fall, a jealousy of their intending to sacrifice the interest of the public to their own private advantage. If they should work it into vessels, or any sort of plate, they fear that the people might grow too fond of it, and so be unwilling to let the plate be run down, if a war made it necessary to

1435   employ it in paying their soldiers. To prevent all these inconveniences, they have fallen upon an expedient, which as it agrees with their other policy, so is it very different from ours, and will scarce gain belief among us, who value gold so much, and lay it up so carefully. They eat and drink out of vessels of earth, or glass, which make an agreeable appearance though formed of brittle materials: while

1440   they make their chamber-pots and close-stools of gold and silver; and that not only in their public halls, but in their private houses: of the same metals they likewise make chains and fetters for their slaves; to some of which, as a badge of infamy, they hang an ear-ring of gold, and make others wear a chain or a coronet of the same metal; and thus they take care, by all possible means, to render gold and

1445   silver of no esteem. And from hence it is, that while other nations part with their gold and silver, as unwillingly as if one tore out their bowels, those of Utopia would look on their giving in all they possess of those (metals, when there were any use for them) but as the parting with a trifle, or as we would esteem the loss of

1450

a penny. They find pearls on their coast; and diamonds and carbuncles on their rocks; they do not look after them, but if they find them by chance, they polish them, and with them they adorn their children, who are delighted with them, and glory in them during their childhood; but when they grow to years, and see that none but children use such baubles, they of their own accord, without being bid by their parents, lay them aside; and would be as much ashamed to use them afterwards, as

1455

children among us, when they come to years, are of their puppets and other toys.

I never saw a clearer instance of the opposite impressions that different customs make on people, than I observed in the ambassadors of the Anemolians, who came to Amaurot when I was there. As they came to treat of affairs of great consequence, the deputies from several towns met together to wait for their coming.

1460

The ambassadors of the nations that lie near Utopia, knowing their customs, and that fine clothes are in no esteem among them, that silk is despised, and gold is a badge of infamy, use to come very modestly clothed; but the Anemolians lying more remote, and having had little commerce with them, understanding that they were coarsely clothed, and all in the same manner, took it for granted that they had none

1465

of those fine things among them of which they made no use; and they being a vain-glorious rather than a wise people, resolved to set themselves out with so much pomp, that they should look like gods, and strike the eyes of the poor Utopians with their splendour. Thus three ambassadors made their entry with an hundred attendants, all clad in garments of different colours, and the greater part in silk;

1470

the ambassadors themselves, who were of the nobility of their country, were in cloth of gold, and adorned with massy chains, ear-rings and rings of gold: their caps were covered with bracelets set full of pearls and other gems: in a word, they were set out with all those things that, among the Utopians, were either the badges of slavery, the marks of infamy, or the playthings of children. It was not

1475

unpleasant to see, on the one side, how they looked big, when they compared their rich habits with the plain clothes of the Utopians, who were come out in great numbers to see them make their entry: and, on the other, to observe how much they were mistaken in the impression which they hoped this pomp would have made on them. It appeared so ridiculous a show to all that had never stirred out of their

1480

country, and had not seen the customs of other nations, that though they paid some reverence to those that were the most meanly clad, as if they had been the ambassadors, yet when they saw the ambassadors themselves, so full of gold and chains, they looked upon them as slaves, and forbore to treat them with reverence. You might have seen the children, who were grown big enough to despise their

1485

playthings, and who had thrown away their jewels, call to their mothers, push them gently, and cry out, "See that great fool that wears pearls and gems, as if he were yet a child." While their mothers very innocently replied, "Hold your peace, this I believe is one of the ambassador's fools." Others censured the fashion of their chains, and observed that they were of no use; for they were too slight to

1490

bind their slaves, who could easily break them; and besides hung so loose about them, that they thought it easy to throw them away, and so get from them. But after the ambassadors had stayed a day among them, and saw so vast a quantity of gold

1495

in their houses, which was as much despised by them as it was esteemed in other nations, and beheld more gold and silver in the chains and fetters of one slave than all their ornaments amounted to, their plumes fell, and they were ashamed of all that glory for which they had formerly valued themselves, and accordingly laid it aside; a resolution that they immediately took, when on their engaging in some free discourse with the Utopians, they discovered their sense of such things and their

1500

other customs. The Utopians wonder how any man should be so much taken with the glaring doubtful lustre of a jewel or a stone, that can look up to a star, or to the sun himself, or how any should value himself because his cloth is made of a finer thread: for how fine soever that thread may be, it was once no better than the fleece of a sheep, and that sheep was a sheep still for all its wearing it. They wonder much to hear that gold which in itself is so useless a thing, should be

1505

everywhere so much esteemed, that even men for whom it was made, and by whom it has its value, should yet be thought of less value than this metal. That a man of lead, who has no more sense than a log of wood, and is as bad as he is foolish, should have many wise and good men to serve him, only because he has a great heap of that metal; and that if it should happen that by some accident or trick of

1510

law (which sometimes produces as great changes as chance itself) all this wealth should pass from the master to the meanest varlet of his whole family, he himself would very soon become one of his servants, as if he were a thing that belonged to his wealth, and so were bound to follow its fortune. But they much more admire and detest the folly of those who when they see a rich man, though they neither

1515

owe him anything, nor are in any sort dependent on his bounty, yet merely because he is rich give him little less than divine honours; even though they know him to be so covetous and base-minded, that notwithstanding all his wealth, he will not part with one farthing of it to them as long as he lives.

1520

These and such like notions has that people imbibed, partly from their education, being bred in a country whose customs and laws are opposite to all such foolish maxims, and partly from their learning and studies; for though there are but few in any town that are so wholly excused from labour as to give themselves entirely up to their studies, these being only such persons as discover from their childhood an extraordinary capacity and disposition for letters; yet

1525

their children, and a great part of the nation, both men and women, are taught to spend those hours in which they are not obliged to work in reading: and this they do through the whole progress of life. They have all their learning in their own tongue, which is both a copious and pleasant language, and in which a man can fully express his mind. It runs over a great tract of many countries, but it is not

1530

equally pure in all places. They had never so much as heard of the names of any of those philosophers that are so famous in these parts of the world, before we went among them; and yet they had made the same discoveries as the Greeks, both in music, logic, arithmetic, and geometry. But as they are almost in everything equal to the ancient philosophers, so they far exceed our modern logicians; for they have

1535

never yet fallen upon the barbarous niceties that our youth are forced to learn in those trifling logical schools that are among us; they are so far from minding

chimeras, and fantastical images made in the mind, that none of them could comprehend what we meant when we talked to them of a man in the abstract, as common to all men in particular (so that though we spoke of him as a thing that we
1540   could point at with our fingers, yet none of them could perceive him), and yet distinct from every one, as if he were some monstrous Colossus or giant. Yet for all this ignorance of these empty notions, they knew astronomy, and were perfectly acquainted with the motions of the heavenly bodies, and have many instruments, well contrived and divided, by which they very accurately compute the course and
1545   positions of the sun, moon, and stars. But for the cheat, of divining by the stars by their oppositions or conjunctions, it has not so much as entered into their thoughts. They have a particular sagacity, founded upon much observation, in judging of the weather, by which they know when they may look for rain, wind, or other alterations in the air; but as to the philosophy of these things, the causes of the
1550   saltness of the sea, of its ebbing and flowing, and of the original and nature both of the heavens and the earth; they dispute of them, partly as our ancient philosophers have done, and partly upon some new hypothesis, in which, as they differ from them, so they do not in all things agree among themselves.

     As to moral philosophy, they have the same disputes among them as we have
1555   here: they examine what are properly good both for the body and the mind, and whether any outward thing can be called truly good, or if that term belong only to the endowments of the soul. They inquire likewise into the nature of virtue and pleasure; but their chief dispute is concerning the happiness of a man, and wherein it consists? Whether in some one thing, or in a great many? They seem, indeed,
1560   more inclinable to that opinion that places, if not the whole, yet the chief part of a man's happiness in pleasure; and, what may seem more strange, they make use of arguments even from religion, notwithstanding its severity and roughness, for the support of that opinion so indulgent to pleasure; for they never dispute concerning happiness without fetching some arguments from the principles of religion, as well
1565   as from natural reason, since without the former they reckon that all our inquiries after happiness must be but conjectural and defective.

     These are their religious principles, that the soul of man is immortal, and that God of His goodness has designed that it should be happy; and that He has therefore appointed rewards for good and virtuous actions, and punishments for
1570   vice, to be distributed after this life. Though these principles of religion are conveyed down among them by tradition, they think that even reason itself determines a man to believe and acknowledge them, and freely confess that if these were taken away no man would be so insensible as not to seek after pleasure by all possible means, lawful or unlawful; using only this caution, that a lesser
1575   pleasure might not stand in the way of a greater, and that no pleasure ought to be pursued that should draw a great deal of pain after it; for they think it the maddest thing in the world to pursue virtue, that is a sour and difficult thing; and not only to renounce the pleasures of life, but willingly to undergo much pain and trouble, if a man has no prospect of a reward. And what reward can there be for one that
1580   has passed his whole life, not only without pleasure, but in pain, if there is

nothing to be expected after death? Yet they do not place happiness in all sorts of pleasures, but only in those that in themselves are good and honest. There is a party among them who place happiness in bare virtue; others think that our natures are conducted by virtue to happiness, as that which is the chief good of man. They define virtue thus, that it is a living according to Nature, and think that we are made by God for that end; they believe that a man then follows the dictates of Nature when he pursues or avoids things according to the direction of reason; they say that the first dictate of reason is the kindling in us a love and reverence for the Divine Majesty, to whom we owe both all that we have, and all that we can ever hope for. In the next place, reason directs us to keep our minds as free from passion and as cheerful as we can, and that we should consider ourselves as bound by the ties of good-nature and humanity to use our utmost endeavours to help forward the happiness of all other persons; for there never was any man such a morose and severe pursuer of virtue, such an enemy to pleasure, that though he set hard rules for men to undergo much pain, many watchings, and other rigours, yet did not at the same time advise them to do all they could, in order to relieve and ease the miserable, and who did not represent gentleness and good-nature as amiable dispositions. And from thence they infer that if a man ought to advance the welfare and comfort of the rest of mankind, there being no virtue more proper and peculiar to our nature, than to ease the miseries of others, to free from trouble and anxiety, in furnishing them with the comforts of life, in which pleasure consists, Nature much more vigorously leads them to do all this for himself. A life of pleasure is either a real evil, and in that case we ought not to assist others in their pursuit of it, but on the contrary, to keep them from it all we can, as from that which is most hurtful and deadly; or if it is a good thing, so that we not only may, but ought to help others to it, why then ought not a man to begin with himself? Since no man can be more bound to look after the good of another than after his own; for Nature cannot direct us to be good and kind to others, and yet at the same time to be unmerciful and cruel to ourselves. Thus, as they define virtue to be living according to Nature, so they imagine that Nature prompts all people on to seek after pleasure, as the end of all they do. They also observe that in order to our supporting the pleasures of life, Nature inclines us to enter into society; for there is no man so much raised above the rest of mankind as to be the only favourite of Nature, who, on the contrary, seems to have placed on a level all those that belong to the same species. Upon this they infer that no man ought to seek his own conveniences so eagerly as to prejudice others; and therefore they think that not only all agreements between private persons ought to be observed; but likewise that all those laws ought to be kept, which either a good prince has published in due form, or to which a people, that is neither oppressed with tyranny nor circumvented by fraud, has consented, for distributing those conveniences of life which afford us all our pleasures.

They think it is an evidence of true wisdom for a man to pursue his own advantages, as far as the laws allow it. They account it piety to prefer the public good to one's private concerns; but they think it unjust for a man to seek for

1625   pleasure, by snatching another man's pleasures from him. And on the contrary, they think it a sign of a gentle and good soul, for a man to dispense with his own advantage for the good of others; and that by this means a good man finds as much pleasure one way, as he parts with another; for as he may expect the like from others when he may come to need it, so if that should fail him, yet the sense of a

1630   good action, and the reflections that he makes on the love and gratitude of those whom he has so obliged, gives the mind more pleasure than the body could have found in that from which it had restrained itself. They are also persuaded that God will make up the loss of those small pleasures, with a vast and endless joy, of which religion easily convinces a good soul.

1635   Thus upon an inquiry into the whole matter, they reckon that all our actions, and even all our virtues, terminate in pleasure, as in our chief end and greatest happiness; and they call every motion or state, either of body or mind, in which Nature teaches us to delight, a pleasure. Thus they cautiously limit pleasure only to those appetites to which Nature leads us; for they say that Nature leads us only

1640   to those delights to which reason as well as sense carries us, and by which we neither injure any other person, nor lose the possession of greater pleasures, and of such as draw no troubles after them; but they look upon those delights which men by a foolish, though common, mistake call pleasure, as if they could change as easily the nature of things as the use of words; as things that greatly obstruct their

1645   real happiness, instead of advancing it, because they so entirely possess the minds of those that are once captivated by them with a false notion of pleasure, that there is no room left for pleasures of a truer or purer kind.

         There are many things that in themselves have nothing that is truly delightful; on the contrary, they have a good deal of bitterness in them: and yet from our

1650   perverse appetites after forbidden objects, are not only ranked among the pleasures, but are made even the greatest designs of life. Among those who pursue these sophisticated pleasures, they reckon such as I mentioned before, who think themselves really the better for having fine clothes; in which they think they are doubly mistaken, both in the opinion that they have of their clothes, and in that

1655   they have of themselves; for if you consider the use of clothes, why should a fine thread be thought better than a coarse one? And yet these men, as if they had some real advantages beyond others, and did not owe them wholly to their mistakes, look big, seem to fancy themselves to be more valuable, and imagine that a respect is due to them for the sake of a rich garment, to which they would not have

1660   pretended if they had been more meanly clothed; and even resent it as an affront, if that respect is not paid them. It is also a great folly to be taken with outward marks of respect, which signify nothing: for what true or real pleasure can one man find in another's standing bare, or making legs to him? Will the bending another man's knees give ease to yours? And will the head's being bare cure the

1665   madness of yours? And yet it is wonderful to see how this false notion of pleasure bewitches many who delight themselves with the fancy of their nobility, and are pleased with this conceit, that they are descended from ancestors, who have been held for some successions rich, and who have had great possessions; for this is all

1670 that makes nobility at present; yet they do not think themselves a whit the less noble, though their immediate parents have left none of this wealth to them, or though they themselves have squandered it away. The Utopians have no better opinion of those who are much taken with gems and precious stones, and who account it a degree of happiness, next to a divine one, if they can purchase one that is very extraordinary; especially if it be of that sort of stones that is then in 1675 greatest request; for the same sort is not at all times universally of the same value; nor will men buy it unless it be dismounted and taken out of the gold; the jeweller is then made to give good security, and required solemnly to swear that the stone is true, that by such an exact caution a false one might not be bought instead of a true: though if you were to examine it, your eye could find no difference between 1680 the counterfeit and that which is true; so that they are all one to you as much as if you were blind. Or can it be thought that they who heap up an useless mass of wealth, not for any use that it is to bring them, but merely to please themselves with the contemplation of it, enjoy any true pleasure in it? The delight they find is only a false shadow of joy. Those are no better whose error is somewhat different 1685 from the former, and who hide it, out of their fear of losing it; for what other name can fit the hiding it in the earth, or rather the restoring it to it again, it being thus cut off from being useful, either to its owner or to the rest of mankind? And yet the owner having hid it carefully, is glad, because he thinks he is now sure of it. If it should be stole, the owner, though he might live perhaps ten years after the theft, of 1690 which he knew nothing, would find no difference between his having or losing it; for both ways it was equally useless to him.

Among those foolish pursuers of pleasure, they reckon all that delight in hunting, in fowling, or gaming: of whose madness they have only heard, for they have no such things among them. But they have asked us, what sort of pleasure is it 1695 that men can find in throwing the dice? For if there were any pleasure in it, they think the doing of it so often should give one a surfeit of it: and what pleasure can one find in hearing the barking and howling of dogs, which seem rather odious than pleasant sounds? Nor can they comprehend the pleasure of seeing dogs run after a hare, more than of seeing one dog run after another, for if the seeing them 1700 run is that which gives the pleasure, you have the same entertainment to the eye on both these occasions; since that is the same in both cases: but if the pleasure lies in seeing the hare killed and torn by the dogs, this ought rather to stir pity, that a weak, harmless and fearful hare should be devoured by strong, fierce, and cruel dogs. Therefore all this business of hunting is, among the Utopians, turned over to 1705 their butchers; and those, as has been already said, are all slaves; and they look on hunting as one of the basest parts of a butcher's work: for they account it both more profitable and more decent to kill those beasts that are more necessary and useful to mankind; whereas the killing and tearing of so small and miserable an animal can only attract the huntsman with a false show of pleasure, from which 1710 he can reap but small advantage. They look on the desire of the bloodshed, even of beasts, as a mark of a mind that is already corrupted with cruelty, or that at least by the frequent returns of so brutal a pleasure must degenerate into it.

Thus, though the rabble of mankind look upon these, and on innumerable other things of the same nature, as pleasures; the Utopians, on the contrary, 1715 observing that there is nothing in them truly pleasant, conclude that they are not to be reckoned among pleasures: for though these things may create some tickling in the senses (which seems to be a true notion of pleasure), yet they imagine that this does not arise from the thing itself, but from a depraved custom, which may so vitiate a man's taste, that bitter things may pass for sweet; as women with child 1720 think pitch or tallow taste sweeter than honey; but as a man's sense when corrupted, either by a disease or some ill habit, does not change the nature of other things, so neither can it change the nature of pleasure.

They reckon up several sorts of pleasures, which they call true ones: some belong to the body and others to the mind. The pleasures of the mind lie in 1725 knowledge, and in that delight which the contemplation of truth carries with it; to which they add the joyful reflections on a well-spent life, and the assured hopes of a future happiness. They divide the pleasures of the body into two sorts; the one is that which gives our senses some real delight, and is performed, either by recruiting nature, and supplying those parts which feed the internal heat of life by 1730 eating and drinking; or when nature is eased of any surcharge that oppresses it; when we are relieved from sudden pain, or that which arises from satisfying the appetite which Nature has wisely given to lead us to the propagation of the species. There is another kind of pleasure that arises neither from our receiving what the body requires, nor its being relieved when overcharged, and yet by a 1735 secret, unseen virtue affects the senses, raises the passions, and strikes the mind with generous impressions; this is the pleasure that arises from music. Another kind of bodily pleasure is that which results from an undisturbed and vigorous constitution of body, when life and active spirits seem to actuate every part. This lively health, when entirely free from all mixture of pain, of itself gives an inward 1740 pleasure, independent of all external objects of delight; and though this pleasure does not so powerfully affect us, nor act so strongly on the senses as some of the others, yet it may be esteemed as the greatest of all pleasures, and almost all the Utopians reckon it the foundation and basis of all the other joys of life; since this alone makes the state of life easy and desirable; and when this is wanting, a man is 1745 really capable of no other pleasure. They look upon freedom from pain, if it does not rise from perfect health, to be a state of stupidity rather than of pleasure. This subject has been very narrowly canvassed among them; and it has been debated whether a firm and entire health could be called a pleasure or not? Some have thought that there was no pleasure but what was excited by some sensible motion 1750 in the body. But this opinion has been long ago excluded from among them, so that now they almost universally agree that health is the greatest of all bodily pleasures; and that as there is a pain in sickness, which is as opposite in its nature to pleasure as sickness itself is to health; so they hold that health is accompanied with pleasure: and if any should say that sickness is not really pain, but that it 1755 only carries pain along with it, they look upon that as a fetch of subtilty, that does not much alter the matter. It is all one, in their opinion, whether it be said that health is in itself a pleasure, or that it begets a pleasure, as fire gives heat; so it be granted, and all those whose health is entire have a true pleasure in the enjoyment of it: and they reason thus—what is the pleasure of eating, but that a man's health which had been weakened, does, with the assistance of food, drive away hunger, and so recruiting itself recovers its former vigour? And being thus refreshed, it finds a pleasure in that conflict; and if the conflict is pleasure, the victory must yet breed a greater pleasure, except we fancy that it becomes stupid as soon as it has obtained that which it pursued, and so neither knows nor rejoices in its own welfare. If it is said that health cannot be felt, they absolutely deny it; for what man is in health that does not perceive it when he is awake? Is there any man that is so dull and stupid as not to acknowledge that he feels a delight in health? And what is delight but another name for pleasure?

But of all pleasures, they esteem those to be most valuable that lie in the mind; the chief of which arises out of true virtue, and the witness of a good conscience. They account health the chief pleasure that belongs to the body; for they think that the pleasure of eating and drinking, and all the other delights of sense, are only so far desirable as they give or maintain health. But they are not pleasant in themselves, otherwise than as they resist those impressions that our natural infirmities are still making upon us: for as a wise man desires rather to avoid diseases than to take physic; and to be freed from pain, rather than to find ease by remedies; so it is more desirable not to need this sort of pleasure, than to be obliged to indulge it. If any man imagines that there is a real happiness in these enjoyments, he must then confess that be would be the happiest of all men if he were to lead his life in perpetual hunger, thirst, and itching, and by consequence in perpetual eating, drinking, and scratching himself; which any one may easily see would be not only a base, but a miserable state of a life. These are indeed the lowest of pleasures, and the least pure; for we can never relish them, but when they are mixed with the contrary pains. The pain of hunger must give us the pleasure of eating; and here the pain outbalances the pleasure; and as the pain is more vehement, so it lasts much longer; for as it begins before the pleasure, so it does not cease but with the pleasure that extinguishes it, and both expire together. They think, therefore, none of those pleasures are to be valued any further than as they are necessary; yet they rejoice in them, and with due gratitude acknowledge the tenderness of the great Author of Nature, who has planted in us appetites, by which those things that are necessary for our preservation are likewise made pleasant to us. For how miserable a thing would life be, if those daily diseases of hunger and thirst were to be carried off by such bitter drugs as we must use for those diseases that return seldomer upon us? And thus these pleasant as well as proper gifts of Nature maintain the strength and the sprightliness of our bodies.

They also entertain themselves with the other delights let in at their eyes, their ears, and their nostrils, as the pleasant relishes and seasonings of life, which Nature seems to have marked out peculiarly for man; since no other sort of animals contemplates the figure and beauty of the universe; nor is delighted with smells, any farther than as they distinguish meats by them; nor do they apprehend the concords or discords of sound; yet in all pleasures whatsoever they take care that a lesser joy does not hinder a greater, and that pleasure may never breed pain, which they think always follows dishonest pleasures. But they think it madness for a man to wear out the beauty of his face, or the force of his natural strength; to

1805 corrupt the sprightliness of his body by sloth and laziness, or to waste it by fasting; that it is madness to weaken the strength of his constitution, and reject the other delights of life; unless by renouncing his own satisfaction, he can either serve the public or promote the happiness of others, for which he expects a greater recompense from God. So that they look on such a course of life as the mark of a

1810 mind that is both cruel to itself, and ungrateful to the Author of Nature, as if we would not be beholden to Him for His favours, and therefore rejects all His blessings; as one who should afflict himself for the empty shadow of virtue; or for no better end than to render himself capable of bearing those misfortunes which possibly will never happen.

1815 This is their notion of virtue and of pleasure; they think that no man's reason can carry him to a truer idea of them, unless some discovery from Heaven should inspire him with sublimer notions. I have not now the leisure to examine whether they think right or wrong in this matter: nor do I judge it necessary, for I have only undertaken to give you an account of their constitution, but not to defend all their

1820 principles. I am sure, that whatsoever may be said of their notions, there is not in the whole world either a better people or a happier government: their bodies are vigorous and lively; and though they are but of a middle stature, and have neither the fruitfullest soil nor the purest air in the world, yet they fortify themselves so well by their temperate course of life, against the unhealthiness of their air, and by

1825 their industry they so cultivate their soil, that there is nowhere to be seen a greater increase both of corn and cattle, nor are there anywhere healthier men, and freer from diseases: for one may there see reduced to practice, not only all the art that the husbandman employs in manuring and improving an ill soil, but whole woods plucked up by the roots, and in other places new ones planted, where there

1830 were none before. Their principal motive for this is the convenience of carriage, that their timber may be either near their towns, or growing on the banks of the sea, or of some rivers, so as to be floated to them; for it is a harder work to carry wood at any distance over land, than corn. The people are industrious, apt to learn, as well as cheerful and pleasant; and none can endure more labour, when it

1835 is necessary; but except in that case they love their ease. They are unwearied pursuers of knowledge; for when we had given them some hints of the learning and discipline of the Greeks, concerning whom we only instructed them (for we know that there was nothing among the Romans, except their historians and their poets, that they would value much), it was strange to see how eagerly they were set on

1840 learning that language. We began to read a little of it to them, rather in compliance with their importunity, than out of any hopes of their reaping from it any great advantage. But after a very short trial we found they made such progress, that we saw our labour was like to be more successful than we could have expected. They learned to write their characters, and to pronounce their language so exactly, had

1845 so quick an apprehension, they remembered it so faithfully, and became so ready and correct in the use of it, that it would have looked like a miracle if the greater part of those whom we taught had not been men both of extraordinary capacity and of a fit age for instruction. They were for the greatest part chosen from among their learned men, by their chief council, though some studied it of their own

1850 accord. In three years' time they became masters of the whole language, so that they read the best of the Greek authors very exactly. I am indeed apt to think that they learned that language the more easily, from its having some relation to their own. I believe that they were a colony of the Greeks; for though their language comes nearer the Persian, yet they retain many names, both for their towns and

1855 magistrates, that are of Greek derivation. I happened to carry a great many books with me, instead of merchandise, when I sailed my fourth voyage; for I was so far from thinking of soon coming back, that I rather thought never to have returned at all, and I gave them all my books, among which were many of Plato's and some of Aristotle's works. I had also Theophrastus on Plants, which, to my great regret,

1860 was imperfect; for having laid it carelessly by, while we were at sea, a monkey had seized upon it, and in many places torn out the leaves. They have no books of grammar but Lascares, for I did not carry Theodorus with me; nor have they any dictionaries but Hesichius and Dioscorides. They esteem Plutarch highly, and were much taken with Lucian's wit, and with his pleasant way of writing. As for

1865 the poets, they have Aristophanes, Homer, Euripides, and Sophocles of Aldus's edition; and for historians Thucydides, Herodotus and Herodian. One of my companions, Thricius Apinatus, happened to carry with him some of Hippocrates's works, and Galen's Microtechne, which they hold in great estimation; for though there is no nation in the world that needs physic so little as

1870 they do, yet there is not any that honours it so much: they reckon the knowledge of it one of the pleasantest and most profitable parts of philosophy, by which, as they search into the secrets of Nature, so they not only find this study highly agreeable, but think that such inquiries are very acceptable to the Author of Nature; and imagine that as He, like the inventors of curious engines amongst

1875 mankind, has exposed this great machine of the universe to the view of the only creatures capable of contemplating it, so an exact and curious observer, who admires His workmanship, is much more acceptable to Him than one of the herd, who like a beast incapable of reason, looks on this glorious scene with the eyes of a dull and unconcerned spectator.

1880 The minds of the Utopians when fenced with a love for learning, are very ingenious in discovering all such arts as are necessary to carry it to perfection. Two things they owe to us, the manufacture of paper, and the art of printing: yet they are not so entirely indebted to us for these discoveries, but that a great part of the invention was their own. We showed them some books printed by Aldus, we

1885 explained to them the way of making paper, and the mystery of printing; but as we had never practised these arts, we described them in a crude and superficial manner. They seized the hints we gave them, and though at first they could not arrive at perfection, yet by making many essays they at last found out and

1890 corrected all their errors, and conquered every difficulty. Before this they only wrote on parchment, on reeds, or on the barks of trees; but now they have established the manufactures of paper, and set up printing-presses, so that if they had but a good number of Greek authors they would be quickly supplied with many copies of them: at present, though they have no more than those I have mentioned, yet by several impressions they have multiplied them into many

1895 thousands. If any man was to go among them that had some extraordinary talent, or that by much travelling had observed the customs of many nations (which made us to be so well received), he would receive a hearty welcome; for they are very desirous to know the state of the whole world. Very few go among them on the account of traffic, for what can a man carry to them but iron, or gold, or silver,

1900 which merchants desire rather to export than import to a strange country: and as for their exportation, they think it better to manage that themselves than to leave it to foreigners, for by this means, as they understand the state of the neighbouring countries better, so they keep up the art of navigation, which cannot be maintained but by much practice.

OF THEIR SLAVES, AND OF THEIR MARRIAGES.

1905 They do not make slaves of prisoners of war, except those that are taken in battle; nor of the sons of their slaves, nor of those of other nations: the slaves among them are only such as are condemned to that state of life for the commission of some crime, or, which is more common, such as their merchants find condemned to die in those parts to which they trade, whom they sometimes redeem at low

1910 rates; and in other places have them for nothing. They are kept at perpetual labour, and are always chained, but with this difference, that their own natives are treated much worse than others; they are considered as more profligate than the rest, and since they could not be restrained by the advantages of so excellent an education, are judged worthy of harder usage. Another sort of slaves are the

1915 poor of the neighbouring countries, who offer of their own accord to come and serve them; they treat these better, and use them in all other respects as well as their own countrymen, except their imposing more labour upon them, which is no hard task to those that have been accustomed to it; and if any of these have a mind to go back to their own country, which indeed falls out but seldom, as they do not

1920 force them to stay, so they do not send them away empty-handed.

I have already told you with what care they look after their sick, so that nothing is left undone that can contribute either to their ease or health: and for those who are taken with fixed and incurable diseases, they use all possible ways to cherish them, and to make their lives as comfortable as possible. They visit them

1925 often, and take great pains to make their time pass off easily: but when any is taken with a torturing and lingering pain, so that there is no hope, either of recovery or ease, the priests and magistrates come and exhort them, that since they are now unable to go on with the business of life, are become a burden to themselves and to all about them, and they have really outlived themselves, they

1930 should no longer nourish such a rooted distemper, but choose rather to die, since they cannot live but in much misery: being assured, that if they thus deliver themselves from torture, or are willing that others should do it, they shall be happy after death. Since by their acting thus, they lose none of the pleasures, but only the troubles of life; they think they behave not only reasonably, but in a

1935 manner consistent with religion and piety; because they follow the advice given them by their priests, who are the expounders of the will of God. Such as are wrought on by these persuasions, either starve themselves of their own accord, or take opium, and by that means die without pain. But no man is forced on this way of ending his life; and if they cannot be persuaded to it, this does not induce them to

1940 fail in their attendance and care of them; but as they believe that a voluntary death, when it is chosen upon such an authority, is very honourable, so if any man takes away his own life, without the approbation of the priests and the Senate, they give him none of the honours of a decent funeral, but throw his body into a ditch.

1945 Their women are not married before eighteen, nor their men before two-and-twenty, and if any of them run into forbidden embraces before marriage they are severely punished, and the privilege of marriage is denied them, unless they can obtain a special warrant from the Prince. Such disorders cast a great reproach upon the master and mistress of the family in which they happen, for it is supposed

1950 that they have failed in their duty. The reason of punishing this so severely is, because they think that if they were not strictly restrained from all vagrant appetites, very few would engage in a state in which they venture the quiet of their whole lives, by being confined to one person, and are obliged to endure all the inconveniences with which it is accompanied. In choosing their wives they use a

1955 method that would appear to us very absurd and ridiculous, but it is constantly observed among them, and is accounted perfectly consistent with wisdom. Before marriage some grave matron presents the bride naked, whether she is a virgin or a widow, to the bridegroom; and after that some grave man presents the bridegroom naked to the bride. We indeed both laughed at this, and condemned it as very

1960 indecent. But they, on the other hand, wondered at the folly of the men of all other nations, who, if they are but to buy a horse of a small value, are so cautious that they will see every part of him, and take off both his saddle and all his other tackle, that there may be no secret ulcer hid under any of them; and that yet in the choice of a wife, on which depends the happiness or unhappiness of the rest of his

1965 life, a man should venture upon trust, and only see about a hand's-breadth of the face, all the rest of the body being covered, under which there may lie hid what may be contagious, as well as loathsome. All men are not so wise as to choose a woman only for her good qualities; and even wise men consider the body as that which adds not a little to the mind: and it is certain there may be some such

1970 deformity covered with the clothes as may totally alienate a man from his wife when it is too late to part with her. If such a thing is discovered after marriage, a man has no remedy but patience. They therefore think it is reasonable that there should be good provision made against such mischievous frauds.

1975 There was so much the more reason for them to make a regulation in this matter, because they are the only people of those parts that neither allow of polygamy, nor of divorces, except in the case of adultery, or insufferable perverseness; for in these cases the Senate dissolves the marriage, and grants the injured person leave to marry again; but the guilty are made infamous, and are never allowed the privilege of a second marriage. None are suffered to put away

1980 their wives against their wills, from any great calamity that may have fallen on their persons; for they look on it as the height of cruelty and treachery to abandon either of the married persons when they need most the tender care of their comfort, and that chiefly in the case of old age, which as it carries many diseases along with it, so it is a disease of itself. But it frequently falls out that when a married

1985 couple do not well agree, they by mutual consent separate, and find out other persons with whom they hope they may live more happily. Yet this is not done without obtaining leave of the Senate, which never admits of a divorce, but upon a strict inquiry made, both by the senators and their wives, into the grounds upon which it is desired; and even when they are satisfied concerning the reasons of it,

1990 they go on but slowly, for they imagine that too great easiness in granting leave for new marriages would very much shake the kindness of married people. They punish severely those that defile the marriage-bed. If both parties are married they are divorced, and the injured persons may marry one another, or whom they please; but the adulterer and the adulteress are condemned to slavery. Yet if either

1995 of the injured persons cannot shake off the love of the married person, they may live with them still in that state, but they must follow them to that labour to which the slaves are condemned; and sometimes the repentance of the condemned, together with the unshaken kindness of the innocent and injured person, has prevailed so far with the Prince that he has taken off the sentence; but those that relapse after

2000 they are once pardoned are punished with death.

Their law does not determine the punishment for other crimes; but that is left to the Senate, to temper it according to the circumstances of the fact. Husbands have power to correct their wives, and parents to chastise their children, unless the fault is so great that a public punishment is thought necessary for striking

2005 terror into others. For the most part, slavery is the punishment even of the greatest crimes; for as that is no less terrible to the criminals themselves than death, so they think the preserving them in a state of servitude is more for the interest of the commonwealth than killing them; since as their labour is a greater benefit to the public than their death could be, so the sight of their misery is a more lasting terror

2010 to other men than that which would be given by their death. If their slaves rebel, and will not bear their yoke, and submit to the labour that is enjoined them, they are treated as wild beasts that cannot be kept in order, neither by a prison, nor by their chains; and are at last put to death. But those who bear their punishment patiently, and are so much wrought on by that pressure that lies so hard on them

2015 that it appears they are really more troubled for the crimes they have committed than for the miseries they suffer, are not out of hope but that at last either the Prince will, by his prerogative, or the people by their intercession, restore them

2020 again to their liberty, or at least very much mitigate their slavery. He that tempts a married woman to adultery, is no less severely punished than he that commits it; for they believe that a deliberate design to commit a crime, is equal to the fact itself: since its not taking effect does not make the person that miscarried in his attempt at all the less guilty.

2025 They take great pleasure in fools, and as it is thought a base and unbecoming thing to use them ill, so they do not think it amiss for people to divert themselves with their folly: and, in their opinion, this is a great advantage to the fools themselves: for if men were so sullen and severe as not at all to please themselves with their ridiculous behaviour and foolish sayings, which is all that they can do to recommend themselves to others, it could not be expected that they would be so well provided for, nor so tenderly used as they must otherwise be. If any man

2030 should reproach another for his being misshaped or imperfect in any part of his body, it would not at all be thought a reflection on the person so treated, but it would be accounted scandalous in him that had upbraided another with what he could not help. It is thought a sign of a sluggish and sordid mind not to preserve carefully one's natural beauty; but it is likewise infamous among them to use

2035 paint. They all see that no beauty recommends a wife so much to her husband as the probity of her life, and her obedience: for as some few are catched and held only by beauty, so all are attracted by the other excellences which charm all the world.

As they fright men from committing crimes by punishments, so they invite them

2040 to the love of virtue by public honours: therefore they erect statues to the memories of such worthy men as have deserved well of their country, and set these in their market-places, both to perpetuate the remembrance of their actions, and to be an incitement to their posterity to follow their example.

If any man aspires to any office, he is sure never to compass it: they all live

2045 easily together, for none of the magistrates are either insolent or cruel to the people: they affect rather to be called fathers, and by being really so, they well deserve the name; and the people pay them all the marks of honour the more freely, because none are exacted from them. The Prince himself has no distinction, either of garments, or of a crown; but is only distinguished by a sheaf of corn carried

2050 before him; as the high priest is also known by his being preceded by a person carrying a wax light.

They have but few laws, and such is their constitution that they need not many. They very much condemn other nations, whose laws, together with the commentaries on them, swell up to so many volumes; for they think it an

2055 unreasonable thing to oblige men to obey a body of laws that are both of such a bulk, and so dark as not to be read and understood by every one of the subjects.

They have no lawyers among them, for they consider them as a sort of people whose profession it is to disguise matters, and to wrest the laws; and therefore they think it is much better that every man should plead his own cause, and trust it

2060 to the judge, as in other places the client trusts it to a counsellor. By this means they both cut off many delays, and find out truth more certainly: for after the

parties have laid open the merits of the cause, without those artifices which lawyers are apt to suggest, the judge examines the whole matter, and supports the simplicity of such well-meaning persons, whom otherwise crafty men would be
2065 sure to run down: and thus they avoid those evils which appear very remarkably among all those nations that labour under a vast load of laws. Every one of them is skilled in their law, for as it is a very short study, so the plainest meaning of which words are capable is always the sense of their laws. And they argue thus: all laws are promulgated for this end, that every man may know his duty; and
2070 therefore the plainest and most obvious sense of the words is that which ought to be put upon them; since a more refined exposition cannot be easily comprehended, and would only serve to make the laws become useless to the greater part of mankind, and especially to those who need most the direction of them: for it is all one, not to make a law at all, or to couch it in such terms that without a quick
2075 apprehension, and much study, a man cannot find out the true meaning of it; since the generality of mankind are both so dull, and so much employed in their several trades, that they have neither the leisure nor the capacity requisite for such an inquiry.

Some of their neighbours, who are masters of their own liberties, having long
2080 ago, by the assistance of the Utopians, shaken off the yoke of tyranny, and being much taken with those virtues which they observe among them, have come to desire that they would send magistrates to govern them; some changing them every year, and others every five years. At the end of their government they bring them back to Utopia, with great expressions of honour and esteem, and carry away others to
2085 govern in their stead. In this they seem to have fallen upon a very good expedient for their own happiness and safety; for since the good or ill condition of a nation depends so much upon their magistrates, they could not have made a better choice than by pitching on men whom no advantages can bias; for wealth is of no use to them, since they must so soon go back to their own country; and they being
2090 strangers among them, are not engaged in any of their heats or animosities; and it is certain that when public judicatories are swayed, either by avarice or partial affections, there must follow a dissolution of justice, the chief sinew of society.

The Utopians call those nations that come and ask magistrates from them, neighbours; but those to whom they have been of more particular service, friends.
2095 And as all other nations are perpetually either making leagues or breaking them, they never enter into an alliance with any state. They think leagues are useless things, and believe that if the common ties of humanity do not knit men together, the faith of promises will have no great effect; and they are the more confirmed in this by what they see among the nations round about them, who are no strict observers
2100 of leagues and treaties. We know how religiously they are observed in Europe, more particularly where the Christian doctrine is received, among whom they are sacred and inviolable. Which is partly owing to the justice and goodness of the princes themselves, and partly to the reverence they pay to the popes; who as they are most religious observers of their own promises, so they exhort all other
2105 princes to perform theirs; and when fainter methods do not prevail, they compel

2110

them to it by the severity of the pastoral censure, and think that it would be the most indecent thing possible if men who are particularly distinguished by the title of the faithful, should not religiously keep the faith of their treaties. But in that new-found world, which is not more distant from us in situation than the people are in their manners and course of life, there is no trusting to leagues, even though they were made with all the pomp of the most sacred ceremonies; on the contrary, they are on this account the sooner broken, some slight pretence being found in the words of the treaties, which are purposely couched in such ambiguous terms that they can never be so strictly bound but they will always find some loophole to

2115

escape at; and thus they break both their leagues and their faith. And this is done with such impudence, that those very men who value themselves on having suggested these expedients to their princes, would with a haughty scorn declaim against such craft, or to speak plainer, such fraud and deceit, if they found private men make use of it in their bargains, and would readily say that they deserved to

2120

be hanged.

By this means it is, that all sort of justice passes in the world for a lowspirited and vulgar virtue, far below the dignity of royal greatness. Or at least, there are set up two sorts of justice; the one is mean, and creeps on the ground, and therefore becomes none but the lower part of mankind, and so must be

2125

kept in severely by many restraints that it may not break out beyond the bounds that are set to it. The other is the peculiar virtue of princes, which as it is more majestic than that which becomes the rabble, so takes a freer compass; and thus lawful and unlawful are only measured by pleasure and interest. These practices of the princes that lie about Utopia, who make so little account of their faith, seem

2130

to be the reasons that determine them to engage in no confederacies; perhaps they would change their mind if they lived among us; but yet though treaties were more religiously observed, they would still dislike the custom of making them; since the world has taken up a false maxim upon it, as if there were no tie of Nature uniting one nation to another, only separated perhaps by a mountain or a river, and that

2135

all were born in a state of hostility, and so might lawfully do all that mischief to their neighbours against which there is no provision made by treaties; and that when treaties are made, they do not cut off the enmity, or restrain the license of preying upon each other, if by the unskilfulness of wording them there are not effectual provisoes made against them. They, on the other hand, judge that no man

2140

is to be esteemed our enemy that has never injured us; and that the partnership of the human nature is instead of a league. And that kindness and good-nature unite men more effectually and with greater strength than any agreements whatsoever; since thereby the engagements of men's hearts become stronger than the bond and obligation of words.

OF THEIR MILITARY DISCIPLINE.

2145

They detest war as a very brutal thing; and which, to the reproach of human nature, is more practised by men than by any sort of beasts. They, in opposition to

the sentiments of almost all other nations, think that there is nothing more inglorious than that glory that is gained by war. And therefore though they accustom themselves daily to military exercises and the discipline of war, in
2150   which not only their men but their women likewise are trained up, that in cases of necessity they may not be quite useless; yet they do not rashly engage in war, unless it be either to defend themselves, or their friends, from any unjust aggressors; or out of good-nature or in compassion assist an oppressed nation in shaking off the yoke of tyranny. They indeed help their friends, not only in
2155   defensive, but also in offensive wars; but they never do that unless they had been consulted before the breach was made, and being satisfied with the grounds on which they went, they had found that all demands of reparation were rejected, so that a war was unavoidable. This they think to be not only just, when one neighbour makes an inroad on another, by public order, and carry away the
2160   spoils; but when the merchants of one country are oppressed in another, either under pretence of some unjust laws, or by the perverse wresting of good ones. This they count a juster cause of war than the other, because those injuries are done under some colour of laws. This was the only ground of that war in which they engaged with the Nephelogetes against the Aleopolitanes, a little before our time;
2165   for the merchants of the former having, as they thought, met with great injustice among the latter, which, whether it was in itself right or wrong, drew on a terrible war, in which many of their neighbours were engaged; and their keenness in carrying it on being supported by their strength in maintaining it, it not only shook some very flourishing states, and very much afflicted others, but after a series of
2170   much mischief ended in the entire conquest and slavery of the Aleopolitanes, who though before the war they were in all respects much superior to the Nephelogetes, were yet subdued; but though the Utopians had assisted them in the war, yet they pretended to no share of the spoil.

But though they so vigorously assist their friends in obtaining reparation for
2175   the injuries they have received in affairs of this nature, yet if any such frauds was committed against themselves, provided no violence was done to their persons, they would only on their being refused satisfaction forbear trading with such a people. This is not because they consider their neighbours more than their own citizens; but since their neighbours trade every one upon his own stock, fraud is a
2180   more sensible injury to them than it is to the Utopians, among whom the public in such a case only suffers. As they expect nothing in return for the merchandises they export but that in which they so much abound, and is of little use to them, the loss does not much affect them; they think therefore it would be too severe to revenge a loss attended with so little inconvenience either to their lives, or their
2185   subsistence, with the death of many persons; but if any of their people is either killed or wounded wrongfully, whether it be done by public authority or only by private men, as soon as they hear of it they send ambassadors, and demand that the guilty persons may be delivered up to them; and if that is denied, they declare war; but if it be complied with, the offenders are condemned either to death or slavery.

2190 They would be both troubled and ashamed of a bloody victory over their enemies, and think it would be as foolish a purchase as to buy the most valuable goods at too high a rate. And in no victory do they glory so much as in that which is gained by dexterity and good conduct, without bloodshed. In such cases they appoint public triumphs, and erect trophies to the honour of those who have

2195 succeeded; for then do they reckon that a man acts suitably to his nature when he conquers his enemy in such a way as that no other creature but a man could be capable of, and that is by the strength of his understanding. Bears, lions, boars, wolves, and dogs, and all other animals employ their bodily force one against another, in which as many of them are superior to men, both in strength and

2200 fierceness, so they are all subdued by his reason and understanding.

 The only design of the Utopians in war is to obtain that by force, which if it had been granted them in time would have prevented the war; or if that cannot be done, to take so severe a revenge on those that have injured them that they may be terrified from doing the like for the time to come. By these ends they measure all

2205 their designs, and manage them so that it is visible that the appetite of fame or vain-glory does not work so much on them as a just care of their own security.

 As soon as they declare war, they take care to have a great many schedules, that are sealed with their common seal, affixed in the most conspicuous places of their enemies' country. This is carried secretly, and done in many places all at

2210 once. In these they promise great rewards to such as shall kill the prince, and lesser in proportion to such as shall kill any other persons, who are those on whom, next to the prince himself, they cast the chief balance of the war. And they double the sum to him that, instead of killing the person so marked out, shall take him alive and put him in their hands. They offer not only indemnity, but rewards,

2215 to such of the persons themselves that are so marked, if they will act against their countrymen: by this means those that are named in their schedules become not only distrustful of their fellow-citizens, but are jealous of one another, and are much distracted by fear and danger; for it has often fallen out that many of them, and even the Prince himself, have been betrayed by those in whom they have trusted

2220 most: for the rewards that the Utopians offer are so unmeasurably great, that there is no sort of crime to which men cannot be drawn by them. They consider the risk that those run who undertake such services, and offer a recompense proportioned to the danger; not only a vast deal of gold, but great revenues in lands, that lie among other nations that are their friends, where they may go and enjoy them very

2225 securely; and they observe the promises they make of this kind most religiously. They very much approve of this way of corrupting their enemies, though it appears to others to be base and cruel; but they look on it as a wise course, to make an end of what would be otherwise a long war, without so much as hazarding one battle to decide it. They think it likewise an act of mercy and love to mankind to prevent

2230 the great slaughter of those that must otherwise be killed in the progress of the war, both on their own side and on that of their enemies, by the death of a few that are most guilty; and that in so doing they are kind even to their enemies, and pity them no less than their own people, as knowing that the greater part of them do not

2235   engage in the war of their own accord, but are driven into it by the passions of their prince.

If this method does not succeed with them, then they sow seeds of contention among their enemies, and animate the prince's brother, or some of the nobility, to aspire to the crown. If they cannot disunite them by domestic broils, then they engage their neighbours against them, and make them set on foot some old

2240   pretensions, which are never wanting to princes when they have occasion for them. These they plentifully supply with money, though but very sparingly with any auxiliary troops: for they are so tender of their own people, that they would not willingly exchange one of them, even with the prince of their enemies' country.

But as they keep their gold and silver only for such an occasion, so when that

2245   offers itself they easily part with it, since it would be no inconvenience to them though they should reserve nothing of it to themselves. For besides the wealth that they have among them at home, they have a vast treasure abroad, many nations round about them being deep in their debt: so that they hire soldiers from all places for carrying on their wars, but chiefly from the Zapolets, who live five hundred

2250   miles east of Utopia. They are a rude, wild, and fierce nation, who delight in the woods and rocks, among which they were born and bred up. They are hardened both against heat, cold and labour, and know nothing of the delicacies of life. They do not apply themselves to agriculture, nor do they care either for their houses or their clothes. Cattle is all that they look after; and for the greatest part

2255   they live either by hunting, or upon rapine; and are made, as it were, only for war. They watch all opportunities of engaging in it, and very readily embrace such as are offered them. Great numbers of them will frequently go out, and offer themselves for a very low pay, to serve any that will employ them: they know none of the arts of life, but those that lead to the taking it away; they serve those that

2260   hire them, both with much courage and great fidelity; but will not engage to serve for any determined time, and agree upon such terms, that the next day they may go over to the enemies of those whom they serve, if they offer them a greater encouragement: and will perhaps return to them the day after that, upon a higher advance of their pay. There are few wars in which they make not a considerable

2265   part of the armies of both sides: so it often falls out that they who are related, and were hired in the same country, and so have lived long and familiarly together, forgetting both their relations and former friendship, kill one another upon no other consideration than that of being hired to it for a little money, by princes of different interests; and such a regard have they for money, that they are easily

2270   wrought on by the difference of one penny a day to change sides. So entirely does their avarice influence them; and yet this money, which they value so highly, is of little use to them; for what they purchase thus with their blood, they quickly waste on luxury, which among them is but of a poor and miserable form.

This nation serves the Utopians against all people whatsoever, for they pay

2275   higher than any other. The Utopians hold this for a maxim, that as they seek out the best sort of men for their own use at home, so they make use of this worst sort of men for the consumption of war, and therefore they hire them with the offers of vast rewards, to expose themselves to all sorts of hazards, out of which the greater part never returns to claim their promises. Yet they make them good most religiously to such as escape. This animates them to adventure again, whenever there is occasion for it; for the Utopians are not at all troubled how many of these happen to be killed, and reckon it a service done to mankind if they could be a means to deliver the world from such a lewd and vicious sort of people, that seem to have run together as to the drain of human nature. Next to these they are served in their wars with those upon whose account they undertake them, and with the auxiliary troops of their other friends, to whom they join a few of their own people, and send some men of eminent and approved virtue to command in chief There are two sent with him, who during his command are but private men, but the first is to succeed him if he should happen to be either killed or taken; and in case of the like misfortune to him, the third comes in his place; and thus they provide against ill events, that such accidents as may befall their generals may not endanger their armies. When they draw out troops of their own people, they take such out of every city as freely offer themselves, for none are forced to go against their wills, since they think that if any man is pressed that wants courage, he will not only act faintly, but by his cowardice dishearten others. But if an invasion is made on their country they make use of such men, if they have good bodies, though they are not brave; and either put them aboard their ships or place them on the walls of their towns, that being so posted they may find no opportunity of flying away; and thus either shame, the heat of action, or the impossibility of flying, bears down their cowardice; they often make a virtue of necessity and behave themselves well, because nothing else is left them. But as they force no man to go into any foreign war against his will, so they do not hinder those women who are willing to go along with their husbands; on the contrary they encourage and praise them, and they stand often next their husbands in the front of the army. They also place together those who are related, parents and children, kindred, and those that are mutually allied, near one another; that those whom Nature has inspired with the greatest zeal for assisting one another, may be the nearest and readiest to do it; and it is matter of great reproach if husband or wife survive one another, or if a child survives his parents, and therefore when they come to be engaged in action they continue to fight to the last man, if their enemies stand before them. And as they use all prudent methods to avoid the endangering their own men, and if it is possible let all the action and danger fall upon the troops that they hire, so if it becomes necessary for themselves to engage, they then charge with as much courage as they avoided it before with prudence: nor is it a fierce charge at first, but it increases by degrees; and as they continue in action, they grow more obstinate and press harder upon the enemy, insomuch that they will much sooner die than give ground; for the certainty that their children will be well looked after when they are dead, frees them from all that anxiety concerning them which often masters men of great courage; and thus they are animated by a noble and invincible resolution. Their skill in military affairs increases their courage; and the wise sentiments which, according to the laws of their country are instilled into them in

their education, give additional vigour to their minds: for as they do not
undervalue life so as prodigally to throw it away, they are not so indecently fond
of it as to preserve it by base and unbecoming methods. In the greatest heat of
2325   action, the bravest of their youth, who have devoted themselves to that service,
single out the general of their enemies, set on him either openly or by ambuscade,
pursue him everywhere, and when spent and wearied out, are relieved by others,
who never give over the pursuit; either attacking him with close weapons when
they can get near him, or with those which wound at a distance, when others get in
2330   between them; so that unless he secures himself by flight, they seldom fail at last to
kill or to take him prisoner. When they have obtained a victory, they kill as few as
possible, and are much more bent on taking many prisoners than on killing those
that fly before them; nor do they ever let their men so loose in the pursuit of their
enemies, as not to retain an entire body still in order; so that if they have been
2335   forced to engage the last of their battalions before they could gain the day, they
will rather let their enemies all escape than pursue them, when their own army is
in disorder; remembering well what has often fallen out to themselves, that when
the main body of their army has been quite defeated and broken, when their
enemies imagining the victory obtained, have let themselves loose into an irregular
2340   pursuit, a few of them that lay for a reserve, waiting a fit opportunity, have fallen
on them in their chase, and when straggling in disorder and apprehensive of no
danger, but counting the day their own, have turned the whole action, and
wresting out of their hands a victory that seemed certain and undoubted, while the
vanquished have suddenly become victorious.
2345   It is hard to tell whether they are more dexterous in laying or avoiding
ambushes. They sometimes seem to fly when it is far from their thoughts; and when
they intend to give ground, they do it so that it is very hard to find out their design.
If they see they are ill posted, or are like to be overpowered by numbers, they then
either march off in the night with great silence, or by some stratagem delude their
2350   enemies: if they retire in the daytime, they do it in such order, that it is no less
dangerous to fall upon them in a retreat than in a march. They fortify their camps
with a deep and large trench, and throw up the earth that is dug out of it for a
wall; nor do they employ only their slaves in this, but the whole army works at it,
except those that are then upon the guard; so that when so many hands are at
2355   work, a great line and a strong fortification is finished in so short a time that it is
scarce credible. Their armour is very strong for defence, and yet is not so heavy as
to make them uneasy in their marches; they can even swim with it. All that are
trained up to war, practise swimming. Both horse and foot make great use of
arrows, and are very expert. They have no swords, but fight with a poleaxe that
2360   is both sharp and heavy, by which they thrust or strike down an enemy. They are
very good at finding out warlike machines, and disguise them so well, that the
enemy does not perceive them till he feels the use of them; so that he cannot prepare
such a defence as would render them useless; the chief consideration had in the
making them, is that they may be easily carried and managed.

2365   If they agree to a truce, they observe it so religiously that no provocations will make them break it. They never lay their enemies' country waste, nor burn their corn, and even in their marches they take all possible care that neither horse nor foot may tread it down, for they do not know but that they may have use for it themselves. They hurt no man whom they find disarmed, unless he is a spy. When a

2370 town is surrendered to them, they take it into their protection: and when they carry a place by storm, they never plunder it, but put those only to the sword that opposed the rendering of it up, and make the rest of the garrison slaves, but for the other inhabitants, they do them no hurt; and if any of them had advised a surrender, they give them good rewards out of the estates of those that they

2375 condemn, and distribute the rest among their auxiliary troops, but they themselves take no share of the spoil.

     When a war is ended, they do not oblige their friends to reimburse their expenses; but they obtain them of the conquered, either in money, which they keep for the next occasion, or in lands, out of which a constant revenue is to be paid

2380 them; by many increases, the revenue which they draw out from several countries on such occasions, is now risen to above 700,000 ducats a year. They send some of their own people to receive these revenues, who have orders to live magnificently, and like princes, by which means they consume much of it upon the place; and either bring over the rest to Utopia, or lend it to that nation in which it lies. This

2385 they most commonly do, unless some great occasion, which falls out but very seldom, should oblige them to call for it all. It is out of these lands that they assign rewards to such as they encourage to adventure on desperate attempts. If any prince that engages in war with them is making preparations for invading their country, they prevent him, and make his country the seat of the war; for they do

2390 not willingly suffer any war to break in upon their island; and if that should happen, they would only defend themselves by their own people, but would not call for auxiliary troops to their assistance.

OF THE RELIGIONS OF THE UTOPIANS.

     There are several sorts of religions, not only in different parts of the island, but even in every town; some worshipping the sun, others the moon, or one of the

2395 planets: some worship such men as have been eminent in former times for virtue, or glory, not only as ordinary deities, but as the supreme God: yet the greater and wiser sort of them worship none of these, but adore one eternal, invisible, infinite, and incomprehensible Deity; as a Being that is far above all our apprehensions, that is spread over the whole universe, not by His bulk, but by His power and

2400 virtue; Him they call the Father of All, and acknowledge that the beginnings, the increase, the progress, the vicissitudes, and the end of all things come only from Him; nor do they offer divine honours to any but to Him alone. And indeed, though they differ concerning other things, yet all agree in this, that they think there is one supreme Being that made and governs the world, whom they call in the language of

2405 their country Mithras. They differ in this, that one thinks the God whom he worships is this supreme Being, and another thinks that his idol is that God; but they all agree in one principle, that whoever is this supreme Being, He is also that great Essence to whose glory and majesty all honours are ascribed by the consent of all nations.

2410   By degrees, they fall off from the various superstitions that are among them, and grow up to that one religion that is the best and most in request; and there is no doubt to be made but that all the others had vanished long ago, if some of those who advised them to lay aside their superstitions had not met with some unhappy accident, which being considered as inflicted by Heaven, made them afraid that the

2415   God whose worship had like to have been abandoned, had interposed, and revenged themselves on those who despised their authority.

     After they had heard from us an account of the doctrine, the course of life, and the miracles of Christ, and of the wonderful constancy of so many martyrs, whose blood, so willingly offered up by them, was the chief occasion of spreading their

2420   religion over a vast number of nations; it is not to be imagined how inclined they were to receive it. I shall not determine whether this proceeded from any secret inspiration of God, or whether it was because it seemed so favourable to that community of goods, which is an opinion so particular as well as so dear to them; since they perceived that Christ and His followers lived by that rule, and that it

2425   was still kept up in some communities among the sincerest sort of Christians. From whichsoever of these motives it might be, true it is that many of them came over to our religion, and were initiated into it by baptism. But as two of our number were dead, so none of the four that survived were in priest's orders; we therefore could only baptize them; so that to our great regret they could not partake of the other

2430   sacraments, that can only be administered by priests; but they are instructed concerning them, and long most vehemently for them. They have had great disputes among themselves, whether one chosen by them to be a priest would not be thereby qualified to do all the things that belong to that character, even though he had no authority derived from the Pope; and they seemed to be resolved to choose some for

2435   that employment, but they had not done it when I left them.

     Those among them that have not received our religion, do not fright any from it, and use none ill that goes over to it; so that all the while I was there, one man was only punished on this occasion. He being newly baptized, did, notwithstanding all that we could say to the contrary, dispute publicly

2440   concerning the Christian religion with more zeal than discretion; and with so much heat, that he not only preferred our worship to theirs, but condemned all their rites as profane; and cried out against all that adhered to them, as impious and sacrilegious persons, that were to be damned to everlasting burnings. Upon his having frequently preached in this manner, he was seized, and after trial he

2445   was condemned to banishment, not for having disparaged their religion, but for his inflaming the people to sedition: for this is one of their most ancient laws, that no man ought to be punished for his religion. At the first constitution of their government, Utopus having understood that before his coming among them the old inhabitants had been engaged in great quarrels concerning religion, by which they

2450 were so divided among themselves, that he found it an easy thing to conquer them, since instead of uniting their forces against him, every different party in religion fought by themselves; after he had subdued them, he made a law that every man might be of what religion he pleased, and might endeavour to draw others to it by the force of argument, and by amicable and modest ways, but without bitterness

2455 against those of other opinions; but that he ought to use no other force but that of persuasion, and was neither to mix with it reproaches nor violence; and such as did otherwise were to be condemned to banishment or slavery.

This law was made by Utopus, not only for preserving the public peace, which he saw suffered much by daily contentions and irreconcilable heats, but

2460 because he thought the interest of religion itself required it. He judged it not fit to determine anything rashly, and seemed to doubt whether those different forms of religion might not all come from God, who might inspire men in a different manner, and be pleased with this variety; he therefore thought it indecent and foolish for any man to threaten and terrify another to make him believe what did not appear

2465 to him to be true. And supposing that only one religion was really true, and the rest false, he imagined that the native force of truth would at last break forth and shine bright, if supported only by the strength of argument, and attended to with a gentle and unprejudiced mind; while, on the other hand, if such debates were carried on with violence and tumults, as the most wicked are always the most

2470 obstinate, so the best and most holy religion might be choked with superstition, as corn is with briars and thorns; he therefore left men wholly to their liberty, that they might be free to believe as they should see cause; only he made a solemn and severe law against such as should so far degenerate from the dignity of human nature as to think that our souls died with our bodies, or that the world was

2475 governed by chance, without a wise overruling Providence: for they all formerly believed that there was a state of rewards and punishments to the good and bad after this life; and they now look on those that think otherwise as scarce fit to be counted men, since they degrade so noble a being as the soul, and reckon it no better than a beast's: thus they are far from looking on such men as fit for human

2480 society, or to be citizens of a well-ordered commonwealth; since a man of such principles must needs, as oft as he dares do it, despise all their laws and customs: for there is no doubt to be made that a man who is afraid of nothing but the law, and apprehends nothing after death, will not scruple to break through all the laws of his country, either by fraud or force, when by this means he may satisfy his

2485 appetites. They never raise any that hold these maxims, either to honours or offices, nor employ them in any public trust, but despise them, as men of base and sordid minds: yet they do not punish them, because they lay this down as a maxim that a man cannot make himself believe anything he pleases; nor do they drive any to dissemble their thoughts by threatenings, so that men are not tempted to lie or

2490 disguise their opinions; which being a sort of fraud, is abhorred by the Utopians. They take care indeed to prevent their disputing in defence of these opinions, especially before the common people; but they suffer, and even encourage them to dispute concerning them in private with their priests and other grave men, being

2495

confident that they will be cured of those mad opinions by having reason laid before them. There are many among them that run far to the other extreme, though it is neither thought an ill nor unreasonable opinion, and therefore is not at all discouraged. They think that the souls of beasts are immortal, though far inferior to the dignity of the human soul, and not capable of so great a happiness. They are almost all of them very firmly persuaded that good men will be infinitely happy in

2500

another state; so that though they are compassionate to all that are sick, yet they lament no man's death, except they see him loth to depart with life; for they look on this as a very ill presage, as if the soul, conscious to itself of guilt, and quite hopeless, was afraid to leave the body, from some secret hints of approaching misery. They think that such a man's appearance before God cannot be acceptable

2505

to Him, who being called on, does not go out cheerfully, but is backward and unwilling, and is, as it were, dragged to it. They are struck with horror when they see any die in this manner, and carry them out in silence and with sorrow, and praying God that He would be merciful to the errors of the departed soul, they lay the body in the ground; but when any die cheerfully, and full of hope, they do not

2510

mourn for them, but sing hymns when they carry out their bodies, and commending their souls very earnestly to God: their whole behaviour is then rather grave than sad, they burn the body, and set up a pillar where the pile was made, with an inscription to the honour of the deceased. When they come from the funeral, they discourse of his good life and worthy actions, but speak of nothing oftener and

2515

with more pleasure than of his serenity at the hour of death. They think such respect paid to the memory of good men is both the greatest incitement to engage others to follow their example, and the most acceptable worship that can be offered them; for they believe that though by the imperfection of human sight they are invisible to us, yet they are present among us, and hear those discourses that

2520

pass concerning themselves. They believe it inconsistent with the happiness of departed souls not to be at liberty to be where they will, and do not imagine them capable of the ingratitude of not desiring to see those friends with whom they lived on earth in the strictest bonds of love and kindness: besides they are persuaded that good men after death have these affections and all other good

2525

dispositions increased rather than diminished, and therefore conclude that they are still among the living and observe all they say or do. From hence they engage in all their affairs with the greater confidence of success, as trusting to their protection; while this opinion of the presence of their ancestors is a restraint that prevents their engaging in ill designs.

2530

They despise and laugh at auguries, and the other vain and superstitious ways of divination, so much observed among other nations; but have great reverence for such miracles as cannot flow from any of the powers of Nature, and look on them as effects and indications of the presence of the supreme Being, of which they saw many instances have occurred among them; and that sometimes

2535

their public prayers, which upon great and dangerous occasions they have solemnly put up to God, with assured confidence of being heard, have been answered in a miraculous manner.

They think the contemplating God in His works, and the adoring Him for them, is a very acceptable piece of worship to Him.

2540   There are many among them, that upon a motive of religion neglect learning, and apply themselves to no sort of study; nor do they allow themselves any leisure time, but are perpetually employed, believing that by the good things that a man does he secures to himself that happiness that comes after death. Some of these visit the sick; others mend highways, cleanse ditches, repair bridges, or dig turf, gravel,

2545   or stones. Others fell and cleave timber, and bring wood, corn, and other necessaries on carts into their towns. Nor do these only serve the public, but they serve even private men, more than the slaves themselves do; for if there is anywhere a rough, hard, and sordid piece of work to be done, from which many are frightened by the labour and loathsomeness of it, if not the despair of

2550   accomplishing it, they cheerfully, and of their own accord, take that to their share; and by that means, as they ease others very much, so they afflict themselves, and spend their whole life in hard labour; and yet they do not value themselves upon this, nor lessen other people's credit to raise their own; but by their stooping to such servile employments, they are so far from being despised, that they are so

2555   much the more esteemed by the whole nation.

    Of these there are two sorts; some live unmarried and chaste, and abstain from eating any sort of flesh; and thus weaning themselves from all the pleasures of the present life, which they account hurtful, they pursue, even by the hardest and painfullest methods possible, that blessedness which they hope for hereafter;

2560   and the nearer they approach to it, they are the more cheerful and earnest in their endeavours after it. Another sort of them is less willing to put themselves to much toil, and therefore prefer a married state to a single one; and as they do not deny themselves the pleasure of it, so they think the begetting of children is a debt which they owe to human nature and to their country; nor do they avoid any pleasure

2565   that does not hinder labour, and therefore eat flesh so much the more willingly, as they find that by this means they are the more able to work; the Utopians look upon these as the wiser sect, but they esteem the others as the most holy. They would indeed laugh at any man, who from the principles of reason would prefer an unmarried state to a married, or a life of labour to an easy life; but they

2570   reverence and admire such as do it from the motives of religion. There is nothing in which they are more cautious than in giving their opinion positively concerning any sort of religion. The men that lead those severe lives are called in the language of their country Brutheskas, which answers to those we call religious orders.

    Their priests are men of eminent piety, and therefore they are but few, for

2575   there are only thirteen in every town, one for every temple; but when they go to war, seven of these go out with their forces, and seven others are chosen to supply their room in their absence; but these enter again upon their employment when they return; and those who served in their absence attend upon the high-priest, till vacancies fall by death; for there is one set over all the rest. They are chosen by

2580   the people as the other magistrates are, by suffrages given in secret, for preventing of factions; and when they are chosen they are consecrated by the college of

priests. The care of all sacred things, the worship of God, and an inspection into
the manners of the people, are committed to them. It is a reproach to a man to be
sent for by any of them, or for them to speak to him in secret, for that always gives
2585   some suspicion. All that is incumbent on them is only to exhort and admonish the
people; for the power of correcting and punishing ill men belongs wholly to the
Prince and to the other magistrates. The severest thing that the priest does, is the
excluding those that are desperately wicked from joining in their worship. There
is not any sort of punishment more dreaded by them than this, for as it loads them
2590   with infamy, so it fills them with secret horrors, such is their reverence to their
religion; nor will their bodies be long exempted from their share of trouble; for if
they do not very quickly satisfy the priests of the truth of their repentance, they
are seized on by the Senate, and punished for their impiety. The education of youth
belongs to the priests, yet they do not take so much care of instructing them in
2595   letters as in forming their minds and manners aright; they use all possible methods
to infuse very early into the tender and flexible minds of children such opinions as
are both good in themselves and will be useful to their country. For when deep
impressions of these things are made at that age, they follow men through the
whole course of their lives, and conduce much to preserve the peace of the
2600   government, which suffers by nothing more than by vices that rise out of ill
opinions. The wives of their priests are the most extraordinary women of the
whole country; sometimes the women themselves are made priests, though that falls
out but seldom, nor are any but ancient widows chosen into that order.

    None of the magistrates have greater honour paid them than is paid the
2605   priests; and if they should happen to commit any crime, they would not be
questioned for it. Their punishment is left to God, and to their own consciences;
for they do not think it lawful to lay hands on any man, how wicked soever he is,
that has been in a peculiar manner dedicated to God; nor do they find any great
inconvenience in this, both because they have so few priests, and because these are
2610   chosen with much caution, so that it must be a very unusual thing to find one who
merely out of regard to his virtue, and for his being esteemed a singularly good
man, was raised up to so great a dignity, degenerate into corruption and vice. And
if such a thing should fall out, for man is a changeable creature, yet there being few
priests, and these having no authority but what rises out of the respect that is paid
2615   them, nothing of great consequence to the public can proceed from the indemnity
that the priests enjoy.

    They have indeed very few of them, lest greater number sharing in the same
honour might make the dignity of that order which they esteem so highly to sink in
its reputation. They also think it difficult to find out many of such an exalted pitch
2620   of goodness, as to be equal to that dignity which demands the exercise of more than
ordinary virtues. Nor are the priests in greater veneration among them than they
are among their neighbouring nations, as you may imagine by that which I think
gives occasion for it.

    When the Utopians engage in battle, the priests who accompany them to the
2625   war, apparelled in their sacred vestments, kneel down during the action, in a place

not far from the field; and lifting up their hands to heaven, pray, first for peace, and then for victory to their own side, and particularly that it may be gained without the effusion of much blood on either side; and when the victory turns to their side, they run in among their own men to restrain their fury; and if any of
2630 their enemies see them, or call to them, they are preserved by that means; and such as can come so near them as to touch their garments, have not only their lives, but their fortunes secured to them; it is upon this account that all the nations round about consider them so much, and treat them with such reverence, that they have been often no less able to preserve their own people from the fury of their enemies,
2635 than to save their enemies from their rage; for it has sometimes fallen out, that when their armies have been in disorder, and forced to fly, so that their enemies were running upon the slaughter and spoil, the priests by interposing have separated them from one another, and stopped the effusion of more blood; so that by their mediation a peace has been concluded on very reasonable terms; nor is
2640 there any nation about them so fierce, cruel, or barbarous as not to look upon their persons as sacred and inviolable.

The first and the last day of the month, and of the year, is a festival. They measure their months by the course of the moon, and their years by the course of the sun. The first days are called in their language the Cynemernes, and the last the
2645 Trapemernes; which answers in our language to the festival that begins, or ends the season.

They have magnificent temples, that are not only nobly built, but extremely spacious; which is the more necessary, as they have so few of them; they are a little dark within, which proceeds not from any error in the architecture, but is done
2650 with design; for their priests think that too much light dissipates the thoughts, and that a more moderate degree of it both recollects the mind and raises devotion. Though there are many different forms of religion among them, yet all these, how various soever, agree in the main point, which is the worshipping the Divine Essence; and therefore there is nothing to be seen or heard in their temples in
2655 which the several persuasions among them may not agree; for every sect performs those rites that are peculiar to it, in their private houses, nor is there anything in the public worship that contradicts the particular ways of those different sects. There are no images for God in their temples, so that every one may represent Him to his thoughts, according to the way of his religion; nor do they call this one God
2660 by any other name but that of Mithras, which is the common name by which they all express the Divine Essence, whatsoever otherwise they think it to be; nor are there any prayers among them but such as every one of them may use without prejudice to his own opinion.

They meet in their temples on the evening of the festival that concludes a
2665 season: and not having yet broke their fast, they thank God for their good success during that year or month, which is then at an end; and the next day being that which begins the new season, they meet early in their temples, to pray for the happy progress of all their affairs during that period upon which they then enter. In the festival which concludes the period, before they go to the temple, both wives

2670 and children fall on their knees before their husbands or parents, and confess everything in which they have either erred or failed in their duty, and beg pardon for it. Thus all little discontents in families are removed, that they may offer up their devotions with a pure and serene mind; for they hold it a great impiety to enter upon them with disturbed thoughts, or with a consciousness of their bearing

2675 hatred or anger in their hearts to any person whatsoever; and think that they should become liable to severe punishments if they presumed to offer sacrifices without cleansing their hearts, and reconciling all their differences. In the temples, the two sexes are separated, the men go to the right hand, and the women to the left; and the males and females all place themselves before the head and master or

2680 mistress of that family to which they belong; so that those who have the government of them at home may see their deportment in public; and they intermingle them so, that the younger and the older may be set by one another; for if the younger sort were all set together, they would perhaps trifle away that time too much in which they ought to beget in themselves that religious dread of the

2685 supreme Being, which is the greatest and almost the only incitement to virtue.

They offer up no living creature in sacrifice, nor do they think it suitable to the divine Being, from whose bounty it is that these creatures have derived their lives, to take pleasure in their deaths, or the offering up their blood. They burn incense and other sweet odours, and have a great number of wax lights during

2690 their worship; not out of any imagination that such oblations can add anything to the divine Nature, which even prayers cannot do; but as it is a harmless and pure way of worshipping God, as they think those sweet savours and lights, together with some other ceremonies, by a secret and unaccountable virtue, elevate men's souls, and inflame them with greater energy and cheerfulness during the divine

2695 worship.

All the people appear in the temples in white garments, but the priest's vestments are parti-coloured, and both the work and colours are wonderful. They are made of no rich materials, for they are neither embroidered nor set with precious stones, but are composed of the plumes of several birds, laid together

2700 with so much art and so neatly, that the true value of them is far beyond the costliest materials. They say that in the ordering and placing those plumes some dark mysteries are represented, which pass down among their priests in a secret tradition concerning them; and that they are as hieroglyphics, putting them in mind of the blessings that they have received from God, and of their duties both to Him

2705 and to their neighbours. As soon as the priest appears in those ornaments, they all fall prostrate on the ground, with so much reverence and so deep a silence that such as look on cannot but be struck with it, as if it were the effect of the appearance of a Deity. After they have been for some time in this posture, they all stand up, upon a sign given by the priest, and sing hymns to the honour of God,

2710 some musical instruments playing all the while. These are quite of another form than those used among us: but as many of them are much sweeter than ours, so others are made use of by us. Yet in one thing they very much exceed us; all their music, both vocal and instrumental, is adapted to imitate and express the passions,

2715 and is so happily suited to every occasion, that whether the subject of the hymn be cheerful or formed to soothe or trouble the mind, or to express grief or remorse, the music takes the impression of whatever is represented, affects and kindles the passions, and works the sentiments deep into the hearts of the hearers. When this is done, both priests and people offer up very solemn prayers to God in a set form of words; and these are so composed, that whatsoever is pronounced by the whole

2720 assembly may be likewise applied by every man in particular to his own condition; in these they acknowledge God to be the author and governor of the world, and the fountain of all the good they receive, and therefore offer up to Him their thanksgiving; and in particular bless Him for His goodness in ordering it so, that they are born under the happiest government in the world, and are of a

2725 religion which they hope is the truest of all others: but if they are mistaken, and if there is either a better government or a religion more acceptable to God, they implore His goodness to let them know it, vowing that they resolve to follow Him whithersoever He leads them. But if their government is the best, and their religion the truest, then they pray that He may fortify them in it, and bring all the world

2730 both to the same rules of life, and to the same opinions concerning himself; unless, according to the unsearchableness of His mind, He is pleased with a variety of religions. Then they pray that God may give them an easy passage at last to himself; not presuming to set limits to Him, how early or late it should be; but if it may be wished for, without derogating from His supreme authority, they desire to

2735 be quickly delivered, and to be taken to himself, though by the most terrible kind of death, rather than to be detained long from seeing Him by the most prosperous course of life. When this prayer is ended, they all fall down again upon the ground, and after a little while they rise up, go home to dinner, and spend the rest of the day in diversion or military exercises.

2740 Thus have I described to you, as particularly as I could, the constitution of that commonwealth, which I do not only think the best in the world, but indeed the only commonwealth that truly deserves that name. In all other places it is visible, that while people talk of a commonwealth, every man only seeks his own wealth; but there, where no man has any property, all men zealously pursue the good of

2745 the public: and, indeed, it is no wonder to see men act so differently; for in other commonwealths, every man knows that unless he provides for himself, how flourishing soever the commonwealth may be, he must die of hunger; so that he sees the necessity of preferring his own concerns to the public; but in Utopia, where every man has a right to everything, they all know that if care is taken to keep the

2750 public stores full, no private man can want anything; for among them there is no unequal distribution, so that no man is poor, none in necessity; and though no man has anything, yet they are all rich; for what can make a man so rich as to lead a serene and cheerful life, free from anxieties; neither apprehending want himself, nor vexed with the endless complaints of his wife? He is not afraid of the misery

2755 of his children, nor is he contriving how to raise a portion for his daughters, but is secure in this, that both he and his wife, his children and grandchildren, to as many generations as he can fancy, will all live both plentifully and happily; since

among them there is no less care taken of those who were once engaged in labour,
but grow afterwards unable to follow it, than there is elsewhere of these that
2760 continue still employed. I would gladly hear any man compare the justice that is
among them with that of all other nations; among whom, may I perish, if I see
anything that looks either like justice or equity: for what justice is there in this,
that a nobleman, a goldsmith, a banker, or any other man, that either does nothing
at all, or at best is employed in things that are of no use to the public, should live
2765 in great luxury and splendour, upon what is so ill acquired; and a mean man, a
carter, a smith, or a ploughman, that works harder even than the beasts
themselves, and is employed in labours so necessary, that no commonwealth could
hold out a year without them, can only earn so poor a livelihood, and must lead so
miserable a life, that the condition of the beasts is much better than theirs? For as
2770 the beasts do not work so constantly, so they feed almost as well, and with more
pleasure; and have no anxiety about what is to come, whilst these men are
depressed by a barren and fruitless employment, and tormented with the
apprehensions of want in their old age; since that which they get by their daily
labour does but maintain them at present, and is consumed as fast as it comes in,
2775 there is no overplus left to lay up for old age.

Is not that government both unjust and ungrateful, that is so prodigal of its
favours to those that are called gentlemen, or goldsmiths, or such others who are
idle, or live either by flattery, or by contriving the arts of vain pleasure; and on
the other hand, takes no care of those of a meaner sort, such as ploughmen, colliers,
2780 and smiths, without whom it could not subsist? But after the public has reaped all
the advantage of their service, and they come to be oppressed with age, sickness,
and want, all their labours and the good they have done is forgotten; and all the
recompense given them is that they are left to die in great misery. The richer sort
are often endeavouring to bring the hire of labourers lower, not only by their
2785 frandulent practices, but by the laws which they procure to be made to that effect;
so that though it is a thing most unjust in itself, to give such small rewards to those
who deserve so well of the public, yet they have given those hardships the name
and colour of justice, by procuring laws to be made for regulating them.

Therefore I must say that, as I hope for mercy, I can have no other notion of all
2790 the other governments that I see or know, than that they are a conspiracy of the
rich, who on pretence of managing the public only pursue their private ends, and
devise all the ways and arts they can find out; first, that they may, without danger,
preserve all that they have so ill acquired, and then that they may engage the poor
to toil and labour for them at as low rates as possible, and oppress them as much
2795 as they please. And if they can but prevail to get these contrivances established by
the show of public authority, which is considered as the representative of the
whole people, then they are accounted laws. Yet these wicked men after they have,
by a most insatiable covetousness, divided that among themselves with which all
the rest might have been well supplied, are far from that happiness that is enjoyed
2800 among the Utopians: for the use as well as the desire of money being extinguished,
much anxiety and great occasions of mischief is cut off with it. And who does not

see that the frauds, thefts, robberies, quarrels, tumults, contentions, seditions, murders, treacheries, and witchcrafts, which are indeed rather punished than restrained by the severities of law, would all fall off, if money were not any more valued by the world? Men's fears, solicitudes, cares, labours, and watchings, would all perish in the same moment with the value of money: even poverty itself, for the relief of which money seems most necessary, would fall. But, in order to the apprehending this aright, take one instance.

Consider any year that has been so unfruitful that many thousands have died of hunger; and yet if at the end of that year a survey was made of the granaries of all the rich men that have hoarded up the corn, it would be found that there was enough among them to have prevented all that consumption of men that perished in misery; and that if it had been distributed among them, none would have felt the terrible effects of that scarcity; so easy a thing would it be to supply all the necessities of life, if that blessed thing called money, which is pretended to be invented for procuring them, was not really the only thing that obstructed their being procured!

I do not doubt but rich men are sensible of this, and that they well know how much a greater happiness it is to want nothing necessary than to abound in many superfluities, and to be rescued out of so much misery than to abound with so much wealth; and I cannot think but the sense of every man's interest, added to the authority of Christ's commands, who as He was infinitely wise, knew what was best, and was not less good in discovering it to us, would have drawn all the world over to the laws of the Utopians, if pride, that plague of human nature, that source of so much misery, did not hinder it; for this vice does not measure happiness so much by its own conveniences as by the miseries of others; and would not be satisfied with being thought a goddess, if none were left that were miserable, over whom she might insult. Pride thinks its own happiness shines the brighter by comparing it with the misfortunes of other persons; that by displaying its own wealth, they may feel their poverty the more sensibly. This is that infernal serpent that creeps into the breasts of mortals, and possesses them too much to be easily drawn out; and therefore I am glad that the Utopians have fallen upon this form of government, in which I wish that all the world could be so wise as to imitate them; for they have indeed laid down such a scheme and foundation of policy, that as men live happily under it, so it is like to be of great continuance; for they having rooted out of the minds of their people all the seeds both of ambition and faction, there is no danger of any commotion at home; which alone has been the ruin of many states, that seemed otherwise to be well secured; but as long as they live in peace at home, and are governed by such good laws, the envy of all their neighbouring princes, who have often though in vain attempted their ruin, will never be able to put their state into any commotion or disorder.

2845

2850

2855

2860

When Raphael had thus made an end of speaking, though many things occurred to me, both concerning the manners and laws of that people, that seemed very absurd, as well as their way of making war, as in their notions of religion and divine matters; together with several other particulars, but chiefly what seemed the foundation of all the rest, their living in common, without the use of money, by which all nobility, magnificence, splendour, and majesty, which, according to the common opinion, are the true ornaments of a nation, would be quite taken away; yet since I perceived that Raphael was weary, and was not sure whether he could easily bear contradiction, remembering that he had taken notice of some who seemed to think they were bound in honour to support the credit of their own wisdom, by finding out something to censure in all other men's inventions, besides their own; I only commended their constitution, and the account he had given of it in general; and so taking him by the hand, carried him to supper, and told him I would find out some other time for examining this subject more particularly, and for discoursing more copiously upon it; and indeed I shall be glad to embrace an opportunity of doing it. In the meanwhile, though it must be confessed that he is both a very learned man, and a person who has obtained a great knowledge of the world, I cannot perfectly agree to everything he has related; however, there are many things in the Commonwealth of Utopia that I rather wish, than hope, to see followed in our governments.

14. THE PRINCE
(1513)

Niccolò Machiavelli
(1469–1527)

(trans. by N. H. Thomson)

The chaotic conditions of Florence and the intellectual ferment of the Renaissance renewed the classical concerns with politics, the art of social living. Machiavelli responded with The Prince, *a manual dedicated to Lorenzo de'Medici, to offer advice as to how princes might gain and maintain power. Unlike other political treatises offering ideal solutions for governance, such as Plato's* Republic *and the yet to be published* Utopia *of Thomas More, Machiavelli, drawing on the example of Rome, presents expedience as the goal, seeing "it better to follow the real truth of things than an imaginary view of them." The "real truth of things" reveals a view of the human person that is controversial, but as the chief goal of government is peace and stability, Machiavelli advocates the "end to justify the means;" the result is a separation of morality and politics so the prince may "use or not use his goodness as necessity requires."*

DEDICATION

TO THE MAGNIFICENT LORENZO DI PIERO DE'MEDICI

It is customary for such as seek a Prince's favour, to present themselves before him with those things of theirs which they themselves most value, or in which they perceive him chiefly to delight. Accordingly, we often see horses, armour, cloth of gold, precious stones, and the like costly gifts, offered to Princes as worthy of their

5   greatness. Desiring in like manner to approach your Magnificence with some token of my devotion, I have found among my possessions none that I so much prize and esteem as a knowledge of the actions of great men, acquired in the course of a long experience of modern affairs and a continual study of antiquity. Which knowledge most carefully and patiently pondered over and sifted by me, and now

10   reduced into this little book, I send to your Magnificence. And though I deem the work unworthy of your greatness, yet am I bold enough to hope that your courtesy will dispose you to accept it, considering that I can offer you no better gift than the means of mastering in a very brief time, all that in the course of so many years, and at the cost of so many hardships and dangers, I have learned, and know.

15   This work I have not adorned or amplified with rounded periods, swelling and high-flown language, or any other of those extrinsic attractions and allurements wherewith many authors are wont to set off and grace their writings;

since it is my desire that it should either pass wholly unhonoured, or that the truth of its matter and the importance of its subject should alone recommend it.

20   Nor would I have it thought presumption that a person of very mean and humble station should venture to discourse and lay down rules concerning the government of Princes. For as those who make maps of countries place themselves low down in the plains to study the character of mountains and elevated lands, and place themselves high up on the mountains to get a better view of the plains, so

25   in like manner to understand the People a man should be a Prince, and to have a clear notion of Princes he should belong to the People.

    Let your Magnificence, then, accept this little gift in the spirit in which I offer it; wherein, if you diligently read and study it, you will recognize my extreme desire that you should attain to that eminence which Fortune and your own merits

30   promise you. Should you from the height of your greatness some time turn your eyes to these humble regions, you will become aware how undeservedly I have to endure the keen and unremitting malignity of Fortune.

CHAPTER I: OF THE VARIOUS KINDS OF PRINCEDOM, AND OF THE WAYS IN WHICH THEY ARE ACQUIRED

    All the States and Governments by which men are or ever have been ruled, have been and are either Republics or Princedoms. Princedoms are either

35   hereditary, in which the sovereignty is derived through an ancient line of ancestors, or they are new. New Princedoms are either wholly new, as that of Milan to Francesco Sforza; or they are like limbs joined on to the hereditary possessions of the Prince who acquires them, as the Kingdom of Naples to the dominions of the King of Spain. The States thus acquired have either been used to

40   live under a Prince or have been free; and he who acquires them does so either by his own arms or by the arms of others, and either by good fortune or by merit.

CHAPTER II: OF HEREDITARY PRINCEDOMS

    Of Republics I shall not now speak, having elsewhere spoken of them at length. Here I shall treat exclusively of Princedoms, and, filling in the outline above traced out, shall proceed to examine how such States are to be governed and

45   maintained.

    I say, then, that hereditary States, accustomed to the family of their Prince, are maintained with far less difficulty than new States, since all that is required is that the Prince shall not depart from the usages of his ancestors, trusting for the rest to deal with events as they arise. So that if an hereditary Prince be of average

50   address, he will always maintain himself in his Princedom, unless deprived of it by some extraordinary and irresistible force; and even if so deprived will recover it, should any, even the least, mishap overtake the usurper. We have in Italy an example of this in the Duke of Ferrara, who never could have withstood the attacks of the Venetians in 1484, nor those of Pope Julius in 1510, had not his

55   authority in that State been consolidated by time. For since a Prince by birth has
      fewer occasions and less need to give offence, he ought to be better loved, and will
      naturally be popular with his subjects unless outrageous vices make him odious.
      Moreover, the very antiquity and continuance of his rule will efface the memories
      and causes which lead to innovation. For one change always leaves a dovetail
60   into which another will fit.

CHAPTER III: OF MIXED PRINCEDOMS

      But in new Princedoms difficulties abound. And, first, if the Princedom be not
      wholly new, but joined on to the ancient dominions of the Prince, so as to form
      with them what may be termed a mixed Princedom, changes will come from a cause
      common to all new States, namely, that men, thinking to better their condition, are
65   always ready to change masters, and in this expectation will take up arms against
      any ruler; wherein they deceive themselves, and find afterwards by experience
      that they are worse off than before. This again results naturally and necessarily
      from the circumstance that the Prince cannot avoid giving offence to his new
      subjects, either in respect of the troops he quarters on them, or of some other of the
70   numberless vexations attendant on a new acquisition. And in this way you may
      find that you have enemies in all those whom you have injured in seizing the
      Princedom, yet cannot keep the friendship of those who helped you to gain it; since
      you can neither reward them as they expect, nor yet, being under obligations to
      them, use violent remedies against them. For however strong you may be in respect
75   of your army, it is essential that in entering a new Province you should have the
      good will of its inhabitants.
      Hence it happened that Louis XII of France, speedily gaining possession of
      Milan, as speedily lost it; and that on the occasion of its first capture, Lodovico
      Sforza was able with his own forces only to take it from him. For the very people
80   who had opened the gates to the French King, when they found themselves
      deceived in their expectations and hopes of future benefits, could not put up with
      the insolence of their new ruler. True it is that when a State rebels and is again got
      under, it will not afterwards be lost so easily. For the Prince, using the rebellion
      as a pretext, will not scruple to secure himself by punishing the guilty, bringing the
85   suspected to trial, and otherwise strengthening his position in the points where it
      was weak. So that if to recover Milan from the French it was enough on the first
      occasion that a Duke Lodovico should raise alarms on the frontiers, to wrest it
      from them a second time the whole world had to be ranged against them, and their
      armies destroyed and driven out of Italy. And this for the reasons above assigned.
90   And yet, for a second time, Milan was lost to the King. The general causes of its
      first loss have been shown. It remains to note the causes of the second, and to point
      out the remedies which the French King had, or which might have been used by
      another in like circumstances to maintain his conquest more successfully than he
      did.

95   I say, then, that those States which upon their acquisition are joined on to the ancient dominions of the Prince who acquires them, are either of the same Province and tongue as the people of these dominions, or they are not. When they are, there is a great ease in retaining them, especially when they have not been accustomed to live in freedom. To hold them securely it is enough to have rooted out the line of the

100 reigning Prince; because if in other respects the old condition of things be continued, and there be no discordance in their customs, men live peaceably with one another, as we see to have been the case in Brittany, Burgundy, Gascony, and Normandy, which have so long been united to France. For although there be some slight difference in their languages, their customs are similar, and they can easily

105 get on together. He, therefore, who acquires such a State, if he mean to keep it, must see to two things; first, that the blood of the ancient line of Princes be destroyed; second, that no change be made in respect of laws or taxes; for in this way the newly acquired State speedily becomes incorporated with the hereditary.

    But when States are acquired in a country differing in language, usages, and

110 laws, difficulties multiply, and great good fortune, as well as address, is needed to overcome them. One of the best and most efficacious methods for dealing with such a State, is for the Prince who acquires it to go and dwell there in person, since this will tend to make his tenure more secure and lasting. This course has been followed by the Turk with regard to Greece, who, had he not, in addition to all his

115 other precautions for securing that Province, himself come to live in it, could never have kept his hold of it. For when you are on the spot, disorders are detected in their beginnings and remedies can be readily applied; but when you are at a distance, they are not heard of until they have gathered strength and the case is past cure. Moreover, the Province in which you take up your abode is not pillaged

120 by your officers; the people are pleased to have a ready recourse to their Prince; and have all the more reason if they are well disposed, to love, if disaffected, to fear him. A foreign enemy desiring to attack that State would be cautious how he did so. In short, where the Prince resides in person, it will be extremely difficult to oust him.

125   Another excellent expedient is to send colonies into one or two places, so that these may become, as it were, the keys of the Province; for you must either do this, or else keep up a numerous force of men-at-arms and foot soldiers. A Prince need not spend much on colonies. He can send them out and support them at little or no charge to himself, and the only persons to whom he gives offence are those whom

130 he deprives of their fields and houses to bestow them on the new inhabitants. Those who are thus injured form but a small part of the community, and remaining scattered and poor can never become dangerous. All others being left unmolested, are in consequence easily quieted, and at the same time are afraid to make a false move, lest they share the fate of those who have been deprived of their

135 possessions. In few words, these colonies cost less than soldiers, are more faithful, and give less offence, while those who are offended, being, as I have said, poor and dispersed, cannot hurt. And let it here be noted that men are either to be kindly treated, or utterly crushed, since they can revenge lighter injuries, but not graver.

140 Wherefore the injury we do to a man should be of a sort to leave no fear of reprisals.

But if instead of colonies you send troops, the cost is vastly greater, and the whole revenues of the country are spent in guarding it; so that the gain becomes a loss, and much deeper offence is given; since in shifting the quarters of your soldiers from place to place the whole country suffers hardship, which as all feel,

145 all are made enemies; and enemies who remaining, although vanquished, in their own homes, have power to hurt. In every way, therefore, this mode of defence is as disadvantageous as that by colonizing is useful.

The Prince who establishes himself in a Province whose laws and language differ from those of his own people, ought also to make himself the head and

150 protector of his feebler neighbours, and endeavour to weaken the stronger, and must see that by no accident shall any other stranger as powerful as himself find an entrance there. For it will always happen that some such person will be called in by those of the Province who are discontented either through ambition or fear; as we see of old the Romans brought into Greece by the Aetolians, and in every

155 other country that they entered, invited there by its inhabitants. And the usual course of things is that so soon as a formidable stranger enters a Province, all the weaker powers side with him, moved thereto by the ill-will they bear towards him who has hitherto kept them in subjection. So that in respect of these lesser powers, no trouble is needed to gain them over, for at once, together, and of their own

160 accord, they throw in their lot with the government of the stranger. The new Prince, therefore, has only to see that they do not increase too much in strength, and with his own forces, aided by their good will, can easily subdue any who are powerful, so as to remain supreme in the Province. He who does not manage this matter well, will soon lose whatever he has gained, and while he retains it will

165 find in it endless troubles and annoyances.

In dealing with the countries of which they took possession the Romans diligently followed the methods I have described. They planted colonies, conciliated weaker powers without adding to their strength, humbled the great, and never suffered a formidable stranger to acquire influence. A single example

170 will suffice to show this. In Greece the Romans took the Achaians and Aetolians into their pay; the Macedonian monarchy was humbled; Antiochus was driven out. But the services of the Achaians and Aetolians never obtained for them any addition to their power; no persuasions on the part of Philip could induce the Romans to be his friends on the condition of sparing him humiliation; nor could all

175 the power of Antiochus bring them to consent to his exercising any authority within that Province. And in thus acting the Romans did as all wise rulers should, who have to consider not only present difficulties but also future, against which they must use all diligence to provide; for these, if they be foreseen while yet remote, admit of easy remedy, but if their approach be awaited, are already past

180 cure, the disorder having become hopeless; realizing what the physicians tell us of hectic fever, that in its beginning it is easy to cure, but hard to recognize; whereas,

after a time, not having been detected and treated at the first, it becomes easy to recognize but impossible to cure.

And so it is with State affairs. For the distempers of a State being discovered
185 while yet inchoate, which can only be done by a sagacious ruler, may easily be dealt with; but when, from not being observed, they are suffered to grow until they are obvious to every one, there is no longer any remedy. The Romans, therefore, foreseeing evils while they were yet far off, always provided against them, and never suffered them to take their course for the sake of avoiding war; since they
190 knew that war is not so to be avoided, but is only postponed to the advantage of the other side. They chose, therefore, to make war with Philip and Antiochus in Greece, that they might not have to make it with them in Italy, although for a while they might have escaped both. This they did not desire, nor did the maxim *leave it to Time*, which the wise men of our own day have always on their lips, ever
195 recommend itself to them. What they looked to enjoy were the fruits of their own valour and foresight. For Time, driving all things before it, may bring with it evil as well as good.

But let us now go back to France and examine whether she has followed any of those methods of which I have made mention. I shall speak of Louis and not of
200 Charles, because from the former having held longer possession of Italy, his manner of acting is more plainly seen. You will find, then, that he has done the direct opposite of what he should have done in order to retain a foreign State.

King Louis was brought into Italy by the ambition of the Venetians, who hoped by his coming to gain for themselves a half of the State of Lombardy. I will
205 not blame this coming, nor the part taken by the King, because, desiring to gain a footing in Italy, where he had no friends, but on the contrary, owing to the conduct of Charles, every door was shut against him, he was driven to accept such friendships as he could get. And his designs might easily have succeeded had he not made mistakes in other particulars of conduct.

210 By the recovery of Lombardy, Louis at once regained the credit which Charles had lost. Genoa made submission; the Florentines came to terms; the Marquis of Mantua, the Duke of Ferrara, the Bentivogli, the Countess of Forlì, the Lords of Faenza, Pesaro, Rimini, Camerino, and Piombino, the citizens of Lucca, Pisa, and Siena, all came forward offering their friendship. The Venetians, who to
215 obtain possession of a couple of towns in Lombardy had made the French King master of two-thirds of Italy, had now cause to repent the rash game they had played.

Let any one, therefore, consider how easily King Louis might have maintained his authority in Italy had he observed the rules which I have noted above, and
220 secured and protected all those friends of his, who being weak, and fearful, some of the Church, some of the Venetians, were of necessity obliged to attach themselves to him, and with whose assistance, for they were many, he might readily have made himself safe against any other powerful State. But no sooner was he in Milan than he took a contrary course, in helping Pope Alexander to
225 occupy Romagna; not perceiving that in seconding this enterprise he weakened

himself by alienating friends and those who had thrown themselves into his arms, while he strengthened the Church by adding great temporal power to the spiritual power which of itself confers so mighty an authority. Making this first mistake, he was forced to follow it up, until at last, in order to curb the ambition of Pope
230 Alexander, and prevent him becoming master of Tuscany, he was obliged to come himself into Italy.

And as though it were not enough for him to have aggrandized the Church and stripped himself of friends, he must needs in his desire to possess the Kingdom of Naples, divide it with the King of Spain; thus bringing into Italy, where before he
235 had been supreme, a rival to whom the ambitious and discontented in that Province might have recourse. And whereas he might have left in Naples a King willing to hold as his tributary, he displaced him to make way for another strong enough to effect his expulsion. The wish to acquire is no doubt a natural and common sentiment, and when men attempt things within their power, they will
240 always be praised rather than blamed. But when they persist in attempts that are beyond their power, mishaps and blame ensue. If France, therefore, with her own forces could have attacked Naples, she should have done so. If she could not, she ought not to have divided it. And if her partition of Lombardy with the Venetians may be excused as the means whereby a footing was gained in Italy, this other
245 partition is to be condemned as not justified by the like necessity.

Louis, then, had made these five blunders. He had destroyed weaker States, he had strengthened a Prince already strong, he had brought into the country a very powerful stranger, he had not come to reside, and he had not sent colonies. And yet all these blunders might not have proved disastrous to him while he lived, had he
250 not added to them a sixth in depriving the Venetians of their dominions. For had he neither aggrandized the Church, nor brought Spain into Italy, it might have been at once reasonable and necessary to humble the Venetians; but after committing himself to these other courses, he should never have consented to the ruin of Venice. For while the Venetians were powerful they would always have kept
255 others back from an attempt on Lombardy, as well because they never would have agreed to that enterprise on any terms save of themselves being made its masters, as because others would never have desired to take it from France in order to hand it over to them, nor would ever have ventured to defy both. And if it be said that King Louis ceded Romagna to Alexander, and Naples to Spain in order to avoid
260 war, I answer that for the reasons already given, you ought never to suffer your designs to be crossed in order to avoid war, since war is not so to be avoided, but is only deferred to your disadvantage. And if others should allege the King's promise to the Pope to undertake that enterprise on his behalf, in return for the dissolution of his marriage, and for the Cardinal's hat conferred on d'Amboise, I
265 answer by referring to what I say further on concerning the faith of Princes and how it is to be kept.

King Louis, therefore, lost Lombardy from not following any one of the methods pursued by others who have taken Provinces with the resolve to keep them. Nor is this anything strange, but only what might reasonably and naturally

270 be looked for. And on this very subject I spoke to d'Amboise at Nantes, at the time when Duke Valentino, as Cesare Borgia, son to Pope Alexander, was vulgarly called, was occupying Romagna. For, on the Cardinal saying to me that the Italians did not understand war, I answered that the French did not understand statecraft, for had they done so, they never would have allowed the Church to grow so

275 powerful. And the event shows that the aggrandizement of the Church and of Spain in Italy has been brought about by France, and that the ruin of France has been wrought by them. Whence we may draw the general axiom, which never or rarely errs, that *he who is the cause of another's greatness is himself undone*, since he must work either by address or force, each of which excites distrust in the

280 person raised to power.

CHAPTER IV: WHY THE KINGDOM OF DARIUS, CONQUERED BY ALEXANDER, DID NOT, ON ALEXANDER'S DEATH, REBEL AGAINST HIS SUCCESSORS

Alexander the Great having achieved the conquest of Asia in a few years, and dying before he had well entered on possession, it might have been expected, having regard to the difficulty of preserving newly acquired States, that on his death the whole country would rise in revolt. Nevertheless, his successors were

285 able to keep their hold, and found in doing so no other difficulty than arose from their own ambition and mutual jealousies.

If any one think this strange and ask the cause, I answer, that all the Princedoms of which we have record have been governed in one or other of two ways, either by a sole Prince, all others being his servants permitted by his grace and favour to assist in governing the kingdom as his ministers; or else, by a Prince

290 with his Barons who hold their rank, not by the favour of a superior Lord, but by antiquity of blood, and who have States and subjects of their own who recognize them as their rulers and entertain for them a natural affection. States governed by a sole Prince and by his servants vest in him a more complete authority; because throughout the land none but he is recognized as sovereign, and if obedience be

295 yielded to any others, it is yielded as to his ministers and officers for whom personally no special love is felt.

Of these two forms of government we have examples in our own days in the Turk and the King of France. The whole Turkish empire is governed by a sole

300 Prince, all others being his slaves. Dividing his kingdom into *sandjaks,* he sends thither different governors whom he shifts and changes at his pleasure. The King of France, on the other hand, is surrounded by a multitude of nobles of ancient descent, each acknowledged and loved by subjects of his own, and each asserting a precedence in rank of which the King can deprive him only at his peril.

305 He, therefore, who considers the different character of these two States, will perceive that it would be difficult to gain possession of that of the Turk, but that once won it might be easily held. The obstacles to its conquest are that the invader cannot be called in by a native nobility, nor expect his enterprise to be aided by

310 the defection of those whom the sovereign has around him. And this for the various reasons already given, namely, that all being slaves and under obligations they are not easily corrupted, or if corrupted can render little assistance, being unable, as I have already explained, to carry the people with them. Whoever, therefore, attacks the Turk must reckon on finding a united people, and must trust rather to his own strength than to divisions on the other side. But were his

315 adversary once overcome and defeated in the field, so that he could not repair his armies, no cause for anxiety would remain, except in the family of the Prince; which being extirpated, there would be none else to fear; for since all beside are without credit with the people, the invader, as before his victory he had nothing to hope from them, so after it has nothing to dread.

320 But the contrary is the case in kingdoms governed like that of France, into which, because men who are discontented and desirous of change are always to be found, you may readily procure an entrance by gaining over some Baron of the Realm. Such persons, for the reasons already given, are able to open the way to you for the invasion of their country and to render its conquest easy. But

325 afterwards the effort to hold your ground involves you in endless difficulties, as well in respect of those who have helped you, as of those whom you have overthrown. Nor will it be enough to have destroyed the family of the Prince, since all those other Lords remain to put themselves at the head of new movements; whom being unable either to content or to destroy, you lose the State whenever

330 occasion serves them.

Now, if you examine the nature of the government of Darius, you will find that it resembled that of the Turk, and, consequently, that it was necessary for Alexander, first of all, to defeat him utterly and strip him of his dominions; after which defeat, Darius having died, the country, for the causes above explained,

335 was permanently secured to Alexander. And had his successors continued united they might have enjoyed it undisturbed, since there arose no disorders in that kingdom save those of their own creating.

But kingdoms ordered like that of France cannot be retained with the same ease. Hence the repeated risings of Spain, Gaul, and Greece against the Romans,

340 resulting from the number of small Princedoms of which these Provinces were made up. For while the memory of these lasted, the Romans could never think their tenure safe. But when that memory was worn out by the authority and long continuance of their rule, they gained a secure hold, and were able afterwards in their contests among themselves, each to carry with him some portion of these

345 Provinces, according as each had acquired influence there; for these, on the extinction of the line of their old Princes, came to recognize no other Lords than the Romans.

Bearing all this in mind, no one need wonder at the ease wherewith Alexander was able to lay a firm hold on Asia, nor that Pyrrhus and many others

350 found difficulty in preserving other acquisitions; since this arose, not from the less or greater merit of the conquerors, but from the different character of the States with which they had to deal.

CHAPTER V: HOW CITIES OR PROVINCES WHICH BEFORE THEIR ACQUISITION HAVE LIVED UNDER THEIR OWN LAWS ARE TO BE GOVERNED

When a newly acquired State has been accustomed, as I have said, to live under its own laws and in freedom, there are three methods whereby it may be
355 held. The first is to destroy it; the second, to go and reside there in person; the third, to suffer it to live on under its own laws, subjecting it to a tribute, and entrusting its government to a few of the inhabitants who will keep the rest your friends. Such a Government, since it is the creature of the new Prince, will see that it cannot stand without his protection and support, and must therefore do all it
360 can to maintain him; and a city accustomed to live in freedom, if it is to be preserved at all, is more easily controlled through its own citizens than in any other way.

We have examples of all these methods in the histories of the Spartans and the Romans. The Spartans held Athens and Thebes by creating oligarchies in these
365 cities, yet lost them in the end. The Romans, to retain Capua, Carthage, and Numantia, destroyed them and never lost them. On the other hand, when they thought to hold Greece as the Spartans had held it, leaving it its freedom and allowing it to be governed by its own laws, they failed, and had to destroy many cities of that Province before they could secure it. For, in truth, there is no sure
370 way of holding other than by destroying, and whoever becomes master of a City accustomed to live in freedom and does not destroy it, may reckon on being destroyed by it. For if it should rebel, it can always screen itself under the name of liberty and its ancient laws, which no length of time, nor any benefits conferred will ever cause it to forget; and do what you will, and take what care you may,
375 unless the inhabitants be scattered and dispersed, this name, and the old order of things, will never cease to be remembered, but will at once be turned against you whenever misfortune overtakes you, as when Pisa rose against the Florentines after a hundred years of servitude.

If, however, the newly acquired City or Province has been accustomed to live
380 under a Prince, and his line is extinguished, it will be impossible for the citizens, used, on the one hand, to obey, and deprived, on the other, of their old ruler, to agree to choose a leader from among themselves; and as they know not how to live as freemen, and are therefore slow to take up arms, a stranger may readily gain them over and attach them to his cause. But in Republics there is a stronger
385 vitality, a fiercer hatred, a keener thirst for revenge. The memory of their former freedom will not let them rest; so that the safest course is either to destroy them, or to go and live in them.

CHAPTER VI: OF NEW PRINCEDOMS WHICH A PRINCE ACQUIRES WITH HIS OWN ARMS AND BY MERIT

Let no man marvel if in what I am about to say concerning Princedoms wholly new, both as regards the Prince and the form of Government, I cite the highest examples. For since men for the most part follow in the footsteps and imitate the actions of others, and yet are unable to adhere exactly to those paths which others have taken, or attain to the virtues of those whom they would resemble, the wise man should always follow the roads that have been trodden by the great, and imitate those who have most excelled, so that if he cannot reach their perfection, he may at least acquire something of its savour. Acting in this like the skilful archer, who seeing that the object he would hit is distant, and knowing the range of his bow, takes aim much above the destined mark; not designing that his arrow should strike so high, but that flying high it may alight at the point intended.

I say, then, that in entirely new Princedoms where the Prince himself is new, the difficulty of maintaining possession varies with the greater or less ability of him who acquires possession. And, because the mere fact of a private person rising to be a Prince presupposes either merit or good fortune, it will be seen that the presence of one or other of these two conditions lessens, to some extent, many difficulties. And yet, he who is less beholden to Fortune has often in the end the better success; and it may be for the advantage of a Prince that, from his having no other territories, he is obliged to reside in person in the State which he has acquired.

Looking first to those who have become Princes by their merit and not by their good fortune, I say that the most excellent among them are Moses, Cyrus, Romulus, Theseus, and the like. And though perhaps I ought not to name Moses, he being merely an instrument for carrying out the Divine commands, he is still to be admired for those qualities which made him worthy to converse with God. But if we consider Cyrus and the others who have acquired or founded kingdoms, they will all be seen to be admirable. And if their actions and the particular institutions of which they were the authors be studied, they will be found not to differ from those of Moses, instructed though he was by so great a teacher. Moreover, on examining their lives and actions, we shall see that they were debtors to Fortune for nothing beyond the opportunity which enabled them to shape things as they pleased, without which the force of their spirit would have been spent in vain; as on the other hand, opportunity would have offered itself in vain, had the capacity for turning it to account been wanting. It was necessary, therefore, that Moses should find the children of Israel in bondage in Egypt, and oppressed by the Egyptians, in order that they might be disposed to follow him, and so escape from their servitude. It was fortunate for Romulus that he found no home in Alba, but was exposed at the time of his birth, to the end that he might become king and founder of the City of Rome. It was necessary that Cyrus should find the Persians discontented with the rule of the Medes, and the Medes enervated and effeminate from a prolonged peace. Nor could Theseus have

displayed his great qualities had he not found the Athenians disunited and
430   dispersed. But while it was their opportunities that made these men fortunate, it
was their own merit that enabled them to recognize these opportunities and turn
them to account, to the glory and prosperity of their country.

They who come to the Princedom, as these did, by virtuous paths, acquire
with difficulty, but keep with ease. The difficulties which they have in acquiring
435   arise mainly from the new laws and institutions which they are forced to
introduce in founding and securing their government. And let it be noted that there
is no more delicate matter to take in hand, nor more dangerous to conduct, nor
more doubtful in its success, than to set up as a leader in the introduction of
changes. For he who innovates will have for his enemies all those who are well
440   off under the existing order of things, and only lukewarm supporters in those who
might be better off under the new. This lukewarm temper arises partly from the
fear of adversaries who have the laws on their side, and partly from the
incredulity of mankind, who will never admit the merit of anything new, until they
have seen it proved by the event. The result, however, is that whenever the enemies
445   of change make an attack, they do so with all the zeal of partisans, while the
others defend themselves so feebly as to endanger both themselves and their cause.

But to get a clearer understanding of this part of our subject, we must look
whether these innovators can stand alone, or whether they depend for aid upon
others; in other words, whether to carry out their ends they must resort to
450   entreaty, or can prevail by force. In the former case they always fare badly and
bring nothing to a successful issue; but when they depend upon their own
resources and can employ force, they seldom fail. Hence it comes that all armed
Prophets have been victorious, and all unarmed Prophets have been destroyed.

For, besides what has been said, it should be borne in mind that the temper of
455   the multitude is fickle, and that while it is easy to persuade them of a thing, it is
hard to fix them in that persuasion. Wherefore, matters should be so ordered that
when men no longer believe of their own accord, they may be compelled to believe
by force. Moses, Cyrus, Theseus, and Romulus could never have made their
ordinances be observed for any length of time had they been unarmed, as was the
460   case, in our own days, with the Friar Girolamo Savonarola, whose new
institutions came to nothing so soon as the multitude began to waver in their faith;
since he had not the means to keep those who had been believers steadfast in their
belief, or to make unbelievers believe.

Such persons, therefore, have great difficulty in carrying out their designs; but
465   all their difficulties are on the road, and may be overcome by courage. Having
conquered these, and coming to be held in reverence, and having destroyed all who
were jealous of their influence, they remain powerful, safe, honoured, and
prosperous.

To the great examples cited above, I would add one other, of less note indeed,
470   but assuredly bearing some proportion to them, and which may stand for all
others of a like character. I mean the example of Hiero the Syracusan. He from a
private station rose to be Prince of Syracuse, and he too was indebted to Fortune

475 only for his opportunity. For the Syracusans being oppressed, chose him to be
their Captain, which office he so discharged as deservedly to be made their King.
For even while a private citizen his merit was so remarkable, that one who writes
of him says, he lacked nothing that a King should have save the Kingdom. Doing
away with the old army, he organized a new, abandoned existing alliances and
assumed new allies, and with an army and allies of his own, was able on that
foundation to build what superstructure he pleased; having trouble enough in
480 acquiring, but none in preserving what he had acquired.

CHAPTER VII: OF NEW PRINCEDOMS ACQUIRED BY THE AID OF OTHERS AND BY GOOD FORTUNE

They who from a private station become Princes by mere good fortune, do so
with little trouble, but have much trouble to maintain themselves. They meet with
no hindrance on their way, being carried as it were on wings to their destination,
but all their difficulties overtake them when they alight. Of this class are those on
485 whom States are conferred either in return for money, or through the favour of him
who confers them; as it happened to many in the Greek cities of Ionia and the
Hellespont to be made Princes by Darius, that they might hold these cities for his
security and glory; and as happened in the case of those Emperors who, from
privacy, attained the Imperial dignity by corrupting the army. Such Princes are
490 wholly dependent on the favour and fortunes of those who have made them great,
than which supports none could be less stable or secure; and they lack both the
knowledge and the power that would enable them to maintain their position. They
lack the knowledge, because unless they have great parts and force of character, it
is not to be expected that having always lived in a private station they should
495 have learned how to command. They lack the power, since they cannot look for
support from attached and faithful troops. Moreover, States suddenly acquired,
like all else that is produced and that grows up rapidly, can never have such root
or hold as that the first storm which strikes them shall not overthrow them; unless,
indeed, as I have said already, they who thus suddenly become Princes have a
500 capacity for learning quickly how to defend what Fortune has placed in their lap,
and can lay those foundations after they rise which by others are laid before.

Of each of these methods of becoming a Prince, namely, by merit and by good
fortune, I shall select an instance from times within my own recollection, and shall
take the cases of Francesco Sforza and Cesare Borgia. By suitable measures and
505 singular ability, Francesco Sforza rose from privacy to be Duke of Milan,
preserving with little trouble what it cost him infinite efforts to gain. On the other
hand, Cesare Borgia, vulgarly spoken of as Duke Valentino, obtained his
Princedom through the favourable fortunes of his father, and with these lost it,
although, so far as in him lay, he used every effort and practised every expedient
510 that a prudent and able man should, who desires to strike root in a State given him
by the arms and fortune of another. For, as I have already said, he who does not
lay his foundations at first, may, if he be of great parts, succeed in laying them

afterwards, though with inconvenience to the builder and risk to the building. And if we consider the various measures taken by Duke Valentino, we shall
515 perceive how broad were the foundations he had laid whereon to rest his future power.

These I think it not superfluous to examine, since I know not what lessons I could teach a new Prince, more useful than the example of his actions. And if the measures taken by him did not profit him in the end , it was through no fault of his,
520 but from the extraordinary and extreme malignity of Fortune.

In his efforts to aggrandize the Duke his son, Alexander VI had to face many difficulties, both immediate and remote. In the first place, he saw no way to make him Lord of any State which was not a State of the Church, while, if he sought to take for him a State belonging to the Church, he knew that the Duke of Milan and
525 the Venetians would withhold their consent; Faenza and Rimini being already under the protection of the latter. Further, he saw that the arms of Italy, and those more especially of which he might have availed himself, were in the hands of men who had reason to fear his aggrandizement, that is, of the Orsini, the Colonnesi, and their followers. These therefore he could not trust. It was consequently
530 necessary that the existing order of things should be changed, and the States of Italy thrown into confusion, in order that he might safely make himself master of some part of them; and this became easy for him when he found that the Venetians, moved by other causes, were plotting to bring the French once more into Italy. This design he accordingly did not oppose, but furthered by annulling the first marriage
535 of the French King.

King Louis therefore came into Italy at the instance of the Venetians, and with the consent of Pope Alexander, and no sooner was he in Milan than the Pope got troops from him to aid him in his enterprise against Romagna, which Province, moved by the reputation of the French arms, at once submitted. After thus
540 obtaining possession of Romagna, and after quelling the Colonnesi, Duke Valentino was desirous to follow up and extend his conquests. Two causes, however, held him back, namely, the doubtful fidelity of his own forces, and the waywardness of France. For he feared that the Orsini, of whose arms he had made use, might fail him, and not merely prove a hindrance to further acquisitions, but
545 take from him what he had gained, and that the King might serve him the same turn. How little he could count on the Orsini was made plain when, after the capture of Faenza, he turned his arms against Bologna, and saw how reluctantly they took part in that enterprise. The King's mind he understood, when, after seizing on the Dukedom of Urbino, he was about to attack Tuscany; from which design Louis
550 compelled him to desist. Whereupon the Duke resolved to depend no longer on the arms or fortune of others. His first step, therefore, was to weaken the factions of the Orsini and Colonnesi in Rome. Those of their following who were of good birth, he gained over by making them his own gentlemen, assigning them a liberal provision, and conferring upon them commands and appointments suited to their
555 rank; so that in a few months their old partisan attachments died out, and the hopes of all rested on the Duke alone.

He then awaited an occasion to crush the chiefs of the Orsini, for those of the house of Colonna he had already scattered, and a good opportunity presenting itself, he turned it to the best account. For when the Orsini came at last to see that the greatness of the Duke and the Church involved their ruin, they assembled a council at Magione in the Perugian territory, whence resulted the revolt of Urbino, commotions in Romagna, and an infinity of dangers to the Duke, all of which he overcame with the help of France. His credit thus restored, the Duke trusting no longer either to the French or to any other foreign aid, that he might not have to confront them openly, resorted to stratagem, and was so well able to dissemble his designs, that the Orsini, through the mediation of Signor Paolo (whom he failed not to secure by every friendly attention, furnishing him with clothes, money, and horses), were so won over as to be drawn in their simplicity into his hands at Sinigaglia. When the leaders were thus disposed of, and their followers made his friends, the Duke had laid sufficiently good foundations for his future power, since he held all Romagna together with the Dukedom of Urbino, and had ingratiated himself with the entire population of these States, who now began to see that they were well off.

And since this part of his conduct merits both attention and imitation, I shall not pass it over in silence. After the Duke had taken Romagna, finding that it had been ruled by feeble Lords, who thought more of plundering than correcting their subjects, and gave them more cause for division than for union, so that the country was overrun with robbery, tumult, and every kind of outrage, he judged it necessary, with a view to render it peaceful and obedient to his authority, to provide it with a good government. Accordingly he set over it Messer Remiro d'Orco, a stern and prompt ruler, who being entrusted with the fullest powers, in a very short time, and with much credit to himself, restored it to tranquillity and order. But afterwards apprehending that such unlimited authority might become odious, the Duke decided that it was no longer needed, and established in the centre of the Province a civil Tribunal, with an excellent President, in which every town was represented by its advocate. And knowing that past severities had generated ill-feeling against himself, in order to purge the minds of the people and gain their good-will, he sought to show them that any cruelty which had been done had not originated with him, but in the harsh disposition of his minister. Availing himself of the pretext which this afforded, he one morning caused Remiro to be beheaded, and exposed in the market place of Cesena with a block and bloody axe by his side. The barbarity of which spectacle at once astounded and satisfied the populace.

But, returning to the point whence we diverged, I say that the Duke, finding himself fairly strong and in a measure secured against present dangers, being furnished with arms of his own choosing and having to a great extent got rid of those which, if left near him, might have caused him trouble, had to consider, if he desired to follow up his conquests, how he was to deal with France, since he saw he could expect no further support from King Louis, whose eyes were at last opened to his mistake. He therefore began to look about for new alliances, and to waver in his adherence to the French, then occupied with their expedition into the kingdom of Naples against the Spaniards, at that time laying siege to Gaeta; his object being to secure himself against France; and in this he would soon have succeeded had Alexander lived.

605 Such was the line he took to meet present exigencies. As regards the future, he had to apprehend that a new Head of the Church might not be his friend, and might even seek to deprive him of what Alexander had given. This he thought to provide against in four ways. First, by exterminating all who were of kin to those Lords whom he had despoiled of their possessions, that they might not become
610 instruments in the hands of a new Pope. Second, by gaining over all the Roman nobles, so as to be able with their help to put a bridle, as the saying is, in the Pope's mouth. Third, by bringing the College of Cardinals, so far as he could, under his control. And fourth, by establishing his authority so firmly before his father's death, as to be able by himself to withstand the shock of a first onset.

615 Of these measures, at the time when Alexander died, he had already effected three, and had almost carried out the fourth. For of the Lords whose possessions he had usurped, he had put to death all whom he could reach, and very few had escaped. He had gained over the Roman nobility, and had the majority in the College of Cardinals on his side.

620 As to further acquisitions, his design was to make himself master of Tuscany. He was already in possession of Perugia and Piombino, and had assumed the protectorship of Pisa, on which city he was about to spring; taking no heed of France, as indeed he no longer had occasion, since the French had been deprived of the kingdom of Naples by the Spaniards under circumstances which made it
625 necessary for both nations to buy his friendship. Pisa taken, Lucca and Siena would soon have yielded, partly through jealousy of Florence, partly through fear, and the position of the Florentines must then have been desperate.

Had he therefore succeeded in these designs, as he was succeeding in that very year in which Alexander died, he would have won such power and reputation
630 that he might afterwards have stood alone, relying on his own strength and resources, without being beholden to the power and fortune of others. But Alexander died five years from the time he first unsheathed the sword, leaving his son with the State of Romagna alone consolidated, with all the rest unsettled, between two powerful hostile armies, and sick almost to death. And yet such were
635 the fire and courage of the Duke, he knew so well how men must either be conciliated or crushed, and so solid were the foundations he had laid in that brief period, that had these armies not been upon his back, or had he been in sound health, he must have surmounted every difficulty.

How strong his foundations were may be seen from this, that Romagna waited
640 for him for more than a month; and that although half dead, he remained in safety in Rome, where though the Baglioni, the Vitelli, and the Orsini came to attack him, they met with no success. Moreover, since he was able if not to make whom he liked Pope, at least to prevent the election of any whom he disliked, had he been in health at the time when Alexander died, all would have been easy for him. But he

645   told me himself on the day on which Julius II was created, that he had foreseen and provided for everything else that could happen on his father's death, but had never anticipated that when his father died he too should be at death's-door.

    Taking all these actions of the Duke together, I can find no fault with him; nay, it seems to me reasonable to put him forward, as I have done, as a pattern for
650   all such as rise to power by good fortune and the help of others. For with his great spirit and high aims he could not act otherwise than he did, and nothing but the shortness of his father's life and his own illness prevented the success of his designs. Whoever, therefore, on entering a new Princedom, judges it necessary to rid himself of enemies, to conciliate friends, to prevail by force or fraud, to make
655   himself feared yet not hated by his subjects, respected and obeyed by his soldiers, to crush those who can or ought to injure him, to introduce changes in the old order of things, to be at once severe and affable, magnanimous and liberal, to do away with a mutinous army and create a new one, to maintain relations with Kings and Princes on such a footing that they must see it for their interest to aid
660   him, and dangerous to offend, can find no brighter example than in the actions of this Prince.

    The one thing for which he may be blamed was the creation of Pope Julius II, in respect of whom he chose badly. Because, as I have said already, though he could not secure the election he desired, he could have prevented any other; and he
665   ought never to have consented to the creation of any one of those Cardinals whom he had injured, or who on becoming Pope would have reason to fear him; for fear is as dangerous an enemy as resentment. Those whom he had offended were, among others, San Pietro ad Vincula, Colonna, San Giorgio, and Ascanio; all the rest, excepting d'Amboise and the Spanish Cardinals (the latter from their connexion
670   and obligations, the former from the power he derived through his relations with the French Court), would on assuming the Pontificate have had reason to fear him. The Duke, therefore, ought, in the first place, to have laboured for the creation of a Spanish Pope; failing in which, he should have agreed to the election of d'Amboise, but never to that of San Pietro ad Vincula. And he deceives himself who believes
675   that with the great, recent benefits cause old wrongs to be forgotten.

    The Duke, therefore, erred in the part he took in this election; and his error was the cause of his ultimate downfall.

CHAPTER VIII: OF THOSE WHO BY THEIR CRIMES COME TO BE PRINCES

    But since from privacy a man may also rise to be a Prince in one or other of two ways, neither of which can be referred wholly either to merit or to fortune, it
680   is fit that I notice them here, though one of them may fall to be discussed more fully in treating of Republics.

    The ways I speak of are, first, when the ascent to power is made by paths of wickedness and crime; and second, when a private person becomes ruler of his country by the favour of his fellow-citizens. The former method I shall make clear

685   by two examples, one ancient, the other modern, without entering further into the merits of the matter, for these, I think, should be enough for any one who is driven to follow them.

       Agathocles the Sicilian came, not merely from a private station, but from the very dregs of the people, to be King of Syracuse. Son of a potter, through all the
690   stages of his fortunes he led a foul life. His vices, however, were conjoined with so great vigour both of mind and body, that becoming a soldier, he rose through the various grades of the service to be Praetor of Syracuse. Once established in that post, he resolved to make himself Prince, and to hold by violence and without obligation to others the authority which had been spontaneously entrusted to him.
695   Accordingly, after imparting his design to Hamilcar, who with the Carthaginian armies was at that time waging war in Sicily, he one morning assembled the people and senate of Syracuse as though to consult with them on matters of public moment, and on a preconcerted signal caused his soldiers to put to death all the senators, and the wealthiest of the commons. These being thus got rid of, he
700   assumed and retained possession of the sovereignty without opposition on the part of the people; and although twice defeated by the Carthaginians, and afterwards besieged, he was able not only to defend his city, but leaving a part of his forces for its protection, to invade Africa with the remainder, and so in a short time to raise the siege of Syracuse, reducing the Carthaginians to the utmost
705   extremities, and compelling them to make terms whereby they abandoned Sicily to him and confined themselves to Africa.

       Whoever examines this man's actions and achievements will discover little or nothing in them which can be ascribed to Fortune, seeing, as has already been said, that it was not through the favour of any, but by the regular steps of the military
710   service, gained at the cost of a thousand hardships and hazards, he reached the Princedom which he afterwards maintained by so many daring and dangerous enterprises. Still, to slaughter fellow-citizens, to betray friends, to be devoid of honour, pity, and religion, cannot be counted as merits, for these are means which may lead to power, but which confer no glory. Wherefore, if in respect of the
715   valour with which he encountered and extricated himself from difficulties, and the constancy of his spirit in supporting and conquering adverse fortune, there seems no reason to judge him inferior to the greatest captains that have ever lived, his unbridled cruelty and inhumanity, together with his countless crimes, forbid us to number him with the greatest men; but, at any rate, we cannot attribute to Fortune
720   or to merit what he accomplished without either.

       In our own times, during the papacy of Alexander VI, Oliverotto of Fermo, who some years before had been left an orphan, and had been brought up by his maternal uncle Giovanni Fogliani, was sent while still a lad to serve under Paolo Vitelli, in the expectation that a thorough training under that commander might
725   qualify him for high rank as a soldier. After the death of Paolo, he served under his brother Vitellozzo, and in a very short time, being of a quick wit, hardy and resolute, he became one of the first soldiers of his company. But thinking it beneath him to serve under others, with the countenance of the Vitelleschi and the

connivance of certain citizens of Fermo who preferred the slavery to the freedom
730   of their country, he formed the design to seize on that town.

He accordingly wrote to Giovanni Fogliani that after many years of absence
from home, he desired to see him and his native city once more, and to look a little
into the condition of his patrimony; and as his one endeavour had been to make
himself a name, in order that his fellow-citizens might see that his time had not
735   been misspent, he proposed to return honourably attended by a hundred horsemen
from among his own friends and followers; and he begged Giovanni graciously to
arrange for his reception by the citizens of Fermo with corresponding marks of
distinction, as this would be creditable not only to himself, but also to the uncle
who had brought him up.

740   Giovanni accordingly did not fail in any proper attention to his nephew, but
caused him to be splendidly received by his fellow-citizens, and lodged him in his
house; where Oliverotto having passed some days, and made the necessary
arrangements for carrying out his wickedness, gave a formal banquet, to which he
invited his uncle and all the first men of Fermo. When the repast and the other
745   entertainments proper to such an occasion had come to an end, Oliverotto artfully
turned the conversation to matters of grave interest, by speaking of the greatness
of Pope Alexander and Cesare his son, and of their enterprises; and when
Giovanni and the others were replying to what he said, he suddenly rose up,
observing that these were matters to be discussed in a more private place, and so
750   withdrew to another chamber; whither his uncle and all the other citizens
followed him, and where they had no sooner seated themselves, than soldiers
rushing out from places of concealment put Giovanni and all the rest to death.

After this butchery, Oliverotto mounted his horse, rode through the streets,
and besieged the chief magistrate in the palace, so that all were constrained by
755   fear to yield obedience and accept a government of which he made himself the head.
And all who from being disaffected were likely to stand in his way, he put to
death, while he strengthened himself with new ordinances, civil and military, to
such purpose, that for the space of a year during which he retained the Princedom,
he not merely kept a firm hold of the city, but grew formidable to all his
760   neighbours. And it would have been as impossible to unseat him as it was to
unseat Agathocles, had he not let himself be overreached by Cesare Borgia on the
occasion when, as has already been told, the Orsini and Vitelli were entrapped at
Sinigaglia; where he too being taken, one year after the commission of his
parricidal crime, was strangled along with Vitellozzo, whom he had assumed for
765   his master in villiany as in valour.

It may be asked how Agathocles and some like him, after numberless acts of
treachery and cruelty, have been able to live long in their own country in safety,
and to defend themselves from foreign enemies, without being plotted against by
their fellow-citizens, whereas, many others, by reason of their cruelty, have failed
770   to maintain their position even in peaceful times, not to speak of the perilous times
of war. I believe that this results from cruelty being well or ill employed. Those
cruelties we may say are well employed, if it be permitted to speak well of things

evil, which are done once for all under the necessity of self-preservation, and are not afterwards persisted in, but so far as possible modified to the advantage of the
775 governed. Ill-employed cruelties, on the other hand, are those which from small beginnings increase rather than diminish with time. They who follow the first of these methods, may, by the grace of God and man, find, as did Agathocles, that their condition is not desperate; but by no possibility can the others maintain themselves.
780   Hence we may learn the lesson that on seizing a State, the usurper should make haste to inflict what injuries he must, at a stroke, that he may not have to renew them daily, but be enabled by their discontinuance to reassure men's minds, and afterwards win them over by benefits. Whosoever, either through timidity or from following bad counsels, adopts a contrary course, must keep the sword
785 always drawn, and can put no trust in his subjects, who suffering from continued and constantly renewed severities, will never yield him their confidence. Injuries, therefore, should be inflicted all at once, that their ill savour being less lasting may the less offend; whereas, benefits should be conferred little by little, that so they may be more fully relished.
790   But, before all things, a Prince should so live with his subjects that no vicissitude of good or evil fortune shall oblige him to alter his behaviour; because, if a need to change come through adversity, it is then too late to resort to severity; while any leniency you may use will be thrown away, for it will be seen to be compulsory and gain you no thanks.

CHAPTER IX: OF THE CIVIL PRINCEDOM

795   I come now to the second case, namely, of the leading citizen who, not by crimes or violence, but by the favour of his fellow-citizens is made Prince of his country. This may be called a Civil Princedom, and its attainment depends not wholly on merit, nor wholly on good fortune, but rather on what may be termed a *fortunate astuteness*. I say then that the road to this Princedom lies either through
800 the favour of the people or of the nobles. For in every city are to be found these two opposed humours having their origin in this, that the people desire not to be domineered over or oppressed by the nobles, while the nobles desire to oppress and domineer over the people. And from these two contrary appetites there arises in cities one of three results, a Princedom, or Liberty, or Licence. A Princedom is
805 created either by the people or by the nobles, according as one or other of these factions has occasion for it. For when the nobles perceive that they cannot withstand the people, they set to work to magnify the reputation of one of their number, and make him their Prince, to the end that under his shadow they may be enabled to indulge their desires. The people, on the other hand, when they see that
810 they cannot make head against the nobles, invest a single citizen with all their influence and make him Prince, that they may have the shelter of his authority.
    He who is made Prince by the favour of the nobles, has greater difficulty to maintain himself than he who comes to the Princedom by aid of the people, since he

finds many about him who think themselves as good as he, and whom, on that
815   account, he cannot guide or govern as he would. But he who reaches the Princedom
by the popular support, finds himself alone, with none, or but a very few about
him who are not ready to obey. Moreover, the demands of the nobles cannot be
satisfied with credit to the Prince, nor without injury to others, while those of the
people well may, the aim of the people being more honourable than that of the
820   nobles, the latter seeking to oppress, the former not to be oppressed. Add to this,
that a Prince can never secure himself against a disaffected people, their number
being too great, while he may against a disaffected nobility, since their number is
small. The worst that a Prince need fear from a disaffected people is, that they may
desert him, whereas when the nobles are his enemies he has to fear not only that
825   they may desert him, but also that they may turn against him; because, as they have
greater craft and foresight, they always choose their time to suit their safety, and
seek favour with the side they think will win. Again, a Prince must always live
with the same people, but need not always live with the same nobles, being able to
make and unmake these from day to day, and give and take away their authority at
830   his pleasure.

But to make this part of the matter clearer, I say that as regards the nobles
there is this first distinction to be made. They either so govern their conduct as to
bind themselves wholly to your fortunes, or they do not. Those who so bind
themselves, and who are not grasping, should be loved and honoured. As to those
835   who do not so bind themselves, there is this further distinction. For the most part
they are held back by pusillanimity and a natural defect of courage, in which case
you should make use of them, and of those among them more especially who are
prudent, for they will do you honour in prosperity, and in adversity give you no
cause for fear. But where they abstain from attaching themselves to you of set
840   purpose and for ambitious ends, it is a sign that they are thinking more of
themselves than of you, and against such men a Prince should be on his guard, and
treat them as though they were declared enemies, for in his adversity they will
always help to ruin him.

He who becomes a Prince through the favour of the people should always
845   keep on good terms with them; which it is easy for him to do, since all they ask is
not to be oppressed. But he who against the will of the people is made a Prince by
the favour of the nobles, must, above all things, seek to conciliate the people,
which he readily may by taking them under his protection. For since men who are
well treated by one whom they expected to treat them ill, feel the more beholden to
850   their benefactor, the people will at once become better disposed to such a Prince
when he protects them, than if he owed his Princedom to them.

There are many ways in which a Prince may gain the good-will of the people,
but, because these vary with circumstances, no certain rule can be laid down
respecting them, and I shall, therefore, say no more about them. But this is the sum
855   of the matter, that it is essential for a Prince to be on a friendly footing with his
people, since, otherwise, he will have no resource in adversity. Nabis, Prince of
Sparta, was attacked by the whole hosts of Greece, and by a Roman army flushed

with victory, and defended his country and crown against them; and when danger approached, there were but few of his subjects against whom he needed to guard himself, whereas had the people been hostile, this would not have been enough.

And what I affirm let no one controvert by citing the old saw that *'he who builds on the people builds on mire,'* for that may be true of a private citizen who presumes on his favour with the people, and counts on being rescued by them when overpowered by his enemies or by the magistrates. In such cases a man may often find himself deceived, as happened to the Gracchi in Rome, and in Florence to Messer Giorgio Scali. But when he who builds on the people is a Prince capable of command, of a spirit not to be cast down by ill-fortune, who, while he animates the whole community by his courage and bearing, neglects no prudent precaution, he will not find himself betrayed by the people, but will be seen to have laid his foundations well.

The most critical juncture for Princedoms of this kind, is at the moment when they are about to pass from the popular to the absolute form of government: and as these Princes exercise their authority either directly or through the agency of the magistrates, in the latter case their position is weaker and more hazardous, since they are wholly in the power of those citizens to whom the magistracies are entrusted, who can, and especially in difficult times, with the greatest ease deprive them of their authority, either by opposing, or by not obeying them. And in times of peril it is too late for a Prince to assume to himself an absolute authority, for the citizens and subjects who are accustomed to take their orders from the magistrates, will not when dangers threaten to take them from the Prince, so that at such seasons there will always be very few in whom he can trust. Such Princes, therefore, must not build on what they see in tranquil times when the citizens feel the need of the State. For then every one is ready to run, to promise, and, danger of death being remote, even to die for the State. But in troubled times, when the State has need of its citizens, few of them are to be found. And the risk of the experiment is the greater in that it can only be made once. Wherefore, a wise Prince should devise means whereby his subjects may at all times, whether favourable or adverse, feel the need of the State and of him, and then they will always be faithful to him.

CHAPTER X: HOW THE STRENGTH OF ALL PRINCEDOMS SHOULD BE MEASURED

In examining the character of these Princedoms, another circumstance has to be considered, namely, whether the Prince is strong enough, if occasion demands, to stand alone, or whether he needs continual help from others. To make the matter clearer, I pronounce those to be able to stand alone who, with the men and money at their disposal, can get together an army fit to take the field against any assailant; and, conversely, I judge those to be in constant need of help who cannot take the field against their enemies, but are obliged to retire behind their walls, and to defend themselves there. Of the former I have already spoken, and shall

900   speak again as occasion may require. As to the latter there is nothing to be said, except to exhort such Princes to strengthen and fortify the towns in which they dwell, and take no heed of the country outside. For whoever has thoroughly fortified his town, and put himself on such a footing with his subjects as I have already indicated and shall hereafter speak of, will always be attacked with much circumspection; for men are always averse to enterprises that are attended with difficulty, and it is impossible not to foresee difficulties in attacking a Prince

905   whose town is strongly fortified and who is not hated by his subjects.

The towns of Germany enjoy great freedom. Having little territory, they render obedience to the Emperor only when so disposed, fearing neither him nor any other neighbouring power. For they are so fortified that it is plain to every one that it would be a tedious and difficult task to reduce them, since all of them

910   are protected by moats and suitable ramparts, are well supplied with artillery, and keep their public magazines constantly stored with victual, drink and fuel, enough to last them for a year. Besides which, in order to support the poorer class of citizens without public loss, they lay in a common stock of materials for these to work on for a year, in the handicrafts which are the life and sinews of such cities,

915   and by which the common people live. Moreover, they esteem military exercises and have many regulations for their maintenance.

A Prince, therefore, who has a strong city, and who does not make himself hated, can not be attacked, or should he be so, his assailant will come badly off; since human affairs are so variable that it is almost impossible for any one to keep

920   an army posted in leaguer for a whole year without interruption of some sort. Should it be objected that if the citizens have possessions outside the town, and see them burned, they will lose patience, and that self-interest, together with the hardships of a protracted siege, will cause them to forget their loyalty; I answer that a capable and courageous Prince will always overcome these difficulties,

925   now, by holding out hopes to his subjects that the evil will not be of long continuance; now, by exciting their fears of the enemy's cruelty; and, again, by dexterously silencing those who seem to him too forward in their complaints. Moreover, it is to be expected that the enemy will burn and lay waste the country immediately on their arrival, at a time when men's minds are still heated and

930   resolute for defence. And for this very reason the Prince ought the less to fear, because after a few days, when the first ardour has abated, the injury is already done and suffered, and cannot be undone; and the people will now, all the more readily, make common cause with their Prince from his seeming to be under obligations to them, their houses having been burned and their lands wasted in his

935   defence. For it is the nature of men to incur obligation as much by the benefits they render as by those they receive.

Wherefore, if the whole matter be well considered, it ought not to be difficult for a prudent Prince, both at the outset and afterwards, to maintain the spirits of his subjects during a siege; provided always that victuals and the other means of

940   defence do not run short.

CHAPTER XI: OF ECCLESIASTICAL PRINCEDOMS

It now only remains for me to treat of Ecclesiastical Princedoms, all the difficulties in respect of which precede their acquisition. For they are acquired by merit or good fortune, but are maintained without either; being upheld by the venerable ordinances of Religion, which are all of such a nature and efficacy that they secure the authority of their Princes in whatever way they may act or live. These Princes alone have territories which they do not defend, and subjects whom they do not govern; yet their territories are not taken from them through not being defended, nor are their subjects concerned at not being governed, or led to think of throwing off their allegiance; nor is it in their power to do so. Accordingly these Princedoms alone are secure and happy. But inasmuch as they are sustained by agencies of a higher nature than the mind of man can reach, I forbear to speak of them: for since they are set up and supported by God himself, he would be a rash and presumptuous man who should venture to discuss them.

Nevertheless, should any one ask me how it comes about that the temporal power of the Church, which before the time of Alexander was looked on with contempt by all the Potentates of Italy, and not only by those so styling themselves, but by every Baron and Lordling however insignificant, has now reached such a pitch of greatness that the King of France trembles before it, and that it has been able to drive him out of Italy and to crush the Venetians; though the causes be known, it seems to me not superfluous to call them in some measure to recollection.

Before Charles of France passed into Italy, that country was under the control of the Pope, the Venetians, the King of Naples, the Duke of Milan, and the Florentines. Two chief objects had to be kept in view by all these powers: first, that no armed foreigner should be allowed to invade Italy; second, that no one of their own number should be suffered to extend his territory. Those whom it was especially needed to guard against, were the Pope and the Venetians. To hold back the Venetians it was necessary that all the other States should combine, as was done for the defence of Ferrara; while to restrain the Pope, use was made of the Roman Barons, who being divided into two factions, the Orsini and Colonnesi, had constant cause for feud with one another, and standing with arms in their hands under the very eyes of the Pontiff, kept the Popedom feeble and insecure.

And although there arose from time to time a courageous Pope like Sixtus, neither his prudence nor his good fortune could free him from these embarrassments. The cause whereof was the shortness of the lives of the Popes. For in the ten years, which was the average duration of a Pope's life, he could barely succeed in humbling one of these factions; so that if, for instance, one Pope had almost exterminated the Colonnesi, he was followed by another, who being the enemy of the Orsini had no time to rid himself of them, but so far from completing the destruction of the Colonnesi, restored them to life. This led to the temporal authority of the Popes being little esteemed in Italy.

Then came Alexander VI, who more than any of his predecessors showed what a Pope could effect with money and arms, achieving by the instrumentality of

985 Duke Valentino, and by taking advantage of the coming of the French into Italy, all those successes which I have already noticed in speaking of the actions of the Duke. And although his object was to aggrandize, not the Church but the Duke, what he did turned to the advantage of the Church, which after his death, and after the Duke had been put out of the way, became the heir of his labours.

990 After him came Pope Julius, who found the Church strengthened by the possession of the whole of Romagna, and the Roman Barons exhausted and their factions shattered under the blows of Pope Alexander. He found also a way opened for the accumulation of wealth, which before the time of Alexander no one had followed. These advantages Julius not only used but added to. He undertook the conquest of Bologna, the overthrow of the Venetians, and the expulsion of the French from Italy; in all which enterprises he succeeded, and with the greater

995 glory to himself in that whatever he did, was done to strengthen the Church and not to aggrandize any private person. He succeeded, moreover, in keeping the factions of the Orsini and Colonnesi within the same limits as he found them; and, though some seeds of insubordination may still have been left among them, two causes operated to hold them in check; first, the great power of the Church, which

1000 overawed them, and second, their being without Cardinals, who had been the cause of all their disorders. For these factions while they have Cardinals among them can never be at rest, since it is they who foment dissension both in Rome and out of it, in which the Barons are forced to take part, the ambition of the Prelates thus giving rise to tumult and discord among the Barons.

1005 His Holiness, Pope Leo, has consequently found the Papacy most powerful; and from him we may hope, that as his predecessors made it great with arms, he will render it still greater and more venerable by his benignity and other countless virtues.

CHAPTER XII: HOW MANY DIFFERENT KINDS OF SOLDIERS THERE ARE, AND OF MERCENARIES

1010 Having spoken particularly of all the various kinds of Princedom whereof at the outset I proposed to treat, considered in some measure what are the causes of their strength and weakness, and pointed out the methods by which men commonly seek to acquire them, it now remains that I should discourse generally concerning the means for attack and defence of which each of these different kinds of Princedom may make use.

1015 I have already said that a Prince must lay solid foundations, since otherwise he will inevitably be destroyed. Now the main foundations of all States, whether new, old, or mixed, are good laws and good arms. But since you cannot have the former without the latter, and where you have the latter, are likely to have the former, I shall here omit all discussion on the subject of laws, and speak only of

1020 arms.

I say then that the arms wherewith a Prince defends his State are either his own subjects, or they are mercenaries, or they are auxiliaries, or they are partly

one and partly another. Mercenaries and auxiliaries are at once useless and dangerous, and he who holds his State by means of mercenary troops can never be
1025 solidly or securely seated. For such troops are disunited, ambitious, insubordinate, treacherous, insolent among friends, cowardly before foes, and without fear of God or faith with man. Whenever they are attacked defeat follows; so that in peace you are plundered by them, in war by your enemies. And this because they have no tie or motive to keep them in the field beyond their paltry
1030 pay, in return for which it would be too much to expect them to give their lives. They are ready enough, therefore, to be your soldiers while you are at peace, but when war is declared they make off and disappear. I ought to have little difficulty in getting this believed, for the present ruin of Italy is due to no other cause than her having for many years trusted to mercenaries, who though heretofore they may
1035 have helped the fortunes of some one man, and made a show of strength when matched with one another, have always revealed themselves in their true colours so soon as foreign enemies appeared. Hence it was that Charles of France was suffered to conquer Italy *with chalk;* and he who said our sins were the cause, said truly, though it was not the sins he meant, but those which I have noticed. And as
1040 these were the sins of Princes, they it is who have paid the penalty.

But I desire to demonstrate still more clearly the untoward character of these forces. Captains of mercenaries are either able men or they are not. If they are, you cannot trust them, since they will always seek their own aggrandizement, either by overthrowing you who are their master, or by the overthrow of others
1045 contrary to your desire. On the other hand, if your captain be not an able man the chances are you will be ruined. And if it be said that whoever has arms in his hands will act in the same way whether he be a mercenary or no, I answer that when arms have to be employed by a Prince or a Republic, the Prince ought to go in person to take command as captain, the Republic should send one of her citizens,
1050 and if he prove incapable should change him, but if he prove capable should by the force of the laws confine him within proper bounds. And we see from experience that both Princes and Republics when they depend on their own arms have the greatest success, whereas from employing mercenaries nothing but loss results. Moreover, a Republic trusting to her own forces, is with greater difficulty than
1055 one which relies on foreign arms brought to yield obedience to a single citizen. Rome and Sparta remained for ages armed and free. The Swiss are at once the best armed and the freest people in the world.

Of mercenary arms in ancient times we have an example in the Carthaginians, who at the close of their first war with Rome, were well-nigh ruined by their
1060 hired troops, although these were commanded by Carthaginian citizens. So too, when, on the death of Epaminondas, the Thebans made Philip of Macedon captain of their army, after gaining a victory for them, he deprived them of their liberty. The Milanese, in like manner, when Duke Filippo died, took Francesco Sforza into their pay to conduct the war against the Venetians. But he, after defeating the
1065 enemy at Caravaggio, combined with them to overthrow the Milanese, his masters. His father too while in the pay of Giovanna, Queen of Naples, suddenly left her

without troops, obliging her, in order to save her kingdom, to throw herself into the arms of the King of Aragon.

And if it be said that in times past the Venetians and the Florentines have 1070 extended their dominions by means of these arms, and that their captains have served them faithfully, without seeking to make themselves their masters, I answer that in this respect the Florentines have been fortunate, because among those valiant captains who might have given them cause for fear, some have not been victorious, some have had rivals, and some have turned their ambition in other 1075 directions.

Among those not victorious, was Giovanni Acuto, whose fidelity, since he was unsuccessful, was not put to the proof but any one may see, that had he been victorious the Florentines must have been entirely in his hands. The Sforzas, again, had constant rivals in the Bracceschi, so that the one following was a check 1080 upon the other; moreover, the ambition of Francesco was directed against Milan, while that of Braccio was directed against the Church and the kingdom of Naples. Let us turn, however, to what took place lately. The Florentines chose for their captain Paolo Vitelli, a most prudent commander, who had raised himself from privacy to the highest renown in arms. Had he been successful in reducing Pisa, 1085 none can deny that the Florentines would have been completely in his power, for they would have been ruined had he gone over to their enemies, while if they retained him they must have submitted to his will.

Again, as to the Venetians, if we consider the growth of their power, it will be seen that they conducted their affairs with glory and safety so long as their 1090 subjects of all ranks, gentle and simple alike, valiantly bore arms in their wars; as they did before they directed their enterprises landwards. But when they took to making war by land, they forsook those methods in which they excelled and were content to follow the customs of Italy.

At first, indeed, in extending their possessions on the mainland, having as yet 1095 but little territory and being held in high repute, they had not much to fear from their captains; but when their territories increased, which they did under Carmagnola, they were taught their mistake. For as they had found him a most valiant and skilful leader when, under his command, they defeated the Duke of Milan, and, on the other hand, saw him slack in carrying on the war, they made up 1100 their minds that no further victories were to be had under him; and because, through fear of losing what they had gained, they could not discharge him, to secure themselves against him they were forced to put him to death. After him they have had for captains, Bartolommeo of Bergamo, Roberto of San Severino, the Count of Pitigliano, and the like, under whom their danger has not been from 1105 victories, but from defeats; as, for instance, at Vaila, where they lost in a single day what it had taken the efforts of eight hundred years to acquire. For the gains resulting from mercenary arms are slow, and late, and inconsiderable, but the losses sudden and astounding.

And since these examples have led me back to Italy, which for many years 1110 past has been defended by mercenary arms, I desire to go somewhat deeper into the matter, in order that the causes which led to the adoption of these arms being seen, they may the more readily be corrected. You are to understand, then, that when in these later times the Imperial control began to be rejected by Italy, and the temporal power of the Pope to be more thought of, Italy suddenly split up into a number of 1115 separate States. For many of the larger cities took up arms against their nobles, who, with the favour of the Emperor, had before kept them in subjection, and were supported by the Church with a view to add to her temporal authority: while in many others of these cities, private citizens became rulers. Hence Italy, having passed almost entirely into the hands of the Church and of certain Republics, the 1120 former made up of priests, the latter of citizens unfamiliar with arms, began to take foreigners into her pay.

The first who gave reputation to this service was Alberigo of Conio in Romagna, from whose school of warlike training descended, among others, Braccio and Sforza, who in their time were the arbiters of Italy; after whom came 1125 all those others who down to the present hour have held similar commands, and to whose merits we owe it that our country has been overrun by Charles, plundered by Louis, wasted by Ferdinand, and insulted by the Swiss.

The first object of these mercenaries was to bring foot soldiers into disrepute, in order to enhance the merit of their own followers; and this they did, because 1130 lacking territory of their own and depending on their profession for their support, a few foot soldiers gave them no importance, while for a large number they were unable to provide. For these reasons they had recourse to horsemen, a less retinue of whom was thought to confer distinction, and could be more easily maintained. And the matter went to such a length, that in an army of twenty thousand men, not 1135 two thousand foot soldiers were to be found. Moreover, they spared no endeavour to relieve themselves and their men from fatigue and danger, not killing one another in battle, but making prisoners who were afterwards released without ransom. They would attack no town by night; those in towns would make no sortie by night against a besieging army. Their camps were without rampart or 1140 trench. They had no winter campaigns. All which arrangements were sanctioned by their military rules, contrived by them, as I have said already, to escape fatigue and danger; but the result of which has been to bring Italy into servitude and contempt.

CHAPTER XIII: OF AUXILIARY, MIXED, AND NATIONAL ARMS

The second sort of unprofitable arms are auxiliaries, by whom I mean, troops 1145 brought to help and protect you by a potentate whom you summon to your aid; as when in recent times, Pope Julius II observing the pitiful behaviour of his mercenaries at the enterprise of Ferrara, betook himself to auxiliaries, and arranged with Ferdinand of Spain to be supplied with horse and foot soldiers.

Auxiliaries may be excellent and useful soldiers for themselves, but are 1150 always hurtful to him who calls them in; for if they are defeated, he is undone, if victorious, he becomes their prisoner. Ancient histories abound with instances of

this, but I shall not pass from the example of Pope Julius, which is still fresh in men's minds. It was the height of rashness for him, in his eagerness to gain Ferrara, to throw himself without reserve into the arms of a stranger. Nevertheless, his
1155   good fortune came to his rescue, and he had not to reap the fruits of his ill-considered conduct. For after his auxiliaries were defeated at Ravenna, the Swiss suddenly descended and, to their own surprise and that of every one else, swept the victors out of the country, so that, he neither remained a prisoner with his enemies, they being put to flight, nor with his auxiliaries, because victory was
1160   won by other arms than theirs. The Florentines, being wholly without soldiers of their own, brought ten thousand French men-at-arms to the siege of Pisa, thereby incurring greater peril than at any previous time of trouble. To protect himself from his neighbours, the Emperor of Constantinople summoned ten thousand Turkish soldiers into Greece, who, when the war was over, refused to leave, and
1165   this was the beginning of the servitude of Greece to the Infidel.

Let him, therefore, who would deprive himself of every chance of success, have recourse to auxiliaries, these being far more dangerous than mercenary arms, bringing ruin with them ready made. For they are united, and wholly under the control of their own officers; whereas, before mercenaries, even after gaining a
1170   victory, can do you hurt, longer time and better opportunities are needed; because, as they are made up of separate companies, raised and paid by you, he whom you place in command cannot at once acquire such authority over them as will be injurious to you. In short, with mercenaries your greatest danger is from their inertness and cowardice, with auxiliaries from their valour. Wise Princes,
1175   therefore, have always eschewed these arms, and trusted rather to their own, and have preferred defeat with the latter to victory with the former, counting that as no true victory which is gained by foreign aid.

I shall never hesitate to cite the example of Cesare Borgia and his actions. He entered Romagna with a force of auxiliaries, all of them French men-at-arms, with
1180   whom he took Imola and Forli. But it appearing to him afterwards that these troops were not to be trusted, he had recourse to mercenaries from whom he thought there would be less danger, and took the Orsini and Vitelli into his pay. But finding these likewise while under his command to be fickle, false, and treacherous, he got rid of them, and fell back on troops of his own raising. And we
1185   may readily discern the difference between these various kinds of arms, by observing the different degrees of reputation in which the Duke stood while he depended upon the French alone, when he took the Orsini and Vitelli into his pay, and when he fell back on his own troops and his own resources; for we find his reputation always increasing, and that he was never so well thought of as when
1190   every one perceived him to be sole master of his own forces.

I am unwilling to leave these examples, drawn from what has taken place in Italy and in recent times; and yet I must not omit to notice the case of Hiero of Syracuse, who is one of those whom I have already named. He, as I have before related, being made captain of their armies by the Syracusans, saw at once that a
1195   force of mercenary soldiers, supplied by men resembling our Italian *condottieri*,

was not serviceable; and as he would not retain and could not disband them, he caused them all to be cut to pieces, and afterwards made war with native soldiers only, without other aid.

And here I would call to mind a passage in the Old Testament as bearing on this point. When David offered himself to Saul to go forth and fight Goliath the Philistine champion, Saul to encourage him armed him with his own armour, which David, so soon as he had put it on, rejected, saying that with these untried arms he could not prevail, and that he chose rather to meet his enemy with only his sling and his sword. In a word, the armour of others is too wide, or too strait for us; it falls off us, or it weighs us down.

Charles VII, the father of Louis XI, who by his good fortune and valour freed France from the English, saw this necessity of strengthening himself with a national army, and drew up ordinances regulating the service both of men-at-arms and of foot soldiers throughout his kingdom. But afterwards his son, King Louis, did away with the national infantry, and began to hire Swiss mercenaries. Which blunder having been followed by subsequent Princes, has been the cause, as the result shows, of the dangers into which the kingdom of France has fallen; for, by enhancing the reputation of the Swiss, the whole of the national troops of France have been deteriorated. For from their infantry being done away with, their men-at-arms are made wholly dependent on foreign assistance, and being accustomed to cooperate with the Swiss, have grown to think they can do nothing without them. Hence the French are no match for the Swiss, and without them cannot succeed against others.

The armies of France, then, are mixed, being partly national and partly mercenary. Armies thus composed are far superior to mere mercenaries or mere auxiliaries, but far inferior to forces purely national. And this example is in itself conclusive, for the realm of France would be invincible if the military ordinances of Charles VII had been retained and extended. But from want of foresight men make changes which relishing well at first do not betray their hidden venom, as I have already observed respecting hectic fever. Nevertheless, the ruler is not truly wise who cannot discern evils before they develop themselves, and this is a faculty given to few.

If we look for the causes which first led to the overthrow of the Roman Empire, they will be found to have had their source in the employment of Gothic mercenaries, for from that hour the strength of the Romans began to wane and all the virtue which went from them passed to the Goths. And, to be brief, I say that without national arms no Princedom is safe, but on the contrary is wholly dependent on Fortune, being without the strength that could defend it in adversity. And it has always been the deliberate opinion of the wise, that nothing is so infirm and fleeting as a reputation for power not founded upon a national army, by which I mean one composed of subjects, citizens, and dependants, all others being mercenary or auxiliary.

The methods to be followed for organizing a national army may readily be ascertained, if the rules above laid down by me, and by which I abide, be well

1240 considered, and attention be given to the manner in which Philip, father of Alexander the Great, and many other Princes and Republics have armed and disposed their forces.

CHAPTER XIV: OF THE DUTY OF A PRINCE IN RESPECT OF MILITARY AFFAIRS

A Prince, therefore, should have no care or thought but for war, and for the regulations and training it requires, and should apply himself exclusively to this
1245 as his peculiar province; for war is the sole art looked for in one who rules, and is of such efficacy that it not merely maintains those who are born Princes, but often enables men to rise to that eminence from a private station; while, on the other hand, we often see that when Princes devote themselves rather to pleasure than to arms, they lose their dominions. And as neglect of this art is the prime cause of
1250 such calamities, so to be a proficient in it is the surest way to acquire power. Francesco Sforza, from his renown in arms, rose from privacy to be Duke of Milan, while his descendants, seeking to avoid the hardships and fatigues of military life, from being Princes fell back into privacy. For among other causes of misfortune which your not being armed brings upon you, it makes you despised,
1255 and this is one of those reproaches against which, as shall presently be explained, a Prince ought most carefully to guard.

Between an armed and an unarmed man no proportion holds, and it is contrary to reason to expect that the armed man should voluntarily submit to him who is unarmed, or that the unarmed man should stand secure among armed
1260 retainers. For with contempt on one side, and distrust on the other, it is impossible that men should work well together. Wherefore, as has already been said, a Prince who is ignorant of military affairs, besides other disadvantages, can neither be respected by his soldiers, nor can he trust them. A Prince, therefore, ought never to allow his attention to be diverted from warlike pursuits, and should occupy
1265 himself with them even more in peace than in war. This he can do in two ways, by practice or by study.

As to the practice, he ought, besides keeping his soldiers well trained and disciplined, to be constantly engaged in the chase, that he may inure his body to hardships and fatigue, and gain at the same time a knowledge of places, by
1270 observing how the mountains slope, the valleys open, and the plains spread; acquainting himself with the characters of rivers and marshes, and giving the greatest attention to this subject. Such knowledge is useful to him in two ways; for first, he learns thereby to know his own country, and to understand better how it may be defended; and next, from his familiar acquaintance with its localities, he
1275 readily comprehends the character of other districts when obliged to observe them for the first time. For the hills, valleys, plains, rivers, and marshes of Tuscany, for example, have a certain resemblance to those elsewhere; so that from a knowledge of the natural features of that province, similar knowledge in respect of other provinces may readily be gained. The Prince who is wanting in this kind of

1280 knowledge, is wanting in the first qualification of a good captain, for by it he is taught how to surprise an enemy, how to choose an encampment, how to lead his army on a march, how to array it for battle, and how to post it to the best advantage for a siege.

1285 Among the commendations which Philopoemon, Prince of the Achaians, has received from historians is this—that in times of peace he was always thinking of methods of warfare, so that when walking in the country with his friends he would often stop and talk with them on the subject. 'If the enemy,' he would say, 'were posted on that hill, and we found ourselves here with our army, which of us would have the better position? How could we most safely and in the best order

1290 advance to meet them? If we had to retreat, what direction should we take? If they retired, how should we pursue?' In this way he put to his friends, as he went along, all the contingencies that can befall an army. He listened to their opinions, stated his own, and supported them with reasons; and from his being constantly occupied with such meditations, it resulted, that when in actual command no

1295 complication could ever present itself with which he was not prepared to deal.

As to the mental training of which we have spoken, a Prince should read histories, and in these should note the actions of great men, observe how they conducted themselves in their wars, and examine the causes of their victories and defeats, so as to avoid the latter and imitate them in the former. And above all, he

1300 should, as many great men of past ages have done, assume for his models those persons who before his time have been renowned and celebrated, whose deeds and achievements he should constantly keep in mind, as it is related that Alexander the Great sought to resemble Achilles, Caesar Alexander, and Scipio Cyrus. And any one who reads the life of this last-named hero, written by Xenophon, recognizes

1305 afterwards in the life of Scipio, how much this imitation was the source of his glory, and how nearly in his chastity, affability, kindliness, and generosity, he conformed to the character of Cyrus as Xenophon describes it.

A wise Prince, therefore, should pursue such methods as these, never resting idle in times of peace, but strenuously seeking to turn them to account, so that he

1310 may derive strength from them in the hour of danger, and find himself ready should Fortune turn against him, to resist her blows.

CHAPTER XV: OF THE QUALITIES IN RESPECT OF WHICH MEN, AND MOST OF ALL PRINCES, ARE PRAISED OR BLAMED

It now remains for us to consider what ought to be the conduct and bearing of a Prince in relation to his subjects and friends. And since I know that many have written on this subject, I fear it may be thought presumptuous in me to write of it

1315 also; the more so, because in my treatment of it I depart from the views that others have taken.

But since it is my object to write what shall be useful to whosoever understands it, it seems to me better to follow the real truth of things than an imaginary view of them. For many Republics and Princedoms have been imagined

1320   that were never seen or known to exist in reality. And the manner in which we live, and that in which we ought to live, are things so wide asunder, that he who quits the one to betake himself to the other is more likely to destroy than to save himself; since any one who would act up to a perfect standard of goodness in everything, must be ruined among so many who are not good. It is essential,

1325   therefore, for a Prince who desires to maintain his position, to have learned how to be other than good, and to use or not to use his goodness as necessity requires.

     Laying aside, therefore, all fanciful notions concerning a Prince, and considering those only that are true, I say that all men when they are spoken of, and Princes more than others from their being set so high, are characterized by

1330   some one of those qualities which attach either praise or blame. Thus one is accounted liberal, another miserly (which word I use, rather than *avaricious*, to denote the man who is too sparing of what is his own, *avarice* being the disposition to take wrongfully what is another's); one is generous, another greedy; one cruel, another tenderhearted; one is faithless, another true to his word;

1335   one effeminate and cowardly, another high-spirited and courageous; one is courteous, another haughty; one impure, another chaste; one simple, another crafty; one firm, another facile; one grave, another frivolous; one devout, another unbelieving; and the like. Every one, I know, will admit that it would be most laudable for a Prince to be endowed with all of the above qualities that are

1340   reckoned good; but since it is impossible for him to possess or constantly practise them all, the conditions of human nature not allowing it, he must be discreet enough to know how to avoid the infamy of those vices that would deprive him of his government, and, if possible, be on his guard also against those which might not deprive him of it; though if he cannot wholly restrain himself, he may with less

1345   scruple indulge in the latter. He need never hesitate, however, to incur the reproach of those vices without which his authority can hardly be preserved; for if he well consider the whole matter, he will find that there may be a line of conduct having the appearance of virtue, to follow which would be his ruin, and that there may be another course having the appearance of vice, by following

1350   which his safety and well-being are secured.

CHAPTER XVI: OF LIBERALITY AND MISERLINESS

     Beginning, then, with the first of the qualities above noticed, I say that it may be a good thing to be reputed liberal, but, nevertheless, that liberality without the reputation of it is hurtful; because, though it be worthily and rightly used, still if it be not known, you escape not the reproach of its opposite vice. Hence, to have

1355   credit for liberality with the world at large, you must neglect no circumstance of sumptuous display; the result being, that a Prince of a liberal disposition will consume his whole substance in things of this sort, and, after all, be obliged, if he would maintain his reputation for liberality, to burden his subjects with extraordinary taxes, and to resort to confiscations and all the other shifts

1360   whereby money is raised. But in this way he becomes hateful to his subjects, and growing impoverished is held in little esteem by any. So that in the end, having by his liberality offended many and obliged few, he is worse off than when he began, and is exposed to all his original dangers. Recognizing this, and endeavouring to retrace his steps, he at once incurs the infamy of miserliness.

1365   A Prince, therefore, since he cannot without injury to himself practise the virtue of liberality so that it may be known, will not, if he be wise, greatly concern himself though he be called miserly. Because in time he will come to be regarded as more and more liberal, when it is seen that through his parsimony his revenues are sufficient; that he is able to defend himself against any who make war on him; that

1370   he can engage in enterprises against others without burdening his subjects; and thus exercise liberality towards all from whom he does not take, whose number is infinite, while he is miserly in respect of those only to whom he does not give, whose number is few.

     In our own days we have seen no Princes accomplish great results save those

1375   who have been accounted miserly. All others have been ruined. Pope Julius II, after availing himself of his reputation for liberality to arrive at the Papacy, made no effort to preserve that reputation when making war on the King of France, but carried on all his numerous campaigns without levying from his subjects a single extraordinary tax, providing for the increased expenditure out of his long-

1380   continued savings. Had the present King of Spain been accounted liberal, he never could have engaged or succeeded in so many enterprises.

     A Prince, therefore, if he is enabled thereby to forbear from plundering his subjects, to defend himself, to escape poverty and contempt, and the necessity of becoming rapacious, ought to care little though he incur the reproach of

1385   miserliness, for this is one of those vices which enable him to reign.

     And should any object that Caesar by his liberality rose to power, and that many others have been advanced to the highest dignities from their having been liberal and so reputed, I reply, 'Either you are already a Prince or you seek to become one; in the former case liberality is hurtful, in the latter it is very necessary

1390   that you be thought liberal; Caesar was one of those who sought the sovereignty of Rome; but if after obtaining it he had lived on without retrenching his expenditure, he must have ruined the Empire.' And if it be further urged that many Princes reputed to have been most liberal have achieved great things with their armies, I answer that a Prince spends either what belongs to himself and his

1395   subjects, or what belongs to others; and that in the former case he ought to be sparing, but in the latter ought not to refrain from any kind of liberality. Because for a Prince who leads his armies in person and maintains them by plunder, pillage, and forced contributions, dealing as he does with the property of others this liberality is necessary, since otherwise he would not be followed by his

1400   soldiers. Of what does not belong to you or to your subjects you should, therefore, be a lavish giver, as were Cyrus, Caesar, and Alexander; for to be liberal with the property of others does not take from your reputation, but adds to it. What injures you is to give away what is your own. And there is no quality so self-destructive as liberality; for while you practise it you lose the means whereby it can be

1405 practised, and become poor and despised, or else, to avoid poverty, you become rapacious and hated. For liberality leads to one or other of these two results, against which, beyond all others, a Prince should guard.

Wherefore it is wiser to put up with the name of being miserly, which breeds ignominy, but without hate, than to be obliged, from the desire to be reckoned 1410 liberal, to incur the reproach of rapacity, which breeds hate as well as ignominy.

CHAPTER XVII: OF CRUELTY AND CLEMENCY, AND WHETHER IT IS BETTER TO BE LOVED OR FEARED

Passing to the other qualities above referred to, I say that every Prince should desire to be accounted merciful and not cruel. Nevertheless, he should be on his guard against the abuse of this quality of mercy. Cesare Borgia was reputed cruel, yet his cruelty restored Romagna, united it, and brought it to order and obedience; 1415 so that if we look at things in their true light, it will be seen that he was in reality far more merciful than the people of Florence, who, to avoid the imputation of cruelty, suffered Pistoja to be torn to pieces by factions.

A Prince should therefore disregard the reproach of being thought cruel where it enables him to keep his subjects united and obedient. For he who quells 1420 disorder by a very few signal examples will in the end be more merciful than he who from too great leniency permits things to take their course and so to result in rapine and bloodshed; for these hurt the whole State, whereas the severities of the Prince injure individuals only.

And for a new Prince, of all others, it is impossible to escape a name for 1425 cruelty, since new States are full of dangers. Wherefore Virgil, by the mouth of Dido, excuses the harshness of her reign on the plea that it was new, saying:

A fate unkind, and newness in my reign
Compel me thus to guard a wide domain.

Nevertheless, the new Prince should not be too ready of belief, nor too easily 1430 set in motion; nor should he himself be the first to raise alarms; but should so temper prudence with kindliness that too great confidence in others shall not throw him off his guard, nor groundless distrust render him insupportable.

And here comes in the question whether it is better to be loved rather than feared, or feared rather than loved. It might perhaps be answered that we should 1435 wish to be both; but since love and fear can hardly exist together, if we must choose between them, it is far safer to be feared than loved. For of men it may generally be affirmed that they are thankless, fickle, false, studious to avoid danger, greedy of gain, devoted to you while you are able to confer benefits upon them, and ready, as I said before, while danger is distant, to shed their blood, and 1440 sacrifice their property, their lives, and their children for you; but in the hour of need they turn against you. The Prince, therefore, who without otherwise securing himself builds wholly on their professions is undone. For the friendships which we buy with a price, and do not gain by greatness and nobility of character, though they be fairly earned are not made good, but fail us when we have occasion to use them.

Moreover, men are less careful how they offend him who makes himself loved than him who makes himself feared. For love is held by the tie of obligation, which, because men are a sorry breed, is broken on every whisper of private interest; but fear is bound by the apprehension of punishment which never relaxes its grasp.

Nevertheless a Prince should inspire fear in such a fashion that if he do not win love he may escape hate. For a man may very well be feared and yet not hated, and this will be the case so long as he does not meddle with the property or with the women of his citizens and subjects. And if constrained to put any to death, he should do so only when there is manifest cause or reasonable justification. But, above all, he must abstain from the property of others. For men will sooner forget the death of their father than the loss of their patrimony. Moreover, pretexts for confiscation are never to seek, and he who has once begun to live by rapine always finds reasons for taking what is not his; whereas reasons for shedding blood are fewer, and sooner exhausted.

But when a Prince is with his army, and has many soldiers under his command, he must needs disregard the reproach of cruelty, for without such a reputation in its Captain, no army can be held together or kept under any kind of control. Among other things remarkable in Hannibal this has been noted, that having a very great army, made up of men of many different nations and brought to fight in a foreign country, no dissension ever arose among the soldiers themselves, nor any mutiny against their leader, either in his good or in his evil fortunes. This we can only ascribe to the transcendent cruelty, which, joined with numberless great qualities, rendered him at once venerable and terrible in the eyes of his soldiers; for without this reputation for cruelty these other virtues would not have produced the like results.

Unreflecting writers, indeed, while they praise his achievements, have condemned the chief cause of them; but that his other merits would not by themselves have been so efficacious we may see from the case of Scipio, one of the greatest Captains, not of his own time only but of all times of which we have record, whose armies rose against him in Spain from no other cause than his too great leniency in allowing them a freedom inconsistent with military strictness. With which weakness Fabius Maximus taxed him in the Senate House, calling him the corrupter of the Roman soldiery. Again, when the Locrians were shamefully outraged by one of his lieutenants, he neither avenged them, nor punished the insolence of his officer; and this from the natural easiness of his disposition. So that it was said in the Senate by one who sought to excuse him, that there were many who knew better how to refrain from doing wrong themselves than how to correct the wrong-doing of others. This temper, however, must in time have marred the name and fame even of Scipio, had he continued in it, and retained his command. But living as he did under the control of the Senate, this hurtful quality was not merely disguised, but came to be regarded as a glory.

Returning to the question of being loved or feared, I sum up by saying, that since his being loved depends upon his subjects, while his being feared depends upon himself, a wise Prince should build on what is his own, and not on what

1490   rests with others. Only, as I have said, he must do his utmost to escape hatred.

CHAPTER XVIII: HOW PRINCES SHOULD KEEP FAITH

Every one understands how praiseworthy it is in a Prince to keep faith, and to live uprightly and not craftily. Nevertheless, we see from what has taken place in our own days that Princes who have set little store by their word, but have known how to overreach men by their cunning, have accomplished great things,

1495   and in the end got the better of those who trusted to honest dealing.

Be it known, then, that there are two ways of contending, one in accordance with the laws, the other by force; the first of which is proper to men, the second to beasts. But since the first method is often ineffectual, it becomes necessary to resort to the second. A Prince should, therefore, understand how to use well both the man

1500   and the beast. And this lesson has been covertly taught by the ancient writers, who relate how Achilles and many others of these old Princes were given over to be brought up and trained by Chiron the Centaur; since the only meaning of their having for instructor one who was half man and half beast is, that it is necessary for a Prince to know how to use both natures, and that the one without the other

1505   has no stability.

But since a Prince should know how to use the beast's nature wisely, he ought of beasts to choose both the lion and the fox; for the lion cannot guard himself from the toils, nor the fox from wolves. He must therefore be a fox to discern toils, and a lion to drive off wolves.

1510   To rely wholly on the lion is unwise; and for this reason a prudent Prince neither can nor ought to keep his word when to keep it is hurtful to him and the causes which led him to pledge it are removed. If all men were good, this would not be good advice, but since they are dishonest and do not keep faith with you, you, in return, need not keep faith with them; and no prince was ever at a loss for

1515   plausible reasons to cloak a breach of faith. Of this numberless recent instances could be given, and it might be shown how many solemn treaties and engagements have been rendered inoperative and idle through want of faith in Princes, and that he who was best known to play the fox has had the best success.

It is necessary, indeed, to put a good colour on this nature, and to be skilful in

1520   simulating and dissembling. But men are so simple, and governed so absolutely by their present needs, that he who wishes to deceive will never fail in finding willing dupes. One recent example I will not omit. Pope Alexander VI had no care or thought but how to deceive, and always found material to work on. No man ever had a more effective manner of asseverating, or made promises with more

1525   solemn protestations, or observed them less. And yet, because he understood this side of human nature, his frauds always succeeded.

It is not essential, then, that a Prince should have all the good qualities which I have enumerated above, but it is most essential that he should seem to have them; I will even venture to affirm that if he has and invariably practises them all, they

1530 are hurtful, whereas the appearance of having them is useful. Thus, it is well to seem merciful, faithful, humane, religious, and upright, and also to be so; but the mind should remain so balanced that were it needful not to be so, you should be able and know how to change to the contrary.

And you are to understand that a Prince, and most of all a new Prince, cannot

1535 observe all those rules of conduct in respect whereof men are accounted good, being often forced, in order to preserve his Princedom, to act in opposition to good faith, charity, humanity, and religion. He must therefore keep his mind ready to shift as the winds and tides of Fortune turn, and, as I have already said, he ought not to quit good courses if he can help it, but should know how to follow evil

1540 courses if he must.

A Prince should therefore be very careful that nothing ever escapes his lips which is not replete with the five qualities above named, so that to see and hear him, one would think him the embodiment of mercy, good faith, integrity, humanity, and religion. And there is no virtue which it is more necessary for him to seem to

1545 possess than this last; because men in general judge rather by the eye than by the hand, for every one can see but few can touch. Every one sees what you seem, but few know what you are, and these few dare not oppose themselves to the opinion of the many who have the majesty of the State to back them up.

Moreover, in the actions of all men, and most of all of Princes, where there is

1550 no tribunal to which we can appeal, we look to results. Wherefore if a Prince succeeds in establishing and maintaining his authority, the means will always be judged honourable and be approved by every one. For the vulgar are always taken by appearances and by results, and the world is made up of the vulgar, the few only finding room when the many have no longer ground to stand on.

1555 A certain Prince of our own days, whose name it is as well not to mention, is always preaching peace and good faith, although the mortal enemy of both; and both, had he practised them as he preaches them, would, oftener than once, have lost him his kingdom and authority.

CHAPTER XIX: THAT A PRINCE SHOULD SEEK TO ESCAPE CONTEMPT AND HATRED

Having now spoken of the chief of the qualities above referred to, the rest I

1560 shall dispose of briefly with these general remarks, that a Prince, as has already in part been said, should consider how he may avoid such courses as would make him hated or despised; and that whenever he succeeds in keeping clear of these, he has performed his part, and runs no risk though he incur other infamies.

A Prince, as I have said before, sooner becomes hated by being rapacious and

1565 by interfering with the property and with the women of his subjects, than in any other way. From these, therefore, he should abstain. For so long as neither their property nor their honour is touched, the mass of mankind live contentedly, and the Prince has only to cope with the ambition of a few, which can in many ways and easily be kept within bounds.

1570   A Prince is despised when he is seen to be fickle, frivolous, effeminate, pusillanimous, or irresolute, against which defects he ought therefore most carefully to guard, striving so to bear himself that greatness, courage, wisdom, and strength may appear in all his actions. In his private dealings with his subjects his decisions should be irrevocable, and his reputation such that no one would dream
1575 of overreaching or cajoling him.

    The Prince who inspires such an opinion of himself is greatly esteemed, and against one who is greatly esteemed conspiracy is difficult; nor, when he is known to be an excellent Prince and held in reverence by his subjects, will it be easy to attack him. For a Prince is exposed to two dangers, from within in respect of his
1580 subjects, from without in respect of foreign powers. Against the latter he will defend himself with good arms and good allies, and if he have good arms he will always have good allies; and when things are settled abroad, they will always be settled at home, unless disturbed by conspiracies; and even should there be hostility from without, if he has taken those measures, and has lived in the way I
1585 have recommended, and if he never abandons hope, he will withstand every attack; as I have said was done by Nabis the Spartan.

    As regards his own subjects, when affairs are quiet abroad, he has to fear they may engage in secret plots; against which a Prince best secures himself when he escapes being hated or despised, and keeps on good terms with his people; and
1590 this, as I have already shown at length, it is essential he should do. Not to be hated or despised by the body of his subjects, is one of the surest safeguards that a Prince can have against conspiracy For he who conspires always reckons on pleasing the people by putting the Prince to death; but when he sees that instead of pleasing he will offend them, he cannot summon courage to carry out his design. For the
1595 difficulties that attend conspirators are infinite, and we know from experience that while there have been many conspiracies, few of them have succeeded.

    He who conspires cannot do so alone, nor can he assume as his companions any save those whom he believes to be discontented; but so soon as you impart your design to a discontented man, you supply him with the means of removing his
1600 discontent, since by betraying you he can procure for himself every advantage; so that seeing on the one hand certain gain, and on the other a doubtful and dangerous risk, he must either be a rare friend to you, or the mortal enemy of his Prince, if he keep your secret.

    To put the matter shortly, I say that on the side of the conspirator there are
1605 distrust, jealousy, and dread of punishment to deter him, while on the side of the Prince there are the laws, the majesty of the throne, the protection of friends and of the government to defend him; to which if the general good-will of the people be added, it is hardly possible that any should be rash enough to conspire. For while in ordinary cases, the conspirator has ground for fear only before the execution of
1610 his villainy, in this case he has also cause to fear after the crime has been

perpetrated, since he has the people for his enemy, and is thus cut off from every hope of shelter.

Of this, endless instances might be given, but I shall content myself with one that happened within the recollection of our fathers. Messer Annibale Bentivoglio, Lord of Bologna and grandfather of the present Messer Annibale, was conspired against and murdered by the Canneschi, leaving behind none belonging to him save Messer Giovanni, then an infant in arms. Immediately upon the murder, the people rose and put all the Canneschi to death. This resulted from the general good-will with which the House of the Bentivogli was then regarded in Bologna; which feeling was so strong, that when upon the death of Messer Annibale no one was left who could govern the State, there being reason to believe that a descendant of the family (who up to that time had been thought to be the son of a smith) was living in Florence, the citizens of Bologna came there for him, and entrusted him with the government of their city; which he retained until Messer Giovanni was old enough to govern.

To be brief, a Prince has little to fear from conspiracies when his subjects are well disposed towards him; but when they are hostile and hold him in detestation, he has then reason to fear everything and every one. And well ordered States and wise Princes have provided with extreme care that the nobility shall not be driven to desperation, and that the commons shall be kept satisfied and contented; for this is one of the most important matters that a Prince has to look to.

Among the well ordered and governed Kingdoms of our day is that of France, wherein we find an infinite number of wise institutions, upon which depend the freedom and the security of the King, and of which the most important are the Parliament and its authority. For he who gave its constitution to this Realm, knowing the ambition and arrogance of the nobles, and judging it necessary to bridle and restrain them, and on the other hand knowing the hatred, originating in fear, entertained against them by the commons, and desiring that they should be safe, was unwilling that the responsibility for this should rest on the King; and to relieve him of the ill-will which he might incur with the nobles by favouring the commons, or with the commons by favouring the nobles, appointed a third party to be arbitrator, who without committing the King, might depress the nobles and uphold the commons. Nor could there be any better, wiser, or surer safeguard for the King and the Kingdom. And hence we may draw another notable lesson, namely, that Princes should devolve on others those matters that entail responsibility, and reserve to themselves those that relate to grace and favour. And again I say that a Prince should esteem the great, but must not make himself odious to the people.

To some it may perhaps appear, that if the lives and deaths of many of the Roman Emperors be considered, they offer examples opposed to the views expressed by me; since we find that some among them who had always lived good lives, and shown themselves possessed of great qualities, were nevertheless deposed and even put to death by their subjects who had conspired against them.

1655

In answer to such objections, I shall examine the characters of several Emperors, and show that the causes of their downfall were in no way different from those which I have indicated. In doing this I shall submit for consideration such matters only as must strike every one who reads the history of these times; and it will be enough for my purpose to take those Emperors who reigned from the time of Marcus the Philosopher to the time of Maximinus, who were, inclusively,

1660

Marcus, Commodus his son, Pertinax, Julianus, Severus, Caracalla his son, Macrinus, Heliogabalus, Alexander, and Maximinus.

In the first place, then, we have to note that while in other Princedoms the Prince has only to contend with the ambition of the nobles and the insubordination of the people, the Roman Emperors had a further difficulty to

1665

encounter in the cruelty and rapacity of their soldiers, which were so distracting as to cause the ruin of many of these Princes. For it was hardly possible for them to satisfy both the soldiers and the people; the latter loving peace and therefore preferring sober Princes, while the former preferred a Prince of a warlike spirit, however harsh, haughty, or rapacious; being willing that he should exercise these

1670

qualities against the people, as the means of procuring for themselves double pay, and indulging their greed and cruelty.

Whence it followed that those Emperors who had not inherited or won for themselves such authority as enabled them to keep both people and soldiers in check, were always ruined. The most of them, and those especially who came to the

1675

Empire new and without experience, seeing the difficulty of dealing with these conflicting humours, set themselves to satisfy the soldiers, and made little account of offending the people. And for them this was a necessary course to take; for as Princes cannot escape being hated by some, they should, in the first place, endeavour not to be hated by a class; failing in which, they must do all they can to

1680

escape the hatred of that class which is the stronger. Wherefore those Emperors who, by reason of their newness, stood in need of extraordinary support, sided with the soldiery rather than with the people; a course which turned out advantageous or otherwise, according as the Prince knew, or did not know, how to maintain his authority over them.

1685

From the causes indicated it resulted that Marcus, Pertinax, and Alexander, being Princes of a temperate disposition, lovers of justice, enemies of cruelty, gentle, and kindly, had all, save Marcus, an unhappy end. Marcus alone lived and died honoured in the highest degree; and this because he had succeeded to the Empire by right of inheritance, and not through the favour either of the soldiery or

1690

of the people; and also because, being endowed with many virtues which made him revered, he kept, while he lived, both factions within bounds, and was never either hated or despised.

But Pertinax was chosen Emperor against the will of the soldiery, who being accustomed to a licentious life under Commodus, could not tolerate the stricter

1695

discipline to which his successor sought to bring them back. And having thus made himself hated, and being at the same time despised by reason of his advanced age, he was ruined at the very outset of his reign.

And here it is to be noted that hatred is incurred as well on account of good actions as of bad; for which reason, as I have already said, a Prince who would maintain his authority is often compelled to be other than good. For when the class, be it the people, the soldiers, or the nobles, on whom you judge it necessary to rely for your support, is corrupt, you must needs adapt yourself to its humours, and satisfy these, in which case virtuous conduct will only prejudice you.

Let us now come to Alexander, who was so just a ruler that among the praises ascribed to him it is recorded, that, during the fourteen years he held the Empire, no man was ever put to death by him without trial. Nevertheless, being accounted effeminate, and thought to be governed by his mother, he fell into contempt, and the army conspiring against him, slew him.

When we turn to consider the characters of Commodus, Severus, and Caracalla, we find them all to have been most cruel and rapacious Princes, who to satisfy the soldiery, scrupled not to inflict every kind of wrong upon the people. And all of them, except Severus, came to a bad end. But in Severus there was such strength of character, that, keeping the soldiers his friends, he was able, although he oppressed the people, to reign on prosperously to the last; because his great qualities made him so admirable in the eyes both of the people and the soldiers, that the former remained in a manner amazed and awestruck, while the latter were respectful and contented.

And because his actions, for one who was a new Prince, were thus remarkable, I will point out shortly how well he understood to play the part both of the lion and of the fox, each of which natures, as I have observed before, a Prince should know how to assume.

Knowing the indolent disposition of the Emperor Julianus, Severus persuaded the army which he commanded in Illyria that it was their duty to go to Rome to avenge the death of Pertinax, who had been slain by the Pretorian guards. Under this pretext, and without disclosing his design on the Empire, he put his army in march, and reached Italy before it was known that he had set out. On his arrival in Rome, the Senate, through fear, elected him Emperor and put Julianus to death. After taking this first step, two obstacles still remained to his becoming sole master of the Empire; one in Asia, where Niger who commanded the armies of the East had caused himself to be proclaimed Emperor; the other in the West, where Albinus, who also aspired to the Empire, was in command. And as Severus judged it dangerous to declare open war against both, he resolved to proceed against Niger by arms, and against Albinus by artifice. To the latter, accordingly, he wrote, that having been chosen Emperor by the Senate, he desired to share the dignity with him; that he therefore sent him the title of Caesar, and in accordance with a resolution of the Senate assumed him as his colleague. All which statements Albinus accepted as true. But so soon as Severus had defeated and slain Niger, and restored tranquillity in the East, returning to Rome he complained in the Senate that Albinus, all unmindful of the favours he had received from him, had treacherously sought to destroy him; for which cause he was compelled to go and punish his ingratitude. Whereupon he set forth to seek Albinus in Gaul, where he at once deprived him of his dignities and his life.

Whoever, therefore, examines carefully the actions of this Emperor, will find in him all the fierceness of the lion and all the craft of the fox, and will note how

1745 he was feared and respected by the people, yet not hated by the army, and will not be surprised that though a new man, he was able to maintain his hold of so great an Empire. For the splendour of his reputation always shielded him from the odium which the people might otherwise have conceived against him by reason of his cruelty and rapacity.

1750 Caracalla, his son, was likewise a man of great parts, endowed with qualities that made him admirable in the sight of the people, and endeared him to the army, being of a warlike spirit, most patient of fatigue, and contemning all luxury in food and every other effeminacy. Nevertheless, his ferocity and cruelty were so extravagant and unheard of (he having put to death a vast number of the

1755 inhabitants of Rome at different times, and the whole of those of Alexandria at a stroke), that he came to be detested by all the world, and so feared even by those whom he had about him, that at the last he was slain by a centurion in the midst of his army.

And here let it be noted that deaths like this which are the result of a

1760 deliberate and fixed resolve, cannot be escaped by Princes, since any one who disregards his own life can effect them. A Prince, however, needs the less to fear them as they are seldom attempted. The only precaution he can take is to avoid doing grave wrong to any of those who serve him, or whom he has near him as officers of his Court, a precaution which Caracalla neglected in putting to a

1765 shameful death the brother of this centurion, and in using daily threats against the man himself, whom he nevertheless retained as one of his bodyguards. This, as the event showed, was a rash and fatal course.

We come next to Commodus, who, as he took the Empire by hereditary right, ought to have held it with much ease. For being the son of Marcus, he had only to

1770 follow in his father's footsteps to content both the people and the soldiery. But being of a cruel and brutal nature, to sate his rapacity at the expense of the people, he sought support from the army, and indulged it in every kind of excess. On the other hand, by an utter disregard of his dignity, in frequently descending into the arena to fight with gladiators, and by other base acts wholly unworthy of the

1775 Imperial station, he became contemptible in the eyes of the soldiery; and being on the one hand hated, on the other despised, was at last conspired against and murdered.

The character of Maximinus remains to be touched upon. He was of a very warlike disposition, and on the death of Alexander, of whom we have already

1780 spoken, was chosen Emperor by the army who had been displeased with the effeminacy of that Prince. But this dignity he did not long enjoy, since two causes concurred to render him at once odious and contemptible; the one the baseness of his origin, he having at one time herded sheep in Thrace, a fact well known to all, and which led all to look on him with disdain; the other that on being proclaimed

1785   Emperor, delaying to repair to Rome and enter on possession of the Imperial throne, he incurred the reputation of excessive cruelty by reason of the many atrocities perpetrated by his prefects in Rome and other parts of the Empire. The result was that the whole world, stirred at once with scorn of his mean birth and with the hatred which the dread of his ferocity inspired, combined against him,

1790   Africa leading the way, the Senate and people of Rome and the whole of Italy following. In which conspiracy his own army joined. For they, being engaged in the siege of Aquileja and finding difficulty in reducing it, disgusted with his cruelty, and less afraid of him when they saw so many against him, put him to death.

1795   I need say nothing of Heliogabalus, Macrinus, or Julianus, all of whom being utterly despicable, came to a speedy downfall, but shall conclude these remarks by observing, that the Princes of our own days are less troubled with the difficulty of having to make constant efforts to keep their soldiers in good humour. For though they must treat them with some indulgence, the need for doing so is soon over, since

1800   none of these Princes possesses a standing army which, like the armies of the Roman Empire, has strengthened with the growth of his government and the administration of his State. And if it was then necessary to satisfy the soldiers rather than the people, because the soldiers were more powerful than the people, now it is more necessary for all Princes, except the Turk and the Soldan, to satisfy

1805   the people rather than the soldiery, since the former are more powerful than the latter.

     I except the Turk because he has always about him some twelve thousand foot soldiers and fifteen thousand horse, on whom depend the security and strength of his kingdom, and with whom he must needs keep on good terms, all regard for the

1810   people being subordinate. The government of the Soldan is similar, so that he too being wholly in the hands of his soldiers, must keep well with them without regard to the people.

     And here you are to note that the State of the Soldan, while it is unlike all other Princedoms, resembles the Christian Pontificate in this, that it can neither be

1815   classed as new, nor as hereditary. For the sons of a Soldan who dies do not succeed to the kingdom as his heirs, but he who is elected to the post by those who have authority to make such elections. And this being the ancient and established order of things, the Princedom cannot be accounted new, since none of the difficulties that attend new Princedoms are found in it. For although the Prince be

1820   new, the institutions of the State are old, and are so contrived that the elected Prince is accepted as though he were an hereditary Sovereign.

     But returning to the matter in hand, I say that whoever reflects on the above reasoning will see that either hatred or contempt was the ruin of the Emperors whom I have named; and will also understand how it happened that some taking

1825   one way and some the opposite, one only by each of these roads came to a happy, and all the rest to an unhappy, end. Because for Pertinax and Alexander, they being new Princes, it was useless and hurtful to try to imitate Marcus, who was an hereditary Prince; and similarly for Caracalla, Commodus, and Maximinus it

1830   was a fatal error to imitate Severus, since they lacked the qualities that would have enabled them to tread in his footsteps.

    In short, a Prince new to the Princedom cannot imitate the actions of Marcus, nor is it necessary that he should imitate all those of Severus; but he should borrow from Severus those parts of his conduct which are needed to serve as a foundation for his government, and from Marcus those suited to maintain it, and

1835   render it glorious when once established.

CHAPTER XX: WHETHER FORTRESSES, AND CERTAIN OTHER EXPEDIENTS TO WHICH PRINCES OFTEN HAVE RECOURSE, ARE PROFITABLE OR HURTFUL

    To govern more securely some Princes have disarmed their subjects, others have kept the towns subject to them divided by factions; some have fostered hostility against themselves, others have sought to gain over those who at the beginning of their reign were looked on with suspicion; some have built fortresses,

1840   others have dismantled and destroyed them; and though no definite judgment can be pronounced respecting any of these methods, without regard to the special circumstances of the State to which it is proposed to apply them, I shall nevertheless speak of them in as comprehensive a way as the nature of the subject will admit.

1845   It has never chanced that any new Prince has disarmed his subjects. On the contrary, when he has found them unarmed he has always armed them. For the arms thus provided become yours, those whom you suspected grow faithful, while those who were faithful at the first, continue so, and from your subjects become your partisans. And though all your subjects cannot be armed, yet if those of them

1850   whom you arm be treated with marked favour, you can deal more securely with the rest. For the difference which those whom you supply with arms perceive in their treatment, will bind them to you, while the others will excuse you, recognizing that those who incur greater risk and responsibility merit greater rewards. But by disarming, you at once give offence, since you show your subjects

1855   that you distrust them, either as doubting their courage, or as doubting their fidelity, each of which imputations begets hatred against you. Moreover, as you cannot maintain yourself without arms you must have recourse to mercenary troops. What these are I have already shown, but even if they were good, they could never avail to defend you, at once against powerful enemies abroad and

1860   against subjects whom you distrust. Wherefore, as I have said already, new Princes in new Princedoms have always provided for their being armed; and of instances of this History is full.

    But when a Prince acquires a new State, which thus becomes joined on like a limb to his old possessions, he must disarm its inhabitants, except such of them as

1865   have taken part with him while he was acquiring it; and even these, as time and occasion serve, he should seek to render soft and effeminate; and he must so manage matters that all the arms of the new State shall be in the hands of his own soldiers who have served under him in his ancient dominions.

Our forefathers, even such among them as were esteemed wise, were wont to say that *'Pistoja was to be held by feuds, and Pisa by fortresses,'* and on this principle used to promote dissensions in various subject towns with a view to retain them with less effort. At a time when Italy was in some measure in equilibrium, this may have been a prudent course to follow; but at the present day it seems impossible to recommend it as a general rule of policy. For I do not believe that divisions purposely caused can ever lead to good; on the contrary, when an enemy approaches, divided cities are lost at once, for the weaker faction will always side with the invader, and the other will not be able to stand alone.

The Venetians, influenced as I believe by the reasons above mentioned, fostered the factions of Guelf and Ghibelline in the cities subject to them; and though they did not suffer blood to be shed, fomented their feuds, in order that the citizens having their minds occupied with these disputes might not conspire against them. But this, as we know, did not turn out to their advantage, for after their defeat at Vaila, one of the two factions, suddenly taking courage, deprived them of the whole of their territory.

Moreover methods like these argue weakness in a Prince, for under a strong government such divisions would never be permitted, since they are profitable only in time of peace as an expedient whereby subjects may be more easily managed; but when war breaks out their insufficiency is demonstrated.

Doubtless, Princes become great by vanquishing difficulties and opposition, and Fortune, on that account, when she desires to aggrandize a new Prince, who has more need than an hereditary Prince to win reputation, causes enemies to spring up, and urges them on to attack him, to the end that he may have opportunities to overcome them, and make his ascent by the very ladder which they have planted. For which reason, many are of the opinion that a wise Prince, when he has the occasion, ought dexterously to promote hostility to himself in certain quarters, in order that his greatness may be enhanced by crushing it.

Princes, and new Princes especially, have found greater fidelity and helpfulness in those whom, at the beginning of their reign, they have held in suspicion, than in those who at the outset have enjoyed their confidence; and Pandolfo Petrucci, Lord of Siena, governed his State by the instrumentality of those whom he had at one time distrusted, in preference to all others. But on this point it is impossible to lay down any general rule, since the course to be followed varies with the circumstances. This only I will say, that those men who at the beginning of a reign have been hostile, if of a sort requiring support to maintain them, may always be won over by the Prince with much ease, and are the more bound to serve him faithfully because they know that they have to efface by their conduct the unfavourable impression he had formed of them; and in this way a Prince always obtains better help from them, than from those who serving him in too complete security neglect his affairs.

1910   And since the subject suggests it, I must not fail to remind the Prince who acquires a new State through the favour of its inhabitants, to weigh well what were the causes which led those who favoured him to do so; and if it be seen that they have acted not from any natural affection for him, but merely out of discontent with the former government, that he will find the greatest difficulty in

1915   keeping them his friends, since it will be impossible for him to content them. Carefully considering the cause of this, with the aid of examples taken from times ancient and modern, he will perceive that it is far easier to secure the friendship of those who being satisfied with things as they stood, were for that very reason his enemies, than of those who sided with him and aided him in his usurpation only

1920   because they were discontented.

It has been customary for Princes, with a view to hold their dominions more securely, to build fortresses which might serve as a curb and restraint on such as have designs against them, and as a safe refuge against a first onset. I approve this custom, because it has been followed from the earliest times. Nevertheless, in our

1925   own days, Messer Niccolò Vitelli thought it prudent to dismantle two fortresses in Città di Castello in order to secure that town: and Guido Ubaldo, Duke of Urbino, on returning to his dominions, whence he had been driven by Cesare Borgia, razed to their foundations the fortresses throughout the Dukedom, judging that if these were removed, it would not again be so easily lost. A like course was

1930   followed by the Bentivogli on their return to Bologna.

Fortresses, therefore, are useful or no, according to circumstances, and if in one way they benefit, in another they injure you. We may state the case thus: the Prince who is more afraid of his subjects than of strangers ought to build fortresses, while he who is more afraid of strangers than of his subjects, should

1935   leave them alone. The citadel built by Francesco Sforza in Milan, has been, and will hereafter prove to be, more dangerous to the House of Sforza than any other disorder of that State. So that, on the whole, the best fortress you can have, is in not being hated by your subjects. If they hate you no fortress will save you; for when once the people take up arms, foreigners are never wanting to assist them.

1940   Within our own time it does not appear that fortresses have been of service to any Prince, unless to the Countess of Forlì after her husband Count Girolamo was murdered; for by this means she was able to escape the first onset of the insurgents, and awaiting succour from Milan, to recover her State; the circumstances of the times not allowing any foreigner to lend assistance to the people. But afterwards,

1945   when she was attacked by Cesare Borgia, and the people, out of hostility to her, took part with the invader, her fortresses were of little avail. So that, both on this and on the former occasion, it would have been safer for her to have had no fortresses, than to have had her subjects for enemies.

All which considerations taken into account, I shall applaud him who builds

1950   fortresses, and him who does not; but I shall blame him who, trusting in them, reckons it a light thing to be held in hatred by his people.

CHAPTER XXI: HOW A PRINCE SHOULD BEAR HIMSELF SO AS TO ACQUIRE REPUTATION

Nothing makes a Prince so well thought of as to undertake great enterprises and give striking proofs of his capacity.

Among the Princes of our time Ferdinand of Aragon, the present King of Spain, may almost be accounted a new Prince, since from one of the weakest he has become, for fame and glory, the foremost King in Christendom. And if you consider his achievements you will find them all great and some extraordinary.

In the beginning of his reign he made war on Granada, which enterprise was the foundation of his power. At first he carried on the war leisurely, without fear of interruption, and kept the attention and thoughts of the Barons of Castile so completely occupied with it, that they had no time to think of changes at home. Meanwhile he insensibly acquired reputation among them and authority over them. With the money of the Church and of his subjects he was able to maintain his armies, and during the prolonged contest to lay the foundations of that military discipline which afterwards made him so famous. Moreover, to enable him to engage in still greater undertakings, always covering himself with the cloak of religion, he had recourse to what may be called *pious cruelty*, in driving out and clearing his Kingdom of the Moors; than which exploit none could be more wonderful or uncommon. Using the same pretext he made war on Africa, invaded Italy, and finally attacked France; and being thus constantly busied in planning and executing vast designs, he kept the minds of his subjects in suspense and admiration, and occupied with the results of his actions, which arose one out of another in such close succession as left neither time nor opportunity to oppose them.

Again, it greatly profits a Prince in conducting the internal government of his State, to follow striking methods, such as are recorded of Messer Bernabò of Milan, whenever the remarkable actions of any one in civil life, whether for good or for evil, afford him occasion; and to choose such ways of rewarding and punishing as cannot fail to be much spoken of. But above all, he should strive by all his actions to inspire a sense of his greatness and goodness.

A Prince is likewise esteemed who is a stanch friend and a thorough foe, that is to say, who without reserve openly declares for one against another, this being always a more advantageous course than to stand neutral. For supposing two of your powerful neighbours come to blows, it must either be that you have, or have not, reason to fear the one who comes off victorious. In either case it will always be well for you to declare yourself, and join in frankly with one side or other. For should you fail to do so you are certain, in the former of the cases put, to become the prey of the victor to the satisfaction and delight of the vanquished, and no reason or circumstance that you may plead will avail to shield or shelter you; for the victor dislikes doubtful friends, and such as will not help him at a pinch; and the vanquished will have nothing to say to you, since you would not share his fortunes sword in hand.

When Antiochus, at the instance of the Aetolians, passed into Greece in order to drive out the Romans, he sent envoys to the Achaians, who were friendly to the Romans, exhorting them to stand neutral. The Romans, on the other hand, urged them to take up arms on their behalf. The matter coming to be discussed in the Council of the Achaians, the legate of Antiochus again urged neutrality, whereupon the Roman envoy answered—'Nothing can be less to your advantage than the course which has been recommended as the best and most useful for your State, namely, to refrain from taking any part in our war, for by standing aloof you will gain neither favour nor fame, but remain the prize of the victor.' And it will always happen that he who is not your friend will invite you to neutrality, while he who is your friend will call on you to declare yourself openly in arms. Irresolute Princes, to escape immediate danger, commonly follow the neutral path, in most instances to their destruction. But when you pronounce valiantly in favour of one side or other, if he to whom you give your adherence conquers, although he be powerful and you are at his mercy, still he is under obligations to you, and has become your friend; and none are so lost to shame as to destroy with manifest ingratitude, one who has helped them. Besides which, victories are never so complete that the victor can afford to disregard all considerations whatsoever, more especially considerations of justice. On the other hand, if he with whom you take part should lose, you will always be favourably regarded by him; while he can he will aid you, and you become his companion in a cause which may recover.

In the second case, namely, when both combatants are of such limited strength that whichever wins you have no cause to fear, it is all the more prudent for you to take a side, for you will then be ruining the one with the help of the other, who were he wise would endeavour to save him. If he whom you help conquers, he remains in your power, and with your aid he cannot but conquer.

And here let it be noted that a Prince should be careful never to join with one stronger than himself in attacking others, unless, as already said, he be driven to it by necessity. For if he whom you join prevails, you are at his mercy; and Princes, so far as in them lies, should avoid placing themselves at the mercy of others. The Venetians, although they might have declined the alliance, joined with France against the Duke of Milan, which brought about their ruin. But when an alliance cannot be avoided, as was the case with the Florentines when the Pope and Spain together led their armies to attack Lombardy, a Prince, for the reasons given, must take a side. Nor let it be supposed that any State can choose for itself a perfectly safe line of policy. On the contrary, it must reckon on every course which it may take being doubtful; for it happens in all human affairs that we never seek to escape one mischief without falling into another. Prudence therefore consists in knowing how to distinguish degrees of disadvantage, and in accepting a less evil as a good.

Again, a Prince should show himself a patron of merit, and should honour those who excel in every art. He ought accordingly to encourage his subjects by enabling them to pursue their callings, whether mercantile, agricultural, or any other, in security, so that this man shall not be deterred from beautifying his possessions from the apprehension that they may be taken from him, or that other refrain from opening a trade through fear of taxes; and he should provide rewards for those who desire so to employ themselves, and for all who are disposed in any way to add to the greatness of his City or State.

He ought, moreover, at suitable seasons of the year to entertain the people with festivals and shows. And because all cities are divided into guilds and companies, he should show attention to these societies, and sometimes take part in their meetings; offering an example of courtesy and munificence, but always maintaining the dignity of his station, which must under no circumstances be compromised.

CHAPTER XXII: OF THE SECRETARIES OF PRINCES

The choice of Ministers is a matter of no small moment to a Prince. Whether they shall be good or no depends on his prudence, so that the readiest conjecture we can form of the character and sagacity of a Prince, is from seeing what sort of men he has about him. When they are at once capable and faithful, we may always account him wise, since he has known to recognize their merit and to retain their fidelity. But if they be otherwise, we must pronounce unfavourably of him, since he has committed a first fault in making this selection.

There was none who knew Messer Antonio of Venafro as Minister of Pandolfo Petrucci, Lord of Siena, but thought Pandolfo a most prudent ruler in having him for his servant. And since there are three scales of intelligence, one which understands by itself, a second which understands what is shown it by others, and a third which understands neither by itself nor on the showing of others, the first of which is most excellent, the second good, but the third worthless, we must needs admit that if Pandolfo was not in the first of these degrees, he was in the second; for when one has the judgment to discern the good from the bad in what another says or does, though he be devoid of invention, he can recognize the merits and demerits of his servant, and will commend the former while he corrects the latter. The servant cannot hope to deceive such a master, and will continue good.

As to how a Prince is to know his Minister, this unerring rule may be laid down. When you see a Minister thinking more of himself than of you, and in all his actions seeking his own ends, that man can never be a good Minister or one that you can trust. For he who has the charge of the State committed to him, ought not to think of himself, but only of his Prince, and should never bring to the notice of the latter what does not directly concern him. On the other hand, to keep his Minister good, the Prince should be considerate of him, dignifying him, enriching him, binding him to himself by benefits, and sharing with him the honours as well as the burthens of the State, so that the abundant honours and wealth bestowed upon him may divert him from seeking them at other hands; while the great responsibilities wherewith he is charged may lead him to dread change, knowing that he cannot stand alone without his master's support. When Prince and

Minister are upon this footing they can mutually trust one another; but when the contrary is the case, it will always fare ill with one or other of them.

CHAPTER XXIII: THAT FLATTERERS SHOULD BE SHUNNED

2080   One error into which Princes, unless very prudent or very fortunate in their choice of friends, are apt to fall, is of so great importance that I must not pass it over. I mean in respect of flatterers. These abound in Courts, because men take such pleasure in their own concerns, and so deceive themselves with regard to them, that they can hardly escape this plague; while even in the effort to escape it
2085   there is risk of their incurring contempt.

There is no way to guard against flattery but by letting it be seen that you take no offence in hearing the truth: but when every one is free to tell you the truth respect falls short. Wherefore a prudent Prince should follow a middle course, by choosing certain discreet men from among his subjects, and allowing them alone
2090   free leave to speak their minds on any matter on which he asks their opinion, and on none other. But he ought to ask their opinion on everything, and after hearing what they have to say, should reflect and judge for himself. And with these counsellors collectively, and with each of them separately, his bearing should be such, that each and all of them may know that the more freely they declare their
2095   thoughts the better they will be liked. Besides these, the Prince should hearken to no others, but should follow the course determined on, and afterwards adhere firmly to his resolves. Whoever acts otherwise is either undone by flatterers, or from continually vacillating as opinions vary, comes to be held in light esteem.

With reference to this matter, I shall cite a recent instance. Father Luke, who
2100   is attached to the Court of the present Emperor Maximilian, in speaking of his Majesty told me, that he seeks advice from none, yet never has his own way; and this from his following a course contrary to that above recommended. For being of a secret disposition, he never discloses his intentions to any, nor asks their opinion; and it is only when his plans are to be carried out that they begin to be
2105   discovered and known, and at the same time they begin to be thwarted by those he has about him, when he being facile gives way. Hence it happens that what he does one day, he undoes the next; that his wishes and designs are never fully ascertained; and that it is impossible to build on his resolves.

A Prince, therefore, ought always to take counsel, but at such times and
2110   seasons only as he himself pleases, and not when it pleases others; nay, he should discourage every one from obtruding advice on matters on which it is not sought. But he should be free in asking advice, and afterwards, as regards the matters on which he has asked it, a patient hearer of the truth, and even displeased should he perceive that any one, from whatever motive, keeps it back.

2115   But those who think that every Prince who has a name for prudence owes it to the wise counsellors he has around him, and not to any merit of his own, are certainly mistaken; since it is an unerring rule and of universal application that a Prince who is not wise himself cannot be well advised by others, unless by chance

2120 he surrender himself to be wholly governed by some one adviser who happens to be supremely prudent; in which case he may, indeed, be well advised; but not for long, since such an adviser will soon deprive him of his Government. If he listen to a multitude of advisers, the Prince who is not wise will never have consistent counsels, nor will he know of himself how to reconcile them. Each of his counsellors will study his own advantage, and the Prince will be unable to detect

2125 or correct them. Nor could it well be otherwise, for men will always grow rogues on your hands unless they find themselves under a necessity to be honest.

Hence it follows that good counsels, whencesoever they come, have their origin in the prudence of the Prince, and not the prudence of the Prince in wise counsels.

CHAPTER XXIV: WHY THE PRINCES OF ITALY HAVE LOST THEIR STATES

2130 The lessons above taught if prudently followed will make a new Prince seem like an old one, and will soon seat him in his place more firmly and securely than if his authority had the sanction of time. For the actions of a new Prince are watched much more closely than those of an hereditary Prince; and when seen to be good are far more effectual than antiquity of blood in gaining men over and

2135 attaching them to his cause. For men are more nearly touched by things present than by things past, and when they find themselves well off as they are, enjoy their felicity and seek no further; nay, are ready to do their utmost in defence of the new Prince, provided he be not wanting to himself in other respects. In this way there accrues to him a twofold glory, in having laid the foundations of the new

2140 Princedom, and in having strengthened and adorned it with good laws and good arms, with faithful friends and great deeds; as, on the other hand, there is a double disgrace in one who has been born to a Princedom losing it by his own want of wisdom.

And if we contemplate those Lords who in our own times have lost their

2145 dominions in Italy, such as the King of Naples, the Duke of Milan, and others, in the first place we shall see, that in respect of arms they have, for reasons already dwelt on, been all alike defective; and next, that some of them have either had the people against them, or if they have had the people with them, have not known how to secure themselves against their nobles. For without such defects as these,

2150 States powerful enough to keep an army in the field are never overthrown.

Philip of Macedon, not the father of Alexander the Great, but he who was vanquished by Titus Quintius, had no great State as compared with the strength of the Romans and Greeks who attacked him. Nevertheless, being a Prince of a warlike spirit, and skilful in gaining the good will of the people and in securing

2155 the fidelity of the nobles, he maintained himself for many years against his assailants, and in the end, though he lost some towns, succeeded in saving his Kingdom.

2160 Let those Princes of ours, therefore, who, after holding them for a length of years, have lost their dominions, blame not Fortune but their own inertness. For never having reflected in tranquil times that there might come a change (and it is human nature when the sea is calm not to think of storms), when adversity overtook them, they thought not of defence but only of escape, hoping that their people, disgusted with the arrogance of the conqueror, would some day recall them.

2165 This course may be a good one to follow when all others fail, but it were the height of folly, trusting to it, to abandon every other; since none would wish to fall on the chance of some one else being found to lift him up. It may not happen that you are recalled by your people, or if it happen, it gives you no security. It is an ignoble resource, since it does not depend on you for its success; and those 2170 modes of defence are alone good, certain and lasting, which depend upon yourself and your own worth.

CHAPTER XXV: WHAT FORTUNE CAN EFFECT IN HUMAN AFFAIRS, AND HOW SHE MAY BE WITHSTOOD

I am not ignorant that many have been and are of the opinion that human affairs are so governed by Fortune and by God, that men cannot alter them by any prudence of theirs, and indeed have no remedy against them; and for this reason 2175 have come to think that it is not worth while to labour much about anything, but that they must leave everything to be determined by chance.

Often when I turn the matter over, I am in part inclined to agree with this opinion, which has had the readier acceptance in our own times from the great changes in things which we have seen, and every day see happen contrary to all 2180 human expectation. Nevertheless, that our free will be not wholly set aside, I think it may be the case that Fortune is the mistress of one half our actions, and yet leaves the control of the other half, or a little less, to ourselves. And I would liken her to one of those wild torrents which, when angry, overflow the plains, sweep away trees and houses, and carry off soil from one bank to throw it down upon 2185 the other. Every one flees before them, and yields to their fury without the least power to resist. And yet, though this be their nature, it does not follow that in seasons of fair weather, men cannot, by constructing weirs and moles, take such precautions as will cause them when again in flood to pass off by some artificial channel, or at least prevent their course from being so uncontrolled and 2190 destructive. And so it is with Fortune, who displays her might where there is no organized strength to resist her, and directs her onset where she knows that there is neither barrier nor embankment to confine her.

And if you look at Italy, which has been at once the seat of these changes and their cause, you will perceive that it is a field without embankment or barrier. For 2195 if, like Germany, France, and Spain, it had been guarded with sufficient skill, this inundation, if it ever came upon us, would never have wrought the violent changes which we have witnessed.

This I think enough to say generally touching resistance to Fortune. But confining myself more closely to the matter in hand, I note that one day we see a Prince prospering and the next day overthrown, without detecting any change in his nature or character. This, I believe, comes chiefly from a cause already dwelt upon, namely, that a Prince who rests wholly on Fortune is ruined when she changes. Moreover, I believe that he will prosper most whose mode of acting best adapts itself to the character of the times; and conversely that he will be unprosperous, with whose mode of acting the times do not accord. For we see that men in these matters which lead to the end that each has before him, namely, glory and wealth, proceed by different ways, one with caution, another with impetuosity, one with violence, another with subtlety, one with patience, another with its contrary; and that by one or other of these different courses each may succeed.

Again, of two who act cautiously, you shall find that one attains his end, the other not, and that two of different temperament, the one cautious, the other impetuous, are equally successful. All which happens from no other cause than that the character of the times accords or does not accord with their methods of acting. And hence it comes, as I have already said, that two operating differently arrive at the same result, and two operating similarly, the one succeeds and the other not. On this likewise depend the vicissitudes of Fortune. For if to one who conducts himself with caution and patience, time and circumstances are propitious, so that his method of acting is good, he goes on prospering; but if these change he is ruined, because he does not change his method of acting.

For no man is found so prudent as to know how to adapt himself to these changes, both because he cannot deviate from the course to which nature inclines him, and because, having always prospered while adhering to one path, he cannot be persuaded that it would be well for him to forsake it. And so when occasion requires the cautious man to act impetuously, he cannot do so and is undone: whereas, had he changed his nature with time and circumstances, his fortune would have been unchanged.

Pope Julius II proceeded with impetuosity in all his undertakings, and found time and circumstances in such harmony with his mode of acting that he always obtained a happy result. Witness his first expedition against Bologna, when Messer Giovanni Bentivoglio was yet living. The Venetians were not favourable to the enterprise; nor was the King of Spain. Negotiations respecting it with the King of France were still open. Nevertheless, the Pope with his wonted hardihood and impetuosity marched in person on the expedition, and by this movement brought the King of Spain and the Venetians to a check, the latter through fear, the former from his eagerness to recover the entire Kingdom of Naples; at the same time, he dragged after him the King of France, who, desiring to have the Pope for an ally in humbling the Venetians, on finding him already in motion saw that he could not refuse him his soldiers without openly offending him. By the impetuosity of his movements, therefore, Julius effected what no other Pontiff endowed with the highest human prudence could. For had he, as any other Pope would have done,

2245

put off his departure from Rome until terms had been settled and everything duly arranged, he never would have succeeded. For the King of France would have found a thousand pretexts to delay him, and the others would have menaced him with a thousand alarms. I shall not touch upon his other actions, which were all of a like character, and all of which had a happy issue, since the shortness of his life did not allow him to experience reverses. But if times had overtaken him, rendering a cautious line of conduct necessary, his ruin must have ensued, since he never could have departed from those methods to which nature inclined him.

2250

2255

To be brief, I say that since Fortune changes and men stand fixed in their old ways, they are prosperous so long as there is congruity between them, and the reverse when there is not. Of this, however, I am well persuaded, that it is better to be impetuous than cautious. For Fortune is a woman who to be kept under must be beaten and roughly handled; and we see that she suffers herself to be more readily mastered by those who so treat her than by those who are more timid in their approaches. And always, like a woman, she favours the young, because they are less scrupulous and fiercer, and command her with greater audacity.

CHAPTER XXVI: AN EXHORTATION TO LIBERATE ITALY FROM THE BARBARIANS

2260

2265

2270

Turning over in my mind all the matters which have above been considered, and debating with myself whether in Italy at the present hour the times are such as might serve to confer honour on a new Prince, and whether a fit opportunity now offers for a prudent and valiant leader to bring about changes glorious for himself and beneficial to the whole Italian people, it seems to me that so many conditions combine to further such an enterprise, that I know of no time so favourable to it as the present. And if, as I have said, it was necessary in order to display the valour of Moses that the children of Israel should be slaves in Egypt, and to know the greatness and courage of Cyrus that the Persians should be oppressed by the Medes, and to illustrate the excellence of Theseus that the Athenians should be scattered and divided, so at this hour, to prove the worth of some Italian hero, it was required that Italy should be brought to her present abject condition, to be more a slave than the Hebrew, more oppressed than the Persian, more disunited than the Athenian, without a head, without order, beaten, spoiled, torn in pieces, over-run and abandoned to destruction in every shape.

2275

2280

But though, heretofore, glimmerings may have been discerned in this man or that, whence it might be conjectured that he was ordained by God for her redemption, nevertheless it has afterwards been seen in the further course of his actions that Fortune has disowned him; so that our country, left almost without life, still waits to know who it is that is to heal her bruises, to put an end to the devastation and plunder of Lombardy, to the exactions and imposts of Naples and Tuscany, and to stanch those wounds of hers which long neglect has changed into running sores.

We see how she prays God to send some one to rescue her from these barbarous cruelties and oppressions. We see too how ready and eager she is to follow any standard were there only some one to raise it. But at present we see no one except in your illustrious House (pre-eminent by its virtues and good fortune, and favoured by God and by the Church whose headship it now holds), who could undertake the part of a deliverer.

But for you this will not be too hard a task, if you keep before your eyes the lives and actions of those whom I have named above. For although these men were singular and extraordinary, after all they were but men, not one of whom had so great an opportunity as now presents itself to you. For their undertakings were not more just than this, nor more easy, nor was God more their friend than yours. The justice of the cause is conspicuous; for that war is just which is necessary, and those arms are sacred from which we derive our only hope. Everywhere there is the strongest disposition to engage in this cause; and where the disposition is strong the difficulty cannot be great, provided you follow the methods observed by those whom I have set before you as models.

But further, we see here extraordinary and unexampled proofs of Divine favour. The sea has been divided; the cloud has attended you on your way; the rock has flowed with water; the manna has rained from heaven; everything has concurred to promote your greatness. What remains to be done must be done by you; since in order not to deprive us of our free will and such share of glory as belongs to us, God will not do everything himself.

Nor is it to be marvelled at if none of those Italians I have named has been able to effect what we hope to see effected by your illustrious House; or that amid so many revolutions and so many warlike movements it should always appear as though the military virtues of Italy were spent; for this comes from her old system being defective, and from no one being found among us capable to strike out a new. Nothing confers such honour on the reformer of a State, as do the new laws and institutions which he devises; for these when they stand on a solid basis and have a greatness in their scope, make him admired and venerated. And in Italy material is not wanting for improvement in every form. If the head be weak the limbs are strong, and we see daily in single combats, or where few are engaged, how superior are the strength, dexterity, and intelligence of Italians. But when it comes to armies, they are nowhere, and this from no other reason than the defects of their leaders. For those who are skilful in arms will not obey, and every one thinks himself skilful, since hitherto we have had none among us so raised by merit or by fortune above his fellows that they should yield him the palm. And hence it happens that for the long period of twenty years, during which so many wars have taken place, whenever there has been an army purely Italian it has always been beaten. To this testify, first Taro, then Alessandria, Capua, Genoa, Vaila, Bologna, Mestri.

If then your illustrious House should seek to follow the example of those great men who have delivered their country in past ages, it is before all things necessary, as the true foundation of every such attempt, to be provided with

2325   national troops, since you can have no braver, truer, or more faithful soldiers; and although every single man of them be good, collectively they will be better, seeing themselves commanded by their own Prince, and honoured and esteemed by him. That you may be able, therefore, to defend yourself against the foreigner with Italian valour, the first step is to provide yourself with an army such as this.

2330   And although the Swiss and the Spanish infantry are each esteemed formidable, there are yet defects in both, by reason of which troops trained on a different system might not merely withstand them, but be certain of defeating them. For the Spaniards cannot resist cavalry and the Swiss will give way before infantry if they find them as resolute as themselves at close quarters. Whence it 2335 has been seen, and may be seen again, that the Spaniards cannot sustain the onset of the French men-at-arms and that the Swiss are broken by the Spanish foot. And although of this last we have no complete instance, we have yet an indication of it in the battle of Ravenna, where the Spanish infantry confronted the German companies who have the same discipline as the Swiss; on which occasion the 2340 Spaniards by their agility and with the aid of their bucklers forced their way under the pikes, and stood ready to close with the Germans, who were no longer in a position to defend themselves; and had they not been charged by cavalry, they must have put the Germans to utter rout. Knowing, then, the defects of each of these kinds of troops, you can train your men on some different system, to withstand 2345 cavalry and not to fear infantry. To effect this, will not require the creation of any new forces, but simply a change in the discipline of the old. And these are matters in reforming which the new Prince acquires reputation and importance.

    This opportunity then, for Italy at last to look on her deliverer, ought not to be allowed to pass away. With what love he would be received in all those 2350 Provinces which have suffered from the foreign inundation, with what thirst for vengeance, with what fixed fidelity, with what devotion, and what tears, no words of mine can declare. What gates would be closed against him? What people would refuse him obedience? What jealousy would stand in his way? What Italian but would yield him homage? This barbarian tyranny stinks in all 2355 nostrils.

    Let your illustrious House therefore take upon itself this enterprise with all the courage and all the hopes with which a just cause is undertaken; so that under your standard this our country may be ennobled, and under your auspices be fulfilled the words of Petrarch:—

2360   Brief will be the strife
When valour arms against barbaric rage;
For the bold spirit of the bygone age
Still warms Italian hearts with life.

15. HAMLET

William Shakespeare
(1564–1616)

Shakespeare's fame as the premier English author is based on his career as narrative and lyric poet, and playwright of thirty-five comedies, tragedies and histories. However, he took little care in preserving his texts and his collected plays were only published after his death (The First Folio *edition of 1623). He earned most of his livelihood from acting and being a principal shareholder in theater companies for which he wrote his plays. His tragedy of* Hamlet *(1601), one of his darker plays, raises issues of utmost concern in the Renaissance: Hamlet's seemingly simple problem of discovering the truth about his father's death involves nothing less than the questioning the capacity of the human person to know anything for certain. Yet Shakespeare's reputation arises from his capacity to convey a multiplicity of moods, views, and situations in richly compressed language; he probes the depths of despair as well as the heights of magical delight, as in his last play,* The Tempest *(1611).*

DRAMATIS PERSONAE

CLAUDIUS, King of Denmark.
HAMLET, son to the late, and nephew to the present king.
POLONIUS, Lord Chamberlain.
HORATIO, friend to Hamlet.
LAERTES, son to Polonius.
VOLTIMAND,
CORNELIUS,
ROSENCRANZ,   courtiers.
GUILDENSTERN,
OSRIC,
A Gentleman,
A Priest.
MARCELLUS,   officers.
BERNARDO,
FRANCISCO, a soldier.
REYNALDO, servant to Polonius.
Players.

Two Clowns, grave-diggers.
FORTINBRAS, Prince of Norway.
A Captain.
English Ambassadors.
GERTRUDE, Queen of Denmark, and mother to Hamlet.
OPHELIA, daughter to Polonius.
Lords, Ladies, Officers, Soldiers, Sailors, Messengers,
and other Attendants.
Ghost of Hamlet's Father.

SCENE: *Denmark*

ACT I.
SCENE I. *Elsinore. A platform before the castle.*

FRANCISCO *at his post. Enter to him* BERNARDO.

	BER.	Who's there?
	FRAN.	Nay, answer me. Stand and unfold yourself.
	BER.	Long live the King!
5	FRAN.	Bernardo?
	BER.	He.
	FRAN.	You come most carefully upon your hour.
	BER.	'Tis now struck twelve. Get thee to bed, Francisco.
	FRAN.	For this relief much thanks. 'Tis bitter cold,
10		And I am sick at heart.
	BER.	Have you had quiet guard?
	FRAN.	Not a mouse stirring.
	BER.	Well, good night.
		If you do meet Horatio and Marcellus,
15		The rivals[1] of my watch, bid them make haste.
	FRAN.	I think I hear them. Stand, ho! Who is there?

Enter HORATIO *and* MARCELLUS.

	HOR.	Friends to this ground.
	MAR.	And liegemen to the Dane.
20	FRAN.	Give you good night.
	MAR.	O, farewell, honest soldier.
		Who hath relieved you?
	FRAN.	Bernardo hath my place.
		Give you good night. [*Exit.*
25	MAR.	Holla, Bernardo!
	BER.	Say,
		What, is Horatio there?

---

[1]*rivals*—partners.

	HOR.	A piece of him.
	BER.	Welcome, Horatio. Welcome, good Marcellus.
30	MAR.	What, has this thing appear'd again tonight?
	BER.	I have seen nothing.
	MAR.	Horatio says 'tis but our fantasy,
		And will not let belief take hold of him
		Touching this dreaded sight, twice seen of us.
35		Therefore I have entreated him along
		With us to watch the minutes of this night,
		That if again this apparition come
		He may approve our eyes[2] and speak to it.
	HOR.	Tush, tush, 'twill not appear.
40	BER.	Sit down awhile,
		And let us once again assail your ears,
		That are so fortified against our story,
		What we have two nights seen.
	HOR.	Well, sit we down,
45		And let us hear Bernardo speak of this.
	BER.	Last night of all,
		When yond same star that's westward from the pole[3]
		Had made his course to illume that part of heaven
		Where now it burns, Marcellus and myself,
50		The bell then beating one—

Enter GHOST.

	MAR.	Peace, break thee off. Look where it comes again.
	BER.	In the same figure like the King that's dead.
	MAR.	Thou art a scholar; speak to it, Horatio.
55	BER.	Looks it not like the King? Mark it, Horatio.
	HOR.	Most like. It harrows me with fear and wonder.
	BER.	It would be spoke to.
	MAR.	Question it, Horatio.
	HOR.	What art thou that usurpst this time of night,
60		Together with that fair and warlike form
		In which the majesty of buried Denmark[4]
		Did sometimes[5] march? By heaven I charge thee, speak!
	MAR.	It is offended.
	BER.	See, it stalks away.
65	HOR.	Stay! speak, speak! I charge thee, speak! [*Exit* GHOST.
	MAR.	'Tis gone, and will not answer.

---

[2]*approve our eyes*—confirm what we have seen.

[3]*pole*—polestar, North star.

[4]*Denmark*—King of Denmark, Hamlet I.

[5]*sometimes*—formerly.

	BER.	How now, Horatio? You tremble and look pale.
		Is not this something more than fantasy?
		What think you on't?
70	HOR.	Before my God, I might not this believe
		Without the sensible and true avouch
		Of mine own eyes.
	MAR.	Is it not like the King?
	HOR.	As thou art to thyself.
75		Such was the very armour he had on
		When he the ambitious Norway combated;
		So frown'd he once, when, in an angry parle,[6]
		He smote the sledded Polacks on the ice.
		'Tis strange.
80	MAR.	Thus twice before, and jump[7] at this dead hour,
		With martial stalk hath he gone by our watch.
	HOR.	In what particular thought to work I know not;
		But, in the gross and scope[8] of my opinion,
		This bodes some strange eruption to our state.
85	MAR.	Good now, sit down, and tell me, he that knows,
		Why this same strict and most observant watch
		So nightly toils the subject[9] of the land,
		And why such daily cast of brazen cannon,
		And foreign mart for implements of war,
90		Why such impress[10] of shipwrights, whose sore task
		Does not divide the Sunday from the week.
		What might be toward,[11] that this sweaty haste
		Doth make the night joint-labourer with the day,
		Who is't that can inform me?
95	HOR.	That can I—
		At least the whisper goes so. Our last King,
		Whose image even but now appear'd to us,
		Was, as you know, by Fortinbras of Norway,
		Thereto prick'd on by a most emulate[12] pride,
100		Dared to the combat; in which our valiant Hamlet—
		For so this side of our known world esteem'd him—
		Did slay this Fortinbras; who by a seal'd compact,
		Well ratified by law and heraldry,

---

[6]*parle*—word (French, parler).

[7]*jump*—just.

[8]*gross and scope*—general drift.

[9]*subject*—subjects, people.

[10]*impress*—conscription.

[11]*toward*—impending.

[12]*emulate*—ambitious.

Did forfeit, with his life, all those his lands
105   Which he stood seized of, to the conqueror;
Against the which, a moiety competent[13]
Was gaged by our King; which had return'd
To the inheritance of Fortinbras,
Had he been vanquisher; as, by the same covenant
110   And carriage[14] of the article design'd,
His fell to Hamlet. Now, sir, young Fortinbras,
Of unimproved[15] metal hot and full,
Hath in the skirts of Norway here and there
Shark'd up[16] a list of lawless resolutes,
115   For food and diet to some enterprise
That hath a stomach in't; which is no other—
As it doth well appear unto our state—
But to recover of us, by strong hand
And terms compulsatory, those foresaid lands
120   So by his father lost. And this, I take it,
Is the main motive of our preparations,
The source of this our watch and the chief head
Of this post-haste and romage[17] in the land.

BER.   I think it be no other but e'en so.
125   Well may it sort[18] that this portentous figure
Comes armed through our watch, so like the King
That was and is the question of these wars.

HOR.   A mote it is to trouble the mind's eye.
In the most high and palmy state of Rome,
130   A little ere the mightiest Julius fell,
The graves stood tenantless, and the sheeted dead
Did squeak and gibber in the Roman streets;
As stars with trains of fire and dews of blood,
Disasters[19] in the sun; and the moist star,[20]
135   Upon whose influence Neptune's empire stands,
Was sick almost to doomsday with eclipse.
And even the like precurse of feared events,
As harbingers preceding still the fates
And prologue to the omen coming on,

---

[13]*moiety competent*—equal portion.
[14]*carriage*—purport.
[15]*unimproved*—unproved.
[16]*Shark'd up*—rounded up, "shanghied."
[17]*romage*—bustle, activity.
[18]*sort*—be fitting.
[19]*Disasters*—ominous signs.
[20]*the moist star*—the moon.

140		Have heaven and earth together demonstrated
		Unto our climatures and countrymen.
		Enter GHOST.
		But soft, behold! Lo, where it comes again.
		I'll cross it; though it blast me. Stay, illusion.
145		If thou hast any sound or use of voice,
		Speak to me;
		If there be any good thing to be done,
		That may to thee do ease and grace to me,
		Speak to me;
150		If thou art privy to thy country's fate,
		Which, happily, foreknowing may avoid,
		O, speak!
		Or if thou hast uphoarded in thy life
		Extorted treasure in the womb of earth,
155		For which, they say, you spirits oft walk in death,
		Speak of it; stay and speak. [*The cock crows.*] Stop it, Marcellus.
	MAR.	Shall I strike at it with my partisan?[21]
	HOR.	Do, if it will not stand.
	BER.	'Tis here.
160	HOR.	'Tis here.
	MAR.	'Tis gone. [*Exit* GHOST.
		We do it wrong, being so majestical,
		To offer it the show of violence;
		For it is, as the air, invulnerable,
165		And our vain blows malicious mockery.
	BER.	It was about to speak, when the cock crew.
	HOR.	And then it started like a guilty thing
		Upon a fearful summons. I have heard,
		The cock, that is the trumpet to the morn,
170		Doth with his lofty and shrill-sounding throat
		Awake the god of day, and at his warning,
		Whether in sea or fire, in earth or air,
		The extravagant and erring spirit hies
		To his confine; and of the truth herein
175		This present object made probation.[22]
	MAR.	It faded on the crowing of the cock.
		Some say that ever 'gainst[23] that season comes
		Wherein our Saviour's birth is celebrated,
		The bird of dawning singeth all night long;

---

[21]*partisan*—spear.
[22]*probation*—proof.
[23]*'gainst*—just before.

180		And then, they say, no spirit dare stir abroad,
		The nights are wholesome, then no planets strike,[24]
		No fairy takes[25] nor witch hath power to charm,
		So hallow'd and so gracious[26] is the time.
	HOR.	So have I heard and do in part believe it.
185		But look, the morn, in russet mantle clad,
		Walks o'er the dew of yon high eastward hill.
		Break we our watch up; and by my advice,
		Let us impart what we have seen tonight
		Unto young Hamlet; for, upon my life,
190		This spirit, dumb to us, will speak to him.
		Do you consent we shall acquaint him with it,
		As needful in our loves, fitting our duty?
	MAR.	Let's do't, I pray; and I this morning know
		Where we shall find him most conveniently. [*Exeunt.*

---

[24]*strike*—blast, destroy.
[25]*takes*—charms.
[26]*gracious*—graced.

ACT I, SCENE II. *A room of state in the castle.*

<table>
<tr><td>195</td><td colspan="2">*Flourish. Enter the* KING, QUEEN, HAMLET, POLONIUS, LAERTES,
VOLTIMAND, CORNELlUS, Lords, *and* Attendants.</td></tr>
<tr><td></td><td>KING.</td><td>Though yet of Hamlet our dear brother's death</td></tr>
<tr><td></td><td></td><td>The memory be green, and that it us befitted</td></tr>
<tr><td></td><td></td><td>To bear our hearts in grief and out whole kingdom</td></tr>
<tr><td>200</td><td></td><td>To be contracted in one brow of woe,</td></tr>
<tr><td></td><td></td><td>Yet so far hath discretion fought with nature</td></tr>
<tr><td></td><td></td><td>That we with wisest sorrow think on him</td></tr>
<tr><td></td><td></td><td>Together with remembrance of ourselves.</td></tr>
<tr><td></td><td></td><td>Therefore our sometime sister, now our queen,</td></tr>
<tr><td>205</td><td></td><td>The imperial jointress to this warlike state,</td></tr>
<tr><td></td><td></td><td>Have we, as 'twere with a defeated joy,</td></tr>
<tr><td></td><td></td><td>With an auspicious and a dropping eye,</td></tr>
<tr><td></td><td></td><td>With mirth in funeral and with dirge in marriage,</td></tr>
<tr><td></td><td></td><td>In equal scale weighing delight and dole,</td></tr>
<tr><td>210</td><td></td><td>Taken to wife. Nor have we herein barr'd</td></tr>
<tr><td></td><td></td><td>Your better wisdoms, which have freely gone</td></tr>
<tr><td></td><td></td><td>With this affair along. For all, our thanks.</td></tr>
<tr><td></td><td></td><td>Now follows, that you know, young Fortinbras,</td></tr>
<tr><td></td><td></td><td>Holding a weak supposal[27] of our worth,</td></tr>
<tr><td>215</td><td></td><td>Or thinking by our late dear brother's death</td></tr>
<tr><td></td><td></td><td>Our state to be disjoint and out of frame,</td></tr>
<tr><td></td><td></td><td>Colleagued with this dream of his advantage,</td></tr>
<tr><td></td><td></td><td>He hath not fail'd to pester us with message,</td></tr>
<tr><td></td><td></td><td>Importing the surrender of those lands</td></tr>
<tr><td>220</td><td></td><td>Lost by his father, with all bonds of law,</td></tr>
<tr><td></td><td></td><td>To our most valiant brother. So much for him.</td></tr>
<tr><td></td><td></td><td>Now for ourself, and for this time of meeting,</td></tr>
<tr><td></td><td></td><td>Thus much the business is: we have here writ</td></tr>
<tr><td></td><td></td><td>To Norway, uncle of young Fortinbras—</td></tr>
<tr><td>225</td><td></td><td>Who, impotent and bed-rid, scarcely hears</td></tr>
<tr><td></td><td></td><td>Of this his nephew's purpose—to suppress</td></tr>
<tr><td></td><td></td><td>His further gait[28] herein, in that the levies,</td></tr>
<tr><td></td><td></td><td>The lists and full proportions, are all made</td></tr>
<tr><td></td><td></td><td>Out of his subject;[29] and we here dispatch</td></tr>
<tr><td>230</td><td></td><td>You, good Cornelius, and you, Voltimand,</td></tr>
<tr><td></td><td></td><td>For bearers of this greeting to old Norway,</td></tr>
<tr><td></td><td></td><td>Giving to you no further personal power</td></tr>
</table>

---

[27]*weak supposal*—low opinion.

[28]*gait*—proceeding.

[29]*subject*—at the expense of his subjects.

		To business with the King more than the scope
		Of these dilated[30] articles allow.
235		Farewell, and let your haste commend your duty.
	COR.	
		In that and all things will we show our duty.
	VOL.	
	KING.	We doubt it nothing. Heartily farewell.
240		[*Exeunt* VOLTIMAND *and* CORNELIUS.
		And now, Laertes, what's the news with you?
		You told us of some suit; what is't, Laertes?
		You cannot speak of reason to the Dane,[31]
		And lose your voice.[32] What wouldst thou beg, Laertes,
245		That shall not be my offer, not thy asking?
		The head is not more native[33] to the heart,
		The hand more instrumental to the mouth,
		Than is the throne of Denmark to thy father.
		What wouldst thou have, Laertes?
250	LAER.	My dread lord,
		Your leave and favour to return to France,
		From whence though willingly I came to Denmark,
		To show my duty in your coronation,
		Yet now, I must confess, that duty done,
255		My thoughts and wishes bend again toward France
		And bow them to your gracious leave and pardon.
	KING.	Have you your father's leave? What says Polonius?
	POL.	He hath, my lord, wrung from me my slow leave
		By laboursome petition, and at last
260		Upon his will I seal'd my hard[34] consent.
		I do beseech you, give him leave to go.
	KING.	Take thy fair hour, Laertes; time be thine,
		And thy best graces spend it at thy will.
		But now, my cousin[35] Hamlet, and my son—
265	HAM.	[*Aside*] A little more than kin, and less than kind.
	KING.	How is it that the clouds still hang on you?
	HAM.	Not so, my lord; I am too much i' the sun.
	QUEEN.	Good Hamlet, cast thy nighted colour off,
		And let thine eye look like a friend on Denmark.
270		Do not for ever with thy vailed lids

---

[30]*dilated*—detailed.
[31]*the Dane*—the King of Denmark.
[32]*lose your voice*—speak in vain.
[33]*native*—closely related.
[34]*hard*—reluctant.
[35]*cousin*—close relation.

		Seek for thy noble father in the dust.
		Thou knowst 'tis common: all that lives must die,
		Passing through nature to eternity.
	HAM.	Ay, madam, it is common.
275	QUEEN.	If it be,
		Why seems it so particular with thee?
	HAM.	Seems, madam? Nay, it is. I know not 'seems.'
		'Tis not alone my inky cloak, good mother,
		Nor customary suits of solemn black,
280		Nor windy suspiration of forced breath,
		No, nor the fruitful river in the eye,
		Nor the dejected haviour of the visage,
		Together with all forms, moods, shapes of grief,
		That can denote me truly. These indeed seem,
285		For they are actions that a man might play;
		But I have that within which passeth show,
		These but the trappings and the suits of woe.
	KING.	'Tis sweet and commendable in your nature, Hamlet,
		To give these mourning duties to your father;
290		But, you must know, your father lost a father,
		That father lost, lost his, and the survivor bound
		In filial obligation for some term
		To do obsequious sorrow.[36] But to persever
		In obstinate condolement is a course
295		Of impious stubbornness; 'tis unmanly grief;
		It shows a will most incorrect to heaven,
		A heart unfortified, a mind impatient,
		An understanding simple and unschool'd;
		For what we know must be and is as common
300		As any the most vulgar thing to sense,
		Why should we in our peevish opposition
		Take it to heart? Fie! 'tis a fault to heaven,
		A fault against the dead, a fault to nature,
		To reason most absurd, whose common theme
305		Is death of fathers, and who still hath cried,
		From the first corse till he that died today,
		'This must be so.' We pray you, throw to earth
		This unprevailing[37] woe, and think of us
		As of a father; for let the world take note,
310		You are the most immediate to our throne,
		And with no less nobility of love

---

[36]*obsequious sorrow*—i.e., dutiful mourning (obsequies).
[37]*unprevailing*—pointless.

		Than that which dearest father bears his son
		Do I impart toward you. For your intent
		In going back to school in Wittenberg,
315		It is most retrograde[38] to our desire,
		And we beseech you, bend you to remain
		Here in the cheer and comfort of our eye,
		Our chiefest courtier, cousin and our son.
	QUEEN.	Let not thy mother lose her prayers, Hamlet.
320		I pray thee, stay with us; go not to Wittenberg.
	HAM.	I shall in all my best obey you, madam.
	KING.	Why, 'tis a loving and a fair reply.
		Be as ourself in Denmark. Madam, come;
		This gentle and unforced accord of Hamlet
325		Sits smiling to my heart; in grace whereof,
		No jocund health that Denmark drinks today,
		But the great cannon to the clouds shall tell,
		And the King's rouse[39] the heaven shall bruit[40] again,
		Re-speaking earthly thunder. Come away.
330		*[Flourish. Exeunt all but* HAMLET.
	HAM.	O, that this too too sullied flesh would melt,
		Thaw and resolve itself into a dew,
		Or that the Everlasting had not fix'd
		His canon[41] 'gainst self-slaughter! O God! God!
335		How weary, stale, flat and unprofitable
		Seem to me all the uses of this world!
		Fie on't! ah fie! 'Tis an unweeded garden
		That grows to seed; things rank and gross in nature
		Possess it merely.[42] That it should come to this!
340		But two months dead—nay, not so much, not two—
		So excellent a king, that was to this
		Hyperion to a satyr, so loving to my mother
		That he might not beteem[43] the winds of heaven
		Visit her face too roughly. Heaven and earth,
345		Must I remember? Why, she would hang on him
		As if increase of appetite had grown
		By what it fed on; and yet, within a month—
		Let me not think on't—Frailty, thy name is woman—
		A little month, or ere those shoes were old

---

[38]*retrograde*—contrary.
[39]*rouse*—drink, carousal.
[40]*bruit*—proclaim.
[41]*canon*—law.
[42]*merely*—entirely.
[43]*beteem*—permit.

350		With which she follow'd my poor father's body,
		Like Niobe, all tears—why she, even she—
		O God! a beast that wants discourse of reason
		Would have mourn'd longer—married with my uncle,
		My father's brother, but no more like my father
355		Than I to Hercules. Within a month,
		Ere yet the salt of most unrighteous tears
		Had left the flushing in her galled eyes,
		She married. O, most wicked speed, to post
		With such dexterity to incestuous sheets!
360		It is not, nor it cannot come to good.
		But break, my heart, for I must hold my tongue.
	Enter HORATIO, MARCELLUS, *and* BERNARDO.	
	HOR.	Hail to your lordship.
	HAM.	I am glad to see you well.
365		Horatio—or I do forget myself.
	HOR.	The same, my lord, and your poor servant ever.
	HAM.	Sir, my good friend; I'll change that name with you.
		And what make you from Wittenberg, Horatio?—
		Marcellus.
370	MAR.	My good lord.
	HAM.	I am very glad to see you. —[*To* BER.] Good even, Sir.—
		But what, in faith, make you from Wittenberg?
	HOR.	A truant disposition, good my lord.
	HAM.	I would not hear your enemy say so,
375		Nor shall you do my ear that violence,
		To make it truster of your own report
		Against yourself. I know you are no truant.
		But what is your affair in Elsinore?
		We'll teach you to drink deep ere you depart.
380	HOR.	My lord, I came to see your father's funeral.
	HAM.	I pray thee, do not mock me, fellow-student;
		I think it was to see my mother's wedding.
	HOR.	Indeed, my lord, it follow'd hard upon.
	HAM.	Thrift, thrift, Horatio. The funeral baked meats
385		Did coldly furnish forth the marriage tables.
		Would I had met my dearest[44] foe in heaven
		Or ever I had seen that day, Horatio.
		My father—Methinks I see my father.
	HOR.	O where, my lord?
390	HAM.	In my mind's eye, Horatio.
	HOR.	I saw him once; he was a goodly king.

---

[44]*dearest*—direst.

	HAM.	He was a man, take him for all in all;
		I shall not look upon his like again.
	HOR.	My lord, I think I saw him yesternight.
395	HAM.	Saw? Who?
	HOR.	My lord, the King your father.
	HAM.	The King my father?
	HOR.	Season your admiration[45] for a while
		With an attent ear, till I may deliver,
400		Upon the witness of these gentlemen,
		This marvel to you.
	HAM.	For God's love, let me hear!
	HOR.	Two nights together had these gentlemen,
		Marcellus and Bernardo, on their watch,
405		In the dead vast and middle of the night,
		Been thus encounter'd. A figure like your father,
		Armed at point exactly, cap-à-pie,[46]
		Appears before them, and with solemn march
		Goes slow and stately by them. Thrice he walk'd
410		By their oppress'd and fear-surprised eyes
		Within his truncheon's length, whilst they, distill'd
		Almost to jelly with the act[47] of fear,
		Stand dumb, and speak not to him. This to me
		In dreadful secrecy impart they did;
415		And I with them the third night kept the watch,
		Where, as they had deliver'd, both in time,
		Form of the thing, each word made true and good,
		The apparition comes. I knew your father;
		These hands are not more like.
420	HAM.	But where was this?
	MAR.	My lord, upon the platform where we watch'd.
	HAM.	Did you not speak to it?
	HOR.	My lord, I did,
		But answer made it none. Yet once methought
425		It lifted up it head and did address
		Itself to motion, like as it would speak.
		But even then the morning cock crew loud,
		And at the sound it shrunk in haste away
		And vanish'd from our sight.
430	HAM.	Tis very strange.
	HOR.	As I do live, my honour'd lord, 'tis true,

---

[45]*Season your admiration*—temper your astonishment.
[46]*cap-à-pie*—head to foot.
[47]*act*—effect.

		And we did think it writ down in our duty
		To let you know of it.
	HAM.	Indeed, indeed, sirs; but this troubles me.
435		Hold you the watch tonight?
	MAR.	
		We do, my lord.
	BER.	
	HAM.	Arm'd, say you?
440	MAR.	
		Arm'd, my lord.
	BER.	
	HAM.	From top to toe?
	MAR.	
445		My lord, from head to foot.
	BER.	
	HAM.	Then saw you not his face?
	HOR.	O, yes, my lord; he wore his beaver[48] up.
	HAM.	What look'd he, frowningly?
450	HOR.	A countenance more in sorrow than in anger.
	HAM.	Pale, or red?
	HOR.	Nay, very pale.
	HAM.	And fix'd his eyes upon you?
	HOR.	Most constantly.
455	HAM.	I would I had been there.
	HOR.	It would have much amazed you.
	HAM.	Very like, very like. Stay'd it long?
	HOR.	While one with moderate haste might tell[49] a hundred.
	MAR.	Longer, longer.
460	BER.	
	HOR.	Not when I saw't.
	HAM.	His beard was grizzled, no?
	HOR.	It was as I have seen it in his life,
		A sable silver'd.
465	HAM.	I will watch tonight;
		Perchance 'twill walk again.
	HOR.	I warrant it will.
	HAM.	If it assume my noble father's person,
		I'll speak to it, though hell itself should gape
470		And bid me hold my peace. I pray you all,
		If you have hitherto conceal'd this sight,
		Let it be tenable in your silence still,

---

[48]*beaver*—visor.

[49]*tell*—count.

		And whatsoever else shall hap tonight,
		Give it an understanding, but no tongue.
475		I will requite your loves, So fare you well.
		Upon the platform, 'twixt eleven and twelve,
		I'll visit you.
	ALL.	Our duty to your honour.
	HAM.	Your loves, as mine to you. Farewell.
480		*[Exeunt all but* HAMLET.
		My father's spirit in arms! All is not well.
		I doubt[50] some foul play. Would the night were come.
		Till then sit still, my soul. Foul deeds will rise,
		Though all the earth o'erwhelm them, to men's eyes.
485		*[Exit.*

---

[50]*doubt*—suspect.

ACT I, SCENE III. *A room in Polonius's house.*

Enter LAERTES *and* OPHELIA.

LAER.   My necessaries are embark'd. Farewell.
And, sister, as the winds give benefit
And convoy[51] is assistant, I do not sleep,

490   But let me hear from you.

OPH.   Do you doubt that?

LAER.   For Hamlet, and the trifling of his favour,
Hold it a fashion,[52] and a toy in blood,
A violet in the youth of primy nature,

495   Forward, not permanent, sweet, not lasting,
The perfume and suppliance[53] of a minute,
No more.

OPH.   No more but so?

LAER.   Think it no more

500   For nature crescent[54] does not grow alone
In thews[55] and bulk, but, as this temple[56] waxes,
The inward service of the mind and soul
Grows wide withal. Perhaps he loves you now,
And now no soil nor cautel[57] doth besmirch

505   The virtue of his will; but you must fear,
His greatness weigh'd,[58] his will is not his own;
For he himself is subject to his birth.
He may not, as unvalued persons do,
Carve for himself, for on his choice depends

510   The safety and health of this whole state;
And therefore must his choice be circumscribed
Unto the voice and yielding of that body
Whereof he is the head. Then if he says he loves you,
It fits your wisdom so far to believe it

515   As he in his particular act and place
May give his saying deed; which is no further
Than the main[59] voice of Denmark goes withal.
Then weigh what loss your honour may sustain

---

[51]*convoy*—transport.
[52]*fashion*—passing whim.
[53]*suppliance*—gratification.
[54]*crescent*—growing.
[55]*thews*—strength.
[56]*temple*—i.e., human body.
[57]*cautel*—deceit.
[58]*His greatness weigh'd*—his important rank considered.
[59]*main*—general.

		If with too credent ear you list[60] his songs,
520		Or lose your heart, or your chaste treasure open
		To his unmaster'd importunity.
		Fear it, Ophelia, fear it, my dear sister,
		And keep you in the rear of your affection,
		Out of the shot and danger of desire.
525		The chariest[61] maid is prodigal enough
		If she unmask her beauty to the moon.
		Virtue itself 'scapes not calumnious strokes.
		The canker galls the infants of the spring
		Too oft before their buttons[62] be disclosed,
530		And in the morn and liquid dew of youth
		Contagious blastments[63] are most imminent.
		Be wary then; best safety lies in fear.
		Youth to itself rebels, though none else near.
	OPH.	I shall the effect of this good lesson keep
535		As watchman to my heart. But, good my brother,
		Do not, as some ungracious pastors do,
		Show me the steep and thorny way to heaven,
		Whilst, like a puff'd and reckless libertine,
		Himself the primrose path of dalliance treads
540		And recks not his own rede.[64]
	LAER.	O, fear me not.
		I stay too long. But here my father comes.

Enter POLONIUS.

		A double blessing is a double grace;
545		Occasion smiles upon a second leave.
	POL.	Yet here, Laertes? Aboard, aboard, for shame!
		The wind sits in the shoulder of your sail,
		And you are stay'd for. There, my blessing with thee.
		And these few precepts in thy memory
550		Look thou character.[65] Give thy thoughts no tongue,
		Nor any unproportion'd thought his act.
		Be thou familiar, but by no means vulgar.
		Those friends thou hast, and their adoption tried,
		Grapple them to thy soul with hoops of steel,
555		But do not dull thy palm[66] with entertainment

[60]*list*—listen to.
[61]*chariest*—wariest.
[62]*buttons*—buds.
[63]*blastments*—blights.
[64]*recks not his own rede*—does not heed his own advice.
[65]*character*—engrave.
[66]*palm*—"glad-hand."

Of each new-hatch'd unfledged comrade. Beware
Of entrance to a quarrel; but being in,
Bear't, that the opposed may beware of thee.
Give every man thy ear, but few thy voice;
560   Take each man's censure,[67] but reserve thy judgement.
Costly thy habit[68] as thy purse can buy,
But not express'd in fancy; rich, not gaudy;
For the apparel oft proclaims the man;
And they in France of the best rank and station
565   Are of a most select and generous chief[69] in that.
Neither a borrower nor a lender be;
For loan oft loses both itself and friend,
And borrowing dulls the edge of husbandry.[70]
This above all: to thine own self be true,
570   And it must follow, as the night the day,
Thou canst not then be false to any man.
Farewell. My blessing season this in thee.

LAER.   Most humbly do I take my leave, my lord.

POL.   The time invites you; go, your servants tend.

575 LAER.   Farewell, Ophelia, and remember well
What I have said to you.

OPH.   'Tis in my memory lock'd,
And you yourself shall keep the key of it.

LAER.   Farewell.   [*Exit.*

580 POL.   What is't, Ophelia, he hath said to you?

OPH.   So please you, something touching the Lord Hamlet.

POL.   Marry, well bethought.
'Tis told me, he hath very oft of late
Given private time to you, and you yourself
585   Have of your audience been most free and bounteous.
If it be so—as so 'tis put on[71] me,
And that in way of caution—I must tell you,
You do not understand yourself so clearly
As it behoves my daughter and your honour.
590   What is between you? Give me up the truth.

OPH.   He hath, my lord, of late made many tenders
Of his affection to me.

POL.   Affection? Pooh! You speak like a green girl,

---

[67]*censure*—opinion.
[68]*habit*—dress.
[69]*chief*—excellence.
[70]*husbandry*—economy, thrift.
[71]*put on*—told.

Unsifted[72] in such perilous circumstance.

595 Do you believe his tenders, as you call them?

OPH. I do not know, my lord, what I should think.

POL. Marry, I'll teach you. Think yourself a baby,
That you have ta'en these tenders for true pay,
Which are not sterling. Tender yourself more dearly;

600 Or—not to crack the wind of the poor phrase,
Running it thus—you'll tender me a fool.

OPH. My lord, he hath importuned me with love
In honourable fashion.

POL. Ay, fashion you may call it. Go to, go to.

605 OPH. And hath given countenance[73] to his speech, my lord,
With almost all the holy vows of heaven.

POL. Ay, springes[74] to catch woodcocks. I do know,
When the blood burns, how prodigal the soul
Lends the tongue vows. These blazes, daughter,

610 Giving more light than heat, extinct in both,
Even in their promise, as it is a-making,
You must not take for fire. From this time
Be something scanter of your maiden presence;
Set your entreatments[75] at a higher rate

615 Than a command to parley. For Lord Hamlet,
Believe so much in him, that he is young,
And with a larger tether may he walk
Than may be given you. In few,[76] Ophelia,
Do not believe his vows; for they are brokers,[77]

620 Not of that dye which their investments[78] show,
But mere implorators[79] of unholy suits,
Breathing like sanctified and pious bawds,
The better to beguile. This is for all:
I would not, in plain terms, from this time forth,

625 Have you so slander any moment leisure,
As to give words or talk with the Lord Hamlet.
Look to't, I charge you. Come your ways.

OPH. I shall obey, my lord. [*Exeunt.*

---

[72]*unsifted*—inexperienced.
[73]*countenance*—authority.
[74]*springes*—snares.
[75]*entreatments*—company.
[76]*In few*—in sum.
[77]*brokers*—procurers.
[78]*investments*—clothes.
[79]*implorators*—implorers.

ACT I, SCENE IV. *The platform.*

Enter HAMLET, HORATIO, *and* MARCELLUS.

630	HAM.	The air bites shrewdly; it is very cold.
	HOR.	It is a nipping and an eager air.
	HAM.	What hour now?
	HOR.	I think it lacks of twelve.
	MAR.	No, it is struck.
635	HOR.	Indeed? I heard it not. It then draws near the season
		Wherein the spirit held his wont to walk.

[*A flourish of trumpets, and ordnance shot off within.*]

		What doth this mean, my lord?
	HAM.	The King doth wake tonight and takes his rouse,[80]
640		Keeps wassail, and the swaggering upspring[81] reels;
		And as he drains his draughts of Rhenish[82] down,
		The kettle-drum and trumpet thus bray out
		The triumph of his pledge.[83]
	HOR.	Is it a custom?
645	HAM.	Ay, marry, is't;
		But to my mind, though I am native here
		And to the manner born, it is a custom
		More honour'd in the breach than the observance.
		This heavy-headed revel east and west
650		Makes us traduced and tax'd of other nations.
		They clepe[84] us drunkards, and with swinish phrase
		Soil our addition;[85] and indeed it takes
		From our achievements, though perform'd at height,
		The pith and marrow of our attribute.
655		So, oft it chances in particular men,
		That for some vicious mole of nature in them,
		As in their birth—wherein they are not guilty,
		Since nature cannot choose his origin—
		By the o'ergrowth of some complexion,[86]
660		Oft breaking down the pales and forts of reason,
		Or by some habit that too much o'er-leavens[87]

---

[80]*takes his rouse*—carouses.

[81]*upspring*—wild dance.

[82]*Rhenish*—Rhine wine.

[83]*pledge*—his drinking toast.

[84]*clepe*—call.

[85]*addition*—sully our reputation.

[86]*complexion*—humor, trait.

[87]*o'er-leavens*—becomes excessive.

		The form of plausive[88] manners, that these men—
		Carrying, I say, the stamp of one defect,
		Being Nature's livery, or Fortune's star—
665		Their virtues else[89]—be they as pure as grace,
		As infinite as man may undergo—
		Shall in the general censure take corruption
		From that particular fault. The dram of evil
		Doth all the noble substance of a doubt[90]
670		To his own scandal.[91]
	Enter GHOST.	
	HOR.	Look, my lord, it comes.
	HAM.	Angels and ministers of grace defend us!
		Be thou a spirit of health or goblin damn'd,
675		Bring with thee airs from heaven or blasts from hell,
		Be thy intents wicked or charitable,
		Thou comest in such a questionable shape
		That I will speak to thee. I'll call thee Hamlet,
		King, father, royal Dane. O, answer me!
680		Let me not burst in ignorance, but tell
		Why thy canonized bones, hearsed in death,
		Have burst their cerements, why the sepulchre,
		Wherein we saw thee quietly inurn'd,
		Hath oped his ponderous and marble jaws,
685		To cast thee up again. What may this mean,
		That thou, dead corse, again, in complete steel,
		Revisits thus the glimpses of the moon,
		Making night hideous, and we fools of nature
		So horridly to shake our disposition
690		With thoughts beyond the reaches of our souls?
		Say, why is this? Wherefore? What should we do?
		[GHOST *beckons* HAMLET.
	HOR.	It beckons you to go away with it,
		As if it some impartment did desire
695		To you alone.
	MAR.	Look, with what courteous action
		It waves you to a more removed ground.
		But do not go with it.
	HOR.	No, by no means.
700	HAM.	It will not speak. Then I will follow it.

---

[88]*plausive*—pleasing.

[89]*virtues else*—their other virtues.

[90]*of a doubt*—often nullify?

[91]*scandal*—harm.

	HOR.	Do not, my lord.
	HAM.	Why, what should be the fear?
		I do not set my life at a pin's fee;
		And for my soul, what can it do to that,
705		Being a thing immortal as itself?
		It waves me forth again. I'll follow it.
	HOR.	What if it tempt you toward the flood, my lord,
		Or to the dreadful summit of the cliff
		That beetles o'er[92] his base into the sea,
710		And there assume some other horrible form,
		Which might deprive your sovereignty of reason
		And draw you into madness? Think of it.
		The very place puts toys of desperation,[93]
		Without more motive, into every brain
715		That looks so many fathoms to the sea
		And hears it roar beneath.
	HAM.	It waves me still.
		Go on; I'll follow thee.
	MAR.	You shall not go, my lord.
720	HAM.	Hold off your hands.
	HOR.	Be ruled; you shall not go.
	HAM.	My fate cries out,
		And makes each petty artery in this body
		As hardy as the Nemean lion's[94] nerve.
725		Still am I call'd. Unhand me, gentlemen.
		By heaven, I'll make a ghost of him that lets[95] me.
		I say, away! Go on; I'll follow thee.
		[*Exeunt* GHOST *and* HAMLET.
	HOR.	He waxes desperate with imagination.
730	MAR.	Let's follow. 'Tis not fit thus to obey him.
	HOR.	Have after. To what issue will this come?
	MAR.	Something is rotten in the state of Denmark.
	HOR.	Heaven will direct it.
	MAR.	Nay, let's follow him. [*Exeunt.*

---

[92]*beetles o'er*—overhangs.

[93]*toys of desperation*—desperate imaginings.

[94]*Nemean lion's*—slain by Hercules as one of his twelve labors.

[95]*lets*—hinders.

ACT I, SCENE V. *Another part of the platform.*

735	*Enter* GHOST *and* HAMLET.	
	HAM.	Whither wilt thou lead me? Speak; I'll go no further.
	GHOST.	Mark me.
	HAM.	I will.
	GHOST.	My hour is almost come,
740		When I to sulphurous and tormenting
		Must render up myself
	HAM.	Alas, poor ghost!
	GHOST.	Pity me not, but lend thy serious hearing
		To what I shall unfold.
745	HAM.	Speak; I am bound to hear.
	GHOST.	So art thou to revenge, when thou shalt hear.
	HAM.	What?
	GHOST.	I am thy father's spirit.
		Doom'd for a certain term to walk the night,
750		And for the day confined to fast in fires,
		Till the foul crimes done in my days of nature.
		Are burnt and purged away. But that I am forbid
		To tell the secrets of my prison-house,
		I could a tale unfold whose lightest word
755		Would harrow up thy soul, freeze thy young blood,
		Make thy two eyes, like stars, start from their spheres,
		Thy knotted and combined locks to part
		And each particular hair to stand an end,
		Like quills upon the fretful porpentine.
760		But this eternal blazon[96] must not be
		To ears of flesh and blood. List, list, O, list!
		If thou didst ever thy dear father love—
	HAM.	O God!
	GHOST.	Revenge his foul and most unnatural murder.
765	HAM.	Murder?
	GHOST.	Murder most foul, as in the best it is,
		But this most foul, strange, and unnatural.
	HAM.	Haste me to know't, that I, with wings as swift
		As meditation or the thoughts of love,
770		May sweep to my revenge.
	GHOST.	I find thee apt;
		And duller shouldst thou be than the fat weed
		That roots itself in ease on Lethe[97] wharf,

---

[96]*eternal blazon*—description of the afterlife.

[97]*Lethe*—the river of forgetfulness in the underworld.

		Wouldst thou not stir in this. Now, Hamlet, hear.
775		'Tis given out that, sleeping in my orchard,
		A serpent stung me; so the whole ear of Denmark
		Is by a forged process of my death
		Rankly abused. But know, thou noble youth,
		The serpent that did sting thy father's life
780		Now wears his crown.
	HAM.	O my prophetic soul! My uncle!
	GHOST.	Ay, that incestuous, that adulterate beast,
		With witchcraft of his wit, with traitorous gifts—
		O wicked wit and gifts that have the power
785		So to seduce!—won to his shameful lust
		The will of my most seeming-virtuous queen.
		O Hamlet, what a falling off was there!
		From me, whose love was of that dignity
		That it went hand in hand even with the vow
790		I made to her in marriage; and to decline
		Upon a wretch, whose natural gifts were poor
		To those of mine.
		But virtue, as it never will be moved,
		Though lewdness court it in a shape of heaven,
795		So lust, though to a radiant angel link'd,
		Will sate itself in a celestial bed
		And prey on garbage.
		But, soft! methinks I scent the morning air;
		Brief let me be. Sleeping within my orchard,
800		My custom always of the afternoon,
		Upon my secure hour thy uncle stole,
		With juice of cursed hebenon in a vial,
		And in the porches of my ears did pour
		The leperous distilment, whose effect
805		Holds such an enmity with blood of man
		That swift as quicksilver it courses through
		The natural gates and alleys of the body,
		And with a sudden vigour it doth posset[98]
		And curd, like eager droppings into milk,
810		The thin and wholesome blood. So did it mine;
		And a most instant tetter[99] bark'd about,
		Most lazar-like,[100] with vile and loathsome crust,
		All my smooth body.

---

[98]*posset*—curdle.
[99]*tetter*—disease that thickens the skin (like tree bark).
[100]*lazar-like*—like a leper.

815		Thus was I, sleeping, by a brother's hand
		Of life, of crown, of queen, at once dispatch'd,
		Cut off even in the blossoms of my sin,
		Unhousel'd, disappointed, unaneled,[101]
		No reckoning made, but sent to my account
		With all my imperfections on my head.
820		O, horrible! O, horrible! most horrible!
		If thou hast nature in thee, bear it not.
		Let not the royal bed of Denmark be
		A couch for luxury[102] and damned incest.
		But, howsoever thou pursuest this act,
825		Taint not thy mind, nor let thy soul contrive
		Against thy mother aught. Leave her to heaven,
		And to those thorns that in her bosom lodge,
		To prick and sting her. Fare thee well at once.
		The glow-worm shows the matin to be near,
830		And 'gins to pale his uneffectual fire.
		Adieu, adieu, adieu. Remember me. [*Exit.*
	HAM.	O all you host of heaven! O earth! What else?
		And shall I couple hell? O, fie! Hold, hold, my heart;
		And you, my sinews, grow not instant old,
835		But bear me stiffly up. Remember thee?
		Ay, thou poor ghost, while memory holds a seat
		In this distracted globe.[103] Remember thee?
		Yea, from the table[104] of my memory
		I'll wipe away all trivial fond[105] records,
840		All saws[106] of books, all forms, all pressures past,
		That youth and observation copied there;
		And thy commandment all alone shall live
		Within the book and volume of my brain,
		Unmix'd with baser matter. Yes, by heaven!
845		O most pernicious woman!
		O villain, villain, smiling, damned villain!
		My tables—meet it is I set it down
		That one may smile, and smile, and be a villain;
		At least I'm sure it may be so in Denmark. [*Writing.*
850		So, uncle, there you are. Now to my word.

[101]*Unhousel'd, disappointed, unaneled*—without sacrament, unprepared and not having received extreme unction.
[102]*luxury*—lechery.
[103]*globe*—head.
[104]*table*—(writing) tablet.
[105]*fond*—foolish.
[106]*saws*—maxims.

It is 'Adieu, adieu, remember me.'

I have sworn't

HOR.

[*Within*] My lord, my lord.

855 MAR.

Enter HORATIO *and* MARCELLUS.

MAR.   Lord Hamlet.

HOR.   Heaven secure him!

HAM.   So be it.

860 MAR.   Illo, ho, ho, my lord.

HAM.   Hillo, ho, ho, boy. Come, bird, come.

MAR.   How is't, my noble lord?

HOR.   What news, my lord?

HAM.   O, wonderful!

865 HOR.   Good my lord, tell it.

HAM.   No; you will reveal it.

HOR.   Not I, my lord, by heaven.

MAR.   Nor I, my lord.

HAM.   How say you, then; would heart of man once think it?

870   But you'll be secret?

HOR.

    Ay, by heaven, my lord.

MAR.

HAM.   There's ne'er a villain dwelling in all Denmark

875   But he's an arrant knave.

HOR.   There needs no ghost, my lord, come from the grave

    To tell us this.

HAM.   Why, right, you are i' the right;

    And so, without more circumstance at all,

880   I hold it fit that we shake hands and part,

    You, as your business and desire shall point you—

    For every man hath business and desire,

    Such as it is—and for my own poor part,

    Look you, I'll go pray.

885 HOR.   These are but wild and whirling words, my lord.

HAM.   I'm sorry they offend you, heartily;

    Yes, faith, heartily.

HOR.   There's no offence, my lord.

HAM.   Yes, by Saint Patrick, but there is, Horatio,

890   And much offence too. Touching this vision here,

    It is an honest[107] ghost that let me tell you.

    For your desire to know what is between us,

---

[107]*honest*—genuine.

	O'ermaster't as you may. And now, good friends,
	As you are friends, scholars and soldiers,
895	Give me one poor request.
HOR.	What is't, my lord? We will.
HAM.	Never make known what you have seen tonight.
HOR.	
	My lord, we will not.
900 MAR.	
HAM.	Nay, but swear't.
HOR.	In faith,
	My lord, not I.
MAR.	Nor I, my lord, in faith.
905 HAM.	Upon my sword.[108]
MAR.	We have sworn, my lord, already.
HAM.	Indeed, upon my sword, indeed.
GHOST.	[*Beneath*] Swear.
HAM.	Ah, ha, boy, say'st thou so? Art thou there, truepenny?[109]
910	Come on. You hear this fellow in the cellarage.
	Consent to swear.
HOR.	Propose the oath, my lord.
HAM.	Never to speak of this that you have seen,
	Swear by my sword.
915 GHOST.	[*Beneath*] Swear.
HAM.	*Hic et ubique?*[110] Then we'll shift our ground.
	Come hither, gentlemen,
	And lay your hands again upon my sword.
	Never to speak of this that you have heard,
920	Swear by my sword.
GHOST.	[*Beneath*] Swear.
HAM.	Well said, old mole. Canst work i' the earth so fast?
	A worthy pioner![111] Once more remove, good friends.
HOR.	O day and night, but this is wondrous strange.
925 HAM.	And therefore as a stranger give it welcome.
	There are more things in heaven and earth, Horatio,
	Than are dreamt of in your philosophy
	But come;
	Here, as before, never, so help you mercy,
930	How strange or odd soe'er I bear myself—
	As I perchance hereafter shall think meet

[108]*sword*—The sword's hilt forms a cross.
[109]*truepenny*—honest fellow.
[110]*Hic et ubique*—here and everywhere.
[111]*pioner*—miner, digger.

To put an antic[112] disposition on—
That you, at such times seeing me, never shall,
With arms encumber'd[113] thus, or this head-shake,
935 Or by pronouncing of some doubtful phrase,
As 'Well, we know'or 'We could, an if we would,'
Or 'If we list to speak,' or 'There be, an if they might,'
Or such ambiguous giving out, to note
That you know aught of me; this not to do,
940 So grace and mercy at your most need help you,
Swear.

GHOST. [*Beneath*] Swear.
HAM. Rest, rest, perturbed spirit. [*They swear.*] So, gentlemen,
With all my love I do commend me to you;
945 And what so poor a man as Hamlet is
May do to express his love and friending to you,
God willing, shall not lack. Let us go in together;
And still your fingers on your lips, I pray.
The time is out of joint. O cursed spite,
950 That ever I was born to set it right!
Nay, come, let's go together. [*Exeunt.*

---

[112]*antic*—odd, strange.
[113]*encumber'd*—folded.

ACT II.

SCENE I. *A room in Polonius's house.*

Enter POLONIUS *and* REYNALDO.

	POL.	Give him this money and these notes, Reynaldo.
	REY.	I will, my lord.
	POL.	You shall do marvellous wisely, good Reynaldo,
5		Before you visit him, to make inquire
		Of his behaviour.
	REY.	My lord, I did intend it.
	POL.	Marry, well said, very well said. Look you, sir,
		Inquire me first what Danskers[114] are in Paris,
10		And how, and who, what means, and where they keep,[115]
		What company, at what expense, and finding
		By this encompassment[116] and drift of question
		That they do know my son, come you more nearer
		Than your particular demands will touch it.[117]
15		Take[118] you, as 'twere, some distant knowledge of him,
		As thus, 'I know his father and his friends,
		'And in part him.' Do you mark this, Reynaldo?
	REY.	Ay, very well, my lord.
	POL.	And in part him; but,' you may say, 'not well;
20		But if't be he I mean, he's very wild,
		Addicted so and so;' and there put on him
		What forgeries you please—marry, none so rank
		As may dishonour him, take heed of that—
		But, sir, such wanton, wild and usual slips
25		As are companions noted and most known
		To youth and liberty.
	REY.	As gaming, my lord?
	POL.	Ay, or drinking, fencing, swearing, quarrelling,
		Drabbing.[119] You may go so far.
30	REY.	My lord, that would dishonour him.
	POL.	'Faith, no; as you may season it in the charge.
		You must not put another scandal on him,
		That he is open to incontinency.[120]

---

[114]*Danskers*—Danes.

[115]*keep*—dwell.

[116]*encompassment*—roundabout way of talking.

[117]*. . . it*—than by specific question.

[118]*Take*—Take on, assume.

[119]*Drabbing*—whoring.

[120]*incontinency*—licentiousness.

		That's not my meaning; but breathe his faults so quaintly[121]
35		That they may seem the taints of liberty,
		The flash and outbreak of a fiery mind,
		A savageness in unreclaimed[122] blood,
		Of general assault.[123]
	REY.	But, my good lord—
40	POL.	Wherefore should you do this?
	REY.	Ay, my lord,
		I would know that.
	POL.	Marry, Sir, here's my drift,
		And I believe it is a fetch of warrant:[124]
45		You laying these slight sullies on my son,
		As 'twere a thing a little soil'd i' the working,
		Mark you,
		Your party in converse,[125] him you would sound,
		Having ever seen in the prenominate[126] crimes
50		The youth you breathe of guilty, be assured
		He closes[127] with you in this consequence:
		'Good Sir,' or so, or 'friend,' or 'gentleman,'
		According to the phrase or the addition[128]
		Of man and country.
55	REY.	Very good, my lord.
	POL.	And then, Sir, does he this—he does—what was I about to say?
		By the mass, I was about to say something. Where did I leave?
	REY.	At 'closes in the consequence,' at 'friend or so,' and 'gentleman.'
	POL.	At 'closes in the consequence,' ay, marry.
60		He closes with you thus: 'I know the gentleman;
		I saw him yesterday,' or t'other day,'
		Or then, or then, with such, or such, 'and, as you say,
		There was a[129] gaming,' 'there o'ertook in's rouse,'[130]
		'There falling out at tennis;' or perchance,
65		'I saw him enter such a house of sale,'
		Videlicet,[131] a brothel, or so forth.

---

[121]*quaintly*—subtly.

[122]*unreclaimed*—untamed.

[123]*Of general assault*—overtaking young men generally.

[124]*fetch of warrant*—justified strategem.

[125]*converse*—conversation.

[126]*prenominate*—aforementioned.

[127]*closes*—agrees.

[128]*addition*—title.

[129]*a*—he.

[130]*o'ertook in's rouse*—overcome by carousel (heavy drinking).

[131]*Videlicet*—namely.

		See you now;	
		Your bait of falsehood takes this carp of truth;	
		And thus do we of wisdom and of reach,[132]	
70		With windlasses[133] and with assays of bias,	
		By indirections find directions out.	
		So, by my former lecture and advice,	
		Shall you my son. You have me, have you not?	
	REY.	My lord, I have.	
75	POL.	God be wi' ye. Fare ye well.	
	REY.	Good my lord.	
	POL.	Observe his inclination in yourself.[134]	
	REY.	I shall, my lord.	
	POL.	And let him ply his music.	
80	REY.	Well, my lord.	
	POL.	Farewell.	[*Exit* REYNALDO.

Enter OPHELIA.

		How now, Ophelia, what's the matter?
	OPH.	O, my lord, my lord, I have been so affrighted.
85	POL.	With what, i' the name of God?
	OPH.	My lord, as I was sewing in my closet,
		Lord Hamlet, with his doublet all unbraced,[135]
		No hat upon his head, his stockings foul'd,
		Ungarter'd and down-gyved[136] to his ankle,
90		Pale as his shirt, his knees knocking each other,
		And with a look so piteous in purport
		As if he had been loosed out of hell
		To speak of horrors, he comes before me.
	POL.	Mad for thy love?
95	OPH.	My lord, I do not know,
		But truly I do fear it.
	POL.	What said he?
	OPH.	He took me by the wrist and held me hard;
		Then goes he to the length of all his arm,
100		He falls to such perusal of my face
		As he would draw it. Long stay'd he so.
		At last, a little shaking of mine arm,
		And thrice his head thus waving up and down,
		He raised a sigh so piteous and profound

---

[132]*reach*—foresight.

[133]*windlasses*—indirect advances.

[134]*Observe . . . yourself*—(?) Behave as he does.

[135]*unbraced*—jacket unbuttoned.

[136]*down-gyved*—fallen down, becoming gyves (fetters).

105		As it did seem to shatter all his bulk
		And end his being. That done, he lets me go,
		And with his head over his shoulder turn'd,
		He seem'd to find his way without his eyes;
		For out o' doors he went without their helps,
110		And to the last bended their light on me.
	POL.	Come, go with me. I will go seek the King.
		This is the very ecstasy of love,
		Whose violent property fordoes itself[137]
		And leads the will to desperate undertakings
115		As oft as any passion under heaven
		That does afflict our natures. I am sorry.
		What, have you given him any hard words of late?
	OPH.	No, my good lord, but, as you did command,
		I did repel his letters and denied
120		His access to me.
	POL.	That hath made him mad.
		I am sorry that with better heed and judgement
		I had not quoted[138] him. I fear'd he did but trifle
		And meant to wrack thee. But beshrew my jealousy![139]
125		By heaven, it is as proper to our age
		To cast beyond ourselves in our opinions
		As it is common for the younger sort
		To lack discretion. Come, go we to the King.
		This must be known, which, being kept close, might move
130		More grief to hide than hate to utter love.[140]
		Come. [*Exeunt.*

---

[137]*Whose . . . itself*—Love's violent nature destroys itself.

[138]*quoted*—observed.

[139]*jealousy*—curse my suspicion.

[140]*. . . love*—than hatred by being exposed as love.

ACT II, SCENE II. A *room in the castle.*

Flourish. Enter KING, QUEEN, ROSENCRANTZ, GUILDENSTERN, *and*
Attendants.

	KING.	Welcome, dear Rosencrantz and Guildenstern.
135		Moreover that we much did long to see you,
		The need we have to use you did provoke
		Our hasty sending. Something have you heard
		Of Hamlet's transformation—so call it,
		Sith[141] nor the exterior nor the inward man
140		Resembles that it was. What it should be,
		More than his father's death, that thus hath put him
		So much from the understanding of himself,
		I cannot dream of. I entreat you both
		That, being of so young days brought up with him
145		And sith so neighbour'd to his youth and haviour,
		That you vouchsafe your rest[142] here in our court
		Some little time: so by your companies
		To draw him on to pleasures, and to gather
		So much as from occasion[143] you may glean,
150		Whether aught to us unknown afflicts him thus
		That open'd lies within our remedy.
	QUEEN.	Good gentlemen, he hath much talk'd of you,
		And sure I am two men there are not living
		To whom he more adheres. If it will please you
155		To show us so much gentry[144] and good will
		As to expend your time with us awhile
		For the supply and profit of our hope,
		Your visitation shall receive such thanks
		As fits a king's remembrance.
160	ROS.	Both your Majesties
		Might, by the sovereign power you have of us,
		Put your dread pleasures more into command
		Than to entreaty.
	GUIL.	But we both obey,
165		And here give up ourselves, in the full bent[145]
		To lay our service freely at your feet,
		To be commanded.

---

[141]*Sith*—since.
[142]*vouchsafe your rest*—agree to stay.
[143]*occasion*—opportunity.
[144]*gentry*—courtesy.
[145]*in the full bent*—full willingness.

	KING.	Thanks, Rosencrantz and gentle Guildenstern.
	QUEEN.	Thanks, Guildenstern and gentle Rosencrantz.
170		And I beseech you instantly to visit
		My too much changed son. Go, some of you,
		And bring these gentlemen where Hamlet is.
	GUIL.	Heavens make our presence and our practices
		Pleasant and helpful to him.
175	QUEEN.	Ay, amen.

[*Exeunt* ROSENCRANTZ, GUILDENSTERN, *and some* Attendants.

Enter POLONIUS.

	POL.	The ambassadors from Norway, my good lord,
		Are joyfully return'd.
180	KING.	Thou still[146] hast been the father of good news.
	POL.	Have I, my lord? I assure my good liege,
		I hold my duty as I hold my soul,
		Both to my God and to my gracious King.
		And I do think, or else this brain of mine
185		Hunts not the trail of policy so sure
		As it hath used to do, that I have found
		The very cause of Hamlet's lunacy.
	KING.	O, speak of that; that do I long to hear.
	POL.	Give first admittance to the ambassadors.
190		Me news shall be the fruit to that great feast.
	KING.	Thyself do grace to them, and bring them in.

[*Exit* POLONIUS.

		He tells me, my dear Gertrude, he hath found
		The head and source of all your son's distemper.
195	QUEEN.	I doubt it is no other but the main:
		His father's death and our o'erhasty marriage.
	KING.	Well, we shall sift him.

Enter POLONIUS, *with* VOLTIMAND *and* CORNELIUS.

		Welcome, my good friends.
200		Say, Voltimand, what from our brother Norway?
	VOLT.	Most fair return of greetings and desires.
		Upon our first,[147] he sent out to suppress
		His nephew's levies, which to him appear'd
		To be a preparation 'gainst the Polack,[148]
205		But better look'd into, he truly found
		It was against your Highness; whereat grieved,
		That so his sickness, age and impotence

---

[146] *still*—always.

[147] *our first*—i.e., our first report of the actions of Fortinbras.

[148] *the Polack*—the King of Poland.

Was falsely borne in hand,[149] sends our arrests
On Fortinbras; which he, in brief, obeys,
210   Receives rebuke from Norway, and in fine
Makes vow before his uncle never more
To give the assay of arms against your Majesty.
Whereon old Norway, overcome with joy,
Gives him three thousand crowns in annual fee
215   And his commission to employ those soldiers,
So levied as before, against the Polack,
With an entreaty, herein further shown,   *[Giving a paper.*
That it might please you to give quiet pass
Through your dominions for this enterprise,
220   On such regards of safety and allowance
As therein are set down.

KING.   It likes us well,
And at our more consider'd time we'll read,
Answer, and think upon this business.
225   Meantime we thank you for your well-took labour.
Go to your rest; at night we'll feast together.
Most welcome home.   *[Exeunt* VOLTIMAND *and* CORNELIUS.

POL.   This business is well ended.
My liege, and madam, to expostulate
230   What majesty should be, what duty is,
Why day is day, night night, and time is time,
Were nothing but to waste night, day and time.
Therefore, since brevity is the soul of wit
And tediousness the limbs and outward flourishes,
235   I will be brief. Your noble son is mad.
Mad call I it; for, to define true madness,
What is't but to be nothing else but mad?
But let that go.

QUEEN.   More matter, with less art.
240   POL.   Madam, I swear I use no art at all.
That he is mad, 'tis true—a foolish figure;
But farewell it, for I will use no art.
Mad let us grant him then. And now remains
That we find out the cause of this effect,
245   Or rather say, the cause of this defect,
For this effect defective comes by cause.
Thus it remains and the remainder thus:
Perpend;[150]

---

[149]*borne in hand*—deluded.
[150]*Perpend*—consider.

250   I have a daughter—have while she is mine—
Who in her duty and obedience, mark,
Hath given me this. Now gather and surmise.   [*Reads.*

To the celestial, and my soul's idol, the most beautiful Ophelia—

That's an ill phrase, a vile phrase; 'beautified' is a vile phrase.
But you shall hear: [*Reads.*

255   In her excellent white bosom, these, &c.

QUEEN.   Came this from Hamlet to her?
POL.   Good madam, stay awhile. I will be faithful.   [*Reads.*

           Doubt thou the stars are fire,
               Doubt that the sun doth move,
260   Doubt truth to be a liar,
               But never doubt I love.

O dear Ophelia, I am ill at these numbers.[151] I have not art to reckon[152] my
groans. But that I love thee best, O most best, believe it. Adieu.

           Thine evermore, most dear lady, whilst this
265   machine[153] is to him, HAMLET.

This in obedience hath my daughter shown me;
And more above, hath his solicitings,
As they fell out by time, by means and place,
All given to mine ear.
270   KING.   But how hath she
Received his love?
POL.   What do you think of me?
KING.   As of a man faithful and honourable.
POL.   I would fain prove so. But what you might think,
275   When I had seen this hot love on the wing—
As I perceived it, I must tell you that,
Before my daughter told me—what might you,
Or my dear Majesty your queen here, think,
If I had play'd the desk or table-book,[154]

---

[151]*ill at these numbers*—not gifted in versifying.
[152]*reckon*—(1) count; (2) tell.
[153]*machine*—body.
[154]*play'd . . . table-book*—noted silently.

280		Or given my heart a winking,[155] mute and dumb,
		Or look'd upon this love with idle sight;[156]
		What might you think? No, I went round[157] to work,
		And my young mistress thus I did bespeak:
		'Lord Hamlet is a prince, out of thy star.
285		This must not be.' And then I prescripts gave her,
		That she should lock herself from his resort,
		Admit no messengers, receive no tokens.
		Which done, she took the fruits of my advice;
		And he, repulsed—a short tale to make—
290		Fell into a sadness, then into a fast,
		Thence to a watch,[158] thence into a weakness,
		Thence to a lightness,[159] and by this declension
		Into the madness wherein he now raves
		And all we mourn for.
295	KING.	Do you think 'tis this?
	QUEEN.	It may be; very like.
	POL.	Hath there been such a time—I'ld fain know that—
		That I have positively said ''Tis so,'
		When it proved otherwise?
300	KING.	Not that I know.
	POL.	[*Pointing to his head and shoulder*] Take this from this, if this
		be otherwise.
		If circumstances lead me, I will find
		Where truth is hid, though it were hid indeed
305		Within the centre.[160]
	KING.	How may we try it further?
	POL.	You know, sometimes he walks four hours together
		Here in the lobby.
	QUEEN.	So he does, indeed.
310	POL.	At such a time I'll loose my daughter to him.
		Be you and I behind an arras[161] then;
		Mark the encounter. If he love her not,
		And be not from his reason fall'n thereon,
		Let me be no assistant for a state,
315		But keep a farm and carters.
	KING.	We will try it.

---

[155]*given . . . winking*—shut my eyes deliberately.

[156]*idle sight*—casually.

[157]*round*—straight.

[158]*a watch*—insomnia.

[159]*lightness*—lightheadedness.

[160]*centre*—i.e., of the earth.

[161]*arras*—tapestry (heavy curtain or screen).

	QUEEN.	But look where sadly the poor wretch comes reading.
	POL.	Away, I do beseech you both, away.
		I'll board[162] him presently. O, give me leave.
320		[*Exeunt* KING, QUEEN, *and* Attendants.

Enter HAMLET, *reading.*

		How does my good Lord Hamlet?
	HAM.	Well, God-a-mercy.
	POL.	Do you know me, my lord?
325	HAM.	Excellent well. You are a fishmonger.
	POL.	Not I, my lord.
	HAM.	Then I would you were so honest a man.
	POL.	Honest, my lord?
	HAM.	Ay, Sir. To be honest, as this world goes, is to be one man picked out
330		of ten thousand.
	POL.	That's very true, my lord.
	HAM.	For if the sun breed maggots in a dead dog, being a good
		kissing carrion[163]—Have you a daughter?
	POL.	I have, my lord.
335	HAM.	Let her not walk i' the sun. Conception is a blessing, but as
		your daughter may conceive—friend, look to't.
	POL.	[*Aside*] How say you by that? Still harping on my daughter. Yet he
		knew me not at first; he said I was a fishmonger. He is far gone. And
		truly in my youth I suffered much extremity for love, very near this.
340		I'll speak to him again.—What do you read, my lord?
	HAM.	Words, words, words.
	POL.	What is the matter, my lord?
	HAM.	Between who?
	POL.	I mean, the matter that you read, my lord.
345	HAM.	Slanders, Sir. For the satirical rogue says here that old men have
		grey beards, that their faces are wrinkled, their eyes purging thick
		amber and plum-tree gum, and that they have a plentiful lack of wit,
		together with most weak hams—all which, sir, though I most
		powerfully and potently believe, yet I hold it not honesty to have it
350		thus set down; for yourself, sir, shall grow old as I am, if like a crab
		you could go backward.
	POL.	[*Aside*] Though this be madness, yet there is method in't.—
		Will you walk out of the air, my lord?
	HAM.	Into my grave?
355	POL.	Indeed, that's out of the air. [*Aside*] How pregnant sometimes his
		replies are!—a happiness[164] that often madness hits on, which

---

[162]*board*—approach.

[163]*a good kissing carrion*—flesh good for kissing.

[164]*a happiness*—aptness of phrasing.

		reason and sanity could not so prosperously be delivered of. I will
		leave him, and suddenly contrive the means of meeting between him
		and my daughter.—My honourable lord, I will take my leave of you.
360	HAM.	You cannot, Sir, take from me anything that I will more wilingly part
		withal—except my life, except my life, except my life.
	POL.	Fare you well, my lord.
	HAM.	These tedious old fools!

Enter ROSENCRANTZ *and* GUILDENSTERN.

365	POL.	You go to seek the Lord Hamlet. There he is.
	ROS.	[*To Polonius*] God save you, sir. [*Exit* POLONIUS.
	GUIL.	My honoured lord.
	ROS.	My most dear lord.
	HAM.	My excellent good friends. How dost thou, Guildenstern?
370		Ah, Rosencrantz. Good lads, how do you both?
	ROS.	As the indifferent[165] children of the earth.
	GUIL.	Happy, in that we are not over-happy; on Fortune's cap we are not
		the very button.
	HAM.	Nor the soles of her shoe?
375	ROS.	Neither, my lord.
	HAM.	Then you live about her waist, or in the middle of her favours?
	GUIL.	Faith, her privates[166] we.
	HAM.	In the secret parts of Fortune? O, most true; she is a strumpet.
		What's the news?
380	ROS.	None, my lord, but that the world's grown honest.
	HAM.	Then is doomsday near. But your news is not true. Let me question
		more in particular. What have you, my good friends, deserved at the
		hands of Fortune that she sends you to prison hither?
	GUIL.	Prison, my lord?
385	HAM.	Denmark's a prison.
	ROS.	Then is the world one.
	HAM.	A goodly one, in which there are many confines, wards and
		dungeons, Denmark being one o' the worst.
	ROS.	We think not so, my lord.
390	HAM.	Why, then 'tis none to you; for there is nothing either good or bad
		but thinking makes it so. To me it is a prison.
	ROS.	Why, then your ambition makes it one: 'tis too narrow for your
		mind.
	HAM.	O God, I could be bounded in a nutshell and count myself a king of
395		infinite space were it not that I have bad dreams.
	GUIL.	Which dreams indeed are ambition; for the very substance of the
		ambitious is merely the shadow of a dream.

---

[165]*indifferent*—ordinary.

[166]*privates*—(1) ordinary persons; (2) genitalia.

	HAM.	A dream itself is but a shadow.
	ROS.	Truly, and I hold ambition of so airy and light a quality that it is
400		but a shadow's shadow.
	HAM.	Then are our beggars bodies, and our monarchs and outstretched
		heroes the beggars' shadows. Shall we to the court?
		For, by my fay, I cannot reason.
	ROS.	
405		We'll wait upon you.
	GUIL.	
	HAM.	No such matter. I will not sort[167] you with the rest of my servants;
		for, to speak to you like an honest man, I am most dreadfully
		attended. But, in the beaten way of friendship, what make you at
410		Elsinore?
	ROS.	To visit you, my lord, no other occasion.
	HAM.	Beggar that I am, I am even poor in thanks, but I thank you. And sure,
		dear friends, my thanks are too dear a halfpenny. Were you not sent
		for? Is it your own inclining? Is it a free visitation? Come, deal
415		justly with me. Come, come. Nay, speak.
	GUIL.	What should we say, my lord?
	HAM.	Why, anything, but to the purpose. You were sent for; and there is a
		kind of confession in your looks which your modesties have not
		craft enough to colour. I know the good King and Queen have sent
420		for you.
	ROS.	To what end, my lord?
	HAM.	That you must teach me. But let me conjure you by the rights of our
		fellowship, by the consonancy of our youth, by the obligation of our
		ever-preserved love, and by what more dear a better proposer could
425		charge you withal, be even[168] and direct with me whether you were
		sent for or no.
	ROS.	[*Aside to* GUIL.] What say you?
	HAM.	[*Aside*] Nay then, I have an eye of[169] you.—If you love me, hold not
		off.
430	GUIL.	My lord, we were sent for.
	HAM.	I will tell you why. So shall my anticipation prevent your
		discovery,[170] and your secrecy to the King and Queen moult no
		feather. I have of late—but wherefore I know not—lost all my mirth,
		forgone all custom of exercises, and indeed it goes so heavily with
435		my disposition that this goodly frame, the earth, seems to me a sterile
		promontory. This most excellent canopy, the air, look you, this brave

---

[167]*sort*—class.

[168]*even*—fair.

[169]*of*—on.

[170]*prevent your discovery*—precede your confession.

o'erhanging firmament, this majestical roof fretted[171] with golden fire, why, it appears no other thing to me than a foul and pestilent congregation of vapours. What a piece of work is a man! How noble in reason, how infinite in faculty, in form and moving how express and admirable, in action how like an angel, in apprehension how like a god—the beauty of the world, the paragon of animals! And yet, to me, what is this quintessence of dust? Man delights not me—no, nor woman neither, though by your smiling you seem to say so.

440

445	ROS.	My lord, there was no such stuff in my thoughts.
	HAM.	Why did you laugh then, when I said man delights not me?
	ROS.	To think, my lord, if you delight not in man, what lenten entertainment[172] the players shall receive from you. We coted[173] them on the way, and hither are they coming to offer you service.
450	HAM.	He that plays the king shall be welcome; his Majesty shall have tribute of me. The adventurous knight shall use his foil and target,[174] the lover shall not sigh gratis, the humorous man[175] shall end his part in peace, the clown shall make those laugh whose lungs are tickle o' the sere,[176] and the lady shall say her mind freely, or the blank verse shall halt for't. What players are they?
455		
	ROS.	Even those you were wont to take such delight in, the tragedians of the city.
	HAM.	How chances it they travel? Their residence, both in reputation and profit, was better both ways.
460	ROS.	I think their inhibition[177] comes by the means of the late innovation.
	HAM.	Do they hold the same estimation they did when I was in the city? Are they so followed?
	ROS.	No, indeed, are they not.
	HAM.	How comes it? Do they grow rusty?
465	ROS.	Nay, their endeavour keeps in the wonted pace. But there is, sir, an eyrie of children, little eyases,[178] that cry out on the top of question and are most tyrannically clapped for't. These are now the fashion, and so berattle the common stages[179]—so they call them—that many wearing rapiers are afraid of goose-quills,[180] and dare scarce come thither.
470		

---

[171]*fretted*—adorned.

[172]*lenten entertainment*—lean reception.

[173]*coted*—passed by.

[174]*foil and target*—fencing sword and targe (light shield).

[175]*humorous man*—character representing one of the four "humours," eccentric.

[176]*are tickle o' the sere*—"will laugh at anything."

[177]*inhibition*—prohibition (from acting in the town).

[178]*eyases*—young hawks.

[179]*berattle the common stages*—berate the public playhouses.

[180]*many . . . goose-quills*—being satirized by poets' pens.

	HAM.	What, are they children? Who maintains 'em? How are they escoted?[181] Will they pursue the quality[182] no longer than they can sing? Will they not say afterwards, if they should grow themselves to common players—as it is most like, if their means are no better—
475		their writers do them wrong to make them exclaim against their own succession?[183]
	ROS.	Faith, there has been much to do on both sides, and the nation holds it no sin to tarre[184] them to controversy There was for a while no money bid for argument[185] unless the poet and the player went to
480		cuffs[186] in the question.
	HAM.	Is't possible?
	GUIL.	O, there has been much throwing about of brains.
	HAM.	Do the boys carry it away?[187]
	ROS.	Ay, that they do, my lord, Hercules and his load[188] too.
485	HAM.	It is not very strange; for my uncle is King of Denmark, and those that would make mows[189] at him while my father lived, give twenty, forty, fifty, a hundred ducats apiece for his picture in little. 'Sblood, there is something in this more than natural, if philosophy could find it out.
490		[*Flourish of trumpets within.*
	GUIL.	There are the players.
	HAM.	Gentlemen, you are welcome to Elsinore. Your hands, come then. The appurtenance of welcome is fashion and ceremony. Let me comply with you in this garb, lest my extent[190] to the players—which, I tell
495		you, must show fairly outwards—should more appear like entertainment than yours. You are welcome. But my uncle-father and aunt-mother are deceived.
	GUIL.	In what, my dear lord?
	HAM.	I am but mad north-north-west. When the wind is southerly I know a
500		hawk from a handsaw.
	Enter POLONIUS.	
	POL.	Well be with you, gentlemen.

---

[181]*escoted*—supported.

[182]*quality*—acting profession.

[183]*succession*—fate.

[184]*tarre*—incite.

[185]*argument*—plots for plays.

[186]*went to cuffs*—"fisticuffs."

[187]*carry it away*—win.

[188]*Hercules and his load*—The Globe theatre has a sign which portrayed Hercules supporting the earth.

[189]*mows*—grimaces.

[190]*extent*—welcome.

15. *Shakespeare*/Hamlet (II. ii)

	HAM.	Hark you, Guildenstern, and you too—at each ear a hearer. That great baby you see there is not yet out of his swaddling clouts.
505	ROS.	Happily he's the second time come to them; for they say an old man is twice a child.
	HAM.	I will prophesy he comes to tell me of the players. Mark it. You say right, sir; o' Monday morning; 'twas so, indeed.[191]
	POL.	My lord, I have news to tell you.
510	HAM.	My lord, I have news to tell you. When Roscius[192] was an actor in Rome—
	POL.	The actors are come hither, my lord.
	HAM.	Buzz, buzz.
	POL.	Upon my honour—
515	HAM.	Then came each actor on his ass—
	POL.	The best actors in the world, either for tragedy, comedy, history, pastoral, pastoral-comical, historical-pastoral, tragical-historical, tragical-comical-historical-pastoral, scene individable, or poem unlimited. Seneca cannot be too heavy, nor Plautus too light. For the
520		law of writ and the liberty, these are the only men.
	HAM.	O Jephthah, judge of Israel,[193] what a treasure hadst thou!
	POL.	What a treasure had he, my lord?
	HAM.	Why,

One fair daughter, and no more,
525 The which he loved passing well.

	POL.	[*Aside*] Still on my daughter.
	HAM.	Am I not i' the right, old Jephthah?
	POL.	If you call me Jephthah, my lord, I have a daughter that I love passing well.
530	HAM.	Nay, that follows not.
	POL.	What follows, then, my lord?
	HAM.	Why,

As by lot God wot,

and then, you know,

535 It came to pass, as most like it was—

---

[191]*I . . . indeed*—Hamlet pretends to be talking of other matters as Polonius nears.

[192]*Roscius*—comic actor of ancient Rome.

[193]*Jephthah, judge of Israel*—a Biblical figure who sacrificed his own daughter.

The first row of the pious chanson[194] will show you more; for look where my abridgement[195] comes.

Enter the Players.

540 You are welcome, masters. Welcome, all. I am glad to see thee well. Welcome, good friends. O, my old friend! Why, thy face is valanced[196] since I saw thee last. Comest thou to beard me in Denmark? What, my young lady and mistress! By'r lady, your ladyship is nearer to heaven than when I saw you last, by the altitude of a chopine.[197] Pray God, your voice, like a piece of

545 uncurrent gold, be not cracked within the ring.[198] Masters, you are all welcome. We'll e'en to't like French falconers, fly at any thing we see. We'll have a speech straight. Come, give us a taste of your quality. Come, a passionate speech.

FIRST PLAY. What speech, my good lord?

550 HAM. I heard thee speak me a speech once, but it was never acted, or, if it was, not above once; for the play, I remember, pleased not the million, 'twas caviare to the general.[199] But it was— as I received it, and others, whose judgements in such matters cried in the top of[200] mine—an excellent play, well digested in the scenes, set down with

555 as much modesty as cunning. I remember, one said there were no sallets[201] in the lines to make the matter savoury, nor no matter in the phrase that might indict the author of affection,[202] but called it an honest method, as wholesome as sweet, and by very much more handsome than fine. One speech in it I chiefly loved: 'twas Æneas'

560 tale to Dido, and thereabout of it especially where he speaks of Priam's slaughter. If it live in your memory, begin at this line—let me see, let me see—

The rugged Pyrrhus,[203] like th' Hyrcanian beast—[204]

It is not so. It begins with Pyrrhus—

565 The rugged Pyrrhus, he whose sable arms,
Black as his purpose, did the night resemble
When he lay couched in the ominous horse,[205]

---

[194]*chanson*—stanza of the song/poem.

[195]*abridgement*—cutting short the conversation with Polonius.

[196]*valanced*—draped (bearded).

[197]*chopine*—thick-soled shoes.

[198]*cracked within the ring*—A coin that had been clipped.

[199]*caviare to the general*—general populace ("pearls before swine").

[200]*in the top of*—with more authority than.

[201]*sallets*—salad, relish; spicy words.

[202]*affection*—affectation.

[203]*Pyrrhus*—Achilles' son who slayed Priam.

[204]*Hyrcanian beast*—tiger.

[205]*the ominous horse*—the Trojan horse.

		Hath now this dread and black complexion smear'd
		With heraldry more dismal. Head to foot
570		Now is he total gules,[206] horridly trick'd[207]
		With blood of fathers, mothers, daughters, sons,
		Baked and impasted with the parching streets,
		That lend a tyrannous and a damned light
		To their lord's murder. Roasted in wrath and fire,
575		And thus o'er-sized[208] with coagulate gore,
		With eyes like carbuncles, the hellish Pyrrhus
		Old grandsire Priam seeks.
		So, proceed you.
	POL.	'Fore God, my lord, well spoken, with good accent and good
580		discretion.
	FIRST PLAY.	Anon he finds him
		Striking too short at Greeks. His antique sword,
		Rebellious to his arm, lies where it falls,
		Repugnant to command. Unequal match'd,
585		Pyrrhus at Priam drives, in rage strikes wide,
		But with the whiff and wind of his fell[209] sword
		The unnerved father falls. Then senseless Ilium,
		Seeming to feel this blow, with flaming top
		Stoops to his base, and with a hideous crash
590		Takes prisoner Pyrrhus' ear. For, lo! his sword,
		Which was declining on the milky head
		Of reverend Priam, seem'd i' the air to stick.
		So, as a painted tyrant, Pyrrhus stood,
		And like a neutral to his will and matter,
595		Did nothing.
		But as we often see, against some storm,
		A silence in the heavens, the rack[210] stand still,
		The bold winds speechless and the orb below
		As hush as death, anon the dreadful thunder
600		Doth rend the region, so after Pyrrhus' pause
		Aroused vengeance sets him new a-work,
		And never did the Cyclops' hammers fall
		On Mars's armour, forged for proof[211] eterne,
		With less remorse than Pyrrhus' bleeding sword
605		Now falls on Priam.

---

[206]*gules*—a heraldic term for red.
[207]*trick'd*—a heraldic term; adorned.
[208]*o'ersized*—covered over.
[209]*fell*—deadly.
[210]*rack*—clouds.
[211]*proof*—tested and proved.

		Out, out, thou strumpet, Fortune! All you gods,
		In general synod take away her power,
		Break all the spokes and fellies[212] from her wheel,
		And bowl the round nave[213] down the hill of heaven
610		As low as to the fiends.
	POL.	This is too long.
	HAM.	It shall to the barber's, with your beard. Prithee, say on. He's for a jig or a tale of bawdry, or he sleeps. Say on; come to Hecuba.
	FIRST PLAY.	But who, O, who had seen the mobled[214] queen—
615	HAM.	'The mobled queen?'
	POL.	That's good; 'mobled queen' is good.
	FIRST PLAY.	Run barefoot up and down, threatening the flames
		With bisson rheum,[215] a clout upon that head
		Where late the diadem stood, and for a robe,
620		About her lank and all o'er-teemed[216] loins,
		A blanket, in the alarm of fear caught up;
		Who this had seen, with tongue in venom steep'd
		'Gainst Fortune's state would treason have pronounced.
		But if the gods themselves did see her then,
625		When she saw Pyrrhus make malicious sport
		In mincing with his sword her husband's limbs,
		The instant burst of clamour that she made,
		Unless things mortal move them[217] not at all,
		Would have made milch[218] the burning eyes of heaven
630		And passion in the gods.
	POL.	Look whether he has not turned his colour and has tears in's eyes. Prithee, no more.
	HAM.	'Tis well. I'll have thee speak out the rest of this soon. Good my lord, will you see the players well bestowed? Do you hear, let them be
635		well used, for they are the abstract[219] and brief chronicles of the time. After your death you were better have a bad epitaph than their ill report while you live.
	POL.	My lord, I will use them according to their desert.
	HAM.	God's bodykins, man, much better. Use every man after his desert,
640		and who shall 'scape whipping? Use them after your own honour

---

212*fellies*—rim.
213*nave*—hub.
214*mobled*—with head muffled.
215*bisson rheum*—blinding tears.
216*o'er-teemed*—worn out by childbearing.
217*them*—the gods.
218*milch*—milky tears.
219*abstract*—summary.

and dignity: the less they deserve, the more merit is in your bounty. Take them in.

POL. Come, sirs.

HAM. Follow him, friends. We'll hear a play tomorrow.
645
[*Exit* POLONIUS *with all the* Players *but the* First.]
Dost thou hear me, old friend? Can you play *The Murder of Gonzago?*

FIRST PLAY. Ay, my lord.

HAM. We'll ha't tomorrow night. You could, for a need,[220] study a speech
650
of some dozen or sixteen lines, which I would set down and insert in't, could you not?

FIRST PLAY. Ay, my lord.

HAM. Very well. Follow that lord, and look you mock him not. [*Exit* FIRST
PLAYER.] My good friends, I'll leave you till night. You are
655
welcome to Elsinore.

ROS. Good my lord.

HAM. Ay, so. God be wi' ye.
[*Exeunt* ROSENCRANTZ *and* GUILDERSTERN.
Now I am alone.
660
O, what a rogue and peasant slave am I!
Is it not monstrous that this player here,
But in a fiction, in a dream of passion,
Could force his soul so to his own conceit
That from her working all his visage wann'd,
665
Tears in his eyes, distraction in's aspect,
A broken voice, and his whole function suiting
With forms to his conceit?[221] And all for nothing!
For Hecuba![222]
What's Hecuba to him, or he to Hecuba,
670
That he should weep for her? What would he do,
Had he the motive and the cue for passion
That I have? He would drown the stage with tears
And cleave the general ear with horrid speech,
Make mad the guilty and appal the free,
675
Confound the ignorant, and amaze indeed
The very faculties of eyes and ears.
Yet I,
A dull and muddy-mettled rascal, peak,[223]

---

[220]*for a need*—if necessary.
[221]*his whole . . . conceit*—gestures matching words.
[222]*Hecuba*—Priam's wife.
[223]*peak*—mope.

	Like John-a-dreams unpregnant of[224] my cause,
680	And can say nothing; no, not for a king,
	Upon whose property and most dear life
	A damn'd defeat was made. Am I a coward?
	Who calls me villain, breaks my pate across,
	Plucks off my beard and blows it in my face,
685	Tweaks me by the nose, gives me the lie i' the throat,
	As deep as to the lungs? Who does me this?
	Ha!
	'Swounds, I should take it: for it cannot be
	But I am pigeon-liver'd and lack gall
690	To make oppression bitter, or ere this
	I should have fatted all the region kites[225]
	With this slave's offal. Bloody, bawdy villain!
	Remorseless, treacherous, lecherous, kindless[226] villain!
	Why, what an ass am I! This is most brave,
695	That I, the son of a dear father murder'd,
	Prompted to my revenge by heaven and hell,
	Must, like a whore, unpack my heart with words,
	And fall a-cursing, like a very drab,[227]
	A scullion![228] Fie upon't! Foh!
700	About,[229] my brain! Hum, I have heard
	That guilty creatures, sitting at a play,
	Have by the very cunning of the scene
	Been struck so to the soul that presently
	They have proclaim'd their malefactions.
705	For murder, though it have no tongue, will speak
	With most miraculous organ. I'll have these players
	Play something like the murder of my father
	Before mine uncle. I'll observe his looks,
	I'll tent[230] him to the quick. If he but blench,
710	I know my course. The spirit that I have seen
	May be the devil, and the devil hath power
	To assume a pleasing shape, yea, and perhaps
	Out of my weakness and my melancholy,
	As he is very potent with such spirits,
715	Abuses me to damn me. I'll have grounds

---

[224]*unpregnant of*—unconscious of.
[225]*region kites*—hawks.
[226]*kindless*—unnatural.
[227]*drab*—prostitute.
[228]*scullion*—kitchen servant.
[229]*About*—Go to!
[230]*tent*—probe.

More relative[231] than this. The play's the thing
Wherein I'll catch the conscience of the King.   [*Exit.*

---

[231]*relative*—to the purpose, relevant.

ACT III.

SCENE I. *A room in the castle.*

Enter KING, QUEEN, POLONIUS, OPHELIA, ROSENCRANZ, *and* GUILDENSTERN.

	KING.	And can you by no drift of conference[232]
		Get from him why he puts on this confusion,
5		Grating so harshly all his days of quiet
		With turbulent and dangerous lunacy?
	ROS.	He does confess he feels himself distracted,
		But from what cause he will by no means speak.
	GUIL.	Nor do we find him forward to be sounded;
10		But, with a crafty madness, keeps aloof,
		When we would bring him on to some confession
		Of his true state.
	QUEEN.	Did he receive you well?
	ROS.	Most like a gentleman.
15	GUIL.	But with much forcing of his disposition.
	ROS.	Niggard of question,[233] but of our demands
		Most free in his reply.
	QUEEN.	Did you assay him[234]
		To any pastime?
20	ROS.	Madam, it so fell out that certain players
		We o'er-raught[235] on the way. Of these we told him,
		And there did seem in him a kind of joy
		To hear of it. They are about the court,
		And, as I think, they have already order
25		This night to play before him.
	POL.	'Tis most true;
		And he beseech'd me to entreat your Majesties
		To hear and see the matter.
	KING.	With all my heart; and it doth much content me
30		To hear him so inclined.
		Good gentlemen, give him a further edge,[236]
		And drive his purpose on to these delights.
	ROS.	We shall, my lord.
		[*Exeunt* ROSENCRANTZ *and* GUILDENSTERN.
35	KING.	Sweet Gertrude, leave us too;

---

[232]*conference*—conversation.

[233]*Niggard of question*—sparing in conversation.

[234]*assay*—tempt him.

[235]*o'er-raught*—overtook.

[236]*edge*—inducement.

For we have closely[237] sent for Hamlet hither,
That he, as 'twere by accident, may here
Affront[238] Ophelia.
Her father and myself, lawful espials,[239]

40   Will so bestow ourselves that, seeing unseen,
We may of their encounter frankly judge,
And gather by him, as he is behaved,
If t be the affliction of his love or no
That thus he suffers for.

45   QUEEN.   I shall obey you.
And for your part, Ophelia, I do wish
That your good beauties be the happy cause
Of Hamlet's wildness; so shall I hope your virtues
Will bring him to his wonted way again,

50   To both your honours.
OPH.   Madam, I wish it may.   [*Exit* QUEEN.
POL.   Ophelia, walk you here. Gracious, so please you,
We will bestow ourselves. [*To* OPHELIA] Read on this book,
That show of such an exercise may colour

55   Your loneliness.[240] We are oft to blame in this—
'Tis too much proved—that with devotion's visage
And pious action we do sugar o'er
The devil himself.
KING.   [*Aside*] O, 'tis too true.

60   How smart a lash that speech doth give my conscience.
The harlot's cheek, beautied with plastering art,
Is not more ugly to the thing that helps it
Than is my deed to my most painted word.
O heavy burden!

65   POL.   I hear him coming. Let's withdraw, my lord.
                    [*Exeunt* KING *and* POLONIUS.

Enter HAMLET.
HAM.   To be, or not to be, that is the question:
Whether 'tis nobler in the mind to suffer

70   The slings and arrows of outrageous fortune,
Or to take arms against a sea of troubles,
And by opposing end them. To die: to sleep;
No more; and by a sleep to say we end
The heart-ache and the thousand natural shocks

---

[237]*closely*—secretly.

[238]*Affront*—encounter.

[239]*espials*—spies.

[240]*colour Your loneliness*—provide reason for being alone.

75		That flesh is heir to; 'tis a consummation
		Devoutly to be wish'd. To die, to sleep;
		To sleep; perchance to dream. Ay, there's the rub;[241]
		For in that sleep of death what dreams may come,
		When we have shuffled off[242] this mortal coil,[243]
80		Must give us pause—there's the respect
		That makes calamity of so long life.
		For who would bear the whips and scorns of time,
		The oppressor's wrong, the proud man's contumely,
		The pangs of disprized[244] love, the law's delay,
85		The insolence of office, and the spurns
		That patient merit of the unworthy takes,
		When he himself might his quietus[245] make
		With a bare bodkin?[246] Who would fardels[247] bear,
		To grunt and sweat under a weary life,
90		But that the dread of something after death,
		The undiscover'd country from whose bourn[248]
		No traveller returns, puzzles the will,
		And makes us rather bear those ills we have
		Than fly to others that we know not of?
95		Thus conscience[249] does make cowards of us all,
		And thus the native hue of resolution
		Is sicklied o'er with the pale cast of thought,
		And enterprises of great pitch[250] and moment
		With this regard their currents turn awry
100		And lose the name of action. Soft you now,
		The fair Ophelia! Nymph; in thy orisons[251]
		Be all my sins remember'd.
	OPH.	Good my lord,
		How does your honour for this many a day?
105	HAM.	I humbly thank you: well.
	OPH.	My lord, I have remembrances of yours
		That I have longed long to redeliver.

---

[241]*rub*—obstacle (a bowling term for anything deflecting the course of the bowl).
[242]*shuffled off*—cast off.
[243]*coil*—(1) turmoil; (2) body.
[244]*disprized*—despised.
[245]*quietus*—final settlement of an account.
[246]*bodkin*—dagger.
[247]*fardels*—burdens, packs.
[248]*bourn*—boundary.
[249]*conscience*—(1) consciousness; (2) conscience.
[250]*pitch*—height.
[251]*orisons*—prayers.

		I pray you, now receive them.
	HAM.	No, not I.
110		I never gave you aught.
	OPH.	My honour'd lord, you know right well you did;
		And with them words of so sweet breath composed
		As made the things more rich. Their perfume lost,
		Take these again; for to the noble mind
115		Rich gifts wax poor when givers prove unkind.
		There, my lord.
	HAM.	Ha, ha! Are you honest?
	OPH.	My lord?
	HAM.	Are you fair?
120	OPH.	What means your lordship?
	HAM.	That if you be honest and fair, your honesty should admit no discourse to your beauty.
	OPH.	Could beauty, my lord, have better commerce than with honesty?
	HAM.	Ay, truly; for the power of beauty will sooner transform honesty
125		from what it is to a bawd than the force of honesty can translate beauty into his likeness. This was sometime a paradox, but now the time gives it proof I did love you once.
	OPH.	Indeed, my lord, you made me believe so.
	HAM.	You should not have believed me; for virtue cannot so inoculate[252]
130		our old stock but we shall relish of it.[253] I loved you not.
	OPH.	I was the more deceived.
	HAM.	Get thee to a nunnery. Why, wouldst thou be a breeder of sinners? I am myself indifferent honest, but yet I could accuse me of such things that it were better my mother had not borne me. I am very proud,
135		revengeful, ambitious, with more offences at my beck than I have thoughts to put them in, imagination to give them shape, or time to act them in. What should such fellows as I do crawling between heaven and earth? We are arrant knaves all. Believe none of us. Go thy ways to a nunnery. Where's your father?
140	OPH.	At home, my lord.
	HAM.	Let the doors be shut upon him, that he may play the fool nowhere but in's own house. Farewell.
	OPH.	O, help him, you sweet heavens!
	HAM.	If thou dost marry, I'll give thee this plague for thy dowry: be thou as
145		chaste as ice, as pure as snow, thou shalt not escape calumny. Get thee to a nunnery, farewell. Or if thou wilt needs marry, marry a

---

[252]*innoculate*—graft.
[253]*it*—sinful nature.

		fool; for wise men know well enough what monsters[254] you make of
		them. To a nunnery, go; and quickly too. Farewell.
	OPH.	O heavenly powers, restore him!
150	HAM.	I have heard of your paintings too, well enough. God hath given you

OPH. O heavenly powers, restore him!

150 HAM. I have heard of your paintings too, well enough. God hath given you
one face, and you make yourselves another. You jig, you amble, and
you lisp, and nickname God's creatures, and make your wantonness
your ignorance. Go to, I'll no more on't; it hath made me mad. I say,
we will have no more marriages. Those that are married already—

155 all but one—shall live; the rest shall keep as they are. To a nunnery,
go.   [*Exit.*

OPH. O, what a noble mind is here o'erthrown!
The courtier's, soldier's, scholar's, eye, tongue, sword,
The expectancy and rose of the fair state,

160 The glass of fashion and the mould of form,
The observed of all observers, quite, quite down!
And I, of ladies most deject and wretched,
That suck'd the honey of his music vows,
Now see that noble and most sovereign reason

165 Like sweet bells jangled out of tune and harsh,
That unmatch'd form and feature of blown[255] youth
Blasted with ecstasy.[256] O, woe is me,
To have seen'what I have seen, see what I see!

Enter KING *and* POLONIUS

170 KING. Love? His affections do not that way tend;
Nor what he spake, though it lack'd form a little,
Was not like madness. There's something in his soul
O'er which his melancholy sits on brood,
And I do doubt[257] the hatch and the disclose

175 Will be some danger; which for to prevent,
I have in quick determination
Thus set it down: he shall with speed to England,
For the demand of our neglected tribute.
Haply the seas and countries different

180 With variable objects shall expel
This something-settled matter in his heart,
Whereon his brains still beating puts him thus
From fashion of himself.[258] What think you on't?

POL. It shall do well. But yet do I believe

---

[254]*monsters*—i.e., cuckolds (having horns), husbands whose wives have been unfaithful.
[255]*blown*—full bloom.
[256]*ecstasy*—madness.
[257]*doubt*—fear.
[258]*From fashion of himself*—out of his normal fashion.

185		The origin and commencement of his grief	
		Sprung from neglected love. How now, Ophelia?	
		You need not tell us what Lord Hamlet said;	
		We heard it all. My lord, do as you please;	
		But, if you hold it fit, after the play,	
190		Let his queen mother all alone entreat him	
		To show his grief. Let her be round[259] with him;	
		And I'll be placed, so please you, in the ear	
		Of all their conference. If she find him not,	
		To England send him, or confine him where	
195		Your wisdom best shall think.	
	KING.	It shall be so.	
		Madness in great ones must not unwatch'd go.	[*Exeunt.*

---

[259]*be round*—direct.

ACT III, SCENE II. *A hall in the castle.*

Enter HAMLET *and* Players.

HAM. Speak the speech, I pray you, as I pronounced it to you, trippingly on
200   the tongue. But if you mouth it, as many of your players do, I had as
       lief the town-crier spoke my lines. Nor do not saw the air too much
       with your hand, thus; but use all gently: for in the very torrent,
       tempest, and, as I may say, whirlwind of your passion, you must
       acquire and beget a temperance that may give it smoothness. O, it
205   offends me to the soul to hear a robustious periwig-pated fellow
       tear a passion to tatters, to very rags, to split the ears of the ground
       lings,[260] who, for the most part, are capable of[261] nothing but
       inexplicable dumb-shows and noise. I would have such a fellow
       whipped for o'erdoing Termagant.[262] It out-Herods Herod.[263] Pray
210   you, avoid it.

FIRST PLAY. I warrant your honour.

HAM. Be not too tame neither, but let your own discretion be your tutor.
       Suit the action to the word, the word to the action, with this special
       observance, that you o'erstep not the modesty of nature. For
215   anything so overdone is from the purpose of playing, whose end,
       both at the first and now, was and is, to hold, as 'twere, the mirror
       up to nature, to show virtue her own feature, scorn her own image,
       and the very age and body of the time his form and pressure.[264] Now
       this overdone or come tardy off though it make the unskilful laugh,
220   cannot but make the judicious grieve, the censure of the which one
       must in your allowance o'erweigh a whole theatre of others. O,
       there be players that I have seen play, and heard others praise, and
       that highly, not to speak it profanely, that neither having the accent
       of Christians nor the gait of Christian, pagan, nor man, have so
225   strutted and bellowed, that I have thought some of Nature's
       journeymen[265] had made men, and not made them well, they imitated
       humanity so abominably.

FIRST PLAY. I hope we have reformed that indifferently[266] with us, sir.

HAM. O, reform it altogether. And let those that play your clowns speak no
230   more than is set down for them; for there be of them that will
       themselves laugh, to set on some quantity of barren spectators to

---

[260]*groundlings*—those spectators who stood or sat on the ground of the theater (cheap seats).

[261]*capable of*—capable of understanding.

[262]*Termagant*—a legendary Muslim deity, presented as a noisy character in morality plays.

[263]*Herod*—Herod was presented as a ranting tyrant in medieval dramas.

[264]*pressure*—imprint.

[265]*journeymen*—apprentices.

[266]*indifferently*—tolerably well.

laugh too, though in the meantime some necessary question of the play be then to be considered. That's villanous, and shows a most pitiful ambition in the fool that uses it. Go, make you ready.

235   [*Exeunt* Players.

Enter POLONIUS, ROSENCRANTZ, *and* GUILDENSTERN.

                 How now, my lord! Will the King hear this piece of work?

POL.   And the Queen too, and that presently.

HAM.   Bid the players make haste.   [*Exit* POLONIUS.

240   Will you two help to hasten them?

ROS.

                 We will, my lord.

GUIL.

                        [*Exeunt* ROSENCRANTZ *and* GUILDENSTERN.

245 HAM.   What ho, Horatio!

Enter HORATIO.

HOR.   Here, sweet lord, at your service.

HAM.   Horatio, thou art e'en as just a man
                 As e'er my conversation coped[267] withal.

250 HOR.   O, my dear lord—

HAM.   Nay, do not think I flatter;
                 For what advancement may I hope from thee,
                 That no revenue hast but thy good spirits,
                 To feed and clothe thee? Why should the poor be flatter'd?

255   No, let the candied tongue lick absurd pomp,
                 And crook the pregnant[268] hinges of the knee
                 Where thrift[269] may follow fawning. Dost thou hear?
                 Since my dear soul was mistress of her choice,
                 And could of men distinguish her election,

260   Sh'hath seal'd thee for herself; for thou hast been
                 As one, in suffering all, that suffers nothing,
                 A man that Fortune's buffets and reward's
                 Hast ta'en with equal thanks; and blest are those
                 Whose blood and judgement are so well commeddled

265   That they are not a pipe for Fortune's finger
                 To sound what stop she please. Give me that man
                 That is not passion's slave, and I will wear him
                 In my heart's core, ay, in my heart of heart,
                 As I do thee. Something too much of this.

270   There is a play tonight before the King.
                 One scene of it comes near the circumstance

---

[267]*coped*—encountered.
[268]*pregnant*—ready.
[269]*thrift*—profit.

Which I have told thee of my father's death.
I prithee, when thou seest that act afoot,
Even with the very comment of thy soul[270]

275   Observe my uncle. If his occulted guilt
Do not itself unkennel in one speech,
It is a damned ghost that we have seen,
And my imaginations are as foul
As Vulcan's stithy.[271] Give him heedful note;

280   For I mine eyes will rivet to his face,
And after we will both our judgements join
In censure of his seeming.[272]

HOR.   Well, my lord.
If he steal aught the whilst this play is playing,

285   And 'scape detecting, I will pay the theft.

HAM.   They are coming to the play. I must be idle.[273]
Get you a place.

Danish march. A flourish. Enter KING, QUEEN, POLONIUS, OPHELIA,
ROSENCRANTZ, GUILDENSTERN, *and other Lords attendant, with the*

290   *Guard carrying torches.*

KING.   How fares our cousin Hamlet?

HAM.   Excellent, i' faith; of the chameleon's dish.[274] I eat the air, promise-crammed. You cannot feed capons so.

KING.   I have nothing with this answer, Hamlet. These words are not
295   mine.[275]

HAM.   No, nor mine now. [*To* POLONIUS] My lord, you played once i' the university, you say?

POL.   That did I, my lord, and was accounted a good actor.

HAM.   What did you enact?

300   POL.   I did enact Julius Caesar. I was killed i' the Capitol. Brutus killed me.

HAM.   It was a brute part of him to kill so capital a calf there. Be the players ready?

ROS.   Ay, my lord; they stay upon your patience.

305   QUEEN. Come hither, my dear Hamlet, sit by me.

HAM.   No, good mother, here's metal more attractive.

POL.   [*To the* KING] O, ho! do you mark that?

HAM.   Lady, shall I lie in your lap? [*Lying down at* OPHELIA's *feet.*

OPH.   No, my lord.

---

[270]*comment of the soul*—the most discerning judgment.

[271]*Vulcan's stithy*—the smithy of Vulcan, god of fire and metalworking.

[272]*In censure of his seeming*—in judgment of his behavior.

[273]*idle*—unoccupied, distracted.

[274]*the chameleon's dish*—Chameleons were said to feed on air.

[275]*are not mine*—do not correspond to my question.

310	HAM.	I mean, my head upon your lap?
	OPH.	Ay, my lord.
	HAM.	Do you think I meant country matters?
	OPH.	I think nothing, my lord.
	HAM.	That's a fair thought to lie between maids' legs.
315	OPH.	What is, my lord?
	HAM.	Nothing.
	OPH.	You are merry, my lord.
	HAM.	Who, I?
	OPH.	Ay, my lord.
320	HAM.	O God, your only jig-maker. What should a man do but be merry? For, look you, how cheerfully my mother looks, and my father died within's two hours.
	OPH.	Nay, 'tis twice two months, my lord.
	HAM.	So long? Nay then, let the devil wear black, for I'll have a suit of
325		sables. O heavens, die two months ago, and not forgotten yet! Then there's hope a great man's memory may outlive his life half a year. But, by'r lady, he must build churches then, or else shall he suffer not thinking on, with the hobby-horse, whose epitaph is, 'For, O, for, O, the hobby-horse is forgot.'
330	*Hautboys play. The dumb-show enters.*
		Enter a King and a Queen very lovingly, the Queen embracing him, and he her. She kneels and makes show of protestation unto him. He takes her up and declines his head upon her neck; lays him down upon a bank of flowers. She, seeing him asleep, leaves him. Anon comes in a fellow, takes off his crown, kisses it, and pours poison in
335		*the King's ears, and exit. The Queen returns, finds the King dead, and makes passionate action. The Poisoner, with some two or three Mutes, comes in again, seeming to lament with her. The dead body is carried away. The Poisoner wooes the Queen with gifts. She seems loath and unwilling awhile, but in the end accepts his love.* [Exeunt.
340	OPH.	What means this, my lord?
	HAM.	Marry, this is miching mallecho.[276] It means mischief.
	OPH.	Belike this show imports the argument[277] of the play.
	Enter PROLOGUE.
	HAM.	We shall know by this fellow. The players cannot keep counsel;
345		they'll tell all.
	OPH.	Will he tell us what this show meant?
	HAM.	Ay, or any show that you'll show him. Be not you ashamed to show, he'll not shame to tell you what it means.
	OPH.	You are naught,[278] you are naught. I'll mark the play.

---

[276]*miching mallecho*—much mischief.

[277]*argument*—theme.

[278]*naught*—naughty.

350	PRO.	For us, and for our tragedy,
		Here stooping to your clemency,
		We beg your hearing patiently.
	HAM.	Is this a prologue, or the posy of a ring?
	OPH.	'Tis brief, my lord.
355	HAM.	As woman's love.

Enter two Players, KING *and* QUEEN.

	P. KING.	Full thirty times hath Phœbus' cart[279] gone round
		Neptune's salt wash and Tellus' orbed ground,[280]
		And thirty dozen moons with borrowed sheen
360		About the world have times twelve thirties been,
		Since love our hearts and Hymen[281] did our hands
		Unite commutual in most sacred bands.
	P. QUEEN.	So many journeys may the sun and moon
		Make us again count o'er ere love be done.
365		But, woe is me, you are so sick of late,
		So far from cheer and from your former state,
		That I distrust[282] you. Yet, though I distrust,
		Discomfort you, my lord, it nothing must.
		For women's fear and love hold quantity,[283]
370		In neither aught, or in extremity.
		Now, what my love is, proof hath made you know,
		And as my love is sized, my fear is so.
		Where love is great, the littlest doubts are fear,
		Where little fears grow great, great love grows there.
375	P. KING.	Faith, I must leave thee, love, and shortly too.
		My operant[284] powers their functions leave[285] to do,
		And thou shalt live in this fair world behind,
		Honour'd, beloved; and haply one as kind
		For husband shalt thou—
380	P. QUEEN.	O, confound the rest!
		Such love must needs be treason in my breast.
		In second husband let me be accurst,
		None wed the second but who kill'd the first.
	HAM.	[*Aside*] Wormwood, wormwood.
385	P. QUEEN.	The instances[286] that second marriage move

---

[279]*Phœbus' cart*—the chariot of the sun-god.
[280]*Tellus' orbed ground*—the earth.
[281]*Hymen*—the god of marriage.
[282]*distrust*—feel concern for.
[283]*hold quantity*—are in balance.
[284]*operant*—active.
[285]*leave*—cease.
[286]*instances*—motives.

		Are base respects of thrift,[287] but none of love.
		A second time I kill my husband dead
		When second husband kisses me in bed.
	P. KING.	I do believe you think what now you speak,
390		But what we do determine oft we break.
		Purpose is but the slave to memory,
		Of violent birth but poor validity,
		Which now, like fruit unripe, sticks on the tree,
		But fall unshaken when they mellow be.
395		Most necessary 'tis that we forget
		To pay ourselves what to ourselves is debt.
		What to ourselves in passion we propose,
		The passion ending, doth the purpose lose.
		The violence of either grief or joy
400		Their own enactures[288] with themselves destroy
		Where joy most revels, grief doth most lament;
		Grief joys, joy grieves, on slender accident.
		This world is not for aye, nor 'tis not strange
		That even our loves should with our fortunes change,
405		For 'tis a question left us yet to prove,
		Whether love lead fortune or else fortune love.
		The great man down, you mark his favourite flies,
		The poor advanced makes friends of enemies.
		And hitherto doth love on fortune tend;
410		For who not needs shall never lack a friend,
		And who in want a hollow friend doth try
		Directly seasons him[289] his enemy.
		But, orderly to end where I begun,
		Our wills and fates do so contrary run,
415		That our devices still are overthrown;
		Our thoughts are ours, their ends none of our own.
		So think thou wilt no second husband wed,
		But die thy thoughts when thy first lord is dead.
	P. QUEEN.	Nor earth to me give food nor heaven light,
420		Sport and repose lock from me day and night,
		To desperation turn my trust and hope,
		An anchor's cheer[290] in prison be my scope,
		Each opposite, that blanks[291] the face of joy,

---

[287]*thrift*—economics.
[288]*enactures*—fulfillment.
[289]*seasons him*—ripens him into.
[290]*anchor's cheer*—anchorite's fare.
[291]*blanks*—makes pale.

		Meet what I would have well and it destroy,

<table>
<tr><td>425</td><td></td><td>Meet what I would have well and it destroy,</td><td></td></tr>
</table>

425		Meet what I would have well and it destroy,	
		Both here and hence pursue me lasting strife,	
		If, once a widow, ever I be wife.	
	HAM.	If she should break it now.	
	P. KING.	'Tis deeply sworn. Sweet, leave me here awhile.	
		My spirits grow dull, and fain I would beguile	
430		The tedious day with sleep.	[*Sleeps.*
	P. QUEEN.	Sleep rock thy brain,	
		And never come mischance between us twain.	[*Exit.*
	HAM.	Madam, how like you this play?	
	QUEEN.	The lady doth protest too much, methinks.	
435	HAM.	O, but she'll keep her word.	
	KING.	Have you heard the argument? Is there no offence in't?	
	HAM.	No, no, they do but jest, poison in jest. No offence i' the world.	
	KING.	What do you call the play?	
	HAM.	*The Mousetrap.* Marry, how? Tropically.[292] This play is the image	
440		of a murder done in Vienna. Gonzago is the Duke's name; his wife,	
		Baptista. You shall see anon. Tis a knavish piece of work, but what	
		o' that? Your Majesty, and we that have free souls, it touches us not.	
		Let the galled jade[293] wince, our withers are unwrung.[294]	

Enter LUCIANUS.

445		This is one Lucianus, nephew to the King.
	OPH.	You are as good as a chorus, my lord.
	HAM.	I could interpret between you and your love, if I could see the puppets dallying.
	OPH.	You are keen, my lord, you are keen.
450	HAM.	It would cost you a groaning to take off my edge.[295]
	OPH.	Still better, and worse.
	HAM.	So you mistake[296] your husbands. Begin, murderer. Pox, leave thy damnable faces and begin. Come, the croaking raven doth bellow for revenge.
455	LUC.	Thoughts black, hands apt, drugs fit, and time agreeing,
		Confederate season, else no creature seeing;
		Thou mixture rank, of midnight weeds collected,
		With Hecate's ban[297] thrice blasted, thrice infected,
		Thy natural magic and dire property,
460		On wholesome life usurp immediately.
		[*Pours the poison into the sleepers ear.*

---

[292]*Tropically*—by a trope, figuratively.

[293]*galled jade*—horse rubbed sore (by a saddle or harness).

[294]*unwrung*—not pinched.

[295]*edge*—i.e., sexual appetite.

[296]*mistake*—mis-take, deceive.

[297]*Hecate's ban*—the curse of Hecate, goddess of magic and the underworld.

	HAM.	He poisons him i' the garden for his estate. His name's Gonzago. The story is extant, and written in very choice Italian. You shall see anon how the murderer gets the love of Gonzago's wife.
465	OPH.	The King rises.
	HAM.	What, frighted with false fire?
	QUEEN.	How fares my lord?
	POL.	Give o'er the play.
	KING.	Give me some light. Away!
470	POL.	Lights, lights, lights! [*Exeunt all but* HAMLET *and* HORATIO.
	HAM.	Why, let the stricken deer go weep,

<blockquote>
Why, let the stricken deer go weep,

The hart ungalled play;

For some must watch, while some must sleep,

Thus runs the world away.
</blockquote>

475   Would not this, sir, and a forest of feathers—if the rest of my fortunes turn Turk with me[298]—with two Provincial roses on my razed shoes,[299] get me a fellowship in a cry[300] of players, sir?

	HOR.	Half a share.
	HAM.	A whole one, I.

<blockquote>
For thou dost know, O Damon dear,

This realm dismantled was

Of Jove himself; and now reigns here

A very, very—pajock.[301]
</blockquote>

	HOR.	You might have rhymed.
485	HAM.	O good Horatio, I'll take the ghost's word for a thousand pound. Didst perceive?
	HOR.	Very well, my lord.
	HAM.	Upon the talk of the poisoning?
	HOR.	I did very well note him.
490	HAM.	Ah, ha! Come, some music; come, the recorders.

<blockquote>
For if the King like not the comedy,

Why then, belike, he likes it not, perdy.[302]
</blockquote>

       Come, some music.

Enter ROSENCRANTZ *and* GUILDENSTERN.

495	GUIL.	Good my lord, vouchsafe me a word with you.
	HAM.	Sir, a whole history.
	GUIL.	The King, sir—
	HAM.	Ay, sir, what of him?
	GUIL.	Is in his retirement marvellous distempered.

---

[298]*turn Turk with me*—betray me.

[299]*razed shoes*—feathers and decorated shoes were regularly part of an actor's costume.

[300]*cry*—pack.

[301]*pajock*—(?) peacock.

[302]*perdy*—a colloquial form of *pardieu*, by god.

500	HAM.	With drink, sir?
	GUIL.	No, my lord, rather with choler.[303]
	HAM.	Your wisdom should show itself more richer to signify this to the doctor; for, for me to put him to his purgation would perhaps plunge him into far more choler.
505	GUIL.	Good my lord, put your discourse into some frame, and start not so wildly from my affair.
	HAM.	I am tame, sir. Pronounce.
	GUIL.	The Queen, your mother, in most great affliction of spirit, hath sent me to you.
510	HAM.	You are welcome.
	GUIL.	Nay, good my lord, this courtesy is not of the right breed. If it shall please you to make me a wholesome answer, I will do your mother's commandment; if not, your pardon and my return shall be the end of my business.
515	HAM.	Sir, I cannot.
	GUIL.	What, my lord?
	HAM.	Make you a wholesome answer. My wit's diseased. But, sir, such answer as I can make, you shall command, or rather, as you say, my mother. Therefore no more, but to the matter. My mother, you say—
520	ROS.	Then thus she says: your behaviour hath struck her into amazement and admiration.[304]
	HAM.	O wonderful son, that can so astonish a mother! But is there no sequel at the heels of this mother's admiration? Impart.
	ROS.	She desires to speak with you in her closet, ere you go to bed.
525	HAM.	We shall obey, were she ten times our mother. Have you any further trade with us?
	ROS.	My lord, you once did love me.
	HAM.	So I do still, by these pickers and stealers.[305]
	ROS.	Good my lord, what is your cause of distemper? You do surely bar the door upon your own liberty if you deny your griefs to your friend.
530		
	HAM.	Sir, I lack advancement.
	ROS.	How can that be, when you have the voice of the King himself for your succession in Denmark?
535	HAM.	Ay, Sir, but 'while the grass grows'—the proverb is something musty.

Enter Players *with recorders.*

---

[303]*choler*—bile, bitterness.
[304]*admiration*—astonishment.
[305]*pickers and stealers*—hands.

O, the recorders! Let me see one. To withdraw[306] with you:— why
do you go about to recover the wind of[307] me, as if you would drive
540 me into a toil?[308]

GUIL. O, my lord, if my duty be too bold, my love is too unmannerly.

HAM. I do not well understand that. Will you play upon this pipe?

GUIL. My lord, I cannot.

HAM. I pray you.

545 GUIL. Believe me, I cannot.

HAM. I do beseech you.

GUIL. I know no touch of it, my lord.

HAM. It is as easy as lying. Govern these ventages[309] with your fingers
and thumb, give it breath with your mouth, and it will discourse
550 most eloquent music. Look you, these are the stops.

GUIL. But these cannot I command to any utterance of harmony I have not
the skill.

HAM. Why, look you now, how unworthy a thing you make of me.
You would play upon me, you would seem to know my stops, you
555 would pluck out the heart of my mystery, you would sound me from
my lowest note to the top of my compass; and there is much music,
excellent voice, in this little organ; yet cannot you make it speak.
'Sblood, do you think I am easier to be played on than a pipe? Call
me what instrument you will, though you can fret me, yet you
560 cannot play upon me.

Enter POLONIUS.

God bless you, Sir.

POL. My lord, the Queen would speak with you, and presently.

HAM. Do you see yonder cloud that's almost in shape of a camel?

565 POL. By the mass, and 'tis like a camel, indeed.

HAM. Methinks it is like a weasel.

POL. It is backed like a weasel.

HAM. Or like a whale?

POL. Very like a whale.

570 HAM. Then I will come to my mother by and by. [*Aside*] They fool me to the
top of my bent.—I will come by and by.

POL. I will say so.   [*Exit* POLONIUS.

HAM. 'By and by' is easily said. Leave me, friends.
                                        [*Exeunt all but* HAMLET.

575 'Tis now the very witching time of night,
When churchyards yawn, and hell itself breathes out

---

[306]*withdraw*—to talk in private.

[307]*recover the wind of*—a hunting metaphor meaning "to get upwind of."

[308]*toil*—net.

[309]*ventages*—wind/breath holes in a reed pipe.

Contagion to this world. Now could I drink hot blood,
And do such bitter business as the day
Would quake to look on. Soft, now to my mother.
580 O heart, lose not thy nature. Let not ever
The soul of Nero[310] enter this firm bosom.
Let me be cruel, not unnatural.
I will speak daggers to her, but use none.
My tongue and soul in this be hypocrites;
585 How in my words soever she be shent,[311]
To give them seals never my soul consent.   [*Exit.*

---

[310]*Nero*—the Roman emperor who put his mother, Agrippina, to death.
[311]*shent*—reproached.

ACT III, SCENE III. *A room in the castle.*

Enter KING, ROSENCRANTZ, and GUILDENSTERN.

	KING.	I like him not, nor stands it safe with us
		To let his madness range. Therefore prepare you.
590		I your commission will forthwith dispatch,
		And he to England shall along with you.
		The terms of our estate may not endure
		Hazard so near us as doth hourly grow
		Out of his brows.
595	GUIL.	We will ourselves provide.
		Most holy and religious fear it is
		To keep those many many bodies safe
		That live and feed upon your Majesty.
	ROS.	The single and peculiar life is bound
600		With all the strength and armour of the mind
		To keep itself from noyance, but much more
		That spirit upon whose weal depends and rests
		The lives of many. The cess[312] of majesty
		Dies not alone, but like a gulf[313] doth draw
605		What's near it with it. It is a massy wheel,
		Fix'd on the summit of the highest mount,
		To whose huge spokes ten thousand lesser things
		Are mortised and adjoin'd; which, when itfalls,
		Each small annexment, petty consequence,
610		Attends the boisterous ruin. Never alone
		Did the King sigh, but with a general groan.
	KING.	Arm you, I pray you, to this speedy voyage,
		For we will fetters put about this fear,
		Which now goes too free-footed.
615	ROS.	We will haste us.
	GUIL.	

[*Exeunt* ROSENCRANTZ *and* GUILDENSTERN.

Enter POLONIUS.

	POL.	My lord, he's going to his mother's closet.
620		Behind the arras I'll convey myself,
		To hear the process. I'll warrant she'll tax him home.
		And, as you said, and wisely was it said,
		'Tis meet that some more audience than a mother,
		Since nature makes them partial, should o'erhear

---

[312]*cess*—decease.
[313]*gulf*—whirlpool.

625		The speech, of vantage.[314] Fare you well, my liege.
		I'll call upon you ere you go to bed,
		And tell you what I, know.
	KING.	Thanks, dear my lord.

[*Exit* POLONIUS.

630   O, my offence is rank, it smells to heaven.
It hath the primal eldest curse upon't,
A brother's murder. Pray can I not,
Though inclination be as sharp as will;
My stronger guilt defeats my strong intent,
635   And, like a man to double business bound,
I stand in pause where I shall first begin,
And both neglect. What if this cursed hand
Were thicker than itself with brother's blood,
Is there not rain enough in the sweet heavens
640   To wash it white as snow? Whereto serves mercy
But to confront the visage of offence?
And what's in prayer but this twofold force,
To be forestalled ere we come to fall,
Or pardon'd being down? Then I'll look up.
645   My fault is past. But O, what form of prayer
Can serve my turn? 'Forgive me my foul murder?'
That cannot be, since I am still possess'd
Of those effects for which I did the murder—
My crown, mine own ambition and my queen.
650   May one be pardon'd and retain the offence?[315]
In the corrupted currents of this world
Offence's gilded hand may shove by justice,
And oft 'tis seen the wicked prize itself
Buys out the law. But 'tis not so above:
655   There is no shuffling, there the action lies
In his[316] true nature, and we ourselves compell'd
Even to the teeth and forehead of our faults
To give in evidence. What then? What rests?
Try what repentance can. What can it not?
660   Yet what can it when one can not repent?
O wretched state, O bosom black as death,
O limed soul, that struggling to be free
Art more engaged! Help, angels! Make assay.[317]

---

[314]*of vantage*—from another vantage point.
[315]*offence*—the fruits of the crime.
[316]*his*—its.
[317]*assay*—attempt.

	Bow, stubborn knees, and, heart with strings of steel,	
665	Be soft as sinews of the new-born babe.	
	All may be well.	[*Retires and kneels.*

Enter HAMLET.

HAM.   Now might I do it pat, now he is praying.
              And now I'll do't. And so he goes to heaven;
670   And so am I revenged. That would be scann'd:[318]
              A villain kills my father, and for that,
              I, his sole son, do this same villain send
              To heaven.
              O, this is hire and salary, not revenge.
675   He took my father grossly, full of bread,
              With all his crimes broad blown,[319] as flush as May;
              And how his audit stands who knows save heaven?
              But in our circumstance[320] I and course of thought,
              Tis heavy with him. And am I then revenged,
680   To take him in the purging of his soul,
              When he is fit and season'd for his passage?
              No.
              Up, sword, and know thou a more horrid hent.[321]
              When he is drunk asleep, or in his rage,
685   Or in the incestuous pleasure of his bed,
              At game, a-swearing, or about some act
              That has no relish of salvation in't,
              Then trip him, that his heels may kick at heaven
              And that his soul may be as damn'd and black
690   As hell, whereto it goes. My mother stays.
              This physic[322] but prolongs thy sickly days.   [*Exit.*

KING.   [*Rising*] My words fly up, my thoughts remain below.
              Words without thoughts never to heaven go.   [*Exit.*

---

[318]*would be scann'd*—understood.
[319]*broad blown*—in full bloom.
[320]*in our circumstance*—viewed from our earthly perspective.
[321]*hent*—grip.
[322]*physic*—remedy (praying).

ACT III, SCENE IV. *The Queen's closet.*[323]

Enter QUEEN *and* POLONIUS.

695	POL.	He will come straight. Look you lay home to him.[324]
		Tell him his pranks have been too broad to bear with,
		And that your grace hath screen'd and stood between
		Much heat and him. I'll silence me even here.
		Pray you, be round[325] with him.
700	QUEEN.	I'll warrant you,
		Fear me not. Withdraw, I hear him coming.

> [POLONIUS *hides behind the arras.*

Enter HAMLET.

	HAM.	Now, mother, what's the matter?
705	QUEEN.	Hamlet, thou hast thy father much offended.
	HAM.	Mother, you have my father much offended.
	QUEEN.	Come, come; you answer with an idle tongue.
	HAM.	Go, go, you question with a wicked tongue.
	QUEEN.	Why, how now, Hamlet?
710	HAM.	What's the matter now?
	QUEEN.	Have you forgot me?
	HAM.	No, by the rood, not so.
		You are the Queen, your husband's brother's wife,
		And—would it were not so—you are my mother.
715	QUEEN.	Nay, then, I'll set those to you that can speak.
	HAM.	Come, come, and sit you down; you shall not budge.
		You go not till I set you up a glass
		Where you may see the inmost part of you.
	QUEEN.	What wilt thou do? Thou wilt not murder me?
720		Help, help, ho!
	POL.	[*Behind*] What, ho! Help, help, help!
	HAM.	[*Drawing*] How now, a rat? Dead for a ducat, dead.

> [*Makes a pass through the arras.*

	POL.	[*Behind*] O, I am slain! [*Falls and dies.*
725	QUEEN.	O me, what hast thou done?
	HAM.	Nay, I know not. Is it the King?
	QUEEN.	O, what a rash and bloody deed is this!
	HAM.	A bloody deed. Almost as bad, good mother,
		As kill a king and marry with his brother.
730	QUEEN.	As kill a king?
	HAM.	Ay, lady, 'twas my word.

> [*Lifts up the arras and discovers* POLONIUS.

---

[323]*closet*—private rooms.
[324]*lay home to him*—be blunt with him.
[325]*round*—direct.

Thou wretched, rash, intruding fool, farewell.
I took thee for thy better. Take thy fortune.

735 Thou findst to be too busy is some danger.—
Leave wringing of your hands. Peace, sit you down,
And let me wring your heart; for so I shall,
If it be made of penetrable stuff,
If damned custom have not braz'd[326] it so,

740 That it be proof[327] and bulwark against sense.[328]

QUEEN.   What have I done, that thou darest wag thy tongue
In noise so rude against me?

HAM.   Such an act
That blurs the grace and blush of modesty,

745 Calls virtue hypocrite, takes off the rose
From the fair forehead of an innocent love,
And sets a blister there, makes marriage vows
As false as dicers' oaths—O, such a deed
As from the body of contraction[329] plucks

750 The very soul, and sweet religion makes
A rhapsody of words. Heaven's face doth glow,[330]
Yea, this solidity and compound mass
With tristful visage, as against the doom,[331]
Is thought-sick at the act.

755 QUEEN.   Ay me, what act,
That roars so loud and thunders in the index?[332]

HAM.   Look here upon this picture, and on this,
The counterfeit presentment of two brothers.
See what a grace was seated on this brow:

760 Hyperion's curls, the front of Jove himself,
An eye like Mars, to threaten and command,
A station[333] like the herald Mercury
New-lighted on a heaven-kissing hill,
A combination and a form indeed

765 Where every god did seem to set his seal
To give the world assurance of a man.
This was your husband. Look you now, what follows.

---

[326]*braz'd*—coated with brass, hardened.
[327]*proof*—impenetrable.
[328]*sense*—reason.
[329]*contraction*—the marriage contract.
[330]*glow*—blush.
[331]*against the doom*—in expectation of the Judgment Day.
[332]*index*—preface, prologue.
[333]*station*—stance.

770	Here is your husband: like a mildew'd ear,[334]
	Blasting his wholesome brother. Have you eyes?
	Could you on this fair mountain leave[335] to feed,
	And batten on this moor?[336] Ha, have you eyes?
	You cannot call it love, for at your age
	The heyday in the blood is tame, it's humble,
	And waits upon the judgement; and what judgement
775	Would step from this to this? Sense sure you have,
	Else could you not have motion, but sure that sense
	Is apoplex'd, for madness would not err,
	Nor sense to ecstasy[337] was ne'er so thrall'd
	But it reserved some quantity of choice,
780	To serve in such a difference. What devil was't
	That thus hath cozen'd you at hoodman-blind?[338]
	Eyes without feeling, feeling without sight,
	Ears without hands or eyes, smelling sans[339] all,
	Or but a sickly part of one true sense
785	Could not so mope.[340]
	O shame, where is thy blush? Rebellious hell,
	If thou canst mutine in a matron's bones,
	To flaming youth let virtue be as wax
	And melt in her own fire. Proclaim no shame
790	When the compulsive ardour gives the charge,
	Since frost itself as actively doth burn,
	And reason panders will.

QUEEN.   O Hamlet, speak no more.
Thou turn'st mine eyes into my very soul,
795   And there I see such black and grained spots
As will not leave their tinct.

HAM.   Nay, but to live
In the rank sweat of an enseamed[341] bed,
Stew'd in corruption, honeying and making love
800   Over the nasty sty—

QUEEN.   O, speak to me no more.
These words like daggers enter in my ears.
No more, sweet Hamlet.

---

[334] *ear*—ear of corn.
[335] *leave*—cease.
[336] *moor*—barren plain.
[337] *ecstasy*—delusion.
[338] *hoodman-blind*—tricked you at blindman's bluff.
[339] *sans*—without.
[340] *mope*—be so senseless.
[341] *enseamed*—seamy, dirty.

	HAM.	A murderer and a villain,
805		A slave that is not twentieth part the tithe[342]
		Of your precedent lord, a vice of kings,
		A cutpurse of the empire and the rule,
		That from a shelf the precious diadem stole
		And put it in his pocket—
810	QUEEN.	No more.
	HAM.	A king of shreds and patches—

Enter GHOST.

		Save me, and hover o'er me with your wings,
		You heavenly guards! What would your gracious figure?
815	QUEEN.	Alas, he's mad.
	HAM.	Do you not come your tardy son to chide,
		That, lapsed in time and passion, lets go by
		The important acting of your dread command?
		O, say!
820	GHOST.	Do not forget. This visitation
		Is but to whet thy almost blunted purpose.
		But look, amazement on thy mother sits.
		O step between her and her fighting soul.
		Conceit[343] in weakest bodies strongest works.
825		Speak to her, Hamlet.
	HAM.	How is it with you, lady?
	QUEEN.	Alas, how is't with you,
		That you do bend your eye on vacancy
		And with the incorporal air do hold discourse?
830		Forth at your eyes your spirits wildly peep,
		And, as the sleeping soldiers in the alarm,
		Your bedded hair, like fife in excrements,
		Start up and stand an end. O gentle son,
		Upon the heat and flame of thy distemper
835		Sprinkle cool patience. Whereon do you look?
	HAM.	On him, on him. Look you how pale he glares.
		His form and cause conjoin'd, preaching to stones,
		Would make them capable.[344]—Do not look upon me,
		Lest with this piteous action you convert
840		My stem effects.[345] Then what I have to do
		Will want true colour—tears perchance for blood.
	QUEEN.	To whom do you speak this?

---

[342]*tithe*—one tenth (traditional annual offering for church maintenance).

[343]*Conceit*—imagination.

[344]*capable*—responsive.

[345]*effects*—intended.

	HAM.	Do you see nothing there?
	QUEEN.	Nothing at all; yet all that is I see.
845	HAM.	Nor did you nothing hear?
	QUEEN.	No, nothing but ourselves.
	HAM.	Why, look you there. Look how it steals away.

My father, in his habit as he lived.

Look where he goes, even now, out at the portal.   [*Exit* GHOST.

850   QUEEN.   This is the very coinage of your brain.

This bodily creation ecstasy

Is very cunning in.

        HAM.   Ecstasy?

My pulse, as yours, doth temperately keep time,

855   And makes as healthful music. It is not madness

That I have utter'd. Bring me to the test,

And I the matter will re-word, which madness

Would gambol[346] from. Mother, for love of grace,

Lay not that flattering unction[347] to your soul,

860   That not your trespass but my madness speaks.

It will but skin[348] and film the ulcerous place,

Whiles rank corruption, mining all within,

Infects unseen. Confess yourself to heaven,

Repent what's past, avoid what is to come,

865   And do not spread the compost on the weeds,

To make them ranker. Forgive me this my virtue,

For in the fatness of these pursy[349] times

Virtue itself of vice must pardon beg,

Yea, curb[350] and woo for leave to do him good.

870   QUEEN.   O Hamlet, thou hast cleft my heart in twain.

        HAM.   O, throw away the worser part of it

And live the purer with the other half.

Good night. But go not to my uncle's bed.

Assume a virtue, if you have it not.

875   That monster, custom, who all sense doth eat,

Of habits evil, is angel yet in this,

That to the use of actions fair and good

He likewise gives a frock or livery,

That aptly is put on. Refrain tonight

880   And that shall lend a kind of easiness

---

[346]*gambol*—skip, shy away.
[347]*unction*—salve.
[348]*skin*—cover with skin.
[349]*pursy*—flabby.
[350]*curb*—bow.

		To the next abstinence, the next more easy;
		For use almost can change the stamp of nature
		And either master the devil, or throw him out
		With wondrous potency. Once more, good night;
885		And when you are desirous to be blest,
		I'll blessing beg of you. For this same lord, [*Pointing to* POLONIUS.
		I do repent. But heaven hath pleased it so,
		To punish me with this, and this with me,
		That I must be their scourge and minister.
890		I will bestow[351] him, and will answer well
		The death I gave him. So, again, good night.
		I must be cruel, only to be kind.
		This bad begins, and worse remains behind.
		One word more, good lady.
895	QUEEN.	What shall I do?
	HAM.	Not this, by no means, that I bid you do:
		Let the bloat[352] King tempt you again to bed,
		Pinch wanton on your cheek, call you his mouse,
		And let him, for a pair of reechy kisses,
900		Or paddling in your neck with his damn'd fingers,
		Make you to ravel all this matter out,
		That I essentially am not in madness,
		But mad in craft. 'Twere good you let him know;
		For who, that's but a queen, fair, sober, wise,
905		Would from a paddock,[353] from a bat, a gib,[354]
		Such dear concernings hide? Who would do so?
		No, in despite of sense and secrecy,
		Unpeg the basket on the house's top,
		Let the birds fly, and like the famous ape,[355]
910		To try conclusions, in the basket creep
		And break your own neck down.
	QUEEN.	Be thou assured, if words be made of breath
		And breath of life, I have no life to breathe
		What thou hast said to me.
915	HAM.	I must to England; you know that?
	QUEEN.	Alack,
		I had forgot. 'Tis so concluded on.
	HAM.	There's letters seal'd, and my two schoolfellows,

---

[351]*bestow*—dispose of.

[352]*bloat*—bloated with drink.

[353]*paddock*—toad.

[354]*gib*—tomcat.

[355]*famous ape*—the ape trying 'to ape' the birds' flight.

Whom I will trust as I will adders fang'd,
920   They bear the mandate. They must sweep my way,
And marshal[356] me to knavery. Let it work;
For 'tis the sport to have the enginer
Hoist[357] with his own petard;[358] and't shall go hard
But I will delve one yard below their mines,
925   And blow them at the moon. O, 'tis most sweet
When in one line two crafts directly meet.
This man shall set me packing.
I'll lug the guts into the neighbour room.
Mother, good night indeed. This counsellor
930   Is now most still, most secret and most grave,
Who was in life a foolish prating knave.
Come, sir, to draw toward an end with you.
Good night, mother.
           [*Exeunt severally;* HAMLET *dragging in* POLONIUS.

---

[356]*marshal*—lead.
[357]*Hoist*—blown up.
[358]*petard*—explosive device.

ACT IV
SCENE I. *A room in the castle.*

Enter KING, QUEEN, ROSENCRANTZ, *and* GUILDENSTERN.

KING.   There's matter in these sighs, these profound heaves;
         You must translate. 'Tis fit we understand them.
5   Where is your son?
QUEEN.   Bestow this place on us[359] a little while.
              [*Exeunt* ROSENCRANTZ *and* GUILDENSTERN.
         Ah, mine own lord, what have I seen tonight!
KING.   What, Gertrude? How does Hamlet?
10 QUEEN. Mad as the sea and wind, when both contend
         Which is the mightier. In his lawless fit,
         Behind the arras hearing something stir,
         Whips out his rapier, cries 'A rat, a rat!'
         And in this brainish apprehension kills
15   The unseen good old man.
KING.   O heavy deed!
         It had been so with us, had we been there.
         His liberty is full of threats to all,
         To you yourself, to us, to everyone.
20   Alas, how shall this bloody deed be answer'd?
         It will be laid to us, whose providence
         Should have kept short,[360] restrain'd and out of haunt,[361]
         This mad young man. But so much was our love,
         We would not understand what was most fit,
25   But, like the owner of a foul disease,
         To keep it from divulging,[362] let it feed
         Even on the pith of life. Where is he gone?
QUEEN.   To draw apart the body he hath kill'd,
         O'er whom—his very madness, like some ore[363]
30   Among a mineral[364] of metals base,
         Shows itself pure—he weeps for what is done.
KING.   O Gertrude, come away.
         The sun no sooner shall the mountains touch,
         But we will, ship him hence; and this vile deed
35   We must, with all our majesty and skill,

---

[359]*Bestow this place on us*—"Leave us alone."
[360]*short*—i.e., close watch.
[361]*out of haunt*—away from public places.
[362]*divulging*—becoming divulged.
[363]*ore*—gold.
[364]*mineral*—mine.

Both countenance and excuse. Ho, Guildenstern!
Enter ROSENCRANTZ *and* GUILDENSTERN.
 Friends both, go join you with some further aid.
 Hamlet in madness hath Polonius slain,
40 And from his mother's closet hath he dragg'd him.
 Go seek him out, speak fair, and bring the body
 Into the chapel. I pray you, haste in this.
    [*Exeunt* ROSENCRANTZ *and* GUILDENSTERN.
 Come, Gertrude, we'll call up our wisest friends,
45 And let them know, both what we mean to do,
 And what's untimely done. So . . . slander,[365]
 Whose whisper o'er the world's diameter
 As level as the cannon to his blank[366]
 Transports his poison'd shot, may miss our name
50 And hit the woundless air. O, come away.
 My soul is full of discord and dismay.   [*Exeunt.*

---

[365]*So . . . slander*—a defective line.
[366]*blank*—target.

ACT IV, SCENE II. *Another room in the castle*

Enter HAMLET.

	HAM.	Safely stowed.
	ROS.	
55		[*Within*] Hamlet! Lord Hamlet!
	GUIL.	
	HAM.	But soft, what noise? Who calls on Hamlet? O, here they come.

Enter ROSENCRANTZ *and* GUILDENSTERN.

	ROS.	What have you done, my lord, with the dead body?
60	HAM.	Compounded it with dust, whereto 'tis kin.
	ROS.	Tell us where 'tis, that we may take it thence and bear it to the chapel.
	HAM.	Do not believe it.
	ROS.	Believe what?
65	HAM.	That I can keep your counsel and not mine own. Besides, to be demanded of a sponge—what replication[367] should be made by the son of a king?
	ROS.	Take you me for a sponge, my lord?
	HAM.	Ay, sir, that soaks up the King's countenance, his rewards, his
70		authorities. But such officers do the King best service in the end. He keeps them, like an ape, in the corner of his jaw—first mouthed, to be last swallowed. When he needs what you have gleaned, it is but squeezing you, and, sponge, you shall be dry again.
	ROS.	I understand you not, my lord.
75	HAM.	I am glad of it. A knavish speech sleeps in a foolish ear.
	ROS.	My lord, you must tell us where the body is, and go with us to the King.
	HAM.	The body is with the King, but the King is not with the body. The King is a thing—
80	GUIL.	A thing, my lord?
	HAM.	Of nothing. Bring me to him. [*Exeunt.*

---

[367]*replication*—reply.

ACT IV, SCENE III. *Another room in the castle.*

Enter KING, *attended.*

| | KING. | I have sent to seek him, and to find the body. |

Enter KING, *attended.*

KING.   I have sent to seek him, and to find the body.
        How dangerous is it that this man goes loose!

85   Yet must not we put the strong law on him.
        He's loved of the distracted[368] multitude,
        Who like not in their judgement, but their eyes;
        And where 'tis so, the offender's scourge is weigh'd,
        But never the offence. To bear all smooth and even,

90   This sudden sending him away must seem
        Deliberate pause.[369] Diseases desperate grown
        By desperate appliance[370] are relieved,
        Or not at all.

Enter ROSENCRANTZ.

95   How now, what hath befall'n?

ROS.   Where the dead body is bestow'd, my lord,
        We cannot get from him.

KING.   But where is he?

ROS.   Without, my lord; guarded, to know your pleasure.

100 KING.   Bring him before us.

ROS.   Ho, Guildenstern! Bring in my lord.

Enter HAMLET *and* GUILDENSTERN.

KING.   Now, Hamlet, where's Polonius?

HAM.   At supper.

105 KING.   At supper? Where?

HAM.   Not where he eats, but where he is eaten. A certain convocation of politic worms are e'en at him. Your worm is your only emperor for diet. We fat all creatures else to fat us, and we fat ourselves for maggots. Your fat king and your lean beggar is but variable

110   service,[371] two dishes, but to one table. Thats the end.

KING.   Alas, alas!

HAM.   A man may fish with the worm that hath eat of a king, and eat of the fish that hath fed of that worm.

KING.   What dost thou mean by this?

115 HAM.   Nothing but to show you how a king may go a progress[372] through the guts of a beggar.

KING.   Where is Polonius?

---

[368]*distracted*—unthinking.
[369]*Deliberate pause*—the result of careful consideration.
[370]*appliance*—treatment.
[371]*service*—serving (of food).
[372]*progress*—royal journey, procession.

	HAM.	In heaven. Send thither to see. If your messenger find him not there,
		seek him i'the other place yourself. But indeed, if you find him not
120		within this month, you shall nose him as you go up the stairs into the
		lobby.
	KING.	[*To some* Attendants] Go seek him there.
	HAM.	He will stay till you come. [*Exeunt* Attendants.
	KING.	Hamlet, this deed, for thine especial safety—
125		Which we do tender,[373] as we dearly grieve
		For that which thou hast done—must send thee hence
		With fiery quickness. Therefore prepare thyself.
		The bark is ready and the wind at help,
		The associates tend,[374] and everything is bent
130		For England.
	HAM.	For England?
	KING.	Ay, Hamlet.
	HAM.	Good.
	KING.	So is it, if thou knew'st our purposes.
135	HAM.	I see a cherub that sees them. But, come; for England. Farewell, dear
		mother.
	KING.	Thy loving father, Hamlet.
	HAM.	My mother. Father and mother is man and wife, man and wife is one
		flesh, and so, my mother. Come for England. [*Exit.*
140	KING.	Follow him at foot. Tempt him with speed aboard.
		Delay it not. I'll have him hence tonight.
		Away, for every thing is seal'd and done
		That else leans on the affair. Pray you, make haste.
		[*Exeunt* ROSENCRANTZ *and* GUILDENSTERN.
145		And, England,[375] if my love thou hold'st at aught—
		As my great power thereof may give thee sense,
		Since yet thy cicatrice looks raw and red
		After the Danish sword, and thy free awe
		Pays homage to us—thou mayst not coldly set[376]
150		Our sovereign process; which imports at full,
		By letters congruing to that effect,
		The present death of Hamlet. Do it, England;
		For like the hectic[377] in my blood he rages,
		And thou must cure me. Till I know 'tis done,
155		Howe'er my haps, my joys were ne'er begun. [*Exit.*

---

[373]*tender*—hold dear.
[374]*tend*—attend.
[375]*England*—the King of England.
[376]*coldly set*—regard with indifference.
[377]*hectic*—fever.

ACT IV, SCENE IV. *A plain in Denmark.*

Enter FORTINBRAS, *a* Captain *and* Soldiers, *marching.*

	FOR.	Go, captain, from me greet the Danish king.
		Tell him that by his license Fortinbras
		Craves the conveyance of a promised march
160		Over his kingdom. You know the rendezvous.
		If that his Majesty would aught with us,
		We shall express our duty in his eye;[378]
		And let him know so.
	CAP.	I will do't, my lord.
165	FOR.	Go softly on. [*Exeunt* FORTINBRAS *and* Soldiers.

Enter HAMLET, ROSENCRANTZ, GUILDENSTERN, *and others.*

	HAM.	Good sir, whose powers are these?
	CAP.	They are of Norway, sir.
	HAM.	How purposed, sir, I pray you?
170	CAP.	Against some part of Poland.
	HAM.	Who commands them, sir?
	CAP.	The nephew to old Norway, Fortinbras.
	HAM.	Goes it against the main of Poland, sir,
		Or for some frontier?
175	CAP.	Truly to speak, and with no addition,
		We go to gain a little patch of ground
		That hath in it no profit but the name.
		To pay five ducats, five, I would not farm it,
		Nor will it yield to Norway or the Pole
180		A ranker rate, should it be sold in fee.[379]
	HAM.	Why, then the Polack never will defend it.
	CAP.	Yes, it is already garrison'd.
	HAM.	Two thousand souls and twenty thousand ducats
		Will not debate the question of this straw!
185		This is the imposthume[380] of much wealth and peace,
		That inward breaks, and shows no cause without
		Why the man dies. I humbly thank you, sir.
	CAP.	God be wi' you, sir. [*Exit.*
	ROS.	Will't please you go, my lord?
190	HAM.	I'll be with you straight. Go a little before.
		[*Exeunt all but* HAMLET.
		How all occasions do inform against me,

---

[378]*his eye*—his presence.
[379]*in fee*—outright, freehold.
[380]*imposthume*—ulcer.

And spur my dull revenge. What is a man,
If his chief good and market of his time
195 Be but to sleep and feed? A beast, no more.
Sure, he that made us with such large discourse,[381]
Looking before and after, gave us not
That capability and godlike reason
To fust[382] in us unused. Now, whether it be
200 Bestial oblivion, or some craven scruple
Of thinking too precisely on the event—
A thought which, quarter'd, hath but one part wisdom
And ever three parts coward— do not know
Why yet I live to say this thing's to do,
205 Sith I have cause, and will, and strength, and means,
To do't. Examples gross as earth exhort me:
Witness this army, of such mass and charge,
Led by a delicate and tender prince,
Whose spirit with divine ambition puff'd
210 Makes mouths at the invisible event,
Exposing what is mortal and unsure
To all that fortune, death and danger dare,
Even for an eggshell. Rightly to be great
Is not to stir without great argument,
215 But greatly to find quarrel in a straw
When honour's at the stake. How stand I then,
That have a father kill'd, a mother stain'd,
Excitements of my reason and my blood,
And let all sleep, while to my shame I see
220 The imminent death of twenty thousand men,
That for a fantasy and trick[383] of fame
Go to their graves like beds, fight for a plot
Whereon the numbers cannot try the cause,[384]
Which is not tomb enough and continent
225 To hide the slain? O, from this time forth,
My thoughts be bloody, or be nothing worth.   [*Exit.*

---

[381]*discourse*—rationality.
[382]*fust*—grow moldy.
[383]*trick*—trifle.
[384]*Whereon . . . cause*—i.e., the territory is not large enough to be the battlefield.

ACT IV, SCENE V. *Elsinore. A room in the castle.*

Enter QUEEN, HORATIO, *and a* Gentleman.

	QUEEN.	I will not speak with her.
	GENT.	She is importunate,
230		Indeed distract. Her mood will needs be pitied.
	QUEEN.	What would she have?
	GENT.	She speaks much of her father, says she hears
		There's tricks i' the world, and hems and beats her heart,
		Spurns enviously at straws,[385] speaks things in doubt,
235		That carry but half sense. Her speech is nothing,
		Yet the unshaped use of it doth move
		The hearers to collection.[386] They aim at it,
		And botch the words up fit to their own thoughts,
		Which, as her winks and nods and gestures yield them,
240		Indeed would make one think there might be thought,
		Though nothing sure, yet much unhappily.
	HOR.	'Twere good she were spoken with, for she may strew
		Dangerous conjectures in ill-breeding minds.
	QUEEN.	Let her come in. [*Exit* Gentleman.
245		[*Aside*] To my sick soul, as sin's true nature is,
		Each toy[387] seems prologue to some great amiss.[388]
		So full of artless jealousy[389] is guilt,
		It spills itself in fearing to be spilt.

Enter Gentleman, *with* OPHELIA.

250	OPH.	Where is the beauteous Majesty of Denmark?
	QUEEN.	How now, Ophelia?
	OPH.	[*Sings*] How should I your true love know
		From another one?
		By his cockle hat and staff
255		And his sandal shoon.[390]
	QUEEN.	Alas, sweet lady, what imports this song?
	OPH.	Say you? Nay, pray you, mark.
		[*Sings*] He is dead and gone, lady,
		He is dead and gone;
260		At his head a grass-green turf,
		At his heels a stone.
		Oh, oh!

---

[385]*at straws*—at trifles.
[386]*collection*—to collect what sense they can.
[387]*toy*—trifle.
[388]*great amiss*—calamity.
[389]*jealousy*—apprehension.
[390]*shoon*—shoes.

	QUEEN.	Nay, but, Ophelia—
	OPH.	Pray you, mark.
265		[*Sings*] White his shroud as the mountain snow—

Enter KING.

	QUEEN.	Alas, look here, my lord.
	OPH.	[Sings] Larded[391] with sweet flowers,
		Which bewept to the grave did go
270		With true-love showers.
	KING.	How do you, pretty lady?
	OPH.	Well, God 'ild you.[392] They say the owl was a baker's daughter.
		Lord, we know what we are, but know not what we may be.
		God be at your table.
275	KING.	Conceit upon her father.
	OPH.	Pray you, let's have no words of this;. but when they ask you what
		it means, say you this:
		[*Sings*] Tomorrow is Saint Valentine's day,
		All in the morning betime,
280		And I a maid at your window,
		To be your Valentine.
		Then up he rose, and donn'd his clothes,
		And dupp'd[393] the chamber door,
		Let in the maid, that out a maid
285		Never departed more.
	KING.	Pretty Ophelia—
	OPH.	Indeed, without an oath, I'll make an end on't.
		[*Sings*] By Gis[394] and by Saint Charity,
		Alack, and fie for shame!
290		Young men will do't, if they come to't,
		By Cock,[395] they are to blame.
		Quoth she, 'Before you tumbled me,
		You promised me to wed.'
295		He answers:
		'So would I ha' done, by yonder sun,
		An thou hadst not come to my bed.'
	KING.	How long hath she been thus?

---

[391]*Larded*—garnished.
[392]*God 'ild you*—God yield (reward) you.
[393]*dupp'd*—opened.
[394]*Gis*—a corruption of "Jesus."
[395]*Cock*—a corruption of "God."

	OPH.	I hope all will be well. We must be patient. But I cannot choose but
300		weep, to think they should lay him i' the cold ground. My brother
		shall know of it. And so I thank you for your good counsel. Come, my
		coach. Good night, ladies; good night, sweet ladies; good night, good
		night. [*Exit.*
	KING.	Follow her close. Give her good watch, I pray you.
305		[*Exit* HORATIO.

O, this is the poison of deep grief; it springs

All from her father's death. O Gertrude, Gertrude,

When sorrows come, they come not single spies,

But in battalions. First, her father slain;

310   Next, your son gone, and he most violent author

Of his own just remove; the people muddied,

Thick and unwholesome in their thoughts and whispers,

For good Polonius' death; and we have done but greenly,[396]

In hugger-mugger[397] to inter him; poor Ophelia

315   Divided from herself and her fair judgement,

Without the which we are pictures, or mere beasts;

Last, and as much containing as all these,

Her brother is in secret come from France,

Feeds on his wonder,[398] keeps himself in clouds,

320   And wants not buzzers[399] to infect his ear

With pestilent speeches of his father's death;

Wherein necessity, of matter beggar'd,

Will nothing stick our person to arraign[400]

In ear and ear. O my dear Gertrude, this,

325   Like to a murdering-piece[401] in many places

Gives me superfluous death.   [*A noise within.*

	QUEEN.	Alack, what noise is this?
	KING.	Where are my Switzers?[402] Let them guard the door.
	Enter another Gentleman.	
330		What is the matter?
	GENT.	Save yourself, my lord.
		The ocean, overpeering of his list,[403]
		Eats not the flats with more impetuous haste

---

[396]*greenly*—foolishly.

[397]*In hugger-mugger*—secret.

[398]*wonder*—bewilderment.

[399]*buzzers*—rumor-mongers.

[400]*arraign*—accuse.

[401]*murdering-piece*—a type of cannon firing schrapnel.

[402]*Switzers*—Swiss bodyguards.

[403]*overpeering of his list*—rising above its high water mark.

Than young Laertes, in a riotous head,[404]

335 O'erbears your officers. The rabble call him lord;

And, as the world were now but to begin,

Antiquity forgot, custom not known—

The ratifiers and props of every word—

They cry 'Choose we! Laertes shall be king.'

340 Caps, hands and tongues applaud it to the clouds,

'Laertes shall be king, Laertes king.'

QUEEN. How cheerfully on the false trail they cry.

O, this is counter, you false Danish dogs! [*Noise within.*

KING. The doors are broke.

345 *Enter* LAERTES, *armed;* Danes *following.*

LAER. Where is this King? Sirs, stand you all without.

DANES. No, let's come in.

LAER. I pray you, give me leave.

DANES. We will, we will.

350 LAER. I thank, you. Keep the door. [*They retire without the door.*

O thou vile king,

Give me my father.

QUEEN. Calmly, good Laertes.

LAER. That drop of blood that's calm proclaims me bastard,

355 Cries cuckold to my father, brands the harlot

Even here, between the chaste unsmirched brows

Of my true mother.

KING. What is the cause, Laertes,

That thy rebellion looks so giant-like?

360 Let him go, Gertrude. Do not fear[405] our person.

There's such divinity doth hedge a king

That treason can but peep to what it would,

Acts little of his will. Tell me, Laertes,

Why thou art thus incensed. Let him go, Gertrude.

365 Speak, man.

LAER. Where is my father?

KING. Dead.

QUEEN. But not by him.

KING. Let him demand his fill.

370 LAER. How came he dead? I'll not be juggled with.

To hell, allegiance! Vows, to the blackest devil!

Conscience and grace, to the profoundest pit!

I dare damnation. To this point I stand,

That both the worlds I give to negligence,

---

[404]*head*—head of a riotous band.

[405]*fear*—fear for.

375		Let come what comes; only I'll be revenged
		Most throughly[406] for my father.
	KING.	Who shall stay you?
	LAER.	My will, not all the world.
		And for my means, I'll husband them so well,
380		They shall go far with little.
	KING.	Good Laertes,
		If you desire to know the certainty
		Of your dear father's death, is't writ in your revenge
		That, swoopstake,[407] you will draw both friend and foe,
385		Winner and loser?
	LAER.	None but his enemies.
	KING.	Will you know them then?
	LAER.	To his good friends thus wide I'll ope my arms,
		And, like the kind life-rendering pelican,[408]
390		Repast them with my blood.
	KiNG.	Why, now you speak
		Like a good child and a true gentleman.
		That I am guiltless of your father's death,
		And am most sensibly in grief for it,
395		It shall as level to your judgement pierce
		As day does to your eye.
	DANES.	[*Within*] Let her come in.
	LAER.	How now, what noise is that?
	Enter OPHELIA.	
400		O heat, dry up my brains! Tears seven times salt,
		Burn out the sense and virtue[409] of mine eye!
		By heaven, thy madness shall be paid with weight,
		Till our scale turn the beam. O rose of May!
		Dear maid, kind sister, sweet Ophelia!
405		O heavens, is't possible a young maid's wits
		Should be as mortal as an old man's life?
		Nature is fine in love, and where 'tis fine
		It sends some precious instance[410] of itself
		After the thing it loves.
410	OPH.	[*Sings*] They bore him barefired on the bier;
		And in his grave rain'd many a tear—
		Fare you well, my dove.

---

[406]*throughly*—thoroughly.

[407]*swoopstake*—sweepstake; i.e., you may sweep up anything.

[408]*kind life-rendering pelican*—behaving in accordance with its nature, to feed its young with its own blood.

[409]*virtue*—power.

[410]*instance*—portion, sample.

	LAER.	Hadst thou thy wits, and didst persuade revenge,
		It could not move thus.
415	OPH.	You must sing 'down a-down,' and you 'Call him a-down-a.'
		O, how the wheel[411] becomes it! It is the false steward that stole his
		master's daughter.
	LAER.	This nothing's more than matter.
	OPH.	There's rosemary, that's for remembrance. Pray you, love, remember.
420		And there is pansies, that's for thoughts.
	LAER.	A document in madness: thoughts and remembrance fitted.
	OPH.	There's fennel for you, and columbines.[412] There's rue for you, and
		here's some for me. We may call it herb of grace[413] o' Sundays. O,
		you must wear your rue with a difference.[414] There's a daisy.[415] I
425		would give you some violets,[416] but they withered all when my
		father died. They say a made a good end—
		[*Sings*] For bonny sweet Robin is all my joy.
	LAER.	Thought and affliction, passion, hell itself,
		She turns to favour and to prettiness.
430	OPH.	[*Sings*] And will a not come again?
		And will a not. come again?
		No, no, he is dead,
		Go to thy death-bed,
		He never will come again.
435		His beard was as white as snow,
		All flaxen was his poll.
		He is gone, he is gone,
		And we cast away moan.
		God ha' mercy on his soul.
440		And of[417] all Christian souls, I pray God. God be wi' you.
		[*Exit.*
	LAER.	Do you see this, O God?
	KING.	Laertes, I must commune with your grief,
		Or you deny me right. Go but apart,
445		Make choice of whom your wisest friends you will,
		And they shall hear and judge 'twixt you and me.
		If by direct or by collateral[418] hand

---

[411]*wheel*—poetic refrain.

[412]*fennel . . . columbines*—plants signifying falsity and infidelity.

[413]*rue . . . herb of grace*—plant signifying repentance.

[414]*a difference*—a mark of distinction.

[415]*daisy*—signifying unhappy love.

[416]*violets*—signifying faithfulness.

[417]*of*—for.

[418]*collateral*—indirect.

They find us touch'd,[419] we will our kingdom give,
Our crown, our life, and all that we call ours,
450   To you in satisfaction. But if not,
Be you content to lend your patience to us,
And we shall jointly labour with your soul
To give it due content.

LAER.   Let this be so.
455   His means of death, his obscure funeral—
No trophy,[420] sword, nor hatchment[421] o'er his bones,
No noble rite nor formal ostentation—[422]
Cry to be heard, as 'twere from heaven to earth,
That I must call't in question.

460   KING.   So you shall.
And where the offence is, let the great axe fall.
I pray you, go with me.   *[Exeunt.*

---

[419]*touch'd*—implicated.
[420]*trophy*—memorial.
[421]*hatchment*—engraved coat of arms.
[422]*ostentation*—ceremony.

ACT IV, SCENE VI. *Another room in the castle.*

Enter HORATIO *and a* Servant.

	HOR.	What are they that would speak with me?
465	SERV.	Seafaring men, sir. They say they have letters for you.
	HOR.	Let them come in. [*Exit* Servant.
		I do not know from what part of the world
		I should be greeted, if not from Lord Hamlet.

Enter Sailors.

470	FIRST SAIL.	God bless you, sir.
	HOR.	Let him bless thee too.
	FIRST SAIL.	He shall, sir, an't please him. There's a letter for you, sir. It comes from the ambassador that was bound for England—if your name be Horatio, as I am let to know it is.
475	HOR.	[*Reads*] Horatio, when thou shalt have overlooked[423] this, give these fellows some means to the King. They have letters for him. Ere we were two days old at sea, a pirate of very warlike appointment gave us chase. Finding ourselves too slow of sail, we put on a compelled valour, and in the grapple I boarded them. On the instant they got clear of our ship; so I alone became their prisoner. They have dealt with me like thieves of mercy; but they knew what they did: I am to do a turn for them. Let the King have the letters I have sent, and repair thou to me with as much speed as thou wouldest fly death. I have words to speak in thine ear will make thee dumb, yet are they much too light for the bore[424] of the matter. These good fellows will bring thee where I am. Rosencrantz and Guildenstern hold their course for England. Of them I have much to tell thee. Farewell.

He that thou knowest thine, HAMLET.

		Come, I will make you way for these your letters,
		And do't the speedier, that you may direct me
490		To him from whom you brought them. [*Exeunt.*

---

[423]*overlooked*—looked over.
[424]*bore*—i.e., Hamlet's words are like shot too light for the caliber of the gun.

ACT IV, SCENE VII. *Another room in the castle.*

Enter KING *and* LAERTES.

	KING.	Now must your conscience my acquittance seal,
		And you must put me in your heart for friend,
		Sith you have heard, and with a knowing ear,
495		That he which hath your noble father slain
		Pursued my life.
	LAER.	It well appears. But tell me
		Why you proceeded not against these feats,[425]
		So crimeful and so capital in nature,
500		As by your safety, wisdom, all things else,
		You mainly[426] were stirr'd up.
	KING.	O, for two special reasons,
		Which may to you perhaps seem much unsinew'd,
		But yet to me they're strong. The Queen his mother
505		Lives almost by his looks; and for myself—
		My virtue or my plague, be it either which—
		She's so conjunctive[427] to my life and soul
		That, as the star moves not but in his sphere,
		I could not but by her. The other motive,
510		Why to a public count[428] I might not go,
		Is the great love the general gender[429] bear him,
		Who, dipping all his faults in their affection,
		Would, like the spring that turneth wood to stone,
		Convert his gyves[430] to graces; so that my arrows,
515		Too slightly timber'd for so loud a wind,
		Would have reverted to my bow again
		And not where I had aim'd them.
	LAER.	And so have I a noble father lost,
		A sister driven into desperate terms,
520		Whose worth, if praises may go back again,
		Stood challenger on mount of all the age
		For her perfections. But my revenge will come.
	KING.	Break not your sleeps for that. You must not think
		That we are made of stuff so flat and dull
525		That we can let our beard be shook with danger
		And think it pastime. You shortly shall hear more.

---

[425] *feats*—wicked deeds.
[426] *mainly*—mightily.
[427] *conjunctive*—closely joined.
[428] *count*—account.
[429] *general gender*—common people.
[430] *gyves*—fetters; character impediments.

I loved your father, and we love ourself.

And that, I hope, will teach you to imagine—

Enter a Messenger, *with letters.*

530 How now? What news?

MESS. Letters, my lord, from Hamlet.

This to your Majesty; this to the Queen.

KING. From Hamlet? Who brought them?

MESS. Sailors, my lord, they say. I saw them not.

535 They were given me by Claudio. He received them

Of him that brought them.

KING. Laertes, you shall hear them.—

Leave us. [*Exit* Messenger.

[*Reads*] High and mighty, you shall know I am set naked[431] on your

540 kingdom. Tomorrow shall I beg leave to see your kingly eyes, when I shall,

first asking your pardon, thereunto recount the occasion of my sudden and

more strange return.

HAMLET.

What should this mean? Are all the rest come back?

545 Or is it some abuse,[432] and no such thing?

LAER. Know you the hand?

KING. 'Tis Hamlet's character.[433] 'Naked'—

And in a postscript here, he says 'Alone.'

Can you advise me?

550 LAER. I'm lost in it, my lord. But let him come.

It warms the very sickness in my heart

That I shall live and tell him to his teeth,

'Thus diest thou.'

KING. If it be so, Laertes—

555 As how should it be so, how otherwise?—

Will you be ruled by me?

LAER. Ay, my lord,

So you will not o'errule me to a peace.

KING. To thine own peace. If he be now return'd,

560 As checking at[434] his voyage, and that he means

No more to undertake it, I will work him

To an exploit now ripe in my device,

Under the which he shall not choose but fall;

And for his death no wind of blame shall breathe,

---

[431]*naked*—destitute.

[432]*abuse*—deception.

[433]*character*—handwriting.

[434]*checking at*—turning from.

565		But even his mother shall uncharge the practice,[435]
		And call it accident.
	LAER.	My lord, I will be ruled;
		The rather, if you could devise it so
		That I might be the organ.
570	KING.	It falls right.
		You have been talk'd of since your travel much,
		And that in Hamlet's hearing, for a quality
		Wherein, they say, you shine. Your sum of parts
		Did not together pluck such envy from him,
575		As did that one, and that in my regard
		Of the unworthiest siege.[436]
	LAER.	What part is that, my lord?
	KING.	A very ribbon in the cap of youth,
		Yet needful too; for youth no less becomes
580		The light and careless livery that it wears
		Than seffled age his sables and his weeds,
		Importing health and graveness. Two months since,
		Here was a gentleman of Normandy—
		I've seen myself, and served against, the French,
585		And they can well on horseback; but this gallant
		Had witchcraft in't. He grew unto his seat,
		And to such wondrous doing brought his horse
		As had he been incorpsed and demi-natured[437]
		With the brave beast. So far he topp'd my thought
590		That I, in forgery of shapes and tricks,
		Come short of what he did.
	LAER.	A Norman was't?
	KING.	A Norman.
	LAER.	Upon my life, Lamord.
595	KING.	The very same.
	LAER.	I know him well. He is the brooch indeed
		And gem of all the nation.
	KING..	He made confession of[438] you,
		And gave you such a masterly report,
600		For art and exercise in your defence,[439]
		And for your rapier most especial,
		That he cried out, 'twould be a sight indeed

---

[435]*practice*—not note the plot.
[436]*siege*—seat, rank.
[437]*demi-natured*—horse and he became one.
[438]*made confession of*—spoke of.
[439]*defence*—fencing skill.

		If one could match you. The scrimers[440] of their nation,
		He swore, had neither motion, guard, nor eye,
605		If you opposed them. Sir, this report of his
		Did Hamlet so envenom with his envy
		That he could nothing do but wish and beg
		Your sudden coming o'er, to play with him.
		Now, out of this—
610	LAER.	What out of this, my lord?
	KING.	Laertes, was your father dear to you?
		Or are you like the painting of a sorrow,
		A face without a heart?
	LAER.	Why ask you this?
615	KING.	Not that I think you did not love your father,
		But that I know love is begun by time,
		And that I see, in passages of proof,[441]
		Time qualifies[442] the spark and fire of it.
		There lives within the very flame of love
620		A kind of wick or snuff that will abate it;
		And nothing is at a like goodness still,
		For goodness, growing to a pleurisy,
		Dies in his own too much. That we would do,
		We should do when we would; for this 'would' changes
625		And hath abatements and delays as many
		As there are tongues, are hands, are accidents,
		And then this 'should' is like a spendthrift sigh
		That hurts by easing. But, to the quick o' the ulcer:
		Hamlet comes back; what would you undertake
630		To show yourself your father's son in deed
		More than in words?
	LAER.	To cut his throat i' the church.
	KING.	No place indeed should murder sanctuarize.
		Revenge should have no bounds. But, good Laertes,
635		Will you do this, keep close within your chamber.
		Hamlet return'd shall know you are come home.
		We'll put on[443] those shall praise your excellence
		And set a double varnish on the fame
		The Frenchman gave you, bring you in fine[444] together
640		And wager on your heads. He, being remiss,[445]

[440]*scrimers*—fencers.
[441]*passages of proof*—reliable instances.
[442]*qualifies*—diminishes.
[443]*put on*—urge on.
[444]*in fine*—in the end.
[445]*remiss*—unsuspecting.

		Most generous and free from all contriving,
		Will not peruse the foils, so that with ease,
		Or with a little shuffling, you may choose
		A sword unbated,[446] and in a pass[447] of practice
645		Requite him for your father.
	LAER.	I will do't.
		And for that purpose I'll anoint my sword.
		I bought an unction[448] of a mountebank,
		So mortal that but dip a knife in it,
650		Where it draws blood no cataplasm[449] so rare,
		Collected from all simples[450] that have virtue
		Under the moon, can save the thing from death
		That is but scratch'd withal. I'll touch my point
		With this contagion that, if I gall[451] him slightly,
655		It may be death.
	KING.	Let's further think of this,
		Weigh what convenience both of time and means
		May fit us to our shape. If this should fail,
		And that our drift[452] look through our bad performance,
660		'Twere better not assay'd. Therefore this project
		Should have a back or second that might hold
		If this did blast in proof.[453] Soft, let me see.
		We'll make a solemn wager on your cunnings—[454]
		I ha't!
665		When in your motion you are hot and dry—
		As make your bouts more violent to that end—
		And that he calls for drink, I'll have prepared him
		A chalice for the nonce; whereon but sipping,
		If he by chance escape'your venom'd stuck,[455]
670		Our purpose may hold there. But stay, what noise?
	Enter QUEEN.	
		How now, sweet Queen?
	QUEEN.	One woe doth tread upon another's heel,
		So fast they follow. Your sister's drown'd, Laertes.

---

[446]*unabated*—unblunted (without its point shielded).

[447]*pass*—thrust.

[448]*unction*—ointment.

[449]*cataplasm*—plaster, poultice.

[450]*simples*—herbs.

[451]*gall*—wound.

[452]*drift*—scheme.

[453]*blast in proof*—fail in the test.

[454]*your cunnings*—your respective skills.

[455]*stuck*—stick, sword.

675	LAER.	Drown'd? O, where?
	QUEEN.	There is a willow grows aslant a brook,
		That shows his hoary leaves in the glassy stream.
		Therewith fantastic garlands did she make
		Of crow-flowers, nettles, daisies, and long purples,
680		That liberal shepherds give a grosser name,
		But our cold maids do dead men's fingers call them.
		There, on the pendent boughs her crownet weeds
		Clambering to hang, an envious sliver broke;
		When down her weedy trophies and herself
685		Fell in the weeping brook. Her clothes spread wide,
		And mermaid-like awhile they bore her up;
		Which time she chanted snatches of old lauds,[456]
		As one incapable[457] of her own distress,
		Or like a creature native and indued
690		Unto[458] that element. But long it could not be
		Till that her garments, heavy with their drink,
		Pull'd the poor wretch from her melodious lay
		To muddy death.
	LAER.	Alas, then she is drown'd.
695	QUEEN.	Drown'd, drown'd.
	LAER.	Too much of water hast thou, poor Ophelia,
		And therefore I forbid my tears. But yet
		It is our trick;[459] nature her custom holds,
		Let shame say what it will. When these are gone,
700		The woman will be out.[460] Adieu, my lord.
		I have a speech of fire that fain would blaze,
		But that this folly douts it.[461] [*Exit.*
	KING.	Let's follow, Gertrude.
		How much I had to do to calm his rage.
705		Now fear I this will give it start again;
		Therefore let's follow. [*Exeunt.*

---

[456]*lauds*—hymns.

[457]*incapable*—unaware.

[458]*indued Unto*—suited to live in.

[459]*our trick*—in our peculiar nature.

[460]*When . . . out*—when these tears are done, so too my softer nature.

[461]*this folly douts it*—this weeping extinguishes it.

ACT V.
SCENE I. *A churchyard.*

Enter two Clowns, *with spades, &c.*

FIRST CLO. Is she to be buried in Christian burial that wilfully seeks her own salvation?

SEC. CLO. I tell thee she is; and therefore make her grave straight. The crowner[462] hath sat on her, and finds it Christian burial.

FIRST CLO. How can that be, unless she drowned herself in her own defence?

SEC. CLO. Why, 'tis found so.

FIRST CLO. It must be *se offendendo*;[463] it cannot be else. For here lies the point: if I drown myself wittingly, it argues an act, and an act hath three branches: it. is to act, to do, and to perform; argal,[464] she drowned herself wittingly.

SEC. CLO. Nay, but hear you, Goodman Delver—

FIRST CLO. Give me leave. Here lies the water—good. Here stands the man—good. If the man go to this water and drown himself, it is, will he, nill he, he goes. Mark you that. But if the water come to him and drown him, he drowns not himself; argal, he that is not guilty of his own death shortens not his own life.

SEC. CLO. But is this law?

FIRST CLO. Ay, marry, is't; crowner's quest[465] law.

SEC. CLO. Will you ha' the truth on't? If this had not been a gentlewoman, she should have been buried out o' Christian burial.

FIRST CLO. Why, there thou say'st. And the more pity that great folk should have countenance in this world to drown or hang themselves, more than their even[466] Christian. Come, my spade. There is no ancient gentlemen but gardeners, ditchers and grave-makers: they hold up[467] Adam's profession.

SEC. CLO. Was he a gentleman?

FIRST CLO. A was the first that ever bore arms.

SEC. CLO. Why, he had none.

FIRST CLO. What, art a heathen? How dost thou understand the Scripture? The Scripture says Adam digged. Could he dig without arms? I'll put another question to thee. If thou answerest me not to the purpose, confess thyself—

SEC. CLO. Go to.

---

[462]*crowner*—coroner.

[463]*se offendendo*—a blunder for *se defendendo* (in self-defense).

[464]*argal*—"ergo," therefore.

[465]*quest*—inquest.

[466]*even*—fellow.

[467]*hold up*—uphold.

35   FIRST CLO.   What is he that builds stronger than either the mason, the shipwright, or the carpenter?

SEC. CLO.   The gallows-maker; for that frame outlives a thousand tenants.

FIRST CLO.   I like thy wit well, in good faith. The gallows does well. But how does it well? It does well to those that do ill. Now, thou dost ill to

40   say the gallows is built stronger than the church; argal, the gallows may do well to thee. To't again, come.

SEC. CLO.   'Who builds stronger than a mason, a shipwright, or a carpenter?'

FIRST CLO.   Ay, tell me that, and unyoke.[468]

SEC. CLO.   Marry, now I can tell.

45   FIRST CLO.   To't.

SEC. CLO.   Mass, I cannot tell.

Enter HAMLET *and* HORATIO, *afar off.*

FIRST CLO.   Cudgel thy brains no more about it, for your dull ass will not mend his pace with beating, and when you are asked this question next,

50   say 'A grave-maker.' The houses that he makes last till doomsday. Go, get thee to Yaughan. Fetch me a stoup of liquor.

> [*Exit Sec. Clown; First Clown* digs, *and sings.*
>
> In youth, when I did love, did love,
> Methought it was very sweet,
55   To contract,[469] O, the time, for-a my behove,[470]
> O, methought, there-a was nothing-a meet.

HAM.   Has this fellow no feeling of his business, that he sings at gravemaking?

HOR.   Custom hath made it in him a property of easiness.[471]

60   HAM.   'Tis e'en so. The hand of little employment hath the daintier sense.

FIRST CLO.   [*Sings*]

> But age, with his stealing steps,
> Hath claw'd me in his clutch,
> And hath shipped me intil[472] the land,
> As if I had never been such.

65   [*Throws up a skull.*]

HAM.   That skull had a tongue in it, and could sing once. How the knave jowls[473] it to the ground, as if it were Cain's jawbone, that did the first murder. It might be the pate of a politician, which this ass now o'er-offices,[474] one that would circumvent God, might it not?

70   HOR.   It might, my lord.

---

[468]*unyoke*—then your work is done.

[469]*contract*—shorten.

[470]*behove*—behoof, advantage.

[471]*property of easiness*—an easy matter.

[472]*intil*—to.

[473]*jowls*—drops.

[474]*o'er-offices*—lords over (by virtue of his office as grave digger).

	HAM.	Or of a courtier, which could say 'Good morrow, sweet lord. How dost thou, sweet lord?' This might be my Lord Such-a-one, that praised my Lord Such-a-one's horse, when he meant to beg it, might it not?
75	HOR.	Ay, my lord.
	HAM.	Why, e'en so; and now my Lady Worm's, chapless,[475] and knocked about the mazard[476] with a sexton's spade. Here's fine revolution, an we had the trick[477] to see't. Did these bones cost no more the breeding, but to play at loggats[478] with 'em? Mine ache to think on't.

80	FIRST CLO.	*[Sings]*

A pickaxe, and a spade, a spade,
For and[479] a shrouding-sheet;
O, a pit of clay for to be made
For such a guest is meet.

[Throws up another skull.]

85	HAM.	There's another. Why may not that be the skull of a lawyer? Where be his quiddities now, his quillets,[480] his cases, his tenures, and his tricks? Why does he suffer this rude knave now to knock him about the sconce with a dirty shovel, and will not tell him of his action of battery?[481] Hum! This fellow might be in's time a great buyer of land, with his statutes, his recognizances, his fines, his double vouchers, his recoveries.[482] Is this the fine of his fines and the recovery of his recoveries, to have his fine pate full of fine dirt? Will his vouchers vouch him no more of his purchases, and double ones too, than the length and breadth of a pair of indentures?[483] The very conveyances of his lands will hardly lie in this box; and must the inheritor himself have no more, ha?
90		
95		
	HOR.	Not a jot more, my lord.
	HAM.	Is not parchment made of sheepskins?
	HOR.	Ay, my lord, and of calfskins too.
100	HAM.	They are sheep and calves which seek out assurance in that. I will speak to this fellow. Whose grave's this, sirrah?
	FIRST CLO.	Mine, Sir.

[Sings] O, a pit of clay for to be made
For such a guest is meet.

105	HAM.	I think it be thine indeed, for thou liest in't.

---

[475]*chapless*—without a jaw.

[476]*mazard*—head (pate).

[477]*trick*—knack, art.

[478]*loggats*—a game in which small logs are thrown at a stake.

[479]*For and*—and also.

[480]*quiddities . . . quillets*—subtle arguments.

[481]*battery*—assault.

[482]*statutes . . . recoveries*—legal terms relating to the transfer and mortgaging of land.

[483]*indentures*—contracts.

	FIRST CLO.	You lie out on't, sir, and therefore 'tis not yours. For my part, I do not lie in't, and yet it is mine.
	HAM.	Thou dost lie in't, to be in't and say 'tis thine. 'Tis for the dead, not for the quick;[484] therefore thou liest.
110	FIRST CLO.	Tis a quick lie, sir; 'twill away again from me to you.
	HAM.	What man dost thou dig it for?
	FIRST CLO.	For no man, sir.
	HAM.	What woman then?
	FIRST CLO.	For none, neither.
115	HAM.	Who is to be buried in't?
	FIRST CLO.	One that was a woman, sir, but, rest her soul, she's dead.
	HAM.	How absolute[485] the knave is! We must speak by the card,[486] or equivocation will undo us. By the Lord, Horatio, this three years I have taken note of it: the age is grown so picked[487] that the toe of the
120		peasant comes so near the heel of the courtier, he galls his kibe.[488] How long hast thou been a grave-maker?
	FIRSTCLO.	Of all the days i'the year, I came to't that day that our last King Hamlet o'ercame Fortinbras.
	HAM.	How long is that since?
125	FIRST CLO.	Cannot you tell that? Every fool can tell that. It was that very day that young Hamlet was born—he that is mad and sent into England.
	HAM.	Ay, marry, why was he sent into England?
	FIRST CLO.	Why, because a was mad. A shall recover his wits there; or, if a
130		do not, 'tis no great matter there.
	HAM.	Why?
	FIRST CLO.	'Twill not be seen in him there. There the men are as mad as he.
	HAM.	How came he mad?
	FIRST CLO.	Very strangely, they say.
135	HAM.	How 'strangely'?
	FIRST CLO.	Faith, e'en with losing his wits.
	HAM.	Upon what ground?
	FIRST CLO.	Why, here in Denmark. I have been sexton here, man and boy, thirty years.
140	HAM.	How long will a man lie i' the earth ere he rot?
	FIRST CLO.	I'faith, if a be not rotten before a die—as we have many pocky corses nowadays that will scarce hold the laying in [489]—a will last you some eight year or nine year. A tanner will last you nine year.

---

[484]*quick*—alive.

[485]*absolute*—expecting.

[486]*by the card*—with the utmost precision.

[487]*picked*—refined.

[488]*galls his kibe*—irritates his sore heel.

[489]*hold the laying in*—remain intact until the burial.

	HAM.	Why he more than another?
145	FIRST CLO.	Why, sir, his hide is so tanned with his trade that a will keep out water a great while; and your water is a sore decayer of your whoreson dead body Here's a skull, now. This skull has lain in the earth three and twenty years.
	HAM.	Whose was it?
150	FIRST CLO.	A whoreson mad fellow's it was. Whose do you think it was?
	HAM.	Nay, I know not.
	FIRST CLO.	A pestilence on him for a mad rogue! A poured a flagon of Rhenish on my head once. This same skull, sir, was Yorick's skull, the King's jester.
155	HAM.	[*Takes the skull*] This?
	FIRST CLO.	E'en that.
	HAM.	Alas, poor Yorick. I knew him, Horatio: a fellow of infinite jest, of most excellent fancy. He hath borne me on his back a thousand times; and now, how abhorred in my imagination it is! My gorge rises at it.
160		Here hung those lips that I have kissed I know not how oft. Where be your gibes now, your gambols, your songs, your flashes of merriment, that were wont to set the table on a roar? Not one now to mock your own grinning? Quite chop[490]-fallen? Now get you to my
165		lady's chamber, and tell her, let her paint an inch thick, to this favour[491] she must come. Make her laugh at that. Prithee, Horatio, tell me one thing.
	HOR.	What's that, my lord?
	HAM.	Dost thou think Alexander looked o' this fashion i' the earth?
	HOR.	E'en so.
170	HAM.	And smelt so? Pah! [*Puts down the skull.*
	HOR.	E'en so, my lord.
	HAM.	To what base uses we may return, Horatio! Why, may not imagination trace the noble dust of Alexander till he find it stopping a bung-hole?
175	HOR.	'Twere to consider too curiously to consider so.
	HAM.	No, faith, not a jot; but to follow him thither with modesty[492] enough and likelihood to lead it, as thus: Alexander died, Alexander was buried, Alexander returneth into dust, the dust is earth, of earth we make loam, and why of that loam, whereto he was converted, might
180		they not stop a beer-barrel?
		Imperious Cæsar, dead and turn'd to clay,
		Might stop a hole to keep the wind away.
		O, that that earth, which kept the world in awe,

---

[490]*chop*—chap, jaw.

[491]*favour*—appearance.

[492]*modesty*—moderation.

		Should patch a wall to expel the winter's flaw!
185		But soft, but soft awhile! Here comes the King,
		The Queen, the courtiers.

Enter Priests, *&c. in procession; the Corpse of Ophelia,* LAERTES, *and* Mourners *following;* KING, QUEEN, *their trains, &c.*

		Who is this they follow?
190		And with such maimed rites? This doth betoken
		The corse they follow did with desperate hand
		Fordo[493] its own life. 'Twas of some estate.[494]
		Couch we[495] awhile and mark. [*Retiring with* HORATIO.
	LAER.	What ceremony else?
195	HAM.	That is Laertes, a very noble youth. Mark.
	LAER.	What ceremony else?
	PRIEST.	Her obsequies have been as far enlarged
		As we have warranty. Her death was doubtful;
		And, but that great command o'ersways the order,
200		She should in ground unsanctified have lodged
		Till the last trumpet; for charitable prayers,
		Shards,[496] flints and pebbles should be thrown on her.
		Yet here she is allow'd her virgin crants,[497]
		Her maiden strewments[498] and the bringing home
205		Of bell and burial.[499]
	LAER.	Must there no more be done?
	PRIEST.	No more be done.
		We should profane the service of the dead
		To sing a requiem and such rest to her
210		As to peace-parted souls.
	LAER.	Lay her i' the earth,
		And from her fair and unpolluted flesh
		May violets spring. I tell thee, churlish priest,
		A ministering angel shall my sister be
215		When thou liest howling.
	HAM.	What, the fair Ophelia!
	QUEEN.	[*Scattering flowers*] Sweets, to the sweet. Farewell.
		I hoped thou shouldst have been my Hamlet's wife;
		I thought thy bride-bed to have deck'd, sweet maid,
220		And not have strew'd thy grave.

---

[493]*Fordo*—destroy.

[494]*estate*—rank.

[495]*Couch we*—let us hide.

[496]*Shards*—fragments.

[497]*crants*—garlands.

[498]*strewments*—strewing of flowers.

[499]*bringing home . . . burial*—laying to rest to the sound of the knell.

	LAER.	O, treble woe
		Fall ten times treble on that cursed head
		Whose wicked deed thy most ingenious sense
		Deprived thee of! Hold off the earth awhile,
225		Till I have caught her once more in mine arms.

[*Leaps into the grave.*

		Now pile your dust upon the quick and dead,
		Till of this flat a mountain you have made
		To o'ertop old Pelion or the skyish head
230		Of blue Olympus.
	HAM.	[*Advancing*] What is he whose grief
		Bears such an emphasis, whose phrase of sorrow
		Conjures the wandering stars and makes them stand
		Like wonder-wounded hearers? This is I,
235		Hamlet the Dane.
	LAER.	The devil take thy soul! [*Grappling with him.*
	HAM.	Thou pray'st not well.
		I prithee, take thy fingers from my throat;
		For, though I am not splenative[500] and rash,
240		Yet have I in me something dangerous,
		Which let thy wisdom fear. Hold off thy hand.
	KING.	Pluck them asunder.
	QUEEN.	Hamlet, Hamlet!
	ALL.	Gentlemen!
245	HOR.	Good my lord, be quiet.
	HAM.	Why, I will fight with him upon this theme
		Until my eyelids will no longer wag.
	QUEEN.	O my son, what theme?
	HAM.	I loved Ophelia. Forty thousand brothers
250		Could not, with all their quantity of love,
		Make up my sum. What wilt thou do for her?
	KING.	O, he is mad, Laertes.
	QUEEN.	For love of God, forbear him.
	HAM.	'Swounds, show me what thou'lt do.
255		Woo't[501] weep, woo't fight, woo't fast, woo't tear thyself,
		Woo't drink up eisel,[502] eat a crocodile?
		I'll do't. Dost thou come here to whine,
		To outface me with leaping in her grave?
		Be buried quick[503] with her, and so will I.

---

[500]*splenative*—hot-tempered, impetuous (spleen).
[501]*Woo't*—would you.
[502]*eisel*—vinegar.
[503]*quick*—alive.

260		And, if thou prate of mountains, let them throw
		Millions of acres on us, till our ground,
		Singeing his pate against the burning zone,
		Make Ossa like a wart. Nay, an thou'lt mouth,
		I'll rant as well as thou.
265	QUEEN.	This is mere madness;
		And thus awhile the fit will work on him.
		Anon, as patient as the female dove
		When that her golden couplets are disclosed,[504]
		His silence will sit drooping.
270	HAM.	Hear you, sir,
		What is the reason that you use me thus?
		I loved you ever. But it is no matter.
		Let Hercules himself do what he may,
		The cat will mew, and dog will have his day. *[Exit.*
275	KING.	I pray thee, good Horatio, wait upon him. *[Exit* HORATIO.
		[*To* LAERTES] Strengthen your patience in our last night's speech;
		We'll put the matter to the present push.—[505]
		Good Gertrude, set some watch over your son.
		This grave shall have a living monument.
280		An hour of quiet shortly shall we see;
		Till then, in patience our proceeding be. *[Exeunt.*

---

[504]*disclosed*—hatched.

[505]*to the present push*—into immediate action.

ACT V, SCENE II. *A hall in the castle.*

Enter HAMLET *and* HORATIO.

	HAM.	So much for this, sir. Now shall you see the other.
		You do remember all the circumstance?
285	HOR.	Remember it, my lord!
	HAM.	Sir, in my heart there was a kind of fighting,
		That would not let me sleep. Methought I lay
		Worse than the mutines in the bilboes.[506] Rashly—
		And praised be rashness for it: let us know
290		Our indiscretion sometime serves us well
		When our deep plots do pall; and that should learn us
		There's a divinity that shapes our ends,
		Rough-hew them how we will—
	HOR.	That is most certain.
295	HAM	Up from my cabin,
		My sea-gown scarf'd about me, in the dark
		Groped I to find out them, had my desire,
		Finger'd their packet, and in fine withdrew
		To mine own room again, making so bold,
300		My fears forgetting manners, to unseal
		Their grand commission, where I found, Horatio—
		O royal knavery!—an exact command,
		Larded with many several sorts of reasons
		Importing Denmark's health and England's too,
305		With, ho! such bugs and goblins in my life,
		That on the supervise,[507] no leisure bated,[508]
		No, not to stay the grinding of the axe,
		My head should be struck off.
	HOR.	Is't possible?
310	HAM.	Here's the commission. Read it at more leisure.
		But wilt thou hear now how I did proceed?
	HOR.	I beseech you.
	HAM.	Being thus benetted round with villanies—
		Or[509] I could make a prologue to my brains,
315		They had begun the play—I sat me down,
		Devised a new commission, wrote it fair.
		I once did hold it, as our statists[510] do,

---

[506]*mutines in the bilboes*—mutineers in shackles.

[507]*supervise*—perusal (of Claudius' missive).

[508]*no leisure bated*—with no delay.

[509]*Or*—before.

[510]*statists*—statesmen.

A baseness to write fair, and labour'd much
How to forget that learning; but, sir, now
320   It did me yeoman's service. Wilt thou know
The effect of what I wrote?

HOR.   Ay, good my lord.

HAM.   An earnest conjuration from the King,
As England was his faithful tributary,
325   As love between them like the palm might flourish,
As peace should still her wheaten garland wear
And stand a comma 'tween their amities,
And many such-like 'As'es of great charge,
That on the view and knowing of these contents,
330   Without debatement further, more or less,
He should the bearers put to sudden death,
Not shriving-time[511] allow'd.

HOR.   How was this seal'd?

HAM.   Why, even in that was heaven ordinant.[512]
335   I had my father's signet in my purse,
Which was the model of that Danish seal;
Folded the writ up in the form of the other,
Subscribed it, gave't the impression, placed it safely,
The changeling never known. Now, the next day
340   Was our sea-fight; and what to this was Sequent
Thou know'st already.

HOR.   So Guildenstern and Rosencrantz go to't.

HAM.   Why, man, they did make love to this employment.
They are not near my conscience. Their defeat
345   Does by their own insinuation grow.
'Tis dangerous when the baser nature comes
Between the pass[513] and fell incensed points
Of mighty opposites.

HOR.   Why, what a king is this!

350 HAM.   Does it not, think thee, stand me now upon—[514]
He that hath kill'd my king and whored my mother,
Popp'd in between the election and my hopes,
Thrown out his angle for my proper[515] life,
And with such cozenage[516]—is't not perfect conscience
355   To quit him with this arm? And is't not to be damn'd

---

[511]*shriving-time*—time for absolution.

[512]*ordinant*—ordaining, directing.

[513]*pass*—sword thrust.

[514]*stand me now upon*—obligate me.

[515]*proper*—own.

[516]*cozenage*—deceit.

		To let this canker of our nature come
		In further evil?
	HOR.	It must be shortly known to him from England
		What is the issue of the business there.
360	HAM.	It will be short. The interim is mine;
		And a man's life's no more than to say 'One.'
		But I am very sorry, good Horatio,
		That to Laertes I forgot myself;
		For by the image of my cause I see
365		The portraiture of his. I'll court his favours.
		But, sure, the bravery[517] of his grief did put me
		Into a towering passion.
	HOR.	Peace, who comes here?

Enter OSRIC.

370	OSR.	Your lordship is right welcome back to Denmark.
	HAM.	I humbly thank you, Sir. Dost know this water-fly?,
	HOR.	No, my good lord.
	HAM.	Thy state is the more gracious,[518] for 'tis a vice to know him. He hath much land, and fertile. Let a beast be lord of beasts, and his crib
375		shall stand at the king's mess.[519] 'Tis a chuff,[520] but, as I say, spacious in the possession of dirt.
	OSR.	Sweet lord, if your lordship were at leisure, I should impart a thing to you from his Majesty.
	HAM.	I will receive it, sir, with all diligence of spirit. Put your bonnet to
380		his right use: 'tis for the head.
	OSR.	I thank your lordship, it is very hot.
	HAM.	No, believe me, 'tis very cold; the wind is northerly.
	OSR.	It is indifferent cold, my lord, indeed.
	HAM.	But yet methinks it is very sultry and hot for my complexion.
385	OSR.	Exceedingly, my lord. It is very sultry, as 'twere—I cannot tell how. But, my lord, his Majesty bade me signify to you that he has laid a great wager on your head. Sir, this is the matter—
	HAM.	I beseech you, remember—
		[HAMLET *moves him to put on his hat.*
390	OSR.	Nay, good my lord; for mine ease, in good faith. Sir, here is newly come to court Laertes—believe me, an absolute gentleman, full of most excellent differences, of very soft society and great showing. Indeed, to speak feelingly of him, he is the card or calendar of

---

[517]*bravery*—bravado.

[518]*gracious*—graced.

[519]*mess*—table.

[520]*chuff*—a wealthy, but dull, person.

395		gentry,[521] for you shall find in him the continent[522] of what part a gentleman would see.
	HAM.	Sir, his definement suffers no perdition[523] in you, though, I know, to divide him inventorially would dizzy the arithmetic of memory, and yet but yaw neither,[524] in respect of his quick sail. But, in the verity of extolment, I take him to be a soul of great article, and his
400		infusion[525] of such dearth[526] and rareness as, to make true diction of him, his semblable is his mirror,[527] and who else would trace[528] him, his umbrage,[529] nothing more.
	OSR.	Your lordship speaks most infallibly of him.
	HAM.	The concernancy,[530] sir? Why do we wrap the gentleman in our
405		more rawer breath?[531]
	OSR.	Sir?
	HOR.	Is't not possible to understand in another tongue?[532] You will do't, sir, really.
	HAM.	What imports the nomination of this gentleman?
410	OSR.	Of Laertes?
	HOR.	His purse is empty already; all's golden words are spent.
	HAM.	Of him, sir.
	OSR.	I know you are not ignorant—
	HAM.	I would you did, sir. Yet, in faith, if you did, it would not much
415		approve[533] me. Well, sir?
	OSR.	You are not ignorant of what excellence Laertes is—
	HAM.	I dare not confess that, lest I should compare with him in excellence; but, to know a man well were to know himself.
	OSR.	I mean, sir, for his weapon; but in the imputation[534] laid on him by
420		them in his meed, he's unfellowed.[535]
	HAM.	What's his weapon?
	OSR.	Rapier and dagger.

---

[521]*card or calendar of gentry*—epitome of courtesy.

[522]*continent*—container.

[523]*perdition*—loss.

[524]*but yaw neither*—steer out of course nevertheless.

[525]*infusion*—quality.

[526]*dearth*—rarity.

[527]*his semblance is his mirror*—the only like is his own reflection.

[528]*trace*—follow.

[529]*umbrage*—shadow.

[530]*concernancy*—significance.

[531]*more rawer breath*—inadequate language.

[532]*another tongue*—simpler terms.

[533]*approve*—commend.

[534]*imputation*—reputation.

[535]*unfellowed*—unequaled (in swordsmanship).

	HAM.	That's two of his weapons. But, well.
	OSR.	The King, sir, hath wagered with him six Barbary horses, against
425		the which he has impawned,[536] as I take it, six French rapiers and
		poniards,[537] with their assigns,[538] as girdle, hanger, and so. Three
		of the carriages,[539] in faith, are very dear to fancy, very
		responsive[540] to the hilts, most delicate carriages, and of very
		liberal conceit.[541]
430	HAM.	What call you the carriages?
	HOR.	I knew you must be edified by the margent[542] ere you had done.
	OSR.	The carriages, sir, are the hangers.
	HAM.	The phrase would be more german[543] to the matter if we could carry
		a cannon by our sides. I would it might be hangers till then. But, on.
435		Six Barbary horses against six French swords, their assigns, and
		three liberal-conceited carriages—that's the French bet against the
		Danish. Why is this 'impawned,' as you call it?
	OSR.	The King, sir, hath laid, sir, that in a dozen passes[544] between
		yourself and him, he shall not exceed you three hits. He hath laid on
440		twelve for nine. And it would come to immediate trial, if your
		lordship would vouchsafe the answer.
	HAM.	How if I answer no?
	OSR.	I mean, my lord, the opposition of your person in trial.
	HAM.	Sir, I will walk here in the hall. If it please his Majesty, it is the
445		breathing time[545] of day with me. Let the foils be brought, the
		gentleman willing, and the King hold his purpose, I will win for him
		an I can. If not, I will gain nothing but my shame and the odd hits.
	OSR.	Shall I redeliver you e'en so?
	HAM.	To this effect, Sir, after what flourish your nature will.
450	OSR.	I commend my duty to your lordship.
	HAM.	Yours, yours. [*Exit* OSRIC.] He does well to commend it himself,
		there are no tongues else for's turn.
	HOR.	This lapwing runs away with the shell on his head.[546]

---

[536]*impawned*—wagered.

[537]*poniards*—daggers.

[538]*assigns*—accessories.

[539]*carriages*—belts, straps.

[540]*responsive*—suited.

[541]*liberal conceit*—ornate design.

[542]*margent*—marginal notes, explanation.

[543]*german*—germane, appropriate.

[544]*passes*—sword parries.

[545]*breathing time*—exercise period.

[546]*This lapwing . . . head*—fly off shortly after hatching, hence "precocious."

455	HAM.	He did comply with his dug[547] before he sucked it. Thus has he—and many more of the same breed that I know the drossy[548] age dotes on—only got the tune of the time and outward habit of encounter, a kind of yesty[549] collection, which carries them through and through the most fanned and winnowed[550] opinions; and do but blow them to their trial, the bubbles are out.
460	*Enter a* Lord.	
	LORD.	My lord, his Majesty commended him to you by young Osric, who brings back to him that you attend him in the hall. He sends to know if your pleasure hold to play with Laertes or that you will take longer time.
465	HAM.	I am congtant to my purposes; they follow the King's pleasure. If his fitness speaks, mine is ready; now or whensoever, provided I be so able as now.
	LORD.	The King and Queen and all are coming down.
	HAM.	In happy time.
470	LORD.	The Queen desires you to use some gentle entertainment to Laertes before you fall to play.
	HAM.	She well instructs me. [*Exit* Lord.
	HOR.	You will lose this wager, my lord.
475	HAM.	I do not think so. Since he went into France, I have been in continual practice. I shall win at the odds. But thou wouldst not think how ill all's here about my heart, but it is no matter.
	HOR.	Nay, good my lord—
	HAM.	It is but foolery; but it is such a kind of gain-giving[551] as would perhaps trouble a woman.
480	HOR.	If your mind dislike anything, obey it. I will forestall their repair hither and say you are not fit.
	HAM.	Not a whit. We defy augury. There is special providence in the fall of a sparrow. If it be now, 'tis not to come; if it be not to come, it will be now; if it be not now, yet it will come. The readiness is all. Since no man has aught of what he leaves, what is't to leave betimes? Let be.
485		
	Enter KING, QUEEN, LAERTES, *and* Lords, OSRIC *and other* Attendants *with foils and gauntlets; a table and flagons of wine on it.*	
	KING.	Come, Hamlet, come, and take this hand from me.
490		[*The* KING *puts* LAERTES' *hand into* HAMLET's.
	HAM.	Give me your pardon, sir. I've done you wrong;

---

[547] *. . . dug*—his mother's breast.

[548] *drossy*—frivolous.

[549] *yesty*—yeasty, frothy.

[550] *fanned and winnowed*—tried and sifted.

[551] *gain-giving*—misgiving.

But pardon't as you are a gentleman.
This presence[552] knows,
And you must needs have heard, how I am punish'd

495 With sore distraction. What I have done
That might your nature, honour and exception[553]
Roughly awake, I here proclaim was madness.
Was't Hamlet wrong'd Laertes? Never Hamlet.
If Hamlet from himself be ta'en away,

500 And when he's not himself does wrong Laertes,
Then Hamlet does it not, Hamlet denies it.
Who does it then? His madness. If't be so
Hamlet is of the faction that is wrong'd;
His madness is poor Hamlet's enemy.

505 Sir, in this audience,
Let my disclaiming from a purposed evil
Free me so far in your most generous thoughts
That I have shot mine arrow o'er the house
And hurt my brother.

510 LAER.   I am satisfied in nature,
Whose motive in this case should stir me most
To my revenge; but in my terms of honour
I stand aloof, and will no reconcilement
Till by some elder masters of known honour

515 I have a voice and precedent[554] of peace
To keep my name ungored. But till that time
I do receive your offer'd love like love
And will not wrong it.

         HAM.   I embrace it freely,
520 And will this brother's wager frankly play.—
Give us the foils. Come on.

         LAER.   Come, one for me.

         HAM.   I'll be your foil, Laertes. In mine ignorance
Your skill shall, like a star i' the darkest night,

525 Stick fiery off[555] indeed.

         LAER.   You mock me, sir.

         HAM.   No, by this hand.

         KING.   Give them the foils, young Osric. Cousin Hamlet,
You know the wager?

530 HAM.   Very well, my lord.

---

[552]*presence*—noble assembly.

[553]*exception*—objection.

[554]*precedent*—authoritative judgment.

[555]*Stick fiery off*—stand out brightly.

		Your Grace has laid the odds o' the weaker side.
	KING.	I do not fear it; I have seen you both,
		But since he is better'd, we have therefore odds.
	LAER.	This is too heavy; let me see another.
535	HAM.	This likes me well. These foils have all a length?
	OSR.	Ay, I my good lord. *[They prepare to play.*
	KING.	Set me the stoups of wine upon that table.
		If Hamlet give the first or second hit,
		Or quit in answer of the third exchange,
540		Let all the battlements their ordnance fire:
		The King shall drink to Hamlet's better breath,
		And in the cup an union[556] shall he throw,
		Richer than that which four successive kings
		In Denmark's crown have worn. Give me the cups;
545		And let the kettle to the trumpet speak,
		The trumpet to the cannoneer without,
		The cannons to the heavens, the heaven to earth,
		'Now the King drinks to Hamlet.' Come, begin.
		And you, the judges, bear a wary eye.
550	HAM.	Come on, sir.
	LAER.	Come, my lord. *[They play.*
	HAM.	One.
	LAER.	No.
	HAM.	Judgement.
555	OSR.	A hit, a very palpable hit.
	LAER.	Well, again.
	KING.	Stay; give me drink. Hamlet, this pearl is thine.
		Here's to thy health.
		[Trumpets sound, and cannon shot off within.
560		Give him the cup.
	HAM.	I'll play this bout first. Set it by awhile.
		Come. *[They play.]* Another hit. What say you?
	LAER.	A touch, a touch, I do confess.
	KING.	Our son shall win.
565	QUEEN.	He's fat[557] and scant of breath.
		Here, Hamlet, take my napkin, rub thy brows.
		The Queen carouses to thy fortune, Hamlet.
	HAM.	Good madam.
	KING.	Gertrude, do not drink.
570	QUEEN.	I will, my lord; I pray you, pardon me.
	KING.	*[Aside]* It is the poison'd cup; it is too late.

---

[556]*union*—pearl.
[557]*fat*—out of shape.

	HAM.	I dare not drink yet, madam—by and by.
	QUEEN.	Come, let me wipe thy face.
	LAER.	My lord, I'll hit him now.
575	KING.	I do not think't.
	LAER.	[*Aside*] And yet it is almost against my conscience.
	HAM.	Come, for the third, Laertes. You but dally.
		I pray you, pass with your best violence.
		I am afeard you make a wanton of me.[558]
580	LAER.	Say you so? Come on. [*They play.*
	OSR.	Nothing, neither way.
	LAER.	Have at you now!
		[LAERTES *wounds* HAMLET; *then, in scuffling, they change rapiers, and* HAMLET *wounds* LAERTES.
585	KING.	Part them; they are incensed.
	HAM.	Nay, come, again. [*The* QUEEN *falls.*
	OSR.	Look to the Queen there, ho!
	HOR.	They bleed on both sides. How is it, my lord?
	OSR.	How is't, Laertes?
590	LAER.	Why, as a woodcock to mine own springe,[559] Osric.
		I am justly kill'd with mine own treachery.
	HAM.	How does the Queen?
	KING.	She swoons to see them bleed.
	QUEEN.	No, no, the drink, the drink—O my dear Hamlet—
595		The drink, the drink! I am poison'd. [*Dies.*
	HAM.	O villany! Ho! Let the door be lock'd.
		Treachery! Seek it out. [*Exit* OSRIC; LAERTES *falls.*
	LAER.	It is here, Hamlet. Hamlet, thou art slain.
		No medicine in the world can do thee good;
600		In thee there is not half an hour of life.
		The treacherous instrument is in thy hand,
		Unbated and envenom'd. The foul practice[560]
		Hath turn'd itself on me. Lo, here I lie,
		Never to rise again. Thy mother's poison'd.
605		I can no more. The King, the King's to blame.
	HAM.	The point envenom'd too? Then, venom, to thy work.
		[*Stabs the* KING.
	ALL.	Treason! treason!
	KING.	O, yet defend me, friends. I am but hurt.
610	HAM.	Here, thou incestuous, murderous, damned Dane,
		Drink off this potion. Is thy union here?

---

[558]*make a wanton of me*—treat me like a weakling.
[559]*springe*—snare.
[560]*practice*—strategem.

		Follow my mother.	[KING *dies.*
	LAER.	He is justly served.	
		It is a poison temper'd[561] by himself	
615		Exchange forgiveness with me, noble Hamlet.	
		Mine and my father's death come not upon thee,	
		Nor thine on me.	[*Dies.*
	HAM.	Heaven make thee free of it. I follow thee.	
		I am dead, Horatio. Wretched Queen, adieu!	
620		You that look pale and tremble at this chance,	
		That are but mutes or audience to this act,	
		Had I but time—as this fell sergeant, Death,	
		Is strict in his arrest—O, I could tell you—	
		But let it be. Horatio, I am dead,	
625		Thou livest. Report me and my cause aright	
		To the unsatisfied.	
	HOR.	Never believe it.	
		I am more an antique Roman than a Dane.	
		Here's yet some liquor left.	
630	HAM.	As thou'rt a man,	
		Give me the cup. Let go. By heaven, I'll have't.	
		O God, Horatio, what a wounded name,	
		Things standing thus unknown, shall live behind me!	
		If thou didst ever hold me in thy heart,	
635		Absent thee from felicity awhile,	
		And in this harsh world draw thy breath in pain	
		To tell my story.	[*March afar off, and shot within.*

Enter OSRIC.

		What warlike noise is this?	
640	OSR.	Young Fortinbras, with conquest come from Poland,	
		To the ambassadors of England gives	
		This warlike volley.	
	HAM.	O, I die, Horatio.	
		The potent poison quite o'er-crows[562] my spirit.	
645		I cannot live to hear the news from England;	
		But I do prophesy the election lights	
		On Fortinbras. He has my dying voice.	
		So tell him, with the occurrents,[563] more and less,	
		Which have solicited.[564] The rest is silence.	[*Dies.*
650	HOR.	Now cracks a noble heart. Good night, sweet prince,	

---

[561]*temper'd*—mixed.

[562]*o'er-crows*—triumphs over.

[563]*occurents*—of the occurences.

[564]*solicited*—solicited (these events).

And flights of angels sing thee to thy rest.   [*March within.*
Why does the drum come hither?
Enter FORTINBRAS, *and the* English Ambassadors, *with drum, colours, and*
Attendants.

655   FORT.   Where is this sight?

    HOR.   What is it you would see?
If aught of woe or wonder, cease your search.

    FORT.   This quarry cries on havoc.[565] O proud Death,
What feast is toward in thine eternal cell,

660   That thou so many princes at a shot
So bloodily hast struck?

    FIRST AMB.   The sight is dismal;
And our affairs from England come too late.
The ears are senseless that should give us hearing

665   To tell him his commandment is fulfill'd,
That Rosencrantz and Guildenstern are dead.
Where should we have our thanks?

    HOR.   Not from his mouth,
Had it the ability of life to thank you.

670   He never gave commandment for their death.
But since so jump upon this bloody question
You from the Polack wars, and you from England,
Are here arrived, give order that these bodies
High on a stage[566] be placed to the view;

675   And let me speak to the yet unknowing world
How these things came about. So shall you hear
Of carnal, bloody and unnatural acts,
Of accidental judgements, casual[567] slaughters,
Of deaths put on[568] by cunning and forced cause,

680   And, in this upshot, purposes mistook
Fall'n on the inventors' heads. All this can I
Truly deliver.

    FORT.   Let us haste to hear it,
And call the noblest to the audience.

685   For me, with sorrow I embrace my fortune.
I have some rights of memory in this kingdom,
Which now to claim my vantage doth invite me.

    HOR.   Of that I shall have also cause to speak,

---

[565]*This quarry cries on havoc*—This heap of corpses speaks of havoc.
[566]*stage*—platform.
[567]*casual*—accidental.
[568]*put on*—instigated.

And from his mouth whose voice will draw on more.[569]

690 But let this same be presently perform'd,
Even while men's minds are wild, lest more mischance
On[570] plots and errors happen.

FORT. Let four captains
Bear Hamlet like a soldier to the stage;

695 For he was likely, had he been put on,
To have proved most royal; and, for his passage,[571]
The soldiers' music and the rites of war
Speak loudly for him.
Take up the bodies. Such a sight as this

700 Becomes the field, but here shows much amiss.
Go, bid the soldiers shoot.

[*A dead march. Exeunt, bearing off the bodies;*
after which a peal of ordnance is shot off.

---

[569]*draw on more*—voices (approving Fortinbras).
[570]*On*—in addition to.
[571]*passages*—passing, death.

16. ESSAYS (SELECTIONS)

Michel de Montaigne
(1533–1592)

(trans. by Donald M. Frame)

Montaigne, born at the outset of the Renaissance in France, was trained as a child to speak only Latin and did not learn French until he was ten. His father had appointed a German tutor for his son, and the strict classical education he administered provided the foundation for Montaigne's habits of thinking and later influential support for the New Learning. After a brief career in law and the death of his father, Montaigne retreated to the family estate in Bordeaux to devote himself to a life of meditation and writing. Though pressed into public service as mayor of Bordeaux (two terms), he once again retired to his library to work on his life project, the Essays. *The title, from the French "essayer" (to test, try), is descriptive of Montaigne's method and the form he invented. Each essay is a compilation of personal thoughts, observations, experiences, with frequent classical allusions and quotations. The subject matter is essentially himself, for the essays exemplify writing as thinking, and were the means by which Montaigne "knew himself" and allowed others to know him. His authorial posture is unique at a time when others were composing instructive manuals on ideal behavior, for Montaigne presents himself as an admittedly flawed creature, inconsistent in views and beliefs, inept in social and political matters, and in sum, as an ordinary human being.*

BOOK I, 31: OF CANNIBALS

When King Pyrrhus passed over into Italy, after he had reconnoitered the formation of the army that the Romans were sending to meet him, he said: "I do not know what barbarians these are" (for so the Greeks called all foreign nations), "but the formation of this army that I see is not at all barbarous." The Greeks said
5 as much of the army that Flamininus brought into their country, and so did Philip, seeing from a knoll the order and distribution of the Roman camp, in his kingdom, under Publius Sulpicius Galba. Thus we should beware of clinging to vulgar opinions, and judge things by reason's way, not by popular say.

I had with me for a long time a man who had lived for ten or twelve years in
10 that other world which has been discovered in our century, in the place where

Villegaignon landed, and which he called Antarctic France.[1] This discovery of a boundless country seems worthy of consideration. I don't know if I can guarantee that some other such discovery will not be made in the future, so many personages greater than ourselves having been mistaken about this one. I am afraid we have eyes bigger than our stomachs, and more curiosity than capacity. We embrace everything, but we clasp only wind.

Plato brings in Solon, telling how he had learned from the priests of the city of Saïs in Egypt that in days of old, before the Flood, there was a great island named Atlantis, right at the mouth of the Strait of Gibraltar, which contained more land than Africa and Asia put together, and that the kings of that country, who not only possessed that island but had stretched out so far on the mainland that they held the breadth of Africa as far as Egypt, and the length of Europe as far as Tuscany, undertook to step over into Asia and subjugate all the nations that border on the Mediterranean, as far as the Black Sea; and for this purpose crossed the Spains, Gaul, Italy, as far as Greece, where the Athenians checked them; but that some time after, both the Athenians and themselves and their island were swallowed up by the Flood.

It is quite likely that that extreme devastation of waters made amazing changes in the habitations of the earth, as people maintain that the sea cut off Sicily from Italy—

> 'Tis said an earthquake once asunder tore
> These lands with dreadful havoc, which before
> Formed but one land, one coast
>
> VIRGIL

—Cyprus from Syria, the island of Euboea from the mainland of Boeotia; and elsewhere joined lands that were divided, filling the channels between them with sand and mud:

> A sterile marsh, long fit for rowing, now
> Feeds neighbor towns, and feels the heavy plow.
>
> HORACE

But there is no great likelihood that that island was the new world which we have just discovered; for it almost touched Spain, and it would be an incredible result of a flood to have forced it away as far as it is, more than twelve hundred leagues; besides, the travels of the moderns have already almost revealed that it is not an island, but a mainland connected with the East Indies on one side, and elsewhere with the lands under the two poles; or, if it is separated from them, it is by so narrow a strait and interval that it does not deserve to be called an island on that account.

---

[1]In Brazil, in 1557.

It seems that there are movements, some natural, others feverish, in these great bodies, just as in our own. When I consider the inroads that my river, the Dordogne, is making in my lifetime into the right bank in its descent, and that in twenty years it has gained so much ground and stolen away the foundations of several buildings, I clearly see that this is an extraordinary disturbance; for if it had always gone at this rate, or was to do so in the future, the face of the world would be turned topsy-turvy. But rivers are subject to changes: now they overflow in one direction, now in another, now they keep to their course. I am not speaking of the sudden inundations whose causes are manifest. In Médoc, along the seashore, my brother, the sieur d'Arsac, can see an estate of his buried under the sands that the sea spews forth; the tops of some buildings are still visible; his farms and domains have changed into very thin pasturage. The inhabitants say that for some time the sea has been pushing toward them so hard that they have lost four leagues of land. These sands are its harbingers; and we see great dunes of moving sand that march half a league ahead of it and keep conquering land.

The other testimony of antiquity with which some would connect this discovery is in Aristotle, at least if that little book *Of Unheard-of Wonders* is by him. He there relates that certain Carthaginians, after setting out upon the Atlantic Ocean from the Strait of Gibraltar and sailing a long time, at last discovered a great fertile island, all clothed in woods and watered by great deep rivers, far remote from any mainland; and that they, and others since, attracted by the goodness and fertility of the soil, went there with their wives and children, and began to settle there. The lords of Carthage, seeing that their country was gradually becoming depopulated, expressly forbade anyone to go there any more, on pain of death, and drove out these new inhabitants, fearing, it is said, that in course of time they might come to multiply so greatly as to supplant their former masters and ruin their state. This story of Aristotle does not fit our new lands any better than the other.

This man I had was a simple, crude fellow[2]—a character fit to bear true witness; for clever people observe more things and more curiously, but they interpret them; and to lend weight and conviction to their interpretation, they cannot help altering history a little. They never show you things as they are, but bend and disguise them according to the way they have seen them; and to give credence to their judgment and attract you to it, they are prone to add something to their matter, to stretch it out and amplify it. We need a man either very honest, or so simple that he has not the stuff to build up false inventions and give them plausibility; and wedded to no theory. Such was my man; and besides this, he at various times brought sailors and merchants, whom he had known on that trip, to see me. So I content myself with his information, without inquiring what the cosmographers say about it.

We ought to have topographers who would give us an exact account of the places where they have been. But because they have over us the advantage of

---

[2]The traveler Montaigne spoke of at the beginning of the chapter.

having seen Palestine, they want to enjoy the privilege of telling us news about all the rest of the world. I would like everyone to write what he knows, and as much as he knows, not only in this, but in all other subjects; for a man may have some special knowledge and experience of the nature of a river or a fountain, who in other matters knows only what everybody knows. However, to circulate this little scrap of knowledge, he will undertake to write the whole of physics. From this vice spring many great abuses.

Now, to return to my subject, I think there is nothing barbarous and savage in that nation, from what I have been told, except that each man calls barbarism whatever is not his own practice; for indeed it seems we have no other test of truth and reason than the example and pattern of the opinions and customs of the country we live in. *There* is always the perfect religion, the perfect government, the perfect and accomplished manners in all things. Those people are wild, just as we call wild the fruits that Nature has produced by herself and in her normal course; whereas really it is those that we have changed artificially and led astray from the common order, that we should rather call wild. The former retain alive and vigorous their genuine, their most useful and natural, virtues and properties, which we have debased in the latter in adapting them to gratify our corrupted taste. And yet for all that, the savor and delicacy of some uncultivated fruits of those countries is quite as excellent, even to our taste, as that of our own. It is not reasonable that art should win the place of honor over our great and powerful mother Nature. We have so overloaded the beauty and richness of her works by our inventions that we have quite smothered her. Yet wherever her purity shines forth, she wonderfully puts to shame our vain and frivolous attempts:

> Ivy comes readier without our care;
> In lonely caves the arbutus grows more fair;
> No art with artless bird song can compare.
> PROPERTIUS

All our efforts cannot even succeed in reproducing the nest of the tiniest little bird, its contexture, its beauty and convenience; or even the web of the puny spider. All things, says Plato, are produced by nature, by fortune, or by art; the greatest and most beautiful by one or the other of the first two, the least and most imperfect by the last.

These nations, then, seem to me barbarous in this sense, that they have been fashioned very little by the human mind, and are still very close to their original naturalness. The laws of nature still rule them, very little corrupted by ours; and they are in such a state of purity that I am sometimes vexed that they were unknown earlier, in the days when there were men able to judge them better than we. I am sorry that Lycurgus and Plato did not know of them; for it seems to me that what we actually see in these nations surpasses not only all the pictures in which poets have idealized the golden age and all their inventions in imagining a happy state of man, but also the conceptions and the very desire of philosophy.

130   They could not imagine a naturalness so pure and simple as we see by experience;
       nor could they believe that our society could be maintained with so little artifice
       and human solder. This is a nation, I should say to Plato, in which there is no sort
       of traffic, no knowledge of letters, no science of numbers, no name for a magistrate
       or for political superiority, no custom of servitude, no riches or poverty, no
135   contracts, no successions, no partitions, no occupations but leisure ones, no care
       for any but common kinship, no clothes, no agriculture, no metal, no use of wine or
       wheat. The very words that signify lying, treachery, dissimulation, avarice, envy,
       belittling, pardon—unbeard of. How far from this perfection would he find the
       republic that he imagined: *Men fresh sprung from the gods* [Seneca].

140   These manners nature first ordained.
                                        VIRGIL

       For the rest, they live in a country with a very pleasant and temperate climate,
       so that according to my witnesses it is rare to see a sick man there; and they have
       assured me that they never saw one palsied, bleary-eyed, toothless, or bent with
       age. They are settled along the sea and shut in on the land side by great high
145   mountains, with a stretch about a hundred leagues wide in between. They have a
       great abundance of fish and flesh which bear no resemblance to ours, and they eat
       them with no other artifice than cooking. The first man who rode a horse there,
       though he had had dealings with them on several other trips, so horrified them in
       this posture that they shot him dead with arrows before they could recognize him.
150   Their buildings are very long, with a capacity of two or three hundred souls;
       they are covered with the bark of great trees, the strips reaching to the ground at
       one end and supporting and leaning on one another at the top, in the manner of
       some of our barns, whose covering hangs down to the ground and acts as a side.
       They have wood so hard that they cut with it and make of it their swords and
155   grills to cook their food. Their beds are of a cotton weave, hung from the roof like
       those in our ships, each man having his own; for the wives sleep apart from their
       husbands.
       They get up with the sun, and eat immediately upon rising, to last them
       through the day; for they take no other meal than that one. Like some other Eastern
160   peoples, of whom Suidas tells us, who drank apart from meals, they do not drink
       then; but they drink several times a day, and to capacity. Their drink is made of
       some root, and is of the color of our claret wines. They drink it only lukewarm.
       This beverage keeps only two or three days; it has a slightly sharp taste, is not at
       all heady, is good for the stomach, and has a laxative effect upon those who are
165   not used to it; it is a very pleasant drink for anyone who is accustomed to it. In
       place of bread they use a certain white substance like preserved coriander. I have
       tried it; it tastes sweet and a little flat.
       The whole day is spent in dancing. The younger men go to hunt animals with
       bows. Some of the women busy themselves meanwhile with warming their drink,
170   which is their chief duty. Some one of the old men, in the morning before they begin

to eat, preaches to the whole barnful in common, walking from one end to the other, and repeating one single sentence several times until he has completed the circuit (for the buildings are fully a hundred paces long). He recommends to them only two things: valor against the enemy and love for their wives. And they never 175 fail to point out this obligation, as their refrain, that it is their wives who keep their drink warm and seasoned.

There may be seen in several places, including my own house, specimens of their beds, of their ropes, of their wooden swords and the bracelets with which they cover their wrists in combats, and of the big canes, open at one end, by whose 180 sound they keep time in their dances. They are close shaven all over, and shave themselves much more cleanly than we, with nothing but a wooden or stone razor. They believe that souls are immortal, and that those who have deserved well of the gods are lodged in that part of heaven where the sun rises, and the damned in the west.

185 They have some sort of priests and prophets, but they rarely appear before the people, having their home in the mountains. On their arrival there is a great feast and solemn assembly of several villages—each barn, as I have described it, makes up a village, and they are about one French league from each other. The prophet speaks to them in public, exhorting them to virtue and their duty; but their 190 whole ethical science contains only these two articles: resoluteness in war and affection for their wives. He prophesies to them things to come and the results they are to expect from their undertakings, and urges them to war or holds them back from it; but this is on the condition that when he fails to prophesy correctly, and if things turn out otherwise than he has predicted, he is cut into a thousand pieces if 195 they catch him, and condemned as a false prophet. For this reason, the prophet who has once been mistaken is never seen again.

Divination is a gift of God; that is why its abuse should be punished as imposture. Among the Scythians, when the soothsayers failed to hit the mark, they were laid, chained hand and foot, on carts full of heather and drawn by oxen, on 200 which they were burned. Those who handle matters subject to the control of human capacity are excusable if they do the best they can. But these others, who come and trick us with assurances of an extraordinary faculty that is beyond our ken, should they not be punished for not making good their promise, and for the temerity of their imposture?

205 They have their wars with the nations beyond the mountains, further inland, to which they go quite naked, with no other arms than bows or wooden swords ending in a sharp point, in the manner of the tongues of our boar spears. It is astonishing what firmness they show in their combats, which never end but in slaughter and bloodshed; for as to routs and terror, they know nothing of either.

210 Each man brings back as his trophy the head of the enemy he has killed, and sets it up at the entrance to his dwelling. After they have treated their prisoners well for a long time with all the hospitality they can think of, each man who has a prisoner calls a great assembly of his acquaintances. He ties a rope to one of the prisoner's arms, by the end of which he holds him, a few steps away, for fear of

215 being hurt, and gives his dearest friend the other arm to hold in the same way; and these two, in the presence of the whole assembly, kill him with their swords. This done, they roast him and eat him in common and send some pieces to their absent friends. This is not, as people think, for nourishment, as of old the Scythians used to do; it is to betoken an extreme revenge. And the proof of this came when they
220 saw the Portuguese, who had joined forces with their adversaries, inflict a different kind of death on them when they took them prisoner, which was to bury them up to the waist, shoot the rest of their body full of arrows, and afterward hang them. They thought that these people from the other world, being men who had sown the knowledge of many vices among their neighbors and were much
225 greater masters than themselves in every sort of wickedness, did not adopt this sort of vengeance without some reason, and that it must be more painful than their own; so they began to give up their old method and to follow this one.

I am not sorry that we notice the barbarous horror of such acts, but I am heartily sorry that, judging their faults rightly, we should be so blind to our own. I
230 think there is more barbarity in eating a man alive than in eating him dead; and in tearing by tortures and the rack a body still full of feeling, in roasting a man bit by bit, in having him bitten and mangled by dogs and swine (as we have not only read but seen within fresh memory, not among ancient enemies, but among neighbors and fellow citizens, and what is worse, on the pretext of piety and religion), than in
235 roasting and eating him after he is dead.

Indeed, Chrysippus and Zeno, heads of the Stoic sect, thought there was nothing wrong in using our carcasses for any purpose in case of need, and getting nourishment from them; just as our ancestors, when besieged by Caesar in the city of Alésia, resolved to relieve their famine by eating old men, women, and other
240 people useless for fighting.

> The Gascons once, 'tis said, their life renewed
> By eating of such food.
>
> JUVENAL

And physicians do not fear to use human flesh in all sorts of ways for our health, applying it either inwardly or outwardly. But there never was any
245 opinion so disordered as to excuse treachery, disloyalty, tyranny, and cruelty, which are our ordinary vices.

So we may well call these people barbarians, in respect to the rules of reason, but not in respect to ourselves, who surpass them in every kind of barbarity.

Their warfare is wholly noble and generous, and as excusable and beautiful
250 as this human disease can be; its only basis among them is their rivalry in valor. They are not fighting for the conquest of new lands, for they still enjoy that natural abundance that provides them without toil and trouble with all necessary things in such profusion that they have no wish to enlarge their boundaries. They are still in that happy state of desiring only as much as their natural needs
255 demand; anything beyond that is superfluous to them.

They generally call those of the same age, brothers; those who are younger, children; and the old men are fathers to all the others. These leave to their heirs in common the full possession of their property, without division or any other title at all than just the one that Nature gives to her creatures in bringing them into the
260 world.

If their neighbors cross the mountains to attack them and win a victory, the gain of the victor is glory, and the advantage of having proved the master in valor and virtue; for apart from this they have no use for the goods of the vanquished, and they return to their own country, where they lack neither anything necessary
265 nor that great thing, the knowledge of how to enjoy their condition happily and be content with it. These men of ours do the same in their turn. They demand of their prisoners no other ransom than that they confess and acknowledge their defeat. But there is not one in a whole century who does not choose to die rather than to relax a single bit, by word or look, from the grandeur of an invincible courage; not
270 one who would not rather be killed and eaten than so much as ask not to be. They treat them very freely, so that life may be all the dearer to them, and usually entertain them with threats of their coming death, of the torments they will have to suffer, the preparations that are being made for that purpose, the cutting up of their limbs, and the feast that will be made at their expense. All this is done for the
275 sole purpose of extorting from their lips some weak or base word, or making them want to flee, so as to gain the advantage of having terrified them and broken down their firmness. For indeed, if you take it the right way, it is in this point alone that true victory lies:

It is no victory
280 Unless the vanquished foe admits your mastery.
CLAUDIAN

The Hungarians, very bellicose fighters, did not in olden times pursue their advantage beyond putting the enemy at their mercy. For having wrung a confession from him to this effect, they let him go unharmed and unransomed, except, at most, for exacting his promise never again to take up arms against them.
285 We win enough advantages over our enemies that are borrowed advantages, not really our own. It is the quality of a porter, not of valor, to have sturdier arms and legs; agility is a dead and corporeal quality; it is a stroke of luck to make our enemy stumble, or dazzle his eyes by the sunlight; it is a trick of art and technique, which may be found in a worthless coward, to be an able fencer. The worth and
290 value of a man is in his heart and his will; there lies his real honor. Valor is the strength, not of legs and arms, but of heart and soul; it consists not in the worth of our horse or our weapons, but in our own. He who falls obstinate in his courage, *if he has fallen, he fights on his knees* [Seneca]. He who relaxes none of his assurance, no matter how great the danger of imminent death; who, giving up his
295 soul, still looks firmly and scornfully at his enemy—he is beaten not by us, but by fortune; he is killed, not conquered.

The most valiant are sometimes the most unfortunate. Thus there are triumphant defeats that rival victories. Nor did those four sister victories, the fairest that the sun ever set eyes on—Salamis, Plataea, Mycale, and Sicily—ever

300   dare match all their combined glory against the glory of the annihilation of King Leonidas and his men at the pass of Thermopylae.

Who ever hastened with more glorious and ambitious desire to win a battle than Captain Ischolas to lose one? Who ever secured his safety more ingeniously and painstakingly than he did his destruction? He was charged to defend a certain

305   pass in the Peloponnesus against the Arcadians. Finding himself wholly incapable of doing this, in view of the nature of the place and the inequality of the forces, he made up his mind that all who confronted the enemy would necessarily have to remain on the field. On the other hand, deeming it unworthy both of his own virtue and magnanimity and of the Lacedaemonian name to fail in his charge, he took a

310   middle course between these two extremes, in this way. The youngest and fittest of his band be preserved for the defense and service of their country, and sent them home; and with those whose loss was less important, he determined to hold this pass, and by their death to make the enemy buy their entry as dearly as he could. And so it turned out. For he was presently surrounded on all sides by the

315   Arcadians, and after slaughtering a large number of them, he and his men were all put to the sword. Is there a trophy dedicated to victors that would not be more due to these vanquished? The role of true victory is in fighting, not in coming off safely; and the honor of valor consists in combating, not in beating.

To return to our story. These prisoners are so far from giving in, in spite of all

320   that is done to them, that on the contrary, during the two or three months that they are kept, they wear a gay expression; they urge their captors to hurry and put them to the test; they defy them, insult them, reproach them with their cowardice and the number of battles they have lost to the prisoners' own people.

I have a song composed by a prisoner which contains this challenge, that they

325   should all come boldly and gather to dine off him, for they will be eating at the same time their own fathers and grandfathers, who have served to feed and nourish his body. "These muscles," he says, "this flesh and these veins are your own, poor fools that you are. You do not recognize that the substance of your ancestors' limbs is still contained in them. Savor them well; you will find in them

330   the taste of your own flesh." An idea that certainly does not smack of barbarity. Those that paint these people dying, and who show the execution, portray the prisoner spitting in the face of his slayers and scowling at them. Indeed, to the last gasp they never stop braving and defying their enemies by word and look. Truly here are real savages by our standards; for either they must be thoroughly so, or

335   we must be; there is an amazing distance between their character and ours.

The men there have several wives, and the higher their reputation for valor the more wives they have. It is a remarkably beautiful thing about their marriages that the same jealousy our wives have to keep us from the affection and kindness of other women, theirs have to win this for them. Being more concerned for their

340   husbands' honor than for anything else, they strive and scheme to have as many companions as they can, since that is a sign of their husbands' valor.

     Our wives will cry "Miracle!" but it is no miracle. It is a properly matrimonial virtue, but one of the highest order. In the Bible, Leah, Rachel, Sarah, and Jacob's wives gave their beautiful handmaids to their husbands; and Livia

345   seconded the appetites of Augustus, to her own disadvantage; and Stratonice, the wife of King Deiotarus, not only lent her husband for his use a very beautiful young chambermaid in her service, but carefully brought up her children, and backed them up to succeed to their father's estates.

     And lest it be thought that all this is done through a simple and servile

350   bondage to usage and through the pressure of the authority of their ancient customs, without reasoning or judgment, and because their minds are so stupid that they cannot take any other course, I must cite some examples of their capacity. Besides the warlike song I have just quoted, I have another, a love song, which begins in this vein: "Adder, stay; stay, adder, that from the pattern of your

355   coloring my sister may draw the fashion and the workmanship of a rich girdle that I may give to my love; so may your beauty and your pattern be forever preferred to all other serpents." This first couplet is the refrain of the song. Now I am familiar enough with poetry to be a judge of this: not only is there nothing barbarous in this fancy, but it is altogether Anacreontic.[3] Their language, moreover, is a soft

360   language, with an agreeable sound, somewhat like Greek in its endings.

     Three of these men, ignorant of the price they will pay some day, in loss of repose and happiness, for gaining knowledge of the corruptions of this side of the ocean; ignorant also of the fact that of this intercourse will come their ruin (which I suppose is already well advanced: poor wretches, to let themselves be tricked by

365   the desire for new things, and to have left the serenity of their own sky to come and see ours!)—three of these men were at Rouen, at the time the late King Charles IX[4] was there. The king talked to them for a long time; they were shown our ways, our splendor, the aspect of a fine city. After that, someone asked their opinion, and wanted to know what they had found most amazing. They mentioned

370   three things, of which I have forgotten the third, and I am very sorry for it; but I still remember two of them. They said that in the first place they thought it very strange that so many grown men, bearded, strong, and armed, who were around the king (it is likely that they were talking about the Swiss of his guard) should submit to obey a child, and that one of them was not chosen to command instead.

375   Second (they have a way in their language of speaking of men as halves of one another), they had noticed that there were among us men full and gorged with all sorts of good things, and that their other halves were beggars at their doors, emaciated with hunger and poverty; and they thought it strange that these needy halves could endure such an injustice, and did not take the others by the throat, or

380   set fire to their houses.

---

[3]Anacreon was a 6th century Greek lyric poet who was much imitated.
[4]In 1562.

I had a very long talk with one of them; but I had an interpreter who followed my meaning so badly, and who was so hindered by his stupidity in taking in my ideas, that I could get hardly any satisfaction from the man. When I asked him what profit he gained from his superior position among his people (for he was a
385   captain, and our sailors called him king), he told me that it was to march foremost in war. How many men followed him? He pointed to a piece of ground, to signify as many as such a space could hold; it might have been four or five thousand men. Did all his authority expire with the war? He said that this much remained, that when he visited the villages dependent on him, they made paths for him through the
390   underbrush by which he might pass quite comfortably.

All this is not too bad—but what's the use? They don't wear breeches.

(1578–1580)

BOOK II, 1: OF THE INCONSISTENCY OF OUR ACTIONS

Those who make a practice of comparing human actions are never so perplexed as when they try to see them as a whole and in the same light; for they commonly contradict each other so strangely that it seems impossible that they have come from the same shop. One moment young Marius is a son of Mars,
5   another moment a son of Venus. Pope Boniface VIII, they say, entered office like a fox, behaved in it like a lion, and died like a dog. And who would believe that it was Nero, that living image of cruelty, who said, when they brought him in customary fashion the sentence of a condemned criminal to sign: "Would to God I had never learned to write!" So much his heart was wrung at condemning a man to
10   death!

Everything is so full of such examples—each man, in fact, can supply himself with so many—that I find it strange to see intelligent men sometimes going to great pains to match these pieces; seeing that irresolution seems to me the most common and apparent defect of our nature, as witness that famous line of Publilius, the
15   farce writer:

Bad is the plan that never can be changed.

PUBLILIUS SYRUS

There is some justification for basing a judgment of a man on the most ordinary acts of his life; but in view of the natural instability of our conduct and opinions, it has often seemed to me that even good authors are wrong to insist on
20   fashioning a consistent and solid fabric out of us. They choose one general characteristic, and go and arrange and interpret all a man's actions to fit their picture; and if they cannot twist them enough, they go and set them down to dissimulation. Augustus has escaped them; for there is in this man throughout the course of his life such an obvious, abrupt, and continual variety of actions that
25   even the boldest judges have had to let him go, intact and unsolved. Nothing is harder for me than to believe in men's consistency, nothing easier than to believe

in their inconsistency. He who would judge them in detail and distinctly, bit by bit, would more often hit upon the truth.

30   In all antiquity it is hard to pick out a dozen men who set their lives to a certain and constant course, which is the principal goal of wisdom. For, to comprise all wisdom in a word, says an ancient [Seneca], and to embrace all the rules of our life in one, it is "always to will the same things, and always to oppose the same things." I would not deign, he says, to add "provided the will is just"; for if it is not just, it cannot always be whole.

35   In truth, I once learned that vice is only unruliness and lack of moderation, and that consequently consistency cannot be attributed to it. It is a maxim of Demosthenes, they say, that the beginning of all virtue is consultation and deliberation; and the end and perfection, consistency. If it were by reasoning that we settled on a particular course of action, we would choose the fairest course—
40 but no one has thought of that:

> He spurns the thing he sought, and seeks anew
> What he just spurned; he seethes, his life's askew.
> HORACE

    Our ordinary practice is to follow the inclinations of our appetite, to the left, to the right, uphill and down, as the wind of circumstance carries us. We think of
45 what we want only at the moment we want it, and we change like that animal which takes the color of the place you set it on. What we have just now planned, we presently change, and presently again we retrace our steps: nothing but oscillation and inconsistency:

> Like puppets we are moved by outside strings.
> HORACE

50   We do not go; we are carried away, like floating objects, now gently, now violently, according as the water is angry or calm:

> Do we not see all humans unaware
> Of what they want, and always searching everywhere,
> And changing place, as if to drop the load they bear?
> LUCRETIUS

55   Every day a new fancy, and our humors shift with the shifts in the weather:

> Such are the minds of men, as is the fertile light
> That Father Jove himself sends down to make earth bright.
> HOMER

We float between different states of mind; we wish nothing freely, nothing absolutely, nothing constantly. If any man could prescribe and establish definite laws and a definite organization in his head, we should see shining throughout his life an evenness of habits, an order, and an infallible relation between his principles and his practice.

Empedocles noticed this inconsistency in the Agrigentines, that they abandoned themselves to pleasures as if they were to die on the morrow, and built as if they were never to die.

This man[5] would be easy to understand, as is shown by the example of the younger Cato: he who has touched one chord of him has touched all; he is a harmony of perfectly concordant sounds, which cannot conflict. With us, it is the opposite: for so many actions, we need so many individual judgments. The surest thing, in my opinion, would be to trace our actions to the neighboring circumstances, without getting into any further research and without drawing from them any other conclusions.

During the disorders of our poor country,[6] I was told that a girl, living near where I then was, had thrown herself out of a high window to avoid the violence of a knavish soldier quartered in her house. Not killed by the fall, she reasserted her purpose by trying to cut her throat with a knife. From this she was prevented, but only after wounding herself gravely. She herself confessed that the soldier had as yet pressed her only with requests, solicitations, and gifts; but she had been afraid, she said, that he would finally resort to force. And all this with such words, such expressions, not to mention the blood that testified to her virtue, as would have become another Lucrece. Now, I learned that as a matter of fact, both before and since, she was a wench not so hard to come to terms with. As the story says: Handsome and gentlemanly as you may be, when you have had no luck, do not promptly conclude that your mistress is inviolably chaste; for all you know, the mule driver may get his will with her.

Antigonus, having taken a liking to one of his soldiers for his virtue and valor, ordered his physicians to treat the man for a persistent internal malady that had long tormented him. After his cure, his master noticed that he was going about his business much less warmly, and asked him what had changed him so and made him such a coward. "You yourself, Sire," he answered, "by delivering me from the ills that made my life indifferent to me." A soldier of Lucullus who had been robbed of everything by the enemy made a bold attack on them to get revenge. When he had retrieved his loss, Lucullus, having formed a good opinion of him, urged him to some dangerous exploit with all the fine expostulations he could think of,

With words that might have stirred a coward's heart.

HORACE

---

[5]The disciplined man in the sentence before last.

[6]The religious civil wars between Catholics and Protestants, which lasted intermittently from 1562 to 1594.

"Urge some poor soldier who has been robbed to do it," he replied;

> Though but a rustic lout,
> "That man will go who's lost his money," he called out;
>   HORACE

and resolutely refused to go.

100   We read that Sultan Mohammed outrageously berated Hassan, leader of his Janissaries, because he saw his troops giving way to the Hungarians and Hassan himself behaving like a coward in the fight. Hassan's only reply was to go and hurl himself furiously—alone, just as he was, arms in hand—into the first body of enemies that he met, by whom he was promptly swallowed up; this was perhaps
105   not so much self-justification as a change of mood, nor so much his natural valor as fresh spite.

    That man whom you saw so adventurous yesterday, do not think it strange to find him just as cowardly today: either anger, or necessity, or company, or wine, or the sound of a trumpet, had put his heart in his belly. His was a courage formed
110   not by reason, but by one of these circumstances; it is no wonder if he has now been made different by other, contrary circumstances.

    These supple variations and contradictions that are seen in us have made some imagine that we have two souls, and others that two powers accompany us and drive us, each in its own way, one toward good, the other toward evil; for
115   such sudden diversity cannot well be reconciled with a simple subject.

    Not only does the wind of accident move me at will, but, besides, I am moved and disturbed as a result merely of my own unstable posture; and anyone who observes carefully can hardly find himself twice in the same state. I give my soul now one face, now another, according to which direction I turn it. If I speak of
120   myself in different ways, that is because I look at myself in different ways. All contradictions may be found in me by some twist and in some fashion. Bashful, insolent; chaste, lascivious; talkative, taciturn; tough, delicate; clever, stupid; surly, affable; lying, truthful; learned, ignorant; liberal, miserly, and prodigal: all this I see in myself to some extent according to how I turn; and whoever studies
125   himself really attentively finds in himself, yes, even in his judgment, this gyration and discord. I have nothing to say about myself absolutely, simply, and solidly, without confusion and without mixture, or in one word. *Distinguo* is the most universal member of my logic.

    Although I am always minded to say good of what is good, and inclined to
130   interpret favorably anything that can be so interpreted, still it is true that the strangeness of our condition makes it happen that we are often driven to do good by vice itself—were it not that doing good is judged by intention alone.

    Therefore one courageous deed must not be taken to prove a man valiant; a man who was really valiant would be so always and on all occasions. If valor
135   were a habit of virtue, and not a sally, it would make a man equally resolute in any contingency, the same alone as in company, the same in single combat as in

battle; for, whatever they say, there is not one valor for the pavement and another for the camp. As bravely would he bear an illness in his bed as a wound in camp, and he would fear death no more in his home than in an assault. We would not see
140 the same man charging into the breach with brave assurance, and later tormenting himself, like a woman, over the loss of a lawsuit or a son. When, though a coward against infamy, he is firm against poverty; when, though weak against the surgeons' knives, he is steadfast against the enemy's swords, the action is praiseworthy, not the man.
145   Many Greeks, says Cicero, cannot look at the enemy, and are brave in sickness; the Cimbrians and Celtiberians, just the opposite; *for nothing can be uniform that does not spring from a firm principle* [Cicero].

    There is no more extreme valor of its kind than Alexander's; but it is only of one kind, and not complete and universal enough. Incomparable though it is, it still
150 has its blemishes; which is why we see him worry so frantically when he conceives the slightest suspicion that his men are plotting against his life, and why he behaves in such matters with such violent and indiscriminate injustice and with a fear that subverts his natural reason. Also superstition, with which he was so strongly tainted, bears some stamp of pusillanimity. And the excessiveness of the
155 penance he did for the murder of Clytus is also evidence of the unevenness of his temper.

    Our actions are nothing but a patchwork—*they despise pleasure, but are too cowardly in pain; they are indifferent to glory, but infamy breaks their spirit* [Cicero]—and we want to gain honor under false colors. Virtue will not be
160 followed except for her own sake; and if we sometimes borrow her mask for some other purpose, she promptly snatches it from our face. It is a strong and vivid dye, once the soul is steeped in it, and will not go without taking the fabric with it. That is why, to judge a man, we must follow his traces long and carefully. If he does not maintain consistency for its own sake, *with a way of life that has been well*
165 *considered and preconcerted* [Cicero]; if changing circumstances make him change his pace (I mean his path, for his pace may be hastened or slowed), let him go: that man goes before the wind, as the motto of our Talbot says.

    It is no wonder, says an ancient [Seneca], that chance has so much power over us, since we live by chance. A man who has not directed his life as a whole
170 toward a definite goal cannot possibly set his particular actions in order. A man who does not have a picture of the whole in his head cannot possibly arrange the pieces. What good does it do a man to lay in a supply of paints if he does not know what he is to paint? No one makes a definite plan of his life; we think about it only piecemeal. The archer must first know what he is aiming at, and then set his
175 hand, his bow, his string, his arrow, and his movements for that goal. Our plans go astray because they have no direction and no aim. No wind works for the man who has no port of destination.

    I do not agree with the judgment given in favor of Sophocles, on the strength of seeing one of his tragedies, that it proved him competent to manage his domestic
180 affairs, against the accusation of his son. Nor do I think that the conjecture of the

Parians sent to reform the Milesians was sufficient ground for the conclusion they drew. Visiting the island, they noticed the best-cultivated lands and the best-run country houses, and noted down the names of their owners. Then they assembled the citizens in the town and appointed these owners the new governors and

185   magistrates, judging that they, who were careful of their private affairs, would be careful of those of the public.

We are all patchwork, and so shapeless and diverse in composition that each bit, each moment, plays its own game. And there is as much difference between us and ourselves as between us and others. *Consider it a great thing to play the part of*

190   *one single man* [Seneca]. Ambition can teach men valor, and temperance, and liberality, and even justice. Greed can implant in the heart of a shop apprentice, brought up in obscurity and idleness, the confidence to cast himself far from hearth and home, in a frail boat at the mercy of the waves and angry Neptune; it also teaches discretion and wisdom. Venus herself supplies resolution and boldness to

195   boys still subject to discipline and the rod, and arms the tender hearts of virgins who are still in their mothers' laps:

> Furtively passing sleeping guards, with Love as guide,
> Alone by night the girl comes to the young man's side.
> TIBULLUS

In view of this, a sound intellect will refuse to judge men simply by their outward actions; we must probe the inside and discover what springs set men in motion. But since this is an arduous and hazardous undertaking, I wish fewer people would meddle with it.

(1572–1574)

BOOK II, 10: OF BOOKS

I have no doubt that I often happen to speak of things that are better treated by the masters of the craft, and more truthfully. This is purely the essay of my natural faculties, and not at all of the acquired ones; and whoever shall catch me in ignorance will do nothing against me, for I should hardly be answerable for my

5   ideas to others, I who am not answerable for them to myself, or satisfied with them. Whoever is in search of knowledge, let him fish for it where it dwells; there is nothing I profess less. These are my fancies, by which I try to give knowledge not of things, but of myself. The things will perhaps be known to me some day, or have been once, according as fortune may have brought me to the places where

10   they were made clear. But I no longer remember them. And if I am a man of some reading, I am a man of no retentiveness.

Thus I guarantee no certainty, unless it be to make known to what point, at this moment, extends the knowledge that I have of myself. Let attention be paid not to the matter, but to the shape I give it.

15   Let people see in what I borrow whether I have known how to choose what would enhance my theme. For I make others say what I cannot say so well, now through the weakness of my language, now through the weakness of my understanding. I do not count my borrowings, I weigh them. And if I had wanted to have them valued by their number, I should have loaded myself with twice as

20   many. They are all, or very nearly all, from such famous and ancient names that they seem to identify themselves enough without me. In the reasonings and inventions that I transplant into my soil and confound with my own, I have sometimes deliberately not indicated the author, in order to hold in check the temerity of those hasty condemnations that are tossed at all sorts of writings,

25   notably recent writings of men still living, and in the vulgar tongue, which invites everyone to talk about them and seems to convict the conception and design of being likewise vulgar. I want them to give Plutarch a fillip on my nose and get burned insulting Seneca in me. I have to hide my weakness under these great authorities. I will love anyone that can unplume me, I mean by clearness of

30   judgement and by the sole distinction of the force and beauty of the remarks. For I who, for lack of memory, fall short at every turn in picking them out by knowledge of their origin, can very well realize, by measuring my capacity, that my soil is not at all capable of producing certain too rich flowers that I find sown there, and that all the fruits of my own growing could not match them.

35   For this I am obliged to be responsible: if I get myself tangled up, if there is vanity and faultiness in my reasonings that I do not perceive or that I am not capable of perceiving when pointed out to me. For faults often escape our eyes; but infirmity of judgment consists in not being able to perceive them when another reveals them to us. Knowledge and truth can lodge in us without judgment, and

40   judgment also without them; indeed the recognition of ignorance is one of the fairest and surest testimonies of judgment that I find.

        I have no other marshal but fortune to arrange my bits. As my fancies present themselves, I pile them up; now they come pressing in a crowd, now dragging single file. I want people to see my natural and ordinary pace, however off the track it is.

45   I let myself go as I am. Besides, these are not matters of which we are forbidden to be ignorant and to speak casually and at random.

        I should certainly like to have a more perfect knowledge of things, but I do not want to buy it as dear as it costs. My intention is to pass pleasantly, and not laboriously, what life I have left. There is nothing for which I want to rack my

50   brain, not even knowledge, however great its value.

        I seek in books only to give myself pleasure by honest amusement; or if I study, I seek only the learning that treats of the knowledge of myself and instructs me in how to die well and live well:

        This is the goal toward which my sweating horse should strain.

                                                        PROPERTIUS

55 If I encounter difficulties in reading, I do not gnaw my nails over them; I leave
them there, after making one or two attacks on them. If I planted myself in them, I
would lose both myself and time; for I have an impulsive mind. What I do not see at
the first attack, I see less by persisting. I do nothing without gaiety; continuation
and too strong contention dazes, depresses, and wearies my judgement. My sight
60 becomes confused and dispersed. I have to withdraw it and apply it again by
starts, just as in order to judge the luster of a scarlet fabric, they tell us to pass our
eyes over it several times, catching it in various quickly renewed and repeated
glimpses.

If this book wearies me, I take up another; and I apply myself to it only at the
65 moments when the boredom of doing nothing begins to grip me. I do not take much
to modern books, because the ancient ones seem to me fuller and stronger; nor to
those in Greek, because my judgement cannot do its work with a childish and
apprentice understanding.

Among the books that are simply entertaining, I find, of the moderns, the
70 *Decameron* of Boccaccio, Rabelais, and *The Kisses* of Johannes Secundus, if they
may be placed under this heading, worth reading for amusement. As for the
Amadises and writings of that sort, they did not have the authority to detain even
my childhood. I will also say this, whether boldly or rashly, that this heavy old
soul of mine no longer lets itself be tickled, not merely by Ariosto, but even by the
75 good Ovid: his facility and inventions, which once enchanted me, hardly entertain
me at all now.

I speak my mind freely on all things, even on those which perhaps exceed my
capacity and which I by no means hold to be within my jurisdiction. And so the
opinion I give of them is to declare the measure of my sight, not the measure of
80 things. When I feel a distaste for Plato's *Axiochus* as a work without power
considering such an author, my judgment does not trust itself: it is not so stupid as
to oppose itself to the authority of so many other famous ancient judgments, which
it considers its tutors and masters, and with which it is rather content to err. It
blames and condemns itself either for stopping at the outer bark, not being able to
85 penetrate to the heart, or for looking at the thing by some false light. It is content
with simply securing itself from confusion and disorder; as for its weakness, it
readily recognizes and admits it. It thinks it gives a correct interpretation to the
appearances that its conception presents to it; but these are weak and imperfect.

Most of Aesop's Fables have many meanings and interpretations. Those who
90 take them allegorically choose some aspect that squares with the fable, but for the
most part this is only the first and superficial aspect; there are others more living,
more essential and internal, to which they have not known how to penetrate; this
is how I read them.

But, to pursue my path, it has always seemed to me that in poetry Virgil,
95 Lucretius, Catullus, and Horace hold the first rank by very far, and especially
Virgil in his *Georgics*, which I consider the most accomplished work in poetry; in
comparison with it one can easily recognize that there are passages in the *Aeneid*
which the author would have brushed up still a little more if he had had the

100 chance. And the fifth book of the *Aeneid* seems to me the most perfect. I also love Lucan and enjoy his company, not so much for his style as for his own worth and the truth of his opinions and judgments. As for the good Terence, the very refinement and charm of the Latin language, I find him admirable at representing to the life the movements of the soul and the state of our characters; at every moment our actions throw me back to him. I cannot read him so often as not to find in him

105 some new beauty and grace.

Those who lived near Virgil's time used to complain that some compared Lucretius to him. I am of the opinion that that is in truth an unequal comparison; but I have much to do to confirm myself in this belief when I find myself fixed on one of the beautiful passages in Lucretius. If they were stung by this comparison,

110 what would they say of the barbarous brutishness and stupidity of those who nowadays compare Ariosto to him? And what would Ariosto himself say?

> O foolish and dull-witted age!
>
> CATULLUS

I think the ancients had still more reason to complain of those who compared Plautus to Terence (the latter savors much more of the gentleman) than of those

115 who compared Lucretius to Virgil. It does much for the esteem and preference of Terence that the father of Roman eloquence[7] has him, and him alone of his class, so often in his mouth; and also the verdict that the first judge among the Roman poets[8] gives of his fellow.

It has often struck my mind how in our time those who set themselves to write

120 comedies (like the Italians, who are rather happy at it) use three or four plots from Terence or Plautus to make one of their own. They pile up in a single comedy five or six stories from Boccaccio. What makes them so load themselves with material is the distrust they have of being able to sustain themselves by their own graces; they have to find a body to lean on; and not having enough of their own to detain

125 us, they want the story to amuse us. It is quite the contrary with my author: the perfections and beauties of his style of expression make us lose our appetite for his subject. His distinction and elegance hold us throughout; he is everywhere so delightful,

> Clear flowing and most like a crystal stream,
>
> HORACE

130 and so fills our soul with his charms, that we forget those of his plot.

This same consideration draws me on further. I observe that the good ancient poets avoided the affectation and the quest, not only of the fantastic Spanish and Petrarchian flights, but even of the milder and more restrained conceits that are the

---

[7]Cicero.
[8]Horace.

adornment of all the poetic works of the succeeding centuries. Yet there is no good
135 judge who misses them in those ancients, and who does not admire incomparably
more the even polish and that perpetual sweetness and flowering beauty of
Catullus' epigrams than all the stings with which Martial sharpens the tails of
his. This is for the same reason that I was stating just now, as Martial says of
himself: *he had less need for the labor of wit, since his subject matter took the place of*
140 *wit.* The former, without getting excited and without goading themselves, make
themselves sufficiently felt: they have matter enough for laughter everywhere, they
don't have to tickle themselves. The latter need outside help: the less wit they have,
the more body they need. They mount on horseback because they are not strong
enough on their legs.
145   Just as at our balls these men of low condition who keep dancing schools, not
being able to imitate the bearing and fitness of our nobility, seek to recommend
themselves by perilous leaps and other strange mountebank's antics. And the
ladies can more cheaply show off their carriage in the dances where there are
various contortions and twistings of the body, than in certain other formal dances
150 where they need only walk with a natural step and display a natural bearing and
their ordinary grace. As I have also seen excellent clowns, in their ordinary dress
and usual face, give us all the pleasure that can be derived from their art, while the
apprentices and those who are not so highly skilled need to flour their faces, dress
up, and counterfeit wild movements and grimaces in order to make us laugh.
155   This idea of mine is easier to recognize in the comparison of the *Aeneid* and
the *Orlando Furioso* than anywhere else. We see the former on outspread wings in
lofty and sustained flight always pursuing his point; the latter fluttering and
hopping from tale to tale as from branch to branch, not trusting his wings except
for a very short hop, and alighting at every turn for fear his breath and strength
160 should fail:

He tries his wings in short excursions.

                                                    VIRGIL

These, then, in this sort of subjects, are the authors I like best.
       As for my other reading, which mingles a little more profit with the pleasure,
and by which I learn to arrange my humors and my ways, the books that serve me
165 for this are Plutarch, since he exists in French, and Seneca. They both have this
notable advantage for my humor, that the knowledge I seek is there treated in
detached pieces that do not demand the obligation of long labor, of which I am
incapable. Such are the *Moral Essays* of Plutarch and the *Epistles* of Seneca,
which are the finest part of his writings, and the most profitable. I need no great
170 enterprise to get at them, and I leave them whenever I like. For they have no
continuity from one to the other.
       These authors agree in most of the opinions that are useful and true; and so
were their fortunes similar: they were born at about the same time, each tutored a
Roman Emperor, both came from foreign countries, both were rich and powerful.

175 Their teaching is the cream of philosophy, and presented in simple and pertinent
     fashion. Plutarch is more uniform and constant, Seneca more undulating and
     diverse. The latter labors, strains, and tenses himself to arm virtue against
     weakness, fear, and vicious appetites; the other seems not to esteem their power so
     much, and to disdain to hurry his step or stand on guard for them. Plutarch's
180 opinions are Platonic, mild, and accommodated to civil society; the other's are
     Stoic and Epicurean, more remote from common use, but in my opinion more
     suitable for private life and more sturdy. In Seneca it seems that he concedes a
     little to the tyranny of the emperors of his time, for I hold it for certain that it is by
     a forced judgment that he condemns the cause of those high-minded murderers of
185 Caesar; Plutarch is free throughout. Seneca is full of witty points and sallies,
     Plutarch of things. The former heats you and moves you more; the latter contents
     you more and pays you better. He guides us, the other pushes us.

     As for Cicero, the works of his that can best serve my purpose are those that
     treat of philosophy, especially moral. But to confess the truth boldly (for once you
190 have crossed over the barriers of impudence there is no more curb), his way of
     writing, and every other similar way, seems to me boring. For his prefaces,
     definitions, partitions, etymologies, consume the greater part of his work; what
     life and marrow there is, is smothered by his long-winded preparations. If I have
     spent an hour in reading him, which is a lot for me, and I remember what juice and
195 substance I have derived, most of the time I find nothing but wind; for he has not
     yet come to the arguments that serve his purpose and the reasons that properly
     touch on the crux, which I am looking for.

     For me, who ask only to become wiser, not more learned or eloquent, these
     logical and Aristotelian arrangements are not to the point. I want a man to begin
200 with the conclusion. I understand well enough what death and pleasure are; let
     him not waste his time anatomizing them. I look for good solid reasons from the
     start, which will instruct me in how to sustain their attack. Neither grammatical
     subtleties nor an ingenious contexture of words and argumentations are any use
     for that. I want reasonings that drive their first attack into the stronghold of the
205 doubt; his languish around the pot. They are good for the school, for the bar, and
     for the sermon, where we have leisure to nap and are still in time a quarter of an
     hour later to pick up the thread of the discourse. It is necessary to speak thus to
     judges, whom we want to win over rightly or wrongly, to children, and to the
     common herd, to whom we have to say everything to see what will carry.

210 I do not want a man to use his strength making me attentive and to shout at me
     fifty times *"Or oyez!"* in the manner of our heralds. The Romans used to say in
     their religion *"Hoc age,"* as we say in ours *"Sursum corda"*:[9] these are so many
     words lost on me. I come fully prepared from my house; I need no allurement or
     sauce; I can perfectly well eat my meat quite raw; and instead of whetting my
215 appetite by these preparations and preliminaries, they pall and weary it.

---

[9] *"Or oyez!"*—"Now listen." *"Hoc age"*—"Give heed." *"Sursum corda"*—"Lift up your
hearts."

Will the license of the times excuse my sacrilegious audacity in considering
that even Plato's dialogues drag and stifle his substance too much, and in
lamenting the time put into these long vain preliminary interlocutions by a man
who had so many better things to say? My ignorance will excuse me better in that
220   I have no perception of the beauty of his language. In general I ask for books that
make use of learning, not those that build it up.

The first two, and Pliny, and their like, have no *Hoc age;* they want to have to
do with men who themselves have told themselves this; or if they have one, it is a
substantial *Hoc age* that has a body of its own.

225   I also like to read the *Letters to Atticus,*[10] not only because they contain a
very ample education in the history and affairs of his time, but much more because
in them I discover his personal humors. For I have a singular curiosity, as I have
said elsewhere, to know the soul and the natural judgments of my authors. We
must indeed judge their capacity, but not their character nor themselves, by that
230   display of their writings that they expose on the stage of the world. I have
regretted a thousand times that we have lost the book that Brutus had written on
virtue: for it is a fine thing to learn the theory from those who well know the
practice. But since the preachings are one thing and the preacher another, I am as
glad to see Brutus in Plutarch as in a book of his own. I would rather choose to
235   know truly the conversation he held in his tent with some one of his intimate
friends on the eve of a battle than the speech he made the next day to his army; and
what he was doing in his study and his chamber than what he was doing in the
public square and in the Senate.

As for Cicero, I am of the common opinion, that except for learning there was
240   not much excellence in his soul. He was a good citizen, of an affable nature, as all
fat jesting men, such as he was, are apt to be; but of softness and ambitious vanity
he had in truth a great deal. And moreover I do not know how to excuse him for
having considered his poetry worth being published. It is not a great imperfection
to write verses badly; but it is a lack of judgment in him not to have felt how
245   unworthy they were of the glory of his name. As for his eloquence, it is entirely
beyond comparison; I believe that no man will ever equal him.

The younger Cicero, who resembled his father only in name, while
commanding in Asia, had several strangers at his table one day, and among others
Cestius, seated at the lower end, as people often push in to the open tables of the
250   great. Cicero inquired who he was of one of his men, who told him his name. But
like a man whose thoughts were elsewhere and who kept forgetting what they
answered him, he asked him that again two or three more times. The servant, in
order not to have the trouble of repeating the same thing so often to him, and to
make him know him by some circumstance, said to him: "It is that Cestius of whom
255   you were told that he sets no great store by your father's eloquence in comparison
with his own." Cicero, suddenly stung by this, ordered them to lay hold of this

[10]By Cicero.

poor Cestius and had him very soundly whipped in his presence. That was a discourteous host!

Even among those who, all things considered, esteemed this eloquence of his as incomparable, there were some who did not fail to note some faults in it; thus the great Brutus, his friend, used to say that it was a broken and weak-loined eloquence, *fractam et elumbem.*[11] The orators who lived near his time also reprehended in him his sedulous care for a certain long cadence at the end of his periods, and noted the words *esse videatur*[12] which he uses so often. As for me, I prefer a cadence that falls shorter, cut into iambics. To be sure, he does sometimes mix up his rhythms quite roughly, but rarely. My ears have noted this passage: "Ego vero me minus diu senem esse mallem, quam esse senem, antequam essem."[13]

The historians come right to my forehand. They are pleasant and easy; and at the same time, man in general, the knowledge of whom I seek, appears in them more alive and entire than in any other place—the diversity and truth of his inner qualities in the mass and in detail, the variety of the ways he is put together, and the accidents that threaten him. Now those who write biographies, since they spend more time on plans than on events, more on what comes from within than on what happens without, are most suited to me. That is why in every way Plutarch is my man. I am very sorry that we do not have a dozen Laertiuses, or that he is not either more receptive or more perceptive. For I consider no less curiously the fortunes and the lives of these great teachers of the world than the diversity of their doctrines and fancies.

In this kind of study of history we must leaf without distinction through all sorts of authors, both old and new, both gibberish and French, in order to learn in them the things of which they variously treat. But it seems to me that Caesar singularly deserves to be studied, not only for the knowledge of history, but for himself, so much perfection and excellence he has above all the others, although Sallust is one of their number. Indeed I read this author with a little more reverence and respect than one reads human works: now considering him in himself by his actions and the miracle of his greatness, now the purity and inimitable polish of his language, which surpassed not only all the historians, as Cicero says, but perhaps Cicero himself. With so much sincerity in his judgments when speaking of his enemies, that except for the false colors with which he tries to cover his evil cause and the filthiness of his pestilential ambition, I think the only fault that can be found in him is that he has been too sparing in speaking of himself. For so many great things cannot have been performed by him without much more of himself having gone into them than he sets down.

I like historians who are either very simple or outstanding. The simple, who have not the wherewithal to mix in anything of their own, and who bring to it only the care and diligence to collect all that comes to their attention and to record

---

[11]"broken and weak"

[12]"It would seem to be."

[13]"For my part, in truth, I would rather be old less long than be old before I am old."

everything faithfully without choice or discrimination, leave our judgment intact
to discern the truth. Such, for example, among others, is the good Froissart, who
has gone along in his undertaking with such frank simplicity that having made a
300 mistake he is not at all afraid to recognize it and correct it at the spot where he
has been made aware of it; and who presents to us even the diversity of the rumors
that were current and the different reports that were made to him. This is the
material of history, naked and unformed; each man can make his profit of it
according to his understanding.
305   The really outstanding ones have the capacity to choose what is worth
knowing; they can pick out of two reports the one that is more likely. From the
nature and humors of princes they infer their intentions and attribute appropriate
words to them. They are right to assume the authority to regulate our belief by
their own; but certainly this privilege belongs to very few people.
310   Those in between (which are the commonest sort) spoil everything for us.
They want to chew our morsels for us; they give themselves the right to judge, and
consequently to slant history to their fancy; for once the judgment leans to one
side, one cannot help turning and twisting the narrative to that bias. They
undertake to choose the things worth knowing, and often conceal from us a given
315 word, a given private action, that would instruct us better; they omit as incredible
the things they do not understand, and perhaps also some things because they do
not know how to say them in good Latin or French. Let them boldly display their
eloquence and their reasonings, let them judge all they like; but let them also leave
us the wherewithal to judge after them, and not alter or arrange by their
320 abridgments and selection anything of the substance of the matter, but pass it on to
us pure and entire in all its dimensions.
Most of the time, especially in these days, people are selected for this work
from among the common herd for the sole consideration of knowing how to speak
well; as if here we were trying to learn grammar! And having been hired only for
325 that and having put on sale only their babble, they are right accordingly to care
chiefly only about that part. Thus with many fine words they go and cook up a
fine concoction of the rumors they pick up in the city squares.
The only good histories are those that have been written by the very men who
were in command in the affairs, or who were participants in the conduct of them,
330 or who at least have had the fortune to conduct others of the same sort. Such are
almost all the Greek and Roman histories. For when several eyewitnesses have
written about the same subject (as it happened in those days that greatness and
learning usually met), if there is a mistake, it must be very slight, and on a very
doubtful incident. What can you expect of a doctor discussing war, or a schoolboy
335 discussing the intentions of princes? If we want to note the scruples the Romans
had in this, we need only this example. Asinius Pollio found in the histories even
of Caesar some mistake into which he had fallen through not having been able to
keep his eyes on every part of his army and having believed individuals who often
reported to him things insufficiently verified; or else through not having been
340 carefully enough informed by his lieutenants about what they had done in his

absence. We can see by this example whether this quest of truth is delicate, when we cannot trust the commander's knowledge of a battle his soldiers have fought, or the soldiers' knowledge of what happened near them, unless, in the manner of a judicial inquiry, we confront the witnesses and hear the objections about the
345 evidence in the slightest details of each incident. Truly, the knowledge we have of our own affairs is much looser. But this has been sufficiently treated by Bodin, and according to my way of thinking.

To compensate a little for the treachery and weakness of my memory, so extreme that it has happened to me more than once to pick up again, as recent and
350 unknown to me, books which I had read carefully a few years before and scribbled over with my notes, I have adopted the habit for some time now of adding at the end of each book (I mean of those that I intend to use only once) the time I finished reading it and the judgment I have derived of it as a whole, so that this may represent to me at least the sense and general idea I had conceived of the
355 author in reading it. I want to transcribe here some of these annotations.

Here is what I put some ten years ago in my Guicciardini (for whatever language my books speak, I speak to them in my own): "He is a diligent historiographer from whom, in my opinion, one can learn the truth about the affairs of his time as exactly as from any other: and indeed in most of them he was
360 an actor himself, and of honorable rank. There is no appearance that through hatred, favor, or vanity, he disguised things; which is attested by the free judgments he gives of the great, and especially of those by whom he had been advanced and employed in responsibilities, like Pope Clement VII. As for the part he seems to want to make most of, which is his digressions and discourses, there
365 are some good ones and enriched with fine traits, but he is too fond of them. For by not wanting to leave anything unsaid, having a subject so full and ample and almost infinite, he becomes diffuse and smacking a bit of scholastic prattle. I have also noted this, that of so many souls and actions that he judges, so many motives and plans, he never refers a single one to virtue, religion, and conscience, as if
370 these qualities were wholly extinct in the world; and of all actions, however fair in appearance they may be of themselves, he throws the cause back onto some vicious motive or some profit. It is impossible to imagine that among the infinite number of actions that he judges there was not a single one produced by the way of reason. No corruption can have seized men so universally that someone would not
375 escape the contagion. This makes me fear that his taste was a bit corrupted; and it may have happened that he judged others by himself."

In my Philippe de Commines there is this: "Here you will find the language pleasant and agreeable, of a natural simplicity; the narrative pure, and the author's good faith showing through it clearly, free from vanity in speaking of
380 himself, and of partiality or envy in speaking of others; his ideas and exhortations accompanied more by good zeal and truth than by any exquisite capacity; and, throughout, authority and gravity, representing the man of good background and brought up in great affairs."

On the *Memoirs* of Monsieur du Bellay:[14] "It is always a pleasure to see
385 things written by people who have experienced how they should be conducted; but
it cannot be denied that there is clearly revealed in these two lords a great falling
off from the frankness and freedom of writing that shine forth in the ancients of
their class, such as the sire de Joinville, intimate friend of Saint Louis; Eginhard,
chancellor of Charlemagne; and, of more recent memory, Philippe de Commines.
390 This is rather a plea for King Francis against the Emperor Charles V, than a
history. I will not believe that they have changed anything in the main facts; but as
for turning the judgment of events to our advantage, often contrary to reason, and
omitting everything that is ticklish in the life of their master, they make a practice
of it: witness the disgrace of Messieurs de Montmorency and de Brion, which are
395 forgotten; indeed the very name of Madame d'Etampes is not to be found. One may
cover up secret actions; but to be silent about what all the world knows, and
about things that have led to public results of such consequence, is an inexcusable
defect. In short, to get a complete knowledge of King Francis and the events of his
time, a man should turn elsewhere, if he takes my advice. The profit one can make
400 here is from the detailed narrative of the battles and exploits of war at which
these gentlemen were present; some private words and actions of certain princes of
their time; and the dealings and negotiations carried on by the seigneur de Langey,
in which there are plenty of things worth knowing, and ideas above the
ordinary."

(1578–1580)

---

[14]These *Memoirs*, which cover the years 1513–47 and were first published in 1569, are
presented by Martin du Bellay but include three books (out of ten) by his brother
Guillaume du Bellay, seigneur de Langey. This explains Montaigne's reference to "these
two lords."

BOOK II, 17: OF PRESUMPTION

There is another kind of vainglory, which is an over-good opinion we form of our own worth. It is an unreasoning affection, by which we cherish ourselves, which represents us to ourselves as other than we are; as the passion of love lends beauties and graces to the object it embraces, and makes its victims, with muddled
5 and unsettled judgment, think that what they love is other and more perfect than it is.

However, I do not want a man to misjudge himself, for fear of erring in that direction, or to think himself less than he is. Judgment must maintain its rights in all matters; it is right that it should see, in this subject as elsewhere, what truth
10 sets before it. If he is Caesar, let him boldly judge himself the greatest captain in the world.

We are nothing but ceremony; ceremony carries us away, and we leave the substance of things; we hang on to the branches and abandon the trunk and body. We have taught the ladies to blush at the mere mention of what they are not at all
15 afraid to do; we dare not call our members by their right names, and we are not afraid to employ them in every kind of debauchery. Ceremony forbids our expressing in words things that are permissible and natural, and we obey it; reason forbids our doing things that are illicit and wicked, and no one obeys it. I find myself here entangled in the laws of ceremony, for she does not allow a man
20 either to speak well of himself, or to speak ill. We shall let her alone for the moment.

Those whom Fortune (whether we should call her good or bad) has caused to spend their lives in some eminent station, can testify to what they are by their public actions. But those whom she has employed only in a mass, and of whom no
25 one will speak unless they do so themselves, may be excused if they have the temerity to speak of themselves to those who have an interest in knowing them, after the example of Lucilius:

He would confide, as unto trusted friends,
His secrets to his notebooks; turn there still,
30 Not elsewhere, whether faring well or ill.
So that the old man's whole life lay revealed
As on a votive tablet.
                                        Horace

That man committed to his paper his actions and thoughts, and portrayed himself there as he felt he was. *Nor did anyone doubt the honesty or disparage the motives of*
35 *Rutilius or Scaurus for doing so* [Tacitus].

So I remember that from my tenderest childhood people noticed in me some indefinable carriage of the body and certain gestures testifying to some vain and stupid pride. I want to say this first, that it is not unbecoming to have characteristics and propensities so much our own and so incorporated into us

40   that we have no way of sensing and recognizing them. And of such natural inclinations the body is likely to retain a certain bent, without our knowledge or consent. It was a certain affectation in keeping with his beauty that made Alexander lean his head a little to one side, and Alcibiades speak softly and with a lisp. Julius Caesar used to scratch his head with one finger, which is the

45   behavior of a man full of troublesome thoughts; and Cicero, it seems to me, was in the habit of wrinkling his nose, which is a sign of a mocking nature. Such gestures can arise in us unperceived.

There are others that are artificial, of which I do not speak, like bows and salutations, by which men gain credit, most often wrongfully, for being very

50   humble and courteous; a man may be humble through vainglory. I am rather prodigal in taking off my hat, especially in summer, and I never receive this salute without returning it, from whatever class of man it may come, unless he is in my pay. I could wish that certain princes I know would be more sparing and just in dispensing these salutes; for when they are thus strewn about indiscriminately,

55   they have no more power. If they are given without consideration, they are given without effect.

Among the extraordinary mannerisms, let us not forget the arrogance of the Emperor Constantius, who in public always held his head straight, without turning or bending it this way or that, not even to look at those who saluted him

60   from the side; keeping his body fixed and motionless, without letting himself move with the swaying of his coach, without daring either to spit, or to blow his nose, or to wipe his face in front of people.

I do not know whether those gestures that people noticed in me were of the first kind, and whether I really had some occult propensity to this fault, as may

65   well be; and I cannot answer for the movement of my body. But as for the movements of my soul, I want to confess here what I am aware of.

There are two parts in this vainglory, namely, to esteem ourselves too highly, and not to esteem others highly enough.

As for the first, it seems to me that first of all, these considerations should be

70   taken into account: that I feel myself oppressed by an error of my soul which I dislike, both as unjust and, even more, as troublesome. I try to correct it, but uproot it I cannot. It is that I lower the value of the things I possess, because I possess them, and raise the value of things when they are foreign, absent, and not mine. This humor spreads very far. As the prerogative of authority makes, husbands

75   regard their own wives, and many fathers their children, with wicked disdain; so it is with me, and between two similar works I should always decide against my own. Not so much that zeal for my progress and improvement disturbs my judgment and keeps me from being satisfied with myself, as that dominion, of itself, breeds contempt of what we hold and control. Far-off governments, customs, and

80   languages delight me; and I realize that Latin, by its dignity, beguiles me more than it should, as it does children and common people. The housekeeping, the house, the horse of my neighbor, if equal in value, seem better than my own, because they are not mine—the more so because I am very ignorant of my affairs. I wonder at the

85 assurance and confidence each man has about himself, whereas there is virtually nothing that I know I know, or that I dare give my word that I can do. I do not have my means catalogued and arranged; and I know about them only after doing something: I am as doubtful of myself as of anything else. Whence it comes about that if I happen to do well in a task, I attribute it more to my luck than to my ability; for I plan them all at random and in fear.

90 Likewise this is generally true of me, that of all the opinions antiquity has held of man as a whole, the ones I embrace most willingly and adhere to most firmly are those that despise, humiliate, and nullify us most. Philosophy seems to me never to have such an easy game as when she combats our presumption and vanity, when she honestly admits her uncertainty, weakness, and ignorance. It

95 seems to me that the nursing mother of the falsest opinions, public and private, is the over-good opinion man has of himself.

These people who perch astride the epicycle of Mercury, who see so far into the heavens, yank out my teeth. For in the study I am making, the subject of which is man, when I find such an extreme variety of judgments, so deep a labyrinth of

100 difficulties one on top of the other, so much diversity and uncertainty in the very school of wisdom, you may well wonder—since these people have not been able to come to an agreement in the knowledge of themselves and their own state, which is ever present before their eyes, which is in them; since they do not know the motion of what they move themselves, or how to depict and decipher to us the springs that

105 they hold and manage themselves—how I should believe them about the cause of the ebb and flow of the river Nile. The curiosity to know things was given to men as a scourge, says the Holy Scripture.

But to come to my own particular case, it would be very difficult, it seems to me, for anyone else to esteem himself less, or indeed for anyone else to esteem me

110 less, than I esteem myself. I consider myself one of the common sort, except in that I consider myself so; guilty of the commoner and humbler faults, but not of faults disavowed or excused; and I value myself only for knowing my value.

If there is vainglory in me, it is infused in me superficially by the treachery of my nature, and has no body of its own to appear before my judgment. I am

115 sprinkled with it, but not dyed.

For in truth, as regards any kind of products of the mind, I have never brought forth anything that satisfied me; and the approbation of others does not repay me. My taste is delicate and hard to please, and especially regarding myself; I am incessantly disowning myself; and I feel myself, in every part, floating and bending

120 with weakness. I have nothing of my own that satisfies my judgment. My sight is clear and controlled enough; but when I put it to work, it grows blurred, as I find most evidently in poetry. I love it infinitely; I am a pretty good judge of other men's works; but in truth, I play the child when I try to set my hand to it; I cannot endure myself. A man may play the fool anywhere else, but not in poetry:

125   For Gods and men and booksellers refuse
          To countenance a mediocre Muse.
HORACE

Would God that maxim were written on the front of all our printers' shops, to deny entrance to so many versifiers:

          No man has more assurance than a bad poet.
MARTIAL

130   Why have we no such nations as these? Dionysius the Elder esteemed nothing of his own so highly as his poetry. At the time of the Olympic games, with chariots surpassing all others in magnificence, he also sent poets and musicians to present his verses, with royally gilded and tapestried tents and pavilions. When they came to deliver his verses, the grace and excellence of the pronunciation at first drew

135 the attention of the people; but when later they came to ponder the ineptitude of the work, they first grew scornful, and, becoming more and more bitter in their judgment, they presently flew into a fury, and ran to all his pavilions and knocked them down and tore them to bits in resentment. And when his chariots did not make any kind of a showing in the races either, and the ship bringing his men back

140 missed Sicily and was driven and shattered by the tempest against the coast of Tarentum, the people felt certain that it was the wrath of the gods, irritated, like themselves, against this bad poem. And even the sailors who escaped from the shipwreck seconded this opinion of the people.

      The oracle that predicted his death also seemed to subscribe to this somewhat.

145 It said that Dionysius would be near his end when he had vanquished men better than himself; which he took to mean the Carthaginians, who surpassed him in power. And in fighting them he often sidestepped victory and tempered it so as not to incur the fate predicted. But he misunderstood it; for the god was referring to the time he gained the award at Athens over better tragic poets than he, by favor and

150 injustice, presenting in the competition his play entitled *The Leneians*; after which victory he suddenly died, partly of the excessive joy that he got from it.

      What I find excusable in my own work I find so not in itself and in reality, but in comparison with other and worse things to which I see people give credit. I am envious of the happiness of those who can rejoice and feel gratified in their

155 work, for it is an easy way to give oneself pleasure, since the source of the pleasure is oneself. Especially so if there is a little firmness in their self-conceit, I know a poet to whom the strong and the weak, in the crowd and in the chamber, and heaven and earth, cry out that he does not know his business. For all that, he will not reduce one bit of the measure for which he has cut himself out; he is

160 always beginning again, always reconsidering, and always persisting, all the stronger and more set in his opinion because it depends on him alone to maintain it. My works are so far from delighting me that as many times as I sample them again, so many times I am vexed with them:

-721-

When I reread I blush, for I see quite enough
Fit to erase, though it was I who wrote the stuff.
OVID

I have always an idea in my mind, and some blurred picture, which offers me as if in a dream a better form than the one I have employed, but I cannot grasp it and exploit it. And that idea itself is on only a mediocre plane. From that I conclude that the productions of those great rich minds of the past are very far beyond the utmost stretch of my imagination and desire. Their writings not only satisfy and fill me, but astound me and transfix me with admiration. I judge their beauty; I see it, if not to the utmost, at least enough so that I cannot aspire to it myself.

Whatever I undertake, I owe a sacrifice to the Graces, as Plutarch says of someone, to curry their favor:

If anything gives pleasure that I write,
If it affects men's senses with delight,
Unto the charming Graces it is due.
AUTHOR UNKNOWN

They abandon me at every turn. Everything I write is crude; it lacks distinction and beauty. I do not know how to make things appear any more precious than they really are; my fashioning is no help to the matter. That is why I need my matter strong, with plenty of grip, and shining by its own light. When I seize on popular and gayer matters, it is so as to go my own way, for I do not love a solemn and gloomy wisdom, as does the world, and to cheer up myself, not my style, which rather prefers grave and austere matters (at least if I should give the name of style to a formless and undisciplined way of talking, a popular jargon, and a way of proceeding without definitions, without divisions, without conclusions, and confused, like that of Amafanius and Rabirius).

I do not know how to please, or delight, or tickle: the best story in the world dries up in my hands and becomes dull. I do not know how to talk except in good earnest, and am wholly devoid of that facility, which I see in several of my acquaintances, of entertaining the first comer and holding the attention of a whole group, or tirelessly amusing the ear of a prince with all kinds of talk, matter never failing them, because of the gift they have of knowing how to use the first subject that comes to mind, and accommodating it to the humor and capacity of the people they are dealing with. Princes are not very fond of serious talk, nor I of telling stories. The first and easiest arguments, which are commonly the best received, I do not know how to use: a bad popular preacher. On all matters I am apt to say the deepest things I know. Cicero thinks that in philosophical treatises the hardest part is the exordium. If that is so, I shall stick to the conclusion.

Yet we must tune the string to all sorts of notes; and the sharpest is the one that least often comes into play. There is at least as great perfection in developing

an empty theme as in sustaining a weighty one. Sometimes we must handle things superficially, sometimes go into them deeply. I well know that most people keep on
205 that low plane, since they grasp things only by that outer bark; but I also know that the greatest masters, both Xenophon and Plato, are often seen relaxing into that humble and popular way of speaking and treating things, sustaining it with the graces that never fail them.

As for the rest, my language has no ease or polish; it is harsh and disdainful,
210 with a free and unruly disposition. And I like it that way, if not by judgment, then by inclination. But I am quite conscious that sometimes I let myself go too far, and that in the effort to avoid art and affectation, I fall back into them in another direction:

I strive to be concise,
215   And grow obscure.
                HORACE

Plato says that length and brevity are properties which neither decrease nor increase the worth of style.

If I should attempt to follow that other style that is even, smooth, and orderly, I could not attain it. And even though the concision and cadences of Sallust are
220 more to my humor, yet I consider Caesar both greater and less easy to imitate. And if my inclination leads me more to imitate Seneca's style, I nonetheless esteem Plutarch's more. As in action, so in speech I simply follow my natural bent; which is perhaps the reason why I can do better in speech than in writing. Movement and action animate words, notably in men who move about briskly, as I do, and
225 become heated.. Bearing, countenance, voice, robe and posture can give value to things which in themselves are nothing but babble. Messala complains, in Tacitus, of certain tight garments of his time, and of the form of the benches where the orators had to speak, which weakened their eloquence.

My French is corrupted, both in pronunciation and in other respects, by the
230 barbarism of my home soil; I never saw a man from the south of France whose accent was not clearly marked and offending to pure French ears. Yet this is not because I am very expert in my Perigordian, for I have no more command of it than of German; and that does not worry me much. It is a language like others around me, on one side or another, those of Poitou, Saintonge, Angournois, Limoges, and
235 Auvergne: soft, drawling, looseboweled. To be sure, there is above us, toward the mountains, a Gascon dialect that I find singularly beautiful, dry, brief, expressive, and indeed a more manly and military language than any that I understand; as sinewy, powerful, and pertinent as French is graceful, delicate, and abundant.

As for Latin, which was given me for my mother tongue, I have lost through
240 lack of practice the ability to use it quickly in speaking; yes, and in writing, in which they used to call me Master John. That is how little I am worth on that side.

Beauty is a great recommendation in dealings with men; it is the prime means of conciliation between them, and there is no man so barbarous and surly as not to

245 be somewhat struck by its charm. The body has a great part in our being, it holds a high rank in it; so its structure and composition are well worth consideration. Those who want to split up our two principal parts and sequester them from each other are wrong. On the contrary, we must couple and join them together again. We must order the soul not to draw aside and entertain itself apart, not to scorn and abandon the body (nor can it do so except by some counterfeit monkey trick), but

250 to rally to the body, embrace it, cherish it, assist it, control it, advise it, set it right and bring it back when it goes astray; in short, to marry it and be a husband to it, so that their actions may appear not different and contrary, but harmonious and uniform.

Christians are particularly instructed about this bond; for they know that

255 divine justice embraces this association and union of body and soul, even to making the body capable of eternal rewards, and that God watches the whole man in action and wills that he receive, in his entirety, punishment or reward, according to his merits.

The Peripatetic sect, of all sects the most sociable, attributes to wisdom this

260 sole care, to provide and procure the common good of these two associated parts. And they show that the other sects, for not having devoted themselves enough to the consideration of this mixture, have taken sides, one for the body, another for the soul, with equal error, and have put aside their subject, which is man, and their guide, which they generally avow is Nature.

265 The first distinction that existed between men, and the first consideration that gave some men preeminence over others, was probably the advantage of beauty:

They portioned out the fields, and gave
To each after his beauty, strength, and intellect;
For then beauty was prized, and strength enjoyed respect.
LUCRETIUS

270 Now I am a little below medium height. This is not only an ugly defect, but also a disadvantage, especially for men in command or office; for the authority given by a fine presence and bodily majesty is lacking. C. Marius was reluctant to accept soldiers who were not six feet in height. The Courtier[15] is quite right to prefer an average height to any other for the gentleman he is training, and to reject

275 any peculiarity that will make people point him out. But as for choosing to have him shorter rather than taller if he fails to be of this medium height, I would not do so for a military man.

Little men, says Aristotle, may well be pretty, but not handsome; and in greatness is a great soul known, as is beauty in a great tall body. The Ethiopians

280 and Indians, he says, in electing their kings and magistrates, considered the beauty and lofty stature of their persons. They were right; for it breeds respect in his

---

[15]*Il Libro del Cortegiano* (1528), by Baldassare Castiglione.

followers and terror in the enemy to see marching at the head of a troop a leader of handsome and majestic stature:

> Turnus himself moves with the foremost, arms in hand,
> Splendid in build, a full head taller than his band.
>
> VIRGIL

Our great, divine, and heavenly King, whose every particular should be carefully, religiously, and reverently noted, did not reject the recommendation of a handsome body: *fairer than the children of men* [Psalms]. And Plato desires beauty, as well as temperance and courage, in the guardians of his Republic.

It is a great annoyance to be addressed in the midst of your servants with the question: "Where is the master?" and to get only the tail end of the salute made to your barber or your secretary. As happened to poor Philopoemen. He was the first of his company to arrive at a house where he was expected, and his hostess, who did not know him and saw his rather unimpressive appearance, set him to work helping her maids draw water and stir up the fire in honor of Philopoemen. The gentlemen of his suite, having arrived and surprised him busy at this fine occupation (for he had not failed to obey the command given him), asked him what he was doing there. "I am paying," he answered them, "the penalty of my ugliness."

The other kinds of beauty are for women; the beauty of stature is the only beauty of men. Where smallness dwells, neither breadth and roundness of forehead, nor clarity and softness of eyes, nor the moderate form of the nose, nor small size of ears and mouth, nor regularity and whiteness of teeth, nor the smooth thickness of a beard brown as the husk of a chestnut, nor curly hair, nor proper roundness of head, nor freshness of color, nor a pleasant facial expression, nor an odorless body, nor just proportion of limbs, can make a handsome man.

For the rest, I have a strong, thick-set body, a face not fat but full, a temperament between the jovial and the melancholy, moderately sanguine and warm—

> My legs are stiff with bristles, my chest with shaggy hair
>
> MARTIAL

—sound and sprightly health, rarely troubled by illnesses, until I was well along in years. Such I was, for I am not considering myself at this moment, when I am well on the road to old age, having long since passed forty:

> Old age shatters their powers, their ripened strength,
> And melts into decrepitude at length.
>
> LUCRETIUS

What I shall be from now on will be nothing but half a being, it will no longer be myself. I escape and steal away from myself every day:

The passing years steal from us all things, one by one.

HORACE

Adroitness and agility I have never had; and yet I am the son of a very nimble
father whose sprightliness lasted him until his extreme old age. He scarcely ever
320   found a man of his condition who was his equal in any bodily exercise; just as I
have scarcely found any who did not surpass me, except in running, in which I
was just fair. Of music, either vocal, for which my voice is very inept, or
instrumental, they never succeeded in teaching me anything. At dancing, tennis,
wrestling, I have never been able to acquire any but very slight and ordinary
325   ability; at swimming, fencing, vaulting, and jumping, none at all. My hands are so
clumsy that I cannot even write so I can read it; so that I would rather do over
what I have scribbled than give myself the trouble of unscrambling it. And I read
hardly any better. I feel that I weigh upon my listeners. Otherwise, a good scholar.
I cannot close a letter the right way, nor could I ever cut a pen, or carve at table
330   worth a rap, or saddle a horse, or properly carry a bird and release it, or talk to
dogs, birds, or horses.
My bodily qualities, in short, are very well matched with those of my soul.
There is no liveliness; there is only a full, firm vigor. I stand up well under hard
work; but I do so only if I go to it of my own will, and as much as my desire leads
335   me to it,

When gently zest beguiles the rigors of the toil.

HORACE

Otherwise, if I am not lured to it by some pleasure, and if I have any other guide
than my own pure free will, I am good for nothing. For I have come to the point
where except for health and life, there is nothing for which I am willing to bite my
340   nails, nothing that I am willing to buy at the price of mental torment and
constraint:

I would not buy at such a fee
All Tagus' sands, and all the gold it rolls to sea.

JUVENAL

Extremely idle, extremely independent, both by nature and by art. I would as soon
345   lend my blood as my pains.
I have a soul all its own, accustomed to conducting itself in its own way.
Having had neither governor nor master forced on me to this day, I have gone just
so far as I pleased, and at my own pace. This has made me soft and useless for
serving others, and no good to anyone but myself. And for my own sake there was
350   no need to force that heavy, lazy, and do-nothing nature. For having found myself
from birth in such a degree of fortune that I had reason to be content with it, and

having as much sense as I felt I had occasion for, I have sought nothing, and have also acquired nothing:

355
> I am not wafted by fair winds with swelling sails;
> Yet neither do I steer my life through adverse gales.
> In strength, wit, beauty, virtue, rank, and wealth, I'm cast
> The last among the first, the first among the last.
> HORACE

360   The only ability I have needed is the ability to content myself with my lot, which, however, if you take it rightly, requires a well-ordered state of mind, equally difficult in every kind of fortune, and which we see by experience is more readily found in want than in abundance; perhaps because, as with our other passions, hunger for riches is sharpened more by the use of them than by the lack of them, and because the virtue of moderation is rarer than that of patience. And all I needed was to enjoy pleasantly the good things that God in his liberality had

365 placed in my hands. I have never tasted of any sort of tedious work. I have had hardly anything to manage but my own affairs; or, if I have, it has been on condition of managing them at my own times and in my own way, commissioned by people who trusted me and knew me, and did not hustle me. For experts get some service out of even a restive and broken-winded horse.

370   Even my childhood was guided in a mild, free fashion, exempt from rigorous subjection. All this has built up in me a delicate disposition, unable to endure worry—to such a point that I like to have the losses and disorders that concern me hidden from me; I put under the heading of expenses what my nonchalance costs me for its food and upkeep:

375
> Things that the master ne'er perceives,
> Superfluous, but a delight to thieves.
> HORACE

I like to be ignorant of the count of what I have, so as to feel my loss less exactly. I ask those who live with me, if they lack affection for me and for honest dealings, to cheat me and pay me with decent appearances. Not having enough fortitude to

380 endure the annoyance of the adverse accidents to which we are subject, and being unable to keep up the tension of regulating and ordering affairs, I foster as best I can this idea: to abandon myself completely to Fortune, expect the worst in everything, and resolve to bear that worst meekly and patiently. It is for that alone that I labor; that is the goal toward which I direct all my reflections.

385   When in danger, I do not think so much how I shall escape, as how little it matters that I escape. Even if I should fall, what would it matter? Not being able to rule events, I rule myself, and adapt myself to them if they do not adapt themselves to me. I have hardly the skill to dodge Fortune and escape her or force her, and to direct and lead things foresightedly to serve my purpose. I have even less patience

390   to stand the arduous and painful care that is needed for that. And the most painful situation for me is to be in suspense about urgent matters, and tossed between fear and hope. Deliberation, even about the slightest things, annoys me; and I feel my mind harder put to it to endure the various shocks and ups and downs of doubt and deliberation, than to settle down and accept any course whatever, after the

395   die is cast. Few passions have troubled my sleep; but as for deliberations, the slightest one troubles it. Even as in roads I like to avoid the sloping and slippery sides, and cast myself into the beaten part, even the muddiest and boggiest, from which I cannot sink lower, and seek security there; just so I like pure misfortunes, which do not try me and worry me any more, once the uncertainty about mending

400   them is over, and which drive me at a single bound directly into suffering:

> Uncertain ills torment us most.
> SENECA

When things happen, I bear myself like a man; in conducting them, like a child. The dread of falling gives me a greater fever than the fall. The game is not worth the candle. The miser is worse off for his passion than the poor man, and the

405   jealous man than the cuckold. And often it is not as bad to lose your vineyard as to go to court for it. The lowest step is the firmest. It is the seat of constancy. There you need nothing but yourself. Constancy is founded there and leans only upon itself.

      Is there not a certain philosophical air about the case of a gentleman known

410   to many? He married well along in years, having spent his youth in gay company, a great storyteller, a merry lad. Remembering how the subject of cuckoldry had given him material for talking and jesting about others, to take cover he married a woman whom he picked up in the place where each man can find one for his money, and made a compact with her that they would use these greetings: "Good

415   morning, whore." "Good morning, cuckold." And there was nothing about which be talked more often and openly to visitors at his home than this arrangement of his; by which he checked the secret gossip of mockers, and blunted the point of this reproach.

      As for ambition, which is neighbor to presumption, or rather daughter, it

420   would have been necessary, to advance me, for Fortune to come and take me by the hand. For as for taking pains for the sake of some uncertain hope, and submitting to all the difficulties that attend those who try to push themselves into favor at the beginning of their career, I could never have done it:

425
> I do not purchase hope with ready cash.
> TERENCE

> I cling to what I see and hold, and do not go far from port:
> Let one oar row in water, the other on the shore.
> PROPERTIUS

And then, a man seldom arrives at these advancements except by first risking what he has. And it is my opinion that if what a man has is enough to maintain the way of life to which he was born and brought up, it is folly to let go of it on the chance of increasing it. The man whom Fortune denies a foothold and the means of arranging a calm and restful life is excusable if he tosses what he has to chance, since in any case necessity sends him questing:

> In evil we must take a risky path.
>
> SENECA

And I sooner excuse a younger son for casting his inheritance to the winds than a man who has the honor of his house in his charge, and cannot become needy without being at fault.

I have certainly found the road shorter and easier, with the advice of my good friends of past days, by getting rid of this desire and keeping quiet;

> Who would enjoy the prize without the dust;
>
> HORACE

also judging very sanely that my powers were not capable of great things, and remembering this saying of the late Chancellor Olivier, that the French are like monkeys who climb to the top of a tree, from branch to branch, and never stop moving until they have reached the highest branch, and show their rear ends when they get there.

> 'Tis shameful to take on a load that is too great,
> Then leave it when our knees buckle beneath its weight.
>
> PROPERTIUS

Even the qualities that are not reproachable in me, I have found useless in this age. My easygoing ways would have been called cowardice and weakness; fidelity and conscience would have been thought squeamish and superstitious; frankness and independence, troublesome, thoughtless, and rash.

Misfortune has its uses. It is good to be born in a very depraved time; for by comparison with others, you are considered virtuous for a cheap price. Anyone who is only a parricide and sacrilegious in our days is a good and honorable man:

> If now a friend denies not what was given him in trust,
> If he restores an ancient purse with all its coins and rust,
> This prodigy of honesty deserves to be enrolled
> In Tuscan books, and with a sacrificial lamb extolled.
>
> JUVENAL

460 And there was never time and place where a surer and greater reward was offered to princes for goodness and justice. The first man who thinks to push himself into favor and credit by that path, I am much mistaken if he will not outstrip his fellows without much effort. Force and violence can do something, but not always everything.

465 We see merchants, village justices, and artisans keeping up with the nobility in valor and military knowledge. They do honorably in both private and public combats; they fight, they defend cities in our wars. A prince's distinction is smothered amid this crowd. Let him shine with humanity, truthfulness, loyalty, moderation, and especially justice, marks that are rare, unknown, and banished. It is only by the will of the people that he can do his job, and no other qualities can

470 flatter their will as much as these, which are much more useful to them than the others. *Nothing is so popular as goodness* [Cicero].

By such a comparison I would have thought myself great and rare, just as I think myself dwarfish and ordinary in comparison with certain past ages, in which it was a commonplace, if other, stronger qualities did not concur, to see a

475 man moderate in his revenge, slow to resent offenses, religious in keeping his word, neither double-dealing nor shifty, nor accommodating his faith to the will of others or to the occasion. Rather would I let affairs break their necks than twist my faith for the sake of them. For as for this new-fangled virtue of hypocrisy and dissimulation, which is so highly honored at present, I mortally hate it; and of all

480 vices, I know none that testifies to so much cowardice and baseness of heart. It is a craven and servile idea to disguise ourselves and hide under a mask, and not to dare to show ourselves as we are. In that way our men train for perfidy; being accustomed to speak false words, they have no scruples about breaking their word. A generous heart should not belie its thoughts; it wants to reveal itself even

485 to its inmost depths. There everything is good, or at least everything is human.

Aristotle considers it the function of magnanimity to hate and love openly, to judge, to speak with complete frankness, and to have no regard for the approbation or reprobation of others in comparison with truth. Apollonius said that it was for slaves to lie, and for free men to speak truth.

490 Truth is the first and fundamental part of virtue. We must love it for itself. He who tells the truth because he has some external obligation to do so and because it serves him, and who does not fear to tell a lie when it is not important to anybody, is not sufficiently truthful.

My soul by nature shuns lying and hates even to think a lie. I feel an inward

495 shame and a stinging remorse if one escapes me, as sometimes it does, for occasions surprise me and move me unpremeditatedly.

We must not always say everything, for that would be folly; but what we say must be what we think; otherwise it is wickedness. I do not know what people expect to gain by incessant feigning and dissimulating, unless it is not to be

500 believed even when they speak truth. That may deceive people once or twice; but to make a profession of covering up, and to boast, as some of our princes have done, that they would throw their shirt in the fire if it were privy to their real

intentions (which is a saying of the ancient Metellus of Macedon), and that a man who does not know how to dissemble does not know how to rule—this is
505   warning those who have to deal with them that all they say is nothing but deceit and lies. *The more artful and cunning a man is, the more he is hated and suspected when he loses his reputation for honesty* [Cicero]. It would be very naïve for a man to let himself be taken in by either the face or the words of one who takes pride in being always different outside and inside, as Tiberius did; and I do not know
510   what part such people can have in human dealings, since they never offer anything that is accepted as good money. He who is disloyal to truth is also disloyal to falsehood.

Those who, in our time, in establishing the duties of a prince,[16] have considered only the good of his affairs, and have preferred that to caring for his
515   fidelity and conscience, would have something to say to a prince whose affairs Fortune had so arranged that he could establish them once and for all by a single breach and betrayal of his word. But that is not the way it goes. You often fall into the same sort of bargain again; you make more than one peace, more than one treaty, in your life. The gain that lures them to the first breach of faith—and
520   almost always there is gain in it, as in all other wicked deeds; sacrilege, murder, rebellion, treachery are always undertaken for some sort of profit—this first gain brings after it endless losses, casting this prince out of all relations and means of negotiation in consequence of this breach of faith.

When, during my childhood, Suleiman, of the Ottoman race, a race not overly
525   careful about observing promises and pacts, landed his army at Otranto, he learned that Mercurino de' Gratinare and the inhabitants of Castro were held prisoners after having surrendered the place, contrary to the terms of capitulation, and sent word that they should be released; and he said that having other great enterprises at hand in that region, such a breach of faith, although it seemed
530   somewhat useful at present, would bring upon him in the future a bad name and a distrust infinitely harmful.

Now for my part I would rather be troublesome and indiscreet than flattering and dissembling. I admit that a touch of pride and stubbornness may enter into keeping me sincere and outspoken without consideration for others; and it seems
535   to me that I restrain myself a little less whenever it would be appropriate to restrain myself more, and that I react against the respect I owe by growing more heated. It may be, too, that I let myself follow my nature for lack of art. When I display to great men the same extreme freedom of tongue and bearing that I exercise in my own house, I feel how much it inclines toward indiscretion and incivility.
540   But besides the fact that I am made that way, I have not a supple enough mind to sidestep a sudden question and escape it by some dodge, or to invent a truth, or a good enough memory to retain something thus invented, and certainly not enough assurance to maintain it; and I put on a bold face because of weakness. Therefore I

---

[16]Machiavelli and his disciples.

545 give myself up to being candid and always saying what I think, by inclination and by reason, leaving it to Fortune to guide the outcome.

Aristippus said that the chief fruit he had gathered from philosophy was that he spoke freely and openly to everyone.

550 Memory is a wonderfully useful tool, and without it judgment does its work with difficulty; it is entirely lacking in me. What anyone wants to propound to me must be propounded piecemeal. For to answer a discourse in which there are several different headings is not in my power. I cannot receive a commission without my writing tablets. And when I have a speech of consequence to make, if it is of some length, I am reduced to the mean and miserable necessity of learning by heart, word for word, what I have to say; otherwise I would have neither manner

555 nor assurance, being in fear that my memory would play me a bad trick. But this way is no less difficult for me. To learn three lines of poetry I need three hours. And then, in a work of my own, the freedom and authority to change the order and alter a word, ever varying the material, makes it harder to keep in mind.

Now, the more I distrust my memory, the more confused it becomes. It serves me

560 better by chance encounter; I have to solicit it nonchalantly. For if I press it, it is stunned; and once it has begun to totter, the more I probe it, the more it gets mixed up and embarrassed. It serves me at its own time, not at mine.

This thing that I feel in my memory, I feel in several other parts. I flee command, obligation, and constraint. What I do easily and naturally, I can no

565 longer do if I order myself to do it by strict and express command. Even as regards my body, the parts that have some particular freedom and jurisdiction over themselves sometimes refuse to obey me when I destine and bind them to a certain time and place for compulsory service. These forced and tyrannical advance orders repel them; they go limp from fear or spite and become paralyzed.

570 Some time ago, being in a place where it is a barbarous discourtesy not to respond to those who invite you to drink, though I was treated with complete freedom, I tried to play the good fellow for the sake of the ladies who were in the party, according to the custom of the country. But then the fun began; for the threat and anticipation of having to force myself beyond my natural habit stopped up my

575 gullet so that I could not swallow a single drop, and was deprived of drink, even as much as my meal required. I found myself brimful and my thirst quenched by all the drink that my imagination had anticipated.

This effect is more apparent in those who have a more ardent and powerful imagination; but for all that, it is natural, and there is no one who does not feel it

580 somewhat. An excellent archer, condemned to death, was offered his life if he would show some notable proof of his skill; he refused to try it, fearing that the excessive tension of his will would make his hand go astray, and that instead of saving his life, he would lose the reputation he had acquired for shooting with the bow.

585 A man whose thoughts are elsewhere will not fail, to the inch, to take always the same number and length of steps in the place where he walks; but if he goes at it

attentively, measuring and counting them, he will find that what he did naturally and by chance, he will not do as exactly by design.

590 My library, which is a handsome one among country libraries, is situated at one corner of my house. If anything enters my fancy that I want to look up or write down there, for fear it may escape me even as I cross my courtyard, I have to give it into someone else's safekeeping. If in speaking I am emboldened to digress however little from my thread, I never fail to lose it; which is the reason I keep myself constrained, dry, and compressed in speaking. The people who serve me I have to

595 call by the name of their job or their province, for it is very hard for me to remember names. To be sure, I will tell you that it has three syllables and a rough sound, that it begins or ends with such and such a letter. And if I were to live a long time, I do not doubt that I would forget my own name, as others have done. Messala Corvinus was two years without any trace of memory, and this is also

600 said of George of Trebizond. And in my own interest I often ruminate about what sort of a life theirs was, and whether without this faculty I shall have enough left to support me with any comfort; and looking at it closely, I fear that this defect, if it is absolute, ruins all the functions of the mind. *It is certain that the memory is the only receptacle, not only of philosophy, but of all that concerns the conduct of life,*

605 *and of all the arts* [Cicero].

I'm full of cracks, and leak out on all sides.
TERENCE

It has happened more than once that I have forgotten the watchword that I had given three hours before, or received from another, and forgotten where I had hidden my purse, in spite of what Cicero says about that. I help myself to lose what I lock up most carefully.

610 Memory is the receptacle and container of knowledge; mine being so defective, I can hardly complain if I do not know much. I know in general the names of the arts and what they treat, but nothing beyond that. I leaf through books, I do not study them. What I retain of them is something I no longer recognize as anyone else's. It is only the material from which my judgment has profited, and the

615 thoughts and ideas with which it has become imbued; the author, the place, the words, and other circumstances, I immediately forget.

And I am so good at forgetting that I forget even my own writings and compositions no less than the rest. People are all the time quoting me to myself without my knowing it. Anyone who would like to know the sources of the verses

620 and examples I have piled up here would put me to great trouble to tell him. And yet I have begged them only at well-known and famous doors, not content with their being rich unless they also came from rich and honorable hands; in them authority and reason concur. It is no great wonder if my book follows the fate of other books, and if my memory lets go of what I write as of what I read, and of

625 what I give as of what I receive.

Besides the defect of my memory I have others which contribute greatly to my ignorance. My mind is slow and dull; it cannot penetrate the slightest cloud, so that, for example, I could never offer it any enigma easy enough for it to unravel. There is no subtlety so empty that it will not stump me. Of games in which the mind 630 has a part—chess, cards, draughts, and others—I understand nothing but the barest rudiments.

My apprehension is slow and muddled; but what it once grasps, it grasps well and embraces most entirely, closely, and deeply for such time as it does grasp it. My sight is long, sound, and whole, but it is easily tired by work and grows 635 blurred; for that reason I cannot have long sessions with books except by the help of others. The younger Pliny will inform those who have not experienced it how important this delay is to those who devote themselves to this occupation.

There is no mind so puny or brutish as not to reveal some particular faculty shining out; there is none so buried but that some bit of it will burst forth. And 640 how it happens that a mind that is blind and asleep to everything else is lively, clear, and excellent in some particular task, we must inquire of the masters. But the fine minds are the universal minds, open and ready for everything; if not will taught, at least teachable. And I say this to accuse my own; for whether by weakness or nonchalance (and to be nonchalant about what lies at our feet, what 645 we have between our hands, what most concerns our use of life, is something far removed from my doctrine), there is no mind as inept as mine and none as ignorant of many such ordinary common things of which a man cannot be ignorant without disgrace. I must cite a few examples.

I was born and brought up in the country and in the midst of farming; I have 650 had affairs and management in my hands ever since my predecessors in the possession of the property I enjoy left me their place. Now I cannot reckon, either with counters or with a pen; most of our coins I do not know; nor do I know the difference between one grain and another, either in the ground or in the barn, unless it is too obvious, and I can scarcely distinguish the difference between the 655 cabbages and lettuces in my garden. I do not even understand the names of the chief household implements or the roughest principles of agriculture, which children know. I know still less of the mechanical arts, of trade and merchandise, of the diversity and nature of fruits, wines, and foods, and of how to train a bird, or doctor a horse or dog. And since I must make my shame quite complete, not a month 660 ago I was caught ignorant that leaven was used to make bread, and what was meant by fermenting wine. Once in Athens people conjectured an aptitude for mathematics in a man who was seen ingeniously arranging a load of brushwood and making it into fagots. Truly they would draw the very opposite conclusion about me; for if you give me all the equipment of a kitchen, I shall starve.

665 From these lines of my confession you can imagine others at my expense. But whatever I make myself known to be, provided I make myself known such as I am, I am carrying out my plan. And so I make no excuse for daring to put into writing such mean and trivial remarks as these. The meanness of my subject forces me to do so. Blame my project if you will, but not my procedure. At all events, I see well

670   enough, without others telling me, how little value and weight all this has, and the folly of my plan. It is enough that my judgment is not unshod, of which these are the essays:

> Be nosy as you will, have such a nose
> That Atlas to support it would refuse;
675   Latinus' self bewilder with your wit:
> Against my trifles you can say no whit
> More than I've said myself. Why use your teeth
> On teeth? If you'd be full, you must have meat.
> Save up your pains, your sting, for those who so
680   Admire themselves; that this is naught, we know.
>   Martial

     I am not obliged not to say stupid things, provided I do not fool myself and that I recognize them as such. And to slip up knowingly is so common for me that I scarcely ever slip up in any other way; I never slip up accidentally. It is a small matter to attribute my silly actions to the rashness of my disposition, since I
685   cannot help commonly attributing my vicious actions to it.

     One day at Bar-le-Duc I saw King Francis II presented, in remembrance of René, king of Sicily, with a portrait that this king had made of himself. Why is it not permissible in the same way for each man to portray himself with the pen, as he portrayed himself with a pencil?

690   So I do not want to forget this further scar, very unfit to produce in public: irresolution, a most harmful failing in negotiating worldly affairs. I do not know which side to take in doubtful enterprises:

> Nor yes nor no my inmost heart will say.
>   Petrarch

     I can easily maintain an opinion, but not choose one.
695   Because in human matters, whatever side we lean to, we find many probabilities to confirm us in it—and the philosopher Chrysippus said that he wanted to learn from Zeno and Cleanthes, his masters, nothing but their tenets, for when it came to proofs and reasons, he would furnish enough by himself—so in whatever direction I turn, I can always provide myself with enough causes and
700   probabilities to keep me that way. So I keep within me doubt and freedom of choice until the occasion is urgent. And then, to confess the truth, I most often toss the feather to the wind, as they say, and abandon myself to the mercy of fortune; a very slight inclination or circumstance carries me away:

> When the mind doubts, a trifle pulls it to and fro.
>   Terence

705 The uncertainty of my judgment is so evenly balanced in most occurrences that I would willingly submit to the decision of chance and of the dice. And I note, with much reflection on our human weakness, the examples that even sacred history has left us of this custom of entrusting to fortune and chance the determination of choice in doubtful cases: *The lot fell upon Matthias* [Acts].

710 Human reason is a two-edged and dangerous sword. And even in the hand of Socrates, its most intimate and familiar friend, see what a many-ended stick it is.

Thus I am fit only to follow, and I let myself be carried away easily by the crowd. I do not trust my own powers enough to undertake to command, or to guide; I am very glad to find my steps traced out by others. If I must run the risk of an

715 uncertain choice, I would rather it should be under some man who is more sure of his opinions and wedded to them than I am to mine, whose foundation and grounds I find slippery.

And yet I am not too easy to change, since I perceive a like weakness in the contrary opinions. *The very habit of assenting seem to be dangerous and slippery*

720 [Cicero]. Notably in political matters, there is a fine field open for vacillation and dispute:

> As when an even scale with equal weights is pressed,
> Neither side rises, neither falls; it stays at rest.
>
> TIBULLUS

Machiavelli's arguments, for example, were solid enough for the subject, yet it

725 was very easy to combat them; and those who did so left it no less easy to combat theirs. In such an argument there would always be matter for answers, rejoinders, replications, triplications, quadruplications, and that infinite web of disputes that our pettifoggers have spun out as far as they could in favor of lawsuits:

> We are hard hit, and hit out hard in turn.
>
> HORACE

730 For the reasons have little other foundation than experience, and the diversity of human events offers us infinite examples in all sorts of forms.

A learned person of our time says that where they say warm in our almanacs, if someone wants to say cold, and wet where they say dry, and always put down the opposite of what they forecast, and if he had to lay a wager on one or the other

735 coming true, he would not care which side he took; except in cases that admit of no uncertainty, such as promising extreme heat at Christmas and the rigors of winter on Midsummer's Day. I have the same opinion about these political arguments: whatever part they give you to play, you have as good a chance as your opponent, provided you do not bump up against principles that are too plain and obvious.

740 And therefore, to my mind, in public affairs there is no course so bad, provided it is old and stable, that it is not better than change and commotion. Our morals are extremely corrupt, and lean with a remarkable inclination toward the

worse; of our laws and customs, many are barbarous and monstrous; however, because of the difficulty of improving our condition and the danger of everything
745 crumbling into bits, if I could put a spoke in our wheel and stop it at this point, I would do so with all my heart:

> Never such shameful, foul examples do we find,
> But that still worse, untold, remain behind.
> JUVENAL

The worst thing I find in our state is instability, and the fact that our laws cannot,
750 any more than our clothes, take any settled form. It is very easy to accuse a government of imperfection, for all mortal things are full of it. It is very easy to engender in a people contempt for their ancient observances; never did a man undertake that without succeeding. But as for establishing a better state in place of the one they have ruined, many of those who have attempted it have achieved
755 nothing for their pains.

I give my prudence small share in my conduct; I readily let myself be led by the general way of the world. Happy the people who do what they are commanded better than those who command, without tormenting themselves about the reasons, who let themselves roll relaxedly with the rolling of the heavens. Obedience is not
760 pure or tranquil in a man who reasons and argues.

All in all, to return to myself, the only thing that makes me think something of myself is the thing in which no man ever thought himself deficient: my recommendation is vulgar, common, and popular, for who ever thought he lacked sense? That would be a proposition implying its own contradiction. It is a disease
765 that is never where it is perceived; it is indeed tenacious and strong, but it is pierced and dispersed by the first glance from the patient's eye, like a dense fog by a glance from the sun. To accuse oneself would be to excuse oneself in that subject, and to condemn oneself would be to absolve oneself. There never was a porter or a silly woman who did not think they had enough sense to take care of themselves.
770 We readily acknowledge in others an advantage in courage, in bodily strength, in experience, in agility, in beauty; but an advantage in judgment we yield to no one. And the arguments that come from simple natural reasoning in others, we think we would have found if we had merely glanced in that direction. As for knowledge, style, and such qualities that we see in the works of others, we sense very easily
775 whether they surpass our own; but as for the simple products of the understanding, each man thinks he had it in him to hit upon the very same things, and does not easily perceive their weight and difficulty, unless—and hardly even then—they are at a great distance and beyond comparison. So this is a kind of exercise for which I must hope for very little commendation and praise, and a kind
780 of composition offering little renown.

And then, for whom do you write? The learned men to whom it falls to pass judgment on books know no other value than that of learning, and admit no other procedure for our minds than that of erudition and art. If you have mistaken one of

785 the Scipios for the other, what is there left for you to say that can be worth while? Anyone who does not know Aristotle, according to them, by the same token does not know himself. Common, ordinary minds do not see the grace and the weight of a lofty and subtle speech. Now, these two types fill the world. The third class into whose hands you come, that of minds regulated and strong in themselves, is so rare that for this very reason it has neither name nor rank among us; it is time half

790 wasted to aspire and strive to please this group.

It is commonly said that the fairest division of her favors Nature has given us is that of sense; for there is no one who is not content with the share of it that she has allotted him. Is that not reasonable? If anyone saw beyond, he would see beyond his sight.

795 I think my opinions are good and sound; but who does not think as much of his? One of the best proofs I have of mine is the little esteem I have for myself; for if these opinions had not been very firm, they would easily have let themselves be fooled by the singular affection I have for myself, being one who concentrates nearly all his affection upon himself and does not squander much of it elsewhere.

800 All the affection that others distribute to an infinite multitude of friends and acquaintances, to their glory, to their greatness, I devote entirely to the repose of my mind and to myself. What escapes in other directions is not properly by command of my reason:

> Trained to live healthily and for myself.
> LUCRETIUS

805 Now I find my opinions infinitely bold and constant in condemning my inadequacy. In truth, this too is a subject on which I exercise my judgment as much as on any other. The world always looks straight ahead; as for me, I turn my gaze inward, I fix it there and keep it busy. Everyone looks in front of him; as for me, I look inside of me; I have no business but with myself; I continually observe myself,

810 I take stock of myself, I taste myself. Others always go elsewhere, if they stop to think about it; they always go forward;

> No man tries to descend into himself;
> PERSIUS

as for me, I roll about in myself.

This capacity for sifting truth, whatever it may amount to in me, and this free

815 will not to enslave my belief easily, I owe principally to myself. For the firmest and most general ideas I have are those which, in a manner of speaking, were born with me. They are natural and all mine. I produced them crude and simple, with a conception bold and strong, but a little confused and imperfect. Since then I have established and fortified them by the authority of others and the sound arguments

820 of the ancients, with whom I found my judgment in agreement. These men have given

me a firmer grip on my ideas and a more complete enjoyment and possession of them.

The recommendation everyone seeks for liveliness and promptness of wit, I aspire to for orderliness; what they seek for a brilliant and signal deed, or for
825 some particular ability, I aspire to for order, consistency, and tranquillity of opinions and conduct. *Certainly, if anything is becoming, it is uniformity in our whole lives and in our individual actions; which you cannot maintain if, imitating the nature of others, you eliminate your own* [Cicero].

Here then you see to what extent I feel guilty of what I said was the first part
830 of the vice of presumption. As for the second, which consists in not esteeming others highly enough, I do not know if I can excuse myself so well; for cost me what it may, I am determined to tell the facts about it.

Whether it may be that the continual association I have with the humors of the ancients, and the idea I have formed of those rich souls of the past, give me a
835 distaste both for others and for myself; or whether we are indeed living in a time which produces only very mediocre things; at any rate, I know of nothing worthy of great admiration. Also, I know scarcely any men intimately enough to be able to judge them; and those I come in contact with most commonly through my situation are for the most part men who have little care for the culture of the soul, and to
840 whom one can suggest no other blessing than honor, and no other perfection than valor.

What beauty I see in others I praise and esteem very gladly. Indeed, I often go farther than what I really think of it, and allow myself to lie to that extent. For I am incapable of inventing anything false. I am glad to testify for my friends to the
845 praiseworthy qualities I find in them; and of one foot of value I am likely to make a foot and a half. But as for lending them qualities that are not there, I cannot, nor can I defend them openly for the imperfections they have.

Even to my enemies I frankly render the testimony of honor that is due. My feelings change; my judgment, no. And I do not confuse my criticism with other
850 circumstances that do not enter into it; and I am so jealous of the liberty of my judgment that I can hardly give it up for any passion whatsoever. I do myself more harm by lying than I do to the person I lie about. This laudable and generous custom is observed of the Persian nation, that they speak of their mortal enemies, and wage war to the death against them, honorably and fairly, so far as their
855 valor deserves it.

I know enough men who have various fine qualities, one wit, another courage, another skill, another conscience, another style, one one science, another another. But as for an all-round great man having all these fine parts together, or one part in such excellent degree as to cause amazement or comparison with the
860 men of the past whom we honor, I have not had the good fortune to find any. And the greatest man I have known in person, I mean for natural qualities of the soul, and the best endowed, was Etienne de La Boétie. He was truly a full soul, handsome from every point of view; a soul of the old stamp, who would have

865 achieved great results if fortune had willed it, for he had added much to this rich nature by learning and study.

But I do not know how it happens—and yet beyond doubt it does happen—that there is as much vanity and weakness of understanding in those who profess to have the greatest capacity, and who meddle with literary occupations and tasks that depend on books, as in any other sort of men; whether because people demand

870 and expect more of them, and cannot excuse ordinary faults in them, or because the thought that they are learned emboldens them to show off and reveal too much of themselves, whereby they ruin and betray themselves. Just as an artisan shows his stupidity much better on some rich material he has in his hands, if he arranges and mixes it foolishly and contrary to the rules of his craft, than on some wretched

875 stuff, and as people are more offended at a defect in a statue of gold than in one that is of plaster; so do these men when they display things that in themselves, and in their place, would be good; for they use them without discretion, doing honor to their memory at the expense of their intelligence: they do honor to Cicero, Galen, Ulpian, and Saint Jerome, and themselves they make ridiculous.

880 I gladly return to the subject of the ineptitude of our education. Its goal has been to make us not good or wise, but learned; it has attained this goal. It has not taught us to follow and embrace virtue and wisdom, but has imprinted in us their derivation and etymology. We know how to decline virtue, if we cannot love it. If we do not know what wisdom is by practice and experience, we know it by jargon

885 and by rote. With our neighbors, we are not content to know their family, their kindred, and their connections; we want to have them as friends and form some association and understanding with them. Education has taught us the definitions, divisions, and partitions of virtue, like the surnames and branches of a genealogy, without any further concern to form between us and virtue any familiar

890 relationship and intimate acquaintance. It has chosen for our instruction not the books that have the soundest and truest opinions, but those that speak the best Greek and Latin; and amid its beautiful words, it has poured into our minds the most inane humors of antiquity.

A good education changes your judgment and conduct, as happened to

895 Polemon, that dissipated young Greek, who, having gone by chance to hear a lecture by Xenocrates, did not notice merely the eloquence and mastery of the teacher, or bring back to his house merely the knowledge of some fine matter, but reaped a more perceptible and solid fruit, which was the sudden change and amendment of his former life. Who has ever felt such an effect from our education?

900
> Will you behave like Polemon,
> When he reformed, one bygone day? Will you lay down
> The badges of disease—wraps, anklets, pads—as he
> Tore from his drunken neck, they say, the wreath of glee,
> When the undinnered sage addressed him chidingly?
>
> HORACE

905   The least contemptible class of people seems to me to be those who, through their simplicity, occupy the lowest rank; and they seem to show greater regularity in their relations. The morals and the talk of peasants I find commonly more obedient to the prescriptions of true philosophy than are those of our philosophers. *The common people are wiser, because they are as wise as they need be*

910   [Lactantius].

The most notable men that I have judged by outward appearances—for to judge them in my own way, I would need more light on them—were, in point of war and military ability, the duke of Guise, who died at Orléans, and the late Marshal Strozzi. As for able men of uncommon virtue, Olivier and L'Hôpital, chancellors

915   of France. It seems to me that poetry too has flourished in our century. We have a wealth of good craftsmen in that trade: Daurat, Beza, Buchanan, L'Hôpital, Montdoré, Turnebus. As for those writing in French, I think they have raised its poetry to the highest point it will ever reach; and in the respects in which Ronsard and Du Bellay excel, I do not consider them far removed from the perfection of the

920   ancients. Adrianus Turnebus knew more, and knew better what he knew, than any man that lived in his time or for many years before.

The lives of the duke of Alva, who died recently, and of our Constable de Montmorency were noble lives that had many rare similarities in fortune. But the beauty and glory of the latter's death, suddenly and in extreme old age, before the

925   eyes of Paris and his king and in their service against his nearest kin, commanding an army victorious through his leadership, deserves, I think, to be placed among the notable events of my time. So do the constant goodness, the gentle conduct, and the conscientious affability of Monsieur de La Noue, amid such injustice of armed factions, true school of treachery, inhumanity, and brigandage, in which he was

930   brought up—a great and very experienced warrior.

I have taken pleasure in making public in several places the hopes I have for Marie de Gournay le Jars, my covenant daughter, whom I love indeed more than a daughter of my own, and cherish in my retirement and solitude as one of the best parts of my own being. She is the only person I still think about in the world. If

935   youthful promise means anything, her soul will some day be capable of the finest things, among others of perfection in that most sacred kind of friendship which, so we read, her sex has not yet been able to attain. The sincerity and firmness of her character are already sufficient, her affection for me more than superabundant, and such, in short, that it leaves nothing to be desired, unless that her

940   apprehension about my end, in view of my fifty-five years when I met her, would not torment her so cruelly. The judgment she made of the first *Essays,* she a woman, and in this age, and so young, and alone in her district, and the remarkable eagerness with which she loved me and wanted my friendship for a long time, simply through the esteem she formed for me before she had seen me, is a

945   phenomenon very worthy of consideration.

The other virtues are given little or no value nowadays; but valor has become common through our civil wars, and in this respect there are among us souls firm to the point of perfection, and in great numbers, so that a choice is impossible.

950   This is all the extraordinary and uncommon greatness that I have known up
to this moment.

(1578–1580)

BOOK II, 23: OF EVIL MEANS EMPLOYED TO A GOOD END

There is a wonderful relation and correspondence in this universal
government of the works of nature, which well shows that it is neither accidental
nor conducted by divers masters. The diseases and conditions of our bodies are
seen also in states and governments: kingdoms and republics are born, flourish,
5   and wither with age, as we do. We are subject to a useless and harmful surfeit of
humors: either of good humors—for even this the doctors fear; and because there is
nothing stable in us, they say that too blithe and vigorous a perfection of health
must be artificially reduced and abated for us, for fear that our nature, unable to
settle in any certain position and having no room for improvement, may retreat in
10   disorder and too suddenly; therefore they order purgings and bleedings for
athletes to draw off this superabundance of health—or of evil humors, which is
the ordinary cause of diseases.

States are often seen to be sick of a similar repletion, and it has been
customary to use various sorts of purgation. Sometimes a great multitude of
15   families are sent away to relieve the country of them, and these go to seek
accommodations elsewhere at the expense of others. In this fashion our ancient
Franks, starting from the depths of Germany, came and took possession of Gaul
and drove out its first inhabitants. Thus was formed that infinite tide of men that
poured into Italy under Brennus and others. Thus the Goths and Vandals, and
20   also the people who are now in possession of Greece, abandoned their native
country to go and settle elsewhere where they had more room. And there are
scarcely two or three corners in the world which have not felt the effect of such
movements.

By this means the Romans built their colonies; for, feeling their city growing
25   immoderately, they would relieve it of the least necessary people and send them to
inhabit and cultivate their conquered lands. Sometimes also they deliberately
fostered wars with certain of their enemies, not only to keep their men in
condition, for fear that idleness, mother of corruption, might bring them some
worse mischief—

30   We bear the evils of long peace: fiercer than war,
Luxury weighs us down

JUVENAL

—but also to serve as a bloodletting for their republic and to cool off a bit the too
vehement heat of their young men, to prune and clear the branches of that too
lustily proliferating stock. To this effect they once used their war against the
Carthaginians.

16. *Montaigne*/Essays ("Of Evil Means Employed to a Good End")

In the treaty of Bretigny, Edward III, king of England, would not include, in the general peace that he made with our king, the question of the contested duchy of Brittany, in order that he might have a place to unload his soldiers, and that the
35 crowd of Englishmen he had employed in his affairs on this side of the Channel might not rush back into England. This was one of the reasons why our King Philip consented to send his son John to the war overseas, so that he would take along with him a great number of hot-blooded young men who were in his armed forces.
40 There are many in our times who reason in like fashion, wishing that this heated passion that is among us might be deflected into some war with our neighbors, for fear that these peccant humors which dominate our body at the moment, if they are not drained off elsewhere may keep our fever still at its height and in the end bring on our total ruin. And indeed a foreign war is a much milder
45 evil than a civil war. But I do not believe that God would favor so unjust an enterprise as to injure and pick a quarrel with others for our own convenience:

> Nothing, O Nemesis, may I so strongly covet
> That I would rob its rightful owner of it.
> CATULLUS

However, the weakness of our condition often pushes us to the necessity of
50 using evil means to a good end. Lycurgus, the most virtuous and perfect lawmaker that ever was, hit upon this very unjust method of teaching his people temperance: to make the Helots, who were their slaves, forcibly drunk, so that the Spartans, seeing them thus lost and buried in wine, should hold the excess of this vice in horror.
55 Those were still more in the wrong who in ancient times allowed that criminals, whatever kind of death they were condemned to, should be cut up alive by the doctors, so that they might see our inner parts in their natural state and thereby establish more certainty in their art. For if we must go to excess, it is more excusable to do so for the health of the soul than for that of the body; as the
60 Romans trained the people to valor and contempt for dangers and death by those furious spectacles of gladiators and fencers who fought to the death and cut up and killed each other in their presence:

> What seeks this impious practice of a savage game,
> This death of youths, this blood-fed lust—what other aim?
> PRUDENTIUS

65 And this custom lasted until the Emperor Theodosius:

> Then seize this honor, Prince, delayed until your days;
> Take what your father left to take, heir to his praise.
> Let none be slain in Rome whose death serves as a thrill.

Let the cruel arena be now content to spill
The blood of beasts alone, not put on homicides.

PRUDENTIUS

70   It was in truth an admirable example, and very fruitful for the education of the people, to see every day before their eyes a hundred, two hundred, even a thousand pairs of men, armed against one another, hack each other to pieces with such extreme firmness of courage that they were observed never to let slip a word of weakness or commiseration, never to turn their back or make even a cowardly
75 movement to avoid their adversary's blow, but rather to extend their neck to his sword and offer themselves to the blow. Many of them, covered with mortal wounds, would send and ask the people if they were content with their performance of their duty, before lying down and giving up the ghost on the spot. They had to fight and die not only steadfastly, but even cheerfully, so that they
80 were booed and cursed if they were even seen to struggle against accepting death.
     Even the girls urged them on:

Each blow makes the modest maiden leap;
And every time the victor thrusts his weapon deep
In the other's throat, she shrieks for joy, and gives command,
85   Thumb down, to rip the bosom of the fallen man.

PRUDENTIUS

     The early Romans used criminals for such examples; but later they used innocent slaves, and even freemen who sold themselves for this purpose; finally Roman senators and knights, and even women:

And now they sell their heads, to die upon the sand,
90   And, with war quiet, each man seeks a foe at hand.

MANILUS

Amid these novel sports and these alarms,
The gentle sex takes part, unskilled in arms,
And manly conflict shamelessly usurps.

STATIUS

     This I should consider very strange and incredible if we were not accustomed to
95 see every day in our wars many thousands of foreigners engaging their blood and their lives for money in quarrels in which they have no concern.

(1578–1580)

17. ESSAYS, NOVUM ORGANUM, NEW ATLANTIS (SELECTIONS)

Sir Francis Bacon
(1561–1626)

Francis Bacon possessed all the characteristics of the Renaissance Man: he was a scientist, philosopher, essayist, lawyer, politician, and had high ambition, rising to be Lord Chancellor of England in 1618. He also had a corresponding ego, declaring, "I have taken all knowledge as my province."

His major contribution rests on his methodology; he pioneered the inductive method (proceeding from particular to general), and, like his classical predecessor, Aristotle, he wished to classify all knowledge and to systematize scientific procedures. First, however, he saw the need to clear the impediments to truth, the biases and habits of mind and language (the "idols" as described in Novum Organum, or "The New Instrument") that led to error. He composed a treatise describing a scientific utopia, The New Atlantis, *which accords research and the life of the mind central position. His literary fame is based on his fifty eight* Essays. *Very unlike Montaigne's loosely constructed personal ruminations, Bacon's* Essays *were designed to be practical and pithy guides to wisdom on a given topic, using his own distilled observations supplemented with wisdom from the classics (he subtitled the collection "Councils Civil and Moral"). He was a thorough going empiricist providing ways and means humans might gain mastery over their lives and over nature.*

ON LOVE

The stage is more beholding to love, than the life of man. For as to the stage, love is ever matter of comedies, and now and then of tragedies; but in life it doth much mischief; sometimes like a siren, sometimes like a fury.

You may observe, that amongst all the great and worthy persons (whereof the memory remaineth, either ancient or recent) there is not one that hath been transported to the mad degree of love which shows that great spirits, and great business, do keep out this weak passion. You must except, nevertheless, Marcus Antonius, the half partner of the empire of Rome, and Appius Claudius, the decemvir[1] and lawgiver; whereof the former was indeed a voluptuous man, and

5

---

[1]Ten member committee which drew up laws.

10   inordinate; but the latter was an austere and wise man: and therefore it seems (though rarely) that love can find entrance, not only into an open heart, but also into a heart well fortified, if watch be not well kept. It is a poor saying of Epicurus, *Satis magnum alter alteri theatrum sumus;*[2] as if man, made for the contemplation of heaven, and all noble objects, should do nothing but kneel before

15   a little idol and make himself a subject, though not of the mouth (as beasts are), yet of the eye; which was given him for higher purposes. It is a strange thing, to note the excess of this passion, and how it braves the nature, and value of things, by this; that the speaking in a perpetual hyperbole is comely in nothing but in love. Neither is it merely in the phrase; for whereas it hath been well said, that the arch-

20   flatterer, with whom all the petty flatterers have intelligence, is a man's self; certainly the lover is more. For there was never proud man thought so absurdly well of himself, as the lover doth of the person loved; and therefore it was well said, That it is impossible to love, and to be wise. Neither doth this weakness appear to others only, and not to the party loved; but to the loved most of all,

25   except the love be reciproque [reciprocal]. For it is a true rule, that love is ever rewarded, either with the reciproque, or with an inward and secret contempt. By how much the more, men ought to beware of this passion, which loseth not only other things, but itself! As for the other losses, the poet's relation doth well figure them: that he that preferred Helena, quitted the gifts of Juno and Pallas. For

30   whosoever esteemeth too much of amorous affection, quitteth both riches and wisdom. This passion hath his floods, in very times of weakness; which are great prosperity, and great adversity; though this latter hath been less observed: both which times kindle love, and make it more fervent, and therefore show it to be the child of folly. They do best, who if they cannot but admit love, yet make it keep

35   quarters; and sever it wholly from their serious affairs, and actions, of life; for if it check once with business, it troubleth men's fortunes, and maketh men, that they can no ways be true to their own ends. I know not how, but martial men are given to love: I think, it is but as they are given to wine; for perils commonly ask to be paid in pleasures. There is in man's nature, a secret inclination and motion,

40   towards love of others, which if it be not spent upon some one or a few, doth naturally spread itself towards many, and maketh men become humane and charitable; as it is seen sometime in friars. Nuptial love maketh mankind; friendly love perfecteth it; but wanton love corrupteth, and embaseth [debase] it.

OF ANGER

    To seek to extinguish anger utterly, is but a bravery of the Stoics. We have

45   better oracles: Be angry, but sin not. Let not the sun go down upon your anger.

    Anger must be limited and confined, both in race and in time. We will first speak how the natural inclination and habit to be angry, may be attempted and calmed. Secondly, how the particular motions of anger may be repressed, or at

---

[2]"Each of us is a great enough spectacle for the other."

least refrained from doing mischief. Thirdly, how to raise anger, or appease anger
in another.

For the first; there is no other way but to meditate, and ruminate well upon
the effects of anger, how it troubles man's life. And the best time to do this, is to
look back upon anger, when the fit is thoroughly over. Seneca saith well, That
anger is like ruin, which breaks itself upon that it falls. The Scripture exhorteth us
to possess our souls in patience. Whosoever is out of patience, is out of possession
of his soul. Men must not turn bees; . . . *animasque in vulnere ponunt.*[3]

Anger is certainly a kind of baseness; as it appears well in the weakness of
those subjects in whom it reigns; children, women, old folks, sick folks. Only men
must beware, that they carry their anger rather with scorn, than with fear; so that
they may seem rather to be above the injury, than below it; which is a thing easily
done, if a man will give law to himself in it.

For the second point; the causes and motives of anger, are chiefly three. First,
to be too sensible of hurt; for no man is angry, that feels not himself hurt; and
therefore tender and delicate persons must needs be oft angry; they have so many
things to trouble them, which more robust natures have little sense of. The next is,
the apprehension and construction of the injury offered, to be, in the circumstances
thereof, full of contempt: for contempt is that, which putteth an edge upon anger, as
much or more than the hurt itself. And therefore, when men are ingenious in
picking out circumstances of contempt, they do kindle their anger much. Lastly,
opinion of the touch of a man's reputation, doth multiply and sharpen anger.
Wherein the remedy is, that a man should have, as Consalvo was wont to say,
telam honoris crassiorem.[4] But in all refrainings of anger, it is the best remedy to
win time; and to make a man's self believe, that the opportunity of his revenge is
not yet come, but that he foresees a time for it; and so to still himself in the
meantime, and reserve it.

To contain anger from mischief, though it take hold of a man, there be two
things, whereof you must have special caution. The one, of extreme bitterness of
words, especially if they be aculeate [pointed, sharp] and proper; for *cummunia
maledicta*[5] are nothing so much; and again, that in anger a man reveal no secrets;
for that makes him not fit for society. The other, that you do not peremptorily
break off, in any business, in a fit of anger; but howsoever you show bitterness, do
not act anything, that is not revocable.

For raising and appeasing anger in another; it is done chiefly by choosing of
times, when men are frowardest [most contrary] and worst disposed, to incense
them. Again, by gathering (as was touched before) all that you can find out, to
aggravate the contempt. And the two remedies are by the contraries. The former to
take good times, when first to relate to a man an angry business; for the first
impression is much; and the other is, to sever, as much as may be, the construction

---

[3]"and they give their minds to bloodshed"
[4]"a thicker spear of honor"
[5]"mutual curses"

90 of the injury from the point of contempt; imputing it to misunderstanding, fear, passion, or what you will.

OF SUPERSTITION

It were better to have no opinion of God at all, than such an opinion, as is unworthy of him. For the one is unbelief, the other is contumely [contempt]; and certainly superstition is the reproach of the Deity.

Plutarch saith well to that purpose: Surely (saith he) I had rather a great deal,
95 men should say, there was no such man at all, as Plutarch, than that they should say, that there was one Plutarch, that would eat his children as soon as they were born; as the poets speak of Saturn. And as the contumely is greater towards God, so the danger is greater towards men. Atheism leaves a man to sense, to philosophy, to natural piety, to laws, to reputation—all which may be guides to
100 an outward moral virtue, though religion were not; but superstition dismounts all these, and erecteth an absolute monarchy, in the minds of men. Therefore theism did never perturb states; for it makes men wary of themselves, as looking no further: and we see the times inclined to atheism (as the time of Augustus Caesar) were civil times. But superstition hath been the confusion of many states, and bringeth
105 in a new primum mobile [prime mover], that ravisheth all the spheres of government. The master of superstition, is the people; and in all superstition, wise men follow fools; and arguments are fitted to practice, in a reversed order. It was gravely said by some of the prelates in the Council of Trent, where the doctrine of the Schoolmen [scholastic philosophers] bare great sway, that the Schoolmen were
110 like astronomers, which did feign eccentrics and epicycles, and such engines of orbs, to save the phenomena; though they knew there were no such things; and in like manner, that the Schoolmen had framed a number of subtle and intricate axioms, and theorems, to save the practice of the church. The causes of superstition are: pleasing and sensual rites and ceremonies; excess of outward and pharisaical
115 holiness; overgreat reverence of traditions, which cannot but load the church; the stratagems of prelates, for their own ambition and lucre; the favoring too much of good intentions, which openeth the gate to conceits and novelties; the taking an aim at divine matters, by human, which cannot but breed mixture of imaginations: and, lastly, barbarous times, especially joined with calamities and disasters.
120 Superstition, without a veil, is a deformed thing; for, as it addeth deformity to an ape, to be so like a man, so the similitude of superstition to religion, makes it the more deformed. And as wholesome meat corrupteth to little worms, so good forms and orders corrupt, into a number of petty observances. There is a superstition in avoiding superstition, when men think to do best, if they go furthest from the
125 superstition, formerly received; therefore care would be had that as it fareth in the good be not taken away with the bad; which commonly is done, when the people is the reformer.

* * * * *

FROM *NOVUM ORGANUM* (SELECTIONS)
The Works of Francis Bacon, 1857–1874

(trans. by Spedding, Ellis, and Heath)

PREFACE

Those who have taken upon them to lay down the law of Nature as a thing already searched out and understood, whether they have spoken in simple assurance or professional affectation, have therein done philosophy and the sciences great injury. For as they have been successful in inducing belief so they
5   have been effective in quenching and stopping inquiry; and have done more harm by spoiling and putting an end to other men's efforts than good by their own. Those on the other hand who have taken a contrary course, and asserted that absolutely nothing can be known,—whether it were from hatred of the ancient sophists, or from uncertainty and fluctuation of mind, or even from a kind of
10   fulness of learning, that they fell upon this opinion,—have certainly advanced reasons for it that are not to be despised; but yet they have neither started from true principles nor rested in the just conclusion, zeal and affectation having carried them much too far. The more ancient of the Greeks (whose writings are lost) took up with better judgment a position between these two extremes,—
15   between the presumption of pronouncing on everything, and the despair of comprehending anything; and though frequently and bitterly complaining of the difficulty of inquiry and the obscurity of things, and like impatient horses champing the bit, they did not the less follow up their object and engage with Nature; thinking (it seems) that this very question,—viz. whether or not any thing
20   can be known, —was to be settled not by arguing, but by trying. And yet they too, trusting entirely to the force of their understanding, applied no rule, but made everything turn upon hard thinking and perpetual working and exercise of the mind.

Now my method, though hard to practise, is easy to explain; and it is this. I
25   propose to establish progressive stages of certainty. The evidence of the sense, helped and guarded by a certain process of correction, I retain. But the mental operation which follows the act of sense I for the most part reject; and instead of it I open and lay out a new and certain path for the mind to proceed in, starting directly from the simple sensuous perception. The necessity of this was felt no
30   doubt by those who attributed so much importance to Logic; showing thereby that they were in search of helps for the understanding, and had no confidence in the native and spontaneous process of the mind. But this remedy comes too late to do any good, when the mind is already, through the daily intercourse and conversation of life, occupied with unsound doctrines and beset on all sides by
35   vain imaginations. And therefore that art of Logic, coming (as I said) too late to the rescue, and no way able to set matters right again, has had the effect of fixing

errors rather than disclosing truth. There remains but one course for the recovery of a sound and healthy condition, namely, that the entire work of the understanding be commenced afresh, and the mind itself be from the very outset not
40 left to take its own course, but guided at every step; and the business be done as if by machinery. Certainly if in things mechanical men had set to work with their naked hands, without help or force of instruments, just as in things intellectual they have set to work with little else than the naked forces of the understanding, very small would the matters have been which, even with their best efforts applied
45 in conjunction, they could have attempted or accomplished. Now (to pause awhile upon this example and look in it as in a glass) let us suppose that some vast obelisk were (for the decoration of a triumph or some such magnificence) to be removed from its place, and that men should set to work upon it with their naked hands; would not any sober spectator think them mad? And if they should then
50 send for more people, thinking that in that way they might manage it, would he not think them all the madder? And if they then proceeded to make a selection, putting away the weaker hands, and using only the strong and vigorous, would he not think them madder than ever? And if lastly, not content with this, they resolved to call in aid the art of athletics, and required all their men to come with hands, arms,
55 and sinews well anointed and medicated according to the rules of art, would he not cry out that they were only taking pains to show a kind of method and discretion in their madness? Yet just so it is that men proceed in matters intellectual, with just the same kind of mad effort and useless combination of forces,—when they hope great things either from the number and co-operation or
60 from the excellency and acuteness of individual wits; yea, and when they endeavour by Logic (which may be considered as a kind of athletic art) to strengthen the sinews of the understanding; and yet with all this study and endeavour it is apparent to any true judgement that they are but applying the naked intellect all the time; whereas in every great work to be done by the hand of
65 man it is manifestly impossible, without instruments and machinery, either for the strength of each to be exerted or the strength of all to be united.

Upon these premises two things occur to me of which, that they may not be overlooked, I would have men reminded. First it falls out fortunately as I think for the allaying of contradictious and heart-burnings, that the honour and reverence
70 due to the ancients remains untouched and undiminished; while I may carry out my designs and at the same time reap the fruit of my modesty. For if I should profess that I, going the same road as the ancients, have something better to produce, there must needs have been some comparison or rivalry between us (not to be avoided by any art of words) in respect of excellency or ability of wit; and though in this
75 there would be nothing unlawful or new (for if there be anything misapprehended by them, or falsely laid down, why may not I, using a liberty common to all, take exception to it?) yet the contest, however just and allowable, would have been an unequal one perhaps, in respect of the measure of my own powers. As it is however, —my object being to open a new way for the understanding, a way by
80 them untried and unknown, —the ease is altered; party zeal and emulation are at

an end; and I appear merely as a guide to point out the road; an office of small authority, and depending more upon a kind of luck than upon any ability or excellency. And thus much relates to the persons only. The other point of which I would have men reminded relates to the matter itself.

85   Be it remembered then that I am far from wishing to interfere with the philosophy which now flourishes, or with any other philosophy more correct and complete than this which has been or may hereafter be propounded. For I do not object to the use of this received philosophy, or others like it, for supplying matter for disputations or ornaments for discourse,—for the professor's lecture and for

90 the business of life. Nay more, I declare openly that for these uses the philosophy which I bring forward will not be much available. It does not lie in the way. It cannot be caught up in passage. It does not flatter the understanding by conformity with preconceived notions. Nor will it come down to the apprehension of the vulgar except by its utility and effects.

95   Let there lie therefore (and may it be for the benefit of both) two streams and two dispensations of knowledge; and in like manner two tribes or kindreds of students in philosophy tribes not hostile or alien to each other, but bound together by mutual services;—let there in short be one method for the cultivation, another for the invention, of knowledge. And for those who prefer the former, either from

100 hurry or from considerations of business or for want of mental power to take in and embrace the other (which must needs be most men's case), I wish that they may succeed to their desire in what they are about, and obtain what they are pursuing. But if any man there be who, not content to rest in and use the knowledge which has already been discovered, aspires to penetrate further; to overcome, not an

105 adversary in argument, but nature in action; to seek, not pretty and probable conjectures, but certain and demonstrable knowledge;—I invite all such to join themselves, as true sons of knowledge, with me, that passing by the outer courts of nature, which numbers have trodden, we may find a way at length into her inner chambers. And to make my meaning clearer and to familiarise the thing by giving it

110 a name, I have chosen to call one of these methods or ways Anticipation of the Mind, the other Interpretation of Nature. Moreover I have one request to make. I have on my own part made it my care and study that the things which I shall propound should not only be true, but should also be presented to men's minds, how strangely soever preoccupied and obstructed, in a manner not harsh or

115 unpleasant. It is but reasonable however, (especially in so great a restoration of learning and knowledge) that I should claim of men one favour in return; which is this: If any one would form an opinion or judgment either out of his own observation, or out of the crowd of authorities, or out of the forms of demonstration (which have now acquired a sanction like that of judicial laws),

120 concerning these speculations of mine, let him not hope that he can do it in passage or by the by; but let him examine the thing thoroughly; let him make some little trial for himself of the way which I describe and lay out; let him familiarise his thoughts with that subtlety of nature to which experience bears witness; let him correct by seasonable patience and due delay the depraved and deep-rooted habits

125   of his mind; and when all this is done and he has begun to be his own master, let him (if he will) use his own judgement.

* * * * *

THE IDOLS

L.

    But by far the greatest hindrance and aberration of the human understanding proceeds from the dullness, incompetency, and deceptions of the senses; in that things which strike the sense outweigh things which do not immediately strike it,

130   though they be more important. Hence it is that speculation commonly ceases where sight ceases; insomuch that of things invisible there is little or no observation. Hence all the working of the spirits inclosed in tangible bodies lies hid and unobserved of men. So also all the more subtle changes of form in the parts of coarser substances (which they commonly call alteration, though it is in truth

135   local motion through exceedingly small spaces) is in like manner unobserved. And yet unless these two things just mentioned be searched out and brought to light, nothing great can be achieved in nature, as far as the production of works is concerned. So again the essential nature of our common air, and of all bodies less dense than air (which are very many), is almost unknown. For the sense by itself is

140   a thing infirm and erring; neither can instruments for enlarging or sharpening the senses do much; but all the truer kind of interpretation of nature is effected by instances and experiments fit and apposite; wherein the sense decides touching the experiment only, and the experiment touching the point in nature and the thing itself.

LI.

145   The human understanding is of its own nature prone to abstractions and gives a substance and reality to things which are fleeting. But to resolve nature into abstractions is less to our purpose than to dissect her into parts; as did the school of Democritus, which went further into nature than the rest. Matter rather than forms should be the object of our attention, its configurations and changes of

150   configuration, and simple action, and law of action or motion; for forms are figments of the human mind, unless you will call those laws of action forms.

LII.

    Such then are the idols which I call Idols of the Tribe; and which take their rise either from the homogeneity of the substance of the human spirit, or from its preoccupation, or from its narrowness, or from its restless motion, or from an

155   infusion of the affections, or from the incompetency of the senses, or from the mode of impression.

LIII.

The Idols of the Cave take their rise in the peculiar constitution, mental or bodily, of each individual; and also in education, habit, and accident. Of this kind there is a great number and variety; but I will instance those the pointing out of which contains the most important caution, and which have most effect in disturbing the clearness of the understanding.

LIV.

Men become attached to certain particular sciences and speculations, either because they fancy themselves the authors and inventors thereof, or because they have bestowed the greatest pains upon them and become most habituated to them. But men of this kind, if they betake themselves to philosophy and contemplations of a general character, distort and colour them in obedience to their former fancies; a thing especially to be noticed in Aristotle, who made his natural philosophy a mere bond-servant to his logic, thereby rendering it contentious and well nigh useless. The race of chemists again out of a few experiments of the furnace have built up a fantastic philosophy, framed with reference to a few things; and Gilbert also, after he had employed himself most laboriously in the study and observation of the loadstone, proceeded at once to construct an entire system in accordance with his favourite subject.

LV.

There is one principal and as it were radical distinction between different minds, in respect of philosophy and the sciences; which is this: that some minds are stronger and apter to mark the differences of things, others to mark their resemblances. The steady and acute mind can fix its contemplations and dwell and fasten on the subtlest distinctions: the lofty and discursive mind recognises and puts together the finest and most general resemblances. Both kinds however easily err in excess, by catching the one at gradations, the other at shadows.

LVI.

There are found some minds given to an extreme admiration of antiquity, others to an extreme love and appetite for novelty: but few so duly tempered that they can hold the mean, neither carping at what has been well laid down by the ancients, nor despising what is well introduced by the moderns. This however turns to the great injury of the sciences and philosophy; since these affectations of antiquity and novelty are the humours of partisans rather than judgments; and truth is to be sought for not in the felicity of any age, which is an unstable thing, but in the light of nature and experience, which is eternal. These factions therefore must be abjured, and care must be taken that the intellect be not hurried by them into assent.

LVII.

Contemplations of nature and of bodies in their simple form break up and distract the understanding, while contemplations of nature and bodies in their composition and configuration overpower and dissolve the understanding: a distinction well seen in the school of Leucippus and Democritus as compared with
195   the other philosophies. For that school is so busied with the particles that it hardly attends to the structure; while the others are so lost in admiration of the structure that they do not penetrate to the simplicity of nature. These kinds of contemplation should therefore be alternated and taken by turns; that so the understanding may be rendered at once penetrating and comprehensive, and the
200   inconveniences above mentioned, with the idols which proceed from them, may be avoided.

LVIII.

Let such then be our provision and contemplative prudence for keeping off and dislodging the Idols of the Cave, which grow for the most part either out of the predominance of a favourite subject, or out of an excessive tendency to compare or
205   to distinguish, or out of partiality for particular ages, or out of the largeness or minuteness of the objects contemplated. And generally let every student of nature take this as a rule, —that whatever his mind seizes and dwells upon with peculiar satisfaction is to be held in suspicion, and that so much the more care is to be taken in dealing with such questions to keep the understanding even and clear.

LIX.

210   But the Idols of the Market-place are the most troublesome of all: idols which have crept into the understanding through the alliances of words and names. For men believe that their reason governs words; but it is also true that words react on the understanding; and this it is that has rendered philosophy and the sciences sophistical and inactive. Now words, being commonly framed and applied
215   according to the capacity of the vulgar, follow those lines of division which are most obvious to the vulgar understanding. And whenever an understanding of greater acuteness or a more diligent observation would alter those lines to suit the true divisions of nature, words stand in the way and resist the change. Whence it comes to pass that the high and formal discussions of learned men end oftentimes in
220   disputes about words and names; with which (according to the use and wisdom of the mathematicians) it would be more prudent to begin, and so by means of definitions reduce them to order. Yet even definitions cannot cure this evil in dealing with natural and material things; since the definitions themselves consist of words, and those words beget others: so that it is necessary to recur to
225   individual instances, and those in due series and order; as I shall say presently when I come to the method and scheme for the formation of notions and axioms.

LX.

The idols imposed by words on the understanding are of two kinds. They are either names of things which do not exist (for as there are things left unnamed through lack of observation, so likewise are there names which result from fantastic suppositions and to which nothing in reality corresponds), or they are names of things which exist, but yet confused and ill-defined, and hastily and irregularly derived from realities. Of the former kind are Fortune, the Prime Mover, Planetary Orbits, Element of Fire, and like fictions which owe their origin to false and idle theories. And this class of idols is more easily expelled, because to get rid of them it is only necessary that all theories should be steadily rejected and dismissed as obsolete.

But the other class, which springs out of a faulty and unskilful abstraction, is intricate and deeply rooted. Let us take for example such a word as humid; and see how far the several things which the word is used to signify agree with each other; and we shall find the word humid to be nothing else than a mark loosely and confusedly applied to denote a variety of actions which will not bear to be reduced to any constant meaning. For it both signifies that which easily spreads itself round any other body; and that which in itself is indeterminate and cannot solidise; and that which readily yields in every direction; and that which easily divides and scatters itself; and that which easily unites and collects itself; and that which readily flows and is put in motion; and that which readily clings to another body and wets it; and that which is easily reduced to a liquid, or being solid easily melts. Accordingly when you come to apply the word,—if you take it in one sense, flame is humid; if in another, air is not humid; if in another, fine dust is humid; if in another, glass is humid. So that it is easy to see that the notion is taken by abstraction only from water and common and ordinary liquids, without any due verification.

There are however in words certain degrees of distortion and error. One of the least faulty kinds is that of names of substances, especially of lowest species and well-deduced (for the notion of chalk and of mud is good, of earth bad); a more faulty kind is that of actions, as to generate, to corrupt, to alter; the most faulty is of qualities (except such as are the immediate objects of the sense) as heavy, light, rare, dense, and the like. Yet in all these cases some notions are of necessity a little better than others, in proportion to the greater variety of subjects that fall within the range of the human sense.

LXI.

But the Idols of the Theatre are not innate, nor do they steal into the understanding secretly, but are plainly impressed and received into the mind from the play-books of philosophical systems and the perverted rules of demonstration. To attempt refutations in this case would be merely inconsistent with what I have already said: for since we agree neither upon principles nor upon demonstrations there is no place for argument. And this is so far well, inasmuch as it leaves the honour of the ancients untouched. For they are no wise disparaged—the question

270   between them and me being only as to the way. For as the saying is, the lame man who keeps the right road outstrips the runner who takes a wrong one. Nay it is obvious that when a man runs the wrong way, the more active and swift he is, the further he will go astray.

     But the course I propose for the discovery of sciences is such as leaves but
275   little to the acuteness and strength of wits, but places all wits and understandings nearly on a level. For as in the drawing of a straight line or a perfect circle, much depends on the steadiness and practice of the hand, if it be done by aim of hand only, but if with the aid of rule or compass, little or nothing; so is it exactly with my plan. But though particular confutations would be of no avail, yet touching the
280   sects and general divisions of such systems I must say something; something also touching the external signs which show that they are unsound; and finally something touching the causes of such great infelicity and of such lasting and general agreement in error; that so the access to truth may be made less difficult, and the human understanding may the more willingly submit to its purgation and
285   dismiss its idols.

LXII.

     Idols of the Theatre, or of Systems, are many, and there can be and perhaps will be yet many more. For were it not that new for many ages men's minds have been busied with religion and theology; and were it not that civil governments, especially monarchies, have been averse to such novelties, even in matters
290   speculative; so that men labour therein to the peril and harming of their fortunes,—not only unrewarded, but exposed also to contempt and envy; doubtless there would have arisen many other philosophical sects like to those which in great variety flourished once among the Greeks. For as on the phenomena of the heavens many hypotheses may be constructed, so likewise (and more also)
295   many various dogmas may be set up and established on the phenomena of philosophy. And in the plays of this philosophical theatre you may observe the same thing which is found in the theatre of the poets, that stories invented for the stage are more compact and elegant, and more as one would wish them to be, than true stories out of history.

300   In general however there is taken for the material of philosophy either a great deal out of a few things, or a very little out of many things; so that on both sides philosophy is based on too narrow a foundation of experiment and natural history, and decides on the authority of too few cases. For the Rational School of philosophers snatches from experience a variety of common instances, neither duly
305   ascertained nor diligently examined and weighed, and leaves all the rest to meditation and agitation of wit.

     There is also another class of philosophers, who having bestowed much diligent and careful labour on a few experiments, have thence made bold to educe and construct systems; wresting all other facts in a strange fashion to conformity
310   therewith.

And there is yet a third class, consisting of those who out of faith and veneration mix their philosophy with theology and traditions; among whom the vanity of some has gone so far aside as to seek the origin of sciences among spirits and genii. So that this parent stock of errors—this false philosophy—is of three

315   kinds; the Sophistical, the Empirical, and the Superstitious.

* * * * *

LXVIII.

So much concerning the several classes of Idols, and their equipage: all of which must be renounced and put away with a fixed and solemn determination, and the understanding thoroughly freed and cleansed; the entrance into the kingdom of man, founded on the sciences, being not much other than the entrance

320   into the kingdom of heaven, where into none may enter except as a little child.

* * * * *

FROM *THE NEW ATLANTIS* [THE HOUSE OF SALOMON]

"Ye are happy men; for the father of Salomon's House taketh knowledge of your being here, and commanded me to tell you that he will admit all your company to his presence, and have private conference with one of you, that ye shall choose; and for this hath appointed the next day after to-morrow. And because he meaneth

5   to give you his blessing, he hath appointed it in the forenoon."

We came at our day and hour, and I was chosen by my fellows for the private access. We found him in a fair chamber, richly hanged, and carpeted under foot, without any degrees to the state; he was set upon a low throne richly adorned, and a rich cloth of state over his head of blue satin embroidered. He was alone,

10   save that he had two pages of honor, on either hand one, finely attired in white. His under-garments were the like that we saw him wear in the chariot; but instead of his gown, he had on him a mantle with a cape, of the same fine black, fastened about him. When we came in, as we were taught, we bowed low at our first entrance; and when we were come near his chair, he stood up, holding forth his

15   hand ungloved, and in posture of blessing; and we every one of us stooped down and kissed the end of his tippet. That done, the rest departed, and I remained. Then he warned the pages forth of the room, and caused me to sit down beside him, and spake to me thus in the Spanish tongue:

"God bless thee, my son; I will give thee the greatest jewel I have. For I will

20   impart unto thee, for the love of God and men, a relation of the true state of Salomon's House. Son, to make you know the true state of Salomon's House, I will keep this order. First, I will set forth unto you the end of our foundation. Secondly, the preparations and instruments we have for our works. Thirdly, the several employments and functions whereto our fellows are assigned. And fourthly, the

25   ordinances and rites which we observe.

"The end of our foundation is the knowledge of causes, and secret motions of things; and the enlarging of the bounds of human empire, to the effecting of all things possible.

"The preparations and instruments are these: We have large and deep caves
30 of several depths; the deepest are sunk 600 fathoms; and some of them are digged and made under great hills and mountains; so that if you reckon together the depth of the hill and the depth of the cave, they are, some of them, above three miles deep. For we find that the depth of a hill and the depth of a cave from the flat are the same thing; both remote alike from the sun and heaven's beams, and from the open
35 air. These caves we call the lower region. And we use them for all coagulations, indurations, refrigerations, and conservations of bodies. We use them likewise for the imitation of natural mines and the producing also of new artificial metals, by compositions and materials which we use and lay there for many years. We use them also sometimes (which may seem strange) for curing of some diseases, and for
40 prolongation of life, in some hermits that choose to live there, well accommodated of all things necessary, and indeed live very long; by whom also we learn many things.

"We have burials in several earths, where we put divers cements, as the Chinese do their porcelain. But we have them in greater variety, and some of them
45 more fine. We also have great variety of composts and soils, for the making of the earth fruitful.

"We have high towers, the highest about half a mile in height, and some of them likewise set upon high mountains, so that the vantage of the hill with the tower is in the highest of them three miles at least. And these places we call the
50 upper region, account the air between the high places and the low as a middle region.

"We have great lakes, both salt and fresh, whereof we have use for the fish and fowl. We use them also for burials of some natural bodies, for we find a difference in things buried in earth, or in air below the earth, and things buried in
55 water. We have also pools, of which some do strain fresh water out of salt, and others by art do turn fresh water into salt. We have also some rocks in the midst of the sea, and some bays upon the shore for some works, wherein are required the air and vapor of the sea. We have likewise violent streams and cataracts, which serve us for many motions; and likewise engines for multiplying and enforcing of
60 winds to set also on divers motions.

"We have also a number of artificial wells and fountains, made in imitation of the natural sources and baths, as tincted upon vitriol, sulphur, steel, brass, lead, nitre, and other minerals; and again, we have little wells for infusions of many things, where the waters take the virtue quicker and better than in vessels or
65 basins. And among them we have a water, which we call water of paradise, being by that we do it made very sovereign for health and prolongation of life.

"We have also great and spacious houses, where we imitate and demonstrate meteors—as snow, hail, rain, some artificial rains of bodies and not of water,

thunders, lightnings; also generations of bodies in air—as frogs, flies, and divers
70   others.

"We have also certain chambers, which we call chambers of health, where we qualify the air as we think good and proper for the cure of divers diseases and preservation of health.

"We have also fair and large baths, of several mixtures, for the cure of
75   diseases, and the restoring of man's body from a refaction; and others for the confirming of it in strength of sinews, vital parts, and the very juice and substance of the body.

"We have also large and various orchards and gardens, wherein we do not so much respect beauty as variety of ground and soil, proper for divers trees and
80   herbs, and some very spacious, where trees and berries are set, whereof we make divers kinds of drinks, beside the vineyards. In these we practise likewise all conclusions of grafting, and inoculating, as well of wild-trees as fruit-trees, which produceth many effects. And we make by art, in the same orchards and gardens, trees and flowers, to come earlier or later than their seasons, and to come up and
85   bear more speedily than by their natural course they do. We make them also by art greater much than their nature; and their fruit greater and sweeter, and of differing taste, smell, color, and figure, from their nature. And many of them we so order as that they become of medicinal use.

"We have also means to make divers plants rise by mixtures of earths without
90   seeds, and likewise to make divers new plants, differing from the vulgar, and to make one tree or plant turn into another.

"We have also parks, and enclosures of all sorts, of beasts and birds; which we use not only for view or rareness, but likewise for dissections and trials, that thereby may take light what may be wrought upon the body of man. Wherein we
95   find many strange effects: as continuing life in them, though divers parts, which you account vital, be perished and taken forth; resuscitating of some that seem dead in appearance, and the like. We try also all poisons, and other medicines upon them, as well of chirurgery as physic. By art likewise we make them greater or smaller than their kind is, and contrariwise dwarf them and stay their growth;
100   we make them more fruitful and bearing than their kind is, and contrariwise barren and not generative. Also we make them differ in color, shape, activity, many ways. We find means to make commixtures and copulations of divers kinds, which have produced many new kinds, and them not barren, as the general opinion is. We make a number of kinds of serpents, worms, flies, fishes of
105   putrefaction, whereof some are advanced (in effect) to be perfect creatures, like beasts or birds, and have sexes, and do propagate. Neither do we this by chance, but we know beforehand of what matter and commixture, what kind of those creatures will arise.

"We have also particular pools where we make trials upon fishes, as we
110   have said before of beasts and birds.

"We have also places for breed and generation of those kinds of worms and flies which are of special use; such as are with you your silkworms and bees.

"I will not hold you long with recounting of our brew-houses, bake-houses, and kitchens, where are made divers drinks, breads, and meats, rare and of special
115 effects. Wines we have of grapes, and drinks of other juice, of fruits, of grains, and of roots, and of mixtures with honey, sugar, manna, and fruits dried and decocted; also of the tears or wounding of trees and of the pulp of canes. And these drinks are of several ages, some to the age or last of forty years. We have drinks also brewed with several herbs and roots and spices; yea, with several fleshes and
120 white meats; whereof some of the drinks are such as they are in effect meat and drink both, so that divers, especially in age, do desire to live with them with little or no meat or bread. And above all we strive to have drinks of extreme thin parts, to insinuate into the body, and yet without all biting, sharpness, or fretting; insomuch as some of them put upon the back of your hand, will with a little stay
125 pass through to the palm, and yet taste mild to the mouth. We have also waters, which we ripen in that fashion, as they become nourishing, so that they are indeed excellent drinks, and many will use no other. Bread we have of several grains, roots, and kernels; yea, and some of flesh, and fish, dried; with divers kinds of leavings and seasonings; so that some do extremely move appetites, some do
130 nourish so as divers do live of them, without any other meat, who live very long. So for meats, we have some of them so beaten, and made tender, and mortified, yet without all corrupting, as a weak heat of the stomach will turn them into good chilus, as well as a strong heat would meat otherwise prepared. We have some meats also and bread, and drinks, which, taken by men, enable them to fast long
135 after; and some other, that used make the very flesh of men's bodies sensibly more hard and tough, and their strength far greater than otherwise it would be.

"We have dispensatories or shops of medicines; wherein you may easily think, if we have such variety of plants, and living creatures, more than you have in Europe (for we know what you have), the simples, drugs, and ingredients of
140 medicines, must likewise be in so much the greater variety. We have them likewise of divers ages, and long fermentations. And for their preparations, we have not only all manner of exquisite distillations, and separations, and especially by gentle heats, and percolations through divers strainers, yea, and substances; but also exact forms of composition, whereby they incorporate almost as they were
145 natural simples.

"We have also divers mechanical arts, which you have not; and stuffs made by them, as papers, linen, silks, tissues, dainty works of feathers of wonderful lustre, excellent dyes, and many others, and shops likewise as well for such as are not brought into vulgar use among us, as for those that are. For you must know,
150 that of the things before recited, many of them are grown into use throughout the kingdom, but yet, if they did flow from our invention, we have of them also for patterns and principals.

"We have also furnaces of great diversities, and that keep great diversity of heats; fierce and quick, strong and constant, soft and mild, blown, quiet, dry, moist,
155 and the like. But above all we have heats, in imitation of the sun's and heavenly bodies' heats, that pass divers inequalities, and as it were orbs, progresses, and

returns whereby we produce admirable effects. Besides, we have heats of dungs, and of bellies and maws of living creatures and of their bloods and bodies, and of hays and herbs laid up moist, of lime unquenched, and such like. Instruments also which generate heat only by motion. And farther, places for strong insulations; and, again, places under the earth, which by nature or art yield heat. These divers heats we use as the nature of the operation which we intend requireth.

"We have also perspective houses, where we make demonstrations of all lights and radiations and of all colors; and out of things uncolored and transparent we can represent unto you all several colors, not in rainbows, as it is in gems and prisms, but of themselves single. We represent also all multiplications of light, which we carry to great distance, and make so sharp as to discern small points and lines. Also all colorations of light: all delusions and deceits of the sight, in figures, magnitudes, motions, colors; all demonstrations of shadows. We find also divers means, yet unknown to you, of producing of light, originally from divers bodies. We procure means of seeing objects afar off, as in the heaven and remote places; and represent things near as afar off, and things afar off as near; making feigned distances. We have also helps for the sight far above spectacles and glasses in use; we have also glasses and means to see small and minute bodies, perfectly and distinctly; as the shapes and colors of small flies and worms, grains, and flaws in gems which cannot otherwise be seen, observations in urine and blood not otherwise to be seen. We make artificial rainbows, halos, and circles about light. We represent also all manner of reflections, refractions, and multiplications of visual beams of objects.

"We have also precious stones, of all kinds, many of them of great beauty and to you unknown, crystals likewise, and glasses of divers kind; and among them some of metals vitrificated, and other materials, besides those of which you make glass. Also a number of fossils and imperfect minerals, which you have not. Likewise loadstones of prodigious virtue, and other rare stones, both natural and artificial.

"We have also sound-houses, where we practise and demonstrate all sounds and their generation. We have harmony which you have not, of quarter-sounds and lesser slides of sounds. Divers instruments of music likewise to you unknown, some sweeter than any you have; with bells and rings that are dainty and sweet. We represent small sounds as great and deep, likewise great sounds extenuate and sharp; we make divers tremblings and warblings of sounds, which in their original are entire. We represent and imitate all articulate sounds and letters, and the voices and notes of beasts and birds. We have certain helps which, set to the ear, do further the hearing greatly; we have also divers strange and artificial echoes, reflecting the voice many times, and, as it were, tossing it; and some that give back the voice louder than it came, some shriller and some deeper; yea, some rendering the voice, differing in the letters or articulate sound from that they receive. We have all means to convey sounds in trunks and pipes, in strange lines and distances.

200   "We have also perfume-houses, wherewith we join also practices of taste. We multiply smells which may seem strange: we imitate smells, making all smells to breathe out of other mixtures than those that give them. We make divers imitations of taste likewise, so that they will deceive any man's taste. And in this house we contain also a confiture-house, where we make all sweatmeats, dry and moist, and
205   divers pleasant wines, milks, broths, and salads, far in greater variety than you have.

    "We have also engine-houses, where are prepared engines and instruments for all sorts of motions. There we imitate and practise to make swifter motions than any you have, either out of your muskets or any engine that you have; and to
210   make them and multiply them more easily and with small force, by wheels and other means, and to make them stronger and more violent than yours are, exceeding your greatest cannons and basilisks. We represent also ordinance and instruments of war and engines of all kinds; and likewise new mixtures and compositions of gunpowder, wild-fires burning in water and unquenchable, also fire-works of all
215   variety, both for pleasure and use. We imitate also flights of birds; we have some degrees of flying in the air. We have ships and boats for going under water and brooking of seas, also swimming-girdles and supporters. We have divers curious clocks and other like motions of return, and some perpetual motions. We imitate also motions of living creatures by images of men, beasts, birds, fishes, and
220   serpents; we have also a great number of other various motions, strange for equality, fineness, and subtilty.

    "We have also a mathematical-house, where are represented all instruments, as well of geometry as astronomy, exquisitely made.

    "We have also houses of deceits of the senses, where we represent all manner
225   of feats of juggling, false apparitions, impostures and illusions, and their fallacies. And surely you will easily believe that we, that have so many things truly natural which induce admiration, could in a world of particulars deceive the senses if we would disguise those things, and labor to make them more miraculous. But we do hate all impostures and lies, insomuch as we have severely forbidden it to all our
230   fellows, under pain of ignomiy and fines, that they do not show any natural work or thing adorned or swelling, but only pure as it is, and without all affectation of strangeness.

    "These are, my son, the riches of Salomon's House.

    "For the several employments and offices of our fellows, we have twelve that
235   sail into foreign countries under the names of other nations (for our own we conceal), who bring us the books and abstracts, and patterns of experiments of all other parts. These we call merchants of light.

    "We have three that collect the experiments which are in all books. These we call depredators.
240   "We have three that collect the experiments of all mechanical arts, and also of liberal sciences, and also of practices which are not brought into arts. These we call mystery-men.

"We have three that try new experiments, such as themselves think good. These we call pioneers or miners.

245 "We have three that draw the experiments of the former four into titles and tables, to give the better light for the drawing of observations and axioms out of them. These we call compilers. We have three that bend themselves, looking into the experiments of their fellows, and cast about how to draw out of them things of use and practice for man's life and knowledge, as well for works as for plain

250 demonstration of causes, means of natural divinations, and the easy and clear discovery of the virtues and parts of bodies. These we call dowry-men or benefactors.

"Then after divers meetings and consults of our whole number, to consider of the former labors and collections, we have three that take care out of them to

255 direct new experiments, of a higher light, more penetrating into nature than the former. These we call lamps.

"We have three others that do execute the experiments so directed, and report them. These we call inoculators.

"Lastly, we have three that raise the former discoveries by experiments into

260 greater observations, axioms, and aphorisms. These we call interpreters of nature.

"We have also, as you must think, novices and apprentices, that the succession of the former employed men do not fail; besides a great number of servants and attendants, men and women. And this we do also: we have consultations, which of the inventions and experiences which we have discovered

265 shall be published, and which not; and take all an oath of secrecy for the concealing of those which we think fit to keep secret; though some of those we do reveal sometime to the State, and some not.

"For our ordinances and rites we have two very long and fair galleries. In one of these we place patterns and samples of all manner of the more rare and

270 excellent inventions; in the other we place the statues of all principal inventors. There we have the statue of your Columbus, that discovered the West Indies, also the inventor of ships, your monk that was the inventor of ordnance and of gunpowder, the inventor of music, the inventor of letters, the inventor of printing, the inventor of observations of astronomy, the inventor of works in metal, the

275 inventor of glass, the inventor of silk of the worm, the inventor of wine, the inventor of corn and bread, the inventor of sugars; and all these by more certain tradition than you have. Then we have divers inventors of our own, of excellent works; which, since you have not seen, it were too long to make descriptions of them; and besides, in the right understanding of those descriptions you might easily

280 err. For upon every invention of value we erect a statue to the inventor, and give him a liberal and honorable reward. These statues are some of brass, some of marble and touchstone, some of cedar and other special woods gilt and adorned; some of iron, some of silver, some of gold.

"We have certain hymns and services, which we say daily, of laud and

285 thanks to God for His marvellous works. And forms of prayers, imploring His aid

and blessing for the illumination of our labors; and turning them into good and holy uses.

"Lastly, we have circuits or visits, of divers principal cities of the kingdom; where as it cometh to pass we do publish such new profitable inventions as we

290 think good. And we do also declare natural divinations of diseases, plagues, swarms of hurtful creatures, scarcity, tempest, earthquakes, great inundations, comets, temperature of the year, and divers other things; and we give counsel thereupon, what the people shall do for the prevention and remedy of them."

And when he had said this he stood up, and I, as I had been taught, knelt

295 down; and he laid his right hand upon my head, and said: "God bless thee, my son, and God bless this relation which I have made. I give thee leave to publish it, for the good of other nations; for we here are in God's bosom, a land unknown." And so he left me; having assigned a value of about 2,000 ducats for a bounty to me and my fellows. For they give great largesses, where they come, upon all occasions.

300 [THE REST WAS NOT PERFECTED.]

18. DON QUIXOTE (SELECTIONS)

Miguel de Cervantes
(1547–1616)

(trans. by John Ormsby)

It is often noted that Cervantes and Shakespeare died on the same day (April 23, 1616), for between the two authors exist the greatest range and depth of human imagination and the truest readings on the human condition. Cervantes joined the military to escape poverty and gain glory, but his heroism was short lived; he was seriously wounded in battle and by ill luck captured by pirates and imprisoned in Algiers. Escapes proved futile, and once ransomed, he decided to switch glory in arms for glory in letters—with about as little success initially. Cervantes tried every manner of writing—poetry, drama, romance, but not until being imprisoned for debt (again, probably unfairly) did he conceive the tale that rang true: Don Quixote, the story of a fool who tried to be a hero. The narrator tells us that Don Quixote's brain dried up from too much reading ('caveat lector'!); as evidence, the poor fellow changes his name, fashions some armor from junk, renames his hack, and sets out to live the chivalric life by righting all manner of wrongs. He is joined by an incongruous squire, Sancho Panza, whose realistic and materialistic perspective initially serves as a corrective, but very soon it becomes apparent that sanity is both relative and slippery. Thus what begins as parody turns into an examination of the nature of reality and the transforming powers of the imagination.

CHAPTER I: WHICH TREATS OF THE CHARACTER AND PURSUITS OF THE FAMOUS GENTLEMAN DON QUIXOTE OF LA MANCHA

In a village of La Mancha, the name of which I have no desire to call to mind, there lived not long since one of those gentlemen that keep a lance in the lance-rack, an old buckler, a lean hack, and a greyhound for coursing. An *olla* of rather more beef than mutton, a salad on most nights, scraps on Saturdays, lentils on
5 Fridays, and a pigeon or so extra on Sundays, made away with three-quarters of his income. The rest of it went in a doublet of fine cloth and velvet breeches and shoes to match for holidays, while on week-days he made a brave figure in his best homespun. He had in his house a housekeeper past forty, a niece under twenty, and a lad for the field and market-place, who used to saddle the hack as well as handle
10 the bill-hook. The age of this gentleman of ours was bordering on fifty; he was of a

hardy habit, spare, gaunt-featured, a very early riser and a great sportsman. They will have it his surname was Quixada or Quesada (for here there is some difference of opinion among the authors who write on the subject), although from reasonable conjectures it seems plain that he was called Quexana. This, however,

15   is of but little importance to our tale; it will be enough not to stray a hair's breadth from the truth in the telling of it.

You must know, then, that the above-named gentleman whenever he was at leisure (which was mostly all the year round) gave himself up to reading books of chivalry with such ardour and avidity that he almost entirely neglected the

20   pursuit of his field-sports, and even the management of his property; and to such a pitch did his eagerness and infatuation go that he sold many an acre of tillageland to buy books of chivalry to read, and brought home as many of them as he could get. But of all there were none he liked so well as those of the famous Feliciano de Silva's composition, for their lucidity of style and complicated conceits were as

25   pearls in his sight, particularly when in his reading he came upon courtships and cartels, where he often found passages like "the reason of the unreason with which my reason is afflicted so weakens my reason that with reason I murmur at your beauty;" or again, "the high heavens, that of your divinity divinely fortify you with the stars, render you deserving of the dessert your greatness deserves."

30   Over conceits of this sort the poor gentleman lost his wits, and used to lie awake striving to understand them and worm the meaning out of them; what Aristotle himself could not have made out or extracted had he come to life again for that special purpose. He was not at all easy about the wounds which Don Belianis gave and took, because it seemed to him that, great as were the surgeons who had

35   cured him, he must have had his face and body covered all over with seams and scars. He commended, however, the author's way of ending his book with the promise of that interminable adventure, and many a time was he tempted to take up his pen and finish it properly as is there proposed, which no doubt he would have done, and made a successful piece of work of it too, had not greater and more

40   absorbing thoughts prevented him.

Many an argument did he have with the curate of his village (a learned man, and a graduate of Siguenza) as to which had been the better knight, Palmerin of England or Amadis of Gaul. Master Nicholas, the village barber, however, used to say that neither of them came up to the Knight of Phoebus, and that if there was

45   any that could compare with him it was Don Galaor, the brother of Amadis of Gaul, because he had a spirit that was equal to every occasion, and was no finikin knight, nor lachrymose like his brother, while in the matter of valour he was not a whit behind him. In short, he became so absorbed in his books that he spent his nights from sunset to sunrise, and his days from dawn to dark, poring

50   over them; and what with little sleep and much reading his brains got so dry that he lost his wits. His fancy grew full of what he used to read about in his books, enchantments, quarrels, battles, challenges, wounds, wooings, loves, agonies, and all sorts of impossible nonsense; and it so possessed his mind that the whole fabric of invention and fancy he read of was true, that to him no history in the world had

55   more reality in it. He used to say the Cid Ruy Diaz was a very good knight, but
that he was not to be compared with the Knight of the Burning Sword who with
one back-stroke cut in half two fierce and monstrous giants. He thought more of
Bernardo del Carpio because at Roncesvalles he slew Roland in spite of
enchantments, availing himself of the artifice of Hercules when he strangled
60   Antaeus the son of Terra in his arms. He approved highly of the giant Morgante,
because, although of the giant breed which is always arrogant and ill-
conditioned, he alone was affable and well-bred. But above all he admired
Reinaldos of Montalban, especially when he saw him sallying forth from his
castle and robbing everyone he met, and when beyond the seas he stole that image
65   of Mahomet which, as his history says, was entirely of gold. To have a bout of
kicking at that traitor of a Ganelon he would have given his housekeeper, and his
niece into the bargain.

        In short, his wits being quite gone, he hit upon the strangest notion that ever
madman in this world hit upon, and that was that he fancied it was right and
70   requisite, as well for the support of his own honour as for the service of his
country, that he should make a knight-errant of himself, roaming the world over in
full armour and on horseback in quest of adventures, and putting in practice
himself all that he had read of as being the usual practices of knights-errant;
righting every kind of wrong, and exposing himself to peril and danger from
75   which, in the issue, he was to reap eternal renown and fame. Already the poor
man saw himself crowned by the might of his arm Emperor of Trebizond at least;
and so, led away by the intense enjoyment he found in these pleasant fancies, he set
himself forthwith to put his scheme into execution.

        The first thing he did was to clean up some armour that had belonged to his
80   great-grandfather, and had been for ages lying forgotten in a corner eaten with
rust and covered with mildew. He scoured and polished it as best he could, but he
perceived one great defect in it, that it had no closed helmet, nothing but a simple
morion.[1] This deficiency, however, his ingenuity supplied, for he contrived a kind
of half-helmet of pasteboard which, fitted on to the morion, looked like a whole
85   one. It is true that, in order to see if it was strong and fit to stand a cut, he drew his
sword and gave it a couple of slashes, the first of which undid in an instant what
had taken him a week to do. The ease with which he had knocked it to pieces
disconcerted him somewhat, and to guard against that danger he set to work again,
fixing bars of iron on the inside until he was satisfied with its strength; and then,
90   not caring to try any more experiments with it, he passed it and adopted it as a
helmet of the most perfect construction.

        He next proceeded to inspect his hack, which, with more *quartos* than a *real*
and more blemishes than the steed of Gonela, that *tantum pellis et ossa fuit*,[2]
surpassed in his eyes the Bucephalus of Alexander or the Babieca of the Cid. Four
95   days were spent in thinking what name to give him, because (as he said to himself)

_____

[1]headpiece of helmet
[2]"all skin and bone"

it was not right that a horse belonging to a knight so famous, and one with such merits of his own, should be without some distinctive name, and he strove to adapt it so as to indicate what he had been before belonging to a knight-errant, and what he then was; for it was only reasonable that, his master taking a new character, he
100   should take a new name, and that it should be a distinguished and full-sounding one, befitting the new order and calling he was about to follow. And so, after having composed, struck out, rejected, added to, unmade, and remade a multitude of names out of his memory and fancy, he decided upon calling him Rocinante, a name, to his thinking, lofty, sonorous, and significant of his condition as a hack before
105   he became what he now was, the first and foremost of all the hacks in the world.

Having got a name for his horse so much to his taste, he was anxious to get one for himself, and he was eight days more pondering over this point, till at last he made up his mind to call himself "Don Quixote," whence, as has been already said, the authors of this veracious history have inferred that his name must have
110   been beyond a doubt Quixada, and not Quesada as others would have it. Recollecting, however, that the valiant Amadis was not content to call himself curtly Amadis and nothing more, but added the name of his kingdom and country to make it famous, and called himself Amadis of Gaul, he, like a good knight, resolved to add on the name of his, and to style himself Don Quixote of La Mancha,
115   whereby, he considered, he described accurately his origin and country, and did honour to it in taking his surname from it.

So then, his armour being furbished, his morion turned into a helmet, his hack christened, and he himself confirmed, he came to the conclusion that nothing more was needed now but to look out for a lady to be in love with; for a knight-errant
120   without love was like a tree without leaves or fruit, or a body without a soul. As he said to himself, "If, for my sins, or by my good fortune, I come across some giant hereabouts, a common occurrence with knights-errant, and overthrow him in one onslaught, or cleave him asunder to the waist, or, in short, vanquish and subdue him, will it not be well to have some one I may send him to as a present, that he may
125   come in and fall on his knees before my sweet lady, and in a humble, submissive voice say, 'I am the giant Caraculiambro, lord of the island of Malindrania, vanquished in single combat by the never sufficiently extolled knight Don Quixote of La Mancha, who has commanded me to present myself before your Grace, that your Highness dispose of me at your pleasure'?" Oh, how our good gentleman
130   enjoyed the delivery of this speech, especially when he had thought of some one to call his Lady! There was, so the story goes, in a village near his own a very good-looking farm-girl with whom he had been at one time in love, though, so far as is known, she never knew it nor gave a thought to the matter. Her name was Aldonza Lorenzo, and upon her he thought fit to confer the title of Lady of his Thoughts;
135   and after some search for a name which should not be out of harmony with her own, and should suggest and indicate that of a princess and great lady, he decided upon calling her Dulcinea del Toboso—she being of El Toboso—a name, to his mind, musical, uncommon, and significant, like all those he had already bestowed upon himself and the things belonging to him.

CHAPTER II: WHICH TREATS OF THE FIRST SALLY THE INGENIOUS DON QUIXOTE MADE FROM HOME

140   These preliminaries settled, he did not care to put off any longer the execution of his design, urged on to it by the thought of all the world was losing by his delay, seeing what wrongs he intended to right, grievances to redress, injustices to repair, abuses to remove, and duties to discharge. So, without giving notice of his intention to anyone, and without anybody seeing him, one morning before the

145   dawning of the day (which was one of the hottest of the month of July) he donned his suit of armour, mounted Rocinante with his patched-up helmet on, braced his buckler, took his lance, and by the back door of the yard sallied forth upon the plain in the highest contentment and satisfaction at seeing with what ease he had made a beginning with his grand purpose. But scarcely did he find himself upon the

150   open plain, when a terrible thought struck him, one all but enough to make him abandon the enterprise at the very outset. It occurred to him that he had not been dubbed a knight, and that according to the law of chivalry he neither could nor ought to bear arms against any knight; and that even if he had been, still he ought, as a novice knight, to wear white armour, without a device upon the shield until

155   by his prowess he had earned one. These reflections made him waver in his purpose, but his craze being stronger than any reasoning, he made up his mind to have himself dubbed a knight by the first one he came across, following the example of others in the same case, as he had read in the books that brought him to this pass. As for white armour, he resolved, on the first opportunity, to scour his

160   until it was whiter than an ermine; and so comforting himself he pursued his way, taking that which his horse chose, for in this he believed lay the essence of adventures.

    Thus setting out, our new-fledged adventurer paced along, talking to himself and saying, "Who knows but that in time to come, when the veracious history of

165   my famous deeds is made known, the sage who writes it, when he has to set forth my first sally in the early morning, will do it after this fashion? 'Scarce had the rubicund Apollo spread o'er the face of the broad spacious earth the golden threads of his bright hair, scarce had the little birds of painted plumage attuned their notes to hail with dulcet and mellifluous harmony the coming of the rosy

170   Dawn, that, deserting the soft couch of her jealous spouse, was appearing to mortals at the gates and balconies of the Manchegan horizon, when the renowned knight Don Quixote of La Mancha, quitting the lazy down, mounted his celebrated steed Rocinante and began to traverse the ancient and famous Campo de Montiel;'" which in fact he was actually traversing. "Happy the age, happy the

175   time," he continued, "in which shall be made known my deeds of fame, worthy to be moulded in brass, carved in marble, limned in pictures, for a memorial for ever. And thou, O sage magician, whoever thou art, to whom it shall fall to be the chronicler of this wondrous history, forget not, I entreat thee, my good Rocinante, the constant companion of my ways and wanderings." Presently he broke out

180   again, as if he were love-stricken in earnest, "O Princess Dulcinea, lady of this

captive heart, a grievous wrong hast thou done me to drive me forth with scorn, and with inexorable obduracy banish me from the presence of thy beauty. O lady, deign to hold in remembrance this heart, thy vassal, that thus in anguish pines for love of thee."

185   So he went on stringing together these and other absurdities, all in the style of those his books had taught him, imitating their language as well as he could; and all the while he rode so slowly and the sun mounted so rapidly and with such fervour that it was enough to melt his brains if he had any. Nearly all day he travelled without anything remarkable happening to him, at which he was in

190   despair, for he was anxious to encounter some one at once upon whom to try the might of his strong arm.

    Writers there are who say the first adventure he met with was that of Puerto Lapice; others say it was that of the windmills; but what I have ascertained on this point, and what I have found written in the annals of La Mancha, is that he

195   was on the road all day, and towards nightfall his hack and he found themselves dead tired and hungry, when, looking all around to see if he could discover any castle or shepherd's shanty where he might refresh himself and relieve his sore wants, he perceived not far out of his road an inn, which was as welcome as a star guiding him to the portals, if not the palaces, of his redemption; and

200   quickening his pace he reached it just as night was setting in. At the door were standing two young women, girls of the district as they call them, on their way to Seville with some carriers who had chanced to halt that night at the inn; and as, happen what might to our adventurer, everything he saw or imagined seemed to him to be and to happen after the fashion of what he read of, the moment he saw

205   the inn he pictured it to himself as a castle with its four turrets and pinnacles of shining silver, not forgetting the drawbridge and moat and all the belongings usually ascribed to castles of the sort. To this inn, which to him seemed a castle, he advanced, and at a short distance from it he checked Rocinante, hoping that some dwarf would show himself upon the battlements, and by sound of trumpet give

210   notice that a knight was approaching the castle. But seeing that they were slow about it, and that Rocinante was in a hurry to reach the stable, he made for the inn door, and perceived the two gay damsels who were standing there, and who seemed to him to be two fair maidens or lovely ladies taking their ease at the castle gate.

215   At this moment it so happened that a swineherd who was going through the stubbles collecting a drove of pigs (for, without any apology, that is what they are called) gave a blast of his horn to bring them together, and forthwith it seemed to Don Quixote to be what he was expecting, the signal of some dwarf announcing his arrival; and so with prodigious satisfaction he rode up to the inn and to the

220   ladies, who, seeing a man of this sort approaching in full armour and with lance and buckler, were turning in dismay into the inn, when Don Quixote, guessing their fear by their flight, raising his pasteboard visor, disclosed his dry dusty visage, and with courteous bearing and gentle voice addressed them, "Your ladyships need not fly or fear any rudeness, for that it belongs not to the order of

225   knighthood which I profess to offer to anyone, much less to highborn maidens as
      your appearance proclaims you to be." The girls were looking at him and
      straining their eyes to make out the features which the clumsy visor obscured, but
      when they heard themselves called maidens, a thing so much out of their line, they
      could not restrain their laughter, which made Don Quixote wax indignant, and
230   say, "Modesty becomes the fair, and moreover laughter that has little cause is
      great silliness; this, however, I say not to pain or anger you, for my desire is none
      other than to serve you."

      The incomprehensible language and the unpromising looks of our cavalier
      only increased the ladies' laughter, and that increased his irritation, and matters
235   might have gone farther if at that moment the landlord had not come out, who,
      being a very fat man, was a very peaceful one. He, seeing this grotesque figure clad
      in armour that did not match any more than his saddle, bridle, lance, buckler, or
      corselet, was not at all indisposed to join the damsels in their manifestations of
      amusement; but, in truth, standing in awe of such a complicated armament, he
240   thought it best to speak him fairly, so he said, "Señor Caballero, if your worship
      wants lodging, bating [barring] the bed (for there is not one in the inn) there is
      plenty of everything else here." Don Quixote, observing the respectful bearing of
      the Alcaide of the fortress (for so innkeeper and inn seemed in his eyes), made
      answer, "Sir Castellan, for me anything will suffice, for

245   'My armour is my only wear,
         My only rest the fray.'"

      The host fancied he called him Castellan because he took him for a "worthy of
      Castile," though he was in fact an Andalusian, and one from the strand of San
      Lucar, as crafty a thief as Cacus and as full of tricks as a student or a page. "In
250   that case," said he,

         "'Your bed is on the flinty rock
         Your sleep to watch alway;'

      and if so, you may dismount and safely reckon upon any quantity of sleeplessness
      under this roof for a twelvemonth, not to say for a single night." So saying, he
255   advanced to hold the stirrup for Don Quixote, who got down with great difficulty
      and exertion (for he had not broken his fast all day), and then charged the host to
      take great care of his horse, as he was the best bit of flesh that ever ate bread in
      this world. The landlord eyed him over but did not find him as good as Don
      Quixote said, nor even half as good; and putting him up in the stable, he returned
260   to see what might be wanted by his guest, whom the damsels, who had by this time
      made their peace with him, were now relieving of his armour. They had taken off
      his breastplate and backpiece, but they neither knew nor saw how to open his
      gorget or remove his make-shift helmet, for he had fastened it with green ribbons,
      which, as there was no untying the knots, required to be cut. This, however, he

265   would not by any means consent to, so he remained all the evening with his helmet on, the drollest and oddest figure that can be imagined; and while they were removing his armour, taking the baggages who were about it for ladies of high degree belonging to the castle, he said to them with great sprightliness:

270
> "Oh, never, surely, was there knight
> So served by hand of dame,
> As served was he, Don Quixote hight,
> When from his town he came;
> With maidens waiting on himself,
> Princesses on his hack—

275   or Rocinante, for that, ladies mine, is my horse's name, and Don Quixote of La Mancha is my own; for though I had no intention of declaring myself until my achievements in your service and honour had made me known, the necessity of adapting that old ballad of Lancelot to the present occasion has given you the knowledge of my name altogether prematurely. A time, however, will come for

280   your ladyships to command and me to obey, and then the might of my arm will show my desire to serve you."

     The girls, who were not used to hearing rhetoric of this sort, had nothing to say in reply; they only asked him if he wanted anything to eat. "I would gladly eat a bit of something," said Don Quixote, "for I feel it would come very seasonably."

285   The day happened to be a Friday, and in the whole inn there was nothing but some pieces of the fish they call in Castile "abadejo," in Andalusia "bacallao," and in some places "curadillo," and in others "troutlet;" so they asked him if he thought he could eat troutlet, for there was no other fish to give him. "If there be troutlets enough," said Don Quixote, "they will be the same thing as a trout; for it is all one

290   to me whether I am given eight reals in small change or a piece of eight; moreover, it may be that these troutlets are like veal, which is better than beef, or kid, which is better than goat. But whatever it be let it come quickly, for the burden and pressure of arms cannot be borne without support to the inside." They laid a table for him at the door of the inn for the sake of the air, and the host brought him a

295   portion of ill-soaked and worse cooked stockfish, and a piece of bread as black and mouldy as his own armour; but a laughable sight it was to see him eating, for having his helmet on and the beaver up, he could not with his own hands put anything into his mouth unless some one else placed it there, and this service one of the ladies rendered him. But to give him anything to drink was impossible, or

300   would have been so had not the landlord bored a reed, and putting one end in his mouth poured the wine into him through the other; all which he bore with patience rather than sever the ribbons of his helmet.

     While this was going on there came up to the inn a sowgelder, who, as he approached, sounded his reed pipe four or five times, and thereby completely

305   convinced Don Quixote that he was in some famous castle, and that they were regaling him with music, and that the stockfish was trout, the bread the whitest,

310 the wenches ladies, and the landlord the castellan of the castle; and consequently he held that his enterprise and sally had been to some purpose. But still it distressed him to think he had not been dubbed a knight, for it was plain to him he could not lawfully engage in any adventure without receiving the order of knighthood.

CHAPTER III: WHEREIN IS RELATED THE DROLL WAY IN WHICH DON QUIXOTE HAD HIMSELF DUBBED A KNIGHT

315 Harassed by this reflection, he made haste with his scanty pothouse supper, and having finished it called the landlord, and shutting himself into the stable with him, fell on his knees before him, saying, "From this spot I rise not, valiant knight, until your courtesy grants me the boon I seek, one that will redound to your praise and the benefit of the human race." The landlord, seeing his guest at his feet and hearing a speech of this kind, stood staring at him in bewilderment, not knowing what to do or say, and entreating him to rise, but all to no purpose until he had agreed to grant the boon demanded of him. "I looked for no less, my lord,

320 from your High Magnificence," replied Don Quixote, "and I have to tell you that the boon I have asked and your liberality has granted is that you shall dub me knight to-morrow morning, and that to-night I shall watch my arms in the chapel of this your castle; thus tomorrow, as I have said, will be accomplished what I so much desire, enabling me lawfully to roam through all the four quarters of the

325 world seeking adventures on behalf of those in distress, as is the duty of chivalry and of knights-errant like myself, whose ambition is directed to such deeds."

The landlord, who, as has been mentioned, was something of a wag, and had already some suspicion of his guest's want of wits, was quite convinced of it on hearing talk of this kind from him, and to make sport for the night he determined to

330 fall in with his humour. So he told him he was quite right in pursuing the object he had in view, and that such a motive was natural and becoming in cavaliers as distinguished as he seemed and his gallant bearing showed him to be; and that he himself in his younger days had followed the same honourable calling, roaming in quest of adventures in various parts of the world, among others the Curing-

335 grounds of Malaga, the Isles of Riaran, the Precinct of Seville, the Little Market of Segovia, the Olivera of Valencia, the Rondilla of Granada, the Strand of San Lucar, the Colt of Cordova, the Taverns of Toledo, and divers other quarters, where he had proved the nimbleness of his feet and the lightness of his fingers, doing many wrongs, cheating many widows, ruining maids and swindling minors,

340 and, in short, bringing himself under the notice of almost every tribunal and court of justice in Spain; until at last he had retired to this castle of his, where he was living upon his property and upon that of others; and where he received all knights-errant of whatever rank or condition they might be, all for the great love he bore them and that they might share their substance with him in return for his

345 benevolence. He told him, moreover, that in this castle of his there was no chapel in which he could watch his armour, as it had been pulled down in order to be

rebuilt, but that in a case of necessity it might, he knew, be watched anywhere, and he might watch it that night in a courtyard of the castle, and in the morning, God willing, the requisite ceremonies might be performed so as to have him dubbed a
350 knight, and so thoroughly dubbed that nobody could be more so. He asked if he had any money with him, to which Don Quixote replied that he had not a farthing, as in the histories of knights-errant he had never read of any of them carrying any. On this point the landlord told him he was mistaken; for, though not recorded in the histories, because in the author's opinion there was no need to mention
355 anything so obvious and necessary as money and clean shirts, it was not to be supposed therefore that they did not carry them, and he might regard it as certain and established that all knights-errant (about whom there were so many full and unimpeachable books) carried well-furnished purses in case of emergency, and likewise carried shirts and a little box of ointment to cure the wounds they
360 received. For in those plains and deserts where they engaged in combat and came out wounded, it was not always that there was some one to cure them, unless indeed they had for a friend some sage magician to succour them at once by fetching through the air upon a cloud some damsel or dwarf with a vial of water of such virtue that by tasting one drop of it they were cured of their hurts and wounds in
365 an instant and left as sound as if they had not received any damage whatever. But in case this should not occur, the knights of old took care to see that their squires were provided with money and other requisites, such as lint and ointments for healing purposes; and when it happened that knights had no squires (which was rarely and seldom the case) they themselves carried everything in cunning saddle-
370 bags that were hardly seen on the horse's croup, as if it were something else of more importance, because, unless for some such reason, carrying saddle-bags was not very favourably regarded among knights-errant. He therefore advised him (and, as his godson so soon to be, he might even command him) never from that time forth to travel without money and the usual requirements, and he would find the
375 advantage of them when he least expected it.

Don Quixote promised to follow his advice scrupulously, and it was arranged forthwith that he should watch his armour in a large yard at one side of the inn; so, collecting it all together, Don Quixote placed it on a trough that stood by the side of a well, and bracing his buckler on his arm he grasped his lance and
380 began with a stately air to march up and down in front of the trough, and as he began his march night began to fall.

The landlord told all the people who were in the inn about the craze of his guest, the watching of the armour, and the dubbing ceremony he contemplated. Full of wonder at so strange a form of madness, they flocked to see it from a distance,
385 and observed with what composure he sometimes paced up and down, or sometimes, leaning on his lance, gazed on his armour without taking his eyes off it for ever so long; and as the night closed in with a light from the moon so brilliant that it might vie with his that lent it, everything the novice knight did was plainly seen by all.

390　　　Meanwhile one of the carriers who were in the inn thought fit to water his team, and it was necessary to remove Don Quixote's armour as it lay on the trough; but he seeing the other approach hailed him in a loud voice, "O thou, whoever thou art, rash knight that comest to lay hands on the armour of the most valorous errant that ever girt on sword, have a care what thou dost; touch it not
395　　unless thou wouldst lay down thy life as the penalty of thy rashness." The carrier gave no heed to these words (and he would have done better to heed them if he had been heedful of his health), but seizing it by the straps flung the armour some distance from him. Seeing this, Don Quixote raised his eyes to heaven, and fixing his thoughts, apparently, upon his lady Dulcinea, exclaimed, "Aid me, lady mine,
400　　in this the first encounter that presents itself to this breast which thou holdest in subjection; let not thy favour and protection fail me in this first jeopardy;" and, with these words and others to the same purpose, dropping his buckler he lifted his lance with both hands and with it smote such a blow on the carrier's head that he stretched him on the ground, so stunned that had he followed it up with a
405　　second there would have been no need of a surgeon to cure him. This done, he picked up his armour and returned to his beat with the same serenity as before.

　　　　Shortly after this, another, not knowing what had happened (for the carrier still lay senseless), came with the same object of giving water to his mules, and was proceeding to remove the armour in order to clear the trough, when Don Quixote,
410　　without uttering a word or imploring aid from anyone, once more dropped his buckler and once more lifted his lance, and without actually breaking the second carrier's head into pieces, made more than three of it, for he laid it open in four. At the noise all the people of the inn ran to the spot, and among them the landlord. Seeing this, Don Quixote braced his buckler on his arm, and with his hand on his
415　　sword exclaimed, "O Lady of Beauty, strength and support of my faint heart, it is time for thee to turn the eyes of thy greatness on this thy captive knight on the brink of so mighty an adventure." By this he felt himself so inspired that he would not have flinched if all the carriers in the world had assailed him. The comrades of the wounded perceiving the plight they were in began from a distance to shower
420　　stones on Don Quixote, who screened himself as best he could with his buckler, not daring to quit the trough and leave his armour unprotected. The landlord shouted to them to leave him alone, for he had already told them that he was mad, and as a madman he would not be accountable even if he killed them all. Still louder shouted Don Quixote, calling them knaves and traitors, and the lord of the
425　　castle, who allowed knights-errant to be treated in this fashion, a villain and a low-born knight whom, had he received the order of knighthood, he would call to account for his treachery. "But of you," he cried, "base and vile rabble, I make no account; fling, strike, come on, do all ye can against me, ye shall see what the reward of your folly and insolence will be." This he uttered with so much spirit
430　　and boldness that he filled his assailants with a terrible fear, and as much for this reason as at the persuasion of the landlord they left off stoning him, and he allowed them to carry off the wounded, and with the same calmness and composure as before resumed the watch over his armour.

But these freaks of his guest were not much to the liking of the landlord, so he
determined to cut matters short and confer upon him at once the unlucky order of
knighthood before any further misadventure could occur; so, going up to him, he
apologised for the rudeness which, without his knowledge, had been offered to
him by these low people, who, however, had been well punished for their
audacity. As he had already told him, he said, there was no chapel in the castle,
nor was it needed for what remained to be done, for, as he understood the
ceremonial of the order, the whole point of being dubbed a knight lay in the
accolade and in the slap on the shoulder, and that could be administered in the
middle of a field; and that he had now done all that was needful as to watching the
armour, for all requirements were satisfied by a watch of two hours only, while
he had been more than four about it. Don Quixote believed it all, and told him he
stood there ready to obey him, and to make an end of it with as much despatch as
possible; for, if he were again attacked, and felt himself to be dubbed knight, he
would not, he thought, leave a soul alive in the castle, except such as out of respect
he might spare at his bidding.

Thus warned and menaced, the castellan forthwith brought out a book in
which he used to enter the straw and barley he served out to the carriers, and,
with a lad carrying a candle-end, and the two damsels already mentioned, he
returned to where Don Quixote stood, and bade him kneel down. Then, reading
from his account-book as if he were repeating some devout prayer, in the middle of
his delivery he raised his hand and gave him a sturdy blow on the neck, and then,
with his own sword, a smart slap on the shoulder, all the while muttering between
his teeth as if he was saying his prayers. Having done this, he directed one of the
ladies to gird on his sword, which she did with great self-possession and gravity,
and not a little was required to prevent a burst of laughter at each stage of the
ceremony; but what they had already seen of the novice knight's prowess kept
their laughter within bounds. On girding him with the sword the worthy lady said
to him, "May God make your worship a very fortunate knight, and grant you
success in battle." Don Quixote asked her name in order that he might from that
time forward know to whom he was beholden for the favour he had received, as
he meant to confer upon her some portion of the honour he acquired by the might of
his arm. She answered with great humility that she was called La Tolosa, and
that she was the daughter of a cobbler of Toledo who lived in the stalls of
Sanchobienaya, and that wherever she might be she would serve and esteem him as
her lord. Don Quixote said in reply that she would do him a favour if
thenceforward she assumed the "Don" and called herself Dona Tolosa. She
promised she would, and then the other buckled on his spur, and with her
followed almost the same conversation as with the lady of the sword. He asked
her name, and she said it was La Molinera, and that she was the daughter of a
respectable miller of Antequera; and of her likewise Don Quixote requested that
she would adopt the "Don" and call herself Dona Molinera, making offers to her
further services and favours.

Having thus, with hot haste and speed, brought to a conclusion these never-till-now-seen ceremonies, Don Quixote was on thorns until he saw himself on horseback sallying forth in quest of adventures; and saddling Rocinante at once he
480   mounted, and embracing his host, as he returned thanks for his kindness in knighting him, he addressed him in language so extraordinary that it is impossible to convey an idea of it or report it. The landlord, to get him out of the inn, replied with no less rhetoric though with shorter words, and without calling upon him to pay the reckoning let him go with a Godspeed.

CHAPTER IV: OF WHAT HAPPENED TO OUR KNIGHT WHEN HE LEFT THE INN [THE FARMER'S LAD]

485   Day was dawning when Don Quixote quitted the inn, so happy, so gay, so exhilarated at finding himself now dubbed a knight, that his joy was like to burst his horse-girths. However, recalling the advice of his host as to the requisites he ought to carry with him, especially that referring to money and shirts, he determined to go home and provide himself with all, and also with a squire, for he
490   reckoned upon securing a farm-labourer, a neighbour of his, a poor man with a family, but very well qualified for the office of squire to a knight. With this object he turned his horse's head towards his village, and Rocinante, thus reminded of his old quarters, stepped out so briskly that he hardly seemed to tread the earth.

He had not gone far, when out of a thicket on his right there seemed to come
495   feeble cries as of some one in distress, and the instant he heard them he exclaimed, "Thanks be to heaven for the favour it accords me, that it so soon offers me an opportunity of fulfilling the obligation I have undertaken, and gathering the fruit of my ambition. These cries, no doubt, come from some man or woman in want of help, and needing my aid and protection;" and wheeling, he turned Rocinante in
500   the direction whence the cries seemed to proceed. He had gone but a few paces into the wood, when he saw a mare tied to an oak, and tied to another, and stripped from the waist upwards, a youth of about fifteen years of age, from whom the cries came. Nor were they without cause, for a lusty farmer was flogging him with a belt and following up every blow with scoldings and commands, repeating, "Your
505   mouth shut and your eyes open!" while the youth made answer, "I won't do it again, master mine; by God's passion I won't do it again, and I'll take more care of the flock another time."

Seeing what was going on, Don Quixote said in an angry voice, "Discourteous knight, it ill becomes you to assail one who cannot defend himself;
510   mount your steed and take your lance" (for there was a lance leaning against the oak to which the mare was tied), "and I will make you know that you are behaving as a coward." The farmer, seeing before him this figure in full armour brandishing a lance over his head, gave himself up for dead, and made answer meekly, "Sir Knight, this youth that I am chastising is my servant, employed by me
515   to watch a flock of sheep that I have hard by, and he is so careless that I lose one every day, and when I punish him for his carelessness and knavery he says I do it

out of niggardliness, to escape paying him the wages I owe him, and before God, and on my soul, he lies."

"Lies before me, base clown!" said Don Quixote. "By the sun that shines on
520 us I have a mind to run you through with this lance. Pay him at once without another word; if not, by the God that rules us I will make an end of you, and annihilate you on the spot; release him instantly."

The farmer hung his head, and without a word untied his servant, of whom Don Quixote asked how much his master owed him.

525 He replied, nine months at seven *reals* a month. Don Quixote added it up, found that it came to sixty-three *reals,* and told the farmer to pay it down immediately, if he did not want to die for it.

The trembling clown replied that as he lived and by the oath he had sworn (though he had not sworn any) it was not so much; for there were to be taken into
530 account and deducted three pairs of shoes he had given him, and a *real* for two blood-lettings when he was sick.

"All that is very well," said Don Quixote; "but let the shoes and the blood-lettings stand as a setoff against the blows you have given him without any cause; for if he spoiled the leather of the shoes you paid for, you have damaged that of his
535 body, and if the barber took blood from him when he was sick, you have drawn it when he was sound; so on that score he owes you nothing."

"The difficulty is, Sir Knight, that I have no money here; let Andres come home with me, and I will pay him all, *real* by *real.*"

"I go with him!" said the youth. "Nay, God forbid! No, señor, not for the
540 world; for once alone with me, he would flay me like a Saint Bartholomew."

"He will do nothing of the kind," said Don Quixote; "I have only to command, and he will obey me; and as he has sworn to me by the order of knighthood which he has received, I leave him free, and I guarantee the payment."

"Consider what you are saying, señor," said the youth; "this master of mine is
545 not a knight, nor has he received any order of knighthood; for he is Juan Haldudo the Rich, of Quintanar."

"That matters little," replied Don Quixote; "there may be Haldudos knights; moreover, everyone is the son of his works."

"That is true," said Andres; "but this master of mine—of what works is he
550 the son, when he refuses me the wages of my sweat and labour?"

"I do not refuse, brother Andres," said the farmer, "be good enough to come along with me, and I swear by all the orders of knighthood there are in the world to pay you as I have agreed, *real* by *real,* and perfumed."

"For the perfumery I excuse you," said Don Quixote; "give it to him in reals,
555 and I shall be satisfied; and see that you do as you have sworn; if not, by the same oath I swear to come back and hunt you out and punish you; and I shall find you though you should lie closer than a lizard. And if you desire to know who it is lays this command upon you, that you be more firmly bound to obey it, know that I am the valorous Don Quixote of La Mancha, the undoer of wrongs and injustices;

560 and so, God be with you, and keep in mind what you have promised and sworn under those penalties that have been already declared to you."

So saying, he gave Rocinante the spur and was soon out of reach. The farmer followed him with his eyes, and when he saw that he had cleared the wood and was no longer in sight, he turned to his boy Andres, and said, "Come here, my son,
565 I want to pay you what I owe you, as that undoer of wrongs has commanded me."

"My oath on it," said Andres, "your worship will be well advised to obey the command of that good knight—may he live a thousand years—for, as he is a valiant and just judge, by [Saint] Roque, if you do not pay me, he will come back and do as he said."

570 "My oath on it, too," said the farmer; "but as I have a strong affection for you, I want to add to the debt in order to add to the payment;" and seizing him by the arm, he tied him up again, and gave him such a flogging that he left him for dead.

"Now, Master Andres," said the farmer, "call on the undoer of wrongs; you will find he won't undo that, though I am not sure that I have quite done with you,
575 for I have a good mind to flay you alive." But at last he untied him, and gave him leave to go look for his judge in order to put the sentence pronounced into execution.

Andres went off rather down in the mouth, swearing he would go to look for the valiant Don Quixote of La Mancha and tell him exactly what had happened,
580 and that all would have to be repaid him sevenfold; but for all that, he went off weeping, while his master stood laughing.

Thus did the valiant Don Quixote right that wrong, and, thoroughly satisfied with what had taken place, as he considered he had made a very happy and noble beginning with his knighthood, he took the road towards his village in perfect
585 self-content, saying in a low voice, "Well mayest thou this day call thyself fortunate above all on earth, O Dulcinea del Toboso, fairest of the fair! since it has fallen to thy lot to hold subject and submissive to thy full will and pleasure a knight so renowned as is and will be Don Quixote of La Mancha, who, as all the world knows, yesterday received the order of knighthood, and hath to-day righted
590 the greatest wrong and grievance that ever injustice conceived and cruelty perpetrated: who hath to-day plucked the rod from the hand of yonder ruthless oppressor so wantonly lashing that tender child."

He now came to a road branching in four directions, and immediately he was reminded of those cross-roads where knights-errant used to stop to consider
595 which road they should take. In imitation of them he halted for a while, and after having deeply considered it, he gave Rocinante his head, submitting his own will to that of his hack, who followed out his first intention, which was to make straight for his own stable. After he had gone about two miles Don Quixote perceived a large party of people, who, as afterwards appeared, were some
600 Toledo traders, on their way to buy silk at Murcia. There were six of them coming along under their sunshades, with four servants mounted, and three muleteers on foot. Scarcely had Don Quixote descried them when the fancy possessed him that this must be some new adventure; and to help him to imitate as far as he could

those passages he had read of in his books, here seemed to come one made on
605   purpose, which he resolved to attempt. So with a lofty bearing and determination
he fixed himself firmly in his stirrups, got his lance ready, brought his buckler
before his breast, and planting himself in the middle of the road, stood waiting the
approach of these knights-errant, for such he now considered and held them to be;
and when they had come near enough to see and hear, he exclaimed with a haughty
610   gesture, "All the world stand, unless all the world confess that in all the world
there is no maiden fairer than the Empress of La Mancha, the peerless Dulcinea
del Toboso."

The traders halted at the sound of this language and the sight of the strange
figure that uttered it, and from both figure and language at once guessed the craze
615   of their owner; they wished, however, to learn quietly what was the object of this
confession that was demanded of them, and one of them, who was rather fond of a
joke and was very sharp-witted, said to him, "Sir Knight, we do not know who
this good lady is that you speak of; show her to us, for, if she be of such beauty as
you suggest, with all our hearts and without any pressure we will confess the
620   truth that is on your part required of us."

"If I were to show her to you," replied Don Quixote, "what merit would you
have in confessing a truth so manifest? The essential point is that without seeing
her you must believe, confess, affirm, swear, and defend it; else ye have to do with
me in battle, ill-conditioned, arrogant rabble that ye are; and come ye on, one by
625   one as the order of knighthood requires, or all together as is the custom and vile
usage of your breed, here do I bide and await you relying on the justice of the
cause I maintain."

"Sir Knight," replied the trader, "I entreat your worship in the name of this
present company of princes, that, to save us from charging our consciences with
630   the confession of a thing we have never seen or heard of, and one moreover so
much to the prejudice of the Empresses and Queens of the Alcarria and
Estremadura, your worship will be pleased to show us some portrait of this lady,
though it be no bigger than a grain of wheat; for by the thread one gets at the ball,
and in this way we shall be satisfied and easy, and you will be content and
635   pleased; nay, I believe we are already so far agreed with you that even though her
portrait should show her blind of one eye, and distilling vermilion and sulphur
from the other, we would nevertheless, to gratify your worship, say all in her
favour that you desire."

"She distils nothing of the kind, vile rabble," said Don Quixote, burning with
640   rage, "nothing of the kind, I say, only ambergris and civet in cotton; nor is she one-
eyed or humpbacked, but straighter than a Guadarrama spindle: but ye must pay
for the blasphemy ye have uttered against beauty like that of my lady."

And so saying, he charged with levelled lance against the one who had
spoken, with such fury and fierceness that, if luck had not contrived that
645   Rocinante should stumble midway and come down, it would have gone hard with
the rash trader. Down went Rocinante, and over went his master, rolling along the
ground for some distance; and when he tried to rise he was unable, so encumbered

was he with lance, buckler, spurs, helmet, and the weight of his old armour; and all the while he was struggling to get up he kept saying, "Fly not, cowards and caitiffs! stay, for not by my fault, but my horse's, am I stretched here."

650

One of the muleteers in attendance, who could not have had much good nature in him, hearing the poor prostrate man blustering in this style, was unable to refrain from giving him an answer on his ribs; and coming up to him he seized his lance, and having broken it in pieces, with one of them he began so to belabour our Don Quixote that, notwithstanding and in spite of his armour, he milled him like a measure of wheat. His masters called out not to lay on so hard and to leave him alone, but the muleteer's blood was up, and he did not care to drop the game until he had vented the rest of his wrath, and gathering up the remaining fragments of the lance he finished with a discharge upon the unhappy victim, who all through the storm of sticks that rained on him never ceased threatening heaven, and earth, and the brigands, for such they seemed to him. At last the muleteer was tired, and the traders continued their journey, taking with them matter for talk about the poor fellow who had been cudgelled. He, when he found himself alone, made another effort to rise; but if he was unable when whole and sound, how was he to rise after having been thrashed and well-nigh knocked to pieces? And yet he esteemed himself fortunate, as it seemed to him that this was a regular knight-errant's mishap, and entirely, he considered, the fault of his horse. However, battered in body as he was, to rise was beyond his power.

655

660

665

CHAPTER V: IN WHICH THE NARRATIVE OF OUR KNIGHT'S MISHAP IS CONTINUED

670

Finding, then, that, in fact he could not move, he thought himself of having recourse to his usual remedy, which was to think of some passage in his books, and his craze brought to his mind that about Baldwin and the Marquis of Mantua, when Carloto left him wounded on the mountain side, a story known by heart by the children, not forgotten by the young men, and lauded and even believed by the old folk; and for all that not a whit truer than the miracles of Mahomet. This seemed to him to fit exactly the case in which he found himself, so, making a show of severe suffering, he began to roll on the ground and with feeble breath repeat the very words which the wounded knight of the wood is said to have uttered:

675

680

"Where art thou, lady mine, that thou
My sorrow dost not rue?
Thou canst not know it, lady mine,
Or else thou art untrue."

And so he went on with the ballad as far as the lines:

"O noble Marquis of Mantua,

685   My Uncle and liege lord!"

As chance would have it, when he had got to this line there happened to come by a peasant from his own village, a neighbour of his, who had been with a load of wheat to the mill, and he, seeing the man stretched there, came up to him and asked him who he was and what was the matter with him that he complained so

690   dolefully.

Don Quixote was firmly persuaded that this was the Marquis of Mantua, his uncle, so the only answer he made was to go on with his ballad, in which he told the tale of his misfortune, and of the loves of the Emperor's son and his wife all exactly as the ballad sings it.

695   The peasant stood amazed at hearing such nonsense, and relieving him of the visor, already battered to pieces by blows, he wiped his face, which was covered with dust, and as soon as he had done so he recognised him and said, "Señor Quixada" (for so he appears to have been called when he was in his senses and had not yet changed from a quiet country gentleman into a knight-errant), "who

700   has brought your worship to this pass?" But to all questions the other only went on with his ballad.

Seeing this, the good man removed as well as he could his breastplate and backpiece to see if he had any wound, but he could perceive no blood nor any mark whatever. He then contrived to raise him from the ground, and with no little

705   difficulty hoisted him upon his ass, which seemed to him to be the easiest mount for him; and collecting the arms, even to the splinters of the lance, he tied them on Rocinante, and leading him by the bridle and the ass by the halter he took the road for the village, very sad to hear what absurd stuff Don Quixote was talking. Nor was Don Quixote less so, for what with blows and bruises he could not sit

710   upright on the ass, and from time to time he sent up sighs to heaven, so that once more he drove the peasant to ask what ailed him. And it could have been only the devil himself that put into his head tales to match his own adventures, for now, forgetting Baldwin, he bethought himself of the Moor Abindarraez, when the Alcaide of Antequera, Rodrigo de Narvaez, took him prisoner and carried him

715   away to his castle; so that when the peasant again asked him how he was and what ailed him, he gave him for reply the same words and phrases that the captive Abindarraez gave to Rodrigo de Narvaez, just as he had read the story in the "Diana" of Jorge de Montemayor where it is written, applying it to his own case so aptly that the peasant went along cursing his fate that he had to listen to such a

720   lot of nonsense; from which, however, he came to the conclusion that his neighbour was mad, and so made all haste to reach the village to escape the wearisomeness of this harangue of Don Quixote's; who, at the end of it, said, "Señor Don Rodrigo de Narvaez, your worship must know that this fair Xarifa I have mentioned is now the lovely Dulcinea del Toboso, for whom I have done, am doing, and will do the

725   most famous deeds of chivalry that in this world have been seen, are to be seen, or ever shall be seen."

To this the peasant answered, "Señor—sinner that I am!—cannot your worship see that I am not Don Rodrigo de Narvaez nor the Marquis of Mantua, but Pedro Alonso your neighbour, and that your worship is neither Baldwin nor
730   Abindarraez, but the worthy gentleman Señor Quixada?"

"I know who I am," replied Don Quixote, "and I know that I may be not only those I have named, but all the Twelve Peers of France and even all the Nine Worthies, since my achievements surpass all that they have done all together and each of them on his own account."

735   With this talk and more of the same kind they reached the village just as night was beginning to fall, but the peasant waited until it was a little later that the belaboured gentleman might not be seen riding in such a miserable trim. When it was what seemed to him the proper time he entered the village and went to Don Quixote's house, which he found all in confusion, and there were the curate and
740   the village barber, who were great friends of Don Quixote, and his housekeeper was saying to them in a loud voice, "What does your worship think can have befallen my master, Señor Licentiate Pero Perez?" for so the curate was called; "it is three days now since anything has been seen of him, or the hack, or the buckler, lance, or armour. Miserable me! I am certain of it, and it is as true as that I was
745   born to die, that these accursed books of chivalry he has, and has got into the way of reading so constantly, have upset his reason; for now I remember having often heard him saying to himself that he would turn knight-errant and go all over the world in quest of adventures. To the devil and Barabbas with such books, that have brought to ruin in this way the finest understanding there was in all La
750   Mancha!"

The niece said the same, and, more: "You must know, Master Nicholas"—for that was the name of the barber—"it was often my uncle's way to stay two days and nights together poring over these unholy books of misventures, after which he would fling the book away and snatch up his sword and fall to slashing the
755   walls; and when he was tired out he would say he had killed four giants like four towers; and the sweat that flowed from him when he was weary he said was the blood of the wounds he had received in battle; and then he would drink a great jug of cold water and become calm and quiet, saying that this water was a most precious potion which the sage Esquife, a great magician and friend of his, had
760   brought him. But I take all the blame upon myself for never having told your worships of my uncle's vagaries, that you might put a stop to them before things had come to this pass, and burn all these accursed books—for he has a great number—that richly deserve to be burned like heretics."

"So say I too," said the curate, "and by my faith to-morrow shall not pass
765   without public judgment upon them, and may they be condemned to the flames lest they lead those that read to behave as my good friend seems to have behaved."

All this the peasant heard, and from it he understood at last what was the matter with his neighbour, so he began calling aloud, "Open, your worships, to Señor Baldwin and to Señor the Marquis of Mantua, who comes badly wounded,

770 and to Señor Abindarraez, the Moor, whom the valiant Rodrigo de Narvaez, the
Alcaide of Antequera, brings captive."

At these words they all hurried out, and when they recognised their friend,
master, and uncle, who had not yet dismounted from the ass because he could not,
they ran to embrace him.

775 "Hold!" said he, "for I am badly wounded through my horse's fault; carry me
to bed, and if possible send for the wise Urganda to cure and see to my wounds."

"See there! plague on it!" cried the housekeeper at this: "did not my heart tell
the truth as to which foot my master went lame of? To bed with your worship at
once, and we will contrive to cure you here without fetching that Hurgada. A

780 curse I say once more, and a hundred times more, on those books of chivalry that
have brought your worship to such a pass."

They carried him to bed at once, and after searching for his wounds could
find none, but he said they were all bruises from having had a severe fall with his
horse Rocinante when in combat with ten giants, the biggest and the boldest to be

785 found on earth.

"So, so!" said the curate, "are there giants in the dance? By the sign of the
Cross I will burn them to-morrow before the day over."

They put a host of questions to Don Quixote, but his only answer to all
was—give him something to eat, and leave him to sleep, for that was what he

790 needed most. They did so, and the curate questioned the peasant at great length as
to how he had found Don Quixote. He told him, and the nonsense he had talked
when found and on the way home, all which made the licentiate the more eager to
do what he did the next day, which was to summon his friend the barber, Master
Nicholas, and go with him to Don Quixote's house.

* * * * *

CHAPTER VII: OF THE SECOND SALLY OF OUR WORTHY KNIGHT DON QUIXOTE OF LA MANCHA

795 At this instant Don Quixote began shouting out, "Here, here, valiant knights!
here is need for you to put forth the might of your strong arms, for they of the Court
are gaining the mastery in the tourney!" Called away by this noise and outcry,
they proceeded no farther with the scrutiny of the remaining books, and so it is
thought that "The Carolea," "The Lion of Spain," and "The Deeds of the

800 Emperor," written by Don Luis de Avila, went to the fire unseen and unheard; for
no doubt they were among those that remained, and perhaps if the curate had seen
them they would not have undergone so severe a sentence.

When they reached Don Quixote he was already out of bed, and was still
shouting and raving, and slashing and cutting all round, as wide awake as if he

805 had never slept.

They closed with him and by force got him back to bed, and when he had
become a little calm, addressing the curate, he said to him, "Of a truth, Señor

Archbishop Turpin, it is a great disgrace for us who call ourselves the Twelve Peers, so carelessly to allow the knights of the Court to gain the victory in this

810   tourney, we the adventurers having carried off the honour on the three former days."

"Hush, gossip," said the curate; "please God, the luck may turn, and what is lost to-day may be won to-morrow; for the present let your worship have a care of your health, for it seems to me that you are over-fatigued, if not badly wounded."

815   "Wounded no," said Don Quixote, "but bruised and battered no doubt, for that bastard Don Roland has cudgelled me with the trunk of an oak tree, and all for envy, because he sees that I alone rival him in his achievements. But I should not call myself Reinaldos of Montalvan did he not pay me for it in spite of all his enchantments as soon as I rise from this bed. For the present let them bring me

820   something to eat, for that, I feel, is what will be more to my purpose, and leave it to me to avenge myself."

They did as he wished; they gave him something to eat, and once more he fell asleep, leaving them marvelling at his madness.

That night the housekeeper burned to ashes all the books that were in the

825   yard and in the whole house; and some must have been consumed that deserved preservation in everlasting archives, but their fate and the laziness of the examiner did not permit it, and so in them was verified the proverb that the innocent suffer for the guilty.

One of the remedies which the curate and the barber immediately applied to

830   their friend's disorder was to wall up and plaster the room where the books were, so that when he got up he should not find them (possibly the cause being removed the effect might cease), and they might say that a magician had carried them off, room and all; and this was done with all despatch. Two days later Don Quixote got up, and the first thing he did was to go and look at his books, and not finding

835   the room where he had left it, he wandered from side to side looking for it. He came to the place where the door used to be, and tried it with his hands, and turned and twisted his eyes in every direction without saying a word; but after a good while he asked his housekeeper whereabouts was the room that held his books.

The housekeeper, who had been already well instructed in what she was to

840   answer, said, "What room or what nothing is it that your worship is looking for? There are neither room nor books in this house now, for the devil himself has carried all away."

"It was not the devil," said the niece, "but a magician who came on a cloud one night after the day your worship left this, and dismounting from a serpent that

845   he rode he entered the room, and what he did there I know not, but after a little while he made off, flying through the roof, and left the house full of smoke; and when we went to see what he had done we saw neither book nor room: but we remember very well, the housekeeper and I, that on leaving, the old villain said in a loud voice that, for a private grudge he owed the owner of the books and the

850   room, he had done mischief in that house that would be discovered by-and-by: he said too that his name was the Sage Munaton."

"I don't know whether he called himself Friston or Friton," said the housekeeper, "I only know that his name ended with 'ton.'"

855 "So it does," said Don Quixote, "and he is a sage magician, a great enemy of mine, who has a spite against me because he knows by his arts and lore that in process of time I am to engage in single combat with a knight whom he befriends and that I am to conquer, and he will be unable to prevent it; and for this reason he endeavours to do me all the ill turns that he can; but I promise him it will be hard for him to oppose or avoid what is decreed by Heaven."

860 "Who doubts that?" said the niece; "but, uncle, who mixes you up in these quarrels? Would it not be better to remain at peace in your own house instead of roaming the world looking for better bread than ever came of wheat, never reflecting that many go for wool and come back shorn?"

"Oh, niece of mine," replied Don Quixote, "how much astray art thou in thy
865 reckoning: ere they shear me I shall have plucked away and stripped off the beards of all who dare to touch only the tip of a hair of mine."

The two were unwilling to make any further answer, as they saw that his anger was kindling.

In short, then, he remained at home fifteen days very quietly without showing
870 any signs of a desire to take up with his former delusions, and during this time he held lively discussions with his two gossips, the curate and the barber, on the point he maintained, that knights-errant were what the world stood most in need of, and that in him was to be accomplished the revival of knight-errantry. The curate sometimes contradicted him, sometimes agreed with him, for if he had not
875 observed this precaution he would have been unable to bring him to reason.

Meanwhile Don Quixote worked upon a farm labourer, a neighbour of his, an honest man (if indeed that title can be given to him who is poor), but with very little wit in his pate. In a word, he so talked him over, and with such persuasions and promises, that the poor clown made up his mind to sally forth with him and
880 serve him as esquire. Don Quixote, among other things, told him he ought to be ready to go with him gladly, because any moment an adventure might occur that might win an island in the twinkling of an eye and leave him governor of it. On these and the like promises Sancho Panza (for so the labourer was called) left wife and children, and engaged himself as esquire to his neighbour. Don Quixote
885 next set about getting some money; and selling one thing and pawning another, and making a bad bargain in every case, he got together a fair sum. He provided himself with a buckler, which he begged as a loan from a friend, and, restoring his battered helmet as best he could, he warned his squire Sancho of the day and hour he meant to set out, that he might provide himself with what he thought most
890 needful. Above all, he charged him to take *alforjas* [saddlebags] with him. The other said he would, and that he meant to take also a very good ass he had, as he was not much given to going on foot. About the ass, Don Quixote hesitated a little, trying whether he could call to mind any knight-errant taking with him an esquire mounted on ass-back, but no instance occurred to his memory. For all that,
895 however, he determined to take him, intending to furnish him with a more

honourable mount when a chance of it presented itself, by appropriating the horse
of the first discourteous knight he encountered. Himself he provided with shirts
and such other things as he could, according to the advice the host had given him;
all which being done, without taking leave, Sancho Panza of his wife and
900   children, or Don Quixote of his housekeeper and niece, they sallied forth unseen
by anybody from the village one night, and made such good way in the course of it
that by daylight they held themselves safe from discovery, even should search be
made for them.

Sancho rode on his ass like a patriarch, with his *alforjas* and *bota* [wineskin],
905   and longing to see himself soon governor of the island his master had promised
him. Don Quixote decided upon taking the same route and road he had taken on his
first journey, that over the Campo de Montiel, which he travelled with less
discomfort than on the last occasion, for, as it was early morning and the rays of
the sun fell on them obliquely, the heat did not distress them.

910   And now said Sancho Panza to his master, "Your worship will take care,
Señor Knight-errant, not to forget about the island you have promised me, for be it
ever so big I'll be equal to governing it."

To which Don Quixote replied, "Thou must know, friend Sancho Panza, that
it was a practice very much in vogue with the knights-errant of old to make their
915   squires governors of the islands or kingdoms they won, and I am determined that
there shall be no failure on my part in so liberal a custom; on the contrary, I mean
to improve upon it, for they sometimes, and perhaps most frequently, waited until
their squires were old, and then when they had had enough of service and hard
days and worse nights, they gave them some title or other, of count, or at the most
920   marquis, of some valley or province more or less; but if thou livest and I live, it
may well be that before six days are over, I may have won some kingdom that has
others dependent upon it, which will be just the thing to enable thee to be crowned
king of one of them. Nor needst thou count this wonderful, for things and chances
fall to the lot of such knights in ways so unexampled and unexpected that I might
925   easily give thee even more than I promise thee."

"In that case," said Sancho Panza, "if I should become a king by one of those
miracles your worship speaks of, even Juana Gutierrez, my old woman, would
come to be queen and my children infantes."

"Well, who doubts it?" said Don Quixote.

930   "I doubt it," replied Sancho Panza, "because for my part I am persuaded that
though God should shower down kingdoms upon earth, not one of them would fit
the head of Mari Gutierrez. Let me tell you, señor, she is not worth two maravedis
for a queen; countess will fit her better, and that only with God's help."

"Leave it to God, Sancho," returned Don Quixote, "for he will give her what
935   suits her best; but do not undervalue thyself so much as to come to be content with
anything less than being governor of a province."

"I will not, señor," answered Sancho, "specially as I have a man of such
quality for a master in your worship, who will know how to give me all that will
be suitable for me and that I can bear."

CHAPTER VIII: OF THE GOOD FORTUNE WHICH THE VALIANT DON QUIXOTE HAD IN THE TERRIBLE AND UNDREAMT-OF ADVENTURE OF THE WINDMILLS, WITH OTHER OCCURRENCES WORTHY TO BE FITLY RECORDED

940 At this point they came in sight of thirty or forty windmills that were on plain, and as soon as Don Quixote saw them he said to his squire, "Fortune is arranging matters for us better than we could have shaped our desires ourselves, for look there, friend Sancho Panza, where thirty or more monstrous giants present themselves, all of whom I mean to engage in battle and slay, and with
945 whose spoils we shall begin to make our fortunes; for this is righteous warfare, and it is God's good service to sweep so evil a breed from off the face of the earth."
"What giants?" said Sancho Panza.
"Those thou seest there," answered his master, "with the long arms, and some have them nearly two leagues long."
950 "Look, your worship," said Sancho; "what we see there are not giants but windmills, and what seem to be their arms are the sails that turned by the wind make the millstone go."
"It is easy to see," replied Don Quixote, "that thou art not used to this business of adventures; those are giants; and if thou art afraid, away with thee
955 out of this and betake thyself to prayer while I engage them in fierce and unequal combat."
So saying, he gave the spur to his steed Rocinante, heedless of the cries his squire Sancho sent after him, warning him that most certainly they were windmills and not giants he was going to attack. He, however, was so positive they were
960 giants that he neither heard the cries of Sancho, nor perceived, near as he was, what they were, but made at them shouting, "Fly not, cowards and vile beings, for a single knight attacks you."
A slight breeze at this moment sprang up, and the great sails began to move, seeing which Don Quixote exclaimed, "Though ye flourish more arms than the
965 giant Briareus, ye have to reckon with me."
So saying, and commending himself with all his heart to his lady Dulcinea, imploring her to support him in such a peril, with lance in rest and covered by his buckler, he charged at Rocinante's fullest gallop and fell upon the first mill that stood in front of him; but as he drove his lance-point into the sail the wind
970 whirled it round with such force that it shivered the lance to pieces, sweeping with it horse and rider, who went rolling over on the plain, in a sorry condition. Sancho hastened to his assistance as fast as his ass could go, and when he came up found him unable to move, with such a shock had Rocinante fallen with him.
"God bless me!" said Sancho, "did I not tell your worship to mind what you
975 were about, for they were only windmills? and no one could have made any mistake about it but one who had something of the same kind in his head."
"Hush, friend Sancho," replied Don Quixote, "the fortunes of war more than any other are liable to frequent fluctuations; and moreover I think, and it is the

truth, that that same sage Friston who carried off my study and books, has turned these giants into mills in order to rob me of the glory of vanquishing them, such is the enmity he bears me; but in the end his wicked arts will avail but little against my good sword."

"God order it as he may," said Sancho Panza, and helping him to rise got him up again on Rocinante, whose shoulder was half out; and then, discussing the late adventure, they followed the road to Puerto Lapice, for there, said Don Quixote, they could not fail to find adventures in abundance and variety, as it was a great thoroughfare. For all that, he was much grieved at the loss of his lance, and saying so to his squire, he added, "I remember having read how a Spanish knight, Diego Perez de Vargas by name, having broken his sword in battle, tore from an oak a ponderous bough or branch, and with it did such things that day, and pounded so many Moors, that he got the surname of Machuca, and he and his descendants from that day forth were called Vargas y Machuca. I mention this because from the first oak I see I mean to rend such another branch, large and stout like that, with which I am determined and resolved to do such deeds that thou mayest deem thyself very fortunate in being found worthy to come and see them, and be an eyewitness of things that will with difficulty be believed."

"Be that as God will," said Sancho, "I believe it all as your worship says it; but straighten yourself a little, for you seem all on one side, may be from the shaking of the fall."

"That is the truth," said Don Quixote, "and if I make no complaint of the pain it is because knights-errant are not permitted to complain of any wound, even though their bowels be coming out through it."

"If so," said Sancho, "I have nothing to say; but God knows I would rather your worship complained when anything ailed you. For my part, I confess I must complain however small the ache may be; unless this rule about not complaining extends to the squires of knights-errant also."

Don Quixote could not help laughing at his squire's simplicity, and he assured him he might complain whenever and however he chose, just as he liked, for, so far, he had never read of anything to the contrary in the order of knighthood.

Sancho bade him remember it was dinner-time, to which his master answered that he wanted nothing himself just then, but that he might eat when he had a mind. With this permission Sancho settled himself as comfortably as he could on his beast, and taking out of the alforjas what he had stowed away in them, he jogged along behind his master munching deliberately, and from time to time taking a pull at the bota with a relish that the thirstiest tapster in Malaga might have envied; and while he went on in this way, gulping down draught after draught, he never gave a thought to any of the promises his master had made him, nor did he rate it as hardship but rather as recreation going in quest of adventures, however dangerous they might be. Finally they passed the night among some trees, from one of which Don Quixote plucked a dry branch to serve him after a fashion as a lance, and fixed on it the head he had removed from the broken one. All that night

Don Quixote lay awake thinking of his lady Dulcinea, in order to conform to what he had read in his books, how many a night in the forests and deserts knights used to lie sleepless supported by the memory of their mistresses. Not so did Sancho Panza spend it, for having his stomach full of something stronger than chicory water he made but one sleep of it, and, if his master had not called him, neither the rays of the sun beating on his face nor all the cheery notes of the birds welcoming the approach of day would have had power to waken him. On getting up he tried the bota and found it somewhat less full than the night before, which grieved his heart because they did not seem to be on the way to remedy the deficiency readily. Don Quixote did not care to break his fast, for, as has been already said, he confined himself to savoury recollections for nourishment.

They returned to the road they had set out with, leading to Puerto Lapice, and at three in the afternoon they came in sight of it. "Here, brother Sancho Panza," said Don Quixote when he saw it, "we may plunge our hands up to the elbows in what they call adventures; but observe, even shouldst thou see me in the greatest danger in the world, thou must not put a hand to thy sword in my defence, unless indeed thou perceivest that those who assail me are rabble or base folk; for in that case thou mayest very properly aid me; but if they be knights it is on no account permitted or allowed thee by the laws of knighthood to help me until thou hast been dubbed a knight."

"Most certainly, señor," replied Sancho, "your worship shall be fully obeyed in this matter; all the more as of myself I am peaceful and no friend to mixing in strife and quarrels: it is true that as regards the defence of my own person I shall not give much heed to those laws, for laws human and divine allow each one to defend himself against any assailant whatever."

"That I grant," said Don Quixote, "but in this matter of aiding me against knights thou must put a restraint upon thy natural impetuosity."

"I will do so, I promise you," answered Sancho, "and will keep this precept as carefully as Sunday."

While they were thus talking there appeared on the road two friars of the order of St. Benedict, mounted on two dromedaries, for not less tall were the two mules they rode on. They wore travelling spectacles and carried sunshades; and behind them came a coach attended by four or five persons on horseback and two muleteers on foot. In the coach there was, as afterwards appeared, a Biscay lady on her way to Seville, where her husband was about to take passage for the Indies with an appointment of high honour. The friars, though going the same road, were not in her company; but the moment Don Quixote perceived them he said to his squire, "Either I am mistaken, or this is going to be the most famous adventure that has ever been seen, for those black bodies we see there must be, and doubtless are, magicians who are carrying off some stolen princess in that coach, and with all my might I must undo this wrong."

"This will be worse than the windmills," said Sancho. "Look, señor; those are friars of St. Benedict, and the coach plainly belongs to some travellers: I tell you to mind well what you are about and don't let the devil mislead you."

"I have told thee already, Sancho," replied Don Quixote, "that on the subject of adventures thou knowest little. What I say is the truth, as thou shalt see presently."

1070 So saying, he advanced and posted himself in the middle of the road along which the friars were coming, and as soon as he thought they had come near enough to hear what he said, he cried aloud, "Devilish and unnatural beings, release instantly the highborn princesses whom you are carrying off by force in this coach, else prepare to meet a speedy death as the just punishment of your evil

1075 deeds."

The friars drew rein and stood wondering at the appearance of Don Quixote as well as at his words, to which they replied, "Señor Caballero, we are not devilish or unnatural, but two brothers of St. Benedict following our road, nor do we know whether or not there are any captive princesses coming in this coach."

1080 "No soft words with me, for I know you, lying rabble," said Don Quixote, and without waiting for a reply he spurred Rocinante and with levelled lance charged the first friar with such fury and determination, that, if the friar had not flung himself off the mule, he would have brought him to the ground against his will, and sore wounded, if not killed outright. The second brother, seeing how his

1085 comrade was treated, drove his heels into his castle of a mule and made off across the country faster than the wind.

Sancho Panza, when he saw the friar on the ground, dismounting briskly from his ass, rushed towards him and began to strip off his gown. At that instant the friars muleteers came up and asked what he was stripping him for. Sancho

1090 answered them that this fell to him lawfully as spoil of the battle which his lord Don Quixote had won. The muleteers, who had no idea of a joke and did not understand all this about battles and spoils, seeing that Don Quixote was some distance off talking to the travellers in the coach, fell upon Sancho, knocked him down, and leaving hardly a hair in his beard, belaboured him with kicks and left

1095 him stretched breathless and senseless on the ground; and without any more delay helped the friar to mount, who, trembling, terrified, and pale, as soon as he found himself in the saddle, spurred after his companion, who was standing at a distance looking on, watching the result of the onslaught; then, not caring to wait for the end of the affair just begun, they pursued their journey making more crosses than if

1100 they had the devil after them.

Don Quixote was, as has been said, speaking to the lady in the coach: "Your beauty, lady mine," said he, "may now dispose of your person as may be most in accordance with your pleasure, for the pride of your ravishers lies prostrate on the ground through this strong arm of mine; and lest you should be pining to know

1105 the name of your deliverer, know that I am called Don Quixote of La Mancha, knight-errant and adventurer, and captive to the peerless and beautiful lady Dulcinea del Toboso: and in return for the service you have received of me I ask no more than that you should return to El Toboso, and on my behalf present yourself before that lady and tell her what I have done to set you free."

1110   One of the squires in attendance upon the coach, a Biscayan, was listening to all Don Quixote was saying, and, perceiving that he would not allow the coach to go on, but was saying it must return at once to El Toboso, he made at him, and seizing his lance addressed him in bad Castilian and worse Biscayan after his fashion, "Begone, caballero, and ill go with thee; by the God that made me, unless

1115   thou quittest coach, slayest thee as art here a Biscayan."

    Don Quixote understood him quite well, and answered him very quietly, "If thou wert a knight, as thou art none, I should have already chastised thy folly and rashness, miserable creature." To which the Biscayan returned, "I no gentleman! I swear to God thou liest as I am Christian: if thou droppest lance and drawest

1120   sword, soon shalt thou see thou art carrying water to the cat: Biscayan on land, hidalgo at sea, hidalgo at the devil, and look, if thou sayest otherwise thou liest."

    "'You will see presently,' said Agrajes,'"[3] replied Don Quixote; and throwing his lance on the ground he drew his sword, braced his buckler on his arm, and attacked the Biscayan, bent upon taking his life.

1125   The Biscayan, when he saw him coming on, though he wished to dismount from his mule, in which, being one of those sorry ones let out for hire, he had no confidence, had no choice but to draw his sword; it was lucky for him, however, that he was near the coach, from which he was able to snatch a cushion that served him for a shield; and they went at one another as if they had been two

1130   mortal enemies. The others strove to make peace between them, but could not, for the Biscayan declared in his disjointed phrase that if they did not let him finish his battle he would kill his mistress and everyone that strove to prevent him. The lady in the coach, amazed and terrified at what she saw, ordered the coachman to draw aside a little, and set herself to watch this severe struggle, in the course of which

1135   the Biscayan smote Don Quixote a mighty stroke on the shoulder over the top of his buckler, which, given to one without armour, would have cleft him to the waist. Don Quixote, feeling the weight of this prodigious blow, cried aloud, saying, "O lady of my soul, Dulcinea, flower of beauty, come to the aid of this your knight, who, in fulfilling his obligations to your beauty, finds himself in this

1140   extreme peril." To say this, to lift his sword, to shelter himself well behind his buckler, and to assail the Biscayan was the work of an instant, determined as he was to venture all upon a single blow. The Biscayan, seeing him come on in this way, was convinced of his courage by his spirited bearing, and resolved to follow his example, so he waited for him keeping well under cover of his cushion, being

1145   unable to execute any sort of manoeuvre with his mule, which, dead tired and never meant for this kind of game, could not stir a step.

    On, then, as aforesaid, came Don Quixote against the wary Biscayan, with uplifted sword and a firm intention of splitting him in half, while on his side the Biscayan waited for him sword in hand, and under the protection of his cushion;

1150   and all present stood trembling, waiting in suspense the result of blows such as

---

[3]Don Quixote is continually quoting chivalric heroes and stories; sometimes the quotation is utterly meaningless, as here.

threatened to fall, and the lady in the coach and the rest of her following were making a thousand vows and offerings to all the images and shrines of Spain, that God might deliver her squire and all of them from this great peril in which they found themselves. But it spoils all, that at this point and crisis the author of the
1155 history leaves this battle impending, giving as excuse that he could find nothing more written about these achievements of Don Quixote than what has been already set forth. It is true the second author of this work was unwilling to believe that a history so curious could have been allowed to fall under the sentence of oblivion, or that the wits of La Mancha could have been so
1160 undiscerning as not to preserve in their archives or registries some documents referring to this famous knight; and this being his persuasion, he did not despair of finding the conclusion of this pleasant history, which, heaven favouring him, he did find in a way that shall be related in the Second Part.

CHAPTER IX: IN WHICH IS CONCLUDED AND FINISHED THE TERRIFIC BATTLE BETWEEN THE GALLANT BISCAYAN AND THE VALIANT MANCHEGAN

In the First Part of this history we left the valiant Biscayan and the renowned
1165 Don Quixote with drawn swords uplifted, ready to deliver two such furious slashing blows that if they had fallen full and fair they would at least have split and cleft them asunder from top to toe and laid them open like a pomegranate; and at this so critical point the delightful history came to a stop and stood cut short without any intimation from the author where what was missing was to be found.
1170 This distressed me greatly, because the pleasure derived from having read such a small portion turned to vexation at the thought of the poor chance that presented itself of finding the large part that, so it seemed to me, was missing of such an interesting tale. It appeared to me to be a thing impossible and contrary to all precedent that so good a knight should have been without some sage to
1175 undertake the task of writing his marvellous achievements; a thing that was never wanting to any of those knights-errant who, they say, went after adventures; for every one of them had one or two sages as if made on purpose, who not only recorded their deeds but described their most trifling thoughts and follies, however secret they might be; and such a good knight could not have been so
1180 unfortunate as not to have what Platir and others like him had in abundance. And so I could not bring myself to believe that such a gallant tale had been left maimed and mutilated, and I laid the blame on Time, the devourer and destroyer of all things, that had either concealed or consumed it.
On the other hand, it struck me that, inasmuch as among his books there had
1185 been found such modern ones as *The Enlightenment of Jealousy* and the *Nymphs and Shepherds of Henares*, his story must likewise be modern, and that though it might not be written, it might exist in the memory of the people of his village and of those in the neighbourhood. This reflection kept me perplexed and longing to know really and truly the whole life and wondrous deeds of our famous Spaniard, Don

1190   Quixote of La Mancha, light and mirror of Manchegan chivalry, and the first that
        in our age and in these so evil days devoted himself to the labour and exercise of
        the arms of knight-errantry, righting wrongs, succouring widows, and protecting
        damsels of that sort that used to ride about, whip in hand, on their palfreys, with
        all their virginity about them, from mountain to mountain and valley to valley—
1195   for, if it were not for some ruffian, or boor with a hood and hatchet, or monstrous
        giant, that forced them, there were in days of yore damsels that at the end of eighty
        years, in all which time they had never slept a day under a roof, went to their
        graves as much maids as the mothers that bore them. I say, then, that in these and
        other respects our gallant Don Quixote is worthy of everlasting and notable
1200   praise, nor should it be withheld even from me for the labour and pains spent in
        searching for the conclusion of this delightful history; though I know well that if
        Heaven, chance and good fortune had not helped me, the world would have
        remained deprived of an entertainment and pleasure that for a couple of hours or
        so may well occupy him who shall read it attentively. The discovery of it occurred
1205   in this way.
            One day, as I was in the Alcana [marketplace] of Toledo, a boy came up to sell
        some pamphlets and old papers to a silk mercer, and, as I am fond of reading even
        the very scraps of paper in the streets, led by this natural bent of mine I took up
        one of the pamphlets the boy had for sale, and saw that it was in characters which
1210   I recognised as Arabic, and as I was unable to read them though I could recognise
        them, I looked about to see if there were any Spanish-speaking Morisco at hand to
        read them for me; nor was there any great difficulty in finding such an interpreter,
        for even had I sought one for an older and better language I should have found him.
        In short, chance provided me with one, who when I told him what I wanted and
1215   put the book into his hands, opened it in the middle and after reading a little in it
        began to laugh. I asked him what he was laughing at, and he replied that it was at
        something the book had written in the margin by way of a note. I bade him tell it to
        me; and he still laughing said, "In the margin, as I told you, this is written: 'This
        Dulcinea del Toboso so often mentioned in this history, had, they say, the best
1220   hand of any woman in all La Mancha for salting pigs.'"
            When I heard Dulcinea del Toboso named, I was struck with surprise and
        amazement, for it occurred to me at once that these pamphlets contained the history
        of Don Quixote. With this idea I pressed him to read the beginning, and doing so,
        turning the Arabic offhand into Castilian, he told me it meant, *History of Don*
1225   *Quixote of La Mancha*, written by Cide Hamete Benengeli, an Arab historian." It
        required great caution to hide the joy I felt when the title of the book reached my
        ears, and snatching it from the silk mercer, I bought all the papers and pamphlets
        from the boy for half a real; and if he had had his wits about him and had known
        how eager I was for them, he might have safely calculated on making more than six
1230   reals by the bargain. I withdrew at once with the Morisco into the cloister of the
        cathedral, and begged him to turn all these pamphlets that related to Don Quixote
        into the Castilian tongue, without omitting or adding anything to them, offering
        him whatever payment he pleased. He was satisfied with two *arrobas* [measure of

weight] of raisins and two bushels of wheat, and promised to translate them faithfully and with all despatch; but to make the matter easier, and not to let such a precious find out of my hands, I took him to my house, where in little more than a month and a half he translated the whole just as it is set down here.

In the first pamphlet the battle between Don Quixote and the Biscayan was drawn to the very life, they planted in the same attitude as the history describes, their swords raised, and the one protected by his buckler, the other by his cushion, and the Biscayan's mule so true to nature that it could be seen to be a hired one a bowshot off. The Biscayan had an inscription under his feet which said, "Don Sancho de Azpeitia," which no doubt must have been his name; and at the feet of Rocinante was another that said, "Don Quixote." Rocinante was marvellously portrayed, so long and thin, so lank and lean, with so much backbone and so far gone in consumption, that he showed plainly with what judgment and propriety the name of Rocinante had been bestowed upon him. Near him was Sancho Panza holding the halter of his ass, at whose feet was another label that said, "Sancho Zancas," and according to the picture, he must have had a big belly, a short body, and long shanks, for which reason, no doubt, the names of Panza and Zancas were given him, for by these two surnames the history several times calls him. Some other trifling particulars might be mentioned, but they are all of slight importance and have nothing to do with the true relation of the history; and no history can be bad so long as it is true.

If against the present one any objection be raised on the score of its truth, it can only be that its author was an Arab, as lying is a very common propensity with those of that nation; though, as they are such enemies of ours, it is conceivable that there were omissions rather than additions made in the course of it. And this is my own opinion; for, where he could and should give freedom to his pen in praise of so worthy a knight, he seems to me deliberately to pass it over in silence; which is ill done and worse contrived, for it is the business and duty of historians to be exact, truthful, and wholly free from passion, and neither interest nor fear, hatred nor love, should make them swerve from the path of truth, whose mother is history, rival of time, storehouse of deeds, witness for the past, example and counsel for the present, and warning for the future. In this I know will be found all that can be desired in the pleasantest, and if it be wanting in any good quality, I maintain it is the fault of its hound of an author and not the fault of the subject. To be brief, its Second Part, according to the translation, began in this way:

With trenchant swords upraised and poised on high, it seemed as though the two valiant and wrathful combatants stood threatening heaven, and earth, and hell, with such resolution and determination did they bear themselves. The fiery Biscayan was the first to strike a blow, which was delivered with such force and fury that had not the sword turned in its course, that single stroke would have sufficed to put an end to the bitter struggle and to all the adventures of our knight; but that good fortune which reserved him for greater things, turned aside the sword of his adversary, so that although it smote him upon the left shoulder, it did

him no more harm than to strip all that side of its armour, carrying away a great part of his helmet with half of his ear, all which with fearful ruin fell to the
1280 ground, leaving him in a sorry plight.

Good God! Who is there that could properly describe the rage that filled the heart of our Manchegan when he saw himself dealt with in this fashion? All that can be said is, it was such that he again raised himself in his stirrups, and, grasping his sword more firmly with both hands, he came down on the Biscayan
1285 with such fury, smiting him full over the cushion and over the head, that—even so good a shield proving useless—as if a mountain had fallen on him, he began to bleed from nose, mouth, and ears, reeling as if about to fall backwards from his mule, as no doubt he would have done had he not flung his arms about its neck; at the same time, however, he slipped his feet out of the stirrups and then unclasped
1290 his arms, and the mule, taking fright at the terrible blow, made off across the plain, and with a few plunges flung its master to the ground. Don Quixote stood looking on very calmly, and, when he saw him fall, leaped from his horse and with great briskness ran to him, and, presenting the point of his sword to his eyes, bade him surrender, or he would cut his head off. The Biscayan was so bewildered that he
1295 was unable to answer a word, and it would have gone hard with him, so blind was Don Quixote, had not the ladies in the coach, who had hitherto been watching the combat in great terror, hastened to where he stood and implored him with earnest entreaties to grant them the great grace and favour of sparing their squire's life; to which Don Quixote replied with much gravity and dignity, "In
1300 truth, fair ladies, I am well content to do what ye ask of me; but it must be on one condition and understanding, which is that this knight promise me to go to the village of El Toboso, and on my behalf present himself before the peerless lady Dulcinea, that she deal with him as shall be most pleasing to her."

The terrified and disconsolate ladies, without discussing Don Quixote's
1305 demand or asking who Dulcinea might be, promised that their squire should do all that had been commanded.

"Then, on the faith of that promise," said Don Quixote, "I shall do him no further harm, though he well deserves it of me."

CHAPTER X: OF THE PLEASANT DISCOURSE THAT PASSED BETWEEN DON QUIXOTE AND HIS SQUIRE SANCHO PANZA

Now by this time Sancho had risen, rather the worse for the handling of the
1310 friars' muleteers, and stood watching the battle of his master, Don Quixote, and praying to God in his heart that it might be his will to grant him the victory, and that he might thereby win some island to make him governor of, as he had promised. Seeing, therefore, that the struggle was now over, and that his master was returning to mount Rocinante, he approached to hold the stirrup for him, and,
1315 before he could mount, he went on his knees before him, and taking his hand, kissed it saying, "May it please your worship, Señor Don Quixote, to give me the government of that island which has been won in this hard fight, for be it ever so

big I feel myself in sufficient force to be able to govern it as much and as well as anyone in the world who has ever governed islands."

1320   To which Don Quixote replied, "Thou must take notice, brother Sancho, that this adventure and those like it are not adventures of islands, but of cross-roads, in which nothing is got except a broken head or an ear the less: have patience, for adventures will present themselves from which I may make you, not only a governor, but something more."

1325   Sancho gave him many thanks, and again kissing his hand and the skirt of his hauberk, helped him to mount Rocinante, and mounting his ass himself, proceeded to follow his master, who at a brisk pace, without taking leave, or saying anything further to the ladies belonging to the coach, turned into a wood that was hard by. Sancho followed him at his ass's best trot, but Rocinante stepped out so

1330 that, seeing himself left behind, he was forced to call to his master to wait for him. Don Quixote did so, reining in Rocinante until his weary squire came up, who on reaching him said, "It seems to me, señor, it would be prudent in us to go and take refuge in some church, for, seeing how mauled he with whom you fought has been left, it will be no wonder if they give information of the affair to the Holy

1335 Brotherhood and arrest us, and, faith, if they do, before we come out of gaol we shall have to sweat for it."

    "Peace," said Don Quixote; "where hast thou ever seen or heard that a knight-errant has been arraigned before a court of justice, however many homicides he may have committed?"

1340   "I know nothing about omecils," answered Sancho, "nor in my life have had anything to do with one; I only know that the Holy Brotherhood looks after those who fight in the fields, and in that other matter I do not meddle."

    "Then thou needst have no uneasiness, my friend," said Don Quixote, "for I will deliver thee out of the hands of the Chaldeans, much more out of those of the

1345 Brotherhood. But tell me, as thou livest, hast thou seen a more valiant knight than I in all the known world; hast thou read in history of any who has or had higher mettle in attack, more spirit in maintaining it, more dexterity in wounding or skill in overthrowing?"

    "The truth is," answered Sancho, "that I have never read any history, for I

1350 can neither read nor write, but what I will venture to bet is that a more daring master than your worship I have never served in all the days of my life, and God grant that this daring be not paid for where I have said; what I beg of your worship is to dress your wound, for a great deal of blood flows from that ear, and I have here some lint and a little white ointment in the *alforjas*."

1355   "All that might be well dispensed with," said Don Quixote, "if I had remembered to make a vial of the balsam of Fierabras, for time and medicine are saved by one single drop."

    "What vial and what balsam is that?" said Sancho Panza.

    "It is a balsam," answered Don Quixote, "the receipt of which I have in my

1360 memory, with which one need have no fear of death, or dread dying of any wound; and so when I make it and give it to thee thou hast nothing to do when in some

battle thou seest they have cut me in half through the middle of the body—as is wont to happen frequently,—but neatly and with great nicety, ere the blood congeal, to place that portion of the body which shall have fallen to the ground
1365   upon the other half which remains in the saddle, taking care to fit it on evenly and exactly. Then thou shalt give me to drink but two drops of the balsam I have mentioned, and thou shalt see me become sounder than an apple."

    "If that be so," said Panza, "I renounce henceforth the government of the promised island, and desire nothing more in payment of my many and faithful
1370   services than that your worship give me the receipt of this supreme liquor, for I am persuaded it will be worth more than two reals an ounce anywhere, and I want no more to pass the rest of my life in ease and honour; but it remains to be told if it costs much to make it."

    "With less than three *reals,* six quarts of it may be made," said Don Quixote.
1375   "Sinner that I am!" said Sancho, "then why does your worship put off making it and teaching it to me?"

    "Peace, friend," answered Don Quixote; "greater secrets I mean to teach thee and greater favours to bestow upon thee; and for the present let us see to the dressing, for my ear pains me more than I could wish."
1380   Sancho took out some lint and ointment from the alforjas; but when Don Quixote came to see his helmet shattered, he was like to lose his senses, and clapping his hand upon his sword and raising his eyes to heaven, be said, "I swear by the Creator of all things and the four Gospels in their fullest extent, to do as the great Marquis of Mantua did when he swore to avenge the death of his
1385   nephew Baldwin (and that was not to eat bread from a table-cloth, nor embrace his wife, and other points which, though I cannot now call them to mind, I here grant as expressed) until I take complete vengeance upon him who has committed such an offence against me."

    Hearing this, Sancho said to him, "Your worship should bear in mind, Señor
1390   Don Quixote, that if the knight has done what was commanded him in going to present himself before my lady Dulcinea del Toboso, he will have done all that he was bound to do, and does not deserve further punishment unless he commits some new offence."

    "Thou hast said well and hit the point," answered Don Quixote; and so I
1395   recall the oath in so far as relates to taking fresh vengeance on him, but I make and confirm it anew to lead the life I have said until such time as I take by force from some knight another helmet such as this and as good; and think not, Sancho, that I am raising smoke with straw in doing so, for I have one to imitate in the matter, since the very same thing to a hair happened in the case of Mambrino's helmet,
1400   which cost Sacripante so dear."

    "Señor," replied Sancho, "let your worship send all such oaths to the devil, for they are very pernicious to salvation and prejudicial to the conscience; just tell me now, if for several days to come we fall in with no man armed with a helmet, what are we to do? Is the oath to be observed in spite of all the inconvenience and
1405   discomfort it will be to sleep in your clothes, and not to sleep in a house, and a

thousand other mortifications contained in the oath of that old fool the Marquis of Mantua, which your worship is now wanting to revive? Let your worship observe that there are no men in armour travelling on any of these roads, nothing but carriers and carters, who not only do not wear helmets, but perhaps never
1410   heard tell of them all their lives."

"Thou art wrong there," said Don Quixote, "for we shall not have been above two hours among these cross-roads before we see more men in armour than came to Albraca to win the fair Angelica."

"Enough," said Sancho; "so be it then, and God grant us success, and that the
1415   time for winning that island which is costing me so dear may soon come, and then let me die."

"I have already told thee, Sancho," said Don Quixote, "not to give thyself any uneasiness on that score; for if an island should fail, there is the kingdom of Denmark, or of Sobradisa, which will fit thee as a ring fits the finger, and all the
1420   more that, being on *terra firma,* thou wilt all the better enjoy thyself. But let us leave that to its own time; see if thou hast anything for us to eat in those alforjas, because we must presently go in quest of some castle where we may lodge to-night and make the balsam I told thee of, for I swear to thee by God, this ear is giving me great pain."

1425   "I have here an onion and a little cheese and a few scraps of bread," said Sancho, "but they are not victuals fit for a valiant knight like your worship."

"How little thou knowest about it," answered Don Quixote; "I would have thee to know, Sancho, that it is the glory of knights-errant to go without eating for a month, and even when they do eat, that it should be of what comes first to hand;
1430   and this would have been clear to thee hadst thou read as many histories as I have, for, though they are very many, among them all I have found no mention made of knights-errant eating, unless by accident or at some sumptuous banquets prepared for them, and the rest of the time they passed in dalliance. And though it is plain they could not do without eating and performing all the other natural
1435   functions, because, in fact, they were men like ourselves, it is plain too that, wandering as they did the most part of their lives through woods and wilds and without a cook, their most usual fare would be rustic viands such as those thou now offer me; so that, friend Sancho, let not that distress thee which pleases me, and do not seek to make a new world or pervert knight-errantry."

1440   "Pardon me, your worship," said Sancho, "for, as I cannot read or write, as I said just now, I neither know nor comprehend the rules of the profession of chivalry: henceforward I will stock the alforjas with every kind of dry fruit for your worship, as you are a knight; and for myself, as I am not one, I will furnish them with poultry and other things more substantial."

1445   "I do not say, Sancho," replied Don Quixote, "that it is imperative on knights-errant not to eat anything else but the fruits thou speakest of; only that their more usual diet must be those, and certain herbs they found in the fields which they knew and I know too."

1450   "A good thing it is," answered Sancho, "to know those herbs, for to my thinking it will be needful some day to put that knowledge into practice."

    And here taking out what he said he had brought, the pair made their repast peaceably and sociably. But anxious to find quarters for the night, they with all despatch made an end of their poor dry fare, mounted at once, and made haste to reach some habitation before night set in; but daylight and the hope of succeeding

1455 in their object failed them close by the huts of some goatherds, so they determined to pass the night there, and it was as much to Sancho's discontent not to have reached a house, as it was to his master's satisfaction to sleep under the open heaven, for he fancied that each time this happened to him he performed an act of ownership that helped to prove his chivalry.

CHAPTER XI: OF WHAT BEFELL DON QUIXOTE WITH CERTAIN GOATHERDS

1460   He was cordially welcomed by the goatherds, and Sancho, having as best he could put up Rocinante and the ass, drew towards the fragrance that came from some pieces of salted goat simmering in a pot on the fire; and though he would have liked at once to try if they were ready to be transferred from the pot to the stomach, he refrained from doing so as the goatherds removed them from the fire,

1465 and laying sheepskins on the ground, quickly spread their rude table, and with signs of hearty good-will invited them both to share what they had. Round the skins six of the men belonging to the fold seated themselves, having first with rough politeness pressed Don Quixote to take a seat upon a trough which they placed for him upside down. Don Quixote seated himself, and Sancho remained

1470 standing to serve the cup, which was made of horn. Seeing him standing, his master said to him:

    "That thou mayest see, Sancho, the good that knight-errantry contains in itself, and how those who fill any office in it are on the high road to be speedily honoured and esteemed by the world, I desire that thou seat thyself here at my side

1475 and in the company of these worthy people, and that thou be one with me who am thy master and natural lord, and that thou eat from my plate and drink from whatever I drink from; for the same may be said of knight-errantry as of love, that it levels all."

    "Great thanks," said Sancho, "but I may tell your worship that provided I

1480 have enough to eat, I can eat it as well, or better, standing, and by myself, than seated alongside of an emperor. And indeed, if the truth is to be told, what I eat in my corner without form or fuss has much more relish for me, even though it be bread and onions, than the turkeys of those other tables where I am forced to chew slowly, drink little, wipe my mouth every minute, and cannot sneeze or cough if I

1485 want or do other things that are the privileges of liberty and solitude. So, señor, as for these honours which your worship would put upon me as a servant and follower of knight-errantry, exchange them for other things which may be of more use and advantage to me; for these, though I fully acknowledge them as received, I renounce from this moment to the end of the world."

1490   "For all that," said Don Quixote, "thou must seat thyself, because him who humbleth himself God exalteth;" and seizing him by the arm he forced him to sit down beside himself.

    The goatherds did not understand this jargon about squires and knights-errant, and all they did was to eat in silence and stare at their guests, who with
1495   great elegance and appetite were stowing away pieces as big as one's fist. The course of meat finished, they spread upon the sheepskins a great heap of parched acorns, and with them they put down a half cheese harder than if it had been made of mortar. All this while the horn was not idle, for it went round so constantly, now full, now empty, like the bucket of a water-wheel, that it soon drained one of
1500   the two wine-skins that were in sight. When Don Quixote had quite appeased his appetite he took up a handful of the acorns, and contemplating them attentively delivered himself somewhat in this fashion:

    "Happy the age, happy the time, to which the ancients gave the name of golden, not because in that fortunate age the gold so coveted in this our iron one was
1505   gained without toil, but because they that lived in it knew not the two words 'mine' and 'thine'! In that blessed age all things were in common; to win the daily food no labour was required of any save to stretch forth his hand and gather it from the sturdy oaks that stood generously inviting him with their sweet ripe fruit. The clear streams and running brooks yielded their savoury limpid waters in
1510   noble abundance. The busy and sagacious bees fixed their republic in the clefts of the rocks and hollows of the trees, offering without usance the plenteous produce of their fragrant toil to every hand. The mighty cork trees, unenforced save of their own courtesy, shed the broad light bark that served at first to roof the houses supported by rude stakes, a protection against the inclemency of heaven alone.
1515   Then all was peace, all friendship, all concord; as yet the dull share of the crooked plough had not dared to rend and pierce the tender bowels of our first mother that without compulsion yielded from every portion of her broad fertile bosom all that could satisfy, sustain, and delight the children that then possessed her. Then was it that the innocent and fair young shepherdess roamed from vale to vale and hill
1520   to hill, with flowing locks, and no more garments than were needful modestly to cover what modesty seeks and ever sought to hide. Nor were their ornaments like those in use today, set off by Tyrian purple, and silk tortured in endless fashions, but the wreathed leaves of the green dock and ivy, wherewith they went as bravely and becomingly decked as our Court dames with all the rare and far-
1525   fetched artifices that idle curiosity has taught them. Then the love-thoughts of the heart clothed themselves simply and naturally as the heart conceived them, nor sought to commend themselves by forced and rambling verbiage. Fraud, deceit, or malice had then not yet mingled with truth and sincerity. Justice held her ground, undisturbed and unassailed by the efforts of favour and of interest, that now so
1530   much impair, pervert, and beset her. Arbitrary law had not yet established itself in the mind of the judge, for then there was no cause to judge and no one to be judged.

Maidens and modesty, as I have said, wandered at will alone and unattended, without fear of insult from lawlessness or libertine assault, and if they were undone it was of their own will and pleasure. But now in this hateful age of ours
1535   not one is safe, not though some new labyrinth like that of Crete conceal and surround her; even there the pestilence of gallantry will make its way to them through chinks or on the air by the zeal of its accursed importunity, and, despite of all seclusion, lead them to ruin. In defence of these, as time advanced and wickedness increased, the order of knights-errant was instituted, to defend
1540   maidens, to protect widows and to succour the orphans and the needy. To this order I belong, brother goatherds, to whom I return thanks for the hospitality and kindly welcome ye offer me and my squire; for though by natural law all living are bound to show favour to knights-errant, yet, seeing that without knowing this obligation ye have welcomed and feasted me, it is right that with all the good-will
1545   in my power I should thank you for yours."

All this long harangue (which might very well have been spared) our knight delivered because the acorns they gave him reminded him of the golden age; and the whim seized him to address all this unnecessary argument to the goatherds, who listened to him gaping in amazement without saying a word in reply. Sancho
1550   likewise held his peace and ate acorns, and paid repeated visits to the second wine-skin, which they had hung up on a cork tree to keep the wine cool.

Don Quixote was longer in talking than the supper in finishing, at the end of which one of the goatherds said, "That your worship, señor knight-errant, may say with more truth that we show you hospitality with ready good-will, we will
1555   give you amusement and pleasure by making one of our comrades sing: he will be here before long, and he is a very intelligent youth and deep in love, and what is more he can read and write and play on the rebeck to perfection."

The goatherd had hardly done speaking, when the notes of the rebeck reached their ears; and shortly after, the player came up, a very good-looking young man of
1560   about two-and-twenty. His comrades asked him if he had supped, and on his replying that he had, he who had already made the offer said to him:

"In that case, Antonio, thou mayest as well do us the pleasure of singing a little, that the gentleman, our guest, may see that even in the mountains and woods there are musicians: we have told him of thy accomplishments, and we want thee to
1565   show them and prove that we say true; so, as thou livest, pray sit down and sing that ballad about thy love that thy uncle the prebendary made thee, and that was so much liked in the town."

"With all my heart," said the young man, and without waiting for more pressing he seated himself on the trunk of a felled oak, and tuning his rebeck,
1570   presently began to sing to these words.

ANTONIO'S BALLAD

"Thou dost love me well, Olalla;
Well I know it, even though
Love's mute tongues, thine eyes, have never
By their glances told me so.

1575   For I know my love thou knowest,
Therefore thine to claim I dare:
Once it ceases to be secret,
Love need never feel despair.

True it is, Olalla, sometimes
1580   Thou hast all too plainly shown
That thy heart is brass in hardness,
And thy snowy bosom stone.

Yet for all that, in thy coyness,
And thy fickle fits between,
1585   Hope is there—at least the border
Of her garment may be seen.

Lures to faith are they, those glimpses,
And to faith in thee I hold;
Kindness cannot make it stronger,
1590   Coldness cannot make it cold.

If it be that love is gentle,
In thy gentleness I see
Something holding out assurance
To the hope of winning thee.

1595   If it be that in devotion
Lies a power hearts to move,
That which every day I show thee,
Helpful to my suit should prove.

Many a time thou must have noticed—
1600   If to notice thou dost care—
How I go about on Monday
Dressed in all my Sunday wear.

Love's eyes love to look on brightness;
Love loves what is gaily drest;

1605   Sunday, Monday, all I care is
     Thou shouldst see me in my best.

     No account I make of dances,
     Or of strains that pleased thee so,
     Keeping thee awake from midnight
1610   Till the cocks began to crow;

     Or of how I roundly swore it
     That there's none so fair as thou;
     True it is, but as I said it,
     By the girls I'm hated now.

1615   For Teresa of the hillside
     At my praise of thee was sore;
     Said, 'You think you love an angel;
     It's a monkey you adore;

     'Caught by all her glittering trinkets,
1620   And her borrowed braids of hair,
     And a host of made-up beauties
     That would Love himself ensnare.'

     'Twas a lie, and so I told her,
     And her cousin at the word
1625   Gave me his defiance for it;
     And what followed thou hast heard.

     Mine is no high-flown affection,
     Mine no passion par amours—
     As they call it—what I offer
1630   Is an honest love, and pure.

     Cunning cords the holy Church has,
     Cords of softest silk they be;
     Put thy neck beneath the yoke, dear;
     Mine will follow, thou wilt see.

1635   Else—and once for all I swear it
     By the saint of most renown—
     If I ever quit the mountains,
     'Twill be in a friar's gown."

Here the goatherd brought his song to an end, and though Don Quixote entreated him to sing more, Sancho had no mind that way, being more inclined for sleep than for listening to songs; so said he to his master, "Your worship will do well to settle at once where you mean to pass the night, for the labour these good men are at all day does not allow them to spend the night in singing."

"I understand thee, Sancho," replied Don Quixote; "I perceive clearly that those visits to the wine-skin demand compensation in sleep rather than in music."

"It's sweet to us all, blessed be God," said Sancho.

"I do not deny it," replied Don Quixote; "but settle thyself where thou wilt; those of my calling are more becomingly employed in watching than in sleeping; still it would be as well if thou wert to dress this ear for me again, for it is giving me more pain than it need."

Sancho did as he bade him, but one of the goatherds, seeing the wound, told him not to be uneasy, as he would apply a remedy with which it would be soon healed; and gathering some leaves of rosemary, of which there was a great quantity there, he chewed them and mixed them with a little salt, and applying them to the ear he secured them firmly with a bandage, assuring him that no other treatment would be required, and so it proved.

CHAPTER XII: OF WHAT A GOATHERD RELATED TO THOSE WITH DON QUIXOTE

Just then another young man, one of those who fetched their provisions from the village, came up and said, "Do you know what is going on in the village, comrades?"

"How could we know it?" replied one of them.

"Well, then, you must know," continued the young man, "this morning that famous student-shepherd called Chrysostom died, and it is rumoured that he died of love for that devil of a village girl, the daughter of Guillermo the Rich, she that wanders about the woods here in the dress of a shepherdess."

"You mean Marcela?" said one.

"Her I mean," answered the goatherd; "and the best of it is, he has directed in his will that he is to be buried in the fields like a Moor, and at the foot of the rock where the Cork-tree spring is, because, as the story goes (and they say he himself said so), that was the place where he first saw her. And he has also left other directions which the clergy of the village say should not and must not be obeyed because they savour of paganism. To all which his great friend Ambrosio the student, he who, like him, also went dressed as a shepherd, replies that everything must be done without any omission according to the directions left by Chrysostom, and about this the village is all in commotion; however, report says that, after all, what Ambrosio and all the shepherds his friends desire will be done, and to-morrow they are coming to bury him with great ceremony where I said. I am sure it will be something worth seeing; at least I will not fail to go and see it even if I knew I should not return to the village tomorrow."

1680 "We will do the same," answered the goatherds, "and cast lots to see who must stay to mind the goats of all."

"Thou sayest well, Pedro," said one, "though there will be no need of taking that trouble, for I will stay behind for all; and don't suppose it is virtue or want of curiosity in me; it is that the splinter that ran into my foot the other day will not let me walk." "For all that, we thank thee," answered Pedro.

1685 Don Quixote asked Pedro to tell him who the dead man was and who the shepherdess, to which Pedro replied that all he knew was that the dead man was a wealthy gentleman belonging to a village in those mountains, who had been a student at Salamanca for many years, at the end of which he returned to his village with the reputation of being very learned and deeply read. "Above all, they said,

1690 he was learned in the science of the stars and of what went on yonder in the heavens and the sun and the moon, for he told us of the cris of the sun and moon to exact time."

"Eclipse it is called, friend, not cris, the darkening of those two luminaries," said Don Quixote; but Pedro, not troubling himself with trifles, went on with his

1695 story, saying, "Also he foretold when the year was going to be one of abundance or estility."

"Sterility, you mean," said Don Quixote.

"Sterility or estility," answered Pedro, "it is all the same in the end. And I can tell you that by this his father and friends who believed him grew very rich

1700 because they did as he advised them, bidding them 'sow barley this year, not wheat; this year you may sow pulse and not barley; the next there will be a full oil crop, and the three following not a drop will be got.'"

"That science is called astrology," said Don Quixote. "I do not know what it is called," replied Pedro, "but I know that he knew all this and more besides. But,

1705 to make an end, not many months had passed after he returned from Salamanca, when one day he appeared dressed as a shepherd with his crook and sheepskin, having put off the long gown he wore as a scholar; and at the same time his great friend, Ambrosio by name, who had been his companion in his studies, took to the shepherd's dress with him. I forgot to say that Chrysostom, who is dead, was a

1710 great man for writing verses, so much so that he made carols for Christmas Eve, and plays for *Corpus Christi*, which the young men of our village acted, and all said they were excellent. When the villagers saw the two scholars so unexpectedly appearing in shepherd's dress, they were lost in wonder, and could not guess what had led them to make so extraordinary a change. About this time

1715 the father of our Chrysostom died, and he was left heir to a large amount of property in chattels as well as in land, no small number of cattle and sheep, and a large sum of money, of all of which the young man was left absolute owner, and indeed he was deserving of it all, for he was a very good comrade, and kind-hearted, and a friend of worthy folk, and had a countenance like a benediction.

1720 Presently it came to be known that he had changed his dress with no other object than to wander about these wastes after that shepherdess Marcela our lad mentioned a while ago, with whom the deceased Chrysostom had fallen in love.

And I must tell you now, for it is well you should know it, who this girl is; perhaps, and even without any perhaps, you will not have heard anything like it all the days of your life, though you should live more years than sarna."[4]

"Say Sarra," said Don Quixote, unable to endure the goatherd's confusion of words.

"The sarna lives long enough," answered Pedro; "and if, señor, you must go finding fault with words at every step, we shall not make an end of it this twelvemonth."

"Pardon me, friend," said Don Quixote; "but, as there is such a difference between sarna and Sarra, I told you of it; however, you have answered very rightly, for sarna lives longer than Sarra: so continue your story, and I will not object any more to anything."

"I say then, my dear sir," said the goatherd, "that in our village there was a farmer even richer than the father of Chrysostom, who was named Guillermo, and upon whom God bestowed, over and above great wealth, a daughter at whose birth her mother died, the most respected woman there was in this neighbourhood; I fancy I can see her now with that countenance which had the sun on one side and the moon on the other; and moreover active, and kind to the poor, for which I trust that at the present moment her soul is in bliss with God in the other world. Her husband Guillermo died of grief at the death of so good a wife, leaving his daughter Marcela, a child and rich, to the care of an uncle of hers, a priest and prebendary in our village. The girl grew up with such beauty that it reminded us of her mother's, which was very great, and yet it was thought that the daughter's would exceed it; and so when she reached the age of fourteen to fifteen years nobody beheld her but blessed God that had made her so beautiful, and the greater number were in love with her past redemption. Her uncle kept her in great seclusion and retirement, but for all that the fame of her great beauty spread so that, as well for it as for her great wealth, her uncle was asked, solicited, and importuned, to give her in marriage not only by those of our town but of those many leagues round, and by the persons of highest quality in them. But he, being a good Christian man, though he desired to give her in marriage at once, seeing her to be old enough, was unwilling to do so without her consent, not that he had any eye to the gain and profit which the custody of the girl's property brought him while he put off her marriage; and, faith, this was said in praise of the good priest in more than one set in the town. For I would have you know, Sir Errant, that in these little villages everything is talked about and everything is carped at, and rest assured, as I am, that the priest must be over and above good who forces his parishioners to speak well of him, especially in villages."

"That is the truth," said Don Quixote; "but go on, for the story is very good, and you, good Pedro, tell it with very good grace."

"May that of the Lord not be wanting to me," said Pedro; "that is the one to have. To proceed; you must know that though the uncle put before his niece and

---

[4]He probably means Sarah, the wife of Abraham.

1765   described to her the qualities of each one in particular of the many who had asked her in marriage, begging her to marry and make a choice according to her own taste, she never gave any other answer than that she had no desire to marry just yet, and that being so young she did not think herself fit to bear the burden of matrimony. At these, to all appearance, reasonable excuses that she made, her

1770   uncle ceased to urge her, and waited till she was somewhat more advanced in age and could mate herself to her own liking. For, said he—and he said quite right— parents are not to settle children in life against their will. But when one least looked for it, lo and behold! one day the demure Marcela makes her appearance turned shepherdess; and, in spite of her uncle and all those of the town that strove

1775   to dissuade her, took to going a-field with the other shepherd-lasses of the village, and tending her own flock. And so, since she appeared in public, and her beauty came to be seen openly, I could not well tell you how many rich youths, gentlemen and peasants, have adopted the costume of Chrysostom, and go about these fields making love to her. One of these, as has been already said, was our deceased

1780   friend, of whom they say that he did not love but adore her. But you must not suppose, because Marcela chose a life of such liberty and independence, and of so little or rather no retirement, that she has given any occasion, or even the semblance of one, for disparagement of her purity and modesty; on the contrary, such and so great is the vigilance with which she watches over her honour, that of

1785   all those that court and woo her not one has boasted, or can with truth boast, that she has given him any hope however small of obtaining his desire. For although she does not avoid or shun the society and conversation of the shepherds, and treats them courteously and kindly, should any one of them come to declare his intention to her, though it be one as proper and holy as that of matrimony, she

1790   flings him from her like a catapult. And with this kind of disposition she does more harm in this country than if the plague had got into it, for her affability and her beauty draw on the hearts of those that associate with her to love her and to court her, but her scorn and her frankness bring them to the brink of despair; and so they know not what to say save to proclaim her aloud cruel and hard-hearted, and

1795   other names of the same sort which well describe the nature of her character; and if you should remain here any time, señor, you would hear these hills and valleys resounding with the laments of the rejected ones who pursue her. Not far from this there is a spot where there are a couple of dozen of tall beeches, and there is not one of them but has carved and written on its smooth bark the name of Marcela,

1800   and above some a crown carved on the same tree as though her lover would say more plainly that Marcela wore and deserved that of all human beauty. Here one shepherd is sighing, there another is lamenting; there love songs are heard, here despairing elegies. One will pass all the hours of the night seated at the foot of some oak or rock, and there, without having closed his weeping eyes, the sun finds

1805   him in the morning bemused and bereft of sense; and another without relief or respite to his sighs, stretched on the burning sand in the full heat of the sultry summer noontide, makes his appeal to the compassionate heavens, and over one and the other, over these and all, the beautiful Marcela triumphs free and careless.

And all of us that know her are waiting to see what her pride will come to, and who is to be the happy man that will succeed in taming a nature so formidable and gaining possession of a beauty so supreme. All that I have told you being such well-established truth, I am persuaded that what they say of the cause of Chrysostom's death, as our lad told us, is the same. And so I advise you, señor, fail not to be present tomorrow at his burial, which will be well worth seeing, for Chrysostom had many friends, and it is not half a league from this place to where he directed he should be buried."

I will make a point of it," said Don Quixote, "and I thank you for the pleasure you have given me by relating so interesting a tale."

"Oh," said the goatherd, "I do not know even the half of what has happened to the lovers of Marcela, but perhaps to-morrow we may fall in with some shepherd on the road who can tell us; and now it will be well for you to go and sleep under cover, for the night air may hurt your wound, though with the remedy I have applied to you there is no fear of an untoward result."

Sancho Panza, who was wishing the goatherd's loquacity at the devil, on his part begged his master to go into Pedro's hut to sleep. He did so, and passed all the rest of the night in thinking of his lady Dulcinea, in imitation of the lovers of Marcela. Sancho Panza settled himself between Rocinante and his ass, and slept, not like a lover who had been discarded, but like a man who had been soundly kicked.

CHAPTER XIII: IN WHICH IS ENDED THE STORY OF THE SHEPHERDESS MARCELA, WITH OTHER INCIDENTS

But hardly had day begun to show itself through the balconies of the east, when five of the six goatherds came to rouse Don Quixote and tell him that if he was still of a mind to go and see the famous burial of Chrysostom they would bear him company. Don Quixote, who desired nothing better, rose and ordered Sancho to saddle and pannel at once, which he did with all despatch, and with the same they all set out forthwith. They had not gone a quarter of a league when at the meeting of two paths they saw coming towards them some six shepherds dressed in black sheepskins and with their heads crowned with garlands of cypress and bitter oleander. Each of them carried a stout holly staff in his hand, and along with them there came two men of quality on horseback in handsome travelling dress, with three servants on foot accompanying them. Courteous salutations were exchanged on meeting, and inquiring one of the other which way each party was going, they learned that all were bound for the scene of the burial, so they went on all together.

One of those on horseback addressing his companion said to him, "It seems to me, Señor Vivaldo, that we may reckon as well spent the delay we shall incur in seeing this remarkable funeral, for remarkable it cannot but be judging by the strange things these shepherds have told us, of both the dead shepherd and homicide shepherdess."

"So I think too," replied Vivaldo, "and I would delay not to say a day, but four, for the sake of seeing it."

1850

Don Quixote asked them what it was they had heard of Marcela and Chrysostom. The traveller answered that the same morning they had met these shepherds, and seeing them dressed in this mournful fashion they had asked them the reason of their appearing in such a guise; which one of them gave, describing

1855 the strange behaviour and beauty of a shepherdess called Marcela, and the loves of many who courted her, together with the death of that Chrysostom to whose burial they were going. In short, he repeated all that Pedro had related to Don Quixote.

This conversation dropped, and another was commenced by him who was

1860 called Vivaldo asking Don Quixote what was the reason that led him to go armed in that fashion in a country so peaceful. To which Don Quixote replied, "The pursuit of my calling does not allow or permit me to go in any other fashion; easy life, enjoyment, and repose were invented for soft courtiers, but toil, unrest, and arms were invented and made for those alone whom the world calls knights-

1865 errant, of whom I, though unworthy, am the least of all."

The instant they heard this all set him down as mad, and the better to settle the point and discover what kind of madness his was, Vivaldo proceeded to ask him what knights-errant meant.

"Have not your worships," replied Don Quixote, "read the annals and

1870 histories of England, in which are recorded the famous deeds of King Arthur, whom we in our popular Castilian invariably call King Artus, with regard to whom it is an ancient tradition, and commonly received all over that kingdom of Great Britain, that this king did not die, but was changed by magic art into a raven, and that in process of time he is to return to reign and recover his kingdom

1875 and sceptre; for which reason it cannot be proved that from that time to this any Englishman ever killed a raven? Well, then, in the time of this good king that famous order of chivalry of the Knights of the Round Table was instituted, and the amour of Don Lancelot of the Lake with the Queen Guinevere occurred, precisely as is there related, the go-between and confidante therein being the highly

1880 honourable dame Quintanona, whence came that ballad so well known and widely spread in our Spain—O never surely was there knight So served by hand of dame, As served was he Sir Lancelot hight When he from Britain came—with all the sweet and delectable course of his achievements in love and war. Handed down from that time, then, this order of chivalry went on extending and spreading

1885 itself over many and various parts of the world; and in it, famous and renowned for their deeds, were the mighty Amadis of Gaul with all his sons and descendants to the fifth generation, and the valiant Felixmarte of Hircania, and the never sufficiently praised Tirante el Blanco, and in our own days almost we have seen and heard and talked with the invincible knight Don Belianis of Greece. This,

1890 then, sirs, is to be a knight-errant, and what I have spoken of is the order of his chivalry, of which, as I have already said, I, though a sinner, have made profession, and what the aforesaid knights professed that same do I profess, and so I go through these solitudes and wilds seeking adventures, resolved in soul to oppose my arm and person to the most perilous that fortune may offer me in aid of the weak and needy."

By these words of his the travellers were able to satisfy themselves of Don Quixote's being out of his senses and of the form of madness that overmastered him, at which they felt the same astonishment that all felt on first becoming acquainted with it; and Vivaldo, who was a person of great shrewdness and of a lively temperament, in order to beguile the short journey which they said was required to reach the mountain, the scene of the burial, sought to give him an opportunity of going on with his absurdities. So he said to him, "It seems to me, Señor Knight-errant, that your worship has made choice of one of the most austere professions in the world, and I imagine even that of the Carthusian monks is not so austere."

"As austere it may perhaps be," replied our Don Quixote, "but so necessary for the world I am very much inclined to doubt. For, if the truth is to be told, the soldier who executes what his captain orders does no less than the captain himself who gives the order. My meaning, is, that churchmen in peace and quiet pray to Heaven for the welfare of the world, but we soldiers and knights carry into effect what they pray for, defending it with the might of our arms and the edge of our swords, not under shelter but in the open air, a target for the intolerable rays of the sun in summer and the piercing frosts of winter. Thus are we God's ministers on earth and the arms by which his justice is done therein. And as the business of war and all that relates and belongs to it cannot be conducted without exceeding great sweat, toil, and exertion, it follows that those who make it their profession have undoubtedly more labour than those who in tranquil peace and quiet are engaged in praying to God to help the weak. I do not mean to say, nor does it enter into my thoughts, that the knight-errant's calling is as good as that of the monk in his cell; I would merely infer from what I endure myself that it is beyond a doubt a more laborious and a more belaboured one, a hungrier and thirstier, a wretcheder, raggeder, and lousier; for there is no reason to doubt that the knights-errant of yore endured much hardship in the course of their lives. And if some of them by the might of their arms did rise to be emperors, in faith it cost them dear in the matter of blood and sweat; and if those who attained to that rank had not had magicians and sages to help them they would have been completely baulked in their ambition and disappointed in their hopes."

"That is my own opinion," replied the traveller; "but one thing among many others seems to me very wrong in knights-errant, and that is that when they find themselves about to engage in some mighty and perilous adventure in which there is manifest danger of losing their lives, they never at the moment of engaging in it think of commending themselves to God, as is the duty of every good Christian in like peril; instead of which they commend themselves to their ladies with as much devotion as if these were their gods, a thing which seems to me to savour somewhat of heathenism."

"Sir," answered Don Quixote, "that cannot be on any account omitted, and the knight-errant would be disgraced who acted otherwise: for it is usual and customary in knight-errantry that the knight-errant, who on engaging in any great feat of arms has his lady before him, should turn his eyes towards her softly and lovingly, as though with them entreating her to favour and protect him in the hazardous venture he is about to undertake, and even though no one hear him, he is bound to say certain words between his teeth, commending himself to her with all his heart, and of this we have innumerable instances in the histories. Nor is it to be supposed from this that they are to omit commending themselves to God, for there will be time and opportunity for doing so while they are engaged in their task."

"For all that," answered the traveller, "I feel some doubt still, because often I have read how words will arise between two knights-errant, and from one thing to another it comes about that their anger kindles and they wheel their horses round and take a good stretch of field, and then without any more ado at the top of their speed they come to the charge, and in mid-career they are wont to commend themselves to their ladies; and what commonly comes of the encounter is that one falls over the haunches of his horse pierced through and through by his antagonist's lance, and as for the other, it is only by holding on to the mane of his horse that he can help falling to the ground; but I know not how the dead man had time to commend himself to God in the course of such rapid work as this; it would have been better if those words which he spent in commending himself to his lady in the midst of his career had been devoted to his duty and obligation as a Christian. Moreover, it is my belief that all knights-errant have not ladies to commend themselves to, for they are not all in love."

"That is impossible," said Don Quixote: "I say it is impossible that there could be a knight-errant without a lady, because to such it is as natural and proper to be in love as to the heavens to have stars: most certainly no history has been seen in which there is to be found a knight-errant without an amore, and for the simple reason that without one he would be held no legitimate knight but a bastard, and one who had gained entrance into the stronghold of the said knighthood, not by the door, but over the wall like a thief and a robber."

"Nevertheless," said the traveller, "if I remember rightly, I think I have read that Don Galaor, the brother of the valiant Amadis of Gaul, never had any special lady to whom he might commend himself, and yet he was not the less esteemed, and was a very stout and famous knight."

To which our Don Quixote made answer, "Sir, one solitary swallow does not make summer; moreover, I know that knight was in secret very deeply in love; besides which, that way of falling in love with all that took his fancy was a natural propensity which he could not control. But, in short, it is very manifest that he had one alone whom he made mistress of his will, to whom he commended himself very frequently and very secretly, for he prided himself on being a reticent knight."

"Then if it be essential that every knight-errant should be in love," said the traveller, "it may be fairly supposed that your worship is so, as you are of the order; and if you do not pride yourself on being as reticent as Don Galaor, I entreat you as earnestly as I can, in the name of all this company and in my own, to inform us of the name, country, rank, and beauty of your lady, for she will esteem herself fortunate if all the world knows that she is loved and served by such a knight as your worship seems to be."

At this Don Quixote heaved a deep sigh and said, "I cannot say positively whether my sweet enemy is pleased or not that the world should know I serve her; I can only say in answer to what has been so courteously asked of me, that her name is Dulcinea, her country El Toboso, a village of La Mancha, her rank must be at least that of a princess, since she is my queen and lady, and her beauty superhuman, since all the impossible and fanciful attributes of beauty which the poets apply to their ladies are verified in her; for her hairs are gold, her forehead Elysian fields, her eyebrows rainbows, her eyes suns, her cheeks roses, her lips coral, her teeth pearls, her neck alabaster, her bosom marble, her hands ivory, her fairness snow, and what modesty conceals from sight such, I think and imagine, as rational reflection can only extol, not compare."

"We should like to know her lineage, race, and ancestry," said Vivaldo.

To which Don Quixote replied, "She is not of the ancient Roman Curtii, Caii, or Scipios, nor of the modern Colonnas or Orsini, nor of the Moncadas or Requesenes of Catalonia, nor yet of the Rebellas or Villanovas of Valencia; Palafoxes, Nuzas, Rocabertis, Corellas, Lunas, Alagones, Urreas, Foces, or Gurreas of Aragon; Cerdas, Manriques, Mendozas, or Guzmans of Castile; Alencastros, Pallas, or Meneses of Portugal; but she is of those of El Toboso of La Mancha, a lineage that though modern, may furnish a source of gentle blood for the most illustrious families of the ages that are to come, and this let none dispute with me save on the condition that Zerbino placed at the foot of the trophy of Orlando's arms, saying, 'These let none move Who dareth not his might with Roland prove.'"

"Although mine is of the Cachopins of Laredo," said the traveller, "I will not venture to compare it with that of El Toboso of La Mancha, though, to tell the truth, no such surname has until now ever reached my ears."

"What!" said Don Quixote, "has that never reached them?"

The rest of the party went along listening with great attention to the conversation of the pair, and even the very goatherds and shepherds perceived how exceedingly out of his wits our Don Quixote was. Sancho Panza alone thought that what his master said was the truth, knowing who he was and having known him from his birth; and all that he felt any difficulty in believing was that about the fair Dulcinea del Toboso, because neither any such name nor any such princess had ever come to his knowledge though he lived so close to El Toboso. They were going along conversing in this way, when they saw descending a gap between two high mountains some twenty shepherds, all clad in sheepskins of black wool, and crowned with garlands which, as afterwards appeared, were, some of them of yew, some of cypress. Six of the number were carrying a bier

covered with a great variety of flowers and branches, on seeing which one of the
goatherds said, "Those who come there are the bearers of Chrysostom's body, and
2025 the foot of that mountain is the place where he ordered them to bury him." They
therefore made haste to reach the spot, and did so by the time those who came had
laid the bier upon the ground, and four of them with sharp pickaxes were digging a
grave by the side of a hard rock. They greeted each other courteously, and then
Don Quixote and those who accompanied him turned to examine the bier, and on
2030 it, covered with flowers, they saw a dead body in the dress of a shepherd, to all
appearance of one thirty years of age, and showing even in death that in life he
had been of comely features and gallant bearing. Around him on the bier itself
were laid some books, and several papers open and folded; and those who were
looking on as well as those who were opening the grave and all the others who
2035 were there preserved a strange silence, until one of those who had borne the body
said to another, "Observe carefully, Ambrosio, if this is the place Chrysostom
spoke of, since you are anxious that what he directed in his will should be so
strictly complied with."

"This is the place," answered Ambrosio, "for in it many a time did my poor
2040 friend tell me the story of his hard fortune. Here it was, he told me, that he saw for
the first time that mortal enemy of the human race, and here, too, for the first time
he declared to her his passion, as honourable as it was devoted, and here it was
that at last Marcela ended by scorning and rejecting him so as to bring the tragedy
of his wretched life to a close; here, in memory of misfortunes so great, he desired
2045 to be laid in the bowels of eternal oblivion."

Then turning to Don Quixote and the travellers he went on to say, "That
body, sirs, on which you are looking with compassionate eyes, was the abode of a
soul on which Heaven bestowed a vast share of its riches. That is the body of
Chrysostom, who was unrivalled in wit, unequalled in courtesy, unapproached in
2050 gentle bearing, a phoenix in friendship, generous without limit, grave without
arrogance, gay without vulgarity, and, in short, first in all that constitutes
goodness and second to none in all that makes up misfortune. He loved deeply, he
was hated; he adored, he was scorned; he wooed a wild beast, he pleaded with
marble, he pursued the wind, he cried to the wilderness, he served ingratitude, and
2055 for reward was made the prey of death in the mid-course of life, cut short by a
shepherdess whom he sought to immortalise in the memory of man, as these papers
which you see could fully prove, had he not commanded me to consign them to the
fire after having consigned his body to the earth."

"You would deal with them more harshly and cruelly than their owner
2060 himself," said Vivaldo, "for it is neither right nor proper to do the will of one who
enjoins what is wholly unreasonable; it would not have been reasonable in
Augustus Caesar had he permitted the directions left by the divine Mantuan in his
will to be carried into effect. So that, Señor Ambrosio, while you consign your
friend's body to the earth, you should not consign his writings to oblivion, for if
2065 he gave the order in bitterness of heart, it is not right that you should irrationally
obey it. On the contrary, by granting life to those papers, let the cruelty of Marcela

live for ever, to serve as a warning in ages to come to all men to shun and avoid falling into like danger; or I and all of us who have come here know already the story of this your love-stricken and heart-broken friend, and we know, too, your
2070 friendship, and the cause of his death, and the directions he gave at the close of his life; from which sad story may be gathered how great was the cruelty of Marcela, the love of Chrysostom, and the loyalty of your friendship, together with the end awaiting those who pursue rashly the path that insane passion opens to their eyes. Last night we learned the death of Chrysostom and that he was to be buried
2075 here, and out of curiosity and pity we left our direct road and resolved to come and see with our eyes that which when heard of had so moved our compassion, and in consideration of that compassion and our desire to prove it if we might by condolence, we beg of you, excellent Ambrosio, or at least I on my own account entreat you, that instead of burning those papers you allow me to carry away
2080 some of them."

And without waiting for the shepherd's answer, he stretched out his hand and took up some of those that were nearest to him; seeing which Ambrosio said, "Out of courtesy, señor, I will grant your request as to those you have taken, but it is idle to expect me to abstain from burning the remainder."

2085 Vivaldo, who was eager to see what the papers contained, opened one of them at once, and saw that its title was *Lay of Despair*. Ambrosio hearing it said, "That is the last paper the unhappy man wrote; and that you may see, señor, to what an end his misfortunes brought him, read it so that you may be heard, for you will have time enough for that while we are waiting for the grave to be dug."

2090 "I will do so very willingly," said Vivaldo; and as all the bystanders were equally eager they gathered round him, and he, reading in a loud voice, found that it ran as follows.

CHAPTER XIV: WHEREIN ARE INSERTED THE DESPAIRING VERSES OF THE DEAD SHEPHERD, TOGETHER WITH OTHER INCIDENTS NOT LOOKED FOR THE LAY OF CHRYSOSTOM

"Since thou dost in thy cruelty desire
The ruthless rigour of thy tyranny
2095 From tongue to tongue, from land to land proclaimed,
The very Hell will I constrain to lend
This stricken breast of mine deep notes of woe
To serve my need of fitting utterance.
And as I strive to body forth the tale
2100 Of all I suffer, all that thou hast done,
Forth shall the dread voice roll, and bear along
Shreds from my vitals torn for greater pain.
Then listen, not to dulcet harmony,
But to a discord wrung by mad despair
2105 Out of this bosom's depths of bitterness,

To ease my heart and plant a sting in thine.
The lion's roar, the fierce wolf's savage howl,
The horrid hissing of the scaly snake,
The awesome cries of monsters yet unnamed,
2110   The crow's ill-boding croak, the hollow moan
Of wild winds wrestling with the restless sea,
The wrathful bellow of the vanquished bull,
The plaintive sobbing of the widowed dove,
The envied owl's sad note, the wail of woe
2115   That rises from the dreary choir of Hell,
Commingled in one sound, confusing sense,
Let all these come to aid my soul's complaint,
For pain like mine demands new modes of song.
No echoes of that discord shall be heard
2120   Where Father Tagus rolls, or on the banks
Of olive-bordered Betis; to the rocks
Or in deep caverns shall my plaint be told,
And by a lifeless tongue in living words;
Or in dark valleys or on lonely shores,
2125   Where neither foot of man nor sunbeam falls;
Or in among the poison-breathing swarms
Of monsters nourished by the sluggish Nile.
For, though it be to solitudes remote
The hoarse vague echoes of my sorrows sound
2130   Thy matchless cruelty, my dismal fate
Shall carry them to all the spacious world.
Disdain hath power to kill, and patience dies
Slain by suspicion, be it false or true;
And deadly is the force of jealousy;
2135   Long absence makes of life a dreary void;
No hope of happiness can give repose
To him that ever fears to be forgot;
And death, inevitable, waits in hall.
But I, by some strange miracle, live on
2140   A prey to absence, jealousy, disdain;
Racked by suspicion as by certainty;
Forgotten, left to feed my flame alone.
And while I suffer thus, there comes no ray
Of hope to gladden me athwart the gloom;
2145   Nor do I look for it in my despair;
But rather clinging to a cureless woe,
All hope do I abjure for evermore.
Can there be hope where fear is? Were it well,
When far more certain are the grounds of fear?

2150 Ought I to shut mine eyes to jealousy,
If through a thousand heart-wounds it appears?
Who would not give free access to distrust,
Seeing disdain unveiled, and—bitter change!—
All his suspicions turned to certainties,
2155 And the fair truth transformed into a lie?
Oh, thou fierce tyrant of the realms of love,
Oh, Jealousy! put chains upon these hands,
And bind me with thy strongest cord, Disdain.
But, woe is me! triumphant over all,
2160 My sufferings drown the memory of you.
And now I die, and since there is no hope
Of happiness for me in life or death,
Still to my fantasy I'll fondly cling.
I'll say that he is wise who loveth well,
2165 And that the soul most free is that most bound
In thraldom to the ancient tyrant Love.
I'll say that she who is mine enemy
In that fair body hath as fair a mind,
And that her coldness is but my desert,
2170 And that by virtue of the pain be sends
Love rules his kingdom with a gentle sway.
Thus, self-deluding, and in bondage sore,
And wearing out the wretched shred of life
To which I am reduced by her disdain,
2175 I'll give this soul and body to the winds,
All hopeless of a crown of bliss in store.
Thou whose injustice hath supplied the cause
That makes me quit the weary life I loathe,
As by this wounded bosom thou canst see
2180 How willingly thy victim I become,
Let not my death, if haply worth a tear,
Cloud the clear heaven that dwells in thy bright eyes;
I would not have thee expiate in aught
The crime of having made my heart thy prey;
2185 But rather let thy laughter gaily ring
And prove my death to be thy festival.
Fool that I am to bid thee! well I know
Thy glory gains by my untimely end.
And now it is the time; from Hell's abyss
2190 Come thirsting Tantalus, come Sisyphus
Heaving the cruel stone, come Tityus
With vulture, and with wheel Ixion come,
And come the sisters of the ceaseless toil;

2195

    And all into this breast transfer their pains,
    And (if such tribute to despair be due)
    Chant in their deepest tones a doleful dirge
    Over a corse unworthy of a shroud.
    Let the three-headed guardian of the gate,
    And all the monstrous progeny of hell,

2200

    The doleful concert join: a lover dead
    Methinks can have no fitter obsequies.
    Lay of despair, grieve not when thou art gone
    Forth from this sorrowing heart: my misery
    Brings fortune to the cause that gave thee birth;

2205

    Then banish sadness even in the tomb."

The *Lay of Chrysostom* met with the approbation of the listeners, though the reader said it did not seem to him to agree with what he had heard of Marcela's reserve and propriety, for Chrysostom complained in it of jealousy, suspicion, and absence, all to the prejudice of the good name and fame of Marcela; to which

2210 Ambrosio replied as one who knew well his friend's most secret thoughts, "Señor, to remove that doubt I should tell you that when the unhappy man wrote this lay he was away from Marcela, from whom be had voluntarily separated himself, to try if absence would act with him as it is wont; and as everything distresses and every fear haunts the banished lover, so imaginary jealousies and suspicions,

2215 dreaded as if they were true, tormented Chrysostom; and thus the truth of what report declares of the virtue of Marcela remains unshaken, and with her envy itself should not and cannot find any fault save that of being cruel, somewhat haughty, and very scornful."

"That is true," said Vivaldo; and as he was about to read another paper of

2220 those he had preserved from the fire, he was stopped by a marvellous vision (for such it seemed) that unexpectedly presented itself to their eyes; for on the summit of the rock where they were digging the grave there appeared the shepherdess Marcela, so beautiful that her beauty exceeded its reputation. Those who had never till then beheld her gazed upon her in wonder and silence, and those who

2225 were accustomed to see her were not less amazed than those who had never seen her before. But the instant Ambrosio saw her he addressed her, with manifest indignation:

"Art thou come, by chance, cruel basilisk of these mountains, to see if in thy presence blood will flow from the wounds of this wretched being thy cruelty has

2230 robbed of life; or is it to exult over the cruel work of thy humours that thou art come; or like another pitiless Nero to look down from that height upon the ruin of his Rome in embers; or in thy arrogance to trample on this ill-fated corpse, as the ungrateful daughter trampled on her father Tarquin's? Tell us quickly for what thou art come, or what it is thou wouldst have, for, as I know the thoughts of

2235 Chrysostom never failed to obey thee in life, I will make all these who call themselves his friends obey thee, though he be dead."

"I come not, Ambrosio for any of the purposes thou hast named," replied Marcela, "but to defend myself and to prove how unreasonable are all those who blame me for their sorrow and for Chrysostom's death; and therefore I ask all of you that are here to give me your attention, for will not take much time or many words to bring the truth home to persons of sense.

"Heaven has made me, so you say, beautiful, and so much so that in spite of yourselves my beauty leads you to love me; and for the love you show me you say, and even urge, that I am bound to love you. By that natural understanding which God has given me I know that everything beautiful attracts love, but I cannot see how, by reason of being loved, that which is loved for its beauty is bound to love that which loves it; besides, it may happen that the lover of that which is beautiful may be ugly, and ugliness being detestable, it is very absurd to say, "I love thee because thou art beautiful, thou must love me though I be ugly." But supposing the beauty equal on both sides, it does not follow that the inclinations must be therefore alike, for it is not every beauty that excites love, some but pleasing the eye without winning the affection; and if every sort of beauty excited love and won the heart, the will would wander vaguely to and fro unable to make choice of any; for as there is an infinity of beautiful objects there must be an infinity of inclinations, and true love, I have heard it said, is indivisible, and must be voluntary and not compelled. If this be so, as I believe it to be, why do you desire me to bend my will by force, for no other reason but that you say you love me? Nay—tell me—had Heaven made me ugly, as it has made me beautiful, could I with justice complain of you for not loving me? Moreover, you must remember that the beauty I possess was no choice of mine, for, be it what it may, Heaven of its bounty gave it me without my asking or choosing it; and as the viper, though it kills with it, does not deserve to be blamed for the poison it carries, as it is a gift of nature, neither do I deserve reproach for being beautiful; for beauty in a modest woman is like fire at a distance or a sharp sword; the one does not burn, the other does not cut, those who do not come too near. Honour and virtue are the ornaments of the mind, without which the body, though it be so, has no right to pass for beautiful; but if modesty is one of the virtues that specially lend a grace and charm to mind and body, why should she who is loved for her beauty part with it to gratify one who for his pleasure alone strives with all his might and energy to rob her of it?

"I was born free, and that I might live in freedom I chose the solitude of the fields; in the trees of the mountains I find society, the clear waters of the brooks are my mirrors, and to the trees and waters I make known my thoughts and charms. I am a fire afar off, a sword laid aside. Those whom I have inspired with love by letting them see me, I have by words undeceived, and if their longings live on hope—and I have given none to Chrysostom or to any other—it cannot justly be said that the death of any is my doing, for it was rather his own obstinacy than my cruelty that killed him; and if it be made a charge against me that his wishes were honourable, and that therefore I was bound to yield to them, I answer that when on this very spot where now his grave is made he declared to me his purity of purpose, I told him that mine was to live in perpetual solitude, and that the earth

2240

2245

2250

2255

2260

2265

2270

2275

2280

alone should enjoy the fruits of my retirement and the spoils of my beauty; and if, after this open avowal, he chose to persist against hope and steer against the wind, what wonder is it that he should sink in the depths of his infatuation? If I had encouraged him, I should be false; if I had gratified him, I should have acted against my own better resolution and purpose. He was persistent in spite of warning, he despaired without being hated. Bethink you now if it be reasonable that his suffering should be laid to my charge. Let him who has been deceived complain, let him give way to despair whose encouraged hopes have proved vain, let him flatter himself whom I shall entice, let him boast whom I shall receive; but let not him call me cruel or homicide to whom I make no promise, upon whom I practise no deception, whom I neither entice nor receive. It has not been so far the will of Heaven that I should love by fate, and to expect me to love by choice is idle.

"Let this general declaration serve for each of my suitors on his own account, and let it be understood from this time forth that if anyone dies for me it is not of jealousy or misery he dies, for she who loves no one can give no cause for jealousy to any, and candour is not to be confounded with scorn. Let him who calls me wild beast and basilisk, leave me alone as something noxious and evil; let him who calls me ungrateful, withhold his service; who calls me wayward, seek not my acquaintance; who calls me cruel, pursue me not; for this wild beast, this basilisk, this ungrateful, cruel, wayward being has no kind of desire to seek, serve, know, or follow them.

"If Chrysostom's impatience and violent passion killed him, why should my modest behaviour and circumspection be blamed? If I preserve my purity in the society of the trees, why should he who would have me preserve it among men, seek to rob me of it? I have, as you know, wealth of my own, and I covet not that of others; my taste is for freedom, and I have no relish for constraint; I neither love nor hate anyone; I do not deceive this one or court that, or trifle with one or play with another. The modest converse of the shepherd girls of these hamlets and the care of my goats are my recreations; my desires are bounded by these mountains, and if they ever wander hence it is to contemplate the beauty of the heavens, steps by which the soul travels to its primeval abode."

With these words, and not waiting to hear a reply, she turned and passed into the thickest part of a wood that was hard by, leaving all who were there lost in admiration as much of her good sense as of her beauty. Some—those wounded by the irresistible shafts launched by her bright eyes—made as though they would follow her, heedless of the frank declaration they had heard; seeing which, and deeming this a fitting occasion for the exercise of his chivalry in aid of distressed damsels, Don Quixote, laying his hand on the hilt of his sword, exclaimed in a loud and distinct voice:

"Let no one, whatever his rank or condition, dare to follow the beautiful Marcela, under pain of incurring my fierce indignation. She has shown by clear and satisfactory arguments that little or no fault is to be found with her for the death of Chrysostom, and also how far she is from yielding to the wishes of any of her lovers, for which reason, instead of being followed and persecuted, she should

2325 in justice be honoured and esteemed by all the good people of the world, for she shows that she is the only woman in it that holds to such a virtuous resolution."

Whether it was because of the threats of Don Quixote, or because Ambrosio told them to fulfil their duty to their good friend, none of the shepherds moved or stirred from the spot until, having finished the grave and burned Chrysostom's 2330 papers, they laid his body in it, not without many tears from those who stood by. They closed the grave with a heavy stone until a slab was ready which Ambrosio said he meant to have prepared, with an epitaph which was to be to this effect:

Beneath the stone before your eyes
The body of a lover lies;
2335 In life he was a shepherd swain,
In death a victim to disdain.
Ungrateful, cruel, coy, and fair,
Was she that drove him to despair,
And Love hath made her his ally
2340 For spreading wide his tyranny.

They then strewed upon the grave a profusion of flowers and branches, and all expressing their condolence with his friend Ambrosio, took their Vivaldo and his companion did the same; and Don Quixote bade farewell to his hosts and to the travellers, who pressed him to come with them to Seville, as being such a 2345 convenient place for finding adventures, for they presented themselves in every street and round every corner oftener than anywhere else. Don Quixote thanked them for their advice and for the disposition they showed to do him a favour, and said that for the present he would not, and must not go to Seville until he had cleared all these mountains of highwaymen and robbers, of whom report said they 2350 were full. Seeing his good intention, the travellers were unwilling to press him further, and once more bidding him farewell, they left him and pursued their journey, in the course of which they did not fail to discuss the story of Marcela and Chrysostom as well as the madness of Don Quixote. He, on his part, resolved to go in quest of the shepherdess Marcela, and make offer to her of all the service 2355 he could render her; but things did not fall out with him as he expected, according to what is related in the course of this veracious history, of which the Second Part ends here.

* * * * *

FROM CHAPTER XVIII: IN WHICH IS RELATED THE DISCOURSE SANCHO PANZA HELD WITH HIS MASTER, DON QUIXOTE, AND OTHER ADVENTURES WORTH RELATING [THE SHEEP ARMIES]

Thus talking, Don Quixote and his squire were going along, when, on the road they were following, Don Quixote perceived approaching them a large and thick cloud of dust, on seeing which he turned to Sancho and said:

"This is the day, Sancho, on which will be seen the boon my fortune is reserving for me; this, I say, is the day on which as much as on any other shall be displayed the might of my arm, and on which I shall do deeds that shall remain written in the book of fame for all ages to come. Seest thou that cloud of dust which rises yonder? Well, then, all that is churned up by a vast army composed of various and countless nations that comes marching there."

"According to that there must be two," said Sancho, "for on this opposite side also there rises just such another cloud of dust."

Don Quixote turned to look and found that it was true, and rejoicing exceedingly, he concluded that they were two armies about to engage and encounter in the midst of that broad plain; for at all times and seasons his fancy was full of the battles, enchantments, adventures, crazy feats, loves, and defiances that are recorded in the books of chivalry, and everything he said, thought, or did had reference to such things. Now the cloud of dust he had seen was raised by two great droves of sheep coming along the same road in opposite directions, which, because of the dust, did not become visible until they drew near, but Don Quixote asserted so positively that they were armies that Sancho was led to believe it and say, "Well, and what are we to do, señor?"

"What?" said Don Quixote: "give aid and assistance to the weak and those who need it; and thou must know, Sancho, that this which comes opposite to us is conducted and led by the mighty emperor Alifanfaron, lord of the great isle of Trapobana; this other that marches behind me is that of his enemy the king of the Garamantas, Pentapolin of the Bare Arm, for he always goes into battle with his right arm bare."

"But why are these two lords such enemies?"

"They are at enmity," replied Don Quixote, "because this Alifanfaron is a furious pagan and is in love with the daughter of Pentapolin, who is a very beautiful and moreover gracious lady, and a Christian, and her father is unwilling to bestow her upon the pagan king unless he first abandons the religion of his false prophet Mahomet, and adopts his own."

"By my beard," said Sancho, "but Pentapolin does quite right, and I will help him as much as I can."

"In that thou wilt do what is thy duty, Sancho," said Don Quixote; "for to engage in battles of this sort it is not requisite to be a dubbed knight."

"That I can well understand," answered Sancho; "but where shall we put this ass where we may be sure to find him after the fray is over? for I believe it has not been the custom so far to go into battle on a beast of this kind."

"That is true," said Don Quixote, "and what you had best do with him is to leave him to take his chance whether he be lost or not, for the horses we shall have when we come out victors will be so many that even Rocinante will run a risk of being changed for another. But attend to me and observe, for I wish to give thee some account of the chief knights who accompany these two armies; and that thou mayest the better see and mark, let us withdraw to that hillock which rises yonder, whence both armies may be seen."

They did so, and placed themselves on a rising ground from which the two droves that Don Quixote made armies of might have been plainly seen if the clouds of dust they raised had not obscured them and blinded the sight; nevertheless, seeing in his imagination what he did not see and what did not exist, he began thus in a loud voice:

"That knight whom thou seest yonder in yellow armour, who bears upon his shield a lion crowned crouching at the feet of a damsel, is the valiant Laurcalco, lord of the Silver Bridge; that one in armour with flowers of gold, who bears on his shield three crowns argent on an azure field, is the dreaded Micocolembo, grand duke of Quirocia; that other of gigantic frame, on his right hand, is the ever dauntless Brandabarbaran de Boliche, lord of the three Arabias, who for armour wears that serpent skin, and has for shield a gate which, according to tradition, is one of those of the temple that Samson brought to the ground when by his death he revenged himself upon his enemies. But turn thine eyes to the other side, and thou shalt see in front and in the van of this other army the ever victorious and never vanquished Timonel of Carcajona, prince of New Biscay, who comes in armour with arms quartered azure, vert, white, and yellow, and bears on his shield a cat or on a field tawny with a motto which says Miau, which is the beginning of the name of his lady, who according to report is the peerless Miaulina, daughter of the duke Alfeniquen of the Algarve; the other, who burdens and presses the loins of that powerful charger and bears arms white as snow and a shield blank and without any device, is a novice knight, a Frenchman by birth, Pierres Papin by name, lord of the baronies of Utrique; that other, who with iron-shod heels strikes the flanks of that nimble parti-coloured zebra, and for arms bears azure vair, is the mighty duke of Nerbia, Espartafilardo del Bosque, who bears for device on his shield an asparagus plant with a motto in Castilian that says, Rastrea mi suerte." And so he went on naming a number of knights of one squadron or the other out of his imagination, and to all he assigned off-hand their arms, colours, devices, and mottoes, carried away by the illusions of his unheard-of craze; and without a pause, he continued, "People of divers nations compose this squadron in front; here are those that drink of the sweet waters of the famous Xanthus, those that scour the woody Massilian plains, those that sift the pure fine gold of Arabia Felix, those that enjoy the famed cool banks of the crystal Thermodon, those that in many and various ways divert the streams of the golden Pactolus, the Numidians, faithless in their promises, the Persians renowned in archery, the Parthians and the Medes that fight as they fly, the Arabs that ever shift their dwellings, the Scythians as cruel as they are fair, the Ethiopians with pierced lips, and an

infinity of other nations whose features I recognise and descry, though I cannot recall their names. In this other squadron there come those that drink of the crystal streams of the olive-bearing Betis, those that make smooth their countenances with
2445   the water of the ever rich and golden Tagus, those that rejoice in the fertilising flow of the divine Genil, those that roam the Tartesian plains abounding in pasture, those that take their pleasure in the Elysian meadows of Jerez, the rich Manchegans crowned with ruddy ears of corn, the wearers of iron, old relics of the Gothic race, those that bathe in the Pisuerga renowned for its gentle current,
2450   those that feed their herds along the spreading pastures of the winding Guadiana famed for its hidden course, those that tremble with the cold of the pineclad Pyrenees or the dazzling snows of the lofty Apennine; in a word, as many as all Europe includes and contains."

Good God! what a number of countries and nations he named! giving to each
2455   its proper attributes with marvellous readiness; brimful and saturated with what he had read in his lying books! Sancho Panza hung upon his words without speaking, and from time to time turned to try if he could see the knights and giants his master was describing, and as he could not make out one of them he said to him:

"Señor, devil take it if there's a sign of any man you talk of, knight or giant, in
2460   the whole thing; maybe it's all enchantment, like the phantoms last night."

"How canst thou say that!" answered Don Quixote; "dost thou not hear the neighing of the steeds, the braying of the trumpets, the roll of the drums?"

"I hear nothing but a great bleating of ewes and sheep," said Sancho; which was true, for by this time the two flocks had come close.

2465   "The fear thou art in, Sancho," said Don Quixote, "prevents thee from seeing or hearing correctly, for one of the effects of fear is to derange the senses and make things appear different from what they are; if thou art in such fear, withdraw to one side and leave me to myself, for alone I suffice to bring victory to that side to which I shall give my aid;" and so saying he gave Rocinante the spur, and putting
2470   the lance in rest, shot down the slope like a thunderbolt.

Sancho shouted after him, crying, "Come back, Señor Don Quixote; I vow to God they are sheep and ewes you are charging! Come back! Unlucky the father that begot me! what madness is this! Look, there is no giant, nor knight, nor cats, nor arms, nor shields quartered or whole, nor vair azure or bedevilled. What are
2475   you about? Sinner that I am before God!"

But not for all these entreaties did Don Quixote turn back; on the contrary he went on shouting out, "Ho, knights, ye who follow and fight under the banners of the valiant emperor Pentapolin of the Bare Arm, follow me all; ye shall see how easily I shall give him his revenge over his enemy Alifanfaron of the Trapobana."
2480   So saying, he dashed into the midst of the squadron of ewes, and began spearing them with as much spirit and intrepidity as if he were transfixing mortal enemies in earnest. The shepherds and drovers accompanying the flock shouted to him to desist; seeing it was no use, they ungirt their slings and began to salute his ears with stones as big as one's fist. Don Quixote gave no heed to the stones, but,
2485   letting drive right and left kept saying:

"Where art thou, proud Alifanfaron? Come before me; I am a single knight who would fain prove thy prowess hand to hand, and make thee yield thy life a penalty for the wrong thou dost to the valiant Pentapolin Garamanta."

Here came a sugar-plum from the brook that struck him on the side and buried a couple of ribs in his body. Feeling himself so smitten, he imagined himself slain or badly wounded for certain, and recollecting his liquor he drew out his flask, and putting it to his mouth began to pour the contents into his stomach; but ere he had succeeded in swallowing what seemed to him enough, there came another almond which struck him on the hand and on the flask so fairly that it smashed it to pieces, knocking three or four teeth and grinders out of his mouth in its course, and sorely crushing two fingers of his hand. Such was the force of the first blow and of the second, that the poor knight in spite of himself came down backwards off his horse. The shepherds came up, and felt sure they had killed him; so in all haste they collected their flock together, took up the dead beasts, of which there were more than seven, and made off without waiting to ascertain anything further.

All this time Sancho stood on the hill watching the crazy feats his master was performing, and tearing his beard and cursing the hour and the occasion when fortune had made him acquainted with him. Seeing him, then, brought to the ground, and that the shepherds had taken themselves off, he ran to him and found him in very bad case, though not unconscious; and said he:

"Did I not tell you to come back, Señor Don Quixote; and that what you were going to attack were not armies but droves of sheep?"

"That's how that thief of a sage, my enemy, can alter and falsify things," answered Don Quixote; "thou must know, Sancho, that it is a very easy matter for those of his sort to make us believe what they choose; and this malignant being who persecutes me, envious of the glory he knew I was to win in this battle, has turned the squadrons of the enemy into droves of sheep. At any rate, do this much, I beg of thee, Sancho, to undeceive thyself, and see that what I say is true; mount thy ass and follow them quietly, and thou shalt see that when they have gone some little distance from this they will return to their original shape and, ceasing to be sheep, become men in all respects as I described them to thee at first. But go not just yet, for I want thy help and assistance; come hither, and see how many of my teeth and grinders are missing, for I feel as if there was not one left in my mouth."

Sancho came so close that he almost put his eyes into his mouth; now just at that moment the balsam had acted on the stomach of Don Quixote, so, at the very instant when Sancho came to examine his mouth, he discharged all its contents with more force than a musket, and full into the beard of the compassionate squire.

"Holy Mary!" cried Sancho, "what is this that has happened me? Clearly this sinner is mortally wounded, as he vomits blood from the mouth;" but considering the matter a little more closely he perceived by the colour, taste, and smell, that it was not blood but the balsam from the flask which he had seen him drink; and he was taken with such a loathing that his stomach turned, and he vomited up his inside over his very master, and both were left in a precious state. Sancho ran to his ass to get something wherewith to clean himself, and relieve his

2530　master, out of his alforjas; but not finding them, he well-nigh took leave of his senses, and cursed himself anew, and in his heart resolved to quit his master and return home, even though he forfeited the wages of his service and all hopes of the promised island.

2535　Don Quixote now rose, and putting his left hand to his mouth to keep his teeth from falling out altogether, with the other he laid hold of the bridle of Rocinante, who had never stirred from his master's side—so loyal and well-behaved was he—and betook himself to where the squire stood leaning over his ass with his hand to his cheek, like one in deep dejection. Seeing him in this mood, looking so sad, Don Quixote said to him:

2540　"Bear in mind, Sancho, that one man is no more than another, unless he does more than another; all these tempests that fall upon us are signs that fair weather is coming shortly, and that things will go well with us, for it is impossible for good or evil to last for ever; and hence it follows that the evil having lasted long, the good must be now nigh at hand; so thou must not distress thyself at the misfortunes

2545　which happen to me, since thou hast no share in them."

"How have I not?" replied Sancho; "was he whom they blanketed yesterday perchance any other than my father's son? and the alforjas that are missing to-day with all my treasures, did they belong to any other but myself?"

"What! are the alforjas missing, Sancho?" said Don Quixote.

2550　"Yes, they are missing," answered Sancho.

"In that case we have nothing to eat to-day," replied Don Quixote.

"It would be so," answered Sancho, "if there were none of the herbs your worship says you know in these meadows, those with which knights-errant as unlucky as your worship are wont to supply such-like shortcomings."

2555　"For all that," answered Don Quixote, "I would rather have just now a quarter of bread, or a loaf and a couple of pilchards' [herring fish] heads, than all the herbs described by Dioscorides, even with Doctor Laguna's notes. Nevertheless, Sancho the Good, mount thy beast and come along with me, for God, who provides for all things, will not fail us (more especially when we are so

2560　active in his service as we are), since he fails not the midges of the air, nor the grubs of the earth, nor the tadpoles of the water, and is so merciful that he maketh his sun to rise on the good and on the evil, and sendeth rain on the unjust and on the just."

"Your worship would make a better preacher than knight-errant," said

2565　Sancho.

"Knights-errant knew and ought to know everything, Sancho," said Don Quixote; "for there were knights—errant in former times as well qualified to deliver a sermon or discourse in the middle of an encampment, as if they had graduated in the University of Paris; whereby we may see that the lance has never

2570　blunted the pen, nor the pen the lance."

"Well, be it as your worship says," replied Sancho; "let us be off now and find some place of shelter for the night, and God grant it may be somewhere where there are no blankets, nor blanketeers, nor phantoms, nor enchanted Moors; for if there are, may the devil take the whole concern."

2575 "Ask that of God, my son," said Don Quixote; and do thou lead on where thou wilt, for this time I leave our lodging to thy choice; but reach me here thy hand, and feel with thy finger, and find out how many of my teeth and grinders are missing from this right side of the upper jaw, for it is there I feel the pain."

Sancho put in his fingers, and feeling about asked him, "How many grinders

2580 used your worship have on this side?"

"Four," replied Don Quixote, "besides the back-tooth, all whole and quite sound."

"Mind what you are saying, señor."

"I say four, if not five," answered Don Quixote, "for never in my life have I

2585 had tooth or grinder drawn, nor has any fallen out or been destroyed by any decay or rheum."

"Well, then," said Sancho, "in this lower side your worship has no more than two grinders and a half, and in the upper neither a half nor any at all, for it is all as smooth as the palm of my hand."

2590 "Luckless that I am!" said Don Quixote, hearing the sad news his squire gave him; "I had rather they despoiled me of an arm, so it were not the sword-arm; for I tell thee, Sancho, a mouth without teeth is like a mill without a millstone, and a tooth is much more to be prized than a diamond; but we who profess the austere order of chivalry are liable to all this. Mount, friend, and lead the way, and I will

2595 follow thee at whatever pace thou wilt."

Sancho did as he bade him, and proceeded in the direction in which he thought he might find refuge without quitting the high road, which was there very much frequented. As they went along, then, at a slow pace—for the pain in Don Quixote's jaws kept him uneasy and ill-disposed for speed—Sancho thought it

2600 well to amuse and divert him by talk of some kind.

* * * * *

CHAPTER XXII: OF THE FREEDOM DON QUIXOTE CONFERRED ON SEVERAL UNFORTUNATES WHO AGAINST THEIR WILL WERE BEING CARRIED WHERE THEY HAD NO WISH TO GO [THE GALLEY SLAVES]

Cide Hamete Benengeli, the Arab and Manchegan author, relates in this most grave, high-sounding, minute, delightful, and original history that after the discussion between the famous Don Quixote of La Mancha and his squire Sancho Panza which is set down at the end of chapter twenty-one, Don Quixote raised his

2605 eyes and saw coming along the road he was following some dozen men on foot strung together by the neck, like beads, on a great iron chain, and all with manacles on their hands. With them there came also two men on horseback and two on foot; those on horseback with wheel-lock muskets, those on foot with javelins and swords, and as soon as Sancho saw them he said:

2610   "That is a chain of galley slaves, on the way to the galleys by force of the king's orders."

    "How by force?" asked Don Quixote; "is it possible that the king uses force against anyone?"

    "I do not say that," answered Sancho, "but that these are people condemned

2615 for their crimes to serve by force in the king's galleys."

    "In fact," replied Don Quixote, "however it may be, these people are going where they are taking them by force, and not of their own will."

    "Just so," said Sancho.

    "Then if so," said Don Quixote, "here is a case for the exercise of my office, to

2620 put down force and to succour and help the wretched."

    "Recollect, your worship," said Sancho, "Justice, which is the king himself, is not using force or doing wrong to such persons, but punishing them for their crimes."

    The chain of galley slaves had by this time come up, and Don Quixote in very

2625 courteous language asked those who were in custody of it to be good enough to tell him the reason or reasons for which they were conducting these people in this manner. One of the guards on horseback answered that they were galley slaves belonging to his majesty, that they were going to the galleys, and that was all that was to be said and all he had any business to know.

2630   "Nevertheless," replied Don Quixote, "I should like to know from each of them separately the reason of his misfortune;" to this he added more to the same effect to induce them to tell him what he wanted so civilly that the other mounted guard said to him:

    "Though we have here the register and certificate of the sentence of every one

2635 of these wretches, this is no time to take them out or read them; come and ask themselves; they can tell if they choose, and they will, for these fellows take a pleasure in doing and talking about rascalities."

    With this permission, which Don Quixote would have taken even had they not granted it, he approached the chain and asked the first for what offences he

2640 was now in such a sorry case.

    He made answer that it was for being a lover.

    "For that only?" replied Don Quixote; "why, if for being lovers they send people to the galleys I might have been rowing in them long ago."

    "The love is not the sort your worship is thinking of," said the galley slave;

2645 "mine was that I loved a washerwoman's basket of clean linen so well, and held it so close in my embrace, that if the arm of the law had not forced it from me, I should never have let it go of my own will to this moment; I was caught in the act, there was no occasion for torture, the case was settled, they treated me to a hundred lashes on the back, and three years of *gurapas* besides, and that was the end of it."

2650   "What are *gurapas*?" asked Don Quixote.

"*Gurapas* are galleys," answered the galley slave, who was a young man of about four-and-twenty, and said he was a native of Piedrahita.

Don Quixote asked the same question of the second, who made no reply, so downcast and melancholy was he; but the first answered for him, and said, "He, sir, goes as a canary, I mean as a musician and a singer."

"What!" said Don Quixote, "for being musicians and singers are people sent to the galleys too?"

"Yes, sir," answered the galley slave, "for there is nothing worse than singing under suffering."

"On the contrary, I have heard say," said Don Quixote, "that he who sings scares away his woes."

"Here it is the reverse," said the galley slave; "for he who sings once weeps all his life."

"I do not understand it," said Don Quixote; but one of the guards said to him, "Sir, to sing under suffering means with the non sancta fraternity to confess under torture; they put this sinner to the torture and he confessed his crime, which was being a *cuatrero,* that is a cattle-stealer, and on his confession they sentenced him to six years in the galleys, besides two hundred lashes that he has already had on the back; and he is always dejected and downcast because the other thieves that were left behind and that march here ill-treat, and snub, and jeer, and despise him for confessing and not having spirit enough to say nay; for, say they, 'nay' has no more letters in it than 'yea,' and a culprit is well off when life or death with him depends on his own tongue and not on that of witnesses or evidence; and to my thinking they are not very far out."

"And I think so too," answered Don Quixote; then passing on to the third he asked him what he had asked the others, and the man answered very readily and unconcernedly, "I am going for five years to their ladyships the *gurapas* for the want of ten ducats."

"I will give twenty with pleasure to get you out of that trouble," said Don Quixote.

"That," said the galley slave, "is like a man having money at sea when he is dying of hunger and has no way of buying what he wants; I say so because if at the right time I had had those twenty ducats that your worship now offers me, I would have greased the notary's pen and freshened up the attorney's wit with them, so that to-day I should be in the middle of the plaza of the Zocodover at Toledo, and not on this road coupled like a greyhound. But God is great; patience—there, that's enough of it."

Don Quixote passed on to the fourth, a man of venerable aspect with a white beard falling below his breast, who on hearing himself asked the reason of his being there began to weep without answering a word, but the fifth acted as his tongue and said, "This worthy man is going to the galleys for four years, after having gone the rounds in ceremony and on horseback."

"That means," said Sancho Panza, "as I take it, to have been exposed to shame in public."

2695   "Just so," replied the galley slave, "and the offence for which they gave him that punishment was having been an ear-broker, nay body-broker; I mean, in short, that this gentleman goes as a pimp, and for having besides a certain touch of the sorcerer about him."

2700   "If that touch had not been thrown in," said Don Quixote, "he would not deserve, for mere pimping, to row in the galleys, but rather to command and be admiral of them; for the office of pimp is no ordinary one, being the office of persons of discretion, one very necessary in a well-ordered state, and only to be exercised by persons of good birth; nay, there ought to be an inspector and overseer of them, as in other offices, and recognised number, as with the brokers

2705   on change; in this way many of the evils would be avoided which are caused by this office and calling being in the hands of stupid and ignorant people, such as women more or less silly, and pages and jesters of little standing and experience, who on the most urgent occasions, and when ingenuity of contrivance is needed, let the crumbs freeze on the way to their mouths, and know not which is their right

2710   hand. I should like to go farther, and give reasons to show that it is advisable to choose those who are to hold so necessary an office in the state, but this is not the fit place for it; some day I will expound the matter to some one able to see to and rectify it; all I say now is, that the additional fact of his being a sorcerer has removed the sorrow it gave me to see these white hairs and this venerable

2715   countenance in so painful a position on account of his being a pimp; though I know well there are no sorceries in the world that can move or compel the will as some simple folk fancy, for our will is free, nor is there herb or charm that can force it. All that certain silly women and quacks do is to turn men mad with potions and poisons, pretending that they have power to cause love, for, as I say, it is an

2720   impossibility to compel the will."

        "It is true," said the good old man, "and indeed, sir, as far as the charge of sorcery goes I was not guilty; as to that of being a pimp I cannot deny it; but I never thought I was doing any harm by it, for my only object was that all the world should enjoy itself and live in peace and quiet, without quarrels or troubles; but

2725   my good intentions were unavailing to save me from going where I never expect to come back from, with this weight of years upon me and a urinary ailment that never gives me a moment's ease;" and again he fell to weeping as before, and such compassion did Sancho feel for him that he took out a *real* from his bosom and gave it to him in alms.

2730   Don Quixote went on and asked another what his crime was, and the man answered with no less but rather much more sprightliness than the last one.

        "I am here because I carried the joke too far with a couple of cousins of mine, and with a couple of other cousins who were none of mine; in short, I carried the joke so far with them all that it ended in such a complicated increase of kindred

2735   that no accountant could make it clear: it was all proved against me, I got no favour, I had no money, I was near having my neck stretched, they sentenced me to the galleys for six years, I accepted my fate, it is the punishment of my fault; I am a young man; let life only last, and with that all will come right. If you, sir, have

2740 anything wherewith to help the poor, God will repay it to you in heaven, and we on earth will take care in our petitions to him to pray for the life and health of your worship, that they may be as long and as good as your amiable appearance deserves."

This one was in the dress of a student, and one of the guards said he was a great talker and a very elegant Latin scholar.

2745 Behind all these there came a man of thirty, a very personable fellow, except that when he looked, his eyes turned in a little one towards the other. He was bound differently from the rest, for he had to his leg a chain so long that it was wound all round his body, and two rings on his neck, one attached to the chain, the other to what they call a "keep-friend" or "friend's foot," from which hung 2750 two irons reaching to his waist with two manacles fixed to them in which his hands were secured by a big padlock, so that he could neither raise his hands to his mouth nor lower his head to his hands. Don Quixote asked why this man carried so many more chains than the others. The guard replied that it was because he alone had committed more crimes than all the rest put together, and was 2755 so daring and such a villain, that though they marched him in that fashion they did not feel sure of him, but were in dread of his making his escape.

"What crimes can he have committed," said Don Quixote, "if they have not deserved a heavier punishment than being sent to the galleys?"

"He goes for ten years," replied the guard, "which is the same thing as civil 2760 death, and all that need be said is that this good fellow is the famous Gines de Pasamonte, otherwise called Ginesillo de Parapilla."

"Gently, señor commissary," said the galley slave at this, "let us have no fixing of names or surnames; my name is Gines, not Ginesillo, and my family name is Pasamonte, not Parapilla as you say; let each one mind his own business, and he 2765 will be doing enough."

"Speak with less impertinence, master thief of extra measure," replied the commissary, "if you don't want me to make you hold your tongue in spite of your teeth."

"It is easy to see," returned the galley slave, "that man goes as God pleases, 2770 but some one shall know some day whether I am called Ginesillo de Parapilla or not."

"Don't they call you so, you liar?" said the guard.

"They do," returned Gines, "but I will make them give over calling me so, or I will be shaved, where, I only say behind my teeth. If you, sir, have anything to give 2775 us, give it to us at once, and God speed you, for you are becoming tiresome with all this inquisitiveness about the lives of others; if you want to know about mine, let me tell you I am Gines de Pasamonte, whose life is written by these fingers."

"He says true," said the commissary, "for he has himself written his story as grand as you please, and has left the book in the prison in pawn for two hundred 2780 *reals.*"

"And I mean to take it out of pawn," said Gines, "though it were in for two hundred ducats."

"Is it so good?" said Don Quixote.

2785 "So good is it," replied Gines, "that a fig for 'Lazarillo de Tormes,' and all of that kind that have been written, or shall be written compared with it: all I will say about it is that it deals with facts, and facts so neat and diverting that no lies could match them."

"And how is the book entitled?" asked Don Quixote.

"The 'Life of Gines de Pasamonte,'" replied the subject of it.

2790 "And is it finished?" asked Don Quixote.

"How can it be finished," said the other, "when my life is not yet finished? All that is written is from my birth down to the point when they sent me to the galleys this last time."

"Then you have been there before?" said Don Quixote.

2795 "In the service of God and the king I have been there for four years before now, and I know by this time what the biscuit and courbash are like," replied Gines; "and it is no great grievance to me to go back to them, for there I shall have time to finish my book; I have still many things left to say, and in the galleys of Spain there is more than enough leisure; though I do not want much for what I

2800 have to write, for I have it by heart."

"You seem a clever fellow," said Don Quixote.

"And an unfortunate one," replied Gines, "for misfortune always persecutes good wit."

"It persecutes rogues," said the commissary.

2805 "I told you already to go gently, master commissary," said Pasamonte; "their lordships yonder never gave you that staff to ill-treat us wretches here, but to conduct and take us where his majesty orders you; if not, by the life of—never mind—; it may be that some day the stains made in the inn will come out in the scouring; let everyone hold his tongue and behave well and speak better; and now

2810 let us march on, for we have had quite enough of this entertainment."

The commissary lifted his staff to strike Pasamonte in return for his threats, but Don Quixote came between them, and begged him not to ill-use him, as it was not too much to allow one who had his hands tied to have his tongue a trifle free; and turning to the whole chain of them he said:

2815 "From all you have told me, dear brethren, make out clearly that though they have punished you for your faults, the punishments you are about to endure do not give you much pleasure, and that you go to them very much against the grain and against your will, and that perhaps this one's want of courage under torture, that one's want of money, the other's want of advocacy, and lastly the perverted

2820 judgment of the judge may have been the cause of your ruin and of your failure to obtain the justice you had on your side. All which presents itself now to my mind, urging, persuading, and even compelling me to demonstrate in your case the purpose for which Heaven sent me into the world and caused me to make profession of the order of chivalry to which I belong, and the vow I took therein to

2825 give aid to those in need and under the oppression of the strong. But as I know that it is a mark of prudence not to do by foul means what may be done by fair, I will ask these gentlemen, the guards and commissary, to be so good as to release you and let you go in peace, as there will be no lack of others to serve the king under more favourable circumstances; for it seems to me a hard case to make slaves of those whom God and nature have made free. Moreover, sirs of the guard," added Don Quixote, "these poor fellows have done nothing to you; let each answer for his own sins yonder; there is a God in Heaven who will not forget to punish the wicked or reward the good; and it is not fitting that honest men should be the instruments of punishment to others, they being therein no way concerned. This request I make thus gently and quietly, that, if you comply with it, I may have reason for thanking you; and, if you will not voluntarily, this lance and sword together with the might of my arm shall compel you to comply with it by force."

"Nice nonsense!" said the commissary; "a fine piece of pleasantry he has come out with at last! He wants us to let the king's prisoners go, as if we had any authority to release them, or he to order us to do so! Go your way, sir, and good luck to you; put that basin straight that you've got on your head, and don't go looking for three feet on a cat."

"'Tis you that are the cat, rat, and rascal," replied Don Quixote, and acting on the word he fell upon him so suddenly that without giving him time to defend himself he brought him to the ground sorely wounded with a lance-thrust; and lucky it was for him that it was the one that had the musket. The other guards stood thunderstruck and amazed at this unexpected event, but recovering presence of mind, those on horseback seized their swords, and those on foot their javelins, and attacked Don Quixote, who was waiting for them with great calmness; and no doubt it would have gone badly with him if the galley slaves, seeing the chance before them of liberating themselves, had not effected it by contriving to break the chain on which they were strung. Such was the confusion, that the guards, now rushing at the galley slaves who were breaking loose, now to attack Don Quixote who was waiting for them, did nothing at all that was of any use. Sancho, on his part, gave a helping hand to release Gines de Pasamonte, who was the first to leap forth upon the plain free and unfettered, and who, attacking the prostrate commissary, took from him his sword and the musket, with which, aiming at one and levelling at another, he, without ever discharging it, drove every one of the guards off the field, for they took to flight, as well to escape Pasamonte's musket, as the showers of stones the now released galley slaves were raining upon them. Sancho was greatly grieved at the affair, because he anticipated that those who had fled would report the matter to the Holy Brotherhood, who at the summons of the alarm-bell would at once sally forth in quest of the offenders; and he said so to his master, and entreated him to leave the place at once, and go into hiding in the sierra that was close by.

"That is all very well," said Don Quixote, "but I know what must be done now;" and calling together all the galley slaves, who were now running riot, and had stripped the commissary to the skin, he collected them round him to hear what he had to say, and addressed them as follows: "To be grateful for benefits received is the part of persons of good birth, and one of the sins most offensive to God is

2875

ingratitude; I say so because, sirs, ye have already seen by manifest proof the benefit ye have received of me; in return for which I desire, and it is my good pleasure that, laden with that chain which I have taken off your necks, ye at once set out and proceed to the city of El Toboso, and there present yourselves before the lady Dulcinea del Toboso, and say to her that her knight, he of the Rueful Countenance, sends to commend himself to her; and that ye recount to her in full detail all the particulars of this notable adventure, up to the recovery of your longed-for liberty; and this done ye may go where ye will, and good fortune attend you."

2880

2885

2890

Gines de Pasamonte made answer for all, saying, "That which you, sir, our deliverer, demand of us, is of all impossibilities the most impossible to comply with, because we cannot go together along the roads, but only singly and separate, and each one his own way, endeavouring to hide ourselves in the bowels of the earth to escape the Holy Brotherhood, which, no doubt, will come out in search of us. What your worship may do, and fairly do, is to change this service and tribute as regards the lady Dulcinea del Toboso for a certain quantity of *ave-marias* and *credos* which we will say for your worship's intention, and this is a condition that can be complied with by night as by day, running or resting, in peace or in war; but to imagine that we are going now to return to the flesh-pots of Egypt, I mean to take up our chain and set out for El Toboso, is to imagine that it is now night, though it is not yet ten in the morning, and to ask this of us is like asking pears of the elm tree."

2895

"Then by all that's good," said Don Quixote (now stirred to wrath), "Don son of a bitch, Don Ginesillo de Paropillo, or whatever your name is, you will have to go yourself alone, with your tail between your legs and the whole chain on your back."

2900

2905

2910

Pasamonte, who was anything but meek (being by this time thoroughly convinced that Don Quixote was not quite right in his head as he had committed such a vagary as to set them free), finding himself abused in this fashion, gave the wink to his companions, and falling back they began to shower stones on Don Quixote at such a rate that he was quite unable to protect himself with his buckler, and poor Rocinante no more heeded the spur than if he had been made of brass. Sancho planted himself behind his ass, and with him sheltered himself from the hailstorm that poured on both of them. Don Quixote was unable to shield himself so well but that more pebbles than I could count struck him full on the body with such force that they brought him to the ground; and the instant he fell the student pounced upon him, snatched the basin from his head, and with it struck three or four blows on his shoulders, and as many more on the ground, knocking it almost to pieces. They then stripped him of a jacket that he wore over his armour, and they would have stripped off his stockings if his greaves had not prevented them. From Sancho they took his coat, leaving him in his shirt-sleeves; and dividing among themselves the remaining spoils of the battle, they went each one his own way, more solicitous about keeping clear of the Holy Brotherhood they dreaded, than about burdening themselves with the chain, or going to present themselves

2915   before the lady Dulcinea del Toboso. The ass and Rocinante, Sancho and Don Quixote, were all that were left upon the spot; the ass with drooping head, serious, shaking his ears from time to time as if he thought the storm of stones that assailed them was not yet over; Rocinante stretched beside his master, for he too had been brought to the ground by a stone; Sancho stripped, and trembling with

2920   fear of the Holy Brotherhood; and Don Quixote fuming to find himself so served by the very persons for whom he had done so much.

* * * * *

FROM CHAPTER LII: OF THE QUARREL THAT DON QUIXOTE HAD WITH THE GOATHERD, TOGETHER WITH THE RARE ADVENTURE OF THE PENITENTS, WHICH WITH AN EXPENDITURE OF SWEAT HE BROUGHT TO A HAPPY CONCLUSION

   The goatherd's tale gave great satisfaction to all the hearers, and the canon especially enjoyed it, for he had remarked with particular attention the manner in which it had been told, which was as unlike the manner of a clownish goatherd as

2925   it was like that of a polished city wit; and he observed that the curate had been quite right in saying that the woods bred men of learning. They all offered their services to Eugenio but he who showed himself most liberal in this way was Don Quixote, who said to him, "Most assuredly, brother goatherd, if I found myself in a position to attempt any adventure, I would, this very instant, set out on your

2930   behalf, and would rescue Leandra from that convent (where no doubt she is kept against her will), in spite of the abbess and all who might try to prevent me, and would place her in your hands to deal with her according to your will and pleasure, observing, however, the laws of chivalry which lay down that no violence of any kind is to be offered to any damsel. But I trust in God our Lord

2935   that the might of one malignant enchanter may not prove so great but that the power of another better disposed may prove superior to it, and then I promise you my support and assistance, as I am bound to do by my profession, which is none other than to give aid to the weak and needy."

   The goatherd eyed him, and noticing Don Quixote's sorry appearance and

2940   looks, he was filled with wonder, and asked the barber, who was next him, "Señor, who is this man who makes such a figure and talks in such a strain?"

   "Who should it be," said the barber, "but the famous Don Quixote of La Mancha, the undoer of injustice, the righter of wrongs, the protector of damsels, the terror of giants, and the winner of battles?"

2945   "That," said the goatherd, "sounds like what one reads in the books of the knights-errant, who did all that you say this man does; though it is my belief that either you are joking, or else this gentleman has empty lodgings in his head."

   "You are a great scoundrel," said Don Quixote, "and it is you who are empty and a fool. I am fuller than ever was the whoreson bitch that bore you;" and

2950   passing from words to deeds, he caught up a loaf that was near him and sent it full in the goatherd's face, with such force that he flattened his nose; but the goatherd, who did not understand jokes, and found himself roughly handled in such good earnest, paying no respect to carpet, tablecloth, or diners, sprang upon Don Quixote, and seizing him by the throat with both hands would no doubt have throttled him, had not Sancho Panza that instant come to the rescue, and grasping him by the shoulders flung him down on the table, smashing plates, breaking glasses, and upsetting and scattering everything on it. Don Quixote, finding himself free, strove to get on top of the goatherd, who, with his face covered with blood, and soundly kicked by Sancho, was on all fours feeling about for one of the table-knives to take a bloody revenge with. The canon and the curate, however, prevented him, but the barber so contrived it that he got Don Quixote under him, and rained down upon him such a shower of fisticuffs that the poor knight's face streamed with blood as freely as his own. The canon and the curate were bursting with laughter, the officers were capering with delight, and both the one and the other hissed them on as they do dogs that are worrying one another in a fight. Sancho alone was frantic, for he could not free himself from the grasp of one of the canon's servants, who kept him from going to his master's assistance.

At last, while they were all, with the exception of the two bruisers who were mauling each other, in high glee and enjoyment, they heard a trumpet sound a note so doleful that it made them all look in the direction whence the sound seemed to come. But the one that was most excited by hearing it was Don Quixote, who though sorely against his will he was under the goatherd, and something more than pretty well pummelled, said to him, "Brother devil (for it is impossible but that thou must be one since thou hast had might and strength enough to overcome mine), I ask thee to agree to a truce for but one hour for the solemn note of yonder trumpet that falls on our ears seems to me to summon me to some new adventure." The goatherd, who was by this time tired of pummelling and being pummelled, released him at once, and Don Quixote rising to his feet and turning his eyes to the quarter where the sound had been heard, suddenly saw coming down the slope of a hill several men clad in white like penitents.

The fact was that the clouds had that year withheld their moisture from the earth, and in all the villages of the district they were organising processions, rogations, and penances, imploring God to open the hands of his mercy and send the rain; and to this end the people of a village that was hard by were going in procession to a holy hermitage there was on one side of that valley. Don Quixote when he saw the strange garb of the penitents, without reflecting how often he had seen it before, took it into his head that this was a case of adventure, and that it fell to him alone as a knight-errant to engage in it; and he was all the more confirmed in this notion, by the idea that an image draped in black they had with them was some illustrious lady that these villains and discourteous thieves were carrying off by force. As soon as this occurred to him he ran with all speed to Rocinante who was grazing at large, and taking the bridle and the buckler from the saddle-bow, he had him bridled in an instant, and calling to Sancho for his sword he mounted Rocinante, braced his buckler on his arm, and in a loud voice

2995 exclaimed to those who stood by, "Now, noble company, ye shall see how important it is that there should be knights in the world professing the order of knight-errantry; now, I say, ye shall see, by the deliverance of that worthy lady who is borne captive there, whether knights-errant deserve to be held in estimation," and so saying he brought his legs to bear on Rocinante—for he had no

3000 spurs—and at a full canter (for in all this veracious history we never read of Rocinante fairly galloping) set off to encounter the penitents, though the curate, the canon, and the barber ran to prevent him. But it was out of their power, nor did he even stop for the shouts of Sancho calling after him, "Where are you going, Señor Don Quixote? What devils have possessed you to set you on against our Catholic

3005 faith? Plague take me! mind, that is a procession of penitents, and the lady they are carrying on that stand there is the blessed image of the immaculate Virgin. Take care what you are doing, señor, for this time it may be safely said you don't know what you are about."

Sancho laboured in vain, for his master was so bent on coming to quarters

3010 with these sheeted figures and releasing the lady in black that he did not hear a word; and even had he heard, he would not have turned back if the king had ordered him. He came up with the procession and reined in Rocinante, who was already anxious enough to slacken speed a little, and in a hoarse, excited voice he exclaimed, "You who hide your faces, perhaps because you are not good subjects,

3015 pay attention and listen to what I am about to say to you." The first to halt were those who were carrying the image, and one of the four ecclesiastics who were chanting the Litany, struck by the strange figure of Don Quixote, the leanness of Rocinante, and the other ludicrous peculiarities he observed, said in reply to him, "Brother, if you have anything to say to us say it quickly, for these brethren are

3020 whipping themselves, and we cannot stop, nor is it reasonable we should stop to hear anything, unless indeed it is short enough to be said in two words."

"I will say it in one," replied Don Quixote, "and it is this; that at once, this very instant, ye release that fair lady whose tears and sad aspect show plainly that ye are carrying her off against her will, and that ye have committed some

3025 scandalous outrage against her; and I, who was born into the world to redress all such like wrongs, will not permit you to advance another step until you have restored to her the liberty she pines for and deserves."

From these words all the hearers concluded that he must be a madman, and began to laugh heartily, and their laughter acted like gunpowder on Don

3030 Quixote's fury, for drawing his sword without another word he made a rush at the stand. One of those who supported it, leaving the burden to his comrades, advanced to meet him, flourishing a forked stick that he had for propping up the stand when resting, and with this he caught a mighty cut Don Quixote made at him that severed it in two; but with the portion that remained in his hand he dealt such

3035 a thwack on the shoulder of Don Quixote's sword arm (which the buckler could not protect against the clownish assault) that poor Don Quixote came to the ground in a sad plight.

Sancho Panza, who was coming on close behind puffing and blowing, seeing him fall, cried out to his assailant not to strike him again, for he was poor
3040   enchanted knight, who had never harmed anyone all the days of his life; but what checked the clown was, not Sancho's shouting, but seeing that Don Quixote did not stir hand or foot; and so, fancying he had killed him, he hastily hitched up his tunic under his girdle and took to his heels across the country like a deer.

By this time all Don Quixote's companions had come up to where he lay; but
3045   the processionists seeing them come running, and with them the officers of the Brotherhood with their crossbows, apprehended mischief, and clustering round the image, raised their hoods, and grasped their scourges, as the priests did their tapers, and awaited the attack, resolved to defend themselves and even to take the offensive against their assailants if they could. Fortune, however, arranged the
3050   matter better than they expected, for all Sancho did was to fling himself on his master's body, raising over him the most doleful and laughable lamentation that ever was heard, for he believed he was dead.

The curate was known to another curate who walked in the procession, and their recognition of one another set at rest the apprehensions of both parties; the
3055   first then told the other in two words who Don Quixote was, and he and the whole troop of penitents went to see if the poor gentleman was dead, and heard Sancho Panza saying, with tears in his eyes, "Oh flower of chivalry, that with one blow of a stick hast ended the course of thy well-spent life! Oh pride of thy race, honour and glory of all La Mancha, nay, of all the world, that for want of
3060   thee will be full of evil-doers, no longer in fear of punishment for their misdeeds! Oh thou, generous above all the Alexanders, since for only eight months of service thou hast given me the best island the sea girds or surrounds! Humble with the proud, haughty with the humble, encounterer of dangers, endurer of outrages, enamoured without reason, imitator of the good, scourge of the wicked, enemy of
3065   the mean, in short, knight-errant, which is all that can be said!"

At the cries and moans of Sancho, Don Quixote came to himself, and the first word he said was, "He who lives separated from you, sweetest Dulcinea, has greater miseries to endure than these. Aid me, friend Sancho, to mount the enchanted cart, for I am not in a condition to press the saddle of Rocinante, as this
3070   shoulder is all knocked to pieces."

"That I will do with all my heart, señor," said Sancho; "and let us return to our village with these gentlemen, who seek your good, and there we will prepare for making another sally, which may turn out more profitable and creditable to us."

3075   "Thou art right, Sancho," returned Don Quixote; "It will be wise to let the malign influence of the stars which now prevails pass off."

The canon, the curate, and the barber told him he would act very wisely in doing as he said; and so, highly amused at Sancho Panza's simplicities, they placed Don Quixote in the cart as before. The procession once more formed itself in order
3080   and proceeded on its road; the goatherd took his leave of the party; the officers of the Brotherhood declined to go any farther, and the curate paid them what was

due to them; the canon begged the curate to let him know how Don Quixote did, whether he was cured of his madness or still suffered from it, and then begged leave to continue his journey; in short, they all separated and went their ways,
3085 leaving to themselves the curate and the barber, Don Quixote, Sancho Panza, and the good Rocinante, who regarded everything with as great resignation as his master. The carter yoked his oxen and made Don Quixote comfortable on a truss of hay, and at his usual deliberate pace took the road the curate directed, and at the end of six days they reached Don Quixote's village, and entered it about the
3090 middle of the day, which it so happened was a Sunday, and the people were all in the plaza, through which Don Quixote's cart passed. They all flocked to see what was in the cart, and when they recognised their townsman they were filled with amazement, and a boy ran off to bring the news to his housekeeper and his niece that their master and uncle had come back all lean and yellow and stretched on a
3095 truss of hay on an ox-cart. It was piteous to hear the cries the two good ladies raised, how they beat their breasts and poured out fresh maledictions on those accursed books of chivalry; all which was renewed when they saw Don Quixote coming in at the gate.
At the news of Don Quixote's arrival Sancho Panza's wife came running, for
3100 she by this time knew that her husband had gone away with him as his squire, and on seeing Sancho, the first thing she asked him was if the ass was well. Sancho replied that he was, better than his master was.
"Thanks be to God," said she, "for being so good to me; but now tell me, my friend, what have you made by your squirings? What gown have you brought me
3105 back? What shoes for your children?"
"I bring nothing of that sort, wife," said Sancho; "though I bring other things of more consequence and value."
"I am very glad of that," returned his wife; "show me these things of more value and consequence, my friend; for I want to see them to cheer my heart that has
3110 been so sad and heavy all these ages that you have been away."
"I will show them to you at home, wife," said Sancho; "be content for the present; for if it please God that we should again go on our travels in search of adventures, you will soon see me a count, or governor of an island, and that not one of those everyday ones, but the best that is to be had."
3115 "Heaven grant it, husband," said she, "for indeed we have need of it. But tell me, what's this about islands, for I don't understand it?"
"Honey is not for the mouth of the ass," returned Sancho; "all in good time thou shalt see, wife—nay, thou wilt be surprised to hear thyself called 'your ladyship' by all thy vassals."
3120 "What are you talking about, Sancho, with your ladyships, islands, and vassals?" returned Teresa Panza—for so Sancho's wife was called, though they were not relations, for in La Mancha it is customary for wives to take their husbands' surnames.
"Don't be in such a hurry to know all this, Teresa," said Sancho; "it is
3125 enough that I am telling you the truth, so shut your mouth. But I may tell you this

much by the way, that there is nothing in the world more delightful than to be a person of consideration, squire to a knight-errant, and a seeker of adventures. To be sure most of those one finds do not end as pleasantly as one could wish, for out of a hundred, ninety-nine will turn out cross and contrary. I know it by

3130   experience, for out of some I came blanketed, and out of others belaboured. Still, for all that, it is a fine thing to be on the look-out for what may happen, crossing mountains, searching woods, climbing rocks, visiting castles, putting up at inns, all at free quarters, and devil take the maravedi to pay."

While this conversation passed between Sancho Panza and his wife, Don

3135   Quixote's housekeeper and niece took him in and undressed him and laid him in his old bed. He eyed them askance, and could not make out where he was. The curate charged his niece to be very careful to make her uncle comfortable and to keep a watch over him lest he should make his escape from them again, telling her what they had been obliged to do to bring him home. On this the pair once more

3140   lifted up their voices and renewed their maledictions upon the books of chivalry, and implored heaven to plunge the authors of such lies and nonsense into the midst of the bottomless pit. They were, in short, kept in anxiety and dread lest their uncle and master should give them the slip the moment he found himself somewhat better, and as they feared so it fell out.

* * * * *

PART II. CHAPTER III: OF THE LAUGHABLE CONVERSATION THAT PASSED BETWEEN DON QUIXOTE, SANCHO PANZA, AND THE BACHELOR SAMSON CARRASCO

3145   Don Quixote remained very deep in thought, waiting for the bachelor Carrasco, from whom he was to hear how he himself had been put into a book as Sancho said; and he could not persuade himself that any such history could be in existence, for the blood of the enemies he had slain was not yet dry on the blade of his sword, and now they wanted to make out that his mighty achievements were

3150   going about in print. For all that, he fancied some sage, either a friend or an enemy, might, by the aid of magic, have given them to the press; if a friend, in order to magnify and exalt them above the most famous ever achieved by any knight-errant; if an enemy, to bring them to naught and degrade them below the meanest ever recorded of any low squire, though as he said to himself, the achievements of

3155   squires never were recorded. If, however, it were the fact that such a history were in existence, it must necessarily, being the story of a knight-errant, be grandiloquent, lofty, imposing, grand and true. With this he comforted himself somewhat, though it made him uncomfortable to think that the author was a Moor, judging by the title of "Cide;" and that no truth was to be looked for from Moors,

3160   as they are all impostors, cheats, and schemers. He was afraid he might have dealt with his love affairs in some indecorous fashion, that might tend to the discredit and prejudice of the purity of his lady Dulcinea del Toboso; he would have had

him set forth the fidelity and respect he had always observed towards her, spurning queens, empresses, and damsels of all sorts, and keeping in check the
3165   impetuosity of his natural impulses. Absorbed and wrapped up in these and divers other cogitations, he was found by Sancho and Carrasco, whom Don Quixote received with great courtesy.

    The bachelor, though he was called Samson, was of no great bodily size, but he was a very great wag; he was of a sallow complexion, but very sharp-witted,
3170   somewhere about four-and-twenty years of age, with a round face, a flat nose, and a large mouth, all indications of a mischievous disposition and a love of fun and jokes; and of this he gave a sample as soon as he saw Don Quixote, by falling on his knees before him and saying, "Let me kiss your mightiness's hand, Señor Don Quixote of La Mancha, for, by the habit of St. Peter that I wear, though I have no
3175   more than the first four orders, your worship is one of the most famous knights-errant that have ever been, or will be, all the world over. A blessing on Cide Hamete Benengeli, who has written the history of your great deeds, and a double blessing on that connoisseur who took the trouble of having it translated out of the Arabic into our Castilian vulgar tongue for the universal entertainment of the
3180   people!"

    Don Quixote made him rise, and said, "So, then, it is true that there is a history of me, and that it was a Moor and a sage who wrote it?"

    "So true is it, señor," said Samson, "that my belief is there are more than twelve thousand volumes of the said history in print this very day. Only ask
3185   Portugal, Barcelona, and Valencia, where they have been printed, and moreover there is a report that it is being printed at Antwerp, and I am persuaded there will not be a country or language in which there will not be a translation of it."

    "One of the things," here observed Don Quixote, "that ought to give most pleasure to a virtuous and eminent man is to find himself in his lifetime in print
3190   and in type, familiar in people's mouths with a good name; I say with a good name, for if it be the opposite, then there is no death to be compared to it."

    "If it goes by good name and fame," said the bachelor, "your worship alone bears away the palm from all the knights-errant; for the Moor in his own language, and the Christian in his, have taken care to set before us your gallantry,
3195   your high courage in encountering dangers, your fortitude in adversity, your patience under misfortunes as well as wounds, the purity and continence of the platonic loves of your worship and my lady Dona Dulcinea del Toboso—"

    "I never heard my lady Dulcinea called Dona," observed Sancho here; "nothing more than the lady Dulcinea del Toboso; so here already the history is
3200   wrong."

    "That is not an objection of any importance," replied Carrasco.

    "Certainly not," said Don Quixote; "but tell me, señor bachelor, what deeds of mine are they that are made most of in this history?"

    "On that point," replied the bachelor, "opinions differ, as tastes do; some
3205   swear by the adventure of the windmills that your worship took to be Briareuses and giants; others by that of the fulling mills; one cries up the description of the

two armies that afterwards took the appearance of two droves of sheep; another that of the dead body on its way to be buried at Segovia; a third says the liberation of the galley slaves is the best of all, and a fourth that nothing comes up

3210 to the affair with the Benedictine giants, and the battle with the valiant Biscayan."

"Tell me, señor bachelor," said Sancho at this point, "does the adventure with the Yanguesans come in, when our good Rocinante went hankering after dainties?"

3215 "The sage has left nothing in the ink-bottle," replied Samson; "he tells all and sets down everything, even to the capers that worthy Sancho cut in the blanket."

"I cut no capers in the blanket," returned Sancho; "in the air I did, and more of them than I liked."

"There is no human history in the world, I suppose," said Don Quixote, "that

3220 has not its ups and downs, but more than others such as deal with chivalry, for they can never be entirely made up of prosperous adventures."

"For all that," replied the bachelor, "there are those who have read the history who say they would have been glad if the author had left out some of the countless cudgellings that were inflicted on Señor Don Quixote in various

3225 encounters."

"That's where the truth of the history comes in," said Sancho.

"At the same time they might fairly have passed them over in silence," observed Don Quixote; "for there is no need of recording events which do not change or affect the truth of a history, if they tend to bring the hero of it into

3230 contempt. Aeneas was not in truth and earnest so pious as Virgil represents him, nor Ulysses so wise as Homer describes him."

"That is true," said Samson; "but it is one thing to write as a poet, another to write as a historian; the poet may describe or sing things, not as they were, but as they ought to have been; but the historian has to write them down, not as they

3235 ought to have been, but as they were, without adding anything to the truth or taking anything from it."

"Well then," said Sancho, "if this señor Moor goes in for telling the truth, no doubt among my master's drubbings mine are to be found; for they never took the measure of his worship's shoulders without doing the same for my whole body;

3240 but I have no right to wonder at that, for, as my master himself says, the members must share the pain of the head."

"You are a sly dog, Sancho," said Don Quixote; "in faith, you have no want of memory when you choose to remember."

"If I were to try to forget the thwacks they gave me," said Sancho, "my weals

3245 [welts] would not let me, for they are still fresh on my ribs."

"Hush, Sancho," said Don Quixote, "and don't interrupt the bachelor, whom I entreat to go on and tell all that is said about me in this history."

"And about me," said Sancho, "for they say, too, that I am one of the principal presonages in it."

3250 "Personages, not presonages, friend Sancho," said Samson.

"What! Another word-catcher!" said Sancho; "if that's to be the way we shall not make an end in a lifetime."

"May God shorten mine, Sancho," returned the bachelor, "if you are not the second person in the history, and there are even some who would rather hear you talk than the cleverest in the whole book; though there are some, too, who say you showed yourself over-credulous in believing there was any possibility in the government of that island offered you by Señor Don Quixote."

"There is still sunshine on the wall," said Don Quixote; "and when Sancho is somewhat more advanced in life, with the experience that years bring, he will be fitter and better qualified for being a governor than he is at present."

"By God, master," said Sancho, "the island that I cannot govern with the years I have, I'll not be able to govern with the years of Methuselah; the difficulty is that the said island keeps its distance somewhere, I know not where; and not that there is any want of head in me to govern it."

"Leave it to God, Sancho," said Don Quixote, "for all will be and perhaps better than you think; no leaf on the tree stirs but by God's will."

"That is true," said Samson; "and if it be God's will, there will not be any want of a thousand islands, much less one, for Sancho to govern."

"I have seen governors in these parts," said Sancho, "that are not to be compared to my shoe-sole; and for all that they are called 'your lordship' and served on silver."

"Those are not governors of islands," observed Samson, "but of other governments of an easier kind: those that govern islands must at least know grammar."

"I could manage the gram well enough," said Sancho; "but for the mar I have neither leaning nor liking, for I don't know what it is; but leaving this matter of the government in God's hands, to send me wherever it may be most to his service, I may tell you, señor bachelor Samson Carrasco, it has pleased me beyond measure that the author of this history should have spoken of me in such a way that what is said of me gives no offence; for, on the faith of a true squire, if he had said anything about me that was at all unbecoming an old Christian, such as I am, the deaf would have heard of it."

"That would be working miracles," said Samson.

"Miracles or no miracles," said Sancho, "let everyone mind how he speaks or writes about people, and not set down at random the first thing that comes into his head."

"One of the faults they find with this history," said the bachelor, "is that its author inserted in it a novel called 'The Ill-advised Curiosity;' not that it is bad or ill-told, but that it is out of place and has nothing to do with the history of his worship Señor Don Quixote."

"I will bet the son of a dog has mixed the cabbages and the baskets," said Sancho.

"Then, I say," said Don Quixote, "the author of my history was no sage, but some ignorant chatterer, who, in a haphazard and heedless way, set about writing

3295   it, let it turn out as it might, just as Orbaneja, the painter of Ubeda, used to do, who, when they asked him what he was painting, answered, 'What it may turn out.' Sometimes he would paint a cock in such a fashion, and so unlike, that he had to write alongside of it in Gothic letters, 'This is a cock;' and so it will be with my history, which will require a commentary to make it intelligible."

3300   "No fear of that," returned Samson, "for it is so plain that there is nothing in it to puzzle over; the children turn its leaves, the young people read it, the grown men understand it, the old folk praise it; in a word, it is so thumbed, and read, and got by heart by people of all sorts, that the instant they see any lean hack, they say, 'There goes Rocinante.' And those that are most given to reading it are the

3305   pages, for there is not a lord's ante-chamber where there is not a 'Don Quixote' to be found; one takes it up if another lays it down; this one pounces upon it, and that begs for it. In short, the said history is the most delightful and least injurious entertainment that has been hitherto seen, for there is not to be found in the whole of it even the semblance of an immodest word, or a thought that is other than

3310   Catholic."

    "To write in any other way," said Don Quixote, "would not be to write truth, but falsehood, and historians who have recourse to falsehood ought to be burned, like those who coin false money; and I know not what could have led the author to have recourse to novels and irrelevant stories, when he had so much to

3315   write about in mine; no doubt he must have gone by the proverb 'with straw or with hay, &c.,' for by merely setting forth my thoughts, my sighs, my tears, my lofty purposes, my enterprises, he might have made a volume as large, or larger than all the works of El Tostado would make up. In fact, the conclusion I arrive at, señor bachelor, is, that to write histories, or books of any kind, there is need of great

3320   judgment and a ripe understanding. To give expression to humour, and write in a strain of graceful pleasantry, is the gift of great geniuses. The cleverest character in comedy is the clown, for he who would make people take him for a fool, must not be one. History is in a measure a sacred thing, for it should be true, and where the truth is, there God is; but notwithstanding this, there are some who write and

3325   fling books broadcast on the world as if they were fritters."

    "There is no book so bad but it has something good in it," said the bachelor.

    "No doubt of that," replied Don Quixote; "but it often happens that those who have acquired and attained a well-deserved reputation by their writings, lose it entirely, or damage it in some degree, when they give them to the press."

3330   "The reason of that," said Samson, "is, that as printed works are examined leisurely, their faults are easily seen; and the greater the fame of the writer, the more closely are they scrutinised. Men famous for their genius, great poets, illustrious historians, are always, or most commonly, envied by those who take a particular delight and pleasure in criticising the writings of others, without

3335   having produced any of their own."

    "That is no wonder," said Don Quixote; "for there are many divines who are no good for the pulpit, but excellent in detecting the defects or excesses of those who preach."

"All that is true, Señor Don Quixote," said Carrasco; "but I wish such fault-
3340   finders were more lenient and less exacting, and did not pay so much attention to
the spots on the bright sun of the work they grumble at; for if *aliquando bonus
dormitat Homerus*,[5] they should remember how long he remained awake to shed the
light of his work with as little shade as possible; and perhaps it may be that what
they find fault with may be moles, that sometimes heighten the beauty of the face
3345   that bears them; and so I say very great is the risk to which he who prints a book
exposes himself, for of all impossibilities the greatest is to write one that will
satisfy and please all readers."

"That which treats of me must have pleased few," said Don Quixote.

"Quite the contrary," said the bachelor; "for, as stultorum infinitum est
3350   numerus, innumerable are those who have relished the said history; but some have
brought a charge against the author's memory, inasmuch as he forgot to say who
the thief was who stole Sancho's Dapple; for it is not stated there, but only to be
inferred from what is set down, that he was stolen, and a little farther on we see
Sancho mounted on the same ass, without any reappearance of it. They say, too,
3355   that he forgot to state what Sancho did with those hundred crowns that he found
in the valise in the Sierra Morena, as he never alludes to them again, and there are
many who would be glad to know what he did with them, or what he spent them
on, for it is one of the serious omissions of the work."

"Señor Samson, I am not in a humour now for going into accounts or
3360   explanations," said Sancho; "for there's a sinking of the stomach come over me,
and unless I doctor it with a couple of sups of the old stuff it will put me on the
thorn of Santa Lucia. I have it at home, and my old woman is waiting for me; after
dinner I'll come back, and will answer you and all the world every question you
may choose to ask, as well about the loss of the ass as about the spending of the
3365   hundred crowns;" and without another word or waiting for a reply he made off
home.

Don Quixote begged and entreated the bachelor to stay and do penance with
him. The bachelor accepted the invitation and remained, a couple of young pigeons
were added to the ordinary fare, at dinner they talked chivalry, Carrasco fell in
3370   with his host's humour, the banquet came to an end, they took their afternoon
sleep, Sancho returned, and their conversation was resumed.

* * * * *

CHAPTER XII: OF THE STRANGE ADVENTURE WHICH BEFELL THE VALIANT DON QUIXOTE WITH THE BOLD KNIGHT OF THE MIRRORS

The night succeeding the day of the encounter with Death, Don Quixote and
his squire passed under some tall shady trees, and Don Quixote at Sancho's
persuasion ate a little from the store carried by Dapple, and over their supper

---

[5]"worthy Homer sometimes nods"

3375　Sancho said to his master, "Señor, what a fool I should have looked if I had chosen for my reward the spoils of the first adventure your worship achieved, instead of the foals of the three mares. After all, 'a sparrow in the hand is better than a vulture on the wing.'"

"At the same time, Sancho," replied Don Quixote, "if thou hadst let me attack
3380　them as I wanted, at the very least the emperor's gold crown and Cupid's painted wings would have fallen to thee as spoils, for I should have taken them by force and given them into thy hands."

"The sceptres and crowns of those play-actor emperors," said Sancho, "were never yet pure gold, but only brass foil or tin."
3385　"That is true," said Don Quixote, "for it would not be right that the accessories of the drama should be real, instead of being mere fictions and semblances, like the drama itself; towards which, Sancho—and, as a necessary consequence, towards those who represent and produce it—I would that thou wert favourably disposed, for they are all instruments of great good to the State,
3390　placing before us at every step a mirror in which we may see vividly displayed what goes on in human life; nor is there any similitude that shows us more faithfully what we are and ought to be than the play and the players. Come, tell me, hast thou not seen a play acted in which kings, emperors, pontiffs, knights, ladies, and divers other personages were introduced? One plays the villain,
3395　another the knave, this one the merchant, that the soldier, one the sharp-witted fool, another the foolish lover; and when the play is over, and they have put off the dresses they wore in it, all the actors become equal."

"Yes, I have seen that," said Sancho.

"Well then," said Don Quixote, "the same thing happens in the comedy and
3400　life of this world, where some play emperors, others popes, and, in short, all the characters that can be brought into a play; but when it is over, that is to say when life ends, death strips them all of the garments that distinguish one from the other, and all are equal in the grave."

"A fine comparison!" said Sancho; "though not so new but that I have heard
3405　it many and many a time, as well as that other one of the game of chess; how, so long as the game lasts, each piece has its own particular office, and when the game is finished they are all mixed, jumbled up and shaken together, and stowed away in the bag, which is much like ending life in the grave."

"Thou art growing less doltish and more shrewd every day, Sancho," said
3410　Don Quixote.

"Ay," said Sancho; "it must be that some of your worship's shrewdness sticks to me; land that, of itself, is barren and dry, will come to yield good fruit if you dung it and till it; what I mean is that your worship's conversation has been the dung that has fallen on the barren soil of my dry wit, and the time I have been
3415　in your service and society has been the tillage; and with the help of this I hope to yield fruit in abundance that will not fall away or slide from those paths of good breeding that your worship has made in my parched understanding."

Don Quixote laughed at Sancho's affected phraseology, and perceived that what he said about his improvement was true, for now and then he spoke in a way that surprised him; though always, or mostly, when Sancho tried to talk fine and attempted polite language, he wound up by toppling over from the summit of his simplicity into the abyss of his ignorance; and where he showed his culture and his memory to the greatest advantage was in dragging in proverbs, no matter whether they had any bearing or not upon the subject in hand, as may have been seen already and will be noticed in the course of this history.

In conversation of this kind they passed a good part of the night, but Sancho felt a desire to let down the curtains of his eyes, as he used to say when he wanted to go to sleep; and stripping Dapple he left him at liberty to graze his fill. He did not remove Rocinante's saddle, as his master's express orders were, that so long as they were in the field or not sleeping under a roof Rocinante was not to be stripped—the ancient usage established and observed by knights-errant being to take off the bridle and hang it on the saddle-bow, but to remove the saddle from the horse—never! Sancho acted accordingly, and gave him the same liberty he had given Dapple, between whom and Rocinante there was a friendship so unequalled and so strong, that it is handed down by tradition from father to son, that the author of this veracious history devoted some special chapters to it, which, in order to preserve the propriety and decorum due to a history so heroic, he did not insert therein; although at times he forgets this resolution of his and describes how eagerly the two beasts would scratch one another when they were together and how, when they were tired or full, Rocinante would lay his neck across Dapple's, stretching half a yard or more on the other side, and the pair would stand thus, gazing thoughtfully on the ground, for three days, or at least so long as they were left alone, or hunger did not drive them to go and look for food. I may add that they say the author left it on record that he likened their friendship to that of Nisus and Euryalus, and Pylades and Orestes; and if that be so, it may be perceived, to the admiration of mankind how firm the friendship must have been between these two peaceful animals, shaming men, who preserve friendships with one another so badly. This was why it was said—

'For friend no longer is there friend;
The reeds turn lances now.'

And some one else has sung—

'Friend to friend the bug, &c.'

And let no one fancy that the author was at all astray when he compared the friendship of these animals to that of men; for men have received many lessons from beasts, and learned many important things, as, for example, the clyster [enema] from the stork, vomit and gratitude from the dog, watchfulness from the crane, foresight from the ant, modesty from the elephant, and loyalty from the horse.

Sancho at last fell asleep at the foot of a cork tree, while Don Quixote dozed at that of a sturdy oak; but a short time only had elapsed when a noise he heard behind him awoke him, and rising up startled, he listened and looked in the direction the noise came from, and perceived two men on horseback, one of whom,

letting himself drop from the saddle, said to the other, "Dismount, my friend, and take the bridles off the horses, for, so far as I can see, this place will furnish grass for them, and the solitude and silence my love-sick thoughts need of." As he said
3465 this he stretched himself upon the ground, and as he flung himself down, the armour in which he was clad rattled, whereby Don Quixote perceived that he must be a knight-errant; and going over to Sancho, who was asleep, he shook him by the arm and with no small difficulty brought him back to his senses, and said in a low voice to him, "Brother Sancho, we have got an adventure."

3470 "God send us a good one," said Sancho; "and where may her ladyship the adventure be?"

"Where, Sancho?" replied Don Quixote; "turn thine eyes and look, and thou wilt see stretched there a knight-errant, who, it strikes me, is not over and above happy, for I saw him fling himself off his horse and throw himself on the ground
3475 with a certain air of dejection, and his armour rattled as he fell."

"Well," said Sancho, "how does your worship make out that to be an adventure?"

"I do not mean to say," returned Don Quixote, "that it is a complete adventure, but that it is the beginning of one, for it is in this way adventures begin.
3480 But listen, for it seems he is tuning a lute or guitar, and from the way he is spitting and clearing his chest he must be getting ready to sing something."

"Faith, you are right," said Sancho, "and no doubt he is some enamoured knight."

"There is no knight-errant that is not," said Don Quixote; "but let us listen to
3485 him, for, if he sings, by that thread we shall extract the ball of his thoughts; because out of the abundance of the heart the mouth speaketh."

Sancho was about to reply to his master, but the Knight of the Grove's voice, which was neither very bad nor very good, stopped him, and listening attentively the pair heard him sing this

SONNET

3490   Your pleasure, prithee, lady mine, unfold;
    Declare the terms that I am to obey;
    My will to yours submissively I mould,
    And from your law my feet shall never stray.
    Would you I die, to silent grief a prey?
3495   Then count me even now as dead and cold;
    Would you I tell my woes in some new way?
    Then shall my tale by Love itself be told.
    The unison of opposites to prove,
    Of the soft wax and diamond hard am I;
3500   But still, obedient to the laws of love,
    Here, hard or soft, I offer you my breast,

Whate'er you grave or stamp thereon shall rest
Indelible for all eternity.

With an "Ah me!" that seemed to be drawn from the inmost recesses of his
3505　heart, the Knight of the Grove brought his lay to an end, and shortly afterwards
exclaimed in a melancholy and piteous voice, "O fairest and most ungrateful
woman on earth! What! can it be, most serene Casildea de Vandalia, that thou
wilt suffer this thy captive knight to waste away and perish in ceaseless
wanderings and rude and arduous toils? It is not enough that I have compelled all
3510　the knights of Navarre, all the Leonese, all the Tartesians, all the Castilians, and
finally all the knights of La Mancha, to confess thee the most beautiful in the
world?"

"Not so," said Don Quixote at this, "for I am of La Mancha, and I have never
confessed anything of the sort, nor could I nor should I confess a thing so much to
3515　the prejudice of my lady's beauty; thou seest how this knight is raving, Sancho. But
let us listen, perhaps he will tell us more about himself."

"That he will," returned Sancho, "for he seems in a mood to bewail himself
for a month at a stretch."

But this was not the case, for the Knight of the Grove, hearing voices near
3520　him, instead of continuing his lamentation, stood up and exclaimed in a distinct but
courteous tone, "Who goes there? What are you? Do you belong to the number of
the happy or of the miserable?"

"Of the miserable," answered Don Quixote.

"Then come to me," said he of the Grove, "and rest assured that it is to woe
3525　itself and affliction itself you come."

Don Quixote, finding himself answered in such a soft and courteous manner,
went over to him, and so did Sancho.

The doleful knight took Don Quixote by the arm, saying, "Sit down here, sir
knight; for, that you are one, and of those that profess knight-errantry, it is to me a
3530　sufficient proof to have found you in this place, where solitude and night, the
natural couch and proper retreat of knights-errant, keep you company."

To which Don made answer, "A knight I am of the profession you mention,
and though sorrows, misfortunes, and calamities have made my heart their abode,
the compassion I feel for the misfortunes of others has not been thereby banished
3535　from it. From what you have just now sung I gather that yours spring from love, I
mean from the love you bear that fair ingrate you named in your lament."

In the meantime, they had seated themselves together on the hard ground
peaceably and sociably, just as if, as soon as day broke, they were not going to
break one another's heads.

3540　"Are you, sir knight, in love perchance?" asked he of the Grove of Don
Quixote.

"By mischance I am," replied Don Quixote; "though the ills arising from well-
bestowed affections should be esteemed favours rather than misfortunes."

3545

"That is true," returned he of the Grove, "if scorn did not unsettle our reason and understanding, for if it be excessive it looks like revenge."

"I was never scorned by my lady," said Don Quixote.

"Certainly not," said Sancho, who stood close by, "for my lady is as a lamb, and softer than a roll of butter."

"Is this your squire?" asked he of the Grove.

3550

"He is," said Don Quixote.

"I never yet saw a squire," said he of the Grove, "who ventured to speak when his master was speaking; at least, there is mine, who is as big as his father, and it cannot be proved that he has ever opened his lips when I am speaking."

3555

"By my faith then," said Sancho, "I have spoken, and am fit to speak, in the presence of one as much, or even—but never mind—it only makes it worse to stir it."

The squire of the Grove took Sancho by the arm, saying to him, "Let us two go where we can talk in squire style as much as we please, and leave these gentlemen our masters to fight it out over the story of their loves; and, depend upon it,

3560

daybreak will find them at it without having made an end of it."

"So be it by all means," said Sancho; "and I will tell your worship who I am, that you may see whether I am to be reckoned among the number of the most talkative squires."

3565

With this the two squires withdrew to one side, and between them there passed a conversation as droll as that which passed between their masters was serious.

CHAPTER XIII: IN WHICH IS CONTINUED THE ADVENTURE OF THE KNIGHT OF THE GROVE, TOGETHER WITH THE SENSIBLE, ORIGINAL, AND TRANQUIL COLLOQUY THAT PASSED BETWEEN THE TWO SQUIRES

3570

The knights and the squires made two parties, these telling the story of their lives, the others the story of their loves; but the history relates first of all the conversation of the servants, and afterwards takes up that of the masters; and it says that, withdrawing a little from the others, he of the Grove said to Sancho, "A hard life it is we lead and live, señor, we that are squires to knights-errant; verily, we eat our bread in the sweat of our faces, which is one of the curses God laid on our first parents."

3575

"It may be said, too," added Sancho, "that we eat it in the chill of our bodies; for who gets more heat and cold than the miserable squires of knight-errantry? Even so it would not be so bad if we had something to eat, for woes are lighter if there's bread; but sometimes we go a day or two without breaking our fast, except with the wind that blows."

3580

"All that," said he of the Grove, "may be endured and put up with when we have hopes of reward; for, unless the knight-errant he serves is excessively unlucky, after a few turns the squire will at least find himself rewarded with a fine government of some island or some fair county."

"I," said Sancho, "have already told my master that I shall be content with the government of some island, and he is so noble and generous that he has promised it to me ever so many times."

"I," said he of the Grove, "shall be satisfied with a canonry for my services, and my master has already assigned me one."

"Your master," said Sancho, "no doubt is a knight in the Church line, and can bestow rewards of that sort on his good squire; but mine is only a layman; though I remember some clever, but, to my mind, designing people, strove to persuade him to try and become an archbishop. He, however, would not be anything but an emperor; but I was trembling all the time lest he should take a fancy to go into the Church, not finding myself fit to hold office in it; for I may tell you, though I seem a man, I am no better than a beast for the Church."

"Well, then, you are wrong there," said he of the Grove; "for those island governments are not all satisfactory; some are awkward, some are poor, some are dull, and, in short, the highest and choicest brings with it a heavy burden of cares and troubles which the unhappy wight [creature] to whose lot it has fallen bears upon his shoulders. Far better would it be for us who have adopted this accursed service to go back to our own houses, and there employ ourselves in pleasanter occupations—in hunting or fishing, for instance; for what squire in the world is there so poor as not to have a hack and a couple of greyhounds and a fishing rod to amuse himself with in his own village?"

"I am not in want of any of those things," said Sancho; "to be sure I have no hack, but I have an ass that is worth my master's horse twice over; God send me a bad Easter, and that the next one I am to see, if I would swap, even if I got four bushels of barley to boot. You will laugh at the value I put on my Dapple—for dapple is the colour of my beast. As to greyhounds, I can't want for them, for there are enough and to spare in my town; and, moreover, there is more pleasure in sport when it is at other people's expense."

"In truth and earnest, sir squire," said he of the Grove, "I have made up my mind and determined to have done with these drunken vagaries of these knights, and go back to my village, and bring up my children; for I have three, like three Oriental pearls."

"I have two," said Sancho, "that might be presented before the Pope himself, especially a girl whom I am breeding up for a countess, please God, though in spite of her mother."

"And how old is this lady that is being bred up for a countess?" asked he of the Grove.

"Fifteen, a couple of years more or less," answered Sancho; "but she is as tall as a lance, and as fresh as an April morning, and as strong as a porter."

"Those are gifts to fit her to be not only a countess but a nymph of the greenwood," said he of the Grove; "whoreson strumpet! what pith the rogue must have!"

3625   To which Sancho made answer, somewhat sulkily, "She's no strumpet, nor was her mother, nor will either of them be, please God, while I live; speak more civilly; for one bred up among knights-errant, who are courtesy itself, your words don't seem to me to be very becoming."

    "O how little you know about compliments, sir squire," returned he of the
3630   Grove. "What! don't you know that when a horseman delivers a good lance thrust at the bull in the plaza, or when anyone does anything very well, the people are wont to say, 'Ha, whoreson rip! how well he has done it!' and that what seems to be abuse in the expression is high praise? Disown sons and daughters, señor, who don't do what deserves that compliments of this sort should be paid to their
3635   parents."

    "I do disown them," replied Sancho, "and in this way, and by the same reasoning, you might call me and my children and my wife all the strumpets in the world, for all they do and say is of a kind that in the highest degree deserves the same praise; and to see them again I pray God to deliver me from mortal sin, or,
3640   what comes to the same thing, to deliver me from this perilous calling of squire into which I have fallen a second time, decayed and beguiled by a purse with a hundred ducats that I found one day in the heart of the Sierra Morena; and the devil is always putting a bag full of doubloons before my eyes, here, there, everywhere, until I fancy at every stop I am putting my hand on it, and hugging it, and carrying
3645   it home with me, and making investments, and getting interest, and living like a prince; and so long as I think of this I make light of all the hardships I endure with this simpleton of a master of mine, who, I well know, is more of a madman than a knight."

    "There's why they say that 'covetousness bursts the bag,'" said he of the
3650   Grove; "but if you come to talk of that sort, there is not a greater one in the world than my master, for he is one of those of whom they say, 'the cares of others kill the ass;' for, in order that another knight may recover the senses he has lost, he makes a madman of himself and goes looking for what, when found, may, for all I know, fly in his own face."

3655   "And is he in love perchance?" asked Sancho.

    "He is," said of the Grove, "with one Casildea de Vandalia, the rawest and best roasted lady the whole world could produce; but that rawness is not the only foot he limps on, for he has greater schemes rumbling in his bowels, as will be seen before many hours are over."

3660   "There's no road so smooth but it has some hole or hindrance in it," said Sancho; "in other houses they cook beans, but in mine it's by the potful; madness will have more followers and hangers-on than sound sense; but if there be any truth in the common saying, that to have companions in trouble gives some relief, I may take consolation from you, inasmuch as you serve a master as crazy as my
3665   own."

    "Crazy but valiant," replied he of the Grove, "and more roguish than crazy or valiant."

"Mine is not that," said Sancho; "I mean he has nothing of the rogue in him; on the contrary, he has the soul of a pitcher; he has no thought of doing harm to anyone, only good to all, nor has he any malice whatever in him; a child might persuade him that it is night at noonday; and for this simplicity I love him as the core of my heart, and I can't bring myself to leave him, let him do ever such foolish things."

"For all that, brother and señor," said he of the Grove, "if the blind lead the blind, both are in danger of falling into the pit. It is better for us to beat a quiet retreat and get back to our own quarters; for those who seek adventures don't always find good ones."

Sancho kept spitting from time to time, and his spittle seemed somewhat ropy and dry, observing which the compassionate squire of the Grove said, "It seems to me that with all this talk of ours our tongues are sticking to the roofs of our mouths; but I have a pretty good loosener hanging from the saddle-bow of my horse," and getting up he came back the next minute with a large *bota* of wine and a pasty half a yard across; and this is no exaggeration, for it was made of a house rabbit so big that Sancho, as he handled it, took it to be made of a goat, not to say a kid, and looking at it he said, "And do you carry this with you, señor?"

"Why, what are you thinking about?" said the other; "do you take me for some paltry squire? I carry a better larder on my horse's croup than a general takes with him when he goes on a march."

Sancho ate without requiring to be pressed, and in the dark bolted mouthfuls like the knots on a tether, and said he, "You are a proper trusty squire, one of the right sort, sumptuous and grand, as this banquet shows, which, if it has not come here by magic art, at any rate has the look of it; not like me, unlucky beggar, that have nothing more in my *alforjas* than a scrap of cheese, so hard that one might brain a giant with it, and, to keep it company, a few dozen carobs and as many more filberts and walnuts; thanks to the austerity of my master, and the idea he has and the rule he follows, that knights-errant must not live or sustain themselves on anything except dried fruits and the herbs of the field."

"By my faith, brother," said he of the Grove, "my stomach is not made for thistles, or wild pears, or roots of the woods; let our masters do as they like, with their chivalry notions and laws, and eat what those enjoin; I carry my food-basket and this *bota* hanging to the saddle-bow, whatever they may say; and it is such an object of worship with me, and I love it so, that there is hardly a moment but I am kissing and embracing it over and over again;" and so saying he thrust it into Sancho's hands, who raising it aloft pointed to his mouth, gazed at the stars for a quarter of an hour; and when he had done drinking let his head fall on one side, and giving a deep sigh, exclaimed, "Ah, whoreson rogue, how catholic it is!"

"There, you see," said he of the Grove, hearing Sancho's exclamation, "how you have called this wine whoreson by way of praise."

"Well," said Sancho, "I own it, and I grant it is no dishonour to call anyone whoreson when it is to be understood as praise. But tell me, señor, by what you love best, is this Ciudad Real wine?"

"O rare wine-taster!" said he of the Grove; "nowhere else indeed does it come from, and it has some years' age too."

"Leave me alone for that," said Sancho; "never fear but I'll hit upon the place it came from somehow. What would you say, sir squire, to my having such a great natural instinct in judging wines that you have only to let me smell one and I can tell positively its country, its kind, its flavour and soundness, the changes it will undergo, and everything that appertains to a wine? But it is no wonder, for I have had in my family, on my father's side, the two best wine-tasters that have been known in La Mancha for many a long year, and to prove it I'll tell you now a thing that happened them. They gave the two of them some wine out of a cask, to try, asking their opinion as to the condition, quality, goodness or badness of the wine. One of them tried it with the tip of his tongue, the other did no more than bring it to his nose. The first said the wine had a flavour of iron, the second said it had a stronger flavour of cordovan. The owner said the cask was clean, and that nothing had been added to the wine from which it could have got a flavour of either iron or leather. Nevertheless, these two great wine-tasters held to what they had said. Time went by, the wine was sold, and when they came to clean out the cask, they found in it a small key hanging to a thong of cordovan; see now if one who comes of the same stock has not a right to give his opinion in such like cases."

"Therefore, I say," said he of the Grove, "let us give up going in quest of adventures, and as we have loaves let us not go looking for cakes, but return to our cribs, for God will find us there if it be his will."

"Until my master reaches Saragossa," said Sancho, "I'll remain in his service; after that we'll see."

The end of it was that the two squires talked so much and drank so much that sleep had to tie their tongues and moderate their thirst, for to quench it was impossible; and so the pair of them fell asleep clinging to the now nearly empty *bota* and with half-chewed morsels in their mouths; and there we will leave them for the present, to relate what passed between the Knight of the Grove and him of the Rueful Countenance.

CHAPTER XIV: WHEREIN IS CONTINUED THE ADVENTURE OF THE KNIGHT OF THE GROVE

Among the things that passed between Don Quixote and the Knight of the Wood, the history tells us he of the Grove said to Don Quixote, "In fine, sir knight, I would have you know that my destiny, or, more properly speaking, my choice led me to fall in love with the peerless Casildea de Vandalia. I call her peerless because she has no peer, whether it be in bodily stature or in the supremacy of rank and beauty. This same Casildea, then, that I speak of, requited my honourable passion and gentle aspirations by compelling me, as his stepmother did Hercules, to engage in many perils of various sorts, at the end of each promising me that, with the end of the next, the object of my hopes should be attained; but my labours have gone on increasing link by link until they are past counting, nor do I know what will be the last one that is to be the beginning of the accomplishment of my chaste desires. On one occasion she bade me go and challenge the famous giantess of Seville, La Giralda by name, who is as mighty and strong as if made of brass, and though never stirring from one spot, is the most restless and changeable woman in the world. I came, I saw, I conquered, and I made her stay quiet and behave herself, for nothing but north winds blew for more than a week.

Another time I was ordered to lift those ancient stones, the mighty bulls of Guisando, an enterprise that might more fitly be entrusted to porters than to knights. Again, she bade me fling myself into the cavern of Cabra—an unparalleled and awful peril—and bring her a minute account of all that is concealed in those gloomy depths. I stopped the motion of the Giralda, I lifted the bulls of Guisando, I flung myself into the cavern and brought to light the secrets of its abyss; and my hopes are as dead as dead can be, and her scorn and her commands as lively as ever. To be brief, last of all she has commanded me to go through all the provinces of Spain and compel all the knights-errant wandering therein to confess that she surpasses all women alive to-day in beauty, and that I am the most valiant and the most deeply enamoured knight on earth; in support of which claim I have already travelled over the greater part of Spain, and have there vanquished several knights who have dared to contradict me; but what I most plume and pride myself upon is having vanquished in single combat that so famous knight Don Quixote of La Mancha, and made him confess that my Casildea is more beautiful than his Dulcinea; and in this one victory I hold myself to have conquered all the knights in the world; for this Don Quixote that I speak of has vanquished them all, and I having vanquished him, his glory, his fame, and his honour have passed and are transferred to my person; for

> The more the vanquished hath of fair renown,
> The greater glory gilds the victor's crown.

Thus the innumerable achievements of the said Don Quixote are now set down to my account and have become mine."

Don Quixote was amazed when he heard the Knight of the Grove, and was a thousand times on the point of telling him he lied, and had the lie direct already on the tip of his tongue; but he restrained himself as well as he could, in order to force him to confess the lie with his own lips; so he said to him quietly, "As to what you say, sir knight, about having vanquished most of the knights of Spain, or even of the whole world, I say nothing; but that you have vanquished Don Quixote of La Mancha I consider doubtful; it may have been some other that resembled him, although there are few like him."

"How! not vanquished?" said he of the Grove; "by the heaven that is above us I fought Don Quixote and overcame him and made him yield; and he is a man of tall stature, gaunt features, long, lank limbs, with hair turning grey, an aquiline nose rather hooked, and large black drooping moustaches; he does battle under the

name of 'The Countenance,' and he has for squire a peasant called Sancho Panza;
3795 he presses the loins and rules the reins of a famous steed called Rocinante; and
lastly, he has for the mistress of his will a certain Dulcinea del Toboso, once upon
a time called Aldonza Lorenzo, just as I call mine Casildea de Vandalia because
her name is Casilda and she is of Andalusia. If all these tokens are not enough to
vindicate the truth of what I say, here is my sword, that will compel incredulity
3800 itself to give credence to it."

"Calm yourself, sir knight," said Don Quixote, "and give ear to what I am
about to say to you. I would have you know that this Don Quixote you speak of is
the greatest friend I have in the world; so much so that I may say I regard him in the
same light as my own person; and from the precise and clear indications you have
3805 given I cannot but think that he must be the very one you have vanquished. On the
other hand, I see with my eyes and feel with my hands that it is impossible it can
have been the same; unless indeed it be that, as he has many enemies who are
enchanters, and one in particular who is always persecuting him, some one of
these may have taken his shape in order to allow himself to be vanquished, so as
3810 to defraud him of the fame that his exalted achievements as a knight have earned
and acquired for him throughout the known world. And in confirmation of this, I
must tell you, too, that it is but ten hours since these said enchanters his enemies
transformed the shape and person of the fair Dulcinea del Toboso into a foul and
mean village lass, and in the same way they must have transformed Don Quixote;
3815 and if all this does not suffice to convince you of the truth of what I say, here is
Don Quixote himself, who will maintain it by arms, on foot or on horseback or in
any way you please."

And so saying he stood up and laid his hand on his sword, waiting to see
what the Knight of the Grove would do, who in an equally calm voice said in
3820 reply, "Pledges don't distress a good player; he who has succeeded in vanquishing
you once when transformed, Sir Don Quixote, may fairly hope to subdue you in
your own proper shape; but as it is not becoming for knights to perform their feats
of arms in the dark, like highwaymen and bullies, let us wait till daylight, that the
sun may behold our deeds; and the conditions of our combat shall be that the
3825 vanquished shall be at the victor's disposal, to do all that he may enjoin, provided
the injunction be such as shall be becoming a knight."

"I am more than satisfied with these conditions and terms," replied Don
Quixote; and so saying, they betook themselves to where their squires lay, and
found them snoring, and in the same posture they were in when sleep fell upon
3830 them. They roused them up, and bade them get the horses ready, as at sunrise they
were to engage in a bloody and arduous single combat; at which intelligence
Sancho was aghast and thunderstruck, trembling for the safety of his master
because of the mighty deeds he had heard the squire of the Grove ascribe to his; but
without a word the two squires went in quest of their cattle; for by this time the
3835 three horses and the ass had smelt one another out, and were all together.

On the way, he of the Grove said to Sancho, "You must know, brother, that it
is the custom with the fighting men of Andalusia, when they are godfathers in any

quarrel, not to stand idle with folded arms while their godsons fight; I say so to remind you that while our masters are fighting, we, too, have to fight, and knock
3840   one another to shivers."

"That custom, sir squire," replied Sancho, "may hold good among those bullies and fighting men you talk of, but certainly not among the squires of knights-errant; at least, I have never heard my master speak of any custom of the sort, and he knows all the laws of knight-errantry by heart; but granting it true that there is
3845   an express law that squires are to fight while their masters are fighting, I don't mean to obey it, but to pay the penalty that may be laid on peacefully minded squires like myself; for I am sure it cannot be more than two pounds of wax, and I would rather pay that, for I know it will cost me less than the lint I shall be at the expense of to mend my head, which I look upon as broken and split already;
3850   there's another thing that makes it impossible for me to fight, that I have no sword, for I never carried one in my life."

"I know a good remedy for that," said he of the Grove; "I have here two linen bags of the same size; you shall take one, and I the other, and we will fight at bag blows with equal arms."
3855   "If that's the way, so be it with all my heart," said Sancho, "for that sort of battle will serve to knock the dust out of us instead of hurting us."

"That will not do," said the other, "for we must put into the bags, to keep the wind from blowing them away, half a dozen nice smooth pebbles, all of the same weight; and in this way we shall be able to baste one another without doing
3860   ourselves any harm or mischief."

"Body of my father!" said Sancho, "see what marten and sable, and pads of carded cotton he is putting into the bags, that our heads may not be broken and our bones beaten to jelly! But even if they are filled with toss silk [cocoons], I can tell you, señor, I am not going to fight; let our masters fight, that's their lookout, and let
3865   us drink and live; for time will take care to ease us of our lives, without our going to look for fillips so that they may be finished off before their proper time comes and they drop from ripeness."

"Still," returned he of the Grove, "we must fight, if it be only for half an hour."
3870   "By no means," said Sancho; "I am not going to be so discourteous or so ungrateful as to have any quarrel, be it ever so small, with one I have eaten and drunk with; besides, who the devil could bring himself to fight in cold blood, without anger or provocation?"

"I can remedy that entirely," said he of the Grove, "and in this way: before
3875   we begin the battle, I will come up to your worship fair and softly, and give you three or four buffets, with which I shall stretch you at my feet and rouse your anger, though it were sleeping sounder than a dormouse."

"To match that plan," said Sancho, "I have another that is not a whit behind it; I will take a cudgel, and before your worship comes near enough to waken my
3880   anger I will send yours so sound to sleep with whacks, that it won't waken unless it be in the other world, where it is known that I am not a man to let my face be

handled by anyone; let each look out for the arrow—though the surer way would
be to let everyone's anger sleep, for nobody knows the heart of anyone, and a man
may come for wool and go back shorn; God gave his blessing to peace and his
3885   curse to quarrels; if a hunted cat, surrounded and hard pressed, turns into a lion,
God knows what I, who am a man, may turn into; and so from this time forth I
warn you, sir squire, that all the harm and mischief that may come of our quarrel
will be put down to your account."

"Very good," said he of the Grove; "God will send the dawn and we shall be
3890   all right."

And now gay-plumaged birds of all sorts began to warble in the trees, and
with their varied and gladsome notes seemed to welcome and salute the fresh morn
that was beginning to show the beauty of her countenance at the gates and
balconies of the east, shaking from her locks a profusion of liquid pearls; in which
3895   dulcet moisture bathed, the plants, too, seemed to shed and shower down a pearly
spray, the willows distilled sweet manna, the fountains laughed, the brooks
babbled, the woods rejoiced, and the meadows arrayed themselves in all their
glory at her coming. But hardly had the light of day made it possible to see and
distinguish things, when the first object that presented itself to the eyes of Sancho
3900   Panza was the squire of the Grove's nose, which was so big that it almost
overshadowed his whole body. It is, in fact, stated, that it was of enormous size,
hooked in the middle, covered with warts, and of a mulberry colour like an egg-
plant; it hung down two fingers' length below his mouth, and the size, the colour,
the warts, and the bend of it, made his face so hideous, that Sancho, as he looked at
3905   him, began to tremble hand and foot like a child in convulsions, and he vowed in
his heart to let himself be given two hundred buffets, sooner than be provoked to
fight that monster. Don Quixote examined his adversary, and found that he
already had his helmet on and visor lowered, so that he could not see his face; he
observed, however, that he was a sturdily built man, but not very tall in stature.
3910   Over his armour he wore a surcoat or cassock of what seemed to be the finest
cloth of gold, all bespangled with glittering mirrors like little moons, which gave
him an extremely gallant and splendid appearance; above his helmet fluttered a
great quantity of plumes, green, yellow, and white, and his lance, which was
leaning against a tree, was very long and stout, and had a steel point more than a
3915   palm in length.

Don Quixote observed all, and took note of all, and from what he saw and
observed he concluded that the said knight must be a man of great strength, but he
did not for all that give way to fear, like Sancho Panza; on the contrary, with a
composed and dauntless air, he said to the Knight of the Mirrors, "If, sir knight,
3920   your great eagerness to fight has not banished your courtesy, by it I would entreat
you to raise your visor a little, in order that I may see if the comeliness of your
countenance corresponds with that of your equipment."

"Whether you come victorious or vanquished out of this emprise, sir knight,"
replied he of the Mirrors, "you will have more than enough time and leisure to see
3925   me; and if now I do not comply with your request, it is because it seems to me I

should do a serious wrong to the fair Casildea de Vandalia in wasting time while I stopped to raise my visor before compelling you to confess what you are already aware I maintain."

3930 "Well then," said Don Quixote, "while we are mounting you can at least tell me if I am that Don Quixote whom you said you vanquished."

"To that we answer you," said he of the Mirrors, "that you are as like the very knight I vanquished as one egg is like another, but as you say enchanters persecute you, I will not venture to say positively whether you are the said person or not."

3935 "That," said Don Quixote, "is enough to convince me that you are under a deception; however, entirely to relieve you of it, let our horses be brought, and in less time than it would take you to raise your visor, if God, my lady, and my arm stand me in good stead, I shall see your face, and you shall see that I am not the vanquished Don Quixote you take me to be."

3940 With this, cutting short the colloquy, they mounted, and Don Quixote wheeled Rocinante round in order to take a proper distance to charge back upon his adversary, and he of the Mirrors did the same; but Don Quixote had not moved away twenty paces when he heard himself called by the other, and, each returning half-way, he of the Mirrors said to him, "Remember, sir knight, that the terms of 3945 our combat are, that the vanquished, as I said before, shall be at the victor's disposal."

"I am aware of it already," said Don Quixote; "provided what is commanded and imposed upon the vanquished be things that do not transgress the limits of chivalry."

3950 "That is understood," replied he of the Mirrors.

At this moment the extraordinary nose of the squire presented itself to Don Quixote's view, and he was no less amazed than Sancho at the sight; insomuch that he set him down as a monster of some kind, or a human being of some new species or unearthly breed. Sancho, seeing his master retiring to run his course, did 3955 not like to be left alone with the nosy man, fearing that with one flap of that nose on his own the battle would be all over for him and he would be left stretched on the ground, either by the blow or with fright; so he ran after his master, holding on to Rocinante's stirrup-leather, and when it seemed to him time to turn about, he said, "I implore of your worship, señor, before you turn to charge, to help me up 3960 into this cork tree, from which I will be able to witness the gallant encounter your worship is going to have with this knight, more to my taste and better than from the ground."

"It seems to me rather, Sancho," said Don Quixote, "that thou wouldst mount a scaffold in order to see the bulls without danger."

3965 "To tell the truth," returned Sancho, "the monstrous nose of that squire has filled me with fear and terror, and I dare not stay near him."

"It is," said Don Quixote, "such a one that were I not what I am it would terrify me too; so, come, I will help thee up where thou wilt."

3970 While Don Quixote waited for Sancho to mount into the cork tree he of the Mirrors took as much ground as he considered requisite, and, supposing Don Quixote to have done the same, without waiting for any sound of trumpet or other signal to direct them, he wheeled his horse, which was not more agile or better-looking than Rocinante, and at his top speed, which was an easy trot, he proceeded to charge his enemy; seeing him, however, engaged in putting Sancho up,

3975 he drew rein, and halted in mid career, for which his horse was very grateful, as he was already unable to go. Don Quixote, fancying that his foe was coming down upon him flying, drove his spurs vigorously into Rocinante's lean flanks and made him scud along in such style that the history tells us that on this occasion only was he known to make something like running, for on all others it was a simple

3980 trot with him; and with this unparalleled fury he bore down where he of the Mirrors stood digging his spurs into his horse up to buttons, without being able to make him stir a finger's length from the spot where he had come to a standstill in his course. At this lucky moment and crisis, Don Quixote came upon his adversary, in trouble with his horse, and embarrassed with his lance, which he either could

3985 not manage, or had no time to lay in rest. Don Quixote, however, paid no attention to these difficulties, and in perfect safety to himself and without any risk encountered him of the Mirrors with such force that he brought him to the ground in spite of himself over the haunches of his horse, and with so heavy a fall that he lay to all appearance dead, not stirring hand or foot. The instant Sancho saw him

3990 fall he slid down from the cork tree, and made all haste to where his master was, who, dismounting from Rocinante, went and stood over him of the Mirrors, and unlacing his helmet to see if he was dead, and to give him air if he should happen to be alive, he saw—who can say what he saw, without filling all who hear it with astonishment, wonder, and awe? He saw, the history says, the very countenance,

3995 the very face, the very look, the very physiognomy, the very effigy, the very image of the bachelor Samson Carrasco! As soon as he saw it he called out in a loud voice, "Make haste here, Sancho, and behold what thou art to see but not to believe; quick, my son, and learn what magic can do, and wizards and enchanters are capable of."

4000 Sancho came up, and when he saw the countenance of the bachelor Carrasco, he fell to crossing himself a thousand times, and blessing himself as many more. All this time the prostrate knight showed no signs of life, and Sancho said to Don Quixote, "It is my opinion, señor, that in any case your worship should take and thrust your sword into the mouth of this one here that looks like the bachelor

4005 Samson Carrasco; perhaps in him you will kill one of your enemies, the enchanters."

"Thy advice is not bad," said Don Quixote, "for of enemies the fewer the better;" and he was drawing his sword to carry into effect Sancho's counsel and suggestion, when the squire of the Mirrors came up, now without the nose which

4010 had made him so hideous, and cried out in a loud voice, "Mind what you are about, Señor Don Quixote; that is your friend, the bachelor Samson Carrasco, you have at your feet, and I am his squire."

"And the nose?" said Sancho, seeing him without the hideous feature he had before; to which he replied, "I have it here in my pocket," and putting his hand into his right pocket, he pulled out a masquerade nose of varnished pasteboard of the make already described; and Sancho, examining him more and more closely, exclaimed aloud in a voice of amazement, "Holy Mary be good to me! Isn't it Tom Cecial, my neighbour and gossip?"

"Why, to be sure I am!" returned the now unnosed squire; "Tom Cecial I am, gossip and friend Sancho Panza; and I'll tell you presently the means and tricks and falsehoods by which I have been brought here; but in the meantime, beg and entreat of your master not to touch, maltreat, wound, or slay the Knight of the Mirrors whom he has at his feet; because, beyond all dispute, it is the rash and ill-advised bachelor Samson Carrasco, our fellow townsman."

At this moment he of the Mirrors came to himself, and Don Quixote perceiving it, held the naked point of his sword over his face, and said to him, "You are a dead man, knight, unless you confess that the peerless Dulcinea del Toboso excels your Casildea de Vandalia in beauty; and in addition to this you must promise, if you should survive this encounter and fall, to go to the city of El Toboso and present yourself before her on my behalf, that she deal with you according to her good pleasure; and if she leaves you free to do yours, you are in like manner to return and seek me out (for the trail of my mighty deeds will serve you as a guide to lead you to where I may be), and tell me what may have passed between you and her—conditions which, in accordance with what we stipulated before our combat, do not transgress the just limits of knight-errantry."

"I confess," said the fallen knight, "that the dirty tattered shoe of the lady Dulcinea del Toboso is better than the ill-combed though clean beard of Casildea; and I promise to go and to return from her presence to yours, and to give you a full and particular account of all you demand of me."

"You must also confess and believe," added Don Quixote, "that the knight you vanquished was not and could not be Don Quixote of La Mancha, but some one else in his likeness, just as I confess and believe that you, though you seem to be the bachelor Samson Carrasco, are not so, but some other resembling him, whom my enemies have here put before me in his shape, in order that I may restrain and moderate the vehemence of my wrath, and make a gentle use of the glory of my victory."

"I confess, hold, and think everything to be as you believe, hold, and think it," said the crippled knight; "let me rise, I entreat you; if, indeed, the shock of my fall will allow me, for it has left me in a sorry plight enough."

Don Quixote helped him to rise, with the assistance of his squire Tom Cecial; from whom Sancho never took his eyes, and to whom he put questions, the replies to which furnished clear proof that he was really and truly the Tom Cecial he said; but the impression made on Sancho's mind by what his master said about the enchanters having changed the face of the Knight of the Mirrors into that of the bachelor Samson Carrasco, would not permit him to believe what he saw with his eyes. In fine, both master and man remained under the delusion; and, down in the mouth, and out of luck, he of the Mirrors and his squire parted from Don Quixote and Sancho, he meaning to go look for some village where he could plaster and strap his ribs. Don Quixote and Sancho resumed their journey to Saragossa, and 4060 on it the history leaves them in order that it may tell who the Knight of the Mirrors and his long-nosed squire were.

CHAPTER XV: WHEREIN IT IS TOLD AND KNOWN WHO THE KNIGHT OF THE MIRRORS AND HIS SQUIRE WERE

Don Quixote went off satisfied, elated, and vain-glorious in the highest degree at having won a victory over such a valiant knight as he fancied him of the Mirrors to be, and one from whose knightly word he expected to learn whether 4065 the enchantment of his lady still continued; inasmuch as the said vanquished knight was bound, under the penalty of ceasing to be one, to return and render him an account of what took place between him and her. But Don Quixote was of one mind, he of the Mirrors of another, for he just then had no thought of anything but finding some village where he could plaster himself, as has been said already. The 4070 history goes on to say, then, that when the bachelor Samson Carrasco recommended Don Quixote to resume his knight-errantry which he had laid aside, it was in consequence of having been previously in conclave with the curate and the barber on the means to be adopted to induce Don Quixote to stay at home in peace and quiet without worrying himself with his ill-starred adventures; at 4075 which consultation it was decided by the unanimous vote of all, and on the special advice of Carrasco, that Don Quixote should be allowed to go, as it seemed impossible to restrain him, and that Samson should sally forth to meet him as a knight-errant, and do battle with him, for there would be no difficulty about a cause, and vanquish him, that being looked upon as an easy matter; and that it 4080 should be agreed and settled that the vanquished was to be at the mercy of the victor. Then, Don Quixote being vanquished, the bachelor knight was to command him to return to his village and his house, and not quit it for two years, or until he received further orders from him; all which it was clear Don Quixote would unhesitatingly obey, rather than contravene or fail to observe the laws of 4085 chivalry; and during the period of his seclusion he might perhaps forget his folly, or there might be an opportunity of discovering some ready remedy for his madness. Carrasco undertook the task, and Tom Cecial, a gossip and neighbour of Sancho Panza's, a lively, feather-headed fellow, offered himself as his squire. Carrasco armed himself in the fashion described, and Tom Cecial, that he might not 4090 be known by his gossip when they met, fitted on over his own natural nose the false masquerade one that has been mentioned; and so they followed the same route Don Quixote took, and almost came up with him in time to be present at the adventure of the cart of Death and finally encountered them in the grove, where all that the sagacious reader has been reading about took place; and had it not been 4095 for the extraordinary fancies of Don Quixote, and his conviction that the bachelor was not the bachelor, señor bachelor would have been incapacitated for ever from taking his degree of licentiate, all through not finding nests where he thought to find birds.

Tom Cecial, seeing how ill they had succeeded, and what a sorry end their expedition had come to, said to the bachelor, "Sure enough, Señor Samson Carrasco, we are served right; it is easy enough to plan and set about an enterprise, but it is often a difficult matter to come well out of it. Don Quixote a madman, and we sane; he goes off laughing, safe, and sound, and you are left sore and sorry! I'd like to know now which is the madder, he who is so because he cannot help it, or he who is so of his own choice?"

To which Samson replied, "The difference between the two sorts of madmen is, that he who is so 'will he nil he,' will be one always, while he who is so of his own accord can leave off being one whenever he likes."

"In that case," said Tom Cecial, "I was a madman of my own accord when I volunteered to become your squire, and, of my own accord, I'll leave off being one and go home."

"That's your affair," returned Samson, "but to suppose that I am going home until I have given Don Quixote a thrashing is absurd; and it is not any wish that he may recover his senses that will make me hunt him out now, but a wish for the sore pain I am in with my ribs won't let me entertain more charitable thoughts."

Thus discoursing, the pair proceeded until they reached a town where it was their good luck to find a bone-setter, with whose help the unfortunate Samson was cured. Tom Cecial left him and went home, while he stayed behind meditating vengeance; and the history will return to him again at the proper time, so as not to omit making merry with Don Quixote now.

CHAPTER XVI: OF WHAT BEFELL DON QUIXOTE WITH A DISCREET GENTLEMAN OF LA MANCHA

Don Quixote pursued his journey in the high spirits, satisfaction, and self-complacency already described, fancying himself the most valorous knight-errant of the age in the world because of his late victory. All the adventures that could befall him from that time forth he regarded as already done and brought to a happy issue; he made light of enchantments and enchanters; he thought no more of the countless drubbings that had been administered to him in the course of his knight-errantry, nor of the volley of stones that had levelled half his teeth, nor of the ingratitude of the galley slaves, nor of the audacity of the Yanguesans and the shower of stakes that fell upon him; in short, he said to himself that could he discover any means, mode, or way of disenchanting his lady Dulcinea, he would not envy the highest fortune that the most fortunate knight-errant of yore ever reached or could reach.

He was going along entirely absorbed in these fancies, when Sancho said to him, "Isn't it odd, señor, that I have still before my eyes that monstrous enormous nose of my gossip, Tom Cecial?"

"And dost thou, then, believe, Sancho," said Don Quixote, "that the Knight of the Mirrors was the bachelor Carrasco, and his squire Tom Cecial thy gossip?"

"I don't know what to say to that," replied Sancho; "all I know is that the tokens he gave me about my own house, wife and children, nobody else but himself

4140   could have given me; and the face, once the nose was off, was the very face of Tom Cecial, as I have seen it many a time in my town and next door to my own house; and the sound of the voice was just the same."

"Let us reason the matter, Sancho," said Don Quixote. "Come now, by what process of thinking can it be supposed that the bachelor Samson Carrasco would

4145   come as a knight-errant, in arms offensive and defensive, to fight with me? Have I ever been by any chance his enemy? Have I ever given him any occasion to owe me a grudge? Am I his rival, or does he profess arms, that he should envy the fame I have acquired in them?"

"Well, but what are we to say, señor," returned Sancho, "about that knight,

4150   whoever he is, being so like the bachelor Carrasco, and his squire so like my gossip, Tom Cecial? And if that be enchantment, as your worship says, was there no other pair in the world for them to take the likeness of?"

"It is all," said Don Quixote, "a scheme and plot of the malignant magicians that persecute me, who, foreseeing that I was to be victorious in the conflict,

4155   arranged that the vanquished knight should display the countenance of my friend the bachelor, in order that the friendship I bear him should interpose to stay the edge of my sword and might of my arm, and temper the just wrath of my heart; so that he who sought to take my life by fraud and falsehood should save his own. And to prove it, thou knowest already, Sancho, by experience which cannot lie or

4160   deceive, how easy it is for enchanters to change one countenance into another, turning fair into foul, and foul into fair; for it is not two days since thou sawest with thine own eyes the beauty and elegance of the peerless Dulcinea in all its perfection and natural harmony, while I saw her in the repulsive and mean form of a coarse country wench, with cataracts in her eyes and a foul smell in her mouth;

4165   and when the perverse enchanter ventured to effect so wicked a transformation, it is no wonder if he effected that of Samson Carrasco and thy gossip in order to snatch the glory of victory out of my grasp. For all that, however, I console myself, because, after all, in whatever shape he may have been, I have victorious over my enemy."

4170   "God knows what's the truth of it all," said Sancho; and knowing as he did that the transformation of Dulcinea had been a device and imposition of his own, his master's illusions were not satisfactory to him; but he did not like to reply lest he should say something that might disclose his trickery.

As they were engaged in this conversation they were overtaken by a man who

4175   was following the same road behind them, mounted on a very handsome flea-bitten mare, and dressed in a *gaban* [cloak] of fine green cloth, with tawny velvet facings, and a *montera* [hood] of the same velvet. The trappings of the mare were of the field and *jineta* fashion, and of mulberry colour and green. He carried a Moorish cutlass hanging from a broad green and gold baldric; the buskins were of the same

4180   make as the baldric; the spurs were not gilt, but lacquered green, and so brightly polished that, matching as they did the rest of his apparel, they looked better than if they had been of pure gold.

    When the traveller came up with them he saluted them courteously, and spurring his mare was passing them without stopping, but Don Quixote called out
4185   to him, "Gallant sir, if so be your worship is going our road, and has no occasion for speed, it would be a pleasure to me if we were to join company."

    "In truth," replied he on the mare, "I would not pass you so hastily but for fear that horse might turn restive in the company of my mare."

    "You may safely hold in your mare, señor," said Sancho in reply to this, "for
4190   our horse is the most virtuous and well-behaved horse in the world; he never does anything wrong on such occasions, and the only time he misbehaved, my master and I suffered for it sevenfold; I say again your worship may pull up if you like; for if she was offered to him between two plates the horse would not hanker after her."

4195   The traveller drew rein, amazed at the trim and features of Don Quixote, who rode without his helmet, which Sancho carried like a valise in front of Dapple's pack-saddle; and if the man in green examined Don Quixote closely, still more closely did Don Quixote examine the man in green, who struck him as being a man of intelligence. In appearance he was about fifty years of age, with but few grey
4200   hairs, an aquiline cast of features, and an expression between grave and gay; and his dress and accoutrements showed him to be a man of good condition. What he in green thought of Don Quixote of La Mancha was that a man of that sort and shape he had never yet seen; he marvelled at the length of his hair, his lofty stature, the lankness and sallowness of his countenance, his armour, his bearing and his
4205   gravity—a figure and picture such as had not been seen in those regions for many a long day.

    Don Quixote saw very plainly the attention with which the traveller was regarding him, and read his curiosity in his astonishment; and courteous as he was and ready to please everybody, before the other could ask him any question he
4210   anticipated him by saying, "The appearance I present to your worship being so strange and so out of the common, I should not be surprised if it filled you with wonder; but you will cease to wonder when I tell you, as I do, that I am one of those knights who, as people say, go seeking adventures. I have left my home, I have mortgaged my estate, I have given up my comforts, and committed myself to the
4215   arms of Fortune, to bear me whithersoever she may please. My desire was to bring to life again knight-errantry, now dead, and for some time past, stumbling here, falling there, now coming down headlong, now raising myself up again, I have carried out a great portion of my design, succouring widows, protecting maidens, and giving aid to wives, orphans, and minors, the proper and natural duty of
4220   knights-errant; and, therefore, because of my many valiant and Christian achievements, I have been already found worthy to make my way in print to well-nigh all, or most, of the nations of the earth. Thirty thousand volumes of my history have been printed, and it is on the high-road to be printed thirty thousand

4225 thousands of times, if heaven does not put a stop to it. In short, to sum up all in a few words, or in a single one, I may tell you I am Don Quixote of La Mancha, otherwise called 'The Knight of the Rueful Countenance;' for though self-praise is degrading, I must perforce sound my own sometimes, that is to say, when there is no one at hand to do it for me. So that, gentle sir, neither this horse, nor this lance, nor this shield, nor this squire, nor all these arms put together, nor the sallowness

4230 of my countenance, nor my gaunt leanness, will henceforth astonish you, now that you know who I am and what profession I follow."

With these words Don Quixote held his peace, and, from the time he took to answer, the man in green seemed to be at a loss for a reply; after a long pause, however, he said to him, "You were right when you saw curiosity in my

4235 amazement, sir knight; but you have not succeeded in removing the astonishment I feel at seeing you; for although you say, señor, that knowing who you are ought to remove it, it has not done so; on the contrary, now that I know, I am left more amazed and astonished than before. What! is it possible that there are knights-errant in the world in these days, and histories of real chivalry printed? I cannot

4240 realise the fact that there can be anyone on earth now-a-days who aids widows, or protects maidens, or defends wives, or succours orphans; nor should I believe it had I not seen it in your worship with my own eyes. Blessed be heaven! for by means of this history of your noble and genuine chivalrous deeds, which you say has been printed, the countless stories of fictitious knights-errant with which the

4245 world is filled, so much to the injury of morality and the prejudice and discredit of good histories, will have been driven into oblivion."

"There is a good deal to be said on that point," said Don Quixote, "as to whether the histories of the knights-errant are fiction or not."

"Why, is there anyone who doubts that those histories are false?" said the

4250 man in green.

"I doubt it," said Don Quixote, "but never mind that just now; if our journey lasts long enough, I trust in God I shall show your worship that you do wrong in going with the stream of those who regard it as a matter of certainty that they are not true."

4255 From this last observation of Don Quixote's, the traveller began to have a suspicion that he was some crazy being, and was waiting him to confirm it by something further; but before they could turn to any new subject Don Quixote begged him to tell him who he was, since he himself had rendered account of his station and life. To this, he in the green *gaban* replied "I, Sir Knight of the Rueful

4260 Countenance, am a gentleman by birth, native of the village where, please God, we are going to dine today; I am more than fairly well off, and my name is Don Diego de Miranda. I pass my life with my wife, children, and friends; my pursuits are hunting and fishing, but I keep neither hawks nor greyhounds, nothing but a tame partridge or a bold ferret or two; I have six dozen or so of books, some in our

4265 mother tongue, some Latin, some of them history, others devotional; those of chivalry have not as yet crossed the threshold of my door; I am more given to turning over the profane than the devotional, so long as they are books of honest entertainment that charm by their style and attract and interest by the invention they display, though of these there are very few in Spain. Sometimes I dine with my neighbours and friends, and often invite them; my entertainments are neat and well served without stint of anything. I have no taste for tattle, nor do I allow tattling in my presence; I pry not into my neighbours' lives, nor have I lynx-eyes for what others do. I hear mass every day; I share my substance with the poor, making no display of good works, lest I let hypocrisy and vainglory, those enemies that subtly take possession of the most watchful heart, find an entrance into mine. I strive to make peace between those whom I know to be at variance; I am the devoted servant of Our Lady, and my trust is ever in the infinite mercy of God our Lord."

Sancho listened with the greatest attention to the account of the gentleman's life and occupation; and thinking it a good and a holy life, and that he who led it ought to work miracles, he threw himself off Dapple, and running in haste seized his right stirrup and kissed his foot again and again with a devout heart and almost with tears.

Seeing this the gentleman asked him, "What are you about, brother? What are these kisses for?"

"Let me kiss," said Sancho, "for I think your worship is the first saint in the saddle I ever saw all the days of my life."

"I am no saint," replied the gentleman, "but a great sinner; but you are, brother, for you must be a good fellow, as your simplicity shows."

Sancho went back and regained his pack-saddle, having extracted a laugh from his master's profound melancholy, and excited fresh amazement in Don Diego. Don Quixote then asked him how many children he had, and observed that one of the things wherein the ancient philosophers, who were without the true knowledge of God, placed the *summum bonum* [greatest good] was in the gifts of nature, in those of fortune, in having many friends, and many and good children.

"I, Señor Don Quixote," answered the gentleman, "have one son, without whom, perhaps, I should count myself happier than I am, not because he is a bad son, but because he is not so good as I could wish. He is eighteen years of age; he has been for six at Salamanca studying Latin and Greek, and when I wished him to turn to the study of other sciences I found him so wrapped up in that of poetry (if that can be called a science) that there is no getting him to take kindly to the law, which I wished him to study, or to theology, the queen of them all. I would like him to be an honour to his family, as we live in days when our kings liberally reward learning that is virtuous and worthy; for learning without virtue is a pearl on a dunghill. He spends the whole day in settling whether Homer expressed himself correctly or not in such and such a line of the *Iliad*, whether Martial was indecent or not in such and such an epigram, whether such and such lines of Virgil are to be understood in this way or in that; in short, all his talk is of the works of these poets, and those of Horace, Perseus, Juvenal, and Tibullus; for of the moderns in our own language he makes no great account; but with all his seeming indifference to Spanish poetry, just now his thoughts are absorbed in making a gloss on four lines that have been sent him from Salamanca, which I suspect are for some poetical tournament."

4315   To all this Don Quixote said in reply, "Children, señor, are portions of their parents' bowels, and therefore, be they good or bad, are to be loved as we love the souls that give us life; it is for the parents to guide them from infancy in the ways of virtue, propriety, and worthy Christian conduct, so that when grown up they may be the staff of their parents' old age, and the glory of their posterity; and to force them to study this or that science I do not think wise, though it may be no

4320   harm to persuade them; and when there is no need to study for the sake of *pane lucrando*,[6] and it is the student's good fortune that heaven has given him parents who provide him with it, it would be my advice to them to let him pursue whatever science they may see him most inclined to; and though that of poetry is less useful than pleasurable, it is not one of those that bring discredit upon the possessor.

4325   Poetry, gentle sir, is, as I take it, like a tender young maiden of supreme beauty, to array, bedeck, and adorn whom is the task of several other maidens, who are all the rest of the sciences; and she must avail herself of the help of all, and all derive their lustre from her. But this maiden will not bear to be handled, nor dragged through the streets, nor exposed either at the corners of the market-places, or in the

4330   closets of palaces. She is the product of an Alchemy of such virtue that he who is able to practise it, will turn her into pure gold of inestimable worth. He that possesses her must keep her within bounds, not permitting her to break out in ribald satires or soulless sonnets. She must on no account be offered for sale, unless, indeed, it be in heroic poems, moving tragedies, or sprightly and ingenious

4335   comedies. She must not be touched by the buffoons, nor by the ignorant vulgar, incapable of comprehending or appreciating her hidden treasures. And do not suppose, señor, that I apply the term vulgar here merely to plebeians and the lower orders; for everyone who is ignorant, be he lord or prince, may and should be included among the vulgar. He, then, who shall embrace and cultivate poetry under

4340   the conditions I have named, shall become famous, and his name honoured throughout all the civilised nations of the earth. And with regard to what you say, señor, of your son having no great opinion of Spanish poetry, I am inclined to think that he is not quite right there, and for this reason: the great poet Homer did not write in Latin, because he was a Greek, nor did Virgil write in Greek, because

4345   he was a Latin; in short, all the ancient poets wrote in the language they imbibed with their mother's milk, and never went in quest of foreign ones to express their sublime conceptions; and that being so, the usage should in justice extend to all nations, and the German poet should not be undervalued because he writes in his own language, nor the Castilian, nor even the Biscayan, for writing in his. But

4350   your son, señor, I suspect, is not prejudiced against Spanish poetry, but against those poets who are mere Spanish verse writers, without any knowledge of other languages or sciences to adorn and give life and vigour to their natural inspiration; and yet even in this he may be wrong; for, according to a true belief, a

---

[6]"by earning bread," i.e., "livelihood"

poet is born one; that is to say, the poet by nature comes forth a poet from his mother's womb; and following the bent that heaven has bestowed upon him, without the aid of study or art, he produces things that show how truly he spoke who said, 'Est Deus in nobis,'[7] &c. At the same time, I say that the poet by nature who calls in art to his aid will be a far better poet, and will surpass him who tries to be one relying upon his knowledge of art alone. The reason is, that art does not surpass nature, but only brings it to perfection; and thus, nature combined with art, and art with nature, will produce a perfect poet. To bring my argument to a close, I would say then, gentle sir, let your son go on as his star leads him, for being so studious as he seems to be, and having already successfully surmounted the first step of the sciences, which is that of the languages, with their help he will by his own exertions reach the summit of polite literature, which so well becomes an independent gentleman, and adorns, honours, and distinguishes him, as much as the mitre does the bishop, or the gown the learned counsellor. If your son write satires reflecting on the honour of others, chide and correct him, and tear them up; but if he compose discourses in which he rebukes vice in general, in the style of Horace, and with elegance like his, commend him; for it is legitimate for a poet to write against envy and lash the envious in his verse, and the other vices too, provided he does not single out individuals; there are, however, poets who, for the sake of saying something spiteful, would run the risk of being banished to the coast of Pontus. If the poet be pure in his morals, he will be pure in his verses too; the pen is the tongue of the mind, and as the thought engendered there, so will be the things that it writes down. And when kings and princes observe this marvellous science of poetry in wise, virtuous, and thoughtful subjects, they honour, value, exalt them, and even crown them with the leaves of that tree which the thunderbolt strikes not, as if to show that they whose brows are honoured and adorned with such a crown are not to be assailed by anyone."

He of the green gaban was filled with astonishment at Don Quixote's argument, so much so that he began to abandon the notion he had taken up about his being crazy. But in the middle of the discourse, it being not very much to his taste, Sancho had turned aside out of the road to beg a little milk from some shepherds, who were milking their ewes hard by; and just as the gentleman, highly pleased, was about to renew the conversation, Don Quixote, raising his head, perceived a cart covered with royal flags coming along the road they were travelling; and persuaded that this must be some new adventure, he called aloud to Sancho to come and bring him his helmet. Sancho, hearing himself called, quitted the shepherds, and, prodding Dapple vigorously, came up to his master, to whom there fell a terrific and desperate adventure.

---

[7]"There is God in us" (Ovid)

CHAPTER XVII: WHEREIN IS SHOWN THE FURTHEST AND HIGHEST POINT WHICH THE UNEXAMPLED COURAGE OF DON QUIXOTE REACHED OR COULD REACH; TOGETHER WITH THE HAPPILY ACHIEVED ADVENTURE OF THE LIONS

The history tells that when Don Quixote called out to Sancho to bring him his helmet, Sancho was buying some curds the shepherds agreed to sell him, and flurried by the great haste his master was in did not know what to do with them
4395   or what to carry them in; so, not to lose them, for he had already paid for them, he thought it best to throw them into his master's helmet, and acting on this bright idea he went to see what his master wanted with him. He, as he approached, exclaimed to him:

"Give me that helmet, my friend, for either I know little of adventures, or what
4400   I observe yonder is one that will, and does, call upon me to arm myself."

He of the green gaban, on hearing this, looked in all directions, but could perceive nothing, except a cart coming towards them with two or three small flags, which led him to conclude it must be carrying treasure of the King's, and he said so to Don Quixote. He, however, would not believe him, being always persuaded and
4405   convinced that all that happened to him must be adventures and still more adventures; so he replied to the gentleman, "He who is prepared has his battle half fought; nothing is lost by my preparing myself, for I know by experience that I have enemies, visible and invisible, and I know not when, or where, or at what moment, or in what shapes they will attack me;" and turning to Sancho he called for his
4410   helmet; and Sancho, as he had no time to take out the curds, had to give it just as it was. Don Quixote took it, and without perceiving what was in it thrust it down in hot haste upon his head; but as the curds were pressed and squeezed the whey began to run all over his face and beard, whereat he was so startled that he cried out to Sancho:
4415   "Sancho, what's this? I think my head is softening, or my brains are melting, or I am sweating from head to foot! If I am sweating it is not indeed from fear. I am convinced beyond a doubt that the adventure which is about to befall me is a terrible one. Give me something to wipe myself with, if thou hast it, for this profuse sweat is blinding me."
4420   Sancho held his tongue, and gave him a cloth, and gave thanks to God at the same time that his master had not found out what was the matter. Don Quixote then wiped himself, and took off his helmet to see what it was that made his head feel so cool, and seeing all that white mash inside his helmet he put it to his nose, and as soon as he had smelt it he exclaimed:
4425   "By the life of my lady Dulcinea del Toboso, but it is curds thou hast put here, thou treacherous, impudent, ill-mannered squire!"

To which, with great composure and pretended innocence, Sancho replied, "If they are curds let me have them, your worship, and I'll eat them; but let the devil eat them, for it must have been he who put them there. I dare to dirty your helmet!
4430   You have guessed the offender finely! Faith, sir, by the light God gives me, it seems I

must have enchanters too, that persecute me as a creature and limb of your worship, and they must have put that nastiness there in order to provoke your patience to anger, and make you baste my ribs as you are wont to do. Well, this time, indeed, they have missed their aim, for I trust to my master's good sense to see that I have got no curds or milk, or anything of the sort; and that if I had it is in my stomach I would put it and not in the helmet."

"May be so," said Don Quixote. All this the gentleman was observing, and with astonishment, more especially when, after having wiped himself clean, his head, face, beard, and helmet, Don Quixote put it on, and settling himself firmly in his stirrups, easing his sword in the scabbard, and grasping his lance, he cried, "Now, come who will, here am I, ready to try conclusions with Satan himself in person!"

By this time the cart with the flags had come up, unattended by anyone except the carter on a mule, and a man sitting in front. Don Quixote planted himself before it and said, "Whither are you going, brothers? What cart is this? What have you got in it? What flags are those?"

To this the carter replied, "The cart is mine; what is in it is a pair of wild caged lions, which the governor of Oran is sending to court as a present to his Majesty; and the flags are our lord the King's, to show that what is here is his property."

"And are the lions large?" asked Don Quixote.

"So large," replied the man who sat at the door of the cart, "that larger, or as large, have never crossed from Africa to Spain; I am the keeper, and I have brought over others, but never any like these. They are male and female; the male is in that first cage and the female in the one behind, and they are hungry now, for they have eaten nothing today, so let your worship stand aside, for we must make haste to the place where we are to feed them."

Hereupon, smiling slightly, Don Quixote exclaimed, "Lion-whelps to me! to me whelps of lions, and at such a time! Then, by God! those gentlemen who send them here shall see if I am a man to be frightened by lions. Get down, my good fellow, and as you are the keeper open the cages, and turn me out those beasts, and in the midst of this plain I will let them know who Don Quixote of La Mancha is, in spite and in the teeth of the enchanters who send them to me."

"So, so," said the gentleman to himself at this; "our worthy knight has shown of what sort he is; the curds, no doubt, have softened his skull and brought his brains to a head."

At this instant Sancho came up to him, saying, "Señor, for God's sake do something to keep my master, Don Quixote, from tackling these lions; for if he does they'll tear us all to pieces here."

"Is your master then so mad," asked the gentleman, "that you believe and are afraid he will engage such fierce animals?"

"He is not mad," said Sancho, "but he is venturesome."

"I will prevent it," said the gentleman; and going over to Don Quixote, who was insisting upon the keeper's opening the cages, he said to him, "Sir knight,

4475   knights-errant should attempt adventures which encourage the hope of a successful issue, not those which entirely withhold it; for valour that trenches upon temerity savours rather of madness than of courage; moreover, these lions do not come to oppose you, nor do they dream of such a thing; they are going as presents to his Majesty, and it will not be right to stop them or delay their

4480   journey."

     "Gentle sir," replied Don Quixote, "you go and mind your tame partridge and your bold ferret, and leave everyone to manage his own business; this is mine, and I know whether these gentlemen the lions come to me or not;" and then turning to the keeper he exclaimed, "By all that's good, sir scoundrel, if you don't open the

4485   cages this very instant, I'll pin you to the cart with this lance."

     The carter, seeing the determination of this apparition in armour, said to him, "Please your worship, for charity's sake, señor, let me unyoke the mules and place myself in safety along with them before the lions are turned out; for if they kill them on me I am ruined for life, for all I possess is this cart and mules."

4490   "O man of little faith," replied Don Quixote, "get down and unyoke; you will soon see that you are exerting yourself for nothing, and that you might have spared yourself the trouble."

     The carter got down and with all speed unyoked the mules, and the keeper called out at the top of his voice, "I call all here to witness that against my will

4495   and under compulsion I open the cages and let the lions loose, and that I warn this gentleman that he will be accountable for all the harm and mischief which these beasts may do, and for my salary and dues as well. You, gentlemen, place yourselves in safety before I open, for I know they will do me no harm."

     Once more the gentleman strove to persuade Don Quixote not to do such a mad

4500   thing, as it was tempting God to engage in such a piece of folly. To this, Don Quixote replied that he knew what he was about. The gentleman in return entreated him to reflect, for he knew he was under a delusion.

     "Well, señor," answered Don Quixote, "if you do not like to be a spectator of this tragedy, as in your opinion it will be, spur your flea-bitten mare, and place

4505   yourself in safety."

     Hearing this, Sancho with tears in his eyes entreated him to give up an enterprise compared with which the one of the windmills, and the awful one of the fulling mills, and, in fact, all the feats he had attempted in the whole course of his life, were cakes and fancy bread. "Look ye, señor," said Sancho, "there's no

4510   enchantment here, nor anything of the sort, for between the bars and chinks of the cage I have seen the paw of a real lion, and judging by that I reckon the lion such a paw could belong to must be bigger than a mountain."

     "Fear at any rate," replied Don Quixote, "will make him look bigger to thee than half the world. Retire, Sancho, and leave me; and if I die here thou knowest

4515   our old compact; thou wilt repair to Dulcinea—I say no more." To these he added some further words that banished all hope of his giving up his insane project. He of the green gaban would have offered resistance, but he found himself ill-matched as to arms, and did not think it prudent to come to blows with a madman, for such

Don Quixote now showed himself to be in every respect; and the latter, renewing
4520 his commands to the keeper and repeating his threats, gave warning to the
gentleman to spur his mare, Sancho his Dapple, and the carter his mules, all
striving to get away from the cart as far as they could before the lions broke loose.
Sancho was weeping over his master's death, for this time he firmly believed it
was in store for him from the claws of the lions; and he cursed his fate and called
4525 it an unlucky hour when he thought of taking service with him again; but with all
his tears and lamentations he did not forget to thrash Dapple so as to put a good
space between himself and the cart. The keeper, seeing that the fugitives were now
some distance off, once more entreated and warned him as before; but he replied
that he heard him, and that he need not trouble himself with any further warnings
4530 or entreaties, as they would be fruitless, and bade him make haste.
     During the delay that occurred while the keeper was opening the first cage,
Don Quixote was considering whether it would not be well to do battle on foot,
instead of on horseback, and finally resolved to fight on foot, fearing that
Rocinante might take fright at the sight of the lions; he therefore sprang off his
4535 horse, flung his lance aside, braced his buckler on his arm, and drawing his
sword, advanced slowly with marvellous intrepidity and resolute courage, to
plant himself in front of the cart, commending himself with all his heart to God and
to his lady Dulcinea.
     It is to be observed, that on coming to this passage, the author of this
4540 veracious history breaks out into exclamations. "O doughty Don Quixote! high-
mettled past extolling! Mirror, wherein all the heroes of the world may see
themselves! Second modern Don Manuel de Leon, once the glory and honour of
Spanish knighthood! In what words shall I describe this dread exploit, by what
language shall I make it credible to ages to come, what eulogies are there unmeet
4545 for thee, though they be hyperboles piled on hyperboles! On foot, alone,
undaunted, high-souled, with but a simple sword, and that no trenchant blade of
the Perrillo brand, a shield, but no bright polished steel one, there stoodst thou,
biding and awaiting the two fiercest lions that Africa's forests ever bred! Thy
own deeds be thy praise, valiant Manchegan, and here I leave them as they stand,
4550 wanting the words wherewith to glorify them!"
     Here the author's outburst came to an end, and he proceeded to take up the
thread of his story, saying that the keeper, seeing that Don Quixote had taken up
his position, and that it was impossible for him to avoid letting out the male
without incurring the enmity of the fiery and daring knight, flung open the doors of
4555 the first cage, containing, as has been said, the lion, which was now seen to be of
enormous size, and grim and hideous mien. The first thing he did was to turn round
in the cage in which he lay, and protrude his claws, and stretch himself
thoroughly; he next opened his mouth, and yawned very leisurely, and with near
two palms' length of tongue that he had thrust forth, he licked the dust out of his
4560 eyes and washed his face; having done this, he put his head out of the cage and
looked all round with eyes like glowing coals, a spectacle and demeanour to strike
terror into temerity itself. Don Quixote merely observed him steadily, longing for

him to leap from the cart and come to close quarters with him, when he hoped to hew him in pieces.

4565 So far did his unparalleled madness go; but the noble lion, more courteous than arrogant, not troubling himself about silly bravado, after having looked all round, as has been said, turned about and presented his hind-quarters to Don Quixote, and very coolly and tranquilly lay down again in the cage. Seeing this, Don Quixote ordered the keeper to take a stick to him and provoke him to make 4570 him come out.

"That I won't," said the keeper; "for if I anger him, the first he'll tear in pieces will be myself. Be satisfied, sir knight, with what you have done, which leaves nothing more to be said on the score of courage, and do not seek to tempt fortune a second time. The lion has the door open; he is free to come out or not to come out; 4575 but as he has not come out so far, he will not come out to-day. Your worship's great courage has been fully manifested already; no brave champion, so it strikes me, is bound to do more than challenge his enemy and wait for him on the field; if his adversary does not come, on him lies the disgrace, and he who waits for him carries off the crown of victory."

4580 "That is true," said Don Quixote; "close the door, my friend, and let me have, in the best form thou canst, what thou hast seen me do, by way of certificate; to wit, that thou didst open for the lion, that I waited for him, that he did not come out, that I still waited for him, and that still he did not come out, and lay down again. I am not bound to do more; enchantments avaunt ["be gone"], and God 4585 uphold the right, the truth, and true chivalry! Close the door as I bade thee, while I make signals to the fugitives that have left us, that they may learn this exploit from thy lips."

The keeper obeyed, and Don Quixote, fixing on the point of his lance the cloth he had wiped his face with after the deluge of curds, proceeded to recall the others, 4590 who still continued to fly, looking back at every step, all in a body, the gentleman bringing up the rear. Sancho, however, happening to observe the signal of the white cloth, exclaimed, "May I die, if my master has not overcome the wild beasts, for he is calling to us."

They all stopped, and perceived that it was Don Quixote who was making 4595 signals, and shaking off their fears to some extent, they approached slowly until they were near enough to hear distinctly Don Quixote's voice calling to them. They returned at length to the cart, and as they came up, Don Quixote said to the carter, "Put your mules to once more, brother, and continue your journey; and do thou, Sancho, give him two gold crowns for himself and the keeper, to compensate 4600 for the delay they have incurred through me."

"That will I give with all my heart," said Sancho; "but what has become of the lions? Are they dead or alive?"

The keeper, then, in full detail, and bit by bit, described the end of the contest, exalting to the best of his power and ability the valour of Don Quixote, at the 4605 sight of whom the lion quailed, and would not and dared not come out of the cage, although he had held the door open ever so long; and showing how, in consequence of his having represented to the knight that it was tempting God to provoke the lion in order to force him out, which he wished to have done, he very reluctantly, and altogether against his will, had allowed the door to be closed.

4610   "What dost thou think of this, Sancho?" said Don Quixote. "Are there any enchantments that can prevail against true valour? The enchanters may be able to rob me of good fortune, but of fortitude and courage they cannot."

     Sancho paid the crowns, the carter put to, the keeper kissed Don Quixote's hands for the bounty bestowed upon him, and promised to give an account of the

4615   valiant exploit to the King himself, as soon as he saw him at court.

     "Then," said Don Quixote, "if his Majesty should happen to ask who performed it, you must say THE KNIGHT OF THE LIONS; for it is my desire that into this the name I have hitherto borne of Knight of the Rueful Countenance be from this time forward changed, altered, transformed, and turned; and in this I

4620   follow the ancient usage of knights-errant, who changed their names when they pleased, or when it suited their purpose."

     The cart went its way, and Don Quixote, Sancho, and he of the green gaban went theirs. All this time, Don Diego de Miranda had not spoken a word, being entirely taken up with observing and noting all that Don Quixote did and said,

4625   and the opinion he formed was that he was a man of brains gone mad, and a madman on the verge of rationality. The first part of his history had not yet reached him, for, had he read it, the amazement with which his words and deeds filled him would have vanished, as he would then have understood the nature of his madness; but knowing nothing of it, he took him to be rational one moment, and

4630   crazy the next, for what he said was sensible, elegant, and well expressed, and what he did, absurd, rash, and foolish; and said he to himself, "What could be madder than putting on a helmet full of curds, and then persuading oneself that enchanters are softening one's skull; or what could be greater rashness and folly than wanting to fight lions tooth and nail?"

4635   Don Quixote roused him from these reflections and this soliloquy by saying, "No doubt, Señor Don Diego de Miranda, you set me down in your mind as a fool and a madman, and it would be no wonder if you did, for my deeds do not argue anything else. But for all that, I would have you take notice that I am neither so mad nor so foolish as I must have seemed to you. A gallant knight shows to

4640   advantage bringing his lance to bear adroitly upon a fierce bull under the eyes of his sovereign, in the midst of a spacious plaza; a knight shows to advantage arrayed in glittering armour, pacing the lists before the ladies in some joyous tournament, and all those knights show to advantage that entertain, divert, and, if we may say so, honour the courts of their princes by warlike exercises, or what

4645   resemble them; but to greater advantage than all these does a knight-errant show when he traverses deserts, solitudes, cross-roads, forests, and mountains, in quest of perilous adventures, bent on bringing them to a happy and successful issue, all to win a glorious and lasting renown. To greater advantage, I maintain, does the knight-errant show bringing aid to some widow in some lonely waste, than the

4650   court knight dallying with some city damsel. All knights have their own special

parts to play; let the courtier devote himself to the ladies, let him add lustre to his sovereign's court by his liveries, let him entertain poor gentlemen with the sumptuous fare of his table, let him arrange joustings, marshal tournaments, and prove himself noble, generous, and magnificent, and above all a good Christian,
4655 and so doing he will fulfil the duties that are especially his; but let the knight-errant explore the corners of the earth and penetrate the most intricate labyrinths, at each step let him attempt impossibilities, on desolate heaths let him endure the burning rays of the midsummer sun, and the bitter inclemency of the winter winds and frosts; let no lions daunt him, no monsters terrify him, no dragons make him
4660 quail; for to seek these, to attack those, and to vanquish all, are in truth his main duties. I, then, as it has fallen to my lot to be a member of knight-errantry, cannot avoid attempting all that to me seems to come within the sphere of my duties; thus it was my bounden duty to attack those lions that I just now attacked, although I knew it to be the height of rashness; for I know well what valour is, that it is a
4665 virtue that occupies a place between two vicious extremes, cowardice and temerity; but it will be a lesser evil for him who is valiant to rise till he reaches the point of rashness, than to sink until he reaches the point of cowardice; for, as it is easier for the prodigal than for the miser to become generous, so it is easier for a rash man to prove truly valiant than for a coward to rise to true valour; and
4670 believe me, Señor Don Diego, in attempting adventures it is better to lose by a card too many than by a card too few; for to hear it said, 'such a knight is rash and daring,' sounds better than 'such a knight is timid and cowardly.'"

"I protest, Señor Don Quixote," said Don Diego, "everything you have said and done is proved correct by the test of reason itself; and I believe, if the laws
4675 and ordinances of knight-errantry should be lost, they might be found in your worship's breast as in their own proper depository and muniment-house; but let us make haste, and reach my village, where you shall take rest after your late exertions; for if they have not been of the body they have been of the spirit, and these sometimes tend to produce bodily fatigue."
4680 "I take the invitation as a great favour and honour, Señor Don Diego," replied Don Quixote; and pressing forward at a better pace than before, at about two in the afternoon they reached the village and house of Don Diego, or, as Don Quixote called him, "The Knight of the Green Gaban."

* * * * *

CHAPTER LXIV: TREATING OF THE ADVENTURE WHICH GAVE DON QUIXOTE MORE UNHAPPINESS THAN ALL THAT HAD HITHERTO BEFALLEN HIM

The wife of Don Antonio Moreno, so the history says, was extremely happy
4685 to see Ana Felix in her house. She welcomed her with great kindness, charmed as well by her beauty as by her intelligence; for in both respects the fair Morisco

was richly endowed, and all the people of the city flocked to see her as though they had been summoned by the ringing of the bells.

4690   Don Quixote told Don Antonio that the plan adopted for releasing Don Gregorio was not a good one, for its risks were greater than its advantages, and that it would be better to land himself with his arms and horse in Barbary; for he would carry him off in spite of the whole Moorish host, as Don Gaiferos carried off his wife Melisendra.

4695   "Remember, your worship," observed Sancho on hearing him say so, "Señor Don Gaiferos carried off his wife from the mainland, and took her to France by land; but in this case, if by chance we carry off Don Gregorio, we have no way of bringing him to Spain, for there's the sea between."

    "There's a remedy for everything except death," said Don Quixote; "if they bring the vessel close to the shore we shall be able to get on board though all the

4700 world strive to prevent us."

    "Your worship hits it off mighty well and mighty easy," said Sancho; "but 'it's a long step from saying to doing;' and I hold to the renegade, for he seems to me an honest good-hearted fellow."

    Don Antonio then said that if the renegade did not prove successful, the

4705 expedient of the great Don Quixote's expedition to Barbary should be adopted. Two days afterwards the renegade put to sea in a light vessel of six oars a-side manned by a stout crew, and two days later the galleys made sail eastward, the general having begged the viceroy to let him know all about the release of Don Gregorio and about Ana Felix, and the viceroy promised to do as he requested.

4710   One morning as Don Quixote went out for a stroll along the beach, arrayed in full armour (for, as he often said, that was "his only gear, his only rest the fray," and he never was without it for a moment), he saw coming towards him a knight, also in full armour, with a shining moon painted on his shield, who, on approaching sufficiently near to be heard, said in a loud voice, addressing himself

4715 to Don Quixote, "Illustrious knight, and never sufficiently extolled Don Quixote of La Mancha, I am the Knight of the White Moon, whose unheard-of achievements will perhaps have recalled him to thy memory. I come to do battle with thee and prove the might of thy arm, to the end that I make thee acknowledge and confess that my lady, let her be who she may, is incomparably fairer than thy

4720 Dulcinea del Toboso. If thou dost acknowledge this fairly and openly, thou shalt escape death and save me the trouble of inflicting it upon thee; if thou fightest and I vanquish thee, I demand no other satisfaction than that, laying aside arms and abstaining from going in quest of adventures, thou withdraw and betake thyself to thine own village for the space of a year, and live there without putting hand to

4725 sword, in peace and quiet and beneficial repose, the same being needful for the increase of thy substance and the salvation of thy soul; and if thou dost vanquish me, my head shall be at thy disposal, my arms and horse thy spoils, and the renown of my deeds transferred and added to thine. Consider which will be thy best course, and give me thy answer speedily, for this day is all the time I have for the

4730 despatch of this business."

Don Quixote was amazed and astonished, as well at the Knight of the White
Moon's arrogance, as at his reason for delivering the defiance, and with calm
dignity he answered him, "Knight of the White Moon, of whose achievements I
have never heard until now, I will venture to swear you have never seen the
illustrious Dulcinea; for had you seen her I know you would have taken care not
to venture yourself upon this issue, because the sight would have removed all
doubt from your mind that there ever has been or can be a beauty to be compared
with hers; and so, not saying you lie, but merely that you are not correct in what
you state, I accept your challenge, with the conditions you have proposed, and at
once, that the day you have fixed may not expire; and from your conditions I
except only that of the renown of your achievements being transferred to me, for I
know not of what sort they are nor what they may amount to; I am satisfied with
my own, such as they be. Take, therefore, the side of the field you choose, and I
will do the same; and to whom God shall give it may Saint Peter add his blessing."

The Knight of the White Moon had been seen from the city, and it was told the
viceroy how he was in conversation with Don Quixote. The viceroy, fancying it
must be some fresh adventure got up by Don Antonio Moreno or some other
gentleman of the city, hurried out at once to the beach accompanied by Don
Antonio and several other gentlemen, just as Don Quixote was wheeling
Rocinante round in order to take up the necessary distance. The viceroy upon this,
seeing that the pair of them were evidently preparing to come to the charge, put
himself between them, asking them what it was that led them to engage in combat
all of a sudden in this way. The Knight of the White Moon replied that it was a
question of precedence of beauty; and briefly told him what he had said to Don
Quixote, and how the conditions of the defiance agreed upon on both sides had
been accepted. The viceroy went over to Don Antonio, and asked in a low voice
did he know who the Knight of the White Moon was, or was it some joke they
were playing on Don Quixote. Don Antonio replied that he neither knew who he
was nor whether the defiance was in joke or in earnest. This answer left the
viceroy in a state of perplexity, not knowing whether he ought to let the combat go
on or not; but unable to persuade himself that it was anything but a joke he fell
back, saying, "If there be no other way out of it, gallant knights, except to confess
or die, and Don Quixote is inflexible, and your worship of the White Moon still
more so, in God's hand be it, and fall on."

He of the White Moon thanked the viceroy in courteous and well-chosen
words for the permission he gave them, and so did Don Quixote, who then,
commending himself with all his heart to heaven and to his Dulcinea, as was his
custom on the eve of any combat that awaited him, proceeded to take a little more
distance, as he saw his antagonist was doing the same; then, without blast of
trumpet or other warlike instrument to give them the signal to charge, both at the
same instant wheeled their horses; and he of the White Moon, being the swifter,
met Don Quixote after having traversed two-thirds of the course, and there
encountered him with such violence that, without touching him with his lance (for
he held it high, to all appearance purposely), he hurled Don Quixote and

4775 Rocinante to the earth, a perilous fall. He sprang upon him at once, and placing the lance over his visor said to him, "You are vanquished, sir knight, nay dead unless you admit the conditions of our defiance."

Don Quixote, bruised and stupefied, without raising his visor said in a weak feeble voice as if he were speaking out of a tomb, "Dulcinea del Toboso is the
4780 fairest woman in the world, and I the most unfortunate knight on earth; it is not fitting that this truth should suffer by my feebleness; drive your lance home, sir knight, and take my life, since you have taken away my honour."

"That will I not, in sooth," said he of the White Moon; "live the fame of the lady Dulcinea's beauty undimmed as ever; all I require is that the great Don
4785 Quixote retire to his own home for a year, or for so long a time as shall by me be enjoined upon him, as we agreed before engaging in this combat."

The viceroy, Don Antonio, and several others who were present heard all this, and heard too how Don Quixote replied that so long as nothing in prejudice of Dulcinea was demanded of him, he would observe all the rest like a true and
4790 loyal knight. The engagement given, he of the White Moon wheeled about, and making obeisance to the viceroy with a movement of the head, rode away into the city at a half gallop. The viceroy bade Don Antonio hasten after him, and by some means or other find out who he was. They raised Don Quixote up and uncovered his face, and found him pale and bathed with sweat. Rocinante from the mere hard
4795 measure he had received lay unable to stir for the present. Sancho, wholly dejected and woebegone, knew not what to say or do. He fancied that all was a dream, that the whole business was a piece of enchantment. Here was his master defeated, and bound not to take up arms for a year. He saw the light of the glory of his achievements obscured; the hopes of the promises lately made him swept away like
4800 smoke before the wind; Rocinante, he feared, was crippled for life, and his master's bones out of joint; for if he were only shaken out of his madness it would be no small luck. In the end they carried him into the city in a hand-chair which the viceroy sent for, and thither the viceroy himself returned, eager to ascertain who this Knight of the White Moon was who had left Don Quixote in such a sad plight.

FROM CHAPTER LXV: WHEREIN IS MADE KNOWN WHO THE KNIGHT OF THE WHITE MOON WAS; LIKEWISE DON GREGORIO'S RELEASE, AND OTHER EVENTS

4805 Don Antonia Moreno followed the Knight of the White Moon, and a number of boys followed him too, nay pursued him, until they had him fairly housed in a hostel in the heart of the city. Don Antonio, eager to make his acquaintance, entered also; a squire came out to meet him and remove his armour, and he shut himself into a lower room, still attended by Don Antonio, whose bread would not
4810 bake until he had found out who he was. He of the White Moon, seeing then that the gentleman would not leave him, said, "I know very well, señor, what you have come for; it is to find out who I am; and as there is no reason why I should conceal it from you, while my servant here is taking off my armour I will tell you the true

state of the case, without leaving out anything. You must know, señor, that I am
called the bachelor Samson Carrasco. I am of the same village as Don Quixote of
La Mancha, whose craze and folly make all of us who know him feel pity for him,
and I am one of those who have felt it most; and persuaded that his chance of
recovery lay in quiet and keeping at home and in his own house, I hit upon a
device for keeping him there. Three months ago, therefore, I went out to meet him as
a knight-errant, under the assumed name of the Knight of the Mirrors, intending to
engage him in combat and overcome him without hurting him, making it the
condition of our combat that the vanquished should be at the disposal of the
victor. What I meant to demand of him (for I regarded him as vanquished already)
was that he should return to his own village, and not leave it for a whole year, by
which time he might be cured. But fate ordered it otherwise, for he vanquished me
and unhorsed me, and so my plan failed. He went his way, and I came back
conquered, covered with shame, and sorely bruised by my fall, which was a
particularly dangerous one. But this did not quench my desire to meet him again
and overcome him, as you have seen to-day. And as he is so scrupulous in his
observance of the laws of knight-errantry, he will, no doubt, in order to keep his
word, obey the injunction I have laid upon him. This, señor, is how the matter
stands, and I have nothing more to tell you. I implore of you not to betray me, or
tell Don Quixote who I am; so that my honest endeavours may be successful, and
that a man of excellent wits—were he only rid of the fooleries of chivalry—may
get them back again."

"O señor," said Don Antonio, "may God forgive you the wrong you have
done the whole world in trying to bring the most amusing madman in it back to his
senses. Do you not see, señor, that the gain by Don Quixote's sanity can never
equal the enjoyment his crazes give? But my belief is that all the señor bachelor's
pains will be of no avail to bring a man so hopelessly cracked to his senses again;
and if it were not uncharitable, I would say may Don Quixote never be cured, for
by his recovery we lose not only his own drolleries, but his squire Sancho
Panza's too, any one of which is enough to turn melancholy itself into merriment.
However, I'll hold my peace and say nothing to him, and we'll see whether I am
right in my suspicion that Señor Carrasco's efforts will be fruitless."

The bachelor replied that at all events the affair promised well, and he hoped
for a happy result from it; and putting his services at Don Antonio's commands he
took his leave of him; and having had his armour packed at once upon a mule, he
rode away from the city the same day on the horse he rode to battle, and returned
to his own country without meeting any adventure calling for record in this
veracious history.

CHAPTER LXXIII: OF THE OMENS DON QUIXOTE HAD AS HE ENTERED HIS OWN VILLAGE, AND OTHER INCIDENTS THAT EMBELLISH AND GIVE A COLOUR TO THIS GREAT HISTORY

At the entrance of the village, so says Cide Hamete, Don Quixote saw two boys quarrelling on the village threshing-floor one of whom said to the other, "Take it easy, Periquillo; thou shalt never see it again as long as thou livest."

4855 Don Quixote heard this, and said he to Sancho, "Dost thou not mark, friend, what that boy said, 'Thou shalt never see it again as long as thou livest'?"

"Well," said Sancho, "what does it matter if the boy said so?"

"What!" said Don Quixote, "dost thou not see that, applied to the object of my desires, the words mean that I am never to see Dulcinea more?"

4860 Sancho was about to answer, when his attention was diverted by seeing a hare come flying across the plain pursued by several greyhounds and sportsmen. In its terror it ran to take shelter and hide itself under Dapple. Sancho caught it alive and presented it to Don Quixote, who was saying, "*Malum signum, malum signum!*[8] a hare flies, greyhounds chase it, Dulcinea appears not."

4865 "Your worship's a strange man," said Sancho; "let's take it for granted that this hare is Dulcinea, and these greyhounds chasing it the malignant enchanters who turned her into a country wench; she flies, and I catch her and put her into your worship's hands, and you hold her in your arms and cherish her; what bad sign is that, or what ill omen is there to be found here?"

4870 The two boys who had been quarrelling came over to look at the hare, and Sancho asked one of them what their quarrel was about. He was answered by the one who had said, "Thou shalt never see it again as long as thou livest," that he had taken a cage full of crickets from the other boy, and did not mean to give it back to him as long as he lived. Sancho took out four *cuartos* from his pocket and

4875 gave them to the boy for the cage, which he placed in Don Quixote's hands, saying, "There, señor! there are the omens broken and destroyed, and they have no more to do with our affairs, to my thinking, fool as I am, than with last year's clouds; and if I remember rightly I have heard the curate of our village say that it does not become Christians or sensible people to give any heed to these silly things; and

4880 even you yourself said the same to me some time ago, telling me that all Christians who minded omens were fools; but there's no need of making words about it; let us push on and go into our village."

The sportsmen came up and asked for their hare, which Don Quixote gave them. They then went on, and upon the green at the entrance of the town they came

4885 upon the curate and the bachelor Samson Carrasco busy with their breviaries. It should be mentioned that Sancho had thrown, by way of a sumpter-cloth [packsaddle cover], over Dapple and over the bundle of armour, the buckram robe painted with flames which they had put upon him at the duke's castle the night Altisidora came back to life. He had also fixed the mitre on Dapple's head, the

---

[8]"a bad sign"

4890   oddest transformation and decoration that ever ass in the world underwent. They were at once recognised by both the curate and the bachelor, who came towards them with open arms. Don Quixote dismounted and received them with a close embrace; and the boys, who are lynxes that nothing escapes, spied out the ass's mitre and came running to see it, calling out to one another, "Come here, boys, and
4895   see Sancho Panza's ass figged out finer than Mingo, and Don Quixote's beast leaner than ever."

     So at length, with the boys capering round them, and accompanied by the curate and the bachelor, they made their entrance into the town, and proceeded to Don Quixote's house, at the door of which they found his housekeeper and niece,
4900   whom the news of his arrival had already reached. It had been brought to Teresa Panza, Sancho's wife, as well, and she with her hair all loose and half naked, dragging Sanchica her daughter by the hand, ran out to meet her husband; but seeing him coming in by no means as good case as she thought a governor ought to be, she said to him, "How is it you come this way, husband? It seems to me you
4905   come tramping and footsore, and looking more like a disorderly vagabond than a governor."

     "Hold your tongue, Teresa," said Sancho; "often 'where there are pegs there are no flitches;' let's go into the house and there you'll hear strange things. I bring money, and that's the main thing, got by my own industry without wronging
4910   anybody."

     "You bring the money, my good husband," said Teresa, "and no matter whether it was got this way or that; for, however you may have got it, you'll not have brought any new practice into the world."

     Sanchica embraced her father and asked him if he brought her anything, for
4915   she had been looking out for him as for the showers of May; and she taking hold of him by the girdle on one side, and his wife by the hand, while the daughter led Dapple, they made for their house, leaving Don Quixote in his, in the hands of his niece and housekeeper, and in the company of the curate and the bachelor.

     Don Quixote at once, without any regard to time or season, withdrew in
4920   private with the bachelor and the curate, and in a few words told them of his defeat, and of the engagement he was under not to quit his village for a year, which he meant to keep to the letter without departing a hair's breadth from it, as became a knight-errant bound by scrupulous good faith and the laws of knight-errantry; and of how he thought of turning shepherd for that year, and taking his diversion
4925   in the solitude of the fields, where he could with perfect freedom give range to his thoughts of love while he followed the virtuous pastoral calling; and he besought them, if they had not a great deal to do and were not prevented by more important business, to consent to be his companions, for he would buy sheep enough to qualify them for shepherds; and the most important point of the whole affair, he
4930   could tell them, was settled, for he had given them names that would fit them to a T. The curate asked what they were. Don Quixote replied that he himself was to be called the shepherd Quixotize and the bachelor the shepherd Carrascon, and the curate the shepherd Curambro, and Sancho Panza the shepherd Pancino.

Both were astounded at Don Quixote's new craze; however, lest he should
4935   once more make off out of the village from them in pursuit of his chivalry, they
trusting that in the course of the year he might be cured, fell in with his new
project, applauded his crazy idea as a bright one, and offered to share the life with
him. "And what's more," said Samson Carrasco, "I am, as all the world knows, a
very famous poet, and I'll be always making verses, pastoral, or courtly, or as it
4940   may come into my head, to pass away our time in those secluded regions where we
shall be roaming. But what is most needful, sirs, is that each of us should choose
the name of the shepherdess he means to glorify in his verses, and that we should
not leave a tree, be it ever so hard, without writing up and carving her name on it,
as is the habit and custom of love-smitten shepherds."

4945   "That's the very thing," said Don Quixote; "though I am relieved from looking
for the name of an imaginary shepherdess, for there's the peerless Dulcinea del
Toboso, the glory of these brooksides, the ornament of these meadows, the
mainstay of beauty, the cream of all the graces, and, in a word, the being to whom
all praise is appropriate, be it ever so hyperbolical."

4950   "Very true," said the curate; "but we the others must look about for
accommodating shepherdesses that will answer our purpose one way or another."

"And," added Samson Carrasco, "if they fail us, we can call them by the
names of the ones in print that the world is filled with, Filidas, Amarilises,
Dianas, Fleridas, Galateas, Belisardas; for as they sell them in the market-places
4955   we may fairly buy them and make them our own. If my lady, or I should say my
shepherdess, happens to be called Ana, I'll sing her praises under the name of
Anarda, and if Francisca, I'll call her Francenia, and if Lucia, Lucinda, for it all
comes to the same thing; and Sancho Panza, if he joins this fraternity, may glorify
his wife Teresa Panza as Teresaina."

4960   Don Quixote laughed at the adaptation of the name, and the curate bestowed
vast praise upon the worthy and honourable resolution he had made, and again
offered to bear him company all the time that he could spare from his imperative
duties. And so they took their leave of him, recommending and beseeching him to
take care of his health and treat himself to a suitable diet.

4965   It so happened his niece and the housekeeper overheard all the three of them
said; and as soon as they were gone they both of them came in to Don Quixote, and
said the niece, "What's this, uncle? Now that we were thinking you had come
back to stay at home and lead a quiet respectable life there, are you going to get
into fresh entanglements, and turn 'young shepherd, thou that comest here, young
4970   shepherd going there?' Nay! indeed 'the straw is too hard now to make pipes of.'"

"And," added the housekeeper, "will your worship be able to bear, out in the
fields, the heats of summer, and the chills of winter, and the howling of the
wolves? Not you; for that's a life and a business for hardy men, bred and
seasoned to such work almost from the time they were in swaddling-clothes. Why,
4975   to make choice of evils, it's better to be a knight-errant than a shepherd! Look
here, señor; take my advice—and I'm not giving it to you full of bread and wine,
but fasting, and with fifty years upon my head—stay at home, look after your

affairs, go often to confession, be good to the poor, and upon my soul be it if any evil comes to you."

4980   "Hold your peace, my daughters," said Don Quixote; "I know very well what my duty is; help me to bed, for I don't feel very well; and rest assured that, knight-errant now or wandering shepherd to be, I shall never fail to have a care for your interests, as you will see in the end." And the good wenches (for that they undoubtedly were), the housekeeper and niece, helped him to bed, where they gave

4985   him something to eat and made him as comfortable as possible.

CHAPTER LXXIV: OF HOW DON QUIXOTE FELL SICK, AND OF THE WILL HE MADE, AND HOW HE DIED

As nothing that is man's can last for ever, but all tends ever downwards from its beginning to its end, and above all man's life, and as Don Quixote's enjoyed no special dispensation from heaven to stay its course, its end and close came when he least looked for it. For—whether it was of the dejection the thought of his

4990   defeat produced, or of heaven's will that so ordered it—a fever settled upon him and kept him in his bed for six days, during which he was often visited by his friends the curate, the bachelor, and the barber, while his good squire Sancho Panza never quitted his bedside. They, persuaded that it was grief at finding himself vanquished, and the object of his heart, the liberation and disenchantment

4995   of Dulcinea, unattained, that kept him in this state, strove by all the means in their power to cheer him up; the bachelor bidding him take heart and get up to begin his pastoral life, for which he himself, he said, had already composed an eclogue that would take the shine out of all Sannazaro had ever written, and had bought with his own money two famous dogs to guard the flock, one called Barcino and the

5000   other Butron, which a herdsman of Quintanar had sold him.

But for all this Don Quixote could not shake off his sadness. His friends called in the doctor, who felt his pulse and was not very well satisfied with it, and said that in any case it would be well for him to attend to the health of his soul, as that of his body was in a bad way. Don Quixote heard this calmly; but not

5005   so his housekeeper, his niece, and his squire, who fell weeping bitterly, as if they had him lying dead before them. The doctor's opinion was that melancholy and depression were bringing him to his end. Don Quixote begged them to leave him to himself, as he had a wish to sleep a little. They obeyed, and he slept at one stretch, as the saying is, more than six hours, so that the housekeeper and niece thought he

5010   was going to sleep for ever. But at the end of that time he woke up, and in a loud voice exclaimed, "Blessed be Almighty God, who has shown me such goodness. In truth his mercies are boundless, and the sins of men can neither limit them nor keep them back!"

The niece listened with attention to her uncle's words, and they struck her as

5015   more coherent than what usually fell from him, at least during his illness, so she asked, "What are you saying, señor? Has anything strange occurred? What mercies or what sins of men are you talking of?"

"The mercies, niece," said Don Quixote, "are those that God has this moment shown me, and with him, as I said, my sins are no impediment to them. My reason is now free and clear, rid of the dark shadows of ignorance that my unhappy constant study of those detestable books of chivalry cast over it. Now I see through their absurdities and deceptions, and it only grieves me that this destruction of my illusions has come so late that it leaves me no time to make some amends by reading other books that might be a light to my soul. Niece, I feel myself at the point of death, and I would fain meet it in such a way as to show that my life has not been so ill that I should leave behind me the name of a madman; for though I have been one, I would not that the fact should be made plainer at my death. Call in to me, my dear, my good friends the curate, the bachelor Samson Carrasco, and Master Nicholas the barber, for I wish to confess and make my will." But his niece was saved the trouble by the entrance of the three. The instant Don Quixote saw them he exclaimed, "Good news for you, good sirs, that I am no longer Don Quixote of La Mancha, but Alonso Quixano, whose way of life won for him the name of Good. Now am I the enemy of Amadis of Gaul and of the whole countless troop of his descendants; odious to me now are all the profane stories of knight-errantry; now I perceive my folly, and the peril into which reading them brought me; now, by God's mercy schooled into my right senses, I loathe them."

When the three heard him speak in this way, they had no doubt whatever that some new craze had taken possession of him; and said Samson, "What? Señor Don Quixote! Now that we have intelligence of the lady Dulcinea being disenchanted, are you taking this line; now, just as we are on the point of becoming shepherds, to pass our lives singing, like princes, are you thinking of turning hermit? Hush, for heaven's sake, be rational and let's have no more nonsense."

"All that nonsense," said Don Quixote, "that until now has been a reality to my hurt, my death will, with heaven's help, turn to my good. I feel, sirs, that I am rapidly drawing near death; a truce to jesting; let me have a confessor to confess me, and a notary to make my will; for in extremities like this, man must not trifle with his soul; and while the curate is confessing me let some one, I beg, go for the notary."

They looked at one another, wondering at Don Quixote's words; but, though uncertain, they were inclined to believe him, and one of the signs by which they came to the conclusion he was dying was this so sudden and complete return to his senses after having been mad; for to the words already quoted he added much more, so well expressed, so devout, and so rational, as to banish all doubt and convince them that he was sound of mind. The curate turned them all out, and left alone with him confessed him. The bachelor went for the notary and returned shortly afterwards with him and with Sancho, who, having already learned from the bachelor the condition his master was in, and finding the housekeeper and niece weeping, began to blubber and shed tears.

The confession over, the curate came out saying, "Alonso Quixano the Good is indeed dying, and is indeed in his right mind; we may now go in to him while he makes his will."

This news gave a tremendous impulse to the brimming eyes of the housekeeper, niece, and Sancho Panza his good squire, making the tears burst from their eyes and a host of sighs from their hearts; for of a truth, as has been said more than once, whether as plain Alonso Quixano the Good, or as Don Quixote of La Mancha, Don Quixote was always of a gentle disposition and kindly in all his ways, and hence he was beloved, not only by those of his own house, but by all who knew him.

The notary came in with the rest, and as soon as the preamble of the will had been set out and Don Quixote had commended his soul to God with all the devout formalities that are usual, coming to the bequests, he said, "Item, it is my will that, touching certain moneys in the hands of Sancho Panza (whom in my madness I made my squire), inasmuch as between him and me there have been certain accounts and debits and credits, no claim be made against him, nor any account demanded of him in respect of them; but that if anything remain over and above, after he has paid himself what I owe him, the balance, which will be but little, shall be his, and much good may it do him; and if, as when I was mad I had a share in giving him the government of an island, so, now that I am in my senses, I could give him that of a kingdom, it should be his, for the simplicity of his character and the fidelity of his conduct deserve it." And then, turning to Sancho, he said, "Forgive me, my friend, that I led thee to seem as mad as myself, making thee fall into the same error I myself fell into, that there were and still are knights-errant in the world."

"Ah!" said Sancho weeping, "don't die, master, but take my advice and live many years; for the foolishest thing a man can do in this life is to let himself die without rhyme or reason, without anybody killing him, or any hands but melancholy's making an end of him. Come, don't be lazy, but get up from your bed and let us take to the fields in shepherd's trim as we agreed. Perhaps behind some bush we shall find the lady Dulcinea disenchanted, as fine as fine can be. If it be that you are dying of vexation at having been vanquished, lay the blame on me, and say you were overthrown because I had girthed Rocinante badly; besides you must have seen in your books of chivalry that it is a common thing for knights to upset one another, and for him who is conquered today to be conqueror tomorrow."

"Very true," said Samson, "and good Sancho Panza's view of these cases is quite right."

"Sirs, not so fast," said Don Quixote, "'in last year's nests there are no birds this year.' I was mad, now I am in my senses; I was Don Quixote of La Mancha, I am now, as I said, Alonso Quixano the Good; and may my repentance and sincerity restore me to the esteem you used to have for me; and now let Master Notary proceed.

"Item, I leave all my property absolutely to Antonia Quixana my niece, here present, after all has been deducted from the most available portion of it that may be required to satisfy the bequests I have made. And the first disbursement I desire to be made is the payment of the wages I owe for the time my housekeeper has served me, with twenty ducats, over and above, for a gown. The curate and the bachelor Samson Carrasco, now present, I appoint my executors.

"Item, it is my wish that if Antonia Quixana, my niece, desires to marry, she shall marry a man of whom it shall be first of all ascertained by information taken that he does not know what books of chivalry are; and if it should be proved that he does, and if, in spite of this, my niece insists upon marrying him, and does marry him, then that she shall forfeit the whole of what I have left her, which my executors shall devote to works of charity as they please.

"Item, I entreat the aforesaid gentlemen my executors, that, if any happy chance should lead them to discover the author who is said to have written a history now going about under the title of 'Second Part of the Achievements of Don Quixote of La Mancha,' they beg of him on my behalf as earnestly as they can to forgive me for having been, without intending it, the cause of his writing so many and such monstrous absurdities as he has written in it; for I am leaving the world with a feeling of compunction at having provoked him to write them."

With this he closed his will, and a faintness coming over him he stretched himself out at full length on the bed. All were in a flutter and made haste to relieve him, and during the three days he lived after that on which he made his will he fainted away very often. The house was all in confusion; but still the niece ate and the housekeeper drank and Sancho Panza enjoyed himself; for inheriting property wipes out or softens down in the heir the feeling of grief the dead man might be expected to leave behind him.

At last Don Quixote's end came, after he had received all the sacraments, and had in full and forcible terms expressed his detestation of books of chivalry. The notary was there at the time, and he said that in no book of chivalry had he ever read of any knight-errant dying in his bed so calmly and so like a Christian as Don Quixote, who amid the tears and lamentations of all present yielded up his spirit, that is to say died. On perceiving it the curate begged the notary to bear witness that Alonso Quixano the Good, commonly called Don Quixote of La Mancha, had passed away from this present life, and died naturally; and said he desired this testimony in order to remove the possibility of any other author save Cide Hamete Benengeli bringing him to life again falsely and making interminable stories out of his achievements.

Such was the end of the Ingenious Gentleman of La Mancha, whose village Cide Hamete would not indicate precisely, in order to leave all the towns and villages of La Mancha to contend among themselves for the right to adopt him and claim him as a son, as the seven cities of Greece contended for Homer. The lamentations of Sancho and the niece and housekeeper are omitted here, as well as the new epitaphs upon his tomb; Samson Carrasco, however, put the following lines:

A doughty gentleman lies here;
A stranger all his life to fear;
Nor in his death could Death prevail,

5150

In that last hour, to make him quail.
He for the world but little cared;
And at his feats the world was scared;
A crazy man his life he passed,
But in his sense died at last.

19. PARADISE LOST (SELECTIONS)

John Milton
(1608–1674)

After his formal education at Cambridge, Milton spent six years in self-directed study, having already decided and begun a career in poetry. He did not, however, remove himself from the political and religious turmoil of his time; rather, as private citizen and then Latin Secretary to Oliver Cromwell, he wrote controversial prose treatises on such radical concepts as divorce, freedom of the press, and political leaders' primary responsibility to their constituents. For the twenty years of the Interregnum (1640–1660), Milton wrote little poetry, but the idea of a great epic never left him, despite his blindness from 1652 on. At the failure of the Cromwellian Commonwealth (1658) and the Restoration of Charles II (1660), Milton was forced to withdraw from public life, an enforced opportunity allowing him to compose his monumental epic, Paradise Lost, *celebrating not merely the English nation, but the human nation, by taking on explication of the whole human condition. In* Paradise Lost, *as in his tragedy,* Samson Agonistes, *Milton writes with his own struggles in mind, yet maintains universality in focus on the big issues: free will, human dignity, integrity, and capacity for deceit and betrayal; he never dodges the difficult theological and philosophical issues of Divine Providence and the nature of evil. His broad humanistic learning fused the classical, Hebraic, and Christian ideals and traditions so thoroughly that his poetry meets the challenge to "justify the ways of God to men" and justifies the ways of humans to one another.*

PARADISE LOST (SELECTIONS)
(1674 edition)

BOOK I
THE ARGUMENT

This first Book proposes, first in brief, the whole Subject, Mans disobedience, and the loss thereupon of Paradise wherein he was plac't: *Then touches* the prime cause of his fall, the Serpent, *or rather* Satan in the Serpent; who revolting from God, and drawing to his side many Legions of Angels, was by the command of God driven out of Heaven with all his Crew into the great Deep. *Which action past over, the Poem hasts into the midst of things, presenting* Satan with his Angels now fallen into Hell, *describ'd here,* not in the Center (for Heaven and Earth may be *suppos'd as yet not made, certainly not yet accurst)* but in a place of utter darkness, fitliest call'd *Chaos:* Here *Satan* with his Angels lying on the burning Lake, thunder-struck and astonisht, after a certain space recovers, as from confusion, calls up him who next in Order and Dignity lay by him; they confer of thir miserable fall. *Satan* awakens all his Legions, who lay till then in the same manner confounded; they rise, thir Numbers, array of Battel, thir chief Leaders nam'd, according to the Idols known afterwards in *Canaan* and the Countries adjoyning. To these *Satan* directs his Speech, comforts them with hope yet of regaining Heaven, but tells them lastly of a new World and new kind of Creature to be created, according to an ancient Prophesie or report in Heaven; *for that Angels were long before this visible Creation, was the opinion of many ancient Fathers.* To find out the truth of this Prophesie, and what to determin thereon he refers to a full Councel. What his Associates thence attempt. *Pandemonium* the Palace of *Satan* rises, suddenly built out of the Deep: The infernal Peers there sit in Councel.

	Of Mans First Disobedience, and the Fruit
	Of that Forbidden Tree, whose mortal tast
	Brought Death into the World, and all our woe,
	With loss of *Eden*, till one greater Man
5	Restore us, and regain the blissful Seat,
	Sing Heav'nly Muse, that on the secret top
	Of *Oreb*, or of *Sinai*, didst inspire
	That Shepherd who first taught the chosen Seed,[1]
	In the Beginning how the Heav'ns and Earth
10	Rose out of *Chaos*: Or if *Sion* Hill
	Delight thee more, and *Siloa's* Brook that flow'd
	Fast by the Oracle of God; I thence
	Invoke thy aid to my adventrous Song,
	That with no middle flight intends to soar
15	Above th' *Aonian* Mount, while it pursues
	Things unattempted yet in Prose or Rime.
	And chiefly Thou O Spirit, that dost prefer
	Before all Temples th' upright heart and pure,
	Instruct me, for Thou know'st; Thou from the first
20	Wast present, and with mighty wings outspread
	Dove-like satst brooding on the vast Abyss
	And mad'st it pregnant: What in me is dark
	Illumin, what is low raise and support;
	That to the highth of this great Argument
25	I may assert Eternal Providence,
	And justifie the wayes of God to men.
	Say first, for Heav'n hides nothing from thy view

---

[1]the chosen Seed—Moses

Nor the deep Tract of Hell, say first what cause
Mov'd our Grand Parents in that happy State,
30 Favour'd of Heav'n so highly, to fall off
From thir Creator, and transgress his Will
For one restraint, Lords of the World besides?
Who first seduc'd them to that foul revolt?
Th' infernal Serpent;[2] he it was, whose guile
35 Stird up with Envy and Revenge, deceiv'd
The Mother of Mankind, what time his Pride
Had cast him out from Heav'n, with all his Host
Of Rebel Angels, by whose aid aspiring
To set himself in Glory above his Peers,
40 He trusted to have equal'd the most High,
If he oppos'd; and with ambitious aim
Against the Throne and Monarchy of God
Rais'd impious War in Heav'n and Battel proud
With vain attempt. Him the Almighty Power
45 Hurld headlong flaming from th' Ethereal Skie
With hideous ruin and combustion down
To bottomless perdition, there to dwell
In Adamantine Chains and penal Fire,
Who durst defie th' Omnipotent to Arms.
50 Nine times the Space that measures Day and Night
To mortal men, he with his horrid crew
Lay vanquisht, rowling in the fiery Gulf
Confounded though immortal: But his doom
Reserv'd him to more wrath; for now the thought
55 Both of lost happiness and lasting pain
Torments him; round he throws his baleful eyes
That witness'd huge affliction and dismay
Mixt with obdurate pride and stedfast hate:
At once as far as Angels kenn he views
60 The dismal Situation waste and wild,
A Dungeon horrible, on all sides round
As one great Furnace flam'd, yet from those flames
No light, but rather darkness visible
Serv'd only to discover sights of woe,
65 Regions of sorrow, doleful shades, where peace
And rest can never dwell, hope never comes
That comes to all; but torture without end
Still urges, and a fiery Deluge, fed
With ever-burning Sulphur unconsum'd:

---

[2]infernal Serpent—Satan

70   Such place Eternal Justice had prepar'd
           For those rebellious, here thir Prison ordain'd
           In utter darkness, and thir portion set
           As far remov'd from God and light of Heav'n
           As from the Center thrice to th' utmost Pole.
75   O how unlike the place from whence they fell!
           There the companions of his fall, o'rewhelm'd
           With Floods and Whirlwinds of tempestuous fire,
           He soon discerns, and weltring by his side
           One next himself in power, and next in crime,
80   Long after known in *Palestine*, and nam'd
           Beëlzebub. To whom th' Arch-Enemy,
           And thence in Heav'n call'd Satan, with bold words
           Breaking the horrid silence thus began.
                    If thou beest he; but O how fall'n! how chang'd
85   From him, who in the happy Realms of Light
           Cloth'd with transcendent brightness didst outshine
           Myriads though bright: If he whom mutual league,
           United thoughts and counsels, equal hope
           And hazard in the Glorious Enterprize,
90   Joynd with me once, now misery hath joynd
           In equal ruin: into what Pit thou seest
           From what highth fall'n, so much the stronger prov'd
           He with his Thunder: and till then who knew
           The force of those dire Arms? yet not for those,
95   Nor what the Potent Victor in his rage
           Can else inflict, do I repent or change,
           Though chang'd in outward lustre; that fixt mind
           And high disdain, from sence of injur'd merit,
           That with the mightiest rais'd me to contend,
100   And to the fierce contention brought along
           Innumerable force to Spirits arm'd
           That durst dislike his reign, and me preferring,
           His utmost power with adverse power oppos'd
           In dubious Battel on the Plains of Heav'n,
105   And shook his throne. What though the field be lost?
           All is not lost; th' unconquerable Will,
           And study of revenge, immortal hate,
           And courage never to submit or yield:
           And what is else not to be overcome?
110   That Glory never shall his wrath or might
           Extort from me. To bow and sue for grace
           With suppliant knee, and deifie his power,
           Who from the terrour of this Arm so late

Doubted his Empire, that were low indeed,
115 That were an ignominy and shame beneath
This downfall; since by Fate the strength of Gods
And this Empyreal substance cannot fail,
Since through experience of this great event
In Arms not worse, in foresight much advanc't,
120 We may with more successful hope resolve
To wage by force or guile eternal Warr
Irreconcileable, to our grand Foe,
Who now triumphs, and in th' excess of joy
Sole reigning holds the Tyranny of Heav'n.
125 So spake th' Apostate Angel, though in pain,
Vaunting aloud, but wrackt with deep despair:
And him thus answer'd soon his bold Compeer.
O Prince, O Chief of many Throned Powers,
That led th' imbattell'd Seraphim to Warr
130 Under thy conduct, and in dreadful deeds
Fearless, endanger'd Heav'ns perpetual King;
And put to proof his high Supremacy,
Whether upheld by strength, or Chance, or Fate,
Too well I see and rue the dire event,
135 That with sad overthrow and foul defeat
Hath lost us Heav'n, and all this mighty Host
In horrible destruction laid thus low,
As far as Gods and Heav'nly Essences
Can perish: for the mind and spirit remains
140 Invincible, and vigour soon returns,
Though all our Glory extinct, and happy state
Here swallow'd up in endless misery.
But what if he our Conquerour (whom I now
Of force believe Almighty, since no less
145 Then such could have orepow'rd such force as ours),
Have left us this our spirit and strength intire
Strongly to suffer and support our pains,
That we may so suffice his vengeful ire,
Or do him mightier service as his thralls
150 By right of Warr, what e're his business be
Here in the heart of Hell to work in Fire,
Or do his Errands in the gloomy Deep;
What can it then avail though yet we feel
Strength undiminisht, or eternal being
155 To undergo eternal punishment?
Whereto with speedy words th' Arch-fiend reply'd.
Fall'n Cherub, to be weak is miserable

Doing or Suffering: but of this be sure,
To do aught good never will be our task,
160   But ever to do ill our sole delight,
As being the contrary to his high will
Whom we resist. If then his Providence
Out of our evil seek to bring forth good,
Our labour must be to pervert that end,
165   And out of good still to find means of evil;
Which oft times may succeed, so as perhaps
Shall grieve him, if I fail not, and disturb
His inmost counsels from thir destind aim.
But see the angry Victor hath recall'd
170   His Ministers of vengeance and pursuit
Back to the Gates of Heav'n: the Sulphurous Hail
Shot after us in storm, oreblown hath laid
The fiery Surge, that from the Precipice
Of Heav'n receiv'd us falling, and the Thunder,
175   Wing'd with red Lightning and impetuous rage,
Perhaps hath spent his shafts, and ceases now
To bellow through the vast and boundless Deep.
Let us not slip th' occasion, whether scorn,
Or satiate fury yield it from our Foe.
180   Seest thou yon dreary Plain, forlorn and wild,
The seat of desolation, voyd of light,
Save what the glimmering of these livid flames
Casts pale and dreadful? Thither let us tend
From off the tossing of these fiery waves,
185   There rest, if any rest can harbour there,
And reassembling our afflicted Powers,
Consult how we may henceforth most offend
Our Enemy, our own loss how repair,
How overcome this dire Calamity,
190   What reinforcement we may gain from Hope,
If not what resolution from despair.
    Thus Satan talking to his neerest Mate
With Head up-lift above the wave, and Eyes
That sparkling blaz'd, his other Parts besides
195   Prone on the Flood, extended long and large
Lay floating many a rood, in bulk as huge
As whom the Fables name of monstrous size,
Titanian, or *Earth-born,* that warr'd on *Jove,*
Briareos or *Typhon,* whom the Den
200   By ancient *Tarsus* held, or that Sea-beast
Leviathan, which God of all his works

Created hugest that swim th' Ocean stream:
Him haply slumbring on the *Norway* foam
The Pilot of some small night-founder'd Skiff,
205 Deeming some Island, oft, as Sea-men tell,
With fixed Anchor in his skaly rind
Moors by his side under the Lee, while Night
Invests the Sea, and wished Morn delayes:
So stretcht out huge in length the Arch-fiend lay
210 Chain'd on the burning Lake, nor ever thence
Had ris'n or heav'd his head, but that the will
And high permission of all-ruling Heav'n
Left him at large to his own dark designs,
That with reiterated crimes he might
215 Heap on himself damnation, while he sought
Evil to others, and enrag'd might see
How all his malice serv'd but to bring forth
Infinite goodness, grace and mercy shewn
On Man by him seduc't, but on himself
220 Treble confusion, wrath and vengeance pour'd.
Forthwith upright he rears from off the Pool
His mighty Stature; on each hand the flames
Drivn backward slope thir pointing spires, and rowl'd
In billows, leave i' th' midst a horrid Vale.
225 Then with expanded wings he stears his flight
Aloft, incumbent on the dusky Air
That felt unusual weight, till on dry Land
He lights, if it were Land that ever burn'd
With solid, as the Lake with liquid fire;
230 And such appear'd in hue, as when the force
Of subterranean wind transports a Hill
Torn from *Pelorus,* or the shatter'd side
Of thundring *Ætna,* whose combustible
And fewel'd entrails thence conceiving Fire,
235 Sublim'd with Mineral fury, aid the Winds,
And leave a singed bottom all involv'd
With stench and smoak: Such resting found the sole
Of unblest feet. Him followed his next Mate,
Both glorying to have scap't the *Stygian* flood
240 As Gods, and by thir own recover'd strength,
Not by the sufferance of supernal Power.
        Is this the Region, this the Soil, the Clime,
Said then the lost Arch-Angel, this the seat
That we must change for Heav'n, this mournful gloom
245 For that celestial light? Be it so, since he

Who now is Sovran can dispose and bid
What shall be right: fardest from him is best
Whom reason hath equald, force hath made supream
Above his equals. Farewel happy Fields
250   Where Joy for ever dwells: Hail horrours, hail
Infernal world, and thou profoundest Hell
Receive thy new Possessor: One who brings
A mind not to be chang'd by Place or Time.
The mind is its own place, and in it self
255   Can make a Heav'n of Hell, a Hell of Heav'n.
What matter where, if I be still the same,
And what I should be, all but less than he
Whom Thunder hath made greater? Here at least
We shall be free; th' Almighty hath not built
260   Here for his envy, will not drive us hence:
Here we may reign secure, and in my choyce
To reign is worth ambition though in Hell:
Better to reign in Hell, then serve in Heav'n.
But wherefore let we then our faithful friends,
265   Th' associates and copartners of our loss
Lye thus astonisht on th' oblivious Pool,
And call them not to share with us their part
In this unhappy Mansion, or once more
With rallied Arms to try what may be yet
270   Regaind in Heav'n, or what more lost in Hell?
       So *Satan* spake, and him *Beëlzebub*
Thus answer'd. Leader of those Armies bright,
Which but th' Omnipotent none could have foyl'd,
If once they hear that voyce, thir liveliest pledge
275   Of hope in fears and dangers, heard so oft
In worst extreams, and on the perilous edge
Of battel when it rag'd, in all assaults
Thir surest signal, they will soon resume
New courage and revive, though now they lye
280   Groveling and prostrate on yon Lake of Fire,
As we erewhile, astounded and amaz'd,
No wonder, fall'n such a pernicious highth.
       He scarce had ceas't when the superiour Fiend
Was moving toward the shoar; his ponderous shield
285   Ethereal temper, massy, large and round,
Behind him cast; the broad circumference
Hung on his shoulders like the Moon, whose Orb

Through Optic Glass the *Tuscan* Artist[3] views
At Ev'ning from the top of *Fesole,*
290   Or in *Valdarno,* to descry new Lands,
Rivers or Mountains in her spotty Globe.
His Spear, to equal which the tallest Pine
Hewn on *Norwegian* hills, to be the Mast
Of some great Ammiral, were but a wand,
295   He walkt with to support uneasie steps
Over the burning Marl, not like those steps
On Heavens Azure, and the torrid Clime
Smote on him sore besides, vaulted with Fire;
Nathless he so endur'd, till on the Beach
300   Of that inflamed Sea, he stood and call'd
His Legions, Angel Forms, who lay intrans't
Thick as Autumnal Leaves that strow the Brooks
In *Vallombrosa,* where th' *Etrurian* shades
High overarch't imbowr; or scatterd sedge
305   Afloat, when with fierce Winds *Orion* arm'd
Hath vext the Red-Sea Coast, whose waves orethrew
Busiris and his *Memphian* Chivalry,
While with perfidious hatred they pursu'd
The Sojourners of *Goshen,* who beheld
310   From the safe shore thir floating Carkases
And broken Chariot Wheels, so thick bestrown
Abject and lost lay these, covering the Flood,
Under amazement of thir hideous change.
He call'd so loud, that all the hollow Deep
315   Of Hell resounded. Princes, Potentates,
Warriers, the Flowr of Heav'n, once yours, now lost,
If such astonishment as this can sieze
Eternal spirits; or have ye chos'n this place
After the toyl of Battel to repose
320   Your wearied vertue, for the ease you find
To slumber here, as in the Vales of Heav'n?
Or in this abject posture have ye sworn
T' adore the Conquerour? who now beholds
Cherub and Seraph rowling in the Flood
325   With scatter'd Arms and Ensigns, till anon
His swift pursuers from Heav'n Gates discern
Th' advantage, and descending tread us down
Thus drooping, or with linked Thunderbolts
Transfix us to the bottom of this Gulf.

---

[3]*Tuscan* Artist—Galileo

330	Awake, arise, or be for ever fall'n.
	They heard, and were abasht, and up they sprung
	Upon the wing, as when men wont to watch
	On duty, sleeping found by whom they dread,
	Rouse and bestir themselves ere well awake.
335	Nor did they not perceave the evil plight
	In which they were, or the fierce pains not feel;
	Yet to thir Generals Voyce they soon obeyd
	Innumerable. As when the potent Rod
	Of *Amrams* Son[4] in *Egypts* evill day
340	Wav'd round the Coast, up call'd a pitchy cloud
	Of *Locusts,* warping on the Eastern Wind,
	That ore the Realm of impious *Pharaoh* hung
	Like Night, and darken'd all the Land of *Nile:*
	So numberless were those bad Angels seen
345	Hovering on wing under the Cope of Hell
	'Twixt upper, nether, and surrounding Fires;
	Till, as a signal giv'n, th' uplifted Spear
	Of thir great Sultan waving to direct
	Thir course, in even ballance down they light
350	On the firm brimstone, and fill all the Plain;
	A multitude, like which the populous North
	Pour'd never from her frozen loyns, to pass
	Rhene or the *Danaw,* when her barbarous Sons
	Came like a Deluge on the South, and spread
355	Beneath *Gibralter* to the *Lybian* sands.
	Forthwith from every Squadron and each Band
	The Heads and Leaders thither hast where stood
	Thir great Commander; Godlike shapes and forms
	Excelling human, Princely Dignities,
360	And Powers that earst in Heaven sat on Thrones;
	Though of thir Names in heav'nly Records now
	Be no memorial blotted out and raz'd
	By thir Rebellion, from the Books of Life.
	Nor had they yet among the Sons of *Eve*
365	Got them new Names, till wandring ore the Earth,
	Through Gods high sufferance for the tryal of man,
	By falsities and lyes the greatest part
	Of Mankind they corrupted to forsake
	God thir Creator, and th' invisible
370	Glory of him that made them, to transform
	Oft to the Image of a Brute, adorn'd

---

[4] *Amrams* Son—Moses

With gay Religions full of Pomp and Gold,
And Devils to adore for Deities:
Then were they known to men by various Names,
375 And various Idols through the Heathen World.
Say, Muse, thir Names then known, who first, who last,
Rous'd from thir slumber, on that fiery Couch,
At thir great Emperors call, as next in worth
Came singly where he stood on the bare strand,
380 While the promiscuous croud stood yet aloof?
The chief were those who from the Pit of Hell
Roaming to seek thir prey on earth, durst fix
Thir Seats long after next the Seat of God,
Thir Altars by his Altar, Gods ador'd
385 Among the Nations round, and durst abide
Jehovah thundring out of *Sion*, thron'd
Between the Cherubim; yea, often plac'd
Within his Sanctuary it self thir Shrines,
Abominations; and with cursed things
390 His holy Rites, and solemn Feasts profan'd,
And with thir darkness durst affront his light.
First *Moloch,* horrid King besmear'd with blood
Of human sacrifice, and parents tears,
Though for the noyse of Drums and Timbrels loud
395 Thir childrens cries unheard, that past through fire
To his grim Idol. Him the *Ammonite*
Worshipt in *Rabba* and her watry Plain,
In *Argob* and in *Basan,* to the stream
Of utmost *Arnon.* Nor content with such
400 Audacious neighbourhood, the wisest heart
Of *Solomon* he led by fraud to build
His Temple right against the Temple of God
On that opprobrious Hill, and made his Grove
The pleasant Vally of *Hinnom, Tophet* thence
405 And black *Gehenna* call'd, the Type of Hell.
Next *Chemos,* th' obscene dread of *Moabs* Sons,
From *Aroar* to *Nebo,* and the wild
Of Southmost *Abarim;* in *Hesebon*
And *Horonaim, Seons* Realm, beyond
410 The flowry Dale of *Sibma* clad with Vines,
And *Eleale* to th' *Asphaltick* Pool.
Peor his other Name, when he entic'd
Israel in *Sittim* on thir march from *Nile*
To do him wanton rites, which cost them woe.
415 Yet thence his lustful Orgies he enlarg'd

Ev'n to that Hill of scandal, by the Grove
Of *Moloch* homicide, lust hard by hate;
Till good *Josiah* drove them thence to Hell.
With these came they, who from the bordring flood
420 Of old *Euphrates* to the Brook that parts
Egypt from *Syrian* ground, had general Names
Of *Baalim* and *Ashtaroth*, those male,
These Feminine. For Spirits when they please
Can either Sex assume, or both; so soft
425 And uncompounded is thir Essence pure,
Not ti'd or manacl'd with joynt or limb,
Nor founded on the brittle strength of bones
Like cumbrous flesh; but in what shape they choose
Dilated or condens't, bright or obscure,
430 Can execute thir aerie purposes,
And works of love or enmity fulfill.
For these the Race of *Israel* oft forsook
Thir living strength, and unfrequented left
His righteous Altar, bowing lowly down
435 To bestial Gods; for which thir heads as low
Bow'd down in Battel, sunk before the Spear
Of despicable foes. With these in troop
Came *Astoreth*, whom the *Phoenicians* call'd
Astarte, Queen of Heav'n, with crescent Horns;
440 To whose bright Image nightly by the Moon
Sidonian Virgins paid thir Vows and Songs,
In *Sion* also not unsung, where stood
Her Temple on th' offensive Mountain, built
By that uxorious King, whose heart though large,
445 Beguil'd by fair Idolatresses, fell
To Idols foul. *Thammuz*, came next behind,
Whose annual wound in *Lebanon* allur'd
The *Syrian* Damsels to lament his fate
In amorous ditties all a Summers day,
450 While smooth *Adonis* from his native Rock
Ran purple to the Sea, suppos'd with blood
Of *Thammuz* yearly wounded: the Love-tale
Infected *Sions* daughters with like heat,
Whose wanton passions in the sacred Porch
455 *Ezekiel* saw, when by the Vision led
His eye survay'd the dark Idolatries
Of alienated *Judah*. Next came one
Who mourn'd in earnest, when the Captive Ark
Maim'd his brute Image, head and hands lopt off

460   In his own Temple, on the grunsel edge,
      Where he fell flat, and sham'd his Worshipers:
      Dagon his Name, Sea Monster, upward Man
      And downward Fish: yet had his Temple high
      Rear'd in *Azotus*, dreaded through the Coast
465   Of *Palestine*, in *Gath* and *Ascalon*
      And *Accaron* and *Gaza*'s frontier bounds.
      Him follow'd *Rimmon*, whose delightful Seat
      Was fair *Damascus*, on the fertil Banks
      Of *Abbana* and *Pharphar*, lucid streams.
470   He also against the house of God was bold:
      A Leper once he lost and gain'd a King,
      Ahaz his sottish Conquerour, whom he drew
      Gods Altar to disparage and displace
      For one of *Syrian* mode, whereon to burn
475   His odious offrings, and adore the Gods
      Whom he had vanquisht. After these appear'd
      A crew who under Names of old Renown,
      Osiris, Isis, Orus and thir Train
      With monstrous shapes and sorceries abus'd
480   Fanatic *Egypt* and her Priests, to seek
      Thir wandring Gods disguis'd in brutish forms
      Rather then human. Nor did *Israel* scape
      Th' infection when thir borrow'd Gold compos'd
      The Calf in *Oreb:* and the Rebel King
485   Doubl'd that sin in *Bethel* and in *Dan*,
      Lik'ning his Maker to the Grazed Ox,
      Jehovah, who in one Night when he pass'd
      From *Egypt* marching, equal'd with one stroke
      Both her first born and all her bleating Gods.
490   *Belial* came last, then whom a Spirit more lewd
      Fell not from Heaven, or more gross to love
      Vice for it self: To him no Temple stood
      Or Altar smoak'd; yet who more oft then hee
      In Temples and at Altars, when the Priest
495   Turns Atheist, as did *Ely*'s Sons, who fill'd
      With lust and violence the house of God.
      In Courts and Palaces he also Reigns
      And in luxurious Cities, where the noyse
      Of riot ascends above thir loftiest Towrs,
500   And injury and outrage: And when Night
      Darkens the Streets, then wander forth the Sons
      Of *Belial*, flown with insolence and wine.
      Witness the Streets of *Sodom*, and that night

In *Gibeah,* when th' hospitable door
505 Expos'd a Matron to avoid worse rape.
These were the prime in order and in might;
The rest were long to tell, though far renown'd,
Th' *Ionian* Gods, of *Javans* Issue held
Gods, yet confest later then Heav'n and Earth
510 Thir boasted Parents; *Titan* Heav'ns first born
With his enormous brood, and birthright seis'd
By younger *Saturn,* lie from mightier *Jove*
His own and *Rhea's* Son like measure found;
So Jove usurping reign'd: these first in *Creet*
515 And *Ida* known, thence on the Snowy top
Of cold *Olympus* rul'd the middle Air
Thir highest Heav'n; or on the *Delphian* Cliff,
Or in *Dodona,* and through all the bounds
Of *Doric* Land; or who with *Saturn* old
520 Fled over *Adria* to th' *Hesperian* Fields,
And ore the *Celtic* roam'd the utmost Isles.
All these and more came flocking; but with looks
Down cast and damp, yet such wherein appear'd
Obscure som glimps of joy, to have found thir chief
525 Not in despair, to have found themselves not lost
In loss it self; which on his count'nance cast
Like doubtful hue: but he his wonted pride
Soon recollecting, with high words, that bore
Semblance of worth, not substance, gently rais'd
530 Thir fainting courage, and dispel'd thir fears.
Then strait commands that at the warlike sound
Of Trumpets loud and Clarions be upreard
His mighty Standard; that proud honour claim'd
Azazel as his right, a Cherub tall:
535 Who forthwith from the glittering Staff unfurld
Th' Imperial Ensign, which full high advanc't
Shon like a Meteor streaming to the Wind
With Gemms and Golden lustre rich imblaz'd,
Seraphic arms and Trophies: all the while
540 Sonorous mettal blowing Martial sounds:
At which the universal Host upsent
A shout that tore Hells Concave, and beyond
Frighted the Reign of *Chaos* and old Night.
All in a moment through the gloom were seen
545 Ten thousand Banners rise into the Air
With Orient Colours waving: with them rose
A Forrest huge of Spears: and thronging Helms

Appear'd, and serried Shields in thick array
Of depth immeasurable: Anon they move
550   In perfect *Phalanx* to the *Dorian* mood
Of Flutes and soft Recorders; such as rais'd
To highth of noblest temper Hero's old
Arming to Battel, and in stead of rage
Deliberate valour breath'd, firm and unmov'd
555   With dread of death to flight or foul retreat,
Nor wanting power to mitigate and swage
With solemn touches, troubl'd thoughts, and chase
Anguish and doubt and fear and sorrow and pain
From mortal or immortal minds. Thus they
560   Breathing united force with fixed thought
Mov'd on in silence to soft Pipes that charm'd
Thir painful steps o're the burnt soyl; and now
Advanc't in view they stand, a horrid Front
Of dreadful length and dazling Arms, in guise
565   Of Warriers old with order'd Spear and Shield,
Awaiting what command thir mighty Chief
Had to impose: He through the armed Files
Darts his experienc't eye, and soon traverse
The whole Battalion views, thir order due,
570   Thir visages and stature as of Gods,
Thir number last he summs. And now his heart
Distends with pride, and hardning in his strength
Glories: For never since created man,
Met such imbodied force, as nam'd with these
575   Could merit more then that small infantry
Warr'd on by Cranes: though all the Giant brood
Of *Phlegra* with th' Heroic Race were joyn'd
That fought at *Thebes* and *Ilium*, on each side
Mixt with auxiliar Gods; and what resounds
580   In Fable or *Romance* of *Uthers* Son
Begirt with *British* and *Armoric* Knights;
And all who since, Baptiz'd or Infidel
Jousted in *Aspramont* or *Montalban*,
Damasco, or *Marocco*, or *Trebisond*,
585   Or whom *Biserta* sent from *Afric* shore
When *Charlemain* with all his Peerage fell
By *Fontarabbia*. Thus far these beyond
Compare of mortal prowess, yet observ'd
Thir dread commander: he above the rest
590   In shape and gesture proudly eminent
Stood like a Towr; his form had yet not lost

All her Original brightness, nor appear'd
Less then Arch Angel ruind, and th' excess
Of Glory obscur'd: As when the Sun new ris'n
595   Looks through the Horizontal misty Air
Shorn of his Beams, or from behind the Moon
In dim Eclips disastrous twilight sheds
On half the Nations, and with fear of change
Perplexes Monarchs. Dark'n'd so, yet shon
600   Above them all th' Arch Angel: but his face
Deep scars of Thunder had intrencht, and care
Sat on his faded cheek, but under Brows
Of dauntless courage, and considerate Pride
Waiting revenge: cruel his eye, but cast
605   Signs of remorse and passion to behold
The fellows of his crime, the followers rather
(Far other once beheld in bliss) condemn'd
For ever now to have thir lot in pain,
Millions of Spirits for his fault amerc't
610   Of Heav'n, and from Eternal Splendors flung
For his revolt, yet faithfull how they stood,
Thir Glory witherd. As when Heavens Fire
Hath scath'd the Forrest Oaks, or Mountain Pines,
With singed top thir stately growth though bare
615   Stands on the blasted Heath. He now prepar'd
To speak; whereat thir doubl'd Ranks they bend
From wing to wing, and half enclose him round
With all his Peers: attention held them mute.
Thrice he assayd, and thrice in spight of scorn,
620   Tears such as Angels weep, burst forth: at last
Words interwove with sighs found out thir way.
      O Myriads of immortal Spirits, O Powers
Matchless, but with th' Almighty, and that strife
Was not inglorious, though th' event was dire,
625   As this place testifies, and this dire change
Hateful to utter: but what power of mind
Foreseeing or presaging, from the Depth
Of knowledge past or present, could have fear'd,
How such united force of Gods, how such
630   As stood like these, could ever know repulse?
For who can yet beleeve, though after loss,
That all these puissant Legions, whose exile
Hath emptied Heav'n, shall fail to re-ascend
Self-rais'd, and repossess thir native seat?
635   For mee be witness all the Host of Heav'n,

If counsels different, or danger shun'd
By mee, have lost our hopes. But he who reigns
Monarch in Heav'n, till then as one secure
Sat on his Throne, upheld by old repute,
640   Consent or custom, and his Regal State
Put forth at full, but still his strength conceal'd,
Which tempted our attempt, and wrought our fall.
Henceforth his might we know, and know our own
So as not either to provoke, or dread
645   New warr, provok't; our better part remains
To work in close design, by fraud or guile
What force effected not: that he no less
At length from us may find, who overcomes
By force, hath overcome but half his foe.
650   Space may produce new Worlds; whereof so rife
There went a fame in Heav'n that he ere long
Intended to create, and therein plant
A generation, whom his choice regard
Should favour equal to the Sons of Heav'n:
655   Thither, if but to pry, shall be perhaps
Our first eruption, thither or elsewhere:
For this Infernal Pit shall never hold
Cælestial Spirits in Bondage, nor th' Abyss
Long under darkness cover. But these thoughts
660   Full Counsel must mature: Peace is despaird,
For who can think Submission? Warr then, Warr
Open or understood must be resolv'd.
       He spake: and to confirm his words, out-flew
Millions of flaming swords, drawn from the thighs
665   Of mighty Cherubim; the sudden blaze
Far round illumin'd hell: highly they rag'd
Against the Highest, and fierce with grasped Arms
Clash'd on thir sounding Shields the din of war,
Hurling defiance toward the Vault of Heav'n.
670   There stood a Hill not far whose griesly top
Belch'd fire and rowling smoak; the rest entire
Shon with a glossie scurff, undoubted sign
That in his womb was hid metallic Ore,
The work of Sulphur. Thither wing'd with speed
675   A numerous Brigad hasten'd. As when Bands
Of Pioners with Spade and Pickax arm'd
Forerun the Royal Camp, to trench a Field,
Or cast a Rampart. *Mammon* led them on,
Mammon, the least erected Spirit that fell

680 From heav'n, for ev'n in heav'n his looks and thoughts
   Were always downward bent, admiring more
   The riches of Heav'ns pavement, trod'n Gold,
   Then aught divine or holy else enjoy'd
   In vision beatific: by him first
685 Men also, and by his suggestion taught,
   Ransack'd the Center, and with impious hands
   Rifl'd the bowels of thir mother Earth
   For Treasures better hid. Soon had his crew
   Op'nd into the Hill a spacious wound
690 And dig'd out ribs of Gold. Let none admire
   That riches grow in Hell; that soyl may best
   Deserve the precious bane. And here let those
   Who boast in mortal things, and wondring tell
   Of *Babel*, and the works of *Memphian* Kings
695 Learn how thir greatest Monuments of Fame,
   And Strength and Art are easily outdone
   By Spirits reprobate, and in an hour
   What in an age they with incessant toyl
   And hands innumerable scarce perform.
700 Nigh on the Plain in many cells prepar'd,
   That underneath had veins of liquid fire
   Sluic'd from the Lake, a second multitude
   With wondrous Art founded the massie Ore,
   Severing each kind, and scum'd the Bullion dross:
705 A third as soon had form'd within the ground
   A various mould, and from the boyling cells
   By strange conveyance fill'd each hollow nook,
   As in an Organ from one blast of wind
   To many a row of Pipes the sound-board breaths.
710 Anon out of the earth a Fabrick huge
   Rose like an Exhalation, with the sound
   Of Dulcet Symphonies and voices sweet,
   Built like a Temple, where *Pilasters* round
   Were set, and Doric pillars overlaid
715 With Golden Architrave; nor did there want
   Cornice or Freeze, with bossy Sculptures grav'n,
   The Roof was fretted Gold. Not *Babilon*,
   Nor great *Alcairo* such magnificence
   Equal'd in all thir glories, to inshrine
720 *Belus* or *Serapis* thir Gods, or seat
   Thir Kings, when *Ægypt* with *Assyria* strove
   In wealth and luxurie. Th' ascending pile
   Stood fixt her stately highth, and strait the dores

Op'ning thir brazen foulds discover wide
725 Within, her ample spaces, o're the smooth
And level pavement: from the arched roof
Pendant by suttle Magic many a row
Of Starry Lamps and blazing Cressets fed
With *Naphtha* and *Asphaltus* yeilded light
730 As from a sky. The hasty multitude
Admiring enter'd, and the work some praise
And some the Architect: his hand was known
In Heav'n by many a Towred structure high,
Where Scepter'd Angels held thir residence,
735 And sat as Princes, whom the supreme King
Exalted to such power, and gave to rule,
Each in his Hierarchie, the Orders bright.
Nor was his name unheard or unador'd
In ancient *Greece*; and in *Ausonian* land
740 Men call'd him *Mulciber*; and how he fell
From Heav'n, they fabl'd, thrown by angry *Jove*
Sheer o're the Chrystal Battlements: from Morn
To Noon he fell, from Noon to dewy Eve,
A Summers day; and with the setting Sun
745 Dropt from the Zenith like a falling Star,
On *Lemnos* th' *Ægæan* Ile: thus they relate,
Erring; for he with this rebellious rout
Fell long before; nor aught avail'd him now
To have built in Heav'n high Towrs; nor did he scape
750 By all his Engins, but was headlong sent
With his industrious crew to build in hell.
Mean while the winged Haralds by command
Of Sovran power, with awful Ceremony
And Trumpets sound throughout the Host proclaim
755 A solemn Councel forthwith to be held
At *Pandæmonium*, the high Capitol
Of Satan and his Peers: thir summons call'd
From every Band and squared Regiment
By place or choice the worthiest; they anon
760 With hunderds and with thousands trooping came
Attended: all access was throng'd, the Gates
And Porches wide, but chief the spacious Hall
(Though like a cover'd field, where Champions bold
Wont ride in arm'd, and at the Soldans chair
765 Defi'd the best of *Paynim* chivalry
To mortal combat or carreer with Lance)
Thick swarm'd, both on the ground and in the air,

Brusht with the hiss of russling wings. As Bees
In spring time, when the Sun with *Taurus* rides,
770   Pour forth thir populous youth about the Hive
In clusters; they among fresh dews and flowers
Flie to and fro, or on the smoothed Plank,
The suburb of thir Straw-built Cittadel,
New rub'd with Baum, expatiate and confer
775   Thir State affairs. So thick the aerie crowd
Swarm'd and were strait'n'd; till the Signal giv'n.
Behold a wonder! they but now who seemd
In bigness to surpass Earths Giant Sons
Now less than smallest Dwarfs, in narrow room
780   Throng numberless, like that Pigmean Race
Beyond the *Indian* Mount, or Faerie Elves,
Whose midnight Revels, by a Forrest side
Or Fountain some belated Peasant sees,
Or dreams he sees, while over-head the Moon
785   Sits Arbitress, and neerer to the Earth
Wheels her pale course, they on thir mirth and dance
Intent, with jocond Music charm his ear;
At once with joy and fear his heart rebounds.
Thus incorporeal Spirits to smallest forms
790   Reduc'd thir shapes immense, and were at large,
Though without number still amidst the Hall
Of that infernal Court. But far within
And in thir own dimensions like themselves
The great Seraphic Lords and Cherubim
795   In close recess and secret conclave sat
A thousand Demy-Gods on golden seats,
Frequent and full. After short silence then
And summons read, the great consult began.

BOOK II
THE ARGUMENT

    The Consultation begun, *Satan* debates whether another Battel be to be hazarded for the recovery of Heaven: some advise it, others dissuade: A third proposal is prefer'd, mention'd before by *Satan*, to search the truth of that Prophesie or Tradition in Heaven concerning another world, and another kind of creature equal or not much inferiour to themselves, about this time to be created: Thir doubt who shall be sent on this difficult search: *Satan* thir chief undertakes alone the voyage, is honourd and applauded. The Councel thus ended, the rest betake them several wayes and to several imployments, as thir inclinations lead them, to entertain the time till *Satan* return. He passes on his journey to Hell Gates, finds them shut, and who sat there to guard them, by whom at length they are op'n'd, and discover to him the great Gulf between Hell and Heaven; with what difficulty he passes through, directed by *Chaos*, the Power of that place, to the sight of this new World which he sought.

High on a Throne of Royal State, which far
Outshon the wealth of *Ormus* and of *Ind*,
Or where the gorgeous East with richest hand
Showrs on her Kings *Barbaric* Pearl and Gold,
5   Satan exalted sat, by merit rais'd
To that bad eminence; and from despair
Thus high uplifted beyond hope, aspires
Beyond thus high, insatiate to pursue
Vain Warr with Heav'n, and by success untaught
10   His proud imaginations thus displaid.
       Powers and Dominions, Deities of Heav'n,
For since no deep within her gulf can hold
Immortal vigor, though opprest and fall'n,
I give not Heav'n for lost. From this descent
15   Celestial vertues rising, will appear
More glorious and more dread then from no fall,
And trust themselves to fear no second fate:
Mee though just right, and the fixt Laws of Heav'n
Did first create your Leader, next, free choice,
20   With what besides, in Counsel or in Fight,
Hath bin achiev'd of merit, yet this loss
Thus farr at least recover'd, hath much more
Establisht in a safe unenvied Throne
Yeilded with full consent. The happier state
25   In Heav'n, which follows dignity, might draw
Envy from each inferior; but who here
Will envy whom the highest place exposes
Formost to stand against the Thunderers aim
Your bulwark, and condemns to greatest share
30   Of endless pain? where there is then no good
For which to strive, no strife can grow up there
From Faction; for none sure will claim in Hell
Precedence, none, whose portion is so small
Of present pain, that with ambitious mind
35   Will covet more. With this advantage then
To union, and firm Faith, and firm accord,
More then can be in Heav'n, we now return
To claim our just inheritance of old,
Surer to prosper then prosperity

40 Could have assur'd us; and by what best way,
  Whether of open Warr or covert guile,
  We now debate; who can advise, may speak.
   He ceas'd, and next him *Moloc*, Scepter'd King
  Stood up, the strongest and the fiercest Spirit
45 That fought in Heav'n; now fiercer by despair:
  His trust was with th' Eternal to be deem'd
  Equal in strength, and rather then be less
  Car'd not to be at all; with that care lost
  Went all his fear: of God, or Hell, or worse
50 He reck'd not, and these words thereafter spake.
   My sentence is for open Warr: Of Wiles,
  More unexpert, I boast not: them let those
  Contrive who need, or when they need, not now.
  For while they sit contriving, shall the rest,
55 Millions that stand in Arms, and longing wait
  The Signal to ascend, sit lingring here
  Heav'ns fugitives, and for thir dwelling place
  Accept this dark opprobrious Den of shame,
  The Prison of his Tyranny who Reigns
60 By our delay? no, let us rather choose
  Arm'd with Hell flames and fury all at once
  O're Heav'ns high Towrs to force resistless way,
  Turning our Tortures into horrid Arms
  Against the Torturer; when to meet the noise
65 Of his Almighty Engin he shall hear
  Infernal Thunder, and for Lightning see
  Black fire and horror shot with equal rage
  Among his Angels; and his Throne it self
  Mixt with *Tartarean* Sulphur, and strange fire,
70 His own invented Torments. But perhaps
  The way seems difficult and steep to scale
  With upright wing against a higher foe.
  Let such bethink them, if the sleepy drench
  Of that forgetful Lake benumm not still,
75 That in our proper motion we ascend
  Up to our native seat: descent and fall
  To us is adverse. Who but felt of late
  When the fierce Foe hung on our brok'n Rear
  Insulting, and pursu'd us through the Deep,
80 With what compulsion and laborious flight
  We sunk thus low? Th' ascent is easie then;
  Th' event is fear'd; should we again provoke
  Our stronger, some worse way his wrath may find

To our destruction: if there be in Hell
85   Fear to be worse destroy'd: what can be worse
Then to dwell here, driv'n out from bliss, condemn'd
In this abhorred deep to utter woe;
Where pain of unextinguishable fire
Must exercise us without hope of end
90   The Vassals of his anger, when the Scourge
Inexorably, and the torturing hour
Calls us to Penance? More destroy'd then thus
We should be quite abolisht and expire.
What fear we then? what doubt we to incense
95   His utmost ire? which to the highth enrag'd,
Will either quite consume us, and reduce
To nothing this essential, happier farr
Then miserable to have eternal being:
Or if our substance be indeed Divine,
100   And cannot cease to be, we are at worst
On this side nothing; and by proof we feel
Our power sufficient to disturb his Heav'n,
And with perpetual inrodes to Allarm,
Though inaccessible, his fatal Throne:
105   Which if not Victory is yet Revenge.
        He ended frowning, and his look denounc'd
Desperate revenge, and Battel dangerous
To less then Gods. On th' other side up rose
Belial, in act more graceful and humane;
110   A fairer person lost not Heav'n; he seemd
For dignity compos'd and high exploit:
But all was false and hollow; though his Tongue
Dropt Manna, and could make the worse appear
The better reason, to perplex and dash
115   Maturest Counsels: for his thoughts were low;
To vice industrious, but to Nobler deeds
Timorous and slothful: yet he pleas'd the ear,
And with perswasive accent thus began.
        I should be much for open Warr, O Peers,
120   As not behind in hate; if what was urg'd
Main reason to perswade immediate Warr,
Did not disswade me most, and seem to cast
Ominous conjecture on the whole success:
When he who most excels in fact of Arms,
125   In what he counsels and in what excels
Mistrustful, grounds his courage on despair
And utter dissolution, as the scope

Of all his aim, after some dire revenge.
First, what Revenge? the Towrs of Heav'n are fill'd
130 With Armed watch, that render all access
Impregnable; oft on the bordering Deep
Encamp thir Legions, or with obscure wing
Scout farr and wide into the Realm of night,
Scorning surprize. Or could we break our way
135 By force, and at our heels all Hell should rise
With blackest Insurrection, to confound
Heav'ns purest Light, yet our great Enemy
All incorruptible would on his Throne
Sit unpolluted, and th' Ethereal mould
140 Incapable of stain would soon expel
Her mischief, and purge off the baser fire
Victorious. Thus repuls'd, our final hope
Is flat despair: we must exasperate
Th' Almighty Victor to spend all his rage,
145 And that must end us, that must be our cure,
To be no more; sad cure; for who would loose,
Though full of pain, this intellectual being,
Those thoughts that wander through Eternity,
To perish rather, swallowd up and lost
150 In the wide womb of uncreated night,
Devoid of sense and motion? and who knows,
Let this be good, whether our angry Foe
Can give it, or will ever? how he can
Is doubtful; that he never will is sure.
155 Will be, so wise, let loose at once his ire,
Belike through impotence, or unaware,
To give his Enemies thir wish, and end
Them in his anger, whom his anger saves
To punish endless? wherefore cease we then?
160 Say they who counsel Warr, we are decreed,
Reserv'd and destin'd to Eternal woe;
Whatever doing, what can we suffer more,
What can we suffer worse? is this then worst,
Thus sitting, thus consulting, thus in Arms?
165 What when we fled amain, pursu'd and strook
With Heav'ns afflicting Thunder, and besought
The Deep to shelter us? this Hell then seem'd
A refuge from those wounds: or when we lay
Chain'd on the burning Lake? that sure was worse.
170 What if the breath that kindl'd those grim fires
Awak'd should blow them into sevenfold rage

And plunge us in the flames? or from above
Should intermitted vengeance arm again
His red right hand to plague us? what if all
175 Her stores were open'd, and this Firmament
Of Hell should spout her Cataracts of Fire,
Impendent horrors, threatning hideous fall
One day upon our heads; while we perhaps
Designing or exhorting glorious warr,
180 Caught in a fierie Tempest shall be hurl'd
Each on his rock transfixt, the sport and prey
Of racking whirlwinds, or for ever sunk
Under yon boyling Ocean, wrapt in Chains;
There to converse with everlasting groans,
185 Unrespited, unpitied, unrepreev'd,
Ages of hopeless end; this would be worse.
Warr therefore, open or conceal'd, alike
My voice disswades; for what can force or guile
With him, or who deceive his mind, whose eye
190 Views all things at one view? he from heav'ns highth
All these our motions vain, sees and derides;
Not more Almighty to resist our might
Then wise to frustrate all our plots and wiles.
Shall we then live thus vile, the Race of Heav'n
195 Thus trampl'd, thus expell'd to suffer here
Chains and these Torments? better these then worse
By my advice; since fate inevitable
Subdues us, and Omnipotent Decree,
The Victors will. To suffer, as to doe,
200 Our strength is equal, nor the Law unjust
That so ordains: this was at first resolv'd,
If we were wise, against so great a foe
Contending, and so doubtful what might fall.
I laugh, when those who at the Spear are bold
205 And vent'rous, if that fail them, shrink and fear
What yet they know must follow, to endure
Exile, or ignominy, or bonds, or pain,
The sentence of thir Conquerour: This is now
Our doom; which if we can sustain and bear,
210 Our Supream Foe in time may much remit
His anger, and perhaps thus farr remov'd
Not mind us not offending, satisfi'd
With what is punish't; whence these raging fires
Will slack'n, if his breath stir not thir flames.
215 Our purer essence then will overcome

Thir noxious vapour, or enur'd not feel,
Or chang'd at length, and to the place conformd
In temper and in nature, will receive
Familiar the fierce heat, and void of pain;
220   This horror will grow mild, this darkness light,
Besides what hope the never-ending flight
Of future dayes may bring, what chance, what change
Worth waiting, since our present lot appeers
For happy though but ill, for ill not worst,
225   If we procure not to our selves more woe.
            Thus *Belial* with words cloath'd in reasons garb
Counsel'd ignoble ease, and peaceful sloath,
Not peace: and after him thus *Mammon* spake.
            Either to disinthrone the King of Heav'n
230   We warr, if warr be best, or to regain
Our own right lost: him to unthrone we then
May hope, when everlasting Fate shall yeild
To fickle Chance, and *Chaos* judge the strife:
The former vain to hope argues as vain
235   The latter: for what place can be for us
Within Heav'ns bound, unless Heav'ns Lord supream
We overpower? Suppose he should relent
And publish Grace to all, on promise made
Of new Subjection; with what eyes could we
240   Stand in his presence humble, and receive
Strict Laws impos'd, to celebrate his Throne
With warbl'd Hymns, and to his Godhead sing
Forc't Halleluiahs; while he Lordly sits
Our envied Sovran, and his Altar breathes
245   Ambrosial Odours and Ambrosial Flowers,
Our servile offerings. This must be our task
In Heav'n, this our delight; how wearisom
Eternity so spent in worship paid
To whom we hate. Let us not then pursue
250   By force impossible, by leave obtain'd
Unacceptable, though in Heav'n, our state
Of splendid vassalage, but rather seek
Our own good from our selves, and from our own
Live to our selves, though in this vast recess,
255   Free, and to none accountable, preferring
Hard liberty before the easie yoke
Of servile Pomp. Our greatness will appear
Then most conspicuous, when great things of small,
Useful of hurtful, prosperous of adverse

260   We can create, and in what place so e're
       Thrive under evil, and work ease out of pain
       Through labour and indurance. This deep world
       Of darkness do we dread? How oft amidst
       Thick clouds and dark doth Heav'ns all-ruling Sire
265   Choose to reside, his Glory unobscur'd,
       And with the Majesty of darkness round
       Covers his Throne; from whence deep thunders roar
       Must'ring thir rage, and Heav'n resembles Hell?
       As he our darkness, cannot we his Light
270   Imitate when we please? This Desart soil
       Wants not her hidden lustre, Gemms and Gold;
       Nor want we skill or Art, from whence to raise
       Magnificence; and what can Heav'n shew more?
       Our torments also may in length of time
275   Become our Elements, these piercing Fires
       As soft as now severe, our temper chang'd
       Into their temper; which must needs remove
       The sensible of pain. All things invite
       To peaceful Counsels, and the settl'd State
280   Of order, how in safety best we may
       Compose our present evils, with regard
       Of what we are and where, dismissing quite
       All thoughts of warr: ye have what I advise.
              He scarce had finisht, when such murmur filld
285   Th' Assembly, as when hollow Rocks retain
       The sound of blustring winds, which all night long
       Had rous'd the Sea, now with hoarse cadence lull
       Sea-faring men orewatcht, whose Bark by chance
       Or Pinnace anchors in a craggy Bay
290   After the Tempest: Such applause was heard
       As *Mammon* ended, and his Sentence pleas'd,
       Advising peace: for such another Field
       They dreaded worse then Hell: so much the fear
       Of Thunder and the Sword of *Michael*
295   Wrought still within them; and no less desire
       To found this nether Empire, which might rise
       By pollicy, and long process of time,
       In emulation opposite to Heav'n.
       Which when *Beëlzebub* perceiv'd, then whom,
300   *Satan* except, none higher sat, with grave
       Aspect he rose, and in his rising seem'd
       A Pillar of State; deep on his Front engrav'n
       Deliberation sat and public care;

And Princely counsel in his face yet shon,
305   Majestic though in ruin: sage he stood
With *Atlantean* shoulders fit to bear
The weight of mightiest Monarchies; his look
Drew audience and attention still as Night
Or Summers Noon-tide air, while thus he spake.
310   Thrones and Imperial Powers, off-spring of heav'n,
Ethereal Vertues; or these Titles now
Must we renounce, and changing stile be call'd
Princes of Hell? for so the popular vote
Inclines, here to continue, and build up here
315   A growing Empire; doubtless; while we dream,
And know not that the King of Heav'n hath doom'd
This place our dungeon, not our safe retreat
Beyond his Potent arm, to live exempt
From Heav'ns high jurisdiction, in new League
320   Banded against his Throne, but to remain
In strictest bondage, though thus far remov'd,
Under th' inevitable curb, reserv'd
His captive multitude: For he, be sure,
In highth or depth, still first and last will Reign
325   Sole King, and of his Kingdom loose no part
By our revolt, but over Hell extend
His Empire, and with Iron Scepter rule
Us here, as with his Golden those in Heav'n.
What sit we then projecting peace and Warr?
330   Warr hath determin'd us, and foild with loss
Irreparable; tearms of peace yet none
Voutsaf't or sought; for what peace will be giv'n
To us enslav'd, but custody severe,
And stripes, and arbitrary punishment
335   Inflicted? and what peace can we return,
But to our power hostility and hate,
Untam'd reluctance, and revenge though slow,
Yet ever plotting how the Conqueror least
May reap his conquest, and may least rejoyce
340   In doing what we most in suffering feel?
Nor will occasion want, nor shall we need
With dangerous expedition to invade
Heav'n, whose high walls fear no assault or Siege,
Or ambush from the Deep. What if we find
345   Some easier enterprize? There is a place
(If ancient and prophetic fame in Heav'n
Err not) another World, the happy seat

Of som new Race call'd *Man*, about this time
To be created like to us, though less
350   In power and excellence, but favour'd more
Of him who rules above; so was his will
Pronounc'd among the Gods, and by an Oath,
That shook Heav'ns whole circumference, confirm'd.
Thither let us bend all our thoughts, to learn
355   What creatures there inhabit, of what mould,
Or substance, how endu'd, and what thir Power,
And where thir weakness, how attempted best,
By force or suttlety: Though Heav'n be shut,
And Heav'ns high Arbitrator sit secure
360   In his own strength, this place may lye expos'd
The utmost border of his Kingdom, left
To their defence who hold it: here perhaps
Som advantagious act may be achiev'd
By sudden onset, either with Hell fire
365   To waste his whole Creation, or possess
All as our own, and drive as we were driv'n,
The punie habitants, or if not drive,
Seduce them to our Party, that thir God
May prove thir foe, and with repenting hand
370   Abolish his own works. This would surpass
Common revenge, and interrupt his joy
In our Confusion, and our Joy upraise
In his disturbance; when his darling Sons
Hurl'd headlong to partake with us, shall curse
375   Thir frail Originals, and faded bliss,
Faded so soon. Advise if this be worth
Attempting, or to sit in darkness here
Hatching vain Empires. Thus *Beëlzebub*
Pleaded his devilish Counsel, first devis'd
380   By *Satan,* and in part propos'd: for whence,
But from the Author of all ill could Spring
So deep a malice, to confound the race
Of mankind in one root, and Earth with Hell
To mingle and involve, done all to spite
385   The great Creatour? But thir spite still serves
His glory to augment. The bold design
Pleas'd highly those infernal States, and joy
Sparkl'd in all thir eyes; with full assent
They vote: whereat his speech he thus renews.
390   Well have ye judg'd, well ended long debate,
Synod of Gods, and like to what ye are,

Great things resolv'd, which from the lowest deep
Will once more lift us up, in spight of Fate,
Neerer our ancient Seat; perhaps in view
395   Of those bright confines, whence with neighbouring Arms
And opportune excursion we may chance
Re-enter Heav'n; or else in some mild Zone
Dwell not unvisited of Heav'ns fair Light
Secure, and at the brightning Orient beam
400   Purge off this gloom; the soft delicious Air,
To heal the scarr of these corrosive Fires
Shall breath her balm. But first whom shall we send
In search of this new world, whom shall we find
Sufficient? who shall tempt with wandring feet
405   The dark unbottom'd infinite Abyss
And through the palpable obscure find out
His uncouth way, or spread his aerie flight
Upborn with indefatigable wings
Over the vast abrupt, ere he arrive
410   The happy Ile; what strength, what art can then
Suffice, or what evasion bear him safe
Through the strict Senteries and Stations thick
Of Angels watching round? Here he had need
All circumspection, and we now no less
415   Choice in our suffrage; for on whom we send,
The weight of all and our last hope relies.
      This said, he sat; and expectation held
His look suspence, awaiting who appeer'd
To second, or oppose, or undertake
420   The perilous attempt: but all sat mute,
Pondering the danger with deep thoughts; and each
In others count'nance read his own dismay
Astonisht: none among the choice and. prime
Of those Heav'n-warring Champions could be found
425   So hardie as to proffer or accept
Alone the dreadful voyage; till at last
Satan, whom now transcendent glory rais'd
Above his fellows, with Monarchal pride
Conscious of highest worth, unmov'd thus spake.
430   O Progeny of Heav'n, Empyreal Thrones,
With reason hath deep silence and demurr
Seis'd us, though undismaid: long is the way
And hard, that out of Hell leads up to light;
Our prison strong, this huge convex of Fire,
435   Outrageous to devour, immures us round

Ninefold, and gates of burning Adamant
Barr'd over us prohibit all egress.
These past, if any pass, the void profound
Of unessential Night receives him next
440   Wide gaping, and with utter loss of being
Threatens him, plung'd in that abortive gulf.
If thence he scape into whatever world,
Or unknown Region, what remains him less
Then unknown dangers and as hard escape.
445   But I should ill become this Throne, O Peers,
And this Imperial Sov'ranty, adorn'd
With splendor, arm'd with power, if aught propos'd
And judg'd of public moment, in the shape
Of difficulty or danger could deterr
450   Mee from attempting. Wherefore do I assume
These Royalties, and not refuse to Reign,
Refusing to accept as great a share
Of hazard as of honour, due alike
To him who Reigns, and so much to him due
455   Of hazard more, as he above the rest
High honourd sits? Go therfore mighty Powers,
Terror of Heav'n, though fall'n; intend at home,
While here shall be our home, what best may ease
The present misery, and render Hell
460   More tollerable; if there be cure or charm
To respite or deceive, or slack the pain
Of this ill Mansion: intermit no watch
Against a wakeful Foe, while I abroad
Through all the coasts of dark destruction seek
465   Deliverance for us all: this enterprize
None shall partake with me. Thus saying rose
The Monarch, and prevented all reply,
Prudent, least from his resolution rais'd
Others among the chief might offer now
470   (Certain to be refus'd) what erst they feard;
And so refus'd might in opinion stand
His rivals, winning cheap the high repute
Which he through hazard huge must earn. But they
Dreaded not more th' adventure then his voice
475   Forbidding; and at once with him they rose;
Thir rising all at once was as the sound
Of Thunder heard remote. Towards him they bend
With awful reverence prone; and as a God
Extoll him equal to the highest in Heav'n:

480   Nor fail'd they to express how much they prais'd,
        That for the general safety he despis'd
        His own: for neither do the Spirits damn'd
        Loose all thir vertue; least bad men should boast
        Thir specious deeds on earth, which glory excites,
485   Or close ambition varnisht o're with zeal.
        Thus they thir doubtful consultations dark
        Ended rejoycing in thir matchless Chief:
        As when from mountain tops the dusky clouds
        Ascending, while the North wind sleeps, o'respread
490   Heav'ns chearful face, the lowring Element
        Scowls ore the dark'n'd lantskip Snow, or showr;
        If chance the radiant Sun with farewell sweet
        Extend his ev'ning beam, the fields revive,
        The birds thir notes renew, and bleating herds
495   Attest thir joy, that hill and valley rings.
        O shame to men! Devil with Devil damn'd
        Firm concord holds, men onely disagree
        Of Creatures rational, though under hope
        Of heav'nly Grace: and God proclaiming peace,
500   Yet live in hatred, emnity, and strife
        Among themselves, and levie cruel warrs,
        Wasting the Earth, each other to destroy:
        As if (which might induce us to accord)
        Man had not hellish foes anow besides,
505   That day and night for his destruction wait.
            The *Stygian* Councel thus dissolv'd; and forth
        In order came the grand infernal Peers,
        Midst came thir mighty Paramount, and seemd
        Alone th' Antagonist of Heav'n, nor less
510   Then Hells dread Emperour with pomp Supream,
        And God-like imitated State; him round
        A Globe of fierie Seraphim inclos'd
        With bright imblazonrie, and horrent Arms.
        Then of thir Session ended they bid cry
515   With Trumpets regal sound the great result:
        Toward the four winds four speedy Cherubim
        Put to thir months the sounding Alchymie
        By Haralds voice explain'd: the hollow Abyss
        Heard farr and wide, and all the host of Hell
520   With deafning shout, return'd them loud acclaim.
        Thence more at ease thir minds and somwhat rais'd
        By false presumptuous hope, the ranged powers
        Disband, and wandring, each his several way

Pursues, as inclination or sad choice
525 Leads him perplext, where he may likeliest find
Truce to his restless thoughts, and entertain
The irksom hours, till his great Chief return.
Part on the Plain, or in the Air sublime
Upon the wing, or in swift race contend,
530 As at th' Olympian Games or *Pythian* fields;
Part curb thir fierie Steeds, or shun the Goal
With rapid wheels, or fronted Brigads form.
As when to warn proud Cities warr appears
Wag'd in the troubl'd Skie, and Armies rush
535 To Battel in the Clouds, before each Van
Prick forth the Aerie Knights, and couch thir spears
Till thickest Legions close; with feats of Arms
From either end of Heav'n the welkin burns.
Others with vast *Typhœan* rage more fell
540 Rend up both Rocks and Hills, and ride the Air
In whirlwind; Hell scarce holds the wild uproar.
As when *Alcides* from *Oechalia* Crown'd
With conquest, felt th' envenom'd robe, and tore
Through pain up by the roots *Thessalian* Pines,
545 And *Lichas* from the top of *Oeta* threw
Into th' *Euboic* Sea. Others more mild,
Retreated in a silent valley, sing
With notes Angelical to many a Harp
Thir own Heroic deeds and hapless fall
550 By doom of Battel; and complain that Fate
Free Vertue should enthrall to Force or Chance.
Thir song was partial, but the harmony
(What could it less when Spirits immortal sing?)
Suspended Hell, and took with ravishment
555 The thronging audience. In discourse more sweet
(For Eloquence the Soul, Song charms the Sense,)
Others apart sat on a Hill retir'd,
In thoughts more elevate, and reason'd high
Of Providence, Foreknowledge, Will and Fate,
560 Fixt Fate, free will, foreknowledge absolute,
And found no end, in wandring mazes lost.
Of good and evil much they argu'd then,
Of happiness and final misery,
Passion and Apathie, and glory and shame,
565 Vain wisdom all, and false Philosophie:
Yet with a pleasing sorcerie could charm
Pain for a while or anguish, and excite

Fallacious hope, or arm th' obdured brest
With stubborn patience as with triple steel.
570   Another part in Squadrons and gross Bands,
On bold adventure to discover wide
That dismal world, if any Clime perhaps
Might yeild them easier habitation, bend
Four ways thir flying March, along the Banks
575   Of four infernal Rivers that disgorge
Into the burning Lake thir baleful streams;
Abhorred *Styx* the flood of deadly hate,
Sad *Acheron* of sorrow, black and deep;
Cocytus, nam'd of lamentation loud
580   Heard on the ruful stream; fierce *Phlegeton*
Whose waves of torrent fire inflame with rage.
Farr off from these a slow and silent stream,
Lethe the River of Oblivion rouls
Her watrie Labyrinth, whereof who drinks,
585   Forthwith his former state and being forgets,
Forgets both joy and grief, pleasure and pain.
Beyond this flood a frozen Continent
Lies dark and wild, beat with perpetual storms
Of Whirlwind and dire Hail, which on firm land
590   Thaws not, but gathers heap, and ruin seems
Of ancient pile; all else deep snow and ice,
A gulf profound as that *Serbonian* Bog
Betwixt *Damiata* and mount *Casius* old,
Where Armies whole have sunk: the parching Air
595   Burns frore, and cold performs th' effect of Fire.
Thither by harpy-footed Furies hail'd,
At certain revolutions all the damn'd
Are brought: and feel by turns the bitter change
Of fierce extreams, extreams by change more fierce,
600   From Beds of raging Fire to starve in Ice
Thir soft Ethereal warmth, and there to pine
Immovable, infixt, and frozen round,
Periods of time, thence hurried back to fire.
They ferry over this *Lethean* Sound
605   Both to and fro, thir sorrow to augment,
And wish and struggle, as they pass, to reach
The tempting stream, with one small drop to loose
In sweet forgetfulness all pain and woe,
All in one moment, and so neer the brink;
610   But Fate withstands, and to oppose th' attempt
Medusa with *Gorgonian* terror guards

The Ford, and of it self the water flies
All taste of living wight, as once it fled
The lip of *Tantalus*. Thus roving on
615 In confus'd march forlorn, th' adventrous Bands
With shuddring horror pale, and eyes agast
View'd first thir lamentable lot, and found
No rest: through many a dark and drearie Vale
They pass'd, and many a Region dolorous,
620 O're many a frozen, many a fierie Alp,
Rocks, Caves, Lakes, Fens, Bogs, Dens, and shades of death,
A Universe of death, which God by curse
Created evil, for evil only good,
Where all life dies, death lives, and nature breeds,
625 Perverse, all monstrous, all prodigious things,
Abominable, inutterable, and worse
Then Fables yet have feign'd, or fear conceiv'd,
Gorgons and *Hydra's,* and *Chimera's* dire.
Mean while the Adversary of God and Man,
630 *Satan* with thoughts inflam'd of highest design,
Puts on swift wings, and towards the Gates of Hell
Explores his solitary flight; som times
He scours the right hand coast, som times the left,
Now shaves with level wing the Deep, then soars
635 Up to the fiery Concave touring high.
As when farr off at Sea a Fleet descri'd
Hangs in the Clouds, by Æquinoctial Winds
Close sailing from *Bengala,* or the Iles
Of *Ternate* and *Tidore,* whence Merchants bring
640 Thir spicie Drugs: they on the Trading Flood
Through the wide *Ethiopian* to the Cape
Ply stemming nightly toward the Pole. So seem'd
Farr off the flying Fiend: at last appeer
Hell bounds high reaching to the horrid Roof,
645 And thrice threefold the Gates; three folds were Brass,
Three Iron, three of Adamantine Rock,
Impenetrable, impal'd with circling fire,
Yet unconsum'd. Before the Gates there sat
On either side a formidable shape;
650 The one seem'd Woman to the waste, and fair,
But ended foul in many a scaly fould
Voluminous and vast, a Serpent arm'd
With mortal sting: about her middle round
A cry of Hell Hounds never ceasing bark'd
655 With wide *Cerberean* mouths full loud, and rung

A hideous Peal: yet, when they list, would creep,
If aught disturb'd thir noyse, into her woomb,
And kennel there, yet there still bark'd and howl'd,
Within unseen. Farr less abhorr'd then these
660   Vex'd *Scylla* bathing in the Sea that parts
Calabria from the hoarce *Trinacrian* shore:
Nor uglier follow the Night-Hag, when call'd
In secret, riding through the Air she comes
Lur'd with the smell of infant blood, to dance
665   With *Lapland* Witches, while the labouring Moon
Eclipses at thir charms. The other shape,
If shape it might be call'd that shape had none
Distinguishable in member, joynt, or limb,
Or substance might be call'd that shadow seem'd,
670   For each seem'd either; black it stood as Night,
Fierce as ten Furies, terrible as Hell,
And shook a dreadful Dart; what seem'd his head
The likeness of a Kingly Crown had on.
Satan was now at hand, and from his seat
675   The Monster moving onward came as fast
With horrid strides, Hell trembled as he strode.
Th' undaunted Fiend what this might be admir'd,
Admir'd, not fear'd; God and his Son except,
Created thing naught valu'd he nor shun'd;
680   And with disdainful look thus first began.
       Whence and what art thou, execrable shape,
That dar'st, though grim and terrible, advance
Thy miscreated Front athwart my way
To yonder Gates? through them I mean to pass,
685   That be assur'd, without leave askt of thee:
Retire, or taste thy folly, and learn by proof,
Hell-born, not to contend with Spirits of Heav'n.
       To whom the Goblin full of wrauth reply'd,
Art thou that Traitor Angel, art thou hee,
690   Who first broke peace in Heav'n and Faith, till then
Unbrok'n, and in proud rebellious Arms
Drew after him the third part of Heav'ns Sons
Conjur'd against the highest, for which both Thou
And they outcast from God, are here condemn'd
695   To waste Eternal dayes in woe and pain?
And reckn'st thou thy self with Spirits of Heav'n,
Hell-doom'd, and breath'st defiance here and scorn,
Where I reign King, and to enrage thee more,
Thy King and Lord? Back to thy punishment,

700 False fugitive, and to thy speed add wings,
    Least with a whip of Scorpions I pursue
    Thy lingring, or with one stroke of this Dart
    Strange horror seise thee, and pangs unfelt before.
        So spake the grieslie terrour, and in shape,
705 So speaking and so threatning, grew tenfold
    More dreadful and deform: on th' other side
    Incenst with indignation *Satan* stood
    Unterrifi'd, and like a Comet burn'd,
    That fires the length of *Ophiucus* huge
710 In th' Artick Sky, and from his horrid hair
    Shakes Pestilence and Warr. Each at the Head
    Level'd his deadly aim; thir fatall hands
    No second stroke intend, and such a frown
    Each cast at th' other, as when two black Clouds
715 With Heav'ns Artillery fraught, come rattling on
    Over the *Caspian*, then stand front to front
    Hov'ring a space, till Winds the signal blow
    To joyn their dark Encounter in mid air:
    So frownd the mighty Combatants, that Hell
720 Grew darker at thir frown, so matcht they stood;
    For never but once more was either like
    To meet so great a foe; and now great deeds
    Had been achiev'd, whereof all Hell had rung,
    Had not the Snakie Sorceress that sat
725 Fast by Hell Gate, and kept the fatal Key,
    Ris'n, and with hideous outcrv rush'd between.
        O Father, what intends thy hand, she cry'd,
    Against thy only Son? What fury O Son,
    Possesses thee to bend that morial Dart
730 Against thy Fathers head? and know'st for whom;
    For him who sits above and laughs the while
    At thee ordain'd his drudge, to execute
    What e're his wrath, which he calls Justice, bids,
    His wrath which one day will destroy ye both.
735   She spake, and at her words the hellish Pest
    Forbore, then these to her *Satan* return'd:
        So strange thy outcry, and thy words so strange
    Thou interposest, that my sudden hand
    Prevented spares to tell thee yet by deeds
740 What it intends; till first I know of thee,
    What thing thou art, thus double-form'd, and why
    In this infernal Vale first met thou call'st
    Me Father, and that Fantasm call'st my Son?

         I know thee not, nor ever saw till now

745   Sight more detestable then him and thee.

             T' whom thus the Portress of Hell Gate reply'd;

         Hast thou forgot me then, and do I seem

         Now in thine eye so foul, once deemd so fair

         In Heav'n, when at th' Assembly, and in sight

750   Of all the Seraphim with thee combin'd

         In bold conspiracy against Heav'ns King,

         All on a sudden miserable pain

         Surpris'd thee, dim thine eyes, and dizzie swumm

         In darkness, while thy head flames thick and fast

755   Threw forth, till on the left side op'ning wide,

         Likest to thee in shape and count'nance bright,

         Then shining heav'nly fair, a Goddess arm'd

         Out of thy head I sprung: amazement seis'd

         All th' Host of Heav'n; back they recoild affraid

760   At first, and call'd me *Sin,* and for a Sign

         Portentous held me; but familiar grown,

         I pleas'd, and with attractive graces won

         The most averse, thee chiefly, who full oft

         Thy self in me thy perfect image viewing

765   Becam'st enamourd, and such joy thou took'st

         With me in secret, that my womb conceiv'd

         A growing burden. Mean while Warr arose,

         And flelds were fought in Heav'n; wherein remaind

         (For what could else) to our Almighty Foe

770   Cleer Victory, to our part loss and rout

         Through all the Empyrean: down they fell

         Driv'n headlong from the Pitch of Heaven, down

         Into this Deep, and in the general fall

         I also; at which time this powerful Key

775   Into my hands was giv'n, with charge to keep

         These Gates for ever shut, which none can pass

         Without my op'ning. Pensive here I sat

         Alone, but long I sat not, till my womb

         Pregnant by thee, and now excessive grown

780   Prodigious motion felt and rueful throes.

         At last this odious offspring whom thou seest

         Thine own begotten, breaking violent way

         Tore through my entrails, that with fear and pain

         Distorted, all my nether shape thus grew

785   Transform'd: but he my inbred enemie

         Forth issu'd, brandishing his fatal Dart

         Made to destroy: I fled, and cry'd out *Death,*

Hell trembl'd at the hideous Name, and sigh'd
From all her Caves, and back resounded *Death*.
790　I fled, but he pursu'd (though more, it seems,
Inflam'd with lust then rage) and swifter far,
Mee overtook his mother all dismaid,
And in embraces forcible and foul
Ingendring with me, of that rape begot
795　These yelling Monsters that with ceasless cry
Surround me, as thou sawst, hourly conceiv'd
And hourly born, with sorrow infinite
To me, for when they list into the womb
That bred them they return, and howl and gnaw
800　My Bowels, thir repast; then bursting forth
Afresh with conscious terrours vex me round,
That rest or intermission none I find.
Before mine eyes in opposition sits
Grim *Death* my Son and foe, who sets them on,
805　And me his Parent would full soon devour
For want of other prey, but that he knows
His end with mine involv'd; and knows that I
Should prove a bitter Morsel, and his bane,
When ever that shall be; so Fate pronounc'd.
810　But thou O Father, I forewarn thee, shun
His deadly arrow; neither vainly hope
To be invulnerable in those bright Arms,
Though temper'd heav'nly, for that mortal dint,
Save he who reigns above, none can resist.
815　　　She finish'd, and the suttle Fiend his lore
Soon learnd, now milder, and thus answerd smooth.
Dear Daughter, since thou claim'st me for thy Sire,
And my fair Son here showst me, the dear pledge
Of dalliance had with thee in Heav'n, and joys
820　Then sweet, now sad to mention, through dire change
Befall'n us unforeseen, unthought of, know
I come no enemie, but to set free
From out this dark and dismal house of pain,
Both him and thee, and all the heav'nly Host
825　Of Spirits that in our just pretenses arm'd
Fell with us from on high: from them I go
This uncouth errand sole, and one for all
My self expose, with lonely steps to tread
Th' unfounded deep, and through the void immense
830　To search with wandring quest a place foretold
Should be, and, by concurring signs, ere now

Created vast and round, a place of bliss
In the Pourlieues of Heav'n, and therein plac't
A race of upstart Creatures, to supply
835 Perhaps our vacant room, though more remov'd,
Least Heav'n surcharg'd with potent multitude
Might hap to move new broils: Be this or aught
Then this more secret now design'd. I haste
To know, and this once known, shall soon return,
840 And bring ye to the place where Thou and Death
Shall dwell at ease, and up and down unseen
Wing silently the buxom Air, imbalm'd
With odours; there ye shall be fed and fill'd
Immeasurably, all things shall be your prey.
845 He ceas'd, for both seemd highly pleas'd, and Death
Grinnd horrible a gastly smile, to hear
His famine should be fill'd, and blest his maw
Destin'd to that good hour: no less rejoyc'd
His mother bad, and thus bespake her Sire.
850   The key of this infernal Pit by due,
And by command of Heav'ns all-powerful King
I keep, by him forbidden to unlock
These Adamantine Gates; against all force
Death ready stands to interpose his dart,
855 Fearless to be o're matcht by living might.
But what ow I to his commands above
Who hates me, and hath hither thrust me down
Into this gloom of *Tartarus* profound,
To sit in hateful Office here confin'd,
860 Inhabitant of Heav'n, and heav'nlie-born,
Here in perpetual agonie and pain,
With terrors and with clamors compasst round
Of mine own brood, that on my bowels feed:
Thou art my Father, thou my Author, thou
865 My being gav'st me; whom should I obey
But thee, whom follow? thou wilt bring me soon
To that new world of light and bliss, among
The Gods who live at ease, where I shall Reign
At thy right hand voluptuous, as beseems
870 Thy daughter and thy darling, without end.
          Thus saying, from her side the fatal Key,
Sad instrument of all our woe, she took;
And towards the Gate rouling her bestial train,
Forthwith the huge Porcullis high up drew,
875 Which but her self not all the *Stygian* powers

Could once have mov'd; then in the key-bole turns
Th' intricate wards, and every Bolt and Bar
Of massie Iron or sollid Rock with ease
Unfast'ns: on a sudden op'n flie
880   With impetuous recoil and jarring sound
Th' infernal dores, and on thir hinges grate
Harsh Thunder, that the lowest bottom shook
Of *Erebus*. She op'nd, but to shut
Excel'd her power; the Gates wide op'n stood,
885   That with extended wings a Bannerd Host
Under spread Ensigns marching might pass through
With Horse and Chariots rankt in loose array;
So wide they stood, and like a Furnace mouth
Cast forth redounding smoak and ruddy flame.
890   Before thir eyes in sudden view appear
The secrets of the hoarie deep, a dark
Illimitable Ocean without bound,
Without dimension, where length, breadth, and highth,
And time and place are lost; where eldest Night
895   And *Chaos*, Ancestors of Nature, hold
Eternal *Anarchie*, amidst the noise
Of endless Warrs, and by confusion stand.
For hot, cold, moist, and dry, four Champions fierce
Strive here for Maistrie, and to Battel bring
900   Thir embryon Atoms; they around the flag
Of each his Faction, in thir several Clanns,
Light-arm'd or heavy, sharp, smooth, swift or slow,
Swarm populous, unnumber'd as the Sands
Of *Barca* or *Cyrene's* torrid soil,
905   Levied to side with warring Winds, and poise
Thir lighter wings. To whom these most adhere,
Hee rules a moment; *Chaos* Umpire sits,
And by decision more imbroils the fray
By which he Reigns: next him high Arbiter
910   *Chance* governs all. Into this wild Abyss,
The Womb of nature and perhaps her Grave,
Of neither Sea, nor Shore, nor Air, nor Fire,
But all these in thir pregnant causes mixt
Confus'dly, and which thus must ever fight,
915   Unless th' Almighty Maker them ordain
His dark materials to create more Worlds,
Into this wild Abyss the warie fiend
Stood on the brink of Hell and look'd a while,
Pondering his Voyage; for no narrow frith

920	He had to cross. Nor was his ear less peal'd
	With noises loud and ruinous (to compare
	Great things with small) then when *Bellona* storms,
	With all her battering Engines bent to rase
	Som Capital City; or less then if this frame
925	Of Heav'n were falling, and these Elements
	In mutinie had from her Axle torn
	The stedfast Earth. At last his Sail-broad Vans
	He spreads for flight, and in the surging smoak
	Uplifted spurns the ground, thence many a League
930	As in a cloudy Chair ascending rides
	Audacious, but that seat soon failing, meets
	A vast vacuitie: all unawares
	Fluttring his pennons vain plumb down he drops
	Ten thousand fadom deep, and to this hour
935	Down had been falling, had not by ill chance
	The strong rebuff of som tumultuous cloud
	Instinct with Fire and Nitre hurried him
	As many miles aloft: that furie stay'd,
	Quencht in a Boggie *Syrtis*, neither Sea,
940	Nor good dry Land: nigh founderd on he fares,
	Treading the crude consistence, half on foot,
	Half flying; behoves him now both Oar and Sail.
	As when a Gryfon through the Wilderness
	With winged course ore Hill or moarie Dale,
945	Pursues the *Arimaspian,* who by stelth
	Had from his wakeful custody purloind
	The guarded Gold: So eagerly the fiend
	Ore bog or steep, through strait, rough, dense, or rare,
	With head, hands, wings or feet pursues his way,
950	And swims or sinks, or wades, or creeps, or flyes:
	At length a universal hubbub wild
	Of stunning sounds and voices all confus'd
	Born through the hollow dark assaults his ear
	With loudest vehemence: thither he plyes,
955	Undaunted to meet there what ever power
	Or Spirit of the nethermost Abyss
	Might in that noise reside, of whom to ask
	Which way the neerest coast of darkness lyes
	Bordering on light; when strait behold the Throne
960	Of *Chaos*, and his dark Pavilion spread
	Wide on the wasteful Deep; with him Enthron'd
	Sat Sable-vested *Night*, eldest of things,
	The Consort of his Reign; and by them stood

Orcus and *Ades,* and the dreaded name
965   Of *Demogorgon; Rumor* next and *Chance,*
And *Tumult* and *Confusion* all imbroild,
And *Discord* with a thousand various mouths.
      T' whom *Satan* turning boldly, thus. Ye Powers
And Spirits of this nethermost Abyss,
970   *Chaos* and ancient *Night,* I come no Spy,
With purpose to explore or to disturb
The secrets of your Realm, but by constraint
Wandring this darksome Desart, as my way
Lies through your spacious Empire up to light,
975   Alone, and without guide, half lost, I seek
What readiest path leads where your gloomie bounds
Confine with Heav'n; or if som other place
From your Dominion won, th' Ethereal King
Possesses lately, thither to arrive
980   I travel this profound, direct my course;
Directed, no mean recompence it brings
To your behoof, if I that Region lost,
All usurpation thence expell'd, reduce
To her original darkness and your sway
985   (Which is my present journey) and once more
Erect the Standard there of ancient *Night,*
Yours be th' advantage all, mine the revenge.
      Thus *Satan;* and him thus the Anarch old
With faultring speech and visage incompos'd
990   Answer'd. I know thee, stranger, who thou art,
That mighty leading Angel, who of late
Made head against Heav'ns King, though overthrown.
I saw and heard, for such a numerous Host
Fled not in silence through the frighted deep
995   With ruin upon ruin, rout on rout,
Confusion worse confounded; and Heav'n Gates
Pourd out by millions her victorious Bands
Pursuing. I upon my Frontiers here
Keep residence; if all I can will serve,
1000   That little which is left so to defend,
Encroacht on still through our intestine broils
Weakning the Scepter of old *Night:* first Hell
Your dungeon stretching far and wide beneath;
Now lately Heav'n and Earth, another World
1005   Hung ore my Realm, link'd in a golden Chain
To that side Heav'n from whence your Legions fell:
If that way be your walk, you have not farr;

So much the neerer danger; go and speed;
Havock and spoil and ruin are my gain.
1010   He ceas'd; and *Satan* staid not to reply,
But glad that now his Sea should find a shore,
With fresh alacritie and force renew'd
Springs upward like a Pyramid of fire
Into the wild expanse, and through the shock
1015 Of fighting Elements, on all sides round
Environ'd wins his way; harder beset
And more endanger'd, then when *Argo* pass'd
Through *Bosporus* betwixt the justling Rocks:
Or when *Ulysses* on the Larbord shunnd
1020 *Charybdis,* and by th' other whirlpool steard.
So he with difficulty and labour hard
Mov'd on, with difficulty and labour hee;
But hee once past, soon after when man fell,
Strange alteration! Sin and Death amain
1025 Following his track, such was the will of Heav'n,
Pav'd after him a broad and beat'n way
Over the dark Abyss, whose boiling Gulf
Tamely endur'd a Bridge of wondrous length
From Hell continu'd reaching th' utmost Orb
1030 Of this frail World; by which the Spirits perverse
With easie intercourse pass to and fro
To tempt or punish mortals, except whom
God and good Angels guard by special grace.
But now at last the sacred influence
1035 Of light appears, and from the walls of Heav'n
Shoots farr into the bosom of dim Night
A glimmering dawn; here Nature first begins
Her fardest verge, and *Chaos* to retire
As from her outmost works a brok'n foe
1040 With tumult less and with less hostile din,
That *Satan* with less toil, and now with ease
Wafts on the calmer wave by dubious light
And like a weather-beaten Vessel holds
Gladly the Port, though Shrouds and Tackle torn;
1045 Or in the emptier waste, resembling Air,
Weighs his spread wings, at leasure to behold
Farr off th' Empyreal Heav'n, extended wide
In circuit, undetermind square or round,
With Opal Towrs and Battlements adorn'd
1050 Of living Saphire, once his native Seat;
And fast by hanging in a golden Chain

This pendant world, in bigness as a Starr
Of smallest Magnitude close by the Moon.
Thither full fraught with mischievous revenge,
1055   Accurst, and in a cursed hour he hies.

BOOK III
THE ARGUMENT

God sitting on his Throne sees *Satan* flying towards this world, then newly created; shews him to the Son who sat at his right hand; foretells the success of *Satan* in perverting man-kind; clears his own Justice and Wisdom from all imputation, having created Man free and able enough to have withstood his Tempter; yet declares his purpose of grace towards him, in regard he fell not of his own malice, as did *Satan*, but by him seduc't. The Son of God renders praises to his Father for the manifestation of his gracious purpose towards Man; but God again declares, that Grace cannot be extended towards Man without the satisfaction of divine Justice; Man hath offended the majesty of God by aspiring to Godhead, and therefore with all his Progeny devoted to death must dye, unless some one can be found sufficient to answer for his offence, and undergo his Punishment. The Son of God freely offers himself a Ransom for Man: the Father accepts him, ordains his incarnation, pronounces his exaltation above all Names in Heaven and Earth; commands all the Angels to adore him; they obey, and hymning to thir Harps in full Quire, celebrate the Father and the Son. Mean while *Satan* alights upon the bar convex of this Worlds outer-most Orb; where wandring he first finds a place since call'd the Lymbo of Vanity; what persons and things fly up thither; thence comes to the Gate of Heaven, describ'd ascending by stairs, and the waters above the Firmament that flow about it: His passage thence to the Orb of the Sun; he finds there *Uriel* the Regent of that Orb, but first changes himself into the shape of a meaner Angel; and pretending a zealous desire to behold the new Creation and Man whom God had plac't here, inquires of him the place of his habitation, and is directed; alights first on Mount *Niphates*.

Hail holy Light, ofspring of Heav'n first-born,
Or of th' Eternal Coeternal beam
May I express thee unblam'd? since God is light,
And never but in unapproached light
5   Dwelt from Eternitie, dwelt then in thee,
Bright effluence of bright essence increate.
Or hear'st thou rather pure Ethereal stream,
Whose Fountain who shall tell? before the Sun,
Before the Heav'ns thou wert, and at the voice
10   Of God, as with a Mantle didst invest
The rising world of waters dark and deep,
Won from the void and formless infinite.

Thee I revisit now with bolder wing,
Escap't the *Stygian* Pool, though long detain'd
15   In that obscure sojourn, while in my flight
Through utter and through middle darkness borne
With other notes then to th' *Orphean* Lyre
I sung of *Chaos* and *Eternal Night,*
Taught by the heav'nly Muse to venture down
20   The dark descent, and up to reascend,
Though hard and rare: thee I revisit safe,
And feel thy sovran vital Lamp; but thou
Revisit'st not these eyes, that rowl in vain
To find thy piercing ray, and find no dawn;
25   So thick a drop serene hath quencht thir Orbs,
Or dim suffusion veild. Yet not the more
Cease I to wander where the Muses haunt
Cleer Spring, or shadie Grove, or Sunnie Hill,
Smit with the love of sacred Song; but chief
30   Thee Sion and the flowrie Brooks beneath
That wash thy hallowd feet, and warbling flow,
Nightly I visit: nor somtimes forget
Those other two equal'd with me in Fate,
So were I equal'd with them in renown,
35   Blind *Thamyris* and blind *Mæonides,*
And *Tiresias* and *Phineus* Prophets old.
Then feed on thoughts, that voluntarie move
Harmonious numbers; as the wakeful Bird
Sings darkling, and in shadiest Covert hid
40   Tunes her nocturnal Note. Thus with the Year
Seasons return, but not to me returns
Day, or the sweet approach of Ev'n or Morn,
Or sight of vernal bloom, or Summers Rose,
Or flocks, or heards, or human face divine;
45   But cloud in stead, and ever-during dark
Surrounds me, from the chearful wayes of men
Cut off, and for the Book of knowledge fair
Presented with a Universal blanc
Of Natures works to mee expung'd and ras'd,
50   And wisdom at one entrance quite shut out.
So much the rather thou Celestial light
Shine inward, and the mind through all her powers
Irradiate, there plant eyes, all mist from thence
Purge and disperse, that I may see and tell
55   Of things invisible to mortal sight.
       Now had th' Almighty Father from above,

From the pure Empyrean where he sits
High Thron'd above all highth, bent down his eye,
His own works and their works at once to view:
60   About him all the Sanctities of Heav'n
Stood thick as Starrs, and from his sight receiv'd
Beatitude past utterance; on his right
The radiant image of his Glory sat,
His onely Son; on Earth he first beheld
65   Our two first Parents, yet the onely two
Of mankind, in the happie Garden plac't,
Reaping immortal fruits of joy and love,
Uninterrupted joy, unrivald love
In blissful solitude; he then survey'd
70   Hell and the Gulf between, and *Satan* there
Coasting the wall of Heav'n on this side Night
In the dun Air sublime, and ready now
To stoop with wearied wings, and willing feet
On the bare outside of this World, that seem'd
75   Firm land imbosom'd without Firmament,
Uncertain which, in Ocean or in Air.
Him God beholding from his prospect high,
Wherein past, present, future he beholds,
Thus to his onely Son foreseeing spake.
80   Onely begotten Son, seest thou what rage
Transports our adversarie, whom no bounds
Prescrib'd, no barrs of Hell, nor all the chains
Heapt on him there, nor yet the main Abyss
Wide interrupt can hold; so bent he seems
85   On desperat revenge, that shall redound
Upon his own rebellious head. And now
Through all restraint broke loose he wings his way
Not farr off Heav'n, in the Precincts of light,
Directly towards the new created World,
90   And Man there plac't, with purpose to assay
If him by force he can destroy, or worse,
By som false guile pervert; and shall pervert;
For man will heark'n to his glozing lyes,
And easily transgress the sole Command,
95   Sole pledge of his obedience: So will fall
Hee and his faithless Progenie: whose fault?
Whose but his own? ingrate, he had of mee
All he could have; I made him just and right,
Sufficient to have stood, though free to fall.
100 Such I created all th' Ethereal Powers

And Spirits, both them who stood and them who faild;
Freely they stood who stood, and fell who fell.
Not free, what proof could they have givn sincere
Of true allegiance, constant Faith or Love,
105 Where onely what they needs must do, appeard,
Not what they would? what praise could they receive?
What pleasure I from such obedience paid,
When Will and Reason (Reason also is choice)
Useless and vain, of freedom both despoild,
110 Made passive both, had serv'd necessitie,
Not mee. They therefore as to right belong'd,
So were created, nor can justly accuse
Thir maker, or thir making, or thir Fate;
As if Predestination over-rul'd
115 Thir will, dispos'd by absolute Decree
Or high foreknowledge; they themselves decreed
Thir own revolt, not I: if I foreknew,
Foreknowledge had no influence on their fault,
Which had no less prov'd certain unforeknown.
120 So without least impulse or shadow of Fate,
Or aught by me immutablie foreseen,
They trespass, Authors to themselves in all
Both what they judge and what they choose; for so
I formd them free, and free they must remain,
125 Till they enthrall themselves: I else must change
Thir nature, and revoke the high Decree
Unchangeable, Eternal, which ordain'd
Thir freedom, they themselves ordain'd thir fall.
The first sort by thir own suggestion fell,
130 Self-tempted, self-deprav'd: Man falls deceiv'd
By the other first: Man therefore shall find grace,
The other none: in Mercy and Justice both,
Through Heav'n and Earth, so shall my glorie excel,
But Mercy first and last shall brightest shine.
135   Thus while God spake, ambrosial fragrance fill'd
All Heav'n, and in the blessed Spirits elect
Sense of new joy ineffable diffus'd:
Beyond compare the Son of God was seen
Most glorious, in him all his Father shon
140 Substantially express'd, and in his face
Divine compassion visibly appeerd,
Love without end, and without measure Grace,
Which uttering thus he to his Father spake.
O Father, gracious was that word which clos'd

145   Thy sovran sentence, that Man should find grace;
        For which both Heav'n and Earth shall high extoll
        Thy praises, with th' innumerable sound
        Of Hymns and sacred Songs, wherewith thy Throne
        Encompass'd shall resound thee ever blest.
150   For should Man finally be lost, should Man
        Thy creature late so lov'd, thy youngest Son
        Fall circumvented thus by fraud, though joynd
        With his own folly? that be from thee farr,
        That farr be from thee, Father, who art Judge
155   Of all things made, and judgest onely right.
        Or shall the Adversarie thus obtain
        His end, and frustrate thine, shall he fulfill
        His malice, and thy goodness bring to naught,
        Or proud return though to his heavier doom,
160   Yet with revenge accomplish't and to Hell
        Draw after him the whole Race of mankind,
        By him corrupted? or wilt thou thy self
        Abolish thy Creation, and unmake,
        For him, what for thy glorie thou hast made?
165   So should thy goodness and thy greatness both
        Be questiond and blaspheam'd without defence.
              To whom the great Creatour thus reply'd.
        O Son, in whom my Soul hath chief delight,
        Son of my bosom, Son who art alone
170   My word, my wisdom, and effectual might,
        All hast thou spok'n as my thoughts are, all
        As my Eternal purpose hath decreed:
        Man shall not quite be lost, but sav'd who will,
        Yet not of will in him, but grace in me
175   Freely voutsaft; once more I will renew
        His lapsed powers, though forfeit and enthrall'd
        By sin to foul exorbitant desires;
        Upheld by me, yet once more he shall stand
        On even ground against his mortal foe,
180   By me upheld, that he may know how frail
        His fall'n condition is, and to me ow
        All his deliv'rance, and to none but me.
        Some I have chosen of peculiar grace
        Elect above the rest; so is my will:
185   The rest shall hear me call, and oft be warnd
        Thir sinful state, and to appease betimes
        Th' incensed Deitie, while offerd grace
        Invites; for I will cleer thir senses dark,

190
What may suffice, and soft'n stonie hearts
To pray, repent, and bring obedience due.
To prayer, repentance, and obedience due,
Though but endevord with sincere intent,
Mine ear shall not be slow, mine eye not shut.
And I will place within them as a guide

195
My Umpire *Conscience*, whom if they will hear,
Light after light well us'd they shall attain,
And to the end persisting, safe arrive.
This my long sufferance and my day of grace
They who neglect and scorn, shall never taste;

200
But hard be hard'n'd, blind be blinded more,
That they may stumble on, and deeper fall;
And none but such from mercy I exclude.
But yet all is not don; Man disobeying,
Disloyal breaks his fealtie, and sinns

205
Against the high Supremacie of Heav'n,
Affecting God-head, and so loosing all,
To expiate his Treason hath naught left,
But to destruction sacred and devote,
He with his whole posteritie must die,

210
Die hee or Justice must; unless for him
Som other able, and as willing, pay
The rigid satisfaction, death for death.
Say Heav'nly Powers, where shall we find such love,
Which of ye will be mortal to redeem

215
Mans mortal crime, and just th' unjust to save,
Dwels in all Heaven charitie so dear?
    He ask'd, but all the Heav'nly Quire stood mute,
And silence was in Heav'n: on mans behalf
Patron or Intercessor none appeerd,

220
Much less that durst upon his own head draw
The deadly forfeiture, and ransom set.
And now without redemption all mankind
Must have bin lost, adjudg'd to Death and Hell
By doom severe, had not the Son of God,

225
In whom the fulness dwels of love divine,
His dearest mediation thus renewd.
    Father, thy word is past, man shall find grace;
And shall grace not find means, that finds her way,
The speediest of thy winged messengers,

230
To visit all thy creatures, and to all
Comes unprevented, unimplor'd, unsought,
Happie for man, so coming; he her aid

Can never seek, once dead in sins and lost;
Attonement for himself, or offering meet,
235   Indebted and undon, hath none to bring:
Behold mee then, mee for him, life for life
I offer, on mee let thine anger fall;
Account mee man; I for his sake will leave
Thy bosom, and this glorie next to thee
240   Freely put off, and for him lastly die
Well pleas'd, on me let Death wreck all his rage;
Under his gloomie power I shall not long
Lie vanquisht; thou hast givn me to possess
Life in my self for ever, by thee I live,
245   Though now to Death I yeild, and am his due
All that of me can die, yet that debt paid,
Thou wilt not leave me in the loathsom grave
His prey, nor suffer my unspotted Soul
For ever with corruption there to dwell;
250   But I shall rise Victorious, and subdue
My Vanquisher, spoild of his vanted spoil;
Death his deaths wound shall then receive, and stoop
Inglorious, of his mortall sting disarm'd.
I through the ample Air in Triumph high
255   Shall lead Hell Captive maugre Hell, and show
The powers of darkness bound. Thou at the sight
Pleas'd, out of Heaven shalt look down and smile,
While by thee rais'd I ruin all my Foes,
Death last, and with his Carcass glut the Grave:
260   Then with the multitude of my redeemd
Shall enter Heav'n long absent, and return,
Father, to see thy face, wherein no cloud
Of anger shall remain, but peace assur'd,
And reconcilement; wrauth shall be no more
265   Thenceforth, but in thy presence Joy entire.
       His words here ended, but his meek aspect
Silent yet spake, and breath'd immortal love
To mortal men, above which only shon
Filial obedience: as a sacrifice
270   Glad to be offer'd, he attends the will
Of his great Father. Admiration seis'd
All Heav'n, what this might mean, and whither tend
Wondring; but soon th' Almighty thus reply'd:
       O thou in Heav'n and Earth the only peace
275   Found out for mankind under wrauth, O thou
My sole complacence! well thou know'st how dear,

To me are all my works, nor Man the least
Though last created, that for him I spare
Thee from my bosom and right hand, to save,

280 By loosing thee a while, the whole Race lost.
Thou therefore whom thou only canst redeem,
Thir Nature also to thy Nature joyn;
And be thy self Man among men on Earth,
Made flesh, when time shall be, of Virgin seed,

285 By wondrous birth: Be thou in *Adams* room
The Head of all mankind, though *Adams* Son.
As in him perish all men, so in thee
As from a second root shall be restor'd,
As many as are restor'd, without thee none.

290 His crime makes guiltie all his Sons, thy merit
Imputed shall absolve them who renounce
Thir own both righteous and unrighteous deeds,
And live in thee transplanted, and from thee
Receive new life. So Man, as is most just,

295 Shall satisfie for Man, be judg'd and die,
And dying rise, and rising with him raise
His Brethren, ransomd with his own dear life.
So Heav'nly love shall outdo Hellish hate,
Giving to death, and dying to redeem,

300 So dearly to redeem what Hellish hate
So easily destroy'd, and still destroyes
In those who, when they may, accept not grace.
Nor shalt thou by descending to assume
Mans Nature, less'n or degrade thine own.

305 Because thou hast, though Thron'd in highest bliss
Equal to God, and equally enjoying
God-like fruition, quitted all to save
A World from utter loss, and hast been found
By Merit more then Birthright Son of God,

310 Found worthiest to be so by being Good,
Farr more then Great or High; because in thee
Love hath abounded more then Glory abounds,
Therefore thy Humiliation shall exalt
With thee thy Manhood also to this Throne;

315 Here shalt thou sit incarnate, here shalt Reign
Both God and Man, Son both of God and Man,
Anointed universal King; all Power
I give thee, reign for ever, and assume
Thy Merits; under thee as Head Supream

320 Thrones, Princedoms, Powers, Dominions I reduce:

All knees to thee shall bow, of them that bide
In Heav'n, or Earth, or under Earth in Hell;
When thou attended gloriously from Heav'n
Shalt in the Sky appeer, and from thee send
325   The summoning Arch-Angels to proclaim
Thy dread Tribunal: forthwith from all Winds
The living, and forthwith the cited dead
Of all past Ages to the general Doom
Shall hast'n, such a peal shall rouse thir sleep.
330   Then all thy Saints assembl'd, thou shalt judge
Bad men and Angels, they arraign'd shall sink
Beneath thy Sentence; Hell her numbers full,
Thenceforth shall be for ever shut. Mean while
The World shall burn, and from her ashes spring
335   New Heav'n and Earth, wherein the just shall dwell
And after all thir tribulations long
See golden days, fruitful of golden deeds,
With Joy and Love triumphing, and fair Truth.
Then thou thy regal Scepter shalt lay by,
340   For regal Scepter then no more shall need,
God shall be All in All. But all ye Gods,
Adore him, who to compass all this dies,
Adore the Son, and honour him as mee.
       No sooner had th' Almighty ceas't, but all
345   The multitude of Angels with a shout
Loud as from numbers without number, sweet
As from blest voices, uttering joy, Heav'n rung
With Jubilee, and loud Hosanna's filld
Th' eternal Regions: lowly reverent
350   Towards either Throne they bow, and to the ground
With solemn adoration down they cast
Thir Crowns inwove with Amarant and Gold,
Immortal Amarant, a Flowr which once
In Paradise, fast by the Tree of Life
355   Began to bloom, but soon for mans offence
To Heav'n remov'd where first it grew, there grows,
And flowrs aloft shading the Fount of Life,
And where the river of Bliss through midst of Heav'n
Rowls o're *Elisian* Flowrs her Amber stream;
360   With these that never fade the Spirits Elect
Bind thir resplendent locks inwreath'd with beams,
Now in loose Garlands thick thrown off, the bright
Pavement that like a Sea of Jasper shon
Impurpl'd with Celestial Roses smil'd.

365	Then Crown'd again thir gold'n Harps they took,
	Harps ever tun'd, that glittering by thir side
	Like Quivers hung, and with Præamble sweet
	Of charming symphonie they introduce
	This sacred Song, and waken raptures high;
370	No voice exempt, no voice but well could join
	Melodious part, such concord is in Heav'n.
	Thee Father first they sung Omnipotent,
	Immutable, Immortal, Infinite,
	Eternal King; thee Author of all being,
375	Fountain of Light, thy self invisible
	Amidst the glorious brightness where thou sit'st
	Thron'd inaccessible, but when thou shad'st
	The full blaze of thy beams, and through a cloud
	Drawn round about thee like a radiant Shrine,
380	Dark with excessive bright thy skirts appeer,
	Yet dazle Heav'n, that brightest Seraphim
	Approach not, but with both wings veil thir eyes.
	Thee next they sang of all Creation first,
	Begotten Son, Divine Similitude,
385	In whose conspicuous count'nance, without cloud
	Made visible, th' Almighty Father shines,
	Whom else no Creature can behold; on thee
	Impress th' effulgence of his Glorie abides,
	Transfus'd on thee his ample Spirit rests.
390	Hee Heav'n of Heav'ns and all the Powers therein
	By thee created, and by thee threw down
	Th' aspiring Dominations: thou that day
	Thy Fathers dreadful Thunder didst not spare,
	Nor stop thy flaming Chariot wheels, that shook
395	Heav'ns everlasting Frame, while o're the necks
	Thou drov'st of warring Angels disarraid.
	Back from pursuit thy Powers with loud acclaim
	Thee only extoll'd, Son of thy Fathers might,
	To execute fierce vengeance on his foes,
400	Not so on Man; him through their malice fall'n,
	Father of Mercie and Grace, thou didst not doom
	So strictly, but much more to pitie encline:
	No sooner did thy dear and onely Son
	Perceive thee purpos'd not to doom frail Man
405	So strictly, but much more to pitie enclin'd,
	He to appease thy wrauth, and end the strife
	Of Mercy and Justice in thy face discern'd,
	Regardless of the Bliss wherein hee sat

410 Second to thee, offerd himself to die
For mans offence. O unexampl'd love,
Love no where to be found less then Divine!
Hail Son of God, Saviour of Men, thy Name
Shall be the copious matter of my Song
415 Henceforth, and never shall my Harp thy praise
Forget, nor from thy Fathers praise disjoin.

* * * * *

BOOK IV
THE ARGUMENT

Satan now in prospect of *Eden*, and nigh the place where he must now attempt the bold enterprize which he undertook alone against God and Man, falls into many doubts with himself, and many passions, fear, envy, and despare; but at length confirms himself in evil; journeys on to Paradise, whose outward prospect and scituation is described, overleaps the bounds, sits in the shape of a Cormorant on the Tree of life, as highest in the Garden to look about him. The Garden describ'd; *Satans* first sight of *Adam* and *Eve*; his wonder at thir excellent form and happy state, but with resolution to work thir fall; overhears thir discourse, thence gathers that the Tree of knowledge was forbidden them to eat of, under penalty of death; and thereon intends to found his Temptation, by seducing them to transgress: then leaves them a while, to know further of thir state by some other means. Mean while *Uriel* descending on a Sun-beam warns *Gabriel*, who had in charge the Gate of Paradise, that some evil spirit had escap'd the Deep, and past at Noon by his Sphere in the shape of a good Angel down to Paradise, discovered after by his furious gestures in the Mount. *Gabriel* promises to find him ere morning. Night coming on, *Adam* and *Eve* discourse of going to thir rest: thir Bower describ'd; thir Evening worship. *Gabriel* drawing forth his Bands of Night-watch to walk the round of Paradise, appoints two strong Angels to *Adams* Bower, least the evill spirit should be there doing some harm to *Adam* or *Eve* sleeping; there they find him at the ear of *Eve*, tempting her in a dream, and bring him, though unwilling, to *Gabriel*; by whom question'd, he scornfully answers, prepares resistance, but hinder'd by a Sign from Heaven, flies out of Paradise.

 O for that warning voice, which he who saw
Th' *Apocalyps*, heard cry in Heaven aloud,
Then when the Dragon, put to second rout,
Came furious down to be reveng'd on men,
5 *Wo to th' inhabitants on Earth!* that now,
While time was, our first Parents had bin warnd
The coming of thir secret foe, and scap'd
Haply so scap'd his mortal snare; for now

Satan, now first inflam'd with rage, came down,

10   The Tempter ere th' Accuser of man-kind,

To wreck on innocent frail man his loss

Of that first Battel, and his flight to Hell:

Yet not rejoycing in his speed, though bold,

Far off and fearless, nor with cause to boast,

15   Begins his dire attempt, which nigh the birth

Now rowling, boils in his tumultuous brest,

And like a devillish Engine back recoils

Upon himself; horror and doubt distract

His troubl'd thoughts, and from the bottom stirr

20   The Hell within him, for within him Hell

He brings, and round about him, nor from Hell

One step no more then from himself can fly

By change of place: Now conscience wakes despair

That slumberd, wakes the bitter memorie

25   Of what he was, what is, and what must be

Worse; of worse deeds worse sufferings must ensue.

Sometimes towards *Eden* which now in his view

Lay pleasant, his griev'd look he fixes sad,

Sometimes towards Heav'n and the full-blazing Sun,

30   Which now sat high in his Meridian Towr:

Then much revolving, thus in sighs began.

       O thou that with surpassing Glory crownd,

Look'st from thy sole Dominion like the God

Of this new World; at whose sight all the Starrs

35   Hide thir diminisht heads; to thee I call,

But with no friendly voice, and add thy name

O Sun, to tell thee how I hate thy beams

That bring to my remembrance from what state

I fell, how glorious once above thy Sphear;

40   Till Pride and worse Ambition threw me down

Warring in Heav'n against Heav'ns matchless King:

Ah wherefore! he deserv'd no such return

From me, whom he created what I was

In that bright eminence, and with his good

45   Upbraided none; nor was his service hard.

What could be less then to afford him praise,

The easiest recompence, and pay him thanks,

How due! yet all his good prov'd ill in me,

And wrought but malice; lifted up so high

50   I sdeind subjection, and thought one step higher

Would set me highest, and in a moment quit

The debt immense of endless gratitude,

So burthensome still paying, still to ow;
Forgetful what from him I still receiv'd,
And understood not that a grateful mind
By owing owes not, but still pays, at once
Indebted and discharg'd; what burden then?
O had his powerful Destiny ordaind
Me some inferiour Angel, I had stood
Then happie; no unbounded hope had rais'd
Ambition. Yet why not? som other Power
As great might have aspir'd, and me though mean
Drawn to his part; but other Powers as great
Fell not, but stand unshak'n, from within
Or from without, to all temptations arm'd.
Hadst thou the same free Will and Power to stand?
Thou hadst: whom hast thou then or what t' accuse,
But Heav'ns free Love dealt equally to all?
Be then his Love accurst, since love or hate,
To me alike, it deals eternal woe.
Nay curs'd be thou; since against his thy will
Chose freely what it now so justly rues.
Me miserable! which way shall I flie
Infinite wrauth, and infinite despair?
Which way I flie is Hell; my self am Hell;
And in the lowest deep a lower deep
Still threatning to devour me opens wide,
To which the Hell I suffer seems a Heav'n.
O then at last relent: is there no place
Left for Repentance, none for Pardon left?
None left but by submission; and that word
Disdain forbids me, and my dread of shame
Among the Spirits beneath, whom I seduc'd
With other promises and other vaunts
Then to submit, boasting I could subdue
Th' Omnipotent. Ay me, they little know
How dearly I abide that boast so vain,
Under what torments inwardly I groan:
While they adore me on the Throne of Hell,
With Diadem and Scepter high advanc't
The lower still I fall, onely supream
In miserie; such joy Ambition finds.
But say I could repent and could obtain
By Act of Grace my former state; how soon
Would highth recall high thoughts, how soon unsay
What feign'd submission swore: ease would recant

Vows made in pain, as violent and void.
For never can true reconcilement grow
Where wounds of deadly hate have peirc'd so deep:
100   Which would but lead me to a worse relapse,
And heavier fall: so should I purchase dear
Short intermission bought with double smart.
This knows my punisher; therefore as farr
From granting hee, as I from begging peace:
105   All hope excluded thus, behold in stead
Of us out-cast, exil'd his new delight,
Mankind created, and for him this World.
So farwell Hope, and with Hope farwell Fear,
Farwell Remorse: all Good to me is lost;
110   Evil be thou my Good; by thee at least
Divided Empire with Heav'ns King I hold
By thee, and more then half perhaps will reigne;
As Man ere long, and this new World shall know.
       Thus while he spake, each passion dimm'd his face
115   Thrice chang'd with pale, ire, envie and despair,
Which marrd his borrow'd visage, and betraid
Him counterfet, if any eye beheld.
For heav'nly minds from such distempers foul
Are ever cleer. Whereof hee soon aware,
120   Each perturbation smooth'd with outward calm,
Artificer of fraud; and was the first
That practis'd falshood under saintly shew,
Deep malice to conceal, couch't with revenge:
Yet not anough had practis'd to deceive
125   *Uriel* once warnd; whose eye pursu'd him down
The way he went, and on th' *Assyrian* mount
Saw him disfigur'd, more then could befall
Spirit of happie sort: his gestures fierce
He mark'd and mad demeanour, then alone,
130   As he suppos'd, all unobserv'd, unseen.
So on he fares, and to the border comes
Of *Eden*, where delicious Paradise,
Now nearer, Crowns with her enclosure green,
As with a rural mound the champain head
135   Of a steep wilderness, whose hairie sides
With thicket overgrown, grottesque and wild,
Access deni'd; and over head up grew
Insuperable highth of loftiest shade,
Cedar, and Pine, and Firr, and branching Palm,
140   A Silvan Scene, and as the ranks ascend

Shade above shade, a woodie Theatre
Of stateliest view. Yet higher then thir tops
The verdurous wall of Paradise up sprung:
Which to our general Sire gave prospect large
145   Into his neather Empire neighbouring round.
And higher then that Wall a circling row
Of goodliest Trees loaden with fairest Fruit,
Blossoms and Fruit at once of golden hue
Appeerd, with gay enameld colours mixt:
150   On which the Sun more glad impress'd his beams
Then in fair Evening Cloud, or humid Bow,
When God hath showrd the earth; so lovely seemd
That Lantskip: And of pure now purer air
Meets his approach, and to the heart inspires
155   Vernal delight and joy, able to drive
All sadness but despair: now gentle gales
Fanning thir odoriferous wings dispense
Native perfumes, and whisper whence they stole
Those balmie spoils. . . .

* * * * *

160   From this *Assyrian* Garden, where the Fiend
Saw undelighted all delight, all kind
Of living Creatures new to sight and strange:
Two of far nobler shape erect and tall,
Godlike erect, with native Honour clad
165   In naked Majestie seemd Lords of all,
And worthie seemd, for in thir looks Divine
The image of thir glorious Maker shon,
Truth, Wisdom, Sanctitude severe and pure,
Severe, but in true filial freedom plac't;
170   Whence true autoritie in men; though both
Not equal, as thir sex not equal seemd;
For contemplation hee and valour formd,
For softness shee and sweet attractive Grace,
Hee for God only, shee for God in him:
175   His fair large Front and Eye sublime declar'd
Absolute rule; and Hyacinthin Locks
Round from his parted forelock manly hung
Clustring, but not beneath his shoulders broad:
Shee as a vail down to the slender waste
180   Her unadorned golden tresses wore
Dissheveld, but in wanton ringlets wav'd

As the Vine curls her tendrils, which impli'd
Subjection, but requir'd with gentle sway,
And by her yeilded, by him best receiv'd,
185   Yeilded with coy submission, modest pride,
And sweet reluctant amorous delay.
Nor those mysterious parts were then conceald,
Then was not guiltie shame, dishonest shame
Of natures works, honor dishonorable,
190   Sin-bred, how have ye troubl'd all mankind
With shews instead, meer shews of seeming pure,
And banisht from mans life his happiest life,
Simplicitie and spotless innocence.
So pass'd they naked on, nor shund the sight
195   Of God or Angel, for they thought no ill:
So hand in hand they pass'd, the loveliest pair
That ever since in loves imbraces met,
Adam the goodliest man of men since born
His Sons, the fairest of her Daughters *Eve.*
200   Under a tuft of shade that on a green
Stood whispering soft, by a fresh Fountain side
They sat them down, and after no more toil
Of thir sweet Gardning labour then suffic'd
To recommend cool *Zephyr,* and made ease
205   More easie, wholsom thirst and appetite
More grateful, to thir Supper Fruits they fell,
Nectarine Fruits which the compliant boughs
Yeilded them, side-long as they sat recline
On the soft downie Bank damaskt with flowrs:
210   The savourie pulp they chew, and in the rind
Still as they thirsted scoop the brimming stream;
Nor gentle purpose, nor endearing smiles
Wanted, nor youthful dalliance as beseems
Fair couple, linkt in happie nuptial League,
215   Alone as they. About them frisking playd
All Beasts of th' Earth, since wild, and of all chase
In Wood or Wilderness, Forrest or Den;
Sporting the Lion ramp'd, and in his paw
Dandl'd the Kid; Bears, Tygers, Ounces, Pards
220   Gambold before them, th' unwieldy Elephant
To make them mirth us'd all his might, and wreath'd
His Lithe Proboscis; close the Serpent sly
Insinuating, wove with Gordian twine
His breaded train, and of his fatal guile
225   Gave proof unheeded; others on the grass

Coucht, and now fild with pasture gazing sat,
Or Bedward ruminating: for the Sun
Declin'd was hasting now with prone carreer
To th' Ocean Iles, and in th' ascending Scale
230   Of Heav'n the Starrs that usher Evening\rose:
When *Satan* still in gaze, as first he stood,
Scarce thus at length faild speech recoverd sad.
       O Hell! what doe mine eyes with grief behold,
Into our room of bliss thus high advanc't
235   Creatures of other mould, earth-born perhaps,
Not Spirits, yet to heav'nly Spirits bright
Little inferior; whom my thoughts pursue
With wonder, and could love, so lively shines
In them Divine resemblance, and such grace
240   The hand that formd them on thir shape hath pourd.
Ah gentle pair, yee little think how nigh
Your change approaches, when all these delights
Will vanish and deliver ye to woe,
More woe, the more your taste is now of joy;
245   Happie, but for so happie ill secur'd
Long to continue, and this high seat your Heav'n
Ill fenc't for Heav'n to keep out such a foe
As now is enterd; yet no purpos'd foe
To you whom I could pittie thus forlorn
250   Though I unpittied: League with you I seek,
And mutual amitie so streight, so close,
That I with you must dwell, or you with me
Henceforth; my dwelling haply may not please
Like this fair Paradise, your sense, yet such
255   Accept your Makers work; he gave it me,
Which I as freely give; Hell shall unfold,
To entertain you two, her widest Gates,
And send forth all her Kings; there will be room,
Not like these narrow limits, to receive
260   Your numerous ofspring; if no better place,
Thank him who puts me loath to this revenge
On you who wrong me not for him who wrong'd.
And should I at your harmless innocence
Melt, as I doe, yet public reason just,
265   Honour and Empire with revenge enlarg'd,
By conquering this new World, compels me now
To do what else though damnd I should abhorr.

* * * * *

Thus at thir shadie Lodge arriv'd, both stood,
Both turnd, and under op'n Skie ador'd
270 The God that made both Skie, Air, Earth and Heav'n
Which they beheld, the Moons resplendent Globe
And starrie Pole: Thou also mad'st the Night,
Maker Omnipotent, and thou the Day,
Which we in our appointed work imployd
275 Have finisht happie in our mutual help
And mutual love, the Crown of all our bliss
Ordaind by thee, and this delicious place
For us too large, where thy abundance wants
Partakers, and uncropt falls to the ground.
280 But thou hast promis'd from us two a Race
To fill the Earth, who shall with us extoll
Thy goodness infinite, both when we wake,
And when we seek, as now, thy gift of sleep.
This said unanimous, and other Rites
285 Observing none, but adoration pure
Which God likes best, into thir inmost bowr
Handed they went; and eas'd the putting off
These troublesom disguises which wee wear,
Strait side by side were laid, nor turnd I ween
290 *Adam* from his fair Spouse, nor *Eve* the Rites
Mysterious of connubial Love refus'd:
Whatever Hypocrites austerely talk
Of puritie and place and innocence,
Defaming as impure what God declares
295 Pure, and commands to som, leaves free to all.
Our Maker bids increase, who bids abstain
But our Destroyer, foe to God and Man?
Hail wedded Love, mysterious Law, true sourse
Of human ofspring, sole proprietie,
300 In Paradise of all things common else.
By thee adulterous lust was driv'n from men
Among the bestial herds to raunge, by thee
Founded in Reason, Loyal, Just, and Pure,
Relations dear, and all the Charities
305 Of Father, Son, and Brother first were known.
Farr be it, that I should write thee sin or blame,
Or think thee unbefitting holiest place,
Perpetual Fountain of Domestic sweets,
Whose bed is undefil'd and chast pronounc't,
310 Present, or past, as Saints and Patriarchs us'd.

Here Love his golden shafts imploies, here lights
His constant Lamp, and waves his purple wings,
Reigns here and revels; not in the bought smile
Of Harlots, loveless, joyless, unindeard,
315   Casual fruition, nor in Court Amours
Mixt Dance, or wanton Mask, or Midnight Ball,
Or Serenate, which the starv'd Lover sings
To his proud fair, best quitted with disdain.
These lulld by Nightingales imbracing slept,
320   And on thir naked limbs the flowrie roof
Showrd Roses, which the Morn repair'd. Sleep on
Blest pair; and O yet happiest if ye seek
No happier state, and know to know no more.

* * * * *

BOOK V
THE ARGUMENT

    Morning approach't, *Eve* relates to *Adam* her troublesome dream; he likes it not, yet comforts her: They come forth to thir day labours: Thir morning Hymn at the Door of thir Bower. God to render Man inexcusable sends *Raphael* to admonish him of his obedience, of his free estate, of his enemy near at hand; who he is, and why his enemy, and whatever else may avail *Adam* to know. *Raphael* comes down to Paradise, his appearance describ'd, his coming discern'd by *Adam* afar off sitting at the door of his Bower; he goes out to meet him, brings him to his lodge, entertains him with the choycest fruits of Paradise got together by *Eve*; thir discourse at Table: *Raphael* performs his message, minds *Adam* of his state and of his enemy; relates at *Adams* request who that enemy is, and how he came to be so, beginning from his first revolt in Heaven, and the occasion thereof; how he drew his Legions after him to the parts of the North, and there incited them to rebel with him, perswading all but only *Abdiel* a Seraph, who in Argument diswades and opposes him, then forsakes him.

    . . . So to the Silvan Lodge
They came, that like *Pomona*'s Arbour smil'd
With flowrets deck't and fragrant smells; but *Eve*
Undeckt, save with her self more lovely fair
5   Then Wood-Nymph, or the fairest Goddess feign'd
Of three that in Mount *Ida* naked strove,
Stood t' entertain her guest from Heav'n; no vail
Shee needed, Vertue-proof, no thought infirm
Alterd her cheek. On whom the Angel *Hail*
10   Bestowd, the holy salutation us'd

Long after to blest *Marie,* second *Eve.*
     Hail Mother of Mankind, whose fruitful Womb
Shall fill the World more numerous with thy Sons
Then with these various fruits the Trees of God
15   Have heap'd this Table. Rais'd of grassie terf
Thir Table was, and mossie seats had round,
And on her ample Square from side to side
All *Autumn* pil'd, though *Spring* and *Autumn* here
Danc'd hand in hand. A while discourse they hold;
20   No fear lest Dinner cool; when thus began
Our Authour. Heav'nly stranger, please to taste
These bounties which our Nourisher, from whom
All perfet good unmeasur'd out, descends,
To us for food and for delight hath caus'd
25   The Earth to yeild; unsavourie food perhaps
To spiritual Natures; only this I know,
That one Celestial Father gives to all.
     To whom the Angel. Therefore what he gives
(Whose praise be ever sung) to man in part
30   Spiritual, may of purest Spirits be found
No ingrateful food: and food alike those pure
Intelligential substances require
As doth your Rational; and both contain
Within them every lower facultie
35   Of sense, whereby they hear, see, smell, touch, taste,
Tasting concoct, digest, assimilate,
And corporeal to incorporeal turn.
For know, whatever was created, needs
To be sustaind and fed; of Elements
40   The grosser feeds the purer, Earth the Sea,
Earth and the Sea feed Air, the Air those Fires
Ethereal, and as lowest first the Moon;
.Whence in her visage round those spots, unpurg'd
Vapours not yet into her substance turn'd.
45   Nor doth the Moon no nourishment exhale
From her moist Continent to higher Orbs.
The Sun that light imparts to all, receives
From all his alimental recompence
In humid exhalations, and at Ev'n
50   Sups with the Ocean: though in Heav'n the Trees
Of life ambrosial fruitage bear, and vines
Yeild Nectar, though from off the boughs each Morn
We brush mellifluous Dews, and find the ground
Cover'd with pearly grain: yet God hath here

55 Varied his bounty so with new delights,
   As may compare with Heaven; and to taste
   Think not I shall be nice. So down they sat,
   And to thir viands fell, nor seemingly
   The Angel, nor in mist, the common gloss
60 Of Theologians, but with keen dispatch
   Of real hunger, and concoctive heat
   To transubstantiate; what redounds, transpires
   Through Spirits with ease; nor wonder; if by fire
   Of sooty coal th' Empiric Alchimist
65 Can turn, or holds it possible to turn
   Metals of drossiest Ore to perfet Gold
   As from the Mine. Mean while at Table *Eve*
   Ministerd naked, and thir flowing cups
   With pleasant liquors crown'd: O innocence
70 Deserving Paradise! if ever, then,
   Then had the Sons of God excuse t' have bin
   Enamour'd at that sight; but in those hearts
   Love unlibidinous reign'd, nor jealousie
   Was understood, the injur'd Lovers Hell.
75   Thus when with meats and drinks they had suffic'd,
   Not burd'nd Nature, sudden mind arose
   In *Adam*, not to let th' occasion pass
   Giv'n him by this great Conference to know
   Of things above his World, and of thir being
80 Who dwell in Heav'n, whose excellence he saw
   Transcend his own so farr, whose radiant forms
   Divine effulgence, whose high Power so far
   Exceeded human, and his wary speech
   Thus to th' Empyreal Minister he fram'd.
85   Inhabitant with God, now know I well
   Thy favour, in this honour done to man,
   Under whose lowly roof thou hast voutsaf't
   To enter, and these earthly fruits to taste,
   Food not of Angels, yet accepted so,
90 As that more willingly thou couldst not seem
   At Heav'ns high feasts t' have fed: yet what compare?
      To whom the winged Hierarch repli'd.
   O *Adam*, one Almightie is, from whom
   All things proceed, and up to him return,
95 If not deprav'd from good, created all
   Such to perfection, one first matter all,
   Indu'd with various forms, various degrees
   Of substance, and in things that live, of life;

But more refin'd, more spiritous, and pure,
100   As neerer to him plac't or neerer tending
Each in thir several active Sphears assign'd,
Till body up to spirit work, in bounds
Proportiond to each kind. So from the root
Springs lighter the green stalk, from thence the leaves
105   More aerie, last the bright consummate flowr
Spirits odorous breathes: flowrs and thir fruit
Mans nourishment, by gradual scale sublim'd
To vital Spirits aspire, to animal,
To intellectual, give both life and sense,
110   Fansie and understanding, whence the Soul
Reason receives, and reason is her being,
Discursive, or Intuitive; discourse
Is oftest yours, the latter most is ours,
Differing but in degree, of kind the same.
115 ·   Wonder not then, what God for you saw good
If I refuse not, but convert, as you,
To proper substance; time may come when men
With Angels may participate, and find
No inconvenient Diet, nor too light Fare:
120   And from these corporal nutriments perhaps
Your bodies may at last turn all to Spirit,
Improv'd by tract of time, and wing'd ascend
Ethereal, as wee, or may at choice
Here or in Heav'nly Paradises dwell;
125   If ye be found obedient, and retain
Unalterably firm his love entire
Whose progenie you are. Mean while enjoy
Your fill what happiness this happie state
Can comprehend, incapable of more.
130   To whom the Patriarch of mankind repli'd.
O favourable spirit, propitious guest,
Well hast thou taught the way that might direct
Our knowledge, and the scale of Nature set
From center to circumference, whereon
135   In contemplation of created things
By steps we may ascend to God. But say,
What meant that caution joind, *if ye be found*
Obedient? can we want obedience then
To him, or possibly his love desert
140   Who formd us from the dust, and plac'd us here
Full to the utmost measure of what bliss
Human desires can seek or apprehend?

To whom the Angel. Son of Heav'n and Earth,
Attend: That thou art happie, owe to God;
145   That thou continu'st such, owe to thy self,
That is, to thy obedience; therein stand.
This was that caution giv'n thee; be advis'd.
God made thee perfet, not immutable;
And good he made thee, but to persevere
150   He left it in thy power, ordaind thy will
By nature free, not over-rul'd by Fate
Inextricable, or strict necessity;
Our voluntarie service he requires,
Not our necessitated, such with him
155   Finds no acceptance, nor can find, for how
Can hearts, not free, be tri'd whether they serve
Willing or no, who will but what they must
By Destinie, and can no other choose?
My self and all th' Angelic Host that stand
160   In sight of God enthron'd, our happie state
Hold, as you yours, while our obedience holds;
On other surety none; freely we serve,
Because wee freely love, as in our will
To love or not; in this we stand or fall:
165   And som are fall'n, to disobedience fall'n,
And so from Heav'n to deepest Hell; O fall
From what high state of bliss into what woe!
    To whom our great Progenitor. Thy words
Attentive, and with more delighted ear,
170   Divine instructer, I have heard, then when
Cherubic Songs by night from neighbouring Hills
Aereal Music send: nor knew I not
To be both will and deed created free;
Yet that we never shall forget to love
175   Our maker, and obey him whose command
Single, is yet so just, my constant thoughts
Assur'd me, and still assure: though what thou tellst
Hath past in Heav'n, som doubt within me move,
But more desire to hear, if thou consent,
180   The full relation, which must needs be strange,
Worthy of Sacred silence to be heard;
And we have yet large day, for scarce the Sun
Hath finisht half his journey, and scarce begins
His other half in the great Zone of Heav'n.
185   Thus *Adam* made request, and *Raphael*
After short pause assenting, thus began.

High matter thou injoinst me, O prime of men,
Sad task and hard, for how shall I relate
To human sense th' invisible exploits
190   Of warring Spirits; how without remorse
The ruin of so many glorious once
And perfet while they stood; how last unfould
The secrets of another world, perhaps
Not lawful to reveal? yet for thy good
195   This is dispenc't, and what surmounts the reach
Of human sense, I shall delineate so,
By lik'ning spiritual to corporal forms,
As may express them best, though what if Earth
Be but the shaddow of Heav'n and things therein
200   Each t' other like, more then on earth is thought?

BOOK VI
THE ARGUMENT

Raphael continues to relate how *Michael* and *Gabriel* were sent forth to battel against *Satan* and his Angels. The first Fight describ'd: *Satan* and his Powers retire under Night: He calls a Councel, invents devilish Engines, which in the second dayes Fight put *Michael* and his Angels to some disorder; but they at length pulling up Mountains overwhelm'd both the force and Machins of *Satan*: Yet the Tumult not so ending, God on the third day sends *Messiah* his Son, for whom he had reserv'd the glory of that Victory: Hee in the Power of his Father coming to the place, and causing all his Legions to stand still on either side, with his Chariot and Thunder driving into the midst of his Enemies, pursues them unable to resist towards the wall of Heaven; which opening, they leap down with horrour and confusion into the place of punishment prepar'd for them in the Deep: *Messiah* returns with triumph to his Father.

So they among themselves in pleasant vein
Stood scoffing, highth'n'd in thir thoughts beyond
All doubt of Victorie, eternal might
To match with thir inventions they presum'd
5   So easie, and of his Thunder made a scorn,
And all his Host derided, while they stood
A while in trouble; but they stood not long,
Rage prompted them at length, and found them arms
Against such hellish mischief fit t' oppose.
10   Forthwith (behold the excellence, the power
Which God hath in his mighty Angels plac'd)
Thir Arms away they threw, and to the Hills
(For Earth hath this variety from Heav'n

Of pleasure situate in Hill and Dale)
15   Light as the Lightning glimps they ran, they flew,
From thir foundations loosning to and fro
They pluckt the seated Hills with all thir load,
Rocks, Waters, Woods, and by the shaggie tops
Up lifting bore them in thir hands: Amaze,
20   Be sure, and terrour seis'd the rebel Host,
When coming towards them so dread they saw
The bottom of the Mountains upward turn'd,
Till on those cursed Engins triple-row
They saw them whelm'd, and all thir confidence
25   Under the weight of Mountains buried deep,
Themselves invaded next, and on thir heads
Main Promontories flung, which in the Air
Came shadowing, and opprest whole Legions arm'd,
Thir armor help'd thir harm, crush't in and bruis'd
30   Into thir substance pent, which wrought them pain
Implacable, and many a dolorous groan,
Long strugling underneath, ere they could wind
Out of such prison, though Spirits of purest light,
Purest at first, now gross by sinning grown.
35   The rest in imitation to like Armes
Betook them, and the neighbouring Hills uptore;
So Hills amid the Air encounterd Hills
Hurl'd to and fro with jaculation dire,
That under ground they fought in dismal shade;
40   Infernal noise; Warr seem'd a civil Game
To this uproar; horrid confusion heapt
Upon confusion rose: and now all Heav'n
Had gon to wrack, with ruin overspred,
Had not th' Almightie Father where he sits
45   Shrin'd in his Sanctuarie of Heav'n secure,
Consulting on the sum of things, foreseen
This tumult, and permitted all, advis'd:
That his great purpose he might so fulfill,
To honour his Anointed Son aveng'd
50   Upon his enemies, and to declare
All power on him transferr'd: whence to his Son
Th' Assessor of his Throne he thus began.
      Effulgence of my Glorie, Son belov'd,
Son in whose face invisible is beheld
55   Visibly, what by Deitie I am,
And in whose hand what by Decree I doe,
Second Omnipotence, two dayes are past,

Two dayes, as we compute the dayes of Heav'n,
Since *Michael* and his Powers went forth to tame
60 These disobedient; sore hath been thir fight,
As likeliest was, when two such Foes met arm'd;
For to themselves I left them, and thou knowst,
Equal in their Creation they were form'd,
Save what sin hath impaird, which yet hath wrought
65 Insensibly, for I suspend thir doom;
Whence in perpetual fight they needs must last
Endless, and no solution will be found:
Warr wearied hath perform'd what Warr can do,
And to disorderd rage let loose the reins,
70 With Mountains as with Weapons arm'd, which makes
Wild work in Heav'n, and dangerous to the main.
Two dayes are therefore past, the third is thine;
For thee I have ordain'd it, and thus farr
Have sufferd, that the Glorie may be thine
75 Of ending this great Warr, since none but Thou
Can end it. Into thee such Vertue and Grace
Immense I have transfus'd, that all may know
In Heav'n and Hell thy Power above compare,
And this perverse Commotion governd thus,
80 To manifest thee worthiest to be Heir
Of all things, to be Heir and to be King
By Sacred Unction, thy deserved right.
Go then thou Mightiest in thy Fathers might,
Ascend my Chariot, guide the rapid Wheels
85 That shake Heav'ns basis, bring forth all my Warr,
My Bow and Thunder, my Almightie Arms
Gird on, and Sword upon thy puissant Thigh;
Pursue these sons of Darkness, drive them out
From all Heav'ns bounds into the utter Deep:
90 There let them learn, as likes them, to despise
God and *Messiah* his anointed King.
    He said, and on his Son with Rayes direct
Shon full, he all his Father full exprest
Ineffably into his face receiv'd,
95 And thus the filial Godhead answering spake.
    O Father, O Supream of heav'nly Thrones,
First, Highest, Holiest, Best, thou alwayes seekst
To glorifie thy Son, I always thee,
As is most just; this I my Glorie account,
100 My exaltation, and my whole delight,
That thou in me well pleas'd, declarst thy will

Fulfill'd, which to fulfil is all my bliss.
Scepter and Power, thy giving, I assume,
And gladlier shall resign, when in the end

105 Thou shalt be All in All, and I in thee
For ever, and in mee all whom thou lov'st:
But whom thou hat'st, I hate, and can put on
Thy terrors, as I put thy mildness on,
Image of thee in all things; and shall soon,

110 Armd with thy might, rid heav'n of these rebell'd,
To thir prepar'd ill Mansion driven down
To chains of darkness, and th' undying Worm,
That from thy just obedience could revolt,
Whom to obey is happiness entire.

115 Then shall thy Saints unmixt, and from th' impure
Farr separate, circling thy holy Mount
Unfained *Halleluiahs* to thee sing,
Hymns of high praise, and I among them chief.
So said, he o're his Scepter bowing, rose

120 From the right hand of Glorie where he sate,
And the third sacred Morn began to shine
Dawning through Heav'n: forth rush'd with whirlwind sound
The Chariot of Paternal Deitie,
Flashing thick flames, Wheel within Wheel undrawn,

125 It self instinct with Spirit, but convoyd
By four Cherubic shapes, four Faces each
Had wondrous, as with Starrs thir bodies all
And Wings were set with Eyes, with Eyes the wheels
Of Beril, and careering Fires between;

130 Over thir heads a chrystal Firmament,
Whereon a Saphir Throne, inlaid with pure
Amber, and colours of the showrie Arch.
Hee in Celestial Panoplie all armd
Of radiant *Urim*, work divinely wrought,

135 Ascended, at his right hand Victorie
Sate Eagle-wing'd, beside him hung his Bow
And Quiver with three-bolted Thunder stor'd,
And from about him fierce Effusion rowld
Of smoak and bickering flame, and sparkles dire;

140 Attended with ten thousand thousand Saints,
He onward came, farr off his coming shon,
And twentie thousand (I thir number heard)
Chariots of God, half on each hand were seen:
Hee on the wings of Cherub rode sublime

145 On the Chrystallin Skie, in Saphir Thron'd.

Illustrious farr and wide, but by his own
First seen, them unexpected joy surpriz'd,
When the great Ensign of *Messiah* blaz'd
Aloft by Angels born, his Sign in Heav'n:
150   Under whose conduct *Michael* soon reduc'd
His Armie, circumfus'd on either Wing,
Under thir Head imbodied all in one.
Before him Power Divine his way prepar'd;
At his command th' uprooted Hills retir'd
155   Each to his place, they heard his voice and went
Obsequious, Heav'n his wonted face renewd,
And with fresh Flowrets Hill and Valley smil'd.
This saw his hapless Foes but stood obdur'd,
And to rebellious fight rallied thir Powers
160   Insensate, hope conceiving from despair.
In heav'nly Spirits could such perverseness dwell?
But to convince the proud what Signs avail,
Or Wonders move th' obdurate to relent?
They hard'n'd more by what might most reclame,
165   Grieving to see his Glorie, at the sight
Took envie, and aspiring to his highth,
Stood reimbattell'd fierce, by force or fraud
Weening to prosper, and at length prevail
Against God and *Messiah*, or to fall
170   In universal ruin last, and now
To final Battel drew, disdaining flight,
Or faint retreat; when the great Son of God
To all his Host on either hand thus spake.
       Stand still in bright array ye Saints, here stand
175   Ye Angels arm'd, this day from Battel rest;
Faithful hath been your warfare, and of God
Accepted, fearless in his righteous Cause,
And as ye have receiv'd, so have ye don
Invincibly; but of this cursed crew
180   The punishment to other hand belongs,
Vengeance is his, or whose he sole appoints;
Number to this dayes work is not ordain'd
Nor multitude, stand onely and behold
Gods indignation on these Godless pourd
185   By mee; not you but mee they have despis'd,
Yet envied; against mee is all thir rage,
Because the Father, t' whom in Heav'n supream,
Kingdom and Power and Glorie appertains,
Hath honourd me according to his will.

190   Therefore to mee thir doom he hath assign'd;
              That they may have thir wish, to trie with mee
              In Battel which the stronger proves, they all,
              Or I alone against them, since by strength
              They measure all, of other excellence
195   Not emulous, nor care who them excells;
              Nor other strife with them do I voutsafe.
                    So spake the Son, and into terrour chang'd
              His count'nance too severe to be beheld
              And full of wrauth bent on his Enemies.
200   At once the Four spred out thir Starrie wings
              With dreadful shade contiguous, and the Orbs
              Of his fierce Chariot rowl'd, as with the sound
              Of torrent Floods, or of a numerous Host.
              Hee on his impious Foes right onward drove,
205   Gloomie as Night; under his burning Wheels
              The stedfast Empyrean shook throughout,
              All but the Throne it self of God. Full soon
              Among them he arriv'd; in his right hand
              Grasping ten thousand Thunders, which he sent
210   Before him, such as in thir Souls infix'd
              Plagues; they astonisht all resistance lost,
              All courage; down thir idle weapons drop'd;
              O're Shields and Helmes, and helmed heads he rode
              Of Thrones and mighty Seraphim prostrate,
215   That wisht the Mountains now might be again
              Thrown on them as a shelter from his ire.
              Nor less on either side tempestuous fell
              His arrows, from the fourfold-visag'd Four,
              Distinct with eyes, and from the living Wheels,
220   Distinct alike with multitude of eyes,
              One Spirit in them rul'd, and every eye
              Glar'd lightning, and shot forth pernicious fire
              Among th' accurst, that witherd all thir strength,
              And of thir wonted vigour left them draind,
225   Exhausted, spiritless, afflicted, fall'n.
              Yet half his strength he put not forth, but check'd
              His Thunder in mid Volie, for he meant
              Not to destroy, but root them out of Heav'n:
              The overthrown he rais'd, and as a Heard
230   Of Goats or timerous flock together throng'd
              Drove them before him Thunder-struck, pursu'd
              With terrors and with furies to the bounds
              And Chrystal wall of Heav'n, which op'ning wide,

Rowl'd inward, and a spacious Gap disclos'd
235 Into the wastful Deep; the monstrous sight
Strook them with horror backward, but far worse
Urg'd them behind; headlong themselvs they threw
Down from the verge of Heav'n, Eternal wrauth
Burnt after them to the bottomless pit.
240   Hell heard th' unsufferable noise, Hell saw
Heav'n ruining from Heav'n and would have fled
Affrighted; but strict Fate had cast too deep
Her dark foundations, and too fast had bound.
Nine dayes they fell; confounded *Chaos* roard,
245 And felt tenfold confusion in thir fall
Through his wild Anarchie, so huge a rout
Incumberd him with ruin; Hell at last
Yawning receav'd them whole, and on them clos'd,
Hell thir fit habitation fraught with fire
250 Unquenchable, the house of woe and pain.
Disburd'n'd Heav'n rejoic'd, and soon repaird
Her mural breach, returning whence it rowl'd.
Sole Victor from th' expulsion of his Foes
Messiah his triumphal Chariot turn'd:
255 To meet him all his Saints, who silent stood
Eye witnesses of his Almightie Acts,
With Jubilie advanc'd; and as they went,
Shaded with branching Palm, each order bright,
Sung Triumph, and him sung Victorious King,
260 Son, Heir, and Lord, to him Dominion giv'n,
Worthiest to Reign: he celebrated rode
Triumphant through mid Heav'n, into the Courts
And Temple of his mightie Father Thron'd
On high: who into Glorie him receav'd,
265 Where now he sits at the right hand of bliss.
      Thus measuring things in Heav'n by things on Earth
At thy request, and that thou maist beware
By what is past, to thee I have reveal'd
What might have else to human Race bin hid;
270 The discord which befell, and Warr in Heav'n
Among th' Angelic Powers, and the deep fall
Of those too high aspiring, who rebell'd
With *Satan,* hee who envies now thy state,
Who now is plotting how he may seduce
275 Thee also from obedience, that with him
Bereav'd of happiness thou maist partake
His punishment, Eternal miserie;

Which would be all his solace and revenge,
As a despite don against the most High,
280   Thee once to gain Companion of his woe.
But list'n not to his Temptations, warn
Thy weaker; let it profit thee t'have heard
By terrible Example the reward
Of disobedience; firm they might have stood,
285   Yet fell; remember, and fear to transgress.

BOOK VII
THE ARGUMENT

Raphael at the request of *Adam* relates how and wherefore this world was first created; that God, after the expelling of *Satan* and his Angels out of Heaven, declar'd his pleasure to create another World and other Creatures to dwell therein; sends his Son with Glory and attendance of Angels to perform the work of Creation in six dayes: the Angels celebrate with Hymns the performance thereof, and his reascention into Heaven.

* * * * *

BOOK VIII
THE ARGUMENT

Adam inquires concerning celestial Motions, is doubtfully answer'd, and exhorted to search rather things more worthy of knowledge: *Adam* assents, and still desirous to detain *Raphael*, relates to him what he remember'd since his own Creation, his placing in Paradise, his talk with God concerning solitude and fit society, his first meeting and Nuptials with *Eve*, his discourse with the Angel thereupon; who after admonitions repeated departs.

* * * * *

BOOK IX
THE ARGUMENT

Satan having compast the Earth, with meditated guile returns as a mist by Night into Paradise, enters into the Serpent sleeping. *Adam* and *Eve* in the Morning go forth to thir labours, which *Eve* proposes to divide in several places, each labouring apart: *Adam* consents not, alledging the danger, lest that Enemy, of whom they were forewarn'd, should attempt her found alone: *Eve* loath to be thought not circumspect or firm enough, urges her going apart, the rather desirous to make tryal of her strength; *Adam* at last yields: The Serpent finds her alone; his subtle approach, first gazing, then speaking, with much flattery extolling *Eve* above all other Creatures. *Eve* wondring to hear the Serpent speak, asks how he attain'd to human speech and such understanding not till now; the Serpent answers, that by tasting of a certain Tree in the Garden he attain'd both to Speech and Reason, till then void of both: *Eve* requires him to bring her to that Tree, and finds it to be the Tree of Knowledge forbidden: The Serpent now grown bolder, with many wiles and arguments induces her at length to eat; she pleas'd with the taste deliberates awhile whether to impart thereof to *Adam* or not, at last brings him of the Fruit, relates what perswaded her to eat thereof: *Adam* at first amaz'd, but perceiving her lost, resolves through vehemence of love to perish with her; and extenuating the trespass eats also of the Fruit: The Effects thereof in them both; they seek to cover thir nakedness; then fall to variance and accusation of one another.

     No more of talk where God or Angel Guest
With Man, as with his Friend, familiar us'd
To sit indulgent, and with him partake
Rural repast, permitting him the while
5   Venial discourse unblam'd: I now must change
Those Notes to Tragic; foul distrust, and breach
Disloyal on the part of Man, revolt,
And disobedience: On the part of Heav'n
Now alienated, distance and distaste,
10   Anger and just rebuke, and judgement giv'n,
That brought into this World a world of woe,
Sin and her shadow Death, and Miserie
Deaths Harbinger: Sad task, yet argument
Not less but more Heroic then the wrauth
15   Of stern *Achilles* on his Foe pursu'd
Thrice Fugitive about *Troy* Wall; or rage
Of *Turnus* for *Lavinia* disespous'd,
Or *Neptun*'s ire or *Juno*'s, that so long
Perplex'd the *Greek* and *Cytherea*'s Son;
20   If answerable style I can obtain
Of my Celestial Patroness, who deignes
Her nightly visitation unimplor'd,
And dictates to me slumbring, or inspires
Easie my unpremeditated Verse:
25   Since first this Subject for Heroic Song
Pleas'd me long choosing, and beginning late;
Not sedulous by Nature to indite
Warrs, hitherto the onely Argument
Heroic deem'd, chief maistrie to dissect
30   With long and tedious havoc fabl'd Knights
In Battels feign'd; the better fortitude

Of Patience and Heroic Martyrdom
Unsung; or to describe Races and Games,
Or tilting Furniture, emblazon'd Shields,
35   Impreses quaint, Caparisons and Steeds;
Bases and tinsel Trappings, gorgious Knights
At Joust and Torneament; then marshal'd Feast
Serv'd up in Hall with Sewers, and Seneshals;
The skill of Artifice or Office mean,
40   Not that which justly gives Heroic name
To Person or to Poem. Mee of these
Nor skill'd nor studious, higher Argument
Remains, sufficient of it self to raise
That name, unless an age too late, or cold
45   Climat, or Years damp my intended wing
Deprest, and much they may, if all be mine,
Not Hers who brings it nightly to my Ear.
        The Sun was sunk, and after him the Starr
Of *Hesperus*, whose Office is to bring
50   Twilight upon the Earth, short Arbiter
Twixt Day and Night, and now from end to end
Nights Hemisphere had veild th' Horizon round:
When *Satan* who late fled before the threats
Of *Gabriel* out of *Eden*, now improv'd
55   In meditated fraud and malice, bent
On mans destruction, maugre what might hap
Of heavier on himself, fearless return'd.
By Night he fled, and at Midnight return'd
From compassing the Earth, cautious of day,
60   Since *Uriel* Regent of the Sun descri'd
His entrance, and forewarnd the Cherubim
That kept thir watch; thence full of anguish driv'n,
The space of seven continu'd Nights he rode
With darkness, thrice the Equinoctial Line
65   He circl'd, four times cross'd the Carr of Night
From Pole to Pole, traversing each Colure;
On th' eighth return'd, and on the Coast averse
From entrance or Cherubic Watch, by stealth
Found unsuspected way. There was a place,
70   Now not, though Sin, not Time, first wraught the change,
Where *Tigris* at the foot of Paradise
Into a Gulf shot under ground, till part
Rose up a Fountain by the Tree of Life;
In with the River sunk, and with it rose
75   Satan involv'd in rising Mist, then sought

Where to lie hid; Sea he had searcht and Land
From *Eden* over *Pontus*, and the Pool
Mæotis, up beyond the River *Ob;*
Downward as farr Antartic; and in length
80   West from *Orontes* to the Ocean barr'd
At *Darien*, thence to the Land where flows
Ganges and *Indus:* thus the Orb he roamd
With narrow search; and with inspection deep
Consider'd every Creature, which of all
85   Most opportune might serve his Wiles, and found
The Serpent suttlest Beast of all the Field.
Him after long debate, irresolute
Of thoughts revolv'd, his final sentence chose
Fit Vessel, fittest Imp of fraud, in whom
90   To enter, and his dark suggestions hide
From sharpest sight: for in the wilie Snake,
Whatever sleights none would suspicious mark,
As from his wit and native suttletie
Proceeding, which in other Beasts observ'd
95   Doubt might beget of Diabolic pow'r
Active within beyond the sense of brute.
Thus be resolv'd, but first from inward grief
His bursting passion into plaints thus pour'd:
     O Earth, how like to Heav'n, if not preferr'd
100   More justly, Seat worthier of Gods, as built
With second thoughts, reforming what was old!
For what God after better worse would build?
Terrestrial Heav'n, danc't round by other Heav'ns
That shine, yet bear thir bright officious Lamps,
105   Light above Light, for thee alone, as seems,
In thee concentring all thir precious beams
Of sacred influence: As God in Heav'n
Is Center, yet extends to all, so thou
Centring receav'st from all those Orbs; in thee,
110   Not in themselves, all thir known vertue appeers
Productive in Herb, Plant, and nobler birth
Of Creatures animate with gradual life
Of Growth, Sense, Reason, all summ'd up in Man.
With what delight could I have walkt thee round,
115   If I could joy in aught, sweet interchange
Of Hill and Vallie, Rivers, Woods and Plains,
Now Land, now Sea, and Shores with Forrest crownd,
Rocks, Dens, and Caves; but I in none of these
Find place or refuge; and the more I see

120   Pleasures about me, so much more I feel
              Torment within me, as from the hateful siege
              Of contraries; all good to me becomes
              Bane, and in Heav'n much worse would be my state.
              But neither here seek I, no nor in Heav'n
125   To dwell, unless by maistring Heav'ns Supream;
              Nor hope to be my self less miserable
              By what I seek, but others to make such
              As I, though thereby worse to me redound:
              For onely in destroying I find ease
130   To my relentless thoughts; and him destroyd,
              Or won to what may work his utter loss,
              For whom all this was made, all this will soon
              Follow, as to him linkt in weal or woe,
              In wo then; that destruction wide may range:
135   To mee shall be the glorie sole among
              Th' infernal Powers, in one day to have marr'd
              What he *Almightie* styl'd, six Nights and Days
              Continu'd making, and who knows how long
              Before had bin contriving, though perhaps
140   Not longer then since I in one Night freed
              From servitude inglorious welnigh half
              Th' Angelic Name, and thinner left the throng
              Of his adorers: hee to be aveng'd,
              And to repair his numbers thus impair'd,
145   Whether such vertue spent of old now faild
              More Angels to Create, if they at least
              Are his Created, or to spite us more,
              Determin'd to advance into our room
              A Creature form'd of Earth, and him endow,
150   Exalted from so base original,
              With Heav'nly spoils, our spoils: What he decreed
              He effected; Man he made, and for him built
              Magnificent this World, and Earth his seat,
              Him Lord pronoune'd, and, O indignitie!
155   Subjected to his service Angel wings,
              And flaming Ministers to watch and tend
              Thir earthy Charge: Of these the vigilance
              I dread, and to elude, thus wrapt in mist
              Of midnight vapor glide obscure, and prie
160   In every Bush and Brake, where hap may find
              The Serpent sleeping, in whose mazie foulds
              To hide me, and the dark intent I bring.
              O foul descent that I who erst contended

With Gods to sit the highest, am now constraind
165 Into a Beast, and mixt with bestial slime,
This essence to incarnate and imbrute,
That to the hight of Deitie aspir'd;
But what will not Ambition and Revenge
Descend to? who aspires must down as low
170 As high he soard, obnoxious first or last
To basest things. Revenge, at first though sweet,
Bitter ere long back on it self recoils;
Let it; I reck not, so it light well aim'd,
Since higher I fall short, on him who next
175 Provokes my envie, this new Favorite
Of Heav'n, this Man of Clay, Son of despite,
Whom us the more to spite his Maker rais'd
From dust: spite then with spite is best repaid.
So saying, through each Thicket Danck or Drie,
180 Like a black mist low creeping, he held on
His midnight search, where soonest he might find
The Serpent: him fast sleeping soon he found
In Labyrinth of many a round self-rowl'd,
His head the midst, well stor'd with suttle wiles:
185 Not yet in horrid Shade or dismal Den,
Nor nocent yet, but on the grassie Herb
Fearless unfeard he slept: in at his Mouth
The Devil enterd, and his brutal sense,
In heart or head, possessing soon inspir'd
190 With act intelligential; but his sleep
Disturb'd not, waiting close th' approach of Morn.
Now when as sacred Light began to dawn
In *Eden* on the humid Flowrs, that breath'd
Thir morning incense, when all things that breath,
195 From th' Earths great Altar send up silent praise
To the Creator, and his Nostrils fill
With grateful Smell, forth came the human pair
And joynd thir vocal Worship to the Quire
Of Creatures wanting voice, that done, partake
200 The season, prime for sweetest Scents and Aires:
Then commune how that day they best may ply
Thir growing work: for much thir work outgrew
The hands dispatch of two Gardning so wide.
And *Eve* first to her Husband thus began.
205 *Adam*, well may we labour still to dress
This Garden, still to tend Plant, Herb and Flowr,
Our pleasant task enjoyn'd, but till more hands

Aid us, the work under our labour grows,
Luxurious by restraint; what we by day
210   Lop overgrown, or prune, or prop, or bind,
One night or two with wanton growth derides
Tending to wild. Thou therefore now advise
Or hear what to my mind first thoughts present,
Let us divide our labours, thou where choice
215   Leads thee, or where most needs, whether to wind
The Woodbine round this Arbour, or direct
The clasping Ivie where to climb, while I
In yonder Spring of Roses intermixt
With Myrtle, find what to redress till Noon:
220   For while so near each other thus all day
Our task we choose, what wonder if so near
Looks intervene and smiles, or object new
Casual discourse draw on, which intermits
Our dayes work brought to little, though begun
225   Early, and th' hour of Supper comes unearn'd.
        To whom mild answer *Adam* thus return'd.
Sole *Eve*, Associate sole, to me beyond
Compare above all living Creatures dear,
Well hast thou motion'd, well thy thoughts imployd
230   How we might best fulfill the work which here
God hath assign'd us, nor of me shalt pass
Unprais'd: for nothing lovelier can be found
In Woman, then to studie houshold good,
And good works in her Husband to promote.
235   Yet not so strictly hath our Lord impos'd
Labour, as to debarr us when we need
Refreshment, whether food, or talk between,
Food of the mind, or this sweet intercourse
Of looks and smiles, for smiles from Reason flow,
240   To brute deni'd, and are of Love the food,
Love not the lowest end of human life.
For not to irksom toil, but to delight
He made us, and delight to Reason joyn'd.
These paths and Bowers doubt not but our joynt hands
245   Will keep from Wilderness with ease, as wide
As we need walk, till younger hands ere long
Assist us: But if much converse perhaps
Thee satiate, to short absence I could yeild.
For solitude somtimes is best societie,
250   And short retirement urges sweet return.
But other doubt possesses me, least harm

Befall thee sever'd from me; for thou knowst
What hath bin warn'd us, what malicious Foe
Envying our happiness, and of his own
255   Despairing, seeks to work us woe and shame
By sly assault; and somwhere nigh at hand
Watches, no doubt, with greedy hope to find
His wish and best advantage, us asunder,
Hopeless to circumvent us joynd, where each
260   To other speedie aid might lend at need;
Whether his first design be to withdraw
Our fealtie from God, or to disturb
Conjugal Love, then which perhaps no bliss
Enjoy'd by us excites his envie more;
265   Or this, or worse, leave not the faithful side
That gave thee being, still shades thee and protects.
The Wife, where danger or dishonour lurks,
Safest and seemliest by her Husband staies,
Who guards her, or with her the worst endures.
270   To whom the Virgin Majestie of *Eve,*
As one who loves, and some unkindness meets,
With sweet austeer composure thus reply'd.
        Ofspring of Heav'n and Earth, and all Earths Lord,
That such an Enemie we have, who seeks
275   Our ruin, both by thee informd I learn,
And from the parting Angel over-heard
As in a shadie nook I stood behind,
Just then return'd at shut of Evening Flowrs.
But that thou shouldst my firmness therfore doubt
280   To God or thee, because we have a foe
May tempt it, I expected not to bear.
His violence thou fearst not, being such,
As wee, not capable of death or pain,
Can either not receave, or can repell.
285   His fraud is then thy fear, which plain inferrs
Thy equal fear that my firm Faith and Love
Can by his fraud be shak'n or seduc't;
Thoughts, which how found they harbour in thy brest,
Adam, misthought of her to thee so dear?
290   To whom with healing words *Adam* reply'd.
Daughter of God and Man, immortal *Eve,*
For such thou art, from sin and blame entire:
Not diffident of thee do I dissuade
Thy absence from my sight, but to avoid
295   Th' attempt it self, intended by our Foe.

For hee who tempts, though in vain, at least asperses
The tempted with dishonour foul, suppos'd
Not incorruptible of Faith, not prooff
Against temptation: thou thy self with scorn
300 And anger wouldst resent the offer'd wrong,
Though ineffectual found: misdeem not then,
If such affront I labour to avert
From thee alone, which on us both at once
The Enemie, though bold, will hardly dare,
305 Or daring, first on mee th' assault shall light.
Nor thou his malice and false guile contemn;
Suttle he needs must be, who could seduce
Angels, nor think superfluous others aid.
I from the influence of thy looks receave
310 Access in every Vertue, in thy sight
More wise, more watchful, stronger, if need were
Of outward strength; while shame, thou looking on,
Shame to be overcome or over-reacht
Would utmost vigor raise, and rais'd unite.
315 Why shouldst not thou like sense within thee feel
When I am present, and thy trial choose
With me, best witness of thy Vertue tri'd.
　　　　So spake domestick *Adam* in his care
And Matrimonial Love; but *Eve*, who thought
320 Less attributed to her Faith sincere,
Thus her reply with accent sweet renewd.
　　　　If this be our condition, thus to dwell
In narrow circuit strait'n'd by a Foe,
Suttle or violent, we not endu'd
325 Single with like defence, wherever met,
How are we happie, still in fear of harm?
But harm precedes not sin: onely our Foe
Tempting affronts us with his foul esteem
Of our integritie: his foul esteem
330 Sticks no dishonor on our Front, but turns
Foul on himself; then wherfore shund or feard
By us? who rather double honour gain
From his surmise prov'd false, find peace within,
Favour from Heav'n, our witness from th' event.
335 And what is Faith, Love, Vertue unassaid
Alone, without exterior help sustaind?
Let us not then suspect our happie State
Left so imperfet by the Maker wise,
As not secure to single or combin'd.

340   Frail is our happiness, if this be so,
     And *Eden* were no *Eden* thus expos'd.
         To whom thus *Adam* fervently repli'd.
     O Woman, best are all things as the will
     Of God ordain'd them, his creating hand
345   Nothing imperfet or deficient left
     Of all that he Created, much less Man,
     Or aught that might his happie State secure,
     Secure from outward force; within himself
     The danger lies, yet lies within his power:
350   Against his will he can receave no harm.
     But God left free the Will, for what obeys
     Reason, is free, and Reason be made right,
     But bid her well beware, and still erect,
     Least by some fair appeering good surpris'd
355   She dictate false, and misinform the Will
     To do what God expresly hath forbid.
     Not then mistrust, but tender love enjoyns,
     That I should mind thee oft, and mind thou me.
     Firm we subsist, yet possible to swerve,
360   Since Reason not impossibly may meet
     Some specious object by the Foe subornd,
     And fall into deception unaware,
     Not keeping strictest watch, as she was warnd.
     Seek not temptation then, which to avoid
365   Were better, and most likelie if from mee
     Thou sever not: Trial will come unsought.
     Wouldst thou approve thy constancie, approve
     First thy obedience; th' other who can know,
     Not seeing thee attempted, who attest?
370   But if thou think, trial unsought may find
     Us both securer then thus warnd thou seemst,
     Go; for thy stay, not free, absents thee more;
     Go in thy native innocence, relie
     On what thou hast of vertue, summon all,
375   For God towards thee hath done his part, do thine.
         So spake the Patriarch of Mankind, but *Eve*
     Persisted, yet submiss, though last, repli'd.
         With thy permission then, and thus forewarnd
     Chiefly by what thy own last reasoning words
380   Touch'd onely, that our trial, when least sought,
     May find us both perhaps farr less prepar'd,
     The willinger I goe, not much expect
     A Foe so proud will first the weaker seek,

So bent, the more shall shame him his repulse.
385   Thus saying, from her Husbands hand her hand
Soft she withdrew, and like a Wood-Nymph light
Oread or *Dryad,* or of *Delia*'s Train,
Betook her to the Groves, but *Delia*'s self
In gate surpass'd and Goddess-like deport,
390   Though not as shee with Bow and Quiver armd,
But with such Gardning Tools as Art yet rude,
Guiltless of fire had formd, or Angels brought.
To *Pales,* or *Pomona* thus adornd,
Likest she seemd, *Pomona* when she fled
395   *Vertumnus,* or to *Ceres* in her Prime,
Yet Virgin of *Proserpina* from *Jove.*
Her long with ardent look his Eye pursu'd
Delighted, but desiring more her stay.
Oft he to her his charge of quick return
400   Repeated, shee to him as oft engag'd
To be returnd by Noon amid the Bowr,
And all things in best order to invite
Noontide repast, or Afternoons repose.
O much deceav'd, much failing, hapless *Eve,*
405   Of thy presum'd return! event perverse!
Thou never from that hour in Paradise
Foundst either sweet repast, or sound repose;
Such ambush hid among sweet Flowrs and Shades
Waited with hellish rancour imminent
410   To intercept thy way, or send thee back
Despoild of Innocence, of Faith, of Bliss.
For now, and since first break of dawn the Fiend,
Meer Serpent in appearance, forth was come,
And on his Quest, where likeliest he might find
415   The onely two of Mankind, but in them
The whole included Race, his purpos'd prey.
In Bowr and Field he sought, where any tuft
Of Grove or Garden-Plot more pleasant lay,
Thir tendance or Plantation for delight,
420   By Fountain or by shadie Rivulet
He sought them both, but wish'd his hap might find
Eve separate, he wish'd, but not with hope
Of what so seldom chanc'd, when to his wish,
Beyond his hope, *Eve* separate he spies,
425   Veild in a Cloud of Fragrance, where she stood,
Half spi'd, so thick the Roses bushing round
About her glowd, oft stooping to support

Each Flowr of slender stalk, whose head though gay
Carnation, Purple, Azure, or spect with Gold,
430   Hung drooping unsustaind, them she upstaies
Gently with Mirtle band, mindless the while,
Her self, though fairest unsupported Flowr,
From her best prop so farr, and storm so nigh.
Neerer he drew, and many a walk travers'd
435   Of stateliest Covert, Cedar, Pine, or Palm,
Then voluble and bold, now hid, now seen
Among thick-wov'n Arborets and Flowrs
Imborderd on each Bank, the hand of *Eve:*
Spot more delicious then those Gardens feign'd
440   Or of reviv'd *Adonis,* or renownd
Alcinous, host of old *Lærtes* Son,
Or that, not Mystic, where the Sapient King
Held dalliance with his fair *Egyptian* Spouse.
Much hee the Place admir'd, the Person more.
445   As one who long in populous City pent,
Where Houses thick and Sewers annoy the Air,
Forth issuing on a Summers Morn to breathe
Among the pleasant Villages and Farmes
Adjoynd, from each thing met conceaves delight,
450   The smell of Grain, or tedded Grass, or Kine,
Or Dairie, each rural sight, each rural sound;
If chance with Nymphlike step fair Virgin pass,
What pleasing seemd, for her now pleases more,
She most, and in her look summs all Delight.
455   Such Pleasure took the Serpent to behold
This Flowrie Plat, the sweet recess of *Eve*
Thus earlie, thus alone; her Heav'nly form
Angelic, but more soft, and Feminine,
Her graceful Innocence, her every Air
460   Of gesture or lest action overawd
His Malice, and with rapine sweet bereav'd
His fierceness of the fierce intent it brought:
That space the Evil one abstracted stood
From his own evil, and for the time remaind
465   Stupidly good, of enmitie disarm'd,
Of guile, of hate, of envie, of revenge;
But the hot Hell that alwayes in him burns,
Though in mid Heav'n, soon ended his delight,
And tortures him now more, the more he sees
470   Of pleasure not for him ordain'd: then soon
Fierce hate he recollects, and all his thoughts

Of mischief, gratulating, thus excites.
　　Thoughts, whither have ye led me, with what sweet
Compulsion thus transported to forget
475　What hither brought us, hate, not love, nor hope
Of Paradise for Hell, hope here to taste
Of pleasure, but all pleasure to destroy,
Save what is in destroying, other joy
To me is lost. Then let me not let pass
480　Occasion which now smiles, behold alone
The Woman, opportune to all attempts,
Her Husband, for I view far round, not nigh,
Whose higher intellectual more I shun,
And strength, of courage hautie, and of limb
485　Heroic built, though of terrestrial mould,
Foe not informidable, exempt from wound,
I not; so much hath Hell debas'd, and pain
Infeebl'd me, to what I was in Heav'n.
Shee fair, divinely fair, fit Love for Gods,
490　Not terrible, though terrour be in Love
And beautie, not approacht by stronger hate,
Hate stronger, under shew of Love well feign'd,
The way which to her ruin now I tend.
　　So spake the Enemie of Mankind, enclos'd
495　In Serpent, Inmate bad, and toward *Eve*
Address'd his way, not with indented wave,
Prone on the ground, as since, but on his rear,
Circular base of rising foulds, that tour'd
Fould above fould a surging Maze, his Head
500　Crested aloft, and Carbuncle his Eyes;
With burnisht Neck of verdant Gold, erect
Amidst his circling Spires, that on the grass
Floted redundant: pleasing was his shape,
And lovely, never since of Serpent kind
505　Lovelier, not those that in *Illyria* chang'd
Hermione and *Cadmus,* or the God
In *Epidaurus;* nor to which transformd
Ammonian Jove, or *Capitoline* was seen,
Hee with *Olympias,* this with her who bore
510　*Scipio* the highth of *Rome.* With tract oblique
At first, as one who sought access, but feard
To interrupt, side-long he works his way.
As when a Ship by skilful Stearsman wrought
Nigh Rivers mouth or Foreland, where the Wind
515　Veres oft, as oft so steers, and shifts her Sail;

So varied hee, and of his tortuous Train
Curld many a wanton wreath in sight of *Eve*,
To lure her Eye; shee busied heard the sound
Of rusling Leaves, but minded not, as us'd
520   To such disport before her through the Field,
From every Beast, more duteous at her call,
Then at *Circean* call the Herd disguis'd.
Hee boulder now, uncall'd before her stood;
But as in gaze admiring: Oft he bowd
525   His turret Crest, and sleek enamel'd Neck,
Fawning, and lick'd the ground whereon she trod.
His gentle dumb expression turn'd at length
The Eye of *Eve* to mark his play; he glad
Of her attention gaind, with Serpent Tongue
530   Organic, or impulse of vocal Air,
His fraudulent temptation thus began.
        Wonder not, sovran Mistress, if perhaps
Thou canst, who art sole Wonder, much less arm
Thy looks, the Heav'n of mildness, with disdain,
535   Displeas'd that I approach thee thus, and gaze
Insatiate, I thus single, nor have feard
Thy awful brow, more awful thus retir'd.
Fairest resemblance of thy Maker fair,
Thee all things living gaze on, all things thine
540   By gift, and thy Celestial Beautie adore
With ravishment beheld, there best beheld
Where universally admir'd; but here
In this enclosure wild, these Beasts among,
Beholders rude, and shallow to discern
545   Half what in thee is fair, one man except,
Who sees thee? (and what is one?) who shouldst be seen
A Goddess among Gods, ador'd and serv'd
By Angels numberless, thy daily Train.
        So gloz'd the Tempter, and his Proem tun'd;
550   Into the Heart of *Eve* his words made way,
Though at the voice much marveling; at length
Not unamaz'd she thus in answer spake.
What may this mean? Language of Man pronounc't
By Tongue of Brute, and human sense exprest?
555   The first at lest of these I thought deni'd
To Beasts, whom God on thir Creation-Day
Created mute to all articulat sound;
The latter I demurr, for in thir looks
Much reason, and in thir actions oft appeers.

560	Thee, Serpent, suttlest beast of all the field
	I knew, but not with human voice endu'd;
	Redouble then this miracle, and say,
	How cam'st thou speakable of mute, and how
	To me so friendly grown above the rest
565	Of brutal kind, that daily are in sight?
	Say, for such wonder claims attention due.
	To whom the guileful Tempter thus reply'd.
	Empress of this fair World, resplendent *Eve,*
	Easie to mee it is to tell thee all
570	What thou commandst, and right thou shouldst be obeyd:
	I was at first as other Beasts that graze
	The trodden Herb, of abject thoughts and low,
	As was my food, nor aught but food discern'd
	Or Sex, and apprehended nothing high:
575	Till on a day roaving the field, I chanc'd
	A goodly Tree farr distant to behold
	Loaden with fruit of fairest colours mixt,
	Ruddie and Gold: I nearer drew to gaze;
	When from the boughs a savorie odour blown,
580	Grateful to appetite, more pleas'd my sense
	Then smell of sweetest Fenel, or the Teats
	Of Ewe or Goat dropping with Milk at Eevn,
	Unsuckt of Lamb or Kid, that tend thir play.
	To satisfie the sharp desire I had
585	Of tasting those fair Apples, I resolv'd
	Not to deferr; hunger and thirst at once,
	Powerful perswaders, quick'n'd at the scent
	Of that alluring fruit, urg'd me so keen.
	About the mossie Trunk I wound me soon,
590	For high from ground the branches would require
	Thy utmost reach or *Adams:* Round the Tree
	All other Beasts that saw, with like desire
	Longing and envying stood, but could not reach.
	Amid the Tree now got, where plenty hung
595	Tempting so nigh, to pluck and eat my fill
	I spar'd not, for such pleasure till that hour
	At Feed or Fountain never had I found.
	Sated at length, ere long I might perceave
	Strange alteration in me, to degree
600	Of Reason in my inward Powers, and Speech
	Wanted not long, though to this shape retain'd.
	Thenceforth to Speculations high or deep
	I turnd my thoughts, and with capacious mind

Considerd all things visible in Heav'n,
605   Or Earth, or Middle, all things fair and good;
But all that fair and good in thy Divine
Semblance, and in thy Beauties heav'nly Ray
United I beheld; no Fair to thine
Equivalent or second, which compel'd
610   Mee thus, though importune perhaps, to come
And gaze, and worship thee of right declar'd
Sovran of Creatures, universal Dame.
      So talk'd the spirited sly Snake; and *Eve*
Yet more amaz'd unwarie thus reply'd.
615   Serpent, thy overpraising leaves in doubt
The vertue of that Fruit, in thee first prov'd:
But say, where grows the Tree, from hence how far?
For many are the Trees of God that grow
In Paradise, and various, yet unknown
620   To us, in such abundance lies our choice,
As leaves a greater store of Fruit untoucht,
Still hanging incorruptible, till men
Grow up to thir provision, and more hands
Help to disburden Nature of her Birth.
625   To whom the wilie Adder, blithe and glad.
Empress, the way is readie, and not long,
Beyond a row of Myrtles, on a Flat,
Fast by a Fountain, one small Thicket past
Of blowing Myrrh and Balm; if thou accept
630   My conduct, I can bring thee thither soon.
      Lead then, said *Eve*. Hee leading swiftly rowld
In tangles, and made intricate seem strait,
To mischief swift. Hope elevates, and joy
Bright'ns his Crest, as when a wandring Fire,
635   Compact of unctuous vapor, which the Night
Condenses, and the cold invirons round,
Kindl'd through agitation to a Flame,
Which oft, they say, some evil Spirit attends,
Hovering and blazing with delusive Light,
640   Misleads th' amaz'd Night-wanderer from his way
To Boggs and Mires, and oft through Pond or Pool,
There swallow'd up and lost, from succour farr.
So glister'd the dire Snake, and into fraud
Led *Eve* our credulous Mother, to the Tree
645   Of prohibition, root of all our woe;
Which when she saw, thus to her guide she spake.
      Serpent, we might have spar'd our coming hither,

Fruitless to mee, though Fruit be here to excess,
The credit of whose vertue rest with thee,
650 Wondrous indeed, if cause of such effects.
But of this Tree we may not taste nor touch;
God so commanded, and left that Command
Sole Daughter of his voice; the rest, we live
Law to our selves, our Reason is our Law.
655   To whom the Tempter guilefully repli'd.
Indeed? hath God then said that of the Fruit
Of all these Garden Trees ye shall not eat,
Yet Lords declar'd of all in Earth or Air?
        To whom thus *Eve* yet sinless. Of the Fruit
660 Of each Tree in the Garden we may eat,
But of the Fruit of this fair Tree amidst
The Garden, God hath said, Ye shall not eat
Thereof, nor shall ye touch it, least ye die.
        She scarse had said, though brief, when now more bold
665 The Tempter, but with shew of Zeal and Love
To Man, and indignation at his wrong,
New part puts on, and as to passion mov'd,
Fluctuats disturb'd, yet comely, and in act
Rais'd, as of som great matter to begin.
670 As when of old som Orator renound
In *Athens* or free *Rome*, where Eloquence
Flourishd, since mute, to som great cause addrest,
Stood in himself collected, while each part,
Motion, each act won audience ere the tongue,
675 Somtimes in highth began, as no delay
Of Preface brooking through his Zeal of Right.
So standing, moving, or to highth upgrown
The Tempter all impassiond thus began.
        Sacred, Wise, and Wisdom-giving Plant,
680 Mother of Science, now I feel thy Power
Within me cleere, not onely to discern
Things in thir Causes, but to trace the wayes
Of highest Agents, deemd however wise.
Queen of this Universe, doe not believe
685 Those rigid threats of Death; ye shall not Die:
How should ye? by the Fruit? it gives you Life
To Knowledge; by the Threatner? look on mee,
Mee who have touch'd and tasted, yet both live,
And life more perfet have attaind then Fate
690 Meant mee, by ventring higher then my Lot.
Shall that be shut to Man, which to the Beast

	Is open? or will God incense his ire
	For such a petty Trespass, and not praise
	Rather your dauntless vertue, whom the pain
695	Of Death denounc't, whatever thing Death be,
	Deterrd not from atchieving what might lead
	To happier life, knowledge of Good and Evil;
	Of good, how just? of evil, if what is evil
	Be real, why not known, since easier shunnd?
700	God therefore cannot hurt ye, and be just;
	Not just, not God; not feard then, nor obeyd:
	Your fear it self of Death removes the fear.
	Why then was this forbid? Why but to awe,
	Why but to keep ye low and ignorant,
705	His worshippers; he knows that in the day
	Ye Eat thereof, your Eyes that seem so cleer,
	Yet are but dim, shall perfetly be then
	Op'n'd and cleerd, and ye shall be as Gods,
	Knowing both Good and Evil as they know.
710	That ye should be as Gods, since I as Man,
	Internal Man, is but proportion meet,
	I of brute human, yee of human Gods.
	So ye shall die perhaps, by putting off
	Human, to put on Gods, death to be wisht,
715	Though threat'n'd, which no worse then this can bring.
	And what are Gods that Man may not become
	As they, participating God-like food?
	The Gods are first, and that advantage use
	On our belief, that all from them proceeds;
720	I question it, for this fair Earth I see,
	Warm'd by the Sun, producing every kind,
	Them nothing: If they all things, who enclos'd
	Knowledge of Good and Evil in this Tree,
	That whoso eats thereof, forthwith attains
725	Wisdom without their leave? and wherein lies
	Th' offence, that Man should thus attain to know?
	What can your knowledge hurt him, or this Tree
	Impart against his will if all be his?
	Or is it envie, and can envie dwell
730	In heav'nly brests? these, these and many more
	Causes import your need of this fair Fruit.
	Goddess humane, reach then, and freely taste.
	He ended, and his words replete with guile
	Into her heart too easie entrance won:
735	Fixt on the Fruit she gaz'd, which to behold

Might tempt alone, and in her ears the sound
Yet rung of his perswasive words, impregn'd
With Reason, to her seeming, and with Truth;
Mean while the hour of Noon drew on, and wak'd
740   An eager appetite, rais'd by the smell
So savorie of that Fruit, which with desire,
Inclinable now grown to touch or taste,
Sollicited her longing eye; yet first
Pausing a while, thus to her self she mus'd.
745   Great are thy Vertues, doubtless, best of Fruits,
Though kept from Man, and worthy to be admir'd,
Whose taste, too long forborn, at first assay
Gave elocution to the mute, and taught
The Tongue not made for Speech to speak thy praise:
750   Thy praise hee also who forbids thy use,
Conceals not from us, naming thee the Tree
Of Knowledge, knowledge both of good and evil;
Forbids us then to taste, but his forbidding
Commends thee more, while it inferrs the good
755   By thee communicated, and our want:
For good unknown, sure is not had, or had
And yet unknown, is as not had at all.
In plain then, what forbids he but to know,
Forbids us good, forbids us to be wise?
760   Such prohibitions bind not. But if Death
Bind us with after-bands, what profits then
Our inward freedom? In the day we eat
Of this fair Fruit, our doom is, we shall die.
How dies the Serpent? hee hath eat'n and lives,
765   And knows, and speaks, and reasons, and discerns,
Irrational till then. For us alone
Was death invented? or to us deni'd
This intellectual food, for beasts reserv'd?
For Beasts it seems: yet that one Beast which first
770   Hath tasted, envies not, but brings with joy
The good befall'n him, Author unsuspect,
Friendly to man, farr from deceit or guile.
What fear I then, rather what know to fear
Under this ignorance of Good and Evil,
775   Of God or Death, of Law or Penaltie?
Here grows the Cure of all, this Fruit Divine,
Fair to the Eye, inviting to the Taste,
Of vertue to make wise: what hinders then
To reach, and feed at once both Bodie and Mind?

780	So saying, her rash hand in evil hour
	Forth reaching to the Fruit, she pluck'd, she eat:
	Earth felt the wound, and Nature from her seat
	Sighing through all her Works gave signs of woe,
	That all was lost. Back to the Thicket slunk
785	The guiltie Serpent, and well might, for *Eve*
	Intent now wholly on her taste, naught else
	Regarded, such delight till then, as seemd,
	In Fruit she never tasted, whether true
	Or fansied so, through expectation high
790	Of knowledge, nor was God-head from her thought.
	Greedily she ingorg'd without restraint,
	And knew not eating Death: Satiate at length,
	And hightn'd as with Wine, jocond and boon,
	Thus to her self she pleasingly began.
795	O Sovran, vertuous, precious of all Trees
	In Paradise, of operation blest
	To Sapience, hitherto obscur'd, infam'd,
	And thy fair Fruit let hang, as to no end
	Created; but henceforth my early care,
800	Not without Song, each Morning, and due praise
	Shall tend thee, and the fertil burden ease
	Of thy full branches offer'd free to all;
	Till dieted by thee I grow mature
	In knowledge, as the Gods who all things know;
805	Though others envie what they cannot give;
	For had the gift bin theirs, it had not here
	Thus grown. Experience, next to thee I owe,
	Best guide; not following thee, I had remaind
	In ignorance, thou op'nst Wisdoms way,
810	And giv'st access, though secret she retire.
	And I perhaps am secret; Heav'n is high,
	High and remote to see from thence distinct
	Each thing on Earth; and other care perhaps
	May have diverted from continual watch
815	Our great Forbidder, safe with all his Spies
	About him. But to *Adam* in what sort
	Shall I appeer? shall I to him make known
	As yet my change, and give him to partake
	Full happiness with me, or rather not,
820	But keep the odds of Knowledge in my power
	Without Copartner? so to add what wants
	In Femal Sex, the more to draw his Love,
	And render me more equal, and perhaps,

A thing not undesirable, somtime
825 Superior; for inferior who is free?
This may be well: but what if God have seen,
And Death ensue? then I shall be no more,
And *Adam* wedded to another *Eve*,
Shall live with her enjoying, I extinct;
830 A death to think. Confirm'd then I resolve,
Adam shall share with me in bliss or woe:
So dear I love him, that with him all deaths
I could endure, without him live no life.
      So saying, from the Tree her step she turnd,
835 But first low Reverence don, as to the power
That dwelt within, whose presence had infus'd
Into the plant sciential sap, deriv'd
From Nectar, drink of Gods. *Adam* the while
Waiting desirous her return, had wove
840 Of choicest Flowrs a Garland to adorn
Her Tresses, and her rural labours crown,
As Reapers oft are wont thir Harvest Queen.
Great joy he promis'd to his thoughts, and new
Solace in her return, so long delay'd;
845 Yet oft his heart, divine of somthing ill,
Misgave him; hee the faultring measure felt;
And forth to meet her went, the way she took
That Morn when first they parted; by the Tree
Of Knowledge he must pass, there he her met,
850 Scarse from the Tree returning; in her hand
A bough of fairest fruit that downie smil'd,
New gatherd, and ambrosial smell diffus'd.
To him she hasted, in her face excuse
Came Prologue, and Apologie to prompt,
855 Which with bland words at will she thus addrest.
      Hast thou not wonderd, *Adam*, at my stay?
Thee I have misst, and thought it long, depriv'd
Thy presence, agonie of love till now
Not felt, nor shall be twice, for never more
860 Mean I to trie, what rash untri'd I sought,
The pain of absence from thy sight. But strange
Hath bin the cause, and wonderful to hear:
This Tree is not as we are told, a Tree
Of danger tasted, nor to evil unknown
865 Op'ning the way, but of Divine effect
To open Eyes, and make them Gods who taste;
And hath bin tasted such: the Serpent wise,

Or not restraind as wee, or not obeying,
Hath eat'n of the fruit, and is become,
870 Not dead, as we are threat'n'd, but thenceforth
Endu'd with human voice and human sense,
Reasoning to admiration, and with mee
Perswasively hath so prevaild, that I
Have also tasted, and have also found
875 Th' effects to correspond, opener mine Eyes,
Dimm erst, dilated Spirits, ampler Heart,
And growing up to Godhead; which for thee
Chiefly I sought, without thee can despise.
For bliss, as thou hast part, to me is bliss,
880 Tedious, unshar'd with thee, and odious soon.
Thou therfore also taste, that equal Lot
May joyn us, equal Joy, as equal Love;
Least thou not tasting, different degree
Disjoyn us, and I then too late renounce
885 Deitie for thee, when Fate will not permit.
　　　Thus *Eve* with Countnance blithe her storie told;
But in her Cheek distemper flushing glowd.
On th' other side, *Adam*, soon as he heard
The fatal Trespass don by *Eve*, amaz'd,
890 Astonied stood and Blank, while horror chill
Ran through his veins, and all his joynts relax'd;
From his slack hand the Garland wreath'd for *Eve*
Down drop'd, and all the faded Roses shed:
Speechless he stood and pale, till thus at length
895 First to himself he inward silence broke.
　　　O fairest of Creation, last and best
Of all Gods works, Creature in whom excell'd
Whatever can to sight or thought be formd,
Holy, divine, good, amiable, or sweet!
900 How art thou lost, how on a sudden lost,
Defac't, deflowrd, and now to Death devote?
Rather how hast thou yeelded to transgress
The strict forbiddance, how to violate
The sacred Fruit forbidd'n! som cursed fraud
905 Of Enemie hath beguil'd thee, yet unknown,
And mee with thee hath ruind, for with thee
Certain my resolution is to Die;
How can I live without thee, how forgoe
Thy sweet Converse and Love so dearly joyn'd,
910 To live again in these wild Woods forlorn?
Should God create another *Eve*, and I

Another Rib afford, yet loss of thee
Would never from my heart; no no, I feel
The Link of Nature draw me: Flesh of Flesh,
915   Bone of my Bone thou art, and from thy State
Mine never shall be parted, bliss or woe.
       So having said, as one from sad dismay
Recomforted, and after thoughts disturb'd
Submitting to what seemd remediless,
920   Thus in calm mood his Words to *Eve* he turnd.
       Bold deed thou hast presumd, adventrous *Eve,*
And peril great provok't, who thus hast dar'd
Had it bin onely coveting to Eye
That sacred Fruit, sacred to abstinence,
925   Much more to taste it under bann to touch.
But past who can recall, or don undoe?
Not God Omnipotent, nor Fate, yet so
Perhaps thou shalt not Die, perhaps the Fact
Is not so hainous now, foretasted Fruit,
930   Profan'd first by the Serpent, by him first
Made common and unhallowd ere our taste;
Nor yet on him found deadly, he yet lives,
Lives, as thou saidst, and gains to live as Man
Higher degree of Life, inducement strong
935   To us, as likely tasting to attain
Proportional ascent, which cannot be
But to be Gods, or Angels Demi-gods.
Nor can I think that God, Creator wise,
Though threatning, will in earnest so destroy
940   Us his prime Creatures, dignifi'd so high,
Set over all his Works, which in our Fall,
For us created, needs with us must fail,
Dependent made; so God shall uncreate,
Be frustrate, do, undo, and labour loose,
945   Not well conceav'd of God, who though his Power
Creation could repeat, yet would be loath
Us to abolish, least the Adversary
Triumph and say; Fickle their State whom God
Most Favors, who can please him long; Mee first
950   He ruind, now Mankind; whom will he next?
Matter of scorn, not to be giv'n the Foe.
However I with thee have fixt my Lot,
Certain to undergoe like doom, if Death
Consort with thee, Death is to mee as Life;
955   So forcible within my heart I feel

The Bond of Nature draw me to my own,
My own in thee, for what thou art is mine;
Our State cannot be severd, we are one,
One Flesh; to loose thee were to loose my self.
960   So *Adam*, and thus *Eve* to him repli'd.
O glorious trial of exceeding Love,
Illustrious evidence, example high!
Ingaging me to emulate, but short
Of thy perfection, how shall I attain,
965   *Adam*, from whose dear side I boast me sprung,
And gladly of our Union hear thee speak,
One Heart, one Soul in both; whereof good prooff
This day affords, declaring thee resolv'd,
Rather then Death or aught then Death more dread
970   Shall separate us, linkt in Love so dear,
To undergoe with mee one Guilt, one Crime,
If any be, of tasting this fair Fruit,
Whose vertue, for of good still good proceeds,
Direct, or by occasion hath presented
975   This happie trial of thy Love, which else
So eminently never had bin known.
Were it I thought Death menac't would ensue
This my attempt, I would sustain alone
The worst, and not perswade thee, rather die
980   Deserted, then oblige thee with a fact
Pernicious to thy Peace, chiefly assur'd
Remarkably so late of thy so true,
So faithful Love unequald; but I feel
Farr otherwise th' event, not Death, but Life
985   Augmented, op'n'd Eyes, new Hopes, new Joyes,
Taste so Divine, that what of sweet before
Hath toucht my sense, flat seems to this, and harsh.
On my experience, *Adam*, freely taste,
And fear of Death deliver to the Winds.
990   So saying, she embrac'd him, and for joy
Tenderly wept, much won that he his Love
Had so enobl'd, as of choice t' incurr
Divine displeasure for her sake, or Death.
In recompence (for such compliance bad
995   Such recompence best merits) from the bough
She gave him of that fair enticing Fruit
With liberal hand: he scrupl'd not to eat
Against his better knowledge, not deceavd,
But fondly overcome with Femal charm.

1000   Earth trembl'd from her entrails, as again

In pangs, and Nature gave a second groan,

Skie lowr'd, and muttering Thunder, som sad drops

Wept at compleating of the mortal Sin

Original; while *Adam* took no thought,

1005   Eating his fill, nor *Eve* to iterate

Her former trespass fear'd, the more to soothe

Him with her lov'd societie, that now

As with new Wine intoxicated both

They swim in mirth, and fansie that they feel

1010   Divinitie within them breeding wings

Wherewith to scorn the Earth: but that false Fruit

Farr other operation first displaid,

Carnal desire enflaming, hee on *Eve*

Began to cast lascivious Eyes, she him

1015   As wantonly repaid; in Lust they burn:

Till *Adam* thus 'gan *Eve* to dalliance move.

       Eve, now I see thou art exact of taste,

And elegant, of Sapience no small part,

Since to each meaning savour we apply,

1020   And Palate call judicious; I the praise

Yeild thee, so well this day thou hast purvey'd.

Much pleasure we have lost, while we abstain'd

From this delightful Fruit, nor known till now

True relish, tasting; if such pleasure be

1025   In things to us forbidden, it might be wishd,

For this one Tree had bin forbidden ten.

But come, so well refresh't, now let us play,

As meet is, after such delicious Fare;

For never did thy Beautie since the day

1030   I saw thee first and wedded thee, adorn'd

With all perfections, so enflame my sense

With ardor to enjoy thee, fairer now

Then ever, bountie of this vertuous Tree.

       So said he, and forbore not glance or toy

1035   Of amorous intent, well understood

Of *Eve,* whose Eye darted contagious Fire.

Her hand he seis'd, and to a shadie bank,

Thick overhead with verdant roof imbowr'd

He led her nothing loath; Flowrs were the Couch,

1040   Pansies, and Violets, and Asphodel,

And Hyacinth, Earths freshest softest lap.

There they thir fill of Love and Loves disport

Took largely, of thir mutual guilt the Seal,

The solace of thir sin, till dewie sleep
1045   Oppress'd them, wearied with thir amorous play.
Soon as the force of that fallacious Fruit,
That with exhilerating vapour bland
About thir spirits had plaid, and inmost powers
Made err, was now exhal'd, and grosser sleep
1050   Bred of unkindly fumes, with conscious dreams
Encumberd, now had left them, up they rose
As from unrest, and each the other viewing,
Soon found thir Eyes how op'n'd, and thir minds
How dark'n'd; innocence, that as a veil
1055   Had shadow'd them from knowing ill, was gon,
Just confidence, and native righteousness,
And honour from about them, naked left
To guiltie shame: hee coverd, but his Robe
Uncover'd more. So rose the *Danite* strong
1060   *Herculean Samson* from the Harlot-lap
Of *Philistean Dalilah*, and wak'd
Shorn of his strength. They destitute and bare
Of all thir vertue: silent, and in face
Confounded long they sate, as struck'n mute,
1065   Till *Adam*, though not less then *Eve* abash't,
At length gave utterance to these words constraind.
        O *Eve*, in evil hour thou didst give ear
To that false Worm, of whomsoever taught
To counterfet Mans voice, true in our Fall,
1070   False in our promis'd Rising; since our Eyes
Op'n'd we find indeed, and find we know
Both Good and Evil, Good lost, and Evil got,
Bad Fruit of Knowledge, if this be to know,
Which leaves us naked thus, of Honour void,
1075   Of Innocence, of Faith, of Puritie,
Our wonted Ornaments now soild and staind,
And in our Faces evident the signes
Of foul concupiscence; whence evil store;
Ev'n shame, the last of evils; of the first
1080   Be sure then. How shall I behold the face
Henceforth of God or Angel, earst with joy
And rapture so oft beheld? those heav'nly shapes
Will dazle now this earthly, with thir blaze
Insufferably bright. O might I here
1085   In solitude live savage, in some glade
Obscur'd, where highest Woods impenetrable
To Starr or Sun-light, spread thir umbrage broad

And brown as Evening: Cover me ye Pines,
Ye Cedars, with innumerable boughs

1090 Hide me, where I may never see them more.
But let us now, as in bad plight, devise
What best may for the present serve to hide
The Parts of each from other, that seem most
To shame obnoxious, and unseemliest seen,

1095 Some Tree whose broad smooth Leaves together sowd,
And girded on our loyns, may cover round
Those middle parts, that this new commer, Shame,
There sit not, and reproach us as unclean.
   So counsel'd hee, and both together went

1100 Into the thickest Wood, there soon they chose
The Figtree, not that kind for Fruit renown'd,
But such as at this day to *Indians* known
In *Malabar* or *Decan* spreds her Armes
Braunching so broad and long, that in the ground

1105 The bended Twigs take root, and Daughters grow
About the Mother Tree, a Pillard shade
High overarch't, and echoing Walks between;
There oft the *Indian* Herdsman shunning heat
Shelters in cool, and tends his pasturing Herds

1110 At Loopholes cut through thickest shade: Those Leaves
They gatherd, broad as *Amazonian* Targe,
And with what skill they had, together sowd,
To gird thir waste, vain Covering if to hide
Thir guilt and dreaded shame; O how unlike

1115 To that first naked Glorie. Such of late
Columbus found th' *American* so girt
With featherd Cincture, naked else and wild
Among the Trees on Iles and woodie Shores.
Thus fenc't, and as they thought, thir shame in part

1120 Coverd, but not at rest or ease of Mind,
They sate them down to weep, nor onely Teares
Raind at thir Eyes, but high Winds worse within
Began to rise, high Passions, Anger, Hate,
Mistrust, Suspicion, Discord, and shook sore

1125 Thir inward State of Mind, calm Region once
And full of Peace, now tost and turbulent:
For Understanding rul'd not, and the Will
Heard not her lore, both in subjection now
To sensual Appetite, who from beneath

1130 Usurping over sovran Reason claimd
Superior sway: from thus distemperd brest,

Adam, estrang'd in look and alterd stile,
Speech intermitted thus to *Eve* renewd.
     Would thou hadst heark'n'd to my words, and stai'd

1135   With me, as I besought thee, when that strange
Desire of wandring this unhappie Morn,
I know not whence possess'd thee; we had then
Remaind still happie, not as now, despoild
Of all our good, sham'd, naked, miserable.

1140   Let none henceforth seek needless cause t' approve
The Faith they owe; when earnestly they seek
Such proof, conclude, they then begin to fail.
     To whom soon mov'd with touch of blame thus *Eve*.
What words have past thy Lips, *Adam* severe,

1145   Imput'st thou that to my default, or will
Of wandring, as thou call'st it, which who knows
But might as ill have happ'n'd thou being by,
Or to thy self perhaps: hadst thou bin there,
Or here th' attempt, thou couldst not have discernd.

1150   Fraud in the Serpent, speaking as he spake;
No ground of enmitie between us known,
Why hee should mean me ill, or seek to harm.
Was I t' have never parted from thy side?
As good have grown there still a liveless Rib.

1155   Being as I am, why didst not thou the Head
Command me absolutely not to go,
Going into such danger as thou saidst?
Too facil then thou didst not much gainsay,
Nay, didst permit, approve, and fair dismiss.

1160   Hadst thou bin firm and fixt in thy dissent,
Neither had I transgress'd, nor thou with mee.
     To whom then first incenst *Adam* repli'd.
Is this the Love, is this the recompence
Of mine to thee, ingrateful *Eve*, exprest

1165   Immutable when thou wert lost, not I,
Who might have liv'd and joyd immortal bliss,
Yet willingly chose rather Death with thee:
And am I now upbraided, as the cause
Of thy transgressing? not enough severe,

1170   It seems, in thy restraint: what could I more?
I warn'd thee, I admonish'd thee, foretold
The danger, and the lurking Enemie
That lay in wait; beyond this had bin force,
And force upon free will hath here no place.

1175   But confidence then bore thee on, secure

> Either to meet no danger, or to find
> Matter of glorious trial; and perhaps
> I also err'd in overmuch admiring
> What seemd in thee so perfet, that I thought
> 1180   No evil durst attempt thee, but I rue
> That errour now, which is become my crime,
> And thou th' accuser. Thus it shall befall
> Him who to worth in Woman overtrusting
> Lets her will rule; restraint she will not brook,
> 1185   And left t' her self, if evil thence ensue,
> Shee first his weak indulgence will accuse.
>   Thus they in mutual accusation spent
> The fruitless hours, but neither self-condemning,
> And of thir vain contest appeer'd no end.

BOOK X
THE ARGUMENT

Mans transgression known, the Guardian Angels forsake Paradise, and return up to Heaven to approve thir vigilance, and are approv'd, God declaring that the entrance of *Satan* could not be by them prevented. He sends his Son to judge the Transgressors, who descends and gives Sentence accordingly; then in pity cloaths them both, and reascends. *Sin* and *Death* sitting till then at the Gates of Hell, by wondrous sympathie feeling the success of *Satan* in this new World, and the sin by Man there committed, resolve to sit no longer confin'd in Hell, but to follow *Satan* thir Sire up to the place of Man: To make the way easier from Hell to this World to and fro, they pave a broad Highway or Bridge over *Chaos*, according to the Track that *Satan* first made; then preparing for Earth, they meet him proud of his success returning to Hell; thir mutual gratulation. *Satan* arrives at *Pandemonium*, in full assembly relates with boasting his success against Man; instead of applause is entertained with a general hiss by all his audience, transform'd with himself also suddenly into Serpents, according to his doom giv'n in Paradise; then deluded with a shew of the forbidden Tree springing up before them, they greedily reaching to taste of the Fruit, chew dust and bitter ashes. The proceedings of *Sin* and *Death*; God foretells the final Victory of his Son over them, and the renewing of all things; but for the present commands his Angels to make several alterations in the Heavens and Elements. *Adam* more and more perceiving his fall'n condition heavily bewails, rejects the condolement of *Eve*; she persists and at length appeases him: then to evade the Curse likely to fall on thir Ofspring, proposes to *Adam* violent wayes which he approves not, but conceiving better hope, puts her in mind of the late Promise made them, that her Seed should be reveng'd on the Serpent, and exhorts her with him to seek Peace of the offended Deity, by repentance and supplication.

* * * * *

Thus *Adam* to himself lamented loud
Through the still Night, not now, as ere man fell,
Wholsom and cool, and mild, but with black Air
Accompanied, with damps and dreadful gloom,
5   Which to his evil Conscience represented
All things with double terror: On the ground
Outstretcht he lay, on the cold ground, and oft
Curs'd his Creation, Death as oft accus'd
Of tardie execution, since denounct
10   The day of his offence. Why comes not Death,
Said hee, with one thrice acceptable stroke
To end me? Shall Truth fail to keep her word,
Justice Divine not hast'n to be just?
But Death comes not at call, Justice Divine
15   Mends not her slowest pace for prayers or cries.
O Woods, O Fountains, Hillocks, Dales and Bowrs,
With other echo late I taught your Shades
To answer, and resound farr other Song.
Whom thus afflicted when sad *Eve* beheld,
20   Desolate where she sate, approaching nigh,
Soft words to his fierce passion she assay'd:
But her with stern regard he thus repell'd.
    Out of my sight, thou Serpent, that name best
Befits thee with him leagu'd, thy self as false
25   And hateful; nothing wants, but that thy shape,
Like his, and colour Serpentine may shew
Thy inward fraud, to warn all Creatures from thee
Henceforth; least that too heav'nly form, pretended
To hellish falshood, snare them. But for thee
30   I had persisted happie, had not thy pride
And wandring vanitie, when lest was safe,
Rejected my forewarning, and disdain'd
Not to be trusted, longing to be seen
Though by the Devil himself, him overweening
35   To over-reach, but with the Serpent meeting
Fool'd and beguil'd, by him thou, I by thee,
To trust thee from my side, imagin'd wise,
Constant, mature, proof against all assaults,
And understood not all was but a shew
40   Rather then solid vertu, all but a Rib
Crooked by nature, bent, as now appears,
More to the part sinister from me drawn,

Well if thrown out, as supernumerarie
To my just number found. O why did God,
45   Creator wise, that peopl'd highest Heav'n
With Spirits Masculine, create at last
This noveltie on Earth, this fair defect
Of Nature, and not fill the World at once
With Men as Angels without Feminine,
50   Or find some other way to generate
Mankind? this mischief had not then befall'n,
And more that shall befall, innumerable
Disturbances on Earth through Femal snares,
And straight conjunction with this Sex: for either
55   He never shall find out fit Mate, but such
As some misfortune brings him, or mistake,
Or whom he wishes most shall seldom gain
Through her perversness, but shall see her gaind
By a farr worse, or if she love, withheld
60   By Parents, or his happiest choice too late
Shall meet, alreadie linkt and Wedlock-bound
To a fell Adversarie, his hate or shame:
Which infinite calamitie shall cause
To Human life, and houshold peace confound.
65   He added not, and from her turn'd, but *Eve*
Not so repulst, with Tears that ceas'd not flowing,
And tresses all disorderd, at his feet
Fell humble, and imbracing them, besaught
His peace, and thus proceeded in her plaint.
70   Forsake me not thus, *Adam*, witness Heav'n
What love sincere, and reverence in my heart
I bear thee, and unweeting have offended,
Unhappilie deceav'd; thy suppliant
I beg, and clasp thy knees; bereave me not,
75   Whereon I live, thy gentle looks, thy aid,
Thy counsel in this uttermost distress,
My onely strength and stay: forlorn of thee,
Whither shall I betake me, where subsist?
While yet we live, scarse one short hour perhaps,
80   Between us two let there be peace, both joyning,
As joyn'd in injuries, one enmitie
Against a Foe by doom express assign'd us,
That cruel Serpent: On me exercise not
Thy hatred for this miserie befall'n,
85   On me already lost, mee then thy self
More miserable; both have sin'd, but thou

Against God onely, I against God and thee,
And to the place of judgment will return,
There with my cries importune Heav'n, that all
90   The sentence from thy head remov'd may light
On me, sole cause to thee of all this woe,
Mee mee onely just object of his ire.
        She ended weeping, and her lowlie plight,
Immoveable till peace obtain'd from fault
95   Acknowledg'd and deplor'd, in *Adam* wraught
Commiseration; soon his heart relented
Towards her, his life so late and sole delight,
Now at his feet submissive in distress,
Creature so fair his reconcilement seeking,
100   His counsel whom she had displeas'd, his aid;
As one disarm'd, his anger all he lost,
And thus with peaceful words uprais'd her soon.

                    * * * * *

... Then let us seek
Som safer resolution, which methinks
105   I have in view, calling to mind with heed
Part of our Sentence, that thy Seed shall bruise
The Serpents head; piteous amends, unless
Be meant, whom I conjecture, our grand Foe
Satan, who in the Serpent hath contriv'd
110   Against us this deceit: to crush his head
Would be revenge indeed; which will be lost
By death brought on our selves, or childless days
Resolv'd, as thou proposest; so our Foe
Shall scape his punishment ordain'd, and wee
115   Instead shall double ours upon our heads.
No more be mention'd then of violence
Against our selves, and wilful barrenness,
That cuts us off from hope, and savours onely
Rancor and pride, impatience and despite,
120   Reluctance against God and his just yoke
Laid on our Necks. Remember with what mild
And gracious temper he both heard and judg'd
Without wrauth or reviling; wee expected
Immediate dissolution, which we thought
125   Was meant by Death that day, when lo, to thee
Pains onely in Child-bearing were foretold,
And bringing forth, soon recompenc't with joy,

Fruit of thy Womb: On mee the Curse aslope
Glanc'd on the ground, with labour I must earn
130 My bread; what harm? Idleness had bin worse;
My labour will sustain me; and least Cold
Or Heat should injure us, his timely care
Hath unbesaught provided, and his hands
Cloath'd us unworthie, pitying while he judg'd;
135 How much more, if we pray him, will his ear
Be open, and his heart to pitie incline,
And teach us further by what means to shun
Th' inclement Seasons, Rain, Ice, Hail and Snow,
Which now the Skie with various Face begins
140 To shew us in this Mountain, while the Winds
Blow moist and keen, shattering the graceful locks
Of these fair spreading Trees; which bids us seek
Som better shroud, som better warmth to cherish
Our Limbs benumm'd, ere this diurnal Starr
145 Leave cold the Night, how we his gather'd beams
Reflected, may with matter sere foment,
Or by collision of two bodies grind
The Air attrite to Fire, as late the Clouds
Justling or pusht with Winds rude in thir shock
150 Tine the slant Lightning, whose thwart flame driv'n down
Kindles the gummie bark of Firr or Pine,
And sends a comfortable heat from farr,
Which might supplie the Sun: such Fire to use,
And what may else be remedie or cure
155 To evils which our own misdeeds have wrought,
Hee will instruct us praying, and of Grace
Beseeching him, so as we need not fear
To pass commodiously this life, sustain'd
By him with many comforts, till we end
160 In dust, our final rest and native home.
What better can we do, then to the place
Repairing where he judg'd us, prostrate fall
Before him reverent, and there confess
Humbly our faults, and pardon beg, with tears
165 Watering the ground, and with our sighs the Air
Frequenting, sent from hearts contrite, in sign
Of sorrow unfeign'd, and humiliation meek.
Undoubtedly he will relent and turn
From his displeasure; in whose look serene,
170 When angry most he seem'd and most severe,
What else but favor, grace, and mercie shon?

So spake our Father penitent, nor *Eve*
Felt less remorse: they forthwith to the place
Repairing where he judg'd them prostrate fell
175 Before him reverent, and both confess'd
Humbly thir faults, and pardon beg'd, with tears
Watering the ground, and with thir sighs the Air
Frequenting, sent from hearts contrite, in sign
Of sorrow unfeign'd, and humiliation meek.

BOOK XI
THE ARGUMENT

The Son of God presents to his Father the Prayers of our first Parents now repenting, and intercedes for them: God accepts them, but declares that they must no longer abide in Paradise; sends *Michael* with a Band of Cherubim to dispossess them; but first to reveal to *Adam* future things: *Michaels* coming down. *Adam* shews to *Eve* certain ominous signs; he discerns *Michaels* approach, goes out to meet him: the Angel denounces thir departure. *Eve's* Lamentation. *Adam* pleads, but submits: The Angel leads him up to a high Hill, sets before him in vision what shall happ'n till the Flood.

* * * * *

BOOK XII
THE ARGUMENT

The Angel *Michael* continues from the Flood to relate what shall succeed; then, in the mention of *Abraham,* comes by degrees to explain, who that Seed of the Woman shall be, which was promised *Adam* and *Eve* in the Fall; his Incarnation, Death, Resurrection, and Ascension; the state of the Church till his second Coming. *Adam* greatly satisfied and recomforted by these Relations and Promises descends the Hill with *Michael;* wakens *Eve,* who all this while had slept, but with gentle dreams compos'd to quietness of mind and submission. *Michael* in either hand leads them out of Paradise, the fiery Sword waving behind them, and the Cherubim taking thir Stations to guard the Place.

* * * * *

Meanwhile they in thir earthly *Canaan* plac't
Long time shall dwell and prosper, but when sins
National interrupt thir public peace,
Provoking God to raise them enemies:
5 From whom as oft he saves them penitent
By Judges first, then under Kings; of whom

The second, both for pietie renownd
And puissant deeds, a promise shall receive
Irrevocable, that his Regal Throne
10 For ever shall endure; the like shall sing
All Prophecie, that of the Royal Stock
Of *David* (so I name this King) shall rise
A Son, the Womans Seed to thee foretold,
Foretold to *Abraham*, as in whom shall trust
15 All Nations, and to Kings foretold, of Kings
The last, for of his Reign shall be no end.
But first a long succession must ensue,
And his next Son for Wealth and Wisdom fam'd,
The clouded Ark of God till then in Tents
20 Wandring, shall in a glorious Temple enshrine.
Such follow him, as shall be registerd
Part good, part bad, of bad the longer scrowl,
Whose foul Idolatries, and other faults
Heapt to the popular sum, will so incense
25 God, as to leave them, and expose thir Land,
Thir Citie, his Temple, and his holy Ark
With all his sacred things, a scorn and prey
To that proud Citie, whose high Walls thou saw'st
Left in confusion, *Babylon* thence call'd.
30 There in captivitie he lets them dwell
The space of seventie years, then brings them back,
Remembring mercie, and his Cov'nant sworn
To *David*, stablisht as the dayes of Heav'n
Returnd from *Babylon* by leave of Kings
35 Thir Lords, whom God dispos'd, the house of God
They first re-edifie, and for a while
In mean estate live moderate, till grown
In wealth and multitude, factious they grow;
But first among the Priests dissension springs,
40 Men who attend the Altar, and should most
Endeavour Peace: thir strife pollution brings
Upon the Temple it self: at last they seise
The Scepter, and regard not *Davids* Sons,
Then loose it to a stranger, that the true
45 Anointed King *Messiah* might be born
Barr'd of his right; yet at his Birth a Starr
Unseen before in Heav'n proclaims him com,
And guides the Eastern Sages, who enquire
His place, to offer Incense, Myrrh, and Gold;
50 His place of birth a solemn Angel tells

To simple Shepherds, keeping watch by night;
They gladly thither haste, and by a Quire
Of squadrond Angels bear his Carol sung.
A Virgin is his Mother, but his Sire
55   The Power of the most High; he shall ascend
The Throne hereditarie, and bound his Reign
With earths wide bounds, his glory with the Heav'ns.
     He ceas'd, discerning *Adam* with such joy
Surcharg'd, as had like grief bin dew'd in tears,
60   Without the vent of words, which these he breath'd.
     O Prophet of glad tidings, finisher
Of utmost hope! now clear I understand
What oft my steddiest thoughts have searcht in vain,
Why our great expectation should be call'd
65   The seed of Woman: Virgin Mother, Hail,
High in the love of Heav'n, yet from my Loyns
Thou shalt proceed, and from thy Womb the Son
Of God most High; so God with man unites.
Needs must the Serpent now his capital bruise
70   Expect with mortal pain: say where and when
Thir fight, what stroke shall bruise the Victors heel.
     To whom thus *Michael.* Dream not of thir fight,
As of a Duel, or the local wounds
Of head or heel: not therefore joyns the Son
75   Manhood to God-head, with more strength to foil
Thy enemie; nor so is overcome
Satan, whose fall from Heav'n, a deadlier bruise,
Disabl'd not to give thee thy deaths wound:
Which hee, who comes thy Saviour, shall recure,
80   Not by destroying *Satan,* but his works
In thee and in thy Seed: nor can this be,
But by fulfilling that which thou didst want,
Obedience to the Law of God, impos'd
On penaltie of death, and suffering death,
85   The penaltie to thy transgression due,
And due to theirs which out of thine will grow:
So onely can high justice rest appaid.
The Law of God exact he shall fulfill
Both by obedience and by love, though love
90   Alone fulfill the Law; thy punishment
He shall endure by coming in the Flesh
To a reproachful life and cursed death,
Proclaiming Life to all who shall believe
In his redemption, and that his obedience

95   Imputed becomes theirs by Faith, his merits
To save them, not thir own, though legal works.
For this he shall live hated, be blasphem'd,
Seis'd on by force, judg'd, and to death conderand
A shameful and accurst, naild to the Cross
100   By his own Nation, slain for bringing Life;
But to the Cross he nails thy Enemies,
The Law that is against thee, and the sins
Of all mankind, with him there crucifi'd,
Never to hurt them more who rightly trust
105   In this his satisfaction; so he dies,
But soon revives, Death over him no power
Shall long usurp; ere the third dawning light
Return, the Starrs of Morn shall see him rise
Out of his grave, fresh as the dawning light,
110   Thy ransom paid, which Man from death redeems,
His death for Man, as many as offerd Life
Neglect not, and the benefit imbrace
By Faith not void of works: this God-like act
Annuls thy doom, the death thou shouldst have dy'd,
115   In sin for ever lost from life; this act
Shall bruise the head of *Satan*, crush his strength
Defeating Sin and Death, his two main armes,
And fix farr deeper in his head thir stings
Then temporal death shall bruise the Victors heel,
120   Or theirs whom he redeems, a death like sleep,
A gentle wafting to immortal Life.
Nor after resurrection shall he stay
Longer on Earth then certain times to appeer
To his Disciples, Men who in his Life
125   Still follow'd him; to them shall leave in charge
To teach all nations what of him they learn'd
And his Salvation, them who shall beleeve
Baptizing in the profluent stream, the signe
Of washing them from guilt of sin to Life
130   Pure, and in mind prepar'd, if so befall,
For death, like that which the redeemer dy'd.
All Nations they shall teach; for from that day
Not onely to the Sons of *Abrahams* Loins
Salvation shall be Preacht, but to the Sons
135   Of *Abrahams* Faith wherever through the world;
So in his seed all Nations shall be blest.
Then to the Heav'n of Heav'ns he shall ascend
With victory, triumphing through the air

140   Over his foes and thine; there shall surprise
The Serpent, Prince of air, and drag in Chains
Through all his Realm, and there confounded leave;
Then enter into glory, and resume
His Seat at Gods right hand, exalted high

145   Above all names in Heav'n; and thence shall come,
When this worlds dissolution shall be ripe,
With glory and power to judge both quick and dead,
To judge th' unfaithful dead, but to reward
His faithful, and receave them into bliss,

150   Whether in Heav'n or Earth, for then the Earth
Shall all be Paradise, far happier place
Then this of *Eden,* and far happier daies.

* * * * *

    ... Truth shall retire
Bestuck with slandrous darts, and works of Faith
Rarely be found: so shall the World goe on,

155   To good malignant, to bad men benigne,
Under her own waight groaning, till the day
Appeer of respiration to the just,
And vengeance to the wicked, at return
Of him so lately promis'd to thy aid,

160   The Womans seed, obscurely then foretold,
Now amplier known thy Saviour and thy Lord,
Last in the Clouds from Heav'n to be reveald
In glory of the Father, to dissolve
Satan with his perverted World, then raise

165   From the conflagrant mass, purg'd and refin'd,
New Heav'ns, new Earth, Ages of endless date
Founded in righteousness and peace and love,
To bring forth fruits Joy and eternal Bliss.
    He ended; and thus *Adam* last reply'd.

170   How soon hath thy prediction, Seer blest,
Measur'd this transient World, the Race of time,
Till time stand fixt: beyond is all abyss,
Eternitie, whose end no eye can reach.
Greatly instructed I shall hence depart,

175   Greatly in peace of thought, and have my fill
Of knowledge, what this Vessel can contain;
Beyond which was my folly to aspire.
Henceforth I learn, that to obey is best,
And love with fear the onely God, to walk

180   As in his presence, ever to observe
         His providence, and on him sole depend,
         Mercifull over all his works, with good
         Still overcoming evil, and by small
         Accomplishing great things, by things deemd weak
185   Subverting worldly strong, and worldly wise
         By simply meek; that suffering for Truths sake
         Is fortitude to highest victorie,
         And to the faithful Death the Gate of Life;
         Taught this by his example whom I now
190   Acknowledge my Redeemer ever blest.
             To whom thus also th' Angel last repli'd:
         This having learnt, thou hast attaind the sum
         Of wisdom; hope no higher, though all the Starrs
         Thou knewst by name, and all th' ethereal Powers,
195   All secrets of the deep, all Natures works,
         Or works of God in Heav'n, Air, Earth, or Sea,
         And all the riches of this World enjoydst,
         And all the rule, one Empire; onely add
         Deeds to thy knowledge answerable, add Faith,
200   Add Vertue, Patience, Temperance, add Love,
         By name to come call'd Charitie, the soul
         Of all the rest: then wilt thou not be loath
         To leave this Paradise, but shalt possess
         A Paradise within thee, happier farr.
205   Let us descend now therefore from this top
         Of Speculation; for the hour precise
         Exacts our parting hence; and see the Guards,
         By mee encampt on yonder Hill, expect
         Thir motion, at whose Front a flaming Sword,
210   In signal of remove, waves fiercely round;
         We may no longer stay: go, waken *Eve*;
         Her also I with gentle Dreams have calm'd
         Portending good, and all her spirits compos'd
         To meek submission: thou at season fit
215   Let her with thee partake what thou hast heard,
         Chiefly what may concern her Faith to know,
         The great deliverance by her Seed to come
         (For by the Womans Seed) on all Mankind.
         That ye may live, which will be many dayes,
220   Both in one Faith unanimous though sad,
         With cause for evils past, yet much more cheer'd
         With meditation on the happie end.
             He ended, and they both descend the Hill;

Descended, Adam to the Bowr where *Eve*
225   Lay sleeping ran before, but found her wak't;
And thus with words not sad she him receav'd.
      Whence thou returnst, and whither wentst, I know;
For God is also in sleep, and Dreams advise,
Which he hath sent propitious, some great good
230   Presaging, since with sorrow and hearts distress
Wearied I fell asleep: but now lead on;
In mee is no delay; with thee to goe,
Is to stay here; without thee here to stay,
Is to go hence unwilling; thou to mee
235   Art all things under Heav'n, all places thou,
Who for my wilful crime art banisht hence.
This further consolation yet secure
I carry hence; though all by mee is lost,
Such favour I unworthie am voutsaft,
240   By mee the Promis'd Seed shall all restore.
      So spake our Mother *Eve*, and *Adam* heard
Well pleas'd, but answer'd not; for now too nigh
Th' Archangel stood, and from the other Hill
To thir fixt Station, all in bright array
245   The Cherubim descended; on the ground
Gliding meteorous, as Ev'ning Mist
Ris'n from a River o're the marish glides,
And gathers ground fast at the Labourers heel
Homeward returning. High in Front advanct,
250   The brandisht Sword of God before them blaz'd
Fierce as a Comet; which with torrid heat,
And vapour as the *Libyan* Air adust,
Began to parch that temperate Clime; whereat
In either hand the hastning Angel caught
255   Our lingring Parents, and to th' Eastern Gate
Led them direct, and down the Cliff as fast
To the subjected Plain; then disappeer'd.
They looking back, all th' Eastern side beheld
Of Paradise, so late thir happie seat,
260   Wav'd over by that flaming Brand, the Gate
With dreadful Faces throng'd and fierie Armes:
Som natural tears they drop'd, but wip'd them soon;
The World was all before them, where to choose
Thir place of rest, and Providence thir guide:
265   They hand in hand with wandring steps and slow,
Through *Eden* took thir solitarie way.